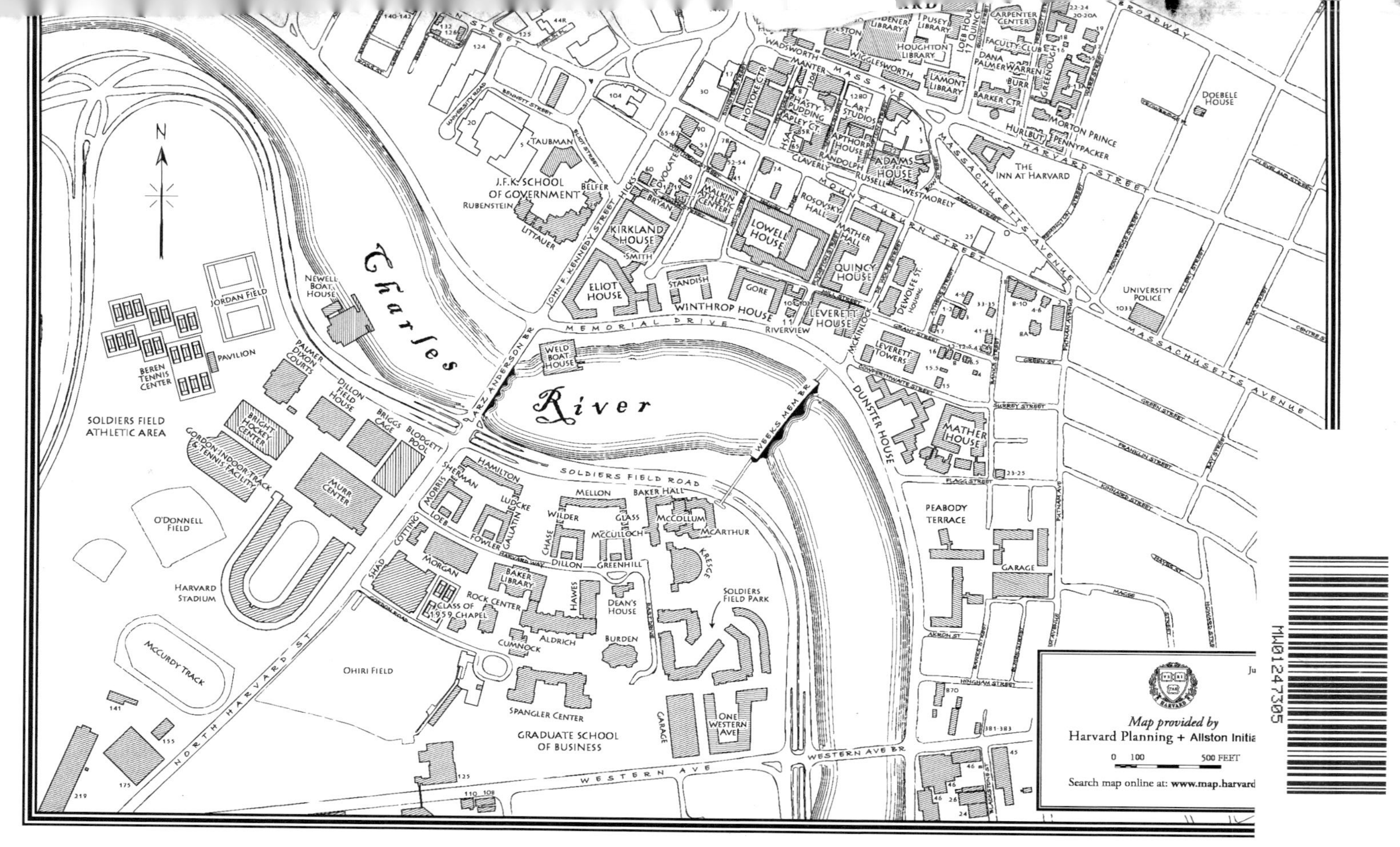

Charles
River
N
SOLDIERS FIELD ATHLETIC AREA
JORDAN FIELD
PAVILION
BEREN TENNIS CENTER
NEWELL BOAT HOUSE
PALMER DIXON COURTS
DILLON FIELD HOUSE
BRIGGS CAGE
BLODGETT POOL
BRIGHT HOCKEY CENTER
GORDON INDOOR TRACK & TENNIS FACILITY
MURR CENTER
O'DONNELL FIELD
HARVARD STADIUM
McCURDY TRACK
NORTH HARVARD ST
OHIRI FIELD
SPANGLER CENTER
GRADUATE SCHOOL OF BUSINESS
WESTERN AVE
WESTERN AVE BR
GARAGE
ONE WESTERN AVE
SOLDIERS FIELD PARK
BURDEN
DEAN'S HOUSE
KRESGE
McARTHUR
McCOLLUM
BAKER HALL
GLASS
MELLON
WILDER
McCULLOCH
CHASE
DILLON
GREENHILL
HAWES
ALDRICH
CUMNOCK
BAKER LIBRARY
ROCK CENTER
CLASS OF 1959 CHAPEL
MORGAN
SHAD
COTTING
LOEB
MORRIS
SHERMAN
HAMILTON
LUDCKE
GALLATIN
FOWLER
SOLDIERS FIELD ROAD
LARZ ANDERSON BR
WELD BOAT HOUSE
WEEKS MEM BR
MEMORIAL DRIVE
RIVERVIEW
J.F.K. SCHOOL OF GOVERNMENT
BELFER
RUBENSTEIN
LITTAUER
TAUBMAN
JOHN F. KENNEDY STREET
KIRKLAND HOUSE
SMITH
ELIOT HOUSE
STANDISH
WINTHROP HOUSE
GORE
LOWELL HOUSE
ROSOVSKY HALL
MATHER HALL
QUINCY HOUSE
LEVERETT HOUSE
McKINLOCK
LEVERETT TOWERS
DEWOLFE ST. HOUSING
DUNSTER HOUSE
MATHER HOUSE
PEABODY TERRACE
GARAGE
MALKIN ATHLETIC CENTER
BRYAN
ADVOCATE
HICKS
CLAVERLY
RANDOLPH
RUSSELL
WESTMORELY
ADAMS HOUSE
APTHORP HOUSE
APLEY CT.
HASTY PUDDING
ART STUDIOS
HOLYOKE CTR
MANTER
WADSWORTH
WIGGLESWORTH
MASS AVE
MOUNT AUBURN STREET
HOUGHTON LIBRARY
LAMONT LIBRARY
PUSEY LIBRARY
LOEB HOUSE
17 QUINCY
CARPENTER CENTER
FACULTY CLUB
DANA PALMER
WARREN
BURR
BARKER CTR
GREENOUGH
HURLBUT
PENNYPACKER
MORTON PRINCE
THE INN AT HARVARD
HARVARD STREET
MASSACHUSETTS AVENUE
UNIVERSITY POLICE
DOEBELE HOUSE
BROADWAY
Map provided by
Harvard Planning + Allston Initia
0 100 500 FEET
Search map online at: www.map.harvard

A gift in honor of

Mary Jo Lees

Pre-Press Supervisor
Flagship Press

Newt

from

The Essay Book Committee

The Harvard College Class of 1957

MJ —
This book would not be so beautiful without you!
Thank you,
Newt

'57

Figure F1 "John Harvard, Founder, 1638"

Bronze statue, 1884, by Daniel Chester French of John Harvard (1607–1638), an English minister who on his deathbed made a bequest of his library and half of his estate to the "schoale or Colledge recently undertaken" by the Massachusetts Bay Colony. The grateful recipients named the college in his honor.

"He gazes for a moment into the future, so dim, so uncertain, yet so full of promise, promise which has been more than realized."

Photo (April 27, 2008) reprinted courtesy of Alain Edouard
Source: https://commons.m.wikimedia.org/wiki/File:John_Harvard_statue.jpg

Figure F2 *University Hall on an early spring evening*

Reprinted courtesy of Harvard University

Harvard College

Class of 1957

RECOLLECTIONS
AND
REFLECTIONS

60th REUNION COMMITTEE

Co-Chairs

James L. Joslin
John A. Simourian
Wallace E. Sisson

Members

Philip J. Andrews
Philip J. Arena
Hugh Blair-Smith
Jeremiah J. Bresnahan
Victor R. Brogna
Geoffrey T. Chalmers
Thomas F. Crowley
Christopher Crowley
Alexander Daley
Peter F. Davis
John E. Dowling
S. Warren Farrell
J. Stephen Friedlaender
Evan M. Geilich
Martin S. Gordon
Harvey J. Grasfield
Peter Gunness
Alan Harwood
Philip C. Haughey
Arthur C. Hodges
Newton E. Hyslop, Jr.
Lawrence A. Joseph
James L. Joslin
Michael D. Kline
Bruce Macdonald
Anthony M. Markella
Neil P. Olken
Carl D. Packer
John Thomas Penniston
Michael S. Robertson
Evan Randolph IV
Edward J. Rolde
George Sadowsky
David W. Scudder
A. Richard Shain
John A. Simourian
Wallace E. Sisson
Charles Steedman
Robert J. Swartz
J. Owen Todd
Thomas H. Townsend
Thomas H. Walsh, Jr.
Ronald M. Weintraub
Philip M. Williams
Thomas B. Worthen

Essay Book Committee

Newton E. Hyslop, Jr.
James L. Joslin
Charles Steedman

Harvard College Class of 1957 logo,
designed in 1982 by architect Peter Chermayeff '57
for the 25th Reunion at the request of Reunion Chairman Wallace Sisson '57

Dedication

In Memory of
Our Classmates
who have passed into the Great Beyond;

to
Our Families
Our lifelong Friends

and
James L. Joslin,
For his 60 years as Secretary of our Class
and Convener of 13 Class Reunions

by
The 60th Reunion Committee
of the Harvard Class of 1957

May 2017

Table of Contents

Chapter Two – HISTORY *(cont'd)*

Chapter Three – EDUCATION *(cont'd)*

Chapter Five – GOVERNMENT *(cont'd)*

Chapter Eight – SCIENCE *(cont'd)*

NATHAN MARSH PUSEY

24th President of Harvard University
Preceded by James Bryant Conant
Succeeded by Derek Curtis Bok

Born in Council Bluffs, Iowa, April 4, 1907
Died in New York City, November 14, 2001, age 94

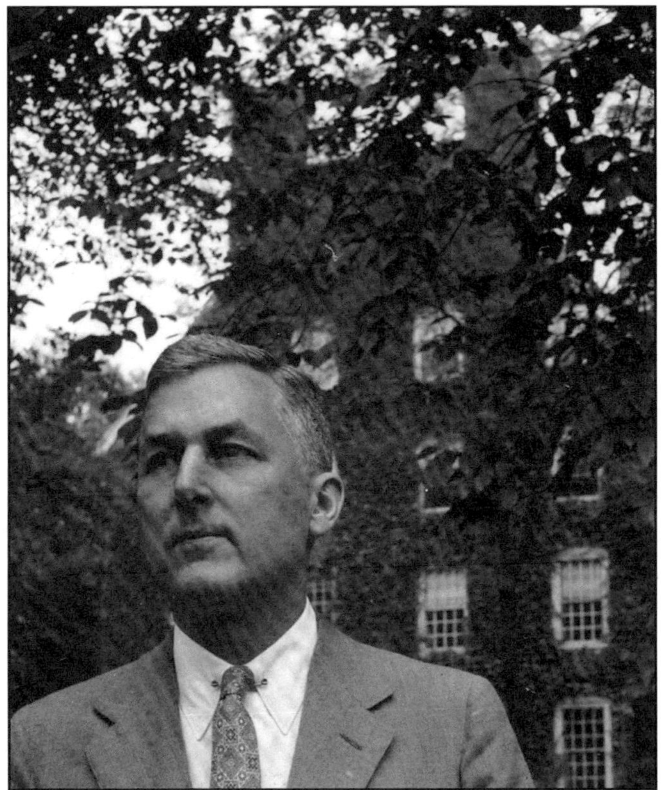

Figure F3 *President Pusey of Lawrence College arrived in Cambridge with the Harvard College Class of 1957 to begin his distinguished tenure as President of Harvard University. In June 1957 he is shown standing in the Yard in front of Massachusetts Hall, which still houses the President's Office as well as students. The College Class of 1957 while all male was geographically, economically, and socially diverse. Over 600 students (53.3%) came from public high schools,*[1] *and although only nine classmates were African-American, many ethnic minorities and immigrant groups were well represented for the times.*

Photograph reprinted courtesy of Harvard University

Nathan Marsh Pusey[2]

President, Harvard University
1953–1971

Arriving in Massachusetts Hall after presiding over Lawrence College, Nathan Marsh Pusey (1907-2001) was the second Harvard president to bring previous presidential experience with him. For Pusey, that meant tangles with the infamous Sen. Joseph R. McCarthy (R-Wis.).

The new president had hardly been confirmed by the Board of Overseers in June when McCarthy took aim at him in a published letter. "When McCarthy's remarks about me are translated, they mean only I didn't vote for him," Pusey wryly replied. The incident made national news, the vast majority of it against McCarthy. In November, after Pusey had spent little more than two months in office, McCarthy attacked Harvard. Pusey parried with the unflappable style that had earlier served so well.

Pusey's firmness of principle reflected his deeply religious nature, and The Memorial Church and the Divinity School benefited from his continuing efforts to enhance Harvard's spiritual fortunes. Nonetheless, Pusey was also one of Harvard's great builders, resuming a scale of new construction to rival that of the Lowell administration.

In 1957, Pusey announced the start of A Program for Harvard College, an $82.5 million effort that actually raised $20 million more and resulted in three additions to the undergraduate House system: Quincy House (1959), Leverett Towers (1960), and Mather House (1970). During the 1960s, the Program for Harvard Medicine raised $58 million. In April 1965, the Harvard endowment exceeded $1 billion for the first time. By 1967, Pusey found himself making the case for yet another major fundraising effort seeking some $160 million for various needs around the University.

Other major structures of the Pusey era include the University Herbaria building (ca. 1954), the Loeb Music Library (1956), Conant Chemistry Laboratory (1959), the Loeb Drama Center (1960), the Center for the Study of World Religions (1960), the Carpenter Center for the Visual Arts (1963), Peabody Terrace (1964), William James Hall (1965), Larsen Hall (1965), the Countway Library of Medicine (1965), and Holyoke Center (1966). A 1960 bequest from art connoisseur Bernard Berenson, Class of 1887, allowed Villa I Tatti (Berenson's great and storied estate near Florence, Italy) to become a special Harvard treasure as the home of the Center for Italian Renaissance Studies. Fundraising for structures such as Pusey Library and the undergraduate Science Center began toward the end of Pusey's term.

Pusey became one of Harvard's most widely traveled chief executives, chalking up official trips to Europe (England, France, Scotland, Switzerland; 1955), East Asia (Hong Kong, India, Japan, Korea, the Philippines, Taiwan; 1961), and Australia and New Zealand (1968).

Toward the end of his term, Pusey found himself once again beset by controversy—this time, from within. Fueled by burning issues such as the Vietnam War, civil rights, economic justice, and the women's movement, student activism escalated to the boiling point by the late 1960s at Harvard and elsewhere. On April 9, 1969, radical students ejected administrators from University Hall and occupied the building to protest Harvard's ROTC program and University expansion into Cambridge and Boston neighborhoods. Early the next morning, many protesters sustained injuries requiring medical treatment after Pusey called in outside police to remove the demonstrators. In response, other students voted to strike and boycott classes. The University almost closed early. The gateway had just opened onto the greatest period of sustained upheaval in Harvard history.

Pusey defended his actions until the end of his long life, but the events of April 1969 undoubtedly shortened his presidency. In February 1970, he made a surprise announcement: he was retiring two years early. Pusey left Harvard in June 1971 to become the second president of New York's Andrew W. Mellon Foundation

* * *

Nathan Marsh Pusey[3]

April 4, 1907 – November 14, 2001

In his habits of character and his presidential style, Nathan Pusey '28, Ph.D '37, LL.D '72, was a figure of transition. The last of a breed in some respects, he did more than perhaps any other man to usher the American research university into the modern age. The last Harvard president to have graduated from the College, he was the first to come from west of New York State. A deeply religious man and a staunch friend of Memorial Church, he was the last Harvard president to read the lesson at services every Sunday. And he was the prototype of today's college presidents, who must feel equally at ease in the world of academe and that of large-scale fundraising.

Still, transitions can be exciting times, requiring a good measure of faith and the courage of one's ideals. Nathan Pusey had both to spare. "This was," he said, "the best time to be a president, almost, in modern history."

A classics scholar with a particular passion for Athenian law, he was only 46 when the Harvard Corporation tapped him to succeed James Bryant Conant as the University's twenty-fourth president, in June 1953. He came to Harvard from Lawrence College, where he had been president for nine very constructive years.

A fellow historian and Midwesterner, Franklin L. Ford, Ph.D. '50, who served as dean of the Faculty of Arts and Sciences under Pusey, thought his friend's experiences in Wisconsin were formative: "At Lawrence he discovered that the person in charge had to be alert to an institution's every need, because the place was depending on him. When he got here, he felt the same way."

Visiting the Yard's laboratories and libraries, offices, and athletic facilities during that first summer, Pusey was appalled by the degree of overcrowding and decrepitude in evidence. He concluded that, without a massive infusion of dollars, Harvard risked failing to meet the opportunities and challenges of a postwar period marked by expansion in nearly every aspect of American society.

His solution was The Program for Harvard College, the most ambitious and successful fundraising effort in the history of higher education to that point. The campaign raised about $100 million from 28,000 donors. As John T. Bethell writes in *Harvard Observed*, "For all of private education, it redefined the art of the possible."

In all, during Pusey's phenomenally progressive tenure as president, Harvard's endowment and budget quadrupled.

The construction of more than 30 buildings—including Mather House, the Science Center, the Countway Library of Medicine, Holyoke Center, Gund Hall, the Loeb Drama Center, and the Carpenter Center for the Visual Arts—almost doubled its floor space. The population of teachers and administrators grew from 3,000 to 8,500.

The student body was transformed as well, with the inception in the 1960s of a "need-blind" admissions policy, which energized the Yard with young people from all sorts of backgrounds. And Pusey bravely started negotiations aimed at a merger between Harvard and Radcliffe, breaking the ice in 1970 with an "experiment" in coresidential living (decried by many alumni at the time). In all these initiatives he was aided by a remarkable cadre of deans, for he worked hard at his appointments and was exceptionally good at finding the right person for a job.

Pusey's dynamism in ensuring a proper physical environment for learning and research was matched by his passion for defending Harvard's intellectual climate against any who dared to threaten civil discourse and academic freedom. He was an early and outspoken adversary of Senator Joseph McCarthy; when McCarthy pressed for dismissal of four faculty members he accused of being Communist sympathizers, Pusey declared:

> *Americanism does not mean enforced and circumscribed belief . . . . Our job is to educate free, independent, and vigorous minds capable of analyzing events, of exercising judgment, of distinguishing facts from propaganda, and truth from half-truths and lies . . . .*

His adamance, which made him a liberal hero in the 1950s, cast him in a less popular light a decade later, in April 1969, when he called in the Cambridge police and state troopers to evict and arrest students who had taken over University Hall to protest the University's perceived role in the military-industrial complex. By his impassive dealings with the protesters, whose behavior he felt was an affront to the civil discourse integral to the culture of a university, Pusey made himself a natural target for criticism. He announced his retirement the following year, but he claimed to have no regrets over his handling of the protest, maintaining that his choice had been a simple one.

In the three decades following his departure from Harvard, Pusey remained true to his ideals. He served for four years as head of the Andrew F. Mellon Foundation, in New York, wrote a book about American higher education, and chaired the Fund for Theological Education.

Visitors to Harvard Yard will find his name emblazoned in the Nathan Marsh and Anne Woodward Pusey Room in Memorial Church and the Nathan Marsh Pusey Library—fitting tributes to a man who feared a *"world without spirit"* above all else, and who *cherished the University as "one of the noblest creations of the mind of man."*

—Deborah Smullyan '72

Endnotes

[1] Editorial: "To Consider and Act", *Harvard Crimson*, November 1, 1957

[2] Reprinted with permission from Harvard University (https://www.harvard.edu/about-harvard/harvard-glance/history-pr)

[3] Reprinted with permission from *Harvard Magazine* (http://harvardmagazine.com/2002/01/nathan-marsh-pusey.html)

Harvard College

Class of 1957

RECOLLECTIONS
AND
REFLECTIONS

A Book of Essays for the 60th Reunion

CAMBRIDGE

Printed for the Class

Harvard Alumni Association
Cambridge, Massachusetts

First printing, May 2017 – 5 copies
Second printing, February 2018 – 1500 copies

ISBN 978-0-9998320-0-4

Printed by

Flagship Press

North Andover • MA • USA

Foreword

A Lost Art

In this era of "*selfies*", three-way conversations with one's grandchild glancing at the "*smart*" phone in his/her lap, and "*messaging*" amongst them/ourselves in 140 characters or less, the essay seems to have become an outdated literary form. In a growing number of *progressive* primary schools cursive handwriting is no longer taught, so some of the current in-school generation cannot read hand written notes from their grandparents. Students communicate with one another, and unknown others, through online "*chat rooms*" controlled by Watson-like artificial intelligence-driven moderators who most participants think are real humans.

Fortunately, as *Gen Ed AHF* was for the Harvard and Radcliffe College Classes of 1957, its equivalent, *Expository Writing Skills*, remains for all first-year students a required full-year discipline. For our class, painful though it might have been for most, whatever creative writing talents were developed in the course of weekly submissions of one thousand word papers were lasting and possibly distinguishing in later life. Seen from our generation's viewpoint, the art of the essay seems to have vanished as one among many of unintended consequences from advances in an information technology which allows us to "keep us in touch" instantaneously and also interrupt our concentration.

So when your editors of this volume sent out a challenge to all classmates—a call to submit essays on a topic of each writer's choice, with final drafts subject only to a few format restrictions—the results proved to be highly gratifying and, ironically, benefitted from the new technology. Interspersed with invited essays, such as the one on the Olympics by Tenley Albright, representing Radcliffe, you will find the collected essays informative, insightful, compelling and often entertaining. Editors Newt Hyslop and Charley Steedman worked with the more than five-score authors to conform matters of syntax and encourage clarity of expression. Newt had served in a similar context for the 55th Reunion of his Harvard Medical School class, and Charley with his background at *The Crimson* retained his mastery in the art of placing the comma and bringing out the best from our stable of authors. Many thanks to both for their extraordinary efforts on our behalf.

In addition to the comments and impressions by Newt and Charley immediately next, as part of the front matter we have placed some preliminary observations by classmate John Dowling, currently Professor of Neuroscience at Harvard, and a Forbes.com article by journalist classmate Bob Lenzner. These pieces set the appropriate tone for the other submissions herein. Bob's article has been circulated widely online in university settings throughout the country. Further, we have reproduced the 2012 *New York Times* article on the principled stand against segregation taken by the Harvard basketball team of 1956–57.

In the *Epilogue* the reader will find an essay written 40 years ago at my invitation by Dr. John Finley for our *20th Anniversary Report* as one of the supplemental articles to that volume. It is included not only because of its timeless commentary, and his observations about our era in Cambridge, but also as an example of the essay as a literary form.

Although our Editors might insist on a few added paragraph breaks in the good Doctor's text, the economy and efficiency of Professor Finley's usage shines through. His conclusion then that

> "*. . . the wonder is not that Harvard changes but that it stays so constant. It is less to be judged relatively to its own past than to other more changing institutions . . .*"

helps as a framework to understand and perhaps accept the inevitability of some of the internal turmoil the University seems to be experiencing presently as it continues to shape its destiny.

James L. Joslin, *Secretary*
Harvard College Class of 1957

Editors' Note

This *Essay Book* was conceived as means of recording elements of the collective wisdom gained by the Harvard College Class of 1957 over the sixty years since our graduation, and also to provide an opportunity for us to offer a perspective on our times.

Life was breathed into this idea in the Fall of 2016 when the Class of 1957 60th Reunion Committee created the *Essay Book Committee* to pursue the possibility of compiling and publishing in a rather short time frame a supplement to the Class Report to consist of essays on a range of topics. This book is the product of two processes: an *Invited Call* to 70 classmates and an *Open Call* issued to everyone in the Class of 1957 possessing a postal and/or e-mail address in the Harvard Alumni Association database.[1]

The Process

To assure a broad range of individual experiences, the *Essay Book Committee* first reviewed all 759 entries, many without essays, as published in the 55th Reunion Class of 1957 Report. Key points were extracted from submitted essays, their content categorized and possible topics and persons identified for essay assignments. In addition, the Class of 1957 HAA Occupational Database of August 2016 was searched to discover those with interesting occupations who had not submitted an essay for the 55th Report. Based on this analysis the Committee next generated a list of 213 living classmates considered to represent many areas of life experience characterizing our Class, and who were considered likely to be willing to write an essay. From this group 70 individuals were selected to be *Invited Essayists*, who were then contacted by personal e-mail and follow-up telephone calls, and were given suggested topic areas for their essays. Although some required gentle persuasion to rise to the challenge, the final acceptance rate of *78%* and the quality of their essays testify to the commitment by the *Invited Essayists* to the theme of *Recollections and Reflections*.

The idea of adding an *Open Call* arose from the 60th Reunion Committee and received its unanimous approval at the full committee meeting in October 2016. In mid-December when invitations to those selected for the *Invited Call* went out by e-mail, a simultaneous *Open*

Call was issued to *all* classmates. They received notification in postal mail first by a letter of invitation, followed by three reminder postcards sent at seven-day intervals.

Each postal mailing was accompanied by an e-mail "blast"[2] which contained copies of the *Open Call* letter of invitation, *Instructions for Authors, FAQs*, a *sample Essay*, and the obligatory optional HAA form for donations towards publication and distribution costs. For the Internet-inclined, the e-mails and postcards noted that all of these materials were continuously accessible on the HAA Class of 1957 web page.

The reminder postcards, hard to overlook at 5½ x 8½ inches and of high-quality stock suitable for framing, carried on one side the full-color reproduction of Solomon Koninck's "*Old Scholar*" (shown on the reverse of the dust jacket of this volume), which was surmounted by the message, "HOW ARE YOU PROGRESSING WITH YOUR ESSAY?" The reverse side carried the mailing addresses, essay instructions, notice of the February 7 deadline, and repeated the following message from the e-mail "blast":

> "Greetings from the Harvard College Class of 1957 Reunion Committee.
>
> Here's another chance to make your mark in Harvard print!
>
> *Put your thinking cap on and write the best essay you ever wrote!*
>
> *You* and our classmates have been deeply involved in all aspects of the immense changes in our world since we entered it. It is time to look back and record our perspective for others.
>
> The goal of the Essay Book is to capture representative views of our classmates on topics from the arts, humanities, sciences, and society, with emphasis on our personal experiences and insights.
>
> The intent is to capture in words and images formative experiences from our professional or vocational lives likely to be of interest to classmates, our families and later generations.
>
> Your entry may best inform future readers by describing an event or period in your life of unusual interest, personal challenge, danger, excitement, or humor, which for you was motivational or influential, or was a life lesson learned from the experience."

Did the notifications alert the class? A survey of 30 attendees at the January 25, 2017 Reunion Committee meeting reassuringly showed that 100% had received both e-mail and postal mailings. Moreover, the Open Call brought forth 77 responses, including from many who had also been on the initial list of 213 considered for selection as *Invited Essayists*.

The Editorial Guidelines for all authors were simple.

> *"Submissions advancing unilateral religious or political views and content outside of legal publishing guidelines (e.g., copyright, fair use, libel, slander, and defamation) are unacceptable.*
>
> *The Committee reserves the right to edit submissions."*[3]

Invited Essayists were allowed up to 4,000 words and asked to provide one or more photographs, especially from their earlier years, which informed the essay. In order to control book size under conditions of an unknown number of responders, *Open Call Essayists* were limited to 2,000 words or its equivalent space. However, when during editorial review it was found that topics addressed in an *Open Call Essay* enhanced the breadth or depth of coverage by *Invited Essays*, *Open Call Essayists* were encouraged to expand and illustrate their essays. All Essayists were requested to submit biographical sketches which also underwent editorial review for consistency of style but not confirmation of statements.

The Result

A total of 138 essays were received and reviewed by the Essay Book Committee. During the editorial phase, Committee members were in regular contact with authors and exchanged drafts until reaching the mutually acceptable final version. Before submission to the publisher, the essays were distributed by content into several broad categories without reference as to whether their authors came from the Invited or Open calls.

The Essay Book opens with President Nathan Marsh Pusey, who began his presidency with us in 1953. It closes with President Drew Gilpin Faust, whose presidency epitomizes the remarkable social changes which characterize our epoch—the sixty years since our graduation in 1957.

Acknowledgements

The *Essay Book Committee* is indebted to *Diane MacDonald,* Senior Associate Director of the Class Report Office of the Harvard Alumni Association, for her encouragement and support of this project from its nascent phase to its completion, and to *Daniel McCarron* of Flagship Press for his enthusiasm, seasoned advice, design skill, adaptability and insistence on production quality, who was ably supported by his excellent colleagues *Mary Jo "M.J." Lees* and *Tony Monteiro. Susan Frodigh* of TFC Financial gave substantial technical support and cheerfully swept up loose ends. *Martin S. "Marty" Gordon '57* reverse-engineered the HAA Home Page server to accept our *Essay Book User Help* pages and, importantly, orchestrated the multiple e-mail "blasts", which process inadvertently uncovered the awkward fact that the HAA e-mail address list labeled as "*Harvard 1957*" included Radcliffe '57![4]

We gratefully acknowledge the support and forbearance of our families from November 2016 through April 2017 when the organizational and editing processes temporarily redefined the nature of our retirement and social lives. But this interval of outreach and intense interchange with classmates, many of them unknown to us in our college years, enriched our own lives and confirmed for us the special nature of our class, as it always did for our predecessor in outreach, *J. Louis Newell '57*.

This project would not have gone forward without the initiative and continuing involvement of *Jim Joslin '57* and the unwavering support of his Co-Chairmen of the 60th Reunion, *John Simourian '57* and *Wally Sisson '57*, who with the approval of the Reunion Committee committed the resources of the Class Treasury to underwrite any losses incurred in printing and distributing the book to every classmate, regardless of donor status.

Most importantly, we wish to thank the 135 members of the Harvard Class of 1957 who responded to the invited and open calls for Essays and then worked patiently with the Essay Book Committee in refining their essays to create this unique book of life experiences recounted and reexamined.

Finally, the quality of this book owes its existence to the excellence of the essays submitted by their authors, whose lives plumbed nearly every depth of human emotions during our times, and who wrote movingly about their experiences.

Respectfully submitted,
Newton E. Hyslop, Jr.

For the *Essay Book Committee:*
Newton E. Hyslop, Jr., *Editor*
James L. Joslin, *Co-Editor*
Charles Steedman, *Co-Editor*

Figure F5 *"Scholar at his Writing Table" [a.k.a. "Scholar at the Lectern"] 1641*
Rembrandt van Rijn (1606–1669)
Royal Castle, Warsaw

Endnotes

1 The HAA Class of 1957 database (*updated August 2016*) available to us had been purged of contact information for more than 100 classmates who had opted-out of receiving Harvard-related mailings. Consequently, to reach Invited Essayists who had elected the "*mailings opt-out*" category, we resorted to contact information published in the 55th Reunion Class Report. Unfortunately for us and them, the other classmates with "mailings opt-out" attached to their names were not sent any Open Call e-mails or postal mailings, since as per their instructions to HAA, their contact information was absent from the database.

2 Not all classmates with postal addresses listed in the HAA database had e-mail addresses. Consequently they received only the permissible version.

3 The statement "*. . . reserves the right to edit submissions . . .*" drew only one written objection, and even that one had potential for expansion into an essay of its own. However, it went unrealized.

4 In November 2016 the *Essay Committee* chose Olympic Gold Medal Winner *Tenley Albright* to represent Radcliffe '57 in this otherwise all-Harvard College Essay Book. At the recommendation of the Harvard '57 Reunion Committee, Radcliffe '57 was left to its own devices, consistent with longstanding policies related to separate Class Reports and Reunion activities except for a joint Memorial Service. However, when the December "e-mail blast" announcing the *Open Call for papers* unexpectedly encompassed Radcliffe '57, it created a period of confusion among Radcliffe recipients and raised the possibility of joint contributions to the *Essay Book*. As a result, in the interval before its resolution by the efforts of Radcliffe '57 Class President Lucia Stein Hatch, Diane MacDonald of HAA and the *Essay Book Committee,* a few R'57 essays were in preparation; those completed are incorporated in the Radcliffe '57 60th Reunion Report.

HOW ARE YOU PROGRESSING WITH YOUR ESSAY?

AN OLD SCHOLAR
Salomon Koninck (1609–1656)
The State Hermitage Museum, St. Petersburg

Figure F4 *Reminder postcard mailed thrice to entire Class of 1957* excellent colleagues *Mary Jo "M.J." Lees* and *Tony Monteiro*. *Susan Frodigh* of TFC Financial gave substantial technical support and cheerfully swept up loose ends. *Martin S. "Marty" Gordon '57* reverse-engineered the HAA Home Page server to accept our *Essay Book User Help* pages and, importantly, orchestrated the multiple e-mail "blasts", which process inadvertently uncovered the awkward fact that the HAA e-mail address list labeled as "*Harvard 1957*" included Radcliffe '57![4]

We gratefully acknowledge the support and forbearance of our families from November 2016 through April 2017 when the organizational and editing processes temporarily redefined the nature of our retirement and social lives. But this interval of outreach and intense interchange with classmates, many of them unknown to us in our college years, enriched our own lives and confirmed for us the special nature of our class, as it always did for our predecessor in outreach, *J. Louis Newell '57*.

This project would not have gone forward without the initiative and continuing involvement of *Jim Joslin '57* and the unwavering support of his Co-Chairmen of the 60th Reunion, *John Simourian '57* and *Wally Sisson '57*, who with the approval of the Reunion Committee committed the resources of the Class Treasury to underwrite any losses incurred in printing and distributing the book to every classmate, regardless of donor status.

Most importantly, we wish to thank the 135 members of the Harvard Class of 1957 who responded to the invited and open calls for Essays and then worked patiently with the Essay Book Committee in refining their essays to create this unique book of life experiences recounted and reexamined.

Finally, the quality of this book owes its existence to the excellence of the essays submitted by their authors, whose lives plumbed nearly every depth of human emotions during our times, and who wrote movingly about their experiences.

Respectfully submitted,
Newton E. Hyslop, Jr.

For the *Essay Book Committee:*
Newton E. Hyslop, Jr., *Editor*
James L. Joslin, *Co-Editor*
Charles Steedman, *Co-Editor*

The Editorial Guidelines for all authors were simple.

> "*Submissions advancing unilateral religious or political views and content outside of legal publishing guidelines (e.g., copyright, fair use, libel, slander, and defamation) are unacceptable.*
>
> *The Committee reserves the right to edit submissions.*"[3]

Invited Essayists were allowed up to 4,000 words and asked to provide one or more photographs, especially from their earlier years, which informed the essay. In order to control book size under conditions of an unknown number of responders, *Open Call Essayists* were limited to 2,000 words or its equivalent space. However, when during editorial review it was found that topics addressed in an *Open Call Essay* enhanced the breadth or depth of coverage by *Invited Essays*, *Open Call Essayists* were encouraged to expand and illustrate their essays. All Essayists were requested to submit biographical sketches which also underwent editorial review for consistency of style but not confirmation of statements.

The Result

A total of 138 essays were received and reviewed by the Essay Book Committee. During the editorial phase, Committee members were in regular contact with authors and exchanged drafts until reaching the mutually acceptable final version. Before submission to the publisher, the essays were distributed by content into several broad categories without reference as to whether their authors came from the Invited or Open calls.

The Essay Book opens with President Nathan Marsh Pusey, who began his presidency with us in 1953. It closes with President Drew Gilpin Faust, whose presidency epitomizes the remarkable social changes which characterize our epoch—the sixty years since our graduation in 1957.

Acknowledgements

The *Essay Book Committee* is indebted to *Diane MacDonald,* Senior Associate Director of the Class Report Office of the Harvard Alumni Association, for her encouragement and support of this project from its nascent phase to its completion, and to *Daniel McCarron* of Flagship Press for his enthusiasm, seasoned advice, design skill, adaptability and insistence on production quality, who was ably supported by his

A Sampling

When the class of 1957 graduated, many of us scattered. Some went into military service; others went to law or medical school. Still others went far afield. If you had picked up *Life* magazine at graduation, you would have read the admonition of our elders, toughened by the Great Depression and World War II. They greatly outnumbered our generation but things would change with the arrival of the Baby Boomers, the first of whom were age 11 when we graduated. The admonition from the editors of *Life* was something like this: "Arise, Class of 1957, you have nothing to lose but your apathy."

To see how badly they misjudged our quietness, our apparent adherence to convention, our willingness to abide by our elders' rules, read the essays in this book. It turns out we were just laying low, waiting to break out and do some amazing things. There was no apathy in the Harvard Class of 1957.

Read into the book to find out how Rod Wolfe reacted when he was suddenly wakened by a collision alarm as his nuclear submarine was gliding under the polar ice pack headed for the North Pole. See what happened to Larry Huntington as he got close to the summit of Mt. Everest on his second attempt. Who was the classmate who played a key role in the creation of the beautiful Zakim Bridge over the Charles River? Which classmate was chief counsel of the Senate's Church Committee investigating America's intelligence agencies in 1975? Who spent more than four months, on two occasions, living and working on frozen sea ice at latitudes between 84 and 85 degrees north?

You will be entertained reading how Peter Davis persuaded Jackie Kennedy Onassis to host a dinner for Eliot House master John Finley. Bernie Gwertzman talks about his travels with Henry Kissinger. Jock McLane, having spent more than 60 years immersed in India, provides revealing insights into the country's politics and culture. Bob Freeman knows what ails our country's symphony orchestras. Nick Platt wades into a mob wearing a bullet-proof vest as ambassador to the Philippines. David Becker worries about legal education, concerned that law students today are not learning the essential problem-solving skills and many cannot write clearly and effectively.

Bob Neer recounts vast changes in medical practice and education, not all for the better. He explains why a formative part of his training—spending many weeks on a hospital medical ward, helping to care for hospitalized patients and querying them about their illnesses—is no longer possible. Bob Lenzner finds that Wall Street is more concentrated today than at any time in US history and concludes that its institutions are too big to manage, too big to regulate, and too opaque for the press, public, and even their regulators to comprehend. Victor McElheny walks us through the fascinating evolutions in science that have occurred since we graduated. John Talbott, home from service in Vietnam in 1968, organizes unknown volunteers, neighbors and friends as well as celebrities from music, art and science in New York City to publicly read the names of those who died in Vietnam.

What was it like to be bombed in Berlin, take refuge in a country town, flee on foot as the Soviet Army approached and then return to the destroyed town where one bartered for scraps of food? Gottfried Brieger tells us. Five times on Frye Island in Sebago Lake, ME, Dick Norris hosts US Navy destroyer crews—up to 100 from each ship, some with wives and children—as each ship nears launch at the Bath Iron Works. The outings start with a police-car siren escort from the ferry landing to the ball field, inspired by our escort to the Boston Pops at our 25th Reunion. Don't miss Murray Levin's account of going from Mattapan to Harvard Square for the first time in his life the day he registered as a freshman, naïvely wondering why one of his Boston Latin School acquaintances was going to live in the Yard.

Imagine young Emile Chi feeling unwittingly and partially responsible for exposing his US-educated father as a highly placed double agent during the war between the Chinese Communists and the Nationalists. Ride the Silk Road with William Bahary as he grows up in Iran and learns firsthand about the opium trade. Accompany newly minted CDC officer Jim Gale on donkeyback to a remote mountain village in Bolivia to investigate a deadly plague outbreak that wiped out the village.

Feel the struggle and pride of the uprooted immigrant families and their descendents in John Simourian's synopsis of the Armenian Genocide; in the adaptations required of William Gray's immigrant father, at 17 asked to change his surname in order to be an acceptable field representative for a high-end clothing company; and in Nino Yannoni's account of growing up Italian in Irish Jamaica Plain. Al Williams tells how he coped with racial segregation growing up in Delaware, and Charles Martin credits his grandmother and mother for uprooting his family from segregation to move north for his educational opportunity.

This is just a small sampling of the treasures your classmates have written. We think you will enjoy them.

Charles Steedman, *Co-Editor*
The Essay Book Committee

Prologues

What Is So Special about the Harvard Class of 1957?

John E. Dowling

What is so special about the Class of 1957? One thing that has always impressed me is the number of our classmates who have earned a PhD degree and have gone on to careers in teaching and research in colleges and universities throughout this country and abroad. In addition, several of our classmates have held most impressive positions as President, Dean, or Provost at various academic institutions. To substantiate some of this, I looked back at our 25th Anniversary Report of 1982. It notes that 14% of our class was involved in education as compared to 10% of Princeton graduates and only 9% of Yale graduate of 1957. Also of interest is that 10% of our class went into law and 19% into medicine. And, of course, many of those in medicine especially, taught as well as carried out research.

A count of those in 1982 who had PhD degrees and held teaching and research professorships in various colleges and universities was 75 and this is clearly an underestimate in that not everyone in the class responded for the report or listed an occupation or position. Virtually all fields were included and were distributed as follows: natural science (18) and math (7), humanities (34) and social science (16). Also several of us stayed at Harvard (at least for a number of years) and not only made substantial contributions to their respective fields, but also to the college and university.

In alphabetical order:

Glen Bowersock: Chairman, Department of Classics, 1972–77; Associate Dean for Undergraduate Education, 1977–80; Acting Senior Fellow of the Society of Fellows, 1979–80. In 1980, Glen moved to the Institute for Advanced Study in Princeton.

John Dowling: Chairman, Department of Biology, 1975–78; Associate Dean for Natural Sciences, 1980–84; Master, Leverett House, 1981–98; Head tutor, Neurobiology Concentration, 2007–12.

Joseph Fletcher: Professor of East Asian Languages and Civilizations. An avid student of languages, but trained especially in Chinese and China's history, Joe specialized in Ch'ing history and the Muslim rebellions of the 18th and 19th centuries. Joe died in 1984.

Edward "Ned" Keenan: Instructor, Lecturer and Professor of History, 1965–2008; Master, North House, 1970–75; Director, Russian Research Center, 1976–77; Dean, Graduate School of Arts and Sciences, 1978–84; Director, Center for Middle Eastern Studies, 1981–94; Director, Dumbarton Oaks (Washington, DC), 1998–2008. Ned died in 2016.

David Mumford: Assistant, Associate and full Professor of Mathematics, 1962–1977; Winner of Fields Medal, 1974 (math's equivalent of the Nobel Prize). David retired and moved to Brown University in 1996.

In addition to those who joined the teaching and research ranks at Harvard, Fred Jewett was (beginning in 1960) Assistant Dean of Freshmen, then Assistant Director of Admissions, Director of Scholarships, and in 1972, Dean of Admissions and Financial Aid. In 1996 Fred became Dean of the College. At one time (1980), four of us held Dean positions in the college; Ned as Dean of Graduate School of Arts and Sciences, Fred as Dean of Admissions and Financial Aid, Glen as

Associate Dean for Undergraduate Education and John as Associate Dean for Natural Sciences.

Two other classmates who held prestigious positions in academic institutions include Jim Freedman (law) who was President of the University of Iowa (1982–87), later Dartmouth College (1987–1998) and finally President of the American Academy of Arts and Sciences beginning in 1998. Jim died in 2006.

Ken Shine (medicine) was Dean and Provost at UCLA School of Medicine (1986–92), President of the Institute of Medicine (now the National Academy of Medicine) (1992–2002) and Executive Vice President for Health Affairs of the University of Texas System for 12 years beginning in 2003.

This brief overview of the accomplishments of our classmates in the area of "higher" education mainly at Harvard does not do justice to the many educators in our class, never mind all of the other areas in which our classmates have chosen to work. In reading earlier class reports, I was struck by all of the accomplishments made by our class. We have done Harvard proud, and I look forward to seeing many of you at our 60th in May.

P1.1 *Widener Library; donated by Eleanor Elkins Widener in memory of her son, Harry Elkins Widener, Class of 1907, who perished in the Atlantic Ocean on the foundering RMS* Titanic *on April 15, 1912.*

Reprinted courtesy of Harvard University

Why There Were No Billionaires in the Harvard Class of 1957

Robert Lenzner
June 12, 2012
Forbes Magazine

We were born during the Great Depression and lived through the shortages and sacrifices of World War II. When we entered Harvard in the fall of 1953, Eisenhower was President and the Dow Jones industrial average had just retraced its 1929–1932 loss; and the index of the 30 major US companies like AT&T, GM and IBM grew by almost 90% before we graduated in 1957. We were blessed by entering our adult years at the very dawn of an industrial boom in America that drove stock prices higher and created many job opportunities.

Many of us served in the military before going to graduate school, which added a layer of national service and maturity to our career choices. Clearly, a huge portion of the class went back to school for advanced degrees—MD, LLB, MBA, PhD—since the most popular professions in our class was to be some area of academia or medicine—in many cases combining both, including the growing profession of psychiatry. Edward J. Rolde, who I don't know, earned five degrees in all from Harvard: BA in Economics, MD, an SM and ScD in public health, as well as a CSS in administration, and spent 30 years on the Harvard Medical School and School of Public Health faculties. An impressive lot of learning.

But the most stunning difference with today is that only 9% of us went into finance, less than went into business administration. We had no Masters of the Universe and the very idea of becoming a billionaire was unknown to us.

We were a serious lot—unlike the *Mad Men* of the HBO series, and hugely monogamous; 72% of those still married are together with their first wives. No alimony and child support draining their finances. In fact, 84% of the 1957 graduates who answered the survey in the Red Book, counted themselves as "satisfied with their overall financial situation, with satisfaction going up to 94% for the 11% who have not retired." (I am one of them, and plan never to retire unless health forces me to.)

On explanation for this sense of comfort is that many of our class—a third of the respondents—reached "a higher level" of professional achievement than they expected." And only 19% or one in five said they would "make major changes in life and work decisions." My friend, John Ratte, an historian of note who taught at Amherst College, and later became head of Loomis Chaffee School for two decades, quotes the late Peter Gomes as warning us five years ago, "Beware of the twin thieves of envy and regret; they seek to rob us of our past and our future."

Truthfully, I was amazed that very nearly one of four of us was of the Jewish faith, even though more than half considered themselves more secular Jew than religious Jew. I was moved in Memorial Church by a phrase in Psalm 121 that reads, "He who keeps Israel will neither slumber nor sleep" and the last verse of "America the Beautiful", which encourages a life of virtue over monetary gain. Good to have had such a spiritual experience. I found the presentations of two Jewish classmates, Roger Graef and Peter Davis, known for their sensitive documentary films as well as socially conscious writings, a model for the expression of a set of ideals that take precedence over fortune.

I was one of the 40% of my class at Phillips Exeter Academy who gained entry to Harvard (St. Paul's School in Concord, NH also sent 40% of their 1953 graduates). I like to think the large number of Jews contributed in part to our class preference for serious careers, and participation now in retirement for civic duties. I think of Michael Cooper, chief of the litigation department at Sullivan & Cromwell, serving as head of the Bar Association.

Non-Jews like Dr. James Gilligan, a professor at NYU, serves as a consultant on issues of violence prevention at the World Health Organization and writes reports for Kofi Annan on violence against children. Charles Brower, a Judge on the Iran-U Claims Tribunal, has been involved in high stakes international arbitration and named one of the world's top ten arbitrators. So much for retirement.

Oh, yes. We were more liberal Republican in 1957, reflecting that era—but now we are more liberal Democrat, with 31% of us choosing Bill Clinton over 30% for Ronald Regan as our favorite president. Was it pure coincidence the stock market rallied substantially during those two presidencies, creating a sense of renewed vitality?

What sticks with me is that though no great famous fortunes were made, or corporate/financial empires built, 85% of those willing to opine said they were financially satisfied with the means their lives had created. We felt fortunate to be at Harvard, and mostly did not put money at the peak priority of our personal goals. Or, many of us had a far less atavistic, insatiable drive to make money over the goals in our hearts and souls. In those years to be a highly successful heart surgeon or corporate lawyer or government bureaucrat or humanities professor carried sufficient financial rewards. This is an enormously important lesson to teach our kids and grandchildren.

P2.1 *The 1725 clock on Massachusetts Hall faces First Parish Church. The clock was recreated by the Electric Time Company of Medfield, MA, architect Dr. Judith Selwyn II, Skylight Studios, Inc., Woburn, MA*

Reprinted courtesy of Harvard University

In 1956, a Racial Law Repelled Harvard's Team

By **BILL PENNINGTON**
New York Times
MARCH 14, 2012

P3.1 *Bob Bowman* (third from left in top row) *graduated before the all-white 1956–57 club decided not to travel to New Orleans.*

Photo source: Harvard Athletic Communications

It has been a long time since anyone in the nation noticed or cared where the Harvard men's basketball team was playing. But Thursday, the Crimson will be among the competitors in the N.C.A.A. tournament for the first time in 66 years. Their dream is to get to the Final Four in New Orleans.

Many Harvard basketball seasons ago, another trip to New Orleans was also something of a dream to the players. In 1956, the team had agreed to play in a New Orleans winter holiday tournament.

"It was pretty exciting," Dick Hurley, a guard on the 1956 team, said. "For us back then, heading south meant Philadelphia."

But the trip to New Orleans never happened, the games disappearing from the official Harvard schedule like an immaterial footnote erased from the bottom of a term paper. The story of the gaping hole in the Harvard basketball schedule from Dec. 21, 1956, to Jan. 8, 1957—big news at the time—has remained almost entirely untold in the intervening years.

"I've told the story from time to time," said Lewis Lowenfels, another guard on the team. "Nobody has ever known what I was talking about."

In mid-July 1956, after Harvard had been invited to the December tournament in New Orleans, the Louisiana legislature—reacting to various federal mandates to integrate its schools and other institutions—voted to bar interracial athletic contests, including activities like dancing and pastimes like cards, dice and checkers. The legislation also ordered segregated seating at athletic events.

The anti-mixing statute, as it came to be known, was one piece of segregationist legislation enacted by several Southern states in the mid-1950s, and the Louisiana sports provision was hardly the most prominent. Still, as classes reconvened at Harvard in September, civil rights debates mushroomed on campus. And in time, it came to the attention of the athletic department that the few African-American athletes on its rosters might be prohibited from playing in some Southern states.

The 1956–57 Harvard basketball team that was planning to travel to New Orleans was all-white. But the center on the team for the previous three years, Bob Bowman, was black.

In October 1956, four months after Bowman graduated from Harvard, the basketball team gathered and was told about Louisiana's new law.

"It was presented to us," said Philip Haughey, a senior on the team. "And our reaction was, 'So Bob wouldn't have been able to come?' There was no debate after that. We weren't going. Yes, we were now an all-white team, but if that was their attitude, then no one was going."

"I remember it was a big deal, as it should have been," Lowenfels said. "It called attention to something that never should have been."

Bowman, 77, now retired in California after 40 years as an orthopedic surgeon, was in medical school when the team decided to forgo its New Orleans trip.

"You have to remember the tenor of those times in America and that these were 19- and 20-year-old college student-athletes," Bowman said. "In that context, it becomes more and more ethically courageous. They should be very proud, and I am very proud, that they took a stance that said, 'If African-Americans can't play, then none of us will play.' "

Harvard, whose teams had played throughout the Midwest, was not the only institution to refuse to play in Louisiana, said Kurt Edward Kemper, author of *College Football and the American Culture in the Cold War Era*. Kemper, a professor of history at Dakota State University, wrote extensively about the Louisiana racial law and its aftereffects.

Things like Harvard's rebuke, which was resistance from a notable place, exerted the kind of public pressure that began to hem in the South in ways it did not expect," Kemper said. "Before that, there had been gentlemen's agreements and Northern schools were complicit in letting segregated schools uphold certain policies. In the 1950s and 1960s, some places were finally willing to say no."

Bowman, who was raised in the South Bronx, said he had hardly ever discussed the episode publicly in the last 56 years. He had not told his children, for example.

P3.2 *Tommy Amaker, the current Harvard coach*

Photo source: Adam Hunger for *The New York Times*

"I did not forget it, I considered it part of the fabric of life then," Bowman said. "I am so glad it's not an issue any longer. Look at how dramatically things have changed. Harvard is in the N.C.A.A. not only with African-American players but an African-American head coach. That means more to me right now."

The 1956 Louisiana law prohibiting interracial sporting activities was invalidated by a court ruling about two years after it passed, although instate universities and colleges almost universally abided by the ban for several years thereafter.

In 1960, Harvard finally traveled south of Philadelphia during the holiday period, playing in a tournament hosted by Furman University in Greenville, S.C. Harvard did not play its first basketball game in New Orleans until 1996, when it played two games in a tournament called the Christmas Classic.

P3.3 *Dr. Martin Luther King, Jr., at the Lincoln Memorial, Washington, DC, overlooks the multitudes at the March on Washington in 1963 before his "I Have a Dream" speech*

Photo: Hulton Archive/Stringer/Getty Images, reprinted with permission

Editors' Note:

Images within this book have been reprinted with the permission of the authors unless indicated otherwise. For those images not in the public domain, every reasonable effort has been made to obtain permission for reproduction.

Table of Illustrations

Front Matter

Prologues

Essays

Chapter One – PHILOSOPHY

Chapter Two – HISTORY *(cont'd)*

Chapter Three – EDUCATION

Chapter Six – ECONOMICS

Chapter Seven – ENVIRONMENT

Chapter Seven – ENVIRONMENT *(cont'd)*

Chapter Eight – SCIENCE

Chapter Eight – SCIENCE *(cont'd)*

Epilogues

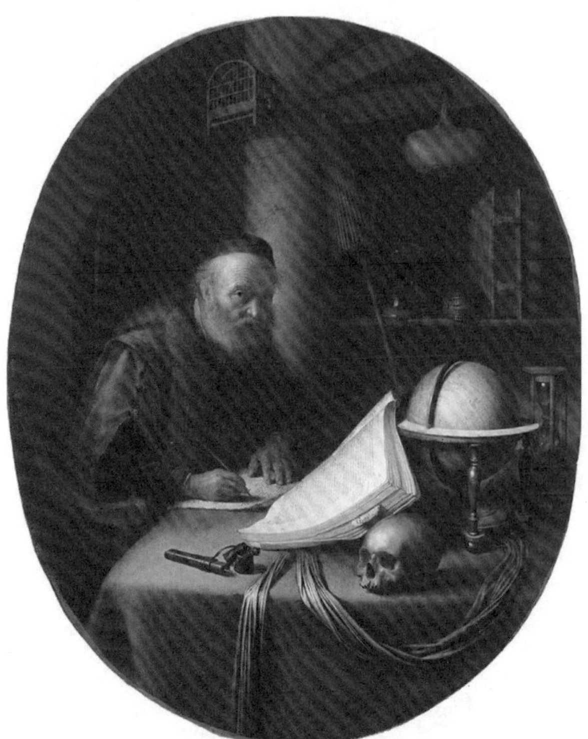

Figure F6 *"Scholar Interrupted at His Writing", ca. 1635*
Gerrit Dou (1613–1675)
The Leiden Collection, New York, GD-102

Essays

Chapter One
PHILOSOPHY

Figure C1 *Everest summit with Camp Six in the foreground—1994*
Photo courtesy of L.S. Huntington

Chapter One
PHILOSOPHY

Vigorous Life

Everest 1994—Alt. 29,002'

Lawrence Huntington

Standing in the airport in Newark, NJ, I was awaiting the arrival of my Australian climbing partner, Michael, to come for an overnight visit on his way to Kathmandu for our next adventure—the 1994 Expedition to climb the North East Ridge of Everest. He and I, both in our high 50s, had become close friends three years before while attempting the same route, and I had come to rely on his advice and experience, gained from his many previous attempts on the north side of the mountain.

His visit brought with it all the apprehensions of the challenge ahead, the three-month separation from my wife, Caroline, the leave from my business responsibilities, and the inherent dangers of such an undertaking. While waiting for Michael, I comforted myself on this latter concern in knowing that he was a person of balance, experience, and good judgement.

Michael and I drove to our house in the country an hour north of New York in time for dinner with Caroline and, incidentally, with our newest family member, a small rabbit with the imposing name of Junior. While catching up on our news, I asked about his close friend, the violin player, whose practice tapes he often listened to as we shared a small tent high on the side of the mountain. He told us that he had broken off his relationship with her because he did not wish to leave any ties back home for his now seventh attempt to climb to the summit. We also learned that he had had an uncharacteristically distressing argument with his Jesuit Priest brother as he was leaving home.

The next morning, the three of us took a stroll in the woods, leaving Junior to his usual daytime activity out of the house eating the grass and other plants. Michael wondered if Junior could get into trouble on his own, but we assured him that there were no predators around. Just then, from ten minutes away, we heard a piercing scream from the rabbit and rushed back to see the neighbor's dog in the process of killing him. Sad.

After Michael's departure, Caroline asked me if the rabbit's death was a sign.

A month later, the expedition members were assembled at Base Camp in Tibet, and the climbing plans began to take shape. As is typical of large expeditions (ours included 20 climbers from around the world and a like number of Sherpas in climbing and support roles), smaller sub-groups of four or six form a team which might last for the duration of the months on the mountain. Knowing this pattern, I assumed that Michael and I would join together, once again.

Prior to actually starting to ascend and establish what would become six separate camps, each a day's climb apart, from Base Camp at 17,000' to Camp Six at 27,200', the Sherpas held their traditional religious ceremony, called a Puja, to bless the mountain and the individuals on the expedition. While standing in the circle around the stone altar-like structure that the Sherpas had built and listening to their chanting, I suddenly had a premonition about Michael's determination to reach the summit at all costs. I decided that I should not place myself with his sub-group and must find a quiet way to change to a different team. This I accomplished by requesting more acclimatization time when he decided he was ready.

After many cycles of climbing for three or four days to ever higher elevations and then retreating all the way to Base Camp for a rest, our team patterns were well established in rotation. One group would be pushing the route higher on the mountain while others would be ferrying loads to equip the camps. By mid-May, we had established Camp Six with tents, sleeping bags, stoves, food and cylinders of oxygen to supplement the very thin air. It was time to plan our summit bids, pending a spell of clear weather. Because of the limitation of space and equipment, only one team could try for the summit at a time. Each left Base Camp one day apart to ascend through the six levels, hoping for perfect weather on the seventh day. Michael's group was one day ahead of ours, and therefore, he was at Six, making his summit bid on the day that we left Five, at 25,500', to climb to occupy the tents at Six. The weather was clear but with very strong winds and very cold, at about zero degrees Fahrenheit.

Climbing at such extreme altitudes is beyond tiring. Each step requires many breaths, even when inhaling some supplemental oxygen, and the pace is probably not better than six or eight steps per minute. The oxygen cylinders are heavy (off-setting some of the value of the extra air), and the mask and goggles limit any peripheral vision. Most of one's thoughts are about wanting the ordeal to be over—to escape the cold, disorientation, and lack of air. Important to ponder is that each step up puts one further from safety, and requires the understanding of how much energy to save for the climb down.

The terrain on the north side of Everest is ever more difficult as one ascends. It is like the inside of a bowl, the higher the steeper. Along with the steepening grade, the slabs of rock poking through the powdery snow angle downward so that most foot placements are precarious, and most of the snow has not consolidated enough to make a firm step. Moving requires great care and concentration.

In the late afternoon, we reached the tents at Camp Six and immediately set about melting snow for liquids to slake the thirst resulting from all the heavy breathing. By about eight o'clock, we settled back to rest, planning to sit up at 10 p.m. to prepare for our midnight departure. (Every movement or task at altitude takes dramatically longer and is more tiring than at sea level).

The radio burst into life. The expedition leader, Eric, came on the air to tell us that Michael had insisted on proceeding to the summit long after a sensible turn-around time, and that he had made the top at 7 p.m., just as darkness had come. He and his partner, Mark, had come down only about 50 feet and were stranded without protection. Eric asked us to abort our summit bid and attempt to climb through the night to rescue our friends. By this time the wind was ferocious, even though the night sky was full of stars. It was bitter cold, and my fingers froze in the short time I removed my mittens to clip on my crampons.

From this time on each of the four in our group was climbing alone in the dark, using the light from a headlamp. I found some comfort in seeing the dots of light around the slope, but I was aware that only I could keep myself safe. After about an hour, I realized that I had no feeling in any of my fingers—I had to deal with that or face their loss. I downclimbed back to the tent, crawled through the doorway and placed by hands in my armpits until the feeling came back. Then I resumed the ascent, returning to the labored breathing on the difficult sloping rock slabs. Soon, it became clear to me that, battling the strong winds, we were not going to be able to make any real progress toward Michael and Mark and that our own safety was back in the tents. I watched all the headlamps descending as well, the others having come to the same conclusion. By dawn, all in our group of four were back at Camp Six. I was spent.

After a short rest and discussion on the radio with Eric and my companions, I decided that my climb was over and that I could not ascend an additional 2,000' to aid Michael and Mark. I started my descent alone and eventually, with only a short break at Camp Four at 24,000', where others were gathered, I reached the bottom of the steep sections of the mountain. There, at Camp Three, I listened in on radio conversations confirming that Michael had reached the summit but had exhausted himself. While his younger partner, Mark, was still able to move, Michael was not ever coming down.

I sat by myself and wept, both for his death and my failure.

As a Harvard freshman in 1953, **Larry Huntington** stood in the back of the Exeter Street Theatre in Boston and listened to Edmund Hillary and Tenzing Norgay describe their ascent of Mt. Everest. "The subject never really left my mind, and at age 40, I decided that I had better get started to gain mountaineering prowess. Fifteen years later, after ascending some of the world's high peaks, including Denali, in Alaska, and Aconcagua, the highest in the Andes, I finally felt ready for the Himalayas. I made two attempts on Everest, each time reaching almost 28,000', before being turned back. Both were profound experiences."

Figure 1.1.1.1 *Larry Huntington, with Everest summit in the background—1994*
Photo courtesy of L.S. Huntington

The Olympic Movement: Yesterday, Today, and Tomorrow

Tenley E. Albright

When I was asked to write an essay on "The Olympic Movement: Yesterday, Today, and Tomorrow", for *Recollections and Reflections*, I was initially hesitant. For one thing, I entered Harvard Medical School after only three years at Radcliffe, so I'm a member of the Class of 1957 on a technicality! Also, figure skating was my first career, but I have gone on to do many things, and I was more interested in discussing my current work as Founder and Director of MIT Collaborative Initiatives. However, I realized that I can do both, as the ideals which make the Olympics an important event are very similar to the principles which have guided my work.

I've been lucky to have had several distinct careers in my life, each of which has been uniquely fulfilling and challenging. I have been an Olympic athlete, a clinical surgeon and health care advocate, and a convener of innovative thinkers and actors to address social change.

I believe that in a complex world we are not going to solve any of the most challenging problems by addressing them in isolation. Collaboration, both with those deeply invested and involved in an issue as well as experts in other fields outside the area of concern, is imperative if we are going to shift the needle of change. These "outside" viewpoints can provide critical perspective and relevant experiences.

Even our broadest concerns; health, environment, economy, education, safety are intertwined and must be addressed in concert for real change to happen. We can't afford to wait for a crisis to act.

The Olympic ideal of nations coming together to compete, the idea of sport as a universal language, is a unique forum for collaboration. As often as politics has interjected itself into the Games on a global scale, the Games have transcended politics on a personal level. Medicine is another universal language. When and where there is human suffering physicians step in to help. Today the discussion of health care has become politicized but the provision of care on an individual level remains the guiding principle of the oath we have all taken.[1]

In my life I have always looked for a way I could make a difference, a way to do things better. I wasn't content to stay within bounds as a young skater or as an older change advocate. How can we innovate and evolve if we are content to let things just stay as they are?

The Olympics have changed since I first competed in 1952 and won a Gold medal in figure skating in 1956. The world has changed a lot since then. However, the ideal of all nations meeting on the common ground of sport is as important today as it ever was. I have been involved in the Olympics as an athlete, a physician, a member of the Executive Committee of the US Olympic Committee and goodwill ambassador—each at different times in my life and different periods of history. Perhaps by analyzing my impressions from these times I can demonstrate the vital role of this unique opportunity for multi-disciplinary collaboration.

An Athlete's View

I began my "working" life as a competitive figure skater. I first put on a pair of skates when I was six, but it wasn't until I was recovering from polio at age 11 that I began to compete. I enjoyed the hard work, the freedom and the creativity that figure skating embodied. When I was 16 the Boston Arena gave me a key and if they hadn't sold the ice for hockey practice the next morning, they allowed me to let myself in and have the ice to myself to practice. I would call after 10 p.m., and they would let me know if the ice was available. It was my favorite time! In the pre-dawn hours, I would get to the rink with my portable record player and music—chase the rats out and clean the hot dogs from the hockey game the night before off the ice!—and skate to my heart's content. I loved the competition and, yes, I loved to win, but the challenge of creating new jumps, picking the right music, choreography and even mastering the discipline of compulsory figures was what kept me going. In truth, I was really competing with myself, always striving to do better.

On my first trip to the Olympics in 1952 at the age of 16, nothing prepared me for the feeling of walking through the gates of the Olympic village, the sight of all the athletes from different countries and different sports, wandering around speaking their own languages but sharing the excitement and anticipation of the occasion. We were in Oslo, and we skated on a cleared rectangle of ice in the middle of a huge field used for speed skating. The edges of the rectangle were marked with 4" mounds of snow, and the judges sat on folding chairs at the edge of the ice. My overriding memory of that competition is that at some point during my free skating program I realized that one judge wasn't even watching me skate. I later learned that the US and Czechoslovakian ice hockey teams had had a fight—based largely on the lack of established international rules—and the Czech judge was not going to watch an American skater. I won a silver medal that year.

By 1956, my second trip to the Olympics, I was a student at Radcliffe and a bit more aware of the world. The Olympics that year were in the small mountain town of Cortina D'Ampezzo, Italy. The entire town was the Olympic village. The music for my long program was the "Barcarolle", from the tales of Hoffman. In a practice ten days before the competition I hit a rut in the ice, and my left heel sliced my right ankle to the bone. My father, Boston-based surgeon and HMS Class of '31, taped me up and although I could barely stand I made it onto the ice to compete. It honestly never occurred to me not to. At one point during the long program I heard an odd sound; moments later I realized that it was the spectators humming along with the music. They literally lifted me up for that performance. And this is perhaps one of the most important aspects of the Olympic experience. In that moment, at that time, it didn't matter that I was American and that we were in Italy competing on an international stage, the audience was transported by the music, by the competition, by the sport.

To provide some context, in 1952 Elizabeth became Queen of England; the Allied occupation of Japan formally ended; and the first open-heart surgery was performed at the University of Minnesota. In 1956, Egypt nationalized the Suez Canal; Morocco gained independence from France; and, Nelson Mandela was arrested in South Africa. In 1952, in particular, we were still very close to the end of World War II. I remember being struck by the fact that in Europe there was butter and other things that were still being rationed in the US. Skating internationally also gave me a first-hand glimpse of the effects of war. I remember skating in Prague, and they had to open a hotel for us to stay in. There was no heat at night so I slept in multiple pairs of skating tights and virtually everything else I had. To witness the devastation of war firsthand gave me new perspective.

Looking at this list, and recognizing that it is only a fraction of what was going on in the world at the time, I find it amazing. I was young, but I have vivid memories of Victory gardens and my father being shipped overseas during the War. However, in those Olympic moments world politics were far from my mind. Many of my competitors from other countries have been lifelong friends, and the moments that stand out greatest are things like sitting in the dining room with other athletes. It was eye opening and awe inspiring. The opportunity to sit down with people who had vastly different life experiences, but were tethered by a common goal, gave me a chance to discuss the things that bind us on a human level. We may have each been competing for our own countries, and I'm sure on a political level there was some sense of gaining national pride, but on an individual level there was far more that brought us together than divided us.

Figure 1.1.2.1 *Italian soldiers observe world champion figure skater Tenley Albright getting ready for training on one of the many ice rinks at the winter resort of Cortina, Italy.*

Photo source: Bettmann/Getty Images, from http://www.achievement.org/achiever/tenley-albright-m-d/#gallery

From Skating to Surgery

After the 1956 Olympics and the subsequent skating season, I left skating to enter Harvard Medical School. Ever since my childhood I had wanted to be a doctor, and my experience with polio at a young age strengthened that. I remember having a spinal tap at that time. A group of men in white coats stood at the end of the bed watching. It was a scary experience for a young child, for anyone really, and I asked if someone would hold my hand. I still remember the startled expressions and the long pause before one of those men stepped forward and held my hand. Perhaps it was that moment that made me determined to provide comfort as well as care. It is interesting to note that, at the time, no one had a clear understanding of what polio was. I was lucky to come out of it without any lasting physical disability, or worse. It wasn't until 1955 that the Salk vaccine[2] became widely used, and the oral vaccine[3] was made available in 1962. Thankfully, due to many wonderful organizations, polio has almost been eradicated across the globe.

I had thought to go into pediatrics but turned to surgery instead. Even as a surgeon, I kept thinking about how I could have kept my patients out of the operating room. What preventive measures could have been applied?

As a skater, in the brief moment before a program would begin, I felt almost hyperaware of my surroundings. I would notice faces in the crowd, small things happening around me, sounds—all while mentally reviewing my program and setting up to begin. It has struck me that this is very similar to the sense I've had in the operating room during surgery. My mind was always in the room, but I had to be aware of any number of things going on around me. The brain is an amazing thing: each of these endeavors required laser focus, but the brain has the capacity to monitor other details simultaneously. In surgery there is something I call the "surgical conscience", the knowledge that you have explored every option, done everything you could to care for the patient. This surgical conscience is what pushes us always forward, always striving to do more, to do better. I was trained for this on the ice.

A Leadership View

Over the years I have been directly involved in the Olympics a number of times, but for this discussion I want to talk about the 1980 Olympics: a year when politics directly intervened in the games. At this time, I was on the Executive Committee of the US Olympic Committee. This was still the era when the Winter and Summer games were held in the same year, and the Winter Games that year were in Lake Placid, NY. Throughout those games President Jimmy Carter's legal counsel, Lloyd Cutler, came to Lake Placid several times to meet with me about the potential impact of a US boycott of the summer Olympics in Moscow. Russia had invaded Afghanistan in December 1979, and

President Carter was exploring the idea of boycotting the Olympics as a means of pressuring them to withdraw their troops.

Again, to put this in context, the American hostages had been taken at the US Embassy in Iran on November 4, 1979, and the Administration was under extreme pressure. When Russia invaded Afghanistan, the Administration needed options. A grain embargo to Russia was enacted in January 1980. On January 20, in a letter to Robert Kane, president of the USOC and in an NBC *Meet the Press* interview, President Carter suggested that the Moscow games "be transferred to another site . . . or to multiple sites, or be cancelled for this year."[4] Further stating,

> "*If the International Olympic Committee rejects such a USOC proposal, I urge the USOC and the Olympic Committees of other like-minded nations not to participate in the Moscow Games.*"[4]

The troops were to be withdrawn "within the next four months" to avoid such action.

The Winter Olympics in Lake Placid were held February 13–24, and the month's deadline was February 20. All through those games discussions regarding what would happen next were going on. In the meanwhile, the US Hockey team defeated the Russian team in what we now know as the "Miracle on Ice".[5] As I was doing a little research to make sure my dates were correct, I came across this interesting bit of trivia: the night before that game, US starting goalie, Jim Craig, and Russian player Sergei Makarov played Centipede at Lake Placid's Olympic Village video arcade. The article states that, "The two communicated with nods and laughs."[6] Here is a dramatic example, in a time of deep political strife, of the value of the Olympic experience.

It was a conflicting time. In his letter, President Carter, stated:

> "*I believe in the desirability of keeping government policy out of the Olympics, but deeper issues are at stake.*"[7]

Looking at athlete opinions from the time, I believe they reflect what I heard. All wanted to compete for their country. Many felt that it was their responsibility to support the President's decision if it would lead to a peaceful resolution of the conflict, while others thought it would be better to compete and beat the Russians on the field. Ultimately, the US boycotted the games. A rally was held in Washington, DC, for the members of that US Olympic Team, and they were each issued a Congressional Gold Medal for their sacrifice.

At the time, I felt that it was important for the athletes to have a voice, and it seemed hard for the athletes, who weren't directly involved, to be the ones to pay the price. There seemed to be a lack of understanding from a political perspective of the value of the Games for the individuals involved. To many this was their only chance to compete on a global scale, to measure their skill across boundaries, to come together—despite the political chaos—and cooperate in the communal language of sport. I understood the thinking on the other side, but I feel that, perhaps, an opportunity was lost.

The Power of Unique Collaboration

In 2010, at the Vancouver Winter Olympics, I hosted a reception at the USA Olympic House near the Athletes Village. In many ways, this represented a confluence of the many roles I have played in my life—as athlete, advocate, surgeon, convener, and perpetual disrupter of the *status quo* in search of a better way.

The reception was titled, "*Sports and Science: A Global Language*" and was attended by athletes, members of the US and foreign delegations, the head of US Health and Human Services and others. Clearly, this brought together my two passions, and the group attending was encouraged to discuss the value of frameworks which unite us as a global community.

The value of sharing diverse experiences to reach a common goal is what inspires my work at *MIT Collaborative Initiatives*. We have tackled health care issues such as Acute Ischemic Stroke, Childhood Obesity, Post-Traumatic Stress in the Active Military, and Clinical Trials, by combining a systems approach—looking at all of the pieces of a broken system and how they interact, with unique collaboration—bringing together experts on an issue with experts from other fields to provide fresh insight. We all have a lot to learn from each other, and you never know where the next best idea will come from.

Summing Up

I am often asked about the relation of skating and surgery in my life. *Yes, it is more than the blades!* Skating was a lesson in perseverance, self-reliance, hard work and determination—all qualities that have stood me well in medical school, as a surgeon, and in my current work. Skating was fun, it was uplifting, and I felt a sense of freedom on the ice, and a kind of responsibility to help the audience hear each note of the music through my performance. While I might not describe surgery as "fun", it was immensely satisfying and rewarding to know that I had done my best to improve a patient's situation.

For me, the Olympics opened the world. It enabled me as an individual to be a part of something bigger, a movement that in the moment transcended what made us, as athletes, different and magnified the qualities we shared. The Olympic Games taught me not to be afraid of being a part of something big and inspired me to take on other challenges.

The Olympic games have grown tremendously. In 1952, there were 694 athletes from 30 countries competing in 22 events.[8] At the Vancouver Games in 2010, there were 2,566 athletes from 82 countries competing in 86 events.[9] The scale of the Olympic Games in terms of size, cost, and visibility has increased dramatically.

Some would argue that, given the current scale of the games, and the political opportunism that often surrounds them, they are no longer relevant. However, I feel that the value of a forum for international cooperation outside the political arena is incredibly important. Without opportunities for people of all backgrounds to come together, where would we be? Working, planning, competing together are all opportunities to learn and appreciate another viewpoint.

While the Olympics will always provide a lightning rod for political action on a national scale, they also provide an opportunity to lay politics at the door and come together on an individual level. We live in a global society, but there are still few opportunities to engage across national boundaries—*the Olympics are a bridge to cooperation and collaboration.*

My strong belief is that it is only through cooperation and collaboration on a grand scale that we will successfully challenge society's biggest concerns: concerns which do not recognize national boundaries.

> "*The goal of the Olympic Movement is to contribute to building a peaceful and better world by educating youth through sport practiced without discrimination of any kind, in a spirit of friendship, solidarity, and fair play.*"[10]
>
> —The International Olympic Committee

Figure 1.1.2.2 *Tenley E. Albright, MD, surrounded by participants of the 2013 Albright Challenge at the Broad Institute in Cambridge, MA*

Photo source: MITCI/D. Sella

Tenley E. Albright, MD, is a Visiting Scientist at MIT and the Founder/Director of MIT Collaborative Initiatives. She is also a faculty member in general surgery at Harvard Medical School. Tenley currently serves on the Board of Research!America and The Bloomberg Philanthropies. She was formerly chairman of the Board of Regents of the National Library of Medicine at the National Institutes of Health, served as a delegate to the World Health Assembly, and was the first woman on the Executive Committee of the US Olympic Committee. She has served on several corporate boards including State Street and West Pharmaceutical Services. Tenley graduated from Harvard Medical School after attending Radcliffe College and has received eight honorary degrees. In 1956, Tenley became the first American woman figure skater to win Olympic Gold. She has been inducted into the US Military Health System Honor Society and was recently inducted into the US National Women's Hall of Fame.

Endnotes

1 Hippocratic Oath

2 Jonas Salk developed the vaccine in 1952

3 The oral vaccine was developed by Albert Sabin.

4 Jimmy Carter: "1980 Summer Olympics Letter to the President of the US Olympic Committee on the Games to Be Held in Moscow", January 20, 1980. Online by Gerhard Peters and John T. Woolley, The American Presidency Project. http://www.presidency.ucsb.edu/ws/?pid=33059

[5] *Miracle on Ice* is a 1981 movie written by Lionel Chetwynd and Directed by Steven Hilliard Stern based on the 1980 US Olympic hockey team's win over the Russian team and subsequent Olympic Gold. However, the label "Miracle on Ice" had been coined almost immediately in response to the amazing win.

[6] Cormier, Roger; "*20 Things You Might Not Know about the "Miracle on Ice*"; http://mentalfloss.com/article/61728/20-things-you-might-not-know-about-miracle-ice

[7] Carter, "*1980 Summer Olympics Letter*"

[8] 1952 Oslo Olympics homepage, https://www.olympic.org/oslo-1952

[9] 2010 Vancouver Olympics homepage, https://www.olympic.org/vancouver-2010

[10] https://www.olympic.org/about-ioc-institution

Editors' Note:

Dr. Albright was honored at the Class of 1957 Reunion Dinner on May 23, 2017, at The Harvard Club of Boston, by her becoming an honorary member of the Harvard Class of 1957. A proclamation signed by the Class Secretary and Class Marshals was presented to her amid general acclaim by attendees, who filled the hall.

My Philosophy, Reflecting on Life's Positives and Negatives

Paul Scher

Descartes said, "*I think, therefore, I am.*" John Paul Sartre said, "*I am, therefore I think.*" Sartre has been my mentor ever since taking three years of French at Harvard.

I am a committed Existentialist. We create our own meaning as we deal with reality. I believe it's important to use both your mind and your experiences to manage through life's difficulties, while remembering your successes to keep you sane.

I'm quite sure that God as we commonly think of him is a creation of Man, and not the other way around. Whether or not there is a source of intelligence that created the universe or universes, I cannot determine. Regardless of what religion one follows, the Ten Commandments are an adequate moral code to serve as a beacon to guide each individual through life if we choose to follow them.

At 82 years old, I have fulfilled most of my life's missions. As with us all, there are both positive and negative situations that informed my worldview and inspired me to become a lifelong learner and an active participant in the great experiences of life.

I will reflect first on the negatives, identifying the major ones.

At an early age I realized I was perceived as different due to my blindness. I was born prematurely in 1934, and with too much oxygen in the incubator I became blind due to retinopathy of prematurity. Throughout my childhood neighborhood kids and schoolmates either taunted me or stayed away from me, and I had few friends.

In addition to being bullied for my disability, I also faced anti-Semitism. My parents, in their continuing effort to help me get the best schooling, sent me to the Illinois State School for the Blind during elementary school. While my disability didn't distinguish me, I was systematically beaten up by my fellow students for being Jewish.

My mother's relatively early death at age 53 left a large void in my life. My parents, Vic and Edith Scher, were my strongest advocates. They provided guidance, moral support and a safe haven that propelled me through life. My strong-willed mother was the driving force. She insisted on getting me released early from the hospital's neonatal ward, which likely ensured I had no additional impairments from the incorrect oxygen levels. She moved the family as needed to get me into the best school districts, she fought to get me placed in sighted classrooms, and she ensured that I had access to special services as needed. Her efforts were the early model for school inclusion, which is an accepted practice today.

Managing schoolwork, especially at the college level and beyond, was challenging. While studying at Harvard, I took Braille notes in class with a slate and stylus. I used volunteer readers to read textbooks and proofread my papers. When working with my readers, I used a Perkins Brailler (Braille typewriter), which was a faster way to take notes. The manual Brailler (still widely used today) is a bit loud, and thus I was provided with private study rooms at the library. After graduating college I had aspirations to be an attorney, but at the University of Chicago I threw in the towel after one semester of law school, as I was overwhelmed with the amount of necessary reading. I transferred to the College of Social Sciences, earning an MS in Political Science. My goal was to enter the Foreign Service, but I was rejected due to my blindness and needed to reassess my career path.

Moving to the positive, there is much in my life that has given me tremendous satisfaction and joy.

My parents taught me that I was expected to live a normal life, demanding academic success, encouraging me in my hobbies, exposing me to culture and travel, and never allowing me to use my blindness as an excuse for not doing my best.

I had the opportunity to attend excellent universities, earning a BA in Government from Harvard, a Master's degree in Political Science from the University of Chicago, and a second Master's degree in Education from the University of Illinois. I have the distinction of being the first blind person to graduate from Harvard. (Helen Keller was ahead of me, although she graduated from Radcliffe.) My goal was to get accepted to a top university; I understood the employment challenges facing blind persons, and I knew that education and credentials would be critical to my success. The impact of what I learned at Harvard as a member of the Class of 1957 continues to represent the backbone from which I make most of life's decisions.

Figure 1.1.3.1 *"I don't think of myself as a blind person. I think of myself as Paul Scher, who is extremely inconvenienced at times."* *Quote from* The Chicago Tribune, *October 9, 1988*

My education led me to secure productive and meaningful work as a Rehabilitation Counselor in both California and Illinois, and then as a Rehabilitation Manager for Sears Merchandise Group for 21 years. I have been involved in my profession and have always strived to make an impact. I served on both the Illinois Governor's Committee and the President's Committee on Employment of the Handicapped (now the Office of Disability Employment Policy), and I was a founding member of the National Association of Rehabilitation Professionals. I serve on the board of directors and remain active with the Chicago Lighthouse for the Blind. I was chosen as a Mary Switzer Scholar in 1990, one of the highest honors given by the National Rehabilitation Association. And I am particularly proud that my input was sought and is reflected in the Title I and Title III regulations enacted under the Americans with Disabilities Act of 1990.

Always learning and actively participating in life has led me to travel the world, with many unique experiences. Highlights include striking three chords on Beethoven's actual piano in his apartment in Vienna; spending the afternoon in Sigmund Freud's apartment; sailing as a crew member on a British tall ship in the Bahamas; riding a dog sled on top of an Alaskan glacier; hanging my head over the edge of the Grand Canyon in order to get a sense of the vast spaciousness of this natural marvel; traveling to China and walking the Great Wall; cruising the Panama Canal and touching the canal walls from our ship with my cane extended; visiting Louis Braille's home outside Paris and using his personal slate and stylus dating from the 1840s; standing on the beaches of Normandy and honoring the soldiers (including my Uncle Bob) who landed there on D-Day.

Family has always been my important to me; my extended family has been my strongest support network. Almost 45 years ago I married Ann, my wife and partner, and I became a stepfather of two young daughters. I enjoy our five grandchildren, watching them mature and fulfill their own dreams and goals. One of my simple joys is spending Sunday afternoons at my daughter's house, catching up with the family, enjoying a good meal, and laying in front of the fire with the three family dogs.

Finally, a tremendous positive in my later life was the decision I made to acquire a guide dog. At the age of 67, after navigating through life (and around the world) with my red-tipped cane, I applied to The Seeing Eye in Morristown, NJ, for a guide dog. I was matched with Aaron, a golden retriever/Labrador mix. While working with a guide dog requires constant training and all the regular responsibilities of dog ownership, it has been a great joy to have a furry navigator and companion. And an unexpected benefit is that I have become more socially connected. While people may be uncomfortable around a blind person with a cane, a dog always attracts attention and conversation. Aaron (one of the great dogs, beloved by all) has since passed, and I now have my second guide dog, a yellow Labrador named Norman.

As I reflect on the positive and negative influencers, both have significantly shaped my identity, my beliefs, and how I respond to challenges. I have strived to live a productive, engaging and meaningful life and I'm proud of my successes. I'm grateful for every day that I can get out of bed feeling well. I don't sweat the small stuff, and at this stage I do not plan far ahead, but I still look forward to tomorrow.

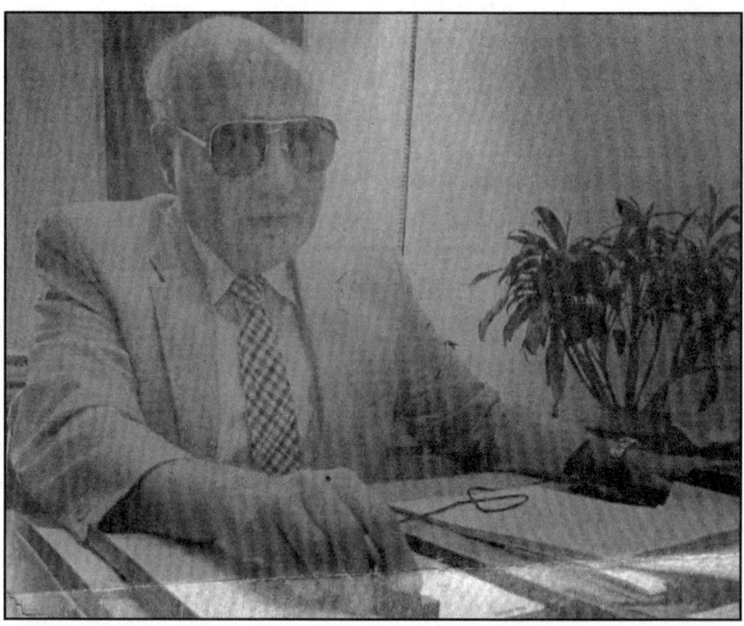

Figure 1.1.3.2 *Paul Scher at his job at Sears, using the Opticon—the device that "reads" print aloud. Paul was the subject of* The Chicago Tribune *October 9, 1988 article by Carol Kleiman on the positive impact of people with disabilities in the workforce.*
Photo by Ernie Cox Jr.

Paul L. Scher, native of Chicago, graduated cum laude with an AB degree in Government. He has the distinction of being the first blind student to graduate from Harvard College. He also holds a Master of Public Administration degree from the University of Chicago, and a Master of Education degree with a concentration in Rehabilitation Counseling from the University of Illinois. He is a nationally recognized human resources executive with significant contributions and accomplishments in the public sector and the private rehabilitation industry. As a certified rehabilitation counselor, he is a recognized spokesperson and advocate for the needs and rights of the disabled.

After graduating from the College, Paul started his career as the Executive Director of the Illinois Governor's Committee on Employment of the Handicapped. He organized a state network of community committees in Illinois to promote the employment of people with disabilities. Upon completing his master's degrees, he worked in San Francisco as a rehabilitation counselor for the California Department of Rehabilitation, carrying a caseload of visually impaired and general clients. Returning to the Midwest, he joined Sears, Roebuck and Company as a Rehabilitation Services executive, developing and managing corporate programs to recruit, employ, train and advance qualified persons who live with a physical, mental or learning disability.

In his 21-year career with Sears, Paul pioneered early-return-to-work and other affirmative action programs for disabled associates. After retirement, he was a founder and partner with Jordan Scher and Associates, providing expertise and guidance to agencies and individuals in the areas of rehabilitation counseling and disability management

Professional contributions include serving on the *President's Committee on Employment of the Handicapped* (now the Office of Disability Employment Policy), and being a founding member of the *National Association of Rehabilitation Professionals*. His input was sought and is reflected in the Title I and Title III regulations enacted under the *Americans with Disabilities Act of 1990*. In 1990 he was chosen as a *Mary Switzer Scholar*, one of the highest honors given by the National Rehabilitation Association. Currently, he serves on the board of the Chicago Lighthouse for the Blind and is a past president.

Paul enjoys the symphony, sailing (including having been a crew member on a tall ship in the Bahamas), worldwide travel, and is an avid lifelong learner, participating in programs at Northwestern University. He resides in Chicago with his wife, Ann; in retirement he has realized his dream of living along the lakefront in a condo on Lake Shore Drive. He has two daughters, five grandchildren, and a seeing eye dog (yellow Labrador) named Norman.

Editors' Note:

In response to the Editors' queries about Paul's technological adaptations, his daughter, Susan Rubin Elfant, wrote:

> "*My father is firmly in the computer era. He typed his essay on the computer in Microsoft Word and sent it to me via e-mail for editing. He has a talking program on his computer called* JAWS. *The JAWS program will read documents, web pages, and e-mails to him. Additionally, the iPhone has an adaptive technology called* Voice Over*: it's available on every iPhone if you choose to enable it. It provides audio, reading what is on the screen.*" *With this* "*adaptive technology, he is using the same tools that other blind people use.*"
>
> "*He learned to type in high school, so he knows the QWERTY keyboard [and] operates similar to a secretary, typing quickly without looking at the keyboard. He previously used an electric typewriter (prior to personal computers) for typing out short notes for sighted people. Now he uses these typing skills at the computer.*"

The Philosophy of Activism

John A. Talbott

I was asked to write about the philosophy of activism, but I am totally ill suited to address such a subject. I know nothing of philosophy; John Rawls is beyond my ken, and although I've been an activist, I've never thought of it academically—my guides were *do-ers* such as the Berrigans and Saul Alinsky.

> One could say I've led an un-examined life, having *done* but never figured out or written why.
>
> Of course I've written books, articles, etc. but always on academic medical scientific areas.

But as I think back on the lessons I've learned as an activist, I think they break down to three things.

1) A passion or cause.

2) An instrument to carry out the passion.

3) And the energy to get into the day-to-day details.

Many change agents have one, or the other, but not all three—see Marx, *The Communist Manifesto*.

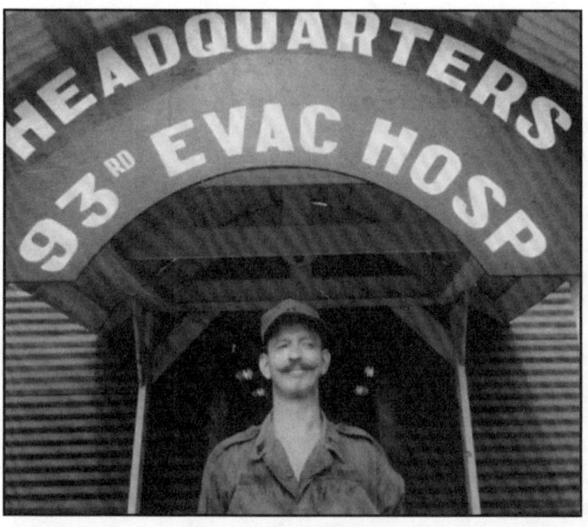

Figure 1.1.4.1 *Captain John Talbott, MD, US Army Medical Corps, at the 93rd Evacuation Hospital, Long Binh, Viet Nam, 1967–1968.*

Figure 1.1.4.2 *The author in his bivouac quarters at the hospital, trying to rest in the sweltering jungle heat and humidity. "A lowly Captain, although the most credentialed psychiatrist in the theater willing to get off my duff, I was a psychiatrist until [the] Tet [Offensive], when I reverted back to an OR scutman."*

My first passionate issue was the Viet Nam war, which I had served in from 1966–68. I didn't believe in it, resisted the draft but wound up serving, getting a Bronze Star, by the way. My wife, Susan, two neighbors, and two architects who designed our New York town houses wanted to protest but didn't know how. We seized upon the idea of reading the names of the war dead (until the war ended) and then had to figure out how to actually do it.

This required our getting noticed. A front page story by R.W. Apple, Jr., a friend from my war days on *The New York Times*, provided that. Then we needed to organize the hundreds of people who saw the article and volunteered. This involved finding space for an office (our basement), hiring a staff, installing telephones, landlines, typewriters, and, most crucially, finding seven "day ladies" who presided over each day of the week, organizing unknown volunteers, neighbors and friends as well as celebrities from music, art and science to do the actual reading of the dead and a czar to oversee it all—Susan, my wife.

Soon afterwards, I was running a huge state mental hospital where few 22- to 28-year-olds identified themselves as Viet Nam vets because they didn't want the stigmatization of the VA or Viet Nam. Through the efforts of two brilliant organizers, Arthur Egendorf and Art Blank, I got together with a bunch of vets, scientists, sociologists and experts, such as Bob Lifton at Yale, who wanted to identify and quantify those whom now we identify as suffering from PTSD. This was tough going, but the result, after hours of interviewing, became the defining work on the differences between Viet Nam vets, resisters and deserters.

This work inevitably led to my concern that vets on the streets of New York often had severe mental illnesses and that they and other non-vets had been dumped from mental hospitals onto the streets, shelters, and prisons with no shelter or care plans.

At this point, I was working my way up the ladder of the American Psychiatric Association and led a new committee on the Chronic Mentally Ill, which got the organization to issue a strongly worded action plan. I then ran for the presidency of the organization and won, which allowed me to appoint one person to each component of the APA; and I chose those members who were fighting for the deinstitutionalized, vets, and chronic mentally ill. I was using my position to promote a policy. (P.S. Unfortunately, those uncared for are less likely to be found on the streets today than to be put into the correctional system, which constitutes another national disaster.)

A lesson learned as well was to seek allies, and the National Alliance for the Mentally Ill (NAMI), the National Institute of Mental Illness (NIMH/NIH) and the national organizations of psychologists, social workers and nurses were trustworthy allies.

So, in sum, my philosophy about activism after 50 years comes down to having a cause or a passion, an instrument to carry it out, and the energy to make it happen.

John A. Talbott, MD, is (still) Professor of Psychiatry at the University of Maryland School of Medicine having stepped down/aside as its Chair in 2000. He earlier worked up the academic ladder at Columbia and Cornell as well as working up his professional organization's steps at the *American Psychiatric Association*, becoming its President and main nudge. He is the author of over 200 books, chapters and peer-reviewed articles. You can help his Amazon.com rating by buying a tattered copy of *The Death of the Asylum*, that solved the problem of chronic mental illness, the homeless mentally ill, deinstitutionalization, the criminalization of the mentally ill and gastric upset. Having perfected his writing style or lack of it at the *Lampoon*, he decided that when everyone else was retiring he would start serious French restaurant food criticism and currently has more followers at John Talbott's Paris (www.johntalbottsparis.typepad.com) than anyone but the so-called Donald Trump. He has also edited, with great enjoyment, the *Psychiatric Quarterly*, *Psychiatric Services* and the *Journal of Nervous and Mental Disorder*. Finally, he returned to Viet Nam this Christmas with all 12 of his family and carried his Bronze Star, although no one asked for it.

Philanthropy

Giving, Getting, and Governing

David Witherspoon Scudder

Preface

In 1966, just after my 30th birthday, I was asked to become a trustee and treasurer of the New England Conservatory of Music in Boston. My wife and I had moved to Ipswich, MA, in 1960 and built a home there very close to Crane Beach, a gorgeous four-to-five-mile stretch of beach, sand dunes and tufts of sea grass. Our house was only about a quarter of a mile away from a neighbor, David Crockett, who had attended Harvard shortly after my father-in-law. This fortuitous circumstance was responsible for 50 years of involvement in non-profits on my part.

David Crockett became a true pioneer in fundraising circles. Right after World War II he returned to his family's home in Ipswich and looked around for a job. David had remarkable powers of persuasion, accompanied by a patrician manner and a style of handsome elegance. He presented himself to the president of the Massachusetts General Hospital (then, as it is today, probably the best and most famous hospital in the country) and was appointed a special assistant to the president. His duties were never defined in the form of a job description, but he understood that he was to bring in funds to the hospital from grateful patients in almost any way he chose.

When I first met David Crockett around 1960, I was only 24, and working at a brokerage firm in Boston, Estabrook & Co. I trained there not to be a broker but rather an investment analyst, a portfolio manager for fee-paying clients and a writer of economic and market essays. Because of his friendship with my in-laws, David decided to try me out, as he was then not only special assistant to the president of Mass General Hospital but also on the boards of the Castle Hill Foundation, the New England Conservatory, and quite probably another institution or two.

He asked me first to join him on the Castle Hill Board. This was a small non-profit engaged in preserving Castle Hill, an enormous piece of property in Ipswich right by Crane Beach, with a 60-room house, ownership of the beach and several thousand surrounding acres. It had been left, with no endowment, to the Trustees of Reservations (the first land preservation organization in the US) in 1949 by Richard T. Crane, Jr., a Chicago industrialist whose summer home it had been until his death. With no endowment, Castle Hill had to raise all its money each year on its own. The Trustees of Reservations created the Castle Hill Foundation as a separate non-profit so as to throw the entire responsibility of Castle Hill's preservation onto that organization's lap. Crockett organized the board of the Foundation, hired a general manager, put the place into the wedding business in order to make money but also ran a concert series every summer so as to justify its non-profit charter.

I began to learn the art of fundraising from Crockett, who served as my mentor. I heard of his legendary successes at Mass General, as he apparently knew every rich person in Boston (especially the widows), and the Hospital's expansion was almost entirely funded by gifts which Crockett had obtained. He would take a widow to tea at the Ritz in Boston; not much later, there would be a new wing at Mass General, named gratefully after the widow's late husband and in honor of her generosity.

Prior to World War II, all fundraising for non-profits was done informally by boards of trustees passing the hat at the end of each year, so as to balance the budget. Crockett changed this informality and this concentration on a small and tight group into a highly professional activity. Now every non-profit with a need to fundraise essentially follows the rules Crockett created: have a professional staff, ensure that the staff researches every single prospect thoroughly, employ the most persuasive people in the administration or on the board of the non-profit to assist the staff in solicitations, and dream up individual campaigns for every major prospect.

Learning avidly from Crockett, I found that not only did I enjoy the art of fundraising but that, much deeper, I became a passionate advocate of non-profits whose mission I both understood and identified with.

I understood that to further the interests of these non-profits, I had to be ready to give (funds, as well as advice and judgment), get (funds from others, as well as persuade volunteers to join boards) and govern (lead a board by example). This is my story.

Early Responsibilities

Music had always been a very serious interest for me, but I had little talent for playing an instrument. Instead, I collected the records of classical music masterpieces, Broadway shows, superb pop singers (especially Ella Fitzgerald and Frank Sinatra) and jazz greats such as Louis Armstrong.

When David Crockett placed me on the board of the Castle Hill Foundation in the early 1960s, I reveled in the magnificent summer concerts which were a combination of classical and popular. Crockett then decided that the New England Conservatory needed a new treasurer and that I should accept that position. Knowing virtually nothing about what a treasurer should do, other than seeing that the books balanced, I accepted the post with enthusiasm and with a blank slate.

A couple of years before I became treasurer of the New England Conservatory, the Board of Trustees had appointed a new president, Gunther Schuller. This was a momentous decision as it turned out. Schuller was a musical wunderkind; as a French horn player, he became first horn of the Cincinnati Orchestra at the age of 20, then joined the Metropolitan Opera orchestra a few years later, and proceeded to compose works of astonishing originality.

Schuller's appointment as president of the New England Conservatory was a calculated gamble. The board of trustees believed correctly that the Conservatory, always a highly regarded institution, had started to lose place to other musical schools and seemed stuck in the past. A jolt was needed, and Schuller provided that jolt, earlier in his tenure and of a much greater magnitude than had been anticipated. Older faculty were encouraged to retire almost immediately. Their replacements were brilliant musicians, some of whom had never taught, but in whose genius Schuller believed. Jazz was introduced as a discipline and the Conservatory became the first music school in the country to grant a degree in jazz.

When I became treasurer in the summer of 1966, I was warned by the retiring treasurer that the financial books were almost hopelessly late and that the systems for financial reporting were rudimentary. Everything he said was true, in fact understated. As a volunteer, I had to spend much more time than I or anyone else had anticipated in assessing the financial staff and trying to get the statements in proper form. Changes had to be made in the staff, and I worked closely with Schuller in selecting a new chief financial officer.

To everyone's shock, it turned out that the Conservatory had way overspent its budget, principally because of the costs of both faculty retirements and new hires. The accounting systems, in that long ago period, were done by hand and by early versions of adding machines. There was no way of keeping on top of the financial situation, except way after the fact.

I, as treasurer, together with the chairman of the board and President Gunther Schuller, traveled to New York on an emergency basis to solicit a very wealthy alumna of the Conservatory to, in effect, bail us out. I was charged with presenting a budget for the upcoming year, and with explaining the reasons for the serious shortfall in the previous year. It worked out. We received the gift which we needed. This was my initial experience in truly serious fundraising. I had passed my first test as treasurer. The thrill of doing a job, for which I had little experience and the rules of which I had to improvise right on the spot, was exhilarating. I was hooked, then and there.

For about ten years, I served as treasurer of the Conservatory (eventually ending up much later as chairman), and I had to keep pace with Schuller's demands for funds which were absolutely necessary to fulfill his mission for the school. More than once, I had to either lead or join with other board members in special fundraising campaigns. I learned to write persuasive appeals and present them persuasively. This was a high-wire act balanced between the threat of financial disaster and the excitement of artistic and educational innovation.

In addition, Crockett then asked me to take over from him as president of the Castle Hill Foundation in the late 1970s, a job which I did for nearly fifteen years. I learned the essentials of governing a board—how to chose and convince friends to take on a role as board member, how to staff committees, how to run a board or a committee meeting, and how to raise funds for the summer programs.

All during these years, my career in the financial service industry also was flourishing and advancing. I found that lessons I learned in both my career and my non-profit world complemented each other. In both, the art of persuasion was necessary, as was the art of explaining yourself clearly and with conviction. Facts had to be communicated appropriately, conclusions drawn convincingly, and other board members had to be organized into a well-working team.

Later Years

Other non-profits asked me to join, and I had a hard time turning any of them down. Over the next 25 years, I became a board member of two small local institutions (a church and an historical society) as well as five larger institutions in the Boston area, though not all of them at the same time. I served as either president or chairman of three (New England Conservatory, Castle Hill Foundation and the Isabella Stewart Gardner Museum), in addition to serving on their various committees. I have chaired committees for four other non-profits (St. Mark's School, the Massachusetts Eye & Ear Infirmary, the Boston Lyric Opera and the Harvard Musical Association). In addition, I have been a member of our Harvard Class reunion fundraising committee ever since our 25th Reunion.

The original lessons learned were confirmed by each and every other board appointment. Non-profits are not that different one from another, except that their mission should be unique. If the mission is clearly stated and if you, as a volunteer, are committed to the success of that mission, then you must give, get and help to govern. Here is one very recent anecdote which shows what board members are sometimes asked to do.

Last June 1, I had a knee replaced exactly seven weeks after I had the other one replaced on April 12. The first one was in pretty good shape by June 1, but I had then to get the other one done. If you have ever had a knee replaced, you will remember that the first several weeks after the operation are full of rigorous physical therapy exercises, many of which take place on your bed. Right at the same time, I was faced with the challenge that a non-profit on which I serve as a board member and fund-raiser was going to have to report a deficit of over $1 million for its year ending June 30, because of unexpected and unusual reverses in what had been thought to be pledges from a small number of donors. So I got to work over the phone, from my bedside, in between physical therapy sessions, and was able to raise in less than three weeks almost $2 million to be divided between fiscal 2016 and fiscal 2017 for this non-profit. By the end of June, my new knee was well along the road to full recovery, I was driving again, and I was able to get in to the office for several hours a day. So, it turned out to be a very productive month.

Summing Up

The most difficult challenge faced by any non-profit is the hiring of a new chief executive officer to run all the day-to-day operations of the organization and to join with the board in long-term planning, fundraising and board development. I have chaired or co-chaired two selection committees. In one, the woman chosen has been a terrific success, and the organization has been brought a long way forward. In the other, the choice turned out to be less successful, though I remain convinced that person chosen at the time had the best credentials and experience of any of the candidates interviewed. All you can try to do is thorough research on a candidate and interview as many times as you think necessary. There is no guarantee that your choice will always work out.

I have had one frustrating experience at Harvard, of all places. Roughly a dozen years ago, a very generous alumna and her husband created a small institute within a graduate school at Harvard, to study non-profits and to try to assist in their proper management and development. This is certainly a worthy goal. I was asked to join an advisory board for this institute as it was being established. Almost immediately, I sensed that I, as a person with plenty of hands-on experience as a practioner but with no credentials as an academic, would be in trouble. The faculty member asked to head up this institute was only interested in two things: had you published books or articles on non-profits (the more scholarly the better), or would you give funds to the institute (the more, the better). Practical experience seemed to be neither desired nor thought to be important. After a year, I quietly resigned.

When I turned 80 last year, I decided that my years of leading a non-profit as either chairman or president were over. Younger people should move into those positions and I would still act as a committee member here and there but others would govern. Today I serve as life trustee of both the Conservatory and the Gardner Museum (which means I can attend all board meetings but have no vote), as trustee for the Boston Lyric Opera, and as a committee member for the Mass Eye & Ear Infirmary, the Harvard Musical Association, St. Mark's School and the Trustees of Reservations. You will note that I have no social service organization on this list. My personal interests and commitments have always leaned strongly towards the arts and education. By restricting myself mostly to those particular fields, I believe that I have been able to bring a sense of passionate commitment to each non-profit board on which I served.

As one grows older, the challenge is to still maintain excitement and interests in various fields (in my case, financial services and non-profits) while stepping back enough to let others take on heavy, full-time responsibilities. Now I go to my office only three or four days a week, take off more time for vacations, and try to act more and more as mentor. I cannot let go of the non-profits I have been committed to but I know I must slowly disengage. I can and will still give what I can, as I know that non-profits have contributed more to my life than I could possibly have thought back in 1966.

Figure 1.2.1.1 *David Crockett*
Photo courtesy of his son, Christopher Y. Crockett

David W. Scudder has spent over four decades in the investment management business. As a partner of Wellington Management Company, from 1968–1998, he managed institutional and individual portfolios, with responsibility for both asset allocation and equity management. At Harvard Management Company, from 1999–2005, he provided overall investment direction for the more than 600 charitable trusts for which Harvard acts as trustee. In 2005, he co-founded Aureus Asset Management, an investment firm specializing in managing family assets, where he remains chairman of the firm's advisory committee.

Additionally, he has served as a trustee for several family groups and for a number of non-profit organizations, including the New England Conservatory (past chairman of the board), the Isabella Stewart Gardner Museum (past chairman of the board), the Massachusetts Eye & Ear Infirmary, the Boston Lyric Opera, the Trustees of Reservations, and St. Mark's School. He has lived in Ipswich, MA, since 1960, with his wife, Marie Louise (Sibley) Scudder, Radcliffe Class of 1959. They have three children and two grandchildren.

Friendship

Finding Harvard

Robert L. Holmes

A 1948 De Soto left Watertown, NY, bound for Cambridge in September of 1953. In front was the 17-year-old driver, his 16-year-old sister and his 17-year-old best friend, who was known as Hamster to some because of the pets he kept, or as Mac to most after his last name, which was McLean, or as David to his mother, because that was his given name. Barely visible in back amid the belongings of three college-bound teens was the father of the brother and sister.

After dropping the 16-year-old off at Russell Sage along the way, the remaining three arrived in Cambridge. Possessing only an artist's rendering of a Harvard graced with trees and lawns for a map, they drove up and down Mass. Avenue in search of such a place. It was nowhere to be found. When they finally parked and asked where Harvard was, they learned they were standing next to it; the Yard was just the other side of those buildings. Like hicks from the north country, they'd found Harvard, but didn't even know it.

Hollis 14 was home to the two for that year. They figured they must be the dumbest kids in the freshman class, but the one known as Hamster to some, as Mac to most, and as David to his mother, was a standout on the undefeated freshman cross-country team. The other one also ran.

They moved to Leverett the next year, rooming with Charlie and Jerry from across the hall and Ray from a floor below. Lacking the foresight to drop out and found Microsoft, they soldiered on, running the Belmont hills endlessly, or so it seemed, and cleaning hundreds of Harvard rooms with dorm crew, as it was called. You get to know the underbelly of Harvard if you vacuum enough rugs and clean enough bathrooms, and they got to know it well. They even learned a thing or two along the way—Mac in English literature, Also Ran in what turned out to be the start of a life sentence in philosophy.

In their third year, Also Ran thought running the Boston Marathon would be a lark—something to tell his grandchildren about. Little did he know that by the time he had grandchildren everyone and his grandmother would run marathons. ("So what else is new, Grandpa?") But he did it, along with Erich, best known for *Love Story*, but who ran and majored in classics long before that. Neither was a Pheidippides, but classics and philosophy had spirited—if something less than Olympic-class—representation in at least one running of that race.

The Watertownians and their fellow cross-country runners were undefeated until the final meet of their senior when, with Mac as captain, they lost to a school from New Haven. Had they known of Alternative Facts, they'd have won that one as well.

Mac, as he was known to most, or Hamster, as he was known to some, or David, as he was known to his mother, taught English until his death from leukemia at 34. He was studying for his PhD at the time. One couldn't have had a better friend, and once they found it, and shook the hayseed out of their hair, the two couldn't have had a better four years than at Harvard.

Robert L. "Bob" Holmes, a.k.a. *Also Ran,* after Harvard took his PhD in philosophy from Michigan, then taught for a year at Texas before moving to the University of Rochester, where he taught philosophy until his retirement in 2009. In addition to the usual tendentious academic articles, he has published several books, including most recently *Pacifism: A Philosophy of Nonviolence* (2017) and *Introduction to Applied Ethics* (forthcoming).

Figure 1.3.1.1 *Johnston Gate (1889) entry into the Old Yard. University Hall is seen in the distance.*

Reprinted courtesy of Harvard University

Seeking Truth through Reason

My Appeal to Reason

Ronald G. Havelock

Like the rest of you, I am about to leave the scene, but before I go, I would like to get a few things off my chest, issues that have bothered me for some years. My life, for as long as I can remember, has been a quest for the truth, the truth about myself, first of all, then my family, then my social milieu starting with the various schools I have attended and then the various career paths I have chosen or been driven to, and the mix of other humans that I have met and associated with and observed along the way.

I could call my life a "*development*" or a "*developing story*" because, at each stage, I learned new stuff that changed me and, I think, made me wiser and more complete as a human being. I kept on growing. I guess we all do that to some extent, but my impression of my fellow human beings, including almost all those I knew at Harvard, is that they stopped growing too early in certain sectors of their lives. They lost curiosity.

So what is this "*truth*" that I seek? It starts with me as a human being. What is a human being and how much do I know? I wanted to know about the body, the mind, the origin of me and everybody else, the earth, the stars, and the universe beyond. I was obsessed in my college years with trying to know who I was. The great General Education Program helped me a lot. I was periodically dumbfounded that most of my classmates didn't know or didn't care. They knew what they wanted. They were career bound. All the big questions were either unknowable or unimportant. Not me. For starters, at Harvard, I was fascinated by Freud. There were whole strata of human experience lying under everything else, the unconscious, and it seemed to explain so much of manifest human behavior. Much later I grew out of that and learned that the mind and the person with the mind were oh so much more complicated than that. Freud was at least half right about a lot of things, but the worlds of psychology and psychiatry were not moving in his direction after all.

I did two involuntary years in the US Army, not all pleasant, but substantial in more learning and growing. Every young person should go through some experience analogous to this. It puts the "*united*" into United States.

I went on to psychology in graduate school and learned, for the first time really, what science was all about (most scientists don't know). I learned and then briefly taught statistics and realized that we can't understand what is going on without statistical inference. It is not boring nor, for the most part, is it really difficult to understand. But it is hugely important for understanding our world and separating out what is important from what is unimportant, and what is real from what is random.

Along the way I also learned that there was very little of Freud's theory or his therapeutic technique that could be supported by empirical evidence (i.e., statistics), so I dropped the idea of becoming a therapist or Freudian practitioner of any sort. As a research social psychologist, there was a lot more I could learn about that was socially important.

Most people spend most of their lives worrying about things that are either unimportant or utterly false while ignoring many other things that *are* really important.

Oddly, this is an affliction that applies equally to intellectual elites like so many Harvard grads assume themselves to be. Take, for example, the idea of "*sustainability*". It is a relatively new fixation, or an old fixation in new clothes, and this meme dominates academia in our times, but what is it, really?

Its true origins are biblical, as in the Garden of Eden, the idea that there was once an ideal time when everything in nature was in balance. It is an utterly false idea, but most humans can't seem to let it go. Then along came "*man*" and his dreaded "*human footprint*". Our habitat was apparently OK for a few thousand years, but when the industrial revolution came along, everything went bad.

Well, anyone who is remotely aware of what has really been going on should know that life for most humans is enormously better than it was in biblical times or even historical times of a few centuries past. We live longer. We eat better. We enjoy an incredible range of entertainments, auditory, visual, sensational, that were never available to our ancestors. Moreover, many of us have the potential of living pain-free lives that are much richer by any standard than our great grandparents could have imagined.

Why do I know this? Statistics! They tell the story in myriad ways: longevity, infant mortality, GDP, food production and consumption per capita, TV sets, refrigerators, cell phones, airline passenger arrivals, indoor plumbing, potable water, electricity, and so much more. There is more of all this for more and more people all around the world, but, somehow, there is also a fixed idea that all this progress is unsustainable. In the very long run, perhaps, but this is emphatically not the story of our lives, '57ers.

There is no evidence of the dreaded unsustainable yet. It is just an assumption, a fixed and nearly pervasive fear that it must all come to an end. The statistics tell an opposite story, but we don't want to hear it.

Sustainability hysteria is pushed by an ever-growing cadre of environmental zealots. More and more identified with my Democratic Party, they are presumed to be liberals; they are not. They are Luddites. Environmentalism began in the 1970s with mostly worthy and laudable goals and achieved much in making our environment healthier for human habitation, e.g., cleaner, more potable water, more breathable air, more careful husbanding of animal and plant resources. Then it went overboard with more and more outrageous claims. It discovered that the more extreme the claim, the more attention it got. Ehrlich's "*Population Bomb*" was an early example. Not one of his outrageous predictions came true, but no matter, tenure at Stanford followed and untold royalty riches.

There's gold in those hysteria hills, so no surprise that less than a decade later came the so-called "*Club of Rome*" with their models (not statistics) that seemed to show that everything we depend on in the modern age is going to run out almost immediately. Alarm bells!!! Millions of copies printed in oh-so-many languages, and because they predicted disaster and showed numbers, the newspapers printed it, and a lot of people believed it. That was 45 years ago, and none of their predictions came true, none.

The gimmick is always the same: "*We are at a turning point,*" and bad things are sure to happen if we don't change our ways with drastic action right away. It may be too late, but if we plunge in with enormous resources, maybe we will save the earth.

Earth was also "*in the balance*" for Al Gore in the late 1990s. Right from the start it was all scare nonsense, but it was told well and it sold well, perhaps distracting Al from all the important liberal causes that Bill Clinton had left undone (health care, poverty, pay equity, black lives matter, do I have to name them all?) Al followed with the profoundly dishonest hyper-alarmist screed, *An Inconvenient Truth,* after the 2000 election debacle (I voted for him, hoping for a truly liberal continuum). The really inconvenient truth about "*Truth*" was that it was a lie, one big scare lie, but it worked. The environmentalists loved it. The liberals fell for it. The clueless United Nations bowed down to it. The Nobel committee oohed and awed over it.

What was their "proof"? The thin scrap of statistical truth was a data stream of very gradual increases in global temperatures, using wobbly measures from a variety of different places on the land surface. They were taken over a roughly 200-year period after an 18th-century phenomenon known as "*the Little Ice Age*". Not only was the increase not alarming (perhaps as much as 1.5 degrees Celsius), but it was also fairly constant from pre-industrial through industrial times. There was no acceleration.

In the last 20 years there has been no statistically significant increase at all (note the shift of terms from "*global warming*" to the meaningless but vaguely ominous "*climate change*"). It is not at all clear what might have caused this gradual increase, and it may be continuing, but it was not and is not harmful (mostly beneficial in fact), and not in any way alarming.

The big pseudo-scientific lie behind the lie was the supposed role played by carbon dioxide, a minor atmospheric contributor that happens to be vital for the survival and advancement of plant life on which all animal life depends. One rule of science is that extraordinary claims require extraordinary evidence, but there is no real evidence that CO2 has anything to do with climate change or global warming, let alone anything extraordinary other than allowing plants to live.

The only supposed proofs are in the familiar "models". These models date back to Malthus. Ehrlich updated them in his outlandish but very popular "*bomb*" screed. They were updated again by the Club of Rome (we will run out of everything very soon—solid predictions nearly 50 years old now, none realized), updated again by Al Gore. Every prediction has failed. There is no serious empirical evidence, and the evidence that exists suggests either no effect or positive effect from the dreaded human footprint.

Nevertheless, the campaign goes on with increasing alarmist vituperation, casting out skeptics like myself with hot code words like "*denialism*". The uber-environmentalists claim to be oh so clean, but they play very dirty. They say over and over again that the "*science*" is settled when there is no evidence to back up their outrageous alarmist claims. Whenever asked for evidence, they assert that the vast majority of "*scientists*" agree. Therefore there is no need to show any actual statistics. They would love to impose a carbon tax, about as regressive as any tax can be, because it would outlaw cheap energy in the form of coal. Coal has nasty environmental side effects if handled poorly, but modern coal-fired electric plants already provide cheap reliable energy in this country, and it could do so for the still desperately needy developing world the way contemporary wind and solar technology cannot do.

Now, the most ghastly of all political outcomes has come upon us from the far right, so I guess I must set aside my anger at the liars and cheats of the pseudo-left, the people who smear true science in the name of science.

Our democratic and tolerant society is under deep threat. They now join us in defense of the open society, but, unfortunately, many have blood on their hands. Like me, they deplore Donald's fake news, even though they have been peddling and profiting greatly from their own version of fake news for years. The media, unfortunately, are their handmaiden, ready and eager to trumpet every storm, drought, tornado, or hurricane as a sure sign that our use of carbon is the culprit.

I greatly admire Barack Obama and voted for him twice with enthusiasm. As a proud liberal. I also voted for Hillary this year, with great foreboding about the alternative. Yet, when I realized last year that Barack's science advisor, Holdren, was one of Ehrlich's disciples, I was shocked; an American Rasputin had my president's ear. Then I heard our former esteemed president spout the environmentalist nonsense about global warming as the greatest looming threat.

No, my dear Obama, it's not! The greatest threat is in the White House right now.

Ronald G. Havelock, PhD, attended Roxbury Latin School and graduated from Phillips Exeter Academy. During his two years in the US Army, he taught mathematics, and then obtained a PhD from Boston University in social and personality psychology. He joined the University of Michigan Institute for Social Research as research psychologist and over the next 13 years rose to Program Director and Research Professor.

From 1978 to 1983 he established and served as Director of the Knowledge Transfer Institute at The American University in Washington, DC. Subsequently he has held a number of positions and served as a consultant to projects related to his special interests.

A recognized authority on knowledge utilization, he has authored many research studies of knowledge use, technology transfer, and the planning of change in a broad range of areas including advanced technology, education, and medicine. His 1969 book, *Planning for Innovation*, was the first conceptual framework and comprehensive literature review on the dissemination and utilization of scientific knowledge, serving as the foundation for many subsequent investigations. His most recent book, *Acceleration* (Prometheus Books, 2011), traces the forces favoring human progress, explaining the intertwining of scientific discovery and technological invention in the upward spiral of the human experience.

Figure 1.4.1.1 *Weeks Footbridge straddles the Charles River. Eliot House tower is in the distance.*

Reprinted courtesy of Harvard University

The Reality Principle

Being 81

Roger Christenfeld

Shouldn't we all by now know the *Meaning of Life*?

But so much of the vaunted wisdom of age seems, at least to me, vaporous and banal. Gathering thoughts, however, for a 60th Reunion—a time for reflection more than pride—one inescapably faces the impact of Time, a concept ambiguous enough that freshman year remains lambent in spirit, while the flesh is challenged—mumbling of friends, smaller print of menus, obduracy of iPhones.

It is time to come to terms with the data: one is neither a world-changer nor a hopeless drone but rather a moderately happy, largely inoffensive Prufrockian creature trying to weigh in—fighting in middleweight division—on what one trusts is the right side, now unexpectedly defending my faith in empirical evidence, in truth.

Not all that many epiphanies so far, slow acceptance that Christenfeld may not be, in this generation, a name to conjure with (although Christenfeld is what Kierkegaard calls his godly, utopian city.) In my own drama I'm not even Rosencrantz or Guildenstern but veering toward Polonius.

In compensation, I've come to meet lots of people more interesting than myself, patients included. About 20 years ago there was a pleasant woman, quite rational except for the delusion that she was married to Donald Trump (which should have been a clue to his mythopoeic power.)

Harvard plays a seminal part, teaching us to think critically, a skill I've been repeatedly surprised to learn is rare in the wider population, one I seek in interviewing Harvard applicants, or trying to teach psychiatry residents, or shepherding Democrats. The adage that *life is a comedy for those who think, a tragedy for those who feel* may, if true, consign some Harvard-trained thinkers to an overdeveloped sense of irony, too sensible of the absurd, particularly in ourselves.

My research endeavors centered mainly on how mental health is affected by milieu. Over time I've seen the *focus of the profession vacillate between mind and brain* (synchronously with the shifts in the culture between liberal and conservative), and I've been in the business long enough to recognize it's cyclical, but I'm old enough to wish the cycles were shorter.

The most interesting phenomena, nonetheless, are the interactions between nature and nurture. If I am remembered at all in my field, I'm afraid it may just be for coining the longest word in the language, amusing British media: Long ago at a conference in Edinburgh I described the reaction against releasing mental patients from hospital as *antideinstitutionalizationism.*

We were taught to think, but feeling is hard impressed on us. Our range of concern expands to encompass a parlous nation and world, and closer by, our circle of coevals diminishes in a game of ultimate musical chairs—chairs constant, but each round fewer players. As Javier Marias wrote, "*Time, too, is constantly driving out people, customs, concepts.*" I am reconciled to this schema by the advent of grandchildren.

In all, I'm not ready for valedictory mode, only autumnal. "*Autumnal?*" I hear one of my sons object, "*Isn't that too optimistic?*"

Roger Christenfeld is as retired as a social psychologist can get. Long ago he gathered an MA from Oxford and a PhD from Michigan and put them to some use as senior psychologist for the US Public Health Service and then as research associate in Columbia's Psychiatry Department and research director at Hudson River Psychiatric Center. He's still Harvardian, as *paterfamilias*, as former president of the Harvard Club of the Hudson Valley, and as director of the Harvard Alumni Association. These days he serves as chairperson of the local Democratic Committee, plotting to overthrow the government.

Ageing

Expectations

You May Soon Have Longer than You Think

Richard L. Veech

At our 50th Reunion we were treated to an urbane lecture on the *limits of life span* by John Dowling.

He elegantly summarized the knowledge of the time which, in essence, restated the aphorism from several past millennia found in *Psalm 90:*

> "*The days of our years are threescore years and ten;*
> *and if by reason of strength they be fourscore years,*
> *yet is their strength labour and sorrow;*
> *for it is soon cut off,*
> *and we fly away.*"

Science tells us we should always be ready for new revelations.

I think we are about to see one.

My advice would be to not spend all your grandchildren's inheritance in anticipation of a departure at 80 years.

You may soon have longer than you think.

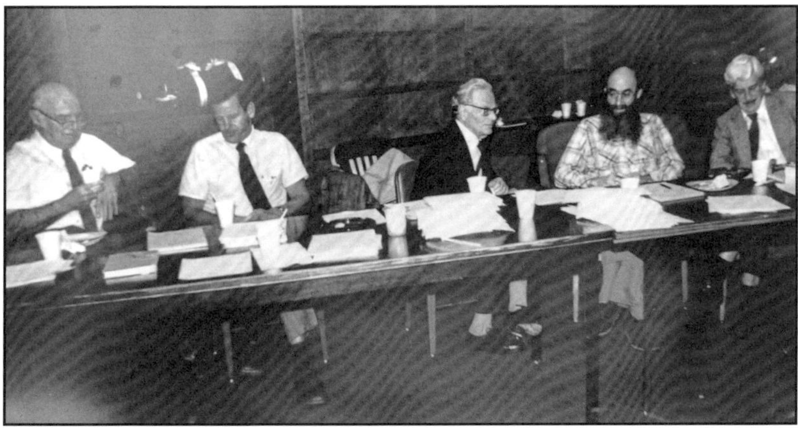

Figure 1.6.1.1 *External Reviewers of the Veech Lab at NIH, composed of world-famous metabolic biochemists, are shown at one of their 13 annual reviews* (left to right): *Merton Utter, Western Reserve; George Cahill, Harvard; Hans Krebs, Oxford; Paul Srere, UT Southwestern; and Edward Rall, Intramural Director, NIH. Krebs and Cahill were particularly influential in shaping the direction of the Veech's unique research on ketone biochemistry.*

Richard Veech, MD, following graduation from Harvard Medical School in 1961 and a post-doctoral year in biochemical research, trained in internal medicine at New York Hospital-Cornell Medical school and from 1964–66 served in the US Public Health Service (USPHS) as a Clinical Fellow at the National Institutes of Health (NIH) in Bethesda, MD.

In 1969 he received his D.Phil. in biochemistry from Oxford University following research training as a USPHS post-doctoral Research Fellow in the laboratory of Nobel Laureate Sir Hans Krebs. He then joined the research staff of the National Institutes of Health, where he has remained for 46 years. He has specialized in biomedical research on metabolic biochemistry and metabolic diseases with a special focus on ketone metabolism and its effects on health and disease. The recipient of the *Blye Foundation Medal* for Research in 1974, the *NIH Director's Award* in 2004 and a *William Douglas French Alzheimer's Foundation* grant from 2004 to 2006, he currently remains head of the Laboratory of Metabolic Control at NIH.

Dr. Veech received the New Hampshire *Hero's Medal* in 1969 for his strenuous efforts to remove injured fellow travelers to safety following a 1968 plane crash in the White Mountains in which he was severely injured, and in which 23 died and only he and eight others survived.

Joie de Vivre

Youngest Day of Your Life

John Appleton

> "*It's not what you gather but what you scatter that tells what kind of life you have lived.*"
> —Helen Walton

> "*Today is the oldest you've ever been, yet the youngest you'll ever be, so enjoy this day while it lasts.*"
> —Eleanor Roosevelt

I first started reading this e-mail and was reading fast until I reached the third sentence. I stopped and started over reading slower and thinking about every word. This e-mail is very thought-provoking. Makes you stop and think. Read slowly!

I found this in the public domain, and would like to have it in the essay book for others to see and appreciate. Cheers!

> You know . . . time has a way of moving quickly and catching you unaware of the passing years. It seems just yesterday that I was young, just married and embarking on my new life with my mate. Yet in a way, it seems like eons ago, and I wonder where all the years went. I know that I lived them all. I have glimpses of how it was back then and of all my hopes and dreams.
>
> But, here it is . . . the "back nine" of my life and it catches me by surprise. . . . How did I get here so fast? Where did the years go and where did my youth go?
>
> I remember well seeing older people through the years and thinking that those older people were years away from me and that "I was only on the first hole" and the "back nine" was so far off that I could not fathom it or imagine fully what it would be like.

Ageing

Joie de Vivre

But, here it is . . . My friends are retired and getting gray . . . they move slower and I see an older person now. Some are in better and some worse shape than me . . . but, I see the great change . . . not like the ones that I remember who were young and vibrant . . . but, like me, their age is beginning to show and we are now those older folks that we used to see and never thought we'd become.

Each day now, I find that just getting a shower is a real target for the day! And taking a nap is not a treat anymore . . . it's mandatory! Cause if I don't on my own free will . . . I just fall asleep where I sit!

And so . . . now I enter into this new season of my life unprepared for all the aches and pains and the loss of strength and ability to go and do things that I wish I had done but never did!! But, at least I know, that though I'm on the "back nine", I'm not sure how long it will last. . . . This I know, that when it's over on this earth . . . a new adventure will begin! Yes, I have regrets. There are things I wish I hadn't done . . . things I should have done, but indeed, there are many things I'm happy to have done. It's all in a lifetime.

So, if you're not on the "back nine" yet . . . let me remind you, that it will be here faster than you think. So, whatever you would like to accomplish in your life please do it quickly! Don't put things off too long! Life goes by quickly. So, do what you can today, as you can never be sure whether you're on the "back nine" or not!

You have no promise that you will see all the seasons of your life . . . so, live for today and say all the things that you want your loved ones to remember . . . and hope that they appreciate and love you for all the things that you have done for them in all the years past!

Lastly, consider this:

(1) Your kids are becoming you . . . but your grandchildren are perfect!

(2) Going out is good . . . coming home is better!

(3) You forget names . . . but it's OK because other people forgot they even knew you!

(4) You realize you're never going to be really good at anything . . . especially golf.

(5) The things you used to care to do, you no longer care to do; but you really do care that you don't care to do them anymore.

(6) You sleep better on a lounge chair with the TV blaring than in bed . . . it's called "pre-sleep".

(7) You miss the days when everything worked with just an "ON" and "OFF" switch.

(8) You tend to use more four-letter words . . . "What?" . . . "When?" . . . "Huhh?"

(9) Now that you can afford expensive jewelry, it's not safe to wear it anywhere.

(10) What used to be freckles are now liver spots.

(11) Everybody whispers.

(12) You have three sizes of clothes in your closet . . . two of which you will never wear.

(13) But Old is good in some things: Old songs, Old movies, and, best of all, OLD FRIENDS!"

"Life" is a gift to you. The way you live your life is your gift to others.

Live it well! Enjoy today! Do something fun! Be happy! Have a great day!

Remember: "*It is health that is real wealth and not pieces of gold and silver.*" Live happy in 2017!

Stay well. Send this on to other "Old Friends" and let them laugh in agreement!

John Appleton is the Senior Partner of his firm, Appleton Associates, but notes that there are no other partners or employees. Even so, he finds that some organizations actually ask (and sometimes pay) for his advice and willingness to work. He thinks that is a blessed place to be for an old codger. He still has a lot of mental energy to enjoy new challenges from eleemosynary, social, and financial organizations.

Experiences

Some Reflections on My Life

Roland Uziel

I'm past my 80th birthday, a good age to reflect on my life. I'm still capable of working, moving, I have all sorts of activities. I am very grateful to God for these blessings. I still work more than 45 hours a week and I enjoy very much what I do.

As I started to write, feelings of nostalgia and sadness overcame me. The values and the goals we set out as young men have all changed. Our generation, the rock 'n roll generation, is fast disappearing. Our world was much larger than it is today, and it was full of excitement and mystery. Today with the Internet, the telephone, and all the communications, the world has shrunk. The ideals we had in our youth have disappeared. The world is more preoccupied with material possessions; trying to better the world is no longer an ideal. After the Second World War all the nations of the world wanted to forget the destruction and the pain that this conflict brought. All the nations of the world wanted to live in peace and prosper. But now the world is again enmeshed in armed conflicts, terrorism and fear in general. The brotherhood is gone.

As a boy of six in 1943 I lived in Morocco, where I was born. I come from a Jewish Sephardic family of immigrants from the countries of the Middle East. We had the hope to eventually come to America. Morocco was at that time a French protectorate and ruled by the fascist Vichy government. As a Jew I had no right to go to school and therefore had no access to a formal education. With the arrival of the American Army in 1943 all these fascist decrees were abolished and I went back to school.

This experience made me worship the values that America stood by. We regarded Roosevelt as a messiah and the American troops as angels sent by God to free us. We then had food on our tables again, and all the racist restrictions were gone. Anything American was good.

For a few months before the American intervention my father served as a volunteer under Montgomery and the British flag. England did not have an Army available, and in North Africa Montgomery raised a Jewish Army, which later fought in Israel in the War of Independence.

In 1943 the British government extended special traveling papers to my father, as a reward for his services to the king. He chose México as his final destination. The document was personal, and he had to leave us behind. He didn't have another choice. The Mexican president at that time was Manuel Ávila Camacho, who had declared war on Germany. His predecessor, President Lázaro Cárdenas, opened up immigration to México. His decrees saved the lives of men of all nationalities. Jews, Spaniards and Europeans of different countries migrated to México.

México, with an incredibly friendly and receptive population, opened its heart to all these immigrants and adopted them as their own.

Figure 1.6.3.1 *1944—Young Rolando Uziel with his mother, Rebecca (28), and sisters Fortuneé (12) and infant Clarissa, at home, in the Atlas Mountains, Morocco*

When we arrived to México in December 1945 we were received with open arms. I registered at that time in a French School, and then a couple of years after that I moved to the American School Foundation to be able to go to university in America. I applied to Harvard and was lucky to be accepted. At Harvard I made many friends with different backgrounds, and I have kept many of those friendships alive through these 60 years. My roommate, Victor Brogna, is like a brother to me. America and the values it had at that time have always been my admiration and love. But México, which received me with open arms, has been my dear home and for which I feel a very deep gratitude and love.

Now coming back to me, I can divide the next 60 years in spans of 20 years each. The first 20 years, as I mentioned before, were those of my schooling, including Harvard, which was like a beam of light. My interaction with my fellow schoolmates, professors, Cambridge, Boston, New York gave me a different vision of life, for which I can only be grateful. The typewriter was our instrument of work, no computers, no Google, no telephone. To learn things we had to rely on our memories and research. Now whenever I have an argument with my grandchildren they just Google the information and correct me. The world our generation knew is gone. The world we all, in a small way, tried to create is gone. The information age has caught me at an old age. I am in a constant war with this technology. I want the machines to think like me and follow my logic, but they have their own logic, which is in battle with mine.

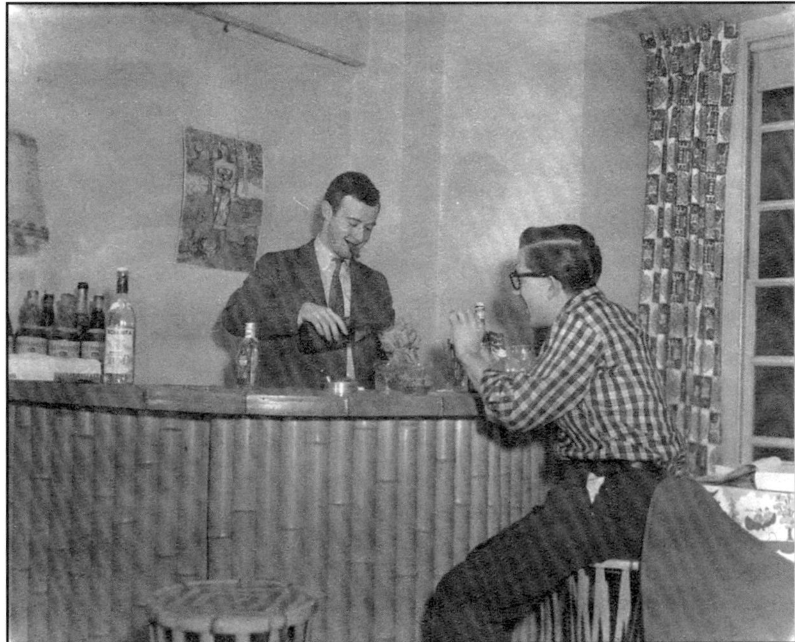

Figure 1.6.3.2 *1956—The author's Eliot House suite with bar*

Figure 1.6.3.3 *1957—Eliot House meeting in Common Room*

After I left Harvard I wanted to become an entrepreneur, not an employee of some large corporation. I had to be my own boss. For a couple of years I worked with my brother-in-law, who had a jewelry manufacturing plant. I saved my salary because I wanted to travel. I traveled by car with a friend for three months all over Europe. One of the cities I went to was Valenza, in Italy. They were very artistic in their designs but very primitive in their knowledge of precious stones. On the way back in New York I met my father, who had all sorts of connections with precious stone dealers. He introduced them to me and, like a flash, I knew this is what I wanted to work in.

The lure of diamonds, pearls and precious stones was for me. I spent the next 20 years traveling all over the world in search of stones and markets for them. I bought stones in Burma, today Myanmar, and sold them in Italy. I bought pearls in Japan and exchanged them for Mexican opals, which were to their liking. The pearls I sold in México and Brazil. I bought semi-precious stones in Brazil and sold them in Europe where they became very popular. India was a must as they started cutting diamonds at very competitive prices. I would go the mines in Siam, today Thailand, bordering Laos, in full war, to buy stones from their mines; in Colombia I was in the middle of a shoot-out between the "esmeralderos". Emeralds were in great demand in Geneva. Even if very dangerous, this was very exciting. I enjoyed these incredible experiences; my grandchildren love these stories when I start talking about them.

Figure 1.6.3.4 *1960—Gemologist Rolando seeking precious jewels in the war zone between Laos and Thailand, at theThailand border*

In the meantime, I got married at 27, and my first daughter was born a year after. Single is okay, but married is an entirely different story, no telephones and no mail. But Sarah endured all these hardships. We have been married now for 52 years; how she can stand me I do not know, but I love her more every day. God must like me to have given me this wife. Sarah is not only my therapist but a very renowned one in México. She has a very large practice. She never stops studying, learning all the new waves, teaching and at the same time holding me and the family together.

I have four incredible daughters, all with University degrees, and two of them are following the footsteps of their mother, all practicing psychologists. Two of my four daughters are twins. One lives in Miami and has a six-year-old boy. She studied cinematography in London and then at the American Film Institute. The youngest of the twins is a graduate museographer; she is actually a homeopath counselor, with an incredible number of patients. They have incredible husbands and I love them as if they were my own sons. I have seven grandchildren, four of them either graduated or studying in American universities. Two of them are university students in México. I am sure that the young one will follow the footsteps of his cousins. All this is the work of Sarah. Every year we invite the whole family to make a trip together. We have been to many countries, as well as many parts of México. Our latest trip was in Cancun, where they all honored me with the celebration of my 80th birthday.

The middle 20 years I spent in México, I got tired of all those trips, and set up a jewelry factory with my nephews. I became very involved in my Jewish community, which I presided over and met many personalities of the Israeli and Jewish world and of México. I was instrumental in building a new school, from kindergarten to preparatory, and I left a thriving community. I am very proud of these accomplishments.

Those 20 years from 40 to 60 were my entrepreneurial years. I started and managed seven different companies; this is where my stomach problems started. I was in the jewelry manufacturing, in the construction industry, I had an industrial where we were the biggest silver industrializers in México (and worked for the likes of Siemens, SquareD, Schneider, Federal Pacific, etc.), in textiles (I had plants to make shirts, and manufactured socks), retail (ten Yves Saint Laurent boutiques). I employed many thousands of people. Slowly I got out of most of these, my health was more important. I started a finance company to give micro-loans to poor people, based on a Hindu model.

When I was in my late 50s I had constant cases of gastritis; obviously something was wrong with me. I was a tennis and squash player, sports which I took up at Harvard since freshmen were required to exercise. Many of us remember that we had to take the famous step test, the 200-yard swimming test, etc. And of course we were required to exercise—excellent requirements. So I kept playing tennis. I was never very good, but socially it was excellent. By the way, I met my wife after a game; it was "shazam", that was it.

One of my sons-in-law, a natural athlete, invited us to see him run in the New York City marathon, an incredible experience. I told him one day I will run this marathon with you. I started training like crazy with a young trainer. He must have been 26 at the time while I was 56. To accomplish this I had to run from 60 to 100 kilometers a week. I never felt better in my life. Sure enough, at 60, I ran the New York City marathon. I ran eight international marathons: New York, Washington, Chicago, Bug Sur, México, Paris, etc. over more than ten years. I participated in more than 100 races, mostly 10k. I have quite a few medals from all these events. Unfortunately, my trainer, a two-hour-twenty minute marathoner, in the prime of life developed liver cancer and passed away.

Running took care of all my emotional problems. I still run about 25k a week but not races. I gave up racing when I could not do 10k in less than an hour. Training helped me change my lifestyle. I owe a lot to these people, my son-in-law and my trainer. I am very proud of this accomplishment.

Figure 1.6.3.5 *Marathoner Uziel crossing the finish line at the Marine Corps Marathon, Washington, DC*

My last 20 years I came back to my old love and became a developer of certain importance in México City. I have built more than 250 different properties during those years. I am publishing a book on this subject, very abundant in photographs. All my work was done in México City. The title is *A Small Footprint in this City*. It should be out in the next two or three weeks. I always had a very large interest in finance, and I joined a small bank as a board member. It has become the seventh bank in the country and will go public, if circumstances will permit it, in the month of May.

Finally, I will mention that I have been an important donor to several institutions in México, the USA, including Harvard, and Israel.

Let us all together sing an "Ode to Joy", and thank God for what he has given us. We are all in our 80s and full of life, and we still can contribute to better our world.

Rolando Uziel as a child emigrated from Morocco to México. His grandparents, members of a Sephardic Jewish family, which for centuries had lived in Turkey like others expelled from Spain and Portugal in 1492, joined the great diaspora with many others who left at the end of the 19th century, oftentimes splitting up the family. Most went to America, and quite a few went to France or its colonies. His great grandmother had gone to Morocco and her sister to America. His father went to Morocco, but two of his sisters joined their boyfriends in New York, and his third sister migrated to Israel. During WWII as a reward for his service to the British, his father received permission to emigrate to México, where the family later joined him. In the interval, his American cousin came to Morocco with the US Navy, searched out Rolando's family and became one of their "savior angels."

After graduation from the College where he was known as Roland (also his name on his French birth certificate based on Napoleonic code), Rolando returned to México and for a period worked in a family jewelry manufacturing company. Early travels to Europe and New York aroused an abiding interest in becoming a dealer in precious stones, a career that subsequently took him all over the world. Around age 40 he settled down in México and set up a jewelry factory with his nephews. After graduating from the Ipade Business School in 1987, he became a real estate developer in México City.

Rolando has been a marathoner, a community leader and supported social work for underprivileged people. He has also been an active supporter of Harvard, and in Israel, where his name in Hebrew is Ben Zion, of the Weizmann Institute and the Yad Washem Museum. With his wife of 52 years, Sarah, he has four daughters and six grandchildren.

Moments of Change

Charles E. Smith

After 50 years of Organization Development coaching, consulting and training with high-level leaders in companies and government agencies, it's my opinion that *the quality, mental, and moral character of leadership is normally distributed*, with 20% at the bottom, 20% at the top, and the rest somewhere in the middle.

Sometimes, I think this comes from the fact that the professional and financial success of senior leaders comes from paying attention to strategy, growth, structure, cost, quality, schedule, and profit. Attention to the humanity of human beings is subsumed within that primary role.

> In Korea and in China, the original meaning of the word "*Economics*" was "*to take care of the world and save people*".
>
> Since then, humans have evolved to where, in most countries, *it's accepted that people who control the most valued resources in business and government consider money and power to be more important than people.*

> Martin Luther King, just before he was assassinated, said, "*When you threaten the way the rich make their money, anything becomes possible.*"
>
> These days, there is a fundamental question never asked. "*Are business and money the primary purposes of my country, or is the primary purpose to take care of the world and save people?*

Star Wars Had It Right

> *The Force is an energy field created by all sentient beings. It surrounds us and penetrates the Universe.*
>
> *People can be with the Force for good and protection. This creates an unspoken cultural energy field that's full of noble purpose, values and accomplishment.*
>
> *People can be with the Dark Side of the Force for ego, greed, self-interest, and domination.*

Education, analysis, good ideas, complaints, and the force of will are not enough to change a paradigm, a fundamental way of operating. Endless strategizing and theorizing does not lead to effective action. General Ulysses S. Grant said,

> "*Great strategy always follows action.*"

* * *

Now, after 81 years, I love where I am in my life with countless blessings, family, friends and accomplishments in work and travel.

In the face of those never-ending failures, incompletions, and thwarted intentions, I'm pleased now because in those years of marrying the wrong women, going to the wrong schools, taking the wrong jobs, living in the wrong places, I finally came to trust my intuition, the little voice in my heart and my head that says,

> "*This doesn't feel right, my reasons for doing it won't overcome the doubt. If there is any doubt, there is no doubt. I know it's scary but get out now.*"

I believe in every single moment there is an aspect of that moment which if trust my gut, ordain it, embrace it as my own, it's connected to the entire universe.

I have learned to trust my intuition as never before. It's never been wrong.

Charles E. Smith is a graduate of Boston Public Latin School, Harvard College, Harvard Business School and Case Western Reserve University, where he received a PhD in *Organizational Behavior* and received a certificate from the Gestalt Institute of Cleveland. He was Visiting Associate Professor of Organizational Behavior at Sir George Williams University in Montreal and taught at the McGill University Centre for Management Education. He is a former President of the Harvard-Radcliffe Club of New Mexico, and Editor of *Transformation Magazine* published in the Library of Professional Coaching.

He lives in Santa Fe, NM, and is a Futurist, Senior Executive Coach, Author, and Leadership Consultant. He has written two books, *The Merlin Factor* and *Navigating from the Future,* and is about to publish *Are You a Noodle in Somebody Else's Soup?*

Charlie is married to Kathryn Grace Smith and has five children and five grandchildren.

Reflections on the End of a World

Simon D. Young

Count me among the deluded fools who long for "the good old days". Take me back to the blissful ignorance I enjoyed in the '40s and '50s, protected by a blanket of warm, reassuring, unquestioned assumptions about how the world is wired up.

Raised in a small industrial city in Massachusetts one generation removed from my Russian-Jewish immigrant grandparents, living in a family of communist-leaning, yet capitalist-striving atheists, my early life was governed by a simple rule: do what is expected of you, and you'll stay out of trouble. It was based on a belief—widely accepted by my peers, and strongly supported by John Wayne and Jimmy Stewart films—that the world is fundamentally fair and rational. That the good guys always win, and even though bad stuff can happen—sooner or later the bad guys always lose.

From that starting point, most of my adult life has been spent like a passenger in a slow-motion train wreck—gradually (and painfully) awakening to the realization that I had been seriously misinformed. Sure, good things happen, and bad stuff happens, but fairness and rationality have nothing to do with it. It's mostly shit luck. Plus—the bad guys are all over the place—and they're not going anywhere soon.

After years of struggling to make peace with this realization, I finally reached a place best described by the philosopher/novelist, Umberto Ecco:

> "*I have come to believe that the whole world is an enigma, a harmless enigma that is made terrible by our own mad attempt to interpret it as though it had an underlying truth.*"

Even more important to me are the final words my father spoke to me shortly before he passed. Frightened, he looked up from his hospital bed, and said, "*So . . . this is the way it ends . . .*" The meaning of this puzzled me for years, in fact right up to the time I sat down to write this essay. But I see now that he was expressing profound disappointment . . . that somehow he expected something more from his life, and perhaps from his death as well. That his *death* could be as simple and undramatic as just turning off a light, may have made him feel that his *life*—after all the effort he had put into it—had no special importance or value, either.

He was wrong, of course. His life had great value for those who loved him. His mistake—that so many of us make—was in *expecting* his life to be something more than what it was . . . and longer than it was about to be. The lesson for me is that you can't be disappointed if you have no investment in expectations beyond what reality finally delivers. So, enjoy the simple pleasures, try not to sweat the small stuff, and remember . . . it's mostly *all* small stuff.

As another great philosopher, George Carlin, wrote:

> "*People who see life as anything more than pure entertainment are missing the point.*"

Simon D. Young, born in Detroit, MI, attended public schools in Brockton, MA before matriculating at Harvard College. Following graduation he served as a 1st Lt. in the US Army from 1958–1960. After Harvard Business School (MBA, 1962), he returned to Brockton to manage the family business. In 1978 he founded a catalog mail-order company, *Wigs by Paula, Inc.*, which became one of America's largest retailers of women's wigs. In 1989 he sold the company and retired in 1995. An active sailor since the '80s in Southern New England waters, he has chartered sailboats in the Virgin Islands, San Juan Islands, Lake Huron, Florida Keys, Bahamas, Maine, and Chesapeake. At 80 he is still playing tennis and racquetball.

He has served the Fuller Museum of Art in Brockton as trustee, chairman and president, and the Massachusetts College of Art as trustee and past chairman of the Board.

Simon and his wife of 60 years, Paula Sims, have two sons. He and Paula still live in Brockton, enjoying theater, live jazz, and walking the family golden-doodle, Miss Daisy.

Counting Blessings

Carlo Zezza

In a time of distressing news, following the dearth of choice for president and the worst-case outcome, with the Middle East on fire, the European Union likely to split up, and a climate catastrophe destined for our children, it seems worthwhile to reflect on how lucky we are to be alive, in the most powerful and prosperous nation on earth, at this moment in history.

At Harvard, we can wonder about the future of tolerance, free expression, and free association. It's ironic that the present leadership's desire for diversity and inclusion should *exclude* misandrists, misogynists, or any student who might seek shelter from the opposite gender.

But we have gained so many benefits in the past sixty years, it's better to count blessings than register complaints. Tasks that were difficult are now easy, and obstacles have disappeared; 40 years ago I offered a prize to anyone in our company, located in Belgium, who could reliably deliver a document overnight to Paris for less than 10,000 Belgian francs; then came the fax, and today we have instant communication to anywhere. A computer file sent to a distant facility can generate a prototype in metal, returned overnight. Books flow easily from keyboard to public, for anyone with time and a mind to write (for me, two on rowing in the past two years). Most important, some loved ones would still be with us if their ailments had come a few years later.

A recent best-seller proposes that, as measured by their leisure time and healthier nourishment, hunter-gatherers of 20,000 years ago lived better than the mass of mankind today. This notion of well-being fails to credit our uniquely human aspirations for improvement. More than ever in history, curiosity, cleverness, and energy can work toward fulfillment of hope—witness Asia, where millions have risen from poverty to middle-class comfort within the past two decades.

We have gained many certainties in the past 60 years, and we like to posit rational causes for predictable effects. But, in retrospect, dame fortune has always come out on top. Saying "so far, so good" gains meaning with every year. I'm reminded of a fellow school alumnus, John Woods, who explained that his ability to compete as a mile runner, at the age of 92, was due to "pure luck". With that thought, I am crossing my fingers for some more lucky years, with books to write, regattas to row, and my family to enjoy.

Carlo Zezza was a naval aviator for four years after graduation. In his business career he was vice president of the J. Walter Thompson advertising agency; president of Samsonite Europe, the luggage company; president of Delsey USA, a subsidiary of the French luggage company; and executive vice president of the Samsonite Corporation.

He is the author of two novels, *The Love Potion* (1975), *Paris 2005* (1990) and two books on rowing—*Winning Head Races* (2015), *Boys in a Box—Why our top varsity crews are rowed by foreigners; Why our men won no medals in Rio; and What to do about it.* (2017). The latter two are available from Amazon.

Be Not Afraid of the Unfamiliar

Robert H. Secrist

The most important lesson I've learned in life is to not overplan: to be not so focused on a pre-determined goal that one is not open to view opportunities and experiences.

The unexpected and unforeseen trajectory of my life—from Pennsylvania to Alaska to Florida—is a case in point.

At first, my family's movements from Pittsburgh to Texas to Seattle were beyond my control, but the move to Alaska was discussed and agreed to by all of us, as a great adventure. Life in "*the frozen North*" was not always pleasant but did provide unusual, interesting and unforeseen experiences—including my becoming the only Alaskan in our class. I had already made other plans for college before the letter from

Harvard arrived, just two hours before my high school graduation, but I leapt at the unexpected opportunity without hesitation.

However, my first year in Cambridge was frustrating, because I was having trouble finding a field of concentration that really interested me until a House-mate suggested Linguistics—which I had never heard of but in which Harvard happened to be one of the only four colleges in the country to have a program at that time!

That one brief conversation resulted in a lifelong career, involving a Fulbright Fellowship at the University of Amsterdam, a MA and PhD from New York University, and a quarter-century teaching career at Youngstown State University in Ohio—none of which I had ever even contemplated before. (Another chance encounter with a stranger on a bus opened new vistas in pleasure and sexuality to my virginal self!)

After retiring and planning to remain in Youngstown, I suddenly had to visit my ailing father in Florida—where I discovered stately palm-lined streets and lush foliage flowering in January. As a result, I immediately purchased a small cottage in which to enjoy the wonderful weather in winter.

However, I eventually grew tired of supporting two residences and driving back and forth. So when a friend-of-a-friend offered to buy my main house (at four times my purchase price), I seized the opportunity to move to Florida full-time (with a much larger house and pool) and never see ice and snow again.

All this is not to imply that my life has been a continuous, uninterrupted pageant of fortunate decisions and great opportunities always grasped. Far from it. I've had a few regrets for bad choices made and unwise actions taken, but those I really remember and regret almost every day are all for missing or rejecting what, in retrospect, was a good opportunity, a "*road not taken*"—not for accepting or drifting into a bad one, i.e., for things *not* done, not for those done unwisely.

Thus, on balance, I can honestly say that whatever successes I have had in these 82 years have been accomplished by not over-planning, i.e., by rigid adherence to a pre-determined course in life, but by being willing at least to *consider* venturing into unexpected or uncharted territory.

As John Lennon said,

> "*Life is what really happens while we're busy making other plans.*"

One should never be so busy making and obsessing over other plans that new choices and opportunities are thoughtlessly cast aside and not experienced.

In the end, that's what life should really be about—an adventure, not a lock-step into eternity.

Just three months after graduation, the future Dr. **Robert Secrist** entered *Universiteit van Amsterdam* on a Fulbright Fellowship to study Germanic linguistics, which involved learning four old languages being taught in three current languages—including Egyptian hieroglyphics in Dutch! Back in New York City, he earned an MA in Foreign Language Education from NYU, taught French at a high school on Long Island, and then joined the founding faculty of Kingsborough Community College in Brooklyn—serving as Head of foreign-language departments at both.

He also spent a summer in Mexico City on an NEA scholarship at *Universidad Ibero-Americana*, with total immersion in Spanish language and culture.

After his PhD in English Linguistics (with the Founders Day Award) from NYU, he spent the rest of his career as Professor of English and Linguistics at Youngstown (Ohio) State University. Since retirement, he's been traveling (to numerous countries) and working on his genealogy, reaching back to many medieval VIPs—and purportedly even to Egyptian Pharaoh Ramses II!

Lately he's been accumulating a very large collection of wood carvings and other sculptural objects (in stone, horn, brass, etc.), for which he is seeking some sort of museum to which to bequeath them eventually.

Belief Systems

Philosophy of Personal Ethics and Living a Joyful Life

Michael S. Robertson

There are two truths in my life; "*Do unto others as you would have them do unto you,*" and "*Do as you are told.*" These form the foundation I have tried to follow on my life's journey.

If you are interested in learning more about my experiences to date, read on.

The Early Years

When we graduated in 1957 I had a pretty clear idea regarding what I wanted to do; namely, work for Robertson Factories, the family curtain and drapery manufacturing business that my father started in 1925.

Following six months of active duty in the Army Reserves, I spent five months in Macy's retail training program in New York City and five months at a J.P. Stevens textile training program in the south. With this unique preparation and my Harvard degree, I went to work in Taunton, MA, opening the mail.

I married Peggy Filoon in 1960, and we moved to Chicago in 1962 to sell Sears, Wards and the State Street stores from our Merchandise Mart office. Sales grew rapidly as did our family (three children in three years).

We moved from a great Chicago apartment to the suburbs in 1964 and became active members of a large church. This led to my becoming involved with the Community Renewal Society and helping set up Leon Sullivan's *Opportunities Industrialization Center (OIC)* job training program in Chicago.

We opened new factories. Sales continued to grow rapidly, and I was traveling constantly with 26 flights in one 25-week stretch. We became the largest privately owned company in our industry as we developed many new products.

In 1969 we moved back to Massachusetts, and our fourth child was born. I assumed various corporate management roles and was elected CEO in 1973. We built a fantastic house overlooking the Taunton River in Berkley, I was Rear Commodore of the Falmouth Yacht Club, a Deacon in our Church, active in community affairs, happily married and the father of four healthy children. Life was good, the company was profitable, sales were growing and the 19 years since graduation were following a predictable path.

Life lesson: *When you get too comfortable look out, because change is coming!*

When no one wanted to run for the US Senate vs. Ted Kennedy in 1976, I agreed to accept the Republican nomination if the Massachusetts Republican Party obtained the necessary signatures. They did, I ran and lost.

It proved to be an educational experience but one that had consequences. The company continued to grow, and the management team seemed to be capable. My leadership role was challenged, and in 1979 I attended the Harvard Business School Advanced Management Program to enhance my management skills.

Shortly after returning I was locked out of my office and fired by my family. My effort to have a family meeting to explain what had happened and why was never accepted, and I was forced to seek legal counsel. So much for a comfortable planned business career.

The following nine years had me owning a boat yard, a retail computer company, serving as a selectman in Berkley, MA, on the boards of the Massachusetts and National Easter Seal Society, Commodore of the Falmouth Yacht Club, the President's Advisory Committee for Trade Negotiations, Candidate for Massachusetts State Auditor and Chairman of the Deacons in my church. With four tuitions to pay to Milton Academy, Colby, Duke, Harvard and St. Lawrence, I was never quite sure these ventures were what I was supposed to be doing, but we were able to pay our bills.

Hearing and Following the Call

In 1989 I decided to do what God wanted me to do. This was a decisive decision but when nothing happened immediately, I continued doing what I had been doing.

In 1991 my life changed in a way I could never have anticipated. After a church service, a church member mentioned that the *National Association of Congregational Christian Churches (NA)* was in the process of hiring an Executive Secretary. Although I had not been involved in the NA, I felt called to look into this and decided to apply.

Much to Peggy's and my surprise I was offered the job after one short interview. This required moving from Massachusetts to Wisconsin, turning the computer company over to management, selling our Berkley home and striking out in a new direction. It was a six-year term-limited position so we knew when accepting the job that in 1997, at age 62, I would once again be unemployed.

With 400 churches in the association, spread out from Alaska to Maine, there was much traveling involved, as the NA provided support and encouragement to our member churches. As an association of member churches and not a denomination, the NA had no ecclesiastical power.

Each church follows its own covenant, and they range theologically from conservative to liberal.

I discovered that I truly enjoyed this diversity and the job. During these six years the NA grew in member churches, and we more than doubled our assets. The NA introduced a three-year lay ministry training program, and since I was visiting churches, preaching and presiding at church events, I enrolled. This training resulted in my becoming licensed in 1998. Congregational polity allows each church to call their minister, but you are not a minister unless you are actually serving a church.

Following a series of back operations, Peggy was diagnosed with terminal Merkel Cell cancer in 1993. She wanted to stay in Milwaukee and for me to continue working here. Classmate Ed Filmanowicz' oncology group provided great medical advice and service during the following three years before Peggy died in 1996. As we celebrated our 40th Harvard Reunion in 1997, I was 62, single after 36 years, and about to become unemployed. According to stress measurements this put me way over the top.

My Life Changes

My experiences visiting over 200 churches had me wondering why urban and suburban churches were not working together. *If we were all seeking the same result, why such a clear separation?*

There were five cities where I thought I might be able to create a working relationship between similar sized churches: Los Angeles, Brooklyn, Detroit, Chicago and Milwaukee. Being able to live anywhere made this search process possible, but as it turned out two churches, North Shore Congregational Church in Fox Point, WI, where Peggy and I were members, and Community Baptist Church in Milwaukee, agreed to create *Community Faith Alliance (CFA).* Community Baptist Church's motto was, "*We're staying in the hood to make it good.*"

In September 1997, as CFA coordinator, I moved into an apartment owned by Community Baptist Church located one block from the church. CFA had a board composed of three members of each church, and I was paid equally by each church. Although the congregations had voted to support this venture, and the pastors were supportive, there were those in both churches who did not believe this was a good idea. The original hope was that by opening up relationships and providing opportunities to know others, barriers would be reduced. The churches, located less than ten miles apart, are culturally, racially and theologically quite different.

I met Emmy Erickson at a North Shore church dinner in October, had my first date in 38 years, fell in love and proposed on a ferry on Vineyard Sound in December. We were married in February with both pastors presiding, bought and renovated a house in the vicinity of Community Baptist Church, sold Emmy's suburban house and moved in as a married couple.

In preparing the budget for 1999 after only one year, the trustees at North Shore decided unilaterally to eliminate funding my position. So much for a working alliance. Rather than making this insult public, Pastor Nabors and the CBC board hired me to become the director of *Community Village*, a 60-block area around the church we hoped to transform into a peace and prosperity zone. Cooperation between the two churches continued in the absence of any formal structure for a number of years before becoming a memory.

I found myself working full-time as a community developer for a Baptist church while living and working in an area most people regarded as being unsafe.

We entered into a relationship with the University of Wisconsin-Milwaukee to help us in the development of this neglected community. The city agreed to donate a library building directly across the street from the church, and Walgreens offered to develop it. An elementary school proposed building a middle school next to the Walgreens that the church would help fund using the lease revenue received from Walgreens.

With support from foundations, we purchased a number of houses and stores to assemble the needed land for the school. We held community meetings and helped develop and lease a parcel for a fast food restaurant and a shoe store. The Community Village office was located in a building we purchased from the city for $300 and renovated. A church-sponsored social services outreach ministry moved into the second floor. The houses were renovated and rented to provide income pending the school construction. Everything seemed to be properly funded, and in 2000 I turned all this over to a long time member of Community Baptist Church.

Homecoming and Ordination

It was time to move back to our home in Falmouth where my neglected sailboat had been holding down my mooring. We sold our Milwaukee house, gave away some furniture to our children, packed up a U-Haul trailer and drove east with no idea what we might be called to do next.

My three-year ministry in the "Hood" enabled me to better understand the challenges facing our society, particularly our minority urban communities. I planned to settle in Falmouth and share this understanding with others by writing articles and/or a book.

When Pilgrim Church, my childhood church, in Taunton needed to call a pastor, the current pastor suggested this might be a position we could share. After much prayer the two of us applied for the job as interim co-ministers and were hired. Imagine what had just happened. In 1989 in Pilgrim Church I had decided I would do what I was told, and 12 years later I was back at that church as their minister. Being ordained at 65, and ministering at the church where I grew up in, in the city where I previously was the CEO of a major employer, confused many, both in and outside the congregation.

Two years at Pilgrim as an interim provided the foundation for my continuing in pastoral ministry as membership and the church's assets grew. While seeking another interim call, I was asked to return to Milwaukee in 2003 to either resurrect Community Village or unravel it.

Because of changes in city politics, some promises that had been made were forgotten, and I spent the next six months closing down Community Village and disposing of the buildings we had purchased. Much of what I had thought might lead to significant social changes in Milwaukee had not taken place. I could only speculate regarding what might happen next and had serious doubts that I understood my calling.

The minister of the Union Church in Braintree, MA, advised he was retiring and suggested I apply to be the interim. I applied, was called and began serving on January 1st, 2004. The 60-mile commute from Falmouth to Braintree was compensated by the truly blessed congregation who welcomed Emmy and me in a way I had not experienced at Pilgrim Church. I was accepted as a pastor. Emmy felt a call to the ministry, applied and was accepted to study for a master's degree at the Episcopal Divinity School in Cambridge. We moved into an apartment on campus, which reduced my commute. My interim ended successfully, Emmy graduated, and I felt called to New Bedford to start a store front church.

With no job in hand, we made purchase offers on two houses that fortunately were not accepted. We were then advised that First Church of Squantum (Quincy) needed a part-time minister. On the Sunday after Easter 2006, I preached and was called by the congregation as their pastor, the following week. This was a church with about eight in regular attendance that was contemplating closing. We moved into the parsonage next to the church, Emmy was ordained as co-minister, and the church began to grow.

Deciding we might want to retire to Cambridge, we asked realtor Eleanor Olken, classmate Neil Olken's wife, to recommend houses, and in 2008 we purchased a single-family house just off Mt. Auburn Street. After all our previous moves this was to be the final one. We sold our Falmouth house and settled in. Our church grew, so closing was no longer a concern, and the members became comfortable. After six years the church could afford to hire a minister with a family who could attract younger members. When we celebrated our 55th Reunion, I knew it was time to move on.

In September 2012 we advised the congregation that our ministry would end following Christmas. The search process took longer than we had anticipated so we stayed on until a great candidate applied. He and his family moved in on August 1st.

Moving furniture from the parsonage and cleaning out my office was painful, since our Cambridge house was only 13 feet wide and very small. Owning one house does indeed reduce expenses and maintenance, and I thought I would become active in Cambridge and at the College and Business School. Emmy wanted us to consider buying a larger house and put Eleanor back to looking. We made offers on two houses in our neighborhood while listing our house, but our offers were turned down, and our house didn't sell.

Back to Wisconsin

On a Saturday in October Emmy said she might like to move back home to Wisconsin to be nearer to her children and grandchildren. After sleeping on this sudden change in direction, I offered, as a birthday present, to fly to Milwaukee on Wednesday. We looked at houses, and the next morning made an offer on one and flew back to Cambridge. On Friday we had an accepted counter, and after a home inspection signed a purchase and sale on Monday. In just eight days we had gone from looking at houses in Cambridge to buying a house in Fox Point, Wisconsin. Three weeks later we loaded up a U-Haul truck and drove to Milwaukee for the closing. Once again I was unemployed and had moved back to Milwaukee after ten years away.

Since the pastor at Community Baptist Church was new, and my mentor was still the minister at North Shore, we thought it made sense for us to be located in the suburbs. This turned out to be a mistake, as we were welcomed back at Community Baptist Church as ministers and as members at North Shore.

Becoming Associate Ministers at Community meant we needed to move into Milwaukee to a safe neighborhood that would be welcoming to all. We began looking and in December bought a large house on the east side next to the University of Wisconsin-Milwaukee. As the Minister of Community Outreach I had returned to exactly where I had been ten years before, and to my dismay nothing much had changed. The same stores and boarded-up houses remained, and the library building we had tried to develop was also empty. It was as if I had been living in a time warp. *Was my return meant to actually cause change or was this wishful thinking on my part?*

I am now entering my third year as minister of community outreach, and it has been hard to patiently wait for the congregation to want to reach out into the neighborhood. If anything, the neighborhood has grown more violent, and past failures to achieve lasting changes seem to discourage new efforts.

At this point you may be wondering what this has to do with *Living a Joyful Life.* The work experiences and the many moves are the result of my not worrying about what may happen next. These dramatic changes in profession and location have been confusing to observers and family. It is virtually impossible to explain, because I have no clear idea regarding what might happen next. There is no clear path laid out for me to follow, and I never receive direct instructions.

Looking back over the past 28 years does not add much insight into what will happen during the coming years. *What is exciting for me is that I continue to think five years into the future just as I always have.* Perhaps this is totally unrealistic at my age, but I have been blessed with excellent health and continue to have ample energy and enthusiasm.

Taking Stock

As I look ahead it is clear that there will be as many life changes in the coming five years as there have been in the past five years. Can I plan for that? Of course not.

Long ago I gave up believing I had any direct control over future events.

Ageing

Belief Systems

The challenge is to live as fully in the present as possible and to spend no time worrying about what might happen.

Ventures we might start may have to be completed by someone else. This is no reason for not continuing to live as if I have all the time in the world, because I do have all the time in the world.

It is harder for me to keep as many things in motion as when I was younger so I am trying to focus on selected ministries. These currently include the *Love Kindness* program, a human trafficking/domestic violence ministry, a public high school transformation effort and a house rehab venture. With all this going on it is exciting to wake up every morning, and these are merely my job-related activities.

My first book has been in the edit stage for a year and still needs work, but I may have copies to give away at our reunion. I took up golf last year and may break 50 for nine holes in 2017. The keyboard Emmy bought me a few years ago sits idle as does the ukulele I bought. My paint supplies and easel sit gathering dust in the basement, while too many books I have vowed to read remain unopened. Trips to places and friends we want to visit will take up time as will graduations, weddings, reunions and memorial services. Some of these events will be scheduled while others will happen suddenly.

It is the not knowing regarding the future that makes each day so very special. When something unexpected happens, and our best laid plans go terribly wrong, there is still tomorrow. As long as we have the capacity to love and be loved, we are truly blessed.

My philosophy of personal ethics means trying to be as kind to everyone as I am able. This is not something I achieve easily, but I keep trying. Cheerful giving of both time and money without expecting anything in return requires my constant attention. Emmy is better at this than I am, although I believe I am improving.

The surprising thing is that whenever we are able to help someone else, we receive more than we give. *A joyful life is filled with acts of kindness beginning with ourselves.* We begin by being as kind to ourselves as possible, and whenever we are able to help someone, we do what we can. Just a smile can make a difference, and a kind word is always welcome. By staying active and involved I can be in a place where I can make a difference.

Kindness is ageless. As a minister I perform memorial services, and the one thing remembered above all else is how the deceased treated others.

We have lived in truly blessed times, and many of our class have made noteworthy contributions that are worthy of mention. We want to be favorably remembered and leave a lasting legacy. I believe the love we share and the kindnesses we do far outweigh everything else.

My life journey has been and continues to be totally unexpected. Many ventures begun with the best intentions and high hopes ended up being failures. These failed campaigns, ministries and businesses have only served to demonstrate to me the endless opportunities we have to serve others.

The words of Micah, "What does the Lord require of you; do justice, love kindness and walk humbly with your God," provide the foundation for my faith.

Love is the most powerful force on earth. I thank God for all the blessings I have received many times every day. I believe each of us is on our own faith journey and are in different places in our relationship with God at any given time. Understanding this allows me to greet each day with the expectation I will be able to make a difference today. What could be more exciting and joyful than that?

I do not worry about what others may or may not do with their day because this day is all mine.

Let me leave you with this prayer.

> *May your days be filled with love received, and love given, and may you experience joy through kind words spoken and kindnesses shared.*

Figure 1.6.4.1 *The Reverends Michael and Emmy Robertson in their ministerial robes at their church in Milwaukee, WI, 2017*

Michael S. Robertson following graduation joined his family-owned Robertson Factories in sales and management until 1980. Following a change of management, he left and invested in and managed three small businesses in Massachusetts, and also served as Selectman in the town of Berkley, MA, 1974–80.

A complete career change took place in 1991 when he and his wife, Peggy, moved to Wisconsin, and he became Executive Secretary of the National Association of Congregational Churches. His commitment ultimately led to his being ordained a Congregational Minister at age 65 in 2000. He has served congregations in coastal Massachusetts and in Wisconsin. He currently serves as minister of community outreach for Community Baptist Church in Milwaukee in an inner-city neighborhood.

Mike and his first wife, Peggy Filoon, had four children. Following her death after 36 years of marriage, he married Emmy Erickson, who like Mike was ordained at a mature age. Together they serve their Milwaukee community as ministers in community outreach to the inner-city neighborhood and its schools where they serve.

Faith – Fantasy, Fiction, or Fundamental[1]

John Fenn

The word "*Faith*", for a third-generation Unitarian boy, was the nearest you could come to using profanity, without actually touching the base. Almighty Google, our 21st-century information deity, defines faith as "complete trust or confidence in someone or something . . . based on spiritual apprehension rather than proof."

"*Proof*" implies REASON, and, if we Unitarians were to believe in anything, sure as shooting it better be based on REASON and proof. Don't lay no "*Faith*" on us. Like Judge Judy, "*Show me some proof!*"

Recently I came to the realization that every human being starts with a belief or Faith. Even Unitarians. The fact is that nobody can totally prove anything. Therefore, we all have to start with something we believe in simply because, based on our observations it seems to be intrinsically valid. In short, we simply must develop our own personal axioms.[2]

So, when my Catholic friends in Boston say, "*Keep the faith*", they simply start with the Faith (axiom), that God exists and sent his only begotten Son to save us all from Original Sin.

> *[Forgive me for a sidebar here: some folks, when asked for proof of this Faith, state that it is in the Bible. Why do you believe that the Bible is infallible? Because it is the word of God. Circular logic? You think?]*

So the bottom line is, no one has any right to challenge, question, or try to refute anybody else's Faith because Faith depends entirely on what is spiritually or self-evidently true *for the individual.* It is an axiom of their lives.

However, as to the Faith in the existence of God, I part company with atheists. They totally discount the existence of God without recognizing the vast civilizing force for the development of civilization that this Faith has produced. It all began when one of the early Pharaohs conceived the idea of one God. Then we hurtled forward from abacus to Artificial Intelligence.

Well then, having removed the stigma from the word "Faith" as a fallen away Unitarian (and if that isn't the neatest trick of the week what is?), I started to explore what my Faiths are.

First, I jumped on the coattails of the venerable Descartes. "*I think, therefore I am.*" Sounds like a pretty self-evident thing to me. But don't ask me to prove it as an absolute truth. Can't be done.

Second Major Faith/Axiom: Because I see things, hear things, smell things, and taste things, there is a separate reality out there to be seen touched, etc.

> *[Another sidebar: Here we can give this Faith/axiom a leg up with a hypothetical experiment. Assemble four people from four different countries.*
>
> *Have a translator write the words on a sign in each participant's language, that says "Please pick up any green object from this table."*
>
> *If they all pick up green objects, at least we have a number of votes for the external reality of the color green.]*

Faith/Axiom Number Three: There is no absolute unchanging eternal truth (including this statement) and whatever there is out there that we call truth is discoverable by the use of reason, which collects our perceptions and forms self-evident conclusions.

So then, armed with my Faiths, I wake up in the morning after a delicious night's rest, to see a bright and beautiful day. I bask in the glorious energy of the sun, see a giant tree, appreciate all its infinite complexity that allows it to grow and change. Then I think of myself, as a human being. "*What piece of work is man,*" said Shakespeare. Just consider the infinite complexity of the atoms and molecules, the energy driving our nervous system, or the billions and trillions of neurons firing in our brains. *If you want something to worship, what else is there but life itself?*

> *[Yet another sidebar: One of the flies in the ointment of life is this death thing. Let's face it, in this universe there ain't no free lunch. If you're going to revel in the excitement and fun of change and growth, you have to be at peace with this death thing. It clears the way for evolutionary change.]*

Finally, I came up with the notion of a universal infinite Chi. Now Chi is roughly defined as energy. So I have sprinkled in some Einsteinian physics, which tells us that matter and energy are the same thing, and that if we could throw a baseball faster than 186,000 miles per second, that "matter" baseball would become energy.

So instead of praying to and worshiping God, my Faith and object of worshipful praise is:

Chi Dayenu[3]

I joyfully celebrate my part in
the Ever Changing Dance of the
Universal Eternal and Infinite Chi
and offer worshipful gratitude
for the abundance of health and mind-power
entrusted to me
to improve the Shining Hour
for myself, my family,
my community and my world.

Chi dayenu,
Chi dayenu.

Thus has it ever been, thus it is now, and evermore shall be:

Chi dayenu, chi dayenu,
Chi dayenu, dayenu,
Chi dayenu, dayenu, dayenu.

John Fenn wrote: "My grandfather (William Wallace Fenn) was Dean of the Harvard Divinity School when Unitarianism was very instrumental at Harvard University.

My career, like Gaul, has been divided into three parts. (1) Work as a production stage manager in New York City with the Shakespeare Festival and numerous other companies; (2) Writing plays and musicals (19 produced with over 70 productions nationwide); (3) Teaching at Circle-in-the-Square Theater School, New York City, as well as all two Minnesota school systems, and as an adjunct professor in three Minnesota colleges.

Although technically retired, I am continuing full speed ahead with writing and teaching. I have informed my doctors that it is my full intention to attend Commencement in Harvard Yard for our 100th Reunion. Heaven only knows how many genetically generated or artificial spare parts I may have on board . . . but most of me will be there, and I sure hope some of you will be joining me."

Endnotes

1 © Copyright 2017 by John Fenn

2 AXIOM: "statement or proposition that is regarded as being established, accepted, or self-evidently true"

3 DAYENU: "Jewish prayer word meaning 'it is enough (sufficient)'"

Wisdom

Report to Iran and America

William S. Bahary

As an introduction, these are my chronicles for my classmates of Harvard Class of 1957 about my opium story, probation at Harvard, and a personal success story.

Growing Up on the Silk Road

As a start, in the middle of the 1800s in order to avoid religious persecution, my great grandfather at the age of two was taken from the eastern Iranian holy city of Mashed on the Silk Road to Kermanshah, Iran, a western city on the Silk Road. About a century later, my family moved to Tehran, the capital of Iran, which was another city on the

Silk Road, and where much else besides silk was traded. My ancestors were traders, as explained below.

Growing up in Tehran, we had a beautiful garden a short distance outside Tehran with a gardener who smoked opium. My family, including my brothers, sister and I, would regularly visit our garden. One day as little kids we visited our gardener in his living room, where he was smoking opium. We sat around the fire of hot coals and took a few breaths of the second hand smoke of opium that our gardener was smoking. It was a social phenomenon, and we thought nothing of it. I felt a little strange, maybe high, and walked away. It was risky, but we did not know better. His wife told us that at times, he would get on the roof of their mud house in the middle of the night and sing at the top of his voice. In that culture it appeared that smoking opium for the plain as well as the rich was a social and inspirational thing to do, and was not an addictive thing to avoid.

Coming back to the Silk Road, my Dad told to me about the opium trade. His father, that is my grandfather, was part of that trade in the early 1900s. The opium exudate would be collected from the poppy flower head, and the workers—who were mostly women—would sit in the hot sun and process the opium. This involved rolling the opium on a board to a firmer consistency in the shape of six inch rolls of one half inch thick, resembling tootsie rolls. These were packaged and shipped along the Silk Road to China. This may not have been as outlandish at the time as it may first appear.

You may recall the *Opium War* of the British with China. This was considered a "respectable" war to preserve their "respectable" trade by ship. The opium trade along the Silk Road with donkeys, horses and camels was also considered a "respectable" trade in the early 1900s. Times have changed.

The Silk Road could have been called the *Opium Road*, but it is still called the Silk Road. This is my understanding of the opium culture in Iran. Heroin and cocaine were not heard of until I came to this country.

My Educational Experiences

Growing up in Tehran, I attended the American Community School, a Presbyterian Mission, which provided the best education in the city, and fortunately it was co-educational and much fun. We immigrated to the United States when I was 15 years old, where I enrolled in the Horace Mann School for Boys. To show the quality of education I had at the Community School in Tehran, I was able to skip a grade at Horace Mann. Academically, Horace Mann was great as it took me to

Harvard, but socially it was amorphous and barren and not much fun. I missed having girls in my classes and at school.

Harvard was a great choice. There were women in my classes and on campus. Once again I felt at home. We also had parietal hours in Lowell House.

It so happened that one Saturday evening I overstayed the parietal hours by 20 minutes. We were supposed to escort our women guests out by 11:00 p.m. on Saturday evenings, but I signed out at 11:20 p.m. A couple of days later I received a call from our Housemaster, Professor Elliot Perkins, for an appointment to see him. In fear and trembling I went to visit him. He said that as this was my first offence, he would put me on probation. I was supposed to go to the gate house to sign the attendance register every evening at exactly 6:00 p.m. for one week. I did that successfully and got off probation. The punishment was not too excessive for him, as he was known to have said that if you can't get in and get out by the parietal time, you don't deserve to get in. I wonder what Prof. Elliot Perkins would say now if he found out that Lowell House was co-educational? I graduated from Harvard in June 1957 without any other nefarious incidents.

My graduate education at Columbia University, and my career doing research and development work, and teaching in chemistry and biochemistry, are for another report, but for now my experiences since retirement are more interesting.

My Experiences since Retirement

Synagogue

One of my noteworthy experiences and accomplishments was my service to our synagogue as an officer. About a year ago, several congregants began leaving the synagogue for another one in our neighborhood. About the same time some of my best friends in the synagogue also left to go to services at another synagogue. I was about to leave the synagogue, where I am an officer, but decided to try to address the issue first. The Rabbi's sermons, after 25 years, had become too orthodox and mystical for a Sephardic congregation.

This was annoying to a good part of the congregants, although some congregants liked them. Some congregants snoozed during the sermons, and others went upstairs to eat and drink. I took it upon myself to address the situation, although my discussion with some close friends did not appear to be promising. However, I discussed the situation with our Rabbi at the end of one of our services in a low-key manner. I asked him if he considered making his sermons more user-friendly. It might help build up our membership. There wasn't much hope that an orthodox Rabbi would change his style, but it was worth a try.

To my surprise, about six months later, I heard sermons that were more relevant to the congregation. He gave sermons on anger management after the presidential elections, and another good one on what constitutes happiness. My discussion may not have influenced our Rabbi, but his sermons became shorter, more interesting, and my spiritual life got a lift.

There is an important lesson I learned here. This confirmed what is known as the *science of personal success*: to build relationships and make friends in order to influence people.

Yoga

Another noteworthy activity in my retirement is practicing yoga and yoga philosophy. I was always interested in philosophy from my college days, but the practice of yoga fascinates me.

It brings together the wisdom of the east, western philosophy, transcendentalism and the self-reliance of Ralph Waldo Emerson and Henry David Thoreau. Toward the end of our yoga session, our yoga instructor prompts us to *breathe* ***in*** *love and gratitude and breathe* ***out*** *a smile.*

So *I breathe* ***out*** *a smile* to my wife, family, friends, my classmates at Harvard, my roots in Iran, and the opportunities and possibilities in America. *Thank you.*

Figure 1.6.10.1 *The author as a teenager in Iran in 1951, soon to depart for Cambridge, MA*

William S. Bahary after graduation received his PhD in chemistry from Columbia University. Subsequently he conducted research and development at several companies, including Duracell and Unilever, and taught at Fairleigh Dickinson University and Stevens Institute of Technology. He is also the holder of several patents and author of publications in his field. He has been a partner with his brothers in Bahary & Company, which invests in real estate, stocks and bonds.

His avocations include tennis, skiing in Vermont and Alta, Utah, for many years as well as gardening and reading biotechnology literature.

His public service includes being an officer at the Manhattan Sephardic Congregation and scientific advisor to *Stop Anellotech*, a citizens group dedicated to preventing the production of toxic benzene and toluene near his country home in Pearl River, NY. He writes: "My spouse of over 30 years is Susan Kurshan Bahary, Vassar '60, to whom I am grateful for her warm companionship and joy to bring us to this date."

A Life in Questions

David Epstein

"Why are we in America?" is the first substantive question that I ever asked. In 1939, I was a four-year-old Texan. My San Antonio neighborhood had modest single-family houses, the residences of multi-generational Texans within a large state that was not far removed from the frontier. This question to my father was conveyed in Yiddish, my home language as well as that of our relatives and the friends of my parents, all of whom had come with their Eastern European Jewish religion and culture. In later years, I would flippantly say that when I was a child I thought everyone in Texas spoke Yiddish. My father, Yudie, arrived in Texas in 1922, at age 18. My mother Sonia and her large family had emigrated from Poland to Mexico in the late 1920s and early 1930s. Mexico was a somewhat exotic country, non-European, soon after its own Revolution with strong remnants of its pre-Columbian past, echoes of Spanish Imperial rule, and a Mestizo present, all filled with its own color, music, foods, smells and traditions. My mother was at that moment in Mexico City to attend the wedding of her youngest sister, leaving my elder brother William and me at home. (Our sister, Eleanor, came along a few years later.) My father responded by writing a poem in Yiddish of how and why first some siblings and then he had migrated to America. Why did I ask this question? I must have sensed that my family circumstances were distinctive to our surroundings.

"Will there still be news after the war?" was the question I posed in the 1940s during World War II. My father would each day drive my brother William and me to our public elementary school. He would not leave the house until after hearing the latest news about the war. We did not have a car radio. I was anxious about getting to school on time. We arrived after the first school bell announcing the beginning of the class day and only a fraction of a minute before the buzzing of the tardy bell. Not only did I later learn that news would still exist but that the concept of news is elastic and ever-expanding, going well beyond great wars.

"What were the causes of the American Civil War?" In the Harvard Yard as a freshman and later at the Adams House dining tables or in the well-worn lecture halls, questions were framed, argued, resolved or left unresolved. Is it the Great Man in History or the combination of social forces that affect the direction of a society? Were the Dark Ages really without learning and culture? What were the consequences of the closing of the American frontier? What is the Greek idea of Tragedy? Why do the righteous suffer and evil prosper? Science posed different questions with precise answers, about how to create compounds, measure weights and understand mass and acceleration.

"Do I want to be a doctor?" was the question that I asked myself after college graduation, in the summer of 1957. A pre-med at the College who was accepted to three respected medical schools, I chose to forego that career on the day before my medical education would have commenced. Days later, I was at Harvard Law School, where the Socratic Method was enshrined and applied in a manner where previously confident students were resigned to humiliation.

"Aye, aye, sir" is the answer of a junior officer in the US Coast Guard, aboard ship or on shore. Follow orders, rules, and military etiquette. I served my country by doing as I was told. No questions asked.

"Ask not what your country can do for you—ask what you can do for your country" proclaimed John F. Kennedy in his 1961 Presidential Inaugural Address. My response was to move to Washington, DC, for these and other reasons. First, as a prosecutor, an Assistant United States Attorney, arising in Court to announce that I, son of the *shtetl*, represent the United States of America. Questions flowed, but of a different nature, to learn and present affirmative facts or challenge those offered by the defense. Then, using these acquired skills in courtrooms around the country in civil litigation or in law school classrooms to teach trial advocacy or as an Arbitrator seeking information that may affect my decision.

"Who is America's most obscure President?" was the question that I asked of Ellen Robinson in May 1971. Her reaction was surprising, agitated excitement. It was our second date. Why this reaction, I asked? Ellen answered that this was the same question that she asked her dates. My response, "If we have that much in common, we should get married." Ten weeks later we were, I, 36, Ellen, 24. We did not then and do not now agree as to who should have the title of "most obscure". I offer "Franklin Pierce". Ellen's candidate is "Chester Alan Arthur". I asked this question because I had years earlier read of a proposal to build a national mausoleum for the interment of all dead Presidents. I thought that there must be a President not worthy of recognition. This led to my published article and an appearance on a national late night television program to argue the reasons why Pierce deserved obscurity. I formed "The Friends of Franklin Pierce", with the motto, "To rescue him from the obscurity he so richly deserves." I was, by design, its sole member. Notwithstanding our disagreement, Ellen and I are in our fifth decade of marriage, with five adult children, their spouses, and now 12 grandchildren.

"What's in this week's Torah?" was the question asked by our then five-year-old son at our traditional Jewish Sabbath Eve Dinner. I had initiated questions with our young children in order to divert them from their antics and introduce content at the dinner table. One week, I forgot to raise any topics. The child's question led to my article by that title, and then an offer from a major publisher for me to write a book. I co-authored *Torah with Love: A Guide for Strengthening Jewish Values within the Family*. A reviewer wrote, "This is one of those books which can change lives." Years later, an author referred to our book as a "classic".

"I wonder what we are missing right now?" is the question that I asked Ellen, who was sitting at my side in the Harvard Yard in 1986 during the weeklong celebration of Harvard's 350th Celebration. The Dean of the JFK School of Government had just noted that in 1936, at the Harvard Tercentenary, not a single one of the speakers made reference to conditions in Europe. Three years later, Europe was aflame in World War II, a war whose consequences took 50 years to resolve. I attest that in 1986 none of the worldly speakers, neither academics nor political nor cultural leaders, offered a single thought to suggest that Europe was on the verge of world-changing events. Again three years later, in 1989, the Berlin Wall, the physical symbol of the divide between the free and the totalitarian, fell. In 1991, the "evil empire" itself, the Soviet Union, collapsed.

"Where shall we go?" led to a high point of my parenting, taking one-on-one travels with each of our five children when teenagers. Our eldest, Jeremy, in 1987 chose to go to countries under Soviet rule over my suggestion to visit Italy and learn about the Roman Empire. The trip ended by visits to both sides of the then-standing Berlin Wall, a contemplation on the blessings of freedom and the meaning of democratic values. Next, Asher, to New Zealand and Australia during the latter's 200th celebration of the arrival of the First Fleet. For Barak, at last the Roman Empire, with our shared reading assignment of Gibbon's *Decline and Fall.* Dina, to Turkey and its multi-layered civilizations, from Hittite, Byzantine, Greek, Roman, Seljuk Turk, Ottoman Turk, then Gallipoli and Ataturk's nation. We walked together up to the ruins of Troy, I, listening anew to Homer's *Iliad* with a faded memory of my first reading in Humanities 3, freshman year. For Kira, the youngest, our trip was across a broad swath of the new South Africa, conceived by Nelson Mandela.

"What do you know now that you didn't know then? What career ambition did you fail to realize?" One part of my decision to have a yearlong 80th Birth Year Celebration in 2015 was to travel around the country to visit individuals with whom I had been friendly decades earlier in high school or college and had seen either infrequently or not at all in the intervening years. In visits with approximately 20 individuals plus many of their spouses, these topics set the tone. We talked about life experience, not current events, resilience after being battered by life, adjustments to a changing world, disappointments and satisfaction in family, career, and community.

"Are you depressed?" was the interview question that I was asked upon entering cardiac rehabilitation during that same 80th year, after an unexpected four-way coronary artery bypass surgery. My response: "No, am I supposed to be?" I was actually exhilarated, amazed at what medical science had done for me though unable to understand how the Medicare system could pay for new medical technology and meet the needs of an aging population. I resumed my activities and travels just three months after the surgery. My only disappointment occurred on the Cunard Line's *Queen Mary II* transatlantic crossing from New York to Southampton, England. I chose this trip with Ellen because it retained the elegance of the 1930s and insisted on black tie dress for three of the dinners. Having lost considerable weight because of the surgery, I fully expected someone to say to me in my tuxedoed elegance, "*You remind me of Cary Grant*" (the mid-20th-century movie actor who epitomized those qualities). I confronted the limits of my imagination when no one on the ship suggested the comparison.

"Where is the conflict?" is what I must provide as a recently self-styled "minor American playwright". My *oeuvre,* a series of plays called "The Lawcycle", in which each presents a challenge of the law. Does the Shakespearean line, "The First Thing that We Do, Let's Kill All the Lawyers" constitute incitement if placed on a billboard, without attribution, and inspires a murderous act?

In another play, will a protagonist suffer more if he complies with a religious law that leads to a detrimental outcome for himself and his loved ones, or should he suppress and betray his commitment to that law? Can satisfaction be derived from using law to exact revenge on an innocent party?

Does Neil Armstrong, the first human to land on the Moon, have authority to negotiate with an unexpected life form on the Moon—who, amazingly, has legal training from auditing law school classes on Earth? The moon creature propounds a list of the Moon's grievances, which, if not satisfied, will result in the obliteration of Armstrong's footprint and all other traces of America's landing.

Finally, if a religiously devout man seeks to avoid sitting next to a woman on a long flight in order to concentrate on religious texts and avoid distracting thoughts about this female neighbor, how should he regard a transgender person, who was once the greatest male athlete of his time and is now a woman?

"What bedrock principles do you seek to convey to your descendants?"

On Character: Integrity is not negotiable.

On Learning: World without end.

On America: Adhere to the aspirations of the Declaration of Independence, the values and restraints of the Constitution, salute the Flag, and stand for the National Anthem.

On Identity: Descendant of the Tribe of Levi, present at Sinai, and indispensible link from generation to generation.

Ageing

Wisdom

David Epstein, born in San Antonio, TX, to Jerome "Yudie" Epstein and Sara "Sonia" Epstein, emigrants from Eastern European Jewish culture, graduated from Thomas Jefferson High School and placed third nationally in the Hearst American History contest. Following college, he graduated from Harvard Law School in 1960. Next, he served as commissioned officer aboard the US Coast Guard Cutter *Rockaway*.

After four years as an Assistant United States Attorney for the District of Columbia, he became a civil lawyer, working nationwide, enjoying the intensity, surprises, drama and stakes involved in trials. His life in the law included: adjunct professor at Georgetown Law; labor arbitrator; opining on lawyer's ethical questions; adjudicating lawyer's professional conduct; officer of the DC Bar; interviewer in Court's oral history project; participant in courthouse design and organization. Epstein has the distinction of four nominations as a candidate for the presidency of the DC Bar. He satisfied his presidential itch in other organizations.

He has authored articles on biblical archaeology, courthouse architecture, President Franklin Pierce, and the Constitution, and was co-author of a book on the rules of criminal procedure. As a self-styled "minor American playwright", his plays are collectively called "Lawcycle".

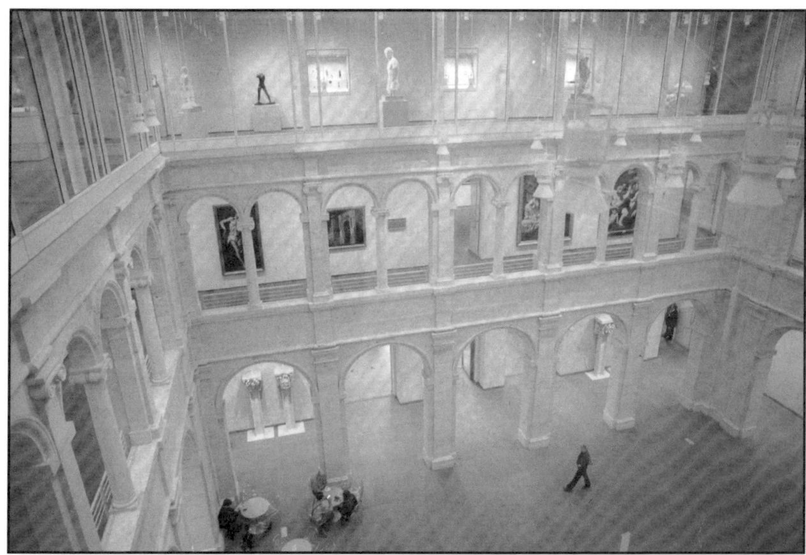

Figure 1.6.10.2 *Fogg courtyard of renovated Harvard Art Museum*

Reprinted courtesy of Harvard University

Figure 1.6.10.3 *Ludwig Josef Johann Wittgenstein (1899–1951), Austrian-British philosopher, in 1930*

An educator and colleague of Bertrand Russell at University of Cambridge from 1929 to 1947, his contributions were mainly in logic, the philosophy of mathematics, the philosophy of mind, and the philosophy of language.

Although during his lifetime he published only one book, the 75-page Tractatus Logico-Philosophicus *(1921), one article, one book review and a children's dictionary, his wider impact came from the influential book* Philosophical Investigations, *compiled and edited from his voluminous manuscripts after his death. Published in 1953, this volume has been acclaimed as one of the most important works of philosophy in the 20th century.*

Sources:

Text: https://en.m.wikipedia.org/wiki/Ludwig_Wittgenstein

Photo: https://en.m.wikipedia.org/wiki/File:Ludwig_Wittgenstein.jpg,
Credit: Moriz Nähr, 1930, Austrian National Library, Accession number Pf 42.805: C (1)

Chapter Two

HISTORY

Figure C2 *A Class Marshal, dressed for his role in the traditional ceremonies of the Happy Observance of Commencement, arrives at dawn in Harvard Yard.*

Reprinted courtesy of Harvard University

Chapter Two
HISTORY

European

Asian

Personal Experience

European

Balkan Wars

1914 and 2014: From Sarajevo to the First World War and the Centennial Controversies

John R. Lampe

Introduction

On June 28, 2014, Sarajevo commemorated the *centennial* of the Archduke Franz Ferdinand's assassination. The somber ceremonies assembled European dignitaries and culminated in a concert by the Vienna Philharmonic Orchestra. I did not attend.

I did, however, make the first of my many visits to Sarajevo many years ago, just after Yugoslavia's media and scholarship had marked the *50th anniversary* of the assassination, celebrating it as a first step in the state's creation. Gavrilo Princip's footprints were still preserved in the sidewalk where he stood, outside a small museum honoring him as a national hero, just across from a small bridge named after Princip. At the time, visitors could travel from the city center into the surrounding hills, on one of the DC streetcars delivered by an American donation, to the Hotel Bosna where the Archduke and his wife had stayed the night before. The dinner menu was still posted in a window near the front door. As for Austria-Hungary, a pamphlet from the same museum of Young Bosnia described the Dual Monarchy as "an anachronism whose disappearance from the scene was an historical necessity."

There was flurry of Western anniversary publication then, but as I will describe shortly, it paid little attention to Bosnia or Serbia.

The controversy of the 1960s centered on German war guilt, a charge that the Second World War helped to revive. Now the wars of Yugoslavia's dissolution in the 1990s and the rise of new terrorist organizations have turned the media's attention back to Bosnia and Serbia for comparisons to 1914.

Already since 1989, new scholarship has encouraged current policy makers to look back on the pre-1914 Habsburg and Ottoman Empires as better frameworks for ordering the mixed populations and religions of the Balkans and the Middle East, better than the set of presumed nation-states put in place by the Paris Peace conference of 1919. These borders did not survive the 1990s in Yugoslavia or Czechoslovakia, and are now under siege in Syria and Iraq.

The most influential scholarly work lamenting the way in which Austria-Hungary was dismantled came from Margaret Macmillan, *Paris 1919, Six Months that Changed the World* ((Random House, 2001). Read the foreword by Richard Holbrooke for a classic example of "retrospective determinism", reading back the failure of the second Yugoslavia to the creation of the first one. Greater Serbian nationalism is the common cause. Macmillan's own account, magisterial in dealing with the leadership of victorious powers, does compare the Serbian prime minister at the Paris conference, Nikola Pasic, to Slobodan Milosevic as equally "deceitful and dangerous".

Now in 2014 we have seen continuing conflict in Syria and Iraq joined by covert Russian military intervention, first in Crimea and then in eastern Ukraine. Hence the current temptation to read back both disruptions to 1914, lamenting the loss of Ottoman order in the Middle East and blaming Russian mobilization in July 1914 for starting the First World War.

Not surprisingly, an historian long based in Turkey, Sean McKeekin, has advanced this thesis in *The Russian Origins of the First World War* (Belknap/Harvard, 2012). Widely reviewed, the volume has been criticized for an anti-Russian agenda and its questionable argument that the Russian leadership initiated the war in order to seize the Straits from the Ottoman Empire. In his majesterial review of the major new volumes in the *New York Review of Books*, R. J. W. Evans calls McKeekin's argument "special pleading".

Special Pleading

In the Balkans itself, the temptation for special pleading has been hard to resist since the 1990s. Most frequent have been moral narratives of victimization, favoring the Bosnian Muslims, and villainy, singling out Serbia and the Bosnian Serbs. And for Bosnia in the 1990s, while no side wore white hats, assigning the Serb side primary responsibility has the incidental value of being true, in Henry Kissinger's phrase. But I have resisted the temptation to read that scenario back to 1914.

I have not, however, resisted the temptation to attract centenary attention. I retitled my recent second edition for Palgrave, *Balkans into Southeastern Europe, 1914–2014, A Century of War and Transition*. Let me draw on that volume and my own recent review of the long historiography addressing the 1914 war, starting during the war itself and since then generating more publications than any other subject in the past century.

Reassessing the Causes of the First World War

Among the dozen new books that have appeared in the past year to reassess the causes of the First World War, three from leading historians and prominent presses have received the most reviews and sold the most copies. They are Margaret Macmillan, *The War that Ended Peace, The Road to 1914* from Harpers, Max Hastings, *Catastrophe 1914, Europe Goes to War* from Knopf, and the bestseller, Christopher Clark, *The Sleepwalkers, How Europe Went to War in 1914* from HarperCollins. Displaying the biographic skills we saw in *Paris 1919*, Macmillan concentrates on tracking the key diplomats and political players from the Great Powers during the 20 years leading up to 1914. We see how the two opposing alliances struggled with their partners but how their rivalry still managed to undo the joint Concert of Europe after a last success in creating Albania in 1912. Only a brief chapter near the end deals with the assassination in Sarajevo. Hastings, well established as a British military historian of the Second World War, covers the June assassination in a Prologue and moves on to concentrate on the failed military plans, incompetent generals, and costly campaigns that did indeed make the catastrophe of the First World War evident before the year had ended.

Only ***Christopher Clark***, an historian of Prussia and imperial Germany, concentrates on the Balkans. Starting with another assassination, the murder of the native Serbian King and his wife in 1903, he devotes a long first chapter to the subsequent history of Serbia under the rival native dynasty as what he calls "a rogue state", locked in "a spiral of economic backwardness" and peasant illiteracy, its military already "steeped in terrorism" before 1914. Then a secret irredentist group of its Army officers, the Black Hand led by the same colonel nicknamed Apis that led the assassination of Aleksandar Obrenovic in 1903, initiates and organizes the plot against Franz Ferdinand. Princip and the other Bosnian Serbs are simply selected and then recruited. Prime Minister Nikola Pasic has full knowledge of Apis's plot but is powerless to stop it. Neither Margaret Macmillan nor Max Hastings goes so far. Hastings notes the same absence of "hard evidence" for this direct Serbian connection which, as we shall see, previous scouring of all written records has not found either.

Clark's Introduction already raised my concern over "retrospective determinism", reading history backward instead of forward. Clark notes the need to re-examine the trajectory of Serbian history in Bosnia "since Srebrenica", the well documented war crime of 1995. There was a rapid reaction in Belgrade to his linking of Milosevic's Serbia to a pre-1914 pattern under Prime Minister Nikola Pasic, while comparing Young Bosnia to Al Qaeda. Already in March, a leading military historian Mile Bjelajac published a book of rebuttal. His longest chapter fairly reviews the long Western and Serbian historiography of pre-1914 Serbian relations with Austria-Hungary. His citations from Serbian archival evidence available since 1980 show no official desire even to risk war. But he does not address the alleged links between the Young Bosnia conspirators and the Black Hand members predominant in Serbian military intelligence. The relationship of its leader, Colonel Apis, to the Army Chief of Staff receives a chapter; relations with Nikola Pasic do not. (In fact, there are few written records from the Black Hand and from a prime minister who typically burned massages in his ashtray after he had read them).

Bjelajac does challenge Clark convincingly on the presumption of predominant Russian influence in Belgrade. This is the same presumption advanced by Sean McKeekin in his aforementioned book blaming Russia for starting the First World War and naming Serbia as its accomplice. While Western reviewers have not been kind to this volume, they have generally praised Clark's work. Still, the bibliographic essay in the new *Cambridge History of the First World War* notes "a bias against Serbia" and in favor of Austria-Hungary as just another Sleepwalker. It should however be noted that Clark visited Belgrade this summer to debate a leading Serbian historian on his overall argument.

And here, before turning back to devils in Balkan details from 1914 and relevance for 2014, I should point out that Clark devotes only two chapters to the pre-1912 decades on which Macmillan spends most of her time. He questions a conscious run-up to an inevitable war and focuses instead on 1914 and the last couple of prewar years.

Most recent scholarship shares this approach, nicely summarized by Gordon Martel in his *The Month That Changed the World, July 1914* (Oxford). Clark uses the second of his two chapters instructively to show how by 1912 the foreign policies of each of the Great Powers had become imbedded in a set of competing, sometimes conflicting centers of, well, great power. Hence the hesitancy and uncertain direction which Clark aptly describes in all of them in July 1914.

Military, diplomatic and political elites all have their say, including naval as well as Army commands for Britain and Germany. Colonial and financial interests are also acknowledged, but as with most recent scholarship they are given less weight than in earlier, sometimes Marxist accounts. Add the uncertainties within the two Great Power alliances, between Germany and Austria-Hungary and between Britain and the earlier Franco-Russian connection, and mix in mobilization plans all demanding immediate offensives. This is the wider military and diplomatic ground for all of them sleepwalking into the wider war that none of the Great Powers desired. And here Clark is, as we shall also see, on well supported ground.

It is the rest of the book that continues to revive the controversy which began with the war itself. Can we still single out the greater responsibility for who started it? Clark returns usefully, as much other work does not, to the immediate Balkan issues and the assassination in Sarajevo. The range of sources consulted and his narrative momentum are indeed impressive. But his claim to avoid the assigning of war guilt seems to rest mainly on exempting Germany and Austria-Hungary even in July 1914—Berlin because the feckless Kaiser kept changing his mind, and Vienna because the assassination justified an ultimatum with terms to which, in Clark's judgment, Belgrade should have accepted. Little wonder that the German translation accounts for over one-third of the half million copies sold. Making Vienna and Berlin only equivalent Sleepwalkers in 1914 brings back and even draws on the German and Austrian disputation in the 1920s against the judgments of the Paris Peace Conference, particularly Article 231 of the Versailles Treaty blaming Germany alone for starting the war.

Assigning or Avoiding Blame Has a Much Longer History

Even before Britain had declared war in August 1914, the German government had published a White Book proclaiming its innocence, quickly followed by a British Blue Book charging German guilt. They were succeeded by a Russian Orange Book, a French Yellow book, and finally an Austrian Red Book.

But with Germany's defeat in 1918 it was ironically a German leader of the new Republic's government, the long eminent Socialist Karl Kautsky, who used his new position in the Foreign Ministry to begin collecting documents to prove that the Kaiser and Imperial Germany had indeed started the war in the interests of economic imperialism, But before the documents could be published, the Paris Peace Conference went ahead with the Versailles Treaty, Article 231 and reparations included. The German Foreign Office responded by creating a War Guilt Section and launching a monthly journal. Soon they surpassed the victorious powers in assembling diplomatic documentation for their innocence, with the 40 volumes of *Die Grosse Politik* stating their case in 1870. Enter the young American historian ***Sidney B. Fay***, standing back from any of the European sides. His initial journal articles singled out the Austrian Foreign Minister Berchtold for particular responsibility. But then in 1928, he drew on all available evidence and published his massive two volume study, *The Origins of the World War*.

Both of Fay's volumes remain important. The second volume concentrated on the assassination of June 28, the responsibility of Serbian nationalism, official involvement unclear, and the official Austrian reaction, without which the wider war could not have started.

But Fay concluded by restating the verdict of his first volume. The decades-long combination of competing alliances, European militarism, nationalism and economic imperialism plus the rise of the popular press had created a rising readiness to risk war shared by all the Great Powers. He therefore rejected the judgment of Versailles against Germany alone. And for the rest of the interwar period, his ***verdict of shared responsibility*** stood up. The American emphasis in the 1930s on the pre-1914 arms race ("the merchants of death") seemed to support this emphasis on common, long-term causes. And indeed the "militarization of diplomacy" in David Stevenson's recent phrase still stands as the most dangerous feature of the prewar decade. It advanced with the set of large standing armies, expanding navies, and sensationalist newspapers in the respective capitols. Their instant coverage shrank time and space in any crisis.

The shift to short-term accountability in the wake of the assassination in Sarajevo started with the post-1945 publication in English of a curious 2,000-page work in three volumes. Assembled by the Italian journalist ***Luigi Albertini*** over the full 20 years of the interwar period, it used interviews as well as the post-1930 French and Russian archival evidence to suggest the central responsibility of diplomatic confusions and contradictions during July 1914, within as well as between the two alliances. They caused a war that otherwise would not have taken place.

Albertini had died in 1941 while working on his conclusions, and we were left with an unconsolidated text in Italian, its repetitive sections reviewing each country's reaction to the same event or proposal. When Oxford finally published a translation in 1952, its initial impact was only to support the Fay thesis that no one power should be singled out, even in July 1914.

Widely cited and rarely read through, its evidence for the war as an ***unintended consequence of the July events***, and therefore hardly inevitable, did not register at the time. It would register after 1989, when the collapse of the second Yugoslavia suggested that creating the first Yugoslavia had been a mistake, and the pre-1914 ordering of the Balkans under Habsburg oversight was preferable.

But first came ***Fritz Fischer*** and with him the start in the 1960s of the close, hard look at the recent past that has distinguished German historiography from its interwar predecessor. Fischer was a younger West German historian whose interest in Berlin's economic motives in 1914 prompted East German authorities to grant to him access their complete archival holdings, beyond the Foreign Ministry records long published. When *Griff nach der Weltmacht*, appeared in 1961, the book created a sensation in the Western world, not just West Germany.

He offered persuasive evidence that German economic plans for incorporating Eastern Europe and Belgium during the First World War looked very much like Nazi plans during the Second World War. From here, however, he jumped to the conclusion that such plans preceded and promoted a German initiative to start the First World War. Facing West German criticism, he responded with a second book, *Krieg der Illusionen* in 1966 to make his case. Here he was not persuasive about economic motivation.

All the same, as Max Hastings notes, ***German responsibility from December 1912 forward to accelerate the buildup of land arms needed for an offensive*** against France before facing a Russian offensive seems to stand up as decisive, even without the economic interest in an expanded land empire. When the German controversy spilled over into Anglo-American scholarship, it did serve the useful purpose of prompting a re-examination of the pre-1914 plans of the other Great Powers as well. They had all sharpened their war plans by the end of 1912. Overall, the consensus on longer-term German responsibility for war in July 1914 continued until 1989.

Since then, both Anglo-American and Austro-German scholarship have moved back to pay more attention to ***pre-1914 Austria-Hungary*** and also to the history of the separate states that emerged from the former Yugoslavia. Serbia's earlier history has suffered by retrospective association with the warfare of the 1990s. But younger scholars from the separate states now make frequent, more detached contributions in recent publications. The biases that mar regional scholarship on the Second World War do not appear here.

This new work on the First World War casts doubt on some of Albertini's evidence from Italian diplomats, evidence on which Clark in particular relies. It also incorporates the Bosnian evidence from the major Yugoslav inquiry, Vladimir Dedijer's *The Road to Sarajevo*, published in English in 1967 and then expanded in 1978 to include more material from the Belgrade archives.

What Problems Does this Body of Work Pose for Clark's Picture of the Settled, Progressive Dual Monarchy and the Balkan Renegade Serbia?

The Vienna government as a "model of administrative modernity" faced mounting internal problems from its ethnic divisions. A Czech-German dispute continued despite the wider franchise in 1907 for the Austrian half of the monarchy and forced the dissolution of parliament in March 1914. Vienna also had to deal with the separate domestic authority of Budapest, its pressures for Magyarization on Slovaks, Romanians and South Slavs, and its successful resistance to the modernization of the joint Army.

Their joint administration of Bosnia-Herzegovina rested its control of the Bosnian Serb plurality there on the exploitative sharecropping framework of Bosnian Muslims left in place from the Ottoman regime. Princip's village was included. Illiteracy still approached 90 percent, while student unrest grew. The General accompanying Franz Ferdinand had already placed Bosnia under martial law in May 1913. He had already joined the Austrian Chief of Staff General Conrad in calling for a "preventive war" against Serbia for several years.

Meanwhile, ***Serbia under the Karadjorjevic dynasty*** since 1903 had become a constitutional monarchy with regular elections under a franchise for all adult males. Law and order ruled in Belgrade, and literacy had climbed past 70 percent by 1905, hardly the 20 percent cited by Clark from a source for Serbia as a whole. Economic growth from agricultural exports survived the Austro-Hungarian Tariff War of 1906–11 by processing meat and sending it on to Germany. French, not Russian, loans allowed the modernization of the Army to go ahead, displacing the Austrian Skoda option and leaving the Monarchy with no economic leverage by 1911.

The constitution, modeled on Belgium's, stated that the "the press is free", and alas in July 1914 the Pasic government was unable to prevent opposition papers from celebrating the Archduke's assassination, while its own *Samouprava* expressed respectful condolence. The popular press in Vienna replied in kind, evidence of the media influence listed by Fay as a shared pressure for war.

The two Serbian victories in the ***Balkan Wars of 1912–13*** had indeed encouraged the Apis group to focus on Bosnia after the heated, official Serbian protests to the Monarchy's annexation in 1908 had failed to overturn the decision. But the Serbian Army was grievously weakened by the losses in men and materiel. Its decision to maintain martial law in Macedonia and Kosovo took more resources and did indeed result in widespread abuse of the non-Serb locals. The Pasic government, supported by the Regent Aleksandar, who took over full royal authority from the aged King Petar in June 1914, wanted to end martial law and thereby also suppress the Apis group, already under investigation for its abuse of authority. (Apis was later tried and shot in 1917).

Irredentist penetration of Serbia's officially sponsored Bosnian cultural organization *Narodna Odbrana*, created after the 1908 annexation, cannot be denied. But, contrary to Clark's assertion, there is no evidence that the three Bosnian Serbs led by Princip were connected to any organization except the Death or Life group of less than 20 formed in the loose student confines of Mlada Bosna.

They read the *Politika* announcement in March of the Archduke's impending visit on June 28, *Vidovdan*, and sought to buy weapons. But they could not afford them and then turned to a lower Black Hand contact who passed them on to the Apis associate, Major Tankosic, for help. Princip had to pawn his overcoat to cover the trip back to Sarajevo. Such details, plus the teenage independence of the *Mlada Bosna* members, persuades Robin Okey, the author of the major new study of the Austrian regime in Bosnia, that speculation about an Apis-initiated plot is unfounded. Knowing and approving is not the same thing as organizing from the start.

For recent parallels to the Middle East, calling the assassins "terrorists" seems to fit despite the current objections from Belgrade. But their aim was what they called ***"tyrannicide"***, killing individual eminences rather than masses of unbelievers, and then themselves. A further distinction from Al Qaeda was the lack of money or technology to go beyond their one, nearly failed action. As for their own beliefs, none including Princip in prison spoke of Greater Serbia but only of some vague South Slav right to separation from Habsburg control.

A second distinction sets the Serbian prime minister apart from Slobodan Milosevic and the flow of arms and financial support with which he stoked the Bosnian Serb side in the warfare of the 1990s. Nikola Pasic wanted no war there in 1914. Distressed to find that "fanatical children" were smuggling weapons into Bosnia, he wanted it stopped. Speculation in a German newspaper in the 1920s by the Serbian Minister of Education, cited by Clark, that Pasic must have known of the plot itself but was powerless to stop it, is not supported by any archival or other accounting.

What about the Russian Connection?

Milosevic had counted on support in Kosovo in 1999 and capitulated to NATO in part after he did not receive it. Clark joins McKeekin in arguing that the assurances of the Russian Ambassador Hartwig after the June 28 assassination pushed Pasic to risk war with Austria-Hungary. Albertini and then Clark rely on the Italian Ambassador's assumption that Pasic's speech at Hartwig's funeral in mid-July reflected such leverage.

Continuing Russian support stiffened the Serbian response to the Austrian ultimatum at the last minute. In fact, promised Russian military supplies did not arrive until late July, and an explicit Russian commitment of support not even then. Belgrade's last changes to its response to the ultimatum softened rather than hardened it. Only Point 6, the demand that Habsburg officials enter Belgrade with police powers to conduct proceedings against Serbian accomplices, was refused. Austrian drafters had inserted this demand forfeiting Serbian sovereignty with the conscious intent of assuring a Serbian refusal. Then a declaration of war could follow.

Finally, I note the neglected relevance of a couple of Sidney Fay's ***pressures building for war in 1914 if the occasion arose*** as in Sarajevo. They were relevant to the wars ofYugoslavia's dissolution in the 1990s but not relevant in 2014. One was the large size of available military forces and arms. The other is a set of alliances or potential allies that promoted the risk of war. Recall that pre-1989 Yugoslavia had a large Army and produced much of its own equipment. By the 1980s, however, each republic, not Kosovo, had a Territorial Defense Force with its own share of those arms.

Then, with the end of other one-party Communist regimes in 1989, Slobodan Milosevic tried to preserve Yugoslavia's regime by adding his control of Kosovo and Vojvodina as autonomous regions to the six republics and thus securing a majority. But his failure to do so, failing to add Bosnia and Macedonia, left the opposing republics of Slovenia and Croatia to go ahead together, as a rival alliance, with a vote for independence. They in turn relied on informal Austrian and Hungarian support and formal German recognition to go ahead and fight for independence, already armed with Territorial Defense equipment.

The Present

In 2014, no paramilitary forces remained, and none of the small armies left in the region showed any inclination to resume the warfare and forced migration of the 1990s. The only associations connecting the successor states were not rival alliances but a regional trade agreement, CEFTA, and membership or aspiration to membership in the European Union. NATO membership was not universal, but not even Serbia had a military connection with Russia.

In 2017, the region's economic challenges since the financial crisis of 2008 continue. But now they are compounded by the political challenges facing the founders of NATO and the European Union, calling into question their relevance to a region that had counted on them.

John R. Lampe is an Emeritus Professor at the University of Maryland, College Park. He retired in 2012 after 40 years in the Department of History. He remains a Senior Scholar at the Woodrow Wilson International Center for Scholars in Washington, DC. From 1986 to 1996, he directed the Center's program in East European Studies, organizing conferences and speakers. He travelled frequently to the region and commented on current events there for the Center and for CNN, PBS, the CBC and the BBC. He has published nine books and a numbers of journal articles and book chapters on Balkan history. He found his regional focus during tours as a Foreign Service Officer at the US Embassies in Belgrade and Sofia in 1965–67, after a post-Harvard year at the London School of Economics, military service in West Berlin and an MA at the University of Minnesota. Leaving the Foreign Service, he entered the doctoral program in History at the University of Wisconsin and received his PhD in 1971.

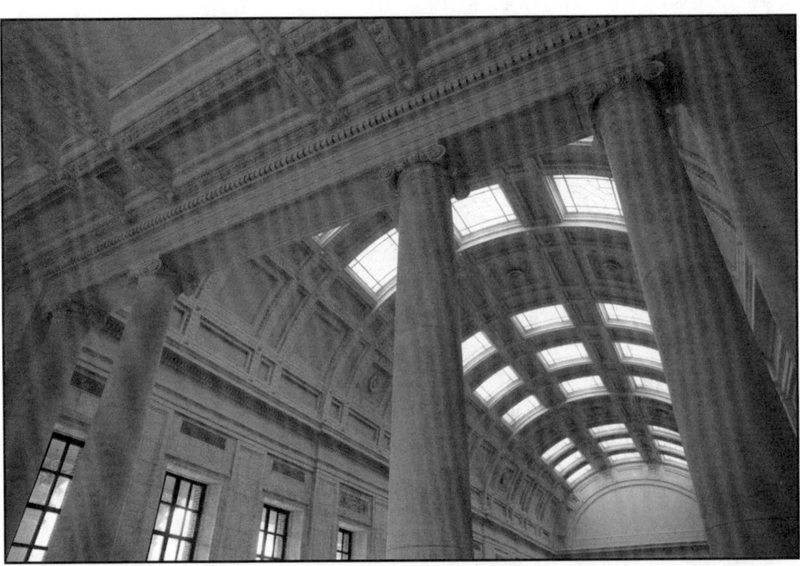

Figure 2.1.1.1 *Vaulted ceiling with skylights in Widener Library Reading Room*
Reprinted courtesy of Harvard University

Asian

India

Sixty Years of Observing India

Jock McLane

Nothing shaped my future more than my trip to India in the fall of my junior year at Harvard. I went on a three-month, non-credit home-stay program run by the *Experiment in International Living*. In 1955, plane travel was still expensive, and therefore our group travelled 30 days on a freighter, the SS *Steel Scientist*, departing from Newport News, VA, and stopping in Beirut, Alexandria, Jeddah, and Aden before disembarking in Karachi. We had Hindi lessons on 78 rpm records, and a library of books about India. Remembering that voyage reminds me what we have lost with air travel.

In boarding school, I struggled with the contrast between my "*townie*" past and my new elite-seeming companions. Liberal teachers, who assumed responsibility for arousing doubts about their students' advantages, talked about and assigned readings on protest movements and revolts against authoritarian rule, colonialism, and racism. Along with many of my classmates I responded positively to these radical themes.

Introduction to Emancipatory Movements

The moment when I first consciously identified with emancipatory movements was when the Reverend Paul Moore spoke at St. Paul's School about his feeling kinship with African-American soldiers in the trenches during World War II and his outrage at racial segregation. He also spoke about his, and his wife, Jenny's, life of service in an inner-city parish in Jersey City beginning in 1949. He belonged to a small group of ministers, mostly Episcopalian but including Martin Luther

King, who were inspired by Gandhi's commitment to non-violent activism on behalf of disadvantaged communities in the US. I remember vividly the effect this had on me. I spent the summer of 1956 in that parish, surrounded by broken pavements and run-down apartment buildings with hallways that reeked of urine, spending time with kids who often seemed to have little hope for the future. A decade later, Jenny Moore wrote about the parish in *The People of Second Street*. She described "The rejected, the hungry, the drunks, the whores, the fools, the exploiters, the has-beens . . . " I met all of them while I was there.

My decision to go to India in my junior year, thus, had a lot to do with my doubts about extreme inequalities and a budding interest in Gandhi, and in non-violent civil disobedience against injustice. Before Harvard, I had a series of summer jobs that widened my social horizons and opened me to the words of Paul Moore and Gandhi. In addition to Jersey City, I had worked on a farm in Franconia, NH, in factory construction in Manchester, NH, and Allston, MA, and in a settlement house in Bethnal Green in the east end of London.

Once in Cambridge, there was no shortage of opportunities to learn about the humiliations of powerlessness. Two summers I went with our late classmate, Tony Sifton, to a United Auto Workers shop stewards' training camp in Port Huron, MI. I worked on a blister rust eradication crew in Yellowstone National Park. At Harvard, I took courses on colonialism, socialism, communism, and immigration. I joined a Marxist discussion group run by a graduate student, Marty Kilson, later Professor of Political Science at Harvard. And I took on a volunteer job in Roxbury, hanging out in the streets, pool halls, and ball fields with a group of adolescent African-Americans who called themselves the Emperors. By my senior year, I was strongly tempted by a career in social activism. But marriage and new interests led me to apply to graduate school in South Asian history instead.

Junior Semester Abroad—India

In my 1955 trip to India, I had found it appallingly poor, as expected. The experience was also intellectually stimulating and physically beautiful, beyond what I had imagined. No doubt my reactions were shaped by my youth, but I seemed to meet one admirable, idealistic person after another—politicians, journalists, social workers, professional men and women. Less than a decade beyond independence, Indians I met seemed delighted by the presence of young Americans and fascinated by the contradictions in American society. Many pumped me about materialism, race, and poverty, and especially about dating, marriage, and family. Many were horrified by practices such as premarital sex, dating, and self-arranged marriages. I found myself in the unfamiliar situation of being required to explain, and sometimes defend, the US from hostile Hindu conservatives or anti-Western leftists. At 19 years old, I suddenly felt like an adult responsible for explaining my own values.

I stayed with an affluent businessman in Bombay who had graduated from Harvard and ran a Willey's Jeep franchise; later, his family manufactured Jeeps. I next stayed in a village with a rural fruit orchard owner who hired labor from local hill tribes who tended his trees while he played ping pong in a shack near the rail crossing just yards from his modest house. Although he was Zoroastrian, he fed an itinerant Hindu ascetic who slept on his tiny porch every night. And I stayed in Ahmedabad, Gujarat, with an idealistic Brahmin school teacher and his family who admired Gandhi, whose ashram had been in Ahmedabad. Each morning before sunrise, an untouchable emptied the metal box in the out-house in the backyard. When I contracted hepatitis, they insisted I practice yoga. They did not take me to a doctor.

Our group visited many Gandhians and Gandhi-inspired institutions. Eight years earlier, Gandhi had been assassinated by a Hindu extremist who resented Gandhi's efforts to include Muslims in the new nation. In 1955, India was still visibly Gandhian in that the ubiquitous Congress party workers still wore the rough, hand-spun white cloth that Gandhi had popularized as a nationalist uniform, as a source of income to impoverished peasants, and as an alternative to the imported fabrics manufactured in the "satanic" factories that Gandhi preached were robbing India of its spirituality and livelihood. Those rough costumes were still associated with Gandhi. In later decades, they came to be identified with Congress Party corruption and nostalgia for an unretrievable past.

We visited numerous villages. Half of India's GNP came from farming, and 70% of the population depended on agriculture. In 1955, industrialization had barely begun, although Prime Minister Nehru and the Congress party government were investing heavily in heavy industry, despite the protests of the Gandhians who wanted to preserve rural handicrafts and village communities. We visited ashrams and agricultural institutes growing the "*miracle rice*" developed in the Philippines with help from the Rockefeller Foundation, and using new, unfamiliar latrines.

I attended a speech by Prime Minister Jawaharlal Nehru, delivered to thousands of peasants squatting on the hot, sandy bottom of a dried out river-bed. Nehru spoke in Hindi to the Gujarati-speaking crowd. I understood few words except the oft-repeated phrase, "*socialist pattern of society*". From my perspective, state investments were a benign, promising action for a country needing to mobilize savings for rapid industrialization and infrastructure, to educate a largely illiterate population, and to promote land reform and other forms of social leveling. I could not tell what peasants thought of Nehru's emphasis on socialism and state intervention. They looked worshipful, more like people in the presence of a deity than a politician.

Indian village society seemed feudal, deferential, stratified. I was strongly drawn to village handicrafts, to pottery, spinning, and weaving. And to the dexterity and ingenuity of peasants who effortlessly fashioned a handle for a hoe, fixed a broken gasoline pump with an improvised part, castrated a goat, or transplanted rice seedlings. Gandhi's desire to preserve these skills and avoid migration to the cities and factories made perfect sense to me. It fit well with what Marx said about the alienation of labor. Marx (and Gandhi, too) had written that when humans worked for others and did not own the product of their labor, they would be estranged from the capitalist, their employer. I often felt I was peering into a society that differed little from what medieval European society had been like. I was hooked! But I had not fully perceived the conflict between my romantic view of the Indian village and the industrializing thrust of Nehru's five-year plans.

Rethinking Gandhism

I returned to Harvard for the second semester of my junior year with a greater appetite for my studies and more skepticism about Marxism and the centrality of class exploitation in our political evolution. The kaleidoscopic complexity of India challenges almost any tendency towards ideological simplicity. Even national heroes such as Gandhi and Nehru are treated with skepticism or scorn by scores of Indian intellectuals. Back in Cambridge, friends like Tony Sifton and Eliot House tutors including Bill Slottman, Adam Ulam, and Martin Malia, all of whom studied Eastern Europe, questioned my admiration for statist solutions to India's problems.

In the fall of 1956, the Soviet Army crushed the Hungarian rising. I found it harder to identify with Indian leftist admiration for Soviet central planning and Soviet support for anti-colonial movements. For a few years, Nehru presented India and the so-called nonaligned bloc as an independent broker between the Soviet Union and the United States. After Hungary, Nehru, Nasser, Nkrumah, and Sukarno no longer seemed likely to end the Cold War. And Gandhian non-violence held little relevance for conflict between the Soviets and the US. And as I read more of Gandhi's writings, I held on to my admiration for his tactics of civil disobedience, but his views on many other issues seemed cranky, archaic, unconvincing.

India nevertheless remained a focus of US Cold War foreign policy and thus a consequential power as I prepared to attend graduate school. India had emerged from British rule in 1947 roughly equal to China in economic backwardness, with an average life expectancy of less than thirty years and little increase for decades in per capita income. But India was committed to democratic rule. US policy makers hoped India would compete with China and demonstrate that rapid economic development was compatible with parliamentary government and democratic freedoms. Many in the US foreign policy and academic establishment over the years articulated enthusiasm for India's democratic possibilities, including Chester Bowles, J. William Fulbright, John Kenneth Galbraith, and employees of the Ford Foundation.

Transition to Academic Life

That was the situation in 1957 when, several months after graduation, I enrolled in the School of Oriental and African Studies *(SOAS)*, University of London. I went to London rather than an American university because foreign area studies programs in the US focusing on South Asia had barely begun. SOAS, by contrast, had a tradition of studying many parts of Africa and Asia in the pre-World War II era to prepare colonial civil servants to rule the Empire, and post-war, to prepare former colonial subjects and other foreigners. such as myself, to teach and do research. The colonial and scholarly functions overlapped in my first year Hindi class at SOAS. For example, a Belgian civil servant from the Belgian Congo enrolled to learn Hindi in order to administer to Indian traders coming into the Belgian Congo from the Swahili coast. At SOAS, I wrote my PhD dissertation on pre-Gandhi Indian nation-building in the early years of the anti-colonial Indian National Congress, the party of Gandhi and the Nehrus which dominated Indian politics in the decades after independence.

In 1961, my wife and I returned to the US with two children. I accepted a teaching position in the history department at Northwestern

University in Evanston, IL, where I worked for 50 years. Private universities afford tenured faculty exceptional security and freedom to pursue different kinds of activity. I loved my job at Northwestern. I mixed teaching, research, and administration in more or less equal proportions.

As the war in Indo-China escalated, I taught numerous courses about Vietnam. This war seemed to be a defining political event in our generation's life. As I saw it, our government lied to its citizens and went to war to prevent self-determination; I embraced the anti-war movement. I marched and participated in teach-ins. Northwestern virtually shut down in 1970 after the Kent State killings when radical students boycotted classes and barricaded the state highway that ran through the campus. Most students took pride in keeping the campus united and free of violence under the leadership of an African-American student president. Even fraternity and sorority houses flew red flags from their windows.

Immersion in India

Research trips to India were a vital part of my teaching and research. I had extended stays in Calcutta in 1964–66, 1974–75, and 1984–85. Calcutta was stimulating in its chaos, multiple cultures, and educated elites. My research stipends allowed us to live in a quasi-colonial style, which meant my wife and I had servants to cook, clean, drive, and look after our two children. Having servants also meant seeing into the lives of people who depended on their employers to pay school fees and doctors' bills. We joined a Quaker Friends Bengali singing group, attended sitar and sarod concerts and poetry readings, socialized with Bengali academics and social workers, as well as with researchers from a Ford Foundation urban research project, a Johns Hopkins medical research group, and US foreign service families.

Living in Calcutta was alternately exhilarating and infuriating. In fact, India was a fascinating place to live, because it surprises with its contradictions, its combining of the new and ancient, its constant originality, and the depth of its spirituality. If you have read William Dalrymple's *Nine Lives: In Search of the Sacred in Modern India*, you will understand what I mean.

Periodically, monsoon floods and Marxist political strikes paralyzed Calcutta. Rarely did a day pass without power outages that shut down fans and air conditioners. Rush hour traffic was so thick, taxis and buses and trams so full, that I often had to walk for an hour or more to reach our flat after a day in the state archives or national library.

Pedestrians were forced to walk in the streets among the moving motor vehicles because sidewalks were packed, including stalls selling all kinds of food—clothing, footwear, pots and pans, furniture, hardware, flowers—as well as homeless families permanently settled into a few square feet of pavement. And the street traffic was stereotypically Indian: foot-drawn rickshaws, coolies balancing *almirahs*, pianos, bundles of cloth, etc. on their heads, stray cows, flocks of goats, buses and trucks spewing diesel exhaust. The sensory experience, of sight, sound, and smell, was hyper-stimulating.

The Evolution of India since 1955

My interest in India's evolution continues. From the time I arrived at Northwestern to the present, I have focused my teaching and research on the crucial processes of national integration and disintegration, the tension between unity and diversity that defines India's recent history. One reason the study of India still engages me is that the recent rise of Hindu self-assertion and extremism, at the expense of Nehru's and Congress secularism, holds so many parallels with what has happened in the Middle East, Europe, and other parts of the world. The rise of religious nationalism and ethnic intolerance seem to be almost universal phenomena; the regional is often global.

Post-Partition India

In certain respects, India makes an unlikely nation, with as much cultural variation as Europe, with states centered around distinct languages, each with its own literature and historical traditions of self-rule. Nothing better illustrates the challenges to the construction of a single nation in South Asia than *the Partition of 1947*, when the British departed, and India split into two rival, hostile countries, India and Pakistan, one with a Hindu majority and the other with a Muslim majority.

The legacy of partition, with ten million migrants and perhaps half a million deaths in the partition riots, still plagues relations between India and Pakistan. Many Indians refuse to forgive Pakistan for breaking apart "the motherland." So one major theme of modern history is grappling with the causes and consequences of partition, including the place of beleaguered Muslims in independent India. India has the third largest Muslim population in the world, behind Indonesia and Pakistan.

Economic Transformation

A second theme centers on the effort to transform an under-developed agrarian, illiterate society into a modern, self-sufficient state. Economic development has competed with identity politics for public attention since Independence. Economic growth was disappointingly modest under the Congress Party governments, with their five-year plans, pursuit of economic independence through investments in heavy industry, and spending on the "green revolutions" which increased rice and wheat productivity. From 1950 until the 1980s, the GNP grew by roughly 3.5% per year, and the per capita income by perhaps 1.5%. Compared to China, this was paltry. By the 1970s and 1980s, discontent with Congress economic performance was widespread, and the Congress Party lost elections in one state after another. Many opposition parties demanded economic liberalization and encouragement for private investments.

Identity Politics

In the same period, identity politics intensified around caste and religious identities. Soon after independence, the Congress Party had drafted India's constitution to guarantee affirmative action for marginalized castes and tribes. Those groups were assigned quotas for seats in the legislatures, admission to institutions of higher education, and jobs in government. The electoral successes of the Congress Party in the early years after independence rested in part on this strategy of positive discrimination. But the strategy failed to diminish the place of caste rivalry in Indian public life. Members of certain middle and high castes came to resent the preferences given to the low status beneficiaries, the so-called untouchables and members of the hill tribes. New political coalitions, often run by the dominant and populous peasant castes which had not qualified for the quotas, successfully challenged the Congress in state elections.

By the 1990s, it was apparent that Congress Party dominance was ending at both the national and state levels. And it was obvious that affirmative action for the backward castes had strengthened caste identities and exacerbated caste rivalries. In fact, castes just above the backward castes, began to demand quotas for themselves. The result of this agitation was that some states gave special quotas to a new category, the *OBCs* or *other backward castes*. Castes competed to win the status of "backward" in order to qualify for the quotas. Today over half the Hindu population qualifies for quotas.

In the 1980s and 1990s, Hindu nationalists successfully exploited the grievances of the OBCs and of a vast array of Indians disaffected with affirmative action, economic stagnation, and Congress corruption. They did so by organizing a vast network of cultural and political organizations and constructing a narrative based on a perception of *Hindu victimhood* at the expense of Muslim and European conquests.

Rise of Hindu Nationalism

Hindu nationalists found in the story of Muslim conquest and rule "*a chosen trauma*", to use the phrase of Vamik Volkan. The narrative seemed designed to forge a new pan-Hindu group-identity to deflect attention from persistent poverty and inequality in the caste system. It sought to convince Hindus that Muslims, Pakistan, and foreign jihadis threatened all Hindus more than gross inequalities within Hindu social systems. Hindu nationalists presented the history of Hindu-Muslim relations as one of perpetual Muslim hostility and violence against the Hindu majority.

The three wars India and Pakistan fought after 1947 reinforced that story. Hindu nationalists questioned the loyalty of Muslims who remained in India after the 1947 partition, suggesting that Indian Muslims, "*the sons of Akbar*", were a fifth column for Pakistan. Hindu nationalists represented Muslims as growing disproportionately rich and populous, even though Muslims are under 14% of India's population and are on average poor, undereducated, and more frequently the victims of violence than Hindus. Hindu nationalists equated *Indian-ness* with the acceptance of Hindu culture, implying that Muslims would be better off if they converted to Hinduism or migrated to Pakistan.

At its extremes, the Hindu nationalist movement stereotyped Muslims as over-sexed, violent, and disloyal. Hindu extremists compiled lists of Muslim mosques that Muslims were said to have built on the sites of Hindu temples destroyed during the Muslim conquests beginning seven or so centuries earlier. In 1992, Hindu mobs tore down the Babri Masjid, a major mosque built by the Mughal Empire in 1528–9. Hindu leaders claimed the mosque had been built on the site of the avatar Rama's birth, and they pledged to build a Hindu temple in its place. This destruction of a former place of worship shocked many Indians, most of whom had lived peacefully with Muslims for generations, and who regarded the rising violence as an unacceptable rejection of the virtues of tolerance and *ahimsa* (non-violence) which Gandhi had said were the essence of Hinduism. Another burst of anti-Muslim violence in Gujarat in 2002 while Hindu police remained inactive raised more doubts about India's future and the security of foreign investments. Not willing to alienate foreign and domestic opinion, *Hindutva* (*Hindu-ness*) leaders increasingly curtailed extremist action, without giving up the goal of making Indian more explicitly Hindu.

In 2014, the Hindu nationalists' limitation on anti-Muslim violence paid off electorally. The 2014 elections signaled clearly the end of the Congress era. The BJP (the *Hindu People's Party* and the political wing of the Hindutva movement), led by Narendra Modi, won a clear majority of the national vote in 2014 for the first time and now governs in New Delhi. (It had governed previously in 1998–2004 as head of a coalition of parties.) Of the 543 seats in the Indian parliament, the Congress Party won only 44 in 2014.

Current Political Status

Prime Minister Modi represents the empowering of the numerically large OBC castes. He belongs to a caste of petty merchants and oil-seed pressers in Gujarat state. Formerly he, like his father, ran a tea stall. This contrasts with the affluence, high (*Brahmin*) caste status, and exclusive education of the Nehru family, which includes the former Prime Ministers Jawaharlal Nehru, Indira Gandhi, and Rajiv Gandhi. Modi's BJP government has extended the liberalizing economic policies initiated by the Congress government in 1991. The government has privatized public industries, including communications; it has encouraged private and foreign investments; it has tried to reduce state subsidies to poor and middle income citizens for food and fertilizers; it has eliminated some government permit and licensing requirements; it has reduced tariffs on imports; and it has built an interstate highway system.

These BJP reforms have received support from most sectors of the public. Performance results have been encouraging. Growth in the GDP has risen from roughly 3.5 percent annually in the first four decades of independence, when the Congress Party dominated, to over seven percent today. Prime Minister Modi has focused on the economy and reigned in the extremist Hindu organizations to which he has been affiliated. In the last decade, they have provoked no major episodes of Hindu-Muslim violence outside Kashmir.

Nevertheless, despite the regularity with which India has held elections and transferred power from one winner to the next, India remains a volatile place. Income distributions are skewed towards the affluent and leave the country vulnerable to long-simmering rebellions among the landless and indebted poor. Tribal populations in the northeast continue to fight for autonomy and protection from the immigrants entering India from Bangladesh and adjoining parts of India. As the first chunks of coastal Bangladesh, India, and Pakistan slide down into rising seas, and as the glaciers in the Himalayas melt, global warming threatens to hasten migration and instability. Much of Bangladesh is low-lying delta and is at particular risk from rising sea levels and erratic storms.

Future Challenges

Most dangerous to India's stability may be Kashmir. India still occupies the Muslim-majority area of Kashmir that Pakistan has claimed since Partition. The Indian Army has exacted a high toll on democratic freedoms and Muslim lives as Kashmiri Muslims seek independence from India, often with cross-border military aid from Pakistan. Pakistan uses Kashmiri Muslim rebelliousness to tie down India's Army and to embarrass India. As long as Pakistani national identity depends on hostility to and fear of more powerful India, and as long as India refuses to compromise on Kashmiri Muslim demands for autonomy, Kashmir threatens South Asian security.

To date, India's Muslim minority of over 180 million has produced relatively few Muslim extremists except in Kashmir, despite provocations and violence by Hindu militants. The major acts of terrorism by Muslims in India, including the attack on the Indian Parliament in 2001 and on the Taj Hotel in Mumbai in 2008, have been sponsored from across the border, from Pakistan. The recent attacks by ISIS jihadis in Bangladesh have not spread to India. If extremists among Hindus or Muslims inside India behave violently, the fragile peace of recent years within India could unravel. Prime Minister Narendra Modi, despite his Hindu chauvinism, has contained the violence since assuming office in 2014.

I feel fortunate to still be engaged by this rich, always complicated, and frequently surprising civilization.

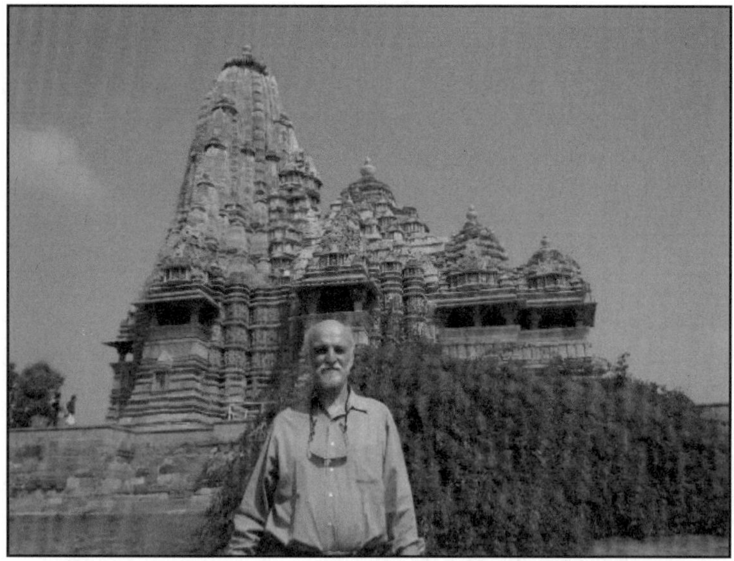

Figure 2.2.1.1 *Historian Jock McLane in 2013 at Vishvanatha temple, Khajaraho Monuments, Chhatarpur, Madhya Pradesh, India*

Jock McLane received his PhD in South Asian History from the School of Oriental and African Studies, University of London, in 1961. His first book, *Indian Nationalism and the Early Congress* (Princeton, 1977), was awarded the Wattamul Prize by the American Historical Association in 1978 as the best book on South Asian history published in the previous two years. He also published *Land and Local Kingship in Eighteenth-Century Bengal*, Cambridge, 1993. He worked at Northwestern University from 1961 until 2011. He served as Master of two residential colleges, as chair of the History department three times, and as Associate Dean for Faculty in the College of Arts and Sciences for eight years. He was a member of the Harvard Board of Overseers visiting committee to the History Department at Harvard, 1992–96. He is married to Joan Brooks McLane, Radcliffe '57, and he is the father of Derek McLane, theater set designer, and Rebecca McLane, who works with victims of domestic abuse.

Personal

Witness to History

Introduction to the Real World – Washington, DC: 1960–1965

Jeremiah Bresnahan

I was a student during the decade of the 1950s, entering Boston College High School in the fall of 1949 and graduating from Harvard Law School in the spring of 1960. During my second year in law school, I suffered a spontaneous pneumothorax (collapsed lung). Although I made a complete recovery, I was nevertheless reclassified as 4F for draft purposes. After passing the Massachusetts Bar Exam, I landed a job as an entry-level lawyer with the United States Securities and Exchange Commission in Washington DC, starting work in October 1960. I left the SEC in November 1965 to accept a position as an associate lawyer with a Boston law firm. My protected years as a student involved few real world responsibilities and were relatively uneventful. The next five years were a different story altogether as several momentous events, some personal, some not, occurred during the period.

Upon arrival in Washington, I was lucky to be able to share the rent on an apartment with a law school classmate and a friend of his. However, I had to buy a bed, which was a traumatic event, as I had never owned an object of that size. This gave me an unwelcome feeling of responsibility for a possession I couldn't just put on my back or in a suitcase, if I had to move again. Somewhere along the line I also acquired my first automobile, a used 1955 Plymouth, which made me mobile, as public transportation in Washington in those years was rudimentary, at best. I borrowed most of the purchase price from the SEC Employees Federal

Credit Union, thus assuming an indebtedness of nearly $500. However, shortly thereafter one of my roommates and I went to the racetrack in Charles Town, West Virginia. We each chipped in $1 and bought a $2 ticket on the "twin double", which meant we had to pick the winners of four consecutive races to collect. We did it! My share came to $600, enough to retire the crushing indebtedness I had recently assumed. I felt like a new man. Eventually, I moved from the Northwest section of Washington to a house in back of the Capitol in Northeast owned by an SEC lawyer who rented rooms, primarily to other SEC personnel. Known to one and all as the "sports palace", it featured inexpensive rent and was within walking distance of the SEC. My last DC move was to a townhouse in a new development in the otherwise desolate Southwest. A few years earlier, the entire Southwest area of Washington had been demolished (except for St. Dominic's Church) in an urban renewal project implementing theories, cutting edge at the time (see Boston's West End) but later discredited.

My admission to the Massachusetts Bar was postponed from a date in October to the Friday following Thanksgiving so that the many Massachusetts Bar inductees who were working in Washington would not need to make two trips. When a Bar member moved our admission, a lawyer present objected on the grounds that we were not going to practice in Massachusetts, at least initially. This unexpected development caused considerable panic before the Supreme Judicial Court Justice presiding overruled the objection and admitted us.

The JFK Years

John F. Kennedy was elected President of the United States that fall and was inaugurated in January 1961. A large snowstorm hit Washington the day preceding the Inauguration, which brought traffic to a standstill. Federal offices were closed on Inauguration Day (sunny and bitterly cold) and government employees were released early the day before, right in the middle of the storm. My bus quickly became stuck in traffic, and I was forced to walk three or four miles through the snow back to my apartment. The JFK years were interesting and exciting, and living in Washington made one feel close to the action. The first family was youthful, vibrant and fascinating. To me, JFK's charismatic quality was best demonstrated by his speech in West Berlin, which concluded with his statement that he took pride in the words "*Ich bin ein Berliner*". It received a tremendous response from the huge audience and, in a nutshell, captured the US position on the Berlin Wall and the Cold War. A good example of his wit was his assertion early in his speech after receiving an honorary degree from Yale in 1962 that "It might be said now that I have the best of both worlds, a Harvard education and a Yale degree."

Cuban Missile Crisis

Sometimes I felt closer to the action than I really wanted. The Cuban-Missile Crisis was unusually stressful. As I recall, the crisis developed gradually, with statements of suspicion and concern, eventually followed by aerial photographs of what were purported to be missile sites and finally shots of the Russian transports. I don't know about the rest of the world or even the rest of the country, but I have never been so frightened in my life. When the Russian missile carrying ships turned back, the relief was enormous. President Kennedy had made it very clear that those ships were never going to reach Cuba.

March on Washington

In the summer of 1963, the "March on Washington" took place. The march was led by Dr. Martin Luther King, Jr. and brought a huge number of visitors to Washington. I can recall looking out an office window, which had a view of the Washington Mall, and seeing bus after endless bus bringing in marchers from all over. Government offices were closed on the day of the march, mainly to eliminate commuter traffic, so I stationed myself at a spot along the route to see the marchers and was able to greet classmate Nino Yannoni as he trooped past. There were dire predictions of unruly crowd behavior, riots, damage and injuries. However, contrary to those predictions and despite the oppressively hot temperature, the throng of marchers was, to a person, orderly and even polite and considerate. Police incidents were, I believe, near zero. The march culminated in a massive rally near the Lincoln Memorial with folk songs by a variety of singers, including Joan Baez, some uninspiring speeches and concluded with Dr. King's famous and very moving "I Have a Dream" speech, which galvanized everyone. The impact of the non-violent movement led by Dr. King was remarkable, resulting as it did in the 1964 passage of the Voting Rights Act. Dr. King was focused, persistent and above all, effective. His success contrasts strikingly with the totally ineffective and counter-productive terrorist tactics of today, where violence is an essential element.

Racial Integration

As I was to discover, Washington was very much a southern city, and living there I came into contact for the first time with large numbers of African Americans. Prejudice was very evident. A friend and I went to a Washington Redskins football game at newly constructed DC Stadium (later named Robert F. Kennedy stadium). After considerable pressure, including likely denial of permission to play in a municipally owned stadium, the team had recently decided to integrate and had traded with the Cleveland Browns for Bobby Mitchell and drafted Charlie Taylor in the first round. They would be the first black players to play for the Redskins since the formation of the team. My friend and I were shocked to encounter a protester at the gate dressed in a gorilla outfit and carrying a sign that said, "Ise wants to play for the Redskins, too." The other tenant at the new stadium was the Washington Senators baseball team, a pretty bad but integrated expansion team, which succeeded the original Senators team, which had moved to Minnesota and become the Twins.

Assassination of JFK

In the early part of 1963, I met Ellen Dunne, also living and working in Washington, and we became engaged in the fall of that year. Ellen was from Richmond, VA, and we arranged to go to Richmond in November so I could meet her parents and siblings. We decided to go on a Saturday in November, stay over night and return to Washington on Sunday. Unfortunately, the Saturday we picked was the day following the assassination of President Kennedy. Understandably, our visit was overshadowed by the shock and the all-day news coverage of the event. I recall watching one of the television stations on Sunday morning to see the transfer of Lee Harvey Oswald from one prison to another and was stunned to see Oswald himself assassinated by Jack Ruby right there on live TV. For a while I thought that civilization, as I knew it, was beginning to collapse.

The President's funeral was held the following Monday and government offices being closed as a result, I decided to go over to Pennsylvania Avenue to watch the procession—a very formal ceremonial event organized by the Army unit charged with such responsibilities. Many dignitaries from around the world, such as Charles de Gaulle were part of the procession. After the funeral Mass at St. Mathew's Cathedral, I followed the procession over Memorial Bridge to Arlington Cemetery. There was a flyover, including a missing-man formation with stealth bombers as well as Air Force One. You could see the graveside flame in the distance as it grew dusk.

Ellen and I enjoyed dancing at the Shoreham hotel and listening to Mark Russell, a comedian whose jokes were always fresh, being based on the ever-changing political scene. Jerry Stiller and Anne Meara and Bill Cosby were young comedians who entertained in Washington, later to become famous (or infamous, in the case of Cosby). We got married in May 1964 and our first child was born a year later.

Securities and Exchange Commission

After a tentative start, I did pretty well at the SEC, moving to more responsible legal positions over the years I was there. The SEC, which was established in 1934, had celebrated its 25th anniversary the year before I arrived. It was located in a "temporary" building, which had been built during World War II and was fairly accurately referred to as a "tar paper shack". Shortly after I began, there was an explosion of filings by companies wishing to "go public", creating a backlog, which took several months to process. This was the major focus of the SEC at that time when markets were less complicated and frauds simpler and not as frequent or as massive. There were no Bernie Madoffs operating then. Excessive markups by broker dealers were the major regulatory concerns. Investment companies were around, but no one foresaw the phenomenal growth of the mutual fund industry that was to take place. About a year after I arrived, our classmate, Bill Joseph, joined the SEC, and we shared an office there until I left. People (employees, members of the public) came and went freely as there were then no significant building security concerns. The metal detectors, picture IDs, escorts, etc. of today were not even on the horizon.

Summing Up

So, to sum up, during the five years following the end of my school years, I got my first permanent full-time job, encountered wholesale urban renewal, witnessed the inauguration of a new President and a massive civil rights demonstration, agonized through the Cuban missile crisis, endured the assassination of the President, followed by the assassination of the assassin, observed the integration of an all-white local sports icon, got engaged, married and became a father.

Jeremiah J. Bresnahan after graduation entered Harvard Law School and received an LLB degree in 1960. He then became an attorney with the United States Securities and Exchange Commission in Washington, DC. While there, he embarked on a part-time post-graduate course of studies at Georgetown Law Center, receiving an LLM in Taxation degree in 1963. He left the SEC in November 1965 to accept a position with the Boston law firm of Gaston, Snow, Motley & Holt, becoming a partner there in 1968. In 1991 he left to become a partner in another Boston law firm, Bingham, Dana & Gould, and remained there until retiring in 2005 at the mandatory retirement age of 70.

Throughout his career he served in various capacities from time to time with non-profit organizations, particularly church-related. Since retirement, he has pursued his interests in travel, reading, theatre attendance and classical music, particularly opera.

Jerry married Ellen Dunne in 1964; they have four children and four grandchildren, the eldest of whom just graduated from Harvard College in the Class of 2016.

A Political Education, Post 1957

Robert McIlwaine

In those undergraduate years in the '50s, we read Edmund Burke's *Reflections on the French Revolution*, which said it had no justification at all, and John Stuart Mill's *On Liberty*, which (as I remember, over 50 years later) said that political change should and could happen by free debate in a parliament, where the best ideas would eventually be adopted, not because an economic group with new clout (like the new-rich manufacturing middle class) demanded more representation with an implicit threat of open revolt, and not as a response to mass marches, protests, violent clashes with police and general civil unrest but, rather, because the light of reason in the parliamentarians' discussions would reveal to them the best law to make.

It was the middle of the Cold War, and all revolutions were bad except ours. Political change should never come except very incrementally and modify but not really change the social order. With Burke (via Wordsworth, I believe), the analogy was with the growth of a great tree adding rings to its girth over eons. When the civil rights movement came, the civil rights laws were not enacted by such a process. Social change about race, women's rights, then gay and lesbian rights has been incremental and will continue to be, but first actions of change were emotionally violent political conflicts that set generations, races and genders against each other with, at times, confrontations in the streets. They didn't happen because of an undisturbing natural social evolution like the growth of a great tree or because the debating society of Congress saw the light of reason on its own. The Supreme Court made its landmark decisions because Martin Luther King, Jr., and his followers battled cops with police dogs and fire hoses, which was seen by everyone in the country, and he appealed his case up to the court. There was certainly debate and Eisenhower, though he angrily regretted appointing Earl Warren to the court by one account, sent federal troops to integrate the schools in Little Rock, AK, when Governor Faubus wouldn't do it.

Burke and Mill did not describe what men in our class faced in our first ten years out of Harvard. You didn't have to be a Marxist to feel that Marx and other more realistic (and less dangerous) thinkers would have prepared us better for this history. Now, and for some years, a leading Marxist literary scholar in English can teach at, of all places, Duke University in North Carolina. Such a thing would have been only a bad joke in the '50s and even the '60s when I was a graduate student there.

A very disturbing memory of the political climate of our college years is the distortions of reality stemming from the overwhelming influence of T.S. Eliot and the so-called *New Criticism*. They created a deep and pervasive blindness to political evils that were not discussed when we read their works. The New Criticism's doctrine was that no historical, biographical or political context for a work of literature should be considered in understanding and judging it.

This supposedly apolitical approach kept out of sight and mind the fact that its leading theorists, John Crowe Ransom, Cleanth Brooks, Allen Tate, and—at that time—Robert Penn Warren were Southern apologists for the old slave-holding South. The radical or progressive politics of the great 19th-century Romantic poets was rejected as extremely idealistic, which it was, by rejecting all their poetry as over-emotional and embarrassing "spilled religion." If you told someone you taught Romantic poetry, they would smile mischievously or even laugh in your face. If you said you liked Whitman, they simply thought you had no taste or "standards". In encounters like these, you had to prove your intelligence some other way.

Probably the most distressing and even frightening memory is the inculcated blindness to the graphic anti-semitism in the poetry of T.S. Eliot. It simply wasn't mentioned when discussing his early poems. I taught them that way myself in the Fifties and Sixties at Duke with at least a few Jewish students in the room. He wrote in his poem about the decay of Western civilization, "Gerontion"—undoubtedly a masterpiece—the "Jew squats on the windowsill, the owner". In "Sweeney among the Nightingales","Rachel, née Rabinovitch/Tears at the grapes with murderous paws".The satiric poem,"Burbank with a Baedeker: Bleistein with a Cigar", contains these lines and others like them.

> But this or such was Bleistein's way:
> A saggy bending of the knees
> And elbows, with the palms turned out,
> Chicago Semite Viennese.
>
> . . .
>
> The rats are underneath the piles.
> The jew is underneath the lot.
> Money in furs.

. . . Because it was a minor work, this poem could be avoided, but with others we stared at the vicious imagery as if it wasn't there; I didn't discuss it or even mention it as I remember.

When our class entered Harvard in 1953, Hitler had been defeated only eight years before when the Holocaust was exposed. But Eliot was one of the gods of modernist literature and our greatest poet. We looked at his anti-semitism in his poetry and prose the way children in Nazi Germany were supposed to have read in their schoolbooks—according to an historian friend—that Hitler had blond hair and blue eyes. They experienced no cognitive dissonance and moved on. We talked about Eliot's ideas of tradition and religion, read his poems, and continued thinking of him as a saintly conservative gentlemen. So far as I know, Eliot never recanted his anti-semitism, as Pound did. My best and only long-time classmate friend is Jewish.

When I spent some time in Germany in the Army in 1962–1964, my naïve view of how the world regarded my country was shaken and the shaking only intensified when I came back to find the civil rights movement and campus protests about race and the Viet Nam war getting violent. The Germans felt no guilt and talked only about the terrible bombing we inflicted on them.

They didn't look at us as the global defender of freedom and democracy but as the richest and most powerful nation. We had defeated them by superior fire power, not our fighting ability—probably true—and because Hitler was a bad general. Now we could occupy their country and tell them what to do. Scores of times Germans berated me and my country for failing to join with them to defeat Stalin. *We* were to blame for the Soviet threat; we had been stupid, they had known all along. "Of course, everything was not so good with our government, but we would've gotten rid of Hitler for you."

They liked us when we defended them against the Soviets, but the usually undereducated teenage *Americanische soldat*, with more money than most of them had ever seen, was notorious. The dollar was worth over four deutsche marks. Young Germans were at times hostile—American soldiers took out German girls—but often neutral or friendly and likable and shadowed by their parents' Nazi past. They were saturated with American pop music, dances, and movies. I became aware how many Germans had relatives in the US from the great migration after the 1848 revolution when Bismarck drove liberals and radicals out of the country. Quite often, Germans would claim proxy pride in our victory by telling me that Americans and Germans had *dasselbe blut* (the same blood). I've kept an interest in Germany and its literature to this day.

The event that I would never have expected myself to experience was a day-and-night sit-down demonstration on the day Martin Luther King, Jr., was shot and killed in Memphis, and the black maintenance workers at Duke went out on strike. They were being paid less than workers were by Southern businessmen in downtown Durham. We marched to the President's class and a leader addressed him. We slept in his home at his invitation and then continued our sit-down in the main quad before Duke cathedral. Young assistant professors of history were the most prominent faculty members in the event. I really just stumbled into it and then stayed the course, cutting classes like the other faculty, and it is a miracle that they and I myself weren't fired, but no one was.

I was given the job to phone William Styron, a Duke graduate, to have him send a message of support, which he did. Joan Baez and Shel Silverstein showed up one evening to speak to us—a very strange pair to see and hear talking to Duke undergraduates sitting around on the familiar quad at night. One day an automaker executive Duke trustee appeared and caused an uproar when he said he thought company unions were better than independent unions, but then he joined hands and we all sang "We Shall Overcome".

A few years later, the president had to resign when there was a take-over of the administration building by black students, imitating black students with guns at Cornell, which brought in the Durham police with tear gas and charges with billy clubs. I stayed uninvolved on that one, never being much of a radical after all.

My demonstration wasn't a life-changing event, even though I was the only member of the English Department, student or faculty, in it. It was just one experience in an ongoing political education since 1957.

I have now lived under 14 presidents. American and world politics are still—indescribable. Now, more than ever.

Bob McIlwaine graduated *magna cum laude* in History and Literature from Harvard. In 1959 he received an MA (with a master's thesis on W. H. Auden) and in 1968 a PhD (with a dissertation on Bernard Shaw) at Duke University. He taught at Duke, Southern Methodist University and Hampden-Sydney College. Since coming to Manhattan in 1972, he has worked as a freelance editor and tutor, writing fiction and plays. One full-length play, *Country Dark*, was produced at the Midtown International Theatre Festival in 2004. Since 2006, Bob has been a professor of English at Touro College, an outreach institution where many students often work one or more jobs, have children, range in age from teenagers to grandmothers, are mostly people of color, Hispanics, or American and immigrant blacks, and represent many religions, including Islam.

Expatriata

Anthony J. Price

From *Syonan; Singapore under Japanese Occupation* (© 1990)

"The Pacific War came to an end in August 1945, not because of an Allied invasion of Syonan or Japan itself (although both were being planned), but because the destruction of Hiroshima and Nagasaki finally made a point to the Japanese that Asia was not to be theirs by force of arms. The local surrender of Syonan's Japanese garrison to Lord Louis Mountbatten didn't take place until September, however, as it took the British many weeks to marshal a liberation force for their faraway former colony. Meanwhile, Japanese soldiers tried halfheartedly to maintain the peace in Syonan-now-Singapore. European POWs continued to sleep in their prison camps, wondering what to do next. Widespread looting took place in the city, and old vendettas were settled. The delay in reoccupation was taken as another sign of British ineffectiveness, and during the month of leaderless existence, Singapore was lost forever to England, though it took until 1962 to formalize a parting of the ways."

From *Casa Crate; a Caribbean Adventure* (© 1994)

"In 1969 we were transferred to Puerto Rico from Mexico City, a place we dearly loved. We had even acquired some land in Mexico with the hope of eventually building a dream house, only to be suddenly packed off to what seemed a backwater province, lacking in either Spanish or American culture. Puerto Rico's dilemma of no clear identity or mission seemed to infect us the same way. Years later, when we returned after a shipwreck in the Mona Passage, we felt warmer about Borrinquen, as the locals call Puerto Rico, but during our first four-year tour we often found the island depressing. Even Puerto Rico's Spanish dialect was odd, and we virtually had to relearn the language after much effort mastering a more 'standard' version in Mexico."

From *Chameleon; Dodging War in the Pacific* (© 2006)

"In 1978 I returned to Singapore, my birthplace, feeling very much a stranger but at the same time oddly in tune with the place. Thirty-eight years had lapsed since leaving the island at age five, when my distraught mother and I sailed to Canada. Behind us we left my father's grave on Dutch Java, a remote place we had moved to from Singapore just eighteen months earlier for an intended new life."

From *Expat: The Episcopal Theatrical Society* (© 2009)

"Introduction: This little book is about coping with and enjoying expatriate life in various foreign environments over several decades—becoming suburban residents of two wonderful cities each in Latin America (Mexico City and San Juan), Southeast Asia (Taipei and Singapore) and Europe (Brussels and London). All or some of our children lived with us throughout; hence we were privileged to observe how a number of fine international schools chose to deal with the local cultures. Moving from country to country, we strove to maintain a tight-knit family nucleus as we developed friendships with people from all over the world, many of whom we still hear from today. Through our children's schools, through the Anglican-Episcopal churches, through business associations, and through expat theatrical groups, we enjoyed meeting people from a variety of origins, and we were honored to be accepted by local people too."

From *Paradise in Ruins; a Novel (View) of the Pacific War* (© 2016)
"If a civilian's house gets blown up in a war, who's to help him rebuild it? Probably not the warring parties."

From *Colonies in Ruins; a Consequence of the Pacific War* (© 2017)
"It was nearly pitch black in the early hours of December 8, 1941, when transport ships among the first of seven Japanese flotillas began dropping landing craft into Siam's offshore waters, and loading infantry to go ashore. Not all flotillas from the original combined fleet would arrive in their target zones at the exact same time, despite best efforts to do so. Accordingly, the earliest wave of barges was fired upon by a Siamese coastal garrison nearly half an hour before the Japanese air attack at Pearl Harbor, Hawaii, seven time-zones away. Fortunately for the faraway Japanese planes, the defenders in Siam were far too preoccupied with battling Japanese troops at the beaches to bother raising an alarm outside the country, thus the US Navy in Hawaii received no warning of its looming disaster, nor did the British Army in Malaya—until the next morning when it was too late.

Anthony Price was born in Singapore of British parents. He attended Fort Street School in Sydney, St. Mark's School in Dallas, then Harvard College and the University of Oklahoma. A US Marine of the late 1950s and a multilingual worldwide resident thereafter, he has authored numerous technical papers, several extensive memoirs, and, in retirement, two historical novels under the pen name Antwyn Price. Selections from these works appear in his Harvard '57 *Recollections and Reflections*.

The American Dream

A Charmed Life in the 20th Century

William S. Gray

Samuel Johnson is often quoted as having said that there is no greater monument to human vanity than a library, and I fear that this Essay Collection represents a good deal of human vanity. What he actually said, by the way, was: "*No place affords a more striking conviction of the vanity of human hopes than a public library.*" Nevertheless, I will bow to my perennial weakness of not wanting to be left out of anything, and proceed.

Along with all my Harvard classmates, I was a "Depression Baby", born in 1936, and, as was not unusual in those days, an only child. But, in a way, I couldn't have been born at a better moment, in a better place, or to better parents. As a child of the Depression, I learned "the value of a buck", as my father would have said, and indeed, although we were comfortably middle class in Paterson, NJ, where I was born, I knew that my parents and grandparents all worked so the family could live as it did. Being aware early on that hard work produced not only creature comforts but satisfaction was a great advantage, and added to that advantage was the fact that, although there was a draft, I was too young to be in either World War II or the Korean War, and too old to be in the Vietnam War. With just a little luck in the next few years, I will likely die in my bed without having experienced hunger or privation or a shot fired at me in anger or battle and among the relatively very few (1/10 of 1%?) people in human history who can say that.

As to place, had my mother's grandparents not emigrated to the US from Germany in 1859, and had my father's parents not emigrated to the US from Hungary in 1903, I would likely have been a victim of the Holocaust. And not only was I fortunate to have been born in the US but further fortunate to have spent my formative years in New York City, to which we moved in 1943, and to experience America in its Golden Age after the war. It was a time when America was the greatest nation on earth, but we are wont to forget that that was because it was the only industrially advanced nation on earth that had virtually everything while the rest of the industrialized world was in shambles and the developing nations impoverished. And, of course it wasn't "great" for everyone. But all in all, for a Jewish boy in New York City, living in the gilded ghetto of the Upper West Side (we weren't rich, but I did live in a nice apartment building three floors over Babe Ruth—who also wasn't rich, by the way), it was indeed great.

Here's a story of "The American Dream":

My father's father, Joseph Grossman, came first to the US and then brought his wife, who was pregnant with my father when she arrived. So my father was born six weeks after his mother arrived in the US, spoke Hungarian and Yiddish before he spoke English, and grew up in abject poverty on the Lower East Side of Manhattan. He started work at age five as a delivery boy, and since he had a beautiful ear for music and language, his English was so good that by the time he was 15, Joseph Grossman decided that my father, Irving (a name thought by immigrant Jews to be very "American" because of Washington Irving!) had to support the family. So my father finished high school at night, and went to work for a very fancy men's clothing store, Finchley Fifth Avenue New York.

Finchley put him on the road when he was 17 and changed his name to "Irving I. Gray" so he could be accepted on the college campuses (including the University of Pennsylvania and the University of Virginia) which were his "territory". So he was "Bob Gray" at work in New York City and "Irving Grossman" at home in Paterson, NJ Because the schools had decided to send report cards to fathers at their business address when I started kindergarten in 1941, the whole family changed its name to "Gray" and I, "Billy Grossman", became "Billy Gray".

My father's dream was to send his son to college, and thankfully he realized his dream: he sent me to Harvard and Harvard Law School and lived to see me graduate from both. He died at 60 in 1964, alas, but 22 years later I came to Charlottesville as a very senior lawyer for the General Electric Company and bought the very elegant house in which we still live, which is only six minutes from the university where my father had to have his name changed in order to sell clothing. So I have lived not only my father's dream, but a large part of The American Dream as well.

I was born at the right time, in the right place, and to the right parents, for it was really my parents who were instrumental in my experiencing "The American Dream", my mother because she taught me that reaching out to others and listening to their stories (everyone has a story) is the most ingratiating and satisfying thing you can do, and my father, who was no less other-directed, by showing me how speaking well and joining to the extent one could in the life experience of others while maintaining one's own identity could make a big difference in one's life.

The result was that I have had a charmed and minor-Zelig-like existence. I got to know Errol Barrow, the first Prime Minister of independent Barbados when I was sent there to be the lawyer for an airline that never got off the ground. Through Barrow I met the then Chairman of British European Airways, Lord (Sholto) Douglas of Kirtleside and Lady Douglas, wound up taking their then five-year-old daughter Katharine and her governess to the zoo in New York City, wrote stories about an imaginary mouse to whom Katharine had introduced me at their penthouse suite at the St. Regis Hotel and am still close friends with the now 58-year-old Katharine, and read stories about "Mouse" to my grandchildren.

What Else?

- I had the sword dance performed and bagpipe played for me by a champion piper of the Scots Guards in Crieff, Scotland, because I met a young man on a train going from Perth to Edinburgh, drank a wee dram with him on our arrival, and at his insistence visited him and his family (which included the piper) in Perth where I was received warmly and virtually became part of the family, which I still keep up with;
- Met a Danish fellow in Copenhagen in 1957 who loved sailing and moved to Rye, NY, as a result of which we owned three sailboats together, became such good friends, that we named our second son, Erik, after him, and became an honorary Dane (I can *helingore* and *halvingore* an *akavit* with the best of them);
- Helped two women in East Harlem, Marge Jenkins and Mary Iemma, get their Upper Park Avenue Community Association building rehab project going, went on their board and found myself involved in the most successful community rehabilitation effort of President Johnson's Great Society program;

- Wound up, because of rejection by Jack Welch of a job in his Group for which the GE General Counsel had nominated me, on the General Counsel's staff and worked on the then-largest acquisition in US industrial history, became counsel to a uranium company, an Emmy-winning entertainment company (which included the operations of my hero, Sol Hurok), General Counsel of the General Electric Supply Company and ultimately Group Counsel of GE's Industrial Electronic Business Group;
- Sailed on a 58-foot ketch acting as second mate from Piraeus to Skiathos, where I and the whole crew were entertained by a Professor of International Law I'd met in Genoa in 1957 and with whom I corresponded for 35 years who had a house there;
- Read to kids in elementary school for the past 17 years, and interviewed applicants for Harvard for the past 40 years, which has always given me great confidence in the future;
- Get together yearly with high-school classmates, one of whom is a well-known cartoonist for *The New Yorker*, another a world famous biographer and a third a physician responsible for the adoption of the cochlear implant;
- And, *above all*, met on her first day in New York on a visit from her home in Brussels, and married Antoinette Goldschmidt, a wonderful woman whose dear and enormously accomplished family (one great-uncle was President of the League of Nations, a great-grandfather was knighted for having designed the Votiv Kirche and a large part of the Ringstrasse in Vienna, her brother was Deputy Director General of the IAEA) immediately adopted me.

I've been happy to sit in the bleachers and clap and always wondered how all this could happen to an NJB (Nice Jewish Boy) from the Upper West Side of New York.

I guess the result of all of this is my conviction that true good fortune in life is to have loving parents and to be a loving parent, for my greatest joy and satisfaction has come from raising, along with my wife, two wonderful sons and seeing them, along with their children, happy.

I've learned that we *give* our children life, they didn't ask for it, and we don't *lend* it to them. So they don't owe us, but rather we *owe* them, namely to provide for them, to love them, to nurture them and to let them go, and the recompense, if you're as lucky as Antoinette and I are, is to have loving children who are our good friends as well.

The other thing I think I've learned is to live by Mark Twain's advice to "*Always do right. It will gratify some people and amaze the rest.*" And when faced with anyone's arrogant conviction that only they are right (arrogance being the most deadly of sins), to follow Sir Roger de Coverly's maxim: "*There's much to be said on both sides of the question.*"

I can only hope that many, if not all, of my classmates' lives have been as eventful and charmed as mine.

Bill Gray's Harvard College and Law degrees got him the MOS of cook and Mess Sergeant in the US Army Reserves, but he did get to practice law for several firms in New York City, specializing in areas as disparate as writing ships' mortgages in an Admiralty Law firm, arguing cases in Land Appropriation and Condemnation in the New York Court of Appeals and co-authoring a book on corporate law, before he became counsel in the IGE Export Division of General Electric Company, from which he went on to be Group Counsel of the Industrial Electronics Business (factory automation) Group in Charlottesville, Virginia. When the Group was abruptly closed down in 1985, Bill opened up a solo practice specializing in International and High Technology Commercial Transactions, a somewhat quixotic undertaking that turned out to be both enjoyable and successful over 14 years, then became a partner in Williams Mullen, a regional firm headquartered in Richmond, and finally Vice-President, Licensing for a biotech firm.

His favorite avocation is reading to kids in elementary school, which is much more important than the several commissions, committees and councils on whose boards he's served and/or chaired.

Hope for Our Children and Grandchildren

Nino Yannoni

I apologize for not writing about something more upbeat, but when I stared at the deadline (February 7, today!), only something which has been on my mind a lot lately got me to writing.

It feels like 1953 when I would put off things I didn't like to do, like slinking off to Lamont Library to read something for Humanities I (or was it Soc. Sci. I?) like "The City of God", which no self-respecting chemistry concentrator should have to read, and then crawling into one of those offices off the Square to meet with a "section man", dreading that he might ask me what I thought.

Since I could be a poster boy of the "*Silent Generation*", I decided to let you know how I feel.

Filling in a little about my background might help understand how I might have come to writing what I have here. Thank, or blame, the Essay Book Committee for that part—thanks to them for urging me on.

My Family

In 1892, my father was sent here from Italy by his mother at the age of 18. He came in through Ellis Island. Apparently how his surname ***(Iannone)*** was spelled meant little to him in comparison to be letting into the United States. For his family, it was a land of promise.

From what little I know, Italians were not all that welcome here, with the result that Italian ghettos were often formed in the cities around Boston. He initially lived with family in Brockton, MA, apprenticing as a tailor. My mother and he got married in 1924 and settled into the "gardener's cottage" on my grandfather's substantial property in Jamaica Plain. Although my grandfather (mother's side) was well off, it seemed that "trickledown" didn't work for our family, especially since my mom and her father definitely did not get along. This resulted in financial struggles since tailors didn't make a lot of money, but I never felt that we were "poor".

I attended parochial school in Jamaica Plain, and then Boston Latin School ("*Boys Latin*"), which was at that time a shoehorn into Harvard. Jamaica Plain was predominantly Irish, and it felt like my family had kind of a siege mentality in that regard, living in an Irish "ghetto". This was the era of James Michael Curley, and my parents felt he was a crook and helped only the Irish.

But their main idea seemed to become as American as possible; as a result, not one of us four learned to speak Italian. My mother made a point that we *should never smell of garlic "like those people who go to St. Leonard's church in the North End*". She was speaking of the very church in which she and my Dad were married.

My parents were relentless about getting an education, and all four of us graduated college. Two of us went way beyond what they were thinking—good jobs—and got our PhD. So the American Dream for us consisted of schooling and being "American".

Politically, from the little I recall in that regard, it was all FDR, the New Deal and the Democrats.

My Adaptation to Harvard

Since I was a commuter at Harvard, I wasn't exposed to much change in my cultural life, since I spent most of my non-school-related hours at Dudley Hall, mostly playing ping-pong in the basement. We were all "*townies*", and I didn't make a big effort to pal around with my friends who did live at Harvard. I clearly remember watching the *Army-McCarthy hearings*, sitting in those overstuffed leather chairs in our common room.

> I heard Mr. Welch, the Army counsel, stand up to Senator McCarthy saying something like, "*Have you no decency, Sir?*"

That stuck in my mind for some reason.

I served as Treasurer of the House Committee and got involved in our battle to get Dudley Hall renamed Dudley House. I recall Charlie Whitlock as our House Master with fondness. Through my political connections at Harvard, namely John Simourian, our Class Marshal and a good friend from NROTC, I was voted in as Class Treasurer. I never did anything but a half-baked job and quit a few years after we graduated.

After Harvard

After Harvard I went into the Navy via NROTC and then in 1959 to graduate school in chemistry at Columbia in the Upper West Side of New York City. Living in New York certainly diluted my "Italianness" but certainly not the liberal, Democratic blood that apparently has flowed in my veins since I don't know when. JFK's election made that blood flow even a little stronger, and the Upper West Side was/is an ever-liberal part of the city. One of my friends, who lived above the West End bar, even got me to the 1963 March on Washington, one of the few public political statements I have made.

In 1966, I married Sue Taylor, a student nurse at Columbia, who spent her formative years in Coral Gables, FL, seeing upfront how blacks were treated in the South in that day. After having two children, Sue wanted to adopt an inter-racial child. We did that and added two more adopted children, one of whom is also inter-racial. In today's world, with the resurgence of white nationalism, we would have had to think a great deal about our children's safety, even though we live in the Bay Area.

I went to work at IBM in Yorktown Heights, NY, until 1971, when we got moved to California. Life went on with some trying times when a couple of our family members got chemically addicted, introducing us to that disease. I am grateful for the insurance-supported rehab programs that existed at that time for those with drinking problems. I cannot say enough about how important a role medical insurance has played in my life, and continues to do so. And I am especially grateful for the 12-step recovery programs that were/are out there for me.

After 23 years of what a nice social worker helping with one of our adoptions called ours an "average" marriage, I was divorced. Four years later, in 1993, I met Pamela Clark, whom I married in 2000. Pam has been the love of my life. She's a nurse practitioner and has an MFCC degree. Pam also has two sons, for a total of seven children. She married into an eclectic Yannoni family and has become a caring maternal influence on the family, not to mention an awesome and loving grandmother. Her lineage is pretty much Anglo-Saxon, and two of her grandparents were immigrants from Europe. Her upbringing and schooling have given her great empathy for the down-trodden, less advantaged members of our society.

We both feel for those who have not had all the advantages we've had, and these liberal tendencies have become enhanced by today's goings-on.

Reflections

So, to what I wrote in the first place to disabuse you about something I said in my 60th Reunion biographical sketch. I wrote:

> "*I am writing this after November 8 and am trying day by day to maintain a positive attitude, despite the fact that I am disappointed in how our country has drifted into negativity. I still hold out hope for a better future for our children and grandchildren.*"

The events that have transpired over the last few weeks have made me much less sanguine about the future of our country. I won't recount them but, like you, I heard stuff throughout the War and the years following about repressive regimes in other countries and what happens to those who live in them. I saw early on what happened while

Senator McCarthy was on the warpath. I'm not expecting that level of regression to happen here, but then again, neither did those in other countries who ended up living with tyranny. It seems like a slow, rather sneaky process.

So my wife and I decided to get involved, admittedly on a kindergarten level. We have started by communicating with our congressmen/women. Even though California is big enough to at least put up a fair amount of resistance, the federal government can certainly put lots of pressure on any state to get its way. We feel that it's essential to keep after our politicians, federal and state, to let them know our feelings about what's happening in Washington. To do this, we feel that we have to do triage by focusing on major issues like the immigration ban, the National Security Council *(NSC)* appointment of Steve Bannon, suppression of the press, attacks on civil rights of any stripe and on separation of church and state. By the time you read this, there will undoubtedly be more such issues.

So there it is, *the freedom which our wonderful country has offered to my grandparents, parents and me. I want that to be there for my children and grandchildren.*

Figure 2.4.2.1 *The Yannoni family in 1943, dressed in clothes made by Nino's father, an expert tailor. Nino, wearing his Eaton cap, is shown with his parents Costantino and Raffaela, his sisters Catherine and Margherita and his brother Nicholas, on the front lawn of the gardener's cottage of his grandfather's farm, situated on a hill overlooking the Arborway in Jamaica Plain, Boston.*

Nino Yannoni, a K-8 graduate of Blessed Sacrament School in Jamaica Plain, MA, before Boston Latin School and Harvard, was a member of Naval Reserve Officers Training Corps (NROTC) during college. He served two years in the Navy before entering graduate school in chemistry at Columbia (1959–1966). After introduction to research chemistry at Union Carbide Research Institute in Tarrytown, NY, he began a 34-year career with IBM as Research Staff Member, first in Yorktown Heights, NY, and then San Jose, CA, until retirement in 2001. He then took on the "nice job" of watching his first grandson grow up every Monday, and after him two other grandsons and three granddaughters. He reports that he has kept active in a 12-step program, plays with his Lionel trains, plays at golf, and shares weekly meals with friends. He and wife, Pam, love spending time together, whether it's over a meal, traveling, or watching the Patriots (yay!!) and her team(s!), the Steelers and Packers.

"Life is good, and much of that I owe to Harvard in ways both tangible and intangible. But I think you might know what I mean."

Figure 2.4.2.2 *Hammerbeam trusses and stenciled ceiling of Annenberg Hall, named in memory of Roger Annenberg, '62, on renovation in 1994 of Memorial Hall, originally completed in 1874.*

Reprinted courtesy of Harvard University

Life-Changing Experiences

How Jackie O. Played Matchmaker to Two of America's Greatest Minds

Peter Frank Davis

Figure 2.5.1.1 *Former First Lady Jackie Kennedy at a picnic sometime in the 1960s*
Photo source: Michael Ochs Archives/Getty Images

Writer Peter F. Davis recalls how the former First Lady hosted an unforgettable evening with Harvard classicist John H. Finley, Jr., journalist I. F. Stone, and the "wallpaper contingent".

Social gaffes curdle an occasion. At a large gathering not long ago in Hollywood, I lost any traction I may have had when I mistook an old friend's young wife for Drew Barrymore and complimented her on her work in *Moneyball*. Of course, Drew Barrymore wasn't in *Moneyball*, she was in an earlier baseball movie, and I wasn't talking to Drew Barrymore. My lifetime-achievement award as an associational dunderhead came in my early 20s, when I spotted the snowy-bearded T. H. White, author of *The Once and Future King* (which became the musical *Camelot*), and rushed up to him with the awestruck declaration that *A Farewell to Arms* had changed my life. At least Hemingway was still alive—barely.

Yet even oafishness can have a holiday. Though this story takes place in 1978, it begins in 1976, when, following an introduction from friends, I was invited to the apartment of Jacqueline Onassis on Fifth Avenue in New York. It was a small gathering that included Lillian Hellman, Felix Rohatyn (who had not long before helped save New York City from bankruptcy), and Dustin Hoffman. The conversation was glittering, smart, at times racy.

For some reason, Dustin Hoffman seemed to want to talk about sex—gossip as well as speculations, grinning hints. He couldn't stop. Felix Rohatyn was becomingly modest about his salvation of New York ("All sides had an interest in the economic survival of the city"), and the acerbic Lillian Hellman threw off the sparks of a Roman candle with every remark she made. I myself, seated at the left hand of our hostess, had nothing to say. Couldn't find a topic. Mrs. Onassis told a sly anecdote about de Gaulle (did she intuit that many years later Rohatyn would be ambassador to France?), but I don't remember it, because I've always had de Gaulle on a very short leash.

I knew I hadn't been invited there to be a mannequin, but I really did have nothing to say. Blinded by the shimmer or simply didn't belong at that table, something. Racing through my mind, helped maybe by the Château Beychevelle, I desperately cherry-picked a piece from that morning's paper. It was about the retirement of an old professor of mine, the great Harvard classicist John H. Finley, Jr. Mrs. Onassis was only a couple of years past her own time in Greece. I asked if she'd seen the article. Luck: she had, was charmed by it. Can you tell me what he was like? A soft pitch into my wheelhouse.

So glad you asked. He was my freshman adviser, steered me as a naïve, intimidated Southern Californian into Harvard's arcane ways, steered me as well into his own memorable course in the humanities that began with his incandescent lectures on Greek and Roman literature. As master of Eliot House, one of Harvard's *über*-dorms, which are like small communities (Mrs. Onassis's first husband had been in Winthrop House), Finley presided longer than any other House master. The professor himself was regarded as an institution within an institution.

It was rumored that Finley had been in the final round before the selection of the new Harvard president, Nathan Pusey, who came in with my freshman class in 1953. No one ever said why Finley hadn't gotten the nod. I finished by telling Mrs. Onassis that Finley was especially famous for saying that Harvard was a conspiracy of alcohol, intellect, and athletics to postpone sex. Take *that*, Dustin. Postponing sex: that's how long ago it was.

I didn't see Mrs. Onassis again and never expected to. A year went by, another half-year and more. In the dreary winter of 1978, I read a piece in *The New York Times Magazine* about how the crusading journalist and essayist I. F. Stone, beginning at the age of 70, taught himself ancient Greek so that he could read the classics. Say, what if these two . . . no, it couldn't happen. Finley seldom left Cambridge, while Stone was retired in Washington, DC. I could hardly bring about a meeting of these two men.

But there was one person, living halfway between them, whose invitation might pull them into the same room. I wrote Jackie—from now on in this story she's not Mrs. Onassis anymore—and asked if she'd seen the piece on Stone, and did she remember our conversation about Finley? Wouldn't it be fascinating if these two men met? Snail mail being quicker then, in less than 24 hours the unmistakable throaty whisper on the phone was telling me what a perfect idea this was.

Stone had once described himself to me as a kosher ham ready to go to the opening of a door, and when I called him he accepted immediately. Finley was tougher—not exactly a recluse but also not known to stray frequently from Cambridge except to go to his summer home in New Hampshire. Yet he'd read the *Times* piece on Stone and said he'd be delighted to come.

Jackie and I discussed who else should be there, and we came up with a couple of Harvard men and their wives whom she knew, men Finley had known as undergraduates. The idea was we'd be comfortable wallpaper decorations for Finley, putting him at ease and making Stone feel like performing to impress us. Yet I was nervous. Finley had been a dazzling conversationalist at Harvard with his pithy comments about life and the college itself—"As a freshman," he told me, "you feel you can do *anything*; as a senior you find out you have to do *something*"–but perhaps this was a talent that didn't travel well.

On the day of the dinner party, I picked up Professor Finley at La Guardia. Izzy and Esther Stone were coming up by train from Washington. I asked Finley if he wanted to go anywhere before I dropped him at the Harvard Club (naturally, the only place where he'd feel even partly at home). He said no—well, perhaps he could briefly see his father. I did a momentary calculation, knowing Finley was in his mid-70s, and arrived at the image of a desiccated centenarian wobbling around in a nursing home. Sure, I said, where do we go? He said to take him to Carl Schurz Park, uptown on the East River.

In the winter, when there are no leaves, you can see Professor Finley's father from East End Avenue even before entering Carl Schurz Park. John Finley Sr. had been president of City College of New York, commissioner of education for New York State, president of the American Geographical Society, and editor of *The New York Times*. I didn't know he was so eminent, because Professor Finley had never mentioned his father to me.

By 1978, Finley senior was, as he is today, a bronze silhouette perched at the top of a pole on the promenade above Carl Schurz Park. In the sculpture he is captured, as if in a photograph, leaning into the breeze with a scarf flowing behind him, bowler hat on his head, walking stick in his hand. Across his upper legs is the silhouette of a fantasy Manhattan skyline, featuring skyscrapers and a bridge. Honoring the quintessential New Yorker of a certain era, an inscription carved above the sculpture announces "JOHN FINLEY WALK."

Figure 2.5.1.2 *Investigative reporter I. F. Stone photographed in 1971* (left)*, and Harvard classicist John H. Finley, Jr., at the University's Commencement, 1978*

Left, from AP Images; *right,* photographer: Lillian Kemp; Schlesinger Library, Radcliffe Institute, Harvard University

I was no less worried than I had been before, because Finley and Stone were so different. To the degree I knew him, I loved Izzy Stone, whose life was devoted to freedom of speech, equality of opportunity, and the exposure of wrongdoing in high places. Elfin and engaging, he could also be extremely contentious. His current contention, about which he later published a book, held that Socrates was not condemned for worshiping false gods or corrupting the youth of Athens, as his follower Plato had claimed. Instead, Stone maintained, Socrates opposed the very democracy he lived in, was even against free speech, and thought society should be run by the wisest aristocrats instead of by common citizens voting for laws and leaders. The Athenian democracy, according to Stone, had to get rid of him because it had already been overthrown twice by aristocrats, and the government feared that Socrates's students could make it happen again.

John Finley actually was an aristocrat, an elite Episcopalian who had spent his whole professional life at Harvard. Izzy Stone was a Jewish maverick who had dropped out of college and essentially taught himself everything he knew. After bouncing around in newspaper jobs, he started his own journal, *I. F. Stone's Weekly*, which became unexpectedly successful, even a kind of bible for young investigative reporters, and ran it until he retired to study ancient Greek. A short, plump, owlish radical with thick-lensed glasses and a conspicuous hearing aid, he presented a stark contrast to the silver-haired Finley, who even in his 70s had the compact physique of an undergraduate on the Harvard lightweight crew.

Yet, for once, opposites actually did attract. Stone and Finley were both relatively short, could have been pixies from different parts of the forest. Neither was fazed by the presence of the other or by the splendor of Jackie Onassis's apartment. By that time, Stone had been around and had even become used to the late honors coming his way, while Finley was more or less to the manner born. With protests of mutual admiration, they engaged immediately. It turned out that the aristocratic Finley was as hospitable to rethinking the legacy of Socrates as Stone was. Esther Stone, as winning in her way as our hostess, ran her eyes around the staggering view of Central Park, the curtains, pictures, glass and silver, mementos of Jackie's first husband but not of her second—all the furnishings. It was not as though she were in awe; rather, she appeared to be tabulating a life, wanting to memorize everything. Esther was the Jewish mother, a woman once told me, everyone wished they'd had.

But what was our hostess wearing? Oafishness was not completely on holiday; I have absolutely no idea what Jackie wore. Whether she glided around the room in a diaphanous gown or a simple blouse over a peasant skirt—in both of which outfits I later saw her—I haven't a clue. She was a sylph; isn't that enough? It will have to suffice that in my memory she was, like Flaubert's idea of an author and God, everywhere present, nowhere visible.

The evening's atmosphere comprised equal parts of light and warmth. You wanted to be there, and you wanted it to go on forever. The talk was not merely sparkling but inspired. Even inspirational. In the presence of Izzy Stone and John Finley, Jackie Onassis transformed herself into the most benign of interviewers—curious, searching, probing, improvising as she went along.

But she was not only a good questioner; in fact, that wasn't her greatest talent. What she did best was listen. In a way this made her a very old-fashioned woman, always alert to absorbing the tales and lessons of men. Yet in her it was different; in her, as she listened, it was clear she was not simply a blotter for others' words but a discerning judge. She raised listening to an art form. Her large shining eyes, glowing from some hidden well, would fix a speaker as though he were in a spotlight. He—yes, it usually was he—had to be brighter, more pointed, concise, with a better dénouement, or at least punch line, than he knew he had in him.

Not that the guests of honor needed much prodding. Especially Izzy. Stone was soon onto his favorite subject, the trial of Socrates. He didn't want Socrates to have been sentenced to death, but he didn't much like the West's first philosopher. An egalitarian himself, Stone regarded Socrates as a class snob. If Socrates had pleaded the right to free speech at his trial, a plea available to him in Athens, he'd have been using the same democratic principles he had contempt for. He might have beaten the charges against him. Almost certainly, Stone said, he allowed himself to be condemned to drink the hemlock.

By this time Jackie had deftly relocated us to the dinner table, where we had a better meal than Socrates ever enjoyed, even when he was the toast of Athens. White truffles were floating on our plates. Accompanied, once again, by Château Beychevelle.

The charge against Socrates of corrupting the youth of Athens, Finley said, didn't have the same meaning then that it has today. He simply didn't accept the state's gods. He also had considerable admiration for the tyrant Agamemnon, who had led the Greek forces in the Trojan War. Finley agreed with Stone that Agamemnon had not been a lovable person, sacrificing his own daughter in order to get favorable winds from the gods for his ships on the way to Troy. Then he mistreated his best warrior, Achilles, and even stole his girlfriend. Finley seemed not to want to counter Stone, especially since the two essentially agreed, so much as to encourage him as he would have an extraordinarily bright PhD candidate. In fact, he might agree with Stone about Socrates's conservative politics, yet he was using the Socratic method itself to draw out his companion. When one of us, the wallpaper for the evening, asked the relevance of the classical period to our own era, Finley and Stone, astonishingly, answered in a duet: "Athens is our yesterday."

I understood that night that, while I'd always regarded Harvard as a kind of religion with John Finley, his true religion was ancient Greece.

He diffidently asked Jackie about what he referred to as her Greek period. She answered diffidently, praising the "incomparable" beauty of Skorpios—Aristotle Onassis's private island—and "every last one" of the people there. She said no more about that part of her life.

Figure 2.5.1.3 *Jackie Kennedy Onassis and Peter Davis at the seventh annual R.F.K. Pro-Celebrity Tennis Tournament in Forest Hills, Queens, 1978*

Photo by Ron Galella/WireImage

At times Finley spoke a little haltingly, appearing reluctant to interrupt the gregarious Stone, who was eager to dispense his newfound wisdom about Socrates's anti-democratic tendencies. The old investigative reporter, captain of all those subversive journalists who did not want to be on any team, was hunting for one final scoop, the revelation of a scandal that had occurred 2,500 years ago. In the city where freedom of speech was born, the Athenians were putting to death their greatest philosopher for exercising free speech.

The second part of the scandal was that Plato, in his account of the trial, lied about what had happened. According to Stone, Plato used the condemnation of Socrates to indict democracy itself, concluding that common citizens were too ignorant to trust with political power. He conveniently left out the fact that Socrates was educating the anti-democratic elements in Athens who wanted to overthrow the democracy. Stone was persuasive, like a lawyer arguing his case, but at one point he was also turning the conversation into a monologue.

When Stone paused for a bite, and Finley proposed something as modest as the fact that Socrates after all bequeathed the very kind of dialogue they were having that evening and that Plato, to his credit, understood that, Stone came right back with the bias against democracy that Plato had shown in his defense of Socrates. At precisely this moment, Esther Stone, like a judge who had heard quite enough from the prosecution, said, "Shush, Izzy, this man *really* knows." The rest of the evening, thanks to Esther, essentially belonged to Finley.

By the time dinner was over and we were in the living room for champagne, Stone was commenting—but now only commenting, not holding forth—on the importance of slavery in democratic Athens. Finley said yes, that was a singular irony in history's first democracy. The presence of slaves was a principal reason the Athenian democracy could exist, since slaves did the work while their masters had time to go to assemblies to vote and debate about the nature of politics or the universe. The advances in statecraft, astronomy, philosophy itself, even the great achievements in the arts—the virtues and legacies we so much admire in the ancient Greeks—were to an often unacknowledged degree underpinned by the institution of slavery. On the other hand, Finley said, a number of Athenians did free their slaves, and the injustice of slavery slowly gained recognition.

Finley was in his element now, gesturing with his hands as though they could buttress his thoughts. He ranged through the Greeks, perceiving resemblances between philosophers and playwrights, sculptors and athletes and troubadours. He said the irony of the world's first democracy's being supported by slaves was furthered by the magisterial Plato's hostility to poets in his ideal society. Was religion soothing to ignorance, or did it inflame creative impulses? Did philosophy goad us to action, or did it encourage us to make peace with the unpleasant aspects of our lives? Was art ennobling or merely distracting? Did it plunge us into the richer strata of ourselves or was it chiefly an escape? Could it lead, as Plato feared, to rebellion against authority?

On he went, none of us, including Izzy Stone, wanting to interrupt or even take a deep breath. The effect was of an electrical current coursing through Jackie's living room; we were not so much being instructed as illuminated. I thought of what it may have been like to sit among the transcendentalists in Concord when Emerson was struck by an idea he wanted to work on among his friends. Finley put us on Mount Olympus among the capricious gods, then hurled us into the underworld, where Odysseus found his mother: "To visit the Greeks is to be half in heaven, half in hell, each half a new half you didn't know could be there." One moment he would declaim, in a flight of imagination about the ancient world; then abruptly he would contradict himself with "on the other hand" and fill the air in the room with ambiguity. He placed us not in a condition of knowing but of thinking. If Homer was especially on his mind that evening, it was because he was about to publish a new book, his last, about *The Odyssey*.

At length Finley began to wind down, and he and Stone conversed easily once again, still concerned with the contradictions that each felt were embodied in Socrates's life and teaching. Although they did not speak in Greek, each used an occasional Greek phrase to make a point. This led one of us in the wallpaper contingent to ask if many ancient Greek words had come down to us in English. What were some cognates?

Izzy Stone offered first. "People have accused me of being a hectoring critic of power," he said, smiling, as he referred to the Trojan prince and military commander. But then John Finley rolled out his artillery.

"Well, let's see," he said. Each of the words he spoke next landed with the force of an insight. "Sympathy, hero, agony, mathematics, economy, euphoria, symphony, politics, synthesis, analysis."

"Oh, yes." Those were the only two words from Jackie.

For a long moment no one else said anything. We looked around the room at one another. Esther Stone broke the silence, speaking for all of us. "That's everything that counts. What else is there anyway that really matters?"

Yes, we all agreed, this was so much of the history and meaning of our culture. Those few ancient Greek words encircled us. Athens was our yesterday, as the guests of honor had said.

It was time to go.

After thanking Jackie with his elegant courtliness, Finley entered the elevator first, followed by the Stones and the rest of us. I brought up the rear, and in the spirit of having put the evening together in the first place, I groped for words, finally fumbling around with something like "I don't know how to express what, I mean, I'll bet the Greeks must have had a word for the kind of occasion this has been, but—" For the only time he interrupted anyone, John Finley rescued me from the back of the elevator. "They did," he said. "Elysium." With that, the elevator door closed, giving the evening its precise punctuation mark.

Professor Finley lived to be 91 and died in his favorite place outside of Harvard itself—his country home in New Hampshire. Izzy Stone died 11 years after the dinner, but not before he had published *The Trial of Socrates*, the very subject of his dialogue with the professor.

The afterglow deserves noting. In Stone's letter to Jackie, he said Esther and he had enjoyed "one of the most wonderful evenings we have ever spent. Meeting Prof. Finley at dinner with your engaging young friends made us think of the 18th century, when great ladies in Paris attracted the *philosophes* to their salons, and in that setting, before an audience of beauty, turned learned debate into an adventure in wit. Your lovely presiding presence was itself an illumination. I. F. Stone."

And, in his own coda, Finley to her from Cambridge: "Shining memories and a general zephyr have wafted me home. You woo the soul into freer skies than it commonly inhabits and which it thinks for the moment its native element—partly rightly, because one will never forget. The Stones were charming, and I am most grateful to have met them. His mind resembles a series of lively but not loud corks leaping from aerated bottles—cases and cases of them. I never saw such conviction matched with such freshness of feeling." Then, in his peroration, still in the midst of winter, he looked ahead to another season. "Where do all those light summer seeds that float in the August wind come to earth? One will never know. They float like thoughts into the future, and one can only give thanks for them and for the breeze that started them, a kindred breeze. Very admiringly and gratefully, John Finley."

Peter Davis is an author and filmmaker whose novel, *Girl of My Dreams*, was published in 2015.

Chaos in Yale Bowl, November 20, 1955

Half-Time Disruption! A Confession

Herbert M. Wyman

At the game of 1955, just as the Yale Band marched onto the field for their half-time performance, three baby pigs appeared from nowhere, and scampered into their carefully formed ranks. A serious mistake was then made by the Yale Band members and the Yale Bowl staff: they attempted to catch the pigs. As any scholar learned in porcine behavior can tell you, this is an impossible task when it comes to baby pigs. The pigs do not have to be "greased". In fact, no grease or any artificial additive was applied to these animals. They simply cannot be caught. They are speedy, nimble, and altogether elusive. So on this occasion they totally disrupted the Yale performance, ran at will up and down the field, evading all efforts to tackle them as if they were Hall of Fame running backs. Every time they crossed a goal line, the crowd cheered as if for a touchdown! This spectacle went on and on until the pigs were finally chased from the field. But by then the damage had been done, and the mission accomplished.

Figure 2.5.2.1 *Headline in* The Harvard Crimson*:*
"Snow, Greased Pigs, Crimson Extras Enliven Weekend"

Charles Steedman wrote: "*The most yards rushed and the most touchdowns scored were both achieved by the three little pigs who, upon their half-time release, disrupted the Yale Band and eluded the groundkeepers by running repeatedly from one end of the field to another to the delight of the 56,000 spectators.*"

Photographer: Ron Kimball/KimballStock

Who put those pigs on the field? For a long time, this has been an unsolved mystery. *The Harvard Lampoon* was, of course, immediately blamed, only because they had recently placed large quantities of liquid detergent in the Harvard Crew practice tank, so that when the crew started rowing they submerged themselves under a tower of suds. Naturally such a record of athletic interference created some suspicions, but on this occasion deniability was—somewhat shakily—maintained.

Now, however, our 60th Reunion is at hand, and the statute of limitations must surely have expired! So yes, of course, it was *The Lampoon*. But we can take particular pride that it was three members of the Harvard Class of 1957 who were directly responsible for this historic achievement: L.D. Hill, R.S. McIlwaine, and myself, H.M. Wyman.

I chose this event for my essay because I learned a lot from it, and also because I haven't done anything earthshaking since then.

First, it required a lot of painstaking research to find a set of pigs of just the right age, and to find a farmer who was willing to part with them. We did finally locate a farmer and a sty in of all places, Wellesley, MA. The lesson here: those pigs you are looking for might be just around the corner.

Then, we had to develop a plan to get the pigs into the Yale Bowl. Here we found valuable allies in the Harvard Band. Al Lourie, the trombone player, was our liason. We knew the Harvard Band would shed no tears for the Yale Band. We owe a profound debt of gratitude to the Harvard Band, whose ingenuity, in fact, provided the solution: Each pig would be carried into the Yale Bowl in a large tuba case. We then worried that the pigs would in the process emit large squeals or snorts, as pigs are wont to do, and so the band members would be challenged by the gatekeepers. Again the band had the right answer: "What noise? We're just tuning up." Another lesson: every great undertaking needs allies.

So we picked up the pigs in Wellesley, packed them in open burlap sacks, inserted them into the trunk of my father's new 1956 Oldsmobile, and set off for New Haven. We left the trunk open a bit for air, which helped out the pigs, but created a constant worry for us that the pigs would somehow fall out of the trunk. It was this worry that resulted in an unfortunate accident on the roller-coaster road that was Route 20 in 1955. I heard a squeal, looked back to check on the pigs, looked forward, and barreled straight into a long line of traffic, setting off a chain of bumping cars. No one was hurt, but my father's car was totaled. The lesson here: don't transport pigs in a passenger car.

Hill, McIlwaine, and the pigs caught rides in other *Lampoon* vehicles passing by, and the plan went forward very successfully. It always helps to have a plan B, and always helps to have a lot of friends.

However, I had to stay behind, to dispose of what was left of my father's car, and also apologetically to console the owners of other damaged cars, whose sense of humor was sorely tried. One of them, however, said to his family: "It's not so bad, I've only been hit by a herd of pigs." Always helps to have a sense of humor.

But now I had to call my father and somehow explain what happened. He knew exactly what we were doing but still had generously lent me his new car, and now I had somehow to work out the exact phraseology of the explanation. It took me quite a while to find those words. By the time I called, he and my mother were, in fact, listening to the Yale Bowl announcer shouting out another pig touchdown! So when my father picked up my call, he spoke first to congratulate me. And then . . . and then . . . I had to tell him what happened. His first words surprised me. I had been expecting one of his loud, endless, and this time quite justified tirades on how his good-for-nothing son was forever fouling things up. Instead he said, what I will never forget, and what patterned the kind of father I wanted to be: "*Are you all right, son?*"

Herbert M. Wyman, MD, writes: "It might be thought, on the basis of his essay, that Wyman was headed straight for a career in the CIA devising failed coup attempts. Indeed, his post-grad wanderings through Europe and the Middle East seemed to promise such a future. But instead, Wyman returned home to follow a traditional cursus honoris, which for him included medical school (Boston University Medical School, '63) rotating internship (Montefiore, 1963–64), Psychiatric Residency (Albert Einstein, 1964–67) and psychoanalytic training (New York Psychoanalytic Institute, 1967–72). He then subsided quietly into the private practice of psychoanalysis which he continues to this day in Manhattan, albeit now on a part-time basis. He has remained active in the Institute, where he has held various academic and executive posts, including Training Analyst, and co-founder of *The Journal of Clinical Psychoanalysis*. Along the way, he married Audrey Schonbrun (1965), with whom he joined in the proud parenthood of three boys and one girl. Currently, the Wyman clan includes five grandchildren, with the sixth scheduled to arrive at the time of the 60th Reunion."

Mid-Life Crisis Revisited

Robert H. King

In the fall of 2002, a few years after my retirement from academia, my wife and I took a trip to northern Wales with a group made up mainly of Episcopalians. Billed as a "Celtic pilgrimage", we followed the route of medieval pilgrims along the Llyn Peninsula to Bardsey Island. This island has been considered from ancient times a "thin place", where the line between the sacred and profane is particularly porous. It was indeed a lovely, quiet place, but I did not find it especially spiritual. Then, in the night following our return to the mainland, I had the most extraordinary series of dreams I've ever had. It felt like *life review*.

The dreams, four in all, came instantaneously, as if downloaded into my brain from some unknown source. I got up immediately and wrote them down as they came to me. The next morning when I read what I had written, two things struck me. Though their meaning was obscure, the dreams seemed to follow a chronological order and to correspond to identifiable moments in my life. On reflection, I concluded that they pointed to periods of transition.

One dream in particular stands out. It is a haunting dream that evokes the year 1968, a time when the country was in upheaval and my life—both personal and professional—was coming apart. Here is the dream: my wife is in our car sitting on the passenger side and I'm on the outside trying to get in. The car is out of control and coasting into the intersection of a busy highway. I'm shouting instructions to her, telling her to shift gears, put on the parking brake, do anything to get the car to stop, but to no avail. Then the car stops of its own accord. Two men show up and look under the hood. They announce that the problem is the crystal. My father appears and confirms this diagnosis. I have no trouble associating the image of the out-of-control car with this time in my life. The crystal is something of a mystery.

That momentous year marked the beginning of the darkest period in my life. Until then my career had been on an upward trajectory: graduation from Harvard with honors, two post-graduate fellowships, a doctorate from Yale, the near-publication of my dissertation (turned down by a major publisher but with a letter of encouragement), and several years of teaching at an upper-tier liberal arts college in the Midwest.

In 1967, I was awarded an NEH fellowship for a year of post-doctoral study at Oxford, where I expected to complete the book that would launch the next phase of my career. For someone pursuing an academic career, it doesn't get much better than that. Yet in 1968, this house of cards collapsed.

The year at Oxford did not produce a book, only an inferior version of my dissertation.

Returning to the college where I had taught for four years, I found myself in the midst of the student revolution sweeping the country. It wasn't just the war in Vietnam that students were protesting, but the educational establishment of which I was a part. Some of my most strongly held assumptions about higher education were being challenged by what came to be called the Boomer generation. Without a major scholarly publication to my credit, I could not expect to move up in the world of higher education, and given this unexpected threat to my educational values, I wasn't sure there was a place for me in the teaching profession. I was thoroughly confused.

To add to my dismay, my wife's health took a serious turn for the worse, just when we thought she was on the road to full recovery. She had suffered a severe depression following the birth of our first child, but her condition had gradually improved. She did quite well the year we were in Oxford. Our daughter was born that year, while our son was a lively, curious two-year-old. Although my work was not going well, we were thriving as a family. Yet once back home in familiar surroundings with a cohort of friends around her, my wife suddenly and unexpectedly went into a psychotic state and had to be hospitalized. We were given no assurance that she would ever fully recover. It was my darkest hour.

It was also the beginning of one of the most fertile periods of my life, though I didn't know it at the time. I put aside my writing project and immersed myself in the student culture, reading authors my students were reading—Paul Goodman, Herbert Marcuse, Malcolm X—and rethinking my approach to teaching. As a teacher I began to pay more attention to my students' personal and intellectual development rather than simply transmitting a body of knowledge. My goal was to help them become independent, critical thinkers. I also became more engaged with the community outside of the college, volunteering for a program of prison visitation and helping start a low-income family clinic in town. It was a time of social ferment and change, and I very much wanted to be a part of it.

I did eventually get back to the writing project, but when I did it was to make a new beginning, since I was no longer the person I had been in Oxford.

My experiences had changed me. My second attempt produced a better book, which was accepted for publication; yet it did not launch the scholarly career I had hoped for. That was a further disappointment, which prompted a reassessment of my career direction. I concluded that my greatest satisfaction came from facilitating the work of others and that pointed me toward college administration, a path I had not seriously considered until then.

So, at age 40 I began to retool. I was offered the position of assistant to the president of the college where I'd been teaching for nearly 15 years. This gave me an opportunity to acquire the administrative experience I lacked, leading eventually to a position as academic dean at a small liberal arts college in the South.

I arrived there at a time when the college was faced with serious financial difficulties. As dean I could not do much for the bottom line, but I could help the faculty re-envision the college curriculum and create a more interactive learning environment for students, incorporating much of what I had learned during the dark days of my descent into self-doubt and uncertainty. My wife also experienced a renaissance of sorts during this time, discovering her talent as a creative artist. Though never entirely free of depression, she was able to live a more productive and satisfying life, while our children flourished. What had seemed to be a low point turned out to be one of the most important and transformative periods in both of our lives.

Returning to the dream that brought up these recollections, I'm wondering why memories of this difficult period should be coming up now, when the problems associated with that time in my life have been largely resolved. Also, there is the matter of the *crystal*. What am I to make of this image in the dream? It does not seem to correspond to anything that was going on then—or any other time for that matter. It is the most puzzling feature of the dream.

Dreams, especially big dreams like this one, are seldom just about the past. They usually have something to say to us in the present. By recalling a time when my life was in crisis, is this dream possibly inviting me to look more deeply into my present condition?

At the time I had the dream I'd recently come through a major life transition—divorce, remarriage, and retirement—so perhaps I'm at a comparable place in my life. There may be something to be learned from the earlier experience that will prepare me for the next stage of life.

For one thing, I'm reminded not to be overly concerned if I do not know what lies ahead. The unknown has its own rewards. Moreover, even a dark period can be a time of healing and renewal. That was true fifty years ago and could be just as true now.

This brings me to the image of the crystal. After looking under the hood of the car, you'd expect the men in the dream to report that the problem had to do with the engine, that it was something mechanical that could be "*fixed*". Instead I'm told "*The problem is the crystal.*"

I can think of a number of associations with the word crystal, including the earliest radios which were called crystal sets, but what comes immediately to mind is New Age spirituality, where crystals are thought to have healing power. I'm not personally disposed toward this kind of spirituality, but I'm prepared to grant that we carry a spiritual power within us that we are not generally aware of, a center of creative energy which we cannot control but which can be a major source of renewal. It is difficult to access, but dreams are one avenue.

By revisiting a time of personal transformation, my dream is telling me to trust my own deeper self, the Mystery within, and so preparing me for the next big transformation, whatever form it might take. At least that's how I see it.

My mid-life crisis, I've concluded, gave me a glimpse into my deeper self. My dreams are now showing me that the journey of self-discovery is not over. Even late in life, there is still more to learn.

Robert H. King earned both a divinity degree (1960) and doctorate (1965) from Yale University. He spent the first half of his career as professor of philosophy and religion at DePauw University in Greencastle, Indiana, and the second half as academic dean of Millsaps College in Jackson, Mississippi. He wrote *The Meaning of God* (1973, Fortress) and co-edited *Christian Theology: Its Traditions and Tasks* (1982, Continuum) during the early part of his career and has written two books on contemplative practice, including one with his wife, Elizabeth, since his retirement in 1997. While in academic administration, he oversaw a major restructuring of the college curriculum to make it more interdisciplinary and to place greater emphasis on writing and critical thinking. He currently resides in a small town at the foot of Pikes Peak in Colorado, where his family vacationed when he was a child. He served two terms on the town council and helped restore an historic town landmark. He hikes, practices Zen meditation, and leads a dream group.

Reflections on a Life of (Nearly) 80 Years

Malcolm S. Mitchell

I think I have led a very interesting and satisfying life, even though I have never been really "famous". (My eldest son as a boy said he thought I was "*sort-of-famous*", because his friends hadn't heard of me, but the people writing for reprints of my scientific papers obviously knew who I was). Even after many newspaper and television interviews about my medical work over the years, that situation hasn't really changed much.

As a 12-year-old (from 1949–50) I spent time on the radio as an NBC "*Quiz Kid*", which gave me some celebrity with my schoolmates and a $50 savings bond as payment for each broadcast. The program was headquartered in Chicago and I lived in New York, so I knew that it was to be short-lived, but I thoroughly enjoyed answering questions on the air very much as in school, even though I badly flubbed one or two that I still remember. I met some real celebrities of the day too: Milton Berle and Perry Como among others, and my radio experience led the school to send me to participate in *The New York Times* Youth Forum (WQXR) and the city-wide World of Science competition (WNYC), both of which I was not really qualified for, but which I navigated satisfactorily, I think.

Perhaps the whole "*radio*" experience taught me that a sense of confidence can be helpful in daunting novel situations—Harvard, for example?

Harvard

Harvard itself was obviously "*formative*" in many ways, including meeting a host of people I had never encountered before. I was an end-of-the-Depression Baby (born in 1937), and never felt deprived growing up.

After attending a very good public high school in Lawrence, NY, I met people whose families the Depression obviously never touched, who had gone to St. Grottlesex or equally fine schools. That was a world I never aspired to enter, but was glad to have seen from the outside.

To learn that FDR was refused admission to the Porcellian quickly disabused me of any pretensions to Harvard high society I might have had. I have always told people that Harvard left me alone to grow up, with no social pressures to join or do anything, and I am happy that there were no "*real*" (State-U) fraternities to consider.

I took the advice of the Harvard Handbook sent to pre-freshmen very seriously, which warned against taking on too many extracurriculars, and joined only the pre-medical society and Phillips Brooks House, where Joel Bernstein (who sang remarkably like Eddie Fisher) and I were itinerant musicians who entertained in the Boston area. Although I would have loved to continue my musical activities if possible, I put my efforts into learning biology, chemistry, etc. and delayed everything else.

Music

Some of you may remember that I played the piano in the Union after dinner, with Leroy Anderson tunes and some classical bits I was working on. An interesting "*low point*" was the theft from a cubby outside Lowell House Dining Room of my Chopin Preludes. Where else but at Harvard would anyone have thought about stealing that?

Fortunately, I have been able to resume my piano playing since college, beginning in my first year of medical school and continuing throughout my career in medicine, as a soloist or member of a chamber ensemble. I have even given a few recitals for friends or small groups. In fact, I believe that I have the unique distinction of having given the first solo piano concert at the Lithonia Baptist Church in Lithonia, Georgia—a moderately remote location before a freeway made it a stone's throw from Atlanta.

Many of our generation were forced to learn to play an instrument, and I am genuinely happy now my parents did that to/for me. Being able to play almost anything classical (perhaps excluding the Rachmaninoff Third Concerto), and also Gershwin, Porter and Kern by ear, has rescued me from feeling rotten many times, and allowed me to celebrate great events, such as engagements (twice), and the birth of my sons (four times).

For those who truly love good music, there is nothing finer than just listening to a great orchestra or soloist, and nothing more torturous than hearing cacophonous rock music—sorry, sons. Two of my sons play the piano well, a third played very well but dropped out to my great regret, while the fourth thankfully stopped playing the trumpet.

Yale and Oxford as a Fulbright Scholar

An immensely formative influence was my year at Oxford after my second year of medical school at Yale. Yale Medical School encourages its students to take a winding path, with time off to study abroad.

At my admission interview that whole topic came up and influenced my decision to go there. Professor John Fulton, a world leader in physiology, helped me secure a research position in Sir Howard Florey's laboratory (The Sir William Dunn School of Pathology). Florey's research team, most of whom were still there when I came, had developed Penicillin, and he had accepted the Nobel Prize for the group in 1945. I was assigned to work with Jim (now Sir James) Gowans, a young, brilliant pioneer in cellular immunology.

I was awarded a Fulbright Scholarship, kindly supplemented monetarily by Yale to equal a US Public Health award I had relinquished.

The work Gowans was doing proved that the lymphocyte was the cell responsible for antibody production and cell-mediated immunity, and I knew even as a neophyte how important that was. Despite some bumbling efforts on my part, Jim kindly offered me a second year, but my first son had just been born, and we felt we had to return home.

The experience of doing real scientific research with precision during that year led me to my career in tumor immunology and immunotherapy—and my new precise mindset made playing Bach inventions thoroughly interesting to me for the only time in my life.

US Public Health Service—CDC

My service time as a Surgeon (Lieutenant Commander) in the US Public Health Service, at the Communicable Disease Center (now called the NCDC) in Atlanta, in 1962–63 was the equivalent of being in the Armed Forces and possibly serving in Viet Nam. (We called ourselves the "Yellow Berets".)

I worked with Bill Cherry, a dedicated career government scientist, who was not only a great scientific mentor but whose example and discussions led me to formally become a Unitarian in my mid-twenties. My outlook on religion was always that of a Unitarian, helped along by several classes at Harvard, but until I met Bill I didn't realize there was a formal designation.

At the CDC I contributed to the rapid diagnosis of bacterial meningitis, a disease that even now is fatal to infants and young adults (particularly college students in close confines) if not treated soon enough, by helping to perfect fluorescent antibody diagnosis within minutes rather than many hours. I also described a new bacterium related to both the meningitis and gonorrhea germs, which is now called *Neisseria lactamicus*, and has been shown to be benign. I could have given it my name, I am told, but I was afraid "*Neisseria mitchelli*" might prove to be the cause of a disgusting venereal disease and let others name it.

Family

Anyone who fails to mention the births of his children as exceedingly important events, does not deserve to have them. I am fortunate to have had four sons, three with my first wife and one with June. She and I have been together for almost 46 years, and married for almost 41 of them.

Each son is different from the others, although there are genetic traces of myself and my wife in each, of course. There is nothing more thrilling or humbling than becoming a father, no matter how many times it happens.

Bringing them up and then letting them go is an altruistic act of giving: to them and to the world. As I see my youngest son, now almost 30, finish his training and start thinking seriously of marriage, I realize just how altruistic and in some ways painful, the process of child rearing is. Nonetheless, I am extremely grateful that I have been given that experience.

Physician-Scientist

Finally, my abilities as a medical scientist—which were nurtured by my educational experiences, but which undoubtedly had something to do with my genes too—allowed me to contribute to medical oncology by introducing cancer "vaccines" that I devised or helped to modify into use in a field where chemotherapy still dominates. (I was once told at an interview for cancer center director that one of my own references wrote I was "out of the mainstream". I didn't get that job.)

I simply wanted to use the research experience I had gained in immunology to treat patients, and I realized early in my fellowship that chemotherapy was curing patients in only a few categories of tumor.

There is no doubt in my mind that I have cured patients (perhaps 5–10%) with my melanoma vaccine, because their metastatic disease disappeared and has remained gone for many years. The time may soon come when immunotherapy with antibodies or vaccines—or another modality to be devised—will replace all of the standard treatments now available to oncologists.

Not as exciting as something from a President or an Academy Award winner, perhaps, but to me a rewarding life nonetheless.

Malcolm Mitchell, MD, has been retired for ten years after an academic medical career spanning over 40 years, having taught at Yale, USC and UC San Diego among other institutions. He combined laboratory research in tumor immunology with clinical research in immunotherapy, a novel approach to cancers. Perhaps his major contribution was a material ("vaccine") called Melacine which was approved for use in Canada for treating melanomas. He also devised a treatment regimen of low-dose Interleukin-2 that was as effective as much higher, toxic doses. Mitchell's still-beautiful wife, June, is a professor of biology at the University of Texas-El Paso, and he has four sons, of whom one was Ambassador to Burma under President Obama. His lifelong pleasure for over 75 years has been to play the piano, which he is grateful he has been able to continue in retirement.

On Thanksgiving 2015, I Died

Charles Hilary King

I was dead for 4½ minutes, while two pediatricians, also at dinner, labored to bring me back to life. My heart started again in Afro-Cuban rhythm, and the docs rushed me to St. Francis hospital, where my heart was shocked into normal rhythm and I was frozen. Several days later I awoke, thinking I was in California flogging my book.

The nurse said, "Maybe we should start with the fact you're on Long Island."

One thing you should know about me is that I was always a writer. I wrote my first story when I was nine years old: about a guy who wakes up before he should and finds out he is the only real person in the world, everybody else is an actor and the buildings across the street from the hotel are mere flats. In my teens I wrote science fiction, and after about 100 rejections slips I got my first story published in *Future Science Fiction* magazine.

After Harvard, I stayed at Harvard and got a job at the computation lab. I worked on the first computer, the *Mark I* and put the first model atmosphere on the *Mark IV*. I stayed at Harvard because my dad would not pay for me to get a PhD, and I wanted to continue my education. Conflicted and unclear about my desire to pursue a math career, I returned to my writing, and did humorous stories for *Gent*, *Dude* and *Escapade* magazines.

Then I met Antoinette Chevigny . . . .

Four years later I was married, living in Manhattan and writing advertising for Foote Cone and Belding. Advertising was like being at a party, a dull party but a party nevertheless. After 19 emotional roller-coaster years I divorced Antoinette. I moved to the East Side of Manhattan and bought the apartment that I thought would be my single pad for the rest of my life. In 1981 I ran into Katharine Rees at a party.

I had seen her years before. She didn't notice me, but I saw her standing in the center of a group of people that seemed to be swirling around her. She had a smile that was so wonderful, it was a revelation. Katharine impressed me in many ways; she had graduated from Oxford University then went to the London School of Economics and got a social work degree. She studied with David Winnicott and Ana Freud. She had a healing quality that helped the children she worked with and also helped me. She became the love of my life, and I moved back to the Upper West Side with her.

Katharine provided the ideal space for my writing; she said, "It's time you quit doing your advertising ditties and write the novel you always thought of." I quit advertising and wrote a thriller that was a big success. It was sold around the world and was optioned a number of times by big names in Hollywood such as the Baldwin brothers, Harrah's Hotel, and Silvester Stallone. It was never made into a movie, but I coined a lot of money from the options. Katherine and I got the house we always wanted in Pine Plains, NY, and I enjoyed the best years of my life there.

The Pine Plains house came with a community sense that NYC had never brought; you can live all your life in an apartment in the city and never know any of your neighbors; you can die unnoticed. We made good lifelong friends with whom we celebrated many dinners, had long talks and who joined us in our traditional 4th of July party every year. The house also was a beautiful frame for our life together. We had the perfect hilltop spot for our Adirondack chairs and had wine, enjoyed sunsets and looked at the whole valley. It was the perfect end of our day. In the house I sat and enjoyed her beautifully laid fires while she cooked dinner, then we would eat on the coffee table in front of the wood stove. Katharine made everything easy.

In December 2012, Katharine started to lose her memory. She was still herself, but her memory loss worried us. At The Neurological Institute she was diagnosed with MCI (minor cognitive impairment) and was medicated to help with the memory loss. Katherine continued practicing until February 2013, when she decided that her condition interfered with work and stopped.

We went to England in June 2013 to celebrate her cousin Mell's 90th birthday. She kept on losing her purse, coat, gloves, and I kept on finding them for her.

After that trip our lives changed. We went to New York Hospital. I knew The Neurological Institute was wrong. After some standard tests and with the wonderful sensitivity that doctors often have, one of them sat in front of us and said, "Of course she has Alzheimer's." Katharine didn't react then. But as we walked down the hall to leave the hospital she held my arm, crying, "No! No! I don't have it!"

Katharine plunged into dementia. I was determined to keep her at our home and made all possible arrangements for that to happen: our door now had a security chain, the oven knob had a lock and I had caregivers in the apartment 24/7. The idea of ever sending her to a nursing home was completely foreign to me. She became more and more violent with the caregivers and me, hitting, scratching, punching and screaming frequently. Even then I thought I would keep her with me in our apartment until the end. It was a strange feeling; Katharine was not Katharine anymore. She was gone. Caregivers constantly encouraged me to go on with my life; the care manager insisted that I go to

Pine Plains and check on the house. When I finally decided to go up to the house, I received an angry call from the care manager asking, "Where did you go?" Katharine was in a locked ward at Mount Sinai, so I immediately rushed back to the city.

Our friends from the city seemed to disappear, while people from the country rallied round. Our friend Amy Rothstein mentioned a doctor at the 80th Street Residence who had helped a family member, so I moved Katharine there. The doctor took a sample from her cheek and sent it to a genetic company which came back with two diagnoses: the first one defined her as a fast metabolizer, and the second one found she was missing a gene that transports psychoactive chemicals to the brain. With these diagnoses the doctor was able to prescribe the best drugs for her. Miraculously, Katharine became friendly and tractable, and I became her boyfriend. She always knew who I was. During the next two years I spent hundreds of hours with her in this place. Sometimes I just stared as she slept; other times I took her to listen to live music which they frequently played on the first floor. She died on February 29th, 2016. (My first wife had died a year before, also suffering from a mental illness. Do you think I have this strange effect on women?)

During 2016 I have been loved and cared for. I have become the patient and not the caregiver; now people look after me 24/7. I have been treated wonderfully by many, but on the whole, I don't recommend dying.

Figure 2.5.5.1 *Sailing with a smiling and loving Katharine before the onset of her Alzheimer's disease*

Charles H. King was a mathematician at the Harvard Computation Laboratory for two years after graduation, a performer and a writer for network radio and a creative writer, supervisor and director at large advertising agencies in New York City from 1962 to 1984. Having written his first story at age nine and published one in 1948, he went on to publish some 20 short stories in national magazines and wrote a thriller in 1992 that sold worldwide. Since 1959 he has lived in New York City, where he met Katharine Rees, the love of his life.

Volunteer Assistance to Syrian Refugees

John A. Grammer, Jr.

In the middle of November 2016 Mary Anne, my wife of 30 years, suggested that she and I should respond to the shocking photographs of Syrian refugee young children in *The New York Times*—one dead on a beach and the other sitting dazed and bloodied in the back of an ambulance. With her long background in special education teaching in the New York City public schools and my lengthy experience in the Middle East and with the Arabic language, perhaps we could make a positive contribution to the Syrian refugee crisis.

John Cheek from the choir of our Episcopal Church recommended I contact the Western Massachusetts regional office of the Church, which referred me to an agency in Westfield, about 45 minutes by car east from our home in Sandisfield, MA, in the Berkshire Hills. Discussion with a refugee coordinator in an office which is among several taking care of the in-flow of refugees from various countries led to our meeting a family from Southern Syria. They had just arrived in the USA after three years in a refugee camp in Jordan.

Mary Anne and I meet with the family once a week at their apartment. The family (mother, father, two boys nine and one and a half, and one girl of seven) is Muslim and is only now beginning to speak English. Therefore, my Arabic language has been crucially important, even though I work hard to recall words and phrases. I started as an undergraduate—in class and with roommates in Adams House from Jordan and Egypt; then travelled throughout the Middle East; then nine months at Army Language School in Monterey, CA; then working with the UN, living in Beirut, Lebanon (United Nations Relief and

Works Agency for Palestine Refugees in the Near East) and travelling around the Near East; then with Citibank in Beirut and Jeddah, Saudi Arabia; and finally as an independent consultant until 2013.

The mother and father are trying to pick up English. This will be vital for them to get jobs and integrate into the local community. Fairly soon they should start English lessons with their sponsor organization. In addition, there are some Arabic-speaking families nearby. The nine-year old son is in third grade and is making slow progress in English. He is making friends better than he did in school in Jordan. The daughter is in first grade and is making some progress in English. The 1½-year-old son is making decent progress in English through television programs such as *Sesame Street*.

Mary Anne continues to tutor the older children and the mother in English and Math. The family receives US government assistance through their sponsor organization. Its office, within walking distance of their apartment, assists them to get Social Security cards, medical care, language classes, job interview skills, and the like. One of our families assembled a package of Arabic foodstuffs including spices for them. We brought a box of utensils to help them stock their kitchen.

The father and I talk in Arabic about problems they are having, and Mary Anne talked with the school administration to make sure that the kids are getting special help. They get one and one-half hours of separate coaching daily. When her English is functional, the mother will be very good, we think and have told her, as a possible pharmacy assistant, doctor's assistant or bilingual teacher's assistant. In Syria the father worked as an administrator in a company. Once his English is operational, he could possibly work in a similar role in Westfield. We understand that jobs in the area are "available", although not plentiful.

We gave them a pocket-sized Arabic-English, English-Arabic dictionary and got the same for us. They have to get into the habit of using the dictionary, as do I. Every new word or every memorized word now recollected is vital.

Soon we hope to visit the parents in the morning, when the older kids are in school, to take them shopping and possibly to visit friends and make new friends. This volunteer work with the Syrian refugee family has been very stimulating for our "little gray cells" and rewarding in the sense of helping the family acclimate better and faster to the USA. It is one family, but one family that we have grown to love and want to see flourish in their new homeland.

John A. Grammer, Jr., in 1954 was fortunate to have two roommates in Adams House from the Middle East—Zaid El-Rifai from Jordan and Nazeeh Habachy from Egypt—who started him in the Arabic language on the first day they met. This had a major impact. Upon graduation, he received a travelling fellowship to the Middle East, where he had interviews with Colonel Abdul Karim Kassem, one of Sadaam Hussein's predecessor's in Iraq, and with David Ben Gurion in Israel. In 1958, John attended a nine-month program in Arabic at Army Language School, Monterey, CA. Following two years service in Germany, he attended the School of International and Public Affairs at Columbia University and received an MIA in 1963. He then moved to Beirut, Lebanon with the United Nations Relief and Works Agency for Palestine Refugees, in the Near East, travelling in Lebanon, Syria, Jordan, and Gaza. Later he joined Citibank, working in New York, Beirut, Jeddah, Manila, and Rio de Janeiro for 17 years. In 1982, John started his own consulting company in risk management, general management, and marketing, with assignments in 31 countries.

Moving to Tennessee

David Hamilton

Imagine, if you can, moving from liberal Minnesota to Tennessee, a state controlled by the Tea Party. Not only that, but the state went overwhelmingly for Trump in the 2016 election.

We try to remain a quiet retired couple and aside from voting openly for Hillary, we have not become involved. It is curious that the city of Knoxville votes Democratic and has a Democratic administration—presumably because of the University and a more liberal student body.

But, although our address is Knoxville, we actually live in Knox country, which is run by the Republicans. We came here because our daughter, son-in-law, and grandkids live here, and we enjoy interacting with them immensely.

I have had a lot of trouble posting this short essay. I hope it gets through.

Best regards to my friends who are still with us.

David Hamilton left Harvard to pursue a PhD in biology as a doctoral research student at Christ's College, Cambridge, England. After obtaining his doctorate, in 1963 he returned to Harvard Medical School as a Research Fellow and progressed to become a Lawrence J. Henderson Associate Professor before moving to the University of Minnesota as head of the Department of Anatomy. He stayed in that position for 18 years, was appointed Interim Vice President for Research and retired in 2007.

In 2012 he and his wife moved to Knoxville to be near grandchildren and his daughter and son-in-law. He is happily living in Knoxville, even though he reports it is very cold at times.

Five All-Important Moments
A Life in Music

Walter L. Chapin

During my adult life I have experienced five events, separated respectively by intervals of five, eight, five, and eight years, that strongly influenced the course of my life and work. Each of them occupied only a moment of time (or a week at most), yet each of them brought lifelong changes.

The First

The first came in 1954, late in the fall term of our Sophomore year, at a time when I realized that I had to deal with the fact that I wasn't doing at all well in the field of concentration I had chosen (anthropology). I knew that I needed to abandon that field and choose another. But which field to choose? And, whatever it would be, how could I know if I would be successful at it?

At that moment I was a member of WHRB, and in that era our way to assemble recordings for a program of music to be broadcast over the radio was to visit a particular record store on what was then Boylston St. (now JFK St.), pull whatever LP albums we needed from its shelves, sign them out, and return them to the store after the broadcast. Although I was primarily doing jazz broadcasts, on one such trip to that record store my eye fell upon a ten-inch LP recording by the combined Harvard Glee Club and Radcliffe Choral Society. Glancing at the list of composers of the choral works on that album, I noticed Randall Thompson's name. Knowing that Thompson was a Harvard professor, and being curious to hear the piece he had written, I took the album into a booth to play it (you'll recall that people could do that in those days). After hearing the first fifteen seconds or so of Thompson's *Alleluia,* as sung by HCG-RCS, I knew that I was experiencing something of incredible beauty. Though I had played classical piano since age nine and jazz piano since age 16, and had done a lot of music in high school (including running a dance band and writing arrangements for it), it had never occurred to me to concentrate in music while at Harvard. But by the time Thompson's piece ended, I had firmly decided to do exactly that. I soon met with the appropriate advisors, selected the prescribed Music Department courses for the second semester and the coming fall, and formally changed my field of concentration.

I later realized why I had not been successful with a scientific concentration, but did find success concentrating in music. While I admired and respected science (and still do, and still read about it a lot), I did not *love* science, and so could not be passionate about it as a concentration. Music was something that I *loved*, and could study with passion. Fortunately, the ear training I had given myself by writing dance band arrangements in high school was excellent preparation for the Music Department's quite tough courses in harmony and counterpoint. Upon graduation, though my overall academic record was far from stellar, I considered my concentration in music to have been a success, and I knew that it could not have been so were it not for the passion I felt for it.

The Second

The second event took place in the early fall of 1959, when, following military service and some music-related but inconsequential employment, I enrolled at the New England Conservatory, in Boston, for additional musical study. Every student at NEC had to be in a performing organization, and those who did not play an orchestral instrument were automatically assigned to the New England Conservatory Chorus, then under the excellent and spirited leadership of Lorna Cooke DeVaron. Even though listening to that LP recording of Randall Thompson's *Alleluia* was what had drawn me to music as a field of study, I had never felt motivated to try out for the Harvard Glee Club, for I didn't think I was much of a singer. But at the very first rehearsal of the New England Conservatory Chorus, I was happy to discover that I seemed to have something of a singing voice, which, soon and fortunately, was nurtured by the excellent voice classes that I attended at NEC. It was at that first choral rehearsal that I found that I loved choral music above all. I began to wonder how successful I might be at choral conducting, and subsequently learned its rudiments in Mrs. DeVaron's introductory choral conducting class at NEC.

The Third

There followed six years during whose winters I taught music at several high schools in the wilds of Maine, and during whose summers I took courses in a graduate program in Music History at Boston University. In the fall of 1967 I entered BU full-time, and took the choral conducting course given by James Cunningham, who then directed both the Boston University Chorus and the Cecilia Society, one of Boston's large choral groups (now known simply as Boston Cecilia). Though I had conducted high school choruses in Maine, I wasn't yet sure if I could make a go of choral directing. I was warmly surprised when Mr. Cunningham once happened to make the offhand remark that I had "real potential" as a choral director. That settled it! That moment was my third life-influencing event. A choral director I would be! A year later I was appointed assistant director of the BU Chorus, was twice director of the BU Summer Chorus, and have directed choral groups, unceasingly, ever since.

The Fourth

The fourth event came in the summer of 1972. Unlike the others, this was not one that changed the course of my life, but it did enhance my life in the direction it was already taking. By that time I had for two years been the director of a community chorus on Boston's South Shore, which I left to found a choral group of my own. A newspaper announced that the Tanglewood Festival Chorus (then under the direction of its founding director, John Oliver, and in only the second year of its existence) had openings for singers. I auditioned, was delighted to be accepted, and first sang with TFC that August out at Tanglewood, in the Berlioz Requiem, with Seiji Ozawa directing the BSO. I remained in TFC (for both the summer and winter seasons) until August of 1976, and during this period had the unique pleasure of participating, as a chorister, in much of the repertory written for chorus and orchestra by Bach, Handel, Haydn, Mozart, Beethoven, Brahms, Berlioz, Liszt, Verdi, Mahler, Schoenberg, Ravel, Ives, Stravinsky, and others—under the batons of the world's great conductors of that decade, including Seiji Ozawa, Leonard Bernstein, Colin Davis, Eugene Ormandy, Michael Tilson Thomas, and Klaus Tennstedt. Although I was later to direct only music written for smaller choral ensembles, this immersion in the world's finest works for large chorus with orchestra was a unique period of my musical life that I could have experienced in no other way, and I am much the richer for it.

(For this experience, I shall eternally owe an immense debt of gratitude to my ever-patient wife and children, who were willing to trek out to Tanglewood with me for five long weekends every summer during those TFC years, and to find things to do in the town of Lenox during the hours that TFC was rehearsing. I suspect that our kids had read every children's book in the Lenox Public Library by the end of those five summers.)

The Fifth

My fifth life-changing experience had nothing at all to do with music. In 1979 I knew that I had had enough of teaching music at the high school level, and looked around for other work. It first occurred not to me, but to my wife, that I ought to try to see if I might be any good at writing computer code. How wise she was! In January of 1980 I enrolled in an introductory course in programming in the Harvard Extension School, and before a week had elapsed, I knew that I was pretty good at it. Hardly ever has a course been such fun! I did so well in the course that the instructor excused me from the final exam, telling me that he didn't want me to skew the curve.

After several more Extension courses I was good enough at the Fortran coding language to be able to program a logical process that my father, a life insurance actuary, had recently developed. He had written a paper about it in the Society of Actuaries' professional journal, and he called it "Adjustable Life". In all my endeavors, I myself have never produced anything that was a game-changer—something that redefined the parameters of an entire field. My father's Adjustable Life was a game-changer. It soon became an insurance industry standard, and I had the honor of being among the first to translate his complicated set of extremely clever algorithms into computer code.

My new skills led to a change of career, in the form of two jobs, over nineteen years, in writing code and designing information systems. During this time I kept up with what in the final decades of the 20th century were new developments in the field, such as database design and client/server coding. Even after retiring, I still design systems and write code. Why was I good at this? I have no idea.

Adjusting to Retirement

My retirement in 2001 from formal employment left me ample time to develop the choral group that had evolved during the directing that I had been doing continually since 1969. This group is the Oriana Consort, which over the past decade or so has become one of the handful of recognized mid-size choral groups in the greater Boston area. Our very stringent auditions have given us a very fine ensemble of about 30 singers, whose ages range from the 20s to the 60s, skewed toward the younger end. I have set no particular date for turning this excellent institution over to a younger hand, though clearly that date will arrive in the not-too-distant future. One of my most fervent wishes is that Oriana continue and thrive without me, far into the future.

Walter L. Chapin for two years after graduation was on active duty in the National Guard. He writes, "I worked indecisively at two inconsequential jobs. I then spent two years earning a B.Mus. at the New England Conservatory, where I discovered a lifelong interest in choral music. For the next six years I directed high school choruses and taught music, followed by three years of graduate study in music history at Boston University, during which time I was assistant director of the BU Chorus, directed the BU Summer Chorus, and married Beth. (We subsequently had three beautiful daughters.) I resumed teaching and briefly directed a community chorus, then organized my own choral group, which over 45 seasons evolved into the Oriana Consort that I still direct today. Along the way I unexpectedly discovered the aptitude for computer programming and systems design that enabled my second career. My lifelong love of carpentry has allowed a low-cost renovation of the Cambridge condominium in which we have lived for four decades."

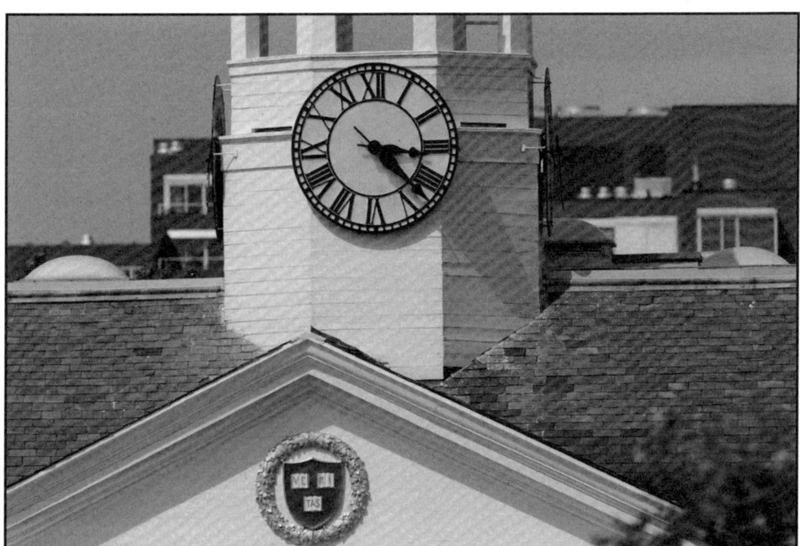

Figure 2.5.8.1 *Dillon Field House clock.*
Harvard Kennedy School and 975 Memorial Drive are in the distance.
Reprinted courtesy of Harvard University

"Called"

JFK and the Peace Corps

Bruce M. Reeves

I met John Kennedy just once, but that was enough for me to quit my job at the Bank of Boston, move to Washington and join the staff of the new Peace Corps. Was it because I graduated from Harvard, or because I was a Democrat? I think both. Of course the exhilaration of the Peace Corps changed forever for me when Kennedy was assassinated. I shifted to the poverty program and traveled across the country, but it never matched the Peace Corps, and I left that to work for George McGovern. (I said I was a Democrat!)

At least I learned how to run for office and was elected to the State Senate in Maine and organized three statewide referendums (won one, lost two).

I ended my political career losing a bid for Congress and then went south to work for the NAACP. At NAACP meetings in Florida I was somewhat suspect—"*Who's that white boy?*", even though I was older than anyone else in the meeting.

Finally I ended up, naturally for ex-politicians, as a consultant.

Bruce Reeves left his position with the First National Bank of Boston and entered the world of government and non-profit organizations, first as the Program Officer for the Peace Corps in Latin America, then as a field officer in the Poverty Program, and finally as a Consultant to the NAACP and community organizations in 15 different states.

Figure 2.6.1.1 *Bruce Reeves says: "This 'political' cartoon appeared in* The Maine Sunday Telegram *at a time when the Central Maine Power Company (CMP), then the state's largest utility, was getting rate increases from the Public Utilities Commission (PUC) for its nuclear power construction, among other useless projects.*

My intervention in the 'rate cases' (with the personal support of Ralph Nader), focused public attention and exposed these and other anti-consumer business practices of the utilities. Today, CMP no longer generates electricity but merely maintains power lines and monthly electric bills. Also, the Bell Telephone Company's scheme to charge for local telephone calls was defeated in a public referendum."

Cartoon reprinted with permission from the *Portland Press Herald/Maine Sunday Telegram.* Reproduction does not imply endorsement.

Figure 2.6.1.2 *The photo of Bruce, taken in East Pittston, ME, dates to c. 1980.*

Figure 2.6.1.3 *Photo portrait of John F. Kennedy, 35th President of the United States, February 20, 1961*

Photo source: White House Press Office

Career Choices

Dropping Law School

Lauren Craig Hickman

"*Elaine May sat her ass here. Mike Nichols over there.*"

It was a hot, sweaty night in Chicago. September 1957. My first week in law school. I was bending an elbow for the first time at the smoky South Side bar where Nichols and May had launched their comedy careers by creating skits for Second City. The other drinkers were mainly grad students like me from the nearby University of Chicago. Young people from the Law, Business and Med schools. Plus assorted PhD aspirants from the Arts, Sciences and Humanities.

A salad bowl.

Me: newly 21 with zilch experience in the bar world.

During the following months, Second City became a nightly stop after the law library closed. I learned the ropes of beer banter and, by the hard way, my drinking limits. Most importantly, I witnessed and jumped into never-ending take-no-prisoner conversations about ideas, philosophy, politics. You name it. We talked about it.

I often describe that year in Chicago—especially those hours in that bar—as the time and place where I digested my Harvard education and came into "*my own.*" Yes, I'd had late night discussions in Cambridge, but the conversations in Chicago—982 miles from Weld Hall and Lowell House—were different somehow. As time moved on, they increasingly made me wonder if I'd chosen the right profession.

I had naively assumed that becoming a lawyer meant learning and applying a set of absolute rules, and that there was always a clear right and wrong.

But the cases we labored to understand in class showed that the Law often cut different ways in the same situation. What was judged legal or non-legal, right or wrong, or good or bad could depend on how well the lawyers argued, or which arguments they advanced. The Law was not a pure absolute world. That was a sad uncomfortable realization, and I became more and more uneasy about becoming a lawyer.

At the same time, and just as importantly, the late-night bar discussions made me realize I didn't know much about life. Or about myself. My years until then had been serious and directed. I had gone to Law School because it was expected of me. And I'd been going to school year after year for 16 years.

It was time to take control of my life.

It was time to fly.

I quit Law School after that first year (despite getting the *Law Review* nod and winning the Moot Court competition), and the rest of my life has been an off-trail parade of sorts.

Wandered through my 20s: Mexico, Marine Corps, Europe, North Africa, and an Atlantic stint in the Merchant Marines. Then in my 30s: marriage, two sons, a serious career (publishing). In mid-life, divorce, relocation from Washington, DC, to San Francisco, where I continued my career and started a new life—tap dancing, accordion, traveling, acting and singing lessons, bar-hopping, poker playing (lasted 12 hours in the 2006 *World Series of Poker*), motorcycling, and, yes, more late-night discussions (which still occur if they're not too late for an 80-year-old). And I'm happily ensconced in a 25-year relationship with a fabulous, scrappy Connecticut woman who also moved to SF in mid-life to "*turn over a page*".

I've collected friendships, memories, lovers, grandchildren, and adventures all along the way. Among my treasured mementos: two pieces of advice which are framed and hang on the dining room wall in our 1878 Victorian flat.

One comes word-for-word from the inscription on an elegant china dinner plate in the Cape Cod Room in Chicago's Drake Hotel. It graced my office walls for 30-plus years and reads:

Aquila non captat muscas.

(If you translate this and think on it, you'll discover it has two different meanings, both of which are very useful in keeping one's cool in business.)

The other was penned in his early 80s by a very good friend. Dean was a full-out lover of life, a skirt-chasing, hard-drinking guy, an occasional nudist, and a committed nonconformist peacenik until his end at 85.

After years of full-tilt living, he concluded living life well and happily boils down to just 13 words in four lines:

Dean's Rules of Life's Road:

Go with Your Heart.
Be Kind.
When in Doubt, Do.
Forgive and Forget.

My life is rich. Full. Rewarding. Hey, I love it. If I hadn't dropped *out of* Law School, I wouldn't be the person I am today. Hooray.

P.S. With a little imagination, Elaine May and Mike Nichols could have cooked up a sketch combining the Cape Cod Room inscription and Dean's advice. It would have been a good one. I'm sure.

Lauren Craig Hickman is a retired (1999) reporter/writer/editor/publisher whose domain primarily included magazines, books and newsletters. He worked for nearly 20 years for McGraw-Hill in Chicago and Washington, DC, and spent his final working years at Miller Freeman, a division of United Business Media, in San Francisco.

Goodbye, Kalifa

Thomas Freed

For all of us there are many forks in the road to our eventual careers. We have little knowledge of any occupation to enable the "right" choice. Briefly, I was an early admission to Harvard Medical School, Nov. 26, 1956, but really did not want to go into medicine and was one of the few to decline admission. Early in 1957, my father, who was a doctor, changed my mind. I called Jack Caughey at Western Reserve in Cleveland, my home, and was admitted to the class of 1961.

During my medical internship, I visited San Francisco, saw the new Stanford Medical School and hospital, decided that this is the place to spend the next four years and switched from MD, PhD in biochemistry, a possible career in academic medicine, to radiology, which a friend there told me was one of Stanford's strong specialties. At that time it was a four-year program, one year each in diagnostic radiology and radiation oncology, and then choice of either for the final two years. "Kalifa" changed my life and career.

Kalifa is not her real name, but the memory is the same. I was a 29-year-old resident in radiation therapy (now termed radiation oncology) when we first met early in 1964. She was a new patient referred from medical oncology—diagnosis, "aggressive undifferentiated lymphoma", had just failed chemotherapy, but her residual tumor appeared confined to the pelvis and possibly treatable by radiation therapy. She was Iranian, the 26-year-old wife of a graduate student in physics. Her husband would receive his PhD in June. Those sad, frightened dark eyes were what I most remember of Kalifa, and why not? How could a 26-year-old comprehend the thought of a fatal disease, worse possibly because of a culture that did not discuss illness, cancer, death? She had a Mediterranean complexion, a bronze tan, very thin—possibly some weight loss from her prior therapy. She sat very quietly as we first talked.

The referral indicated that, although her only residual disease was in the pelvis, there was enough bulk from the residual tumor to cause discomfort by size alone. When we started to talk, Kalifa spoke softly in a British accent, British schooling, but less pronounced than the accent of my 28-year-old British wife. I was uncomfortable both about the extent of her disease and also the thought of multiple pelvic exams in a young, already nervous and frightened woman of a different culture and religion. Surprisingly, she sensed my discomfort, and this seemed to help her. She perked up and tried to make small talk to comfort her apprehensive doctor, which she did. After I did the pelvic exam, it was apparent how extensive the tumor was. Although she had no medical background, it was apparent that she understood both the seriousness of her condition as well as my consultants' guarded outlook for the outcome of her treatment. Unfortunately, her husband, a physicist, perhaps impressed by the array of technology, maybe denial about the seriousness of his wife's disease, did not appear to understand the prognosis for Kalifa. He was very anxious that treatment be started immediately so "she could be cured in three months" to return to Iran. Optimism and denial can both be very helpful in dealing with cancer, but too much of both can make it so hard when treatment fails—as was likely with Kalifa.

The plus of aggressive tumors is that they are frequently very responsive to therapy, as was true with Kalifa. In a matter of a few weeks, the tumor had begun to shrink. As I did my weekly exam, she talked more and more, sometimes even laughing. More importantly, those dark eyes which gauged her feelings were now bright as she told me about her family and Iran. I, too, became much more cheerful when I examined her because of the gratifying tumor response. She no longer had pain, and by a month most of the tumor bulk was gone. We then began to compare lives, my English wife living here for seven years, she for three, the cursed "green cards" and the other commonalties of the "foreign" student wives.

By eight weeks, as her treatment ended, she had no palpable tumor, x-rays were clear, lab work negative. It was a joyful goodbye as she was discharged to follow-up.

I should have known and really did know, it was too good to be true. Aggressive tumors often melt like magic with radiation, only to rapidly recur. When one is young, early in training, one always holds out hope that this tumor will be different. When I saw Kalifa for her first follow-up a month after completion of treatment, she said she was fine, looked happy and relaxed. Unfortunately, when I examined her, I thought there was a slight, but definite abnormality on the pelvic exam. Kalifa knew my concern immediately. I told her it was much too soon to consider the thought of any tumor recurrence but thought it best if my consultant examined her as well so we both had a "good baseline" for future exams. Although he told her there was no definite abnormality, we both sensed that, inconceivably after only a month, a tumor had recurred. Even aggressive tumors rarely occur in such a short time frame. In 1964, there were no CT scans or MRI to confirm our suspicions. The only option was a further follow-up exam.

The next follow-up interval was shortened to two weeks, and even in that short time it was apparent that the tumor had recurred. Kalifa said she still felt well, but those eyes again reflected that she also knew. I was heartbroken having to tell her. She would be sent to medical oncology for an attempt at further palliative chemotherapy, but she knew as well as I what the outcome would be. Her poor husband could not and would not believe that her treatment had failed—the massive linear accelerator, at that time the state-of-the-art cancer treatment that people came for from all over the world, had failed his wife.

Kalifa never returned to radiation therapy. Less than a month later, early on a May morning, I was called from examining a patient by the head nurse on the Medical Oncology ward. Kalifa had been admitted the night before, was terminal and asked to see me. "Could I come soon, that morning if possible?"

In less than an hour, I was in her room. She had the usual IVs running, a little breathless from metastases to her lungs but looked remarkably the same, other than those sad eyes. She asked whether I could sit with her and look out the window. It was a California May day, sunny, cloudless, brilliant blue. Stanford Hospital had been designed by Edward Durell Stone, an architectural masterpiece at the time for a hospital. Patient rooms were ringed by large outdoor corridors with extensive hanging bougainvillea. We both looked together at the red bougainvillea framed by the brilliant blue sky.

She asked whether I could hold her hand. We both just sat quietly looking at the sky. Kalifa said she would never see the sky and flowers again and then cried. I did too—just for a few minutes, very unprofessional. All I could say was something to the effect, "Kalifa, we will meet again—in a better place. I am glad to have known you." We held hands for one final moment and both cried again as we said goodbye.

I turned, walked out—did not want to look at Kalifa again. I went to a men's room at the end of the corridor, washed my face, and wiped my eyes, returned to radiation therapy to see my next patient. I did not say anything to anyone. In those days, we never showed any emotion. It was not correct, very unprofessional. That night, I told my wife that I was very sad, that a patient of mine was about to die. She did not seem to take it in, why should she? She had heard this often before, but it was just too hard to tell her that this was the 26-year-old from Iran.

Kalifa died the next day. I continued my career—but changed to diagnostic radiology. I lacked the emotional maturity to continue in radiation oncology, partly because I could not bear another Kalifa. Now, over 50 years later, when I see the bougainvillea against the blue California sky, I still think of Kalifa.

Thomas Freed, MD, is a retired radiologist and Fellow of the American College of Radiology. A graduate of Case Western Reserve Medical School, he trained in Internal Medicine at University Hospitals, Cleveland, and in Radiology at Stanford Medical School. He has held academic positions in cardiac radiology and angiography at the Medical College of Virginia, and Stanford Medical Center. From 1967–69 he was a Senior Surgeon in the US Public Health Service while serving as cardiac radiologist for the National Heart Institute at the National Institutes of Health in Bethesda, MD. Married to Sally J. Twist in 1963, they have two children and four grandchildren.

Professor Beer and My Career

Charles T. Martin

In my sophomore year at Harvard, I took a required course in social science. It was a history course, and it turned out to be the most memorable course of my undergraduate experience. This was in spite of the fact that I was a natural science major (i.e., engineering science and applied physics), and that I disliked history as it had been taught in high school. The Harvard course was taught by Professor Samuel Beer. What made it so memorable was rather than simply presenting history as a series of events, Prof. Beer had his students analyzing the decisions and actions of historical figures that were largely influenced by what was happening around them. These historical figures were then instrumental somehow in creating the events or conditions that followed in time. As a science major, I'm thinking now that I responded especially well to this "cause and effect" approach to studying history. So why do I tell this now? It's because it has helped me understand and appreciate how I became a Harvard graduate and then came to experience such a satisfying career. This is my story.

Like many of my Harvard classmates, I was born in 1935 in the midst of the historic great economic depression. However, unlike all but nine of my 1,100-plus classmates, I was born an African-American. Furthermore I was born in the racially segregated south—in Winston-Salem, NC. Therefore the likelihood was that my formal education would be in the racially segregated public school system followed by a far less productive and enjoyable career. For the record, my Harvard freshmen register shows that only one of my African-American classmates resided in the south, and he attended a private high school in the north. The fact that I was relocated north and thus was able to benefit from a non-segregated educational experience is the story I now want to tell. It's a classic case of actions taken in response to current happenings that largely determine future happenings. So what were those "current happenings", and how did I learn about them?

In 2000, the year of my retirement from my profession, I had become a fledging genealogist. I then began researching my mother's family. Because of my parents' divorce, my mother's family was the only family I knew. I had never asked any questions about my family's past. And since my mother was the last surviving member of her generation and was suffering from advanced dementia, I could then no longer ask her anything about family history. What I've now learned, I learned the hard way—by researching both family and historical documents.

My maternal grandfather died four years before I was born. He had been a minister in the African Methodist Episcopal Zion Church and in 1920 had been appointed Presiding Elder of its Winston-Salem District. In late 1930 he suffered a stroke and died in June 1931. His death occurred during the early days of the Great Depression, and my grandmother then needed to go to work, probably for the first time in her life. She was then in her early 50s. On the other hand, my mother, who had been a student at a black college in Alabama, had dropped out during her father's illness. So after his death, she also had to go to work. Both my mother and grandmother became domestics.

Eventually in the mid-1930s, my grandmother came north looking for better-paying employment opportunities. She came to Cambridge at the suggestion of my grandfather's niece who co-owned a house on Dana Street. Meanwhile, back in Winston-Salem, my mother met my father-to-be, married him, and I was born. Soon thereafter, my parents were divorced, and my mother somehow was able to resume her college education at Winston-Salem Teachers College (also a black college). She graduated in 1939 with a bachelor's degree in education. My mother was the first one in the family to graduate from college—and 18 years later, I would be only the second one.

After my mother's graduation and with me in tow, my mother joined her mother who had settled in Cambridge for what would be the rest of her life. The year was 1941, meaning I was able to start first grade at age six in the Cambridge Public Schools. Now although my mother was a trained teacher, she could not get a teaching position in Cambridge. The city had a prohibition against married female teachers at that time. Besides, there were almost no black teachers in the entire school system. However, I must have been her "private" student because, although I was the only black child in my school, I was one of their top students in all of my eight grades there! In fact, the school's administrators wanted me to skip second grade, but my mother would not let them do it. I graduated from the Wellington School in 1949 and moved on to Cambridge High and Latin School, the city's one co-ed public high school. I enrolled in their college preparatory program, although I had no idea what college I was preparing for, or what I wanted to become when I grew up . . . Enter Mr. Cohen, my freshman algebra teacher!

Math was by far my best subject. Therefore, I caught Alan Cohen's attention immediately (I was one of only three black students in his class). He took the time to find out what kinds of things I liked to do. He learned that I liked to design and build things. He also could see I was good in math and in solving logic problems. So he told me I could be an engineer, and that I could go to MIT. My high school algebra teacher had named a profession that corresponded to the things I liked to do! So at the beginning of my freshmen year in high school and only because of Mr. Cohen, I set the goal of becoming an engineer and going to MIT. I set this career goal without me or my mother or grandmother knowing anything at all about engineering or about MIT (except that MIT was a college and was in Cambridge). I finished the year as Mr. Cohen's top math student.

After my high school freshmen year, Alan Cohen passed me on to Mr. Sheehan, the boys' master, presumably to shepherd me. In my junior year, the high school headmaster died, and Mr. Sheehan became the new headmaster. Since I continued to excel academically, Mr. Sheehan began talking to me about going to Harvard. Thus, in my senior year I applied for admission to both MIT and Harvard—the only two colleges to which I applied! Since my mother was only able to get a World War II job at the Boston Navy Yard and was the only household breadwinner, we had no money for college. So I applied for scholarships to both schools.

Without substantial scholarship assistance I definitely could not afford college. I was interviewed first by MIT and then by Harvard. At both interviews, I was asked the same two questions: what schools I had applied to and which would I attend if I were admitted to all. At both interviews I gave the same honest answer: I applied only to Harvard and MIT, and if admitted to both I would attend MIT! The result was I was admitted to both. I was offered a full-tuition four-year scholarship by MIT, but amazingly, I was offered a full-tuition plus room & board four-year scholarship by Harvard. Harvard had out-bid MIT, and that is how and why I became a member of the Class of 1957! I graduated from my high school third in a class of over 400, but first among the boys.

At Harvard, I majored in Engineering Sciences & Applied Physics and was also a member of the Air Force ROTC. I was commissioned an Air Force second lieutenant at graduation, and my wife-to-be, Leona Langford, pinned the bars on my uniform. (Leona and I have been happily married for 59 years.) While awaiting my call to Air Force active duty, I was able to begin my engineering career at Philco in

Philadelphia, where I worked on development of what was to be the first transistorized computer for the commercial market. Because I had a pending military obligation, I worked there for only six months. I credit my Harvard credentials for even getting such a short-term job. Supposedly I was the only black engineer at the Philco Government & Industrial Division.

When called to active duty, I was assigned to an engineering position in the Radar Lab at Rome Air Development Center (RADC) at Griffiss Air Force Base, Rome, NY. There I oversaw microwave transmitter tube development work by both universities and corporations.

Figure 2.7.3.1 *Lt. Charles Martin, USAF*

In fact, throughout my career, I found myself at the cutting edge of new technology, and that's why I so thoroughly enjoyed the profession that Mr. Cohen had led me to. Black engineers were indeed a rarity in those days. In fact, I was a practicing engineer for six years and in my third place of employment before I met another black engineer. African-American engineers proved to be a rarity during most of my career, but being one has never knowingly impeded my success or my advancement. I have never regretted my career choice—not even for a second.

Following Philco and RADC, I returned to civilian life in Massachusetts and worked, in turn, at Sylvania Electronics Systems Division, Microtek Electronic, NASA's Electronics Research Center, Raytheon's Equipment Division and finally at Raytheon's Executive Offices. Although each employer was thriving when I left them, only my last employer still exists. I guess that says something about the speed of technology changes and my excellent timing (LOL).

At that first job at Philco, I was a junior engineer engaged in the development of magnetic core memory system for what was to be the first-ever commercial transistorized (i.e., solid-state) computer system.

This was before the invention of the integrated circuit (i.e., "chip"). At that second job at Rome Air Development Center, I was on active military duty and was engaged in directing the development of advanced high power microwave transmission technology for radar system applications. But after three years of active duty, I decided to return to civilian life.

At my third job at Sylvania's Electronics Systems Division, I was engaged in microcircuit design and applications engineering during the emergence of microelectronics as a new technology. At Microtek Electronics, I was the lead electrical design engineer in this start-up company which produced custom microelectronic modules. At NASA's Electronics Research Center, I was a senior member of technical staff engaged in research and development of new biomedical instrumentation for space applications and employing microelectronics technology.

At Raytheon's Equipment Division, I began as a senior engineer engaged in microelectronics technology development and application but eventually rose to become manager of the Microelectronics Engineering Section, where I directed an organization engaged in work that supported major US government programs.

In my last position at Raytheon, before my retirement, I was the corporate Director of Engineering Education and College Liaison Programs in the Executive Offices. This was a staff position to the company's Vice President of Engineering, and I was responsible for developing and managing strategic relationships with numerous colleges of engineering involving sponsored research, education and diversity initiatives.

The bottom line is that my career involved two distinctly different phases: initially technology development and eventually engineering education. I had so much fun at both that not a single day passed that I did not want to go to work. In fact, it never seemed like "work". Rather it was an adult version of the things I liked to do as a child—design things, build things, solve logic problems, use math, and continually learn new things.

Indeed I was fortunate to have had a teacher at a formative stage of my life who equated those things to an engineering profession. My good fortune continued when he passed me on to someone in a position of authority who saw that I was Harvard material.

However, absolutely none of this would have been possible if my widowed grandmother had decided differently when faced with a seriously depressed economy in combination with a racially segregated society. Instead of staying in North Carolina where all seven of her children still lived, she relocated to Cambridge. My divorced mother then followed her with me in tow. Recalling what Professor Beer taught us in 1955, I have come to recognize and appreciate my ultimate good fortune.

The decisions that my mother and grandmother made in the 1930s unquestionably led to my becoming a member of the Harvard Class of 1957 and subsequently my highly satisfying engineering career. Such occurrences were during an era when each was extremely rare for African-Americans but combined they were non-existent.

That is the story I want to record for posterity.

Figure 2.7.3.2 *In his post-retirement education program to encourage girls to enter engineering, Charlie Martin is shown in 2006 training an all-women team of eight teachers and two women engineers preparing for teaching Lego robotics in an* all-female environment *to fifth-grade girls enrolled in a girls-only afterschool engineering club at the Wilson Elementary School in Natick, MA.*

Charles T. Martin holds a bachelor's degree in engineering sciences and applied physics from Harvard University (1957) and a master's degree in electrical engineering from Northeastern University (1966). He has over 40 years' experience as a design and development engineer in several companies and government agencies. His specialty was hybrid microelectronics, which was then an emerging technology.

Following retirement in 2000, for the next decade he served as a part-time independent consultant with a focus on developing and operating programs aimed at increasing ethnic and gender diversity in the pre-college pipeline to engineering careers. To accomplish this goal he successfully led several corporate and college efforts in planning, developing and operating programs that involved students ranging from elementary through high school. He also served on multiple engineering college advisory boards that addressed issues involving both engineering education and increasing ethnic and gender diversity in engineering careers.

His primary avocation since retirement has been and continues to be genealogy, thus leveraging his research skills to discover and document his family history.

Figure 2.7.3.3 *Samuel Hutchison "Sam" Beer (1911–2009)*
Eaton Professor of the Science of Government

Photograph reprinted courtesy of Harvard University

Ohio native, graduate of the University of Michigan, Beer was a Rhodes Scholar in history at Oxford. Before beginning his PhD in political science at Harvard, for three years he worked for the Democratic National Committee, wrote speeches for FDR, articles for Fortune *and was a police reporter.*

During World War II, Army Artillery Captain Beer served in Europe from 1942–1945 in the Normandy invasion and the allied military government of Germany.

*His famous course—*Social Studies 2, Western Thought and Institutions*—concentrated on six key moments in the development of Western civilization as viewed through the lenses of history, political theory, and comparative government. By debating alternatives before offering his own interpretation, Beer mesmerized his undergraduate students.*

In recognition of his scholarship and decades of teaching, in 1997 Harvard awarded him an honorary doctorate.

Source: Harvard Archives—Beer, Samuel H. (Samuel Hutchison), 1911–2009

Identity

"Summer of 1989"

Lowell J. Rubin

It is hard to explain.
That summer was about something different.
All summer long we were on trains
going east.

You remember the rumbling of the train cars
in the movie SHOAH,
the relentless clicking, hour after hour,
that journey . . . to the end of the world.

We boarded the train in Amsterdam,
after climbing the stairs
to see where Anne Frank's family
tried to hide.
We were on our way back to Berlin.
The wall was still there.
That spiritual rent
in the soul of a people,
who never quite saw it that way.

That summer Berlin was like Limbo,
but there was disagreement about
which way to Hell.
I finally understood.
Limbo is crowded, mysterious, full of intrigue,
an air of tension hanging over it.

We walked through the Tiergarten on a Sunday,
after an outdoor piano concert.
The park was filled with old men in wheel chairs
or, hobbling on crutches, leaning
on their upright wives, in 1930's dresses.
It was such a peaceful scene.

Why do I still have trouble going to Germany
and trouble not going to Germany.
Why do I think about how old everyone is
who I am talking to.
Why did we go to Germany that summer
and continue eastward.
We had explanations for it.

We wanted to see Old Europe.
We wanted to see what was not destroyed.
We wanted to see what was destroyed.

We rode on
to the outer rim of the Austro-Hungarian Empire,
where it was still possible to use German
with a few of the old people,
to Prague and Budapest and then Cracow.

The Jews were sent far away.
No one should see this barbarism.
No one should know where it came from.

As the train rumbled on, walls were falling
all over Eastern Europe.
It was a strange summer.
In one month
we made our way through the 20th Century.

Czechoslovakia was as tight as a drum.
You felt faint, the atmosphere was so thick,
about to explode.
We telephoned Jiri. We could never reach him.
Our "Franz Kafka", in the guise of a mechanical
engineer, who worked in a clock factory,
whom we met our first time in Prague.

Identity

In the end we didn't go to the beautiful,
contorted, Art Deco restaurant that night.
You couldn't face it.
Instead we had an expensive dinner wheeled to our room.
Champagne, Filet Mignon, white table cloth and silver.
We needed to escape.
Several times that summer, when it was too much,
we let ourselves be "rich" Americans,
as when we finally flew out of Warsaw, in desperation,
on Swiss Air,
back to Budapest,
where we had left some luggage.

We had not meant it to be that way.
The first time, when we boarded the train to leave Poland,
our new found Polish friends from the art gallery
told us, push, don't worry. This isn't civilization any more.

At the Czech border other Poles and some Czechs whom
we had met on the train translated to the passport control.
Your mother was dying, we had to get back.
But they wouldn't listen.
They threw us off the train
in the middle of the night
at the border.
They would not let us through Czechoslovakia
with all our visas,
so painstakingly obtained.

Was it the conversation in our hotel room
a week before in Prague.
Igor, the young Czech we met was fearless
in his conversation, even though we knew
the room must be bugged.
Did someone see me slip him
a volume of Winnicott,
in the lobby of the Hotel Inter-Continental
to bring to his girlfriend, who was studying psychology.

Being American can protect you only so much.
That was one of the things we learned that summer
on the ride back to Cracow from the Czech border,
sitting in the aisle on upturned plastic milk racks,
the trainman let us use as seats
for two American dollars.
We huddled together in the madness
that came with each stop,
people rushing in and down the aisles,
trying to sell anything, the shirt off their back,
even old plastic bags.

We played dumb in every language that we knew,
threw up our hands.
But even with all that desperation
somehow, now it was different.
We had been to Auschwitz.

It is a simple trip from Cracow.
A taxi will take you there.
The camp was divided into two parts,
you remember.
Birkenau, where the train platforms are.
In the surrounding fields a farmer was haying.
The long simple buildings
which stand like decaying barns,
a trench down the middle, the wooden racks
at the sides.

I lay down for a moment
on the wooden planks.
I remember how it felt months later
when I awoke from my sleep, naked,
shivering, freezing from the terrible cold.

The other part of the camp, Auschwitz,
one desolate brick building after the other
and here and there the ovens.
We descended into the changing rooms,
the "showers".

Why were we there. Why had we come.
"A strange way to celebrate your 25th Wedding
Anniversary", our children said. "Why not Italy,
you know . . ."

Identity

I remember the people of Budapest lining the banks
of the Danube, singing, as the fireworks went off
to celebrate freedom, on that St. Stephen's Eve.
One long ordeal was over.
It was happening everywhere, gradually, and then
in a torrent.
I kept wondering.
What did we come to witness.
Why were we there.

Then I realized, I was a survivor,
more than I knew.
Though only a child
during a war far away,
something was burned into my flesh.
I could remember
names they had called me,
"Kike", "Yid".

Now I knew why
we had to go together
to make that journey into Death
and come back.

Lowell Rubin, MD, born in New Haven, CT, attended Putney School in Vermont before Harvard. After graduation he took pre-med courses at Columbia before entering medical school in London and graduating from what is now the Imperial College of Medicine. After serving as House Physician at Westminster Hospital, London, he returned to the US for a rotating internship at Barnes Hospital of Washington University of St. Louis.

During the Vietnam War, he served in the US Army Medical Corps as doctor to the Headquarters of the Fourth Infantry Division in the Central Highlands. Following military service, he completed a Psychiatric Residency at Mount Sinai Hospital in N.Y. and psychoanalytic training at the New York Psychoanalytic Institute.

After ten years in New York he moved his family to Providence, RI, where he has been in private practice of psychiatry and psychoanalysis. Affiliated with the Brown University Medical School, he has also been a faculty member of the Boston Psychoanalytic Institute and been President of the Rhode Island Psychiatric Society and the Rhode Island Association of Psychoanalytic Psychologies.

He has published one book of poems, *In the Shadow of a Yellow Star* (Amazon). He and his wife, Margot Landcastle Rubin (Vassar 1961), have two sons and three grandchildren.

Escaping Genocide

My Armenian Heritage

John A. Simourian

"*What kind of name is that?*" As an incoming freshman, that was a question I often heard, which was not surprising since there are only five to seven million Armenians in the world and approximately one million in the United States. Even today, Armenians are presented with that question often. Let me try to answer the question by explaining who the Armenians are.

Armenia is one of the oldest countries in the world and dates back to 5000 BC. Its civilization had its beginnings in the Biblical mountains of Ararat, where Noah's Ark came to rest in the Great Flood in 2400 BC. Armenian tradition says Armenia was the site of The Garden of Eden. Yerevan, the capital of modern Armenia, was founded in 782 BC.

At its apex, 95–55 BC, Armenia stretched from the Caspian Sea in the north, to the Mediterranean Sea, including Syria and Lebanon, and south to Persia (Iran) and Babylon (in Iraq). It was the strongest state in Asia Minor and one of the most culturally advanced.

Armenia's history was dominated by tortuous and turbulent periods of war. For centuries it was on the edge of physical annihilation as it occupied an area between the Greeks and Romans to the west and Persians and Arabs to the east. At various times it was at war with the Turks, Persians, Egyptians, and Romans. In spite of these wars, Armenia managed to develop its own national and religious culture. In 301 AD, Armenia became the first Christian state in the world. Christianity was officially recognized in the Roman Empire 12 years later. Moreover, Armenia was the tenth nation in the world to put its language into print.

The Ottoman Empire eventually conquered Armenia in the 16th century and ruled it until the end of World War I (1914–1918). The Ottoman rulers were Muslim, as were most of their subjects except the Armenians, who were Christian. The authorities questioned the

Armenians loyalty to the Sultan and the Empire, viewed them with suspicion, and occasionally subjected them to pogroms even before the War.

On April 24, 1915, the Turkish Government, in an effort to resolve "the Armenian Question", systematically executed several hundred Armenian intellectuals. Over the next two and a half years, the Turks murdered, starved and raped 1.5 million Armenians—50% of the Armenian population—in the first Genocide of the 20th century. In the Versailles Peace Treaty at the end of WWI, the Ottoman Empire was dissolved, and Armenia was annexed by Russia, at that time also nominally Christian.

My grandparents on both sides left Turkey in 1905 because of earlier massacres in 1895. My wife's (Michele) grandparents weren't so fortunate, as both her grandfathers were executed between 1915 and 1917. During this period, Michele's parents, as infants, fled with family members to France. Her parents settled in Lyon, married, had three children, and emigrated to America in 1955 because of Michele's father's illness and the political chaos in France. Her father wanted his children to have the benefits of the opportunities in America. He, unfortunately, succumbed to his illness in 1967.

My father, who was born in Turkey, and was fatherless from the age of 11, grew up poor and humble in Roxbury, a section of Boston. Later, he and his family moved to Watertown, which had attracted a large number of Armenians who were drawn to jobs provided by the Hood Rubber Company. Watertown became the cultural center for Armenians in New England and is the site of the Armenian Library and Museum of America.

My immigrant father started his own business during WWII. Watertown, a next-door neighbor to Cambridge, was our home, and its vibrant Armenian culture shaped me as I was growing up. Sending me to Harvard was my father's dream and his way of telling the Turks that, although they had tried to exterminate the Armenian people, they would not, and could not destroy his life and his family. Thousands of Armenian families have similar stories.

The Armenian Genocide also brought Michele and me together, because without it, our paths would not have crossed. Our Armenian culture also played an important role. Our generation was always told to "marry one of your own". True to tradition, my cousin insisted that I meet her. We married soon after. Michele and I are 100% Armenian, meaning no one in our families has ever married a non-Armenian. Most Armenians look like me—dark complexion, brown eyes, and black hair. But a very few have a light complexion, blue or green eyes and blond hair—features that are traced to the migrants who inhabited ancient Armenia and referred to as "pure" Armenians. Michele is a "pure" Armenian.

In our culture, family and church are supreme. A special effort is made to put family ahead of other relationships and celebrate births, birthdays, anniversaries, graduations, weddings and especially Christmas and Easter with the entire family. Weekly church attendance is expected. Delicious home-prepared Armenian food at all these occasions is always present. On a rotating basis, each family within the greater family takes the responsibility for hosting these special days.

Today, modern Armenia, which became an independent nation with the fall of the Soviet Union in 1991, has a population of three million and encompasses only 29,000 square miles, about the size of Maryland. But only half of the world's Armenians live in Armenia.

Of the one million Armenians living in America, many have distinguished themselves in academia, arts, sports and business. Some of the more famous are Vartan Gregorian, former president of Brown; Kirk Kerkorian, investor and philanthropist; Alex Manoogian, CEO of Delta Faucet; Ara Parseghian, legendary Notre Dame football coach and Andre Agassi, world champion tennis player. All have risen from humble backgrounds to achieve success and build pride in all Armenians.

Our defiant spirit, will to succeed, and resolve is best described by the Pulitzer Prize and Academy Award Winning novelist and author, William Saroyan, in this writing:

> "*I should like to see any power of the world destroy this race, this small tribe of important people, whose wars have all been fought and lost. Whose structures have crumbled, literature is unread, music is unheard and prayers are no more answered.*
>
> *Go ahead, destroy Armenia. See if you can do it. Send them into the desert without bread or water. Burn their homes and churches. Then see if they will not laugh, sing and pray again. For when two of them meet anywhere in the world, see if they will not create a New Armenia.*"

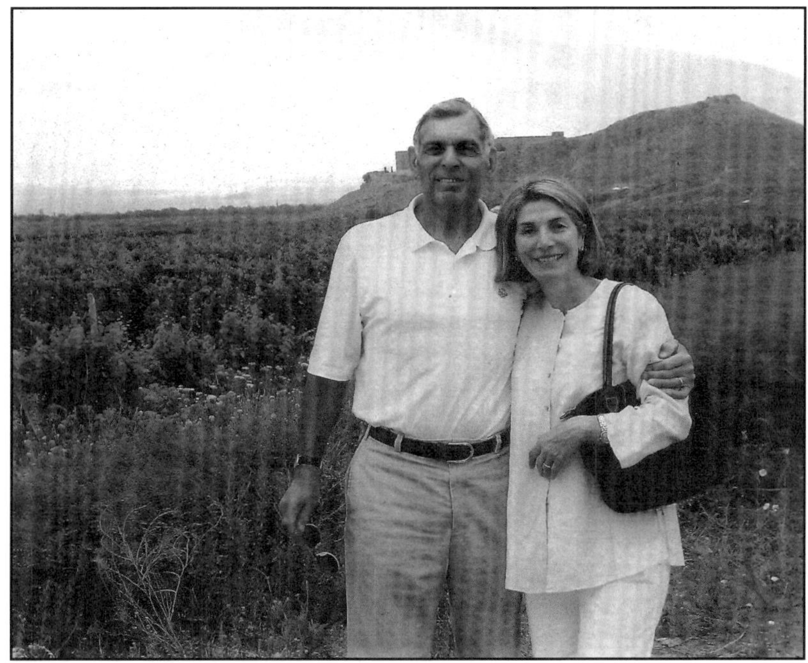

2.8.1.1 *John and Michele Simourian in Armenia in 2010, with Mt. Ararat in the background*

John A. Simourian is a former trustee of the Armenian Library and Museum of America and past chairman of the trustees of the First Armenian Church. His wife, Michele, is the co-founder of the Armenian Missionary Association of America Orphan Childcare Committee, a member of the board of the Armenian Missionary Association of America, and former trustee of the First Armenian Church. For her many years of service to the Armenian community, in 1996 she was honored as woman of the year by the Armenian Library and Museum. John and Michele support the education and well-being of several children and students in Armenia and are benefactors of the Armenian Library and Museum of America, the Armenian Missionary Association of America and the Armenian Heritage Park on the Rose Kennedy Greenway in Boston. John and Michele have visited Armenia twice in connection with their philanthropic efforts.

Life Lessons

A Turning Point or Not

Edward L. Burlingame

In 1951, my parents sent me off to Exeter. The circumstances aren't clear, but I don't remember even visiting the school before arriving for my first day. I was just sent. In those days, extensive consultation between parent and child over such decisions was unknown, at least in my family. You did what your parents instructed you to do. My father had attended Exeter, so that is where I was sent.

I found the school a bruising, tough environment. You sank or swam. Relations between faculty and students were chilly and distant, though many of the teachers were excellent at their work. Fortunately, I was good at sports, which kept me more or less afloat.

During the week, the last class of the day was held in the late afternoon from about 5 to 6. In the winter of my junior year—at Exeter called my upper year—I had an English class with Mr. Leonard at that hour. On the cold, dark and gloomy afternoon that I am remembering, I came to class unprepared. I had not done the assigned reading. At Exeter, the class, about 12 of us, sat around a large, oval wooden table. This arrangement was called The Harkness Plan and was designed to facilitate discussion and learning. (I think it did.) It also meant there was nowhere to hide. I was, of course, hoping on that day that our discussion of the assigned book would be carried along by my classmates, and that I could wear an expression of informed interest without having to speak.

Mr. Leonard called for the class to begin. He then turned to me and said: "Burlingame, why don't you get us started this afternoon by commenting on some of the themes the author is exploring in the book we have just read?"

Decision time! Come clean or wing it.

I made the wrong decision.

I had been struck, I announced, by the author's interesting treatment of opposing elements: youth and age, dreams and reality, loneliness and the bonds of friendship and love. No doubt I threw life and death in there too. As I spoke, I noticed the eyes of my classmates growing wider. I was going down. I stopped speaking, and a long silence followed.

Mr. Leonard then made the short statement that has remained in my memory ever since.

"Burlingame, I don't know what's going to become of you in life, but I advise you to stay far, far away from books."

After college, I spent two years in the Navy, but following that I have devoted my entire working life to reading, editing and publishing books. Is it possible, I sometimes wonder, that I have spent 40–50 years of my life trying to prove Mr. Leonard wrong about me? His remark, which amused the class greatly, seems now comparatively harmless, but at the time it evidently cut deep. Otherwise, I would not remember it so clearly after all these years. But perhaps I have it completely backwards? Is it conceivable that Mr. Leonard was shrewdly perceptive and was goading me onto a path he thought might lead somewhere for me?

We all like causality. We like to believe that A will lead to B, and we do not enjoy the thought that pure chance plays such an important role in our lives. In all probability, my future life working with writers and their books had nothing to do with Mr. Leonard. I'll never know, but one lesson does seem clear: if you shame someone publicly, they'll not soon forget it.

Figure 2.10.1.1 *Ed Burlingame with his wife, Perdita, celebrating his victory in the 75+ division at the 2010 National Squash Championships in Newport, RI.*

Edward Burlingame, now retired, was an editor and publisher of books for over 45 years at New American Library, J.B. Lippincott, and Harper and Row, which became HarperCollins. There he was editor-in-chief and publisher. He worked with a wide range of writers including Edward Abbey, Saul Bellow, Amy Bloom, Leon Edel, Allen Ginsberg, Leon Panetta, Jonathan Raban, Piers Read and Roxana Robinson. He also served as Chairman of the General Publishing Division of the Association of American Publishers and on the Executive Board of the American Center of P.E.N. (the international writers' organization). Apart from editing and publishing, he has remained an avid squash player and has won four National titles in his age group. His wife, Perdita, is a book editor at Little Brown & Company.

Personal Experiences and Insights/ Lessons Learned

Philip C. Berolzheimer

First Wife *(and Present after 58 Years)*

Let's start with the US Army 1958–1960, where I was stationed in Tokyo earning $72/month. Since I majored in geology (rocks in my head), they put me in the US Army Corps of Engineers making maps. I was engaged, so at $72/mo I made a collect phone call to my fiancée, Anne Watkin, just before she was to enter her junior year at Wellesley. She flew to Japan, and we were married on October 10, 1958. We slept a lot on *tatami* and futon floors, and I taught her to be an obedient Japanese-style wife following ten paces behind. I refer to her as my First Wife.

In 1975 we visited Beirut, Lebanon, and met an Arabian Oxford-educated customer who owned a pencil company in Baghdad, Iraq. On the walk from the hotel to a restaurant the men preceded the women. After a half hour at the bar:

> Omar Sharif said: "*I say, Mr. Berolzheimer, you certainly have a very nice wife for an American. Most unusual!*"
>
> Phil: "*Thank you very much. I can explain why.*"
>
> Omar: "*Oh, that would be most interesting.*"

Phil: "*Well, Anne and I were married in Japan, and during our stay I taught her to be an obedient Japanese-style wife. For example, did you notice on the way to the restaurant our wives remained ten paces behind us?*"

Omar: "*Ah, Mr. Berolzheimer, I know that stupid Japanese custom. Here in the Arab countries, our wives walk in front of us in case there is a bomb in the ground!*"

Lesson Learned? Compliment customers on their imaginative proclamations. Always have First Wife walk in front of you. By the way, I am a collector of Plains Indian artifacts and also an honorary member of the Blackfeet tribe that used to have a pencil factory. I recently learned that the First Wife of a Blackfoot was the "*Woman Sitting Beside Him Wife*".

Business

After the Army in 1960 I returned to California and before joining our family companies in 1970 was involved with sailboat racing and sales, a lumber wholesale company and other activities. One year we went into the sawmill business and lost our shirt.

I then went to the PMD 6 program at the Harvard Business School in 1963 (to remove the rocks in my head). When I returned to Stockton, CA, one of the partners said, "*Welcome back to the office. What did you learn?*" I replied, "*Beginning immediately, we are going to liquidate this corporation.*"

Lesson Learned? It's a lot easier to get into rather than out of something. Before you get into a new business, analyze it from all angles—typical HBS stuff. If you do get into a new business, and it was a wrong decision, get out as fast as possible. In a small business always own at least 50 to 51% so you can make a quick decision.

How to Meet Important People

A Japanese customer visited us in 1968 and brought an interpreter who was an English teacher at Keio University who said he was very famous.

Phil: "*How did you get to become famous?*"

He: "*During Second World War, I kamikaze pilot!*"

Phil: "*I thought all kamikaze pilots died bombing our ships.*"

> He: "*Not all! Top ten percent of class becomes Instructor! Big incentive to become Instructor! I became famous and gave lectures at universities and schools and then teach English.*"
>
> *Do you know why Americans won Second World War? Because American men henpecked and want to get away from wife for four years! Problem was that there were too many henpecked men! But I was not famous enough.*"
>
> Phil: "*How did you become more famous?*"
>
> He: "*Well, you know you need invitation to go to wedding but no need invitation to go to funeral. Every day I read obituaries in Tokyo* Shimbun *and when famous person die, I go to famous person's funeral, mix with other famous people, and become even more famous myself.*"

Evidently he was not famous enough. Around 1972, he hijacked a JAL airliner and became the most famous person in Japan! Within 24 hours, we received a telegram from the customer apologizing for having brought this man to a dinner four years ago.

Lesson Learned? Work hard to be in the top 10% of your class or industry. It's a waste of time to go to weddings. It's a waste of time to go to funerals because most of the time famous people won't stick around to chat.

Be diligent when you learn to fly so you won't crash by mistake. (I only crashed once without a problem. I have a Commercial, Instrument, Single- and Twin-Engine and Seaplane ratings.) Don't take the whole family in a plane (or airliner) a second time. Don't get henpecked! Remember customers who remember you.

Courtesy in Different Cultures

During my first visit to Musgrave Pencil Company in the early 1970s in Shelbyville, TN, the attractive receptionist mentioned that I looked a lot different than my brother. She noticed that I had black hair, and Mike's was red. I said, "*Who do you think is younger?*" She replied that I looked much younger than my brother! (I am five years older.) I told her I was falling in love with her! Of course, after this visit, I told this story as often as possible—especially in front of my brother!

Well, about ten years later, in the 1980s, Mr. Kitada, Mr. Sassama, and two Japanese customers visited Stockton, and we were in my brother's office. Somehow the question of our age came up, and I immediately asked Mr. Kitada, "*Which brother do you think is younger?*"

There ensued a five-minute lively conversation among the Japanese, of course in Japanese, about this subject. They put their hands over their mouths, took deep breaths, inhaled and exhaled, and exclaimed "*Ano Ne's*" several times.

Finally Mr. Kitada looked at me and said,

> "*After consultation we determine it is very easy to tell—but difficult question to answer*!"

Practical Joke—*National Pencil Company*

One of the most amusing experiences and Machiavellian ideas by a customer occurred when I met with the new president and various executives of the National Pencil Company in Tennessee. We entered the conference room. I was told to sit at the head of the table. Near the head of the table was a very large Slurpee-type cup turned upside-down.

This was the first meeting with this new president, so we discussed the forest industry, logging, slat manufacturing and the worldwide pencil industry. Their foreman asked a few technical questions about machining pencil slats and also a bleeding problem with lacquering some pencils. I estimate about an hour had passed.

In a few minutes while discussing future orders, I could not stand it anymore and so picked up the inverted Slurpee cup. Out came hundreds of marbles. The marbles went all over the table, they fell on the floor, and rolled all over the floor. There were more marbles in that Slurpee than I had ever seen or owned as a kid. Everyone was laughing.

The president looked at me and asked,

> "*Mr. Berolzheimer, are you here to play marbles or to talk business?*"

Luckily that was one of a few days in my life I was quick on my feet and replied,

> "*I guess we've already discussed a lot of business, so let's play marbles!*"

Unemployment Insurance

This story was published in *Time* magazine.

During the 1960s I was a partner in *Boom Boom Enterprises*, which sold Trepidation Contest records. The partners would eventually have the idea to make fire logs, and after research produced the Duraflame fire log in 1969. Boom Boom became the Northern California distributor.

The three main partners were: Frank Romero—President, a truck driver in San Francisco; Peter "Boom Boom/Boomer" Hermes—VP, a mirror salesman; and Bob Kenyon—a Wells Fargo Bank Manager. Early on, they decided they could stop their salaries after the fire log season (winter) was over. They eliminated their salaries around March and then started them in October and in the meantime drew unemployment insurance.

After the first visit to the California Dept. of Employment, a lady asked The Boomer,

> "*Mr. Hermes, how is it possible for a Vice President of a corporation to ask for unemployment benefits?*"
>
> Boomer: "*Madam, if you think that's strange, then just wait until you talk to the President standing right behind me!*"

Lessons Learned? In your personal and business life, consciously insert as much humor as possible. It helps with relationships, morale, and success. If you start early in life, then it becomes unconscious. Everyone cannot become a Bob Hope, Johnny Carson, etc., but try. Your objective is to be spontaneously amusing.

Summing Up

Of course, you may say after 60 years out of college, it's too late. *Never too late.* Always laugh at yourself if someone else, especially a customer, pulls off a marble joke or does something he thinks is amusing.

If you're in between jobs and/or can think outside the box, then draw unemployment. You pay ridiculous fees to the system, so you might as well take advantage of it. Same for Social Security. Take it out early and live a long time until the system is bankrupt. (Which is about now?)

One of the lessons learned in the last 60 years is the importance of a lot of extracurricular activities, especially physical. I'm still active on boards of directors, including a bank, former trustee and president of a museum, and sail, fly-fish, golf, and play jazz on the piano.

Don't ask me about politics unless you want an hour-long soliloquy.

Don't ask me for a donation to Harvard College. *Too liberal and politically correct.* Once banned ROTC and is discriminating against private clubs, and last week Harvard could not tolerate even a few months' moratorium of visitors from *some* Mid-Eastern countries.

Life is short; smile while you still have teeth.

Philip C. "Phil" Berolzheimer grew up as a part river rat on the San Joaquin River racing sailboats, building ship models, and water skiing. After graduation, he served from 1958 to 1960 in the US Army Corps of Engineers, mostly in Japan. Back in the USA, he worked in a wholesale lumber company and started a sailing yacht dealership. In 1963 he took the Harvard Business School Program for Management Development. He returned to Stockton and became the general manager of a mirror manufacturing factory. In 1970 he joined the family business, California Cedar Products Company (manufacturer of incense-cedar slats for the wooden pencil industry), and held positions of Data Processing Manager, VP, Sales, President, and eventually Chairman. Concurrently, he was involved with Duraflame fire logs. Phil is presently Chairman Emeritus of Duraflame. He is on the board of the Bank of Stockton, a member of Trustee Council and former president of the board of trustees of the Haggin Museum, and president of the Coastal Barrier Island Foundation. He keeps in shape with skiing, tennis, golf, fly-fishing, and keeping up with his first wife, Anne, of over five decades.

Time and Retirement

Gary L. Robertson

Since retiring some ten years ago, my basic beliefs and values have not changed much, but my views on human nature and its impact on life have intensified and become more realistic.

This change is due partly to having more time to think and read on a wider range of subjects previously displaced by the pressures of a career. It also resulted from discoveries about myself and others resulting from the challenges of moving to a different environment.

On leaving the cloistered world of academia, one of my objectives was to reconnect with the larger community that I left behind when I entered Harvard some 60-plus years ago. That goal has been realized to some extent, although I have also managed to keep one foot in the door by continuing to read, write and consult in the specialized area of medicine that kept me occupied and financially comfortable for most of my life. However, as I became more engaged in my new community, I also have learned or, perhaps, relearned some valuable lessons about myself and my fellow citizens.

My most important lesson has to do with the wide variations in human nature and the reasons for them.

I have become much more aware of the power and influence of deeply entrenched human instincts, impulses and yearnings, and the extent to which they can distort perceptions and influence behaviors, often in self-destructive ways.

I used to believe that people were mostly rationale and would behave accordingly. Though evidence to the contrary was all around me, I failed to see it clearly until I was able to step back from the preoccupations and demands of a career and think more deeply about human motivation.

In this regard, I was helped by reading Horace Gregory's translation of Ovid's *Metamorphoses,* an unsparing, poetic depiction of the virtues and vices of the high and mighty in the known world 2,000 years ago.

At the same time, as I became involved in the affairs of my new community, I also became more aware of the basic decency, kindness and common sense of the less powerful and less exalted classes of humanity, a point also made briefly by Ovid.

Notwithstanding current beliefs in progress, it is now clear to me that human nature has not changed in at least 2,000 years. As contemporary studies of monozygotic and dizygotic twins indicate, that is because our behaviors and beliefs are determined largely by genes which vary from person to person, but change little from generation to generation. And, as Darwin indicated, many if not most of those genes have the sole purpose of producing behaviors that serve to ensure their own reproduction.

The most that humanity can claim to have achieved is that we have managed to forge some social arrangements that serve to maximize the positive and minimize the negative impact of all the basic drives inherited from our animal progenitors. And even those mitigating arrangements are in constant danger of breaking down, because we often forget or refuse to see the reasons they were created in the first place.

One of the mitigating social arrangements that may be breaking down now is confidence in democratic forms of government. Upon moving to my new community in the rural Midwest, I became involved in a controversy over plans to construct a 540-KV electric transmission line from windmills in Iowa through one of the most beautiful agricultural areas in the "driftless" part of Wisconsin.

Pushed by a powerful consortium of construction companies and the Obama administration, the plan is supported by most of the University faculty and other government employees who live and work in one of the counties most affected. However, it has been just as strongly opposed by most of the farmers and other long term residents who are skeptical of the need for the transmission line and see the plan as a way to take their land and boost the power and income of the proponents.

Apart from all the uninformed and misleading arguments about the "science" of man-made global warming, the most depressing aspect of the controversy for me is the fatalistic attitude of the citizenry toward government and their ability to influence it. Many now believe that government does not serve their interests, and that there is little they can do about it since the political class, their employees, academia, financial supporters and the news media are part of a large, entrenched, self-serving clique focused on their own agenda. All the others can do is hunker down with family and friends, accept the consequences and hope for a break now and then. If this attitude continues to prevail, I seriously doubt that our democracy and quality of life can long survive.

Responsibility for the loss of faith in democratic government falls at many doors, one of which is academia. It has become almost a branch of government that indoctrinates more than it educates. Even many "private" schools and universities, now depend heavily on government funding in exchange for which they must submit to a lot of government oversight and regulation. As always, he who pays the piper calls the tune.

This situation stands in contrast to the past where universities were supported by religious or other private entities. Though many of them also strove to indoctrinate, their viewpoints tended to be more diverse and independent of those preferred by the king.

Given the current decrease in independence, it's not surprising that most schools and universities now tend to promote the idea that government is best when it is big and should be left to a class of self-anointed "experts". In fact, the opposite is probably true.

More than ever, I now believe that education should teach basic intellectual skills while presenting different points of view and making clear the limitations of human nature and knowledge. It would also be helpful to recognize the practical wisdom of people who learn from experience rather than long years in the library or classroom.

The best way to achieve these educational goals would be to restore a greater degree of academic independence by finding alternatives to direct funding by government. Reducing costs by eliminating non-essential and wasteful spending, such as documentation of compliance with government edicts, would help. So would more support from alumni and other private sources. However, it probably would not suffice in many instances.

So methods of indirect funding by government, such as grants, scholarships or loans direct to students for use at a private school of their choice, may also be necessary. These changes would serve to make the schools more competitive for the customer's dollar and therefore more efficient and diverse. They may not be easy and probably would be opposed by many in the academy as well as government. However, the end result would almost certainly be better for us all.

Gary L. Robertson was born and raised in the Pacific Northwest. After Harvard College, he received his MD from Harvard Medical School. Then followed internship and residency in Medicine at the University of Louisville and post graduate training in Endocrinology at Harvard and the National Institutes of Health. Subsequently, he held positions as Professor of Medicine at the University of Illinois, Indiana, the University of Chicago and Northwestern University, where he taught, practiced medicine and did research pertaining to the regulation of salt and water balance in health and disease. He was also Director of the General Clinical Research Center at the University of Chicago and Northwestern, served on the editorial boards of several medical journals as well as scientific review committees of the Veteran's Administration, National Institute of Health and several private research foundations. He is a member of several professional societies including the Association of American Physicians. After a three-year leave of absence to live and work in Denmark as consultant to a pharmaceutical firm, he retired in 2006, remarried Hsiu Ling Lin, acquired two stepdaughters and moved to a "farm" in Wisconsin, where he now spends his time reading, writing, consulting, and learning how to make wine and grow blueberries.

A Small College in New England: A Harvard Story

Thomas Wilson Burrows II

I have always felt that for me a liberal education would have something to do with the question: "*What shall I do when I retire?*"

When I was a struggling freshman and sophomore student at Harvard (this was 1953–1955), I had planned that I would go to medical school. For these two years I was "pre-med" and had chosen biology as my major.

Many things happened during these two years. One of these was in the summer after my freshman year. I had just completed a year of inorganic chemistry. That summer I returned to Harvard for organic chemistry, taught by a visiting professor from the University of Wisconsin. I was quite overwhelmed by the mass of material to memorize and by the required three to four hours in the organic chemistry lab five days a week—and, as I recall, 15 hours of lectures a week, with an additional "section" class weekly. All of this proved too much for a modest memory—and quite above any interest that I had initially thought that I might have for the subject.

I left Harvard after eight weeks of organic chemistry with the first major failure in my life. But I had resolved on a career in medicine; after all my father was a general surgeon, my uncle a physician and attorney, and my grandfather—for whom I was named—a surgeon and country doctor in Ottawa, LaSalle County, IL. My father, with his brother and one sister, owned a small, private hospital on Chicago's North Side. With all of this it was rather assumed that I would follow in my father's path and eventually practice medicine as my father and grandfather before me.

My second year at Harvard, now in Leverett House, saw me again enrolled in organic chemistry and also taking first year general biology; a double dose of scientific material to remember and to memorize. I took a math class the subject of which I had never liked, except for geometry, which I found only a little more appealing. I also took a review course in Latin (Cicero) during my second year.

My second year's attempt to study organic chemistry again ended in failure, and I believe that I did not take the final exam. Following these shortcomings the University sent me home to Chicago for a year to work. A letter from the Dean said that I could return to Harvard after a year off, but noted that there were other roads to success in life than going to Harvard, or, in fact, to college.

During my year off I found a job working for Rand McNally in their shipping department, where I packed globes. I was several minutes late the second day. I told my supervisor that I was not a "time-clock" person, but that I was interested in the job and would be happy to work extra time if the work demanded, and without any extra pay. After a week in the shipping department I resigned and went home to work on our old house on Sheridan Road across from the Lake—it always needed work, and there was no one else. I chose to begin my academic year by reading R.R. Palmer's *History of the Modern World*. I was a college dropout and a not very good student who was beginning to have academic interests.

I returned to Cambridge to begin my third year and a very interesting thing happened. I was assigned to the first floor of Leverett House and had a roommate. We met just before dinner on my first day back. My roommate's parents were in the Foreign Service, either in the Philippines, or in India. Henry, which I will call him, was sitting on the floor in the middle of our living room, surrounded by luggage, millinery boxes, and Pacific-island artifacts from a life lived mostly abroad, and in strange and far-off countries. He was pleasant and a fine person, I decided. I asked whether he would like to go to dinner together, but he wanted to finish his unpacking and so I went to the dining room alone.

When I got back from dinner in Leverett House, Henry was not there. That was the last time that I saw him at the University. A month or so later, I was able to track him down and found that he was in a psychopathic hospital in Boston. I went to see Henry several times, but then got so busy with my classes that I lost track of him. His luggage remained in the basement of Leverett House for the rest of my junior year. The University tried to reassign my room to a visiting scholar, but I prevailed and had a double room all to myself for my last two years. My father had to pay more.

My first year, too, in Massachusetts Hall, I was able to move to a single room on the fourth floor, sharing a bath with a rich and colorful student who had spent his summers working in the oil fields outside Houston. John was a geology major, oil geology. We were quite the opposite, but I cared for John, and we got along well together. He had a strong romantic streak and a great love for Texas. Some evenings I can hear the plaintive strains of the cowboy songs like "Red River Valley" and "Across the Alley from the Alamo."[1] John preferred to take his dinners at the Continental Hotel, and sometimes he invited me. On one occasion I rode on the back of his large Harley Davidson motorcycle, roaring around Harvard Yard in the middle of the night, in winter.

I was scared, afraid that I might fall off. John had skidded on some gravel not too long before and had come home a bit scraped and banged up. On another night, it was dark and rainy. We drove a hundred and eight miles an hour along black, wet, and winding country roads to an isolated cabin in Maine to deliver a term paper in naval history which was due that day. John was the Jay Gatsby in my life at Harvard.

I went back to Harvard Summer School after my year off. I was becoming committed to studying classics. I enrolled in elementary Greek with Eric A. Havelock. Our text was Alston Hurd Chase and Henry Phillips, Jr., *A New Introduction to Greek* (1954). I also took a course in medieval love taught by Professor John Mundy of Barnard College. I was learning to write papers for my courses and felt a sense of achievement.

My last year I took two more courses in Greek, one with Professor Havelock in the Greek lyric poets. I also took a class in Homer's *Iliad*. When I went home for Christmas that year I was proud to be able to read to my mother the opening lines of the *Iliad* in Greek.

I also had a tutor in classics for a brief time. I was not particularly gifted in languages, but I recognized how important they were to me and to the humanistic tradition of learning. I had always desired to have the classical education of English schoolboys, which I had read about in *Tom Brown's Schooldays*. By the end of my fourth year I had taken enough courses in history and several in English to receive the AB.

For four years I had worried about the draft and dreaded the thought of being drafted into the Army. A few days after graduation I took the Selective Service exam in Boston. By this time I was becoming reconciled to going into the Army. There was one other young man among the hundred or more at the Selective Service center who was not from Massachusetts. At the physical exam the physician asked what I was interested in. I told him Latin and Greek classics. He asked me about Latin deponent verbs. Fortunately, I was able to say *something*. The physician rejected me for Korea. The other student from out-of-state was also rejected. We were the only two in our group of draftees to be rejected that day. The physician told me to go back to school! I was 4-F. My military career thus ended before it began.

I returned home to Chicago and continued to do manual labor on our house and enrolled at Loyola, which was practically in our back yard. I started again from the beginning in a Latin course for pre-seminarians.

Latin was then a requirement in Catholic seminaries, and all of my forty-two classmates were destined for seminary. They had been sent there by their bishops from all over the country to be in what was called "pre-seminary Latin": four years of high-school Latin taught every spring by Fr. Lawrence E. Henderson, SJ. We had class weekdays, every afternoon for three hours, where we learned to read and orate the language of the Roman orators. Since I was not a seminarian and not even Roman Catholic, I considered it a privilege to be in this class. I was later to take more than fifteen classes with Fr. Henderson along with other courses in classics, ancient history, and philosophy.

I drifted about for several years while I taught school as a substitute teacher in the Chicago Public Schools. I continued to go to school, working a year for a title company in Chicago doing legal research. I took classes at the University of Chicago, Rosary College (Dominican University) in River Forest, and Northwestern.

Twenty-seven years after my Cambridge graduation, supported by the sacrifices of an ever-marvelous spouse, KATHLEEN LAY, art director, graphic and visual designer, and now abstract expressionist painter, I received a diploma from Northwestern. It read: "*PhD in Classics*". It would have been the fulfillment of my father's dream. Kathy made my life possible. It is not perhaps what I had planned. My classes at Harvard, at Northwestern, at the University of Chicago have informed my life and made me what I am.

But there is still something else. After 20-some years as a librarian and book cataloguer I am retired. Shortly after this I decided to begin the study of Italian. And now I am the most fortunate of men to be a student of Professoressa Daniela de Vincenti Marchese, teacher, humanist, and lover of learning. Daily she inspires her students to love Italy and the Italian language, and all learning. It is the great gift of my retirement. I come back each week renewed, refreshed, and eager to immerse myself more in the life of learning, and in the language of Dante and Petrarch.

My father, Dr. Sam, who loved medicine and surgery, went around the world in 1921 and studied surgery in Rome and Genoa for a year. He spoke and loved the Italian language and people. In the first years of his practice most of his patients were Italian immigrants in Chicago.

Today, the grandchildren of these first patients are doctors, lawyers, and business people.

I did not study medicine, but I love many of the things which he loved, and I think that he would be pleased to know that his eldest son, in some small way, shares in his love of learning, and in the Italian language, in other ancient languages, and in the peoples of Italy.

* * *

images

music from the dance floor
and the colored lights
and carefree talk
of youths and maids
away at an eastern college
were not for me
I somehow told myself
but why do these images
still remain
in the harbor of my mind
and return
at late hours
from the past
the images of another man
or rather, boy,
that once I was
on a weekend long ago
walking alone

Thomas Wilson Burrows II is a retired librarian devoting himself to studying Italian and English literature. He has lived in Downers Grove, IL, for 40 years. His dream is to be a hermit in Maine or Vermont, or to be a Carthusian. He and his wife, Kathy Lay-Burrows, have been married for 47 years.

Endnotes

1 For these two songs, see: https://www.youtube.com/watch?v=gooN9iu4Ebm ("Red River Valley"); and: https://www.youtube.com/watch?v=snJNTgwYUyo ("Across the Alley from the Alamo").

Personal Life Lessons: America in 2037—Getting There

Philip "Pete" Palmer

OK, I'll offer the events of 40 years or so ago that threatened—and delivered—professional and personal challenge (clouding of reputation), danger (financial wipeout), and the life lesson of how to get along on much less income while educating three kids in private schools and colleges. Some of our coping mechanisms included: sell home for 5X and buy another home (entirely adequate) for X; liquidate all but core pension-type assets; take on a seemingly less responsible and less glamorous job (which worked out great); gear down by half to a new lifestyle (use parents' suburban homes for vacations instead of country house in NYC orbit); shift from housewife and mother to outside work (tough on youngest, eight-year-old kid, but also turned out great); older kids take on summer and student jobs that look mundane on resumes but produce helpful income.

Background

Our firm, an investment partnership with six general partners, was sued by a United States executive agency. The agency had a strong prima facie case, triggered by sensational front page lead columns in *The New York Times* and *The Wall Street Journal*, and buttressed by law suits against us by major Wall Street banks. After a couple months of investigation, these private law suits were dropped. Industry professionals, who had bought the securities we had sold, realized we had done better legitimate (non-insider) investigation than anyone else. But the government hung in.

Following two years of discovery, I believe the executive agency also came to understand the real situation. They offered a consent agreement, with no penalties attached. That was: we would neither admit nor deny their definition of insider trading, but we would agree not to do it again! We refused to sign.

The Government wanted to de-legitimize the so-called "*Mosaic Rule*". That's the concept that a person who finally (not via inside information) pieces together a puzzle or mosaic that makes the mosaic intelligible—"aha, it's a horse, not an elephant"—must publicly disclose that information before buying or selling relevant securities based on that info.

What was our key insight, missed at first by others, that led to the wrath of other securities owners and the US government? When the then revolutionary "soft lens" was undergoing review by the FDA in the early 1970s, three of us had signed up, years ahead, in the US and abroad, as patients in Phase Two and Three Trials.

We learned from our doctors that many patients were sloppy in following the daily sterilization required for safe use. We were alert to the fact that, shortly after the acclaimed public introduction of soft lens, many patients began to experience dangerous eye infections. We took fast action, and retained big profits for our clients. The manufacturer appeared not to know as much as we did, at least in public.

A life and death problem for us was that the government persisted in deferring our pleas to go to trial, even within their in-house agency judiciary, let alone enter the civil court system. What was their motive? It was clear that they wanted to discredit the Mosaic Rule as a defense to accusations of insider trading. Every scoundrel trader tends to claim the Mosaic Rule as a first defense. (See Raj Rajaratnam, and others, on Wikipedia.) It takes a huge amount of prosecutorial time, effort and expense to prove that many Mosaic Rule defenses are bogus.

Outcomes

After two more years of sparring and wrangling, the agency signed a "Discontinued with Prejudice" order. Under the circumstances, that amounted to an admission of "Oops, we thought we had a case, but we got it wrong." Meanwhile, we had bled pension asset clients, bled personal and partnership financial assets in our defense, and merged our firm out of existence for a song.

Another Life Lesson

If I had been one of the ambitious enforcers, or an executive agency or congressional overseer of these proceedings,

> *I probably would have allowed this case to unfold just as it did. That's a scary part of the Administrative State.*

A Third Life Lesson

> *A law firm with an established practice with a government agency generally should not be expected to fight tooth & nail on behalf of a client against a policy that the government agency considers vital to its mission.*
>
> *At least not for a small client.*

The Aftermath

Over the past 35 years, our resilient family has enjoyed good health and good fortune in our great country.

> *America is a city on a hill, despite our many shortcomings.*

As for the Mosaic Rule, the agency charged another small firm under essentially the same circumstances. The individual involved forced and fought the issue to the Supreme Court and won! The Mosaic Rule now is established as a legitimate defense in defending against accusations of insider trading.

America in 2037—*Getting There*

Half the current job descriptions in America will barely exist in 20 years. The Digital Revolution will only accelerate from now to 2037. Scientific/technical advances will be exponentially greater than occurred from 1990 to now. Schumpeter's *Creative Destruction* will advance from gale to hurricane force.

Of course, vast numbers of new types of jobs and opportunities will open up. But the timing will not match the fearsome jobs losses and related social upheaval now about to happen.

So who knows how we'll navigate the storm? In addition to brilliant invention and entrepreneurship to replenish jobs, we'll need a resilient social structure.

For me that structure will include a wide regard for such writings as:

- ***The Golden Rule***.
- ***The United States Constitution*** (the rules by which elected governments govern), including the Ninth and Tenth Amendments, which define division of powers between the Federal and state governments, and the people.
- ***Kipling's "If"*** (If you can keep your head when all others about you . . . Are losing theirs and blaming it on you . . .).
- ***Washington's Farewell Address***.
- ***Yeats' "The Second Coming"*** (. . . The best lack all conviction, while the worst, Are full of passionate intensity . . .).

Daniel Moynihan posed our great dilemma:

> "*The central conservative truth is that it is culture, not politics that determines the success of a society.*
>
> *The central liberal truth is that politics can change culture, and save it from itself.*"

Philip "Pete" Palmer following graduation began three years of anti-submarine service in the North Atlantic, then followed by two years at Harvard Business School. In 1962 he, his wife, Louisa, and the first of their three children moved to Brooklyn. In 1989, after 27 years of widely (and wildly) varied investment banking and investment management experience, he and his primary partner founded Palmer Brennan LLC. Under that umbrella, they managed MidCap Partners LP and other related limited partnerships through 2007.

Pete writes: "In recent decades, I have participated, at times intensely, with Parks New York (oversight and protection of the smaller 1,185 of NYC's more than 1,200 public parks); Golden Seeds (early-stage venture capital); The Manhattan Institute for Policy Research (right-of-center think tank); and the Mountain Top Arboretum (25 acres of curated horticultural collections, plus 150 acres and growing of forests, meadows, swamps & streams) in Upstate New York."

Wisdom's Folly

A Brief Reflection on Life's Lessons Learned

Gottfried Brieger

Here, my prolix classmates, is my current understanding of immortality. It is indeed the written transcription of our thoughts, to be temporarily rendered in our native language, and sent to the archives of our class, the otherwise "Silent Generation". Using the currently fashionable language of science, our renderings may be considered quanta which can indeed extend into the distant future, but will unfortunately be subject to Heisenberg's Uncertainty Principle; that is, the more closely we examine the quanta for meaning, the more elusive they will be.

All this is prologue. The greatest harvest from my years at our alma mater was the introduction to the Age of Enlightenment. It was a real pleasure to learn that Messrs.' Hume, Voltaire, Rousseau, Diderot, and others actually supported my incipient conclusions regarding the operations of the human enterprise; that ignorance, prejudice, and overwrought emotions were rife, and that only reason would bring order to this chaos. Just as it did for many of my 18th-century predecessors, reason necessarily leads to the conclusion that there is no God, since many believers will not hesitate to kill one another on a large scale, a direct contradiction of God's supposed benign influence in the world. Accordingly, I have cultivated my own garden assiduously.

Now, 60 years later, I ruefully declare that I was naïve. Aggression, Power-seeking, Cupidity, and Competition are the true currency of the realm. Peace is a mere brief interlude between wars. Having taken a bite of the fateful apple, having enjoyed my cultural snacks, I must leave it to others to sing of mankind's great achievements. I have enjoyed them and am grateful to have had this opportunity.

As even the ruined temples and monuments of our proud predecessors are being ground down in yet other wars, I can only hope that millennia of evolution will produce a better species. Progress is not guaranteed, however. This is another 18th-century illusion.

Immigrant to Harvard

Standing on the deck of the SS *Marine Marlin*, a troop transport converted to emigration shipping in Bremerhaven, Germany, in 1946, I am contemplating the journey ahead to a distant land called America. I am 11 years old and traveling alone. I don't speak a word of English, and I know nothing about America, except that my father is there, living in a place called Lansdowne, which I pronounce LansDOVne. It is nighttime, I am worried—will I become seasick? I am determined that I will not become seasick. In the morning the ship sails.

I am definitely ready to travel somewhere. The two weeks in a quarantine camp are very dull. There isn't much to do, the food is terrible, and, of course, visitors are not allowed. Over the loudspeakers, as I am swinging on the swing set, I hear a melody, again and again. Years later, I learn that it was "Sentimental Journey".

My fellow emigrants are a polyglot mix, but principally Jewish. From them I hear for the first time and first-hand the horrors of the concentration camps. I am astounded. Actually, it is not the first time. I recall a playmate, who once threatened, for some minor offense, that I would wind up in a KZ, or concentration camp. I did not bother to ask what it was, as he mentioned it in a conspiratorial whisper. Later, during the voyage, a Jewish woman asks me repeatedly whether I really have a father waiting for me in America. I believe she was ready to take me under her wing, although I was not Jewish.

When we arrive in New York, the ship anchored on the Hudson overnight. In the morning, I am among the first to dash up to the deck. It is still dark, but along the shoreline, a string of lights moves along slowly. I ask a crew member what I am seeing. He laughs and says that it is a bunch of cars. It is four days before Christmas in New York, 1946.

The SS *Marine Marlin* docks, and the passengers are let off. I suddenly realize that I have not seen my father for seven years. I am not sure whether I will recognize him. I have no picture along. I wait aboard until most of the passengers and greeters are gone from the wharf. There stands a formally dressed man in a long grey coat and hat. Alone. I go to him with my tiny suitcase. There is something familiar about his eyes. Yes, this is my father, Dr. Heinrich Brieger. He had arrived on the *Queen Mary* in 1939.

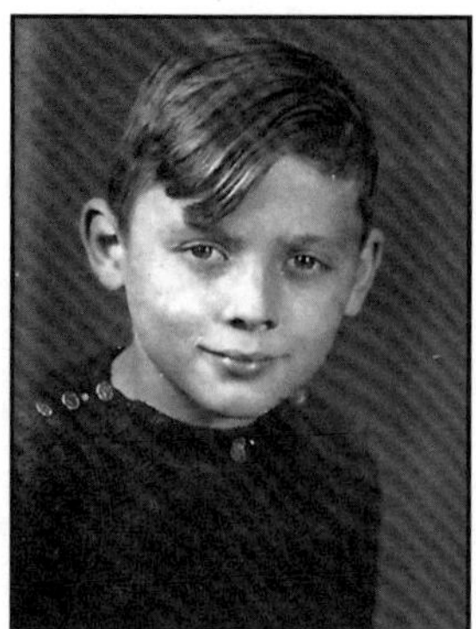

Figure 2.10.6.1 *My passport picture. If I remember correctly, I arrived in the traditional short pants and long woolen stockings.*

I was born on October 27, 1935, in Berlin, Germany. My father had been in the Federal Health Service, and had advanced to the provincial level in the region of Lower Silesia. However he had been arrested and held incommunicado for ten days, for alleged conspiracy with his landlord, a Social Democrat. The charges were eventually dropped, but he began to be serially demoted, winding up in Berlin, where he was informed that he could no longer be a physician. The reason—his parents were converted Jews. He was, however, allowed to run a clinical laboratory until 1939, when, belatedly, he realized that he needed to emigrate. There was also the problem of my four older siblings. They were secretly transported to England and became members of the *Kindertransport* operation.

My mother, Anna Frieda Dorothea von Klaeden, was not Jewish. However, the persecution and dissolution of the family brought about depression and eventually sufficient mental illness to prevent her from emigrating. She was hospitalized, and, except for occasional visits, I would never see her again. She was "euthanized" by the Nazis in 1944, along with thousands of other mentally ill patients. Nevertheless, she learned English and did what she could to obtain permission to emigrate. I was left in the care of a maiden aunt, Tante Editha, who loved me dearly.

The bombing of Berlin started in 1940, and the whining of the warning sirens rings forever in my ears. As the initial air raids were at night, it meant out of bed and into a basement bunk along with others, sometimes even twice in a night. The attendant whistling of bombs and their explosions shook the building. Fires erupted from the apartment building across the street, which was bombed more than once. Children like me found things to do in the morning after raids, however. Exploded bombs would leave behind shrapnel; bright, sharp, twisted bits of metal. Who could find the most, the biggest, the shiniest?

We needed to move to the country, and made our way to my great-aunt Sophie's home in Silesia. Strehlen was a country town of about 20,000 souls, with farm buildings still very common. My great-aunt Sophie's home had plenty for me to do. There was an ample garden to weed, fruits and berries, and each side of the house had a different type of grapes. Next door was a large machine shop for agricultural equipment, and a good friend of similar age. Across the way was a truck garden operation, where I gained my first job. My pay was a choice of a plant or money. I generally chose plants.

The war moved closer. Looking overhead one day, two planes approached each other. Suddenly there were shots, and one plane came down in smoke and flames. Luckily, the town was never bombed. Schools were, nevertheless, closed, and I missed three grades. However, there was home schooling, and I always was an eager reader, devouring whatever came into my hands. Thus, besides the Bible, I read Fennimore Cooper's *Leather Stocking Tales*.

The war was audibly approaching. Not only were the streets congested with military units and equipment moving through, the sounds of battle echoed like distant but approaching thunder.

The military was displaced by endless columns of refugees moving through with whatever means of transportation were available: horse and wagons, buggies, bicycles, rarely a truck or car.

Eventually we joined the throng, Great-aunt Sophie, Aunt Editha, and myself pulling a little wagon with meager belongings. Great-aunt Sophie was extremely thrifty and insisted on taking only the absolute minimum. A blanket I coveted had to be returned to the house. Our trek brought us to farms as we moved west, who eagerly offered us overnight shelter. Since they were afraid of the coming invaders, they offered us almost anything in the way of meals and provisions. Even long-hidden preserved hams came forth!

After a week on the road, we wound up in a health resort town on the Sudentenland border and were assigned a basement room in an abandoned villa. As the Russian front drew near, the remaining Nazis in town, as well as the police, departed in buses. Radio propaganda regarding forthcoming Russian brutalities were rife.

An eerie silence descended on the town, and then, with many shops closed or looted, there was a struggle for survival, which included scavenging, and I saw it as my role to contribute to the household.

Then the war was over suddenly, and the Russian troops were ready to enter the town. What would a nosy ten-year-old do? I noted that every house had a white sheet of surrender. Secretly, I went up to the second floor, and watched out of the window, hidden behind the curtains. Suddenly a Russian officer appeared, wearing enormous epaulets, but otherwise not heavily armed—on a bicycle! He cycled down the main street, grandstanding to the fearful residents! It was my first encounter with Russian soldiers. They were not significantly different from the German soldiers who had previously occupied the barracks in town.

Childhood play does not stop in wartime. Some friends and I took advantage of the lull between the absence of law and order and the arrival of the Russians to appropriate some helmets and swords from a closed local historical museum. Our play was shortly interrupted by the Russian arrival and the announcement that anyone with weapons would be summarily shot. Our illegal armaments were quickly sunk in the local river. Incredibly, the meandering mountain river in town became a long parade of discarded Nazi paraphernalia, flags, Hitler pictures, books, etc. I noted in passing that the Russians were fishing for trout with their automatic rifles.

After about a month, we were required to head home, again on foot. This time, we entered a devastated wasteland of burned-out buildings, abandoned tanks, and other military vehicles. Periodically, there was a wooden cross next to the road where a soldier had fallen and been hastily buried. Often, the fields and even the roads were mined, and we had to tread very carefully. Occasionally, a rest stop with soup and straw beds would be provided.

When we finally returned to Strehlen, the town was almost totally in ruins. The City Hall had been blown up, and the surrounding market square, so familiar to me, lay in ruins. Great-aunt Sophie's house was totally in ashes as well. Great-aunt Sophie was in tears, but, as a devout member of the Old Lutheran church, affirmed that even this had been God's will. We were able to move into the rectory of a church, which belonged to a close but absent relative, along with three other families.

Now the real struggle for survival began. The German currency no longer had any value, and the necessary goods could only be obtained by barter. The staples, such as bread, had to be gotten the hard way. As it was now summer, the harvest had been brought in. We were permitted to enter the fields and glean what grain heads had fallen by the wayside. We would thresh primitively, and then it was my assignment to take the hard-earned grain to the miller, who would turn it into flour in return for a portion of the grain. The next stop was the bakery, where an analogous trade was made for a loaf or two of bread in return for a share of the flour. Vegetables were eaten in the form of common weeds like dandelion and sheep sorrel. It was a hungry time for me, and I ate whatever seemed edible, such as the leftover roasted grain that had served as a coffee substitute. Eventually, it was necessary to beg.

Luckily, one of the other residents at the rectory was a former corset sales lady, whose customers were mostly rural. She took me along on foraging expeditions to her former clients, and after the requisite dialogue on corsets and conquests, she would pop the question for an extra potato or an egg. Then she would turn to me and ask the hostess whether the hungry boy might have something to eat. This usually resulted in a nice sandwich.

Normalcy never returned. Silesia was turned over to Poles who had been displaced by Russians on their frontier. One day, we were told to appear at the railroad station with one suitcase per person.

As we arrived at the depot, tables were set up for "inspection". Naturally, people had brought only those items that were deemed most useful. Many of these were now extracted and kept by the inspectors. I angrily tossed a few worthless coins from my pocket.

Standing in the railroad yard were a series of freight cars, our transportation. I recall writing in the air with a glowing stick from a small bonfire we had lit to keep warm. The railroad cars were lined with straw and very full. Our car had a caboose, however, about the size of a telephone booth. The aunties allowed me to sleep there instead, and off we went! The train traveled at a random pace, sometimes very slowly, so that one could walk beside it, other times, fast, or simply not moving at all. No one knew where we were headed. After a week of such travel, we wound up in former military barracks outside Delmenhorst near Bremen in northern Germany. There my uncle located us, and, before the month was over, I was in the quarantine camp near Bremerhaven.

From New York, it was on to Philadelphia, and Lansdowne, to Friends Select, a Quaker School, which kindly allowed me to spend the entire sixth grade learning English. After three years, transfer to Mt. Hermon Preparatory School, an ordeal for a highly independent and motivated student. I did my job. The school did its job. My next choice was Harvard, Princeton, or Yale. I chose Harvard because Mr. von Stade did not present me with a four-year curriculum in chemistry, my chosen field of study, whereas the Princeton and Yale representatives did. In retrospect, Oberlin would have suited me better, but I had never heard of it then. Thus I became a member of the Class!

Gottfried Brieger, now Professor Emeritus after 50 years of teaching (1963–2013) at Oakland University in Rochester, MI, was born in Berlin, Germany, and emigrated to America after World War II. Following graduation from Harvard College in 1957 with a BA in Chemistry, he received his PhD in Organic Chemistry from the University of Wisconsin in 1961. He and his wife, Ingetraud v. Rennenkampff, are the parents of two children.

In his concise outline of his life, he arranged the parts he played as follows, although he advises they are not necessarily in strict chronological order.

> Quasi-orphan in WWII, immigrant, prep school student, summer biker, Harvard student, resort handyman, bellboy, farmer, graduate student, husband, father, junior professor, professor, chemical researcher, restaurateur, political activist, campus politician, prison counselor, immigrant guide, Quaker, hospital board member, genealogist, archaeologist, grandfather, world traveler, consultant, clinical lab director, poet, editor, hobbyist, anti-race discrimination activist.

Should anyone want a more extensive sketch, he has published one entitled *My Curious Life* (2015), which can be found in the archives of the Signet Society.

Figure 2.10.6.2 *Nuremberg in Ruins, 1945*

Overcoming Discrimination

My Lifetime of Pride and Prejudice before, during, and after Harvard

Richard Allen Williams

I was reflecting recently on my parents and how my experiences as a well-educated, somewhat privileged member of the black medical community and intelligentsia who had done fairly well in life as an accomplished doctor, author, musician, and bon vivant, compared with their lives as dirt-poor, relatively uneducated, unskilled residents of the ghetto who had no time for recreational activities outside of raising eight children, of whom I was the youngest. Was I truly better off than they were? Indeed, was I even *better* than they were, by comparison?

Those questions are at the core of my deliberations as I go about writing this essay about my life experiences relative to attending Harvard—before, during, and after matriculating at and graduating from what is arguably the world's best university. So prior to delving into the particulars of my successes and accomplishments, I need to explain some things about my background that most of my colleagues in the Class of 1957 may not be familiar with, since most of them had not rubbed elbows with folks from the ghetto. I will try to describe the impact that prejudice had on me and how it modified the pride that I was eventually able to feel.

The Background

I was jolted into realizing what it meant to be a poor black male in America at the tender age of 12, when a white man driving a car deliberately ran me off the road as I was riding my bike in my hometown of Wilmington, DE. Up to that time, I was oblivious to the racial discrimination and segregation that existed in this lazy mid-sized industrial town located midway between Philadelphia and Baltimore. It didn't matter to me that I was already being programmed for a certain educational fate in which I was to attend all-black schools from K through 12 with almost no contact with whites except in athletic contests or musical events, and that I was expected to graduate and take some type of menial job or perhaps be lucky enough to get into a small black college in the South where my father came from. I was doing very well in my studies despite having to use second-hand books and other materials that were handed down from the white schools.

My teachers recognized some academic talent in me, and they gave me extra instruction which would lead to my getting almost perfect scores on the standardized tests and eventually on the College Boards. It didn't matter that much to me that I couldn't go to the white movie theaters or eat in the restaurants or at the lunch counters in the stores downtown. Although I didn't understand at that time why my mother would not allow me to try on caps, shoes, and other clothes in those stores, it really didn't disturb me. I was a happy-go-lucky little colored kid who was just cruising through life without a care in the world. That is, until that white man ran me off the road and caused me to fall and injure my head, after which he laughed and called me some racial epithets as he drove away.

To add insult to injury quite literally, when I got back on my bike and rode to the local police station to report the incident and turn in the driver's license plate number, I was actually attacked by the white desk sergeant for having the nerve to accuse a white person of committing an offense against a black person. In fact, he physically threw me out of the police station, and again I heard those racial epithets.

This is when I had an epiphany: for the first time in my life, I saw the ugly face of prejudice and realized that there was a racial divide between blacks and whites, with blacks being in a powerless position. Later I would learn of the *Dred Scott decision* of the US Supreme Court, in which it was declared by Chief Justice Roger Taney in 1847 that a black man amounted to only three-fifths of a white man and therefore had no rights that a white person was bound to respect. That decision from long ago was what allowed the white policeman to deny me the right to lodge a complaint against a white person; it established a culture of prejudice, lack of respect, and justification of bias against blacks which still resounds to this day.

It also helped me to understand that this societal attitude underlies the police violence and use of force against black males that we have witnessed so much in this country. It is not seen in other countries because they have not had the racist history that we have had in the

United States. I could have been the Treyvon Martin or Michael Brown of my day but for the grace of God.

Realizing the powerless position that Negroes occupied, the great African American educator and orator Booker T. Washington delivered an impassioned speech at the Cotton States and International Exposition in Atlanta, Georgia in 1895 imploring his people to go slow, lay low, and be subservient and submissive rather than aggressive and progressive. It was called the *Atlanta Compromise*, and I believe that Mr. Washington intended it to be protective of the freed slaves who were possibly placing themselves in harm's way by attempting to press for full equality in all things.

The trend of prejudice and discrimination was further extended in 1896 by another US Supreme Court decision called *Plessy v. Ferguson* in which it was declared that separate public facilities and educational arrangements were allowable as long as they were equal (which of course they never were). So it should be evident that there was a direct line of prejudice stretching from the Dred Scott decision of 1847 to the Atlanta Compromise of 1895, to the Plessy decision in 1896 to what happened to me at that police station.

Everything was connected. Prejudice, intolerance and bigotry had become implanted within our social fabric, and this is what motivated me to become a lifelong combatant against these evils. As I entered Harvard a few years after suffering my incident and other indignities, I was already conditioned by the impact of racial prejudice on me for whatever battles that lay ahead, and I prepared myself to deal with this invisible adversary while I buried myself in my pre-med studies. I doubt that many of my classmates were burdened by such a distraction.

Before going forward about my experiences, I will describe what my parents and their forebears endured, so that we can compare their lives with mine.

My father was born in rural Georgia into a family of ex-slaves who were brought to America from Africa through the Middle Passage on slave ships. After slavery was ended by the *Emancipation Proclamation* in 1863, his family was able to acquire some land and property in Georgia in the late 19th century. When he was a child around the turn of the 20th century, they were threatened by night riders of the Ku Klux Klan for having the audacity of being landholders, and were forced to leave all of their property and possessions and travel north to avoid being lynched. They decided to keep going until they crossed the Mason-Dixon Line that divides North and South, and they stopped in Delaware, the first state across this mythical line, and settled there.

Meanwhile, my mother was growing up in rural Maryland where her father owned a farm. She and her sisters occasionally traveled to Wilmington, DE, to socialize at dances and gatherings, and that is where she met and eventually married my father. They had eight children, of which I was the last, and they took menial jobs to support us. There was no money to pay for medical care, and all of the children were delivered by midwives at home.

Our house in the ghetto was what was called a "shotgun house", meaning that it was one of a series of row houses where you could stand at the front door and fire a shotgun straight through the back door. That was the way they were made. The toilet was outside, which was pretty rough to use in the winter. There were no supermarkets, gas stations, or other conveniences or accommodations in the neighborhood, and the nearest school was a two-mile walk away, which was also very difficult to manage in winter. Almost no one had a car, but there was bus and trolley service if you could pay the fare. There always was a strong police presence

The cops were on every corner or were constantly driving through or walking their beats, ostensibly to protect us. However, we knew better: they were there to harass us, to make sure that we knew who was in charge, and to continue to stress their dominance. They frequently arrested young men just for gathering on the street corner on a hot summer evening for what they called *loitering*. I believe that it was planned to keep us constantly off balance and therefore unable to commit any crimes. I always wondered why they were trying to keep us from stealing, when there was really nothing of any value to steal where we lived.

My mother was the best cook in the neighborhood, and she made some extra money to support us by selling food from out of our home. Later, my father opened a small store which was an early version of the 7/11 convenience stores, and I was allowed to run it after school and on weekends. I loved doing this because it gave me a sense of entrepreneurship and a feeling of ownership. The other kids in the area looked up to me because we owned "Mildred's Confectionary Store." That was my father's way of teaching me business methods. None of my siblings were interested, so I had complete freedom to operate this little store at the age of 14.

Although he was not able to complete high school, my father was very intelligent and was recognized as the "brains" in the neighborhood. Whenever someone had legal, business, or personal troubles, they consulted Walter Sinclair Williams, or "Saint Clair", as he was called. He would even go to court with some of our black residents, acting as a sort of grass-roots *amicus curiae* for them. He had an extensive collection of law, medical, and history books as well as many classics of literature which I used to read in the private sanctuary of his bedroom. He gave me my first exposure to black history, which definitely influenced my outlook on the world from adolescence forward.

My mother, on the other hand, was recognized as the community expert on the subjects of beauty, health, fashion, food, and dealing with men. All of the women and young girls came to her for advice. She loved going to occasional events with the higher class black women, who were astounded by what she knew about life and they did not. During the Great Depression she devised unique ways of feeding and clothing us, especially when my father was out of work.

When I was at Harvard, she started a company called Mildred's Employment Agency, in which she focused on providing domestic workers for the very wealthy whites of Wilmington including the DuPonts, Carpenters, and others, who just loved "Millie". If they obtained a worker through my mother, they knew they could trust that person. Her little business was very successful and was eventually taken over by two of my sisters. So you may say that we capitalized on the grave unemployment situation by dealing in the employment field, and we were proud of helping a lot of people find some work and to feed themselves. Everyone in the neighborhood knew that Mildred Williams would get you a job if you wanted one. The important lesson here is how my parents used their creativity to survive and to help others to do so as well, even though society treated us in a discriminatory way.

Going to Harvard

I will bet that not many of my Harvard classmates entered to engagement with Harvard in the rather unusual way that I did.

As I continued to make excellent progress at Howard High School, thanks to my dedicated teachers, I came to the attention of some members of the local Harvard Club of Delaware who were looking to find a black student to become the first of his race to attend Harvard College from our state. And so, at the age of 15, I was placed under a sort of surveillance by representatives of the Harvard Club, as I was to find out later. One gentleman in particular, Dr. A. Judson Wells, a chemist with the DuPont Company, checked me out at my track meets, band concerts, performances in plays, and other public appearances. Eventually, he came up to me at a track meet, introduced himself, and told me that Harvard was interested in me. However, he made no promises or commitments to indicate that I was going to be selected by Harvard, nor did I ask for any.

When I was 16, I did very well on the College Boards, and based on the excellent scores that I achieved and a 4.0 GPA, I was admitted to several elite schools, including Harvard. Along with admission came a full scholarship. I became a sort of celebrity in the neighborhood and also a curiosity in the larger community, because I was going to be the first Negro student from the state of Delaware admitted to this great school in its illustrious history. I was even featured on the front page of the Wilmington, Delaware Evening Journal newspaper, along with Wilmington High School graduate Bob McGinnis who was also admitted to the Harvard Class of 1957 as the only other student recruited by the Harvard Club.

When I reached the campus in September 1953, I received a warm welcome from classmates, one of whom was the late Judge Gordon Martin, Jr., who became a lawyer with the US Justice Department and was the leader in the Federal lawsuit *US Justice Department v. Lyden* in Mississippi in 1961 which opened up voter registration for blacks in that state and ultimately helped to get the Voting Rights Act of 1965 passed. His book, *Count Them One by One,* is a classic in the annals of civil rights literature. I was also welcomed by Dean of Students John Usher Munro, who was a close friend of my mentor Jud Wells, and who later left Harvard to become a civil rights activist in the South.

I checked into my room in Mathews Hall 43 and immediately began to experience living in a dorm with all-white classmates except for Dick Wharton of Boston, another black student who became one of my teammates on the cross country and track teams and a lifelong friend (he was intimidating to me not only because of his athletic prowess and physical stature but also because he was fluent in Latin and German!). My two white roommates were as uncomfortable initially as I was, because neither of us had ever been as close as this to a person of the other race, and now we were sleeping in the same room. I soon met some African American upperclass students, including Paul Wright, Tom Wilson, Ken Simmons, Nolan Williams, Clifford Alexander, and Paul Brown, and also more of the black students in my class such as Bob Haygood, Vaughn Payne, Charles Martin, and Milt Campbell.

Of course, Harvard was not co-ed at that time, although Radcliffe had some black students including Lena Horne's daughter, Gail Horne Jones, and Mary Bunton, who was a talented violinist. (We found out about the Cliffies through the *Confy Guide*, which was a little pictorial journal that contained descriptions—and ratings—of the ladies of Radcliffe.)

The black students congregated occasionally in Tom Wilson's suite at Adams House, where freshman were given information about life at Harvard that was a sort of survival guide. We were told what to avoid, like the racist defrocked priest Father Feeny, whose church was situated right across the street from Adams House, and whose followers were known to attack black students. (I recall an incident in which this group picketed Ethiopian Emperor Haile Selassie as he and President Pusey walked across Harvard Yard during the Emperor's visit.) Tom's place was where you went to find out about the latest things in jazz and about the social scene. That's how I discovered 558 Mass Ave., a gathering place in Boston for black collegians. I met my lifetime companion GiGi at one of the Saturday night dances held there. (She will be with me at the 60th Reunion.)

I also learned about Harvard's past history of racism, including the fact that several of the past presidents had been slaveholders (Wadsworth, Mather, Holyoke), and that a cross had been burned in front of the black student residence where Max Bond and others were forced to live until full integration occurred around 1950. The specter of racism connected to slavery still hangs over the University and was recently brought back to our conscious minds and consciences when there was debate about the crest of Harvard Law School which was created as an honor to a Mr. Royall, who donated the money in the 18th century that was used to build that part of Harvard. His fortune was amassed from slave labor, and just last year, the Harvard Corporation wisely voted to replace the crest with another that was more representative of VERITAS!

I became immersed in my studies and at the end of the first semester, I was on the Dean's List. This enabled me to keep my Harvard Club scholarship, and when I visited the Club at the semester break, Jud Wells and his colleagues were very proud that their "Experiment" was going so well. They were not only impressed with my grades, but also with the fact that I was participating in the social life on campus. My main extra-curricular activity was band, which was very strenuous but also gave me great pleasure. One racial incident that occurred was when we were marching through the Princeton campus, and some jerk poured a waste basket full of ink on me as we marched under his dorm window. He had targeted me, the only black person in the band. My fellow bandies ran up to his room, pulled him out, and beat the shit out of him.

As time went on, I had more and more opportunities to hone my jazz trumpet-playing skills by playing in a quartet with Walter Chapin on piano, Bob Haygood on bass, and Dick Cottle on drums. Wally Sisson and I occasionally played together, too. The group played gigs on weekends at smokers and dances on campus and at Boston University and other schools. I also sat in on jam sessions at Wally's Paradise, Morley's, the Jazz Workshop, the Stables on Huntington Ave, and Paul's Mall.

Figure 2.11.1.1 *Jazz trumpeter and bandleader Al Williams at Birdland*

It was at the Stables where I met Miles Davis, the famous trumpet player that some people called "The Prince of Darkness". I had been sent there on assignment by the Harvard New Jazz Society to try to convince him to come to our campus to perform at Sanders Theatre while he was in the area. This tactic had worked before, and we had been successful in soliciting groups like the Modern Jazz Quartet. Miles eventually did come to Harvard, and I stayed in touch with him over the years, keeping our friendship alive well past my graduation from medical school and into my years of practicing Cardiology at UCLA when I provided occasional medical care to him as well as other musicians like drummer Art Blakey. I was often a guest of Miles and his wife, Cicely Tyson, at his concerts and at dinners and public appearances.

As a freshman, I petitioned to get into world-famous psychologist B.F. Skinner's course on Experimental Psychology, which was designed for upperclassmen. I had felt challenged by a statement made by Professor Pitirim Sorokin that Negroes had no intellectual abilities, and that the black race had never accomplished anything except for developing a few boxing champions and musicians. Skinner's course had a reputation of being very difficult, but I handled it well and aced it, which led Professor Skinner to summon me to his office in the catacombs of Memorial Hall. So I went there among all the pigeons and rats to meet the great man, who wanted to know how a little black kid from the ghetto was able to do so well in his vaunted course. I assured him that I didn't cheat, and that my achievement was due simply to hard work and my determination to show Sorokin and others that blacks could be great scholars if given a chance.

During my freshman year, it seemed that there was always some faculty member who was interested in finding out more about me. One was Professor Gordon Allport, whose blockbuster book, *The Nature of Prejudice*, had a huge impact on me, and was to become an important reference used by the United States Supreme Court in their unanimous 9–0 decision against segregated schools in the *Brown v. Board of Education* case in 1954.

Another notable academic experience occurred as a result of my taking a graduate-level class at the Harvard-affiliated Massachusetts Mental Health Center in my junior year. The title of my honors thesis that grew out of this course was "*Alcohol and d-lysergic acid Diethylamide Tartrate (LSD-25): a Comparison and Method of Classification of their Effects upon Psychic Processes and Interpersonal Relations*". My senior tutor was—you guessed it—Dr. Timothy Leary, who later became infamous for his use of LSD, or acid, as it came to be called, to influence students on the Harvard campus and elsewhere in the late '50s and into the '60s to get high and to "*turn on, tune in, and drop out*". Fortunately, he did not convince me to do so. He was eventually dismissed from the Harvard faculty and went on to become the leader of the psychedelic drug culture during the *Beat Generation.*

I faced a number of other situations involving prejudice as I continued through Harvard, but they did not derail my ambition to complete my studies. I lived at Kirkland House, which was a fairly liberal place, but I had few close friends. Most of my white classmates seemed to be more comfortable hanging out with guys of their own race, and there was no chance for me to be accepted into one of the tony eating clubs. Meal times were very lonely times, and I ate alone more often than not, although I was considered a popular guy. I didn't get invited to go to beer busts or to watering holes like Cronin's, and I almost never went to any private parties.

During my junior year I was interviewed by Marya Mannes, the noted journalist from *The Reporter* magazine, who came to Cambridge specifically to see me and to find out how the "Experiment" was going. In her subsequent article she described me as being relaxed and doing well as a black undergraduate surrounded by a sea of whiteness, and stated that I had adjusted adequately to what was initially an uncomfortable situation. In other words, I had been assimilated into the white Harvard culture. She noted that I had overcome a number of obstacles and had become very accepted by my Caucasian schoolmates, but seemed to be relatively isolated, and not by my own choice.

What she didn't appreciate was that I had become an independent, strong black man who was confident of his own identity and was satisfied with the skin that I was in. I had managed to become a part of Harvard and to love my *alma mater* without being swallowed up and brain-washed by its overwhelming influence.

Life after Harvard

I graduated from Harvard with honors in 1957, and went on to medical school at the SUNY Downstate, internship at UC San Francisco, Internal Medicine residency at USC, and Cardiology Fellowship at Brigham and Women's Hospital and Harvard Medical School, where I subsequently joined the faculty under the great Dr. George Widmer

Thorn. He encouraged me to follow my interest in health problems of blacks by writing my first of nine books, the 900-page *Textbook of Black-Related Diseases*, which was published by McGraw-Hill Book Company in 1975. It was only the second medical textbook ever published by an African American: Dr. William A. Hinton, a professor at Harvard Medical School, was the first.

My book was significant in that for the first time it called attention to differences in the disease process and in the expression of illness between blacks and whites. This has led to the recognition that although we are all one species, there are special characteristics in medical conditions that run along racial and ethnic lines, and doctors must first consider the race and ethnicity of the patient, which may have important diagnostic and therapeutic implications. As is sometimes stated, *one size does not fit all.*

While I was in my Cardiology training at Harvard Medical School, I noted that there were no other black interns, residents, or fellows in any of the 20 hospitals under its control, and further research revealed that there had never been any before me. I also found out that the first three black students admitted to Harvard Medical School in 1868 were expelled after one year of matriculation by Dean Oliver Wendell Holmes on the grounds that they were incompatible with the white students. While they were there, they had been forced to sit in a sequestered area of the lecture hall during classes which segregated them from their Caucasian classmates.

All of this and the assassination of Dr. Martin Luther King, Jr., the same year impelled me to start an action in 1968 to recruit black students and postgraduate trainees, and I became basically a civil rights activist attempting to achieve equity and justice for blacks in the Harvard hospital system and, ultimately, at Tufts and Boston University as well. Along the way, I founded the Central Recruitment Council of Boston Hospitals, which seamlessly and dramatically increased the level of diversity over the next few years, thanks to the concurrence and cooperation of the late Dean Robert Ebert.

My efforts were rewarded when I was awarded a Lifetime Achievement Award in a special testimonial ceremony at Harvard Medical School on April 23, 2004. This was one of the highest points of my life, and I must say that pride had indeed trumped prejudice.

I also received the key to the city from the Mayor of my hometown of Wilmington, DE, in 2016; this is another distinction of which I am proud. (I wish that abusive policeman from long ago could have been there to witness this.)

Another organization that I founded is the Association of Black Cardiologists, which I started in 1974 to address inequities in cardiovascular care between blacks and whites. One of the things that stimulated me to form this organization was the fact that blacks were being misunderstood by whites in medicine, and there were demeaning publications in peer-reviewed medical journals stating that black patients did not experience chest pain as whites did because blacks lack the intellectual capacity to perceive pain!

Conclusion

At this point, as we prepare to celebrate the 60th anniversary of our graduation from Harvard, I can look back on my time there with the conviction that I extracted a great deal from my beloved school that helped me to become the person that I am today.

In the same sense, I believe that I added something of value to Harvard by making it realize that black students not only deserve the opportunity to study there, but also that we have to be respected for our special characteristics and talents.

In his book, *The Philadelphia Negro* (1899), the eminent Harvard alumnus W.E.B. DuBois was the first to study a black community in the United States, and his later essay, "The Talented Tenth" in the book *The Negro Problem* (1903), focused on a mythical subset of blacks whom he felt should to be selected for classic training as an elite cadre of blacks to be leaders in our society.

DuBois's approach was in direct contrast to the recommendation enunciated by Booker T. Washington in the *Atlanta Compromise* that blacks should be obsequious and supportive of and submissive to whites in all respects rather than being confrontational and insistent on those inalienable rights and the pursuit of life, liberty, and happiness guaranteed in the Constitution.

I may have been an unknowing member of this group. I can point to my career and the numerous accomplishments that have accrued to my credit with the feeling that I have disproved Professor Pitirim Sorokin's pronouncements about the intellectual deficiencies of blacks. I often say that I now have more yesterdays than tomorrows, and that it is important for me not to rest on my laurels but to continue to push for more positive change in the limited time that I have left.

There is still a great deal of prejudice in this country, and the reset of the government on November 8, 2016, does not auger well for improving the situation. From my position as the 117th president of the National Medical Association, the world's largest (50,000 adherents) and oldest (established 1895) medical organization dedicated to improving health care delivery for people of color, I pledge to continue fighting for justice and equity in health care delivery, and to be a pit bull in this bully pulpit, as it were. I intend to follow the splendid tradition set by President Barack Obama when he signed the *Affordable Care Act* into law on March 23, 2010. This historic legislation is in jeopardy of being repealed by the new administration, which will risk the lives and health of over 20 million people who depend on the health care coverage that it provides.

Future generations will look back on this time to determine if being black in America has continued to be a condition that incites prejudice, as it did for me and my parents, who in the final analysis may be said to have been better than I was because they survived so many more abuses than I did and emerged from their experiences with the utmost dignity. They are my heroes, and whatever I am is completely attributable to their example.

I am also confident that although there still is ill will in the world, as Dr. King stated, the arc of the universe is long, and it eventually curves toward justice. Keeping this in mind, I firmly believe that we shall overcome.

Figure 2.11.1.2 *Dr. Richard Allen Williams with President Barack Obama, 2007*

Richard Allen Williams, MD, FACC, FAHA, FACP, current President of the National Medical Association, is Clinical Professor of Medicine at UCLA School of Medicine and President/CEO of Minority Health Institute, Inc., in Los Angeles. A graduate of State University of New York Downstate Medical Center, he trained in Internal Medicine at UC San Francisco and Los Angeles County-USC Medical Center, and in Cardiology at Harvard Medical School (HMS) and Boston's Brigham & Women's Hospital. While at HMS he successfully initiated the first recruitment of minority medical trainees to Boston hospitals. Following specialty training he became Assistant Medical Director at Dr. Martin Luther King, Jr. Hospital in the Watts neighborhood of Los Angeles, CA. Recruited to West Los Angeles VA Hospital as Chief of the Heart Station and Coronary Care Unit, he rose to Chief of Cardiology.

A founder in 1974 and former president of the Association of Black Cardiologists (ABC), he is also a founding Board member and former Chair of the Institute for the Advancement of Multicultural and Minority Medicine.

Author of *Textbook of Black-related Diseases* (McGraw-Hill, 1975), his latest book is *Blacks in Medicine: Clinical, Demographic, and Socioeconomic Correlations* (Springer, 2017).

His expertise has been recognized by invitations to serve as Visiting Professor at Harvard, Yale, Stanford, University of North Carolina, and University of the West Indies in Jamaica.

I have a dream
that
my four children
will one day
live in a nation
where
they will not be judged
by the color
of their skin
but the content
of their character.

Figure 2.11.1.3 *Dr. Martin Luther King, Jr.*

An excerpt from his "I Have a Dream" speech at the Lincoln Memorial, Washington, DC, on August 28, 1963, on the occasion of the March on Washington for Jobs and Freedom.

Photograph by Julian Wasser, Time Life Pictures/Getty Images, reprinted with permission

The Silent Generation

Are You Now or Have You Ever Been? Not All of Us Were Silent

Emile Chungtien Chi

The Communist

My father Ch'ao-ting Chi (Ji Chaoding) 1904–1963 was a Communist (party member); my mother Harriet Levine Chi 1906–1996 was a Communist (true believer); so I am a double red diaper baby. I was not actually aware of this until I was 11. My father graduated from Tsinghua (Qinghua) University, Beijing, in 1924. At that time Tsinghua was the official prep school for the Boxer Indemnity Scholarship program.[1] While at Tsinghua, influenced by the May 4th Movement,[2] he became socially and politically aware and was an active left wing student leader, viewing China's economic and political problems as largely due to Western Imperialism. He received his BA from the University of Chicago in 1926. While at Chicago he became increasingly radicalized and joined the Anti Imperialist League and the Communist Party which, at that time, was allied with the Kuomintang (Nationalist Party) with the dual goals of modernizing China and freeing it from imperialism.

He started law school at Chicago, but finding real estate law too feudal, switched to economics at Columbia, where he received his PhD. While at Columbia, my father supplemented his Boxer scholarship by acting, starring in *Roar China*[3,4] on Broadway in 1930.

My parents met in 1928 while my father was on his way to the 6th Congress of the Comintern[5] (Communist International) in Moscow and my mother on her way to visit friends in Paris. They met on board the *Carinthia* en route from New York, and considered themselves married when the ship reached Le Havre. They did not in fact marry until their attorney (also a Communist) told them that as a legal, documented, but red alien with a bastard child on the way (me), he was likely to be deported unless married to an American citizen. In 1940 my father publicly renounced his belief in communism and returned to China as "confidential secretary" to H. H. Kung, a banker and brother-in-law of Chiang Kai-shek, head of the Nationalist Government. He served the Nationalist government in the Ministry of Finance under Finance Minister Kung, scion of a Shansi province banking family, and also governor of the Central Bank of China. My grandfather, Chi Kungchuan was Minister of Education in Shansi. These were two prominent Shansi families; the sons were automatically connected, and my father called H. H. Kung "uncle". In Chinese tradition this demonstrates a strong family bond. One's father's best friend is always one's uncle. In 1944 when I was nine, Kung fell ill and was hospitalized in New York. My father took me along on a visit. He rehearsed me to say: "I hope that you get well very soon, Uncle Kung." He was furious when I failed him in this simple task. He demanded to know why. "He looks much too mean and nasty to be my uncle" was my limp but honest reply.

I hardly knew that my disobeying my father could have cost him his cover and his career. In fact, he was still a Communist, working under Zhou Enlai's orders for Kung. (From 1949 until his death in 1976, Zhou was Premier of the People's Republic of China). Kung eventually discovered that his confidential secretary was a Communist agent, but fearing the consequences to himself, did not expose my father. Quite the opposite, in 1948 he sent my father to Peiping (Beijing) to serve as economic advisor to Fu Tsoyi,[6] commander of the Nationalist Army defending the city against the coming Communist invasion. My father's assignment was to control the hyper-inflation of the Yuan. (In order to fly to Peiping from Shanghai, my father ordered the cargo handlers to dump a crate of worthless currency from the full plane). Instead he served as negotiator between Zhou and Fu, travelling secretly during the night to meet with Zhou, then encamped outside the city wall; then meeting with Fu in the Chi family compound in Peiping. A visit to my grandfather was Fu's cover for the sessions.

The result was Fu's peaceful surrender of his Nationalist troops, saving thousands of lives. Fu's reward was his appointment as deputy chairman of the Chinese People's Consultative Conference, and Minister of Water Management in the newly constituted Peoples' Republic of China.

The Red Diapers

My partner and spouse of 57 years, Barrie Alix Chi, née Kleinman, is also a red diaper baby. Her godfather and mother's employer at

International Publishers, Alexander Trachtenberg,[7] was convicted in 1953 for violating the Alien Registration Act of 1940 (Smith Act), which made it illegal to advocate the violent overthrow of the US Government.[8] He was imprisoned for three months, after which his conviction was overturned due to witness perjury. A second conviction in 1956 was voided by the US Circuit Court of Appeals in 1958.

So what happened to our parents' dream? What happened after the Liberation of China in 1949 by the Communists has little resemblance to what Karl Marx intended. My parents' communism (and my lifelong belief in their cause) is hardly what we find in China (or anywhere else today). "Socialism with Chinese characteristics"[9], in fact capitalism with Chinese characteristics, is far from what they dreamed of. "*Jeder nach seinen Fähigkeiten, jedem nach seinen Bedürfnissen.*" (From each according to his ability. To each according to his needs.)[10] is what they were after.

I do not know how to achieve their dream, but I did try political activism for a while. At Stuyvesant High School, I joined the Labor Youth League, a Communist front organization.[11] As a freshman, in 1953 I joined and chaired the underground Harvard chapter of the LYL.

Harvard

I decided on Harvard after visiting my uncle Chi Chao-chu '52[12] in Eliot House. Harvard impressed me more than the many colleges I visited, as a place when there is room for every idea and shade of thought. Chao, as his classmates and friends called him, is not exactly a red diaper baby; not his father, but his sibling, my father, being the diaper supplier. Ch'ao left Harvard after sophomore year, became a Communist and joined China's revolution. He was a translator at the truce talks which ended the Korean War, China's ambassador to the U.K. and under secretary general of the U.N. He is the first generation in our family to bask on the banks of the Charles. Daughter Carlin Li-an Chi '91[12] is the third (and hopefully counting).

After sophomore year, I dropped out of Harvard for two years, returning to graduate with the class of 1960. During this period, my brother and I met my father in Paris in 1956—we had not seen him in nine years. A Chinese Communist leader could not travel to the United States, and US passports were stamped with "Not valid for travel to Communist-controlled portions of China . . ." When we were together, I told him of my plans to follow his example; to work for revolution in the United States. His response: absolutely not. You will never be trusted by either side. China will not fully trust you because you are a native-born United States citizen; America will not fully trust you because you are the son of a Chinese Communist. Become a scientist and work for humanity as a college professor. He was right. This time I did obey.

We Were Not, and Are Not, *Silent*

For political action, I joined the Harvard Society for Minority Rights (HSMR), together with a few other red diaper class of '57 freshmen.[14] In 1955 we sponsored a concert by Pete Seeger '40, who had been "blacklisted"and was unable to perform in his usual venues.[15]

Before giving us a permit to use a Harvard facility, Dean John U. Monro '34 called me into his office and demanded assurance that we were not packing the hall with union members. In fact, we sold it out, mostly to Harvard and Radcliffe students.

Before our 25th Reunion in 1982, the same group of classmates got together again and with our Radcliffe radical colleagues, helped to found HRAAA, Harvard Radcliffe Alumni Against Apartheid.[16] We supported Bishop Desmond Tutu who won election to the Board of Overseers in 1989.[17]

For our 50th Reunion, we assembled once more to sponsor the forum: *Global Warming/Climate Change: Our Issue, Our Legacy*, and again, we filled the room, Science Center D.

So are we indeed the Silent Generation?

Not all of us, I argue. Has our political action had an effect? Yes, I argue. Helping to break the blacklist did. Helping to elect Desmond Tutu a Harvard Overseer did. Increasing awareness of climate change did.

At age 80-plus, is there anything we can do now?

I think so. Do what we can, while we still can, to support Thomas Jefferson's belief:

> "*We hold these truths to be self-evident, that all men are created equal, that they are endowed by their Creator with certain unalienable Rights, that among these are Life, Liberty and the pursuit of Happiness.*"[18]

And apply this to all people.

Figure 2.12.1.1 *The Chi family in Shanghai, 1947.*
L to R: *Carl Chungming Chi (brother), Ch'ao-ting Chi (father), Emile Chungtien Chi (author), and Harriet Levine Chi (mother)*

Emile Chungtien Chi did graduate work in mathematics at Harvard and Columbia, taught math at NYU for three years and then Computer Science at CSI/CUNY since 1970. When he retired in 2016, he went back to work the next day as part-time emeritus professor of Computer Science at the College of Staten Island, City University of NY at a salary less than his commuting cost from Novato, CA.

He writes, "I am slowly switching back to photography, my first and now second career. At Harvard I was on the photo board of *The Crimson* but, despite some commercial success, realized that photography was not really a career for me.

In 1978–79 my spouse, Barrie A. Chi, and I were the first American professors to teach at Tsinghua, Beijing, after the 1949 revolution. Our three daughters all attended local primary schools and became fluent in Chinese, while Barrie and I struggled with it. I have also been visiting professor at Shanghai University, and both of us at Shanghai Open University.

I have found teaching and mentoring my students far more fulfilling than research, which recently has been in hierarchical structures of management and assessment."

Endnotes

1 MIT Drupal Cloud https://earlychinesemit.mit.edu/three-waves/boxer-indemnity-scholarship-program

2 *Encyclopedia Britannica* https://www.britannica.com/event/May-Fourth-Movement

3 IBDB *Roar China* https://www.ibdb.com/broadway-production/roar-china-11246

4 *Biographical Dictionary of Republican China*, Vol. 1, Howard L Boorman, Columbia Univ. Press, 1968

5 Marxists Internet Archive https://www.marxists.org/history/international/comintern/

6 *The New York Times* April 25, 1974 http://www.nytimes.com/1974/04/25/archives/fu-tsoyi-who-surrendered-peking-in-49-dies-nationalist-general.html?_r=0

7 *Red Scare: Memories of the American Inquisition*, Griffin Fariello https://books.google.com/books?id=vv29CQAAQBAJ&pg=PT76&lpg=PT76&dq=trachtenberg+smith+act&source=bl&ots=7cPNNOWWJP&sig=i8sGcZzlAsaKbpfBYFHvpZclqZM&hl=en&sa=X&ved=0ahUKEwiInvmCr_zRAhVTwWMKHVGOCd0Q6AEINjAF#v=onepage&q=trachtenberg%20smith%20act&f=false

8 *The Columbia Electronic Encyclopedia*, 6th ed., 2012 http://www.infoplease.com/encyclopedia/history/smith-act.html

9 Deng Xiaoping http://newlearningonline.com/new-learning/chapter-4/deng-xiaoping-socialism-with-chinese-characteristics

10 Karl Marx, *Critique of the Gotha Program*, 1875 https://simple.wikipedia.org/wiki/From_each_according_to_his_ability,_to_each_according_to_his_need

11 *JUSTIA US Law* http://law.justia.com/cases/federal/appellate-courts/F2/322/364/413494/

12 Chi Chao-chu '52 (Ji Chaozhu) https://www.cambridge.org/core/journals/china-quarterly/article/div-classtitlethe-man-on-maoandaposs-right-from-harvard-yard-to-tiananmen-square-my-life-inside-chinaandaposs-foreign-ministry-chaozhuji-new-york-random-house-2008-xix-354-pp-2800-isbn-978–1–4000–6584–4div/F8964A74EB5D4F7B12C74A586256ABE4

13 Carlin Li-an Chi '91 http://health.usnews.com/doctors/carlin-chi-71263

14 Princeton https://www.princeton.edu/~cggross/Boulevard_09.pdf

15 *The New York Times* Jan 28, 2014 https://www.nytimes.com/2014/01/29/arts/music/pete-seeger-songwriter-and-champion-of-folk-music-dies-at-94.html

16 *The Harvard Crimson* June 4, 1992 http://www.thecrimson.com/article/1992/6/4/the-last-hurrah-pwhen-harvard-radcliffe-alumni/?page=

17 *The Harvard Crimson* June 26, 1989 http://www.thecrimson.com/article/1989/6/26/toward-non-issue-overseers-pbdbespite-this-years/

18 Declaration of Independence

Most Exciting Moment—*Joie de Vivre*

Sealing Rigoletto's Fate

Joel M. Bernstein

After having sung in many musicals in both public school and high school, I also sang in the Harvard Glee Club. I had the honor of being selected the class Chorister in 1957 and sang "Oh Harvard" at the commencement ceremonies in 1957. After Medical School around age 28, I sang lead roles in many Broadway Musicals at the Jewish Center of Buffalo, including *Guys and Dolls* and the King in the *The King and I.* At about the age of 32, I started to take the singing career very seriously and while still practicing Medicine, I enrolled in the School of Music at the University at Buffalo. I spent five years with Heinz Rehfuss, a world famous bass-baritone and Gary Burgess a famous operatic tenor.

With this training, I developed a richer, fuller baritone voice and started to take roles in opera in the Western New York area. At that time the New York City Opera came to Artpark in Lewiston, NY. The Opera Company recruited local talent to sing in the choruses of the operas and occasionally used local talent for small roles. In 1976, the baritone who played the lead role of Escamillo, the Toreador in *Carmen,* decided he did not want to sing the small role of Monterone in Verdi's *Rigoletto,* the opera that was also being staged at that time along with *Carmen.* By serendipity, the chorus director asked me if I would take the role of Monterone. I had only one week to prepare for that role, and the rest is history.

I also sang in a number of operas taking the lead baritone roles in (1) *Sampson and Delilah,* (2) *L'Enfant Du Christ* by Berlioz, and (3) Gian Carlo Menotti's opera, *The Old Maid and the Thief.*

Religious and cantorial music was also an important part of my singing career, as I was the cantor at Temple Beth Zion from 1976 to 1980. I continue to sing at my local Synagogue and occasionally have the honor of giving sermons when the rabbi is on vacation.

The event that was most exciting for me was when I was given the small but incredibly important role of Monterone in *Rigoletto.* Briefly, the role is critical to the outcome of the opera even though it is a small role. Rigoletto makes fun of me in Act I, Scene I, because I have severely criticized the Duke for fooling around with my daughter. I give Rigoletto the Italian "finger", and forever in the opera he knows that he has been cursed. He sings in the next scene "*That old man cursed me.*" At the end of the opera, when Rigoletto's daughter, Gilda, sacrifices herself to save the Duke, Rigoletto sings as the final words of the opera, "Il Maledetto" (The Curse).

I cannot tell you the excitement and the thrill that I had in those five performances knowing that in that famous opera, I had sealed Rigoletto's fate in that five-minute solo that I sang in center stage when the whole cast, leading players and chorus, were focused on me. I write this because it was a "personal challenge" in which both danger and excitement co-existed for me.

It was one of my greatest moments in my brief but wonderful career as a singer.

Joel Bernstein, MD, has been an Otolaryngologist (ear, nose, and throat surgeon) for about 50 years and is still in active practice. He obtained a PhD in Microbiology-Immunology at State University at Buffalo in 1979, where he also received his medical degree in 1961. Joel has published over 140 original articles in his field and has edited three textbooks on *Immunology of the Ear* and one on *Immunology of Nasal Polyposis*. He has been married for 59 years to Sheila Jaffe Bernstein and has three sons. He is still in contact with his roommate from Winthrop House, Dr. Peter Banks.

Figure 2.13.1.1 *Costumes for Rigoletto by Giuseppe Verdi (1813–1901)*
*Watercolor drawings of costumes created by Ludovic Napoleon Lepic (1839–1889) for Rigoletto (*left*) and Count Monterone (*right)
for first performance at the Paris Opera, February 27, 1885, France

Source: Bibliothèque nationale de France
http://gallica.bnf.fr/m/ark:/12148/btv1b84558972/f1.planchecontact

Chapter Three

EDUCATION

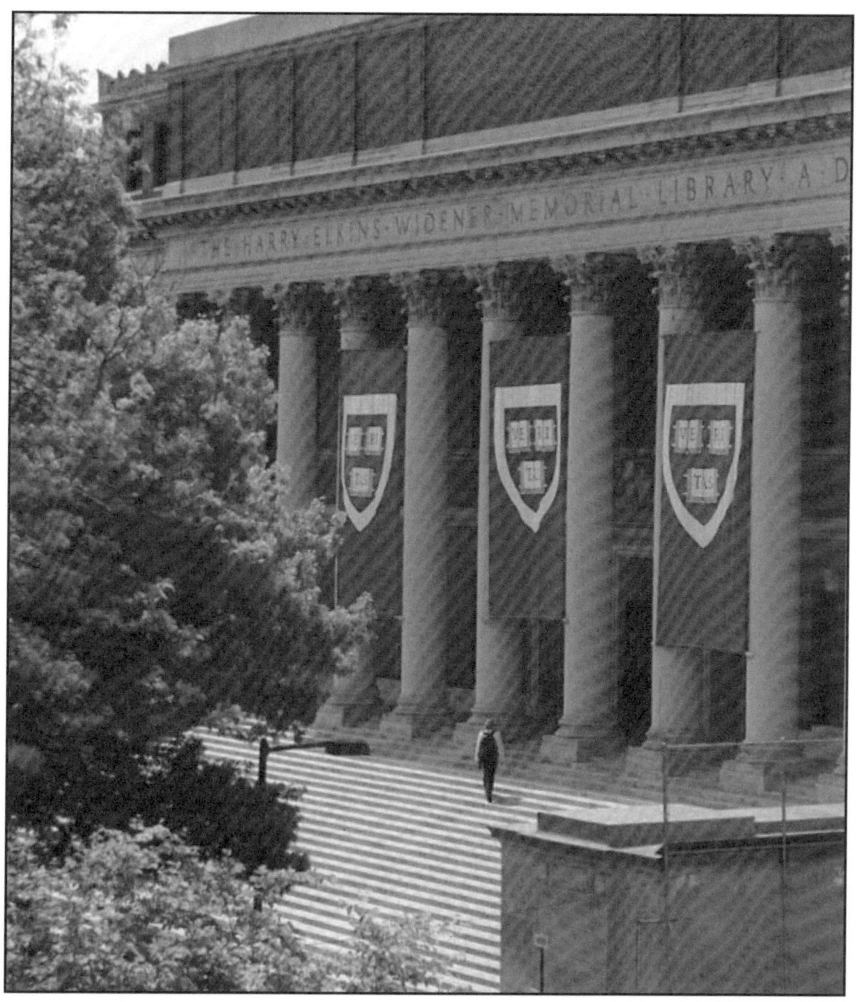

Figure C3 *Widener Library prepared for Commencement*

Reprinted courtesy of Harvard University

Chapter Three

EDUCATION

Secondary School

Leadership

Life as an Educator of Youth

Recollections and Reflections

William C. Prescott, Jr.

I am the product of an era when most—if not all—of the important decisions about my educational life were made by my parents. That could not be said of the decisions regarding my professional life, but as far as my schooling went, I was destined at birth to attend Friends Academy, St. George's School, and Harvard College, all of which had been attended by my father. Similarly, though I haven't really thought of it this way, most of the avocational passions which have shaped my personal life were also introduced to me by my parents. Waterfowl hunting, fishing, and a general love of/appreciation for the outdoors were thanks to my father. Classical music, thanks to my mother. (Vegetable) gardening, which I took up much later in life, I learned about via our WWII Victory Garden. Golf I somehow discovered on my own! In any case, life decisions seemed so much less complicated in my youth and early adulthood.

Peregrinations of a School Master

The above having been said, I don't think there was ever much doubt, even before I became a college graduate, that I would devote my professional life to education. A summer job in Boston in my father's brokerage firm, countered by another summer experience—teaching summer school at St. George's—sealed the deal. Stocks and bonds—anything that had to do with (the business of) numbers—was not for me. My professional chronology started at St. George's, teaching summer school, and then, right out of Harvard, I returned to that same high school preparatory school to teach English, coach (whatever!), and supervise a dormitory of young men. The year following found me at Brown University to earn a Master's degree (in English), followed by two years teaching, coaching, etc. at Lake Forest Academy, and then back to St. George's for seven more years of the typical independent boarding school "triple-threat" experience. In 1962 I married, and our son was born in 1966, but our marriage struggled, and in an attempt to save it, we moved out to Michigan to Grosse Pointe University School in 1968, where I took on a variety of tasks, including teaching, admissions and alumni work, and whatever else the headmaster asked me to do. (In my first year at GPUS, the school merged with the Liggett School to become University Liggett School [ULS], which is what it is known by today.)

The eight years I spent at US represented an extraordinary blend of triumph and tragedy, as it were, in my personal and professional life. My wife and I parted, and she moved back to Newport, RI, with our son. In the meantime, the headmaster of US left the school, the head of the upper school also departed, and I became the assistant head of the upper school, then after two or three years the upper school head. In the meantime, my now ex-wife suffered a horrendous automobile accident, and almost simultaneously my father was diagnosed with inoperable bladder cancer. I have indelible memories of that summer when I was back in the East, driving my dad to the hospital in Providence for radiation treatments while my former wife was in a coma on an upper level of the same hospital. In September of that year she died, and my son, then age five, came out to Michigan to live with me. In October my dad died.

I recount this history because it seems to be so illustrative of how personal and professional lives intersect in extraordinary ways. My failed marriage forced me to leave St. George's, which I loved dearly, but it enabled me to take on professional challenges which might never have come my way, had I not been forced into that change of venue. An even better part of the story is that a year or so after these tragedies, my single dad days came to an end as I met and married Suzie Wardwell, who was then and is to this day the real star of this show! (Ironically, I knew Suzie's parents on a first-name basis, as two of her brothers attended University Liggett.)

A few more historical notes to complete the narrative. At some point in the mid to late '70s, having watched and learned from four heads of school with whom I had worked over almost 20 years, I decided that I wanted to become a head myself. (At that point I did not know that two of our Class of 1957 classmates—Peter Gunness and John

Ratté—would also become school heads and would grow to veritable giants in the field. Fortunately, I got to know them both, over time, and it would not be overstating the fact that they both became models and mentors, acknowledged or unacknowledged.) So I started throwing my hat into various rings. Wet behind the years, I was no threat to Tony Jarvis's candidacy at Roxbury Latin when I interviewed at that great school. (But *voila*, give it time and *voila*, another mentor!) Similarly, I was certainly not ready to become Jim Wickenden's successor at Tabor Academy. But I kept at it, and came very close (but no ceegar!) to the headship of Tower Hill School in Wilmington, DE. Having narrowly missed this opportunity, I was forced to reassess. Consoled by search consultants that my name was out there, and I would eventually get the nod to become a head, I determined that I needed to broaden my search beyond the East Coast, and with the advice and counsel of my "boss", Ray Robbins, who confided that he was not looking forward to the uncertainty—year after year—of whether or not he was going to have to look for an upper school head, I told Ray that "next year will be my last at US. I would bank on receiving an offer somewhere.

Becoming Headmaster

Not-so-fast forward to two months thereafter, the Head of School at Kingswood Cranbrook departed precipitously, and after a quick series of interviews, I was appointed head there, ironically to work alongside my dear friend Chris Corkery, who was the head at Cranbrook and with whom I had taught and coached at St. George's. So we moved from one side of Detroit to the other. It was not the East Coast (no salt water, which I can assure folks does not exist in Michigan), but it was a great opportunity. I found that whether I was really aware of it or not, I was remarkably well prepared for a headship, and I loved my four years there. But then in the fall of 1979 the Wheeler School position opened up in Providence, the chance to "go home", and I did that.

Twenty-three years at Wheeler brought all kinds of professional and personal milestones, which leads into some practical if not philosophical observations. Although I would not have been able to articulate precisely what my M.O. as a school head would become, over time, there were a few undeniable principles that I lived by from the beginning. The most important of whatever talents I could claim was the *ability to recognize effective people and good ideas when I saw/heard them.*

Looking back, I have often wondered whether I ever had an original idea! As silly as it sounds when expressed that way, the point is/was,

I believed that hiring and retaining good people was priority number one, and that understanding and supporting creative efforts, in other words fostering a culture of innovation, was at the heart of what could result in a terrific school. I believed then and still do that *heads of school are essentially conductors of the symphony.* They cannot play most—if any—of the instruments, nor should they. The music is made by the musicians, and the head of school—the music director—needs not just to accept that reality but to celebrate it.

And so in my first year at Wheeler I "discovered" Mark Harris, a fifth-grade teacher who had come to Wheeler right out of Brown University a few years previous to my arrival. Mark was demonstrating his genius by providing a variety of enrichment opportunities to students, activities that ranged from ham radio to electron microscopy to a roof-top botanical garden (one of his few failures!). I marveled at the breadth and depth of his imagination with this fledgling program, which he dubbed AERIE (the eagle's nest vs. an acronym), and which he managed without compensation or, for that matter, recognition. In my second year I made perhaps the best decision of my Wheeler tenure: I appointed him to take this program—full-time—and run with it. To be honest, I had no idea where the program would go, but I know that he did, and it seemed like a better-than risky gamble. Now, pushing up on 40 years, the AERIE program has three full-time staff members, serves the entire school, and is a magnet for students in the admission process. I often expressed the observation—both to Mark's face and behind his back—that in all my years in schools, no one had more influenced my own approach to education than Mark Harris. If he had a motto, it would be, "All Things Are Possible." Thanks to him, that became my own mantra. I believed it, and I loved it!

Children with Learning Differences

One other example of my administrative "brilliance"! In the late '80s the School was offered the right of first refusal on the only building on our city block that we did not own. It was owned at the time by a dentist and a few of his colleagues. He was planning to retire, and despite a fairly hefty price tag, it was an offer we couldn't refuse, even though we were not at all sure how we would use it. After several failed attempts to rent the building out, fortuitousness struck (again?). An educational colleague, known to me but not well, was working on a project to found a school for children with language-based learning differences, and on her planning committee were some former Wheeler parents (whose children had been counseled out for academic reasons) and the Wheeler head of the lower school. At one of my weekly conferences with this lower school head, I asked the innocent question, "How is Emi's new school project going?" Great, came the answer, but we are having trouble figuring out where we will locate it. Bingo! The proverbial light went on. "Do you think Emi would like to house this school in our (recently purchased) building?"

And that is how The Hamilton School at Wheeler, a school for students with language-based learning differences, was born. Its major feature, aside from providing an educational program for a seriously under-served student population, was that it became a school-within-a-school for high-potential dyslexic students in grades one through six. Now, some 30 years later, with a middle school component, its identity is as much a part of the Wheeler program as anything else the school offers. Even more significant, the Hamilton approach to teaching students with learning differences has translated itself across all divisions, and although its original focus was on younger students, it is fair to say that now no secondary school program is more sensitive to the reality that *all* students learn differently from one another. Good teaching of Hamilton students is just plain good teaching, and this school-within-a-school model encourages good teaching, period!

Parenthetically, I should note that one of my goals—from the outset—in creating this school-within-a-school, was that I hoped the model would be replicable, that other schools would follow suit. It has taken a lot longer than I had hoped, but there are two schools—on whose board I once served—which now offer similar programs, one at Friends Academy in North Dartmouth (MA) and the other at Bancroft School in Worcester (MA).

There are more stories similar to the AERIE and Hamilton programs, like Providence Summerbridge (now the Breakthrough Collaborative), which is housed at Wheeler and provides intensive summer academic work (over two summers) for Providence public middle school children, a program taught by high school and college students. This national collaborative program prepares its students for a college-preparatory high school experience, culminating ultimately in college. In addition to its goal of providing its students with the tools to enable them to be successful in secondary and post-secondary education, the Breakthrough program encourages its teachers, a significant number of whom are people of color, to consider careers in teaching. The thread of similarity that runs through all three of these initiatives is that now each of them is embedded in the culture of The Wheeler School. Each has become institutionalized, as it were.

Lessons from Experience

Twenty-three years at a school for a head is undeniably a long stretch, and as I closed in on the end of my second decade at Wheeler, I was often asked, "How can you stay (as head) at the same school for 20 years?" My answer was simple, although in some ways hard to explain.

> "*First, I'm not the same head that I was 20 years ago. I have reinvented myself at least twice since I arrived and hope that I will reinvent myself at least once more before I leave.*
>
> *Secondly, The Wheeler School is not the same school it was when I arrived. It, too, has reinvented itself, and I hope it will continue to do so.*"

That somewhat whimsical response/notion probably calls for some explication. Aside from hiring and retaining terrific people as fellow teachers and colleagues, doubtless some of my behaviors were at least a little idiosyncratic. I was a joiner, almost from the moment I became a school head. NAIS (the National Association of Independent Schools) and NAPSG (the National Association of Principals of Schools for Girls) were two very important organizations for me. At NAIS, I served eight years on the board of directors, and my role eventually saw me as a board liaison with the NAIS Government Relations office in Washington, DC. Early on at Wheeler I joined the Head Mistresses Association of the East, which often elicited droll comments from the uninformed! (Like NAPSG, HMAE was initially a girls' school organization, but as more schools became coeducational, its membership became inclusive of any schools which enrolled girls.)

In the '90s I became a Regent of the *Cum Laude Society*, which meets annually at the Harvard Club of Boston, by the way. The Regents (essentially the board of directors of the Society) convene on the Friday afternoon/Saturday morning of the H-Y football weekend and stay overnight at the Eliot Hotel, next door to the Harvard Club. Every other year, when THE GAME was in Cambridge, we would sneak down the stairs from our meeting room to hear the Whiffenpoofs serenade the Yale Club, which used to—and probably still does—rent the main dining room for that special occasion.

Later in the '90s and into the 2000s, I served on the Commission on Independent Schools of the New England Association of Schools & Colleges, the accrediting body for independent schools in New England. I actually succeeded John Ratté as chair of that board, although nobody could really follow John Ratté!

So truth to tell, all of this joining, this attendance at conferences, serving on boards, etc. contributed to my master plan, which was to find out what was happening across the independent school world, and if someone else had a good idea, steal it! That's not exactly accurate, but it's not all that far from the truth either. There was then, and there is now, so much excitement, so much happening in education, and hearing from and knowing the best practitioners in the field was heady stuff.

I am struggling with the best way to segue toward the end of this tome, so bear with me. . . .

There were perhaps two or three trademark behaviors which I think helped define my "leadership style", and I offer them here. First, I was blessed to have my three children go through their school years tuition-free, by virtue of tuition-remission policies at the schools where I worked. That said, having your children in the school where you are Headmaster presents unique challenges, both for the children and for their parents! My son was passively aggressive in indicating that he was not crazy about being the offspring of the Head, and he managed to flunk himself out of Wheeler at the end of grade ten. Fortunately, my colleague Evan West at Providence Country Day welcomed him there, and he graduated on schedule. (My son's checkered educational experiences are another story, but he is flourishing in the current chapter of that story. A self-taught "techie", he is now Marketing Producer for Major League Baseball, assigned to the Cincinnati Reds. So who needs college??) My elder daughter would reluctantly acknowledge my existence when she saw me at school, but my younger daughter seemed to delight in glimpsing me from time to time. In any case, regardless of the way they expressed—or not—their relationship to the head of school, I was determined to be consistent in establishing my role as parent—vs. employer of their teachers—of my children at Wheeler. I supported their teachers' dealings with my children, for good or ill. The teacher is always right is not necessarily the easiest code to live by, but I found it was an important behavior for me to espouse. Anyway, it seemed to work. (Fortunately, none of my six grandchildren have had that head of school relationship to worry about!)

A second practice which I honored religiously through all of my years as a head of school was that on my frequent times away from school for conferences and/or meetings of various organizations, I *never* called school to "check in". My belief was that in the eventuality of any problem, my administrative colleagues in charge of the school in my absence were far better qualified to deal with the problem than I, from whatever distance I would be calling. If the problem were serious enough—and interestingly there never was such a situation—my colleagues knew where they could reach me. Moreover, my calling in to ask, "How are things going?" would suggest either an absence of trust in their abilities or an inflated trust in mine!

My third practice was enabled by the Wheeler trustee leadership and my family. I wrote about it once in a submission to *The Head's Letter*, a periodical produced by a company—still going strong—called Educational Directions. It was titled "Leaving the Office Behind", and I offered it as a reason why I continued to love the school and my work after double-digit years as head. In this article I suggested that a major contributor to a head's (long) tenure is his/her ability to cultivate passions far removed from the life of the school, and I cited my personal calendar of activities at our summer house in South Dartmouth (MA), activities that included tending a substantial vegetable garden, not to mention routine but often exhausting maintenance of the property, a serious salt-water fishing disease that infected me over roughly five months a year, and an even more serious waterfowl hunting addiction. Weekends and summer vacation times were more than filled with tasks related to one or more of these activities. While some readers of this article were supportive of the concept it represented, others wrote in with a "harrumph, it's all very well for you to describe your profligate life of recreation, but some of us have to take care of our home lives as well as our schools. . . ." Good point and I probably should have acknowledged even more graciously the contribution that my wife made to allow this family life-style. Nevertheless, I still believe that the balance between one's professional and personal life is crucial. I have known head-colleagues whose life is the school, period. For me, routine separations were essential, and they inspired me to an even greater commitment to my vocation when most of the time I was, in fact, in the office.

Retirement?

I welcomed retirement in 2003. At 67, although I still felt energized by my school work, I also felt that it was time to literally "leave the office behind". But again, as much as I loved Wheeler and especially its people, I wanted to use however much time I have left on this planet to control my own full-time calendar. And that translated to a commitment *not* to become a consultant and/or to get into the head-hunting business. So what are you doing now, you ask? Yup. Sometimes so busy that I have been known to complain: "I need to get a job so that I will have some free time!"

What I have been doing the most in these past fourteen years is volunteer work in/for schools. I have served on the Board at St. George's for the past ten years, I am on the Advisory Board for Providence Summerbridge (Breakthrough), and I am still connected to Friends Academy on a variety of fronts.

But most exciting is a new venture on which I will end this essay. Almost ten years ago I was approached by some friends who wanted to tell me about a project they were exploring. Having visited Nativity Prep, a boys' tuition-free middle school in New Bedford, they were blown away by its program, but, they asked (themselves), "Where are the girls?" That was what they wanted to talk to me about. "You don't have to get involved," they said. Yeah, right.

Now, eight years after it opened, Our Sisters' School is a thriving, tuition-free middle school for girls in New Bedford, and as a founding trustee, I couldn't be prouder. The School gets its name from a cohort of women who shipped aboard the whaling vessels during the heyday of the New Bedford whaling era. They were called "sister sailors", and we have adopted the metaphor of the sailors, the ships, and the voyage. There are currently 67 girls at OSS in grades five through eight. The graduates of the first two eighth grade classes have completed high school, having attended—on full scholarship—some of the most selective independent secondary schools in New England, as well as enrolled in honors tracks in local public and parochial schools. *All of them* are attending four-year colleges. An incredibly supportive board of trustees has been raising approximately $2M each year, so that we have created a substantial "Sustainability Fund" (aka endowment). In 2018 OSS will celebrate its tenth anniversary, and our goal will be to surpass the $10M mark in the Sustainability Fund.

The story of OSS and the difference it is making in the lives of underserved New Bedford children seems to be as good a place as any to end this biopic. It has been a pleasure to write it, even though at the outset I was wondering what I would say. Not to worry. Enough said, however.

Figures 3.1.1.1 *Headmaster Bill Prescott handing out diplomas to graduating seniors at the 1998 Commencement of The Wheeler School, Providence, RI*

Bill Prescott began his career in education as a teacher/coach/dormitory master at St. George's School (RI) in 1957–58. After getting a master's degree in English at Brown University, he taught and coached at Lake Forest Academy (IL) before returning to St. George's in 1962. He moved in 1968 to Grosse Pointe, MI, where he taught English and eventually became head of the upper school at University Liggett School. His first headship was at Kingswood Cranbrook School in Bloomfield Hills, MI. In 1980 he became the headmaster of The Wheeler School in Providence, RI, and retired after 23 years as head. He served as a trustee at three private schools in Massachusetts. He also served on the board of directors of the National Association of Independent Schools, on the board of the Association of Independent Schools in New England, on the Commission on Independent Schools of the New England Association of Schools & Colleges, and on the Board of Regents of the Cum Laude Society. Now residing in South Dartmouth, MA, he continues to be active, serving on the boards of trustees at St. George's and at Our Sisters' School in New Bedford, MA.

Secondary School

Leadership

Be Thoreau

Peter Gunness

> *"I don't think that anyone stays in this field of education—I've been at it at Harvard for forty years—unless her temperament and stance are hopeful and determined, unless she can find a way to resist cynicisms and blame, and cultivate searching questions and imaginative thinking.*
>
> *I, for one, refuse to be cynical about teachers and children and about the capacity of these folks to do good work."*
>
> —Sara Lawrence Lightfoot

Although I disclaim any belief in coincidences, let me try this one on for what it's worth. In today's mail I received a letter from the Concord Museum announcing the 200th anniversary of Henry Thoreau's birth date. The first essay I wrote at Harvard College was an essay on Thoreau's "Walden". It was required in General Education A. Max Bluestone was the section man. It was perhaps the first written piece labeled "essay" I had written (there were numerous written reports at Fargo High School but no essays). As it turns out, that Walden paper was the most successful paper I wrote that semester.

Continuing the coincidence, my wife, Peggy, and I have retired to Concord, MA, in a retirement community overlooking the Sudbury River to the east. Farther to the east, Walden Woods and Walden Pond are located. Coincidences be damned.

I have struggled with this essay for the "Class of '57" essay book as much as that one. My time at Harvard, as is true for so many of us, has informed so much of my life. I entered Harvard expecting to go to Harvard Business School, as had my elder brother. Little did I expect the journey that was to follow.

An Educator's Journey

My journey in education started in 1957 when William Perry, Skiddy Von Stade, and George Buttrick encouraged me to consider going to the School of Education. Thus began a journey of over 50 years in variety educational ventures. My journey involved ten years in Harvard Administration: Director of Financial Aid, Assistant Dean, and first Resident Advisor of Peabody Terrace, (Harvard's 500-unit married student housing on the Charles). I spent 23 years at Buckingham

Browne & Nichols School (BB&N) as Headmaster and 20 years as a Search Consultant working with independent schools and trustees conducting searches for Heads of Schools and other top administrative positions. I participated in over 100 searches for school heads and numerous boards of trustee retreats. This work took me all over the US, France, Greece, Turkey, Italy, and Jordan.

Mastering Being a School Headmaster

On the morning of May 4th, 1970, following the killing of four students at Kent State University by National Guard Troops on duty to calm student protests, a teacher at (then) Browne & Nichols School got up and said, "Boys, that's what happens when you break the rules." This shocking comment was the coda to the end of my first year as Headmaster. There had been many upsetting events in the 1960s, such as the assassinations of JFK, Martin Luther King, Malcom X, and Robert Kennedy. But that May morning comment was a statement of the utter despair felt by otherwise reasonable men who could no longer control their anger. There were to be 22 more years at BB&N, but none was imprinted more forcefully on my memory as that morning.

Those next years as Headmaster involved a merger between Browne & Nichols and Buckingham. That meant building a stronger academic program, hiring an outstanding faculty and learning the joys and challenges of co-education. The merger brought unexpected challenges. Our boards decided, after a brief and focused conversation, to forgo detailed negotiations and merge, trusting that we could work together to resolve problems and issues as they arose. The schools merged on January 1, 1974. In the next four months we had to develop a unified budget, merge academic departments with single leadership and make a plan to reconfigure which grades would be housed in which buildings of our new three-campus school. There were numerous other tasks to accomplish: our new school needed a unified color scheme, a crest, a motto and all the trappings. That's when we choose as a motto, "Honor, Scholarship, Kindness." Whoever heard of a school with kindness as one of its key values? That phrase was a favorite expression of a Browne & Nichols teacher in the 1930s.

Feelings ran strong as we pursued each step of this process. It was slow, and we took our time. For instance, in 1988, 14 years after the merger, a set of parents came up to me after graduation. Their daughter had just graduated, and the mother said "Peter, I want you to know as much as I respect you, I sent my daughter to a girl's school at age four, and I wish it had stayed that way." This was a strong reminder to me how these kinds of changes take time.

It was also a time of innovation. We started a senior project program, the curriculum broadened, we experimented with different schedules, off campus activities were increased and we even closed the smoking room. The fact that there was a smoking room seems rather incredible from our current understanding.

Challenges to Authority and Building Trust

The most significant challenge was rebuilding the trust between and among the various constituents: school and students, teachers and students, parents and school, and even students and their parents. The '60s and early '70s had left many residual broken relations. We all remembered the slogans of the '60s: "Don't trust anyone over 30," "Challenge Authority", "Power to the People".

It was a time when the students were protesting for civil rights for African Americans and other minorities, the Vietnam War and all symbols of authority including "private schools". My predecessor Headmaster and other school leaders, many of whom had been important leaders of education, could not understand—even abide—the way authority was being tested. Rules became absurd. For instance, this school had a dress and appearance committee which measured the length of students' hair each day when they came to school. Some boys were sent home because their hair was too long, or their dress too careless, and contrarian Cambridge parents would send them right back to school. All the symbols of rebellion enraged otherwise reasonable leaders, headmasters, teachers, and parents.

Many of us today, as we may despair over the divisions in our country, forget how divided our country was at that time and the powerful feelings that were aroused. Even though the times were so different, the divisions were equally as deep as now. Our children were challenging us and the order of our society.

The challenge we faced in bridging these feelings, and the practical aspect of the merger, tested the patience and good will of all involved, including me. In the larger scheme, mergers only work when conditions are right and good, and that was truly the case in this one. After 40 years we can see that the merger was meant to be. BB&N is one of the very successful schools in the country. The school that emerged, with roots back to the late 19th-century Cambridge, has proven to be remarkably resilient and adaptive. Perhaps the greatest learning for me was to not take the strong emotions expressed as personal attacks. The issues were important and mattered. There was an ill-advised war, denied civil rights were intolerable and had been neglected for too long.

Lessons from the First Headmastership

My success at BB&N was mostly due to four things: a supportive board chairman and boards of trustees; outstanding faculty; my entrepreneurial energy; and my commitment to preserving as much of the two schools' ethos as was possible. These were important because we were building a new school on a solid foundation, and my talents were best at that stage. In retrospect, I recognized I wasn't so strong at the polishing and fine-tuning needed to take a school to the next level. Future leaders could do that. I appreciated the importance of making serious efforts to preserve the many fine qualities of those two schools, while building a new one.

Rebalancing Family Priorities and New Opportunities

During my tenure at BB&N, my wife, Peggy, attended the Episcopal Divinity School in Cambridge, graduated, was ordained in the Episcopal Church, and became a priest serving at Christ Church in Cambridge. Her decision was the right one for her and our family. At that time, Headmasters' wives were considered appendages to their husbands' work. As a result of Peggy's ordination, she and I were asked to speak at workshops about what it was like to have two public careers in one family while running a school. That seems almost laughable by today's standards, but at the time it wasn't. Peggy and I made an agreement that involved planning our schedule around major school and church events one year in advance. Whenever both of us were needed in one place or the other, those dates became fixed times on the calendar around which our other schedule revolved. It really worked well, and we both grew significantly as a result.

In the fall of 1984, Peggy served on a diocesan committee that developed a companion relationship with the diocese of Harare, Zimbabwe. One aspect of the relationship with Zimbabwe was to work collaboratively with the diocese in select areas; one of which was education. There were several diocesan schools in Zimbabwe at that time.

Going to Zimbabwe. Peggy, with me as her companion, was asked to visit those schools and report back to the Massachusetts diocese. We were in Zimbabwe for over two months and visited six schools. The time was just following the end of the war that they called their "War for Independence". Schools were dynamic places bustling with optimism and hope. Education was seen as the key to the future. One school in particular which stands out in my mind was St. Patrick School, Earamobi. The ride through the far reaches of Zimbabwe is etched upon my spine as we rode on the bed of a small Toyota pickup on a narrow single track road. We were running about an hour late. The students who were to greet us had been waiting with a large brass school bell to signal our arrival. The school had been seriously damaged during the recently ended war. Many of the buildings were in rubble, the beautiful chapel was damaged but not destroyed, and as Grace would have it, the altar and cross remained partially covered by a section of the roof. The schoolyard was neat. and the rubble was stacked in a fashion so as to make an outdoor arena for the students to sit during assemblies.

We were welcomed by the Headmaster, a man of straight stature and a deep strong voice. Peggy wrote the following in her journal, "He spoke in English, and a colleague translated his comments into Shona language." Expressing his gratitude for her visit, he says, "We all need visitors: it helps us to know ourselves. Just as I go into your classrooms and say 'how are things with you', these visitors have come from America to say 'hello, and how are things with you'. They help us to know ourselves better. We need to see beyond ourselves; we need a broader vision."

He was a thoughtful, sensitive, hope-filled man. He referred to Peggy as "mother". She was the first woman priest he had met. Then he asked if she would bless them. She offered the following blessing, which was translated into Shona for the students:

> "*As long as there is life,*
> *As long as there are children,*
> *As long as there is love,*
> *We can all be one.*
> *The Lord bless you and keep you.*"

The assembly concluded with the children singing *Ishe Komborera Africa*, Zimbabwe's first national anthem. It was a time of great optimism in Zimbabwe, the war had just ended, and spirits were high. Future troubles were on the horizon, but it was a safe and wonderful time for us to be there.

Going to New Jersey. In 1991, Peggy was elected Rector of Christ Church, Ridgewood, NJ. It was an important call for her, and we decided she should answer it. Also, it proved the impetus to call an end to my tenure at BB&N: 23 years was long enough, maybe even too long.

Going Home. In 2004, Peggy and I drove her 1989 Volvo from Belmont to Emigrant, MT, where our son Per and his wife run a small lamb and wool business on the Wolf Ridge Ranch. It was a great trip that included many stops at my various childhood haunts (but that's another paper).

One stop illustrates a point I want to make.

During the 1940s there was little money available for travel, and gasoline was rationed, so trips were virtually nonexistent. Nevertheless, every Sunday in the summer our family and other families joined for a picnic at the Fort Abraham Lincoln Park 15 miles west of Bismarck over the Missouri River. That old fort was located at the confluence of the Heart and Missouri rivers. There was a stockade and reconstructed "Indian Mounds" built by WPA workers in the '30s. This was a bit of a children's paradise for play at that time. Fort Abraham was the place where Louis and Clark met Sacagawea, and General Custer left on his ill-fated final mission.

As I sat looking over the scene, I realized how little had changed, aside from a new interpretive center and more developed surrounding area. We sat mulling over our trip, and I was boring Peggy with tales of my childhood. A woman ranger came by and sat down with us. It was a quiet day. She was in Native American dress. She had beautiful brown skin, salt-and-pepper hair in a braid, and her face had strong crow's-feet wrinkles around her eyes.

She asked where we were from and what we were up to. I explained how I had not been to this site in 60 years. She exuded a moment of unforgettable calm and a warm smile. Then she said,

> "*You know, you have to maintain and water your roots, or you will wither.*"

That was pretty straight and to the point; we talked further, then she gave us a hug and sent us on our way.

The School Consultant Years

For the final leg of my journey, I spent 20 years as a consultant to independent schools and their boards. I ran executive searches for over 100 schools. During those years there were changes in the process of selecting new leadership. It became more inclusive and process-oriented. That's another reminder of the dynamic nature of education.

The first three heads I placed were still in their positions until recently. I know why. Those three boards knew what they wanted for their school and were willing to risk keeping the decision-making to a small committee. They also actively solicited my opinion, which I freely offered. They consulted with their constituencies and took those thoughts into consideration, but kept a tight rein on the decision-making process. Over time, searches became more broadly inclusive and even though the ultimate decision remained with the board, the other constituents have gained greater influence than was true in earlier stages.

A search, if you think about it, is like a pee wee hockey game (I coached in a pee wee league at six in the morning in an outdoor rink in Belmont in the '70s). I would set up the boys: the right wing, the left wing, the center and the defense in the back. I'd drop the puck, and everyone would scramble toward it. A search is like that: everyone wants to be near the action and to make the decision. Good boards and good process can allow input and set clear boundaries for the roles of all the players. A well-managed search can build community and reinforce positive aspects of the school.

Independent schools are very special places on the American education scene, even though they educate a very small percentage of students. These schools have provided strong innovative leadership and models for all schools. At an earlier time we called them private schools. That word of privilege was anathema to the democratic fervor of the 1960s. In fact, in the early '70s, private education was at its nadir. Some schools closed, others changed their character, and others merged for both good and for survival reasons.

Summing Up

I learned a lot about leadership by doing this work, much of which would have helped me in the early stages of my own career. I have come to understand that the leadership skills needed are hard to define.

Certain skills are learnable: budgeting, reading a balance sheet, etc. Those are useful tools. Good leaders solve problems once they have been defined. Great leaders anticipate what is coming, what is just over the horizon.

I always told board of trustees the skill most needed is the ability to see around corners. The point here is that once problems are identified, they can be solved; that's the easy job. *The ability to prepare for the next generation of problems makes great leaders succeed.*

* * *

The journey from Fargo to Walden has been deeply fulfilling and complete.

Included in that letter I received from the Concord Museum was a sticker which read:

"*BE THOREAU.*"

I put the sticker on the bumper of my 2004 Volvo this morning. Perhaps I'm preparing for another trip west?

Figure 3.1.2.1 *Peter Gunness and his wife, Rev. Peggy Gunness, the first ordained woman Priest on the staff of Trinity Church, Boston. Peter is shown in the 1980s in his regalia as a member of the* Committee for the Happy Observance of Commencement. *Peggy, in 1990, is seated in the Trinity Cloister Garden in Copley Square.*

Peter Gunness' career in education encapsulates three distinct phases. From 1959–1969 he served in various administrative posts in Harvard College. In 1969, after completing a Master of Arts Teaching degree at Harvard Graduate School of Education, he was elected Headmaster of the Browne & Nichols School. In 1974, after leading Browne & Nichols through a merger with the Buckingham School, he served from 1974 to 1992 as Headmaster of the combined schools, Buckingham Browne & Nichols. In 1992, with three colleagues, he joined Educators Collaborative, an executive search and general consultant to Boards of Trustee to Independent Schools. He has conducted over 100 searches in the US and Western Europe.

In 1981, his wife, Peggy, was ordained a priest in the Episcopal Church, and they lived two very public lives during the remainder of their careers. Peter was awarded the Ames Memorial Award at Class Day in 1957.

Learning

Basing Good Learning on Good Thinking

Robert Swartz

I. In 1976, the Direction of My Professional Life Changed Forever

I was a full professor with tenure at the new Boston campus of the University of Massachusetts. I went there in 1972 as Philosophy Department chairman, redesigned the philosophy program to ground it more in important concepts that speak to the lives of our students. We had a traditional philosophy major that was sending students off to graduate school to get their PhDs and go on to some university to teach philosophy. But we added a Moral and Social Issues track along and a combined philosophy/ psychology major. Our student enrollment expanded considerably, we hired new faculty, and were moving along smoothly, when a friend of mine, Kevin O'Reilly, a high school history teacher, invited me to join his 11th grade history class for "something new" that he was planning to do. So I went there.

Kevin's students were learning about the Revolutionary War, and following their textbooks, which focused on names and dates, but occasionally threw in something else. This time it was a passage that said that the British soldiers stationed in Boston and settled in a camp had found out that the colonial militia, who had been formed to challenge the British, had been accumulating arms in a barn in Concord, MA, about 50 miles away. They decided to launch a surprise attack, so they left at midnight and marched through the night. But when they passed through the town of Lexington, a short distance from Concord, the sun was rising, and they ran into a group of colonists who had collected on the village green. So the British commander, General Gage, who was on horseback, rode up and said, "Disperse you rebels immediately. Fire!" And the British troops opened fire "killing eight patriots". The British then rode on to Concord. Then the text book says "It was not long before the swift-riding Paul Revere spread the news of this new atrocity to the neighboring colonies, which then rose up against the British. Then "Even in far away North Carolina the Colonists rose up against the British."

Wow. Patriots, rebels, Paul Revere, North Carolina 800 miles to the south, and those disciplined British. I supposed that my own history textbook was like that when I went to school, but I didn't remember a word of it. I wondered what they were going to be asked on the test. And I wondered why Kevin had asked me to come and visit.

But then Kevin answered my silent wonderings. He told his class that the night before he had been looking at some other books about this period and came across another one about this famous 1775 "Battle of Lexington". He read it to the students. It said pretty much the same thing as their textbook up to the British commander telling the people to disperse (with no use of the word "rebels"). But in the text he didn't say "Fire!" Instead the text said "The colonial committees were very anxious not to provoke open conflict with the British", which I supposed made sense because this was on the heels of the Boston Massacre trial. Then it said: "But in the confusion someone fired. The British then returned the fire and killed some colonists. They then marched on to Concord."

I then had an inkling of what Kevin was doing. He put the book down, scratched his head, and said, "I don't know who to believe. Who fired that first shot?" I thought that nobody cared about that any more. But I knew what Kevin was doing, and I realized how important that question was.

Some students then asked "why" and one of them said that the second passage only says that someone fired, not who it was. But another student said that it must have been a colonist because it says that the British *returned* the fire. I thought, "Good for you!" Then a student asked, "What is that second book?" and Kevin told them that this new text was from Winston Churchill, *History of the English Speaking Peoples.* They had no idea who Winston Churchill was but when they heard that he was English and the book was published in Great Britain, well, they said, *it must be the one that was wrong*. But Kevin said, "Wait a minute" and asked them if they had ever read anything published in the USA that was wrong, and sure they had. So now they perked up. Kevin then said, "Let's think about this a little. Let's make a list of things we will want to find out to determine which of these two is more reliable." And they did: first they asked who the authors were, including their background and profession. And one student said, "Maybe we want to find out where these guys got their information about these things that happened 200 years earlier."

Interestingly enough Kevin was drawing upon a little sourcebook published a few years earlier called *What Happened on Lexington Green?* in which the editor collected all the sources he could find, from the 18th century to the 20th century. So Kevin then cleverly produced some written eyewitness reports of the battle. "Maybe these were what the 20th-century authors used," he said. "I got curious about the same thing and I found these. And I photocopied them for you." So they looked at these and found that they broke down along "party lines" as well—except for a British soldier who testified that the British fired first. Some students said that that proved it—that the American textbook is correct. But Kevin asked them to wait and read them a note that said that this soldier said this when he was a *prisoner of the Colonists*. These students were now deflated. So what next?

Well, Kevin had them work in small groups of three and then share their ideas so that soon they had developed a well-organized check list that they thought of as questions that had to be answered before they could judge whether the original authors were reliable. Here's their list:

JUDGING THE RELIABILITY OF WRITTEN SOURCES

The Author

- ☐ Who?
- ☐ Background?
- ☐ Job or profession?
- ☐ Bias or special interest?

The Writing

- ☐ Where published?
- ☐ Reputation of publication?
- ☐ When did it appear in print?
- ☐ What is the genre of the print source?

The Source of the Information

- ☐ Was the author the observer?
- ☐ If so, how was the observation conducted?
- ☐ If not, where did the author get the information?
- ☐ Is that source trustworthy?

Others/Corroboration

- ☐ Has anyone else said the same thing?
- ☐ Is there any other evidence besides these statements? What and how strong?

Things weren't over yet. They needed to get answers for their questions. So Kevin helped them track down what information they could find about the various accounts, primarily through the use of the sourcebook about what happened on Lexington Green. I was amazed at the way this group of students had become motivated by the challenge of resolving this conflict, to my mind not the most interesting disagreement of this sort in the annals of the recorded history of man's adventures on this planet. But I was even more amazed when they all agreed that you couldn't tell who started this fighting. The information that was available, especially about the eyewitness accounts, was very inconclusive. One student said, "Both of these guys are making up stories. How can they know?" And he said, "They should have said: 'A shot rang out and to this day no one knows who fired that shot.'"... This student was saying that in this case the right answer to who fired the first short was that "We don't know."

What was I thinking? Two things. One was that Kevin, in this one class, had helped students free themselves from the tyranny of text books. They could now gather information and make their own judgments. That thrilled me. I knew all along, of course, something that was obvious: in the history of the Revolutionary War it really doesn't matter who fired the first shot. But more important, I realized that Kevin, in one short class period, had armed these students with something that they could use for the rest of their lives because this issue of reliability is always there in most things that they will be reading. This was exciting.

As I had put it many times since then, these students had just started to develop an extremely important and empowering critical thinking skill, and they would need it. Today when I think about this I think how the Internet and the development of iPhones and iPads has given these students the ability to access in a flash a tremendous amount of information that ten years earlier could only be found in a library search that usually took hours. But at the same time I recognize that, as many teachers know, the standard mode of operation for students using iPads when they search for information is to go to Google, get a bunch of links, access one of them, and copy it, without ever thinking that maybe it is cleverly disguised but false information. Anyone can put anything they want on the Internet and make it sound authentic. Kevin's way needs to be part of learning how to use any new tool that allows us to access information we are looking for.

Of course Kevin closed the door to his classroom when I came in, and I was the only one to see this wonder. I thought: "I need to tell every teacher in the world about this."

II. January 2017, Colegio Aixa, Palma de Mallorca, Spain

Just last month I visited a classroom in Palma de Mallorca in Spain. I have been working with the teachers there on how to restructure classroom teaching to infuse the use of important forms of skillful thinking. I watched a fifth grade teacher, Fatima, work with students who were learning about the early years of space exploration. She showed them the famous video of Neil Armstrong descending the ladder to plant "One great step for mankind" on the moon. They had never seen that. Their "wows" filled the room.

But then she showed them another video clip with the heading "Moon landing is a hoax!" and it went on to say that this was staged by actors in the Arizona desert in order for NASA to get more money from Congress. Many of the students laughed. But then Fatima did what Kevin did. She shifted the center of the classroom to the students and helped them not only think about how they can really tell which is a more reliable source, but how they can develop a plan that they can use whenever that question arises. "What questions do you need to get answers to in order to judge how reliable these accounts are," she asked the students. The students used a special "question organizing graphic organizer" to write questions that they generated in small collaborative groups. They then put the questions in categories and developed a checklist very much like the one that Kevin's students developed without ever having seen it. And, guided by the teacher, they set about to use it. I had shown the teachers in this school what Kevin did in a workshop we did a month earlier. I remember clearly one girl who said to the class: "We need to find out where this piece of writing was published. And we shouldn't forget to find out the reputation of the publisher!" Like in Kevin's classroom Fatima's question had activated some prior experience that this girl had and that was stored in that great web in her brain, and probably would have remained there forever were it not for the fact that Fatima's question has created an analogical connection that brought it out. That's a key learning connection that is rarely made in classrooms where rote learning is the norm.

III. 1976–2017, Thinking-Based Learning

"Telling the world about Kevin" in my life since 1976 has had an interesting history. I found other faculty who were really interested in what made Kevin's excursion into critical thinking with his students so successful. We looked into the "new" work that researchers like Benjamin Bloom, and Robert Ennis had done to start the "teaching thinking" movement, but especially to move the center of gravity of instruction in critical thinking away from logic and argument to the recognition that critical thinking, as practiced in our lives, involves the necessity to use a number of special critical thinking *skills*, like judging the reliability of sources carefully, with the objective of trying to find out what we should believe to develop the most reasonable picture of what is happening in the real world. Included in this conception of the domain of thinking was a shift also to include, as a key focus, the world of action, and not just belief, by emphasizing how important critical thinking is in good decision making and problem solving.

Through this research I developed a broader conceptualization of the kinds of thinking skills that we needed to focus on for pre-university students, using some of the categories of Benjamin Bloom—*analysis, synthesis, and evaluation*—but identifying, in those categories, specific types of thinking that people use every day like accepting sources as reliable, judging what caused something to happen, predicting things, making decisions, and solving problems. The idea was that these types of thinking are used by people world-wide every day, but not used well. Our mission should then be to help them use these types of thinking carefully and with skill. This is the framework that I and my associates now use for teacher-development, K–12.

But as important as this framework is, it does not include anything about the instructional methodology teachers need to practice to make teaching for skillful thinking effective. And in this we, too, searched the literature and research about new instructional methods, and developed a body of research ourselves about shifting to student-centered classrooms, making collaborative learning/thinking groups a classroom norm, using special questioning techniques that can replace lecturing in this context, and especially how important it was to help students learn constructive ways of using metacognition. Teachers using this instructional methodology are, in fact, modeling how good thinkers go about their thinking when the situation calls for it.

But there is also the question of what teachers help their students use these types of skillful thinking to think about. The challenge is, again following Kevin, how the norm in every classroom could be students not just learning how to do these kinds of thinking skillfully but also *using these thinking skills to engage with what they are learning in the regular curriculum*—what I call "***Thinking-Based Learning***". Now plenty of research that has been done about teaching thinking that has shown how ineffective teaching critical thinking is when taught in a separate course and how effective infusing it into content instruction is, when measured by its actual use in the lives of the students.

IV. Don't Ignore Creative Thinking

Amongst those whose initial work on teaching thinking I explored were Paul Torrance, Donald Treffinger, and David Perkins—three important figures in the initiative to make creativity and creative thinking something emphasized in education. In fact I got to know Donald and David, worked with them, and continue to work with David. What I learned was that creative thinking—thinking that yields new and original ideas—in no way conflicts with the use of critical thinking skills, but complements it. Any serious attempt to develop something new to solve problems or just advance our lives needs to be subject to the real world of facts through careful critical thinking if it is ever to be turned into something useful or to be transformed into an invention that can better our lives. But I also recognized that creativity needs to be conceived as much broader than aiming at real inventions—creative expression is an important domain of its own. In Bloom's earlier terminology, types of thinking that aim at creative products fall into the category of *Synthesis.*

V. Let's Go Back to 1996 and a Fifth-Grade Classroom in Lubbock, TX

A book is a roller coaster
Taking you up and lifting your spirits to the sky
Making your stomach churn
Something you will never forget
Taking you through different emotions, reaching the top
The next step is unknown, like the next page in a book
Surprised by where it takes you and where it might leave you
You're nervous, hands trembling, fists clenched as you wonder
What will happen next.
A book is a roller coaster.

Poetry, we are told, is born of inspiration, the poet "touched by the muse", and thinking can only interfere with this process. So, it seems, this poet, too, is carried away by these powerful images and conveys these feelings to us as we read what he wrote. Admittedly, this is not Shakespeare, Neruda, Paz, or Lorca. But perhaps the seeds of poetic inspiration have started to grow and may, with good cultivation, someday produce an equal to Shakespeare, Neruda, Paz, or Lorca.

Actually, this is a fifth-grade student who has been working with his classmates on how to produce effective metaphors, an enterprise that is an important variety of creative thinking. He has come up with a roller-coaster as a metaphor for reading a book. And it is clear that he knows the power of good metaphors. They don't tell us anything literally about their objects, but they do tell us things that are not only informative but also carry with them feelings, sometimes deep and exciting. We worked with the teachers in this school on how they can teach students to identify, create, and use good metaphors.

In this instance the teacher is Rebecca Reagan, and she introduces her fifth-grade students to the topic of metaphors by saying things like: "Metaphors are all around us, 'He's a real dynamo!' 'She's the light of my life!', 'Put that file in the trash.'"And we use them a lot. Can you think of any?" She wants her students to recognize that metaphors are the prime mode of expression in figurative language, and while metaphors are the creative backbone of fine poetry and literature, she wants her students to see that they are all around us.

Often teachers provide no instruction in how to create effective and powerful metaphors. Students just do it and some students seem to do this more naturally than others. One important thing that I have learned since my visit to Kevin is that *all students can learn how to develop effective and powerful metaphors, and to use them to communicate their ideas effectively and powerfully.*

VI. 2009, at Colegio Montserrat, in Barcelona, Spain

I showed the teachers at Colegio Montserrat how Rebecca had helped her students develop a thinking strategy that yielded writing like in the poem "Reading". I focused on how Rebecca first focused on metaphors in the life of the students and on how they convey what they say to us. But then she worked with them on techniques for coming up with new and good metaphors that they could express in words. She had done this in the style that went back to Kevin's classroom 20 years earlier. She was teaching them to stop, ask, think, and answer some important questions before they jump in with a metaphor. What questions?

"Let's think. What does the metaphor 'He's a real dynamo!' tell us?" Monika, a teacher at Colegio Montserrat, asked her students. "Well, certainly not that he is lazy and sloughs things off all the time. So what?" Some students respond: "He's a hard worker, keeps at it till he gets the job done." Another student says, "Not just that he keeps at it but does that with energy."

Monika continues. "What more does this metaphor do?" A student responded: "It stiffened me us up, like I was becoming a dynamo and really moving along with great energy. It almost *feels* that way." Monika adds: "Think about 'She's as radiant as a sunny day:' yes, bright, smiling, giving off wonderful feelings towards you, but feelings that you, too, feel! You smile, feel uplifted, and happy. Metaphors not only tell us things, they do so in a way that projects feelings, often strong feelings. Try 'He's a real skunk!' What feelings does that bring up in you?" One student responded: "Yuk."

So let's try finding a metaphor to use to say something. First, *What do you want to develop a metaphor about?* It could be reading a book, it could be living in a dysfunctional family, or it could be something we all know, like Spain. Just describing these things is often dull and does not convey the feelings they generate.

Next: "*Let's continue thinking: now let's think about what we want to say about the object.* 'Suppose the object is Spain. What do you want to say about Spain? Spain is what?'" Some students respond: "It is a country that loves music and dance." "It is a country of culture and art." "It is a country that produces outstanding and delicious food?" "What else???? Maybe it isn't something so nice. Maybe it's Spain is a backward country? or Years of dictatorship have ruined Spain."

People don't often stop and think about these things. But thinking further can make a big difference. Because now we can ask, and the teacher does:

"*What other things display these characteristics?*" From the students: "A huge art gallery?" "A painter's easel?" "Bacchus' dining room table?" "A food-lover's envy?" "A sinking ship."

"*Pick one that stirs you up! And let's think about the details.*"

Monika used a simple device to bring out this thinking. "*Let's first write down the details that we want to emphasize in what we want to say.*" So "outstanding variety of delicious food" may be elaborated by "people love to eat in Spain", "prepared in many ways", etc. and then let's do the same for the metaphor, say, "a food-lover's envy".

Now thinking about details that the metaphor you've chosen displays.

Then: "*Do they match significantly?*" Of course here we are emphasizing the need for a significant amount of similarity between the object and the metaphor.

From the students: "Hey, 'a food lover's envy' is a really good metaphor!!" From Monika: "Good thinking!"

Monika has shown them the poem "Reading". "But what about then creating a piece of writing like "Reading"? The metaphor is stated in the 1st sentence. What about the rest of the poem?" One student said: "It's in our list of details!" More good thinking!

Take another look at the poem "Reading" again with this in mind.

As I watched all of this I knew that all this organized explicit thinking and its results are a starter. Soon these students will do this with the skill of a concert violinist.

VII. 2016, Five-year-olds in Lima, Peru

What about drawing, painting, and sculpting—the traditional domains of creative expression? Well, I also remember visiting a classroom of five-year old students a few years ago. The students were asked by the teacher to use colored crayons to draw a picture of someone that shows something about that person. What? They said: "She's happy." Or maybe "She's sad." Or maybe "He's mad."

"*Well, OK, how are you going to do that with colors and shapes? First, find some colors that you think are like being happy. Some that are like being mad.*" And, of course, the students who said "happy" selected soft colors: yellows and pinks, while the students who were picturing being mad selected bright red, and black. And sad: grey, brown, and dull green. Then she said: "*And what are some shapes that are happy shapes, and some shapes that are mad shapes? And sad shapes. What are they like?*" They of course drew hearts and flowers for happy, and lightning bolts and heavy lines for mad, using the colors they had selected. Then she said: "*Now think about the shape of the person.*" Some did a smiley face, a face with firm lips and dark wide eyes, a shouting mouth. But one student drew one heavy but wavy gently curved vertical line ending with, at the top, a pronounced curve to the left. She asked: "Why is this sad?" Then he said: "It is an old man who is sick and worried that he may die soon." All the students heard this and there was silence. One little girl cried.

These, too, are metaphors. But they are the result of the teacher guiding the students *to think* before they drew. I could see some of these very young students, again with the right cultivation, learning, and experience, becoming someday like Velasquez or Goya, in which *everything* in their paintings is a metaphor in a way that says something powerful, important, and moving to us. Think about Goya's "The Third of May, 1808". This is not just an ordinary representation of something that happened on just another day in the war with France. It says something much more powerful. It is a complex and powerful metaphor for what? Injustice? Inhumanity? Mortality? The dark side? All of these and more? Look at the eyes of the man about to meet his death in contrast to the routine killing machine of the French. And remember, what it says to us is there planted in this painting deliberatively by using figures and images to represent with color and force something that never gets conveyed by "The Third of May 1803". Just another execution? No way.

Figure 3.1.3.1 *Francisco Goya, "The Third of May, 1808", Museo del Prado, Madrid, Spain*

I continue to think that the seeds have been planted in these young five-year-olds which, if cultivated well by subsequent teachers, can give us 21st-century Goyas. And I continue to think that this kind of talent can be drawn out of all children by good teachers. I think of the doors that have been opened for these children that are never opened if their teachers only show them how to fill in the numbered spaces on an outline with colors or splash paint on paper.

Or am I just an unfettered optimist about the power of good thinking?

Figure 3.1.3.2 *Bob Swartz surrounded by students and a teacher at La Vall School in Bellaterra, a small town near Barcelona, Spain, January 2017*

Robert J. Swartz is Director of the National Center for Teaching Thinking, USA, with branch offices in Spain and Peru. He received his doctorate from Harvard University in 1963 and is an emeritus faculty member at the University of Massachusetts at Boston (retired in 2002), where he was chairman of the Philosophy Department and founded a special interdisciplinary program on Law and Justice, and a master's program on Critical and Creative Thinking.

He has worked extensively over the past thirty years with teachers, schools, school districts, and colleges internationally in staff-development projects on restructuring curriculum and instruction by infusing critical and creative thinking into content teaching.

He is the lead developer of the Thinking-Based Learning Project and has authored ten books about this experience, including *Teaching Thinking: Issues and Approaches*, co-authored with David Perkins (1989, reissued in 2016, Routledge) and a series of five books of TBL model lessons, with commentaries (1995–2002, Critical Thinking Press).

His International Center for Teaching Thinking (CTT), a non-profit service organization for educators, is dedicated to providing educational programs of excellence on both teaching and assessing the skills of critical and creative thinking in K–12 schools and colleges in the US and around the world. The Center's remarkable history, collaborators, and international educational programs are described on its website at http://teach-think.org/.

College

Philosophy

On the Role of Philosophy in Education

William Alfred Wilder

The essay which follows is not primarily a presentation of what the role of philosophy in education in recent decades actually has been, but of my convictions on what that role should be.

Moreover, my undergraduate studies at Harvard were not crucial in forming the convictions to be set forth on this matter. I did take at least one course in philosophy while I was studying at Harvard. I remember it as a solid and informative course, but it was a course on the *history of philosophy*, not on *the role which philosophy should have in education.*

To be sure, there is today in educational centers in philosophy a powerful strain which maintains that the history of philosophy, the study of what qualified people have done and said in philosophy, is "the" way in which this subject can be entered into and studied. I do not share this conviction. To know what others have thought in philosophy is a deeply useful, indeed a continually and largely irreplaceable part of education in philosophy, but education in this field, in my conviction, can and must be carried out in a manner that is much more satisfying. It can and must be carried out in a way that *seeks to know the way things "are"*.

Insights from Studying and Teaching Philosophy

My convictions on the role of the history of philosophy and the role of philosophy in education were formed not at Harvard, but during subsequent studies preparing for ordination to the Catholic priesthood in the *Dominican Order* and during a good number of years teaching philosophy at the *Pontifical University of St. Thomas Aquinas* in Rome, this institution being itself a work of the Dominican Order.

My initial formation of convictions on the matters at hand occurred in a *House of Studies of the Dominican Order* located at River Forest, Illinois, a suburb of Chicago. In this center there was an unusually active and competent concentration of men attempting to explore and carry out the role of philosophy in education who, in addition to not relying solely on the history of philosophy, looked to an *Aristotelian* strain of thought in the matters at hand. More particularly, the House of Studies at River Forest looked to an understanding of the Aristotelian manner of education in philosophy as developed by St. Thomas Aquinas and the school of this doctor. The dedication of the River Forest House of Studies was outstanding, even in comparison to other Houses of Studies in the Dominican Order.

Apart from the role of the study of the history of philosophy, I think the most significant convictions of the River Forest School on education in philosophy were twofold. They involved the *relation of philosophy to logic* and the *relation of philosophy to science.*

> In regard to the first relation the convictions were these*: logic is not philosophy. Logic is a necessary instrument for philosophy*. It indicates to the latter what to do in order to know the way things are. Because human knowledge directly grasps things in the human intellect, and because as things stand as grasped in the human intellect they are universal, in a state of being general but not singular (the only way anything can exist outside the consideration of the intellect), the *proper object of logic is reasonal, unreal being.*
>
> Philosophy, however, by reference to the sensibly known real, which is indicated in a universal way in the intellect, can know the extra-intellectual, real. *Philosophy can know real being*. It knows it, however, *under the guidance of logic.*

Here it seems appropriate to point out that the classical texts for logic in the Aristotelian tradition are the "*Prior Analytics*" and the "*Posterior Analytics*" of the Stagirite. The first sets forth in an abstract manner the *techniques of logic.* This body of logic is termed "*formal.*" The latter sets forth the way in which abstract logical techniques can, in general, *be applied to guide the mind in coming to know real beings*. This latter part of logic is termed "*material.*" It is to be mentioned, however, that any minimally adequate *education in formal logic* must be supplemented by some mastery of basic texts on what has been accomplished in recent centuries in that field which bears the name of "*symbolic*" or (less acceptably) "*mathematical*" logic.

Given the convictions about the relation of logic and philosophy just set forth, after a rather lengthy development in medieval thought in general (not just in the Thomistic strain of that thought), a more detailed notion of the preparation for doing philosophy through the study of logic, that is a *theory of education for philosophy*, developed. It was expressed in the famous notions of the "*trivium*" and "*quadrivium.*"

> The"*trivium*" consists in the study of *logic itself* plus two secondary ways of leading the intellect to conviction, namely *rhetoric* and *poetics*. Rhetoric is seen as leading to conviction, not only by evidence of the matter at hand but by a consideration of *goodness* were the matter at hand the case. Poetics is seen as leading to conviction, not only by evidence of the matter at hand but by a consideration of the *beauty* and accompanying *delight* were the matter at hand the case.
>
> The "*quadrivium*" consists in using logic to try to reach *evident truth and science* in four of the less difficult fields of investigation in philosophy. Science is understood as certain knowledge based on the causes of things. The four less difficult fields of philosophy which make up the "quadrivium" are *arithmetic* and *geometry* (parts respectively concerned simply with quantity and with quantity spatially extended of the basic philosophical field of mathematics) and *astronomy* and *music* (these latter parts respectively of natures considered simply, and natures considered in movement of another basic philosophical field of philosophy, that precisely of the philosophy of nature).

Once the "trivium" and "quadrivium" have been mastered in the education of a student, he is ready to devote himself to the various fields of philosophy as a whole. Education in the "trivium" and "quadrivium" bring about the *acquisition of the liberal arts.* They are so called because they are *bases for the intelligent freedom of the human being.*

At this point it must be said that the characterization of *music* and *astronomy* as easier parts of philosophy in which to practice the application of logic is pitifully scant.

> When in regard to *music*, for instance, one considers the magnificent richness of music theory, of the history of musical composition, of the mechanical skills required to sing or to play a musical instrument well or even to build musical instruments (and all of these things in various cultures of mankind),

one sees what is meant in regard to the *poverty of content* alluded to in *its treatment in the "trivium."*

The same is true in regard to *astronomy*.

The extent of the parts of philosophy is not exhausted by the subjects of the "quadrivium."

In addition to *mathematics* (the study of *quantitative being*) and the philosophy of *nature* (the study of *mobile being*), philosophy includes *metaphysics* (the study of *real being* in general). These parts of philosophy are said to be *speculative*, that is, they *know simply what is true*.

There are as well, however, many other parts of philosophy which seek to know not just what is true but *what are true things to do*. These are first of all *ethics*.

This philosophy seeks to know what in regard to all instances of the good are the *good actions to perform*. (Curiously, although ethics is in a most radical way of liberating the human being, it is not said to be one of the liberal arts.)

There are, however, many other good things (each-together with the good and goods sought in ethics—constituting a "*bonumhonestum*"). Knowledge of *how to act rightly* in regard to these other goods constitutes a whole series *of practical arts*, and they are themselves a part of philosophy.

Examples of such practical skills would include *medical, legal, and engineering matters*, but it would not exclude the knowledge involved in *cooking, sewing, and building bridges*.

As a final indication of the fields of philosophy one must take note of those "*mixed sciences*" which seek *to understand natural, real things according to mathematical characteristics associated with them*. These mixed, mathematical branches of philosophy were recognized already in Aristotle and in the middle ages, but they form, of course, central realities in modern and contemporary science.

Revealed Truth and Theological Science

At this point I would be remiss and untrue to my convictions on education and the sciences if I failed to mention that quite distinct from, beyond, and far more important than all of the philosophical sciences there is *another way of knowing which can also be scientific*. I refer to the knowing which is *based on what God, infinitely knowing and morally perfect, says to us*.

This way of knowing at a most primitive level is understood to consist of *elementary, "kerygmatic" content* imparted initially to a recipient. As the recipient is able to grasp the content with some better understanding it is said to *be "catechetical"*.

Finally, however, as the recipient is able, to some extent, to *understand* the content of what has been said by God *in an ordered way* and according to its own causal situations, this knowledge is said to constitute *theology*. As such it is said to attain in some way to the *status of a science, a science quite distinct from any philosophical science.*

Theology as a science does not see its content but *must rely always on faith*, in believing what has been said. Because, according to Christian conviction, those saved through Christ will "see" God as He is after their life in this world, faith will give way to sight, the theology practiced under the discipline of faith does not constitute the highest way of knowing Him.

> As a clarification on this matter it needs to be pointed out that in the *Thomistic* tradition, it is contended that in this world it is normal that the life of faith be supplemented *by "mystical" experience*, a knowing that is described not as seeing God but (using the term analogously to a basic knowledge of sensation) as "*feeling*" the divine.
>
> As a final clarification on the matter of theological science it should be noted that theology is said to contain a branch, called *apologetics*, in which evident indications in nature and certainly knowable historical events are relied upon to indicate the existence of properly divine revelation. It remains, however, that the faith which is salvific and authentic must be initiated by supernatural grace at work in the believer.

Philosophy, Science, and Education

I return now to further considerations about philosophy, science, and education.

The process of *learning and practicing logic* as outlined in the understanding of the "trivium" and "quadrivium", which I have described, can be coordinated with a division in education almost universally acknowledged in the past and still present today in Western civilization. I refer to the division in that activity between *elementary, secondary, and university levels.*

The elementary level of this pursuit consists in acquiring with a minimum of reflection the ability to read, to write, and to perform elementary mathematical operations. Then at the secondary level of education one might be thought to take up the tasks of logic and first attempts at its use just outlined in this essay as the work of the "trivium" and "quadrivium."Education, using the tools of logic, in the whole field of philosophy would then be seen as the task of the university.

This assignment of tasks to various levels of education just outlined can hardly be said, however, to correspond exactly to the tasks actually undertaken at the three levels in schools under discussion in the past or today. Moreover, even on the level of notions of what ought to be the tasks of various levels of education the scheme I have indicated in the previous paragraph as suggested can hardly be accepted in simple detail.

On the level of *what ought to be the case*, there are various reasons for dissatisfaction. One problem here focuses on the "trivium."

> In the Thomistic tradition set forth in this essay, the poetics and rhetoric that appear alongside logic in the" trivium" are seen as inferior insofar as they are ways of bringing conviction in ways other than the evidential manner proper to logic. Rhetoric and poetics do possess powers of persuasion not present in logic, but these powers alone are seen as not fully justified.
>
> Historically, however, the role of poetics and rhetoric were often seen as worthy of far more attention than that given them in a Thomistic framework. Poetics (and well-constructed literature in general) have been seen by many outside the Thomistic tradition as possessing higher and entirely honest means of expression and persuasion simply not accessible to logical discourse. Thus, beginning in the late medieval period, and continuing especially in the Renaissance and post-Renaissance periods, *interest in poetics and rhetoric tended to overshadow interest in logic.*
>
> In that context, I think it could be said that in the history of the curriculum *for education in the liberal arts at Harvard*, we can at one point recognize the situation described. In re-reading recently Samuel Eliot Morrison's "*Three Centuries of Harvard: 1636–1936*", I think I detected the typical Renaissance attitude described in the parties involved in the great debate on the content of the undergraduate curriculum and education in the liberal arts that occurred at Harvard, as described by Morrison during the presidency of William Eliot.

Scientific Philosophical Knowledge

I return now to a point not about actual historical practice in the liberal arts, science, and education in philosophy but about *my convictions about what should be the case* in these fields.

I have mentioned the conviction that *philosophy* in its various parts can, through the *guidance of logic*, reach certain *knowledge of the real* that deserves to be called *scientific*. This is true not only in *ethics* and *metaphysics*, but also in the philosophy of *nature* (and the parts of this last, that is, in physics, chemistry, and biology). What examples of such putative scientific philosophical knowledge are to be seen?

> The best attempt to respond to this question that I know of is to be found in William Wallace's "*Principal Demonstrations in Natural Science*." This study presents convincing arguments to show the existence of science present in *natural philosophy*, complete with *syllogisms* and indications of whether the middle terms of the syllogisms are properties or causes (formal, material, efficient, or final) of the subject of the conclusions of the syllogisms. Unfortunately this brilliant study has never been published. There is, however, something similar to be found in the public domain in Benedict Ashley's *The Arts of Learning and Communication* (The Priory Press, Dubuque, 1958, pp. 578–599).

There is a final point to be considered about the commonly used *divisions of education and philosophy*. Can one assign the logically directed pursuit of all philosophy (with its scientific possibilities) to *an undifferentiated level of education termed that of the university?* Clearly this cannot be done. There would be entirely too much material to cover.

> This is why already in the high Middle Ages a distinction was drawn between the level of undergraduate and graduate university studies.
>
> On an *undergraduate level* one had to be content with studying philosophy in survey courses of general content in its various fields.
>
> Then in *further years of study* one could choose this or that important area of philosophy, ordinarily as a basis for subsequent life-supporting work, to be done by a student.
>
> Thus, it was that, apart from specialized study of theological science, one could study *medicine* and *law*, or other parts of philosophical knowledge.

This *division of philosophical education at the university level* has not been in the past and is not today always observed. In particular, the initial few years of university education can attempt to cover the survey courses in philosophy (and even of logic and practice in its application to easier philosophical materials) and specialized courses of philosophical science as well.

An alternative to this just-mentioned educational distribution is to *bypass explicit training in logic* and survey courses in logically directed *philosophical sciences* and to devote one's post-secondary education to study aimed at future life-supporting work. This can be attempted even entirely outside any formal school setting in on-the-job training traditionally known as *apprenticeship*.

> These alternative approaches to education and philosophy (or its absence) in university education or in apprenticeships are by no means impossible, but I think that the division of materials studied which has been identified as that of the Thomistic tradition is a generally more satisfying proposal.

I cannot, however, conclude this matter without mention of a characteristic present in effectively all undergraduate curricula today. This is the requirement that *every student must have some field of study in which he "majors."* Whether this major coincides with some field of postgraduate university studies or an area of future life work or not, it seems to me *that its presence is neither ruinous nor essential* to the content of undergraduate studies which I advocate in this essay.

Attainment of Scientific Surety

In regard to the attainment of scientific surety, which I am convinced philosophy can attain, it must be made clear that in fact *only a limited amount of philosophical discourse can reach the dignity of certainly known truth*. Much, indeed most, of this discourse doesn't go beyond the "*dialectical*" *status of consistency* which would be *explanatory hypotheses*.

In the state of "precertain" dialectical thought in philosophy, it is crucial to note that the *study of the history of philosophy* relevant to the material under consideration is a most useful, perhaps indispensable, element.

> Certainly, such a use of the history of philosophy was present in Aristotle and in thinkers throughout the years inspired by him. Moreover, it is clear that courses in the *history of philosophy* as a whole, following the lines of related development in the field, *must form a part of any adequate curriculum in liberal education*.

Finally it is clear than any adequate education must include an awareness of the *history of the species and varieties of natural things (evolution)* and of the history of the *cosmological and geological settings* in which the history of nature has taken place.

A consideration of the history of philosophy reveals that contemporary endeavors in the field are notably divided into two strands.

> The first consists of an *essentialist phenomenological trend* (stemming in large part from Edmund Husserl), which has morphed into what is called *existentialism* and, in the second place, various philosophical efforts designated as *linguistic analysis.*
>
> From the standpoint of the nature and division of philosophy which I favor, it is to be said that the *search for essential insight* at the origins of the first important movement in contemporary philosophy is altogether important in any *Aristotelian-Thomistic* tradition.

This is the case even though Husserl himself was hampered by a *nonrealist epistemology* that radically hampered his thought. (In fact, however, many of the most distinguished pupils and associates of Husserl were not in agreement with his ruinous epistemology.)

In regard to the many-faceted efforts to be seen in contemporary philosophy under title of *linguistic analysis,* the reader might wonder at the fact that the type of philosophy favored in this paper has not spoken of *the role of words and of language in human thought.*

> In answer to this query, I would say first that in the philosophy favored in this essay it is clear that *words and language are not primordial in thought.* They are *expressions of thought*, which is distinct from them. This is the case even though, somewhat confusingly, in the Thomistic and Aristotelian tradition there is an identification of the universal concept and content as an "*internal word.*" The term is used quite analogously here, however.
>
> The analogy is justified because, like the *ordinary, "external" word*, the *universal is something conceived*, produced by the abstraction of the intellect from the content of sense knowledge. It remains, however, that the *ordinary word and that language are not primordial in human thought and philosophy.*
>
> All this granted, it remains that the study of linguistics is a revealing and important part of human, indeed philosophical thought.

Summing Up

I close my considerations *on limitations of scientific accomplishment in philosophy* by reference to an uncompleted task.

I refer to the question of a certain, philosophical understanding of what is involved in the *theories of relativity* associated with Albert Einstein and what is involved in the theories of *quantum mechanics* associated with Werner Heisenberg.

Although I have not studied this question very thoroughly, my impression is that even the best writers in the field of Thomistic thought about science and philosophy (including members of the River Forest School) are rather skittish and *not even clear on what the truth is here.*

That said, I feel duty bound to say, once again, that I remain convinced that the philosophical accomplishments and ambitions set forth in this tradition are sound and should be reflected throughout any sound education.

Figure 3.2.1.1 *Fr. William Wilder, OP* (left), *with Pope John Paul II* (right) *at the Pontifical University of St. Thomas in Rome (Angelicum) on the occasion of the Pope's visit to the university*

College
Philosophy

William A. Wilder was ordained to the Catholic priesthood as a Dominican in 1965 and received a doctorate in philosophy from *Fordham University* in 1976. He was a member and several times dean of the Faculty of Philosophy of the *Dominican Pontifical University of St. Thomas Aquinas* in Rome from 1975 until 2010. He also served as a consultor of the Congregation for the Causes of Saints of the Holy See. He retired and returned to the United States in 2010. He now serves as house chaplain of the motherhouse of the Dominican Sisters of Nashville, Tennessee. He is also a member of Dominican Province of St. Martin de Porres in New Orleans.

Harvard

Harvard Athletics

Philip Haughey, Sr.

Most of the topics covered in this book are likely more esoteric and more abstract than the focus of the piece you are about to read. But I have chosen to dive into the more mundane, unvarying world of Harvard athletics because of the deep and personal significance that world has held for me over the past 64 years.

Harvard athletics are an important and essential part of the lifelong Harvard experience. Harvard is the oldest institution of higher education in the United States—over 380 years old. And although the proud history of sports at Harvard doesn't go quite that far back, Harvard's first intercollegiate sporting event took place in 1852 and was fittingly a competition in rowing against Yale. Even years later, however, the wonderful team experiences undergraduates have access to today would not be possible without the Department of Athletics' first-class leadership, together with the coaches, staff, students and alumni who make up Harvard athletics.

I have been involved with Harvard athletics since my first day on campus as a freshman. My time as an undergraduate resulted in freshman numerals in football, baseball and basketball; varsity letters in football, baseball and basketball; and the position of undergraduate President of the Harvard Varsity Club. I was highly involved myself, but it makes me proud to say that today more than four out of five undergraduates participate in some form of Harvard Athletics.

Over the past six decades, I've had the pleasure of participating in Harvard athletic programs under five University Presidents and six different Directors of Athletics. I have played for three freshmen coaches, three varsity coaches and worked with upwards of thirty assistant coaches. All were first-class people, although some were better coaches than others. All, however, were proud to be at Harvard and influenced the lives of hundreds of young men over the years. Of course, today's coaches and staff help shape the futures of both young men *and* young women, thanks to Title IX of the Education Amendments Act of 1972.

Post-college, I discovered alumni participation initially as President and Chairman of the Harvard Varsity Club, and later as Chairman of the Friends of Harvard Football. Later still I became Chairman of the Friends of Harvard Baseball, and Chairman of the University Visiting Committee for the Department of Harvard Athletics. Each of these opportunities has provided me with an even deeper perspective on the role of Harvard athletics within the University community.

Sports are a key part of a student's education here at Harvard. I can't state it any better than Bob Scalise, The John D. Nichols '53 Family Director of Athletics, when he said:

> "*The athletes in our broad-based programs are representative of the entire student body and are provided the same academic resources as their peers.*
>
> *This partnership with the College to support its mission helps in developing student-athletes into leaders in the community. Through the pursuit of excellence in the playing arena, players are gaining skills that aid their growth in the classroom and that are applicable long after graduation.*"

The Department of Athletics affords a wide array of opportunities to undergraduate students. Harvard College fields 42 intercollegiate sports—the largest Division I program in the United States. The College is home to 1,145 varsity athletes and 4,500+ club and intramural participants, spread across 66 club sports and 32 intramural sports. Our teams have brought home 381 Ivy League Championships over the years, and 142 National or NCAA Championships. Director of Athletics Bob Scalise and his staff of dedicated men and women make "*Athletics For All*" a reality at Harvard—whether those students are playing "quidditch" as part of a club team, or are one of the 236 Olympic athletes fielded by Harvard who have collectively brought home 103 Olympic medals. Over the years, our athletic fields and other venues have undergone renovations, rebuilds and upgrades. In 2017, our teams and facilities are among the best in the country—and among the very best in the Ivy League.

Of course, the Athletic Department cannot make all of these successes happen alone. It is fortunate to receive welcome cooperation, leadership and financial support from "across the River"—the Harvard Administration. Faculty oversight and guidance provide invaluable support to the Department and its programs. In addition, The Harvard Varsity Club (strong partner of the Department of Athletics) leads the way when it comes to setting up various "Friends Groups", hosting the annual Senior Letter Winner Dinner on the eve of Commencement, and publishing the popular "News and Views" of Harvard athletics. Bob Glatz, Broadbent Family Executive Director of the Harvard Varsity Club, and his highly capable staff deserve significant credit for creating this key part of Harvard athletics. Perhaps most importantly of all, however, my involvement has provided me with the opportunity to become more familiar with and appreciative of the "good people" Harvard athletics enables our undergraduates to meet, be supported by and learn from during their undergraduate tenure. Harvard's equipment personnel at the various venues on campus provide clean and safe equipment and Crimson uniforms to the teams that represent Harvard in its 42 intercollegiate sports. Many of us familiar with Harvard athletics warmly recall Jim Farrell, Richie Dwyer, George Ward, Jimmy Cunniff and later Chet Stone as very significant influences during our undergraduate tenures. They will always be missed over at the Field House.

The University's medical staff, trainers and coaching assistants provide quality medical care to our athletes day in and day out. Some—including the over 400 alumni who have gone on to play professionally—will remember all too well the names of Dr. Bart Quigley, Dr. Gus Thorndike or, more recently, Dr. Art Boland and Dr. Mark Steiner. But it is everyone combined—including the grounds crew, the maintenance folks, the parking attendants and game-day ushers—who make the athletic complex what it is and help contribute to a very special experience for our students.

Although I've had opportunities to serve the Harvard community in other areas of administration, including as Former President of the Harvard Club of Boston, Board Member of *Harvard Magazine*, Chairman of the Committee to Nominate Overseers and Directors, and as Chairman of the Alumni Committee on Shareholder Responsibility, it is my involvement in Harvard athletics which stands out as the most significant in my life. The value of my exposure to the best teachers of sport in the world, and to a faculty and administration that places just the right emphasis on a sports program for its exceptional student-athletes, cannot be overstated. Harvard does athletics better than all the rest. Today as I approach our 60th Reunion, it is an honor to still be part of that tradition and remain active serving such a worthy institution and its mission. I am proud to continue my work in order to ensure that Harvard's philosophy of athletics stays constant, and that we continue to approach winning with the pride and sportsmanship befitting of such a time-honored program.

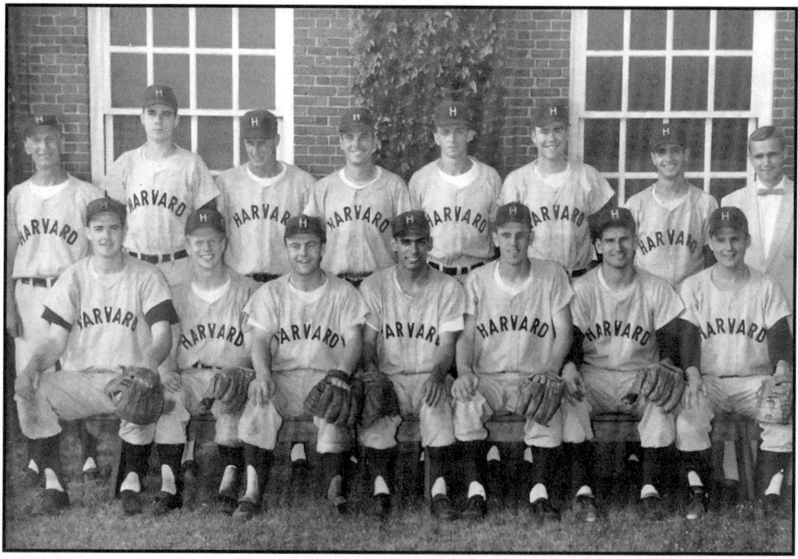

Figure 3.2.2.1 *Harvard baseball team 1957 lettermen*
Front (L-R): *Haughey, P. '57; Botsford, M. '57; Cleary, R. '58; Simourian, J. '57* (Captain)*; Hastings, R. '57; Repetto, D. '57; McGinnis, R. '57.*
Back (L-R): *Shepard, N.* (Coach)*; McGarrity, G. '57; Stahura, W. '58; Fisher, R. '57; Getch, J. '56; Hathaway, K. '58; Bergantino, T. '58; Hyslop, N. '57* (Manager)

Reprinted courtesy of Harvard University

My years associated with Harvard, and particularly with Harvard athletics, have enriched my life. I consider athletics to be an additional vertical subject matter alongside all the other important subjects covered by a Harvard University education. Through athletics, my eyes were opened to knowledge and experiences I otherwise likely never would have had. I learned many valuable lessons on the playing field that have been applicable to my whole life experience, including how to deal with and overcome adversity. Most importantly, I made many lifetime friends along the way whose gift of friendship I have so enjoyed.

We have a motto at the Harvard Varsity Club that the Club is "*Your Team for Life*". And whatever one's interests are, I feel that the Harvard College and Harvard University community can be *any* Harvard graduate's "*Team for Life*", too.

Phil Haughey has been involved with Harvard athletics and other activities for 64 years. He heads a small family real estate company that invests in, develops and manages properties throughout Massachusetts and Maine. He lives in Newton with his wife, Peggy.

How Harvard Influenced Me

Murray L. Levin

In September 1953, I took the MBTA (now the T) to Harvard Square from my home in Mattapan. I was 17, a recent graduate of Boston Latin School along with so many of my classmates, had lived in Boston all my life, and had never been to Harvard Square before. Even my Harvard interview had taken place at Latin School. My naïve and insular life had been spent commuting back and forth to Latin School, going to the Boston Public Library for an occasional reference, going to Fenway Park and Braves Field (there was a team called the Boston Braves that had won the NL Pennant in 1948), and going to the local movies. I had been to New York City a few times to visit relatives. That sums up my insularity. Oh, one more thing—I never had a non-Jewish friend until high school. Francis Murphy, who went to Holy Cross, and

I became good friends. Tom Hegarty and Bill Coyne actually took me to Midnight Mass on Christmas Eve, but that was in college. Unfortunately, all three of these good friends are gone.

That day, when I climbed the stairs at the Harvard Square Station, was the day of our registration for Freshman Year. My naiveté was so extreme that I couldn't understand why one of my Latin School acquaintances was going to live in the Yard. Why should anyone want to live away from home? I found the answer quickly, but to my disappointment even now, I never lived in a college room because of family finances. I did buy a used car sophomore year and drove other commuters for the same fee as the MTA would have charged them. The payments paid for the grease and oil for the car.

I should mention that I had entered Latin School in the ninth grade (Class IVB in the BLS terminology) because my parents thought that the daily transportation might be too difficult for me, a modest asthma sufferer. Most students entered in the seventh grade (Class VI). It was only in retrospect that I realized that those who started in Class VI had the best teachers who also demanded the most from their students. This resulted in a somewhat lesser preparation for Harvard. I memorized well, but thought little. I am certain that my own immaturity and lack of intellectual curiosity contributed the larger fraction of my surface thinking.

Whatever the reason(s), I was overwhelmed by having to write an in-depth essay on Bruegel's "Fall of Icarus" in Gen Ed A, and write an even more lengthy one on comparing Ortega Y Gasset and Thucydides on their views of the masses in Hum 3. Speaking of that Gen Ed A paper, one of my fellow students in the section asked if we could read each other's papers. I knew I was in deep trouble when I couldn't understand his at all. He turned out to be Junior Eight. My writing style was abysmal, and my analytical skills superficial at best. Thus began a less than stellar Harvard academic career.

Much of the reason for my mediocre academic showing was my own inability to turn on intellectually except in my field of concentration. I concentrated in Chemistry for two reasons—I liked it, and I knew I could do reasonably well in it. Nonetheless, I took many great courses and was influenced considerably by Faculty members Harold Martin, Eugene Rochow, J.J. Lingane, George Kistiakowsky, Howard Mumford Jones, Samuel Huntington, and Zbigniew Brzezinski (he filled in during Fainsod's sabbatical from Russian Government), and a visiting

Professor named Johnson from the University of Wisconsin who filled in during Louis Fieser's sabbatical from Chem. 20.

Perhaps it was Nobel laureate Konrad Bloch, my advisor and teacher, who influenced my approach most. He exposed me to a rational and sequential approach to solving problems that, when I remembered to use it, helped me to perform better in my professional life. All of these wonderful teachers tried to get me to be intellectually curious, to think in depth, to think analytically, and never to accept surface thought. I like to think that they had a modicum of success at times.

Whatever the reasons, I turned on academically as soon as I entered Tufts University School of Medicine. My appetite for learning medicine was even greater than my appetite for pizza and Chinese food. I had success, graduating cum laude and third in my Class. The intellectual curiosity and attempts to think analytically engendered by the Harvard Faculty and by the lunch-time bull sessions with very bright compatriots in the Dudley House dining room had tremendous influence on my development (such as it has been) and my approach to life.

I am convinced that the intellectual lessons I learned at Harvard helped me to succeed in my career, becoming a full Professor of Medicine, and in my love of the arts and literature.

I have been extraordinarily lucky to have married Joan, a woman with whom I have shared so much of life's enjoyments—whether music or art or literature or travel. Of great importance, she has put up with my aberrancies and peccadilloes with great patience. We have had a marvelous marriage. Without the love of the arts, literature, and history that Harvard fostered, I doubt that Joan and I could have shared so much.

There still remains a question to which the answer is impossible. Would my attendance at another college have given me the same intellectually curious attempts at in-depth thought as my limited capabilities permitted? It is a question, of course, that is impossible to answer. I attended Harvard College only. It is impossible to answer the unanswerable. I am only sure that whatever positive effects on my maturation and development that occurred were at Harvard. I shall also be grateful for the friendships I have had with classmates. Some of those go back to my days as a Boston Latin student and have been sustained. Others go back to Harvard undergraduate days. What is remarkable is the many friendships I have made with classmates I never knew until long after 1957. They are many and continue to be cherished.

So, how did Harvard influence me? It brought the life of the intellect and curiosity to my consciousness, it gave me an approach to life that I have found satisfying, it gave me the ability to share so much with the woman I have loved dearly for 56 years, and it has given me friendships that I cherish despite separating distances. Finally, it has given me sadness when I reminisce about the friends who are no longer with us.

Our Alma Mater has continued to influence my intellect, such as it may be, as well. Several years ago, I took the live online course on Justice given by Michael Sandel that Harvard offered to alumni(ae). I read much, from Aristotle through Bentham through Kant and Rawls and the Friedmans and Hayek, etc. In fact, this was the first time in my involvement with Harvard that I did all the reading and finished on time! I was exposed to concepts that tickled my curiosity to the point that I began to wonder whether there were roots to some, such as Kant and Rawls, in our western religious teachings and traditions.

Ergo, I read the Old Testament in full. I admit that I skipped a lot of the begats and the measurements of the Temple and of the Ark of the Covenant. I did learn all over again that we should care for the widowed, the orphaned, the poor, and the strangers in our midst. I reread the Golden Rule. I have since reconfirmed that every eastern and western religion of significance teaches a version of the Golden Rule. Perhaps more of us should remember that.

As a final shot, I would like to share several aphorisms that are, I think, *sui generis*.

(1) A human being's largest and most sensitive organ is the ego.

(2) The major messenger that the human male brain recognizes is testosterone.

(3) A corollary to Parkinson's Law that applied to my lecture style—Bull expands to fill the hour.

(4) Jews invented guilt, Catholics perfected it, and fundamentalists of all religions inflict it.

(5) To sum up my financial skills, if I invested in oxygen, human beings would stop breathing.

(6) I never pontificate when acting a bit all-knowing and pompous. Instead, I rabbinicate since there are no pontiffs in my religion.

(7) I dub less than intelligent thought as *cauda equina* thought. The *cauda equina* is that bundle of nerves (looking like a horse's tail) leaving the spinal cord at its bottom. It lies just behind the rectum. Therefore, *cauda equina* thought's quality is equal to its anatomic neighbor's.

ENOUGH! This is now much longer than a Gen Ed A paper.

I have written this with enormous gratitude for those four years, what came after, and for the great friendships formed with classmates.

Murray Levin has spent his professional life in medicine. A *cum laude* graduate of Tufts University School of Medicine in 1961, he did his internship and residency in Internal Medicine at Beth Israel Hospital in Boston and a two-year Fellowship in Nephrology at the University of Texas Southwestern Medical School in Dallas. He joined the Faculty at Northwestern University Feinberg School of Medicine in 1966 where he became Professor of Medicine and remained throughout his career. Currently Professor *Emeritus,* he served the Department of Medicine as Chief of Nephrology and Chief of Medicine at Lakeside VA Hospital, Chief of the Division of Nephrology/Hypertension at Northwestern McGaw Medical Center, and as a Teaching Firm Chief. He has been an officer in several medical research societies, published many papers, chapters and editorials, received teaching awards, and served on many university, medical school and hospital committees. He is still publishing and teaching at Medical Center conferences. His wife says he is still weaning.

Looking Back on My Education at Harvard College

David Folkman

While I compose these comments, I have been rereading a book by Thomas Kuhn, whose class I took during freshman year at Harvard.

I continue to be amazed by the impact my undergraduate education has had on my life in the succeeding years. Although careers in retailing and venture capital benefited from a Harvard Business School

(HBS) MBA as well, the liberal arts from my undergraduate years enriched my perspective and my effectiveness throughout my career.

My wife and I met at Harvard Summer School and now, after raising four children, three of whom are partnered and parents themselves, we are once again enjoying school together, taking continuing education classes at nearby Stanford University each quarter.

Much to my delight, one of the first Stanford classes we enrolled in was about the trials of Galileo. Our texts included Thomas Kuhn's, *The Copernican Revolution* and *The Structure of Scientific Revolutions.* As a freshman, I read much of Kuhn's work in mimeographed, pre-publication form. Kuhn co-taught, with Leonard K. Nash, the General Education course known as *Natural Sciences 4.* This course took place in the then beautiful and relatively new Allston Burr Lecture Hall, a structure that was completely replaced in 1985 by the Sackler Museum.

College—Lasting Friendships

In September 1953, my brother, Judah (HMS '57), and I drove from our home town, Columbus, OH, to Cambridge so Judah could drop me off at the gate nearest Wigglesworth I-31. Judah then went off to Vanderbilt Hall at Harvard Medical School. During that freshman year I met five classmates who would become my suitemates in Eliot House, I-21 and I-22: Irv Fuller, David Terris, Steve Lieberman, Lou Klein, and Bob Israel. All six of us remained friends after graduation, and attended the 25th reunion. Irv passed away before our 50th, but Bonnie Fuller joined all of us for that reunion. One highlight of that week was a special dinner in a private room at the Faculty Club including Bonnie Fuller, Steve and Sheila Lieberman, Susan and David Terris, Lou and Linda Klein, and the then fiancée of Bob Israel, Jennifer Dizon, and, of course, my wife, Susan, and me. Bob and Jenn were married a month after this fabulous reunion dinner evening.

Learning Business in the Field

After graduation I worked in a Houston department store for a year. Susan and I married in June, 1958, and three months later I entered Harvard Business School. Our next move was back to Houston where I returned to the same store and spent a number of years as a buyer and a merchandise manager for ladies' ready-to-wear. It was during this period that we adopted four wonderful children, and in 1969 the six of us moved to St. Louis, where I became a vice president and general merchandise manager in a large department store. Susan earned a master's degree in St. Louis before we made another move, this time to San Francisco where I joined Macy's in 1974 as a senior vice president for merchandising. Eight years later I moved about a block away to take the position of president and CEO of a large department store, Emporium-Capwell, to lead a turnaround.

From Business Operations to Venture Capitalism

After some 30 years in the department store field I became a partner in a venture capital firm in Menlo Park. Four of twelve partners focused on retail and consumer start-ups, some of which are today well-known enterprises: Ross Stores, Gymboree, PetSmart, and Callaway Golf. My next career step was to become president and CEO of Esprit US, once again in a turnaround situation, designing and manufacturing young women's and kids' apparel and accessories that we sold to most of the major American department stores. Then I joined a San Francisco–based consulting firm focused primarily on turnaround management. After some years, I became an independent consultant for a variety of retail and consumer products businesses and eventually began to do pro-bono consulting for interesting consumer businesses and mentoring MBA students at Stanford Business School.

Stress and Coping Skills

Shortly after we moved to San Francisco, Susan enrolled in doctoral program in educational psychology at University of California, Berkeley. She earned her PhD in 1979 and launched a career in research on stress and coping, first at Berkeley and then, from 1988 to 2010 at University of California San Francisco. At US she was appointed Professor of Medicine and the Osher Foundation Distinguished Professor of Integrative Medicine and served as the founding director of the Osher Center for Integrative Medicine. The four children scattered, settling in Minnesota, Massachusetts, Oregon, and Napa, CA. The three older children married and each has two children—so there are six grandkids as well.

Our Times

I recognize how fortunate my classmates and I were in the mid '50s to be at Harvard. It's with great pleasure that I remain in contact with many classmates, although there is the bittersweet memory of loss of two roommates, David Terris and Irv Fuller, and the many other classmates whom we remember during reunion memorial services.

I am struck by the contrast between our relatively conventional lives and the extraordinary social context in which our lives have unfolded. We were born during the Great Depression and began our schooling during WWII. We lived through the social upheavals of the '60s, the sexual revolution in the '70s, and the beginning of the digital age.

And now we have lived through the challenging Obama years in which our country moved from the brink of national and worldwide economic failure to a point of a relatively stable and favorable economic climate.

Now we face great uncertainty as the Trump administration completes its first month in office.

My hope is that the outlook will be more positive and happier at the time of our 65th Reunion.

David Folkman as a former general partner with US Venture Partners has experience with start-up investing in retail enterprises and a venture capital portfolio that included Ross Stores, Gymboree, PetSmart, Imaginarium, and Callaway Golf. He is known as a senior retail, wholesale, and consumer products executive with 35 years of general management experience in department stores, specialty stores, consumer products and services, and branded wholesale fashion apparel and accessories. David has held CEO positions with Esprit US and for The Emporium, a 22-location department store chain (now owned by R.H. Macy & Co., Inc.) and the position of Senior VP for Merchandising, Macy's West. David is also recognized for his turnaround experience.

Although retired, David continues to do pro-bono consulting with young entrepreneurs working on start-up business planning. He is active with the Harvard Schools Committee, interviewing applicants to the College each year, and with the Harvard Business School Community Partners in the San Francisco Bay Area.

Recollections and Reflections

John B. Read, Jr.

After 60 years since graduation from Harvard, Class of 1957, I, John Read, wish to share a few thoughts.

First, I wish to thank Harvard College's administration for the support in helping me pay for my four years at Harvard College. Due to a family financial crisis, I was left with the responsibility of paying for my four-year education at Harvard College, which then amounted to about $1,000 per year. Due to the help and sensitivity of Harvard College's administration, I was able to undertake three different work assignments for pay at the College while there, in addition to other work, more particularly a summer job delivering milk for Hood Milk on Cape Cod and odd job work for residents in Cambridge.

The educational process at Harvard College did much to prepare me for my work engagements in the years to follow to the present day, 60 years later, which included working for financial institutions and in my later 30 years to the present time, engaging in the business of restoring and selling antiques.

Finally, the other benefit of my education at Harvard College was my meeting classmates with whom I have continued to maintain contact and benefit from their support. At present, if any members of the Class of 1957 are engaged in the sale or distribution of antiques, I would look forward to being in communication.

At this point in life, I wish you all good health and continued good fortune.

John Read, Jr., joined Hanson Handicraft, an importer of Swedish fine items, after graduation. He then went to the New England Trust Company of Boston. When it merged with Merchants National Bank of Boston, he took a sales manager position at Nuclear Metals/Tube Division in Somerville, MA, until 1964. John earned an MBA degree from Columbia in 1966. He then worked at First National Bank of Boston but left to establish Read Associates, a banking consulting business, which was stimulating and rewarding. In the 1990s, he stopped consulting to establish Blue Butter Churn Antiques.

Interesting Times for the Meritocracy

Nelson W. Aldrich, Jr.

"Reunions have some quality of what one hopes is the Kingdom of Heaven—not, I mean, in the euphoria of drinks and doings but in a tone of something like the ultimate democracy in which everyone has something, no one has everything, and there is a mood of sharing and valuing . . .

People have obviously to make a living and may not all convey the ultimate in taste or learning, yet are strangely reflective, have read and thought about things, and looked around them.

So I am all for Reunions and hope that you and your family will somehow manage [to come to] yours. It would be splendid to see you for old and new times sake."

– John H. Finley, Jr., letter to TK, 1950s

* * *

Meritocracy came to Harvard during WWII, and by the early '50s—by 1953, say—it began to pinch some of us. You may remember that each autumn incoming freshmen were greeted by barely muted boasts, issued by the Administration, published in *The Crimson*, repeated by authority figures at various gatherings, that very soon public high school graduates would outnumber the graduates of private schools. Why this news should have been a source of pride to Harvard was never explicitly explained, even to those of us who might have been expected to need an explanation, people we would *soon* learn to label preppies, clubbies, and only recently, legacies—in a word, the "***privileged***".

None of this entitled us to an explanation. Especially, perhaps, as our only ground for needing one was that the coming ascendency of the public school types represented a descendency, let's call it, for the private school types. Harvard's comparison of the two was invidious: it was wounding. Harvard, in this respect a synecdoche for America, considered the children of privilege on average as dumber than other children. *The Crimson* published proof of it: relative scores on the SAT would show for decades that, despite the frantic efforts of the private schools to keep the children of privilege up to the mark, the mark kept moving higher.

"*Let's have a look at your safety schools,*" the college counselors at the New England boarding schools learned to say.

Out in the real world, however, the meritocracy was carrying all before it. Like Jim Joslin's footwork on the field, the very word dazzles opponents. No wonder, as a system of promotion, it fits neatly with other shibboleths that guide our civilization—our capitalist economy (efficiency), our governments (transparency and open access), and, rather less neatly, liberal democracy itself (equality). And while the children of meritocracy may not always be so much better than the children of other systems, those other children can be horribly worse.

Since November, however, my mind has been helplessly drawn to another category of Americans, the near majority who are thought to be (not least by themselves) as without merit. I mean the poor, in spirit if not in everything else, specifically the white(!) urban and rural underemployed. An ancient reflex labels these folks "forgotten". And, true enough, until they and the party hacks and donors of the GOP levitated Donald J. Trump to the White House, they were forgotten.

But why so easily? I think the reason is that American meritocrats expect that, so long as the algorithms of the great American sweepstakes seem fair, *the losers will accept their fate.* Why shouldn't they? How many times did they have a chance to take the exams, from the sixth grade on, and then flunked, and flunked, and flunked again?

A stunning misunderstanding enters the drama here. Like other scorned human beings, the forgotten ones looked around them to find something to blame. In the 1950s many meritocrats thought it was "the rich". All authorities from Karl Marx, who theorized the myth, to the busy little election calculators of the Democratic Party, who feared the myth might come true, believed that inequality of wealth and income was what gave point and substance to left-of-center political parties. The election of Trump proved otherwise. The poor, as David Brooks noted with relief, love the rich.

We have known whom they hate all our lives, and, to quote Pogo, they are us: the smart asses, the bitches, the Harvard fairies, the people who got as far as they could go by doing better than other people at exams.

I got in a fight with one of these guys in Harvard Square. I learned his name later: it was Moose. We'd been drinking—in separate booths of course—in the after-hours bar over the *Wursthaus*, and at closing time, on the way down the long steep stairs to Boylston Street, I heard him call me, precisely, a fucking Harvard fairy.

I chose to take offense for a ridiculously Harvard fairy reason. I'd been in a high-toned argument with a friend, Fred Kimball '54, on the virtues of physical courage. Kimball thought it hadn't any; I thought of honor, and so Moose and I came to blows in the street. We were arrested almost instantly, locked up separately in the Central Square station, and arraigned in court that morning. Even there we couldn't get free of ideology. The judge, a palpable Harvard man (tweeds, mid-Atlantic accent), showed his solidarity with the meritocracy by chastising a rising member of it "*for his own good*". Me he fined $100, no small sum even for a rich kid; Moose he fined $15.

We meritocrats began pulling away from guys like Moose around the sixth grade, after which it became unthinkable for us to drop out of the game. The stakes were so very high. So for almost 75 years, we worked harder and harder on the high road to merit. We worked so hard that we forgot the boys and girls we were leaving behind, one grade after another—if we ever knew them. We forgot even our competitors, friends perhaps, who failed to keep the pace. But these are merely the "externalities" that we learned to ignore as we rushed to gather the material and spiritual rewards that a meritocratic society prepares for its hard, hard workers.

I now have to bring one of our House masters, John H. Finley, Jr., into this essay. He is relevant principally because he knew so well the ideological struggle between the meritocratic and the legacy principles, and stood, nimbly and gracefully, with one foot in each camp. He could do this because his own invidious principle antedated both, and contributed indispensably to both. His principle was *arête*, the normative Greek idea of personal human excellence. For him, as for all cultivated meritocrats, I'm sure, *arête* is a worthy standpoint from which to criticize meritocracy without doing it too much damage. This is so because the idea of human excellence immediately puts a lot of pressure on the weakest point of the meritocratic case, the notion of "*merit*" itself, its irredeemable squishiness. In short, Mr. Finley wanted "*merit*" to be awarded to possessors of excellent human qualities other than the ability to pass standardized tests.

Many of his other qualities are favored by meritocrats: leadership ability, some obvious talent or other, athleticism, intelligence, honesty, good character, maybe good looks and charisma (grace). But there was one quality he looked for which would stick in the craw of any true meritocrat, a quality more worried over in the fifties than today: *family background.* He meant by that a Harvard pedigree (Mr. Finley was self-consciously an institutional man), but he also meant the whole cluster of desiderata that, to be frank, we all want to know about each other in our social lives.

An amusing story about Mr. Finley illustrates the point: it involved the dean of a law school who had just read one Mr. Finley's famously effective letters of recommendation. This one, like others on occasion, dwelled lovingly on the virtues of the applicant's family. The dean couldn't resist reading it aloud in the office, and burst out: "*The guy just wants to get into a law school, for God's sake; he's not looking to make it into a stud book*!" In some sense, the personal/social sense, the two were not that different to Mr. Finley.

Facts should play a role in admissions judgments as in most others, the Master believed, but he could never discount the power and uses of myth. After all, myths are built up on facts by belief, and crucially by particular human *needs to believe.* This was especially true in students' endless struggles to find "the best", all kinds of best. Each year, he was proud to remark, whole rafts of students fretted to be admitted to Eliot House, drawn by the need to believe in a "best" House.

Incidentally, this is the proper context for Mr. Finley's widely alleged snobbery. The allegation was not wrong, but student gossip was far too tightly focused on his snobbery about family background. This stuff was naturally scorned by the meritocratic contingent in the House, and mortified the legacy contingent. But the fact is that every Dining Hall in the college, at every meal, in every age, seethes with snobbery. That's one of the things that adolescents do: they fight over who and what is the "best", and in every domain of judgment. I remember one argument I heard at lunch, about the greatest artist in history. Was it Rembrandt of the late portraits or Beethoven of the late quartets? (What do you say about *that*, Moose?)

All this might just go to show that Mr. Finley was an unabashed elitist, and he was. So was virtually everyone else at Harvard, not to mention the institution itself. Until just the other day "elite", like meritocracy, also seemed to fit quite comfortably into American notions of democracy, equality of opportunity, the American Dream, and the rest of it. But for Mr. Finely, when the two didn't fit, the discord caused a good deal of trouble throughout his Mastership.

It began in the corner of University Hall where the office of Student Housing toiled away, unhappily aware that Eliot House, as one bureaucrat of the day told me, had become "a Harvard within Harvard." This was outrageous, he said. "Students who had worked so terribly hard to get into Harvard no sooner got in than they discovered they had to strive again to get into Eliot House." It would be ever thus, needless to say, in the meritocratic life. But my informant evidently believed that Harvard students deserved to be protected from this harsh reality as long as possible. Elitism was intolerable, unfair, undemocratic, even perhaps unmeritocratic—at least when it troubled the ideological equanimity of Harvard College.

The same hilarious tangle is entrapping Harvard even now, in the fracas over the clubs. But for Mr. Finley, University Hall became a serious threat to his ideals of excellence, and inevitably to his institutional power. The latter, known as *Masters' Choice* (choice of students for the House), was chipped away in the course of his tenure. By 1969, when he was succeeded by Alan Heimert, the power was gone. This left the larger conflict to be resolved by democracy's solution to many stubborn contradictions: a lottery. But there was a problem: Mr. Finley was, by background and conviction, a democrat, and the fight over *Masters' Choice* undoubtedly caused him some ideological pain.

What would Mr. Finley have to say about Trump and his base? I have no idea. He was a fastidious man, allergic to violence of any kind. (His daughter Corinna Hammond never understood how he could disdain the street violence reported in the *Boston Globe*, then unconcernedly turn to parsing a truly grisly passage in the *Iliad*.) Trump himself, whom many meritocrats believe to be a monstrous piece of projectile vomit sculpted deep in the bowels of our commercial culture, would leave the Master speechless with disgust and horror. But Trump's wretched supporters would be quite another matter, deserving the pity and terror that Aristotle taught to see in great tragic drama. Marx and Nietzsche tossed the urban and countryside poor into their sacks of deplorables: the one saw a lumpen proletariat of rural idiots, the other saw "*a whole tremulous realm of subterranean revenge, inexhaustible and insatiable . . .*"

But Mr. Finley, given the chance, would see his neighbors in Tamworth, N.H. Folded sweetly into the White Mountains, Tamworth was the summer home that he missed, by only a few weeks, being able to call his birthplace. It had its share of summer meritocrats; a larger one of legacies, including the Finleys; an increasingly discouraged native middle class (the one mill in town failed less dramatically than others in the Merrimac Valley, but the jobs went south regardless); and a large group of contingent workers and wives who made a precarious living off the summer people. *Cognoscenti* called this latter group "*Swamp Yankees*", upland cousins of Maine's *"Down Easters"*, so beloved of upper class collectors of quaint folkways and accents. He knew these people well and in his way treasured their friendship: raising scholarship money to make meritocrats of their children; and in his charming fashion clothing them in Greek or Brahmin Boston mythology.

The American tragedy of Trumpism has few roles for the rural poor, but "***Victim***"—the role of supporters seduced and betrayed—is emphatically one of them; the mills will never open again. Yet the final accounting of the revolt against the meritocracy will show that it wasn't "jobs" that set it off. It will be seen as a tragedy of democratic education, the meritocracy's failure to educate all the people in democratic ideals and mechanics, to stop lying to them, and finally somehow to include them, after so many centuries, in the polis.

It is probably fair to say that, of all the mythic figures Mr. Finley conjured out of his life and reading, his best beloved was Huck Finn. They make an improbable pair, for sure: the dapper figure of the Master of Eliot, a brilliant adept at what he called "*the champagne of languages*", promoting into his pantheon an abused, defiantly filthy son of the Mississippi swamps as perhaps the "truest" American (at least as true as Tom Sawyer, a rising meritocratic salesman if there ever was one). But he did: he even seriously proposed that a statue of the boy be erected in Harvard Yard.

Then, in June, 1952, he went to California, the "territory" Huck probably intended to "light out for", to deliver the graduation speech at Pomona College. It was possibly the best speech he ever wrote.

In his peroration he summoned Huck, as if to introduce one of the "forgotten" to some of the better-favored meritocrats in the territory.

Here is what he said:

> "*Some of you may meet [Huck] in Korea, all will run into him someplace.*
>
> *He is the insecurity of the safe living room at home, the wind of doubt and boredom that ruffles the shrubbery of the quiet suburbs.*
>
> *He is loneliness, and no one is ever at home in the wide world, or with himself, who has not made friends with him.*"

Nelson W. Aldrich, Jr., began his checkered career in 1957 at *Paris Review*, and went thence to The Congress for Cultural Freedom, an overly maligned clandestine operation of the CIA. After three extremely pleasant years in Paris, he returned to Boston and was a reporter for *The Boston Globe*, which was also most agreeable. He was then invited to join WGBH-TV as news director, which proved quite disagreeable (much too collegial). Then it was off to teach fifth-graders in Harlem, an excruciating exercise in *noblesse oblige* for him and a disaster for his pupils. This was followed by a flurry of editorial jobs in NYC, culminating in a five-year post at *Harper's*, which he enjoyed very much, perhaps too much, until he was fired by his great friend, to this day, actually, Lewis Lapham. Then followed an anxious but otherwise happy time as a freelancer, writing for every magazine he wanted to write for, except one. He also wrote or edited three books, two of which—*Old Money* and *George, Being George* (Plimpton, that is)—did well, critically and commercially.

Humanities—Shakespeare

My Teaching Odyssey

Alan Dessen

My first stab at recollections and reflections drew a blank, though in 2007 at the request of someone on the staff of *The Harvard Crimson* I had written something that never made it into the newspaper. These days, having retired in 2005, I am happy to sit back and enjoy watching the accomplishments of our two children: our daughter, Sarah, has her 13th Young Adult novel coming out in June; and our son, Michael, is currently Chair of the Music Department at University of California Irvine but still manages to make music as an "improv jazz" trombonist and composer.

To provide a semi-coherent narrative, I have decided to supply an anecdotal account of my 50 years in the classroom in six different venues.

The Hopkins Years

First, during my four years as a graduate student (Johns Hopkins, 1959–63) I served as a Teaching Assistant (*TA*) who initially stumbled into a composition course for freshmen (I had no training in rhetoric or pedagogy) and then spent three years teaching a variety of items from English and American literature. Some of the works on the syllabus set by the professor were new to me, so at times I was barely one step ahead of my students, with the seniors among them only a few years younger than I was (though, of course, I had the *Power of the Grade*). My major discovery was that I enjoyed the give and take of discussion even when an unexpected question or comment interrupted a so-called lesson plan.

The Wisconsin Years

Then, with PhD in hand (and newly married to Cynthia) I headed off to my first real job at University of Wisconsin (1963–69), blissfully unaware of the troubles that lay ahead. In 1963, there was already tension between the University at one end of State Street in Madison and the State Legislature at the other, with a few legislators trying to build reputations as heirs to Senator Joe McCarthy by getting students to report back on controversial comments delivered by faculty. In a class on More's *Utopia*, I trotted out the usual interpretation—that the author was, to some extent, building on early Christian teachings about community—at which point a show-off undergrad asked me: "Are you saying that Christ was a Communist?" I was bailed out by a nun (an MA candidate) who gave an informed response that would have been beyond me. I soon inherited a Shakespeare course that in its second semester had 400 students and seven TAs. Given the size, I never got to know most of the students, as typified by an experience in Florence when, leaving the Uffizi in a rush to meet Cynthia for lunch, I passed by a young lady rapidly going by in the opposite direction who said: "Hi, Dr. Dessen." I never found out who she was.

The late 1960s was a time of turmoil on college campuses linked to the draft, Viet Nam, and race relations. I had my large class interrupted by a polite group of African-American students seeking to present their demands—and the event turned out to be relevant to the play at hand, *Julius Caesar* (in today's jargon, a teachable moment). Our lecture room in Bascom Hall was opposite the Chancellor's office, a flash point for protests, so that during one tense period to get to class my students had to walk between two lines of National Guardsmen carrying fixed bayonets. On a lighter note, a young lady came up to me after a final class and revealed that she had been bringing her deftly hidden tiny dog to my lectures for the entire term. She added: "He enjoys your lectures." When I asked, "How do you know?" she replied that during her Psych class the previous hour he growled the whole time but was peaceful, perhaps content, when I was talking. Maybe that's the highest compliment I got in my teaching career.

The Northwestern Years

I next moved to a smaller campus (Northwestern University, 1969–73) just in time for a retirement party for a senior colleague. One of his friends said to me wistfully: "There goes 40 years of teaching experience," but a junior colleague, not a fan of the retiree, whispered in my ear: "Not true. There goes one year's teaching experience repeated 40 times." I never forgot that comment, particularly when I myself passed that 40-year mark.

At Northwestern, I did know my students and often learned from them. One of my brightest undergrads absented himself from the two weeks we spent on Donne's poetry but subsequently turned in perhaps the best paper on that poet I have ever received. Clearly, he had no stomach for hearing me mess around with lines and images he had fully digested for himself. My favorite moment came in a course devoted to plays by Shakespeare's contemporaries that had a mix of undergrads and grads when, after a class, two grad students apologized that they would have to leave the next session early because they were graders in a large lecture class and had to pick up the bluebooks. I made the mistake of saying "OK, but this is a drama course, so make a good exit." Midway in the next session, one of them slammed his textbook against his desk and said: "I've had enough!!" and stormed out of the room, leaving the undergrads flabbergasted. The effect was spoiled a bit by his colleague, who paused at the door to deliver a short Epilogue in couplets, but that previous moment was one of the most electric in all my years of teaching.

Settling in at the University of North Carolina

In 1973 I moved to the University of North Carolina (*UNC*), Chapel Hill, where basketball trumps Shakespeare and everything else. Starting in 1974 I also started teaching or co-teaching short summer courses at the Oregon Shakespeare Festival and became addicted to seeing the plays not solely as words on a page but also as words and images to be performed. Here, and in annual trips to the UK that started in 1980, I got a post-graduate-school education thanks to interactions with talented and highly committed actors and directors whose take on what they were doing was very different from mine, a set of alternatives that laid the groundwork for my scholarly work as a theatre historian.

That development in my thinking was enhanced by the arrival in the late 1970s of both the early unwieldy VCRs and ¾-inch cassettes, and the beginning of the BBC-TV Shakespeare series where eventually versions of the entire canon were available. I had never found a way to use the already available Shakespeare movies, for to show them outside of scheduled class times was impractical owing to students' complex schedules. Pedagogically, I discovered the huge advantage of the *pause* button, so that I could show part of a scene and stop for discussion, especially if the choices made did not correspond to a reading of the text presented in the intimidating double columns of a complete works edition.

Classroom technology increased during my roughly 33 years at UNC so that cassettes and cassette-players were phased out in favor of DVDs and overhead projectors. The most welcome change was the appearance of more movies and TV productions that could be used in class—and having two or more versions of the same scene (e.g., the prayer scene in *Hamlet,* the final sequence of *Twelfth Night*) became one of my favorite ploys. However, the same cannot be said about the plays of Shakespeare's contemporaries where the pickings were (and remain) slim.

During over three decades at UNC, I did have some classroom experience with adult clientele. As already noted, between 1974 and 1993 I taught or co-taught (with an actor or director) a short course at the Oregon Shakespeare Festival linked to that summer's offerings. Students included high school teachers, retirees, and regular festival playgoers who wanted to get more out of what they were seeing, so that their comments and evaluations were significantly different from what I had come to expect from undergrads and even grad students. My favorite moment was a reaction to an anecdote I regularly use when dealing with the chaste Isabella's problematic choice in *Measure for Measure,* when Angelo tells her she must sleep with him or her brother dies. A famous Shakespeare professor after his official retirement decided to take this play and its problem on the road to area high schools but was taken aback when female students asked him: "Well, what did Angelo look like?" When I recounted this story, a high school teacher from California responded that her students would not have reacted that way. Rather, their question would have been: "What kind of car does he drive?" Situational ethic?

Another intensive program with an adult group came in 1995–96 at the Folger Shakespeare Library, where director Audrey Stanley and I ran a National Endowment for the Humanities (*NEH*) funded Institute entitled "Shakespeare Examined through Performance" that once a month brought 16 college teachers from both English and Theatre departments to DC. Each session we saw and dissected a professional production and did exercises and scene work, and to that mix I contributed material on theatre history and what we know (or think we know) about the original performances. The participants were talented and outspoken, so that sessions were unpredictable, arguments were not limited to the classroom, and the atmosphere could be electric. From this experience I learned as much as the supposed students and have kept up with this group via e-mail for 20 years.

Approaching Retirement

By 2004 I was ready for retirement. I was still okay in the classroom (and new teachable DVDs were turning up), but much of the time I found myself recycling previous preparations rather than coming up with fresh material. My students may not have known the difference, but I did. Moreover, the bane of teachers in English Departments—providing grades for exams and papers—had struck home, to the point that my complaints became a standing joke among my colleagues. As one with an active academic conscience, I still felt compelled to put comments on a student's independent work, but doing so for over four decades had taken a toll. In May 2005, I was greatly relieved that I managed to get through my last set of papers and exams without hitting the marathoner's wall.

Returning to the Fray—Teaching in Lifelong Learning Programs

I would not describe myself as burned out, but at that point I assumed that my teaching days were over. I did attempt a short Shakespeare course in Spring 2007 in Duke's Institute for Learning in Retirement (*DILR*) program for retirees, but found I was not yet ready to return to the classroom. However, in Fall 2010 that program had come under the umbrella of the national Osher Lifelong Learning Institute (*OLLI*) program, so five years after my official retirement I got back in the saddle and am currently teaching my 14th course. If my offering devoted to five Shakespeare comedies planned for fall 2017 does materialize, I will have taught 35 of the 37 items in the traditional canon (left out in the cold are *Timon of Athens* and *Henry VIII*).

Teaching Shakespeare's plays at OLLI has been a delight. First and foremost, there are no grades, no papers, no exams, and no administration. During my years at Northwestern and UNC, I had managed to sidestep being a department chair or dean, but as a result I ended up taking on more than my share of other tasks (so that for me *committee* became a four-letter word). What OLLI offered was all the joy of being in the classroom without the hassle. Yes, there remained problems with malfunctioning equipment and weather-related class cancellations during winter sessions, but the clientele is forgiving, and we muddled through. As in Oregon, participants put down their money and signed up because they wanted to be there, so that the major problem in teaching undergraduates (establishing the value of your course to those merely trying to fulfill a requirement or an empty slot) is eliminated.

The "students" vary widely. I have had queries or complaints from some who want more time spent on close analysis of the text and prefer reading plays as poems in dramatic form—that is the way I was taught by Harry Levin at Harvard, who had a keen eye for iterated verbal imagery—but my regulars (a dozen or more) enjoy what I am doing. Most important, presenting these plays to people with life experience can make a huge difference. I have taught *The Tempest* twice over these six years and both times have had the best experience in my career with that wonderful play. Miranda's line "O brave new world / That hath such people in it" is justly famous, but we have had some intense and fruitful discussions of Prospero's easily ignored response: "'Tis new to thee." Two of my regulars are retired lawyers who on occasion provide expert commentary. One of them told us he had used Portia's undoing of Shylock in the trial scene in a workshop for would-be trial lawyers. He also clarified a distinction important in Act 2 of *Henry VI* Part 1, between a nobleman being *attached* or *attainted* for treason against the king. I got some expert testimony from a retired pathologist on the possibility of poisoning through the ear in *Hamlet* (he was dubious, though here symbolism-imagery trumps real world practice).

I put a lot more work into these sessions than I need to, so that I send off long detailed e-mails in advance of each class with questions drawn from my reading and playgoing that do not have easy answers. Some of the clientele have a lot of experience with these plays, but others struggle, especially with the history plays, but putting on screen pivotal scenes levels the playing field and elicits reactions that regularly surprise me. In a recent class, one of my favorite students, a contrarian who always has her own take on issues, took offense at another whose remark she deemed sexist, and threw her glasses case across the room (he caught it deftly)—another electric moment that I really enjoyed. Being in a room with people who actually care a lot about these plays is a high point of my teaching career.

I have no idea how long this final phase will last. My voice is sometimes unreliable; my hearing is no longer what it should be; my memory is not to be trusted; and at the end of the day after a ninety-minute class I sometimes feel brain dead. Still, if the in-class adrenalin keeps kicking in, I hope to continue. In Touchstone's words: "much virtue in *if*".

Alan C. Dessen, Peter G. Phialas Professor (Emeritus) at the University of North Carolina, Chapel Hill, is the author of eight books, four of them with Cambridge University Press: *Elizabethan Stage Conventions and Modern Interpreters* (1984); *Recovering Shakespeare's Theatrical Vocabulary* (1995); *Rescripting Shakespeare* (2002); and, co-authored with Leslie Thomson, *A Dictionary of Stage Directions in English Drama*, 1580–1642 (1999). In 2005, he gave the annual British Academy Shakespeare lecture. Between 1994 and 2001, he was the director of ACTER (A Center for Teaching, Education, and Research), a program (now renamed Actors from the London Stage), which brings groups of five British actors for one-week residencies at US college campuses. Between 1994 and 2009, he was editor or co-editor of the "Shakespeare Performed" section of *Shakespeare Quarterly*.

Figure 3.2.6.1 *William Shakespeare (1546–1616)*
The Chandos portrait, artist and authenticity unconfirmed
Courtesy of the National Portrait Gallery, London

The extant works of the "Bard of Avon", including collaborations, consist of approximately 38 plays, 154 sonnets, two long narrative poems, and a few other verses, some of uncertain authorship. His plays have been translated into every major living language and are performed more often than those of any other playwright.

Source: https://en.m.wikipedia.org/wiki/William_Shakespeare

Postgraduate

Law

A Unique Teaching Experience

Lewis David Lowenfels

I have been practicing law for 55 years and continue to practice. Concurrently I co-author an eight-volume treatise on corporate securities law and teach a course at Seton Hall Law School entitled *Advanced Corporate and Securities Practice.*

It is my role as a professor that I would like to discuss briefly.

For many of us who have law degrees, we can recall the courses we took in law school as almost completely based upon analyzing statutes, cases and law review articles. In essence, you study cases and statutes, take notes and then discuss the contents and ramifications of the statutes and cases in class.

In recent years criticism has arisen over the limitations of this approach to learning the practice of law or, for that matter, learning the practice of any number of professions. I agree with this criticism and have attempted to create a law course that covers not only important and relevant statutes and judicial decisions, but also introduces students to the real world of practicing law. I believe readers might find it interesting as to how I conduct this course and the student responses.

Understanding "The Media"

As a first example, we all know the important role that the press plays with respect to major issues, and that role includes corporate and business related issues. There is not a day that goes by where there are not dozens of articles in newspapers, extensive TV coverage, not to mention broad coverage on social media and corporate related media, that address issues involving businesses, the stock exchanges and the interplay between the private sector and government agencies such as the SEC, state regulators or self-regulatory institutions. It is an area which I could cover by assigning my students to study related articles that analyze these issues. We would then discuss these issues in class and examine the extraordinary role that media plays in business and corporate affairs; the students would get the message.

However, instead of confining this topic to class discussion, I take my class directly to *The New York Times* and meet with Pulitzer Prize winning business reporter and author Gretchen Morgenson. My students come to *The Times* with prepared questions, and Ms. Morgenson addresses these questions and then goes well beyond. The crux of what Ms. Morgenson emphasizes is exactly how lawyers should interface with the press and the mutual advantages of this interface.

For lawyers, a public profile is invaluable in advancing public policy initiatives, achieving successful results in professional engagements and in attracting clients. It took me many years of experience to learn, digest and apply the wisdom which Ms. Morgenson conveys to my students. Students leave this class with an extraordinary perception of the role of the press and media that is reality based.

Understanding Stock Exchanges

As a second example, a course in corporate securities law and practice obviously includes lessons with respect to listing and trading securities on the stock exchanges, much of which focuses on the New York Stock Exchange (NYSE). Again, we could study case law and articles describing corporate and stock exchange matters.

Instead, however, of only lecturing to my class with respect to these matters, I take my students directly to the trading floor of the NYSE where they meet and converse with the market-makers who show them exactly how securities trading is conducted on a trade by trade basis.

The class is also guided by a former market-maker and attorney who spent many years actively involved on the NYSE trading floor. The students are stimulated to ask astute and penetrating questions with respect to the trading activity which they are privileged to observe in real time.

The students also see the give and take between human beings and the electronic systems which at a certain level are the very heartbeat of capitalism.

As a former public governor of the American Stock Exchange, I know how valuable it is for the students to have this picture of market reality in mind when they are advising clients in the future with respect to a wide spectrum of corporate and securities legal issues.

Understanding Over-the-Counter Trading

As a third example, shortly after our visit to the stock exchange our next class is an in person visit to the "over-the-counter" trading floor of one of the world's largest securities firms. Here the students meet with the trading personnel and focus upon high-speed trading in "black pools" and "algorithms" as well as cyber security—vital issues in our contemporary securities markets. Again students are able to focus upon the interplay of human efforts and computers and compare this "upstairs" trading with the trading on the stock exchange floor which they have just witnessed in the previous class.

Other important foci in this class are the compliance issues and the tension from the federal, state and self-regulatory authorities which is constant throughout the entire trading day. Indeed, a failure of compliance in existing investment banking firms can put a firm out of business as well as lead to criminal charges against individuals in top management positions. After graduation, a number of my students have gone to work in the compliance departments at these firms and in the regulatory institutions overseeing these firms. The insights which the students are exposed to from their discussions with the compliance attorneys employed by this intensely regulated private firm are invaluable.

Understanding Financial Regulatory Agencies

As a fourth example, today much of corporate America must deal with government agencies such as the SEC and the Financial Industry Regulatory Authority, (FINRA) not only as regulators, but also as overseers of the arbitrations and mediations of disputes involving the securities industry and the investing public.

By law, all of these disputes must be litigated in securities arbitration forums. In particular, we read articles regarding FINRA arbitration and mediation involving customers suing brokers and their firms as well as the latter suing customers.

I take my class to meet with the Director of the FINRA arbitration program which resolves over 99% of contemporary private disputes between and among customers and securities firms and brokers. Present at the class are leading arbitrators and mediators who explain to students exactly how the arbitration and mediation systems work.

The class is held at FINRA headquarters on Wall Street where actual arbitration sessions are conducted. The students receive input from top people in securities arbitration and securities mediation as well as a real-life picture of the arbitration process in action and how this process differs from contemporary court litigation. Again, many of my students go on to represent parties in securities arbitrations and mediation proceedings after graduation.

One additional result of the class "field trips" described above is that my students meet people who I have known during a significant part of my professional life. And some of these individuals are receptive to offering my students (all of whom are third-year law students on the cusp of graduation) much coveted job opportunities after graduation.

Lessons Learned

In closing, I have been teaching this class for 30 years, and the feedback from former students has been very gratifying. Many of my students have emphasized the value of these classes in their later careers in law, business and the judiciary.

Hopefully, my approach to this combination of book learning and reality in teaching the practice of law will provide some thoughts for professors not only in my profession but in other professions as well.

Figure 3.3.1.1 *Lewis D. Lowenfels* (right) *in 2002 reviews his securities law treatise in his Manhattan office with his research assistant.*

Lewis D. Lowenfels graduated from Harvard Law School in 1961 and in 1967 with a partner founded his own law firm specializing in corporate and securities law, from which he developed expertise in fraudulent activities related to securities and commodities. In 1979 he and co-author Alan Bromberg, HC '54, published Bromberg and Lowenfels' *Securities Fraud and Commodities Fraud*, which over time has grown from four to eight volumes. Lew keeps his standard treatise current with timely updates and interpretations in the field of securities law, continues to practice law on a full-time basis, and contributes articles to various related law publications. Both the treatise and the articles are regularly cited by state and federal courts, including the US Supreme Court.

Lew, who served in the US Army Reserve from 1957–1963, has been a public governor of the American Stock Exchange and continues teaching corporate and securities law as an adjunct professor at Seton Hall University Law School. His wife, Fern, retired teacher and dean in New York City schools, now teaches future teachers and counsels school chapters for the United Federation of Teachers. They have two children and grandchildren who live close by, enrich their lives and join them in domestic and overseas travel. Lew, a former varsity basketball letterman, claims he still has an edge on his grandchildren in shooting baskets.

Danger Signs Ahead for Legal Education:

David M. Becker

I am now a retired law teacher after having taught for over 51 years. Although I know I will not be teaching for another 50 years, I frequently wonder what those years will be like.

When I contemplate the future of legal education, I am somewhat saddened, not because I will not be a part of it, but because I worry that the best of what law schools have accomplished during the last century will be abandoned and disappear completely over time. I express this opinion with caution because every generation tends to extol the virtues of the past, denigrate the present, and forecast further decline for the future. Perhaps I am no different.

I also am cautious because, during my time as a teacher, change has often brought great improvements. At the top of the list is undoubtedly diversity. When I began teaching, women were a token among the students and usually unrepresented on the faculty. Today, at least at my school, women constitute 50 percent of the student body and over one-third of the tenure-track faculty. Beyond diversity there has been extraordinary growth in the curriculum. New areas of law have emerged, and with them have come new courses, programs, and even degrees. The most significant curricular change has been in the training of professional skills, particularly clinical education.

When I began teaching, clinical training was essentially nonexistent. Today it dominates the curricular offerings at many schools, and with it there is an effort to integrate professional responsibility into a broad spectrum of courses. In addition to professional skills training, law schools now look frequently to other disciplines to inform their research. In recent years this has led to many new courses and programs in which faculty from other schools and departments often share teaching responsibilities. Technology has also revolutionized certain aspects of legal education. Among them is the manner in which information is retrieved from cases, statutes, regulations, and periodicals. Not only is more information available; often it can be retrieved in a matter of seconds as opposed to hours.

The treatment of students has also changed tremendously. Admission standards have risen, and because of that flunk-out rates at many schools have dropped precipitously. Grade curves have emerged in individual courses, and the treatment of grades, averages, and class ranks has been changed to present student transcripts in the most favorable light. The school calendar has changed so that students now have fall breaks and exam periods that end before the winter vacation. Further, students now serve on law school committees, including one devoted exclusively to student relations, and they regularly interview prospective deans as well as faculty. Many forms of harassment outside of the classroom are now forbidden by faculty rules and often by law. And verbal harassment within the classroom, epitomized by the fictional Professor Kingsfield, has declined if not disappeared. These are some of the good things that have happened to legal education during the last 50 years.

Nevertheless, I find ominous storm warnings on the horizon. Most people would agree that the cost of a legal education stands at the top of any list of serious warnings, and it is a problem that has already arrived. At my law school the average debt load for college and law school education among our graduating students exceeds $100,000. Our tuition cost alone is $53,500. Unbelievably, it is 53 times the tuition that students paid when I began teaching at Washington University in 1963, and there is no expectation that it will shrink. And both tuition and debt often become insurmountable problems when the market place has not offered jobs that make legal education a wise choice.

Many educators would also include somewhere on this list of warnings the pervasive race to come out ahead in school rankings, particularly those of *US News and World Report*. There are serious questions as to the validity of these rankings—questions concerning their methodology and their relevance to an individual applicant's choice of school. Equally important, however, is what law schools often do to ascend in these rankings; they may undertake measures that achieve superior numbers but do not make them better law schools and, perhaps, make them worse. And beyond that, some schools may game the system or even cheat.

Although I do not intend to diminish the importance of these causes for alarm, this essay concerns other things. It focuses on pedagogy and the underlying objectives of legal education. But it also touches on today's students and the basics that one can no longer take for granted.

The Substance of My Concerns—about Teaching

For me the best of my Harvard College education was that I learned to think carefully and critically and to write clearly and effectively. And for me, law school was merely an upgrade in levels of scrutiny, precision and difficulty. This was the essence of legal education. That's it. Critical thought was the best part of all of my higher education, but now I fear it's at risk, at least in law schools. Lawyers are not, and should never become, encyclopedias of legal information. Instead, they are first and foremost problem solvers, and their legal education must be about the skill-set required to do exactly that.

Teaching Problem Solving

The solutions to problems require information, but more importantly they require analytic skills. Law schools must impart these skills and thereby enable their graduates to solve problems on their own. These are the skills that distinguish lawyers from other professionals and often enable them to solve problems that transcend the law itself. These skills are really what legal education has been and must be about. To be sure, solutions to problems depend upon the application of rules. Without command of the rules, a lawyer is unable to forge a solution and perhaps unable even to recognize the problem. Rules are important, but they change over a professional lifetime—sometimes slowly, sometimes overnight.

Teaching Essential Skills

Skills are the one constant from law school. Skills enable a lawyer to elicit the story (the facts), to identify within the story relevant problems and issues, to discover and master rules and principles that may affect these problems and issues, and to develop a strategy or solution that reflects what the lawyer thinks is the law, might be the law, and should be the law. Indeed, it is this skill-set that enables a lawyer to problem-solve when all established precedent seems impossible to overcome or when there is no precedent at all. Quite simply, these are the skills that empower lawyers to think outside the box. Once mastered, these skills endure beyond law school, and they always transcend information that is merely transitory. They distinguish the craft of lawyering; indeed, they are at its core. Consequently, teaching these skills must always be central to the mission of legal education. The mission is not about information delivery. Rather it is about teaching the skills of critical analysis and legal reasoning.

How then have law teachers imparted these critical skills to students? If legal education were simply a matter of information, straight lecture would suffice. And if the course readings were clear and fully explanatory, even lectures might be unnecessary. If not, well-designed lectures can always clarify, punctuate, amplify, and illustrate important rules and concepts. Yet the mission of legal education has not been about information alone, and because of that classroom teaching of the last century has not been conducted merely by lecture.

What have law teachers typically done instead? Students read a case, and their teacher asks them to state the issue. The teacher or the course book may also present a problem or a hypothetical that again asks students to identify the issue or, often, issues. Sometimes the court will recite the issue, but sometimes it is plainly wrong. Whenever a student has difficulty, a skilled teacher will *not* immediately look to others; instead, she will attempt to elicit the correct issue from the same student through repeated questions that reflect the precise problem experienced by the student and ultimately lead him to the correct or preferred understanding.

The emphasis is upon the repetition of cases, problems, and hypothetical questions and the issues they present, because over time nearly everyone gets the hang of it, almost as if these skills were to be acquired by osmosis. And over time these repeated exercises enable incipient lawyers to do all of this on their own, without a teacher leading them or looking over their shoulder and giving them guidance. This process amounts to more than pedagogical technique. It teaches analytic skills essential to what lawyers do by repeated modeling of these skills and their application. Of necessity students must accomplish some of this process vicariously by observing the work of others. But anyone who has ever struggled with this knows that real learning of skills is accomplished experientially: one acquires problem-solving skills only by attempting to perform them. It is not a spectator sport.

Case Method and Problem Method

I am describing a process that is often labeled Socratic, and the illustration concerning issue identification occurs within the context of the Case Method. But the process is not really tied to either the Socratic or the Case Method. Because the subject of our classes is law, it only makes sense that the focus consists of cases, statutes, regulations, and constitutions. The Problem Method really involves the same thing as the Case Method, only it is more advanced. It focuses on the application of the law—cases, statutes, etc.—within the context of a specific problem lawyers must resolve. Presentation of a problem may test one's understanding of the law, or it may assume that one has already mastered it. In either instance, one must take the next step and apply that understanding toward a solution. Along the way, one may discover that there are different understandings and different solutions for consideration. Indeed, the Problem Method achieves what teachers of the Case Method frequently try to accomplish with their hypothetical questions.

Socratic Dialogue—Interactive Discussion

As for the Socratic label, it is really a misnomer. What I am describing is a method of rigorous inquiry that need not be strictly Socratic. It does involve Interactive Discussion that forces students to think critically and carefully. It requires them to formulate an understanding, justify that understanding, apply their understanding, and defend that application. It forces them to integrate, synthesize, critique, and explain. It forces them to examine things logically and to elaborate policy. The forum can be a classroom discussion with cases, or a seminar paper that develops and critiques a body of law, or a clinical practicum or simulation that specifically addresses a client's problem. Above all, it must be interactive—with teachers, but also with students. The process requires students to formulate an idea that is then subjected to careful scrutiny. Next, in light of that scrutiny, it requires students to improve on that idea or understanding. And if one does this enough times, eventually students master the skill of critical thinking and analyze the rule or problems—carefully and comprehensively—on their own.

Experiential Learning

Experiential learning requires extraordinary patience on the part of both teacher and student. A student response requires scrutiny through a teacher's thoughtful reply. And, when necessary, teacher and student must resume the process with a principle and question that are more elementary. Ideally, the student must always see and achieve the light herself. This consumes time, often lots of time. Inevitably, experiential learning must sacrifice coverage and information. Information begets vast knowledge and expertise, but without problem-solving skills both are meaningless.

Sadly, as one interviews entry-level faculty candidates these days, more and more we see people from outstanding law schools with little or even no acquaintance with the kind of experiential learning just described. Many of their classes did have discussions, but the discussions did not include the rigorous examination or scrutiny that enables the student and the class to move to a higher level of skill and understanding. Undoubtedly, some people can master these skills on their own, or at least with minimal experience. These are the best and the brightest, and they are the people we often interview. They caught on, but only time and experience will teach them that this is not the way most of us learn and, therefore, must be taught these critical skills. I fear that in ten to twenty years there may be fewer and fewer teachers who recognize the importance of these problem-solving skills and know how to teach them. I am worried that there will no longer be models for this kind of experiential learning that are a part of a faculty's recent memory and their own personal history. And when this happens, experiential learning as we have known it will disappear.

Economic Pressures

Beyond the absence of faculty memory and experience, there are the pressures for economy and the stabilization of tuition. Interactive class discussion requires student participation, ideally repeated participation. Classes with enrollments of several hundred save costs because they translate into fewer sections of existing courses, and ultimately fewer teachers, and they also work well for straight lecture and delivery of information. But they are not an effective vehicle for teaching problem-solving skills. Straight lecture is also the most efficient way to deliver information, and information and its instantaneous delivery is at the heart of the technology revolution and craze of the 21st century.

Critical Thinking Is Worth all Inherent Discomfort
Critical analysis of problems conducted through interactive dialogue creates unease among students. Conversely, straight lecture is always accompanied by a comfort zone. For many lawyers, memories of the former are synonymous with terror, partly because of its abuse, but mainly because of its pressure and intensity and also the public nature of mastering difficult skills in a classroom performance before others. But lawyers are not encyclopedias, and their training should not be focused on making them such. Memories of being called upon and interrogated in class may not be pretty or comfortable no matter how gentle the process. Nevertheless, the recurrent theme at reunions for nearly all of my thousands of former students is their full appreciation of being "taught to think like a lawyer", which is their way of describing the skill-set needed to problem solve and their acceptance of the discomfort that often accompanied mastering it.

The Substance of My Concerns—about Students

Law students have been the best part of my life as a teacher. They have become my friends, and many are like family. They have challenged me with their intellect, their ideas, their imagination, and their curiosity. They have inspired me with their courage, their tenacity, their resilience, and their ability to sometimes overcome the impossible. And after graduation, they have rewarded me with their accomplishments and the good lives they have lived both professionally and beyond. Indeed, almost every important idea I have had which became the cornerstone of published articles or books began with a student question in the classroom or in my office. For many, I am willing to admit that they gave to me more than I gave to them. Finally, I am eternally grateful for the honors they have bestowed upon me and the generous gifts conferred in my name. Nevertheless, I do have important concerns about students of the recent past and, therefore, of the future.

At reunions, especially for those celebrating 25 or more years, I am frequently asked: If admitted to Washington University School of Law today, which I know I would not be, would I be able to compete with today's students? My reply always begins with: You betcha! And you would be successful despite the fact that your entering grade point averages and law school aptitude scores were lower than theirs. Then I explain, and here are some of the reasons.

Writing Skills

On balance, I firmly believe that students of the twentieth century write better than those of the twenty-first. I will never forget the admonition of my Gen. Ed. teacher at Harvard:

> "*If you can't write clearly, you can't think clearly.*"

To achieve the latter, you must be able to achieve the former. Unfortunately, many students of today cannot write clearly and effectively, even though they come to law school from excellent colleges and universities with outstanding records and aptitude test scores.

For over thirty years I taught a research and writing seminar that required a major paper that was the equivalent of a published law review article. Some students could not readily find a topic, often because they failed to recognize that this required preliminary research that could not be done at the last minute. Others encountered paralysis when it came to putting ideas onto paper. They had no difficulties with writing assignments of 500 words or less, and these were their customary writing experiences in undergraduate school. But given something longer, they would freeze up while living from one extension to another. One student told me that at his college he and many friends never turned in a paper on time. And in law school they expected the same. (A colleague, while visiting at a top-five law school, told me that there was a school expectation that papers would always be accepted and graded even if turned in two semesters late.) These students did not understand, or maybe ignored, that the real world of law practice had time lines and absolute limits.

Other students had no difficulties finding a topic, doing the research, and getting started with a major draft. But they had no sense of the necessary ingredients of a major paper; indeed, ingredients relevant to many forms of writing. These included the importance of developing a thesis; that each section of the paper must relate to the thesis and hopefully appear in some logical order; that each paragraph of a section must advance the purpose of that section; and that each sentence within a paragraph must advance the purpose of that paragraph. Indeed, these students would present drafts sometimes impossible to understand.

Finally there were papers that contained the informality, abbreviations, and disregard of grammar often present in e-mails, texts, and tweets. And I am describing final drafts!

> *These problems I had not seen in my early years as a teacher. Why now?*

Postgraduate

Law

Undergraduate Training in Writing

Not long ago my law school included two questions on its application intended to gather information on the state of writing exercises in undergraduate education. "Please identify the courses in which you had a timed essay test. Please identify the courses in which you had a major paper to write with feedback from the instructor." Seldom did I see an answer of more than two and two (almost always the same two courses). And it was two and two even for majors in English Literature, Political Science, and History! As a Government major at Harvard, I would have answered, "All of my courses except for chemistry, physics and two courses in Latin."

Quite simply, one cannot become comfortable with serious writing without doing it again and again. And today's students are not getting that experience. Why? I am not certain. I do know, however, that writing assignments—even essay tests—are teacher intensive and costly. Today's examinations feature more and more standardized multiple choice tests. At some law schools they dominate and make possible larger courses, fewer teachers, and reduced costs.

Changes in Student/Teacher Dialogue

In addition to the decline in writing experience, I am troubled by a shift in student-teacher engagement beyond the classroom from in-person discussion to the Internet. This can be attributed to both students and teachers. Many teachers encourage and prefer tweets, texts, and e-mails because they can answer questions when convenient to them, reduce or eliminate office hours, and increase time for research and writing. Students prefer it because it saves time, is convenient, and invariably yields answers and not more questions.

As a teacher, however, I insisted that e-mails be limited to administrative kinds of questions because the best learning and teaching experiences occurred during office hours one-on-one or in small groups. Very often a student's question was not the real question because the question reflected inadequate understanding of an important concept, and if I had answered the question the student's problem would have been exacerbated. Yet even when the question was a sound one, or better yet one I never anticipated, an answer by e-mail would have deprived both student and teacher of a superior and fulfilling learning experience—a dialogue in which the teacher guides the student towards resolution of his own question. Perhaps this could be accomplished through a series of e-mails. However, without all of the significant body cues one gives and receives face-to-face, it never would be as successful or rewarding.

For most of my 50 years of teaching my office would be filled with students each afternoon, but my later years were not. Quite simply, students informed me that they much preferred the Internet. They could then ask questions on their terms and time.

Common Sense and Courtesy

Finally, and perhaps most important, I have observed a decline among millennial students in common sense, especially when it comes to human interaction and its importance to all phases of life including building relationships.

I have two very successful former students in the business of advising lawyers. One has written a book on rules for good lawyering, and the other, after a career as a tax attorney, is now a full-time paid coach of very promising associates and even partners from large firms throughout the country.

One of the first rules of good lawyering for young associates concerns respect for assistants/secretaries because they can make you or break you or both. Yet I know of recent graduates who will deliver an onerous, if not painful, assignment by e-mail instead of softening their request by walking ten feet to the assistant's office and demonstrating full appreciation and gratitude respecting the awful problem dumped on the assistant.

The Coach is involved in improving writing skills of many associates, but she is also concerned with client relationships and development. She asked one associate about his conversation with a successful young client who had just returned from vacation with his family. The associate said: "I was all business." She then said: "Did you inquire—I hope you had a good time on vacation?" The answer was: "NO, why do you ask?" She replied: "That's not how you develop a client base, and it's why you need a coach!"

Additionally, I have had outstanding students whom I introduce over lunch to partners of firms from whom they seek jobs. And often that partner will go out of her way to secure an offer. Sometimes that student will reject the offer and accept another. And much too often a student will do so without even calling or writing the partner who made the opportunity happen. No effort is made to preserve a bridge instead of burning it. The consequence is inevitable loss of goodwill that affects both the school and future students.

Further, I will get e-mail requests to write letters of recommendation from students, sometimes repeat requests months or years after graduation. Each request gets to the point immediately after "Dear Professor" and asks for the letter within a very short time frame. Although there is a simple "thank you", there is no "how are you". It's almost as if they expect me to be waiting for their e-mail, in good health, not busy, and ready to respond at a moment's notice.

Summing Up

Well, these are my concerns about students. I hope they do not appear trivial or peevish. I do believe, however, that this decline in the basics of human connection is here to stay and is the unavoidable consequence of the way technology has taken over our lives. Electronic communication for most everything, especially in short bursts without the nuance of face-to-face connection, has a huge cost, not the least of which is incivility. It's all around us, even in law schools. But that's another story. I guess enough is enough.

Figure 3.3.2.1 *The Law Professor in his den—the lecture hall*

Figure 3.3.2.2 *David Becker: 50 years at Washington University of St. Louis Law School, from Instructor to Dean*

Figure 3.3.2.3 *David Becker at student reception in his early years and at his retirement reception with his wife, Sandi*

David Becker received his JD from the University of Chicago in 1960. After practicing law for two years in Chicago, he began teaching at the University of Michigan Law School. One year later he joined the Washington University School of Law, where he taught for 50 years. Now he is the Joseph H. Zumbalen *Emeritus* Professor of Property Law and a consultant to the Dean of the Law school and to Alumni and Development. For many years he was also the Associate Dean for External Relations. Among his awards are the University Founders Day Award for Distinguished Teaching (1973) and as the first recipient (1988) of the Distinguished Teaching Award, Washington University Law Alumni. In 2012, Washington University awarded him an honorary doctorate in Humane Letters.

Sixty Years in Academic Medicine

Robert M. Neer

Following college graduation until I retired at the end of 2013, I spent my life in the world of academic medicine, typically 80–90 hours/week, decreasing to 30–40 when I began working half-time in 2006. As a result, I am only partly informed about the broader world of medical care, but classmates may be interested in my report of changes inside the complex world of academic medicine.

When I entered this world, we were taught that we had three responsibilities: *patient care* first; *teaching* second; and *medical research* third. All three changed markedly during my 56 years, usually but not always for the better.

Patient Care Changes

Female Doctors

The most dramatic change in patient care during my professional life has been the remarkable increase in the number of women doctors. When I was a medical student, my class had 100 men and seven women. Two years later, when my late wife was a medical student, the ratio was 100 to 8. Later, when I was a medical intern, resident, and endocrinology trainee, all my co-interns, residents and endocrine trainees were men. When I was at the National Institutes of Health for two years of research training, all my co-trainees were men. Today is completely different: in medical schools, half or more of the students are women. Interns, residents, trainees, and researchers are frequently women, both in medicine and in surgery. This change reflects social changes, not changes in medicine. When my late wife was considering medical school, her family, I, and my family all encouraged her, but almost everyone else discouraged her, for the multiple reasons that have been widely discussed and debated. Women today are encouraged to fill many social roles that were widely considered inappropriate for women in the 1950s.

Purpose of Hospitals

A second dramatic change has been the consistent sickness of patients admitted to acute care hospitals. Before I started college, I spent the summer working as a hospital orderly in a community hospital. In those days, it was common to hospitalize patients there "for tests", because it was faster and easier to complete multiple x-rays and blood tests in the hospital. Six years later, when I was a medical student, hospitalization "for tests" remained common on the private practice floors of my medical school's hospital, and in the Veterans Administration hospital where I received some of my student training, but the practice had disappeared from the hospital floors where we students received most of our teaching. Today, patients are admitted to hospitals only when they are quite sick. There are no more admissions for tests.

Today's patient must be sicker to get into an acute care hospital, and sicker to stay, and is often transferred to an "intermediate care facility" while s/he is still sick. Intermediate care facilities lack some of the expensive diagnostic equipment and expertise of acute care hospitals, but provide more diagnostic equipment and expertise than nursing homes and rest homes. They are therefore economically efficient, at least in theory. Because medicine and illness, like life, are only somewhat predictable, patients transferred to an intermediate care facility occasionally take a turn for the worse and require transfer back to the acute care hospital.

When I graduated from medical school in 1961, intermediate care facilities did not exist. When they first appeared in the '80s and '90s, some lacked the expertise needed to care properly for the sick patients they received. Most had previously been hospitals for incapacitated patients with slowly evolving chronic illnesses; they were chronic nursing facilities with chronic care doctors on-location. Such institutions were ill-equipped to handle the rapidly changing needs of patients recovering (or not recovering) from a severe illness. I saw this problem first-hand when I served for several years as a consultant physician at an intermediate care facility.

How could such a mismatch evolve? In part, because acute care hospitals were overoptimistic about their ability to select appropriate patients for transfer; in part because intermediate care hospitals were overoptimistic about the expertise of their professional staff.

But driving a change was money: government and private insurers pressured acute care hospitals to reduce costs, and government and private insurers promised intermediate care hospitals more money to care for sicker patients. Time has diminished this mis-match, and I describe it only because it typifies one of the most dramatic changes in patient care during my lifetime: the intrusion of medical insurers as arbiters of care, displacing physicians.

Today's patients must also be quite sick to remain in an acute care hospital. An illustrative example is the treatment of uncomplicated myocardial infarctions (which after a day or two leave the patient frightened but asymptomatic). When I was a medical student, we were taught that several weeks of absolute bed rest were essential after every myocardial infarction (even when it was uncomplicated), to prevent ballooning out of the weakened heart wall in response to physical exertion. Consequently, when I was a medical student, intern, and resident in different acute care hospitals, many of my patients were asymptomatic men convalescing in hospital beds after a myocardial infarction, but angry, restless, and fretful to escape the hospital before they lost their jobs or their livelihood.

Shortly after I joined the staff at Massachusetts General Hospital (where I spent most of my professional life), colleagues there proved that patients with an uncomplicated myocardial infarction fared just as well if they were discharged from the hospital much earlier; prolonged bed rest was unnecessary, inefficient, and ridiculously expensive. Similar meticulously controlled studies 40–50 years ago showed that bed rest, in-hospital or out, helps few illnesses, contrary to Hippocrates and Galen. Because of these and other changes, stays in acute care hospitals are now much shorter: 13.8 days on average for US Medicare recipients in 1967 versus 5.5 days in 2014.

Medical Insurance

Changes in medical care financing, especially Medicare, have had many positive effects. Insurance now protects patients from declaring bankruptcy or selling their home to satisfy medical bills. This was a change for the better. Patients covered by Medicare or other insurance can seek medical care for symptoms before they become emergencies. This was another change for the better, which saved both lives and money. A change peculiar to academic teaching hospitals was the disappearance of large hospital 'wards' housing 12–24 patients together in one large room, helping to care for and encourage each other, while observing each other's recovery or death. These large wards, with their frightful lack of privacy and touching altruism, have been replaced by two-bed or four-bed rooms everywhere, even among charity patients. This was also a change for the better, made possible by changes in medical care financing.

But these changes in financing have had hidden costs, such as a dramatic slowing in the rate of innovation. When I began my medical career, the introduction of a new diagnostic test was a simple matter. If physicians judged a new test valuable for patient care, payment was automatic. Forty years ago, my colleagues and I introduced the first bone density tests, and the first blood tests for vitamin D and important hormones, into medical care at our hospital in just that way. Today, getting a new test approved for payment by medical insurers is so expensive and prolonged that it is often not pursued. As a result, it is now common for academic and commercial researchers to use innovative blood and urine tests in patients for several decades, while the tests remain unavailable for routine care because medical insurers won't pay for them.

An alarming consequence of changes in medical care financing has been the conversion of every patient medical record from a memory aid and communication device for caregivers to a billing document. Medicare and other insurers have decided that doctors only do things they document in the patient medical record. That is why some physicians spend so much time looking at their computer when meeting with a patient: if they don't type the necessary information into their computer, they won't get paid. But this has a serious side effect: excessive focus on writing or typing to document an encounter with a patient makes it difficult to establish a bond of emotion and trust with that patient. Patients' complaints about their physician's illegible writing have now been replaced by complaints about their physician's focus on the computer rather than the patient. This is a good example of what J.W. Forrester called the *counter-intuitive behavior of complex systems*.

A third undesirable side effect of changes in health care financing, and related increases in regulation, is a dramatic growth in hospital bureaucracies. When I came to my large urban teaching hospital in 1966, its telephone directory had one small page with large type for the entire hospital administration. Now the hospital administration is three-four times bigger, even though the number of hospitalized patients is smaller. The administrative costs of health care in the US are far higher than in any other country, which is one reason our costs are higher.

Technology

Although it is expensive to convince Medicare and other insurers to pay for new medical technologies, commercial sponsors of a technology will come up with the money if the financial rewards are sufficient and the information generated is highly valued. Thus every academic hospital is now stuffed with ultrasound machines, CT machines, and MRI machines. When I was a medical student, ultrasound (sonar) produced one-dimensional images that distinguished fluid-filled lumps (cysts) from solid lumps (benign or malignant tumors), but was not good for much else. X-ray images had advanced little since the 19th century, and were recorded on large silver negatives we sometimes developed ourselves. A daily medical student ritual was a trip to the x-ray film library, to retrieve the day's x-ray negatives for our patients. Success required staying on the good side of the film librarians, in each hospital a cluster of wise-cracking heroic women with phenomenal memories, who could find lost x-ray folders among towers of identical-looking x-ray folders waiting to be filed. These silver negatives were so heavy the x-ray film library was always located in a basement, or a specially-braced higher floor.

The past 60 years have revolutionized medical imaging. Mathematical analysis of ultrasound data has converted them into two-dimensional images which can distinguish stiff from pliant heart valves, measure the efficacy and consistency of the heart muscle's contractions, reveal the exact location of a gall bladder stone or a kidney stone, or the sex of a tiny fetus. Replacing x-ray films with electronic detectors eliminated the film library, and replaced its colorful librarians with a computer. Adding mathematical deconvolution techniques converted the 19th century's two-dimensional x-ray images into three-dimensional images. MRI machines added a new level of image information, by distinguishing tissue fat from tissue water. The result of these changes is an astonishing ability to visualize every part of the body, impressive improvements in diagnostic accuracy, and appalling increases in costs—just as a Maserati costs more than a bicycle.

Apart from the cost, an unwelcome side effect is physicians' decreased interest in and reliance on physical examinations of their patients. In my recent experience, today's medical students and doctors in training are fixated upon the results of blood tests and imaging procedures, because these powerful tests can provide critical information about their patients. In contrast, physical examination of the patient is considered less reliable and less informative. Unfortunately, or fortunately, physical examination of a patient involves more than gaining information; it also involves a symbolic laying-on-of-hands. Only a masseuse or a Turkish bath attendant has such intimate contact with most patients.

A careful physical examination demonstrates vividly to the patient the personal interest and concern of the physician. This, plus a careful and detailed conversation about the patient's illness, is the way physicians learn about the patient and simultaneously demonstrate an intense interest in the patient. That is how physicians gain a patient's trust. Neglecting the physical examination makes it harder to gain that trust. Patients who do not trust their doctor do not follow their doctor's advice, no matter how expert and correct it may be. Electronic physical examinations may suffice for robots, but not for humans.

Medical Education Changes

Curriculum

During my first two years of medical school, our professors were paid by the university to teach the sciences that underlie medicine, and to do research. Such arrangements continue, although today's medical school professors put more emphasis on biochemistry and genetics, and less emphasis on anatomy, histology, physiology, and pharmacology. For example, Harvard Medical School no longer has a Department of Physiology or a Department of Pharmacology. Both have been subsumed into other departments, and teaching of those subjects, previously the responsibility of basic science faculty, is now assigned to hospital-based medical specialists. As a result, when today's students reach hospitals, they are better informed about the chemistry of organ function in health and disease, and less informed about the function itself. Learning basic science during medical school has simultaneously become more abstract: I put needles into frog muscles and drugs into frog hearts; today's students read about such things, and watch videos in which everything always works as expected.

Altruism

During my last two years of medical school, half our professors were paid by the government or foundations to do research, and were expected to teach for a small percentage of their time. That small percentage was paid by a supplement the university added to the government or foundation salary. This arrangement continues today. The other half of our faculty during the last two years of my medical school were volunteer practitioners, who taught for the love of it, with little or no salary. These volunteer practitioners were superb doctors, superb teachers, and often very colorful personalities. Some could afford to teach without pay because their life style was monastic; others could afford it because they were independently wealthy. The rest taught part-time, and accepted the reduction in an already-comfortable income from medical or surgical practice in exchange for the satisfaction and stimulation of teaching bright students. Sixty years later, these volunteer practitioners have almost entirely disappeared as teachers. They have been replaced by practitioners who are paid to care for patients, and teach on the side. The reasons are multiple, and the consequences for medical students, interns, and residents are at best controversial.

One obvious consequence is that medical students are no longer taught by example that passing on the arts of medicine without pay is an imperative. The Hippocratic Oath required such donations; but that Oath is now ignored by medical schools, or that part of it is deleted. At the same time, personal charity by faculty physicians has been replaced by institutional charity by hospitals, or by tax-funded insurance (Medicare, Medicaid). As a result, today's medical students do not see the examples of altruism I saw daily when I was a medical student.

Simultaneously, increases in the cost of college and medical school have left most of today's medical students with frightening debts. In 2014, the median debt of US medical students at graduation was $180,000, according to the Association of American Medical Colleges; ten percent owed more than $300,000. It is perhaps not surprising that today's medical students more often pursue high-paying specialties like interventional radiology, and less often pursue low-paying activities like primary care and pediatrics.

When I was a medical student, we spent many weeks on a hospital medical ward, helping to care for hospitalized patients, and querying them about their illnesses. Three afternoons a week, we met in groups of five for two hours with an experienced senior professor, to whom two or three of us related the details of a patient and his/her illness, organized around what we conceived to be the causes of that patient's illness. The professor praised, criticized, and corrected each student's presentation, while the other students listened. That was how we learned to integrate data, and communicate it concisely and comprehensibly. The exercise was difficult and rewarding; many students considered it the high point of medical school.

That kind of teaching is now impossible: patients are too sick and too briefly present to have multiple interviews by a medical student, and senior physicians are no longer available three afternoons a week. Today, more teaching is done with ambulatory patients, and more of the teaching is done by junior physicians. The new arrangements work fine for most students, but some suffer. In my experience, Harvard Medical students in their fourth and final year of medical school are now less consistently able to describe a patient's illness coherently and concisely. This deficiency must be a result of the changes in the teaching program, because these students are some of the country's brightest.

Medical Research Changes

Revolution in Biology

The hospital where I worked has more research funding than almost any other hospital in the US. In the 47 years I worked there, I devoted most of my time to, and got most of my salary from, medical research. My career coincided with the revolution in biology that is one of the 20th century's great cultural achievements. Although my late wife and most of my academic peers participated in this revolution by becoming cell biologists, molecular biologists, or geneticists, I stubbornly devoted myself to patient-oriented research. For 20 years I used, and simultaneously administered, a section of my hospital set aside for such research since 1930. I did this because I thought it was important, and because it was interesting and challenging and fun. For most of my career, patient-oriented research was out of fashion: it is slow, difficult, and expensive, whereas modern biology is fast, easy, and cheap. Fashions shifted around the year 2000, and patient-oriented research is now fashionable. I judged these fashion trends by asking our fellowship applicants what they wanted to study. Experimental genetic manipulations have made whole animal research once again fascinating, and patient-oriented research has become fashionable as a way to delineate new genetic diseases and explore the relevance to humans of physiologic puzzles unscrambled in animals with the help of genetic modifications.

AIDS

A dramatic change to which I contributed nothing, but experienced with awe, was the AIDS epidemic and its arrest by medical research. When that epidemic began, we had patients with unexplained chronic diarrhea, then patients with odd infections, until doctors in New York and San Francisco delineated the new illness, and researchers in Paris and at the National Institutes of Health established its cause. That was a time when the hospital floors where I taught and helped care for patients were filled with young men and women dying slowly from AIDS-related infections, and a generation of young physicians confronted slow death among numerous patients their age. I felt afresh the 19th century's morbid preoccupation with widespread death of its youth.

Today, AIDS has become a chronic disease that can usually be controlled with medications, although the demands upon the patient's attention to detail and diligence remain formidable. Terribly sick patients with AIDS still exist in our acute hospital beds, but they are far less numerous. No longer do all of them face an early death. That is astonishingly rapid progress, even more so when one considers that we had almost no effective treatment for any viral illness before AIDS appeared. But scientists knew how other viruses invaded cells, and how other viruses replicated, and could imagine ways to prevent cell invasion and prevent virus replication. When a disease is almost always fatal, it becomes ethical and feasible to test innovative treatments that would ordinarily be considered too risky; in fact, AIDS victims demanded that. Furthermore, when a disease kills so many young people, society devotes large amounts of money to understanding and controlling it.

Bayh-Dole Amendment

A much more far-reaching change in medical research was the December 12, 1980 signing into law of the Bayh-Dole Amendment, which allowed universities to patent discoveries made with US government funds, retain ownership of the patents, and license them with few restrictions to commercial entities. This law was designed to foster the utilization and commercialization of such patents, and dissemination of their complex technologies. Prior to that date, the US government had retained ownership of all such patents, and they languished: of 28,000 such patents owned by the US government in 1980, fewer than five percent had ever been commercialized. This law has gradually transformed Cambridge, where I have lived for 50 years, because large and small bio-tech companies have flocked here to be near Harvard, MIT, BU, and Boston's three medical schools, hire their experts as consultants, tempt them to cross over into industry, and understand what they are patenting and what they are investigating.

Shortly before this law was adopted, my colleagues and I had reported in a leading medical journal a new treatment for osteoporosis, which reconstituted its depleted bone structure, as proven by biopsies of the pelvis before and after six months of treatment. Because much of our work had been done with US government funds, it could not be patented, and we did not try to patent it before we published it in June 1980. This was a time when patient-oriented research was not popular and the US government funded little therapeutic research. The National Institutes of Health, which had funded all the basic research that led to this new treatment, considered its further evaluation a job for industry.

But 12 different pharmaceutical companies turned us down, because our synthetic hormone was not patented, and its use to increase bone mass and reverse osteoporosis was not patented. In addition, our medicine required a daily injection, and had to be refrigerated. Because insulin shared these three disadvantages, we tried to interest Eli Lilly Co., a major manufacturer of insulin. They also demurred, because they were not then treating osteoporosis. By 1993, Eli Lilly Co. had become interested in osteoporosis, and decided to test this drug's ability to reduce fractures (a multi-million-dollar endeavor). It proved so effective that it is now marketed worldwide, with gross sales exceeding $1 billion/year (a "super-drug").

Because commercialization of most drugs is very expensive, and we are a capitalist society, a candidate for commercialization must have both a high probability of medical success and a high probability of profitability. Lack of a patent can be fatal or (as in this instance) severely retarding. This personal experience, plus the transformation of my city, has made me an admirer of the Bayh-Dole Amendment, and the bipartisan vision that produced it. If it been enacted earlier, my colleagues and I and our hospital might have profited financially, rather than just intellectually.

Disclaimers

Because Massachusetts General Hospital treats anyone who enters the door, I have never had to confront the financial reality of uninsured patients. But it is very clear to me that lack of income causes people to delay medical consultation until medical problems become incapacitating, by which time effective treatment may no longer be feasible. Lack of medical insurance therefore leads to otherwise-preventable illnesses and even death. Delays in treatment were less material when treatments were less effective. Improvements in medical treatment have made delays in treatment more consequential.

Massachusetts General Hospital is Massachusetts' most expensive hospital. Partly that is because Boston is the state's most expensive city, and everything is more expensive here. Partly it is because we treat sicker patients. Partly it is because we have many doctors in training, whose inexperience and insecurity cause them to order too many tests, or treat dying patients too aggressively. But partly it is because we have more specialists (like me), and specialists generally spend more money. We specialists think we also get better results, but we don't really know that, because we haven't tested the hypothesis.

* * *

My wife, Ann Eldridge, Radcliffe 1957, asked me whether I would choose the same career again.

My answer is "*Yes!*" I cannot imagine a career more challenging, more interesting, and more worthwhile.

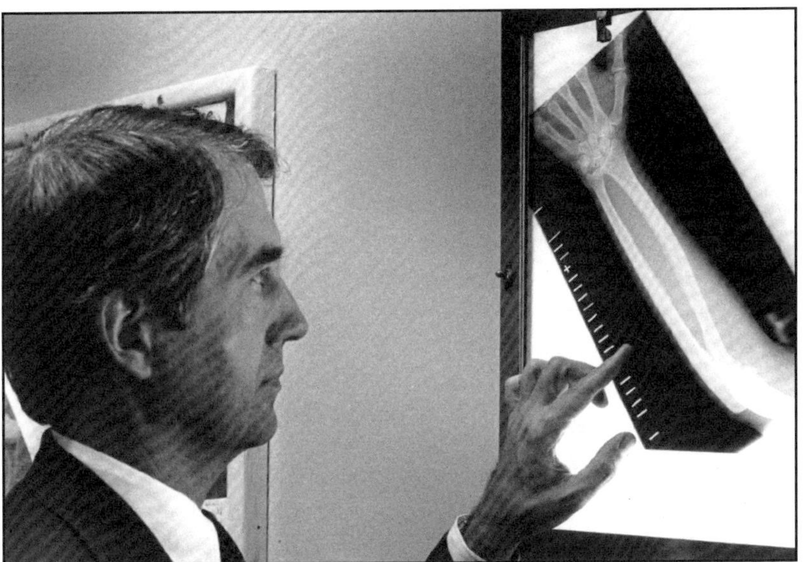

Figure 3.3.3.1 *Endocrinologist Robert Neer, MD, in 1978 examines forearm x-ray of patient participating in his clinical research on bone diseases.*

Figure 3.3.3.2 *The Endocrine Unit of the MGH in 1979 on the Bulfinch steps: Bob Neer* (top row left, indicated by arrow) *is shown in insert.*

Figure 3.3.3.3 *MGH Resident Teaching Rounds,* al fresco *in June 1990, on the Bulfinch Lawn*

Photo by N.E. Hyslop

Postgraduate

Medicine

Robert Neer, MD, attended Columbia medical school, had clinical training in New York and New Haven, research training at the National Institutes of Health and endocrinology training at Massachusetts General Hospital, where he remained for 46 years as a practicing physician, teacher and researcher with a special interest in calcium metabolism. He participated in the first administration of synthetic salmon calcitonin to humans (for Paget's disease of bone or *hyper*calcemia), the first administration of synthetic hPTH 1–34 to humans (to diagnose causes of *hypo*calcemia), and pioneered the use of hPTH 1–34 to increase humans' bone formation, mass, and strength. One of the first researchers to administer 1,25-(OH)2 vitamin D3 to humans for treatment of *hypo*calcemia, he also reported the first use of DXA bone density measurements to diagnose osteoporosis, and invented the widely-used T-score method of reporting the results.

From 1968 to 1990, he directed a ten-bed MGH unit set aside for research on patients, and from 1990 to 2014 directed MGH's Osteoporosis and Bone Density Center. He was Consultant to the Food and Drug Administration, the National Institutes of Health, the Navy, and numerous pharmaceutical companies.

Widowed in 2000, in 2002 he married longtime friend Ann Eldridge, Radcliffe '57. They live in Cambridge.

My Foray into Online Teaching: A Personal Challenge

Stanton Smullens

> "*Hi, Professor Smullens,*
>
> *I have not completed the* ***integrated orientation 2017*** *quiz in my account. It disappeared from my account. What should I do?*"

This is the first e-mail I received on January 9, 2017, the first day that I began to teach an online course at the Jefferson College of Population Health (JCPH). *I had no idea how to answer my student.* So began my foray into the new world of online teaching.

Backdrop to a Professional Adventure

My professional career has been in Medicine. After leaving Harvard in 1957, I enrolled at Jefferson Medical College (now the Sidney Kimmel

Medical College of Thomas Jefferson University) in Philadelphia. Most of my surgical residency training was at Jefferson. Later, as a clinical professor concentrating in thoracic and vascular surgery, I had the privilege of teaching students *live.*

Four years earlier, due to dramatically changing times, the dean and I agreed that the development of a physician hospital organization (PHO), which we called JeffCare, was a necessity, and I was asked to become its first president and CEO.

In 1997, after almost 30 years of clinical practice, I closed the surgical door permanently. Indeed, it was a wrench. However, the Jefferson Health System (JHS) was formed, and I became its first chief medical officer (CMO), a position I held until 2014 when JHS morphed into the Delaware Valley Accountable Care Organization (DVACO). Although planning to retire, unexpectedly I was asked to remain and become the first CMO of this emerging organization.

The journey from clinician to administrator grew to involve two other dimensions: a founding board member in 2002 of the Pennsylvania Patient Safety Authority, where I remain as vice-chair, and a position on the Health Care Advisory Board of Drexel Law School, where I continue to lecture.

In January 2016, two months shy of my 80th birthday, I decided it was time to stop full-time work, and my wife, SaraKay, and I excitedly looked forward to what we called "two months of Sundays." Although we were able to carve out much more free time together, SaraKay had continued to work as a family therapist and writer. Before this decision, at the end of 2015 SaraKay had published a well-received book on burnout and self-care for mental health professionals, which kept her very busy.

After about a month of Sundays, I started to get restless. A subsequent back injury gave me time to think, and I decided to once again carve out something professionally purposeful in health care.

A colleague, the Dean of the Jefferson College of Population Health, had asked me in the past to consider online teaching at his school—a course in Quality Improvement and Patient Safety, areas of interest and expertise. Now was the time. Because one of our granddaughters had a Bat Mitzvah in Berlin, Germany, in late August (but that's another story), I didn't start preparing to teach until mid September 2016.

A New Direction: How Does It Work?

Having never even taken an online course in the past, I approached the knowledge requirements and technology of online teaching with much trepidation. I knew I needed help, and a plan was developed for me to "audit" the course I was to teach.

Auditing the online course showed how times had changed. Everything was asynchronous. No face-to-face contact. I was given access to the material, followed online what the students were doing and writing, and learned to manipulate the software product known as *Blackboard Learn*, which both challenged and frustrated me.

I have to say that in its entirety this was a very anxiety producing time, not only technologically! The course students, working for masters' degrees, were physicians, advanced practice nurses, lawyers, and hospital administrators, a most high powered and knowledgeable group. Yes, I "knew" the material, but I was teaching in a new and awkward setting and did not want to be unprepared when "asked" questions online. So it was back to student days for me too: rereading the basic materials (far more than once) and pouring over numerous old presentations, both others and mine.

What I gradually began to see was a very well thought out methodology to the teaching and structuring of the weekly assignments, one based on sound and impressive educational theory.

A very well-received book, *Empowering Online Learning*, by Bong and Zhang (2008), was the theoretical model for the course. Briefly stated, it is based on the concept of R2D2: *Read, Reflect, Display, and Do*. These four phases are geared to the various types of learners: auditory, verbal, reflective, observational, visual, kinesthetic, and tactile.

Basically it encourages courses to be designed using the R2D2 methodology, to integrate the *four types of learning activities*: (1) reading, (2) reflecting (including reflective writing), (3) displaying, and (4) doing.

Fortunately for me, a professional colleague had set up the course outline and selected readings several years ago. Through this direction, I gradually got used to the format and flow of the weekly assignments.

The course was 14 weeks in length. Each week had a recorded lecture and slides based on the topic of the week. There was assigned reading from a textbook, *The Healthcare Quality Book* (Third Edition 2014), as well as original articles and published papers, websites, synopses of important health care books, and even YouTube videos.

The central learning activities were the students' written responses to two discussion questions that were posted to the *Discussion Board.* There was also a requirement to respond to other students' and instructor's posts and comments. But not just a simple response to the posts was sufficient: it had to be reflective, nuanced, and referenced to appropriate literature.

Additionally, there was a weekly project: writing a reflective journal article, a short paper, or even a template for the course's major performance improvement plan.

The instructor, using a well-constructed rubric, also available to the students, graded each of these activities.

The discussion board activity represented about 55% of the course grade. Feedback on all weekly activities was given to each student with their grades. Students picked teams of three or four, and over the course of the semester, developed a comprehensive and sophisticated performance improvement plan to answer the problem of reducing preventable hospital readmissions.

Every week the students took a quiz to see how well they understood the week's work. They also were asked to judge the best and worst of the week's activities, how much time they spent on the course work: average ten hours, but from three to 20 for some. I was spending at least 15 hours just to keep up! Whew!

During all this time, I would not have recognized any of the students if I had passed them on the street, but I knew their "voices" through the extensive activities required of them. Also, I had the pleasure of hearing their real voices (shades of teaching past) through several conference calls that were set up during the term.

In the midst of all of this, it was necessary to learn how to record a lecture, using a tool called *Panopto*. Another major challenge! Preparing and giving a live lecture is one thing, but recording it for posterity, without the normal give and take of the classroom, is something else again. Finally, I figured that one out, again not without a lot of anxiety and retakes.

My turn to prepare for my course arrived in early December 2016. First I had to record my *Welcoming Video*. I then had to record all 14 of the lectures on Panopto. Fortunately, I was able to use the prepared lectures, with some updated additions. This was a real stretch for me, since each presentation took hours to prepare and record. I finally completed them by the third week of December, a big push, I assure you.

Where Am I Now?

As of right now (February 4, 2017), I have recovered from that first e-mail as I conclude Week 4. I am much more comfortable and getting into the rhythm of the week. There are 13 students in the class I am teaching, all training to be physician assistants (PAs). It's a required course for them, and there are two other sections (taught by others) of PAs taking the course. I am still spending about 15 hours a week on this, but truthfully, much less than the first weeks of January. I can see the time commitment beginning to decrease as I gain more confidence in using *Blackboard Learn*. As you can see, as a former surgeon, my strongest learning method is "doing."

How Does This Approach Compare to Classroom Teaching?

There has been a lot written about how well students learn online vs. classroom teaching. Studies have shown that "It depends." It basically depends on the student and the student's needs and personality. It turns out that the two methods can each give a great education.

Here are some of the variables (Nikotina 2016):

Online

- Convenience and flexibility
- The individual is the focus
- Global reach: anytime, anyplace conversation
- Teaches self-motivation and discipline

In-Class

- "Security" of a longer-standing format
- More "real" face-to-face interaction
- "College experience": social interaction at on-campus clubs and extracurricular activities
- Hands-on training for some professions (Nursing or Home Inspection)

Another aspect that has gained traction has been a "blended" approach of both online and in-class. It is definitely a different world than we knew. But, as Heraclitus said: "*Change is the only constant in life.*"

Extent of Online Teaching

Believe it or not, for eight years *US News and World Report* has ranked online learning institutions in eight different categories including bachelor degrees, MBAs, Masters in Education, Nursing and four more.

Approximately 5.8M students were enrolled in online learning last year. The majority of universities and colleges today offer online learning. Harvard has an extensive program of offerings. From its website: "Explore Harvard's extensive, world-class online learning opportunities. We invite you to follow your intellectual curiosity, from podcasts and lectures to fully interactive courses and programs."

Conclusion: From Trepidation to Conversion

Increasingly, it has become more fun to teach online. Although I could theoretically be anywhere there is an Internet connection to run the course, I have stayed pretty close to home in this my initial try (this way I don't have to shave or even dress to teach—as you can imagine, jacket and tie had been my norm). My course runs until mid-April 2017. Yes, I plan to continue. My next class is scheduled to begin in October of this year.

A looming concern, before the next class starts, is what will happen to the Patient Protection and Affordable Care Act ("Obamacare") with the new administration. A great deal of what is in the ACA is taught since much of it relates to improving the quality and the value proposition (quality/cost) of health care. We may have to change the syllabus for the next class. Time will tell.

By the way, if you go on the Web to look at online teaching jobs, you will find many opportunities available. It might be of interest to some of you who want part-time work to complement your "Sundays." Since I am a convert, please don't hesitate to be in touch.

Stanton N. Smullens, MD, FACS, is a graduate of Thomas Jefferson Medical School in Philadelphia, PA, where he remained for the rest of his medical career, becoming Clinical Professor of Surgery at Jefferson Medical College and founding President and CEO of JeffCare, the Physician Hospital Organization of Thomas Jefferson University Hospital. From 1997 to 2015 he was the Chief Medical Officer of Jefferson Health System and its descendent Delaware Valley

Accountable Care Organization (DVACO), and subsequently Medical Director of Network Performance and Quality until 2016. In 2002, Dr. Smullens was appointed to the Pennsylvania Patient Safety Authority Board and elected Vice Chairman of the Authority, a position he currently holds. He served as Acting Chair (2011–2013). In 2016 he was appointed to the Advisory Board of the Health Law Institute of Drexel Law School.

He has been honored as President of the Hospital Medical Staff. The Jefferson Alumni Association presented Dr. Smullens' portrait to the University in 2010. He is a member of many local and national medical societies and has published widely in the medical literature.

He is currently a Lecturer in the Jefferson College of Population Health, teaching an online course.

Figure 3.4.1.1 *The author at his computer in his home office in 2017, interacting with his online students*

References

Bong, C.J. and K. Zhang (2008). *Empowering Online Learning: 100+ activities for reading, reflecting, displaying, and doing.* San Francisco, Jossey-Bass.

Harvard University Website: http://online-learning.harvard.edu.

M.S. Joshi, et al. (Third Edition 2014). *The Healthcare Quality Book: vision, strategy, and* tools. Chicago, AUPHA.

Nikotina, A. (2016). Online vs In-Class: Are We Asking the Wrong Question? Online Learning Consortium: https://onlinelearningconsortium.org/online-vs-class-asking-wrong-question/.

US News and World Report: http://www.usnews.com/education/online-education/articles/us-news-ranks-best-online-programs.

"Don't Blame the Editor"

William W. Parmley

This brief essay is written to future editors and faculty submitting a manuscript to a medical journal.

During my 30-plus years as a faculty member at the University of California San Francisco (UCSF) I had the opportunity to serve as chief of cardiology for 23 years. During ten of those years I also served as Editor-in-Chief of the *Journal of the American College of Cardiology* (JACC). At the time it was the most widely read cardiology journal in the world. We received about 2,000 scientific manuscripts per year for consideration of publication. After a peer review process by two or three experts in the field, our acceptance rate was about 20%. And of course, nothing is more frustrating to an author than to have his/her manuscript rejected.

So the first part of this essay is directed to frustrated authors in whatever field, whose manuscripts have been rejected.

At our weekly board meeting of the editor, five associate editors, and staff, there were bound to be different perceptions of the value of a given manuscript. After discussion, approximately 80% were rejected, and 20% sent back to the authors for revisions suggested by the reviewers and the editor handling the manuscript.

To rejected authors, I would advise them not to just make the revisions suggested by the reviewers and return it for further consideration. Such a manuscript rarely if ever gets accepted and just further clogs up the workload of the journal. Furthermore, authors do not have the benefit of the discussion at the weekly editorial board meeting, nor the bigger picture of all the manuscripts being reviewed.

So in the eyes of the author, the reason for the rejection would be the editor's misperception of the importance of the manuscript. My plea is DON'T BLAME THE EDITOR!

In the publish-or-perish atmosphere of academic medicine, there can be great pressures on a faculty member to publish many articles which will help him or her get promoted.

Having served on the academic committee that considers all such promotions at my institution, I am only too familiar with the scenario. An outstanding record of teaching, clinical competence and university and public service are necessary—but no longer sufficient—criteria for promotion. Invariably the discussion of candidates focuses on peer-reviewed grant support and publications.

The members of such a committee may come from a wide range of disciplines and thus it is not possible for each member to critically evaluate the overall scientific worth of each study. But the papers are easy to count!

Because of this impetus, there have been an increasing number of coauthors on manuscripts, in part to help each author increase the number of publications in their *curriculum vitae*. An unfortunate side effect of this strategy is the dividing up of data to obtain two manuscripts rather than one, and submit them to different journals. In a worse scenario, data has occasionally been falsified, or plagiarized and used as the illegitimate basis of a manuscript.

During our tenure on the *Journal*, there was even one manuscript which had been lifted intact from another journal years ago and submitted as a *de novo* manuscript. Fortunately a reviewer recognized this so that we could inform the author and the dean of his medical school about this event. In this circumstance, one can BLAME THE EDITOR.

To summarize, we used the **criteria for authorship on a scientific publication** recommended by the International Committee of Medical Journal Editors (N Engl J Med 1991; 324:424–8).

> "*Each author should have participated sufficiently in the work to take public responsibility for the content.*
>
> *Authorship credit should be based on substantial contributions to (a) conception and design, or analysis and interpretation of data; and to (b) drafting the article or revising it critically for important intellectual content; and on (c) final approval of the version to be published. Conditions (a), (b) and (c) must all be met.*"

Clinical trials of procedures or pharmaceuticals form the basis for approval of new techniques or medicines for use in patients. There are so many clinical trials going on that it is virtually impossible to keep track of all of them. ***Each trial is given a specific acronym***. A few years ago I put together some of these acronyms as a paragraph:

> DEFIANT HAL BARI SURE PUTS TOTAL SALT on HIS BIG-MAC and SALAD. By CHOICE, HIS ACUTE LIPID ANZ FATS MUST IMPACT HIS ALIVE HEART. FLUENT GESICA BARI WHAS UST WITH HERS LIPID LIFE. U-CARE so STOP IT. WHAT MITI CARDIAC REGRESS can PROTECT and SAVE HIS and HERS HART—TRUST and ACCEPT SMART, VALID RISC REDUCT to PREVENT and VANQUISH DISTRESS and DEATH. HELP, ACHIEVE, ANS SAVE AVID, AMIABLE LIFE WITH GUSTO, HOPE, PEACE, RADIANCE, SPIRIT, and QUIET.

As you can guess, I'm not a great fan of this chaotic ABC. Avoid this if you can, but DON'T BLAME THE EDITOR.

One of the real challenges associated with a positive study is how best to interact with the media in reporting it. When a study has undergone rigorous peer review and is published, that seems to me to be the best time to involve the media if the study justifies it. Unfortunately there have been examples where an abstract presented at a small or regional meeting has been picked up by the press and its contents greatly magnified. Without the ability to judge the data, and the assurance that the paper has undergone rigorous peer review, such abstracts only muddy the scientific waters. One must be very careful that a positive study is not being "pushed" by a pharmaceutical company which funded the study. If the subsequent published manuscript is not as positive as the original abstract, or even contradicted by other data or studies, "DON'T BLAME THE EDITOR".

One of the discouraging aspects of having one's manuscript rejected is a poor review rather than an insightful peer review. In some cases the reviews are very short, miss the mark, or focus on trivial aspects of the study. It is self evident that the peer review process is less than perfect, inconsistent, and sometimes even capricious.

By having our editors carefully review each manuscript and having it discussed at the weekly editors' meeting, we avoided some of the aspects of a poor review. Over the ten-year period of our tenure at JACC it was clear that the peer review process has become more perfunctory. *What used to be a high duty of the scientific community is becoming more of a bother to the busy faculty member.* It is critical to the editorial process that reviewers act in a timely and thorough manner in reviewing manuscripts. To protect against bias, it is also important to have reviewers (and authors) reveal conflicts of interest.

An interesting question to ask oneself about potential conflicts of interest is: *Would I be willing to have these arrangements generally known?*

We also found that statistical methods frequently were done incorrectly. We had every manuscript reviewed by a knowledgeable statistician in order to avoid inappropriate statistical tests being employed. Overall, despite instances of poor review, we hope that authors will not "BLAME THE EDITOR".

Let me summarize a few thoughts.

First of all it was a great privilege to serve as editor of a medical specialty journal. It certainly does allow one to keep abreast of the latest research in one's given field. It also makes one vulnerable to criticism. If an author has to submit an average of five manuscripts before getting one published, it is difficult not to blame the editor for not understanding the importance of each study. (Hence, the title of this essay).

It goes without saying that it is absolutely essential to have superb associate editors and a committed and talented staff. The flow of manuscripts never stops! Of course, the occasional manuscript submitted from our own cardiology group was handled entirely by a guest editor who was totally separate from our institution.

It is obviously important to maintain transparency about all procedures involved in the editorial process.

This overall experience was one of the greatest of my academic career. So perhaps it *is* appropriate to BLAME THE EDITOR for having such a fulfilling and exciting time.

William W. Parmley, MD, is an emeritus Professor of Medicine at the University of California, San Francisco, where he served as chief of cardiology for 23 years. He is a graduate of Johns Hopkins School of Medicine. His cardiology training was carried out at Johns Hopkins, the National Heart Institute and Harvard. He is also a past president of the American College of Cardiology. For ten years he was editor-in-chief of the *Journal of the American College of Cardiology*, the most widely read cardiology journal in the world at that time. He is author and co-author of over 300 scientific manuscripts. He is also editor-in-chief of a three-volume textbook of cardiology. After retirement he and his wife spent ten years in missionary and humanitarian work, five years of which were in Africa.

Media—Journalism

A Life in Journalism

Bernard Gwertzman

I must confess that I have had a love affair with newspapers ever since I was a young boy, growing up in the Bronx, in New York City. I can remember as a boy about ten years old, listening to the weekly radio program on NBC called *The Big Story*, which each week rewarded an enterprising reporter with a $500 award from Pall Mall cigarettes, the program's sponsor. During World War II, I read the papers with intense interest, from the early days of setbacks to the final victory.

When my family moved to New Rochelle, NY, a nearby suburb of New York City, I was made managing editor of the junior high school paper, and my job included making sure the monthly paper got published correctly by the local print shop—my first introduction to "printers' ink".

When I went to New Rochelle High School in the tenth grade, I was an assistant manager of the school's basketball team. The coach, Dan O'Brien, told me toward the end of the season that he wanted to make me "manager" the next year, but I surprised him by saying that I hoped to win the job of sports reporter for NRHS at *The New Rochelle Standard-Star,* a daily newspaper for the city (now, of course, defunct). O'Brien was surprised and asked me to submit a sample of my writing—covering the high school's entry—a mile relay team—in the Millrose Games the next night in Madison Square Garden.

I turned in my report to him and a few days later, he told me that I had the job as the next sports reporter. Apparently, he spoke to Elmer Miller, the paper's editor, and I got the job. That meant for the next two and a half years, I wrote up all the sports teams at this big high school. When I look over the writing that appeared in print some 63 years ago, I smile at the cliché-ridden prose that the sports editor of *The Star*, Pat McGowan, allowed me to get away with.

In any event, as 1953 rolled around, and graduation was in the offing, I decided then that I wanted a newspaper career, and to that end, I only applied to colleges with daily newspapers. The city editor of *The Star* was a Harvard grad, who also went to Columbia Journalism School. He persuaded me to apply to Harvard. I did, but was put on the waiting list for the Class of 1957. This so infuriated the city editor that he resigned as treasurer of the Harvard Club of Westchester County. Whether his resignation did it, or just my luck, I was finally admitted to Harvard.

I can remember in my first days at Harvard being interviewed by someone from the radio station on why I wanted to go to Harvard, and I replied, "to work on *The Crimson*." In those days, *The Harvard Crimson*, which then as now was located on Plympton Street, took itself extremely seriously. It had on its staff people like David Halberstam, Jack Rosenthal, J. Anthony Lewis, and Arthur J. Langguth, all of whom won Pulitzer Prizes, and all of whom at one time or other worked for *The New York Times*.

I eventually became managing editor of *The Crimson* for the 1956–57 year. It was a time of considerable world tension. There was a Middle East war in 1956, the Soviet invasion of Hungary, and on the domestic front, Eisenhower easily won re-election. Stalin, the long-time tyrannical leader of the Soviet Union, had died in March 1953, and I was fascinated by the man's history and how he was an ally of ours during the war, even though he was so evil. In my freshman year, I took Merle Fainsod's course on Soviet government, and after I was elected to *The Crimson*, I did a series of articles on the Russian Research Center in 1954, interviewing a number of scholars, including Marshall D. Shulman, who was then the deputy director of the Center. Shulman was a former newsman, and told me that he was hoping to get more newspaper people involved in the center so that the country would have a better informed public about Soviet-American tensions.

During my senior year, Newbold Noyes, Jr., the editor of *The Washington Evening Star* in DC, came to Harvard looking for candidates to hire. *The Star*, an afternoon paper, was feeling heavy competition from *The Washington Post*, and wanted to enlarge its coverage from being just a hometown afternoon paper. Later that spring, I received a telegram from Noyes which said: "Subject to solution of problem of your military obligation am happy to inform you of your selection from among 25 college applicants as news department trainee under terms you and I discussed. We would like you to report for work around January 1 after completing six months of active service with National Guard or Reserve."

I accepted his offer, and enlisted in an Army Reserve unit in Boston. I did my six months (there still was a draft in those days), and reported to work in January 1958. *The Star* was a very traditional newspaper for its time. It was located in the heart of DC in an imposing high-rise building. Almost everyone smoked, and everyone of course wrote their stories on typewriters. Copy was edited at copy desks and then sent to the composing room where stories were put into type on linotype machines. I loved the atmosphere, and I enjoyed the work immensely. I was promoted to full staff in the summer, but decided I wanted to go back to Harvard to study Russian affairs, as I had been prompted by Shulman.

I went to night school at George Washington University in DC to study Russian, and showed up in Cambridge again to start the two-year program. In the summer of 1959, I went with a group of about 25 American youth—mostly recent graduates or graduate students—on a two-month visit to the Soviet Union. We went as part of a recently signed US-Soviet cultural exchange which had a provision for an exchange of youth. I wrote a series of articles for *The Star* on the trip after we got back, and *The Star* hired me to help cover Nikita S. Khrushchev's visit to the US in early September. The high point for me on that trip to the Soviet Union was in Leningrad [now St. Petersburg]. Vice President Richard Nixon had arrived in Moscow at about the same time we were there and opened an American exhibition in Sokolniki Park, the main park in Moscow. At the opening, Nixon and Khrushchev got into a debate in a pavilion meant to depict a typical American kitchen. It got massive publicity for Nixon. We got to the exhibition the next day, and I remember the huge throng of Russians looking at everything they did not have then—cars, consumer goods, et al. Nixon arrived in Leningrad about the same time we did, and we went to a big park in the city to celebrate White Nights. Because the city was so far north, it hardly got dark at night in the summer. There I met a young Russian student and we chatted for quite a while. We agreed to meet the next night for dinner.

The next day, I went to the Hotel Astoria, hoping to meet some of the American correspondents traveling with Nixon. Instead, a young woman from Intourist came up to me, asked if I were American and when I said, "Yes," handed me two tickets to the Kirov [now Marinsky] ballet that night. I knew Russians loved ballet, and so was happy to take my "date" there. When we arrived, I was surprised to see the audience seemed to be 90 percent Westerners. It seemed the Soviet authorities were loathe to have Nixon "contaminate" the audience. We watched Khachaturian's "Spartacus", and at intermission, I went, with my Russian friend, up to the mezzanine outside Nixon's Royal Box. When he emerged, reporters asked if he liked the ballet, and when he said he did, he followed up by saying "But where are the Russians?" At that point, I brought my date forward and introduced her to Nixon.

There is a sequel. In November 1980, when I was diplomatic correspondent for *The New York Times*, I went to the annual Soviet embassy party in honor of the November 7th Bolshevik takeover of Russia. Nixon, who by now had become the disgraced former president, showed up with his former Secretary of State Henry Kissinger. Nixon was surrounded by other guests who wanted to remind him of times they had met in the past. I then recalled for him his visit to the Kirov. He then looked me in the eye, and said "What was the ballet that night?" I answered correctly, "Spartacus". Nixon then smiled, said, "Correct", and shook my hand.

In the summer of 1960, I returned to *The Star*, which raised my salary from $58 a week to $85. *The Star* had me do stories about Soviet tourists in DC and a number of city stories. That year, of course, was an important presidential election, and *The Star* sent me to Harvard to do stories about John F. Kennedy's time there. He was not much of a student. My friend and colleague Haynes Johnson and I were assigned to cover inaugural planning after JFK won the election over Nixon that November. I was assigned to help cover the actual inauguration in January 1961, a day marked by a huge snowfall the night before.

Eventually, I was assigned to the "Week in Review" section where I wrote about foreign affairs every Sunday. That gave me a chance to catch up on the brewing crises in Southeast Asia, Laos and Vietnam. *The Star* also encouraged me to write stories about the Soviet Union based on my reporting in DC and from reading the Soviet press. By the middle of 1962, I was freed from the "Week in Review" and made a foreign affairs writer. Also, because I was single and only 28, I was pushed into becoming head of *The Star*'s Newspaper Guild unit.

The Star's contract with its reporters was coming up for renewal in December, 1963, and the demands from the staff were for a $200 a week minimum for experienced reporters. I was preparing my materials for a meeting that afternoon with *The Star* management on November 22, when I noticed a crowd surging around the AP ticker in the front of the newsroom. I rushed up to find out what was going on, only to learn about the assassination of John F. Kennedy in Dallas. My negotiating meeting scrubbed, I was asked to prepare a biography of Lyndon B. Johnson, the new president, which I completed in time for the "extra" edition, which hit the streets about 6 p.m.

I also did a biography of Lee Harvey Oswald for Sunday's paper, based in large part on an interview done with Oswald during the time he was living in Moscow. The death of Kennedy struck me deeply since I could easily connect with the young president, our Harvard connections, and my thinking that he was doing a good job as president. The Guild negotiations went down to the wire, with Federal mediators stepping in. In the climactic round, Samuel Kauffmann, the business manager of *The Star*, said to me: "You are a Harvard graduate. How can you put up with that guy?", meaning the Guild's business manager. who did not shy away from profanities in the negotiations. Finally *The Star* agreed to the $200 minimum, and I was able to announce it to the staff the next day at a meeting at the Hilton Hotel. I was a hero for a day.

The Star sent me on my first trip to Eastern Europe in the first months of 1964. I went to Poland, Czechoslovakia, Hungary, and Romania, as well as the Soviet Union. *The Star* gave my reports tremendous publicity, with a banner: "The Parting Curtain, Ties Breaking in Red Bloc." That was the first of many trips like that which I made for *The Star*. My last was in November 1967, when I went to Moscow to cover the 50th anniversary of the Revolution. As something of a Communist expert, I wrote several pieces about the emerging liberalization in Czechoslovakia and the dangers that posed for Russia. Finally, in August 1968, the invasion happened. I was unhappy I could not have been there. But I dutifully reported the events from afar. In July 1968, Seymour Topping, the foreign editor of *The Times*, had invited me to New York for an interview. *The Times* had one of its Moscow correspondents expelled, and it was looking for a replacement.

When I did not hear anything more in the following weeks, I assumed I was passed over. But on August 30, the start of the Labor Day weekend, I got a call from Topping offering me the job. I took it a few days later, and *The Times* kept me in Washington for several months so I could become familiar with the paper. Finally, in February 1969, I went over to Moscow. I had gotten engaged to Marie-Jeanne Marcouyeux, a State Department French interpreter, at the end of January, and I returned in mid-April for our wedding. This year we will have celebrated our 48th anniversary.

My time in Moscow was during a rather dull period in relations. Arms control talks began in Helsinki, but the big news was the tension between Russia and China, which had included armed clashes along the Far Eastern borders. M.J. and I returned home in September 1971, my last stories from Moscow being the death of Khrushchev and his funeral.

Over the next 15 years, I became *The Times*' chief diplomatic correspondent—I earned my picture in *The Washingtonian* magazine in 1978 as one of the capital's top 50 journalists—and spent a good deal of the time in the Middle East. In 1973, Kissinger had been promoted to Secretary of State by Nixon, who by then was embroiled in the Watergate scandal. In the fall, Kissinger met with the State Department regular correspondents and told us he would be making a trip to Beijing and would take us, in distinction from his secret trip that eventually led to Nixon's trip there in February 1972. But before we could travel with Kissinger, Egypt and Syria launched a surprise attack on Israel in October 1973 on Yom Kippur. This caught everyone by surprise and for me set in motion months of continual travel with Kissinger.

The first trip was a long one, starting in Morocco, going to several Arab countries and Israel, and then on to Pakistan and China, with a brief stopover in Tokyo before returning home. Then in December 1973, we went to Geneva for what was supposed to be a Middle East peace conference, but Syria did not show up. This led in January 1974 to Kissinger's first Middle East shuttle between Israel and Egypt which led to an initial Israeli withdrawal in the Sinai. In May, we all set out again, this time to Syria, which led to a long, 33-day shuttle between Jerusalem and Damascus which produced a disengagement agreement. Those were glorious days for diplomatic correspondents. In February 1973 there also was a Vietnam peace accord sandwiched in, but of course that did not last.

These were tough times for family life, however. My two sons, James and Michael, were born in 1973 and 1975, respectively, and this put a lot of pressure on M.J. to carry on alone. I have always appreciated her indulgence during those times.

The Carter administration came to office, also focused on the Middle East. And President Carter succeeded in his Camp David diplomacy, getting a tentative peace agreement between Anwar el-Sadat of Egypt and Prime Minister Menachem Begin of Israel in September 1978. It took another several months of intense diplomacy, however, to nail down the peace treaty. I covered the signing on the White House lawn on March 26, 1979, and I remember thinking that this would usher in years of peace in the Middle East. Unfortunately, a second part of the Camp David accord, calling for agreement between Israel and Palestinians has yet to be implemented.

Of course, the achievements of the Carter administration came to a shattering halt when, following the Shah's leaving Iran, rampaging students seized the American embassy in Tehran on November 4, 1979. I then spent some 444 days, the length of the takeover, writing almost every day about the crisis. I was convinced that the United States would not use force to try and free the hostages, but I was wrong. On the night of April 24, 1980, I was awakened by the foreign desk and told about a failed rescue attempt being reported on the wires. I immediately confirmed this with the White House. And a few days later we learned that Secretary of State Cyrus Vance had resigned because he was so opposed to the use of force to try to rescue the hostages. Negotiations eventually began later in the year, and the hostages were released on the Inauguration Day of President Ronald Reagan, January 20, 1980.

I continued to cover the diplomacy of the Reagan years, which started out as seemingly opposed to any dealings with the Russians, changing to a complete turnaround when Mikhail Gorbachev took over. My last "big story" as a reporter was covering the initial Reagan-Gorbachev meeting in Iceland in October 1986. What had initially seemed a routine get-together turned into a historic meeting in which the two sides came close to abolishing all nuclear weapons.

In May 1985, Marie-Jeanne threw a big 50th birthday party for me in our house in Foxhall Village. I enjoyed the party, but afterwards I had a bit of depression, thinking my career would soon be over, now that I had turned 50. But soon thereafter, I agreed to go to New York and become deputy foreign editor. My wife and I eventually found a house in the Riverdale section of the Bronx, which was close to the Horace Mann School, which both my sons attended. I found I loved being an editor, and enjoyed the team effort needed to get a story out. In the summer of 1989, I was promoted to foreign editor, and the next six years were amazing for me.

In August 1989, my first month in the new job, I remember sending out a note to all correspondents saying we were in need of stories. Little did I realize at the time that East Germany was soon to collapse. It started with East Germans crossing legally into Hungary but then having sit-ins at the West German embassy, saying they would only leave when Hungary let them depart via the border with Austria. The

Hungarians relented and thousands of East Germans poured into the West via Hungary. More left via Czechoslovakia, and protests mounted in East Germany. Finally on November 9, 1989, the Wall was opened. Serge Schmemann, *The Times'* West German correspondent, was in West Berlin, and he phoned me at the foreign desk to tell me the Wall was open, and when I asked how he knew, he said our East German stringer had just walked into his room at the Hotel Kampinski in West Berlin and told him that he and his wife had walked through it.

We then had liberation in Czechoslovakia, and the slow deterioration of the Soviet Union. One humorous side light: I was curious about Bulgaria, a country we paid no attention to normally. I asked Clyde Haberman, our correspondent in Rome, to make a quick trip to Sofia and report what was going on there. I expected a story saying in effect, everything is quiet in this Communist outpost ruled for years by Todor Zhivkov. Haberman did not want to go, but I finally persuaded him to drop in. Wouldn't you know it? The day he arrived, November 10, 1989, Zhivkov was forced out.

As we neared the Christmas break, there was word of big protests in Bucharest, and an uprising in Timisoara, close to the border with Hungary. Early in the morning of December 24, I got a phone call telling me that John Tagliabue had been shot and wounded when a car he was in was ambushed in Timisoara. That led to frantic efforts in New York and elsewhere to get him evacuated to the West. Our Bonn bureau, led by Schmemann, arranged for a German Red Cross plane to get John to a hospital in Munich. John eventually recovered. I flew to Munich to see him, and then Schmemann and I went to East Berlin to talk about opening a bureau there. We never did, because on October 3, 1990, East Germany disappeared and was merged into one Germany.

Meanwhile, Gorbachev's efforts to liberalize the Soviet Union ran into many problems. The Baltic states all wanted their own independence, and states like Georgia, Armenia and Ukraine wanted independence as well. Finally, on December 25, 1991, despite the Christmas holiday here, the foreign desk was on full alert as Schmemann filed from Moscow that Gorbachev had resigned, and that now there would be one state, Russia, to incorporate the huge land mass of that "country".

We had other big stories in the years I was on the desk. South Africa ended its apartheid rule, and in 1990, Iraq invaded Kuwait, leading to a dispersal of our correspondents to Saudi Arabia awaiting the eventual invasion by allied forces in 1991. In China, Nick Kristof and his wife covered the Tiananmen Square protests in Beijing, which led to the massacre in June of some 400 students.

Early in 1995, I was told that I had had a great run as foreign editor, but what did I want to do next?

In 1993 my elder son, James, then a Harvard student, class of 1995, had shown me the World Wide Web for the first time and I saw the early website of the Library of Congress. That led me to speculate: Why not *The Times* on the web? So I told the top brass that I would like to work on Internet aspects of news. That led me eventually in 1995 to be present for the launch of *The New York Times* on the web in January 1996. I eventually became editor and given the unfamiliarity of people with the web, I hired many young people fresh out of college to staff our publication.

I don't think anyone on *The New York Times* could have foreseen that the web would eventually become the main source of circulation for the paper, and a place where the paper was now resting its hopes for the future. It still is an open question, however, whether major newspapers can survive in the future in print, or whether everything will be on the web. And more importantly, can organizations like *The New York Times* survive economically without a print product.

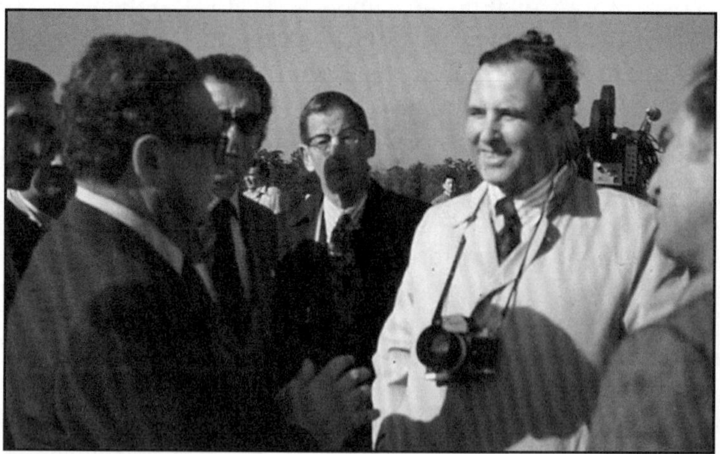

Figure 3.5.1.1 *Bernard Gwertzman (*The New York Times*) with Secretary of State Henry A. Kissinger in Beijing, China, November 1973.*
*To the left of Kissinger are Bruce Van Voorst (*Newsweek*), Richard Valeriani (NBC), Murray Marder (*The Washington Post*) and an unidentified person on the far right.*
Photo source: Unpublished personal photo by a colleague

Figure 3.5.1.2 *Group picture during Secretary's Kissinger's lengthy trip in November 1973 to Middle Eastern countries, Pakistan, China, and Japan following the October 1973 Egyptian-Syrian-Israeli war.*

Front row, l to r: *Darius Jhabvala (*The Boston Globe*); Helen Thomas (UPI); Henry Kissinger; unidentified person; and Marvin Kalb (CBS)*

Back row, l to r: *Bernard Gwertzman (*The New York Times*) and unidentified person*

Standing: *Stan Carter (*The New York Daily News*) and unidentified person*

Photo source: Unpublished personal photo by a colleague and later published in *Bernard Gwertzman, My Memoirs; Fifty Years of Journalism, from Print to the Internet*, 2016.

Bernard Gwertzman's long and distinguished career in journalism began in 1958. Starting as a staff writer for *The Washington Star*, he took time off to get an MA in Russian Studies at Harvard, joined *The New York Times* in 1968 and soon became Moscow bureau chief. After two years he went to the paper's Washington bureau where he was diplomatic correspondent. He was promoted to deputy foreign editor, then foreign editor in 1989. By 1995 he was digital editor before editing the *The New York Times* on the web. Retiring in 2002, he became consulting editor at the Council on Foreign Relations until 2014. He published a memoir in 2016, *Fifty Years of Journalism: From Print to the Internet.*

Figure 3.4.1.3 *G. Wallace "Woody" Woodworth (1902–1969)*

Source: http://www.thecrimson.com/article/1969/7/22/woody-poh-may-i-join-the
Photo: Courtesy of Harvard University

Oh may I join the choir invisible
Of those immortal dead who live again
In minds made better by their presence . . .
So to live is heaven:
To make undying music in the world.
– George Eliot[1]

Woody, the great teacher of the Music Department, as a Harvard undergraduate concentrated not in music but in history, which might account for his commitment to musical education of the amateur and the non-specialist, where he spent decades teaching hundreds of non-concentrators each year in the introductory survey course, Music 1.

Paradoxically, although the Glee Club rejected him an undergraduate as having a poor voice, in his career he became one of the greatest choral conductors in the country. He believed that amateurs could be taught to make music—and make music well—through singing.

As conductor of the Harvard Glee Club and Radcliffe Choral Society for more than three decades, he elicited a level of performance that made these institutions world-renowned—and he did this without any concessions to his singers for degree of difficulty.

Footnote

1 "O May I Join the Choir Invisible" (1867) *Longum illud tempus, quum non ero, magis me move t quam hoc exiguum.* – CICERO, ad Att., xii. 18.

Chapter Four

HUMANITIES

Figure C4 *Summer Pops Orchestra rehearsing in restored Sanders Theatre*
Reprinted courtesy of Harvard University

Chapter Four

HUMANITIES

Poetry

Three poems[1] by
Frederick Seidel

"Arnold Toynbee, Mac Bundy, Hercules Bellville"

Seventy-two hours literally without sleep.
Don't ask.
I found myself standing at the back
Of Sanders Theatre
For a lecture by Arnold Toynbee.

Standing room only.
Oxford had just published
With great fanfare Volume X of his interminable
Magnum opus, *A Study of History*.
McGeorge Bundy, the dean of the faculty,

Later JFK's
National Security Adviser, then LBJ's, came out onstage
To invite all those standing in the back
To come up onstage and use
The dozen rows of folding chairs already

Set out for the Harvard Choral Society
Performance the next day.
Bundy was the extreme of Brahmin excellence.
I floated up there in a trance.
His penis was a frosted cocktail shaker pouring out a cocktail,

But out came jellied napalm.
The best and the brightest
Drank the fairy tale.
The Groton School and Skull and Bones plucked his lyre.
Hercules Bellville died today.

He apparently said to friends:
"Tut, tut, no long faces now."
He got married on his deathbed,
Having set one condition for the little ceremony: no hats.
I knew I would lapse

Into a coma in full view of the Harvard audience.
I would struggle to stay awake
And start to fall asleep.
I would jerk awake in my chair
And almost fall on the floor. I put Hercky

In a poem of mine called "Fucking" thirty-one years ago, only
I called him Pericles in my poem.
At the end of "Fucking," as he had in life,
Hercules pulled out a sterling-silver-plated revolver
At a dinner party in London,

And pointed it at people, who smiled.
I had fallen in love at first sight
With a woman there I was about to meet.
One didn't know if the thing could be fired.
That was the poem.

"School Days"

I

John Updike

Updike is dead.
I remember his big nose at Harvard
When he was a kid.
Someone pointed him out on the street
As a pooh-bah at the Lampoon

As he disappeared into the Lampoon building
On Mt. Auburn.
The building should have seemed
Odd and amusing instead of intimidating,
But everything was intimidating,

Though one never let on.
Here was this strangely
Glamorous geek from New England,
With a spinnaker of a nose billowing out
From a skinny mast,

Only he was actually
Not from New England.
Those were the days when
One often didn't say hello even to a friend.
One just walked past.

I was a freshman in Wigglesworth
When I visited Ezra Pound
At St. Elizabeth's,
And Updike was about to be *summa cum laude*
And go off to Oxford.

These were the days of Archibald MacLeish
And his writers' class in his office
In Widener for the elite.
I remember I put taps on my shoes
To walk out loud the long Widener reading room.

II

House Master

Mr. Finley sat cross-legged
On top of a desk
Reciting from memory Sappho in Greek
In his galoshes, administering an IV drip of nectar
While hovering like a hummingbird.

That was Finley, magical, a bit fruity,
Warbling like a bird while the snow outside
Silenced the Yard.
We were in a Romanesque redbrick
H. H. Richardson building, Sever Hall.

I was an auditor
In a Greek lyric poetry seminar
That was somewhere over the rainbow.
Certainly it was the only time
I heard a hummingbird sing.

I remember everything.
I remember nothing.
I remember ancient Greek sparkles like a diamond ring.
Professors were called mister.
To address someone as professor was deemed vulgar.

It was good sport to refer
To one's inferiors as N.O.C.D. (Not our class, dear.)
Biddies still cleaned the student rooms.
I had a living room with a fireplace that worked.
Finley was the master of Eliot House, my house.

Somewhere else, Senator Joseph McCarthy
Of Wisconsin was chasing American communists,
But despite that, he was evil.
The snow kept falling on the world,
Big white flakes like white gloves.

III

Pretending to Translate Sappho

The mother of the woman I currently
Like to spank, I'm not kidding,
Was my girlfriend at Harvard.
The mother looked like a goddess
And as a matter of fact majored at Radcliffe in Greek.

Or as we would say then,
That was her field of concentration.
Please don't tell me
Anyone reading this
Believes what I'm saying or doesn't, it's irrelevant.

But anyway it's all true.
I don't believe in biographies.
I don't believe in autobiography.
It's a sort of pornography
To display oneself swollen

Into bigger-than-life
Meat-eating flies.
I remember the mother on her bicycle
Flying across Harvard Yard
All legs.

Goddesses still wore skirts.
I'm still up to the same old tricks,
But now I'm always on time.
One time, I kept her waiting for me in the old
Hayes-Bickford Cafeteria on Mass. Ave. three hours.

When I finally got the goddess
Into my student bed,
The beauty of her nineteen-year-old body
Practically made me deaf, so loud
I leaked. My arrogant boy burst into tears.

"Charlie"

In Memory of Charles P. Sifton (1935–2009)[2]

I remember the judge in a particular
Light brown chalk-stripe suit
In which he looked like a boy,
Half hayseed, half long face, half wild horse on the plains,
Half the poet Boris Pasternak with a banjo pick,
Plucking a twanging banjo and singing Pete Seeger labor songs.

I remember a particular color of
American hair,
A kind of American original orange,
Except it was rather red, the dark colors of fire,
In a Tom Sawyer hairstyle,
Which I guess means naturally

Unjudicial and in a boyish
Will Rogers waterfall
Over the forehead,
And then we both got bald . . .
My Harvard roommate, part of my heart,
The Honorable Charles Proctor Sifton of the Eastern District.

Charlie,
Harvard sweet-talked you and me into living in Claverly
Sophomore year, where no one wanted to be.
We were the elect, stars in our class selected
To try to make this palace for losers respected.
The privileged would light the working fireplaces of the rejected.

Everyone called you Tony except me, and finally—
After years—you told me you had put up with years of "Charlie"
From me, but it had been hard!
Yes, but when now
I made an effort to call you Tony, it sounded so odd to you,
You begged me to come back home. Your Honor,

The women firefighters you ruled in favor of lift their hoses high,
Lift their hoses high,
Like elephants raising their trunks trumpeting.
Flame will never be the same. Sifton, row the boat ashore.
Then you'll hear the trumpet blow.
Hallelujah!

Then you'll hear the trumpet sound.
Trumpet sound
The world around.
Flame will never be the same!
Sifton, row the boat ashore.
Tony and Charlie is walking through that door.

Frederick Seidel has published 15 books of poems, including *Ooga-Booga, The Cosmos Trilogy, Poems 1959–1979, Nice Weather*, and, most recently, *Widening Income Inequality*. His poems frequently appear in *The New York Review of Books*. He has received many awards for his poetry. In its issue of January 19, 2017, *The New York Review* published his article on Formula One auto racing entitled "Start Your Engines!"

Endnotes

1 From Frederick Seidel's book of poems, *Nice Weather*, New York: Farrar, Straus and Giroux, 2012, with permission of the author and the publisher.

The first poem, "Arnold Toynbee, Mac Bundy, Hercules Bellville", references the rising protest against the Vietnam War during the Johnson Administration.

2 Charles "Tony" Sifton, '57

Obituary from The New York Times:

Nov. 13, 2009: NEW YORK—Charles P. Sifton, a federal judge in Brooklyn whose rulings paved the way for women to join the New York Fire Department and for Mayor Michael R. Bloomberg to run for a third term, died Monday at his home in Brooklyn.

Judge Sifton handled many major cases in more than 30 years on the bench, many of them as chief judge of the US District Court for the Eastern District of New York.

He presided over civil rights and school desegregation cases, as well as trials of Mafia chieftains, Irish terrorists, and Joseph M. Margiotta, the Nassau County Republican leader convicted in 1983 of mail fraud.

In 1982, Judge Sifton ruled that a Fire Department test of physical strength and speed discriminated against women. He ordered that a new test be developed and that 45 women who had sued the city be hired.

The judge's term-limit ruling, in January, stands out for its impact on recent New York City politics, including the mayor's reelection last week. Judge Sifton's decision upheld a law passed last fall by the City Council to allow incumbents to run for a third term.

Judge Sifton ruled that officials elected by voters are entitled to reverse direct referendums. "To hold that overturning a law enacted by referendum infringed on First Amendment rights would effectively bar repeal, amendment, or revision of all laws initiated by the people," he wrote in his 64-page opinion.

Obituary from The Brooklyn Daily Eagle:

Dec. 9, 2009: CADMAN PLAZA EAST. Brooklyn Bids Farewell to Beloved Federal Judge. Despite Being Known for Historic Decisions, It Was the "Everyman" who Captured Judge Sifton's Heart

Charles Proctor Sifton, born in Manhattan on March 18, 1935, graduated from Harvard, studied in Germany as a Fulbright Scholar, and earned his law degree at Columbia Law School. Staff counsel to the Senate Foreign Relations Committee, then assistant US attorney for the Southern District of New York, he then worked in private practice until appointed to US District Court for the Eastern District of New York by President Jimmy Carter in 1977. He was Chief Judge from 1995 to 2000.

At his memorial service, friends, family and fellow jurists described the many different sides of the man they affectionately knew as "Tony": the man who inspired colleagues with his keen and exacting legal mind; and the nature-loving father remembered by his sons, who playfully recalled fishing trips to Maine where their father may have poached a lobster or two. "He lived a life of the mind, but taught us the love of nature," said Sam Sifton, the restaurant critic for *The New York Times*.

"Judge Sifton and I studied evidence together at Columbia—and then he taught all of us what it meant to be a federal judge," stated US District Judge Jack Weinstein. "He fully appreciated that every case, every person was unique. And from over the horizon, Judge Sifton's great light illuminates us and guides us still."

One of the most moving tributes came from retired firefighter Capt. Brenda Berkman, a plaintiff in the historic lawsuit over whether the FDNY's physical examination discriminated against women. Judge Sifton's 1982 ruling that the FDNY adopt a new test emphasizing stamina and agility instead of speed and strength was revolutionary and caused a ripple effect for firefighters across the world, but in New York, it was extremely unpopular.

"Judge Sifton and women like myself were ridiculed." Besides the harassment and bullying she endured as a leader of the movement to allow women into the FDNY, she even received death threats. Sifton and his family were also harassed and subjected to protests.

Numerous friends and colleagues spoke about Sifton's character, including his two sons who spoke about how Sifton grew up with Marxist sympathies but, as a judge, upheld the American rule of law.

Chief Judge Raymond J. Dearie spoke of Sifton's compassion for defendants trapped in criminal activity, saying that Sifton once said to him in conversation, "We judges—we just pick up the pieces." Sifton "decided to be someone who did something about it" by starting the first federal drug court. "It was a passion for him."

Editors' Note

The above obituaries are edited extracts from the originals.

"Charles"

To the memory of Charles "Tony" Sifton '57

Roger S. Mitchell

I looked in on his room now and then.
Dirty sheets, like mine, a tie across a chair.
We were room-mates, first year in college,
and if we talked more than a dozen times,
I can't imagine what it was about,
he already suave at eighteen, at home
in life. I stared up at some craggy peak
for which I had the wrong equipment
and little interest to climb. I was maybe
fourteen. Developmentally, that is.
He tried out for the "lit mag" before I knew
what "lit" was. He and his friends read books,
the same ones so it seemed. I hadn't, as yet,
hadn't a glimmer of what to do or be
except what my parents had in mind,
which I had no way not to say no to.
A cavernous stairway, always dimly lit,
led up five flights to the top. By the door,
a framed list naming all who had roomed there,
year after year, none of whom I recognized.
Ours, I presumed, would be added next year.
I wrote a paper on the origin of God.
Hopelessly earnest, I'm sure; logical.
At least trying to be. My instructor
had me in for a look-see then, possibly
merely amused at a boy, another one,
who'd figured the big one out, or at least
took it on, a lamb caged with a tiger.
Gamov was pushing the Big Bang in those days.
It was a paper I had to write in a course
I can't remember a sentence of, a book,
the prof, the room we sat in, day after day,
but the grunt instructor asking me up
to his office, smiling and leaning back
in his chair, happy, I think, with his work,
as I would be years later explaining

the reasons for things or why reason failed
to explain very much of what we did or were.
You can live a whole year with a ghost,
a phantom much like yourself, marking
his manners and distance and the soiled sheets
and never forget his name and so ask
when you heard it at parties or meetings
if the stranger knew him. It came to be
a game of sorts, a test, until the night
a woman I'd just met said, yes, I do,
he's my husband, we're about to divorce,
and Charles, she called him Charles, has done
important work for us all. I told her
I knew him, really only his aura, his slow
passing in and out of the door. She said, yes,
I know, and looked away. I meant to write her,
meant to explain, but what? So, I didn't.
What could I say to a woman about to divorce
an oddity, to me an oddity, who must have
thought me the same, with twenty or more years
headed all our ways of unreadable
silence before he died, as the paper said,
honored and old, learned and wise,
the day before yesterday.

* * *

"Charles" is a poem written on the occasion of the death of my freshman room-mate, whom many of you might have known, Charles, or as he called himself, Tony Sifton. I did not know him well. We were as different as room-mates could be, but he was for me something of a remote eminence, a person who came from a very different world. His was in or bordered on a literary world, about which he seemed quite knowledgeable. Mine was then the world of science, and I was headed toward a major in Biochemistry and eventually medical school.

My years at Harvard slowly but surely changed all that. I "discovered" literature, as well as an interest in writing poetry while I was an undergraduate, and to make a long story short, wound up as a poet and a professor of English and American Literature.

Do I have Tony Sifton to thank for that in any way? My poem doesn't say that in so many words, but the answer to that question today is, perhaps, very possibly. I just know that the announcement of Tony's death, which I read in *The New York Times*, "made" me write this poem almost at once.

Roger Mitchell, author of 11 books of poetry, directed the Creative Writing Program at Indiana University and held the Ruth Lilly Chair of Poetry. In retirement he is Poetry Editor of *The Hamilton Stone Review* and writing a biography of poet Jean Garrigue. He has been a Fellow of Indiana Arts Commission and the National Endowment for the Arts. His poetry and non-fictional writing have won numerous awards, including the Akron Prize, the Midland Poetry, John Ben Snow, River Styx International Poetry, and Red Hen Press's Ruskin Art Club awards. Currently, he and his wife, the fiction writer Dorian Gossy, live in Jay, NY.

Recapturing Clarity

Joseph Poindexter

In the spring of 1957, my one and only published poem appeared (with a necessary assist from Fred Seidel) in *The Advocate.*

Since then: two years in the Army; two wives (sequentially); two sons (and the audacious presumption they would welcome their existence); four decades of magazine deadlines; mountains (and a book about mountains).

And now, back to poems—and a reach for the clarity all of us breathed in 1957:

"Sound"

That there is sound,
That there are ribbons of sound unspooling
From the copse of trees above the house,
Their mantel of leaves rippling with melody,
That there is robin song and frog song,
The whir of hummingbird
And the wingbeat of heron
And the great clamorous urgency of geese
Cresting the ridge in miraculous formation,
That there is the hush of mist,
The long sigh of an evening rain,
The measured rush of water over stone,
The ocean's passacaglia,
Its reach and draw of now and now and now,

(We stepped outdoors.
John said listen, and I listened.
Beautiful, he said; what, I said.
The plane, he said—there was one passing overhead.
Is there a sound, I said, that has no beauty?
A pause, then, no, he said.)
That there is sound,
Sometimes no more than the quiet hum among the stars,
Is all we need to know of deity—
It is scripture enough.

"Bridge"

Stone bridges once carried the farm road
Twice across the brook,
But the upper bridge had washed out long ago,
And the lower was giving way,
Its great granite slab collapsing.

We wrapped this stone in chain,
And Paul's machine,
Growling above the rift like an ancient beast,
Lifted, then lowered it to the ledge of rock
I'd built beneath.

The bridge, its dislocated joint reset,
Shuddered into place.
We paused, both of us I like to think,
Basking in the sunlit joy of regeneration,

(It is this putting right an old intention
That shelters us from dread.)

We are neighbors now:
He who farmed this land and we
Who decades later wandered by,
Not knowing we'd be this day forever joined,
Our hand once more upon his stone,
His bridge once more beneath our feet.

"Geese"

Here is a page
Awaiting words as swift and certain
As the skein of geese
That just now cleaves
The western sky.

Joseph Poindexter is retired from a career in writing and editing for magazines (*Business Week, Money, People, Life*). His wife, Holly, a former book designer (Dial Press, Knopf), and he divide their time between Brooklyn and New Marlborough, MA, where he is president of the historical society and writes for the town newspaper. They have two sons and a grandson.

Essay on Haiku

Steve Addiss

I came to haiku primarily through translating traditional Japanese poems, and I soon realized that I couldn't maintain 5–7-5 structures without making the English versions bulky and wordy.

For example, to reach 5–7-5 we would have to add unneeded verbiage to the first two segments of Basho's famous haiku:

[there is an] old pond
(*furu ike ya*)
[suddenly] a frog jumps in
(*kawazu tobikomu*)
the sound of water
(*mizu no oto*)

In my own haiku, I started with the idea of staying near 5–7-5, an early example being a poem that appeared in two Japanese newspapers in 1996:

old pond paved over
into a parking lot –
one frog still singing

Although people have said they liked this haiku in its original state, it now seems a little intellectual to me, even when I give it an image. It was some years before I decided that it could be made more succinct:

old pond
paved over –
one frog still singing

In any case, I now prefer my poems that are more observation and less concept.

coral needles
stitching
the honeysuckle trail

distant rainclouds
darken
her eyes

dozing
the flutter
of hummingbirds

this morning
even the garbage pail
angelic

The haiku and haiga of **Stephen Addiss** have appeared widely. His books include *Cloud Calligraphy, A Haiku Menagerie, The Art of Zen, Haiga: Haiku-Painting, The Art of Chinese Calligraphy, Haiku People, A Haiku Garden, Haiku Humor, Tao Te Ching, Japanese Calligraphy, Haiku: An Anthology,* and *The Art of Haiku.*

Figure 4.1.4.1 *An Ancient Chinese Poet, facsimile of original Chinese scroll*
Photo source: http://www.mhpbooks.com/granta-goes-to-china/

Theater

Playwright

"God Bless America"

David A. Rakov

Blake: *Career counselor and drivers' education coordinator*
Mallory: *Student*
Sylvia: *Student*
William: *Student*
Robert: *Student*

(Blake's office with door open. Mallory enters.)

Mallory: Good morning, Sir.

Blake: Good morning *(looks at file)*—Mallory. Are you here for driver training or career counseling?

Mallory: Career counseling, Sir.

Blake: Career counseling, yes. *(Looks at file.)* I see you've taken the Advance Placement curriculum.

Mallory: Yes, Sir. My parents wanted me to have every opportunity to have a head start toward getting into all the best schools.

Blake: But it seems you've gotten mediocre grades in the all of the AP courses. Why did you get such ordinary grades?

Mallory: That's the question everyone seems to ask. They usually conclude that I was too lazy to do the work. Such a conclusion seems easier for them to accept than the alternative—that I might be just a bit dim.

Blake: Dim?

Mallory: You know—dim—not bright; slightly slow; not the quickest of studies.

Blake: A tad retarded?

Mallory: No need to go overboard, Sir.

Blake: No. Sorry. Well, what are thinking about doing now that Yale, Stanford and East Limerick U seem out of the picture?

Mallory: I was rather hoping that you might be able to give me some advice on that subject, Sir, you being a career counselor and all.

Blake: Yes, yes. You've taken all the personality profiling tests, I assume?

Mallory: Oh, yes, Sir. I was hoping you might have the results there in your files.

(Blake hunts through papers.)

Blake: Ah, here we are. Well, this is quite interesting. As introverted as you seem from these results, any career in sales seems a poor choice.

Mallory: I think that's spot on, Sir. I really don't like pushing people to do something they wouldn't otherwise want to do.

Blake: Scientific careers appear to be out also, given your grades in biology, chemistry and math.

Mallory: I couldn't agree more, Sir. Science and I appear to dwell in independent universes. Science seems overtly academic to me, like teaching. I realize that my dimness would not preclude a career in teaching, but I just would not enjoy it.

Blake: If academics put you off, what about pursuing a technician type of job or a trade?

Mallory: The parents, Sir. They wouldn't hear of my being a tradesman.

Blake: You seem well trained in rejecting ideas, but I don't see that as the basis of a career, other than as a legislator. But have you had any ideas of your own concerning what you might like to do?

Mallory: Well, the thought has crossed my mind that I might be quite successful as a procurer.

Blake: You mean buyer.

Mallory: No, Sir, procurer. You know, pimp. I have a rather wide circle of friends, and I enjoy getting people together to do things that please them. It would sort of be like being the social director on a cruise ship, but you would not need a boat.

Blake: Have you really considered the problems of such a career choice?

Mallory: Oh, yes, Sir. I've evaluated the advantages and disadvantages. The main advantages seem to be social and economic (serving people's needs, low capital investment, high rate of return, social status) and the main disadvantages seem minor (irregular hours, ersatz illegality). Given the people I already know, I think I could get the enterprise underway quite rapidly

Blake: What do you think your parents would say about your choice?

Mallory: Well, as Dad is a professional political campaign adviser, I guess he would feel that I am following in his footsteps. Mom would be proud that I avoid work that excludes women. I guess you could say that I would be replacing the glass ceiling with a mirrored ceiling. Oh—I just noticed the time—I've got an economics course at eleven that I wouldn't want to miss. Thank you for your help. It's good to have positive feedback on my line of thinking

Blake: But, wait . . .

Mallory: Sorry, Sir, I really must go now.

(Mallory leaves. Sylvia approaches the desk.)

Sylvia: Sorry, I don't have an appointment, but could you spare me a few moments?

Blake: Yes I suppose so—but it will have to be brief because I have another appointment in a few minutes. What careers seem to interest you the most?

Sylvia: Modeling looks great to me. But I'm not here about careers. I'm here about driver training.

Blake: Well, you have to go to the registrar's office and set up a series of lessons; then you will take the exam when you are ready.

Sylvia: No, you don't understand. I've already done all that. I want to know how I appeal my failing the exam.

Blake: Appeal?

Sylvia: Yeah. I took the exam yesterday and I didn't pass.

Blake: You don't appeal when you flunk a driver's test. You take some more classes and take the test again. Why did you fail?

Sylvia: Well, the examiner said it was because I hit those cones backing up, but I know it was because of racial and gender prejudice, so I should have a right to appeal. Or maybe sue because of a denial of my civil rights.

Blake: It's just a driver's test.

Sylvia: That's what they used to say about voting. I know my rights; you can't bulldoze me.

Blake: Look, you ought to calm down. Who was your examiner?

Sylvia: Barbara Jeffers.

Blake: I could be wrong and I'm not trying to make any assumptions, but you seem to be female and Caucasian and Barbara also seems to be female and Caucasian. Isn't that going to make a gender/racial complaint unlikely to succeed?

Sylvia: I don't know why I came to talk to you. You're just like all the rest. You're so busy protecting the rights of minorities that we get screwed. I think I'll include you as a defendant.

(Sylvia stalks off. Blake sits stunned, looking in the direction where Sylvia walked off. Wilma enters.)

Wilma: Mr. Blake?

(Blake recovers himself.)

Blake: Yes.

Wilma: I'm Wilma Stevenson. I have an appointment with you.

Blake: Yes; sorry—I was a bit distracted.

Wilma: Have you had a difficult morning?

Blake: Yes, you might well say that.

Wilma: I guess it's a tough job, trying to counsel people in making choices of careers, when the wrong choice could effectively sentence one to a lifetime of doing what he or she might grow to hate.

Blake: You got that right.

Wilma: I remember someone saying that he didn't want to be a 40-year-old lawyer, sitting miserably in his office at ten at night because some idiot 20-year-old thought the law was going to be fascinating.

Blake: Yeah.

Wilma: Did you go into this work because you liked to work with high school students?

Blake: Partly. And also partly because I thought it was the only job open and I needed a job.

Wilma: Looking back, do you feel as if you took enough time to evaluate the alternatives, or did the economic and psychological pressures force you into a possibly overly hasty decision?

Blake: I guess I panicked. And after I got here, the weekly paycheck, although not large, gave me enough security that I didn't really think about leaving.

Wilma: If you recognize your basic unhappiness now, have you developed sufficient self-esteem to reevaluate and perhaps dare to reconsider other positions, to risk change?

Blake: I doubt it. I know I'm in a rut, but it's a comfortable rut—the job doesn't give me much satisfaction, but at least the money comes in regularly. Now, what can I help you with?

Wilma: I'm trying to make a choice between two careers.

Blake: What are they?

Wilma: I need to decide if I should be waiter or a public toilet attendant.

Blake: Oh, that's easy. A toilet attendant. The hours are better.

Wilma: Thank you very much. Even after having done the research and after having analyzed every possible aspect of a problem and come to a tentative resolution, it's always wise to consult an expert in the field and get his or her informed opinion. I can't thank you enough for your guidance.

Blake: No trouble, Wilma. After all, it's my job.

(Wilma leaves. Robert enters.)

Robert: Excuse me, Sir, but I believe I have an appointment with you. My name is Robert Harrison.

Blake: Driver training?

Robert: No, Sir, I have already passed my driving test. This is about career counseling. Would you please review my records, Sir?

Blake: Yes, I have them here. (Goes through papers.) Well, it seems that you have taken every possible advanced placement course and have gotten As in all of them as well as in your regular classes. Your national test scores are at the 99th percentile, it seems. You look familiar. You are captain of the football team, aren't you? (*Robert nods.*) and it says here that you are President of the class. (*Robert nods again.*) And aren't you the Harrison who volunteers at the Hospice four afternoons a week, after athletic practice? (*He nods again.*) What do you do on the fifth day?

Robert: That's the day I tutor the kids at the local leper colony. I'd do more for them, but the doctors won't let me.

Blake: Well, what can I do for you, Robert? It seems to me that, with your record, you can write your own ticket for any school you wish to go to.

Robert: Oh, yes, Sir, I am perfectly aware of that.

Blake: Then why have you come to see me?

Robert: Oh, just to satisfy my ego, Sir. You cannot imagine how satisfying it is to hear someone reciting all your marvelous accomplishments to you and telling you that the world is your oyster.

By the way, you also know, don't you, that I come from a family with enormous amounts of money and that all the best-looking, smartest girls in my class are always throwing themselves at me, offering me money, sex, anything to please me.

Blake: That's all well and good, Robert, but don't you feel that is a bit of an imposition on me as I have responsibilities to serve other students who are more in need of career counseling than you are?

Robert: Oh, Sir, think about it. Why should I, a person who has such an assured, bright future, why should I give a shit about other students, let alone a nonentity like you?

Blake: A point well taken. Good thinking. And good luck to you, not that you'll need it.

Theater

Performing Arts

David Rakov, after graduation, went to Harvard Law School and practiced law in Boston for six years. He then spent five years as a Peace Corps administrator, one year in Washington, DC, and the following four years in Niger, Ivory Coast and Benin. Subsequently he served as General Counsel for the welfare agency in Illinois and then as General Counsel for the University of Chicago Hospitals. After an unsuccessful stab at retirement, he worked part-time for the Sargent Shriver National Center on Poverty Law and Mount Sinai Hospital in Chicago. Now fully retired, he spends his time traveling and writing doggerel.

Performing Arts

Tomorrow and Tomorrow and Tomorrow[1]

Terrence Currier

He was 55, beginning his 17th season at Arena Stage, blessed with stability in a famously unstable profession. Then he hitched his wagon to Annie 2.

From my journal: Sunday morning, January 21, 1990:

The show that was to mark my debut on Broadway closed at the Kennedy Center last night. Doug Baker, the company manager for the ill-fated production of *Annie 2*, hand-delivered my last paycheck to me in my dressing room on Thursday. No sooner had I added the money to my bank account, than I subtracted it for my mortgage payment. I am a conduit through which money flows, or, more accurately, flowed. After 17 years of uninterrupted gainful employment as a member of the Arena Stage Acting Company, I am without a job. The important thing now is to produce income, generate some cash flow. Tomorrow, I'll pay a visit to the Unemployment Office.

And it was as I sat in that pale green, ungodly hot waiting room surrounded by other people down on their luck—a construction worker on my right and a guy talking to himself on my left—that I asked myself one more time: *How, with such dizzying speed, had I been transported from the bright lights of Broadway to the fluorescent drabness of the DC unemployment office?*

It all began in mid-July of 1989 when "On the Town" closed, marking the end of my 16th season as a resident actor at Washington's Arena Stage, the flagship of American regional theaters. On the whole, they had been rewarding years, years of relative stability in a chronically unstable profession, during which my four children, two dogs and several cats had grown to a healthy maturity.

Late July, the powers that be announced that director Liviu Ciulei had been chosen to open the season with his production of *A Midsummer Night's Dream*. Ciulei offered me a role I had no interest in, so I declined. My season would begin with the first rehearsal of *The Man Who Came to Dinner* on October 10, 1989.

In the nick of time an offer came to play Hector Malone in George Bernard Shaw's *Man and Superman* at Baltimore's Center Stage. Things were looking up.

Just after I had begun *Man and Superman* rehearsals, my New York agent called with an appointment for me to audition for *Annie 2*, the sequel to the hugely successful *Annie*.

I caught the early morning Amtrak Acela to New York and fast walked from Penn Station to 890 Broadway—an eight-story audition and rehearsal hall where many Broadway shows begin—I strode into the high-ceilinged audition chamber with a smile and an unmistakable air of confidence, and jauntily greeted the table of judges—the producers, the choreographer, the director and other luminaries. Without further ceremony, I launched into the old pop standard, "Come Rain or Come Shine", instructing the accompanist to be loose and follow me.

I wailed, I wobbled, I set the hardwood floor afire with a display of old-style hoofing and finished with a fervid vow that "*I'm with you always / I'm with you rain or shine.*"

Director Martin Charnin wanted to know more about me and asked if I would mind coming back next week to read for them.

On Monday I received by overnight delivery two scenes—one for Drake the butler, the other for the male lead, Daddy Warbucks, which, the accompanying note informed me, they might want me to understudy. I decided to impress them by committing both scenes to memory.

When I returned to the audition room at 890 Broadway the following Wednesday, Martin said, "*Why don't you do the Warbucks scene for us first?*" I glanced briefly at the scene and then set it aside, remarking that I knew it well enough to do it without the script. Everything went swimmingly.

Again the unmistakable mood of approval. When I finished the number, Martin asked, "Would you be willing to shave your head?"

"*Sure,*" I answered. "*Absolutely.*"

Then he smiled at me with his boyish grin and said, "*Would you mind waiting outside for just a minute while I consult with my associates?*" No problem, I assured him, throwing my backpack over my shoulder and retrieving my music from the pianist. No sooner had I settled into one of the old theater chairs in the lobby than Martin came charging out of the room.

"*We want you to be in our Broadway show, very much.*"

Phew.

"*We want you to understudy Daddy Warbucks and possibly play Drake,*" he said, then went on to explain that they still had some other people to see, but that they would definitely have a role for me in the show.

I assured him that I was mightily pleased, but then I explained my dilemma: I would soon be signing my seasonal contract with Arena Stage and would appreciate a consultation with my agent so that any problems might be resolved.

On Friday, October 6, 1989, Francis Del Duca called to say that he had rejected the first offer from the producers. It would be foolhardy, he had told them, for me to leave Arena Stage in order to lose money in New York.

I expressed my fear that the producers might be offended, but Del Duca assured me that if they really wanted me, they'd make a better offer. They were still uncertain about the role of Drake and wanted to list me only as "ensemble." This, Del Duca felt, was unsatisfactory. At my age, and with my experience, he advised, I should hold out for a featured role and considerably more money. I was persuaded.

Del Duca's strategy worked. I would play Drake the butler, understudy Daddy Warbucks and be handsomely compensated for my efforts. The contract would be for a year, unless the show closed early. Since I hadn't signed the Arena contract, I was able to accept their offer.

The risk seemed minimal. The same artistic team that had created the enormously successful *Annie* was back intact for *Annie 2.* Dorothy Loudon, the Tony Award-winning actress, would be playing Miss Hannigan. Harve Presnell, the gentle giant with the extraordinary voice, would be Daddy Warbucks.

Heels up, into the abyss.

Rehearsals for *Annie 2* were to begin in New York on November 6, but I wasn't scheduled to finish at Center Stage until November 12, which meant round-trip rail fare for four days. Plus parking, taxis and meals. Another piece of cake. I'd tap what little was left in my savings account and restore it when the big bucks started coming in.

Monday morning, November 6, 1989: I was on the 6:50 a.m. Amtrak Express to New York. I had turned 55 the day before.

The rehearsal hall at 890 Broadway was crowded with people milling about. Many of them seemed to know each other and were gathered in small groups exchanging embraces and laughing. I sauntered through the crowd seeking a familiar face. A hand grasped mine. "*Welcome aboard.*" It was Martin Charnin with his disarming smile, resilient dark forelock and anachronous white beard.

He guided me to a pair of men standing nearby. "*This is Tom Meehan, our writer, and Charles Strouse, the composer,*" Martin said. Meehan, a small roundish man with gentle blue eyes, stood in sharp contrast to the dour, circumspect Strouse, who resembled a pool shark. I knew instinctively that I would like them both.

Soon the proceedings began with an introductory message from Martin, followed by an interminable lecture from a representative of Actors Equity, the actors union, on the duties and responsibilities of Equity actors and the recent gains made by Equity in negotiating the new Broadway contract. Then it was time for lunch, and an hour of picture taking and interviews with the stars of the show—most notably Danielle Findley, the young actress playing Annie. Finally, for the first time, we read through the play.

The reading produced enough laughter to warrant optimism in those of us who had not read the script before signing our contracts. The score and lyrics raised our spirits even more. In the ensuing discussions, the words "hit" and "Tony Awards" played prominent roles.

I returned to Baltimore in time to make my 9:30 call at Center Stage for a 10:55 entrance in the fourth act of *Man and Superman.* Or so I thought. As it turned out, the anxiety and exhaustion of the previous week produced a genuine actor's nightmare.

Frazzled by the uncertainties of my life, I donned my running gear in my apartment and set out for a therapeutic jog down to Baltimore's Inner Harbor and around the charming Federal Hill district. After showering, dining alone and a bit of reading, I set the alarm for 9 p.m., slid between the sheets and drifted swiftly into glorious sleep. I awoke feeling refreshed and rested and rolled over to check the time.

Holy Godzilla! 10:50 p.m. My entrance was in five minutes. Thank God my apartment was only one block from the theater. I threw on my sweat suit, slipped my feet into my running shoes and bolted into the rain-driven night.

Several people were standing outside the theater. My God, I thought, they've canceled the show. Then I was in the lobby. The television monitor revealed them to be minutes away from the scene change before my entrance. The dressing rooms were three flights up. I took the steps three at a time, rushed in with the act-change music pouring ominously from the monitor overhead. The folks coming off the stage, suddenly aware of my plight, were all over me. One tied my laces, another my tie.

The music stopped, signaling the end of the scene change. "*Mr. Currier on stage please . . . immediately . . . Mr. Currier on stage.*" They were holding the curtain. Down the three flights of stairs I flew like a man afire. John Krupp, the young actor playing Straker, was waiting uneasily in the wings. We charged onto the stage and the scene began.

E.G. Marshall, playing Roebuck Ramsden, delivered his first line to me with so much transparent relish that I was momentarily shaken from my distracted state. "*It's an unexpected pleasure,*" he said, arching an eyebrow, "*to find you in this part of the world, Mr. Malone.*"

The Investors

With three huge halls at his disposal, Martin divided rehearsals into dance, music and scene work. Once the scenes were blocked, that is, the basic movements were established, the focus moved immediately to the music and dancing. This surprised me. There was no exploration of the text, no discussion of the historical context of the play or moment-to-moment realities. The order of the day seemed to be: Just get it on its feet and run through it as soon as possible. I didn't understand the logic of this process until later.

Sometime during the second week of rehearsals, Martin informed the cast that we would be doing a run-through for some people in the afternoon session. A run-through? We'd never even rehearsed the book scenes (spoken dialogue), never worked through them. In my experience, premature run-throughs are a sure-fire way to incorporate tension and uncertainty into a character or a scene. Martin assured us the run-through wasn't so much for us as it was for the producers, who were bringing some people in to see what we had.

People, what kind of people? *Investors*? I thought the show was already capitalized; that the $7 million was already in the bank. Well, what did I know? I'd been in the ivory tower of institutional theater for 30 years.

For the next two weeks the major emphasis remained on the music and dance. Those with more experience in Broadway musicals assured me that we would eventually work the book scenes. Book scenes, I was told, don't sell tickets.

On Sunday, November 19, a full-page ad appeared in *The New York Times*. My name was the same size as the dog's. But I was a full four spaces ahead of him. As a result of that one ad, Martin told us, we sold about $5 million worth of advance tickets.

Martin and choreographer Danny Daniels drilled the musical numbers relentlessly, leaving me with hours to idle away. Determined to master the Warbucks role early, I had devoted most of my considerable spare time to that task only to find daily changes in lyrics, lines and blocking. It seemed an exercise in futility, but I persevered, replacing old pages with new—white with green, green with blue, blue with pink, pink with salmon, salmon with mauve—always in search of a quiet place.

On Friday, December 1, Martin handed out a ten-page distillation of the script and announced that we would be presenting this to 1,600 ticket brokers at the Marquis Theater on Monday night. The thought of performing before an audience at this stage of the rehearsal process was terrifying and unprecedented in my experience.

The next two days were spent rehearsing this truncated version of the show. On Monday night we all assembled in the green room of the Marquis Theater for a final briefing. Having neither words to speak nor a song to sing in this version, I was noticeably relaxed and buoyant. The rest of the cast huddled tensely in the stage-left wings as Martin made his introductory remarks. "*We hope that you receive as much joy from this evening as we will experience in presenting it.*"

"*Yeah,*" quipped Ronny Graham, who played Dorothy Loudon's boyfriend. "*My joy is running down my leg.*" Those within earshot were thrown into muffled hysteria. Others followed as the quip was repeated. The tension was released, and the show was received with great enthusiasm. That night, the producers treated the cast to dinner at Sam's Restaurant, just a few doors away from the theater.

The next day, it was reported that somewhere in the vicinity of $5 million worth of tickets had been purchased. "*Looks as if you'll all be fulfilling your one-year contracts,*" Martin announced.

Sweeter words were never spoken. And now I understood what the rehearsal process was about.

As had been predicted by my more savvy colleagues, work soon began on the book scenes. The work, however, was hurried and cramped by Martin's style of directing: a no-nonsense, hard-driving, off-the-top-of-the-head style that left little room for protracted discussion. On occasion, when the frustration peaked, he would stop, stride onto the stage and deal slowly and meticulously with the problem until a satisfactory solution could be found. Then he'd charge ahead again. Though his collaborators, Meehan and Strouse, were almost always present at rehearsals, there was no mistaking who was commander in chief.

Not that I wasn't sympathetic to his problems. Martin had a job of Brobdingnagian proportions before him, mounting one of the largest productions in the history of Broadway and attempting to repeat the phenomenal success of *Annie*, which had earned untold millions on Broadway, on the road, in stock and on film.

Mention the Hollywood version, however, and you'd inevitably draw sneers of contempt from all three collaborators and the question, "*What film?*"

Christmas was only a few days away and spirits were high as we prepared for our first preview at the national monument to the Muses, the Kennedy Center. We'd heard that an invitation to the White House was probable; after all, the cast of *Annie* had been invited. Now, the elements missing in the rehearsal in New York would be added—the orchestra, costumes, scenery, lights and, finally, the audience.

Martin's presence was raised to a higher power when we arrived at the Kennedy Center by the addition of what we all referred to as "*the God mike.*" The size of the Opera House made it necessary to add a microphone to Martin's already impressive arsenal of directing techniques. From somewhere near the center of the roseate rotunda would boom the amplified litany. "*Stop! Hold it! Go back! Go back! Shh! Shh! Hold it!*" Abrasive as this was, it succeeded in keeping 35 actors and actresses from falling into instant chaos and minimized the barrage of well-meaning suggestions and inappropriate questions that can paralyze progress. To be honest, I rather admired the boldness of his style and took comfort in the knowledge that, come what may, we had a skipper at the helm who knew how to get the job done.

I marveled at his equanimity in the face of so much pressure and was mystified that a man who was undoubtedly a millionaire several times over and who had suffered a heart attack and undergone triple bypass surgery would willingly subject himself to the enormous stresses of mounting a Broadway musical. By the same token, it would not have been inappropriate to ask what a 55-year-old actor with a modest but steady income was doing risking the little security he had on a chancy theatrical venture. Perhaps the answer would explain the strange bond I felt with Martin. We were kindred spirits. Adventurers.

Truth to tell, we were all adventurers, and my admiration and respect for most of the cast, the sense of camaraderie and cheerfulness they brought to the work, helped to keep my spirits high. We were in it together. Sink or swim.

On December 20, we gave our first preview at the Kennedy Center. It was 3 hours and 30 minutes long. There weren't enough laughs. The audience reaction was not enthusiastic. The following day, the official opening was put off from December 28 to January 4. It was obvious there was much work to do, the most important part of which was to cut an hour out of the show.

On December 28, Martin gathered the troops and, quoting Emlyn Williams, said, "*In the theater you have to be able to drown your own children.*" Then the carnage began. Scenes were to be cut or blended with other scenes, lyrics were to be changed, decent roles were to be reduced to bit parts, songs were to be axed and dances drastically altered. The crew, we were informed, had already restructured cues to accommodate the changes, which would have to go into effect that night.

Little anxious glances were exchanged. "*I don't want any questions,*" Martin said, "*except 'Which side of the stage do I enter from?'*"

Thus began one of the most intriguing and bewildering experiences of my theatrical career. Over the next few weeks, lines that had belonged to some were given to others, leading to moments of terrified confusion on stage. People appeared on stage when they shouldn't have; exits were delayed or ignored. And compressed scenes sometimes led to premature dramatic revelations. For example: I walked on stage one night to reveal information intended to be kept secret from Daddy Warbucks, only to find myself face to face with the man himself. We stared helplessly at each other for a few moments, whereupon Lauren Mitchell, playing Daddy Warbucks's secretary, interjected, "*I think you're wanted out there, Mr. Warbucks,*" pointing off-stage.

"*Yesss . . . ah, right,*" Harve Presnell replied. And to our relief, charged into the wings.

On January 4, the show finally opened, and the results were disastrous. The audience didn't seem to like the show, and the critics were very, well, critical. David Richards of *The Washington Post* wrote:

> "*The plot cooked up by Thomas Meehan is preposterous. The score by Charles Strouse and Martin Charnin is dull. And this decade's Annie, Danielle Findley, while possessed of a voice that can no doubt be heard in West Virginia, seems to have acquired a bratty side now that she's living in the lap of luxury.*"

A reviewer for *Variety* wrote that *Annie 2* "*disappoints on every front*" and "*is a fancily dressed but greatly irritating show.*" Other reviews were uniformly negative. The entire concept of the show was questioned, and little hope was held out that it could be salvaged.

Nonetheless, the jettisoning of unwanted cargo continued. The day after opening we were called for a meeting at 4:30 in the afternoon. The dancers in the big production number, "Coney Island", had been summoned earlier to make some cuts and adjustments. Choreographer Danny Daniels wanted to cut two bars of music out because, he said, "*the opening-night audience was more exuberant than future audiences are likely to be.*" Our leading lady, Dorothy Loudon, with a look of limp-jawed astonishment, replied, "*Exuberant? That was exuberant? What theater were you in?*"

Danny ignored the remark. Dorothy was tired. She had been carrying the greatest burden, and it's likely that she had never done the same script two nights running. It was beginning to get to her. While we waited for Martin's arrival, musical director Peter Howard and Harve Presnell amused the company with a wonderful parody of the opening song of the show, "1934". Someone remarked, "*They oughta have more songs like that in the show.*" What remarkable creatures we were, making sport of the impending disaster.

Why was I laughing? I had hitched my rickety little wagon to a star that was in imminent danger of crashing.

Martin finally arrived, entering through the neatly concealed side doors of the Opera House to enthusiastic applause from the cast. "*If they can't take a joke,*" he said, flashing that ingratiating smile of his, and then he proceeded to tell us what the show's detractors could do if they couldn't take a joke. He went on to defend the basic premise of the play but assured us that things would be changing even more drastically in the weeks and months ahead. I was pleased to hear the word "months." Had a nice sound. Months.

He praised the resilience of the actors and thanked us for our courage and dedication. He assured us that the opening in New York would be delayed by at least a month.

Once again, fervid applause. Dorothy Loudon burst into tears of relief. The meeting ended with Danielle Findley, our spunky little Annie, singing another parody. Later, waiting in the wings for our entrance, Harve Presnell, a marvel of cool under fire, asked, "*What the hell is the next scene and what do I say?*" I gave assistance. "*Hmph,*" he grunted. "*Damn good thing I've got the right ingredients for being an actor. I'm not too smart, but I'm brave.*"

In the ensuring rehearsals Martin was noticeably tired. His coruscating baritone became a muttered monotone. He confessed that he was tired. Not of the show, or the process; just physically tired. There were just not enough hours in the day to do all the things that had to be done. At one rehearsal, Martin lost his patience with the children and shouted at them angrily. A few moments later, as I entered the theater from the side door and stood to accustom my eyes to the darkness, I realized that I was standing next to Martin, who was leaning on the seat in front of him speaking in hushed tones to famed writer and director Garson Kanin, who was frequently at rehearsals.

For propriety's sake, I moved a bit further away. Martin made a move to leave and was beckoned back by Garson, who put a sympathetic hand around Martin's neck and drew him close. "*Patience, Martin . . . be patient,*" Garson whispered. Martin smiled affectionately, scurried down the center aisle and dropped wearily into a seat behind his "God mike."

I went back to my dressing room. A gargantuan cockroach was having an afternoon stroll through the red plush carpet tufts while another defied the laws of gravity on the creamy wall. Lacking the killer instinct, but retaining the inherent cruelty of my species, I sprayed them with hair spray. It had no apparent effect as they scurried to safety all lustrous and gleaming.

A rumor was confirmed over a bowl of cheesecake yogurt in the cafeteria the next day. One actor had talked to a friend in New York, and she'd read it in *The Times*. Mike Nichols would be coming down to give Martin some assistance. Nothing wrong with that, we all agreed. We moved on to other subjects: The review in *Variety* was a hatchet job. One of the chorus girls said she had heard another rumor that we might close in Washington. Bite your tongue, I thought. How could we close in Washington? What about that $10 million advance? But then someone pointed out that *Legs Diamond* also had had a $10 million advance, and it had closed in a few weeks.

From my journal, January 11, 1990:
Threw my back out playing ping pong yesterday. The Fates are having a heyday. But a breakthrough tonight. The new script and structure are better. Hope re-emerges. Stage Manager Bill Buxton says over the intercom: "*Noble effort, commendable, folks. Wonderful show.*" Up by the bootstraps. Spirits are high. Martin gets on the intercom. Praises everyone for their heroism and professionalism. He ends with a tremulous, "*I love you all.*"

The company was called for rehearsal at 1 p.m. Bill Buxton asked us all to wait in the theater. None of the big shots were anywhere to be seen—a bad sign. At 1:20 the side door opened, and Martin strolled down the aisle, followed by Meehan, Strouse and two producers—Lewis Allen and Karen Goodwin. Martin lifted the "God mike", blew into it as a test and began speaking, softly at first, then louder.

He spoke of the painstaking "*molecule by molecule*" labor of making a Broadway musical, of the joys of success and of the pain of failure—the pain that he and his associates were feeling at their inability to bring their vision to reality in a way that would produce commercial success. "I'm going to give you all some bad news, which will be followed by some good news," he said. "*The bad news is that we will close the show after Saturday night's performance at the Kennedy Center.*"

Grim silence.

Then Martin handed the mike to Allen, who proceeded to explain to us the unprecedented attempt the producers were making, with the approval of the investors, to convert the remaining money from *Annie 2* into a revival of the original Annie, using many of the sets, costumes and personnel from *Annie 2*. The revised play would be worked on and remounted at the Goodspeed Opera House in East Haddam, CT, in the summer of 1990.

The "good news" was received with polite applause, barely enough to veil the underlying skepticism of the majority. Most of us in the audience were still reeling, and I didn't really listen to everything Allen said because I was wondering how, and why, they would close a show that had been capitalized at $7 million and had sold an estimated $10 million worth of advance tickets. Later a Broadway veteran would explain it to me. "*Those are all weekend tickets,*" he said. "*You can't run an expensive show like this with revenue for only three of the eight shows a week.*"

One of the children who had just been hired as an orphan burst into tears, and her mother's attempt to comfort her failed. Would the sun come out tomorrow? I had my own concerns about the future. I'd given up steady work to take this risk, and the whole thing was falling apart. Later in the day, I met with Martin to discuss the future. He said they were very pleased with the work that I'd done, and they wanted me to play Drake and understudy Warbucks in the revival.

We sat, side by side, on a white sofa in his office. He put his hand around my neck and drew my face next to his, the way a father comforts a child. Then he released his grip, sat back abruptly and with a dazzling smile asked, "*Well, how are you?*"

For the life of me, I couldn't speak.

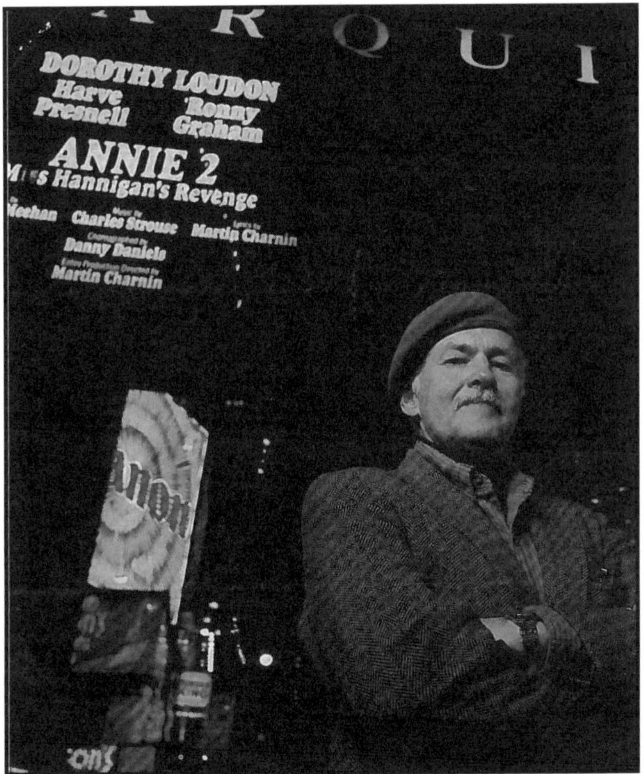

Figure 4.2.1.1 *Author, actor and theatrical producer Terrence Currier standing under the premature marquee for* Annie 2 *in New York City*

Photo source: *The Washington Post Sunday Magazine*, March 18,1990, reprinted courtesy of the author

---

Terrence Currier writes: "It wasn't what might be considered the traditional trajectory of a recent Harvard graduate; graduate school, medicine, science, finance, law etc. I wasn't sure what I wanted, but I knew what I didn't want, and then one day I saw a help-wanted ad in *The Boston Globe*: 'Actors wanted for Charles Playhouse production.' I responded, auditioned and got the job in Brendan Behan's wonderful play, *The Hostage*. It was the beginning of a career in the theater. After ten years as a resident actor at the Charles Playhouse, I joined the acting company in Washington, DC's prestigious *Arena Stage*, where I remained for 23 years and over 80 productions, capped by two years in the Broadway revival of *Damn Yankees*."

Endnote

1 Reprinted with permission from his article in *The Washington Post Sunday Magazine*, March 18, 1990

Arts

Music

Music in My Later Years

Stephen Friedlaender

Overture

During my four years in college and later at the Graduate School of Design, music, specifically western classical music, was not an essential part of my daily existence. Viewed from the perspective of my 60th Reunion, this now appears to me as both sad and surprising. When I entered Harvard in 1953, I had behind me eight years of violin lessons and two years in the Exeter student orchestra that were central to both my musical and social life. It was while leading the 2nd violins at Exeter that I developed a working familiarity with Handel's *Messiah, HMS Pinafore* and Robert Schumann's *Piano Concerto* as well as with a number of young ladies from sister institutions who performed with us in joint concerts that were the high points of an admittedly limited social calendar.

Yet I have no memory of bringing my violin with me to Harvard and, even if I did, I am absolutely certain that it stayed in its case most of the time. This may be due in part to the fact that **Ed Filmanowicz ('57)** and **Dick Bogomolny ('57),** both of whom were serious and accomplished violinists who flirted with careers in music before going on to medicine and business respectively, lived directly beneath me on the first floor of Grays Hall Middle Entry during my freshman year and quickly made me aware of my musical shortcomings, at least as a performer. As a result, I did not even audition for the *Pierian Sodality* (now the Harvard-Radcliffe Orchestra) and did not attend many of its concerts, despite knowing quite a few of the players. My visits to Symphony Hall were infrequent and sporadic and I never set foot, during those years, in New England Conservatory's Jordan Hall. While on campus, I did try to catch **Findlay Cockrell's ('57)** piano performances when possible and rarely missed the concerts in Eliot House featuring **Ed Filmanowicz**, **Charlie Forbes ('58)** and their chamber ensemble.

My three years in Lowell House were equally devoid of active participation in musical events, although it was during that time that the recently established Lowell House Opera put on truly memorable and enlightening performances of Kurt Weil and Berthold Brecht's *Threepenny Opera* and John LaTouche and Jerome Moross' *The Golden Apple*, neither of which had yet entered the standard repertoire. As for recorded music in our suite, I have vivid memories of listening over and over to *Bei Mir Bist Du Schoen,* as performed by Benny Goodman and his Sextet at the legendary Carnegie Hall concert in 1938, but not much else. Across the hall, in a suite occupied by **Tony Lamport ('57), Alan Goodridge ('57), Ned Marcus ('57)** and **David Wiesen ('57)**, the musical offerings consisted mainly of the four operas that make up Wagner's *Der Ring Des Niebelungen,* all sixteen hours of them, repeated so frequently that, if one were so inclined, one might even have begun to make sense of the libretto by graduation time. In my case, it took me exactly 40 years after graduation to summon the courage and stamina needed to attend a live performance of the entire *Ring cycle* at the Metropolitan Opera, after which I became a *Wagner groupie*, having now experienced two complete performances in San Francisco, one in Copenhagen and another at the home of it all, Bayreuth.

Architecture school was even more barren from a musical standpoint. In fact, I do not believe there was a single fellow student who showed any interest in classical music and no one played an instrument. But, several years after I received my M.Arch., things began to change. Upon returning to Cambridge in the summer of 1965 from a 20-month stint in a Finnish architectural firm, I was invited by **Daphne Abeel (R'57)** to bring my violin to her home on a number of occasions in order to read through a large part of the piano trio repertoire with Daphne as pianist and a young undergraduate whose name I do not recall on cello. Truth to tell, I was the weakest of the three and am happy, in retrospect, that we did not attempt to record ourselves. Nonetheless, I was introduced both to many of the gems of the chamber music literature as well as to the intense pleasure of playing great music (no matter how badly) in a small chamber ensemble. To be sure, these evenings at Daphne's aroused my interest in performing and listening to classical music, although it took more than 25 years for this to become a true passion, given the pressures of raising a family and building an architectural practice in the intervening years.

Act One—The Boston Chamber Music Society

My true musical re-awakening, as it were, occurred in late 1982 shortly after our 25th Reunion (which I missed, due to illness). My wife, **Ann Lindsay Fetter (R'60)**, had recently been appointed Dean of the School of Humanities, Arts and Social Sciences (SHASS) at MIT and was in the process of preparing a tenure case for a young violist in the Music Department named Marcus Thompson when he informed her that he and a group of like-minded musical friends were about to organize themselves as The Boston Chamber Music Society and begin a six-concert subscription season at Sanders Theater. She and I dutifully (and enthusiastically) agreed to purchase two tickets to the first season of concerts, the first time in our marriage that we had taken out a season subscription to any Boston musical group. Thirty-four years later, I am not only still a BCMS subscriber but also, as you will learn later, the president of its board.

I must admit that, for the first ten years of its existence—indeed, until Nan's untimely death in 1992—we were simply very satisfied members of the BCMS audience with no active involvement in its governance or financial affairs. Eight more years of passive enjoyment followed before it became apparent to those who concern themselves with this sort of thing that I, as an 18-year subscriber, should be approached to see if I would be interested in becoming a member of the BCMS Board of Directors. My initial response was to refuse the invitation on the grounds of having very limited evenings to attend board meetings because my architectural practice required me to be available for municipal building committee meetings that met only after normal working hours when their volunteer members were able to carry out their civic duties. But, in 2000, I was persuaded to join the Board of Overseers because that group met only three evenings per year. I have since learned that being invited to join the Board of Overseers is simply the first step toward membership in an organization's Board of Directors for those who show any competence whatever. So it was with me: two years after joining the Overseers, I was asked to become a director. This led, eventually, to my becoming Board President during the 25th Anniversary Season of the Boston Chamber Music Society, a year that began blissfully enough but ended with the forced resignation of the founding artistic director. It has thus been my lot to guide this organization through ten years of intermittent turmoil and peace, beginning with the selection of a new artistic director, followed several years later by the resignation of four of the original musicians. At present, I hope it is on course for a triumphant 35th Anniversary Season in 2017–18. More on that later.

Act Two—New England Conservatory

To step back a few years for a moment, it might be relevant to mention here, particularly for those who knew me at Harvard College as a Southerner, that my parents left North Carolina in 1958 for New York City and then, in 1965, took up residency in Cambridge, where they lived for the rest of their lives. One of the more amusing aspects of having my mother and father as neighbors is that, on more than one occasion, I have been taken for a native New Englander rather than a transplanted North Carolinian. But my parents' move to Cambridge had a much more significant impact upon my later life, specifically upon my musical activities, due to my mother's involvement with the New England Conservatory, on whose board she served from 1971–1991. On the occasion of her 85th birthday, she turned to me and said: "I am getting too old to drive over to those NEC Board meetings—and they don't give me a free parking spot anyway. Why don't you take my place on the Board and join your Harvard classmate **David Scudder ('57)** and his friends **Joe Bower ('58)** and **Harry Pratt ('58)**? They run the place!"

Well, it wasn't quite that easy, but I was duly elected to the NEC Board of Overseers, on which I served three three-year terms. During my last term as an overseer, I had the pleasure of working with our classmate **Bob Freeman ('57)** during his short tenure as president of the institution, as well as the pain of being present when the board terminated his contract. I was pleased, therefore, when Bob landed squarely on his feet at the University of Texas–Austin and even more pleased when David Scudder announced to the Board of Trustees (at my very first meeting as a member of that board) that **Daniel Steiner ('55)** had agreed to become our next president. This inaugurated the ascendency of New England Conservatory from a respected local music school into the world-class institution it has now become. And it has been my great good fortune to be actively involved with NEC during and after the exciting years that followed Daniel's appointment as president.

My personal ascension from overseer to trustee was due, in large part, to the truism that architect members of boards are invariably asked, at some point during their tenure, to take over the House Committee, or in the case of NEC, to chair the Facilities Committee. I think there is no question that I was asked to join the NEC Board of Trustees because my architectural background was seen as crucial to the Conservatory's ability to address the continuing deterioration of its physical plant. Jordan Hall, the "gem in the Conservatory's crown", was built in 1903. The NEC residence hall, located directly across Gainsborough Street from the entrance to Jordan Hall, was constructed in 1957, the year of our graduation from Harvard College, and will, after 60 years of service, be taken off-line as a residence hall in September of this year when the new Student Life and Performance Center (SLPC) is to be dedicated. In all humility, I regard the new SLPC as my legacy to NEC (as do, I am pleased to report, my fellow trustees) and confess to a tremendous sense of accomplishment and satisfaction as it approaches completion.

I am not the architect of record for this new building, but I chaired the committee that selected Ann Beha's firm to design it and worked closely with her team as the plans took shape and then with the construction manager and his team as the dream became a reality. Equally important, if not more so, is the fact that my vision for this building dates back to 1997 when, still an overseer, I made a presentation to the NEC Trustees on the various possibilities of combining the sound archives and the printed scores and books that make up the NEC Library into a single facility. Even at that time, it was apparent that the only way to accomplish this was to erect a new building on what was then a 55-car parking lot. But it took several false steps and the efforts of three different presidents over the course of the ensuing 17 years before the money was raised and the commitment made to enable the actual construction to begin.

My experience "on the other side of the table" during all phases of this project has convinced me that all architects would be well-advised, at some point during their professional careers, to serve on a building committee that is working with another design professional, and I have passed this suggestion on to those who have taken over at the firm of which I was one of the four founders and the first president. Perhaps my most important contribution to the SLPC project during the design and construction phases has been my ability to facilitate communication between all parties and keep the process moving forward. Happily, as we approach the building's completion in May, it is on budget, on schedule, and quite likely to transform the student experience at New England Conservatory. Most importantly, I have high hopes that it will finally lift the institution's physical plant to the same level of excellence it currently enjoys as one of the world's great musical conservatories.

During the past 25 years, as I have moved from overseer to trustee to board chair, I have gained a new appreciation of music's important role in facilitating communication between different cultures and an even greater respect for those who devote their lives to the teaching and making of music. Daniel Steiner, who spent the better part of his career as general counsel to Harvard University and who knew the University well, often remarked during his tenure as president of New England Conservatory that NEC students are required to work much more diligently and with more discipline than their counterparts across the river. It is impossible to fake a good musical performance and there is no such thing as a "gentleman's C" at New England Conservatory.

I carry with me a lasting memory of an August evening several years ago as I reclined on the grassy slope behind Seiji Ozawa Hall in Tanglewood. Looking up at the moon and stars while listening to a live performance of a Brahms piano quintet, I was struck by the appreciation of being fortunate enough to hear sounds that no creature on earth had ever heard prior to their composition in the mid-1880s, and I silently promised myself that I would do all I can to make certain that those sounds will always be available to succeeding generations. This is why, as I approach my 60th reunion at Harvard, I find myself increasingly committed to activities that contribute to the support of those individuals and institutions most likely to ensure the long-term survival of western classical music, which brings me back to my current efforts on behalf of the Boston Chamber Music Society.

Act Three—Creating the Audience of the Future

As it happens, 2017 is, in addition to being the year in which we celebrate our 60th Harvard Reunion, as well as the year in which the New England Conservatory celebrates its 150th birthday, the 35th Anniversary Season of the Boston Chamber Music Society. I, as president of the BCMS board, find myself involved in a surprisingly heated debate regarding the most effective way to celebrate the occasion. I agree, of course, that the long-term goal of the 35th Anniversary Celebration should be a significant increase in the size of the Society's endowment, given that its current assets do not come close to generating the annual income needed to reduce its dependence upon individuals and foundations for contributed revenue. If BCMS had to rely upon ticket sales and program book advertisements as the sole means of defraying its annual operating expenses, the cost of tickets would have to be so high that no one would buy them (putting one in mind ofYogi Berra's famous remark that "no one goes there anymore because it's too crowded). No classical music ensemble has ever been able to survive on earned revenue alone: patrons, in the form of royalty, the church, the state, and/or the city have always been crucial to its survival. In today's world and in especially in this country, performing arts organizations like BCMS can rely upon direct ticket sales to cover no more than 40% of operating costs, with the balance coming from private individual and foundation support. The only sure means of survival is to build an endowment of sufficient size to reduce the organization's reliance upon annual fund-raising efforts and direct ticket sales. But I am doubtful of any musical organization's ability to raise significant endowment funds unless it can forcefully and effectively assure those potential donors who, before they commit significant funds, will want to make certain of its long-term survival, delivering exemplary performances to future audiences that appreciate and value the concert-going experience.

This will not be an easy task, because it can no longer be assumed that such an audience will simply continue to exist as a matter of course. We read almost daily reports of the fragile health of most of our major orchestras and performing ensembles, and the Boston Chamber Music Society is not immune to the larger forces that have brought this about. The audience for classical music is ageing and shrinking and, in my opinion, will continue to do so until those organizations that have thought of themselves primarily as "presenters" realize that they now have a basic need to educate and renew the audience to whom they will present in the future.

This was not always so. The data seem to support the view that an overwhelming majority of current concert-goers were regularly taken to concerts at an early age, as I certainly was. There are many reasons why this is much less likely to happen today than it was sixty years ago, and our schools are not equipped and/or funded to step in and take an active role in arts education. Unfortunately, it appears to be a truism that, if one has not formed an attachment to classical music and a desire to attend classical music performances by the time one graduates from high school, one is not likely to join the classical music audience, at least not until much later in life. Given this, presenting organizations such as BCMS must do more than simply open their doors to the concert-going public. They will have to devote a good part of their time and resources to the long-term preservation and growth of that concert-going public—and these efforts should begin when the potential members of the audience of the future are still young.

For many years, major orchestras have been in the habit of offering "youth concerts" and, while BCMS has never formally done so, it has frequently gone into schools and performed for this "target" age group. But, just as current educational trends emphasize hands-on learning and group projects instead of the traditional omniscient teacher delivering lectures from the front of the classroom, the optimum method for instilling an appreciation of classical music in young people is not to ask them to sit and listen to someone else perform it but to engage them in making music themselves. Failure to do so will leave the majority of students in the audience watching others perform. As Thomas H. Walters, the president of the Massachusetts Music Educators Association, recently wrote in the January 7, 2017 issue of *The Boston Globe:*

> *"The arts are essentially process learning and skill building that benefit all students. That's a fundamental misunderstanding by some school leaders at all levels, who only see our results and assume, wrongly, that performances, art pieces, and films magically come together at concert or exhibition time. Those performances and exhibitions are the reflections of learning—understanding of essential concepts, building of physical and intellectual skills—and hard work that have preceded them."*

This is why I have developed and promoted a proposal for the Boston Chamber Music Society to engage with a local public high school orchestra in an effort that is designed to increase BCMS's visibility within its core community and to stress the importance of creating a broader and younger audience for classical music in general and chamber music in particular.

What makes this particularly appealing to me is the fact that this orchestra comprises 46 students in grades 9–12 who have enthusiastically chosen to participate in the program for a variety of reasons, not the least of which is that it offers them a non-verbal way to bond and communicate with their classmates. Nearly two-thirds of the orchestra members come from homes in which English is the second language and a number of them are in their first year at an American high school. Few of them have had any formal musical training and none of them own their own instruments: the violins, violas, cellos and double basses upon which they play are furnished to them by the school's Music Department. Most importantly, there are no auditions for places in this ensemble: participation in the orchestra program is open to anyone and everyone who is eager and willing to spend four hours per week making music together. This is truly a case of music creating its own community.

The orchestra is conducted by a graduate of the New England Conservatory assisted by two professional free-lance violinists who, during rehearsals, move from desk to desk helping the young musicians with their fingering, their bowing and their intonation. This is really as close as most of the students come to receiving individual instruction, but it is not nearly enough. As a result, there is general agreement that the most critical need is for a small group of "musical coaches" to attend the orchestra rehearsals on a frequent basis so as to facilitate sectional rehearsals.

Clearly, the professional member musicians of the Boston Chamber Music Society could not be expected to commit to attending these weekly orchestra rehearsals. Furthermore, few of the young musicians in this high school orchestra are sufficiently advanced to appreciate what seasoned professionals might offer in terms of musicianship or the fine points of playing a violin or a viola. But a good case can be made, I think, for BCMS to solicit for and engage recent conservatory graduates who are just beginning their professional careers to participate as coaches in this program. In addition, BCMS would be responsible for raising the funds necessary to pay them to do so.

Most musical ensembles approach community outreach simply as an opportunity/obligation to perform in schools and hospitals and other civic venues without compensation. This proposal focuses on coaching rather than performing, with the result that the BCMS member musicians and its artistic director would not be the primary participants; but that does not, in my view, make this any less of a Boston Chamber Music Society effort. Many of my fellow board members, who are unwilling to support an outreach effort that does not directly involve BCMS musicians, find this hard to countenance; but I believe this is precisely the type of challenge that BCMS and other similar presenting organizations must be prepared to accept if they are serious about taking on the task of creating the future audience for classical music.

Coda

This essay would not be complete without a brief mention of my membership in and involvement with The Harvard Musical Association. This venerable Boston institution, of whose existence I was unaware until shortly before I was elected to membership in 1997, began its life as the *de facto* Harvard music department in 1837 and continued in that capacity until the University established its own Music Department in1863. At that point, the members of the Association received permission to keep the Harvard name while evolving into a private club dedicated to the performance and appreciation of classical music. As such, the HMA was perhaps the most important musical institution on the Boston musical scene during the last third of the nineteenth century. It had the distinction of presenting the first public performance of classical chamber music in the United States, and its own HMA orchestra was the immediate precursor of the Boston Symphony Orchestra. Today, although its importance in Boston musical life is considerably diminished, the HMA continues to offer its 300 members an opportunity to enjoy performances by outstanding chamber music ensembles from around the world.

My activities as a member of the Harvard Musical Association established the "career path" that I was later to follow at the Boston Chamber Music Society and the New England Conservatory. Immediately upon becoming a member in 1997, I was impressed into service as the chair of the House Committee, a position I still hold some twenty years later. I also served as president of the Association during 2003–2006 and have worked diligently in the ensuing years to forge a meaningful bond linking the HMA to the New England Conservatory.

But my real reason for including the Harvard Musical Association in this essay is to acknowledge its role in re-introducing me to our classmate **Jim Joslin ('57)**, whom I knew only from afar as an undergraduate and subsequently simply as our class secretary, but who has become a valued friend and advisor during the past 20 years. Jim served as treasurer of the HMA during the years when I was responsible for most House Committee improvements to the Association's historic house on Beacon Hill and, in this capacity, he provided both wise counsel and the funds required to undertake these projects. He also recruited me to provide appropriate musical fare for our 50th and 55th Harvard Reunions and has made certain that I am still at it as our 60th Reunion approaches in May of this year.

It is in this spirit and with deep gratitude that I dedicate this 60th Reunion Essay to my friend and classmate, James Lippitt Joslin. Without his encouragement, it would never have seen the light of day.

Figure 4.3.1.1 *Steve Friedlaender in front of the New England Conservatory's new Student Life and Performance Center, February 2017. Steve considers this project to be his legacy to the institution that he has served as overseer, trustee and board chair over the past 25 years.*

Stephen Friedlaender is Principal Emeritus of HMFH Architects, Inc. in Cambridge, a firm he co-founded in 1969 and served as president for 30 years. He was elevated to Fellowship in the American Institute of Architects in 1996. His firm has won both local and national distinction for its educational projects, which include public and private schools as well as college and university projects. Stephen joined the Board of Overseers of New England Conservatory of Music in 1991, became a trustee in 2000 and was elected board chair for a four-year term in 2008. He has also served as a board member and chair of the Boston Chamber Music Society and the Harvard Musical Association. He lives with his partner, Nancy Ellen O'Connell, in Cambridge and is the father of two sons and seven grandchildren.

Travels with the Chicago Symphony Orchestra[1]

C. Anderson "Andy" Hedberg

For 27 years, I was a physician for the Chicago Symphony Orchestra's world tours, led by Maestros George Solti and, later, Daniel Barenboim. My wife travelled with me.

Why take a doctor on such a tour? The tour moves rapidly, and finding a readily available physician in a foreign city is difficult. Our basic role is to "*keep the show on the road*". The show is big, with about 250 participants, including performers, accompanying spouses and friends, administrative staff, stage hands and patrons, and 17 tons of instruments and equipment, all transported to the great music halls of the world to meet the maestro's downbeat at a precise moment.

Since I started this adventure, the CSO has been to Europe, Japan, Australia, the US and South America. I travelled with truly remarkable people who are devoted to their art, and have diverse personalities and interests. They are highly motivated professionals at the very top of their field.

They practice constantly during the tour, at the hotels and backstage. They play hurt. A cellist performed with bronchitis and a 103-degree fever because two other members of the section were sicker and couldn't leave the Madrid hotel. And a violinist painfully dragged a recovering fractured leg through Russia because "*my parents walked out of Russia in 1932, and I have to go back*".

I attend all rehearsals and concerts, and whatever other events are planned for the group, and I am available for urgent problems anytime. I offer daily office hours in my room at the hotel, and I take the first bus to the hall about two hours before the concert, where I am provided with a rehearsal room backstage as an office to see the musicians.

I carry a black doctors' bag with the usual equipment, and an aliquot of commonly needed medications. At the hall, transported with the orchestral equipment, is a steamer trunk filled with about 50 medications, bandages, a portable EKG machine, and everything needed to practice in an internist's medical office.

Each day, there are often minor situations, such as blood pressure checks or abrasions to be attended to at various sites wherever we may be. I prepare for more serious problems before the tour by arranging physician contacts who are connected with the best hospitals in each city that we visit. The promise of two tickets for the usually sold out concerts works wonders! I may need x-rays and specialty consultation—for example, to set a minor fracture, obtain a blood analysis or a culture, and rarely to arrange for a hospitalization

The medical problems that arise are usually routine and common for travelers, such as upper respiratory infections, gastrointestinal disturbances, and minor rashes.

Besides playing their instruments, musicians love to eat! They can demolish a buffet with amazing rapidity! I am an expert on examining buffets. Musicians are often entertained on the road, and I cringe every time I see a lavish gustatory display.

We had only one mini-epidemic on the road—following a typical European whipped cream and mayonnaise extravaganza in Budapest. It was a challenge to pull the group together for the next night's work in Vienna. I warned the orchestra about tropical water precautions for a South American trip, but when we arrived at our first stop in Rio, the hotel provided cooling drinks with ice cubes, which were promptly consumed. Fortunately, nothing untoward happened.

Improvisation may be necessary. On my first trip, encountering a musician with a late-night lower-bowel dysfunction, I realized that we did not carry enemas. To describe what I needed, I had to do a pantomime for a concierge in the Brussels hotel lobby. Moments later, an elegant attendant in full formal dress arrived at the room door with a huge, covered silver tray. He ceremoniously removed the cover, and I have not before or since seen such a beautiful display of a Fleets enema! I had an immediately grateful patient, and now I never leave home on these trips without one.

Emergencies are rare. Some hospitalizations have been necessary over the years, and can be an adventure in a foreign country, but have worked out satisfactorily. I have had to leave hospitalized patients behind to recover from an appendectomy, a heart condition, and a kidney stone. Always, the Orchestra leaves a staff person to be with the stricken individual, and I stay in touch by phone.

I am constantly amazed at the resilience and stamina of the maestros and musicians. At the start of the first Japan concert, which was nationally televised, I looked at my watch, which was still set on Chicago time, and it said 5 a.m. What we call jet lag must have been present, yet the performers gave a superb account of the Mahler 1st Symphony. This was an example of agile and focused minds overcoming fatigue to accomplish a common goal.

There are of course many unpredictable events that can occur on the road, and the trip to the US in November 1990 encountered many. This was a politically and economically chaotic time there. The Mikhail Gorbachev era of glasnost was collapsing, and catastrophic civil unrest was feared. To ensure that the CSO would have maximum control, the musicians, support party, accompanying family members and patrons, and all the instruments and cargo were transported to the US together on a Swissair 747 plane. Avoiding hospitalization was a must, because of the unsatisfactory condition of medical facilities, so we had a contract with an airborne medical evacuation team located in Geneva.

One of the most fascinating aspects of the tours is observing performance halls. Backstage accommodations for musicians vary greatly. It seems that in the older halls the needs and comfort of the musicians were not considered when the halls were built. In Moscow, the CSO musicians dressed behind curtains in the back of the main lobby. At the *Theatre Colon* in Buenos Aries, trunks and performers were cramped into narrow aisles of an area that looked like it had not been dusted since the hall was built at the turn of the last century. At the *Royal Albert Hall* in London, performers are crowded into a few small rooms in the basement. By contrast, the new halls in Japan, Lucerne and Manchester have extensive backstage areas with large modern dressing rooms and abundant rehearsal space. Arriving to set up at the halls, the stage crew often has to struggle to find adequate backstage space, labeling the corridors and stairs with signs telling everyone where they should be, including the doctor.

There is amazing variation in the appearance of the performance spaces of the halls, and each has its own distinctive architecture such as the small jewel-like ornate wooden baroque hall in Hamburg which seats 1,500 people, or the cavernous red-draped Victorian *Royal Albert Hall* in London seating 5,400, or Barcelona's wood interior with carved faces and flowers protruding from the walls.

Acoustics are much discussed on tour. Musicians are concerned about how well they can hear each other on the stage, how bright or dull the reflected sound seems. Sometimes musicians are surprised by a hall that has unexpected, excellent acoustics, such as a mammoth stone train-station lobby converted into a concert hall in São Paulo, Brazil.

Drama. While serving on the support group for these orchestral tours, there is the opportunity to witness many dramatic occasions that reflect the impact of music on culture and people. In Berlin at the beginning of my first tour in 1978, I was struck by the significance of an American orchestra presenting German music, led by a Jewish conductor (Solti) who had been driven from his Hungarian homeland by the Nazis. Present also were at least two members of the CSO who were survivors of concentration camps.

When Solti conducted a movement of the Shostakovich 8th Symphony in Leningrad, a work whose thematic material portrays the German siege of that city, it was a poignant moment for the Russians who had lived through that time.

After performing in the US, the tour moved to Budapest, and for the first time since leaving his homeland, the Maestro returned to his native city with his own orchestra. Although he had guest conducted there before, this was regarded as his real homecoming, and declared a national day of recognition. Television interviews were held, at which Solti emphasized the failures of tyranny and the importance of freedom, and the concert of Bartok music was nationally televised.

Another homecoming that I witnessed was the return of Daniel Barenboim to Argentina in 2001. He was born in Buenos Aires, and as a child prodigy performed his first public piano recital at the age of eight. When he was ten, his family emigrated to Israel, and he spent several years studying piano and conducting in Germany, Austria, and France. Having achieved worldwide eminence as a soloist and conductor, he brought his prized instrument, the Chicago Symphony Orchestra, to his hometown to celebrate his 50th year of performing. It was a glorious occasion at the elegant 19th Century opera house, the *Theatre Colon.*

Barenboim travels widely and speaks at least six languages. He rarely conducts from a score, only when pieces are newly composed or the works are unusual. During many performances, there was not one printed note of music in front of him. I asked him how he was able to remember all this material. "*Doctor,*" he replied, "I have known these pieces since I was 16 years old." This, of course, was not an explanation, this was genius. I said that this was like memorizing *War and Peace*, including paragraphs and punctuation. "*No,*" he replied, "*music is much more logical.*" Barenboim, as did Maestro Solti, sees music as intimately connected to the human condition.

On 9/11, the CSO was in Lucerne, Switzerland. It was close to 3 p.m. in Europe when the tragic events occurred in New York. The musicians met to discuss whether the tour, which had one more week of concerts in Lucerne and Vienna, should continue. It was decided to carry on, and that night before the concert, Maestro Barenboim addressed the audience at the Lucerne Festival Hall in German and English with the following remarks:

> "*The events of today are so shocking that no words can express what every one of us feels. We have all had many discussions—long discussions—and I want to express my gratitude to my colleagues for deciding to play this evening.*
>
> *Somehow without saying so directly, I think we feel that music is what we can express ourselves best with; maybe, when words are inadequate, music can express the feelings that we all have.*
>
> *I must again express my special gratitude to my colleagues because I can only imagine what a group of American musicians—far away from home—are feeling right now.*
>
> *Several of my colleagues have asked that we begin the concert tonight with the American national anthem, and that is what we will do, for tonight we are all of us Americans.*"

In these moving words, the Maestro is describing music as a unique language, which serves to describe emotions that cannot be expressed adequately in words. He presents music as a healing and sustaining force, and I believe that this inspires his artistic life.

* * *

My experiences with the orchestra have brought to me the realization that music and medicine have much in common. They are hard-earned endeavors that require dedication, lifelong study, and continuous practice. Both are an art, which probes deeply into the human condition.

My life has been enriched by the opportunity to serve great musicians, to listen to great music played by a superb orchestra in many different venues before a variety of peoples, and to see the positive effects on the human spirit. It has been a marvelous journey.

Besides, I always thought I had a little show business in me, and what can top being on the road with a show like this?

Carl Anderson "Andy" Hedberg, MD, MACP, graduated from Cornell Medical School and completed internship and residency in Internal Medicine at New York Hospital. In 1964, he began a two-year Fellowship in Gastroenterology at the University of Chicago. In 1966, he entered the Navy at Charleston Naval Base where he served for two years. In 1968, he returned to Chicago to practice medicine with his father for 17 years, after which he moved to Rush University Medical School and Hospital where he practiced for over 25 years. Andy was President of the Chicago Institute of Medicine, Chicago Society of Internal Medicine, Chicago Society of Gastroenterology, the staff of Rush, and the American College of Physicians (ACP). Serving as a consultant for World Book Encyclopedia, and Board member of the Harvard Club of Chicago, for 27 years he was a tour physician for the Chicago Symphony Orchestra. Married since 1960 to Junia Gratiot Hedberg, they have two adult children and two grandchildren.

Endnote

1 Adapted from *Notes from a Road Show*, delivered to the Chicago Literary Club, February 3, 2003

Saving America's Symphony Orchestras

Robert Freeman

While it is true that, immediately after World War II, America's symphony orchestras were the best in the world, in the meantime they have become an endangered species, especially since the nation's budget collapse in 2008.

Although it used to be said that an American city could not aspire to life as a real city without a fine orchestra of its own, there are now several major cities, including Sacramento, Albuquerque, and San Jose, that exist without one.

The development of the National Endowment for the Arts (NEA) in 1964 and the Ford Foundation's $85 million generosity of 1966 resulted in larger orchestras, higher salaries, and 52-week seasons, thus producing more orchestral services than many of the orchestras are able to sell while fulfilling a prediction put forward in 1966 by William Baumol and William Bowen, in their book, *The Performing Arts; the Economic Dilemma.* There two distinguished Princeton economists sensibly warn that, in an inflationary economy, one cannot sustain economies of scale by playing a Mahler symphony with half the number of performers or by doubling the speed of the tempo.

Stanford economist Robert Flanagan's recent book, *The Perilous Life of Orchestras; Artistic Triumphs and Economic Challenges*, published in 2012, presents a clear summary of what has happened since 1966. Though symphony ticket prices have escalated rapidly, especially in recent years, the size of the auditoria in which the music is performed has remained the same, while orchestral budgets rely more and more on annual fundraising and dangerously increasing draws on endowment.

The symphony audience is smaller and aging, the result of increased competition for diminished leisure time at a point in our history when many of the women who used to want an evening out with their husbands are now in the workplace themselves, yearning for a quiet evening at home, where the whole of the symphonic literature is available on the Internet.

The Post Great Recession Budgetary Crisis

The seasons 2010–13 brought a sense of budgetary crisis for many American orchestras, with extended lock-outs for the orchestras of Atlanta, Indianapolis, and Minnesota, and extended strikes for the orchestras of Detroit, Pittsburgh, St. Paul, and Fort Worth, while the Philadelphia Orchestra filed for Chapter 11 bankruptcy, and the New York City Center Opera, founded in 1943, went out of business altogether. The Detroit strike, ending in April 2011, finished with the Orchestra $53 million in debt, an endowment a little more than a third of the $60 million it had been, and with salary cuts of 25% for the players. In Atlanta the number of musicians was reduced from 95 to 88, with a 17% salary cut for the musicians in the first year of a two-year contract, and an additional 14% cut in the second. One can imagine the bitterness that resulted in Atlanta when the CEO's salary, three times that of one of the players, was visited with but a 6% salary cut.

After a 15-month lockout the Minnesota Orchestra was obliged to cut its number of players from 95 to 84 while each of the musicians' salaries was reduced by 15%, as were the salaries of the players of the Pittsburgh Symphony Orchestra.

Salary cuts for the members of the Fort Worth Symphony were reduced by 15%, while in Indianapolis the combined cuts amounted to 32%.

One can easily imagine the pain of players saddled with home mortgages, credit card balances, and college indebtedness, trapped in too many cases by very narrow educations that make it next to impossible for them to find employment in other parts of the economy.

Needed Organizational Reforms in American Symphonic Orchestras

In what follows I have tried to list a number of changes in American orchestras that would mitigate at least some of the pressure.

(1) **Write contracts for music directors that oblige them to live in the city of their Orchestra**, requiring that the conductors spend 75% (85%?) of their working seasons in the city of the orchestra, while owning a home there. Such conductors would play a role not unlike that of university presidents in fundraising and in representing the Orchestra to the community.

(2) **Encourage professional music schools to see to it that each graduate take a one-semester course in elementary business practices**, including accounting, fundraising, public relations, and marketing, thereby reducing the number of full-time staff members required by an orchestra. (There are 100 players in the Boston Symphony these days in addition to 200 staff members.) In addition, the curriculum should be revamped with a focus on helping students become articulate, informed advocates for the music they are studying.

(3) **Prospective orchestra members should not only be auditioned but interviewed** as well. Wonderful performers who insist on sleeping with their colleagues or adding several members of their immediate family to the ensemble do as much harm as good. Young people with excellent interpersonal skills who are excellent players are worth their weight in gold.

(4) **In an orchestra of 100 players, fully 15% play in only 25% of the repertory.** Though it is often claimed that orchestral players do lots of practicing when they are not on stage, in fact almost all of the practicing goes on before a player is auditioned. Hiring young musicians who are also interested in solo or chamber music performance, or in spending part of their time fulfilling work now done by staff members, reduces administrative bloat.

(5) **All of the players need to be advocates of the orchestra**. Imagine an ensemble in which each of 100 players was tasked with selling even two annual subscriptions or with making half a dozen

unpaid appearances on behalf of the orchestra in area schools and colleges. Music faculties whose salary increases are tied in part to their entrepreneurial activities in a college's behalf bring new life blood to an institution. The fact that orchestral players have so minimal a role in deciding who will them lead them, where and what they will perform, and how, does a great deal to deaden the joy they might otherwise take in their work.

(6) **Working with the students of a business school in the home city of an orchestra on researching who the audience is and why it is motivated to attend** is the sort of market research which any organization selling cars, airplane seats, or toothpaste will routinely undertake in order to succeed in a competitive marketplace.

Orchestras have marketed themselves only by implying that *a symphonic experience is morally and socially good for the audience,* introducing them at intermission to other leading members of the community.

Imagine how many ticket buyers we could lure to a baseball game if the only attraction there were the greenness of the grass and the taste of the hotdogs. Realizing this, organized baseball sees to it that their television and radio broadcasts not only report what is taking place at a ballgame, but between every pair of pitches educates its audience on what just happened and what may happen next. (Keith Hernandez's wonderful book, *Pure Baseball,* represents in my view the *ne plus ultra* of this approach.)

A good friend of mine, who recently concluded a very successful term as president of a major university, responded when I asked **what he thought he derived from a symphonic concert**,

"*My wife was a music minor in college, and she appreciates my going to occasional concerts with her.*

The music dean, the music faculty, and the music students are always glad to see me, and thus concert attendance helps me feel as though I am doing a good job as university CEO.

And now that we are in the third movement of a Brahms symphony, I know that there are four of them, that each of the four is in four movements, that the first two are longer than the last two, and that since we are now in the middle of the third movement, the whole thing will be over in less than ten minutes, during which I can reflect on a physics lecture I will give tomorrow, without anyone knowing that I am doing so."

When I asked how many university presidents might respond similarly to my question, he responded, "*Oh, about 99% of us.*"

Those who supported music before the French Revolution were almost always members of the aristocracy and the Church, and trained themselves as amateur musicians. When their numbers and power began to wane in the 19th century, Beethoven wrote that his *Pastorale* Symphony did not depict life in the country but made one *feel* as though he were in the country. When Berlioz printed 2,000 copies of his original program for his *Symphony Fantastique*, he did so in order to provide his audience with a point of departure for a work of art quite unlike anything any of them had ever heard before. Franz Liszt and Richard Strauss went further still with program music, no matter that Mendelssohn had once written to a lady admirer that there were no words for his *Songs without Words*, because music is a self-referential language.

The Future of Music Appreciation and Building Audiences

Since retiring from a chaired professorship at the University Texas at Austin a year and half ago, I have been collaborating with Robert Winter, Distinguished Professor of Music at UCLA, on *Music in the Air (MITA)*, a brilliant computer-mediated means of his invention for integrating the teaching of music history, theory, and performance. Because MITA's annotated interactive scores makes it possible to follow and understand a complex score as the music streams, even a moderately informed listener is soon "reading" scores as though he were Leonard Bernstein.

Listening to a piece of music, like watching a baseball game, is not bimodal but spectral. Just as my late mother was bored by baseball because she had no idea what the players were trying to accomplish, I imagine that the restaurant waiters unable to sing "Happy Birthday" to their customers can't really be expected to get much out of a Beethoven symphony. Similarly, just as Terry Francona, manager of the Cleveland Indians, follows and manages a baseball game with an acuity that I will never be able to bring to the task, the late Pierre Boulez could read a musical score with aural skills that I shall never be able to master.

But the joy of understanding aurally where a piece of music is going, and how it succeeds in getting there, is, along with love of family, the greatest pleasure of my life, the sort of joy one experiences in comparing the beginning of the Brahms *Third Symphony* with its conclusion, or the beginning of the Brahms *Violin Concerto* with the music that appears immediately after the cadenza of the first movement. Robert Winter and his team will go public with MITA in China and worldwide sometime later in 2017, making it possible for the first time in musical history to develop a musical audience that follows the unfolding of a piece of music with skills similar to those of participating in the development of a great novel or of a Shakespeare tragedy.

Summing Up

The primary economic danger to the survival of the great orchestras America built in the first half of the 20th century is the rebalancing of expenses and revenues that are bound to occur in inflationary times. This means, clearly, limiting unnecessary expense while finding new sources of revenue.

Most important, the musicians must themselves learn that the answer is not to blame the board and the management but, like the members of the Berlin Philharmonic, they must escape the inhibiting force of the musicians' union and take control of the orchestra themselves.

They must come to understand collectively that if they personally cannot on a regular basis make a compelling case for what they do to potential attendees, then they have little reason to assume that an audience will materialize out of the ether. Activities such as children's concerts and pop concerts are no longer adequate to stimulate the needed community engagement.

> *What is it about this extraordinary repertory that offers spiritual solace in these troubled times?*

What used to be a self-evident answer today requires the music director and the players to become a marketing juggernaut on their own, willing to make their case in the face of fierce competition for the time of the citizenry. Failing that, the steady decline now being felt could turn into an avalanche.

* * *

This essay is dedicated to Paul R. Judy, orchestral champion. He is an alumnus of Harvard and of the Harvard Business School, former CEO of A.G.Becker and Co., founder of the Orchestral Musician Forum at the Eastman School of Music, former board member of the Chicago Symphony Orchestra and founder of the new Chicago Philharmonic.

Robert Freeman, the son of a Boston Symphony double bassist and grandson of a cornet player in Sousa's Band, graduated from Harvard *summa cum laude*, with a concurrent diploma in piano playing from the Longy School. After a year in Europe on a Harvard Sheldon Traveling Fellowship, he took MFA and PhD degrees in musicology at Princeton, where he joined the junior faculty from 1963–68 and conducted the University Orchestra. In 1969 he joined MIT and made tenure in 1972, shortly before his appointment as director of the Eastman School, which he led to first place in the national rankings of music schools, 1972–96. After a two-year stint as president of the New England Conservatory, he moved to the University of Texas at Austin, where he served as dean of the College of Fine Arts for seven years and as Susan Menefee Ragan Professor of Fine Arts for nine, retiring in 2015 at age 80. He holds honorary degrees from Eastman and from Hamilton College, as well as Rochester's Civic Medal for his work on its downtown revitalization. Eastman School created a website in his honor [http//www.eastman.freeman.edu].

Visual Arts

A Life in the Arts

Samuel Sachs II

Clearly there is something momentous about our 60th anniversary, but a recent event made perhaps a slightly deeper impression: I applied for my passport renewal. The connection resides in the fact that my career in Museums and Art has afforded me with opportunities for wide travel throughout the world, but it is clear that this renewal will likely be the last I will require and this sort of punctuation mark is not entirely welcome. My first passport coincided with our freshman year.

In the fall of 1953 I came to Cambridge, like most of the rest of us, with no idea whatsoever what I specifically wanted to do. Other, that is, than shop as broadly as possible amongst the myriad offerings in the catalog. Forced to declare, I chose chemistry. Not because I loved it particularly but because at the time I was rather good at it, at least until I had a nose-to-nose confrontation with the "organic" variety. I also realized that the department demanded some 90% of my attention and that caused me to look for a place to hide. Art history was my refuge. It became far more than the familiar "darkness at noon" and before I knew it, I was facing graduation with an honors degree and no idea what to do with it.

Given the state of the world, I applied to and was accepted at law school. But prior to matriculating I received an unsolicited offer of a job in a museum and determined that this might be far more fun in the interim; the law school agreed to a one-year deferment. After that first year (of a steep learning curve and riotous good fun), I was granted a considerably more reluctant second year of deferment and stayed in Minneapolis where I had begun at the bottom of the museum ladder. It was clear, however, at the end of year two that it was time to return to school, but it was no longer going to be "law" but rather the Institute of Fine Arts at New York University.

This decision shocked many of my colleagues in Cambridge, but NYU was arguably at the center of the art world and for someone intent on a museum career rather than academe it was made for me. Aside from my required coursework I managed to make the rounds of 20 or more galleries per week, learning all I could about both the contemporary and old master offerings. Not only does one make invaluable contacts, but in the process you train your eye far better than any library of books.

I should insert here that between the time of leaving Minneapolis and matriculating in New York I had managed to squeeze in a *wander-yahr* in Europe attempting to visit all the major museum and dealing centers for further visual immersion. On reflection it was one of the smartest things I ever did, and I'm not sure still to this day where the idea came from. It was a time when one could buy a new Mercedes in Stuttgart and bring it home at a tremendous saving, saying nothing about traveling in style. Let us also not forget that these were the years of "Europe on five dollars a day".

The graduate years flew by, and almost simultaneously with the arrival of my thesis was that of our first of eventually four children (did I forget to mention that like so many of us, I was married shortly after graduation in 1957.) I then did exactly what I said I would never do: I took a job in academe. I moved to Ann Arbor, MI, and became an occupational "schizophrenic" by accepting a joint appointment in both the art history department and the Museum of Art. It afforded a remarkable opportunity to try my hand at teaching and maintaining a museum regimen. I found I liked it far better than I ever imagined. But within three years the long arm of Minneapolis reached out and made me an offer I could not refuse. At the age of 26 I became the Chief Curator of the museum where I had begun selling postcards in the museum shop at night.

Imagining I might stay five or six years before moving on, it was in fact 22 years later that I departed; ten years as curator and 12 as director. These were exciting years in the museum field as well as challenging ones. Major acquisitions were still available at prices commensurate with the museum's purchase endowment, and building on an outstanding permanent collection was one of my great joys. These were also the beginnings of the culture wars as well as serious international museum exchanges. Travel, as mentioned above, was a major part of my activity, and organizing exhibitions for the remarkably culturally hungry audience challenged the staff at all times.

One of the most exciting unfortunately never came to be. For a number of years in the 1980s I worked with colleagues from the National Gallery of Art and San Francisco Museum to create what would've been the first ever "diagonal slice" view of the Hermitage Museum in St. Petersburg. One of the extraordinary collections in the world, the Hermitage is far more than a paintings gallery and contains objects beginning with the Altai peoples from the fourth century BC to Impressionist and Russian modern painting. The exhibition was destined to be "a blockbuster", and its catalog was in galley form when the Soviets invaded Afghanistan. That was the end of that.

Intending to take a sabbatical after my long sojourn in Minnesota, I made the mistake of accepting a dinner invitation with a headhunter. The next thing I knew I was announcing that I would become the next director of the Detroit Institute of Arts. Suffice it to say that Detroit presented itself as "a challenge to management". The physical building is the fifth largest museum in the United States and has a collection to match. The governance, however, was unique, as it is municipal governance and as Director I was head of the Arts Department—a co-equal with the Fire and Police departments. Suffice it to say this caused some unusual problems. Problems which, after my watch, were largely resolved in the recent bankruptcy proceedings of the city wherein the Museum regained self-governance for the first time since 1919.

Figure 4.3.3.1 *Sam Sachs II, the new Director in his museum, The Frick Collection, in 1998*

Photo by Fernando Bengoechea, for *Town & Country* magazine, 1999; courtesy of the author

In 1997, after 12 years at the helm, another headhunter appeared, this time with an offer to return to the city of my birth and become Director of The Frick Collection. It would be difficult to find three more different museums than those with which I have been involved. One, a preeminent Midwestern midsize institution; the next a major urban relic maintaining relevance in a region which had failed to keep up with the times culturally; and finally a gem "preserved in amber" where one of my stated goals was to overhear visitors say, "You know, the Frick is much better now, but nothing has changed."

Presently I can say that I flunked retirement. In 2003 I stepped down after 40 years in the field and became president of the Pollock-Krasner Foundation. I am now giving away money rather than begging for it, and had I only known how much more fun that is, I would've done it a long time ago. We support artists, worldwide, who are needy and worthy and do so with funds which derive from the estates of the artist Jackson Pollock and his wife, Lee Krasner. Our history relates that we have given more than $60 million in 77 countries, and we certainly hope there is no end in sight. There certainly is no shortage of need.

Another interlude occurred in 2007. I was invited to be a Visiting Fellow at Oriel College, Oxford. My wife, Beth, and our then teenaged daughter decamped and spent a year in England. Being a Visiting Fellow is akin to falling into the proverbial "tub of butter": many perks and few obligations other than mentoring and the occasional lecture. One can research and/or travel to ones heart's delight. But the glorious English countryside has many distractions to offer, and two books I had imagined working on still lie unfinished. I was astonished to learn, however, that Oxford did not until recently offer Art History as an undergraduate field of study—only at the graduate level. I rather imagine they assumed you would learn the basics at mother's knee.

Finally, I would be remiss if I did not here include a short screed in support of the Arts in general. It is no secret that they are historically underfunded and over politicized. More people attend museums annually than all sporting events combined! But in spite of this enormous popularity, the National Endowment for the Arts, which costs you, the taxpayer, about the equivalent of one postage stamp, still seems to stick in many a craw. American art museums protect and preserve over 16 million items in their collections for present and future generations. They are worth it.

Figure 4.3.3.2 *Visiting Fellow Sachs at Oxford with Professor Sir John Elliott, Oxford, 2008*

Samuel Sachs II is a native New Yorker, an honors graduate of Harvard College with an MA from the Institute of Fine Arts at New York University and currently President of the Pollock-Krasner Foundation. Choosing to make directing American museums his professional career, in his early positions as Director of The Minneapolis Institute of Arts (1973 to 1985) and The Detroit Institute of Arts (1985 to 1997), he sought to extend their impact on their communities while enriching their collections by gifts and purchases. At The Frick Collection in New York City from 1997 to 2003, he further improved a respected institution.

Sachs's contributions to other cultural and educational institutions have included serving as member and President of the Association of Art Museum Directors and in several positions with the Japan Society, including on the Executive Committee and as Chair of the Society's Exhibition Committee. A past Chairman of the Board of the Isamu Noguchi Foundation, he has also been decorated by Sweden and Denmark for his outstanding contributions to culture.

An author and scholar, he has taught at the University of Michigan, Wayne State University, and the University of Minnesota, and in 2007 to 2008 was Visiting Fellow at Oriel College, Oxford University.

He lives with his wife, Elizabeth, and family in New York.

The Education of Geoffrey Chalmers

Geoffrey T. Chalmers

> "*Seldom, very seldom, does complete truth belong to any human disclosure; seldom can it happen that something is not a little disguised or a little mistaken.*"
>
> —Jane Austin

From the first, it was always about light. "See the light" were my very first words. "*And the light shineth in darkness; and the darkness comprehended it not.*" So, what does it mean to "see" the light? Our English word subsumes both a visual and a cognitive process. To say "I see it" inevitably conveys that I understand it whether object or thought. But do I really?

It is hard enough to actualize what you "see", let alone to convey it. From birth, rigorously trained in connotative symbiosis, our untutored minds are educated (literally "led out") of darkness into the clear light of reason, shining unerringly upon ordered structures, ever more close-tailored to fit over our raw experience, an intellectual "wet suit" designed for confident navigation in the discordant waters of experience.

Young and naïve, I joyously embraced this challenging mental exercise. As one trained one's unruly body to athletic exactitude, so one could, day by day, push up by push up, forge a sleekly powerful instrument for converting experience to manageable, human, utilitarian effort.

> "*Every valley shall be exalted, and every mountain and hill shall be made low: and the crooked shall be made straight, and the rough places plain.*"

Thus it was that I entered Harvard with a raw, inquisitive, scattered intelligence, easily distracted by the irrelevant and prone to inexplicable conclusions. From it all, four years later, I emerged, smugly satisfied and feeling so superior with my newly acquired analytical abilities, all eager to turn them on, crank them up and take on the world.

In those years, painting was for me a fitful exercise, undertaken as a distraction. But in the summer of my last year I came up against a new kind of mental discipline never before experienced by me. I started to learn how to paint.

Now, painting at Harvard in the 1950s was a problematic thing. I remember discovering that there were in fact painting studios on the second floor of the Fogg Museum. One day I presented myself to the Director who occupied a nearby small office. Boldly I walked up to his desk and inquired if I, a mere undergraduate, could access studio space to paint indoors. "No," he politely replied, "the studios are reserved for those studying art history. You would have to take a class." I glanced up at the wall. I said, "That's a Lionel Feininger painting, is it not?" "Yes," he replied, "I am his son." Thoroughly disgusted, I left.

I was to learn, as did Eugene O'Neil, that as an institution of higher learning Harvard did not include artistic pursuits as part of its curriculum. College was for improving the mind. That meant, strictly, symbolics. Those mental push-ups honed the mind to razor-sharp control of symbols in the service of the ever-imperative process of *analysis*, the process of breaking down experience into manageable, malleable pieces. These could be manipulated, reconfigured and rebuilt into extensive, compelling efficient and satisfying structures. Far, far from this was the intuitive, sloppy, irrational process of *synthesis*, whining and sitting like a little orphaned animal outside the academic door, tolerated in General Education courses, undergraduate entertainments and weekend museum teas. No real, purposeful and meaningful intellectual development could be coaxed out of practicing an art.

Not that I really cared much in those days, mind you. Dutifully, I went about garnering grades, moving on, learning the legal trade and pouring whatever creative energies I had into crafting contracts, negotiating deals, forming companies, faithful servant of those who build and those who run things.

And yet, what I had encountered in that brief summer of my senior year haunted me. As I moved, settled down and had a family I began finding more and more time to paint. Surprisingly, in that exercise, I encountered something strange indeed: *I discovered that what I was looking at I was never truly seeing.* What was emerging was basically a regurgitation of what I had been taught to expect and routinely trained to duplicate.

Now, truth be told, I then recalled what I had seen and learned in 1956. During that summer I had studied with a "hard core" impressionist painter in Provincetown named Henry Hensche (1899–1992). Henry was born in Germany, studied at the Chicago Art Institute and, in New York, became a pupil of Charles W. Hawthorne (1872–1930), a prominent New York portrait painter and pupil of William Merritt Chase (1849–1916). Hawthorne enthusiastically espoused the impressionist principles developed in France by Claude Monet (1840–1926) and a slew of his followers, including, for example, the New England painter Childe Hassam (1859–1925).

True revolutionaries, the impressionists had ushered in a whole new way of painting, focused on the study of light. New discoveries such as the invention of paint in tubes and bright, artificial oil colors enabled painters to move outside *en plein air,* escaping the tyranny of studio light and encountering the illuminative mysteries of the great outdoors. New discoveries of the physiology of human sight sparked intense interest in replicating the whole visual experience on canvas rather than simply that of object recognition. In the hands of Hawthorne and his pupil Hensche, impressionist innovations were corralled into an academic discipline based on a careful, methodical translation of visual experience, piece by piece, to the canvas and re-assembling it into a glowing whole. Now, anyone with a modicum of talent could actually learn how to paint like an impressionist in short order.

The whole exercise, which I began to call "*the calculus of color*", consisted of a disciplined, meticulous examination of contiguous large elements of the overall image, calibrating their color relationships to one another with near-fanatical accuracy and only then, *once this was satisfactorily achieved*, breaking these areas down into smaller and smaller segments until the segmentation disappeared and—voila!—a beautiful three-dimensional image emerged, shimmering, and seeming to live within the four walls of the frame. Viewing through this window, the viewer was bidden to look into the scene and marvel at its verisimilitude.

So then to return to the beginning of all this, what becomes of the act of *seeing*?

For me, in the hands of my impressionist teacher, the humble, laborious exercise of color analysis had devolved into one of purposefully "not seeing." It engendered "*a semblance of truth sufficient to procure for these shadows of imagination that willing suspension of disbelief for the moment, which constitutes poetic faith.*" The consciousness of the artist seemingly disappears and becomes one with the universe itself, seamlessly recreating for the human eye a raw experience which uncannily mimics the very process of our human vision.

I had stumbled upon an intellectual tool every bit as sophisticated as those symbolic exercises I had mastered at Harvard. Indeed, I found that I could focus to the same level of intensity I had experienced, for which I had been so well trained at Harvard, on the creative process itself. What a discovery!

Through the inspiration of Monet and the hardy application of Henry Hensche's methods, the patient, meticulous juncture of harmonic surfaces yields an astonishingly three-dimensional image that, holographically, floats in space beyond the confines of the frame. The effect is stereographic, much as that provoked by the stereopticons of old. Or, as in music, the effect produced by placing concurrent microphones and speakers to weave their feeds and output into three-dimensional tracks of sound so you seem to be sitting there among the musicians themselves.

From being a dogged student of mental discipline with a hunger for creative freedom, I found new joy in focusing on subdividing the incomprehensible, ineffable, unknowable visual experience, picking it up off the landscape like a rare, fragile specimen and lovingly depositing it, fresh and immediate, on a two-dimensional surface. *Veritas* indeed!

Armed with this discipline I am able to undergo and communicate a visual experience of the material world that defies scientific or mechanical explanation. On numerous occasions I have stood "*at the still point of the turning world*", a space abandoned, out of time that "*doth tease us out of thought*" and from which, returning, like an exhausted climber, I stop, rubbing my eyes in disbelief.

I.A. Richards abjured us, like Mencius, to "*cultivate a vast chi*" within which we could experience immortality. So, in that spirit, every painting becomes a mysterious voyage of exploration, ridden with discoveries large and small. What I thought I saw, what I thought I knew, regularly up-ended. I feel like Renoir, whose last words were: "*I learned a little something new today.*"

"*I was blind but now I see.*" Suddenly, every surface, seen through the atmosphere, is a vibrating pastiche of reflections, molecules excited by light, quintessentially locked in vibrant motion onto one another. Mere replication of all this through symbolic analysis can never bring to life how my mind reacts, with an abiding passion, to capture the moment. Not analytically, but inspirationally. I am minded of Edward Hopper, who, when asked what was his greatest goal as a painter, answered: "*To truly recreate the light on the side of a house.*"

Since then, I have had many happy experiences sharing my visions with others. I even managed to make a second career for myself out of it all, as the reader may readily discover. Merely Google my name.

So I can't, in the end, say enough about what a Harvard education has done to empower my inquiring mind to harness those creative energies. Through it I was enabled to "see" in both senses of the word, to translate my vision in a disciplined way and to leave behind something beautiful and more permanent than the mere detritus of my brief passage upon this planet.

Henry Adams never had it so good!

Figure 4.3.5.1 *Painting "HEAD OF THE CHARLES—CATCH UP!", © Geoffrey Teale Chalmers, 2013*

Geoffrey Teale Chalmers is an attorney and Boston-based painter of American scenes since the early 1980s. He specializes in impressionist landscapes and seascapes from New England, Florida and the West Coast. He was chosen to provide the 1993 *Boston Marathon* poster image and has provided the image for a number of other events, including the *Head of the Charles*, the Boston US Pro tennis tournament and Fenway Park (Dom DiMaggio Foundation).

Many of Mr. Chalmers' paintings are reproduced as posters and prints sold in retail stores around the country. His paintings are also in a number of corporate collections as well as numerous private collections.

Mr. Chalmers is a graduate of Columbia Law School and NYU (MBA finance). He started law practice with Cravath, Swaine & Moore in New York and later worked for the US Securities and Exchange Commission in Washington, DC. Moving to Boston in 1972, he served as counsel for several Boston-area companies. He also established the Finance for Lawyers course at Suffolk Law School, Boston. He has since 1996 been engaged in the private practice of law and consulting to the financial services industry and serves on a number of corporate and private boards.

The Best Game Ever

Howard Harrison Glaser

I've had a wonderful life . . . or a not-so-wonderful life, depending on the moment or observer assessment: client, employer, family member, friend, etc. Surprise of surprises: I'm still here playing the best game ever—life. Wins are never guaranteed, but continual play ever offers potential.

College years birthed my skills as a writer covering Crimson sports for the *Herald Traveler.* Shockingly, those skills didn't qualify me for a Madison Ave. ad career. However, ambitions and a classmate's connection landed me a job as an editor/staff writer with a publisher specializing in automotive titles. A fun job. It celebrated Detroit's worship of chrome, heavy metal and power, oblivious to the future onslaught of imports.

That job exploded after seven months as my independent ambitions clashed with the publisher's bridle on my energies. Bad news . . . or maybe good news . . . as it launched a 43-year career as freelance creative entrepreneur. My original photographic images fleshed out my articles. Self-taught graphic design skills enabled complete brochure production, four-color printing, trade show booths, studio construction, music videos and opportunities to photograph and dance with "the world's most beautiful" (models).

When asked what I did professionally, the response was, "What do you need done?" When asked if I had experience filling said need, the response was, "*Never done exactly that, but have a consistent success with first-time efforts.*" Projects resulted.

Clearly, my work was as much lifestyle as it was labor. Assignments provided insider status; credentialed connection at major events; access to Gasoline Alley at the Indy 500; a Bell Helicopter perch to record the Daytona 500's inaugural high-speed banked track; photo ops with famed rock-and-rollers, contrasting with an IBM-assigned portrait of an early System 360 installation.

Different days and nights were filled with utterly varied challenge and reward. Lots of excitement tempered by questionable financial or job security. Client loyalty was often corroded by the need for a new look or a better price. Garnering future projects demanded financial creativity (or sacrifice) as much as professional skills.

A four-year participation with the Harvard hockey team had likely conditioned me to myriad ups and downs. Some nights we out-shot the opponent by a high margin yet lost. Our game-tying goal versus Yale at 20:00 of the third period was disallowed by a quick whistle. Alas, our magnificent coach, Ralph "Cooney" Weiland, taught the team "*Keep it simple, keep skating and keep out of hot cars*" (just another practicality of the keep skating mantra).

Coach Weiland wisely suggested team members forgo skiing, so I abandoned a winter love commenced as a youngster. Several years post graduation delivered sufficient finances to rekindle that passion. Serendipity gifted me an assignment to photograph a classic Maserati in the Catskills. Noting a number of small ski areas there, I added ski gear to my photo kit. Thus launched a 55-year Catskills connection and professional association with the National Ski Patrol and eventually, as a ski pro, to the Professional Ski Instructors of America. The 2000 closure of my NYC studio provided ample time to profit in ski world adventure.

As a kid I had typical dreams of becoming a pro athlete—earning money and affirmation from physical sport. Election to varsity hockey manager resulted from ambition and dedication, not size. However, on skis, small stature grants definite advantages. And, certainly, most Harvardians are well prepared to teach, influenced by professorial brilliance or a great coach like Cooney.

A pro ski career has two downsides: its seasonality and the whimsy of snow conditions.

Eventually, stilled creative juices awakened and there was time aplenty. The structure of commercial protocols was long gone. Standards and subjects were to be self-imposed, not client-defined. Infinite artistic freedom was the new bully.

The digital revolution presented practical challenges. Traditional methodology lost value. Craftsmanship became adulterated (or glorified) by the ubiquity of Photoshop. Equipment long ago acquired and exotic craft skills painstakingly mastered crashed onto the trash heap of obsolescence.

The true artist (or hero) can regard each challenge as new opportunity. And the few gerontologists we read promote learning new skills as youthful opportunity. All good.

The images of my most recent output have reached stunning height in their intense color, artful composition and unique capture of a typical subject, the flower.[1]

Commercial success doesn't necessarily mirror the aesthetic quality. "Fine art", no matter how well respected, is neither a necessity for sustenance nor a profit center of bawdy commercial entertainment. No matter that often the two are curiously interchanged by some.

So, you may ask,

"How does this all connect . . . to the Yard and its environment physically and academically . . . to the 'silent generation' . . . to the mainstream . . . to a completion of the circle of thought?"

My readings of class reports, reunion books, etc., more or less implicate my path has been less similar than that of my fellow classmates. In that sense *I may represent Harvard's belief in diversity.*

I chose a realm of endeavor detached from my field of study, Social Relations. Yet, my minglings with individuals from a multitude of cultures, attitudes, affinities and interests could provide rich reward to the social anthropologists.

Survival and ambition expressed through flexibility and innovation enabled a positive response to ever-changing circumstances. Learning at Harvard and being at Harvard reinforced the values and skills required even though there was little formal transfer of the academics.

While these words focus on me and Harvard, their substance has been well implanted on my wife of 32 years and three grown boys. They see and accept my good and not-so-good and ride on their own journeys, all for the better.

I'm still in the game of life . . . a win or two more? We'll see. But I'll keep playing!

Howard Harrison Glaser landed in NYC four days post graduation. There he began a lifelong independent career in creative services. Projects ranged from writing to graphic design and photography to high-end photo lab and studio services. Clients ranged from small fashion designers to blue-chip corporations. The variety of work and range of patronage was dictated by the need to adapt and survive as times changed. The frenetic urban workaday world was balanced by acquisition of a quiet sanctuary in the central Catskills. It became residence for an early (but brief) 1970s retirement and a year 2000 retirement. The term retirement is a misnomer, as photographic work continues, with the focus being strictly artistic rather than commercial. Another major artwork is an overhaul/renovation of the property's carriage house/barn. It has become a praiseworthy listing on Airbnb as well as a gallery for his photography.

Endnote

[1] To view a selection of images, please e-mail myfotogarde@gmail.com.

Figure 4.3.6.1 *Ansel Easton Adams (1902–1984), American photographer and environmentalist*

Beginning at age 14 with a Kodak Brownie box camera, he helped elevate photography to an art comparable with painting and music, and equally capable of expressing emotion and beauty.

During his adolescence the piano was Adams's primary occupation and intended profession. Although he ultimately gave up music for photography, the piano brought him substance, discipline, and structure, and its exacting craft informed his visual artistry as well as his influential writings and teachings on photography.[1]

He told his students, "It is easy to take a photograph, but it is harder to make a masterpiece in photography than in any other art medium."[2]

Art critic John Szarkowski wrote:

> *"Ansel Adams attuned himself more precisely than any photographer before him to a visual understanding of the specific quality of the light that fell on a specific place at a specific moment.*
>
> *For Adams the natural landscape is not a fixed and solid sculpture but an insubstantial image, as transient as the light that continually redefines it.*
>
> *This sensibility to the specificity of light was the motive that forced Adams to develop his legendary photographic technique."*[3]

With Fred Archer, Adams developed the Zone System as a way to determine proper exposure and adjust the contrast of the final print. The resulting clarity and depth characterized his photographs. He primarily used large-format cameras because the large film used with these cameras (primarily 5x4 and 8x10) contributed to sharpness in his prints.

His black-and-white landscape photographs of the American West have been widely reproduced on calendars, posters, books, and the Internet.

Footnotes

1 Wikipedia https://en.m.wikipedia.org/wiki/Ansel_Adams 4/25

2 Alinder, Mary; Stillman, Andrea; Adams, Ansel; Stegner, Wallace (1988). *Ansel Adams: Letters and Images 1916–1984*, p 396. Boston: Little, Brown. ISBN 0-8212-1691-0.

3 Szarkowski, John (1976). *Looking at Photographs: 100 Pictures from the Collection of the Museum of Modern Art.* New York: N.Y. Graphic Society.

Chapter Five

GOVERNMENT

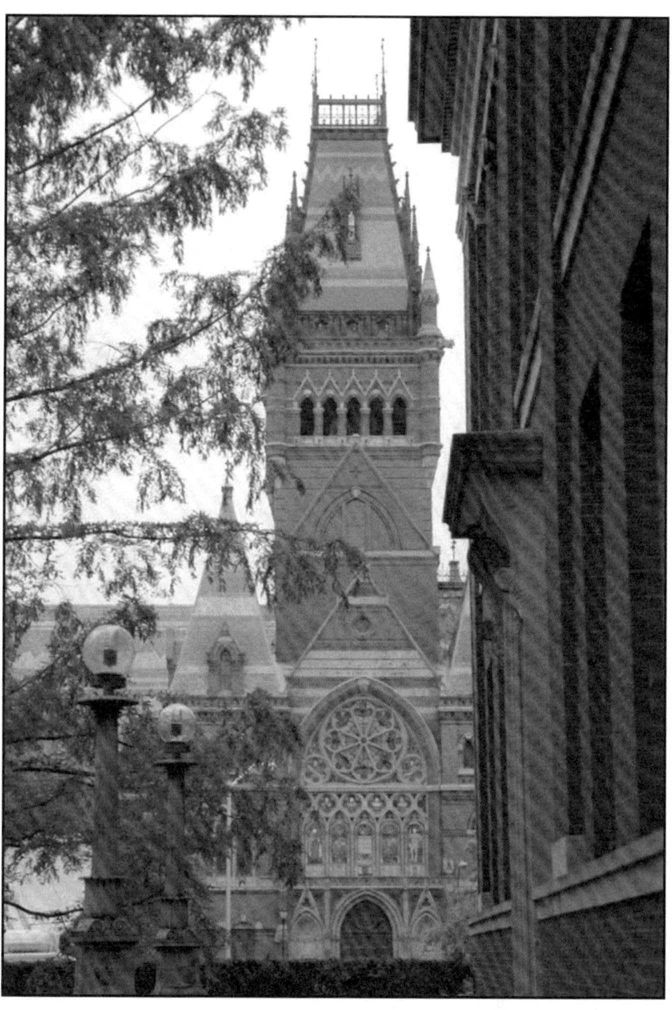

Figure C5 *Memorial Hall: monument to Harvard Alumni serving in the Union Army who died in the Civil War*
Reprinted courtesy of Harvard University

Chapter Five

GOVERNMENT

International

Foreign Service

Diplomacy

Commemorating the 70th Anniversary of the End of World War II

Tatsuo Arima

The following is the text of a statement I gave in September 2015 in Washington, DC, at a special seminar, "*US–Japan Partnership: The Next Seventy Years*", hosted by the *US–Japan Conference on Cultural and Educational Interchange (CULCON)*. CULCON was established in 1961 by an agreement between President Kennedy and Prime Minister Ikeda.

The themes of the seminar commemorating the 70th anniversary of the end of World War II were: "*Passing the Torch to the Next Generation*" and "*Embracing Diversity and Opportunities for Japan and the United States*".

Here is the text:

> "I am honored to share my thoughts on the Japan-U.S. relationship and reflections on my American experiences. Allow me to go back to the beginning.
>
> I arrived at Concord, New Hampshire, to enter a prep school called St. Paul's in September 1951. A few days earlier, the San Francisco Peace Treaty was signed. The Korean War had been going on for more than a year and lasted another two years to save the Republic of Korea at a great cost to American and other lives. I had just finished a journey from Tokyo

lasting three weeks, first on a cargo ship from Yokohama to Seattle, and then on a continental railway across America. I was greeted at the station by Dr. William Oates, later the Rector of the school, with a true sense of welcome. It was before the start of the school, so his family took me into his home. Many years later he wrote that they remembered me as their sons' adopted brother. It was an incipient case of the home-stay now widely practiced across the Pacific. My grandson home-stayed with a family in Michigan a few years back.

The reason I attended St. Paul's was Mr. Minoru Makihara, class of '54, my lifelong friend. He had gone to St. Paul's two years earlier and was there for only one year, but he did so well that the school decided to invite another student from his school in Tokyo, Seikei, where I was a student. I was chosen to follow in his footsteps. This was to be the start of the ties between St. Paul's and Seikei which has since evolved into an unbroken program of annual student exchanges that continues to this day.

At St. Paul's, on one side of the corridor leading to the chapel were the new plaques affixed each bearing the name of the alumnus killed in World War II. It was only six years after the war had ended, and the unfathomable sorrows of their families, particularly of their parents, were still fresh. And yet I experienced no harsh words or gestures.

My life at St. Paul's and subsequently at Harvard totaling more than ten years taught me the goodwill of the American people. This is the original cause of my abiding optimism about our long-lasting relationship.

I think the 20th century was the American century because it succeeded in achieving a multiethnic society to a degree unthinkable when I first arrived here in the United States. The diversity of the student body at St. Paul's today reflects that achievement.

You finally elected President Obama, twice. The moral courage of the Americans has prevailed, though, of course, difficulties remain. For these reasons, I believe you are quietly respected throughout the world.

On the whole, Japan and the United States have managed their relationship reasonably well, best exemplified by the reversion of Okinawa islands, which had been under American administration since the end of World War II, in the midst of the Vietnam War. For the American military, the free use of its bases must have been of strategic importance. And yet, the long-term view prevailed that the return of the islands would strengthen the mutual trust and friendship, the essence of a credible alliance. I was deeply involved in the grueling negotiations for more than two and a half years, but in the end the diplomats on both sides were pleased.

All has not always been well with our relationship. Perhaps the nadir hit in the mid-1980s over our trade disputes. Around this time, I happened upon a book called *America versus Japan* edited by Professor Thomas McCraw of Harvard Business School. In the conclusion, he wrote:

"*In the last analysis Japanese and American friendship represents a pearl beyond price, a hard-won achievement far too valuable to place in jeopardy merely because of short political inertia.*"

I was thankful to read this.

Here are a few thoughts on our alliance and its deterrence.

It is stated in the preamble to our security treaty that together we uphold the principles of democracy, individual liberty and the rule of law. This shared commitment of ours to securing, in short, the individual's dignity is the core value of our alliance.

I believe the quality of our alliance should remain such that no one should ever feel tempted to test its credibility or behave in disregard of it. With this dictate in mind, we should always be vigilant in managing and nurturing our relationship across the board, including our security cooperation.

But it is not enough.

To make our relationship truly resilient and respected, we have to go beyond the confines of our bilateral interests in what Professor Joseph Nye calls the world of transnational interdependence and act as the catalyst for solving global problems, each a threat to the individual wellbeing. To solve them together, we have to further strengthen our environment of consultation and cooperation in all areas and at all levels.

Facing each other across the Pacific, we are bonded by our shared commitment to securing human dignity. The history

> of the Japan-U.S. relationship after the war shows us that the blessing of democracy which is the condition of securing human dignity can be reached beyond borders and even over civilizational divides.
>
> I firmly believe that Japan and the United States can continue to cooperate in the future to make the world a better place. I am happy that I have spent a better part of my life to strengthen our bilateral relationship.
>
> Harvard was an essential part of my life which I will always fondly remember."

I continue to believe in what I wrote in our Fiftieth Anniversary Class Report as follows.

> ". . . the twentieth century was the American Century, because the United States has struggled to prove that liberal democracy is not the exclusive prerogative of any particular race or culture, while having succeeded in creating a truly multi-ethnic society, 'a pearl beyond price'.
>
> The process has been difficult, at times even violent. Still, the American courage and decency prevailed."

I have an empirical faith in the courage and decency of the American people nurtured over more than 60 years.

Figure 5.1.1.1 *Tatsuo Arima, after his ceremonial decoration by His Majesty the Emperor at the Court, November 2008*

Foreign Service

Diplomacy

Figure 5.1.1.2 *Tatsuo and Fumiko, in traditional kimono, at a garden party given by Their Majesties in the spring of 2009*

Tatsuo Arima, PhD, President, Middle East Research Institute of Japan, was honored in 2008 for his exemplary accomplishments as a civil servant and his contributions to peace through diplomacy in a ceremonial decoration by H.M. the Emperor at the Court. During his time in government, he served as Ambassador to the Kingdom of the Netherlands; Ambassador to the Federal Republic of Germany; Consul General, San Francisco; Political Counselor in Washington, DC; Chief Councilor for External Affairs in the Prime Minister's Office; and Director General, North American Affairs Bureau of the Ministry of Foreign Affairs. After he returned from Germany, he was appointed Ambassador at Large, Special Envoy of the Government and also Representative to the Middle East Peace Process.

After receiving his AB in Government, he continued on to doctoral studies in Government at Harvard and received his PhD in 1962. His doctoral thesis, "The Failure of Freedom, A Portrait of Modern Japanese Intellectuals", published by Harvard University Press in 1969, has been used as a textbook in courses on Japanese politics. In 2014 he published in Japanese a well-received two-volume autobiography entitled *Reminiscences of Japan's Diplomacy to Europe and America*, based on a university-designed oral history project. For six years, he also taught the course "Contemporary Diplomacy" at the School of Political Science and Economics of Waseda University, one of the major private universities in Japan.

He and his wife, Fumiko, live in Tokyo and are the parents of two Harvard-educated sons with three grandchildren. Fumiko remains actively engaged in various women's exchange programs with the United States, Holland, and Germany.

What Ambassadors Really Worry About

Nicholas Platt

Introduction

I wrote about my career in China and Japan in a book called *China Boys*, published in 2010 (available on Amazon). This essay will draw on my experiences as a United States ambassador abroad—Zambia (1982–84), the Philippines (1987–91), and Pakistan (1991–92)—during the last ten years of my Foreign Service career. A host of books and articles tell us that ambassadors and their staffs abroad negotiate agreements, further US business interests, protect American citizens, gather information about the host country, and issue visas for travel and residence in the United States.

Here are a few stories which illustrate some worries I had as a chief of mission overseas.

Staying Safe

A fitting for a bulletproof vest was my first appointment after being chosen as ambassador to the Philippines in 1987. Ambassadors' work is dangerous. More US ambassadors have been killed in the line of duty than generals during World War II.

As it turned out, I wore my vest only once in four turbulent years. Manila was too hot, and vests too visible under the transparent dress shirt everyone wore much of the time. The Barong Tagalog, as it is known, was originally designed by Spanish colonial authorities to reveal hidden weapons. Though gun violence is a daily occurrence throughout the Philippines, vests are scorned in this macho society.

A huge street rally and mass was organized in early December 1989 to celebrate Cory Aquino's survival after the most serious coup attempt of her presidency. (There were six in all.) US Embassy security was dead set against my attending. The US had flown fighter planes from Clark Air Force Base to demonstrate support of Mrs. Aquino's government during the coup fighting. I was therefore a prime target, they argued, for assassination by angry Army rightists hidden in the enormous crowd. I replied that not appearing would contradict the prominent US backing for Aquino. It was imperative that I attend. At least wear your vest, they insisted.

The day was cool, so I hid the vest under a blazer, shirt and tie and walked slowly but quite safely a half mile through a huge, rejoicing throng. A truckload of nuns stopped to thank me for sending the fighter planes. On the dais after the ceremony, Cardinal Sin approached to offer congratulations and enveloped me in his ample bear hug. "Aha," he uttered softly in my ear after feeling the vest. I assured him I would never speak to him again if he revealed my secret. He did not.

In fact, bulletproof vests are not what keep US ambassadors safe. What worked was a combination of psychology, logistics, and, most important of all, good intelligence. I was number one on the target list for the communist National People's Army (NPA) from the first day I arrived in August 1987. Later, Army rightists working to overthrow Mrs. Aquino also increasingly wanted to kill me. Nothing personal, of course. Just the symbolism of the office.

NPA "sparrow" death squads liked a sure thing. They studied their targets' daily habits and travel routes, planned meticulously, and usually killed with one shot from a .45 automatic. They were, like most Filipinos, Roman Catholics and not Muslim martyrs thirsting for virgins in paradise. Their ideal was to make their kill, go home and watch the basketball game.

Our first objective, then, was to assure assassins that there was no way to avoid a serious fire fight if they went after the US ambassador. I never drove anywhere without a lead car and a follow van with a total of eight discreetly armed men, some with UZI submachine guns folded into briefcases. An additional guard sat in the front seat of my armored Cadillac with a .357 magnum revolver tucked in the seat pocket behind him for my use. We made sure the NPA knew about it. I also knew if I ever used it in that confined space, I would be deaf for life.

Every six months or so, my entire detail would drive downtown to a public outdoor shooting range, where we would discharge noisily every weapon we had. My men were all retired Philippine Constabulary officers, knowledgeable about the look and ways of local streets. My driver knew all the different routes across Manila from the residence in Makati to the chancery on the bay and all the tricks of defensive driving. I felt safer with them than with a special detail sent from Washington during one period of particularly high alert. Nervous and jumpy, the US agents were incidents waiting to happen. I sent them home with relief at the earliest opportunity.

What kept me safest was intelligence. Our CIA station had penetrated the NPA inner circle and knew when they were studying my movements, preparing an attack. We were warned to use extra vigilance and a wider variety of different routes. In addition a special unit "watched the watchers" and told us when we were actually being followed. After a while the hit men would give up in frustration, to return again in a few months and try again. I was concerned that the tight cordon around me would force the NPA to go after other embassy officials. They did, in fact, murder one Army attaché on his way to work.

Periodic coup attempts by the Army rebels were less predictable. The most serious of these in November 1989 required us to evacuate the residence until the week-long rebellion was over. One truckload of rebel soldiers came after me shortly after we left, but ran head on, like keystone cops, into another vehicle bent on the same mission.

Security requirements vary for every ambassadorial post, and change along with the political situation on the ground. Zambia in 1982–84 offered no threat and required no security detail. In 1991–92, our embassy compound in Pakistan was under regular threat from Muslim mobs inflamed by extremist mullahs at Friday prayers. (They had succeeded in setting fire to the chancery in 1979, and had attacked the USIS center downtown in 1991.) But the person of the ambassador was not a target. My detail was one small Pakistani constable packing an old revolver, with whom we travelled widely without incident. Nowadays, our chiefs of mission in Islamabad have a detail the size and intensity of mine in Manila. As it was for me, the quality of our intelligence is what keeps them safe.

Staying in Command

All ambassadors carry abroad a letter from the president of the United States saying that he/she is his personal representative and is in charge of the operations of all US agency operations in the country of assignment. The ambassador exercises authority through a "Country Team" consisting of the heads of those agencies on his staff. The agencies represented are generally much bigger than the State Department, and all have independent channels of communication with their staffs abroad.

Ambassadors must establish authority from the outset and take every opportunity to underline that authority throughout their term of office. Everyone on the Country Team knows about the ambassador's letter, but if he/she ever has to cite it explicitly, they have lost their authority. The ambassador must know how to take command and exercise it.

Manila was one of the largest embassies abroad in the years I was there. More than 20 agencies worked under its roof, guided by 500 American staff with 2,500 locals helping them. During the first weeks of my tenure I made a point of visiting each agency head and their top staffs. Making the effort to show up and learn how the members of the Country Team view their work was an important way to establish command.

The Country Team meeting is the key instrument for exercising authority. It must be held frequently (weekly), and kept as small and as short (one hour) as possible. The short part is hard. One way is to have everyone stand during the meeting. Informing the ambassador what he/she needs to know (and nothing more) to make decisions is the ideal work of the Country Team meeting. Asking for advice is not a sign of weakness. Choosing the right advice to take is the essence of command.

Crises help concentrate the mind and establish authority. Five days after I presented my credentials in August 1987, a charismatic young Army colonel named Gringo Honasan tried to shoot his way into Malacanang Palace, then occupied Armed Forces headquarters, and could only be dislodged by the government bombing its own building with ancient biplanes. The Army command remained loyal to the elected president, but it became imperative for the embassy to reach Honasan and tell him the US was totally opposed to his action. We had already prepared a message from President Reagan for immediate release that all US assistance would cease immediately to any force that overthrew a democratically elected government. This was established policy but a direct channel to those operating the coup was urgently needed.

"Did anyone in the embassy know Honasan?" I asked the Country Team? "Why, yes," replied our assistant Army attaché. "I am the godfather of his youngest child and send him diapers every month." "Do we know his phone number?" "Of course." "Then call Gringo up and read him Reagan's message."

We spent the next two days reading that message to everyone in the Philippine government, an excellent way for the new ambassador to introduce himself. Honasan fled, not to be caught during the next four years. (He is now a senator.)

It being the Philippines, I was blamed for the coup. Immediately, "Ambassador Plot" tee shirts appeared on the streets, snapped up by conspiracy-prone Filipinos inclined to believe that the US is behind everything bad that happens,

I sent the assistant Army attaché home soon after. Against my orders, he kept up contact with Honasan's family. An excellent officer, his removal did not harm his career but helped me establish authority.

Showing Up

Eighty percent of life is showing up, Woody Allen tells us. The percentage for diplomacy is even higher. American ambassadors are in high profile demand at their posts the instant they arrive. They become the top people to meet, persuade, criticize, feed, and even kill. Their presence at any meeting, whether it be political, economic, social or athletic, bears significance equal to any substantive contribution they may be in a position to make.

I arrived in Pakistan in August '91 with hands both empty and tied. The Pakistani military had completed development of a nuclear weapon in recent months and, as threatened for many years, the US had cut off all military and economic assistance. The move coincided roughly with the end of the Cold War and the collapse of the Soviet Union, leading to a general perception among Pakistanis that the US had simply discarded them, "like a used condom" when no longer needed. I expected to be shunned as a pariah. Not so. Not at all so. I found out that Pakistanis wanted to maintain a relationship with the US, and that I was the convenient vehicle for that. If I showed up and took interest, I was more than welcome. So, having nothing material to offer, Sheila and I showed up all over the country during our 13 months there. Boar hunts in Sind, business banquets in Karachi, polo matches in mountainous Gilgit, weddings in Islamabad, picnics in the foothills of the Himalayas, kebab feasts in Peshawar, kite-flying parties in Lahore; no opportunity was missed.

Pakistani politicians were new to democracy. Officials representing the president, the prime minister and the chief of Army staff, the competing centers of power in the executive branch, were at each other's throats. All felt it worthwhile to show up separately for tea at my residence to complain about each other. It was worthwhile for me to know their issues and sometimes build bridges between them.

A smart and friendly wife adds immeasurably to ones' effectiveness at showing up, particularly in a Muslim country. In any home one visited, particularly in conservative North West Frontier province, the women of the house were sequestered in a separate wing called the *zenana*. No men allowed, but Sheila was welcome and gleaned the juicy news and gossip of the family and the district.

Showing up can be tedious. We classified receptions as follows: (1) substantive—stay and talk; (2) "GTO—grace the occasion", go through the receiving line and then peel off; (3) "grip and grin", what we do when hosting our own diplomatic receptions. We recognized the receptions were workplaces where serious information and analysis could be exchanged, protected by the hubbub from electronic eavesdropping. So we went, and went, and hosted and hosted.

Complex and cumbersome as they were, I did not let security concerns keep me from doing my job. Sheila and I showed up at every event worth attending and travelled widely throughout the Islands. The future status of the huge military bases in the Philippines was the major US preoccupation during my tenure. Endless negotiations sopped up much of my time. The need to reach an agreement that the Philippine Senate would approve required me to travel constantly, drumming up popular support for a continued US presence, opening schools built with US base-related assistance, giving speeches, kissing babies and behaving like a US politician running for office.

It is particularly important to show up when disaster strikes. The Philippines had more than its share of these. But offering of assistance was a delicate matter, given nationalist sensitivity about the wide gap between the Philippine governments' shortage of food and logistical equipment, particularly helicopters, and the plenty available at our bases.

Showing up in the Philippines often involved performing. Filipinos love to sing and invite everyone to join them and do solo renditions. It was our misfortune to be practiced folksingers. Perhaps the only memory of my tenure that will last is a 12-bar blues I wrote about how difficult it was to negotiate with Foreign Secretary Raul Manglapus. He loved the song and accompanied me on drums when I sang it at Malacanang Palace during President Aquino's New Year's Day reception in 1988. The Filipinos also remember that I had two guitars, including a black one for formal occasions.

Performing as an adjunct to showing up is special to the Philippines. Elsewhere, an ambassador who sang a song at a state function complaining about the foreign minister would instantly be declared *persona non grata*. Zambians and Pakistanis did not expect envoys to burst into song and would have been puzzled if I had.

Staying Fit

Every ambassadorial post is a marathon. One should train for it. Regular physical exercise is a must, to dissipate the pressures that build inexorably. Squash was my main device, ideal for intensity, brevity, and the enclosed spaced beloved of security officers. During the grueling years of base negotiations I took comfort in imagining Foreign Secretary Manglapus' head to be the ball as I hit it full strength. Manglapus, in fact, was a difficult interlocutor, slippery, procrastinating, often forgetful, and stooped under the weight of a large nationalist chip on his shoulder.

Squash is not for everyone, however. Any regular activity will do. Tennis and golf are great diplomatic games, affording opportunities for bonding and discussion. I solved many problems with Defense Secretary (and later President) Ramos when struggling together out of rough and bunkers.

President Kaunda of Zambia, a 14-handicap golfer, loved nothing better than to beat the American ambassador at golf. I liked nothing better than spending four-plus hours with the head of state, and developed a strong relationship playing by the odd rules of his private statehouse course. (Examples: a free drop out of hippo hoofprints; permission to tee up your ball on guinea fowl droppings; striking a gazelle cost you the hole, unless you were Kaunda and your shot hit one and bounced onto the green.)

Staying Corrected and Connected

Anyone who reaches the rank of ambassador risks losing touch with reality. All of a sudden everyone agrees with you and laughs at your jokes. It is vital to gather people around you who question your judgment and will tell you when you are wrong. Wives, partners, longtime secretaries or friends often fill these roles and should be sought out and prized. I chose deputy chiefs of mission with strong independent points of view.

Encourage your staff to level with you. I made it a point to tell everyone who worked for me:

- You will never be punished saying something you know I do not want to hear. I will be angry, but not for very long, particularly if it concerns an issue that would become serious if kept hidden.
- You will be severely punished if you do not tell me something you know I do not want to hear and it develops into serious problem.

A candid connection to your staff is crucial to crisis management. Your credibility will determine the degree of community responsiveness in times of maximum danger.

I had plenty of practice. Between August 1987 and July 1991, the embassy in Manila coped with two violent coup attempts against the Aquino government, the assassination of ten American citizens, the kidnapping of a Peace Corps volunteer by Communist rebels and the subsequent evacuation of the entire Peace Corps contingent, a killer earthquake, four super typhoons, and finally the eruption of Mount Pinatubo, which destroyed Clark Air Force Base and required the relocation of 29,000 American service personnel.

Here is a dramatic example of the connection between candor and crisis management. We learned at 2 a.m. one morning toward the end of the 1989 coup attempt that the government was planning to attack rebels holed up in the business district and drive them into a neighborhood where Americans and other diplomats lived. I phoned President Aquino and asked for a delay of two hours to get people out. She agreed. Embassy staffers then tuned up our extensive emergency radio network to alert the community. In the next 90 minutes some 3,000 people moved from their homes into safer parts of the city. Not a peep of complaint or question except perhaps "Can we bring the dog?", to which the answer was "No". We had been straight with the community over the years. They did what we said when we most wanted them to.

Staying in Touch

Ambassadors' communications with Washington are unique within the American bureaucracy. As George Shultz' Executive Secretary (1985–87), I made sure that every proposal he received was cleared by every office which had a legitimate stake in the policy. As a member of Zbigniew Brzezinski's NSC Staff (1978–79), I did the same for President Carter on issues relating to the areas of Asia for which I was responsible. But telegrams from ambassadors abroad can go direct to the President or Secretary of State without being cleared by anyone.

This is a privilege that must be reserved for only the most important matters. Overuse will kill an ambassador's credibility and reputation. Written communications with Washington are often preceded by daily phone calls, usually to the country desk, to check out the environment for policy or personnel recommendations. This is normally the realm of the Deputy Chief of Mission, an official the ambassador must carefully choose and totally trust. Normally, an ambassador waiting for confirmation spends weeks or even months in an office within the country desk. This time is best spent getting to know the desk, the bureau and the department as a whole, finding the officers on whom one can rely. The desk officers serve as the forward spotters for your written artillery.

I was in charge of the Japan Desk during the first years of Ambassador Mike Mansfield's tenure (1977–78). I knew him quite well from visits to Tokyo as a senator, and could plot the trajectory of his messages onto the desks of policy makers in the national security agencies and the White House. I made a point when I reached the level of ambassadorial appointment to cultivate the desks and the bureaus and to identify just the right DCM.

I found out during my tours in the Secretariat that the most effective policy papers were short and pointed. It was not always so, when communications were slower and officials had more time to read. George Kennan's influential "Long Telegram" from Moscow in 1946 was 5,500 words long. Later published in Foreign Affairs under the pseudonym "X", it shaped US policy throughout the Cold War. Today, against the pressure of the daily flood of instant digital mail, well-argued brevity is at a premium.

E-mail has become a prevalent medium and is frequent and uncleared between members of the Country Team and their agencies. The ambassador must emphasize from the beginning that proposals out of line with the policies set in the embassy will result in the rapid removal of the official involved.

It is crucial for any ambassador to return to Washington as frequently as possible. Face-to-face consultations with national security officials and concerned Members of Congress are an essential adjunct to their written communications with the capital. Every excuse to make this happen should be employed.

Staying on Top of Things

To know what is going on, who is doing what, to have easy access to its leaders, and to relate all this to US interests, these are the reasons why ambassadors and their staffs are at their posts. Some people think that jet travel and instant digital communications have rendered ambassadors and embassies obsolete. The facts are just the opposite. Travelling officials from Washington usually arrive in a haze of jet lag. They need to know what day it is, the latest developments on issues that concern them, who they will see, what they are supposed to say, how local leaders will respond, and what their responses will really mean. The ambassador's job is to know the answers, guide the visit, and help the visitor be successful in furthering US interests.

Vice President Dan Quayle visited the Philippines in 1989. Just as he was about to arrive, NPA hit men assassinated two US military contractors as a gesture of welcome, sacrifices on the altar of US-Philippine relations. Briefed on arrival, he and his staff, in a state of shock, sought guidance on how to proceed. We advised him to leverage the tragedy to emphasize the closeness of ties with the US and the importance of the bases. He made special calls at our bases and on families of the victims as well as conferring with President Aquino how best to manage an awful situation. We prepared a special "pothole memo" to help him deal with the most difficult questions the press might throw at him. He followed the advice to the letter. Quayle proved much smarter than his press notices. His movie star good looks enabled him to sail past ambush interviews with the ladies of the palace press corps, who could be vicious. Quayle left the Philippines having made a strong positive impression. We had done our job.

Leaving a Legacy

Ambassadors' legacies depend on the history they share with the countries where they serve. I saw the Philippines through nearly four turbulent years of restoring democracy after decades of dictatorship. My instructions were to support the process without looking like I was doing very much. That proved impossible. To find out what Filipinos remember, ask our classmate Jaime Zobel de Ayala, whom I never knew at college but became a close friend after living through our years in Manila. I was only in Pakistan about a year, but experienced the impact of the end of Soviet rule in Afghanistan on local and international politics. Zambia under Kaunda, where I learned how to be an ambassador, was the Geneva of Southern African politics.

These are topics for other books. In truth, legacies are not as much the stuff of daily worries for ambassadors as are those discussed in this paper. These are what face us getting through the days, weeks and months of our assignments, as we work to advance US interests, stay in charge and stay alive.

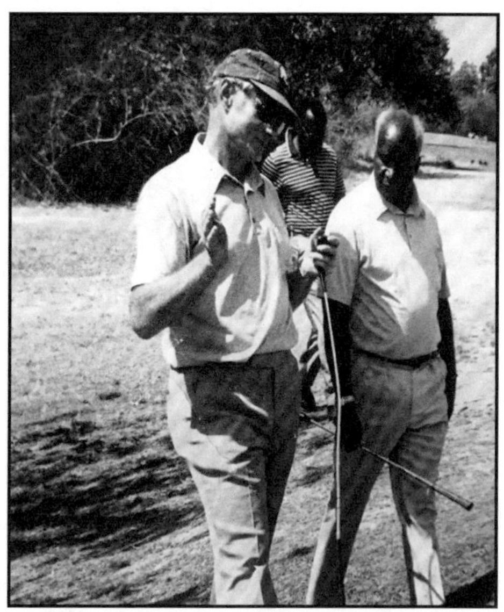

Figure 5.1.2.1 *1983—US Ambassador to Zambia Nicholas Platt discusses policy with Zambian President Kenneth Kaunda*

Figure 5.1.2.2 *1988—US Ambassador to the Philippines Nicholas Platt in the White House with President George H. W. Bush*

Foreign Service

Diplomacy

Figure 5.1.2.3 *1983—Platt in Zambia*

Nicholas Platt has spent most of his life working on relations between the US and Asia. Thirty-four years as a career diplomat, culminating in service as US Ambassador to Zambia (1982–84), the Philippines (1987–91), and Pakistan (1991–92), were followed by 12 years as President of the Asia Society, beginning in 1992. He became President Emeritus following his retirement July 1, 2004. Since 2011 he has advised the Philadelphia Orchestra on China Programming.

Ambassador Platt's involvement with Asia began as a student of the Chinese language in Taiwan in the early '60s, and continued with Foreign Service assignments in Hong Kong (1964–68), Beijing (1973–74), and Tokyo (1974–77). In 1972 he accompanied President Nixon on the historic trip to Beijing that signaled the resumption of relations between the United States and China. He was one of the first members of the US Liaison Office in Beijing when the United States established a mission there in 1973.

He served in several capacities in Washington, including Director of Japanese Affairs, National Security Council Staff; Deputy Assistant Secretary of Defense; Acting Assistant Secretary of State for UN Affairs and Executive Secretary of the Department of State. He and wife, Sheila, have three sons and eight grandchildren.

"Multilateralism Matters"

Luigi Einaudi

Introduction

My career, a mix of teaching, research and diplomacy, is extensively detailed in our many class reports. Since retiring from the State Department in 1998 and completing my elected term of office at the Organization of American States (OAS) in 2005, I have split my time between Italy and the United States, and since 2007 have been a fellow at the Institute for National Strategic Studies at the National Defense University.

The essay that follows is based on my remarks accepting the *2016 William J. Perry Award for Excellence in Security and Defense Education* at a ceremony held at Fort McNair, Washington, DC, on January 12, 2017. Sponsored by the Center for Hemispheric Defense Studies, the award ceremony symbolized State-Defense cooperation by including Ambassador Thomas A. Shannon, Undersecretary of State for Political Affairs, and was attended by some 200 persons, including some 40 US and foreign ambassadors and flag officers.

* * *

I am proud to accept this award. I met Bill Perry when he was Secretary of Defense, and have just finished reading what he calls his "selective memoir". With a forward by my old boss George Shultz, Perry writes how honored he was to have this Center named for him, and makes a passionate plea to eliminate nuclear weapons before they eliminate us. It is a good read, and I recommend it.

My values have been shaped by a belief in Western civilization. That bold phrase *Civis romanus sum* (I am a Roman citizen) is its cornerstone. I was born in the United States and am a citizen of the United States alone. But I believe the rights and obligations of citizenship that began in Rome are at the heart of mankind's progress.

Diplomacy Today and Tomorrow—The OAS Example

I would like to share some thoughts about where we are now and what may lie ahead.

Foreign Service

Diplomacy

The last 20 years or so have been hard on the international order. So much so that disorder increasin*gly seems a better description.*

> The current *Foreign Affairs* asks whether the situation should simply be seen as "*Out of Order*". Governing has become harder and more complicated. Citizen demands for a better life have grown, but disparities in power and cultural differences have not been erased; in some cases, they have sharpened.
>
> World War II ended with winners and losers; the Cold War had blocs and anti-blocs; in contrast, with what has been called the "*end of ideology*", shared reference points and perspectives are fewer than ever.

These conditions hamper international understanding and disrupt long-held concepts. My professional career has focused on United States relations with countries in the Western Hemisphere. In my service on the Policy Planning Staff for Secretaries of State from two different parties, I always tried to see our neighbors in the Americas in a global context.

In that spirit, I will use the Organization of American States, the world's oldest regional organization, to exemplify the difficulties of today's international scene.

The OAS is a multilateral organization of the sovereign states of the Western Hemisphere. This simple definition combines three concepts.

- Multilateralism, based on "generalized principles of conduct"—the creation of predictable universal rules rather than a temporary coalition of a few countries on a specific problem.
- Sovereignty, the sovereign equality of states, the organizing principle of the international system since the 1648 Peace of Westphalia.
- Geography, as in the proposition that "the peoples of this Hemisphere stand in a special relationship to one another which sets them apart from the rest of the world".

Today, these three concepts are all operationally challenged.

> ***Multilateralism*** is associated with inefficiency more than order. International law has been weakened by repeated failures to ratify treaties or abide by their obligations. A cynic might argue that multilateralism is now just an idealistic illusion in an increasingly Hobbesian world.

> ***Sovereignty*** has long meant that individual states are inviolate from outside intervention and free to decide whether or not to participate in any particular activity. The problem is that our times *require* cooperation. Cyberspace, illegal drugs, weapons from small arms to drones and nukes, migration, terrorism, disease, climate and most economic activity cannot be dealt with by any one state acting alone. Does this mean *sovereignty is obsolete?*

Finally, in the age of the jet and the Internet, ***does geography still matter?*** Twenty years ago, a senior administration official told me flatly that geography was no longer relevant to foreign policy.

My colleagues at the Perry Center and the National Defense University are among those who know better. *War is intimately related to sovereignty, geography and even multilateralism.*

> The *League of Nations* was created to end war but had no military authority.
>
> The *United Nations Charter* authorized the use of force in Chapter VII.
>
> The *OAS Charter* purposely conveyed no coercive authority.

These formulas are all incomplete. *Neither force nor diplomacy can work alone.* What is needed, of course, is to *integrate* the various elements of power.

> You can't say "*We'll deal with this militarily, or just economically, or just diplomatically.*"
>
> You can't say "*We'll deal with this multilaterally, that bilaterally, and this unilaterally.*"

Major problems require the application in some form of *all elements of power, civil and military, hard and soft, multilateral, bilateral and unilateral*.

Integrating Power

Trying to integrate power by making the inter-agency system work is how I survived in Washington. My mentors at the State Department all served on the National Security Council. One of them conditioned his acceptance of becoming Assistant Secretary on also chairing the NSC Inter-Departmental Group, then promptly appointed me its Executive Secretary. Years later, in 1995, when I was asked to represent the United States in the effort to end fighting between Ecuador and Peru,

I did the same thing so as to have the authority to team with US Southern Command.

In a dispute that went back to colonial times, 5,000 Special Forces soldiers from the two countries had become entangled in mountainous jungle terrain. To prevent escalation, Brazil, Argentina, Chile and the United States—all guarantors of an earlier treaty—contributed soldiers to a military observation mission, known as *MOMEP*, to separate forces and give diplomacy a chance.

My counterparts from the *guarantor countries*, all of us senior diplomats, and I would share intelligence, listen to each other's views and meet until we hammered out a course our governments could all support. We approached things from different perspectives and different interests. But the give-and-take was mutual. Often our *guarantor meetings* led to a course different from anything any one of us had started with.

> One example was our decision to invite Peru and Ecuador to send soldiers to join the observation mission, a potentially risky move, but one designed to build confidence between the antagonists and demonstrate our position as honest brokers.
>
> Another was our decision to ask our four guarantor presidents to consult and reach a joint decision on issues the two parties felt they could not resolve themselves.

Whenever innovations like these took place, interagency coordination was key to keeping Washington (and of course the other capitals) in sync as well. Sometimes I felt as though I was dealing with two wars, one abroad, and the other here at home.

> The NSC had initially authorized the military deployment for a maximum of 90 days, fearing that any US military casualties in the Amazon would lead to a political backlash at home.
>
> Others feared MOMEP would drag our forces into a Cyprus-like eternal deadlock. Each 90-day extension had to be approved—and each approval was won only because State and Defense kept on the same page.
>
> The *peace agreements* ultimately *settled the land boundaries* at the origins of the conflict, but extended also to *river navigation, trade, parks, burial of casualties, human rights, and economic development.* It took almost four years, but we succeeded where few believed we could.

The peace between Ecuador and Peru has now lasted almost a generation. It resolved the last active territorial conflict on the South American mainland and removed the arms race contagion in the region. *Conventional war among states in the Americas today is almost unthinkable.*

Security

In this lower threat environment, collective security obligations have given way to a concept championed initially by the countries of the Commonwealth Caribbean that security should be understood as "*multidimensional*". This approach expanded security concerns from traditional defense matters like weapons acquisitions and confidence building measures to trafficking in persons, drug abuse and the special security concerns of small island states.

Yet even with this more consensual approach, security and defense matters remain problematic. Uncertainty about military and police roles creates confusion. Asymmetries in power breed illusions and distrust. Tensions among neighbors still flare up. The end of the Cold War reduced but did not eliminate concerns about the activities of countries outside the hemisphere. The variety and complexity of contemporary security issues makes clear that no one policy fits all. Every country has tended to set its own course. Nothing is automatic.

Principles of Diplomatic Strategy

So what should we do in the midst of this uncertainty?

First, multilateral consultations should be part of any strategy.

Multilateralism was the core of the international order the United States led in creating after World War II. The United States today is more focused inward and faces competition from many quarters. The multilateral order has eroded, and US participation has been reduced. Yet even when agreement is elusive, broad consultation can reduce confusion and set the stage for future cooperation.

> The excellent lead article in the *Foreign Affairs* issue cited earlier calls for a system of "Sovereign obligation" to deal with the world's growing common problems. I was amused, however, that the author suggests the United States consult only half a dozen "other major powers". I was delighted to read that the powerful have obligations as well as rights. But in my experience, *democracy is as important among countries as within them.* If smaller countries do not receive respect, they are unlikely to be part of the solution. Democracy is as important among countries as within them.

Our Founding Fathers set a good example in our *Declaration of Independence*: "*a decent respect to the opinions of mankind*" requires that all be heard. Idealism quite aside, success is harder if you don't consult.

Second, respect the law and support local institutions.

In the Peru-Ecuador conflict, the Rio Protocol authorized the guarantors only to "assist" the parties, not to decide. Peru and Ecuador had to agree; and a Terms of Reference had to be negotiated for the military observers. Once the rules were agreed, however, everything could be dealt with.

> Early on, MOMEP helicopters maneuvering to find ways to separate the hostile intertwined forces found that they had been locked in upon by radar that could have targeted them for being shot down. Later, both parties at different moments secretly built up fresh forces near the conflict area. Both activities were in contravention of explicit agreements and when discovered were reversed.

Using the law gradually enabled the parties of peace within Peru and Ecuador to seize the initiative. A key dispute was resolved by a panel headed by the Chief Justice of Brazil's Supreme Court. That Chief Justice, Nelson Jobim, later became Brazil's Minister of Defense. Jobim received the Perry Award in 2011.

But just as the peace between Ecuador and Peru was proving the value of the law, the *United States Senate stopped ratifying key international treaties.*

> We have not ratified the global *Law of the Sea*, even after it was re-written to help meet US objections.
>
> We have also not ratified *conventions* that advance US regional interests in *human rights* or in fighting drugs by *controlling illegal firearms.*

Laws are obviously not self-enforcing, but they do provide agreed goals legitimating international cooperation. Sandra Day O'Connor summarized the consequences of US absenteeism:

> "*The decision **not** to sign on to legal frameworks the rest of the world supports is central to the **decline in American influence in the world**.*"

In 1991, OAS Resolution 1080 established common grounds for *action against interruptions of the democratic process.* But it also called for proposals and *incentives to support democracy*, a call that was never followed up with resources or specifics.

The current tragedy in Venezuela is due to failures in implementation by the member states, starting with Venezuela, rather than to a failure of multilateralism.

> The Inter-American Charter stipulates in Article 3 that the "*essential elements of representative democracy include, inter alia, respect for human rights and fundamental freedoms, access to and the exercise of power in accordance with the rule of law, the holding of periodic, free, and fair elections based on secret balloting and universal suffrage as an expression of the sovereignty of the people, the pluralistic system of political parties and organizations, and the separation of powers and independence of the branches of government.*"
>
> Despite the clarity of the language, specifics are still subject to interpretation and challenge. What is striking is that no serious independent multilateral effort has been made to reconcile differing interpretations or to seek ways to reward good performance.

Much the same principle should apply to other hot-button issues like *migration* and *trade*. Sovereign nations have the right to decide who and what enters and leaves their territory. A wall that channels people and goods to an entry/exit point at which clear rules are enforced is fine, but if the wall is breached or circumvented, or if there are no rules, even a beautiful wall becomes a Maginot line, impressive but ineffectual.

The world needs laws and relationship-building, not walls or nation-building. Lectures and barriers are less effective than relations built on respect and shared rules. Nothing will last unless all concerned feel at least some of their interests are being advanced.

Which brings me to my third and last point:

Prepare professionals to cooperate across cultures.

Even if interagency differences were all miraculously resolved here in the United States, we would still need to work efficiently with other countries.

To reconcile different national interests requires knowledge. Institutional ties maintained by a network of professionals who know how to work together can help contain issues that might otherwise escalate into conflict—in effect, a valuable insurance policy for progress and peace.

> Bill Perry understood this. As Secretary of Defense in the years after the fall of the Berlin wall, he supported the establishment of the *Marshall Center* in Germany to help military and civilian officials from both NATO and the Warsaw Pact learn to work together. And because he understood that geography matters, he then supported the creation of similar centers for other parts of the world.

The *Center for Hemispheric Defense Studies* or CHDS, now known simply as the Perry Center, has an *international faculty and students*, ties to countries and institutions large and small, and an annual fall program that examines US security and defense structures and policy.

For years, the graduates of the *Inter-American Course in International Law* in Rio de Janeiro and of the *Inter-American Defense College* here at Fort McNair have had enviable records.

Between them, the OAS and the Perry Center are forging relationships and cadres of public servants who can help turn a difficult world to mutual advantage. They provide a unique foundation for a safe neighborhood.

And this brings me to a personnel recommendation.

In this increasingly disorderly world, we in the United States might do well *to link cultural sensitivity and knowledge of how to make things work to eligibility for promotion*. In 1986, the Goldwater-Nichols Act established that to be eligible for promotion to General or Flag Officer, a military officer had to have both senior education and a completed Joint Duty Tour. Stealing a page from Goldwater-Nichols, might *a tour in the UN, the OAS, the IMF, or some other international organization become a requirement for promotion to the Senior Executive Service and the Senior Foreign Service?*

Summing Up

Times have changed, but some old truths still apply. *Geography* and *neighborhood* still matter. *Sovereignty* still matters. Yet in today's world, we can no longer retreat like Voltaire to cultivate our own garden. To take care of ourselves, we must also deal with the outside world, our neighbors perhaps most of all.

In international politics and security, there is no MapQuest to click for directions. There is just a lot of time-consuming and necessarily inclusive hard work. It will not be easy.

The logo at the bottom of the Perry Center's crest—***Mens et Fides Mutua*** (**Mutual Understanding and Trust**)—has guided the Center during 20 years of progress.

It must continue.

Figure 5.1.3.1 *The intimate relationship between law, multilateralism and cooperation was symbolized in this 1992 Headquarters Agreement signing giving the Organization of American States (OAS) legal status for the first time since its founding in 1948. Ambassador Luigi R. Einaudi* (left)*, Permanent Representative from the US to the OAS, and Ambassador João Baena Soares of Brazil, Secretary General of the OAS, are shown signing the agreement at the OAS Main Historical Building in Washington, DC. The Headquarters Agreement set forth the legal status of the OAS properties and employees in the US.*

Courtesy of Columbus Memorial Library, Organization of American States

---

Luigi R. Einaudi, drafted into the Army after graduation, returned to Harvard for his PhD and taught at Harvard and Wesleyan before joining the RAND Corporation for 11 years, teaching also at UCLA. Einaudi joined State in 1974 on Henry Kissinger's policy planning staff. For 15 years he coordinated policies toward Latin America, then became Ambassador to the OAS in the successful effort to extricate the United States from the Central American wars. In 1995–1998, he led the peace talks that settled Ecuador and Peru's centuries-old territorial conflict. In 2000, Ambassador Einaudi became the first US citizen elected to office in the OAS, then served as Acting Secretary General in 2004–2005.

He has been a Distinguished Visiting Fellow at the National Defense University in Washington, DC, a member of the Council on Foreign Relations and the American Academy of Diplomacy. A former fellow (1980–81) at the Woodrow Wilson International Center for Scholars, he is now on the board of its Brazil Institute.

In retirement Einaudi has taught at Georgetown, Cornell, the National Defense University and the Woodrow Wilson Center's Brazil Institute. He and his wife, Carol P. Einaudi, Esq., have four children and ten grandchildren. They live in Washington and Italy, where he writes and teaches for the Fondazione Luigi Einaudi in Turin.

Diplomacy, Peace Corps

Three Great Jobs

Charles Steedman

USS *Cacapon* (AO-52)

As I walked up Divinity Avenue our second day at Harvard, I had no intention of joining NROTC. My father, being afraid I would be drafted out of college, pressured me to join. I did want to follow the example of seven cousins who had served in WWII by joining the Navy but after graduation. Reluctantly, I agreed to talk to NROTC. Lieutenant Bellinger, a naval aviator just back from flying combat missions in Korea, interviewed me. I don't remember what was said, but he impressed me greatly. I made a bad impression because I didn't want to join. In dismissing me, he said, "*Steedman, if you decide to join, there is a sign-up book in the passageway, but I will do my best to forget your name!*" I raced out and signed up.

The fall of sophomore year I tried out for *The Crimson* and was fortunate to become an editor. Surrounded in the newsroom by very talented future journalists, I thought I wanted to be one too, after I got out of the Navy. Joining the Navy via NROTC was one of three best decisions in my life. I was assigned to a ship with terrific officers and a good crew, USS *Cacapon* (AO-52). If the name doesn't resonate, it is because she was a fleet oiler, a tanker, whose job it was to fuel other ships at sea. It was the working, "blue collar" Navy. We had a job to do and we did it.

After six weeks of training in San Diego I reported to the ship in Long Beach, California, her home port. Immediately I was invited for coffee in the wardroom by two ensigns. They asked me where I went to college. "*Harvard,*" I said. They gave me a blank look. "*Where is that?*" one of them said. "*It's in the East,*" I weakly replied, puzzled. Ernie Kolowrat (Yale) and Doug Stafford (Cornell) laughed. The joke was on me. The three of us, along with Jim Piper (UVA) and Jack Binns (Annapolis) became great friends. Since the mid-'90s we and our wives have had a reunion every year, along with Harvard NROTC classmates Ed Burlingame, Peter Swords and their wives.

The first few evenings on *Cacapon*, as I sat at the wardroom table, presided over by the Exec, LCDR Bliss, a jovial former merchant mariner, I thought I was going deaf. I couldn't understand the swift exchanges whizzing around the table. It was all inside talk about people and places I didn't know, but soon I caught on. This was a very comradely group of a dozen officers who could let loose in the absence of the skipper, a captain, who ate alone in his stateroom one deck above. Our wardroom included five junior and five older officers who had each been to sea over more than 20 years. The Exec was one. The others had risen through the ranks to become warrant officers (with a specialty) or a line officer. They connected us to WWII. One of them, Tom Gorman, the Bosun, had been a shipmate of Samuel Eliot Morison. In class I called Morison "Professor"; the Bosun called him "Sam".

One might expect some tension between the old salts and the green ensigns. (At officers' call, where we lined up by seniority, the Exec, seeing ensigns jostle, would say, "*Seniority among ensigns is like virtue among whores!*") In fact, the old salts took us under their wings, coached us, became good friends and made us better officers. We got along famously. I wish someone had recorded the joking, the kidding, the repartee, the story-telling that went on around that table. Our closeness mattered during the five months in 1958 we spent in the Marshall Islands as the refueling ship for *Operation Hardtack*, which conducted nuclear bomb tests. We witnessed several tests from about 20 miles away. The only time we got off the ship was for two hours on rare afternoons. We rode a LCM landing craft to Enyu Island, a tiny speck in Bikini Lagoon consisting of sand and a few palm trees. We could play volleyball, swim in the lagoon inside shark nets, or drink. We drank.

When we were at sea, we were all business. As the communications officer, I was in charge in charge of radiomen, quartermasters, electronics technicians and signalmen. I was also the cryptographer, coding and decoding encrypted messages in a tiny, locked space. The chief radioman and I were the only ones allowed. Since the captain couldn't enter, I posted a sign inside the door: *Illegitimi Non Carborundum*.

I was also officer of the deck (OD) during underway refueling, a process that could last up to three hours. At an appointed time *Cacapon* went to a designated spot and headed into the wind at 12 knots. Over the horizon came combat ships. Carriers and cruisers went alongside to port and destroyers to starboard. Our desk crew threw lines across with a "monkey fist" and after the lines would flow cables and hoses—four to port for carriers and two to starboard. As we refueled ships, we played music on loudspeakers ("China Night" was a favorite) and flew our "house flag"—a rooster chasing a hen with our motto underneath: "*Find 'em, Fuel 'em, Forget 'em.*" That is what we did.

I stood countless four-hour bridge watches as OD. *Cacapon* steamed independently, so one officer could handle it, and ensigns could qualify rather quickly. It was a sobering responsibility to stand 12–4 a.m. and 4–8 a.m. watches when every other officer was asleep. We hated to think of the result if our miscalculation caused a collision at sea since the ship contained highly volatile aviation gasoline up forward. Once, on a mid-watch in the East China Sea, we were steaming at our full 16 knots in a pea-soup fog. The captain wanted it that way. The radar was working, he said, but I had nervous moments as small fishing boats swarmed around the ship and some bounced along our 553-foot hull. There were times as OD when mini-crisis seemed to follow mini-crisis, and in the middle of it a seaman would ask permission to dump trash and garbage!

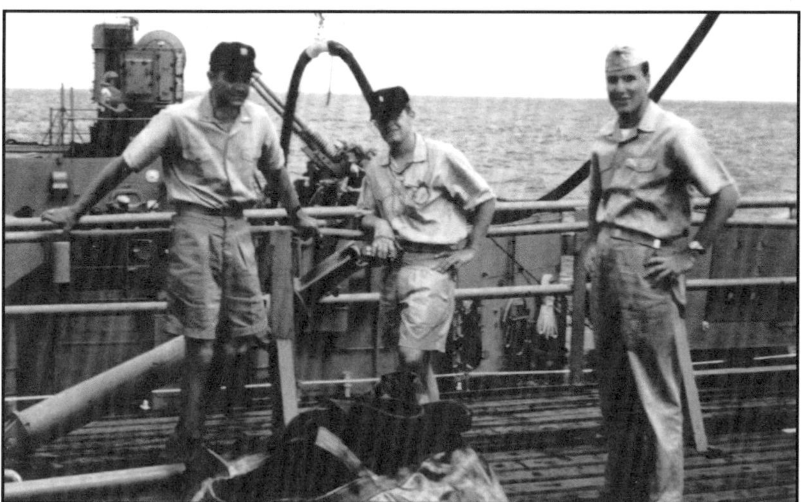

Figure 5.1.4.1 *Charley Steedman* (right) *on the deck of* Cacapon *near Bikini atoll in 1958 with fellow officers Ernie Kolowrat* (left) *and Jack Binns* (center). *A destroyer being refueled is in the background.*

In 1959 we sailed to Japan, Okinawa, and the Philippines, spending a lot of time in and out of Sasebo, Japan. The country charmed me when I went ashore. Ernie and I took leave to travel by train to Tokyo, Kyoto, and Nagasaki. Being in Japan got me thinking about being a foreign correspondent when I got out of the Navy. Then I read *The Ugly American* by Lederer and Burdick. Suddenly I thought that I should try to do something for our country overseas rather than write about what others did. I decided to take the Foreign Service written exam in December 1959.

After living on the ship for over 21 months, it was time for release from active duty. I sailed back to San Diego on a destroyer escort. The wardroom atmosphere on that ship was depressingly far from the camaraderie we had on *Cacapon*. I realized how lucky I had been. I made lifelong friends, gained self-confidence and could be proud that I served, following the tradition of my cousins. We had sea duty in a time of peace, but we did a fine job fueling ships that stood ready if combat were ever required.

The Foreign Service

To pass the written exam I had to fill some gaps in my education such as economics. An academic year at the London School of Economics and Political Science (LSE) definitely helped me pass the written and oral exams. Waiting to be called to Washington, I got a part-time job as research assistant at the new Harvard Center for International Affairs. Very happily for me, Julie Solmssen was assistant librarian at the center.

I became a Foreign Service Officer (FSO) five days after John Kennedy's inauguration. Kennedy believed that working for the government was an honorable profession, which made my entering class proud to become FSOs. Very different from what it must be today, our class consisted of 29 white males and one white female. Fred Shoup '57 was also a member of that A-100 class. Julie and I were married in July, two months before we left for the Philippines, my first post.

We enjoyed the Philippines and Filipinos. I did consular work in the embassy, mainly in the passport and citizenship office and then in charge of helping American citizens in trouble. Asia was appealing but my interest was turning to Africa, where a number of countries had just achieved independence. Several of them were former French colonies, and French was my foreign language.

When the Peace Corps began in 1961, I was already an FSO. One day my Filipino consular section colleague and I drove our jeep into the tiny town of Baguio on the very northern tip of Luzon. At the entrance to the town a large crowd of citizens greeted us with enthusiasm. They thought we were the Peace Corps arriving! We were sorry to let them down, but it sparked an interest in what Peace Corps was doing. When we left Manila in 1963 I had been assigned to study African languages at the Foreign Service Institute and then to report to the embassy at Bamako, Mali, the following year.

US Embassy, Bamako, Republic of Mali

My position was economic and consular officer in the embassy. Diplomats from communist countries, however, wondered if I were with the CIA. The new CIA station chief, Clair George, had arrived a week ahead of me in August 1964, using "economic officer" as his cover. He was duly introduced as such to the foreign ministry and other embassies. About to depart was his predecessor, whose cover was "consular officer". When I made calls on officials, some said, "*We just met the new economic officer! Who are you?*" The Soviets were confused enough to invite me to a stag "spook party" where the guests were intelligence types from various embassies.

In fact I had a great diplomatic job in an interesting country at a fascinating time. Mali had been independent barely four years. The French colonial types had left en masse, along with Lebanese merchants. All the communist countries were represented but there were only four embassies from the West. Mali had "taken its socialist option" and was introducing government control of essential commercial activities, even though it had virtually no capacity to do so. I started reporting to the State Department on the economy and on the aid projects of communist countries. To divine what China was doing, I conferred with my Soviet counterpart because neither of us could talk to the Chinese. I traveled alone in the countryside as often as the ambassador would let me. Once I was told by an official, "*you can't go there because no one speaks French.*" I was able to reply in Bambara that I could manage.

Mali's landlocked isolation had gotten worse two months after independence in 1960. The country's federation with Senegal collapsed, and the Senegalese cut the vital rail line from Dakar to Bamako, eliminating foreign trade through the port for a few years. Mali itself then withdrew from the French franc zone, creating the Malian franc, which was worthless outside the country. What was the result? Once a month, the one "modern" food store in Bamako received a small shipment of butter, cheese and other edibles that non-Malians liked. The Soviets always knew in advance. Soviet wives were the first to line up. Basics like hardware weren't available either. I got to play soccer (badly) with young men from the native *quartier* where Julie and I lived, because I bought a soccer ball for them in Abidjan, Ivory Coast, when I went there to buy basic hardware for the embassy. In a country crazy about soccer, soccer balls were unobtainable.

Conditions at the embassy were much simpler and more open than they are today. When I arrived there wasn't even a receptionist at the front door of our quaint former French bank building. The next year a young Malian was posted there to direct visitors. After a US ambassador was slain in Sudan a few years later, however, Marine guards arrived and security got much tighter.

My office was moved to the second floor next to that of Clair George as the embassy began to send Malian soldiers to the US for flight training in C-47 aircraft. They needed visas. Sergeant Ba of the Malian Army would bring two or three at a time to my office to get them. I didn't think much of it at the time, but Sgt. Ba would slip out while I got busy with passports. It turned out he was an "asset" for Clair and was going next door. The Malian government soon discovered it, and Clair was given 48 hours to leave the country. His career prospered, but Sgt. Ba was not so lucky. He got sealed orders to take to the Army's desert outpost in Kidal. The orders were to execute him on arrival.

It was heady stuff, working in a brand new country that was cozy with communist countries but was full of solid, hard working, friendly people. Chilly official relations did not get in the way of cordial private ones. Julie and I made a great friend in a young school teacher. When I went back to Mali a few times in later years as a consultant, Mamadou Sacko insisted that I spend as much time as possible in his compound, eating from a common bowl with him and his wife, or just sitting of an evening with him and his friends, drinking strong mint tea.

Peace Corps/Chad

After serving in Mali, I became Mali desk officer in the State Department. I saw Mali from a different angle and had a chance to work collaboratively with colleagues in the US Agency for International Development (USAID), the Pentagon, Treasury and other departments. I even chaired a low-level negotiation session with Malian officials. I spent a night in the Department's Crisis Center when a fluke communications failure caused Sekou Touré, the president of Guinea, to cancel PanAm landing rights in Conakry, make the Peace Corps leave the country within 48 hours and incite a mob to invade the embassy and sack the ground floor of the ambassador's residence.

In early 1968 friends at Peace Corps headquarters told me that the agency was looking for staff with experience in French-speaking Africa. Encouraged by them, I obtained an interview. C. Payne Lucas, the charismatic head of the Africa section, liked my resumé and said Peace Corps could "borrow" me from State for three years. I would spend six months in the Francophone Africa division and then have a normal 30-month tour as deputy director in a French-speaking country. State was happy to let me go. Classmate David Rakov was already in the division when I joined.

After six months under Bill Tatge, the best boss I ever had, I suddenly found myself director, not deputy, in Chad. That was because no one with qualifications wanted to go to a country bordering Libya and Sudan, where the first director had been removed for gross incompetence the year before. The current Volunteers (PCVs) had also resisted a nominee for director who had run their training program in Louisiana, and who, when he was sent out to conciliate them, refused to admit he had made any mistakes. He withdrew his candidacy, and Peace Corps was left with me, *faute de mieux*.

Figure 5.1.4.2 *Charley Steedman, Peace Corps Director for Chad, lending a hand to a well-drilling team in southern Chad, 1971*

This was the most exciting and best job ever. Here I was, 33 years old, in a vast, poor country in the middle of Africa where 45 Volunteers were widely scattered. My staff consisted of a deputy and a doctor. A new doctor, Dr. Jerry Morey, who had abandoned his Park Avenue surgery practice to help Peace Corps, soon arrived. Jerry was a wonderful person, warm and friendly, older and wiser than the rest of us. My deputy, John Eriksen, a former PCV in Niger, became my best friend and was really a co-director. Most of the time one of us was traveling to visit PCVs while the other manned the fort in, yes, Fort Lamy. We could only fly to the towns in the desert north because they were surrounded by rebels. Some PCVs were living on the sand dunes next to Lake Chad, in miniscule villages whose inhabitants spoke only Kanembou. We got there by driving a Land Rover six or more hours, at the end going up one sand dune and down another.

Several PCVs were English (TEFL) teachers, assigned singly to small towns, many in the south. Others were on well-drilling teams working with Chadian counterparts to install hand-pump tube wells in villages to provide clean, easily accessible water. Some Volunteers trained school teachers to teach health classes. A few worked on small-scale irrigation. Nurse Volunteers trained Chadian nurses in Fort Lamy. One PCV worked in the Ministry of Planning.

A serious constraint was funding. The Chadian government had very limited budgets. In those days Peace Corps, as a matter of policy, did not provide funding for things like vehicles, equipment and construction. The host government had to do that. We badly wanted to work with the Chadian agricultural extension service, for example, but could not because they had no budget for it. The PCVs themselves got around on motorbikes, which Peace Corps did provide. They had a lonely existence in small remote towns. There were no laptop computers or cell phones to allow them to connect with the outside world, let alone our office in Fort Lamy. We communicated by letter and telegram. Peace Corps gave each of them a "book locker" with paperback versions of various classic titles. They had to immerse themselves in local culture, speak the local language and entertain themselves, all on a meager "living allowance". Peace Corps also put aside $75 for each month of service, paid on completion.

The group we had in Chad was remarkable in their ability to adapt, do their job and persevere in difficult circumstances. We often found that, once the initial newness and excitement of being "on the frontier" had given way to routine and hardship, morale dipped markedly, and PCVs wondered if they should "terminate early". However, we also found that if PCVs stuck with it and got into the second year, their morale rebounded, and they often had a great year. I have the greatest respect, admiration and fondness for those who served in Chad. For many of them their experience in Chad changed their career paths. A number have been quite successful and/or dedicated themselves to serving others. Today, almost half a century since we all were in Chad, a large group of those who served in the 1968–72 time period are in frequent touch with each other through an e-mail list. We have had two great reunions.

As director I worked with Chadian government ministers, prefects, sub-prefects, ministry officials, school superintendents and principals, even the president himself on one occasion. John Eriksen, Dick Wall—who later joined us as a TEFL expert—and I got to know the countryside quite well. We all have many stories to tell. Jim Diamond wrote a book, *I Did What I Had to Do!*, about the incredible things he and his wife, Betty, did in the president's village. In his thirties, Jim had been a sheep farmer, livestock judge and vocational agriculture teacher. He thus had farming and livestock skills to go with an enthusiastic, outgoing personality. His French was not very fluent, his Sara Madjingay basic, but Chadians hung on his every word. Despite much skepticism, he successfully introduced pit silos that provided great silage for farm animals at the height of the dry season at virtually no cost. He later became a professor at Penn State as well as a consultant to several developing countries.

In 1970 I visited TEFL teacher Steve Boswell in Faya Largeau, a tiny oasis in the Sahara. The only way I could get there was via a French military plane. With the rebel situation deteriorating, the French Foreign Legion had recently arrived to help in northern Chad. I called on the prefect, whom I had known as director of public health. He told me he was being relieved by a Chadian Army colonel, who wanted me to come for dinner that evening. I misunderstood the time and got there half an hour early. The colonel graciously came out to sit with me in the very dark, large courtyard. He asked if I had heard the mourning cries from the market. I had. "*If it is just vengeance for a killing,*" he said, "*it is normal, but if it is not . . . .*" At that point I looked through the darkness of the courtyard to the exterior wall and could imagine rebels aiming their guns at the colonel and me! However, the lights soon went up, the other guests arrived and we had dinner.

After I left Chad, rebels did shoot their way into Faya. While I was still there, they shot their way into Am-Timan, a tiny town on the Sudan border. We telegraphed Ray Bilodeau, a TEFL teacher, to come immediately to Fort Lamy. Ray was an incredible teacher. When I visited his classroom I was amazed by the excitement he inspired in kids learning *English* in a remote corner of Chad. He was furious that he had been called in. He said he was fine, the rebels had left and he wanted to get back to his students!

It wasn't all about rebels when I was in Chad. In fact, as I left in 1971, the government seemed close to peace with the rebels. However, Libyan secret agents were caught in Fort Lamy not long afterward. The president became paranoid, turned violently on his closest colleagues and was overthrown in 1973.

The excitement and challenge of working at ground level with people in a developing country spoiled me. I wanted to do more of that. After a year back in the State Department, I was offered the position of deputy director for Africa in charge of programs and training in Peace Corps headquarters. The Peace Corps Act limited staff to five years of service so as to avoid having the permanent bureaucracy. Hence I would be allowed only two years on top of my previous three. Despite this restriction, I resigned from the Foreign Service and took the job in mid 1972.

The Nixon White House did not like Peace Corps. They decreed that country directors had to be registered Republicans and claimed that Peace Corps staff, which probably leaned 90 percent Democratic, did not know how to manage. Republicans did. Senior staff in headquarters turned Republican. New "experts", having no clue what PCVs actually did, wanted to micromanage them through quantitative methods. As a result, I decided I had to protect PCVs and field staff from Washington meddling.

Near the end the second year a chance phone call offered me an opportunity to get an MA in economics while working half-time at a research center at the University of Michigan. The center had grants, and later contracts, from USAID that focused on French-speaking Africa—just what I wanted. Our family spent 17 wonderful years in Ann Arbor, a great place to raise a family. I was 39, yet daughter Sarah asked me what I was going to do when I grew up! It turned out to be managing as well as doing research on economic development, particularly agricultural development, in Africa. I had no formal education in agriculture but managed to lead teams that did sector assessments and to do a number of consulting assignments for the World Bank and USAID. I spent time in every West African country but Sierra Leone and in East and Southern Africa as well. Mali and Madagascar were my favorites.

Charles Steedman became assistant director of the University of Michigan's Center for Research on Economic Development in 1977. He managed field research in Africa under USAID contracts and on occasion led or participated in consulting missions in French-speaking Africa for USAID and the World Bank. Most assignments focused on agricultural sector development, but he also led teams designing renewable energy projects in the late '70s. On a two-year leave of absence he managed a $24-million USAID rural development project in Senegal, 1980–82. For seven years he taught a development economics course for Michigan undergraduate and graduate students. He also co-directed a summer seminar on development economics for mid-career French-speaking Africans during which he taught macro economics in French. He left the center in 1993 to join the international consulting firm ARD, becoming senior vice president.

In 2002, he retired to York, ME, where he has been president of the historical society, a member of the land trust board and chair of the elected town budget committee.

Figure 5.1.4.3 *The Peace Corps*

Established on March 1, 1961, by an executive order signed by newly elected President John F. Kennedy, under its first Director, R. Sargent Shriver, within six years 14,500 volunteers were serving in programs in 55 countries.

Source: https://www.peacecorps.gov/about/history/founding-moment

International Law

From Exploding Beer Bottles to the International Court of Justice

Charles N. Brower

I was always interested in politics and international affairs.

The two mentors of my early life—my father, a giant of the advertising business, and my first Government Honors Program Tutor, George W. Jaeger, who as an early teenager in Austria was put on the Quaker-organized 1930s "*Kindertransport*" to England—were of immense influence. Knowing of my father's friendship with the then junior Senator from our home State of New Jersey, Clifford P. Case, from the time the two were classmates at Rutgers University, George said "*Why don't you ask your father if he can fix you up with a summer job with Senator Case?*" Why hadn't I thought of that? So I asked, and the summer of 1956 in Washington, DC, in the Senate was an unforgettable, eye-opening experience. At the end of it I said to myself, "*I just know I will be coming back here some day!*"

Weighing Career Choices

By the time of our graduation I had passed all of the exams for entrance into the United States Foreign Service, but was able to defer it for the year I then spent in West Germany on a Fulbright Scholarship. Along the way, however, I was persuaded to enter Harvard Law School by those two mentors. My father said, "*The CEOs of all of my clients are lawyers. If you go to law school you can do anything: politics, the Foreign Service, business, whatever you want.*"

George, who had spent four years as a civil servant in the State Department before seeking his PhD at Harvard, said: "*Look! We have been living through the McCarthy era, and a lot of bad things have happened to good men in the Foreign Service as a result. I think you should do well in the Foreign Service, but you should get either a PhD or a law degree so that if something bad happens to you, you will have alternatives.*" (George was doing just that, and following Harvard enjoyed a long and successful career in the Foreign Service.) I took my mentors' advice.

Finishing "The Law School" I was still interested in the Foreign Service. I had, however, the opportunity to join a famous Wall Street law firm, now White & Case LLP. Since I had not served in the military and in June of 1961 was "draft proof"—I turned 26 a week before our graduation, thanks to the US Government-financed Fulbright Scholarship year in Germany, and no draft board in the country was taking anyone over the age of 25—I figured, "*I'd be foolish not to punch this ticket for two years, and at 28 I'll not be too old to enter the Foreign Service.*" So off to Wall Street I went.

Claimed by "The Law"

In short order Holmes' "*jealous mistress*", "The Law" had me locked in its embrace. I fell in love with litigation, trial work, appeals, cross-examination, etc. And so I became a general commercial litigator trying cases in the State and Federal Courts of New York City, never traveling beyond Schenectady to the North, Philadelphia to the West, and Washington, DC, to the South, for eight years.

Hence the "*exploding beer bottles*" of the title, against which personal injury claims I defended Anheuser-Busch and the F. & M. Schaefer Brewing Company. Also defamation cases for Dun & Bradstreet and McGraw-Hill. You name it, I did it. Also Federal Court assignments to front-page indigent criminal defendants: a black Catholic yeoman first class with 17 years' service in the Navy indicted for conspiracy to commit espionage for the Soviet Union, and the 1950's "*Wizard of Wall Street*", the greatest stock fraud artist of that era. No international litigation, as there was none in that era.

Testing Politics

Politics in New Jersey called, too, and by the time Nixon was elected in 1968, I had held elective municipal office as a "*liberal Republican*", been a member of the Republican County Committee and was well wired, and totally eager, to return to Washington, DC, as I had sworn to do a dozen years before. Seeing that all the Nixon appointees had worked as youngsters in the Eisenhower Administration, I judged that "*It was now or very likely never.*" While I was campaigning for something in the State Department, the law firm made me a partner. In the meantime, our classmate Wilmot R. Hastings, until then Deputy Attorney General of the Commonwealth of Massachusetts, had followed his Attorney General, Elliot Richardson, to Foggy Bottom, the latter becoming what is now known as Deputy Secretary of State. "Will" was quite instrumental in my landing there. So, four months after becoming a partner in my firm I resigned to join the State Department.

The State Department

State and DC were the beginning of the rest of my life. I was lucky to acquire two mentors in the State Department, the first being John R. Stevenson, the Legal Adviser of the Department, who hired me and advanced me by leaps and bounds. Thanks to him, apart from the four years' service (1969–1973) there, first as Assistant Legal Adviser in charge of European Affairs, then as Deputy Legal Adviser, and finally as Acting Legal Adviser, I fulfilled certain White House functions, was seconded to the Secretary of Commerce to negotiate with the Soviet Union, lobbied Congress extensively and altogether acquired a very wide-ranging experience. I loved every minute of it.

That total experience, however, completely overcame my earlier interest in elective political office. Having seen so much of the world of foreign affairs and the operations of the Executive Branch, I knew that I would never be satisfied in elective office, e.g., in Congress. Too little knowledge of what actually happens in foreign affairs, too little intellectual content, all for too little pay, and, not being a Rockefeller, too much financial dependence upon others. Thus we sold the home in New Jersey, choosing to practice in Washington, DC, again and always with White & Case LLP, and to be as involved in both international affairs and politics as opportunities would present themselves.

Thanks to the other mentor I had gained at the State Department, David M. Abshire, who had come into the Department as Assistant Secretary for Congressional Relations while I was there, having founded the Center for Strategic and International Studies, I became a member of the President Ford Political Strategy Team at the 1976 Republican Convention and also handled some litigation brought against the President.

When President Reagan was elected in 1980 I was made a member of his State Department Transition Team.

The Hague and International Arbitration

Ultimately, in 1983 I was appointed by the United States as Judge of the *Iran-United States Claims Tribunal* in The Hague, which Tribunal was a key element of the "*Algiers Accords*", which released the 52 American hostages held for 444 days in Tehran just at the moment that President Reagan was being inaugurated.

Since 1983 I have alternated full-time service on that tribunal with part-time service, while pursuing an active and successful career as international judge, advocate before international courts and arbitral tribunals, and international arbitrator.

In 1987 I was called to the White House to serve as Deputy Special Counsellor to the Cabinet-rank Special Counsellor to President Reagan, the same David M. Abshire, with the mission to advise Reagan personally as to how to politically survive the Iran-Contra affair cooked up by Oliver North and Admiral Poindexter.

I have served as Judge *ad hoc* on the Inter-American Court of Human Rights, have argued before the International Court of Justice, and currently am serving as Judge *ad hoc* on the International Court of Justice ("The World Court").

I have learned that The Rule of Law is essential to civilized life, and that **The Rule of International Law is essential to such peace as humanity is capable of achieving**. That is the dream I have pursued.

The lessons to be passed on to the next generation from all of this?

I. Have, if you can, *a dream, a passion, a guiding star*, and always, always follow it. Anything less is just "a job."

II. Never forget, however, that *the journey itself is the constant reward*, in the pursuit is the happiness.

III. Don't listen to anyone who says, "*It's not what you know, but who you know.*"

It's both. If you don't have the goods, no introduction will get you anywhere beyond the threshold.

But having the goods and knowing, or getting to know, people whose appreciation of your work will motivate them to advance you are both critical to your progress towards achievement of your goal.

IV. *Achieving your dream requires four things:*

(1) Intelligence and the gifts to employ it wisely;

(2) Hard, and even harder, work (no one achieved anything without a lot of hard work, some of it certainly unpleasant);

(3) A sharp eye for opportunity; and

(4) Luck, which is heavily dependent upon coincidence—being in the right place at the right time with the required skills and attributes—and which therefore may never come your way.

Charles Nelson Brower received his Harvard Law School degree in 1961, following a year in Germany on a Fulbright Scholarship. He then joined White & Case LLP in New York City. Four months after becoming a partner in 1969 he resigned to spend four years in the Department of State, concluding as Acting Legal Adviser. Thereafter he co-founded the Washington, DC, office of the same firm. In 1983 he was appointed by the Reagan Administration a Judge of the Iran-United States Claims Tribunal in The Hague, taking leave in 1987 to serve in the White House as Deputy Special Counsellor to the President. After resigning from the Tribunal in 1988 he rejoined his firm in Washington, DC. In 1999 he was appointed Judge *ad hoc* of the Inter-American Court of Human rights.

In 2000 he was reappointed to the Iran-United States Claims Tribunal by the Clinton administration, where he serves still, while acting also as Judge *ad hoc* of the International Court of Justice (the "*World Court*") and frequently as international arbitrator. He has been awarded numerous national and international honors.

Foreign Affairs—Middle East

Concerning Colonial Settler States and Ignoble Wars

Lessons from Algeria

Clement M. Henry

We were the "*Silent Generation*", as our class editors note, "*our silence and obedience . . . [being] in contrast to the political and social uproars of some other generations*", because, born shortly before the proclamation of the American Century in 1941, we grew up in a comfortable bipartisan consensus of liberal internationalism.

We were also the Cold War generation. The Iron Curtain descended on Eastern Europe during our pre-teens, dividing the world into the children of light and the children of darkness, and the United States was on the right side of history, the unquestioned leader of the Free World. We graduated at the height of America's postwar power as true believers in a beneficent liberal world order led by the United States.

Youthful Hubris

Upon graduation I immediately in the summer of 1957 joined a special seminar on international student relations conducted by the United States *National Student Association* and, after attending *NSA*'s national congress in August, became its representative in Paris focused on our bilateral contacts with overseas student associations, principally those from France's African colonies.

Algeria was a particular focus of attention. As a sort of junior ambassador I felt I was contributing my share to the Cold War, contesting international Communist influence over Third World students by offering our support in their struggles for national self-determination. Clandestine financing from CIA did not disturb me; quite the contrary, secret financing by an agency apparently run by former student leaders confirmed that we were on the right track, ahead of our official diplomacy paralyzed even after the Suez crisis between support for our traditional NATO European allies and our classic Wilsonian ideals.

The only American public figure of note to be supporting the Algerian revolution in 1957 was Senator John F. Kennedy. I was proud to be following his footsteps and contributing at the NSA congress to drafting a resolution on behalf of Algerian students.

Expelled from France

The day after Christmas, 1957, I represented NSA at the annual congress of the *Fédération des Etudiants d'Afrique Noire en France (FEANF)* and gave my first formal speech in French.

One talking point was to express NSA's solidarity, shared with FEANF, with all the students suffering under the yoke of colonialism, and notably the Algerians. In keeping with the "*syndicalist*" or trade union traditions of national student associations, I had to embed any political stances in material or academic student concerns. Consequently I spoke of the "*ignoble consequences of French colonialism*" for the rights of Algerian students as well as expressing my sympathies with their aspirations for independence.

About two weeks later, the French police knocked on my door in the winter darkness at 8 a.m. They drove me down to police headquarters where the supervisor politely told me that I had abused French hospitality and had 48 hours to leave the country. It seems it was that term *ignoble,* reported in a brief excerpt of *Le Monde,* that did me in.

To me the term *ignoble* was just a throwaway, a term I had heard before that sounded good in French. I should have remembered from a course I had taken a year or two earlier from Louis Hartz, "*Democratic Theory and its Critics*", that only Americans laugh at ignobility: for lack of a feudal past we are blessed to be liberal in the tradition of John Locke.

I spent the rest of the academic year in London but kept up with the Algerians. Shortly after my expulsion the French authorities dissolved their student association, and so in London we organized an international meeting in solidarity with the Algerians and in protest against the arbitrary infringement of their right of student association.

On a personal note, I decided to turn down my admission to the Harvard Law School, already postponed by a year, and enroll instead in graduate school to pursue studies of North African politics. Upon completing my PhD dissertation field work in Tunisia I was finally able to drive my VW across North Africa just a couple of weeks after Algerian independence in the summer of 1962. With me, working on his dissertation about Tunisian labor, was Eqbal Ahmed, who would become a brilliant public intellectual and activist against the war in Vietnam.

Modernizing Vietnam by Carpet Bombing?

Eqbal and I already knew by 1962 that South Vietnam was a lost cause.

Algerian nationalists, inspired in part by the French defeat at Dien Bien Phu in 1954, had just won their war against far greater odds. Unlike distant Vietnam, which had attracted relatively few French settlers, Algeria had been part of France, occupied in 1955 by well over one million settlers out of a total population of almost ten million.

The fact that the Vietnamese nationalists were also Communists was unfortunate from my Cold War perspective but did not justify the massive increase in American troops on the ground in 1965, comparable in my mind with the futile French mobilization of some 600,000 conscripts to fight for "*French Algeria*" in the late 1950s. As an assistant professor at Berkeley I joined many of my colleagues and students protesting against the war in the mid-1960s.

I also worked with Samuel P. Huntington on a conference and eventually a book about the evolution of established single-party systems despite being appalled by his argument, stated in a different context, that the United States was contributing to the urbanization and hence modernization of Vietnam by carpet bombing, forcing its peasants into internment camps.[1]

Arab-Israeli Wars and Post-1967 Attrition

From studying and writing about Algeria and Morocco as well as Tunisia, I moved to the American University in Cairo in 1969 in time to witness some of the speeches and then the funeral of Gamal Abdel Nasser. Only then did I become particularly concerned about another colonial settler state, Israel.

In my NSA year of student politicking, the Middle East had been off limits. In Tunisia, too, where I spent two years doing field work, my Tunisian friends, under the spell of President Habib Bourguiba, used to view Egypt and its Arab neighbors to the East as "*oriental*" and politically as well as economically underdeveloped. In June 1967 the

Democratic and Popular Republic of Algeria even broke off relations with Egypt (as well as the United States) for surrendering to Israel.

Once in Cairo, however, I was exposed to Egyptian perceptions of the Arab-Israeli conflict and began to see the Middle East differently. Israel seemed less like the embattled little democracy depicted by American media. It had invaded Egypt twice, once in 1956 and again in 1967. In 1956 President Eisenhower had obliged Israel as well as Britain and France to withdraw from all their occupied territories, whereas in 1967 President Johnson permitted Israel to keep the territories occupied as a result of the Six-Day War, pending negotiations that have never concluded.

Israel's West Bank and Gaza: A Colonial Settler Mini-State and Open-Air Prison, Respectively?

I left Cairo in 1973, before the outbreak of the October (Yom Kippur) War. While Egypt and Israel eventually made formal peace, the Palestinian-Israeli conflict persists. Fifty years after the Israeli occupation of the West Bank and East Jerusalem in 1967, the territories are peppered with illegal settlements, transforming these parts of Palestine into a mini colonial settler state reminiscent of French Algeria.

Although they withdrew their settlers from Gaza in 2005, the Israelis asphyxiate its 1.8 million inhabitants, most of them refugees from the 1948 war, with a tight blockade and periodic bombardments, sometimes casually referred to as "*mowing the lawn*", with American-supplied F-16s.

The entire area of the former British Mandate of Palestine consists of Israel, Gaza, and the occupied territories of the West Bank and East Jerusalem. Just about half the population is Jewish, the rest being Arab, including Christians as well as Muslims and Druze.

Without any two-state resolution of the Israeli-Palestinian conflict the whole area will in time come demographically to resemble other colonial settler states, with a minority of Jews, the huge majority of whom immigrated to Palestine after 1882, dominating a Palestinian majority. Jimmy Carter and others call it apartheid.

America's Military Overreach in Punishing Aggressors: Parallels between 1950 and Desert Shield

I am concerned not only about America's blind support for Israel, intensified by our new president who apparently endorses Israel's illegal settlement building on occupied territories, but also about the growing militarization of US foreign policy.

It began well before September 11, 2001. When Saddam Hussein occupied Kuwait on August 2, 1990, the United States chose to eject him by force rather than encourage an Arab political solution that would have taken into account some of Iraq's legitimate grievances in exchange for military withdrawal. It is clear from George H.W. Bush's memoirs that he was determined on principle to prevent any Arab compromise short of unconditional Iraqi withdrawal from Kuwait.

On reading these memoirs recently, I remembered another story about the dangers of American overreach, using military force to punish aggressors. Professor McGeorge Bundy lectured us in his US foreign policy course at Harvard about how Truman had unnecessarily extended the Korean War by two years. After brilliantly cutting off the North Korean invaders, who had occupied all but the southern tip of Korea by June 1950, General MacArthur pushed beyond the 38th parallel into North Korea, reaching the border with China to punish the Communists for their aggression. Consequently the Chinese intervened to push the United Nations forces back to a long see-saw struggle around the 38th parallel.

As the appalling events of 9/11 demonstrated, military overreach had consequences. Osama Bin Laden committed his atrocities in response to "*Desert Shield*", the huge American military buildup in Saudi Arabia in 1990 followed by "*Desert Storm*". He also claimed, "*The Palestinian cause has been the main factor that, since my early childhood, fueled my desire, and that of the 19 freemen (Sept. 11 bombers), to stand by the oppressed, and punish the oppressive Jews and their allies.*"[2]

Not only America's invasion of Iraq in 2003 but also unrelenting support for Israel has turned much Arab and Muslim public opinion against the United States. Our "*soft power*" has become negative, in the sense that violent fanatics are able to mobilize support for their insurrections by deliberately attacking our citizens abroad to provoke US counterattacks.

We fell into the trap of generating further support for these fanatics. Perhaps inadvertently, we also armed ISIS by supporting our allies in the region, notably Saudi Arabia and Qatar. Furthermore we have become accomplices in the Saudi destruction of Yemen. Who knows what backlashes these involvements may provoke?

"*America First*" for War against Islam?

Today much is yet to be seen about President Trump's policy in the Middle East and more broadly. But the indications are worrisome. I worry about President Trump's apparent intentions to support Israel unconditionally, settlements and all, further alienating Arab Christian as well as Muslim public opinion. "America First" should stop all aid to Israel if the latter's leadership persists in building settlements in East Jerusalem and on the West Bank.

I worry even more about never-ending wars in the Greater Middle East. Reading *The Field of Fight* by National Security Adviser Michael Flynn and Michael Ledeen, I am reminded of Sam Huntington's culturally parochial *Clash of Civilizations*, now being reduced to real war. As I write, President Trump in his first week in office has issued a reckless Executive Order suspending the entry of Syrian refugees and of other people literally in midair coming from certain Muslim majority countries.

How better to confirm the propaganda of Bin Laden's successors that America is at war with Islam?[3]

Clement M. Henry, who at Harvard and until 1995 wrote under the name of Clement Henry Moore, has written extensively about political development, the engineering profession, and financial institutions in various parts of the Middle East and North Africa over more than five decades. After receiving his doctorate in political science from Harvard in 1963 he taught at the University of California, Berkeley until 1969 when he joined the American University in Cairo (AUC). He returned to the United States just before the October War of 1973 to teach at the University of Michigan, where he also obtained an MBA that enabled him to direct the Business School at the American University of Beirut from 1981 to 1984, at the height of Lebanon's civil war. After serving as visiting professor at UCLA and *Sciences Po*, Paris, he taught at the University of Texas at Austin from 1987 to 2011.[4]

Just retired, he returned during the Arab Spring to AUC to chair its political science department until 2014, when he took up a research professorship at the National University of Singapore, completed in May 2016.

Endnotes

1 Samuel P. Huntington, "The Bases of Accommodation", *Foreign Affairs*, Vol. 46, No. 4 (Jul., 1968), pp. 642–656. Our co-edited book, *Authoritarian Politics in Modern Societies: The Dynamics of Established One-Party Systems* (New York: Basic Books, 1970), may still have some relevance to China and some of its neighbors.

2 "Bin Laden: Palestinian Cause Prompted 9/11", CBS News, May 16, 2008: http://www.cbsnews.com/news/bin-laden-palestinian-cause-prompted-9-11/ (accessed Jan. 31, 2017). Further evidence of the salience of the Palestine issue is revealed in his lengthy "Letter to America", *The Guardian*, Nov. 24, 2002: https://www.theguardian.com/world/2002/nov/24/theobserver (accessed Jan. 31, 2017). See also Thomas Hegghammer, "Osama bin Laden's True Priorities", *The Guardian*, Dec. 3, 2007: https://www.theguardian.com/commentisfree/2007/dec/03/ osamabinladenstruepriorities (accessed Jan. 31, 2017).

3 As reconfirmed after I wrote these lines, in "Trump Pushes Dark View of Islam to Center of US Policy-Making", *The New York Times*, Feb. 1, 2017.

4 Biography of Clement N. Henry: http://liberalarts.utexas.edu/government/faculty/henrycm; http://www.la.utexas.edu/users/chenry/public_html/vitae.html.

Figure 5.3.1.1 *Arab scholars at an Abbasid library in Baghdad. Maqamat of al-Hariri. Illustration by Yahyá al-Wasiti, 1237*

The House of Wisdom (Arabic: بيت الحكمة *; Bayt al-Hikma) was a major intellectual center during the Islamic Golden Age.*

During the reign of al-Ma'mun, astronomical observatories were set up, and the House was an unrivalled center for the study of humanities and for science in medieval Islam, including mathematics, astronomy, medicine, alchemy and chemistry, zoology, and geography and cartography. Drawing primarily on Greek, but also Syriac, Indian and Persian texts, the scholars accumulated a great collection of world knowledge, and built on it through their own discoveries.

By the middle of the ninth century, the House of Wisdom had the largest selection of books in the world. It was destroyed in the sack of the city following the Mongol siege of Baghdad (1258).

Text: https://en.wikipedia.org/wiki/House_of_Wisdom
Image: https://en.wikipedia.org/wiki/File:Maqamat_hariri.jpg

People-to-People; Private/Public Partnership

Marshall Plan – Study Tour Experience in Ukraine

Leland "Lee" Milnor Cole

Ukraine

For the past few years, Ukraine has figured prominently in US and world affairs. Originally, Ukraine was a province of Russia—in both the Russian Empire and the Soviet Union. The word Ukraine means "borderland" in Russian. The Russian Premier Nikita Khrushchev, who came from Kharkiv, later established Ukraine as a separate Republic. With the fall of the Soviet Union in 1991, Ukraine became a separate nation and not a legal official part of Russia. Ukraine inherited Crimea and its warm water ports. Many Russians still consider Ukraine as a part of Russia—including Vladimir Putin!

Cincinnati—Kharkiv *Sister City* Project

In 1993 my previous employer was no longer in business and I was asked to head up the Business Committee of the Cincinnati Kharkiv Sister City Project. This group was already actively engaged in people-to-people exchanges between citizens of Cincinnati and Kharkov, the second-largest city in Ukraine. They were both manufacturing cities of similar size situated in agricultural regions. Cincinnati business people had tried to conduct business in Ukraine after the fall of the Soviet Union, but the cultural and business climates were just too different. We needed a different approach!

The Marshall Plan—Still Alive and Active

Then I read an article in *Foreign Affairs Magazine* entitled "Jump Starting Ex-Communist Economies" written by James M. Silberman and others. It suggested a Marshall Plan program. I contacted Mr. Silberman and soon visited him in Washington to discuss the details. We ended up laying out an approach which we were to follow over the next several years.

The first step was to verify that the Marshall Plan approach could be used effectively in Ukraine. We received a small grant from a Foundation in New York which provided funds to enable Jim and me to visit Kharkov for three weeks. We were warmly welcomed by the local government officials and received a great deal of publicity. No doubt, the government expected us to bring significant funding—which of course we did not. During that trip we visited many Kharkov businesses and learned how business was currently conducted. It was significantly different from business as practiced in the "West", and it was immediately apparent that a significant Marshall Plan Program was badly needed. We prepared a report outlining these findings and submitted it to USAID.

On our first trips to Ukraine, the spoken and written language was Russian. On subsequent trips, the official language became Ukrainian—the language spoken in Western Ukraine. Many Easterners did not like the change—it was tolerable but a constant source of irritation. The only way it affected us was that in Russian there is no letter "i", while there is in Ukrainian. Thus, Kharkov became Kharkiv. This is how we could distinguish between the languages—despite not being able to read either.

Over the next few years Jim Silberman and I worked together very closely. We traveled together to Ukraine and Germany. We stayed at each other's houses and had many interesting discussions.

Figure 5.4.1.1 *Author Leland Cole* (left) *with Marshall Plan mentor James Silberman in Kharkov/Kharkiv*

After World War II, Jim Silberman was working at the US Department of Labor Statistics in Washington, DC, and had been asked to join the Marshall Plan project as the head of the Technical Assistance Program. The Marshall Plan Program consisted of two main parts: *Capital Assistance* and *Technical Assistance.*

> ***Capital Assistance*** was the most famous and the costlier component at 98.5% of the total program cost of over $12 billion. The US sent grain, steel, foodstuffs, and other raw materials to Europe, which had been devastated.
>
> ***Technical Assistance*** brought over 24,000 business leaders to the United States on 5,000 study tours. They were to learn how to manage and grow their industries. At a subsequent meeting of many European participants in Cambridge, MA, it was stated that the Technical Assistance and Capital Assistance programs had equal impacts on the European economy!

During Jim's early experiences with the Marshall Plan Program, the overall head was Paul Hoffmann, who had worked at Chrysler. Early on, Jim was sent by Hoffman to Europe to study the condition of their economies. In France, he eventually became known as the "*Father of the French Supermarket*" and received the French *Legion of Honor*.

Jim was also sent to England to study their post-war industry. There he visited many companies and industries. He was not impressed! Before returning home, he was invited to meet Prime Minister Bevan, who asked for his impressions. Jim told him that British Industry was in very bad shape and without a massive re-training program, there was little hope for Britain. Bevan replied that he would not accept that report, and that Jim should not give it to Hoffman. Bevan also said that Britain would NOT participate in any subsequent technical assistance program.

Upon Jim's return to the US, he met with Paul Hoffman and gave him the original report and Bevan's response, saying that they would not need to participate in the Technical Assistance Program.

Later, after Marshall Plan funding had been approved by Congress, funding started to be distributed. Soon thereafter, Hoffman received a phone call from Bevan saying their funding had not yet been received. Hoffman said it must have been a clerical error. The second month, when funds again did not arrive in Britain, Hoffman told Bevan he would check into it. Nothing arrived! The third month Britain accepted the Technical Assistance Program, and funding started to arrive. So much for the need for any high-level diplomacy.

When we think of the Marshall Plan program, we tend to assume it applied only to Western Europe. Actually, it had been offered to many different countries, including Japan, India, Iran and others. Russia was also invited to participate, but Stalin turned it down.

A few years later, after the Marshall Plan had proven to be so effective in resuscitating post-war recoveries, while in the lavatory in Vienna, Jim was approached by a Russian. Stalin has changed his mind and wanted the program! Jim reported the approach to his superiors in Washington, and the request was ignored. Years later, Jim and associates did propose the program to Russia, and it was turned down by Russia. My organization, the Center for Economic Initiatives *(CEI)*, later also proposed a similar program to Russia, and it was also ignored, with no reasons given.

Creating the Cincinnati-Karkiv, Ukraine Marshall Plan Program

Our first step was to find funding for such a program. We were fortunate to receive backing from Charles Flickner in the House Foreign Affairs office in the Capitol and whom Jim had met earlier. House Report 106–254 was issued, and we received a USAID grant for two initial study tour programs: *Meat & Dairy* and *Fruit & Vegetables*. In the meantime, in Cincinnati we had re-organized our business group as the Center for Economic Initiatives *(CEI)*. On our Board of Directors I was the President and Jim Silberman was a Director.

Several of us then returned to Kharkiv for the selection of participants for the first two study tours, assisted by a local company we had hired. During this trip, I was approached by a local government official saying that he needed to select half the participants (no doubt so he could extract bribes). I told him that we would lose the grant if that happened. He tried valiantly to get me to change our position, but in the end, we were successful in avoiding government "assistance".

One of our major objectives was to select people who could make a difference after they returned home. This meant business owners, managers, etc. USAID also suggested we select 50% women. This was difficult to do in a male-dominated society, although we did have some success. As for overcoming the language barrier, we made extensive use of interpreters, since only a few of the Americans spoke Russian or Ukrainian.

Needs Assessment through Study Tours

Each study tour included 16 participants and one interpreter. This was the largest practical group size. One person was selected as Group Leader or spokesman. The tour groups traveled first from Kharkiv to Kiev in Ukraine, and then by US carrier to Cincinnati. The groups always traveled within the US by bus, from Ohio to Iowa to New York, and all places in between.

Meanwhile, back in Ohio, CEI selected a Tour Director who arranged the tours and made all the appointments. Fortunately, US businesses were very interested to meet the Ukrainians and to learn about this former Soviet country. No doubt, some hoped to do mutual business, but this seldom happened. Differences in language, time zone, telephone/Fax communications, and business practices were too great at that time. With the passage of time, all these problems have been overcome and future study tour projects can look forward to great success.

The Study Tour Program focused on *Management, Technology* and *Marketing,* as improvements in all three areas were badly needed in Ukraine. Here are some examples.

> ***Management.*** In the Soviet Union, there was little or no formal Management education. Management was generally on-the-job training, so management skills were missing. On study tours where Ukrainians visited the US, these differences became apparent to them by meeting, observing and talking (though interpreters) with American managers.
>
> ***Technology.*** Most participants had received technical training in Ukraine. However, several were heard to say, "We knew how to do that at home, but had never thought of doing it that way". An example was a Keebler biscuit factory in Cincinnati, where they saw long production lines turning out crackers and biscuits. In Ukraine, most meat and other food products were sold in the open market.
>
> ***Marketing***. This was the area with the largest differences. When we first went to Ukraine, markets were regional—often limited to their immediate city or town. No one we met sold throughout the region or nation. We asked them about advertising. They explained that advertising was only used to dispose of defective goods. This contrasted with street cars that were emblazoned with logos of international firms such as Lucky Strike, Camels and Marlboro. Milk was delivered in olive-drab Army surplus trucks with the word "Milk" (in Russian) hand painted on the side. Bakery trucks said, in Russian, "Bread"

We explained that a truck was a moving billboard and should be used as such. Eventually we started to see this change in Ukraine—and it is now universal!

Figure 5.4.1.2 *Ukranian bread delivery truck, labeled in Russian, "Bread"*

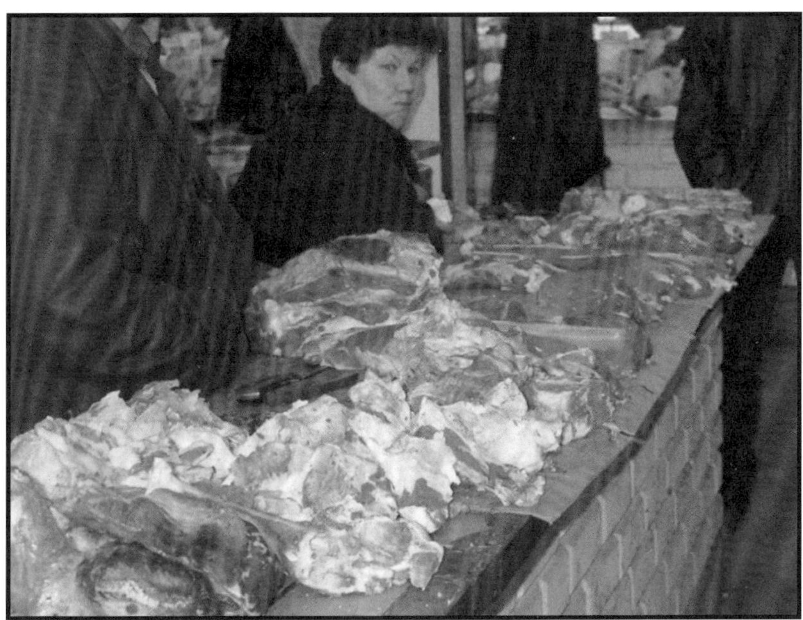

Figure 5.4.1.3 *Typical Ukranian meat market*

At the end of each study tour we met individually with each participant and the interpreter. That was when we learned about their greatest benefits from the US tour. For example, on the Construction tour they liked best the organization of the work site. In Kharkiv, they might have had up to 50 people on a construction site. It would take months to construct a typical building. In the US, there were usually only five workers, and they finished the job significantly quicker. And the cost/benefits were obvious!

Expanding the Kharkiv Program to Include Chernobyl and Slavutych

The initial grant program was targeted at the city and region of Kharkiv. However, part-way through the program, it was extended to include Chernobyl and the neighboring residential city of Slavutych.

For obvious reasons, Chernobyl was a priority for the US government as they tried to rebuild the area after the 1986 disaster. There had been four nuclear reactors, and number four had blown up, contaminating the entire area. Housing for the remaining workers was critical. When we were there, over 5,000 workers were still employed. We were carefully screened for radiation when entering and leaving the area. It was very interesting to see the wildlife in the area, since no-one was permitted to hunt or harvest radioactive items. Carp, growing in the lake at the Power Plant, grew up to six feet in length! Numbers on our wrist watches began to glow again!

Past Industry-Focused Programs and the Future

We had a total of 17 study tours—two of which were from Chernobyl. The others were from the Kharkiv Oblast (Region). The following industries were included in the program.

Agriculture: Grain Production, Livestock Production, Aquaculture, Meat & Dairy Production, Fruit & Vegetable Production, Bakery

Heavy Industry: Agricultural Equipment, Household Goods, Information Technology

Construction: Building Design and Construction (Chernobyl), Interior Design

CEI has capabilities to implement study tours in additional areas of Ukraine and former Soviet states and many developing countries in Africa, Latin America and Asia.

Program Evaluation and Return on Investment

Six months after the Study Tour participants returned home, CEI personnel visited Ukraine to meet with the participants to learn and document the program benefits. Before they returned home, we had encouraged each participant to disseminate the information they had gained. We found they had written papers, given lectures and some had even developed a website. Each had passed the information learned on to over 300 others in their industry.

We also organized reunions of participants so they could exchange experiences. The participants all welcomed us back and were anxious to show us the changes they had introduced. We saw new products, new marketing methods, and organizational changes.

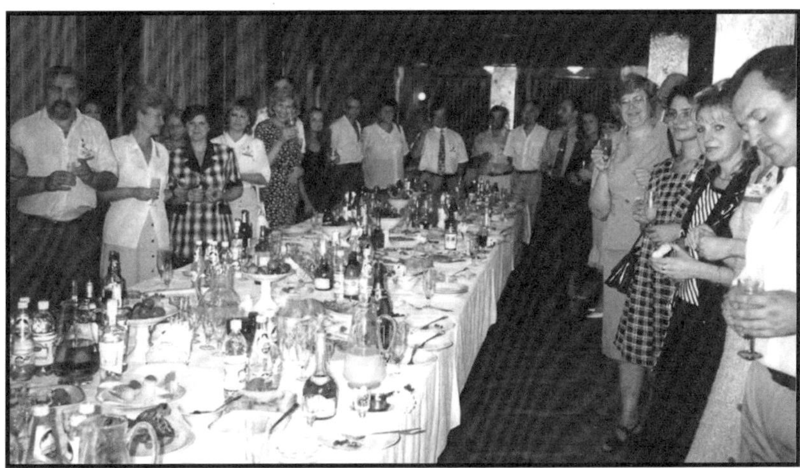

Figure 5.4.1.4 *Study Tour follow-up and reunion in Ukraine*

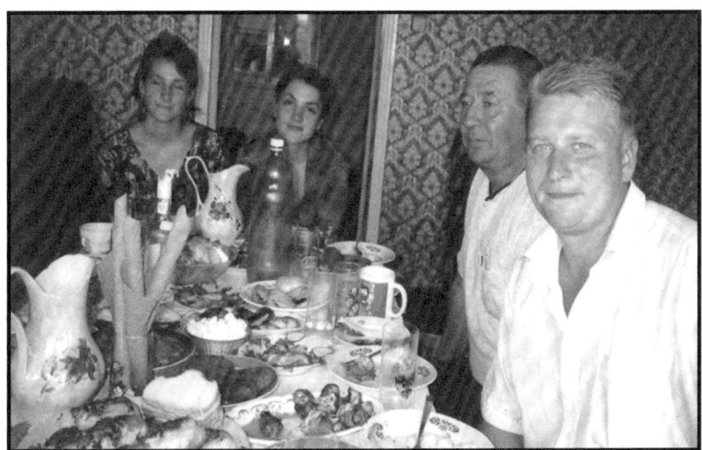

Figure 5.4.1.5 *American evaluators entertained by Study Tour participants in their homes*

Frequently we were invited into their homes to meet the families who were anxious to meet their first "American" and to ask questions about life in America, including schooling, and other activities. The only downside was that we drank too much vodka!

Of course, we documented all our findings in Tour Reports to USAID, which influenced how much funding the program would continue to receive.

In assessing the results of USAID's investment in our Ukraine Marshall Plan, we found the cost/benefit ratio was over 18 to1, based on sales, cost decreases, profit increases, and productivity increases as provided by each of the participants. In fact, we believe 18:1 may be the highest benefit figure in Ukraine when compared with a 10:1 figure calculated by the US Government's SABIT program. While we were active in Ukraine, and based on Ukraine government figures, the Kharkiv region moved in rank from number 16 to number 3 in agriculture. This was due to several factors, including the introduction of soy farming and no-till farming for grain and wheat.

Beyond the economic benefits to Ukraine, the Marshall Plan program generated a great deal of good will for the United States, and members of CEI and others in US gained many long-term friends in Ukraine.

Summing Up

The long-standing Center for Economic Initiatives (CEI) Ukraine-focused Cincinnati-based program has been a great success! We provided significant cost and revenue benefits to Ukraine. We helped individuals and firms who participated. This Marshall Plan Program for Ukraine was also in our national interest by bringing these benefits to Ukraine and not just by being "nice" and helping people. It brought the two countries and peoples closer together.

Life in Ukraine in recent years has not been easy, and continuation of support of Marshall Plan programs such as this one is urgently needed. CEI is still actively seeking new funding for additional study tour programs. I have stepped down as President, but remain active on the Board as Treasurer.

Leland M. "Lee" Cole after graduating with a BA in Applied Science from Harvard in 1957, he and classmate Bart Hoebel drove to Alaska. Afterwards he joined Honeywell's aeronautical division before the Government decided missiles would replace airplanes. At Cincinnati Milling Machine Company, now Milacron, he learned computer programming, received an MBA from Xavier and became manager of Milacron's computer department. Later, he set up the Computer Programming Department in Biggleswade, England, and undertook additional marketing responsibilities.

"After eight years in England, we returned to Cincinnati. Milacron exited the computer industry, and I joined Sentinel Computer as VP, International Marketing, traveling around the world several times and meeting several significant clients. Later, the Cincinnati-Kharkiv Sister City organization asked me to head its business operation. This became The Center for Economic Initiatives. As President, I ran Marshall Plan type study tours. We received USAID and World Bank grants to assist Ukraine, Moldova, and Kazakhstan."

In 2012, Lee became treasurer of CEI and also concentrated on his genealogy and giving associated talks. He and Carol Cronk married in 1958 and have three daughters and four grandchildren.

Figure 5.4.1.6 *The Marshall Plan—Birth of a peaceful Europe*

*George C. Marshall (*third from right*), honorary degree recipient on June 5, 1947 with Gen. Omar N. Bradley and Sen. James W. Wadsworth at Harvard Commencement, stands in front row next to Harvard President James B. Conant (*center*).*

In his 11-minute speech, US Secretary of State and retired five-star general Marshall outlined the United States post-WWII European Recovery Program, soon known as the Marshall Plan, which over the next four years delivered economic assistance approximating $122 billion in 2017 dollars to participating European nations, stabilized their economies, laid the foundation for the European Union and for prosperity with security for war-torn Western Europe.

Reprinted with permission, *Harvard Gazette*

Private Citizen in Foreign Affairs

Preventing a War

Excerpt from his book, *Memories*[1]

David N. Levinson

The Call

The phone call came from Moscow as I was sitting in my chair in the insurance commissioner's office in the state of Delaware.

It was from Dan Koch, an extraordinarily capable member of my staff at the insurance department, who was in Moscow as part of an adoption program being established by my department and the Pearl Buck foundation.

Our department was also writing the insurance regulatory codes of Russia, Latvia, Estonia, Ukraine, and Romania just as the Soviet Union was breaking up.

Dan said, "Commissioner, you have to get on a plane right away and come over here. There has been an attack by the Russian troops in Lithuania on a television tower. There is talk of a conflict, perhaps war breaking out as Russia tries to regain the Baltics, and that could escalate into a major worldwide conflict. I'm told that the Russians say, '*Levinson is the only hope in stopping this, so you have to come over right away.*'"

I got on the next plane and arrived in Moscow the next day.

Preventing a War in the Baltic States

The problem stemmed from all of the Soviet Army personnel (mostly Russian) billeted in the Baltic States. When the Soviet Union broke up, there was no place that Russia had to house them in Russia proper. They could send the kids back to live with their parents, but what to do with the Army officers? The governments of the Baltics were rather moderate, but now that it was a democracy, they had opposition, and the hardliners in the parliaments said, "Get those Russian troops out of here." But Russia had no place to put them. Russia would have been willing to, but they had no place.

So the Russia troops attacked a Lithuanian television tower as a warning to both sides.

Being friendly with top people in Latvia, Estonia, and Russia, I had written a proposal to get the troops out of the Baltics. It was, at its core, a simple proposal. Russia was planning to build two new cities, one next to Tver, between Saint Petersburg and Moscow.

Now, when the Russians built a city, they just threw up hideous block buildings, and that's where people lived. I suggested that the Tver project be turned over to the Russian troops in the Baltics to build. After all, the Russian officers are often engineers and builders.

The wives of these officers could then be organized to determine what they wanted in a home, the floor plans and exteriors. They could create nice subdivisions just like in America. The advantage to the plan was that if the building of the city was turned over to the Russian officers, the moderate governments of the Baltics could say to the hardliners, "They're going to go. There's a plan. Here's the plan. They're building it."

And, in my plan, when they went, the money that the Baltics had already agreed to spend to help with the transition would be spent to buy the housing that was being vacated for the people of the Baltics. They had a perfect answer. Moreover, the Russian military would have to agree to the plan because it was obvious that their own government was now solving their problem as quickly and as well as it could.

Dan Koch had been in a meeting conducted by the number two person in the Russian military. And several of Yeltsin's cabinet members were around the table. Now, Dan didn't speak Russian, but his interpreter, Lev, who had a Harvard Business School master's degree, took him into the meeting and said he wanted him to *see* the meeting. Dan said the only word he understood was Levinson, which was said several times, as the military man pounded on the table.

Lev said that the message of the military man was that the Yeltsin government had to adopt the Levinson plan, or they would bring down the government. The problem was how to get all the countries to agree to the plan. The Russians felt if they presented the plan to the Baltics, the Baltic governments would have to reject it as a Russian plan. And the Baltic countries would feel that if they presented the plan, the Russians would reject it. But I would know that the Russians would accept it. So the Russians concluded that the person to present it to the Baltics was me.

Well, I could present it to the top people in Russia and Latvia and Estonia, but I didn't know anyone in Lithuania. So when I flew to Moscow the Russians told me that I was to go to meetings that were set up by them for me in Latvia and Estonia. I was to go over and convince them that this plan should be adopted. The Baltic governments would tell me that if they presented a plan, the Russians would reject it. But I would know that the Russians would accept it.

I was to fly to Riga on Aeroflot the next day. Now every time I flew on Aeroflot, it was like being on a Mexican bus. There were dogs in the aisle, chicken coops, the overhead racks were nets, and things were constantly falling out of it. The smells were terrible. It was a mess. But it was the way to get there quickly.

That night a reception was given for me in the Russian White House. Halfway through the reception, Lev, our interpreter, rushed into the room, and I could see he had my suitcase with him. He had packed my things and told me that to make these meetings, I would have to take an all-night Russian train because Aeroflot did not have enough fuel to fly to Riga.

When we did business in the Russian White House, we had to bring our own copiers and printers with us because there were only two in the Russian White House, and one of them was always broken. Russia was in much worse shape than I think most people in America imagined.

Lev took me to the train station. I was fully dressed in coat and tie. Each car on the train had a woman in charge of it, a big woman. Lev talked to her at length, and with much emphasis. And I said, "What did you say to her, Lev?" He said, "I told her you were a very important person on a mission for the Russian government, and if anything bad happened to you, I'd have to kill myself". There wasn't much that woman could do.

I was put in a first-class compartment about the size of a king size bed, with three other people who had packed their own food. There were two bunks on either side, one upper and one lower, both very narrow. The hallways on the train were very narrow too, but they had seats that you could bend down, and lights. I thought, "The worst that can happen, I'll spend all night reading in the hallway." But at 11:00 all the lights went out. So I lay on my tiny bunk in my full suit, and arrived, 12 hours later, in Riga with the buttons on my suit broken. Fortunately, I had another suit with me. There was no running water on the train. The bathrooms looked like they belonged in a shack that had been abandoned for forty years with rust all over everything. I don't know what was worse, Aeroflot or the train.

I arrived in time for a shower and a change of clothes, and then met with the foreign secretary of Latvia. He told me that the plan sounded wonderful. He was sure Prime Minister Godmanis and Foreign Minister Jurkans would approve of it, but they were out of the country. I said, "Tell them it is the Levinson plan. They'll accept it." And, of course, they did.

I then went to Estonia where I met with the young defense minister. He said, "I have another very important meeting now, and this is above my pay grade. You'll have to meet with the foreign minister." As I walked out, three or four very large men in naval uniforms walked in. They were the Russian military.

The Secretary of State was in the last month of his term. He was to retire and become the ambassador to Finland, a real honor in Estonia. His name was Lennart Meri. He was the wisest, most thoughtful and intelligent person I have ever met in public life. He spoke with me for two hours. We stood and looked out the window. He talked about the right Russian policy. And when I had finished my presentation. and we finished talking, I told him the truth about Russia accepting the plan. He said, "David, your plan is excellent. I will take care of Lithuania for you. You can count on that."

I went back to Moscow, told them the plan was accepted by all the Baltics.

I was told that the parties met two weeks later in Helsinki, worked it out, and a conflict was averted. I feel this was a very important step because if conflict had broken out at that time between Russia and the Baltics, no doubt the United States would have gotten involved, and it might have been a major war.

* * *

Epilogue—*for My Classmates Only*

For my efforts I was the honored guest at many banquets, appointed an advisor to the Russian Duma, and received a very large medal from Latvia. The United States, however, never in any way acknowledged my efforts. Only those few Americans who were involved have ever known what was done.

The peace between the Baltics and Russia has held until today. But for the first time, there is fear that Putin may attempt to invade the Baltics, as he did Ukraine. And several years ago Putin ended US adoption of Russian children that the Pearl Buck foundation and my insurance department had established.

There are certain principles that I have adopted which I pass on for consideration.

One, do what you believe is right even when there is a price to be paid for it, because the price that you will pay for failing to do what is right is much greater. I won a book prize at age 16 and was quoted (but not named) in *The Organization Man* by William H. Whyte, Jr. (pg. 275) as saying:

> "Is a man justified in doing what he truly thinks is right under any circumstances?
>
> A man must realize that a wrong decision, however sincere, will leave him open to criticism and to probable punishment.
>
> Nevertheless, and after weighing all the facts, it is his moral duty to act as he thinks best."

Two, encourage people to do their best but never insist that someone do something that they are incapable of doing; that is cruel.

Three, in all negotiations be guided by *your* determination of what the other side is (a) willing to do and (b) able to do.

> Whether in the smallest commercial or interpersonal transaction, or the most significant international transaction, this is the first and most important determination to make.
>
> Failing to make that determination accurately results in much wasted time and the inability to structure a deal that can be made.
>
> In international relations the failure to follow this principle and act accordingly will lead to chaos, a process which has unfortunately already begun.

I have attempted to live my life governed by these three principles and hope that I have been successful.

Figure 5.5.1.1 *David Levinson in [A]: Tallinn, Estonia with Leonard Meri, Foreign Minister (later President), Republic of Estonia; [B] Riga, Latvia with Ivars Godmanis, Prime Minister of Latvia; [C] Moscow, with Nikolai Ryabov, Chairman of the Supreme Soviet of the Russian Federation; [D] Moscow, addressing the Commission on Planning, Budget, and Trade, Supreme Soviet of Russia*

Figure 5.5.1.2 *The author in Moscow, with Mikhail Roinsky, Economic Advisor to Boris Yeltsin, President of the Russian Federation; Leonid Gurevich, Chairman of the Subcommittee on Foreign Economic Relations, Supreme Soviet of Russian Federation; and Edvard V'dernikov, Vice Chairman of the Commission on Planning, Budget & Trade in the Supreme Soviet of Russia Federation*

David Levinson received a JD degree from Harvard Law School in 1960. He has been a candidate for the US Senate from Delaware; a two-term Delaware Insurance Commissioner; a member of the Board of Governors of the Middle East Forum; Associate National Commissioner of the Anti-Defamation League; a multi-state real estate developer; founder and chairman of Anderson Creek Academy, a charter school; and is now developing a 4,000-home community, the Anderson Creek Club in North Carolina.

Endnote

1 Excerpts from Chapter 15 of the book *Memories*, a book in progress by David N. Levinson, AB '57, JD '60

National Defense

Military Service

My Career in Nuclear Submarines

Roderic Wolfe

I was fortunate enough to have attended Harvard College on a Naval Reserve Officer Training Corp (NROTC) scholarship; otherwise, I could not have afforded the tuition.

After graduation and commissioning, I was assigned to an old World War II vintage destroyer, USS *Harold J. Ellison* (DD-864) stationed in Norfolk, VA.

While deployed to the Mediterranean, I realized that "showing the (US) flag" had value in terms of international relationships and was more important than my simply learning how to be a better naval officer. I felt that I was, in some very small way, contributing to our National Defense and to world peace. That provided me an incentive to make the Navy a career. As a result of that decision, I applied for submarine training, to which I was eventually assigned.

Because I was available before my Submarine School class convened, I was assigned to USS *Piper* (SS-409), a diesel submarine in New London, Connecticut, for temporary duty, awaiting the start of my class. While there, I made an effort to do what I could to help. The ship was frequently assigned to take Submarine School student officers to sea to train them to dive and surface a submarine. Then at night, the ship spent all night on the surface charging the batteries. Since I had been qualified as an Officer of the Deck (OOD) on my first ship, I stood OOD surfaced watches at night on *Piper*. I also was able to qualify as an In-Port Duty Officer, somewhat unusual for an officer not yet Qualified in Submarines.

Prior to being assigned to submarine training, I had to take a physical to determine whether or not I was qualified for submarine duty, which I passed easily. One of the requirements for submarines was 20/20 vision. I was on the ragged edge of that requirement. After reporting to Sub School, they checked students' vision again. While doing so, the Doctor said "Quit squinting!" He came over to me and, using two fingers on one hand, pried my eye open. I told him that I couldn't read the eye chart with his fingers in my eye! The end result of that exam was that he determined, in his opinion, that my vision was 20/100 in one eye and 20/200 in the other!! My vision might have been 20/25 or even 20/30, but it was never close to 20/100 or 20/200. Thus in order to stay in sub school, I needed a waiver! I immediately went back to *Piper*, and asked the Captain to write a letter of recommendation, requesting a waiver in my case. He said that he would be happy to do so. Apparently he was willing to reward my extra effort to help out the wardroom. Fortunately, the waiver was granted, and I was able to continue my submarine training.

While assigned to the *Ellison*, I had read about the requirements to be selected for the Navy's Nuclear Power Program. I was not qualified because 1) I had not served a tour of duty in the Engineering Department, and 2) my college major was neither math nor science related. However, while at sub school, one day the instructor said, "By the way, if you guys ever want to be Commanding Officers (CO), you need to apply for the Nuclear Power Program, because there won't be any diesel boats when you get to CO seniority." So I thought, Oh, great! Now I need to apply for, and successfully compete in, a program for which I am neither qualified nor academically prepared! Better get used to the idea.

For sub school classes prior to mine, students needed to be in the top 10% of their respective classes in order to be considered for an interview with Admiral Hyman G. Rickover, the head of the Office of Naval Reactors, which was a prerequisite to being accepted into his program. But for my class, because the Ballistic Missile Submarine building program had just begun, with each wardroom requiring two crews, they planned to interview the top 50% of our class. When it came time to go to Washington, DC, for our interviews, I was ninth in a class of 113.

The Prospective Commanding Officers (PCOs), each of whom was assigned to 13 weeks of "Charm School" in Rickover's offices, were assigned to shepherd interviewees from one place to another. The

Commander who was assigned to me told me to "Listen to the question that the Admiral asks you, and answer that question." I thought to myself, "What am I, a first-grader that I need such simplistic instructions?" But I kept my mouth shut and went into my interview with the Admiral. One of his first questions was, "How many hours a week do you study?" I responded, "Two or three hours a night, Admiral." At which point the Admiral jumped all over the PCO for not teaching me to answer the question I had been asked! Then I realized that the Admiral probably wasn't going to multiply "two or three" times five or maybe six or perhaps even seven days in a week. That would be my job, not his. Consequently I have become known in my family as a stickler for insisting that my children listen to the question that was asked and answering that particular question!

Then the Admiral asked me, "If you do nothing but eat, sleep and study, what class standing could you achieve?" As mentioned previously I was at 9th, and I told the Admiral that I thought I could be 7th. My answer was based on the fact that we were two-thirds of the way through the course, and there was a limited amount of time remaining in which to improve.

It was the practice in the Office of Naval Reactors that those who had completed their interviews were segregated from those who had not spoken to the Admiral. So after my interview, I joined those who had also finished their interviews. Immediately, when I walked into the room, they all broke out in peals of laughter. I wondered if I had forgotten to zip up or something. The spokesman said to me, "What did you tell him?" I asked what he was talking about. He said "Well, you see those 12 guys over there? They all told him they would be first. Those 15 guys over there are planning on being second." As it turned out, I was able to improve from ninth to eighth, and was quite happy with that result when school was over.

However, Nuclear Power School was another story for this liberal arts graduate. You will remember that Rickover had chosen from the top 50% of sub school students, so there was a somewhat lower academic potential. Our first exam was in math. While 2.5 was a passing grade, the class average was less than that. The Officer in Charge came to the class room, read us the riot act and told us to prepare for a re-exam on Saturday, which was normally a day off. I had gotten a 2.04 on the first exam, so I studied hard and dis-improved to a 1.96 on the re-exam! I realized early on that I needed all the help I could find, so I went to the math instructor and tried to explain to him all that I didn't know. It was rumored that he had been first in the nation on the Graduate

Records Exam in Mathematics and second in the nation in Aeronautical Engineering. He could not conceive of someone with my lack of understanding of mathematics. We just could not communicate on the subject of mathematics, so as a result, Math became one of the classes I failed.

As you can imagine, I was very near the bottom in class standing, to say the least. I buckled down and moved up to about fifth from the bottom. One day there was a knock on the classroom door, and those with class standing worse than mine were summoned to report to the office of the Officer in Charge. They left, but never came back to class! After that happened again I said to myself, "I got it! I'm the cut score! If I keep my nose clean and work as hard as I can, I'll survive!" I failed four of the seven courses offered, but passed each of the re-exams.

The night before the last exam in Nuclear Power School, I took time to calculate my grade point average. It was a 2.496. I figured that, if I passed the final exam, I would probably pass the course, and somehow I did!

The next phase of our training was at the prototype, an actual shore-based nuclear power plant where we would open and close valves, learn systems and operate the plant under the close supervision of qualified enlisted operators. This was more to my liking. I could understand what to do, when and why. There was no esoteric theory. I made good progress and completed all the required qualifications ahead of most of my contemporaries.

Upon completion of the prototype training, I received orders to USS *Skate* (SSN-578) in New London. When I reported to *Skate* there were only four nuclear subs in New London and perhaps two or three in Pearl Harbor. We worked hard and didn't socialize a lot, but we knew almost every nuclear-trained officer in New London, at least by reputation. There were eight to ten officers on each boat. It was a very small community.

Several weeks after reporting to *Skate*, we left New London to make a classified trip to the North Pole to conduct the first joint operations in the Arctic with the USS *Seadragon* (SSN-584), which came from Pearl Harbor, HI. One night while we were between Greenland and Canada on our way to the North Pole, I was awakened by the sound of the Collision Alarm and the announcement of "Flooding in the Engineering spaces".

That may strike fear in the hearts of the civilians reading this account, but I was not at all afraid. Some will say that I was so naïve that I didn't realize how serious that was, when you are under the ice, or that I was too inexperienced to appreciate the danger involved. On the other hand, I want to say to those of you who don't have a military background that we train extensively for these potentially dangerous events, and when they occur we realize that: (1) there is no mystery about what needs to be done, or (2) whose responsibility it is to take that action, and (3) those responsible take the required action promptly *every time*. His shipmates' lives may depend on his knowing what to do, and so he is prepared to do it.

In this particular instance, the visual evidence was somewhat misleading, making it more difficult to diagnose and correct the flooding casualty. We were, of course, submerged, so the sea pressure made the water entering the boat cascade forcefully. The failure was in a silver-brazed joint in a sea water system at about the level of the deck plates in the lower level Auxiliary Machinery Room (AMR). But the force of sea pressure caused the stream of water to gush out of the failure like a fire hose. It was forced straight up, following the curvature of the hull, and raining down from the overhead as though the failure was above the upper level. Nevertheless, the AMR watch stander determined where the failure was almost immediately and isolated the rupture promptly. At the same time, the Officer of the Deck ordered the ship to a somewhat shallower depth, below the deepest reaches of the ice overhead, and the weight of water taken in had almost no effect on the ballast of the ship. Just another day at the office!!

After meeting up with *Seadragon*, it was planned that we would both surface in the same "*polynya*". *Polynya* is a Russian word meaning open water surrounded by sea ice. When ocean currents and winds create various forces on different "ice floes", it is possible for an opening in the surface of the ice to appear. These can be quite large on occasion. The intent was that both ships would surface in the same *polynya*. Since our CO was senior to the *Seadragon*'s, we surfaced first. For safety's sake, the plan was for *Seadragon* to launch a green smoke out of her forward and aft signal ejectors so that it was apparent where she was before surfacing. We quickly saw the first green smoke off our starboard (right hand) side. We waited and waited and didn't see another smoke. Finally someone turned around and, sure enough, there was the second green smoke very visible on the PORT (left hand) SIDE. It was at this point that we used the underwater telephone to tell *Seadragon* to STOP her efforts to surface, to reposition to a location NOT under us, and to begin the process over again. Civilians who hear this story think it sounds rather harrowing. It was not. We took the necessary precautions and had everything under control at each step of the process, but it makes for good storytelling!

After successfully getting both boats surfaced, we set about to conduct a ceremony. Each CO had a plaque from his Submarine Force Commander, Commander, Submarine Forces, Atlantic and Pacific Fleets respectively. Each sub mustered a military color guard, consisting of two riflemen, a Navy flag bearer and an American flag bearer. This event took place in bright sunlight. The Uniform of the Day for all participants was full Arctic foul weather gear. The only problem was that on this particular day the sun was HOT, and the air temperature was probably in the 50s or 60s. But everything was staged to make it appear that we were all freezing to death!

Figure 5.6.1.1 *Submerged under ice in the Arctic Sea, USN nuclear submarines USS* Skate *(SSN-578) and USS* Seadragon *(SSN-584) surfaced together in a* polynya *at the North Pole and held ceremonies with their color guard.*

Following our Joint Operations, both boats returned to our respective home ports and, much to our children's delight, we had persuaded Santa Claus to return to New London with us!

Upon reporting to *Skate*, my main responsibility, aside from watch qualifications, was to complete my submarine qualification notebook and other associated tasks in order to become "Qualified in Submarines." After an appropriate period of study, each candidate needs to be subjected to an oral interview, or inquisition, on all aspects of the subject at hand. Most of those "subjects" were one of the vital systems on the submarine. Each officer, when qualified, needs to know enough about each of those vital systems so that in the event of an emergency, he could take charge of whatever compartment he found himself in if he were the senior qualified man. He would need to order systems operated to provide for the safety of the personnel in that compartment and of the entire ship. This process normally takes the better part of a year to accomplish.

After an officer completes his written and oral work from his notebook, his Commanding Officer submits a recommendation for his qualification to the Submarine Division Commander (DivCom). The DivCom in turn arranged for the candidate to ride another submarine in his Division. During that ride, the candidate was expected to get the ship underway from the pier, submerge the ship, stand watches and do whatever other tasks that CO might ask him to do to demonstrate his proficiency. Finally, on returning to port the candidate was expected to conn the ship, that is to give orders to make the landing on the pier.

My Division Commander arranged for me to ride the USS *Seawolf* (SSN-575) for my qualification underway. During our underway time, we received word that the USS *Thresher* (SSN-593) was down. They had been on sea trials after a Post Shipyard Availability (PSA) to repair items that needed to be corrected from the ship's post-commissioning trials. Coincidentally, the Thresher's Executive Officer was LCDR Pat Garner, who had been the *Skate*'s Engineer Officer when I reported aboard *Skate*. Therefore, Pat and I had been shipmates, and this was a personal loss for me. *Seawolf* was not far from where *Thresher* went down, so we were directed to proceed to the last known location of the *Thresher* and attempt to establish communication in an effort to see if there were any survivors. At the time, we knew very little about what had happened to *Thresher*, but we were not optimistic about what we might find. We spent some time without any response "at depth", that is to say, below the thermal layer, which could have inhibited underwater communications. Eventually we were detached to resume our original operations. It was a sad time, not wanting to believe that we had lost friends and ex-shipmates in such an abrupt and tragic way. Although I successfully completed my underway assignment, it was a very subdued completion.

Upon returning to New London, we learned that the press, in their typical modus operandi, had announced over the radio that "A US nuclear submarine had sunk" but they didn't know which one so they couldn't specify which submarine had been lost. That announcement struck fear in the hearts of EVERY FAMILY MEMBER of the US submarine community in the area. That radio station got the scoop, and the family members paid the price for their scoop!

In 1965, following my tour on *Skate*, I was assigned to be the Engineer Officer on USS *Robert E. Lee* (SSBN-601). This was a ballistic missile sub, operating out of Holy Loch, Scotland. After my first deterrent patrol, we went through the Panama Canal en route to Mare Island Naval Shipyard for our first nuclear refueling, which was scheduled for 18 months. The overhaul was completed approximately on time, and we transited back through the Panama Canal en route to Cape Canaveral, Florida, for missile testing. Then we went to Charleston, South Carolina, for missile load out before our next deterrent patrol.

After my Engineer Officer tour, we went to Norfolk, VA, where I attended Armed Forces Staff College. After the 13-week course, we were sent back to New London, where I was assigned to be the Executive officer of the USS *Dace* (SSN-607). Our Commanding Officer on *Dace* was Commander Kinnard R. McKee. He had the reputation of being the premier CO in the Atlantic Submarine Fleet. I learned a lot from McKee. He was so well respected that he eventually was tapped to replace Admiral Hyman G. Rickover after Congress forced him to retire. You can read more about US submarine operations in general, and *Dace*'s exploits in particular, in a book entitled *Blind Man's Bluff: The untold Story of American Submarine Espionage* by Sherry Sontag and Christopher Drew. It makes for interesting reading.

In 1969, following my tour on *Dace*, we moved again, this time to Pearl Harbor, Hawaii, where I was assigned to the Nuclear Propulsion Examining Board. We were tasked with conducting annual safeguards exams on each nuclear-powered ship in the Pacific Fleet. Most of our inspections were conducted on subs, but we also went to each nuclear-powered cruiser and aircraft carrier. Our purpose was to assure Rickover that each ship we examined was operating its reactor(s) safely and properly. The Engineer Officers who did well on the exam were among the candidates considered for assignment to the Board. It was my responsibility to examine each ship on those areas with which I had struggled when in Nuclear Power School. Perhaps I had worked harder in those areas after completion of my schooling!

Following my several years on the Board, we moved back to the continental US in 1973. My first assignment was to study in Rickover's offices for 13 weeks of "Charm School", where his staff made it clear what we were expected to do, and what we were expected NOT to do vis-à-vis operation of the nuclear power plant. I was ordered to be the Prospective Commanding Officer of the *L. Mendel Rivers*, which would be constructed at Newport News Shipbuilding and Dry

Dock Company in Newport News, VA. On some weekends while in Charm School, I traveled to Newport News in search of a house for my family. When I found something that would be suitable, I bought it and arranged for my family to take possession and manage the move-in while I was still in school.

After reporting to the pre-commissioning unit, I and a few other prospective crew members were able to ride the ship down the building ways at the launching of the ship. The story is that the speed reached that day, sliding down the ways, was the greatest speed the ship would ever reach, going backwards!

The shipyard had been a family business for years but had recently been sold to the Tenneco Corporation. Tenneco made a concerted effort to make the operations more profitable and, in the process, made some very serious mistakes that failed to comply with the Submarine Safety Program that grew out of the Navy's review of the loss of the Thresher. After a few abortive attempts by the shipyard to circumvent the resulting problems, the Navy's agent, the Supervisor of Shipbuilding, had to instruct the shipyard as to the required action to rectify the problem. That constituted a Letter of Direction, or an un-priced amendment to the shipbuilding contract which allowed the shipbuilder to charge the Government for rectifying the problem that he had created, and the taxpayers picked up the tab for his errors! As a result, our relationship with the shipyard was something less than cordial.

The first acceptance sea trial is the Government's propulsion plant trial. Since Rickover and his office were the designers, he always rode the first sea trial. While I would love to regale you with the particulars of those three days, there is not enough space remaining to give a blow-by-blow account of how the trial went. Suffice it to say, when Rickover left the ship following the trial, he looked at me and said, "Good trial." As my mother would have said, "That's praise from Sir Hubert," or in other words, that's about the highest compliment you would ever receive from Admiral Rickover.

In an effort to develop goodwill with the citizens of Charleston, where we were ultimately to be homeported, we used the local newspaper to advertise an open competition, inviting the citizenry to submit their designs for the ship's plaque. When the time came to select the winner, I traveled to Charleston to participate in that decision. While there, I visited my prospective Submarine Squadron Commander. I told him that I did not want to have the Commissioning Ceremony in the shipyard because of their lack of cooperation, and that I was thinking of taking the ship to the Norfolk Naval Station for Commissioning. He countered with the suggestion that the USS *L. Mendel Rivers* (SSN-686) should be commissioned in Congressman Rivers' hometown of Charleston. That sounded like a great public relations victory to me. But I soon realized that agreeing to that idea was the WORST DECISION of my entire Naval Career! The ship's wardroom, about 12 officers, traditionally hosts the post-commissioning reception. But when we decided to have the commissioning in Charleston, it became necessary to ask the South Carolina Congressional Delegation for their suggestions as to a guest list. Politics being what they were, we were expected to invite each and every elected and appointed official in the entire state of South Carolina to the Commissioning! Now the Navy had a fund to help the wardrooms with some of those expenses, but at the end of the fiscal year, those funds had been expended, and there was no help in sight! Fortunately, the Officer's Club Manager came up with some creative ways to help, and we were able to avoid having any of the officers declare bankruptcy!

Mendel Rivers' widow, Margaret Rivers, and her daughters were the sponsors of the ship. Naturally we invited them to the ship's party after the commissioning. Mrs. Rivers was a very elegant and gracious woman. She was rather upset to learn that not every member of the crew was able to attend the party, because about one third of the crew was onboard the ship. They had the duty and could not leave the ship until relieved the next day. She wanted to reciprocate and invite the entire crew to her home for an open house. When she did so, she hosted it on both Friday and Saturday nights, so that each and every member of the crew was afforded the opportunity to attend one of those nights! She was a very classy lady.

The original crew (i.e., new construction crew) that was assigned to *Rivers* was, by far, the most capable bunch of guys with which I ever had the good fortune to serve. Many of them became Commissioned Warrant Officers or Limited Duty Officers later in their careers. There was excellence from the top to the bottom. While it was inevitable, I was saddened when I watched those guys rotate off, and they were replaced by newer, less experienced crew men. But it was our responsibility to take those young men and train them to make them as good as the guys they were replacing. At each level of responsibility in the Navy, the principal job of the supervisor was to train each of his subordinates to take his job and assume the responsibilities of the guy for whom they worked.

So, in 1982, after 25 years of active duty and 13 moves, I decided to retire from the Navy.

Following my retirement from the Navy, I found the customs in civilian industry to be quite contrary to the way the Navy did business. I worked at the San Onofre Nuclear Generating Station (SONGS) while they were going through the process of bringing two new reactors to the point of starting to generate electricity. There was little or no training to teach subordinates to grow into the next level of responsibility. Quite to the contrary, what I observed surprised me. Supervisors often would not promote a subordinate when that person was doing such a good job that the supervisor was afraid to lose his team's productivity. On the other side of the coin, inept subordinates were "promoted" back to the Engineering Headquarters in order to get rid of them. As a result, those "promoted" would sometimes come back one or two echelons higher in the organization, where they were better able to cause more damage to the organization. After the two units were "on line" generating electricity, I got a job offer closer to home and left SONGS. But ineptness has a way of rearing its ugly head.

Several years later, SONGS was shut down because their engineers had approved a proposed redesign of their steam generators which did not provide an adequate safety margin.

* * *

These anecdotes are not intended to impress the reader with my life's trials and tribulations, but rather to outline the stumbling blocks it was necessary for me to overcome in order to reach the point where I could make a contribution to our National Defense.

A number of years after my retirement, I went to a *Robert E. Lee* reunion in Las Vegas. I ran into Sam Adams, an officer with whom I had served on the *Lee*. He looked me in the eye and asked, "We really did make a difference, didn't we?" I agreed with him. He was saying that our efforts to make the world a safer place did make a difference and was worth the effort.

I was satisfied that making a career of the Navy had, indeed, helped my fellow man, and made my life's work worthwhile.

Captain **Rod Wolfe**, United States Navy (USN) retired, is the author of *My Career in Nuclear Submarines*. He served in the Navy for 25 years, attaining the rank of Captain and having commanded two ships: the USS *L. Mendel Rivers* (SSN-686) and the USS *Dixon* (AS-37).

Our US Navy

Richard C. Norris

I was never in the military. We, of the Class of '57, were born too late for Korea, and I managed to avoid Viet Nam by being a graduate student, a technical worker, and then a father. So, my exposure to the US Navy came much later in life.

It all started with the daughter of my Dunster House roommate, Don Acheson. After backing out of her wedding at the last moment, she went and enlisted in the Navy, much to her parents' distress. She started out as an electrician's mate, but after a couple of years found that she could qualify for a program to go back to college and then become an officer. It was then that she started her climb up the officer ladder of the surface Navy.

I didn't follow her career all that closely in the first few years. It just seemed that she would take one training program after another between tours at sea. But then, in 2004, I learned that there would be a Tiger Cruise (for family and friends) aboard the USS *Mason,* DDG 87, a guided missile destroyer, where Lynn was the XO. After much lobbying, I was able to secure an invitation to go on this three-day cruise from Norfolk, VA, down to Mayport, FL.

What an experience! The cruise itself was fascinating, but what was most impressive was the conduct of the crew. All were so proud to show off their ship to their loved ones. They all walked around with their heads held high and smiles on their faces, asking time and again what they could do for us. The CO, David Gale, was particularly impressive. He was just about to rotate out of this command after taking it on when the ship was under construction at the Bath Iron Works in Maine. He told Don that this command was the high point of his career, enabling him to take on a brand-new crew and develop it into one that stood high in all of its proficiency tests. (He is now a Vice Admiral, continuing in a very successful career indeed.)

One thing I observed in both CO Gale and XO Acheson was their quiet but firm command presence, care for their crew, and competence in their functions. Turns out that Lynn had found a perfect calling.

Several years later, in 2010, Lynn became the CO of another destroyer, the USS *Freddie Gonzales,* DDG 66. I attended her change-of-command ceremony and met the mother of Freddie, who was celebrating her 80th birthday. She was an elegant woman who had brought up Freddie right, the first Mexican American to win the Medal of Honor. The retiring CO had flown her in for the ceremony, which turned out to be 75% birthday party and 25% change of command. It was so elegant. The Navy sure knows how to do these things. At the time, both Don and I pressed Lynn on when she was going to have a Tiger Cruise. She promised that she would work on that and, sure enough, had one the following March.

This cruise was similar to the first and equally impressive. At one point, there was a burial at sea ceremony where the ashes of about eight retired sailors or their spouses were scattered with great solemnity. Included was one husband and wife, where the dispersal was done simultaneously. Very moving. The other memorable event was when Lynn introduced me to two young sailors on temporary assignment to her ship. In June, both would join their own ship, the USS *Jason Dunham*, under construction at the Bath Iron Works. I spend the warm months nearby at my summer cottage on Frye Island in the middle of Lake Sebago, so I immediately extended an invitation to them to come over for a swim and barbecue that summer.

Figure 5.6.2.1 *USS* Jason Dunham, *Arleigh Burke–class guided-missile destroyer, ready to launch in 2010 at Bath Iron Works (BIW), Bath, ME*

Photo source: US Navy

Once the Island opened in May, I got talking to my friends there about my Tiger Cruise experience. In talking about my invitation to two sailors joining their ship in Bath, I suddenly thought that it would be really special to invite the whole crew over to the island for a day of R&R. They all thought that that would be a terrific idea, so I e-mailed Lynn, noting that I wasn't sure about Navy protocols but wondered whether such a day might be a good idea. Her response was immediate. Yes, it would be a terrific idea, and she knew the CO, Scott Sciretta, and would have him get back to me. At first, the Selectmen on the island were very nervous about bringing a large crew of young sailors to run around the island. (Images of them raping their daughters?) However, a senior chief with great command presence talked to them and assured them that the chiefs would watch over the sailors and keep everything under control. The result: the decision to bring over 75.

So, that's how it started, and now we have entertained the crews from five different Bath-built destroyers. With each, we bring from 75 to 100 crew members, with some wives and children, to the island. We start with a fire engine and police car siren escort from the ferry landing to the ball field. (I learned this trick from our 25th and 50th Reunions, where I remember so fondly the siren escorts we had to Symphony Hall for the Pops concert.) Following a color guard and welcoming ceremony, we hold a softball game, followed by a noontime barbecue. The afternoon is devoted to various forms of informal recreation, including kayaking, swimming, golf, basketball, and just plain loafing. The highpoint of the day has turned out to be the suppers, where we split the guests up into groups of two, three, or four, and assign each to a host family. Living in temporary quarters in the Bath area and then moving aboard ship as it nears completion leaves the sailors somewhat adrift. Many of them are quite young, 18 to 21, and to have a home-cooked meal with a warm, welcoming family really hits the spot.

While the sailors have loved the day on the island, the islanders have loved the sailors they have hosted. Many have inspiring and moving stories. A good number are persons brought up in dead-end locations, where opportunities are limited. The Navy offers a means for getting out and on with their lives, developing skills and seeing new places. (One sailor from the South Bronx noted that it was either getting out with the Navy or being sucked into a life of gangs and drugs.) The volunteer Navy, in turn, is able to skim the cream and select attractive candidates. It's a beautiful arrangement.

Figure 5.6.2.2 *Launch in 2011 of the USS* Spruance, *Arleigh Burke–class guided-missile destroyer, at BIW*

Photo source: US Navy

One of my favorite experiences was finding a star. With the first ship, I got a request late Friday afternoon to broadcast "The Star-Spangled Banner" for the color guard ceremony the next morning. After much scrambling, I was able to pull this off. So, the next year in going over the program, I asked the organizing chief if I should play "The Star-Spangled Banner" for his color guard. His response was negative. The ship had done color guard ceremonies for many events, such as Red Sox, Celtics, and Portland Sea Dogs games, all without music. I then had an idea: Did the ship have someone who could sing the national anthem?. He replied that they had never done that before, but it was rumored that there was a good singer aboard. The chief would check it out.

So on the day, little Marnie Santiago, all five feet of her, stood up to the mike. She was a Filipino who had come to the US six years before, had joined the Navy a couple of years later and was the Baby Doc on the ship. Little Marnie proceeded to belt out *a capella* the most marvelous rendition of "The Star-Spangled Banner" I had heard in years. After the event, the chief remarked that he had had no idea that the ship had such a talent and that she should surely perform at the ship's commissioning in the fall. Sure enough, there she was at the commissioning in Key West that fall performing again. But this time, just as she hit and held the high note in "the land of the *free*", a pair of F-18 fighter jets did a low-altitude, high-speed fly by, perfectly synchronized. At the reception following, I found Marnie and congratulated her. I then said that I only had one complaint: that she didn't have a fly by when she sang on Frye Island. We all laughed.

During these R&R days, I have always hosted the chiefs at my place for the evening dinner. I so admire them. These are the senior enlisted men and women who have chosen the Navy as their lifetime career and have been good enough to qualify. Here, we find the functional expertise needed to make a ship run. And here we find persons who are devoted to developing the young sailors working under them. They are very positive people.

In reflecting on my experiences with the Navy, I can't help but compare it with the many companies and organizations that I have been exposed to over 35 years of consulting in the field of operations management and supply chain logistics. Being a functional consultant, I have worked in many industry sectors and many different countries.

Enterprises I have worked with have had a wide range of characteristics, with different sets of dynamics and success factors. In the process, I have seen a few that are mediocre and negative, many that are average, and some that are truly outstanding. Some firms, especially those that succeed through marketing, tend to be very political, with individuals all competing with each other for career advancement success and with a lot of intrigue. But others are remarkable and positive.

Among them are a number that are successful in competitive industries that provide operations-intensive services or are very close to their customers. Here, the good guys win. Examples are the major parcel carriers such as UPS and FedEx as well as many supermarket chains. Trader Joe's and Costco are my favorites. Aren't their employees wonderful? What a contrast to many of the branded consumer products companies, where the corporate offices are so elegant but so cold.

Here are some of the characteristics of the enterprises I admire that I have also found in the US Navy.

(1) A great deal of attention and effort is devoted to individual training. There is one training program after another, with opportunities to attend outside institutes and universities. (Lynn even took a special course in CO leadership before she took command of the *Gonzales*.)

(2) Substantial attention is paid to evaluating the performance and capabilities of individual sailors and officers, in guiding their career development, and in moving them upward in their careers.

(3) Performance of the working unit is evaluated and measured with great intensity, with the findings fed back for improvement.

(4) Considerable effort is devoted to publicly recognizing noteworthy achievements of individual sailors and officers, as well as operational units..

(5) When problems occur, special task forces are convened to determine what went wrong and to work out corrective actions. These reviews are carried out as objectively as possible without consideration for the ranks of the players.

(6) There is great concern for the welfare of sailors and their families.

(7) The Navy's customer is, of course, the citizenry of the USA, whom they serve by providing military security. As a result, a fair amount of effort is devoted to public service in a wide variety of ways, as well as to showing the Flag through public ceremonies. (Hence, the Tiger cruises.)

(8) A high premium is placed on quality leadership and much is done to develop this attribute.

(9) Finally, there is pride. People who work for outstanding organizations take great pride in their work, their team, and the enterprise itself.

In conclusion, my exposure to the US Navy in recent years has been very positive. The Navy is an impressive enterprise, with a grand history and proud tradition indeed.

Figure 5.6.2.3 *Night view in the Kennebec River of USS* Zumwalt*, the first of the* Zumwalt *class to be built at BIW, 2014.*

Photo source: US Navy

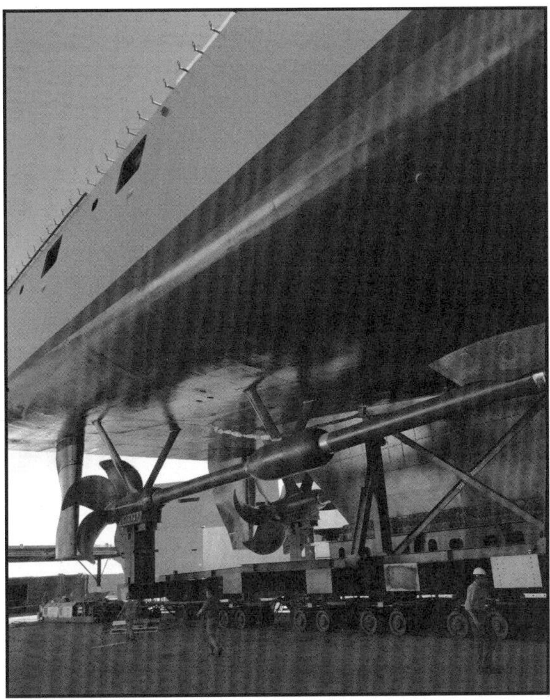

Figure 5.6.2.4 *Propulsion and steering gear of next Zumwalt class at BIW: 600 feet long with a crew of 50*

Photo source: J. L. Joslin, 2016

Richard C. Norris, after receiving his doctorate in operations research at MIT, worked his entire career of 35 years as a management consultant at Arthur D. Little, Inc. His specialty was logistics, operations management, and supporting computer technology. He worked in a wide variety of industries, as diverse as airframe manufacturing, consumer products, pharmaceuticals, textiles, petroleum, grocery retailing, and container shipping. Beyond the domestic, his projects took him to many countries in the Middle and Far East, Europe, and Latin America, exposing him to a wide variety of cultures and practices. Dick especially enjoyed working on unique problems with collaborative, multidisciplinary teams.

Beyond Reasonableness

Stephen Leavitt

The reasonable course of action would have been to follow the path of medicine which I had begun after college; but I wandered off from time to time. I went to NYU Medical School followed by medical internship and residency at The Mary Imogene Bassett Hospital in Cooperstown, NY, followed by residency in neurology at Brigham and Women's Hospital in Boston.

I was on track to the National Institutes of Health when I received the kind of letter that changes peoples' lives.

"Dear Dr. Leavitt"... it began.

"But, Colonel," I declaimed to the officer in charge of my life at that moment. "Look at these letters. I am off to the National Institutes of Health."

"Where is your commission in the Public Health Service?"

"I don't have it yet."

"Then you have two choices. One, you can go to Fort Sam Houston as a physician. Two, I will send you to Fort Dix as a private in the infantry. Or you can go to jail."

* * *

"I see you are a Harvard boy," said Col. Lyle Wright, now my commanding officer at the second battalion 15th Armor, sitting at his desk in a Quonset hut in an encampment called Thunderbolt Valley, in the hills of South Korea about five miles south of the DMZ.

"Have you ever heard a shot fired in anger?" continued the Colonel.

"No, Sir."

"I thought not, Harvard. But here is your job. You have to shape up your 25 troopers and their broken-down vehicles and give my tankers the medical support they need."

I looked out the window onto a valley of dirt bisected by the dirt road over which I had come. On one side were rows of Quonset huts.

Pencil-thin lines of smoke drifted up from their metal smoke stacks. On the other side of the road were lines of tanks and armored personnel carriers

The Colonel continued:"You have to gain the trust of those troopers so that if one of them has to lose a leg, he will look at you, ask if he must lose his leg, and if you say it is so, he will say, "Yes, Sir."

"Understood, Captain?" "Yes, Sir." I answered

* * *

After my 18 months with Colonel Wright and those who became wonderful colleagues and friends—Sgt. Kimmelman, who ran the motor pool and had been with US troops liberating the concentration camps; Tom Tait, a six-foot-five captain; Smitty, another roommate, along with the dentist, Carlos Del Rio Cartagena—I had the choice to return stateside.

My choice was Fort Ord, CA, where with two other physicians we oversaw the new recruits.

* * *

I stayed in California, first as a resident in psychiatry at the Langley Porter Institute of the University of California, then as resident in social psychiatry—a new field which hoped to apply psychological knowledge to big social problems. I became a consultant at the Moffitt Hospital at the University of California Medical Center.

There I entered a strange period of my life during which I encountered the field of operations research and began study with Professor William Jewell at UC Berkley. At the same time I joined a consulting firm and sold contracts to three workers compensation insurance companies in the belief that I could develop a proactive case management model that could get injured workers back to work faster and with less cost. The programs worked, but we and our Data General equipment got swept away by IBM about 18 months later.

In 1969, I fell in love with Maribelle Bryde, a professor of nursing science at the University of California. And that was that. That "... was a love that was more than aft love, me and my Maribelle Bryde". She became my new life and has remained my life for the last 44 years. We had two sons.

In 1968 we spent two years in Washington, DC. I was a consultant to the US Department of Labor on workers compensation issues, and Maribelle began work on her book, *Families at Risk*, for Little Brown.

In 1970 my career moved back to California and my original consulting company. There my role was to start new companies around our ability to get consulting contracts for software in the financial services industry, telecommunications, education, and health care. I would say that the results, though taking anywhere from five to eight years, were quite good. Today I oversee two companies, hoping that they will become robust enough to sell, as the others have.

I was at a parents' meeting at the San Francisco Jewish Community Center, perhaps ten years ago. A young blond woman next to me was wearing a small gold cross on a chain. I asked her why she was at the JCC. She explained it was because Jewish people understand how to nourish others.

I came to believe that Judaism was important not only to Jews, but to the world. I felt it needed expression; and to that end got behind the construction and birth of what is now the Contemporary Jewish Museum in San Francisco, a 45-thousand-square-foot building designed by Daniel Libeskind to present contemporary Jewish thought through works of art. The opening exhibit, for example, was called "In the Beginning", an exhibit by contemporary artists expressing their response to the Torah.

And now I walk the plateau of the 80th year. According to survival statistics, the plateau ends at an inevitable cliff. In the meantime, we are at the Montage Ski Resort in Utah waiting for the weather to clear. Then we will get a chance to meet up with our son, who is on the ski patrol.

Stephen Leavitt, MD, returned to civilian life after his military service in the US Army Medical Corps in Korea in the 1960s, where he received the Army Commendation Medal for developing systems of medical evacuation for tank battalions. Following further medical training, his first career in social psychiatry at the University of California in San Francisco was followed by studies on operations research at the University of California, Berkeley. As a principal of a consulting firm in Berkley, he was responsible for selecting young entrepreneurs who went on to create their own enterprises in software for the telecommunications, securities trading, manufacturing, and medical records industries. He is the owner of *Aprima* medical records corporation in Dallas, TX. He and his wife, retired professor of Nursing Sciences at the University of California, the parents of two sons, live in San Francisco.

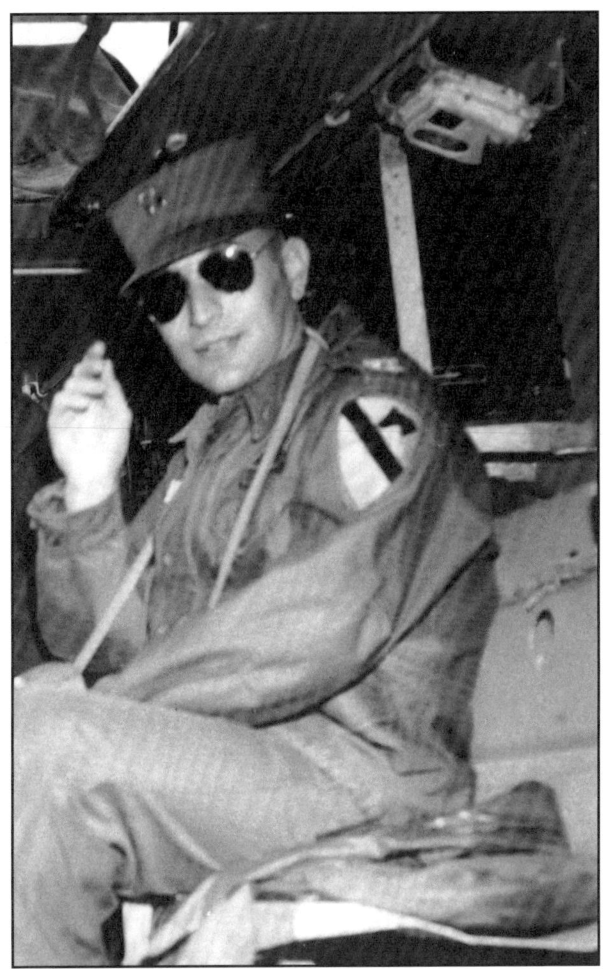

Figure 5.6.3.1 *Captain Stephen Leavitt, MD, US Army Medical Corps, in 1963 with the 2nd Battalion 15th Armor tank corps in South Korea, five miles south of the DMZ border with North Korea*

From Harvard to the Hot Tarmac

Steven T. Susman

"*Are you a chicken-shit or a Marine?*" The Marine Corps Drill Instructor ("DI") hovered over my prostrate body. I was lying face-down on the hot tarmac of the Marine Corps Recruit Depot in San Diego, June 1960. With about 30 other enlistees from Denver, I had just arrived at the San Diego airport; been hauled off the commercial flight; and shoved into a Marine Corps bus. That was 14 minutes ago. Yanked off the bus, in civilian clothes, we were ordered—then and there—to do ten push-ups. I did one; my elbows folded.

Apparently, the correct answer was to say, "*Sir, I'm a Marine!*" My response to that question followed my ridiculous performance on the tarmac: "Apparently, I'm a chicken-shit, because I could do only one push-up." As in a *Tom & Jerry* animated cartoon that preceded movies in that era, he lifted me by my collar; pulled me up from the tarmac; and carried me (as one would pick up a cat by its neck) to the 2nd Lieutenant.

The 2nd Lieutenant, obviously, was fresh out of Marine Corps Officer Candidate School or had been a recent ROTC graduate. I don't think he was old enough to shave, but his uniform was immaculate; his posture erect; his new gold bars shiny. Asking about my education, he was unimpressed. I explained that my local draft board had given me the option to enlist in the Navy JAG program, which entailed a 40-month commitment. It came with the perks of a handsome all-white dress uniform and the silver bars of a Lt. Junior Grade (after graduating from the four-month JAG school in Rhode Island).

I had a very attractive job offer with a prominent Denver law firm, but there was no assurance that the position would await my return in 40+ months. Hence, my only other option (the "easy" National Guard programs were filled) was to enlist in the Marine Corps. The basic training was six months, after which I could return home and begin my career. I would be reassigned to 5½ years in the Marine Corps Active Reserves. That extended commitment included my devoting one weekend per month at an Army base 70 miles south of Denver—from 6 a.m. on Saturday until Sunday night. Also, two weeks for five consecutive summers, reporting to and rejoining with the regular Marines at "summer camp". This servitude took place at the Marine base at Twenty-Nine Palms, CA, in the Mojave Desert, amid the scorpions and average daily temperatures of 115 degrees F.

In those days (1960–61), the Marine Corps apparently did not require enlistees to have a high school diploma or its equivalent. There were several guys in my platoon (ages 18–21) who came directly from rural jails. The daily fare in those slammers typically consisted of at least one baloney sandwich, sometimes concocted by the local sheriff's wife. But these young men enabled me to survive the rigors of the six-month boot camp. Harvard Law (1957–1960) didn't yet offer a course on Negotiating. I improvised a barter system.

Part of the training involved instructional movies, showing (for example) how to disassemble and reassemble the M-1 rifle, the 35-caliber machine gun, and the .45 pistol (skills bearing no similarity to lugging *Prosser on Torts* and other heavy tomes to and from my apartment in north Cambridge). Many of my comrades slept through those movies and had no clue what was taught. As I *usually* did in *Humanities 4* in College, or in *Property* in Law School, I paid attention. When the DI tested us on our weapons dissections (in a dark room), he didn't know that I surreptitiously had performed these operations for several of my colleagues. In return, these guys would a) toss me over the high walls of the obstacle course; b) ride "double" with me on the rope as I swung over a stream; and c) carry my backpack part of the way on long, forced marches.

In retrospect, my choice was not the better one: The "*Cuban missile crisis*" and "*Bay of Pigs*" fiascos were then the major military events for the US. I could visualize myself on a god-forsaken Cuban beach, pinned down by Russian machine-guns, reminiscent of Omaha Beach in June 1944. That crisis for me and for our country did pass. However, one of my Harvard College/Harvard Law classmates took that Navy JAG option. He retired as a one-star admiral at a young age, and lived happily ever after.

Some Reflections on this Post-Harvard Experience

(1) At least since the glory days of ancient Greece and Rome, the peons have been the front-line grist for the military. Many of my Harvard College and Law School classmates, who had not previously served in our military or ROTC, were bypassed

by their local draft board. The inherent randomness and unfairness of previous draft systems have probably been the rule, not the exception, for about 4,000-plus years. Yes, some of my contemporaries had minor physical problems and were classified "4F", but most of those maladies were insignificant. Today, our all-volunteer military attracts these (primarily) low-socioeconomic enlistees.

(2) That supports the idea of a universal draft, as in Israel. Young Israelis, both genders, just "build in" their obligation (two years' active military or noncombatant duty, plus a reserve component). Of course, that country's geo-strategic considerations are much different from ours. But there are so many useful positions that a noncombatant can fill, in or outside US military services. This concept, much studied, has many pros and cons—both for our country and for our 18-year-olds.

(3) The present-day claim of our new Administration's Secretary of Defense, a much-respected, retired Marine Corps four-star general, echoes his colleagues: The equipment of our military is frighteningly old; some is obsolete, not warfare ready. In 1960–65, our rifles and pistols, our self-propelled 155-mm. guns (like tanks), were World War I vintage. Too much of our land, sea, and air equipment and weapons, and our nuclear capabilities, are woefully inadequate. The primary purposes of a strong military are only twofold: (a) project an overwhelming offensive capability; and (b) in battle, kill the other guy before he kills you. We aren't properly equipped to do the former, which, of course, increases the probability of having to deal with the latter.

Epilogue

Invited to a Halloween party in October 2016, I tried to fit myself into my preserved, cleaned, ironed Marine uniform. The bottom part of the fatigues couldn't be pulled above my knees; the blouse suffered a similar inadequacy. But my friends think I'm slim. I hear that the food at the refurbished Dunster House dining room and at the new Harvard Law School Taj Mahal is excellent.

Stephen T. Susman writes: "My family settled in Denver in 1906. I was born near my mother's home; attended Denver public schools, our senior class numbering over 900. One day, a teacher, acting as the school's de facto college counselor, summoned me: "Susman, I'm busy. You can apply to either Amherst or Harvard. Both are excellent. Give me your decision tomorrow." I had vaguely heard of both. My next life-event was riding on the California Zephyr train for two days, to Boston. During Freshman Week, I quickly realized that my new suit—plaid, with a two-button wide-lapel—had to be jettisoned. Off to Central Square, to Max Keezer's Used Clothing emporium. Thence, to J. August (three shirts for $10) and the Coop (2nd floor) for replacements.

I was initially shocked that Matthews Hall was a couple hundred years older than the State of Colorado. Waiting in the freshman line to engage Gordon Linen Service (two sheets, two towels, one pillow case, one week), I overheard repartee such as "Which collection of Beethoven's nine symphonies did you bring—the RCA version or the Deutsche Grammophon?" Was I a fish out of water? Soon, though, the hay fell from my ears.

Seven years later, graduating from Harvard Law and a stint in the Active Reserves of the Marine Corps, I returned to Denver; began practicing law. My 27-year law career took me through firms of different sizes and styles; a great variety of experiences. I most enjoyed civil litigation and "putting business deals together" or picking up their pieces if they failed. I endured a modest measure of notoriety (some good; some not so good). A divorce. I founded and operated for ten years a high-risk business, Rent-A-Cheap Heap—renting jalopies (and having to repossess a few from trailer parks at night) to persons (usually) without credit cards. Customers ranged from local politicians (seeking some anonymity); law-enforcement undercover agents; to ladies-of-the-street. I was a principal in other business ventures, some profitable, one a financial disaster.

After ten years of being single again (before the era of Match.com), I married Fran in 1997. We both retired from our various occupations in 2012. We have extensively traveled the world. I finally relinquished my (serial) responsibilities as director, president, and manager of our 191-unit townhome association—no longer having to deal with dog-waste violations.

I sired two loving children, one a magna graduate of Harvard College; the other a cum laude graduate of Brandeis. I served for several years interviewing high school seniors for the College. More recently, I've been gratified to solicit my College and Law School classmates for the respective Annual Giving Programs. I've been so fortunate for my Harvard experiences and deep-lasting friendships, especially at the College—and especially for a Western kid with his new wide-lapel suit.

I am but a grain of sand on the 381-year-old beach of Harvard, for which I am forever grateful.

The 1962 America Cup Races

A Recollection

James S. Eilberg[1]

In September of 1962, while serving as the senior Supply Officer aboard USS *Blandy* (DD 943) out of Newport, RI, I was detailed to the destroyer USS *Joseph P. Kennedy, Jr.* for the duration of the America Cup Races being held that year off Narragansett Bay. The *Kennedy*, named for the President's eldest brother killed in World War II, had only a very junior Supply Officer aboard and the Cruiser Destroyer *Atlantic Command* wanted to give him an assist because President John F. Kennedy '40, his family, and many of his White House staff would be observing the races each day from the destroyer *Kennedy*. By then, I was a Lieutenant whose job it was to oversee the Field Food Service Team's efforts to keep the press corps well fed during the daily sail and attend to any other of their needs. The Team was composed of four very accomplished chief commissary men, so my job was far from demanding.

Each morning, the press came aboard between 0800 and 0900. Shortly thereafter, the President and his party were piped aboard. They pretty much confined themselves to the forward part of the ship, the CO's quarters and Wardroom, which had been reconfigured for their use. That is, all except for the President's children, Caroline, almost five, and John-John, almost two, who seemed to have the run of the ship, particularly Caroline who kept the Secret Service folks challenged as she scampered around the 01 deck (one above the main deck) at will.

Lunch was served on the 01 level each noon and was well attended. I suspected the Press Secretary, Pierre Salinger, dined with the Presidential Party up forward and then came aft for a second luncheon. He was a hearty eater. Mrs. Jacqueline Kennedy came back to speak with everyone on several occasions, and I had the good fortune to speak with her more than once. Initially she told me, in her very breathless and beguiling voice, just how much she and the President enjoyed the Navy Mess at the White House. She could not have been nicer.

Robert Pierpoint, one of the several correspondents on board, would ask me each day what I thought the sea state was, and how many knots of wind speed we were experiencing. I made an educated guess. and that's what went into the evening papers that day. It didn't matter that I was a Supply Officer and never ventured onto the bridge that week to ascertain that information.

You must remember this was prior to cell phones and e-mail. So each day as the race was concluding about three in the afternoon, the reporters tapped out their stories on their typewriters, placed them in watertight bags with floatation devices attached and then dropped them from the fantail into the ocean. Each of the major news services had a speedboat tailing us, and they would retrieve the bags with boathooks and immediately head for shore at breakneck speed so the stories could be entered into that night's newscasts and the newspapers.

Well, one evening that week as my wife and I were just finishing up our dinner, I received a call from the assistant to the President's Naval Attaché, who held the rank of a Line Captain. He seriously outranked me. It seemed that Caroline was having a group of her friends on board the following day for the sail, and she had been very impressed with the Boatswain's piping aboard of her dad each day. She thought it would be a marvelous idea if she could give each of her friends a boatswain's pipe as a keepsake of their visit.

Obviously, the Attaché needed them immediately. Where does one get eight boatswains pipes at eight o'clock in the evening? Pipes were not stocked in a destroyer's ship's store. Thankfully, I knew one of the congregants at the Touro Synagogue in Newport who owned a local Army/Navy store. Fortunately, he was at home that night, and he had at least a dozen pipes in stock. He was flattered to be asked to furnish eight for the President's daughter. He agreed to meet me downtown at his store within the hour. He didn't even give me an invoice, and I never knew the price. Just before 10 p.m. I rolled up to the gates at Hammersmith Farm where the Kennedys were staying. I turned over the pipes to the Naval Attaché. He never asked where I had located them or how much they cost. Sometime later I wrote a very appreciative letter to the shop owner for his kindness. I never did find out if anyone reimbursed him.

A ship's boatswain spent much of the following day giving instruction to Caroline and her friends on the use of boatswain's pipes. And at the conclusion of the races each of us who had assisted with the Presidential visit was given a PT 109 tie clasp as a memento. I still have mine.

Incidentally, the New York Yacht Club boat *Weatherly* defeated the Australian yacht *Gretel* four races to one.

James S. Eilberg attended Navy Officer Candidate School immediately after graduation and was commissioned as a Line Ensign. He served on a Fletcher-class destroyer for two years and then on a destroyer escort before switching into the Supply Corps. His subsequent assignments were to the destroyer *Blandy*, staff of the cruiser destroyer *Force Atlantic* and the Norfolk Naval Shipyard. After promotion to Lieutenant Commander, he decided to leave active duty in 1967 and enter business in Portsmouth, VA. In the Reserves he was the Executive Officer and Commanding Officer of Reserve units, retiring in 1988 with the rank of Captain. He sold his salvage business in Portsmouth in 1991.

Endnote

1 Captain, Supply Corps, US Navy, retired

Figure 5.6.5.1 *Sever Hall, designed by H.H. Richardson AB 1849, and erected 1878–80, is seen through snowflakes.*

Reprinted courtesy of Harvard University

US Public Health Service

Conversation with Myself

Edward J. Rolde

Introduction

From July 1963 to June 1965, I did my military service in the US Public Health Service, assigned to an interdisciplinary group at the Harvard School of Public Health. These two years came in the middle of my medical training and education. This experience reinforced my already active interests in the relationship between health and economics, and was very influential in my personal development and my future career. I am going to describe some aspects of these two years in this essay. I will begin by describing a specific conversation and interaction I had during this time that I have always thought of as the symbolic dividing line between my "*younger self*" and my "*older self*". I will then describe the general circumstances of the two years.

The Conversation

In December 1963, in the fifth month of assignment to the School of Public Health, I was on a commercial flight from Cairo, Egypt, to Entebbe, Uganda. I was planning to find and investigate examples of the relationship of health and education to economic change in Uganda and Ethiopia. I had complete discretion to plan my trips, to make contacts, and to choose and look at specific situations. On my flight from Cairo to Entebbe, I had to change planes in Khartoum in the Sudan. The airport in Khartoum had an area for those awaiting connections to ongoing flights. In the waiting area, I noticed three men who had been seated near me on the plane from Cairo. They were sitting at a table in the café. They invited me to join them. All three were very buoyant, talking in excited tones. I quickly found out that they had been part of a delegation from Zanzibar that had gone to London to arrange and finalize negotiations for independence for their country from the UK. They were returning in triumph to Zanzibar. The negotiations had been successful and Zanzibar was now an independent country. My three companions were three of the ministers of the newly created Zanzibar government. I was with the new ministers of health, of economic affairs, and of education.

We talked about issues of health, education, and finances, but our conversation centered on their plans and the excitement involved in launching a new country. The men spoke of opportunities and gave little focus to the difficulties. I had never been to Zanzibar. I knew a little about its general culture and history but very little about the specific current events. I did have a degree of general knowledge about the differing cultural and historical groups across areas of east, north, and central Africa, and the general tensions between a variety of black and Arab African communities. Uganda, where I was headed, had been granted its independence by Britain in 1962; I knew that the situation there was complex and tense, and was rapidly changing.

As our conversation progressed, I began to feel and understand that these three gentlemen, with all their buoyancy and enthusiasm, were most likely headed for a troubled situation. It seemed to me that any doubts they might have about the success of their country's and their personal futures were overwhelmed by their recent success and accomplishments and by their focus on the positive aspects of their future plans.

> As we spoke, I began increasingly to believe that their country was going to move into a period of major instability, and that the political structure they envisaged was not likely to survive. Moreover, I actually began to suspect that they themselves were in personal danger. I clearly remember the contrast between my growing certainty that they would not survive, and their complete unawareness of that "fact" (as I began to think of it).

I did not express my feelings of concern to them. I felt it was inappropriate for me to make disruptive predictions during our relatively brief conversation about Zanzibar, which was their home, and which I had never even visited. After an hour or so they were called to board their plane for Zanzibar, and I went on to board my plane for Entebbe.

> About three weeks later I read in the newspapers that there had been a revolution in Zanzibar and that members of the government, including the three ministers I had met, had been killed.
>
> The facts of the situation were complex. Articles described that on December 10 (1963), Zanzibar had received its independence from the United Kingdom. The democratically elected government had been overthrown on January 12, 1964, in what has been termed "*the Zanzibar Revolution*".

> Several thousand ethnic Arab (5,000–12,000 Zanzibaris of Arabic descent) and Indian civilians had been murdered, and thousands more detained or expelled.

It struck me deeply that while I was still thinking of myself as a student, relatively young and inexperienced, I had realized that my ministerial companions would not survive, whereas they, men considerably older and more experienced than I, had had no inkling of this outcome.

> This event occurred 53 years ago, a month after my 28th birthday. Since that time, I have come to think of *that incident as the dividing line between my "younger self" and my "adult self".*

The General Circumstances of My Two Years in the Public Health Service

My major at Harvard College was Economics. My thesis was titled "*A comparison of heavy industrial development in India and China from 1949 to 1955*". During my college years, I focused increasingly on the relationship of economic and social development in developing countries.

I then entered Harvard Medical School, graduating in 1961. I interned in internal medicine at the Beth Israel Hospital (1961–62) and then began my psychiatric residency at the Mass Mental Health Center ('62–63). Both hospitals were Harvard teaching hospitals, and were adjacent to Harvard Medical School *(HMS)* and the Harvard School of Public Health *(HSPH).* Especially during medical school, I spent a lot of time with faculty at the School of Public Health, developed a number of projects, and made numerous trips to developing countries. One of the HSPH faculty I spent time with was Professor Robert Hamlin. He had been US Assistant Secretary of Health, Education and Welfare, and the US delegate to UNESCO. He came to HPSH in 1959 and became a full professor in 1962 and Director of the Department of Public Health Practice.

In June of 1963, my life took a sudden turn. The years of my internship and early residency, 1961–1963, were active years of confusion during the developing Vietnam War. The United States' involvement in the war waxed and waned rapidly. The number of draftees went up and down from year to year, parallel to the US activity in the war. Doctors could join the "*Berry Plan*", where they would be draft-deferred in their training, and then spend two years in the service after training was completed. I joined the Berry Plan in 1961, during my internship when it looked like doctors were going to be drafted. In 1962 the war situation cooled down for a while, the draft decreased, and it looked like doctors were unlikely to be drafted. I then resigned from the Berry plan in the beginning of my psychiatric residency in 1962. In 1963, as the war and the draft picked up, it appeared that I was once again at risk of being drafted.

When I told Dr. Hamlin about my status, he said that he and five other senior and prominent professors from differing faculties at Harvard had just formed a consortium to expand Harvard's role and interest in *the relationship between economic development and health and education in the developing world*. Dr. Hamlin called me in the following week and asked me if I would be willing to take a leave from my residency to spend the next two years working internationally with the Harvard group in fulfillment of my military service. The reader may not be surprised to hear that I agreed.

Within a few weeks, it had been arranged. I was told that Leona Baumgartner, the Director of Technical Cooperation and Research at AID, had arranged for a position to be funded for me at the Public Health Service, and that the Public Health Service had commissioned me and assigned me to the Harvard School of Public Health. I made arrangements to take a leave of absence from my psychiatric residency when the first year ended in June. I became an officer in the Public Health Service assigned to the HSPH with Dr. Hamlin as my commanding officer. In this capacity he wrote official orders for me which read, "*I order Dr. Edward J. Rolde to travel at his discretion throughout the world.*"

The group Dr. Hamlin had mentioned to me consisted of six major figures at Harvard at the time. In addition to Dr. Hamlin there was one other faculty member of the School of Public Health and one Faculty member at the School of Education. The other faculty member at the HSPH was Dr. John Snyder, Dean of the School of Public Health and known as the major developer HSPH's role in world health. As the project developed Dr. Snyder and I met frequently in Boston, and he visited us in Tunis along with Dr. Daggy, then Associate Dean of HSPH. The School of Education was represented by Professor Adam Curle, who had come to Harvard in 1961 as co-founder of the Center for Studies in Education and Development. For many years he had consulted and developed programs in many parts of the world. Dr. Curle is the subject of the 2016 book, *Adam Curle: Radical Peacemaker* by Tim Woodhouse and John Paul Lederach.

The group also included three members of the Faculty of Arts and Sciences. Professor John Dunlop was chairman of the Economics Department. (He was chairman of the Economics Department from '61–66 and Dean of Arts and Sciences '69–73.) He was the most prominent labor economist in the US and was the labor advisor to eleven American presidents from FDR through Bill Clinton. There were years when he would have as many as 50 visits to Washington DC. When I was on the project I met with him at a restaurant near the White House. The second member from Arts and Sciences was Dr. David McClelland, chairman of the Department of Psychology and Social Relations. Dr. McClelland was active in international consulting. He took a sabbatical during 1963. During 1963–64, I met with him in Tokyo, and subsequently in Nairobi, and then worked with him when we were both based in Tunis. The third Arts and Sciences Faculty member was Professor A.J. Meyer, an economist specializing in the Middle East. He published a book called *The Economy of Cyprus* in January 1962.

In 1963, when I met this group, they were very determined to expand Harvard's involvement in interdisciplinary programs dealing with the relationship of economic development to health and education in the developing world. I was fortunate to be able to develop relationships with all six men. This kind of interdisciplinary international work is very common today; in 1963 it was uncommon. The opportunity to work with this group was certainly one of the privileges and formative experiences of my life.

My Consultation to Pakistan

Near the end of my first year of psychiatric residency in June, my life changed dramatically. Dr. Hamlin called me into his office. He introduced me to two professors at the School of Public Health: Norman Scotch, a medical anthropologist, who a few years later was to become the founding dean of the B.U. School of Public Health; and Sol Levine, arguably the most prominent medical sociologist of the time, who was the director of the Social Science program at HSPH and a few years later established the Department of Behavioral Sciences at Johns Hopkins School of Public Health. Dr. Hamlin informed us that he had arranged for the three of us to go to Pakistan as consultants from Harvard to the government of Pakistan on the subject of the economic effects of malaria eradication programs. At that time Pakistan was composed of West and East Pakistan. Our mission involved both regions. About ten years later East Pakistan became Bangladesh, at the time of its creation the seventh most populous nation in the world and one of the poorest and least stable.

We made our trip in late June. We stopped in Geneva on the way to Pakistan to meet with relevant staff at the World Health Organization. A State Department officer met us in Karachi and stayed with us during our time in West and East Pakistan. We were there for about two or three weeks, combining meetings with public health officials and visits to countryside villages and medical facilities. At one point we drove along the Pakistan-India border from Lahore to the then capital of Pakistan, Rawalpindi to meet with the Minister of Health. We stopped in a number of villages along the way. In 1947 when Britain left the "*subcontinent*" and India and Pakistan became independent, the border regions became the site of both massive migration and violence, with Muslims, Hindus, and Sikhs needing to establish settlements on the appropriate side of the new border and to uproot themselves and claim new territory for their homes.

By 1948 when the great migration ended, it is estimated that more than fifteen million people had been uprooted, and between one and two million had died. I had been in communities in the underdeveloped world on many occasions during the ten years of my college, medical school and medical training. These villages along the India-Pakistan border had very poor economic and health conditions, but this came as nothing new to me after my past experience. I found myself much more affected by the poverty, however, due to my knowledge of the horrific conditions that these families had faced at the time of the great migration. I was also impressed by the nobility and complexity of the culture that we were privileged to see.

A Chance Meeting in Widener

One little story I often recount. In 1961 during my last year of medical school I would occasionally read in the Widener Library. One day a gentleman came over to me in the library and said, "*I am here from a foreign country.*" I did not focus at the time on the specific country he had named. "*I see you are reading a medical book. Could you tell me how I might get to see some of the Boston hospitals?*" I stopped my reading and drove him around Boston to see the Brigham, Mass General and other hospitals. A year or two later, arriving in Rawalpindi with Norm Scotch and Sol Levine, we walked into our meeting with the Minister of Health of Pakistan. As we entered his office, the minister looked at me in surprise, and said, "*I know you.*" He was the gentleman I had met at Widener Library and had driven around to see the hospitals of Boston. After the meeting he invited us to his home to meet his family—an unusual gesture at the time in this traditional Muslim society.

After ending our stay in Dacca, East Pakistan, we flew to Calcutta in India, meeting with an anthropological group from Harvard. At the time the United States ambassador to India was Harvard economist John Kenneth Galbraith, with whom I had studied at Harvard a few years before while writing my thesis on China and India. Norm, Sol and I then proceeded to Tokyo where we met with Professor McClelland.

As I have said, I was in my mid-20s during this trip, and Sol Levine and Norm Scotch were in their mid-40s. During the trip we all got along very well, had a good time together and remained friends afterwards. They had been taken aback however at our first meeting, when Dr. Hamlin called us in together a month or so before and introduced me as the third person on their mission to Pakistan. They were close colleagues, established faculty members, and saw me as young and inexperienced and perhaps a little out of place. They were used to working with colleagues their own age and status. Actually I had met Norm two years before. He had brought his ailing mother into the Beth Israel Hospital Emergency Ward in the middle of the night. The BIH is a big-time hospital, but I had been the doctor (in my internship) on call who had been the one to care for his mother. He said that I did very well, but that I was a little young for the job.

On this trip related to health and economics, I was both the economist and the MD for the team. I tended to be outspoken in our professional meetings because, as we all agreed, it was my job. I also will admit that I tend to be a little outspoken in my personal interactions as well, and that at that time I did not have the life experience that matched theirs. During the trip they gave me the nickname "*Red Chief*", which they and our state department escort occasionally used in referring to me. Their nickname "*Red Chief*" referred to the short story by O'Henry, "*The Ransom of Red Chief*". The story is about kidnappers of a young boy who demand ransom from his parents. The young boy is so difficult for them to handle that when the parents refuse to pay a ransom to the kidnappers, the kidnappers eventually pay the parents to take him back.

Our Tunisian Base of Operations

The base of operations for our multidisciplinary project during these two years was established as Tunis, the capital of Tunisia. Dr. McClelland lived with his family in Tunis during the first year as his sabbatical leave and functioned as the interdisciplinary project director. During the second year Dr. George Goethals, the assistant director of the Department of Psychology and Social Relations, lived in Tunis with his family during his sabbatical and took over as project director. We became good friends. After returning from the trip to Pakistan with Norm Scotch and Sol Levine and working on the submission of our report, I went to Tunis to help set up the logistics for our Tunisian base.

Professor A.J. Meyer had recruited a woman living in Tangiers to move to Tunis to be our project administrative assistant. Her name was Carla. I flew from Boston to Tangiers to meet her and proceed to Tunis with her. When I arrived in Tangiers she and I decided to buy ourselves cars in nearby Gibraltar (at Rock Motors) and drive across Morocco and Algeria to Tunisia: we felt it would not be easy to get cars in Tunisia at the time. There was a significant problem however: the country of Algeria was in chaos. Algeria had been declared independent by France in July 1962. The new constitution was adopted and Ahmed Ben Bella had been elected President in September 1963. The battle of Algiers, the battle for independence from France had been one of the most bloody and chaotic in history. Fighting had ceased when we began our travel, but the aftermath of the revolutionary war was chaos and disorganization.

Because of the chaos we were heading into in Algeria I bought myself a handgun, the only time in my life that I have possessed one, and practiced shooting at rocks till I gained a small amount of confidence in my shooting. Carla and I went down to Rabat, checked in at the US Embassy, and headed out for Tunis. We had about 1,200 miles to travel, about the same distance as from Boston to Florida. Much of our travel was through the windy roads of the Atlas Mountains. I drove ahead, and Carla followed. Fortunately, we did not encounter any areas of active conflict. In fact, people did not pay much attention to us. We kept moving because of the uncertain conditions. The biggest event was when Carla, who was following me in her car, drove off the edge of a windy mountain road and traveled a short distance down the mountainside. She was not hurt, only a little startled. I got into her car and drove it back up to the road; it wasn't damaged, and we continued our journey.

When we reached Algiers, the capitol and largest city of Algeria, we checked into the largest hotel in the city at the time. Again there was no active fighting to be seen, but the city was in chaos. We were the only guests in the hotel. There was no running water in the hotel, or, it appeared, in most of the city. Often, when we used the bathroom in one of our rooms, we would move to two other rooms.

The other city I remember most in Algeria at the time is Constantine. The city is dramatically striking. A *Wikipedia* article describes it as "*one of the grand spectacles of the north, made by nature and embellished by men. Over time the Oued Rhumel (the river running through the city) carved out a deep gorge around an outcrop of rock, creating a natural fortress that was already occupied in Neolithic times.*" I remember the impressive city surrounded by the dramatic gorge. Here too there was little or no sanitation in the city, and the gorge was a sad sight with its walls completely encased in garbage.

Consulting and Reconnaissance Trips

During the two years I was based in Tunis, most often during the first year, I made a number of consulting and reconnaissance trips to different countries. The most memorable for me was a time I spent based in Beirut, Lebanon, in the role of a consultant from the United Nations, visiting a number of Palestinian refugee camps and communities in "Palestine", in Jordan, in Lebanon and some other locations. I looked at economic conditions and health and education programs in the communities. When I arrived at a site, a delegation of the local Palestinian group would take me around each day.

One day the leader of the group on that day said to me: "*Dr. Rolde, you are the kind of person that we need here from the United States. You listen to us, look at what is happening, and understand us. The Jewish people have not forgotten their origins in over 1,000 years, and the world cannot expect us to forget our origins in 30 years.*" There was obviously a lot of tension in the region at the time.

On another day the Chief of Police from Cyprus served as my guide in the area. This was in the era when there was active fighting between Turkey and Cyprus.

I made other trips during the time I was based in Tunis, either sequentially or individually. I went to Saudi Arabia to look at the relationship between the Aramco company compounds and the rest of country. I flew down to Sebha in central Libya with a State Department escort to see central Libya where Khadafy was commanding a rebel force at the time. I was escorted by a State Department representative to look at some of Tito's functioning in Belgrade. On a trip to Ankara, Turkey, I arranged for the Medical School Library in Ankara to get a subscription to the *New England Journal of Medicine*. I went at one point with Norm and Sol, who came over from Boston for the occasion, to consult with Israel on the development of its heart and cardiovascular programs. During much of the time when I was based in Tunis, I had two United States passports, arranged by the State Department, because it would not have been possible for me to travel easily in Israel and in some regional countries with passport stamps from both sides of the tensions.

During the second year of the project, Professor George Goethals and I worked together as consultants and visited various regions of Tunisia. We studied an area within the city of Tunis where the population consisted of migrants from rural areas of the country. I worked most of the time in colloquial Arabic and French. The average household in the community had between two and three children who died before the age of five. In the course of this project, Dr. Goethals and I became lifelong friends, and after our return to the US, we got together weekly for lunch or breakfast for the next 35 years.

Continuing On with My Education

When my two years in the project and the Public Health Service were finished in June 1965, I returned to my psychiatric residency at Harvard and the Mass. Mental Health Center. During those two years, I also earned my MS degree at the School of Public Health. I then received a career development grant from NIH, and during that time finished a Sc.D. at the School of Public Health.

In the years that followed, I continued my career interest in the *relationship between health and economics* and also maintained a very strong interest in *regions of marked and dramatic social change*.

Ed Rolde's career relating economics to health has involved teaching, administration and clinical practice. The holder of five Harvard Degrees (BA, Economics, 1957; MD, 1961; MS, Public Health, 1967; DSc, Public Health, 1974; and CSS, Administration and Finance, 1992), he taught at Harvard for over 30 years. While his major faculty appointment was in the Medical School, he also taught courses at the School of Public Health and the Extension School, and held appointments in the Faculty of Arts and Sciences and the School of Education. He consulted in the US and globally, including Africa, Asia and Latin America.

In the health care field he has held administrative positions as Medical Director and Vice President Blue Cross of NE Pennsylvania; Director of Medical Management at Blue Cross of Massachusetts; Associate Medical Director and

Director of Mental Health at the Dartmouth Hitchcock Clinic; and Medical Director of Physician Hospital Organization of Maine. He practiced clinical psychiatry combined with administrative functions when serving as Director of Court Clinics of Massachusetts and Medical Director of Southern Middlesex Opportunity Center, a major antipoverty center in Framingham, Massachusetts. A Boston native, he never abandoned his home base of metropolitan Boston while traveling the world.

A Career in Public Health

James L. Gale

Like some of our classmates, I had little idea what I would do after four years of undergraduate life at Harvard. I had taken one premedical course each year, in the event I decided to try medical school, but that course was far from certain.

When the time came for some action, however, I had no clear plan. I decided to fill out the medical school applications and send off packets to four schools. If I failed to be admitted, I would "get a job teaching in Turkey", my fallback plan. I also requested a letter of recommendation from my House master, John Finley. One phrase passed on to me from Dr. Finley's letter was that I was a "diamond in the rough". I've often wondered how that accolade was received.

I was pleased to be accepted at Columbia's College of Physicians and Surgeons in New York City. Aside from diffuse excitement about the project, I had few specific ideas about what my forthcoming experience might be like.

I had never lived outside of Massachusetts. My father had lost his job after the 1929 Crash, and did not offer any professional role models to follow. I had no physicians in my family. This was an advantage, as I felt no pressure to follow any particular course after medical school.

Choosing a Career within Medicine

In 1957, male medical students were deferred from the Selective Service Draft until they had finished both medical school and a clinical residency. Their Draft Boards usually called them up at the end of this training period, however. During my internship, a clinician-epidemiologist from Sloan Kettering Hospital addressed our house staff group (about 30 residents and interns) about his experience in the US Public Health Service. The service requirement was for a minimum of two years, included training in epidemiology, and working either at the Center for Disease Control in Atlanta, GA, or one of the then 48 state health departments. The job description included participating/leading outbreak investigations, keeping track of known disease conditions (surveillance), and other duties as assigned, with plenty of autonomy. This service satisfied the Selective Service requirement and did not appear to bar any further clinical training following discharge.

At a time when everyone was attempting to find the best situation they could in which to fulfill their Draft time, this sounded like an interesting alternative, so I chose it.

Epidemic Intelligence Service at CDC

We were called to visit Atlanta in April of 1964. I was introduced to grits for breakfast, and a week's presentation of 15 minute talks about epidemic investigations, surveillance projects, problems in hospital infections, and other responsibilities and workings of Epidemic Intelligence Officers (as we were called) in state health departments. I could see that this assignment was going to call both on my medical knowledge and on analytic skills with numbers in ways I had not encountered in medical school.

Four months later I started my federal service with a month's training in investigating and analyzing epidemics. Little did I anticipate the two outbreaks in which I was to participate before the end of the year.

The first was in Houston in September: an outbreak of St. Louis encephalitis. Birds migrating from Central America carried this infection. When they reached the Houston area, mosquitoes bit the birds, became infected, and then bit other local birds, including pigeons and sparrows. Mosquitoes biting these non-migrating birds then bit and infected humans. Interrupting the mosquito cycle was the most effective way to intervene to end the outbreak.

By the end of the year over 700 persons were thought infected, with over 30 deaths, mostly in the elderly.

The CDC mobilized over 50 US Public Health Service workers, including physician epidemiologists like myself, nurses, statisticians, sanitarians, ornithologists, and entomologists. I did not realize the Government had such a diversity of professionals it could mobilize in such short notice. Through the course of the outbreak I realized how much responsibility field epidemiologists took on. My tasks included interviewing patients and their families, calling hospitals to keep tabs on the extent of the epidemic, and analyzing data to determine where prevention efforts could best be directed. For example, infection rates were higher in poorer parts of the city. Many of the houses here were by open drainage ditches, which provided places for mosquitoes to breed. These areas were then targeted for mosquito spraying.

Investigating an Outbreak of Plague in Bolivia

My second outbreak assignment that year was to travel to Bolivia to attempt to bring back a culture of the Plague bacteria, which was rumored to be causing an epidemic of pneumonic plague (a much more deadly illness than the more common bubonic plague, caused by the same organism).

After a three-day field trip to the US Public Field Plague station for a crash course in "plague ecology and bacteriology", we flew to Washington, DC, to get our red "Official Passports", and left for Lima, Peru, to check in with the regional WHO office. I was learning about government protocol the fast way, on the job.

We proceeded to La Paz, Bolivia, where we spotted a small article on the back pages of an English newspaper. This item described the outbreak we had been hoping to find and investigate. After introductions through the United States embassy, the Bolivian national oil company lent us the services of a senior English-speaking company physician. An in-country plane hop, an eight-hour truck ride, and a three-day donkey ride up the eastern slopes of the Andes brought us to the very remote village of Descargadero, original population 31.

By the time we arrived 27 persons had died of the plague, and the remaining three inhabitants had moved away. High susceptibility owing to crowded living conditions, and malnutrition combined with local burial ceremonies near deceased family members, resulted in respiratory spread and this high mortality rate.

Exploring the village, we found a solitary herdsman who showed us the grave of the most recently deceased inhabitant. We exhumed the grave to the point where we could remove a fifth finger, having learned that bone marrow was the part of the body most likely to preserve the organism in these infections. Retracing our steps, with burros and truck, we returned to a regional public health laboratory to inoculate ground-up bone tissue into guinea pigs. They became infected, and their frozen organs, as requested, were shipped back to the United States for laboratory studies. All this had occurred in under six months after I had enrolled in the Public Health Service.

Figure 5.7.2.1 *US Public Health Service team from Atlanta arriving by donkey in decimated Bolivian village on Andes eastern slope to investigate pneumonic plague outbreak and exhume remains to recover specimens for processing at special pathogens laboratory at Fort Detrick, MD*

Photo by the author, who is not shown

From Virus Hunter to Epidemiologist to Public Health Practitioner and Educator

Subsequent decisions and opportunities took me to a National Institutes of Health (NIH) virus laboratory attached to the Gorgas Hospital in Panama for the remaining years of my government service. Although the investigations were not quite so dramatic, they were still interesting. I spent two and a half years learning about viruses, and how they were isolated in cell culture. I also traveled up and down the Central American isthmus to collect laboratory specimens from hospitalized persons with presumed encephalitis or meningitis (including polio), and investigated several outbreaks.

At the end of this period I decided I liked epidemiology well enough to make it my career. Choosing a fellowship in preventive medicine in

Seattle precluded my accepting a clinical infectious disease fellowship in Boston. In retrospect, this was an important turning point.

During this time at the University of Washington, I participated in field studies testing rubella vaccine in Taiwan and subsequently accepted an offer to join the University of Washington faculty. Within a year, however, our Preventive Medicine department had transformed itself into a School of Public Health, with our own dean.

My progression up the academic ladder over the next 35 years, teaching and publishing, corresponded with the emergence of public health/prevention/wellness in the nation's consciousness.

In 1988 the National Institute of Medicine published a report, "The Future of Public Health". It was intended to wake up both academic public health and public health practice to greater collaboration. The preface by Richard Remington summed up the problem:

> "In recent years, there has been a growing sense that public health, as a profession, as a governmental activity, and as a commitment of society is neither clearly defined, adequately supported, nor fully understood. Concerns for chronic diseases, geriatric disorders, substance abuse, teen pregnancy, and toxic substances in the environment seem to some critics of public health, both within and outside government, to be inadequately addressed by a public health apparatus originally conceived and constructed to meet a different set of concerns. . . . This very complexity, when added to the perceived potential vulnerability to new epidemics and environmental hazards of virtually the entire population, lead many observers to conclude that a governmental presence, perhaps an expanded presence, in health has never been more necessary."

Up to this time a large part of the public thought that good health was synonymous with good clinical care and effective medicine. A Seattle focus group, when asked what came to mind when they heard, "public health", immediately said, "public toilets". A Washington State public health official stated that health spending by the United States went 95% to clinical medicine and only 5% to public health and prevention services.

In 1991 a respected Eastern Washington public health practitioner approached our School looking for a faculty member who could take the job of part-time health officer of a rural eastern Washington county. This county, two hours drive from Seattle, over the Cascade Mountains had a population of 31,000, with 7,000 living in the county seat. This new job would allow me an to participate in the effort to bring local and state health departments closer to academic institutions and to put some of the ideas set forth in the Institute of Medicine report into practice in a rural setting, unlike where I lived and worked. These included making the public aware of a pubic health "system" which started with personal responsibility for healthy lifestyle, to community responsibility to educate citizens about healthier lifestyles, providing safer streets, air, and water, to state responsibility to provide expertise and training to local professional personnel.

I took the job, without having to give up my position at the University. I was able to drive to the county health department in two hours, two to three days a month, and additionally supervise physician preventive medicine residents who drove over weekly.

Modeling Needs Assessments in Designing Public Health Projects

One of the first projects we undertook in 1991 was a community public health assessment project to identify strengths and needs in the community. A small free clinic for the county's small population of migrant workers, a free dental clinic, and pre-natal classes for low-income mothers were some of the results of this process. In addition a community group of influential citizens formed a permanent Board of Health Advisory group to work with our elected three-member Board of County Commissioners, which was also our Board of Health.

This group was able to get endorsement for implementing sex education at appropriate grade level in the public school to reduce unwanted pregnancies in teenage girls, promote gun safety measures, HIV prevention efforts, and provide counseling and services for young mothers. The county commissioners were willing to listen to local citizens taking the time to explore these controversial issues. In addition, the advisory board was able to raise health department salaries by 20% after surveying comparable counties and finding that our county was at least that far behind in pay levels.

These ideas played out in my local community with numerous local partnerships with private and non-profit entities. These included health fairs and public school curriculum revisions. Help came from state agencies with expertise in a variety of areas, and critical funding of program from federal grants to my university, as well as to the state agencies, which then made distributions to the 39 Washington counties through their local public health agencies.

I retired from the Health Officer job in 2002, with the added satisfaction of having made many friends in those years among health professionals and citizens of that county.

Summing Up

Although I resigned from my final teaching at the University in 2014, I considered my years at the health department some of the richest years of my later career.

Looking back, I consider myself lucky to have found such an interesting professional life: exciting, dangerous at times, challenging, stimulating and satisfying.

James L. Gale, MD, a Boston native, grew up in Andover, MA, where he attended Phillips Academy as a day student before entering Harvard. In 1961, after receiving his MD degree from the College of Physicians and Surgeons at Columbia University, he began his internship and residency in internal medicine on the Cornell service at Bellevue Hospital and Memorial Sloan Kettering Hospital in New York City. From 1964 until 1967 he served in the US Public Health Service as Epidemic Intelligence Service Officer in the Centers for Disease Control (CDC), and was stationed primarily in the Panama Canal Zone. He also served as head of the Department of Microbiology at a US Naval Reserach Laboratory (NAMRU-2) for three years. His subsequent education included a fellowship in Preventive Medicine at the University of Washington and a Master's degree in Preventive Medicine before he joined its faculty.

His career in Seattle consisted of research in infectious diseases, teaching epidemiology, and serving as a part-time Health Officer in a rural Eastern Washington county. In 2004 Jim became an emeritus faculty member at the rank of Professor, and continued to teach part-time until 2014.

Intelligence Service

The Snowden Revelations with Comments from a Former NSA Officer

Eugene Yeates

I propose in this essay to describe my career at the National Security Agency *(NSA)* and to provide you with my views on what I'll call the ***Snowden situation***—the fall-out from the series of revelations concerning NSA by Edward Snowden, a former NSA contract employee, which first appeared in the press in June 2013.

The National Security Agency (NSA)

When I was about to graduate from college in 1957, all of us were subject to the draft, and we were all thinking hard about the least painful way to satisfy our military obligation. In my case I chose the US Navy and went about finding out how to go to Officer's Candidate School *(OCS)*. However, when I went to take my physical at the Boston Navy Yard, I was shocked to learn that I was color blind and therefore unable to be admitted to OCS. I was later contemplating

Figure 5.8.1.1 *Ensign Eugene Yeates, USNR, 1958, before leaving for duty in the Aleutian Islands*

a dreaded two years as an Army private when the Navy changed its mind and said I could go to OCS after all but that I would be assigned to a part of the Navy that was so secret that no one could tell me what they did. I accepted their offer and started on the path to NSA.

My association with the National Security Agency lasted over 30 years. I'm proud to have been an NSA employee and I believe that agency has made enormous contributions to the security of our country since its creation in 1952 and going back to its earlier roots in World War II.

When I arrived at NSA in 1959 there was a saying that the initials "NSA" stood for "No Such Agency". Though it was larger in terms of personnel and budget than the CIA, it was virtually unknown to the public then and made every effort to keep its highly classified and sensitive activities under wraps. As employees we were told to tell anyone who asked that we worked for the Department of Defense and I reflexively find myself doing that to this day.

Shortly after I began my first tour in 1959, we were all shocked when two young NSA mathematicians, who worked in the highly secret office at NSA charged with analyzing and breaking Soviet codes and ciphers, defected to the Soviet Union. Their last names were Martin and Mitchell. At the time, those of us working at NSA found it difficult to imagine a more devastating blow to NSA's mission and to the country's national security interests. Today I believe that the damage to US interests caused by Edward Snowden far exceeds that caused over 50 years ago by Martin and Mitchell.

I'll begin by stating that Americans are proud and thankful for the rights provided to us by the Constitution but at the same time we are mindful of the need to protect ourselves against adversaries that threaten our well-being. The Snowden revelations have among other things caused a situation where we need to examine these two sometimes competing issues and create a balance between them. This is a difficult task but I am confident that we will be able to complete it in a way that addresses the concerns of those on both sides of the debate. I will attempt to at least shed some new light on some of the key issues involved.

I would also say I do not believe the public has been well served by many of the press accounts dealing with the Snowden revelations. In the case of *The Guardian* newspaper I think the problem may be that the authors of articles based on the revelations seem to be motivated more by political objectives than by a desire to report the facts and that it is therefore good if NSA is made to look like a culprit. On the other hand, reports in *The Washington Post* and the *The New York Times* often seem to reflect the fact the authors have trouble interpreting the rather complicated and difficult-to-understand PowerPoint presentations Snowden seems to favor in his releases. In any event it appears to me a large number of press reports either charge or imply that NSA spends much of its time collecting the content of phone calls of US citizens. That is simply not correct.

NSA's Mission

I want to turn now to NSA's mission, how I came to work there, and some of the things I did during my 30-year career.

President Harry Truman created NSA in a top secret memorandum dated November 4, 1952 entitled "Communications Intelligence Activities". That day also happened to be my 17th birthday, and I was a senior at the Blake School in Minneapolis. The Truman memo established NSA as an element of the Department of Defense to unify under a single military director the squabbling, competing, and uncoordinated activities of the three service signals intelligence elements—the Army Security Agency, the Air Force Security Service and the Naval Security Group.

Although NSA was established in the Department of Defense, it was created as a national foreign intelligence agency to—quoting from the Truman memo—"*satisfy the legitimate foreign intelligence requirements*" of all executive departments and agencies of the US government.

NSA was given a very specific foreign intelligence mission "*to provide an effective, unified organization and control of the communications intelligence activities of the United States conducted against foreign governments, to provide for integrated operations policies and procedures pertaining thereto*".

NSA does not decide what foreign information it will try to collect. A national process managed by the Director of National Intelligence [James Clapper] on behalf of the President and the National Security Council, determines what the collection objectives and priorities are.

It is NSA's mission to satisfy those foreign intelligence requirements through the acquisition of foreign communications used by foreign countries, powers, intelligence organizations, armies and, especially since 9/11, terrorist organizations and individuals.

I want to stress here that despite what some in the media would like their readers to believe, *NSA's mission is foreign intelligence, not domestic.*

NSA has neither the authority nor the responsibility to intercept domestic communications exclusively between US citizens. In fact it is strictly illegal for it to do so. Neither NSA nor any other element of the Intelligence Community—except for the FBI—may undertake any intelligence collection for the purpose of acquiring information concerning the domestic activities of US citizens.

My Introduction to Signals Intelligence *(SIGINT)*

Having described how NSA was created and its mission, I want to move on to how I first became exposed to NSA operations. After completing four months of Navy OCS and two months of communications school, I received orders to proceed to my first duty station, the Naval Communications Station on the Aleutian Island of Adak, Alaska. In the Bering Sea roughly 1,000 miles west of Kodiak, Alaska, Adak is remembered by the 6,000 US troops stationed there during World War II as cold, foggy, windy, lots of mud, Quonset huts to live in, but no women and no trees.

It hadn't changed much when I arrived in September of 1958, except that we were able to move into a BOQ *(Bachelor Officers' Quarters)* constructed of poured concrete rather than the deteriorating Quonset huts that were still scattered across the island. There were school teachers whom we could date if we were lucky. Adak measures approximately 22 by 40 miles and is credited with being the 25th largest island in the US, more than twice as big as Nantucket, which I have been visiting for over 40 years, but I can assure you that it certainly is not as charming as Nantucket.

During the Cold War the entire island was controlled by the US Navy and was used as a base of operations for performing surveillance activities against the Soviet Union. Naval reconnaissance aircraft flew missions against the Soviets from Adak's airfield and, as I will describe in more detail, the Naval Communications Station monitored and collected data from various Soviet military communications targets. At the height of the Cold War, NSA had about 30 such intercept stations located around the world.

When I arrived at the "*Comm*" Station, as we called it, I found a compound surrounded by barbed wire, guarded by armed marines and with lots of locked doors that were off limits to anyone without the proper security clearance. That turned out to include me, since my security clearance had not yet been granted. I was therefore assigned to be the base Special Services Officer with responsibilities for running the bowling alley and the commissary. Not exactly my idea of why I had joined the Navy. After about a month, that all changed when my special top secret clearance came through and I was allowed to pass through the locked doors into what is the completely different and fascinating world of collecting, analyzing, and reporting communications intelligence.

On my first visit to the operational space in which those functions were performed I still vividly remember finding a dimly lit room filled with Navy enlisted men wearing ear phones and sitting at individual positions filled with electronic gear that allowed them to intercept and process the various Soviet military targets to which they were assigned. I could hear the sound of Morse code being sent by Soviet operators. I was able to give up my Special Services duties and became for the next year the Assistant Officer in Charge of the Adak signals collection operation, and I became hooked by the novelty of the tasks being performed and the importance of that mission to US national security. It was the beginning of what became a 30-year career with the National Security Agency.

My Next Stop—NSA Headquarters

When my year-long tour on Adak was complete in September 1959, I was transferred to NSA headquarters in its new building (remember NSA was created in 1952 and was therefore only seven years old at that time) at Fort George G. Meade, MD, on the Baltimore–Washington Parkway about halfway between those two cities.

Unless they had special engineering or linguistic backgrounds, most junior officers ordered to NSA were assigned to an analytic organization covering a specific area such as the Soviet Army, Navy or Air Force. I was lucky and got assigned as a watch officer in something called the Production Intelligence Watch Office. The bad news was we often found ourselves having to come to work at 4 p.m. in the afternoon or at midnight. The good news was that our job was to read all of the intelligence traffic coming into or leaving NSA, compile interesting information into a daily report distributed throughout the agency, and, taking turns, brief the NSA Director and his senior staff each weekday morning.

What that really meant is that I and my seven junior officer colleagues received a top-down education in the broad areas which NSA covered and were involved directly in helping to manage crisis events as they occurred. For example, I was the officer on duty the night in May

1960 when our U2 reconnaissance aircraft was shot down over the Soviet Union creating an international incident of gigantic proportions and embarrassment for President Eisenhower and the United States, and as such I was one of the very few Americans who knew what was going on while the event was actually occurring. I participated that night in the preparation of the message that informed the CIA, who were the mission sponsors, along with the Defense and State Departments and the White House, as to what had occurred. This was a heady and very educational experience for a young naval officer.

I learned so much about the workings of NSA and of its tremendous contributions to the security of the country that, as my Navy tour was drawing to a close in 1961, I barely hesitated when my supervisor asked if I would consider converting to civilian status, which I did in August 1961. I was also getting married in September of '61 and my wife, Nancy, and I decided rather than return to Minneapolis and my job at Cargill, which I had left to join the Navy, we would spend a year more in Washington and then return to Minnesota. Once the year was up, however, I was really hooked by the work at NSA and I continued on with them for 27 more years. I might say I am extremely proud of the work I did while at NSA and have never regretted my decision to stay on.

Snowden

Turning now to the subject of Edward Snowden, I will describe some actions I and some former NSA colleagues took and the oversight environment in which NSA operates. I will also comment on some of the revelations and how they were portrayed in the press and, finally, provide my personal assessment of what this all means for the future of NSA and our country's national security.

To begin this discussion I want to draw on some thoughts from an author named Edward Lucas who was a senior editor at the *Economist* and who describes himself as a former foreign correspondent with 30 years' experience in Russian and east European affairs.

In a book entitled *The Snowden Operation: Inside the West's Greatest Intelligence Disaster*, published in January 2014, Lucas begins as follows:

> "Some of my most respected colleagues tell a story that goes like this: Edward Snowden had a well-paid post inside American intelligence, as a contractor for the NSA. *Disillusioned by the discovery that his employers and their allies engaged in mass*

> *collection of details of private communications, he took a cache of secret documents detailing this appalling behavior and shared them with media outlets across the world.* The noble crusader was bravely risking his career and freedom in the pursuit of truth and transparency—a sacrifice that has made him a worthy candidate for man of the year awards and for canonization as a secular saint."

Lucas continues as follows. He says: "This book tells a different story. My reading of the facts is that *Snowden is a 'useful idiot'*. His theft of documents should be seen not as a heroic campaign but as a reckless act that has jeopardized our safety and played into our enemies' hands."

Lucas goes on to say: "*The damage wrought by Snowden's revelations takes five forms.* It weakens America's relations with Europe and other allies; it harms security relationships between those allies particularly in Europe; it corrodes Western public opinion's trust in their countries' security and intelligence services; it undermines the West's standing in the eyes of the rest of the world; *and it has paralyzed Western intelligence agencies.*"

Whether you agree with either of the opposing views of Snowden as described by Edward Lucas or come down somewhere in the middle, I think Lucas has provided some useful boundaries for examining the Snowden revelations and their implications in more detail.

Since 2000 I have lived in a region of the country called the Upper Connecticut River Valley which has Hanover and Dartmouth College as its cultural center and includes many smaller towns in both Vermont and New Hampshire. Living near me are two old friends and former NSA colleagues. We meet periodically in Hanover for lunch and, not surprisingly, a principal topic of discussion over the past few years has been Edward Snowden.

In November 2013, I and one of those colleagues made a presentation on Snowden to about 80 mostly retired individuals at a symposium sponsored by Dartmouth's continuing education organization. I want to share some of our thoughts with you.

In my friend's presentation, he described NSA's mission and the extensive set of laws and regulations that governs its operations, particularly as they relate to the protections they provide for the privacy and rights of US citizens in regard to unreasonable searches and seizures as specified in the fourth amendment of the US Constitution.

He cited the following four documents and explained their relevance:

(1) **The Foreign Intelligence Surveillance Act of 1978** *(called the **FISA Act**)*

(2) **Executive Order 12333**

(3) **The Patriot Act of 2001**

(4) **The Foreign Intelligence Surveillance Act of 1978** ***Amendments Act of 2008***

Each of these four documents authorized new intelligence tools, some of which became the focus of the debate centering on the National Security Agency. I'll focus here on *one key issue* that was being discussed in Washington.

The Snowden controversy introduced a new term into the mainstream of the discussion and that is the word "*metadata*", which can be described as details about a communication, but not involving the actual content of the communication. For a mobile phone call, this could be the number dialed and the duration of the call. For an e-mail, metadata could include the size, date, addressee and details about the sender such as his Internet connection.

Section 215 of the **Patriot Act** amended the Foreign Intelligence Surveillance Act of 1978 to permit the government to obtain from the Foreign Intelligence Surveillance Court, which was also created in the 1978 law, an *order directing US communications carriers to provide the government with metadata from calls made between the US and a foreign country, and calls made entirely within the US.*

NSA is not allowed to obtain the content of the call, the identity of any party to the call, or any cell-site locational information relating to the call. The **FISA Court**, all of whose judges are appointed by the Chief Justice of the Supreme Court, first authorized the Section 215 Program in 2006, and it has been renewed 34 times by 14 different judges. All of these judges have found the program legal and constitutional.

NSA's purpose in collecting and analyzing this metadata is to determine whether known or suspected terrorist operatives have been in contact with other persons who may be engaged in terrorist activities, including persons and activities within the United States.

When NSA's analysis results in a "*reasonable suspicion*" that a foreign terrorist element may be operating in the US, it provides a tip-off to the FBI, which then attempts to identify and investigate the subscriber. This may also include the FBI's own application to the FISA Court for a warrant to authorize interception of the contents of communications to and from this number.

NSA does *not* intercept the content of any domestic phone calls under this Section 215 program.

Because of the sensitive nature of the Section 215 Program and its 4th amendment implications, there exists an extensive *oversight process* to ensure that neither the law nor the constitutional rights of US citizens are being violated. Internal to NSA the process is monitored by the Inspector General, the General Counsel and the relatively new NSA Director of Compliance, supported by a staff of 300 people monitoring the process 24 hours a day, seven days a week. External to NSA the program is monitored by elements of the Department of Justice, the Director of National Intelligence, the Foreign Intelligence Surveillance Court, and the two intelligence committees of the Congress.

I've spent so much time describing the 215 program because I wanted to try to present a picture of the kind of thing NSA is actually doing in the *war on terror*, as opposed to the many negative and sometimes unbalanced reports in the press on the operational activities and capabilities of the NSA that have been based on the voluminous data stolen by Edward Snowden from NSA's files.

Again, too many of these reports, either in their headlines or in the body of the article, are worded in a manner that creates deep suspicion that NSA is deliberately spying on Americans.

Some Recent Activities

On June 2, 2015, the US Senate passed, and President Obama signed, the "**USA Freedom Act**" which restored in modified forms several provisions of the Patriot Act that had expired the day before, while for the first time imposing some limits on the bulk collection of telecommunications data on US citizens by American intelligence agencies. The restrictions were seen by many as stemming from Snowden's revelations.

One of the many films/documentaries on Edward Snowden is Oliver Stone's *Snowden* released in 2016. The film pictures Snowden as a likeable computer genius who made enormous contributions to the NSA where he was a contract employee. It then went on about his courageous act as a whistleblower who exposed how NSA was spying on US citizens.

Shortly before the film's release, Stone said Snowden should be pardoned, calling him a "*patriot above all*" and suggesting that he should run the NSA himself. After the movie opened, a number of full-page advertisements appeared in the *NY Times* and elsewhere calling on President Obama to grant a pardon to Snowden.

Summary of the *Snowden Situation*

Described in Wikipedia as *an acknowledged subject of great controversy,* Edward Snowden has been variously called a hero, a whistleblower, a dissident, a traitor and a patriot. His disclosures have fueled debates over mass surveillance, government secrecy, and the balance between national security and information privacy. He was granted asylum in Russia in 2013 and remains there to this day (January 2017). It is likely that he will be the subject of worldwide attention for many years to come.

Concluding Remarks

I want to conclude this essay with two observations:

First, there is no doubt in my mind that *our country is less safe* as a result of Snowden's actions. I therefore believe that Edward Snowden should be tried in a US court for the criminal act of releasing highly sensitive intelligence information to the press.

Second, in the four years since Snowden first released the stolen materials to the press, the Obama administration and the Congress have made a number of *changes regarding some NSA operations*. I assume the Trump administration will continue that process going forward.

I hope any discussions over rules that would govern certain NSA operations are approached in a way which considers *both protection of civil liberties* and the continued maintenance of a robust and *capable intelligence collection system* to protect our country.

We would be very foolish, in my opinion, to try to wage a successful war against enemies who are committed to do us harm with one arm tied behind our back.

Figure 5.8.1.2 *Gene Yeates in the Oval Office with President George H.W. Bush in December 1992 shortly before he left office, on the occasion of the President's Foreign Intelligence Advisory Board's visit to the White House.*

Gene Yeates, awarded the National Intelligence Distinguished Service Medal by the Director of Central Intelligence in 1995, was born and raised in Minneapolis and has been a resident of Orford, NH, since 2000. A graduate of the Blake School, Harvard College, George Washington University and the National War College, he worked for nearly 50 years in the fields of intelligence and national security, including 30 years with the National Security Agency.

Some key NSA assignments were Chief, Office of Legislative Affairs; Director of Policy; and Associate Deputy Director of Operations. He had external NSA assignments at the Naval Communications Station in Adak, AK (as a naval officer); the European Command Headquarters in Stuttgart, Germany; the Joint Chiefs of Staff in the Pentagon; and the Director of Central Intelligence's staff in Washington, DC.

In 1992 he was appointed by President George H.W. Bush as Executive Director of the President's Foreign Intelligence Advisory Board; asked to stay on by President Clinton, he continued in that position at the White House until 1995.

In the private sector, Gene held positions with Cargill, Inc. (1957–58); United Technologies Corporation (1985–90); and with Science Applications International Corporation (SAIC), from which he retired after 13 years in 2006 as a Senior Vice President.

Law

Federal Justice Department—Ethics

To Disclose or Not to Disclose—That Still Is the Question

Earl Silbert

FBI Director James Comey's public disclosures relating to the FBI's investigation into Hillary Clinton's e-mails created an uproar. The disclosures occurred in 2016 from July to three days before the national election. Many Democrats were convinced that Comey's disclosures cost Clinton the election. The disclosures, critics claimed, were contrary to longstanding Department of Justice policies not to discuss pending criminal investigations and not to permit politics to have any role on investigative decisions. The Inspector General of the Department of Justice under the former administration opened an investigation, which as of February 2017 had yet to issue a report and is now under a new administration.

The uproar from Comey's disclosures reminded me of the very troublesome disclosure dilemma I confronted when serving as the first Watergate prosecutor. To this day, I am not completely confident that my proposed resolution of the dilemma, as described below, was appropriate.

* * *

At the time, in June 1972, I was serving as the First Assistant US Attorney in the US Attorney's Office in Washington, DC. I had been assigned to direct the grand jury investigation into the burglary of the offices of the Democratic National Committee in the Watergate Office Building. Five men had been arrested in the offices, caught red-handed.

Four were Cuban Americans. The fifth was James McCord. He was director of security for the Committee to Re-Elect the President, Nixon. McCord had previously worked for the CIA.

The investigation by the FBI and my two fellow prosecutors, Don Campbell and Seymour Glanzer, quickly implicated two more suspects, one working in the Finance Committee to Re-elect the President (G. Gordon Liddy) and a part-time White House employee (Howard Hunt). Here the investigation stalled. Witnesses were not in our view telling us the truth, and the seven known co-conspirators created a ring of silence based on assertions of their Fifth Amendment rights.

Time was passing. Election Day, November 7, 1972, was fast approaching. The Democrats were critical of the investigation I was conducting. They were demanding the most exhaustive investigation in the shortest possible time, standards that were plainly impossible, being mutually exclusive. Henry Petersen, the Assistant Attorney General for the Criminal Division of the Department of Justice, told me that the Attorney General, responding to public pressure, asked if we could have the indictment by Labor Day, September 4. I told him "No." I needed at least another week to complete our investigation.

After an extraordinarily hectic week, the grand jury indictment of the Watergate seven: Liddy, Hunt, McCord, and the four Cuban-Americans, was filed on September 15. I recognized that there was a compelling public interest in discovering, prior to the presidential election, whether the burglary was directed by Republican leadership. Or was it a scheme of mid-level types such as McCord, Hunt and Liddy? We prosecutors did not know the answer. The evidence from our investigation was ambiguous: some of it indicated that higher-ups were involved, some of that responsibility ended with the seven defendants. We prosecutors had to be alert and careful that our investigation was not being used to serve political ends, even though the investigative end might overlap with political interests. Neither national party's political interest could dominate our investigation. But the way the legal process works, there was no way the results of a trial would be in before the presidential election.

One possible way to try to determine if there were higher-ups, in advance of the election, was to use a new prosecutorial statute known as "use immunity". This would compel Liddy, Hunt or McCord to testify despite assertions of their Fifth Amendment rights. I knew that Petersen, my boss in the Department of Justice, would never approve its use unless I was prepared not to prosecute the person immunized.

This I was definitely not prepared to do because of the unacceptable risk that there were no higher-ups, and that we were immunizing the most culpable persons in our investigation. This use of the new statute meant that we would not be able to prosecute them.

The other and potentially more attractive solution I considered was to grant either Hunt, Liddy or McCord a very lenient plea agreement in return for cooperation with our grand jury investigation. This cooperation would require the willing defendant to disclose what he knew about the involvement of higher-ups. The agreement would require a plea to only one charge, conspiracy, carrying a maximum possible sentence of five years imprisonment. Absent cooperation with the plea, our offer would be far less lenient: three felony charges carrying a maximum jail sentence of twenty-five years. I was going to make our plea offer with cooperation about higher-ups as attractive as I responsibly could. The question for me was whether I was making this unusually lenient plea offer to get the information out for political and not law enforcement purposes. I felt that the answer was yes, that I would not have made such a lenient offer at that point in time if the election weren't around the corner, but I also felt that I just couldn't sit on the information.

I also concluded that if we made the offer, it should go to McCord. Liddy would not talk to anyone. Hunt appeared, based on what we knew, to be unreliable. McCord, to the contrary, appeared to be a family man who would want to do what he could to avoid a substantial prison sentence.

Here is where the disclosure restrictions on federal prosecutors loomed large and formidable.

If I made the offer I was contemplating in this politically charged case, disclosure of higher up involvement, if it existed, could have enormous political impact on the imminent presidential election. It might seem that politics would be mixed with law enforcement and would likely appear to have a major role in the investigative decisions we were making. But not pursuing this plea offer or some other action to disclose all there was to know would be depriving the political victim, the DNC, of the chance to obtain redress for the violation of its rights. We might appear to be taking sides in the political contest. Not to act was also to act.

This simply did not seem right. I wrestled with the dilemma, changing my mind nearly every time I considered it. Our office had a proud tradition and reputation of keeping politics out of our decisions. I certainly did not want to do anything to undermine or damage our politically neutral position.

After vacillating back and forth again and again, I finally decided that I could not silently sit on possible critical information of enormous potential importance to the electorate and do nothing. I at least had to pursue my plan.

I described my proposed plea agreement to Campbell and Glanzer. They approved it. I telephoned Petersen. He readily agreed, directing only that I keep him advised. I contacted McCord's lawyers and invited them to my office after a court hearing the next day, October 25. I described our proposed plea agreement. They listened and said only they would bring it to the attention of their client. The next day McCord's lawyer called and told me they presented our offer to McCord and he squarely rejected it. The plan I had agonized over had come to naught.

We had no choice but to go to trial, two months later, in January 1973. After the three-week trial, McCord was convicted but then took his own steps relating to disclosure of higher-ups to avoid or limit jail-time. That's another story. The appropriateness of the disclosure in the plea agreement I proposed before the election was never tested and thus had no bearing on the election of President Nixon.

* * *

Currently, I hope that some clarity on what can be disclosed and under what circumstances will come to light in the report of the Inspector General conducting the ongoing Comey investigation. I look forward to seeing that report.

I do believe that *law enforcement officials of all levels need to be aware of the extreme pressures that a highly charged political environment can have on their work.* My experience in the Watergate case made me doubly aware of the potential mistakes that can be made and that will alter history.

Figure 5.9.1.1 *Earl Silbert* (second from right) *at a reception celebrating his appointment as US Attorney for the District of Columbia, 1975*

Earl Silbert, a 1960 graduate of Harvard Law School, joined the United States Department of Justice in its Tax Division before moving to the US Attorney's Office in DC in 1964. In the year 1972–73 he was the first Watergate prosecutor until succeeded by the Special Prosecutor in June 1973. Subsequently he served as US Attorney for 5½ years before entering private practice with Schwalb, Donnenfelt, Bray and Silbert, where he remained for 19 years until joining the international law firm DLA Piper. He remains active in the firm, still practicing law in Washington, DC.

Currently Earl is writing a book on his prosecution of the Watergate-Seven defendants. The initial Watergate prosecutor, he succeeded in convicting the defendants which led to the unraveling of the Watergate cover-up.

He is also deeply involved with pro bono activities and for 20 years has served on the Board of Directors of The Fishing School, a large after-school program for underprivileged youth.

Earl is married to Pat Silbert, an artist and partner in a Maryland art gallery. They have two grown daughters and three grandchildren. Every summer the whole family enjoys being together—swimming, kayaking, and generally hanging out in Jaffrey, NH.

Civil Rights

Cast Your Bread upon the Waters

Frederick A.O. "Fritz" Schwarz, Jr.

Some material in this paper comes from previous writings including *Democracy in the Dark: The Seduction of Government Secrecy* (New Press, 2015) and "An Awakening: How the Civil Rights Movement Helped Shape My Life", *New York Law School Law Review*, Vol. 59, No. 1 (2014–15).

"*And ye shall know the truth and the truth shall make you free.*"

These words, from the Gospel according to Saint John, are carved on the marble wall of the huge entrance lobby to the CIA's headquarters. I walked through that lobby in early 1975 on my way to meet CIA Director William Colby. A young litigator, without previous ties to any Senator or to the intelligence community, I had just been appointed Chief Counsel of the United States Senate's Select Committee created to investigate America's intelligence agencies—commonly known as the *Church Committee* after its Chair, Idaho Sen. Frank Church.

I met Colby at a formal lunch in his conference room. A careful man who revealed little, Colby was sizing me up. By contrast, my first visit to the FBI's fortress-like headquarters had no such subtlety. No genial probing. No fancy meal. Instead, at the start, I was shown photos of severed Black heads on an American city street. The implication was clear: this was done by vicious killers; we protect America against such enemies; stay away from our secrets.

As it turned out, the FBI, the CIA, and the rest of the Ford Administration, eventually cooperated with us as we conducted the most extensive investigation of a government's secret activities ever, in this country or elsewhere.

More on the Church Committee later. But, first, how was a 39-year-old so lucky as to have such a responsible position?

Perhaps there was less competition because the year most of us were born (1935) had the lowest birth rate in American history. A good education helped, beginning at home with conversations about history and government, and reading *The Times*, from age seven, on the rug on the floor of my parents' dining room. Subsequent good education included our classes at Harvard.[1] And I was lucky in my early work experience.

But luck is the residue of desire.[2] By the time I left Harvard Law School in 1960, I had a powerful desire with two parts: to succeed as a private lawyer—an aim probably influenced by my father having done so—and to play a part in public issues. In the years since, I have had some chances to try to help our country move toward fulfillment of the aspirations of the Declaration of Independence[3] and to comply with the restraints and observe the checks and balances of the Constitution.

Entering Public Affairs

I first began to try to participate in public affairs at law school. In February 1960, sit-ins had started in Greensboro, NC, at Woolworth's and other stores that barred blacks from eating at their lunch counters. Young blacks (along with a few white supporters) sat at the counters and were refused food, abused, and arrested. Even though a law student, it was the unfairness—really the inhumanity—more than any legal question, that motivated me to organize sympathy picketing of the Woolworth's on Brattle Street next to Harvard Yard. On several cold February days, we attracted many supporters. But not everyone agreed. Antonin "Nino" Scalia, a *Law Review* friend, who even then was noted for his conservatism, declined, saying that since Woolworth's was run as a franchise, we would first be hurting the franchise holder. Yes. But we would second be hurting the company. And, anyway, the issue was too important to ignore.

The struggle of Africans for independence from colonial rule paralleled the same struggle for fairness and freedom being waged in America by the Civil Rights Movement. And so it was that, after clerking, I worked for the (largely Muslim) Northern Region of the newly independent West African nation of Nigeria. I went as part of a non-government precursor to the Peace Corps: the MIT Fellows in Africa Program, funded by the Ford Foundation. My job was to be Assistant Commissioner for Law Revision.

Africa

Going to Nigeria comes with a story. The offer came after I had accepted an offer to work at Cravath, Swaine and Moore, a firm at the top of New York's establishment law firms. Several distinguished New York lawyers advised against going to Nigeria because, if I did, I "never would become a real lawyer." Although unpersuaded, I decided to check the advice with Judge Learned Hand, with whom I had become friendly and whose office was across the hall from Chief Judge J. Edward Lumbard for whom I was clerking. After I asked Hand what he thought, he paused, and then boomed out "sounds like pure bullshit to me."

I often use this story with young people, and others, as part of advice to be bold and take chances.

Working in Nigeria also contributed to later opportunities for public service. After I started at Cravath, the *Harvard Law School Bulletin* published a speech I had made to young African graduate students. It urged the new generation of African leaders to get rid of the "colonial mentality" so "the yoke of colonialism is thrown off and not merely disguised."[4] But to do so without losing faith in bills of rights. "Why rid your countries and your people of the colonial mentality? To be free. And ultimately that means to be free as individuals, which freedom can be both protected and inspired by a bill of rights."

The speech was read by Peter Weiss, Chair of the American Committee on Africa (ACOA), the most important American organization fighting South Africa's apartheid. Peter asked me to join its board. At ACOA, I worked with three fellow board members closely tied to Dr. King: Bayard Rustin, Clarence Jones, and Stanley Levison.

The most useful thing I did for ACOA was to write an early (1966) magazine article describing apartheid's evils and urging US companies to leave South Africa. The article exposed apartheid's harm to South Africa's blacks and other non-whites. The harm was facilitated by American companies that had "a substantial stake in the status quo." Moreover:

> "*[T]he apparent hypocrisy of the [US] Government and the increasing association of [US] business with the symbol of world racism exacerbates race relations in this country.*
>
> *Present policy supports the charges of those who characterize this nation as racist when the chips are down, white power indifferent to black misery.*"

Early Private Practice and Pro-Bono Public Work

Many Cravath clients did business in South Africa. Vindicating my belief that I should join Cravath because I would be judged by the quality of my work and not by other factors, nobody at Cravath questioned my anti-apartheid activities. And I was made a partner three years later, after six years at the firm.

Cravath gave me real responsibility before making me partner. When Attorney-General Ramsey Clark was deciding whether the Government would file a massive antitrust case accusing IBM of monopolizing the computer industry, IBM's General Counsel, Burke Marshall, and Cravath selected me to make the argument to Clark just a few days before the Johnson Administration was replaced by the Nixon Administration.[5]

I also got to know Burke, who had been the Justice Department's Assistant A.G. for Civil Rights under Robert Kennedy, when I did pro-bono work for the Vera Institute of Justice which he then chaired. One job was to write guidelines for the City's Police Department on reducing the "Use of Deadly Force by Police Officers". The guidelines were preceded by a series of speeches that Police Commissioner Howard Leary asked me to write for him. He wanted to reduce police killings, including getting rid of the "fleeing felon" rule—a rule that allowed a police officer to shoot and kill a suspected felon even if the person (if arrested and then convicted) might be sentenced to only a few years in prison. On behalf of Vera, I also wrote the Police Department's new "Guidelines for Demonstrations" for Commissioner Patrick Murphy.

The Select *Church* Committee of the US Senate, Created to Investigate America's Intelligence Agencies

A few years later, I was asked to be the Church Committee's Chief Counsel. It was, I believe, Burke Marshall who proposed me although he never told me and I never asked him. But the general point is that if you cast your bread upon the waters by doing good work, in addition to the satisfaction of doing work to help others and to help us live up to our ideals, it may open other doors.

Among the many things the Church Committee unearthed was that the FBI tried to induce Dr. King to commit suicide, the CIA hired the Mafia to aid its efforts to kill Cuba's Fidel Castro, and the NSA for 30 years obtained copies of every single telegram that left America. Our hearings and written reports disclosed gobs of previously secret information about these and other agencies. Our most fundamental conclusion, however, was that every President from Franklin Roosevelt to Richard Nixon—four Democrats and two Republicans—had abused their secret powers. This conclusion reflected the Committee's non-partisan nature. It also bolstered our internal cohesion and magnified our external influence.

One of my early roles was to push to focus our work on improper and unethical activity. Others urged us to emphasize "wise men's" opinions on what was wrong with the intelligence agencies and what reforms were needed. My view was that unless we exposed shocking secret abuses there would be no groundswell for reform. We took the debate to Senator Church, who sided with an aggressive investigation.

While I knew nothing about the secret world of intelligence before coming to the Church Committee, my years as a litigator had taught me some important lessons about how to "know the truth", which—as the CIA's entrance lobby says—"shall make you free." Facts point toward the truth. To get facts, you have to get secret documents and examine witnesses. (Ten minutes before our first witness—CIA Director William Colby—Senator Church told me that, before the Senators engaged in questioning, I would first examine the witnesses who came before the Committee.)

So, along with a sensational staff, and excellent, hardworking Senators (including Democrat Walter ("Fritz") Mondale,[6] and Republican Howard Baker), I had to focus on getting the agencies' secret documents, examining witnesses, and drafting several reports. In addition to presenting the facts that led to our conclusions and recommendations for reform, our reports had to invoke American values. I was particularly proud of one piece I drafted the day before one of our many lengthy reports was printed. Because of the lateness, Senator Church said it was okay to add it so long as the assistant to Vice Chair Sen. John Tower, agreed—as he did:

> "*The United States must not adopt the tactics of the enemy. Means are as important as ends. Crisis makes it tempting to ignore the wise restraints that make [men] free. But each time we do so, each time the means we use are wrong, our inner strength, the strength that makes us free, is lessened.*

> *"Despite our distaste for what we have seen, we have great faith in this country. The story is sad, but this country has the strength to hear the story and to learn from it.*
>
> *"We must remain a people who confront our mistakes and resolve not to repeat them. If we do not, we will decline; but, if we do, our future will be worthy of the best of our past."*[7]

Paul Light's recent book, *Government by Investigation: Congress, Presidents, and the Search for Answers, 1945–2012*, which analyzes 100 congressional investigations since 1945, concludes that while

> *"[i]t is impossible to single out one investigation . . . as the best of the best, I often return to the Church Committee's investigation of intelligence agency abuses as a model of a high-impact investigation."*

The Church Committee opened more doors for me, the first of which was nomination and election as a Harvard Overseer.[8] After the Committee, I had two more stints as a litigator at Cravath, 1977–1981, and 1987–2001, and, in 2002 I started my current job as Chief Counsel at the Brennan Center for Justice at NYU Law School. Interspersed have been a number of government jobs: New York City Corporation Counsel, the City's head lawyer (1982–86); Chair of the City's Charter Revision Commission that proposed and persuaded the city voters to adopt the most far-reaching changes in City Government since its establishment (1989); Chair of the City's Campaign Finance Board (2003–2008); and Chair of the Commission that sets pay for City elected officials (2015). (The last two were part-time). When not in government on a full-time basis, I have also been deeply involved with the boards of several non-profits.

Summing Up

These roles all could be covered at the same length as the Church Committee, but that could exhaust readers' patience. So I will just touch on a few points.

Comparisons between Government Work and Private Legal Practice

Consider three possible pleasures: quality performance of one's craft; helping individuals; and making a difference. On the first two, there are no inherent differences between private and public practice. A good cross-examination, brief, or oral argument is satisfying and stimulating whether for a private or public client. As far as helping people, I got, for example, the same pleasure helping CEOs faced with emotionally difficult challenges—such as Dr. Edwin Land of Polaroid or Thomas Watson of IBM—as I got with helping Mayor Ed Koch when he was faced with a difficult personal and political challenge. But where public service is unmatched is in opportunities to serve the nation and its people.

Helping Land, Watson, and Koch. With Land, Polaroid was facing a major class action lawsuit relating to the introduction of its SX70 camera. Land had gotten used to my preparing him for his testimony by asking him either friendly or hostile questions, then critiquing his answers, and then trying again. However, just a couple of days before the trial started, I told him I was going to give him a question that would be the last I would ask him on the stand, but I did *not* want to hear his answer until he gave it on the stand. The question was: "Dr. Land: how does it feel to be accused of defrauding the shareholders of the company you and your wife founded decades ago?" After I asked Dr. Land that question at the end of his testimony, he gave a ten-minute answer in which he cried two or three times. All the jurors were crying, and even the tough-as-nails judge had moist eyes. I knew we could not lose the case.

With Watson, we were defending IBM in the massive computer monopoly case. Watson, whose father had founded the company, was IBM's CEO. And IBM was Cravath's largest client. I was preparing Watson for testimony when, out of the blue, he said Cravath had failed to protect some (harmful) privileged documents in order to—lucratively—string out the case. With anger—which I don't often show—I slammed my hand on the table and energetically responded for a fair time. What was interesting is that this episode substantially strengthened my relationship with Watson.

With Koch, in addition to running the massive New York City Legal Department, I soon also became an advisor on a wide-range of policy issues. At the end of Koch's second term, the City was confronted with a serious corruption crisis. Koch was personally honest. But Rudy Giuliani blew his hot breath on him and the press was in pursuit. Koch was depressed. I had planned to return to Cravath after arguing a Supreme Court case early in my fifth year with the City. But I told

Koch I would stay until he was free of the corruption crisis. (Koch teared up.) Then, using my father's favorite Shakespeare quote—"sweet are the uses of adversity"—I devised a strategy that would help the City and help Koch. We would use the corruption crisis to drive major reforms. Koch embraced them all. The most noteworthy led to the City's landmark campaign finance law based on small-donor matching funds.

The Quality of People Who Work for Government

Most Americans don't recognize that, while there are a few bad apples, most people who work for government are hard working and very talented. Those of us who come into government from the private sector should always stress this.

Facts and Songs

As with the Church Committee, using the facts is vital. One of many other examples arose in a case I brought when I was doing all of Time, Inc.'s major litigation. On behalf of *Sports Illustrated* and its reporter Melissa Ludtke, I brought the case that required professional sports teams to allow female reporters in locker rooms. Our opponents thought it would help them to show our lawsuit was controversial. So they introduced all the comments about the case that *S.I.* had received. One subscriber's letter had said that he was shocked at the lawsuit and was about to cancel his subscription when *S.I.*'s annual swimsuit issue arrived and he realized the magazine understood the proper position of women. We used the quote several times in our reply brief that led to our summary judgment victory.

Persuasion also comes from reaching the emotions. You can do that in many ways. So, for example, I have used lines from Bob Dylan and the Rolling Stones in oral arguments. And in the keynote speech for a Law School reunion weekend, I used Woody Guthrie as part of my argument for why the School should have an environmental program.

Perhaps the general point is that persuasion should not be pedantic or stilted. *Reaching the heart helps reach the head.*

Non-Profits

I have been lucky enough to work for a long time on the boards of several non-profits, most extensively for the Natural Resources Defense Council (NRDC) and the Vera Institute of Justice.[9] For NRDC, some of the enjoyment has been trying to capsulize policy questions such as "Are We to Be the First Generation in Human History to *Knowingly*

Make the World a Worse Place for Our Children and Grandchildren?" and "Why Are We Winning the Battles but Losing the War?" Vera focuses on issues of fairness and efficiency in criminal justice, with major concentration recently on reducing mass incarceration.

A vibrant non-profit sector is uniquely important to America because, in addition to good works, it provides both a check on and an inspiration for government.

Senior Work

I started an "encore" career at the Brennan Center by becoming its Chief Counsel when I reached the "retirement" age at Cravath. In my 15 years at Brennan, I have tried three cases, argued in the Supreme Court, written two books, many op eds, and several Center Reports, and testified frequently before Congress, as well as trying to help guide our people and their work.

While some other Americans are choosing to have "encore" careers, I am surprised there isn't a bigger wave. But it will come.

The Centrality of the Civil Rights Movement

The Civil Rights Movement triggered my public policy efforts. And the aims and tactics of the Civil Rights Movement inspired many other movements, for example by women and the LGBT community. Throughout all my jobs, these issues have always been a part of my focus. Just one vignette.

> On November 4, 2008, after CNN announced that Barack Obama had been elected as president, I sat sobbing on my living room sofa. Leaving aside occasional flashes of choking up, this was the first time I had really cried since my father died 34 years earlier.
>
> Two very different causes for tears spilling out. This time it was the emotions ignited by Dr. King and the other heroes of the Civil Rights Movement, all the hurts and harms that blacks had suffered, and my own caring about the issues. All this reached very deep within me.

* * *

Perhaps what is embedded early lasts longest.

Today's graduates may well find fighting climate change is the flame that lights up their lives.

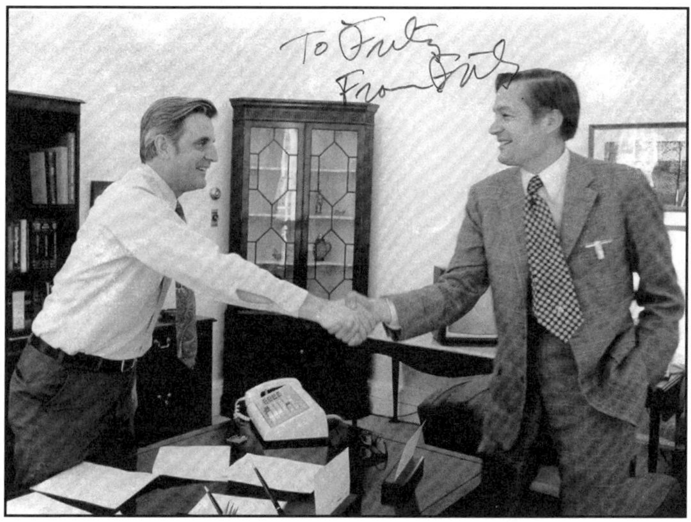

Figure 5.10.1.1 *Fritz Schwarz in the White House with Vice President Walter Mondale, Spring 1977*

Frederick A. O. "Fritz" Schwarz, Jr., received his LLB from Harvard Law School in 1960. He clerked for Chief Judge J. Edward Lumbard of the Second Circuit and then went to work for the Government of Northern Nigeria as Assistant Commissioner for Law Revision (1961–62). He thereafter worked for Cravath, Swaine & Moore, soon became a partner and remains Senior Counsel. He was Chief Counsel for the Select Committee on Intelligence (the "Church Committee") from 1975 to 1976. He was Corporation Counsel of the City of New York, 1982–86, and is now Chief Counsel of the Brennan Center for Justice at NYU Law School. He also chaired three New York City committees—the Charter Revision Commission, the Campaign Finance Board and an advisory commission on pay for elected officials. He has received honorary degrees from the New York Law School and CUNY.

Endnotes

1 Apparently, over 50% of the applicants to our class were admitted, compared to about 5% today. Harvard was open to far fewer students. This was a minus to us—and the country. Some say America was "great" in the 1950s. In some ways it was. But in others—as reflected in the narrowness of the lens applied to our admission—it was not.

2 This expression is attributed to Branch Rickey, the Brooklyn Dodgers General Manager who brought Jackie Robinson to the major leagues as the first black player. (In April 1947, I saw Robinson's first game in New York City.)

3 It is no accident that two of the greatest speeches in American history—Dr. King's "I Have a Dream" speech in 1963 (which I was fortunate to see and hear) and Abraham Lincoln's Gettysburg Address one hundred years earlier—flow from the Declaration of Independence and not from the original Constitution's formulae for government.

4 The colonial mentality was the feeling of many Africans that they lacked the capacity of their former colonial masters. This was coupled with little things that suggested British was better: for example, use of wool wigs for lawyers in sweltering courtrooms, as well as names of streets and institutions that needed to be changed, just as we changed Kings College to Columbia University. One personal experience is revealing: my then-wife and I were the only whites at the wedding of two Nigerian friends. After the ceremony, the twenty or so men settled into a circle, and I was then asked to speak first, even though I knew the groom least well of any of the guests.

5 After the argument, Clark said you have persuaded me that we don't know what we are doing in defining the market for computers. But if it turns out we should have brought the case and didn't, I could not defend our failure to my grandchildren.

6 In the years after Fritz Mondale was thumped by Ronald Reagan in the presidential election of 1984, I have often teased him by saying the only reason he lost was because he ran using the name Walter, rather than Fritz.

7 Senator Church read these words as part of his presentation to a closed session of the full Senate (to which I was invited) convened to learn about this report before it was released to the public. His comments were then interrupted by applause which made me proud and happy. (Several years later, when my appointment as New York City Corporation Counsel was announced, Arthur Sulzberger, Jr., now the publisher of *The New York Times* but then a City Hall reporter, quoted these paragraphs in a profile he wrote of me.)

8 The most useful thing I did as an Overseer was as Chair of the Committee to visit Harvard College. Our Committee produced a report suggesting "increased incentives for good teaching and disincentives for bad teaching." The report was resented by faculty panjandrums who were defensive. A decade or so later, I discovered that the reforms we proposed had been adopted—although I am not sure of a causal connection.

9 In each case, I was Chair for almost 20 years and then continued on as a regular board member. (While there are arguments on both sides, I oppose term limits, but only if the organization has a vigorous nominating process to weed out weak board members at the end of their three-year terms.)

A Lawyer's Growth

Peter Swords

My father (H'29) was a lawyer who practiced in a Wall Street law firm and I followed him into that life. In those days Wall Street lawyers did well (overwhelmingly well by any world standards) but were not, in that particular world, exactly rich—that was the domain of the investment bankers, corporate CEOs and the lot. These, and the wealthy, tended to be our clients. I was told that these folks, working within the freedom of the market system, produced huge product and thus lifted all boats. Comparing America to much of the rest of the world, there seemed to be something to this, and perhaps there still is. It has, however, always struck me as too bad that the incentive of huge personal gains seems to be needed to produce bountiful results, and furthermore their distribution has never seemed right to me.

By the time I was 11 I developed a love for jazz music. It has lasted all my life. I was fortunate enough to have heard Louis Armstrong, Bennie Goodman, Dave Brubeck and John Coltrane, among many others, and more fortunate to have heard and met Charlie Parker, Dizzy Gillespie, Miles Davis, Charlie Mingus and Duke Ellington. Most of these artists were black. At eleven I became a Brooklyn Dodger fan and fell in love with Jackie Robinson. (The only time I have ever wept in the New York subway was in reading about Pee Wee Reece (an Alabamian) going out to second base and standing by Robinson as the racists in the crowd howled.)

I believe that it was this background that directed my interest to civil rights. Soon after the four girls were killed in the Birmingham bombing in 1963, President Kennedy urged the Wall Street firms, and their Philadelphia equivalents, to let their young associates go down to Mississippi to provide legal help to the movement. I went. Each firm provided for two young lawyers to go. I was late in the pick, but our classmate Tony Sifton made the draw. It turned out he was unable to go down, and he then urged me to. It didn't take much. (Tony later became a superb federal court judge.)

In June of 1966 I traveled to Jackson, MS, to volunteer with the Lawyers Committee for Civil Rights Under Law. For the young lawyers, as I remember it, our principal job was to help get movement leaders who were working on voter registration campaigns out of jail after they had been busted on utterly bogus charges. We lost every case but were nearly always able to raise bail money to get them released so that they could return to their work. I also was involved in efforts to rid Mississippi of Jim Crow, and my finest hour was getting 14 young kids out of jail in Grenada, a town in northern Mississippi. They had been arrested and jailed for attempting to integrate the town's movie theater. In 1966 blacks were assigned to the mezzanine. My clients bought tickets for orchestra seats. Sherriff Snugs Ingram, one of the bully cops straight out of central casting, had learned it was going to happen and arranged to have them all picked up and packed off to the city jail. Because under a recent law it was a federal crime to interfere with folks asserting their civil (anti-Jim Crow) rights, it did not take much to persuade the Mayor to release them.

As I recall this glorious time there were a number of key aspects at play. First, we encountered extreme hostility, and it did not take long before we identified with our clients and experienced in our gut the obscenities of Jim Crow segregation and vicious discrimination. It was also dangerous and from time to time very scary. None of my friends got hurt, but there were a lot of guns around and constant threats. Then there was the strong bonding among us young lawyers that we forged together as we went out each day to we knew not what. For me, and most of my compatriots, it was perhaps the only time in our life we lived without any moral ambiguity. We knew we were doing the right thing. Finally, for most of those with whom I have kept up, this commitment, now 51 years ago, was the high point of our lives.

When I returned to New York, I could no longer engage in the commercial practice I had started with. The taste of public service was too strong. I did a little government work (John Lindsay administration) and then worked for a Ford Foundation spin-off, the Council on Legal Education for Professional Responsibility (CLEPR). CLEPR promoted and funded clinical education at law schools all throughout the country. Most of the clinics in those days served the poor, and that seemed to me a good thing for young lawyers to be exposed to.

Then I returned to Columbia Law School as an associate dean and after awhile started teaching nonprofit law—the law that applies to social service and health care groups, schools and universities, churches, advocacy groups and a myriad of arts groups.

I left my administrative post at Columbia in 1987 to set up and run the Nonprofit Coordinating Committee of New York, an advocacy group that promotes and protects the groups I was teaching about. It has always seemed to me that these groups were doing things for the public, the whole public, and whether it was taking care of the indigent, fighting for the environment or producing beauty, I have always thought these groups were doing the right thing, and I think this more strongly than ever today. I continued teaching until May 2016 and still represent pro bono a number of nonprofit clients.

There are many lawyers today doing good things and I hope I can be counted among that group.

For me, it started in Mississippi, and what happened there to me has never gone away.

Peter Swords after graduating from the Columbia Law School joined the firm of Cadwalader, Wickersham and Taft. After his experience as a civil rights lawyer in Mississippi, he left the commercial practice and joined the administration of New York Mayor John Lindsay, where he helped set up the city's income tax system. He then worked for a Ford Foundation spin-off, The Council on Legal Education for Professional Responsibility, that successfully promoted clinical legal education in virtually all American law schools. Next Swords returned to Columbia Law School as an Associate Dean and after a short time began teaching a course on nonprofit law, which he continued to do until the spring of 2016. In 1987 he left Columbia full-time to start and head up the Nonprofit Coordinating Committee of New York, an advocacy group that promotes and protects the interests of New York 501(c)(3) nonprofit organizations. He serves on the boards of and continues to offer pro bono advice to various nonprofits.

Environmental Law

My Fifteen Years as a Trustee of the Manville Personal Injury Settlement Trust, 1992–2007

An Overview of the Trials, Tribulations, and Triumphs of the Trust

Louis Klein, Jr.

In 1982, Johns-Manville (JM) was an important industrial corporation in the United States, ranking 181st on the *Fortune* 500 list. With $2.2 billion of sales, JM was one of the 30 companies whose stock price comprised the Dow Jones Industrial average, and was highly regarded in industrial and financial circles. However, by the end of that year, JM had filed for reorganization under Chapter 11 of the US Bankruptcy Code, burdened by the weight of personal injury lawsuits that started slowly but grew to huge numbers very quickly.

Concerned that claims would continue rising, that assets and insurance proceeds would soon become inadequate to fund awards and settlements and that JM's debt covenants would be breached, the Company's auditors issued a qualified Accountant's Certificate. The only reasonable action to be taken was the bankruptcy filing.

Asbestos is a mineral that had been mined for over 100 years and was used extensively as a fire retardant and insulator in products ranging from ceiling and floor tiles to the construction of naval vessels, where it was specified for use by the US Government. Its popularity was so great that asbestos was referred to as "the magic mineral" at the 1939 World's Fair. However, research increasingly showed that asbestos was harmful to one's health. The link between asbestos exposure and lung cancer and asbestosis rates among insulation installers, for example, was established as early as 1964 by Dr. Irving Selikoff of Mount Sinai Hospital in New York City.

In the intervening years between the 1982 bankruptcy filing and the 1988 formation of the Manville Personal Injury Settlement Trust (MPIST), there was heated discussion among plaintiffs' lawyers, corporate officers, and judges as to the future of JM. One faction sought to liquidate the entire Company and just distribute the proceeds to present and future claimants. Another faction won the argument with a plan to create a new claims-paying facility designed to handle all claims and to protect JM from future personal injury lawsuits by a Court-imposed injunction. A Board of Trustees was selected and given the mandate to use its control position of JM to enhance its value as a means of increasing available assets and thus build up future distributions.

The Trust was funded with cash, insurance proceeds and 90% ownership of the Company's common stock, amounting to about $2.5 billion. The Trust created a claims processing and settlement facility, and categories of illness were established with mesothelioma ("meso") at the top. Meso is a fatal cancer caused only by lengthy exposure to asbestos, and has a latency period of up to 40 years. Other categories of illness were also established, ranging from less serious injuries down to impaired breathing.

There were a number of miscalculations and unforeseen problems which required major adjustments and refinements along the way:

- At the end of 1988, "experts" estimated that the total number of claims over the life of the Trust would be between 88,000 and 100,000. Less than two years later, the Trust had already received over 200,000 claims, and has received over one million claims to date.
- On January 1, 1992, the original group of Trustees was replaced by four new members of the Board, as it became increasingly apparent that a new approach to payouts was needed. The new Trustees were Robert Falise, a prominent corporate lawyer; Frank Macciarola, previously Chancellor of the New York City School system and Dean of the Cardozo School of Law; Christian Markey, formerly chief legal counsel at the University of Southern California; and the author.
- The basic problem was to balance future liabilities (i.e., claims) against the changing value of liquidating assets, as the basis for the Trust to set a payout percentage for claims. Initially, the payment was 100% of liquidated value for each illness category. Under the new Board of Trustees, the payment percentage was sharply reduced to 10% and later to 5%. Subsequently increased to 7.5%, it was recently cut back to 5.1% to reflect the imbalance of assets

and claims. This could only have been accomplished by the Federal District Courts' agreement with the findings of a Special Master that there is a "substantial probability" that estimated future assets of the Trust will be insufficient to pay in full all claims that are projected to be asserted against the Trust. Thus the determination that MPIST is a "limited fund".

- The Trust's governing documents direct the Trustees to "enhance and preserve the Trust's assets". To meet this directive, the Trustees hired Goldman Sachs as its investment banker, and executed a series of corporate changes at JM. Non-traditional debt issued by JM was restructured into corporate bonds in suitable form for resale to the public, raising needed capital for business expansion. A very profitable JM subsidiary named Riverwood International (one of two dominant producers of coated board used for soft drink and beer carriers) was partially sold in a public offering, and the balance of shares was later sold to an equity investment firm. JM's remaining fiberglass business, which ranked second in size in its industry, was sold for cash to Berkshire Hathaway in 2001.

- The Trust had been contacted in 2001 by Berkshire's CEO Warren Buffet with an offer to purchase all the JM shares for $13 each in cash (thus eliminating any financing contingency), without using an investment banker, without the need for further due diligence and with a closing in a matter of weeks not months. After internal debate, as fiduciaries we sought to achieve a somewhat higher price. The answer was a reiteration of the offer as made, with a polite but firm decline of our counter-offer. We accepted. In summary, the value of JM's stock more than quadrupled in the nine years following the appointment of new Trustees in 1992.

- The Trust was inundated with claims, as plaintiffs' lawyers found new and creative ways to build an asbestos litigation industry. Legal services were heavily advertised, mass screenings were sponsored by plaintiffs' attorneys to seek clients, new deep pockets were sought beyond JM and other manufacturers, meso claims were bundled with less serious injuries to facilitate payments by the 40 or so trusts that had been formed, etc. The Manville Trust was put on the defensive by such actions, which together led to a cascade of new claims, a veritable feeding frenzy.

- As part of the directive to enhance its ever-depleting asset base, the Trust also went on offense. There was unchallenged evidence that not only was asbestos injurious to one's health, but that the risk of injury was substantially higher when an individual worker smoked a pack of cigarettes daily. Thus, a lawsuit was brought by the Trustees of MPIST (representing the Trust) against a group of the largest tobacco manufacturers, seeking several billion dollars in damages on behalf of all the beneficiaries of the Trust. Despite intense preparation and non-contested facts and statistics, the Federal District Court judge dismissed the case during trial; the decision stated that although individual claimants clearly had a right to sue the tobacco industry, the Trust was only a third party without standing to do so. The decision was particularly disappointing to the Trustees, as three of us were graduates of Columbia Law School where the judge was previously a professor teaching the law of evidence to us.
- Committed to paying out as much money to beneficiaries as allowed by circumstances, we nevertheless adopted a set of conservative investment guidelines and objectives for the Trust's portfolio. This was the investment management side of the MPIST, involving several billion dollars of assets. Needless to say, the plaintiffs' lawyers were wary and watchful, as they carefully observed the level of expenses incurred in running the Trust as well as the rate of return earned on the portfolio. Several prominent investment management firms were hired for distinct segments of the portfolio. It was a source of great pride for our team that the cash received from the sale of JM in 2001 was very conservatively invested at a time of market turbulence, emphasizing preservation of assets over enhancement of value during a difficult period for the market. Starting with about $2 billion of assets at the beginning of 1992, the Trust has paid out over $5 billion to claimants, due primarily to the increase in value of the JM shares held by the MPIST, reflecting corporate developments. Today, MPIST still has almost $700 million in net Claimants Equity for the future claim payments.

The experience of being a Trustee of the MPIST for over 15 years was both challenging and rewarding. We were directly involved in a confluence of legal, financial, and medical considerations, subject to constant oversight and second-guessing. Our tenure dated from almost the beginning of the Trust and took place during a period of great change.

It is sobering to remember that the Trust will continue its role as a claims-paying facility for many years to come. It automatically terminates on a date that is 90 days after the occurrence, among other events, of the following event (language in the original documents to deal with the Rule Against Perpetuities that existed in the 1980s):

> "*. . . 21 years less 91 days after the death of the last survivor of all the descendants of Joseph P. Kennedy living on the date hereof (November 28, 1988).*"

I am hopeful that someone at that time, whenever that might be, can determine whether we among others managed to accomplish the primary purpose of the Trust, namely:

> "*to use the assets in the Trust to deliver fair, adequate and equitable compensation to bona fide beneficiaries, whether presently known or unknown, without overpaying or underpaying any claims and with settlement to be preferred over arbitration, arbitration to be preferred over resort to the tort system, and fair and efficient resolution of claims to be preferred over all else.*"

Like everything else in the saga of the MPIST, that language is perfectly clear and straightforward, explicit and understandable. Isn't it?

Louis Klein, Jr., after graduating from College and Columbia Law School, passed the Bar Exam and went to work on Wall Street: first, investment banking at Lazard Freres, next, equity investing at Warburg Pincus & Co, and then corporate advisory at Ardshiel Associates. He subsequently served as a director or trustee of several listed companies and as a Trustee of the Manville Personal Injury Settlement Trust. He gradually retired from all but one of his board seats and will soon retire as a trustee of the CRM Group of Mutual Funds.

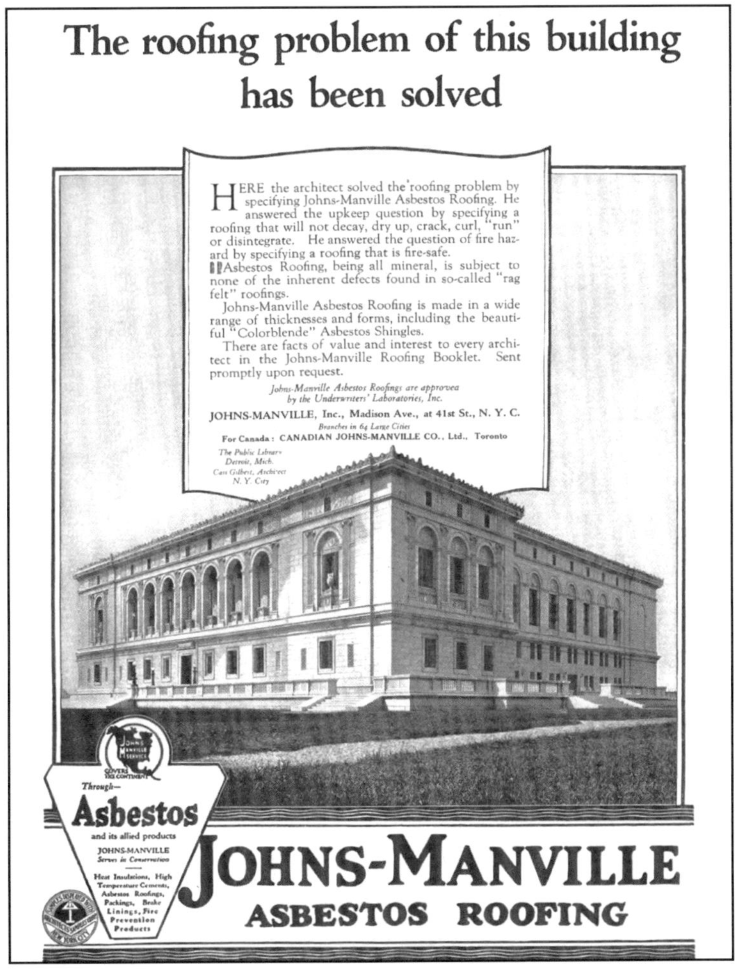

Figure 5.11.1.1 *Advertisement for asbestos roofing by Johns-Manville Inc. depicting the Detroit Public Library,* Architectural Forum, *Vol. 35, Issue 1, page 35, 1921*

Photo courtesy of Johns-Manville

Legal Practice

Life after Harvard

Peter L. Gale

When we arrived at Harvard in 1953, McCarthyism was in its prime. Anti-Communism was used as a cudgel to minimize progressive voices. People were afraid to speak out for fear of being labeled a Communist or "fellow traveler". Harvard was called the "*Kremlin on the Charles*". One day in our freshman year, Professor Wendell H. Furry did not appear to teach our physics class. He had been called to testify before Senator Joseph McCarthy's *Subcommittee on Investigations.* When he came to class the next day, he was applauded by the students. This made a big impression on me. Although McCarthy was eventually censured by the Senate, the "*Red Scare*" had a big effect on our country, and for many years, Americans were cautious about expressing liberal or progressive opinions.

I am not a Harvard alumnus, unlike many of us. I left Harvard after my junior year. I graduated from Wilkes College, now Wilkes University. I went to Cornell Graduate School in the Mathematics Department. At Cornell, I quickly became active in progressive political matters.

A group of us started a Cornell student magazine called *Controversy.* We were involved in *civil rights* causes, in the *anti-Vietnam War movement*, and other matters. The Math Department at Cornell was full of progressives.

After four(!) years in mathematics, and being a teaching assistant, *I decided that my life and occupation should be more in tune with my beliefs.* I went to Cornell Law School, helping finance my way by continuing as a math teaching assistant. I graduated in 1965 and went to Philadelphia to start practicing law.

I worked for a solo practitioner for three years handling estate, trust, and tax matters. I then changed jobs, working with a liberal lawyer who was as interested in progressive causes as I was. I was quite active in the anti-Vietnam War movement and various civil liberties matters.

My practice in Philadelphia was largely in *three areas of law*—representing *plaintiffs in personal injury cases*, representing *defendants in criminal cases*, and, no doubt springing from my speaking out against the war in Vietnam, *representing young men who were trying to avoid the military draft or, after induction, trying to be discharged from military service.*

Some of these young men, would-be draftees, had refused induction and were indicted, and I would represent them as defendants in Federal Court. I was one of a group of lawyers, about 25 of us on the East Coast, mostly members of the *National Lawyers Guild*, who became specialists in *Military* and *Selective Service Law*. We had remarkable success in getting people out of the draft, on a conscientious objector status or other claims, or obtaining acquittals or dismissals if the young men were indicted. I handled about eight or ten cases of young men who were indicted, and only three were convicted.

> The most remarkable case was one which I lost. The young man, who had been granted *conscientious objector status*, refused to report for induction anyway, because he did not want to help the military in any way, even in a non-military job. He was convicted, but his *sentence was to continue the work that he had been doing, for three more years*, working for a peace advocacy group.

In Philadelphia, I married in 1967 and divorced a few years later. In 1972, I met Sheila Kavanagh. We married in 1976. We recently celebrated our 40th anniversary. She is the light of my life. My wife is a pianist. We have three grown children and four grandchildren.

We moved to New York City in 1978. I eventually joined a small law firm, representing plaintiffs in personal injury cases, mostly *medical malpractice.* However, I still handled cases of various *dissidents.* I spent a lot of time representing transit workers in conflicts with management and representing *militant subway workers* who were trying to take over Local 100 of the Transport Workers Union. They were eventually successful.

In the 1990s, I was the attorney in a fascinating case. I represented the *Communist Party in a will contest.* A member of the Communist Party had died, leaving most of her estate to three supposedly trusted members of the Communist Party. The decedent wrote letters, separate from her will, directing the three to give the money to the Communist Party, which they consented to do. However, sometime before her death, two of the three had left the Party. After her death, these two changed their minds, and wanted to give the money to other political groups. I filed a complaint, claiming that there was a *constructive trust*, with the Communist Party as a beneficiary. Although McCarthy was long since dead, I was still concerned that the court might be prejudiced against the Communist Party to the degree that my legal arguments would be ignored. After about three years of litigation, several depositions, and defeating a motion for summary judgment, I obtained a very favorable settlement. *After the case was concluded, it finally sunk into my head that the "Red Scare" was finished.*

In 2003, I represented several people who were *arrested at a large demonstration in New York City protesting the forthcoming United States invasion of Iraq*. I was one of about a dozen lawyers representing about 50 to 75 people arrested. The lawyers worked together, in most cases getting acquittals, dismissals, or other favorable outcomes.

I left the small firm in 2014. At this time, practicing on my own, I am only working part-time, handling only a few (nonpolitical) cases. I still am very active politically. In the last year and one-half, I worked hard for Bernie Sanders for President. After Hillary Clinton won the nomination, I campaigned for her twice in Pennsylvania. After Donald Trump won the presidency, I have been involved in various protests against his policies and programs. I will always be active in left-wing political causes, so long as I am healthy.

The only Harvard classmates with whom I have stayed in contact were my friends Ed Lottick, who died in 2015, Bill Collier, and Hugh Blair-Smith.

To this day, *I think like a mathematician, but my heart is in political stuff.*

Peter L. Gale left Harvard at the end of his junior year and graduated from Wilkes College. He spent four years in graduate school in mathematics at Cornell before transferring to its Law School and graduating in 1965. He moved to Philadelphia to practice law, remaining there for 13 years, practicing with small firms. He then found an interesting opportunity in New York City and moved there to practice law, again only with small law firms. He now works in a small solo practice, slowly easing off.

Title IX and Consent for Sex

The Title IX Pendulum

J. Owen Todd

Introduction

In previous decades, an alarming crisis of sexual misconduct and sexual violence developed on college and university campuses across the country. The objective of this essay is to discuss this problem which, like a pendulum, has swung from neglect by the schools and federal government to an overcorrection resulting in too many instances of unfairness and injustice to the students accused of this abhorrent conduct. Is there a solution or syntheses; are there policies and procedures that schools can implement and that the federal government can monitor which punish sexual misconduct but produce adjudications which are less likely to be catastrophically unjust to the parties involved?

In the spirit of fair disclosure, it should be known that my law firm represents several students each year, predominantly those accused of sexual misconduct, in appealing their school's adverse decisions.

* * *

The Problem

Clearly, unwanted sexual assaults on college campuses, predominantly upon women and commonly fueled by overindulging in alcohol or drugs, has been a crisis for many years. The ready access to parties, alcohol and drugs which relax social tensions and self-discipline result in a significant segment of students engaging in consensual sex, non-consensual sex and, not uncommonly, sexual conduct somewhere between the two categories. The biochemical effect of drugs, including alcohol, diminishes an individual's ability to recognize whether consent was given or implied and to misread or misinterpret the signals being given. All three of these scenarios have led to individuals, after reflection or remorse, voicing complaints to friends, college counselors or administrators that they were victims of unwanted (or regretted) sexual conduct.

It is said that sexual victimization rates are higher in the college student population than in the general population. The estimates appearing in the Association of Universities Survey range as high as one in four female college students will have been the recipient of unwanted sexual aggression. The Campus Sexual Assault Study authored by PhDs Krebs, Linquist, Warner, Fisher and Martin in 2007 and financially funded by the US Department of Justice found that the majority of victims of sexual misconduct on our nation's campuses were freshmen and sophomores, were assaulted in the Fall when school began, after midnight on weekends at or after fraternity or sorority parties.

Many sexual assaults were not reported to the school by the victim for personal reasons, including fear of retaliation, shame, guilt and concern about how they will be regarded after the incident is made public. Others who did report the sexual misconduct to administrators were discouraged or not sufficiently encouraged to proceed as complainants. As a result, colleges and universities were blithely reporting to governmental authorities lower instances of sexual assaults on their campuses than was, in reality, the fact. Obviously, the schools do not wish to create the impression in the minds of parents or potential applicants that their campus is a dangerous place. It has been estimated that between five and ten percent of sexual violence incidents on campuses are reported to the school or to the police.

The horrific impact of sexual violence on its victims discussed in the research suggests that four of five rape victims subsequently suffer from chronic physical and psychological conditions and that rape victims are thirteen times more likely to attempt suicide than non-criminal victims.

Consensual Sex or Sexual Assault?

In the past, it was considered on campus, in the courts of law and in the court of public opinion that women who sought redress for sexual assaults were at fault or complicit because of the way they dressed, acted, drank or did not fight their attacker. This outdated and stereotypical attitude may have contributed to the benign neglect exhibited in addressing the crises of sexual violence being experienced by college students.

Beginning in 2010, the pendulum swung from this benighted state of affairs to the application of increasing pressure on colleges and the federal government for change. Of course, the female college students knew that a fearsome situation was escaping needed attention. Student activists, student victims of sexual abuse and outraged feminist advocates raised the volume of the discussion. They called upon the federal government to focus on this growing national crisis and to employ the powerful legislative tools at its disposal to incentivize the schools.

Erica Kinsman, a former student at Florida State University, filed a lawsuit against the University, charging that she had been raped in 2012 by James Winston, the school's star quarterback, but that her alma mater had been "deliberately indifferent toward her complaint and obstructed the investigation of the incident so that Winston could continue to play football." The University paid $950,000 to settle the lawsuit.

A female student at Tufts University (Tufts) accused her former boyfriend of rape. The College determined that the girl had mislead the investigation and sanctioned her. The student brought a lawsuit against Tufts which led to the Office of Civil Rights of the United States Department of Education conducting its own investigation of the school's sexual misconduct policy and procedures which it found to be deficient. Faced with the threat of losing its federal funding if it did not pay money to the student, change its policy and admit its trespasses, Tufts caved. A similar experience involving Occidental College is described by Emily Yoffe in her article *"The College Rape Overcorrection"*.

The drumbeat caught the attention of the media, which produced alarming stories of the gang rape of a professional stripper by the Duke University varsity lacrosse team which were subsequently debunked. Later, the *Rolling Stone* newspaper published an under-investigated exposé of the rape of a female student at the Phi Kappa Psi fraternity at the University of Virginia, which under later scrutiny could not be substantiated. Indeed, the underlying allegations were shown to have been total fiction and the entire story a hoax.

Still later in November of 2015, CNN produced a controversial documentary called *The Hunting Ground* which was advertised as shedding new light on the "*Campus Rape Epidemic*" through the narrations of a number of female former college students who claimed that their accusations that they were sexually assaulted were ignored. The presentation was criticized as slanted in favor of the accusers by Jeannie Suk, an avowed feminist and a Harvard Law School professor.

At this point, it is my belief that the public's former attitude of cynicism toward persons alleging that they had been raped or sexually assaulted was replaced, in large part, with the notion that only a person who had been truly sexually attacked would take on the burden and psychic costs of coming forward publicly. All circumstances being equal, the tendency is now to believe the accuser in a "she said—he said" situation.

Intervention of the Federal Government and Its Consequences

Inspired by the outcry of student victims, the lawsuits which they brought against their schools, the intervention of the US Department of Education's Office of Civil Rights and media support, student activists and the women's civil rights groups that supported them realized that they had powerful weapons and allies available to them to sensitize colleges and universities to the crisis of insufficiently controlled sexual misconduct among students.

Title IX of The Education Amendments of 1972, as amended, reads, in part, that ". . . no person in The United States shall, on the basis of sex, be excluded from participation in, be denied the benefits of, or be subject to discrimination under any educational program or activity receiving federal financial assistance."The original emphasis of The Act was to correct the imbalance of opportunity and resources for women's athletics and social activities. Later gender discrimination under the Act was interpreted to include sexual harassment, misconduct and assaults. Sexual violence was defined to include attempted and completed rape, sexual assaults, stalking, voyeurism, exhibitionism, verbal or physical sexually based threats or abuse and intimate partner violence.

In addition, Title IX requires that every school must have a Title IX coordinator who manages complaints, implements procedures for handling complaints, investigates complaints and adjudicates the complaints within sixty days of the conclusion of the investigation. The federal government agency overseeing adherence to Title IX mandates, as dictated in its "Dear Colleague Letter" addressed to every college and university president, that the sexual misconduct adjudications employ "the preponderance of the evidence" quantum of proof, i.e., more probable than not, 50.1% degree of certainty rather than the "clear and convincing evidence standard" which is a higher standard or the "beyond a reasonable doubt" standard which our system of justice requires in criminal cases such as rape and sexual assault.

The accused is not allowed any meaningful assistance of an attorney and cannot cross-examine or confront his accuser. That the university's university employees are charged with protecting the university from Title IX violations with the accompanying heavy financial sanctions and bad press while also serving as the investigator—prosecutor—and judge of a student charged with a serious sexual offense raises the stark specter of a conflict of interest.

In 2012 Congress enacted a revised "Clery Act (20 USC 1092 (f))". This legislation was the product of the concerted and persistent efforts of parents to honor their daughter, Jeanne Clery, who was raped and murdered by another student while sleeping in her dorm room at Lehigh University.

The Clery Act obligates all institutions of higher education receiving federal funding to compile and report to The Department of Education all criminal acts involving sexual violence as well as all prevention and security measures in place to control the problem.

Unfortunately, in the words of Nancy Gertner, a retired United States district court judge for Massachusetts and currently a Harvard Law School professor, ". . . until recently, Title IX was dormant and largely ignored. The federal government had been a paper tiger. Universities were not reporting, much less dealing with, either sexual harassment or explicit sexual violence."

Now that the Office of Civil Rights was in the game in response to student lawsuits, public outcry and the high profile and salacious stories appearing in the media, with the investigations of the targeted schools, it did what bureaucracies do. It expanded and exerted its power through regulations it propounded to implement its authorizing legislation. For example, The Violence Against Women Reauthorization Act (VAWA) of 2013 added new, more complex reporting requirements for sexual assaults, violence and stalking.

The White House Task Force to Protect Students from Sexual Assaults

Additional pressure and notoriety was visited upon educational institutions when President Obama in 2014 held a public press conference during which he announced the appointment of The White House Task Force to Protect Students from Sexual Assaults. In April of that year the Task Force issued its report called "*Not Alone*", which painted a very alarming picture of the extent of sexual misconduct and violence on American campuses.

The Obama administration released a list of 55 colleges and universities under investigation for their alleged mishandling of sexual assault complaints. Later that year the Office of Civil Rights website added another 50 names to the list of schools being investigated as shirkers of their responsibilities regarding the handling of sexual misconduct claims.

Janet Napolitano, former Governor of Arizona, United States Secretary of Homeland Security and since 2014 the President of the University of California, describes in her article "Only Yes Means Yes" that investigations by a federal agency go on for years, prompt investigations by other state and federal agencies and require huge outlays of resources of time to produce documents and money to compensate attorneys and outside experts. This onerous expense, the lengthy period of suspicion, and the exposure to ruinous sanctions predictably results in schools just agreeing to do or say what the federal agency feels is appropriate.

Unfortunately, what began as an effort by the government to motivate and assist colleges to protect their students from non-consensual sexual overtures and attacks has devolved into mandated policies and processes which are predicated on the presumption of guilt on the part of the accused.

How Federal Citations and Risk of Penalties Affected Harvard's Procedures

Perhaps emblematic of this "Catch 22" situation that the nation's schools of higher education found themselves in is the story of Harvard University. Harvard, while in the throes of a federal investigation based on a 2010 complaint to The Office of Civil Rights for being too soft on sexual assaults, created a new program establishing new procedures for addressing complaints of sexual misconduct by its students. The new program was to encompass all the schools comprising the university.

Judge Gertner, in an article appearing in the Winter 2015 issue of *American Prospect* criticized Harvard University's new sexual harassment policy for denying effective assistance of counsel to accused students, for the failure to provide a meaningful sharing of information, and for the absence of hearings, as such, given that there is no confrontation between accused and accuser or examination of witnesses and documentary evidence allowed.

Twenty-eight professors at Harvard Law School, including Janet Halley and Jeannie Suk, avowed feminists, signed an Open Letter to the Board of Overseers of the university denouncing the new policy. The Open Letter, which was published by *The Boston Globe*, stated that Harvard's new construct lacked the most basic elements of fairness and due process. Thereafter, Harvard Law School developed a separate process which permitted live hearings with the participation of counsel for the parties, confrontation and cross-examination and, most importantly, a division and separation in the roles of investigation, adjudication and appeals.

Establishing Rules for Consent to Sexual Conduct

The continuing expansion and refining of its regulations and guidance of The Office of Civil Rights has introduced additional inequities in the sexual misconduct policies of colleges and universities.

Two examples are the impact of alcohol and whether there was valid consent given for the sexual conduct.

Impairment by Alcohol: Respected health care groups have warned that "*young women are willingly drinking heavily and using powerful drugs. So are young men. It is an immense public health problem.*" The Obama administration, the Department of Education and schools have shied away from emphasizing the dangers of student intoxication due to the notion that linking excessive drinking by females to nonconsensual sex is a form of "victim blaming".

Since the abuse of alcohol and/or drugs is a common component in instances of campus sexual encounters, the Office of Civil Rights has prodded colleges and universities to deal with the issue in their sexual misconduct policies. It is the policy of Harvard University that if a person is impaired or incapacitated by alcohol or drugs when conduct of a sexual nature occurs that conduct is deemed "unwelcome", i.e., nonconsensual. However, the respondent's impairment for the same reasons when the sexual incident occurs does not diminish the responsibility of the respondent.

> If both parties are intoxicated but not unconscious or incapacitated and they have sex, only the male is responsible under Harvard's policy.

This is a bias in favor of the accuser, critics have argued.

Brown University's policy states "A charged student's use of any drug, including alcohol, judged to be related to an offense will be considered an exacerbating rather than a mitigating circumstance". This policy is harsher to an accused than Massachusetts criminal law where voluntary intoxication is not regarded as an excuse for the crime but can be considered in mitigation.

Affirmative Consent: In the second area of consent or no consent, Janet Halley in her article "Move to Affirmative Consent" (2015) observes that "In a vigorous new trend, supported by many feminists, affirmative consent requirements are appearing in campus sexual conduct codes. California and New York have passed legislation requiring colleges and universities to adopt an affirmative consent standard in their sexual assault policies". Professors Jacob Gerson and Jeannie Suk in a *Columbia University Law Review* article entitled "The Sex Bureaucracy" write:

> "*The United States Department of Justice in an April 2, 2015 pronouncement stated that sexual assault is any type of sexual conduct or behavior that occurs without the* explicit *consent of the recipient (*emphasis supplied*). An absence of 'no', silence, a smile or a nod is not enough. As non-consent increasingly becomes the line separating legal and illegal sexual conduct we see the concept of non-consent expanding.*"

Yale University disclosed in its 2013 ASR that its prevention program tells students that consent is not enough—"*hold out for enthusiasm*". Glendale Community College in California, as disclosed in its 2014 ASR, defined consent to a sexual activity as "voluntary, sober, imaginative, enthusiastic, creative, wanted, informed, mutual, and verbal agreement". Anything else is sexual assault. So much for spontaneity! College students are treated differently than adults in other settings. Consent cannot be presumed even by couples in an established relationship.

Interpreting Post Hoc Reversal of Apparent Consent for Consensual Sex

While requiring affirmative consent may be a step in the right direction for many reasons, it is difficult to perceive how it will be helpful in a "he said—she said" situation in the current atmosphere of bias against the accused.

In the Occidental College case, a student couple engaged in undisputed consensual sex which was a first-time experience for the young lady. Feeling profound remorse the next day, she filed a complaint against the young man which resulted in his expulsion.

In the presently pending case of *Doe v. Amherst College*, a classmate Sarah Jones accused Doe of sexually assaulting her during an evening two years before when she willingly performed oral sex on Doe, her roommate's boyfriend, when he was in a "blackout" from the over-drinking of alcohol. The Hearing Board credited that she had withdrawn her consent and that Doe's expulsion was based entirely on his failure to terminate the interaction at this point. The Amherst Student Handbook defined a "blackout" as incapacitated, in a state beyond drunkenness or intoxication. Megyn Kelly, an attorney and journalist, devoted a portion of three episodes of the Kelly File castigating the absurdity of Amherst's finding against Michael Chang, including its disregard of exculpatory evidence and denying his appeal as untimely.

In *Jack Montague v. Yale University* et al., the female accuser and Jack Montague, the captain of Yale's basketball team which went to the NCAA playoffs, went to her dorm room on three occasions where she voluntarily undressed, engaged in sexual foreplay and then got into the bed and had sex with Jack Montague. On a fourth occasion the same ritual was followed, but when they got into bed she claimed that she said "No" but does not believe that he heard her. Jack Montague was expelled from Yale. It could certainly be argued that in each of these cases affirmative consent was given, by word or by deed, but it did not avail the accused.

Reaction to Problems Created by the Overextension of Title IX

As the lawsuits referenced above suggest, as well as at least three dozen similar cases against colleges and universities, male students accused or found guilty of sexual assault are appealing to courts of law arguing that their schools did not afford them the "fair and impartial" decisions that Title IX requires.

In the past, courts have refused to interfere with the academic freedom and administration of private educational institutions or even to impose upon them the requisite of "due process". Now judges are rendering stinging decisions faulting lack of due process in breach of the school's contractual duties to its students and in breach of the duty imposed by Title IX not to discriminate on the basis of gender.

One such decision was authored by US District Judge for Massachusetts, Dennis Saylor, in the case of *Francis v. Brandeis University* in which the judge commented quizzically, "I don't understand how a university, much less one named after Louis Brandeis, could possibly think that that was a fair procedure to not allow the accused to see the accusation." Later the judge added, "Our constitution provides a right of confrontation, a public proceeding in which you confront your accuser, the right of cross-examination. . . . Most of these schools have this one-sided procedure. I don't understand how a college could set this up. I don't understand it."

The University of Southern California, the University of California at San Diego, University of Tennessee, Middleburg College, George Mason University and Brandeis are some of the schools which have felt the lash of these decisions. Insurers of educational institutions have had to pay out millions of dollars, mostly to the accused students.

Again we see a reversal of the pendulum. In reaction to use of the lowest standard of proof of guilt mandated by the Office of Civil Rights and one person adjudications by Title IX Coordinators, many institutions are expanding in number of members the adjudicatory panels. Others are populating the panels with faculty members, administrators and students. Since an adverse finding on a sexual assault charge is so serious and its effects so lasting, a number of institutions are requiring supermajority decisions. In 2015 Stanford imposed a supermajority decision of four out of five. Currently that has been changed to a unanimous decision of a three-person panel. Duke has also gone from a supermajority to unanimity for a valid decision.

Some schools, rather than trying to train administrators to act as prosecutors, are outsourcing the task to persons with professional prosecutorial and investigatory experience. Law firms with a white collar crime practice, companies of professional mediators and arbitrators and former law enforcement personnel are frequently engaged to conduct the investigation and adjudication of sexual misconduct complaints on the school's behalf.

Suggestions for Remedying the Dilemma

"***What is to be done?*** How can the government and institutions of higher learning address sexual assault, support victims, identify predators and not unfairly punish innocent students?" asks University President Janet Napolitano. She suggests that a good place to start would be scaling back the powers of the Department of Education's Office of Civil Rights, which has overstepped its bounds in micromanaging university policies and enforcing draconian rules that infringe on the rights of the accused.

If the definition of sexual misconduct were narrowed, and there was a return to the "clear and convincing evidence" standard, there would be fewer miscarriages of justice. Affirmative consent regulations which tell people how to conduct their sex lives should be struck.

President Napolitano counsels that schools should emphasize to students the need to exercise good decision-making, including the decision whether to abuse alcohol to the extent that decision-making is impaired or obliterated.

Professor Janet Halley adds the recommendation that colleges and universities reduce their Title IX office to a compliance monitoring role and get it out of the business of adjudicating cases.

In the end, the Title IX experience seems to have proven the immutability of the *law of unintended consequences*. Perhaps the most beneficial allocation of roles is that the government require and monitor the colleges in their role of comforting, counseling and, if necessary, treating the victims of sexual assaults, and if accountability is considered constructive for the victim, that role might best be handled by the parties, their parents, their attorneys and, if necessary and appropriate, the law enforcement authorities which have more powerful investigatory tools and greater truth-detecting technology.

Figure 5.13.1.1 *J. Owen Todd presents his client's case in TW Courtroom, 1989*

J. Owen Todd, a Fellow of The American College of Trial Lawyers, is a graduate of St. Sebastian's Preparatory School, Harvard College and Boston College Law School, and recipient of an Honorary Degree in Law and Letters from New England School of Law. Following his appointment as law clerk to Justice Jacob J. Spiegel of the Massachusetts Supreme Judicial Court, he joined the Boston law firm of Hale and Dorr, where he practiced for 28 years, became a Senior Partner and among other positions served as Chairman of the Executive Committee. In 1988 Governor Dukakis appointed Mr. Todd a Justice of Massachusetts Superior Court. Upon his retirement he co-founded the litigation law firm of Todd & Weld LLP in Boston.

Mr. Todd, a former Massachusetts State Ethics Commissioner and former President of the Massachusetts Trial Lawyers Association, served for ten years as Town Moderator for the Town of Sudbury. He is also a Trustee of the Austin Jones Foundation and the J. Owen Todd Charitable Foundation. He and his wife, Eileen Marie "Lee", have four children and seven grandchildren.

Federal

Transportation Policy

Funding Our Federal Infrastructure

Robin Hood[1]

The Sheriff of Nottingham is up to his old ways. Despite numerous and voluminous studies by the Department of Transportation, the Association of State and Highway Transportation Officials, the American Trucking Association and the American Road and Transportation Builders Association that have warned that the quality and quantity of US transportation infrastructure is deficient and in dire need of permanent long term funding, Congress has been incapable of agreeing on a financial plan that would restore our infrastructure to world class status. Its current status, as reported in a recent Ernst and Young survey,[2] is an embarrassing 25th in the world. Experts like the American Society of Civil Engineers and Ernst and Young estimate a maximum of $1.5 trillion spread over ten years is required to rebuild our infrastructure. The Trump administration, which took office in 2017, proposed a lower target of $1 trillion.

Over the past two decades there has been a plethora of discussions and reports written about the need for long-term funding solution for US infrastructure. These studies have proposed options such as public-private partnerships (*PPPs*), vehicle miles travelled (*VMTs*), infrastructure banks and increasing the current fuel tax. The fuel tax, which in 2017 stands at 24.4 cents for diesel and 18.4 cents for gasoline, has not increased since 1993. All of these options have failed to gain political traction because of significant downsides: PPPs have been disappointing in Indiana, Spain and the United Kingdom; infrastructure banks have tax and governing complications; VMTs are expensive to implement and administer, and are intrusive; and raising fuel taxes has little political or public support. The common thread in all these proposals is user pay and/or increasing the federal debt, all culminating in a regressive tax levied by tolls or debt on those least able to pay.

Former Speaker of the US House of Representatives John Boehner said: "We've got to find a way to deal with America's crumbling infrastructure in a long-term program that is in fact permanently funded."[3] Senator Robert Corker echoed the same sentiment, saying in exasperation, "there is not enough money coming in".[4]

Republicans and Democrats disagree vehemently over taxes. But if this infrastructure problem is to be resolved, they must find a way to reconcile their ideologies in order to permanently fund infrastructure through the Highway Trust Fund. However, devising a plan that permanently funds infrastructure investment, does not increase the federal debt, nor impose a regressive tax on the majority of Americans, has been an elusive objective. Perhaps the answer is to reach back to historical lore and adopt the philosophy of my namesake, Robin Hood: take from the rich, and give to the less fortunate for the greater good.

Let's overlay Robin Hood's legendary actions onto the infrastructure funding problem and see how it might work. To do so, let's focus on the payroll tax which for 2017 taxes earned income up to $127,200 at 6.2%. It is a classic regressive tax because there is no tax on income exceeding the cap.

Here is what Robin Hood would do today, based on recent expert economic research:

First: Remove the payroll tax cap for those with earned incomes of $500k and greater—the so-called "1%ers" who represent that 1% of tax payers whose combined incomes equal the other 99% of US taxpayers. Removing the cap for those earning $500k or more would yield $120 billion per year and regardless of whether they pay any income tax.[5]

Second: Invest the $120 billion per year for ten years to create a world-class infrastructure—bridges, roads, airports, water and flood control systems.

Third: The $120 billion will create three million jobs, as each billion invested in infrastructure will create 25,000 jobs.[6]

Fourth: The additional three million jobs will decrease the 2016 unemployment rate by 1.9 points to 3.6% and also boost the US stock market. According to David Rosenberg, chief economist at Gluskin Sheff of Toronto,[7] a one-percentage drop in the unemployment rate boosts the Standard and Poor's 500 Index annual return by 3.4 percentage points. Using his formula, a 1.9 % reduction in unemployment from three million new jobs would increase the S & P 500 by 6.5%.

Fifth: According to Fidelity Investments,[8] people with earned income of $500k or greater on average have investable assets of $5 million. Removing the Payroll Tax Cap paradoxically will increase these assets 6.5% or $325,000 because of increased return on investments secondary to events following creation of new jobs.

Our Robin Hood analysis predicts that removing the payroll tax cap for the 1%ers will create a positive sequence of events—yield $120 billion per year to be invested in infrastructure, which creates three million jobs, which boosts the S&P 500 6.5%, and translates into a $325,000 gain in assets for the 1%ers who will pay, on average, a payroll tax increase of $23,000 annually.

Not a bad trade for them, or for America!

Thank you, ancestor Robin Hood!

John A. Simourian is the Founder and Chairman of Lily Transportation Corp.; past chairman of the National Truck Leasing Association and the Truck Leasing and Rental Association of America; and former board member of CD&L Delivery System. He has served his community as former board member of the New England Sports Museum, past chairman of trustees of the First Armenian Church, Belmont, MA; and as co-founder of Three Million Jobs Now!

Endnotes

1 *Robin Hood* is the pseudonym of John A. Simourian, HC 1957 and HBS 1961, a national transportation executive.

2 Ernst and Young/Urban Land institute, *Annual Report* 2013.

3 Former Speaker of the US House of Representatives John Boehner as quoted in *Infrastructure Report*, Political Economic Research Institute (PERI), University of Massachusetts, 2009.

4 U.S. Senator Robert Corker as quoted in *Infrastructure Report*, PERI, University of Massachusetts, Amherst, 2009.

5 Personal communication from Heidi Garret-Peltier, Assistant Research Professor, PERI, University of Massachusetts, Amherst.

6 Personal communication from Heidi Garret-Peltier, Assistant Research Professor, PERI, University of Massachusetts, Amherst.

7 Personal communications from David Rosenberg, Chief Economist at Gluskin Sheff Research, Toronto, ONT, Canada, 2015–16.

8 Fidelity *Millionaire Outlook Survey*, 2014.

State

Legislature

Comments on Legislation

Paul Aizley

In 2013, as a Nevada State Assemblyman, I introduced *AB 326.*

The bill addressed what happens when one agrees to conditions on a contract without reading the contract.

> *AB 326* made *binding arbitration unenforceable unless* one specifically agreed to the arbitration described in the agreement.
>
> The governor signed the bill, and it was recently challenged in a Washoe County, NV, court. There may be conflict with federal legislation. Unfortunately, I do not know how that played out.

Agreeing to a contract without reading the agreement is becoming a common practice.

> Yes, everyone should read what they are agreeing to but they don't. There is the man who bought a cellphone, and the cellphone exploded and burned his leg. He had the option of opting out of binding arbitration, but he had to do that within 30 days of purchase.
>
> The way I read the story, he did not receive adequate compensation. But that's not the issue. He should have had the right to sue.

Why all these agreements?

> They seem to be there only to allow the manufacturer to build an inferior product and not get sued. A cellphone should not explode. The car's air bag should not spray shrapnel nor should it decapitate a young passenger.

> On the other hand, if I buy a horse, I cannot sue the breeder when the horse cannot fly. There are normal expectations of buyer and seller.
>
> Contracts and agreements, *whether they are read or not,* should contain only reasonable and relevant conditions.

If *AB 326* fails in Washoe County, the next step would be to strengthen the rules of arbitration in Nevada so that the consumer can know that the process is fair.

Unfortunately, the younger generation knocked me out of the Assembly in an undemocratic act of ageism.

Figure 5.15.1.1 *Candidate for re-election to the Nevada Assembly, Paul Aizley, in 2015*

Paul Aizley, a Boston native, attended Boston English High before Harvard, earned an MS in mathematics from the University of Arizona in 1959, and then returned to Boston as Instructor of Mathematics at Tufts University. Needing a PhD to continue college teaching, Paul spent four miserable wet years in Seattle and then went back to Arizona to earn a PhD in Mathematics from Arizona State University. The degree was completed during the 1968–69 academic year while Paul was an assistant professor at University of Nevada, Las Vegas, where he remained until retirement in 2008.

During the 40 years of wandering in academia, Paul was Faculty Senate Chairman (twice), the president's assistant (five years), Dean of Continuing Education and Summer Term (13 years). Off campus, he was the president of the Nevada Affiliate of ACLU (four years) and delegate to the national ACLU board.

Paul served three terms (six years) in the Nevada Assembly where, he reports, he was one of the most progressive legislators in Nevada. In 2009 he sponsored one bill for legalizing medical marijuana and another to protect transgender persons in the workplace. Both failed in 2009 but were signed by the Governor in 2011.

Paul and Sari Aizley have been married for 35 years. Most of Paul's community activism can be attributed to Sari's more outgoing personality. Together they created a newspaper called *CLASS!*, which survived for 16 years. Free to the 40,000 high school students in Clark County, it included *Diganos,* several pages in Spanish. Paul has seven stepchildren from two marriages: four from Sari and three (one stepson is deceased) from a previous marriage, ten grandchildren, and four great-granddaughters.

Figure 5.15.1.2 *The Nevada State Legislative Building in Carson City, viewed from the Senate side. The Assembly is housed in the far wing. The building, completed in 1915, was added to the original capitol building built in 1871.*

Photo credit: Dave Parker, 2007; Wikimedia Commons

Courts

Reflections on the Jury System

Daniel Johnedis

After graduating from college I served in the Air Force for a few years and then attended law school. My first job was law clerk to a justice of the Massachusetts Supreme Judicial Court, where I developed a love of the law and an abiding interest in the legal process. After my one-year appointment there, I spent the next decade handling civil cases in a firm and the state Attorney General's Office. The part of my practice I enjoyed most was drafting appellate briefs and arguing before the Supreme Judicial Court. I returned to the court as its staff counsel, a position I held for 18 years. Once again, I had the opportunity to work on cases that had been appealed. While there I taught trial advocacy and wrote a number of articles on the appellate process. In the final decade before retirement, I returned to the private practice of law, focusing on civil and criminal appeals. During this period I taught appellate process.

Our System of Justice: Judges and Juries

Throughout my career I have grown to appreciate our system of justice. We follow the common law, inherited from England. The beauty of it is that it evolves, gradually, from the facts of the cases decided by the appellate courts. Typically, when a case is reviewed by the high court, it determines if the facts are supported by the evidence, and if the law, as developed from prior cases, has been correctly applied. When the trial judge in the case is the adjudicator, the system works well, for the judge is learned in the law and experienced in the adjudication of cases. The appellate court can determine if the facts (usually found by the trial judge) are supported by the evidence. The court can then decide if the trial judge's rulings of law and application of them to the facts are correct. In most cases, the outcome is fairly predictable. When the adjudicator is a jury, however, the system does not work as well. Jurors are ordinary people, not usually educated in the law and not experienced in the rigors of careful analysis of evidence and painstaking application of the law to the facts. The findings of fact they make and the rulings of law they apply to those findings are shrouded in the secrecy of the jury deliberation room. It is this feature of our great judicial system—which fosters open and public trials—that is defective. This defect has been recognized by legal scholars for over 200 years.

Appellate Court Reviews of Jury Cases

When a jury case is presented to the appellate court for review, the justices make many assumptions to uphold the verdict, for the jury need not make findings of fact or rulings of law; in fact, jurors are not obligated to explain how they arrived at their decision. To be sure, the trial judge instructs the jury on the law, but the reviewing court has no way to determine if the jury accepted the law as given by the trial judge, correctly applied the law to the facts, or, indeed, if the jury even understood the law. The appellate court is constrained to examine the law as charged by the trial judge to determine if he or she correctly stated the law. If the court decides the judge's instructions were correct, it assumes the jury understood the law and correctly applied it to the facts. If the court decides the instructions were erroneous in a material way, the only relief available is a new trial before a different jury.

During the course of the trial, the judge gives many cautionary and limiting instructions to guide the jury in examining the evidence and making findings. She may, for example, warn the jury not to give any weight to the defendant's past criminal convictions, introduced solely to attack his credibility, when considering whether he committed the offence for which he is being tried. Or the trial judge may direct the jury to disregard prejudicial testimony erroneously admitted but stricken from the record. The appellate court assumes that the jurors followed the judge's instructions in these and in the many other instances of limiting and cautionary instructions.

Moreover, when confronted with conflicting evidence, the reviewing court assumes the jury accepted the version that supports the verdict.

The appellate court makes these assumptions because it is barred from the secret deliberations in the jury room. Jury deliberations are not recorded; therefore, the court has no record to examine. Major decisions regarding parties' lives, liberties, relationships, property and other significant rights are made without opportunity for fair and complete review.

Secrecy in Jury Deliberations

Many studies have been done about jury deliberations. What they reveal is eye-opening. In personal injury cases, jurors have been shown to consider the availability of liability insurance in deciding whether the defendant was negligent, even though the trial judge has instructed them not to do so. Some studies showed that jurors had hard time comprehending scientific evidence, and tended to give too little weight to evidence they did not understand. Results of studies done in criminal cases are especially disturbing. Studies reveal that jurors who hear about the defendant's criminal record, introduced solely for impeachment purposes, have considered it in deciding whether he committed the offense for which he was being tried. Some studies disclosed that many jurors did not understand the government's burden of proof, guilt beyond *a reasonable doubt,* some thinking the burden was to prove guilt beyond *any doubt*. One study disclosed that many jurors, in deciding whether to impose the death penalty, confused the heavy burden of proof borne by the government (proof of aggravating factors *beyond a reasonable doubt*) with the lighter burden borne by the defendant (proof of mitigating factors by *a preponderance of the evidence*). The jurors switched these burdens, thus making the death penalty more likely than if the burdens of proof were correctly allocated.

While some of the studies concluded that the jurors understanding of the law was adequate, others showed that some jurors misunderstood the law, were confused about it, or were unable to follow it.

Can Juries Ignore the Law?

Because jurors deliberate in secret and do not have to give reasons for their verdicts, they have the power, though not the right, to ignore the law. Thus, a non-elected tiny segment of the community can override laws enacted by the legislature or declared by the courts. This power may have had its place in colonial America, where the people opposed laws passed by a foreign power, but it has no place in present-day America. More than 100 years ago juries were allowed to decide the law, as well as the facts, but today juries are required to accept the law as given by the trial judge. However, the reviewing court has no way to determine if the jury has, in fact, followed the law.

Trial judges have little, if any, means of helping the jury to analyze the evidence. Until the 20th century, judges commented on the evidence to aid the jury in their fact-finding function. This practice, considered an invasion of the jury's exclusive right to decide the facts, has been greatly curtailed or abandoned. There is no opportunity for the appellate court to determine the findings, if any, that the jury made in reaching its decision. There are some procedures available to the trial courts to compel the jury to make findings of particular, material facts, but these procedures are not mandatory and are not routinely used.

There is a seldom used procedure for enabling counsel to peek into the jury room: if a juror reveals to the trial judge, on his or her own initiative, or through an attorney, that there has been juror misconduct in the deliberations room. Courts are reluctant to consider such claims, but will do so if the alleged misconduct is sufficiently egregious to affect the integrity of the verdict. Usually, the claims involve outside influences, such as consulting third parties or conducting experiments about a matter under consideration. They also may involve jurors relating personal experiences or exhibiting biases concerning issues being decided. This narrow avenue of relief from improper juror conduct is not usually available because jurors are rarely willing to come forward. Moreover, this type of challenge rarely reaches the questions whether the jury understood, followed or correctly applied the law, and whether the jury properly analyzed the evidence in accordance with the trial judge's instructions in finding the facts. Only the attorneys, educated in the law and experienced in analyzing and applying it, are equipped with the skills essential for uncovering serious errors the jury may have made in adjudicating the case in the closed jury room.

The Right to Trial by Jury: Does It Require Secret Deliberations?

For centuries the right to trial by jury has been preserved in the United States Constitution and in the Massachusetts Constitution. This right is considered sacred. However, neither constitution declares that juries must decide cases in secret and thus shield their deliberations from appellate scrutiny. Secrecy has been a feature of jury trials for many years, but it is not essential to a jury trial. Two centuries ago jurors heard several criminal cases in a day and returned verdicts of some without retiring in private to consider them.

Courts and legal scholars advance several reasons justifying secrecy. Some argue it fosters full and frank discussion without fear of public ridicule and contempt. Others have stated that secrecy ensures finality and community trust in the verdicts. These grounds for maintaining a system of secret discussions—for example, as to whether a defendant will go to prison, or an accident victim will be compensated for his injuries—do not withstand close scrutiny. Today, transparency in making important decisions is favored over secrecy. Highly sophisticated technology is available to make recording deliberations unobtrusive. Confidentiality could be maintained. Jurors, aware their proceedings are being recorded, would be less likely to express biases and more likely to try to follow the trial judge's instructions. Most important, attorneys and their clients would know whether their case was fairly decided by the jury.

As to finality and public trust, the verdict would be no less final than a verdict rendered in secret. Furthermore, the verdict would be subject to a fairer and a more meaningful review by the appellate court justices, who would know if the jury decided the case in accordance with the rules of law. I believe, that, in time, this process would promote the community's trust in our system of justice.

Daniel Johnedis, former Special Master and Commissioner of the Massachusetts Appeals Court, has been a member of appellate practice committees of the American Bar Association, the Massachusetts Bar Association and the Boston Bar Association. A graduate of Boston College Law School, he served as Law Clerk for the Massachusetts Supreme Judicial Court before joining the Boston firm of Lyne, Woodworth & Evarts. After serving as Massachusetts Assistant Attorney General from 1970–1972, he joined the Massachusetts Supreme Judicial Court as Staff Counsel for 18 years before moving to the Appeals Court in 1990. After retiring from the Court in 1992, he returned to private practice with Roche, Carens & DeGiacomo for six years before entering solo practice.

He has taught trial advocacy, legal ethics and the appellate process at Boston University, New England School of Law, Massachusetts Continuing Legal Education, Inc., and other legal venues. He has served as editor of the Massachusetts Law Review and authored articles on appellate practice for the Supreme Judicial Court Historical Society and contributed chapters to *The History of the Law in Massachusetts: The Supreme Judicial Court 1692–1992* and *Summary of Basic Law*.

An Air Force veteran, he and his wife of 58 years, Anna Marie (DeSisto), have three children.

Fifty-One Years at Bridgewater State Hospital

John M. Russell, Jr.

With civil liberties under challenge following the outcome of the presidential election of 2016, it seemed like a good idea to write about a case illustrating what can happen when civil rights are ignored. So here goes.

This is the case of Mike Popendy.

Records from Bridgewater State Hospital dated June 26, 1917, include the following:

> "Patient was born Oct. 10, 1891, in Austria. He learned to read and write in the Polish language. In 1913 he came to the US entering at New York. He was employed as a miner at Glassport, PA, for 2½ years, and then for six months in Wendber, PA. Afterward he was for ten days in Albany, NY. He then came to Worcester, MA. Where after one day he asked the police for a night's lodging and was sent to the State Farm Prison as a vagrant."

Records from Worcester District Court indicate that the day after he asked for a night's lodging he was brought to court, found guilty of the crime of vagrancy and sentenced to two years at Concord Reformatory.

For reasons that are not clear, after a few months he was transferred to Bridgewater. It should be noted that Bridgewater was primarily a prison and not a hospital.

> On November 2, 1917, he was interviewed with another inmate acting as interpreter. The record reads "quiet, well behaved . . . answers many questions directly and with clearness . . . no hallucinations . . . oriented for time and place".

A year later, on November 15, 1918, he was seen by Dr. Farrar, who wrote the following:

> "Continues to get along in a quiet and comfortable manner. States that he has been there 19 months, gives date and name of institution, the names of three physicians correctly. Says his sentence will be completed on the 15th of December for two years and is anxious to be discharged at that time. Never causes the slightest disturbances, not untidy in habits or particularly careless of dress though rather apathetic."

He was never diagnosed with a mental illness and was never considered dangerous. Nevertheless, he remained at Bridgewater for 51 years, together with more than 200 other men who had been convicted of either vagrancy or drunkenness.

An associate and I represented these men at Superior Court hearings in 1968. Until then none of them had ever had an attorney. They had been at Bridgewater for an average of over 40 years; one had been there since 1906.

By 1968 almost all of these men had become senile. In each case the Court ruled that they were being held illegally. Almost all, including Mike Popendy, were sent to a civilian hospital with a geriatric ward. A few were discharged to relatives.

After the hearings my associate and I believed that in the future no one would be held without charges and without a trial or a hearing.

Sadly, Guantanamo has proven that we were wrong.

* * *

Addendum

The Committee has asked me to provide some additional information, and I'll do my best to do so.

The Forgotten Men of Bridgewater. In 1968 I was employed by the Massachusetts Defenders Committee as a trial attorney. In that year the State Supreme Court appointed the MDC to represent the forgotten men of Bridgewater. Chief Counsel of the Defenders assigned the cases to me and to Attorney Mark Witkin, who was also employed by the MDC.

I do not have the docket numbers of these cases, but the hearings were held in the Norfolk Superior Court sitting at Bridgewater in the spring of 1968. We represented the inmates and an Assistant Attorney General represented the hospital. Superior Court Judge Alan Hale presided.

In each case a finding was made that the inmate was being confined illegally, after which a hearing, sometimes lengthy, was held to determine if the inmate should be considered dangerous and committed to a facility with high security. As best I can recall, no inmates were found to be dangerous.

Reforms at Bridgewater. In 1959 Charles Gaughan '37 became Superintendent at Bridgewater, and he held that position until 1985. I found him to be intelligent, compassionate and dedicated to improving conditions at Bridgewater. Beyond that, I do not feel that I am competent to discuss conditions at Bridgewater.

Legal Basis for Long-Term Incarceration. The Committee asks *on what basis the men were held for such a long time.* The short answer is that there was no basis for confining them. As noted above, their confinement was found to be illegal.

Comparison to Guantanamo Bay Detention Camp. Finally, the Committee asks that I provide some information on Guantanamo. Wikipedia has an excellent article on the subject, which begins as follows:

> "*Guantanamo Bay Detention Camp* is a US Military Prison located in Guantanamo Bay Naval Base. . . . Since the inmates have been detained indefinitely without trial and several inmates were severely tortured, this camp is considered as a major breach of human rights by great parts of the world."

John Russell, a native of Watertown, MA, entered Harvard in 1953. He writes, "After a dismal freshman year, I spent nearly two years in the Army. I served as a radio operator and am an 'overseas veteran' of the Korean conflict by virtue of serving 30 days in the Bahamas. War is hell. I returned to Harvard, graduating in 1959, by this time with a wife and child. After a year in St. Thomas, I entered Boston College Law School where, for the first time in my academic career, I did very well. After graduation I took a job with the Massachusetts Defenders Committee and spent the next five years defending people charged with all sorts of crimes. The pay was terrible, but I loved the work." The next 30-plus years consisted of private practice, probably the high point of which was securing a *not guilty* verdict in a very high-profile murder case in Worcester County in 1991.

In 1971 he moved to Hull, MA, served on Town of Hull Finance Committee for four years—one year as chairman. In 1977 he was elected Town Moderator and then reelected, serving 20 years until retiring in 2007. He says, "I miss the job." He served a term as president of the Massachusetts Moderators Association and was an editor of *Town Meeting Time,* a manual of parliamentary procedure used by most New England towns.

He and his wife, Marilyn, "the love of my life", have two children and two grandchildren. For the past 15 years they have divided their time between Florida and Hull, and also attended Elderhostel—now Road Scholar—programs. As to avocations, he writes, "Ten years ago I was a mediocre golfer. Now I'm terrible."

Chapter Six

ECONOMICS

Figure C6 *Harvard Yard in winter's grip, seen through Holworthy Gate, when demand for heat and light drives up energy consumption, and the University modulates energy costs by imposing a January recess during the academic year.*

Reprinted courtesy of Harvard University

Chapter Six

ECONOMICS

Theory

Connecting the Dots

Hugh Blair-Smith

My project for a second book is at heart a continuation of the *Big Thoughts* I shared in our 55th Report in 2012, a connect-the-dots exercise involving *productivity, employment, the limits of ecological exploitation, the nature and purpose of money, world population,* and *prospects for the global economy*.

The funny thing is, I hated Economics courses, probably because they were full of things that looked like function graphs and equations but were too qualitative to satisfy my mathematical and engineering sense. Maybe if there had been a course in "quanting", I'd have liked that better. But anyway, somehow I got over it.

What follows here is a summary of the ideas on which the book will be based. Although these ideas inevitably consider questions of polity, this is not a political document. It does not conform to the platform of any party; I'm quite certain that any partisan will find here some things to appreciate and some to deprecate.

Dot #1 is ***the paradox of accelerating productivity***, which makes more and more wage-paying jobs unnecessary (that's bad) while multiplying the volume and availability of goods and services (that's good). Or maybe it isn't quite that Manichean.

Our longstanding principle, that *all capable people of working age must either hold wage-paying jobs or be despised as good-for-nothing freeloaders*, is increasingly out of step with today's productive world and with tomorrow's more productive world. Look outside that principle, and you can see that most of those "freeloaders" would gladly do things that are thoroughly worthwhile, but for which no business model can create a "job." Put another way, *the number and effectiveness of volunteers would increase radically if people could afford to volunteer.*

I said "longstanding", but that principle underwent a sea change in World War II, before which time wage-paying jobs were allocated almost entirely to men, leaving women to do the world's non-business-model work: *homemaking* and *care giving* primarily. The proximate cause of the change to more-equal opportunity for women was the severe labor shortage in war-production factories when so many men entered the armed forces. But this solution was aided by two other factors: machines that had raised the productivity of homemaking, and the spread of institutions that had increased the productivity of high-maintenance care giving. More women could afford the time and energy to take wage-paying jobs.

In this essay, "*wages*" includes salaries, stock benefits, etc.—every transaction in which money is exchanged for work under the terms of an employment contract. Also, "*wealth*" includes food, clothing, shelter, etc.—everything that directly promotes well-being—but *excludes money and monetary instruments.*

In my 2012 report, I traced a broad ***history of employment and productivity*** thus:

Leaving aside hunter-gatherers (including fishermen, who have their own productivity-vs.-sustainability issues), *the invention of agriculture* raised the first full set of productivity issues. Most everybody had to be engaged in herding and/or farming, leaving a small minority to make clothing, shelter, tools, and social organization. As a general rule, employment was kept full by the ability to make some productive use of anybody who was available, even if the production in question was sometimes only to lay up stores against famines to come.

The *Industrial Revolution* did two things at once: it provided tools that enormously increased agricultural productivity (so that now only a tiny minority is sufficient to work the land), and it demanded large numbers of factory hands to make the tools, thereby neatly solving the unemployment problem it had just created.

Then in the 20th century, another revolution—*automation*—enormously increased the productivity of manufacturing, while at the same time demanding a vast increase in engineers to design the automation, thus again creating and solving an employment problem simultaneously.

More recently, we see a *service economy* expanding to take up people as *automation itself becomes more automated*, and we can't be sure that this is a complete solution, nor can we see clearly whether a further "revolution" is desirable or even possible.

Dot #2 is ***the essence and purpose of money,*** which was originally created as a *medium of exchange* and has worked very well in that role. But with the accelerating rise of people who create huge amounts of money simply by *manipulating other peoples' money*, it has become a tool for concentrating political-economic power in the hands of a tiny band of oligarchs.

Defining *money* as a *commodity in limited supply*, which can be cornered by crafty oligarchs, seems to go logically with a world of scarcity. If there isn't enough real wealth for everybody, then some people will have enough wealth to survive, but the rest will suffer or die prematurely.

The invention of money, in a deliberately finite supply to match the finite supply of wealth, was an improvement on the cave-man approach where *wealth accumulation*, and therefore survival, was achieved generally by brute physical violence. This more civil conduct of *wealth allocation* required money to be recognizable, fungible, durable, measurable, dividable, and portable. In a world without sufficient information systems to support the wonderfully abstract construct we call "*credit*", it made sense to dictate that only precious metals (an actual commodity) would be considered to be "real" money.

That sense led to extreme events like President Grant's demolition of treaties with the Lakota Indians, to open their territory to miners who would produce "*specie*", the gold and silver then felt to be required for the United States to play a role in world economics. But the creation of *credit* and *fiat money* (and finally the utterly frivolous fiat of *BitCoin*) has made that, too, an obsolete principle.

We need to *restore money's function as primarily a medium of exchange*, developing some way to place adequate amounts in the hands of ordinary consumers without mandating the (ultimately) insurmountable obstacle of "*full employment.*"

Not to deprecate full employment generally; it will continue to be achievable in specific places and times (like Cape Cod as I write), but in the global aggregate and the long term, no, not sustainable. Anyway, present employment looks a lot less full if we account more truly for underemployment, for chronically underpaid jobs that more resemble slavery than employment, and for those who just gave up and settled for "freeloader" status.

The global economy is close to producing enough of everything for everyone, even food, as ingenious innovations counter the damaging effects of climate change, leaving the considerable problem of fixing the flaws in the distribution system. Dictators and corrupt inner circles snatch up wealth that should go to their own people—logical, if nasty, in a world of scarcity.

In other places, there are already oversupplies of some forms of wealth. These trigger paroxysms of advertising, pushing excess products and services on people who may or may not be able to afford them, but who can be bullied into concentrating their life's attention on "*buying stuff.*" Such artificial stimulation of demand is not sustainable.

Some years ago I developed an amusing exercise (almost certainly inspired by Sam Hayakawa's textbook in semantics, *Language in Thought and Action*): whenever you see, in an advertisement, some form of the word "*save*", mentally substitute the corresponding form of the word "*spend.*" You'll be astonished at how often the text makes *more* sense that way—closer perhaps to the sense the advertiser secretly intended: "*Now! Your chance to spend even more!!*"

Dots #1 and #2 are already starting to be connected in parts of the developed world, under the umbrella phrase **"Universal Basic Income"** *(UBI)*. In its purest form, **UBI is a *scheme to give everybody in a community enough money to live on, with no strings attached—especially, no means test involving government officials.***

One of the best articles I've seen on UBI is in *The New York Times*, **"Free Cash in Finland. Must Be Jobless"**, by Peter S. Goodman, Dec. 17, 2016, online at https://nytimes/2hRYiSH. Goodman describes an experiment being developed in Finland, as well as referring to the failed UBI plebiscite in Switzerland. As so often happens, the headline focuses only on the most eyeball-grabbing part of the story, the experiment (possibly underway as you read this) of randomly selecting 2,000 unemployed Finnish workers to receive a Basic Income, to see how well they handle it.

For that less-than-Universal population, *BI differs from unemployment compensation in three significant ways*:

- Any BI recipient *may take a job without losing their BI*, removing the powerful incentive to remain unemployed rather than take a job that pays less than the BI.

- BI recipients are *relieved* of the tedious and everlasting burdens of demonstrating to government officials that they are totally unemployed and *are making continual efforts to find work.*
- BI recipients *get regular money*, not scrip like food stamps, and are relieved of the morale-destroying evidence that unemployment marks them as lower-class citizens.

Most of Goodman's article goes beyond the terms of the Finnish experiment to explore aspects of a UBI scheme along the same principles, including the *beneficial effects on employers*, who would be able to hire people as they need them and lay them off when they don't, without being deterred from hiring by the burden of entering a sort of *in loco parentis* relationship. Hiring would lose the dramatic flavor of resembling commutation of a sentence, and layoffs would lose their atmosphere of warlike hostility, instead causing some pain but not actually threatening survival.

While I will reiterate some of the arguments for UBI, the main purpose of this essay is to connect other relevant dots that have not usually entered into these discussions.

Dot #3 is ***global economic growth***. Corporate chieftains are sometimes heard to say, in effect, "*Just stop taxing and regulating us and we'll create more jobs, so that everybody will be employed in building unlimited and accelerating growth of the global economy.*" Setting aside the observation that such speeches are often followed by the purchase of more robots instead, let's focus on the growth aspect.

If we consider substantial growth of the global economy to be essential, how does that interact with global population? Has anyone done a factor analysis showing, over a multi-decade-long term, the extent to which economic growth depends on population growth? We see in first-world countries a declining birth rate, even failures to maintain population. Apparently, a highly productive global economy will initially bring many more countries into that first world, with a secondary effect of slowing down or reversing population growth. How then will the global economy have a growing pool of customers to keep expanding? Or must producers bully a static pool of customers to buy more and more of goods and services that they need less and less?

Don't lose sight of the continuing facts of *growth and decay in smaller economic arenas*. Individual firms and particular industries are born, grow, mature, decay, and die in response to market forces and (to a lesser degree) varying levels of competence and luck in management.

As long as people have the money and freedom to make choices, those choices will continue to help some enterprises and local economies, and hurt others. But the *global aggregate economy*, the arena in which the mightiest multinational enterprises play, doesn't and shouldn't work that way.

We have learned something over many centuries: against the catastrophic meltdown of the ancient Roman Empire plunging Europe into the Dark Ages, contrast the civil devolution of the British Empire into the British Commonwealth, or the remarkably peaceful end of the Cold War. Toynbee's view of the breakdown of civilizations, written prior to these latter two phenomena, makes grim reading but seems not to be the whole truth.

Dot #4 is ***the physical health of our planet***. We are increasingly aware that *many parts of our world are tapped out and cannot support much further exploitation.*

The oceans, long regarded as both an inexhaustible seafood factory and an infinite toilet for everything we wanted to get "rid" of, are now understood to be fragile systems requiring care and good management.

Our atmosphere, the "skin" that keeps our planet viable in the hostile environment of space, is now seen as vulnerable to surprisingly small offenses such as the release of fluorocarbons and a variety of greenhouse gases. And if the planet comes down with "skin cancer", unprecedented migrations will flee regions no longer tenable, triggering wars over territory that may be adequate to support only a much smaller world population.

On land, the true cost of fracking is far from being accounted for accurately or even understood—not in terms of money, but in terms of true wealth like water resources and security against earthquakes. Even activities achieving modest amounts of economic growth will increasingly have to acknowledge such costs and work with or around them.

Dot #5 is ***the increasing life expectancy of people***, even as the total amount of wage-earning work for them to do is on the decrease. *The system of independence in retirement relies on global economic growth to generate the dividends and capital gains to fuel it.*

Put another way, the retirement system is an arrangement whereby everybody in wage-paying jobs uses some of their income to buy promises of future money generated by global economic growth. To make that work, the global economy must grow at a percentage rate related to the percentage of asset value that retired people need as income.

If global growth slows and stops on a plateau, where do sufficient capital gains come from? Investment may become a specialty somewhat like a gambling casino, where small or great gains do happen, but in the aggregate, money flows steadily from the players to the house: not an effective behavior for retirement assets.

Another side of the *retirement economy* is a *dilemma*: should we encourage people to retire later in life, so as to experience a shorter and less expensive retirement . . . or should we encourage people to retire earlier in life, thus creating openings in the wage-earning labor force for younger workers?

Dot #6 is ***a pair of contradictory notions***, one occasionally expressed and one hardly ever mentioned. The overt one, **"*government must be run like a business*",** suggests that the business of government is to create value for shareholders by exploiting employees and customers.

Are the shareholders the whole nation as the Constitution says, or a small set of powerful individuals? And *who are the customers*, if not, again, the whole nation? The employees, being part of the nation, are necessarily also customers and shareholders.

So who exactly is to be exploited for the benefit of whom? Any individual will naturally think of almost all businesses as "them", but our Constitution makes it clear that our government is "us", despite the widespread foolish tendency to hate and fear the national government as a greedy and hostile "them."

The more tacit notion in this pair, **"*businesses must function like government*",** reflects the practice of *shirking governmental duties by passing them off to businesses*. Such vital responsibilities as *pensions* and *health care insurance* were handed over to employers, especially during World War II, as a way to offer fringe benefits, helping them compete for scarce workers when wages were frozen. As long as employment is full, and as long as employers have an incentive to offer such benefits, it works about as well as equivalent government programs, but *fractional employment opens a large and increasing gap that government must scramble to fill.* Even Social Security, the poster-child program of government support, was designed to help only long-term wage-earners, and only in proportion to how much money they earned; there and in Medicare, the employers' role is to make sure the money is set aside.

Enforcement of laws and standards has also been passed off. Every state has civil penalties for bad driving, but the significant penalties are exacted by insurance companies. While it's not simple to define medical malpractice penalties to work like other civil penalties, passing the responsibility off to insurance companies has become effectively a way to sell fear to doctors and nurses at horrific prices.

* * *

Those are the dots. *How shall we connect them to make the world economy work better?*

To bring about *improved behavior* for any system, the engineers must perform *two main tasks*: *define the new behavior* in enough breadth and depth to be confident of its utility and stability, and *map out a viable path and schedule* to get from here to (eventually) there.

The ambitious creation of Soviet, and would-be world, communism failed horribly at both tasks: the stable state was flawed as so lucidly communicated by George Orwell in *1984*, and the gory Leninist-Stalinist path to it was built on millions of corpses of Russian citizens.

Here, I am focusing on ***Universal Basic Income, UBI***, *within a given nation-state that has the ability to formulate monetary policy*, as the best way I am aware of to resolve the mismatch between wage-paying jobs and available workers. But I'm not an expert in designing it and must struggle to raise the *relevant questions* to be addressed.

For starters, what exactly does **"*Universal*"** mean? Citizens undoubtedly, but what about other residents, legally documented or not? Is it sufficient to disqualify undocumented residents, and should there be a higher level of UBI for citizens than for legal residents?

Then what exactly does **"*Basic*"** mean? Should it be a rock-bottom survival stipend, or should it have enough wiggle room to allow recipients to make meaningful economic choices and do their part in the capitalist dynamic? Will it in fact put non-jobholders into a position where they'll be willing to take up volunteer work? How should it vary around the country to apply with equal effect to more expensive places and less expensive ones? Should it be strictly per capita, for people of any age, or should it recognize the economies of scale in family life?

The meaning of **"*Income*"** is easier: it should be *regular money*, indistinguishable in use from money earned from wages. Probably the distribution itself should be digital, via bank accounts or at least debit cards, implying that people who refuse to have either one are effectively opting out of the system.

Next, ***where does the money come from?*** My suggestion is a radical one, which I've hinted at above. We have long since gotten used to the way in which banks create money by lending a multiple of the reserves they hold, always in ways they judge to be sound investments in economic growth. In a *new world of plenty* (or at least, *sufficiency*) *it is time to invest in people for their own sake*, without the old fear of making too much money chase too little wealth. National governments have long exercised the power to make monetary policy for their own currency, and the European Union has taken that power a step further for an explicitly multinational currency.

I suggest that a nation (or the EU) *can take the fiat-currency concept to the next level*, and simply "*print*" *enough currency to cover the UBI*. It doesn't materially change the fiat concept, which is still the principle that the money is backed by the full faith and credit of the nation itself. That *faith and credit is founded*, ultimately if somewhat implicitly, *on the productivity of the nation*. This may be the way to convert the problem into a solution.

To my knowledge, the most spectacular case of *hyperinflation* (the bogeyman that scares people away from fiat currency) is Germany in the years after World War I. But I think the main cause of that trouble was the insupportable penalties imposed on Germany by the Versailles treaty, penalties that ensured critical shortages of everything those hapless marks were chasing.

In our present and future, it may take very little government action to *keep the nation's production at a level where it can function as the standard supporting the currency*. Adam Smith's invisible hand will still make entrepreneurs and capitalists take risks to improve production and make more money for the daring.

Given a UBI scheme approximately as described above, ***what happens to wages?*** As in the Finnish experiment, *wage-paying jobs would continue to exist*, available to *any interested person*, though not simultaneously to *all interested persons*.

One possible transitional step would be to mandate an initial reduction in wages by the amount of each worker's UBI, but (obviously) not reducing anyone's income below the UBI level. To do such a thing suddenly would surely be unwise, and should probably be phased in over time. What's wanted is a *renegotiation, for each paying job, of what its (now incremental) wage level should be.*

Or to put it another way, every employment contract would be restarted as an even-handed agreement between a willing seller (employee) and a willing buyer (employer). *Wages would no longer be a survival strategy, but a premium for anyone willing to commit to employment conditions for whatever "extra" money the market will bear.* Minimum wage laws could disappear because the UBI would be doing their job. Some results would be remarkable from today's point of view: jobs involving the cleaning of toilets might be better paid than the sort of R&D work I did for Apollo and the Space Shuttle guidance and navigation systems. I remember some of my colleagues in those days observing that "If it weren't for the groceries and the rent and all, I'd do this for nothing."

And what would become of taxes? It would be idiotic to tax UBI money; that would be just a fraudulent pretense that the UBI level was higher than it is. Given a *monetary policy that redefines most income money as simply some numbers injected into each person's balance*, we'd have to re-imagine what taxes are for.

As an initial guess, I'd focus on a finite amount of tax money (whether collected from trans-UBI wage income, value-added, or whatever) as a way to allocate the productive resources of the public sector according to cost-benefit analysis. That is, *tax receipts would continue to be a way to allow—and oblige—the public sector to make choices like any consumer.*

Another purpose would be to limit the accumulation of money by successful entrepreneurs, *taxing the rich just to stop them from cornering the money market* and perverting the link between their country's money and its actual domestic product.

How would insurance be handled? In today's world, a "*living wage*" is enough to cover ordinary predictable expenses, including some money used to buy promises of monetary rescue from insurance companies, for catastrophic events that would otherwise destroy the quality of life.

A UBI scheme would make *life insurance optional*, needed only to maintain widows/widowers and orphans at some level above UBI levels; it would likely be bought with trans-UBI wage money rather than with UBI money. Similarly, *annuities and other retirement assets* would be an optional way to maintain lifestyles above UBI levels. These long-term insurance instruments would need some redesign to cope with a global economy that is nearly static rather than experiencing secular growth.

Auto and homeowner's insurance would continue much as it is now, with insurance companies setting price points according to their estimations of disaster risk in individual categories. *Medical insurance* could be aligned more toward exceptional expenses such as childbirth and serious diseases, since the formula for UBI would include consideration of ordinary health expenses. These short-term insurance instruments would continue to be funded by current premiums paid by *all members of each risk class,* with a backup at the national or world level for medical catastrophes like pandemics.

What would be meant, in the public sector, by deficits and debt? Given the arbitrary generation of money for UBI, these concepts may become meaningful only for non-UBI public expenses, those to be supported by taxes. As such, they may become a much less significant (and less stressful) factor in the well-being of citizens generally.

* * *

These are just a sample of the **design tasks required to define a highly automated UBI-based world** scraping the ceilings of achievable global population and economic growth, and to create a manageable path to it.

My final question in this essay is, **who will work on this design and how much time and other crucial resources will they need**?

The project is too vast for small groups of activists funded by grants. Among other things, I imagine that understanding how people will respond to such substantial changes in economic practice, and adjusting the design accordingly, will require a monumental "*sim game*"—a *crowd-implemented simulation involving many thousands of ordinary people* in addition to the experts. It will surpass other simulations by an enormous margin of complexity, somewhat as the human-genome project surpassed prior biological research, and may well trigger the same kind of powerful methodological innovations.

The *necessary time scale* extends well beyond the two-to-four-year horizon of political leaders, not to mention the three-to-18-month horizon of most corporate chieftains.

I believe that only a major research university, or a consortium of several of them, can put together a multi-disciplinary program to research the ways all these factors interact now and how their interaction will have to develop over the coming decades.

And on that basis, I offer these thoughts for publication by Harvard's Class of 1957, and *urge creation and leadership of the project itself by Harvard University.*

Figure 6.1.1.1 *Hugh Blair-Smith—Harvard 1957 graduation portrait*

Figure 6.1.1.2 *The author in the library of the Aigas Field Centre, Beauly, Invernessshire, Scotland, during a one-week expedition as a naturalist in May 2015*

Hugh Blair-Smith began his half-century career in computers in 1957, programming a water resources simulation for a Harvard graduate seminar while consuming Harvard's few remaining computer courses and earning a SB. Recruited to MIT's Instrumentation Lab in 1959, he participated in both hardware and software development for Apollo and Space Shuttle guidance computers. In 1982, he shifted to joining startup companies pioneering touch screen technology for graphical user interfaces. Retirement (2005) was interrupted (2007) to develop diagnostic software for the Lunar Reconnaissance Orbiter. He published a history/memoir in 2015, *Left Brains for the Right Stuff: Computers, Space, and History*, and is working on a second book.

The End of Work

Ronald M. Weintraub

As an academic surgeon, and decidedly not an early adopter, I finally gained some proficiency in Microsoft's PowerPoint. By the early 2000s I was making my own slides. It was a great timesaver, and significantly reduced the cost of slides for presentations, and figures and charts for manuscripts. A couple of years ago, though, I ran into the medical illustrator who had made my slides at the Beth Israel Hospital. We exchanged pleasantries and histories. I learned that her practice had essentially disappeared with the advent of PowerPoint. In my then role as surgical safety officer, one of whose duties was reviewing medical charts, I could, quite literally, see how voice recognition was making illegible handwriting a thing of the past and a boon for physicians. But it would surely put many transcribers out of work. I realized how even American physicians were being made redundant by the growth of radiology "nighthawks" (radiologists in distant time zones who could read our night-time x-ray studies).

Figure 6.1.2.1 *Cardiac surgeon Ronald Weintraub explains the functional anatomy of the heart.*

So I was really intrigued when the July/August (2015) issue of *The Atlantic* arrived in the mail. This featured a long-form cover article by Derek Thompson, a senior editor of the magazine, and a sophisticated observer/reporter of business and the economy ("A Life Without Work?"). This superb essay starts by describing the closing of the steel mills in Youngstown, OH, on September 19, 1977. It ends with the barely hopeful interview with a former steelworker's son, in college on that Black Friday. Now at 60, after years of hanging on selling products to construction companies devastated by the great recession, returning to the University to get a master's degree in teaching, doing something he had always really wanted to do.

After reading this powerful piece, what was an old, about to retire doc—an old History and Lit major—to do? Go to the library, of course. What did I have practically at my doorstep? The Cambridge Public Library . . . and Widener. I started by reading authors whom Thompson had cited.

The fears of new technology extend back to the beginning of the industrial revolution. Ned Ludd, a weaver's apprentice, was said to have destroyed new knitting machines because of their threat to his livelihood. The story is probably either apocryphal or an embellishment, but it demonstrates an almost primeval fear of technology as a disruptor.

Traditional economists have always believed that every new machine that took the job performed by a person's hands and muscles *increased* the demand for complementary human skills, that is, those performed by eyes, ears, or brains. In other words, that capital—from land and lathes to computers and cyclotrons—is complementary to labor. Lately, though, Porter, DeLong and others have begun to question the Robert Solow "canon" that labor, capital and technological progress contribute to economic growth, and that the share of the economy's rewards accruing to labor and capital would be roughly equal. But there is now evidence emerging—though not universally accepted—that this may no longer be true. For instance, in the US, the share of national income that goes to workers in salary and benefits has been falling for almost half a century! Just to name a few economists that now have their doubts about *Solow's canon*:

> *Brad Delong (UC Berkeley)*: "No law of nature ensures that this will always be the case.
>
> ". . . as information technology creeps into occupations that have historically relied mostly on brainpower, it threatens to leave many fewer good jobs for people to do."

> *Loukas Karabarounis and Brent Neiman (U. of Chicago):* "As the cost of capital investments has fallen relative to the cost of labor, businesses have rushed to replace workers with technology . . . from the mid-1970s onwards. There is evidence that capital and labor are more substitutable than what standard economic models would suggest . . . . This is happening all over the place. It is a major global trend."
>
> *Even Robert Solow*: Although he stressed that technology is probably not the only cause of labor's declining share, and that everyday reasons including the erosion of the minimum wage, the decimation of the unions, and anti-union legislation is more important,
>
> ". . . technology clearly plays a role. We will know better in ten or 15 years, but if I had to interpret the data now, I would guess that as the economy becomes more capital intensive, capital's share of income will rise."

What does this all mean for the problem that everyone is acknowledging—the growing inequality between those at the top and those at the bottom of the income ladder? Where formerly capital and labor together increased productivity, the new paradigm, where capital (technology, machines, robots, land, natural resources) is replacing labor, the fruits of the rising productivity increasingly biases to the owners or managers of capital, that is, the top 10% of the population (this certainly includes us), and really, in terms of influence, the top 1% or 0.1% of the population.

In 2013, Former President Lawrence Summers delivered the Martin Feldstein Lecture. It's worth reading in its entirety, but here are a few key quotes:

> "First there were the bookstores, then there were the superstores, then there was Amazon, and now there are the Kindle and e-books. And at every stage it was better to be a reader, better to be an author and worse to be an ordinary person involved in the intermediation between the author and reader", in other words, those in the actual making and selling of books.
>
> "Larry Katz has famously remarked that computer programs do not do empathy, but there have existed for many years those that actually do a creditable job of providing psychotherapy. In response to confessionals, they prompt with

> responses like: 'tell me a little bit more about what's distressing you. That must have been hard for you. Can you explain a little more fully?' On at least some occasions these programs have been an important source of solace."

Parenthetically, the 2014 movie *The Imitation Game* was about Alan Turing and the dawn of artificial intelligence. People have asked me what the name of the movie meant. It's actually about a thought experiment in which a subject tries to guess the source of the voice with which he is conversing and asking questions. Is it a computer or a real human? In real life tests, subjects were able to identify their interlocutor less than 50% of the time. Apple's Siri and Amazon's Alexa are today's distant descendants.

> Summers continues: "The non-employment rate for men 25 to 54 and then adjusted for trend and cycle. . . . I summarize by saying that in the 1950s and '60s one in 20 men between 24 and 54 were not working. In a simple extrapolation to the period a decade from now, between one in six and one in seven men between 25 and 54 will not be workings. . . . In any case, though, it's clear that this cohort of males appears to be underperforming in terms of employment.
>
> "One of the worrisome issues for the future is that there is usually a time gap between the introduction of new technology and its effect on job replacement, because employers take years to embrace new machines that displace workers. For example factory robots in the '70s didn't really replace the floor workers until 20-plus years later. And as we have seen in the past decade, a recession often encourages that progression."

In this excellent paper, Summers points out that classic economic theory has been somewhat upended. The theory holds that in a company making widgets,—firms producing a ***thing*** with workers with increasing marginal costs, such as durables, clothes, and cars—we've seen a very substantial growth in real wages as measured by the purchasing power of those wages in things our economy produces.

Of course some of that is due to competition on the basis of economies of scale and overseas competition (e.g., Walmart). The reason that wages *in aggregate* have stagnated is that much of what people buy are things where there are issues of fundamental scarcity: energy, the land under the houses we buy, and goods and services that are produced in complicated, heavily public-sector-inflected ways, for example medical care and educational services.

He illustrates this in an interesting way. He compares the cost of various commodities and services by considering the changes in CPI *(Consumer Price Index)* over the past 30 years. Using the CPI *baseline in 1982–84 as 100,* he documents today's prices of TV sets at 5 or 5% the price of the same item in 1982–84 in constant dollars. Toys are about half the price, apparel and durable goods are about the same price. Energy and food come in at about 2½ times the price when compared to the early 1980s. *But medical care at over five times, and college tuition and fees over seven times the price.*

In other words, as the ***cost*** of widgets has fallen, the prices in sectors that are thought of as widgets produced by competing firms have stayed the same or have fallen. On the other hand, in sectors where property rights, scarcities, intellectual property, and the like are of fundamental importance, prices have increased dramatically. When the Bureau of Labor Statistics next does its analysis, he posits, we'll find out that projections on growth in the widget world—retail trade, transportation and warehousing and wholesale trade—are going to have come down given the trends. He points out that a *great deal of productivity growth can occur,* but ***that it is self-limited by demand***.

On the other hand, the sectors involving property and intellectual rights, scarcities, and the like (based on capital-rich productivity) will continue to reward capital at the expense of wages.

Take, for example, Apple. The originators especially, but also some early stockholders have become enormously wealthy, while the actual number of American workers employed by the company has never exceeded 35,000. Compare this to the hundreds of thousands of American workers associated with the making and selling of General Motors cars in the latter part of the 20th century.

Another revolution that is occurring at the same time is the displacement of salaried employment by contract workers. Uber is the classic weapon of creative destruction, not only for personal transportation, but currently imitators are delivering your wish for a pâté at your door. Consider how many people are currently employed as drivers of one type or another. Pity the poor taxi driver, but consider the Army of (mostly) men employed in the transportation industry. The Google personal transportation vehicle is already here. I believe there will be in the future of our grandchildren driverless transportation of a panoply of goods currently moved by human-driven 18-wheelers. Just think how the world-wide economy of distribution has been changed for longshoremen and allied workers by the advent of the container ship.

And another problem for the future: *Moynihan's corollary* to *Baumol's Law* may hold: There is a propensity for slow-growing sectors, where productivity is less influenced by increased input, to end up in the public sector; e.g., health care and education. A primary care doctor can only see one patient at a time; a public school teacher's room size (number of students) has a limit.

> A few years ago my wife and I were in Singapore. Starting at the wonderful Botanical Garden, I walked the length of Orchard Street towards the Harbor. I had lost a favorite small folding umbrella, and thought to replace it while walking about town. As I walked along the main drag into the heart of the town, I passed and explored a few of the countless many-storied department stores and small mom-and-pop basement level stores. Although I never found that umbrella, I was astonished by the amazing amount of "*stuff*" displayed, the modest number of tourists, and the numberless bored clerks who attended them. "*Who,*" I thought, "*would ever buy all this stuff?*"

Fast forward a few years to last month when I came upon an interview by our friend Derek Thompson, with Ryan Avent, an editor of my favorite newsmagazine *The Economist*. Avent's new book *The Wealth of Humans*—that I immediately downloaded to my Kindle—deals directly with the problem I sensed in Singapore years ago. A play on Adam Smith's masterpiece, he contends that we are in the early years of a third industrial revolution in which capital (machines, technology, and command of transportation and communication), and a highly skilled creative class control "rents", and in which human labor as classically defined is a *glut* on the market.

He makes a convincing argument that the "*secular stagnation*" we are currently experiencing is a product of inadequate demand from the former working class whose buying capacity has been degraded. He defines the problem extraordinarily well, recognizes that our fixation on offshored jobs is misplaced, and ponders possible partial solutions to a future in which a large number of people in "*The Rich West*" will remain underemployed. He, like Thompson in the earlier essay cited, tries his hand at such possibilities as artisanal entrepreneurship in wines, beer, cheeses, etc., but admits this has its limits.

For several "post-work" writers, the disappearance of jobs offers opportunity. Again, Uber offers an example where self-actuated workers can schedule their "work" around other activities. Unfortunately, these jobs may be the leading edge of the "*precariat*", a working class that swings from task to task in order to make ends meet, suffering a loss of labor rights, bargaining rights, and job security.

There are other possibilities. Both Thompson and Avent describe the springing up of artist and artisan cooperatives.

> My son and his wife are surviving in this new economy. They're glass artists, and there seems to be a market for their wares. But the mass of former worker bees will have few artists and artisans among them. For some lucky people like ourselves, our work defined us in some major way, and most of us continued to work beyond the usual 65 years of age.

We are fortunate to have had the luxury of good educations, still have more or less intact minds, and continue to enjoy the world of ideas and physical activity. For some, the end of work may lead to new careers.

Another personal example: my elder son works for a major commercial real estate company, and is doing comfortably well as a financial analyst, a job that could ultimately fall to technology. When I asked him where he thought he might be in ten or 20 years, he responded, "*Teaching*". He's always had a knack for teaching, continues to do mentoring at The Home for Little Wanderers, and teaches a class at the Sloan School. He'll have opportunities when his work days are over.

But what of the great mass of people with decreasing hours of work? Will society be able to subsidize them in some way?

Thompson and Avent leave us with more questions than answers. But I come away thinking that the full employment consumer society that we have lived in throughout our lives will likely pass away with us.

Figure 6.1.2.2 *Ron Weintraub listens with interest at the ceremony honoring his retirement from the Cambridge Health Alliance in 2015.*

Ronald Weintraub, MD, is the David Ginsburg Associate Professor (*emeritus*) in Cardiothoracic Surgery at the Harvard Medical School He served as chief of the cardiothoracic surgery at the Beth Israel Hospital, and retired from active surgical practice in 2001. He was named chief of surgery at the Cambridge Health Alliance (CHA) in 2003, stepping down after restructuring the surgical department. At his successor's request he stayed on as surgical safety officer from which position he retired in 2015. He is on the board of the CHA Foundation.

He writes: "This essay began as an oral presentation about 18 months ago to a group that I call '*The Old Guys*', docs, lawyers, businessmen, all of our age cohort, who meet every Wednesday for presentations and discussions. I became so interested in the topic that I expanded the brief oral presentation into an essay, updating it over the ensuing months, using the excellent Cambridge Public Library, so different from those we knew as students. When the call came for Essays from the Reunion Committee, I turned it into a term paper.

"Though not particularly personal, I think the Essay describes a real *inflection point in American, and more generally Western society*, as it struggles with nationalism, the struggles of the middle class, and great changes from the society into which we were born and educated."

In retirement Ron takes courses at Harvard College and the Beacon Hill Seminars, and contributes essays and presentations in a local discussion group. His non-professional life is occupied by music, cycling, and attempting to keep up with his wife, Margo Howard, a writer and journalist.

Recollections and Reflections on the Roots of the Great Recession

Philip Morrison Williams

In the spring of 2011, I was a member of the Harvard Club of Boston, and we invited Lawrence H. Summers to be our honored guest at the Club's Annual Meeting.

Larry Summers was an economist. Fresh from his stint as Harvard's President, he had been yanked into President Obama's inner circle to confront the unfathomable forces driving the 2006 financial unruliness into the *2008 meltdown*, which remains to this day unsolved and barely contained. But one cannot contain by regulation the dimensions of something that has not yet fully appeared. We might recall that traffic was not regulated with traffic lights until the horse and buggy was overwhelmed by the automobile.

The forces swirling through finance were only tangential to economic theory, but exploiting those forces was raw meat to those traders who had an inkling of financial potentials inherent in the digital computer's ability to deal with properties at speeds that had been the stuff of quantum theorists. Heisenberg's Uncertainty Principle, Schrodlinger's Cat, and Photon Entanglement were more aligned with physics experiments than lectures in Economics One.

In fact, in late 1956, or in 1957, John Von Neumann, was giving a series of lectures at Yale on his seminal topic,"*The Computer and The Brain*". Those lectures, his final work, addressed phenomena consistent with our brain's ability to entertain two contrary outcomes simultaneously. If one asks, "*Do you want to go out for a walk?*" and the other replies, "*I must change my clothes,*" he, or she, can live comfortably with the puzzle. From that point of view, Von Neumann posits that our brain accepts the quantum computer's ability to be off (zero) and on (one) at the same time.

The financial collapse of 2008 was reflected in the housing mortgage bubble, but we relish real property. Housing was the victim, not the cause. Theory predicts that if one buys low and sells high, one gains a profit. Many speculators did so. Theory affirms that broad markets and limited merchandise make for a seller's market.

The advent of faxed (electronic) information accepted as a legal mortgage document was the first action that brought about the disjoint in housing mortgages. While the house stays in place, its mortgage no longer stays in the issuing bank's vault. Its electronic existence morphed via the digital computer into a series of binomial numbers, or bits, that travel around the world at close to light-speed, 186,000 miles a second. This ease of transfer made any housing mortgage available to any willing buyer throughout the world. Alan Greenspan's "*irrational exuberance*" was enabled by electronic convenience replacing pen and ink.

The earthbound reality of a property mortgage was further eroded by electronically gathering a bunch of binominal bits of mortgages, bundling them together with other bits, and then dividing those bundles into tranches, which were sold. It is difficult for an individual to look up into the sky, and say to himself, "there goes my mortgage, made up into bits, streaming through whatever the physicists make of the world: the aether, or chaos, or string, or other theories of equal quantum gravity."

Nick Leeson was not the cause of the failure of Baring's Bank. One feels nostalgic for Baring's Bank. Years ago, Baring's Bank was instrumental in our ability to consummate *The Louisiana Purchase*, as they advanced us the gold and accepted our bonds so we could buy real property, and Napoleon could finance his dream of invading England. Rather than leaving gold in the vault, investing a bank's money in different currencies to take advantage of their relative value has been an arcane niche for more than a century. It was a leisurely affair. The bank's trader would discuss possibilities with higher officials. If they approved, he would invest money, go to his club for dinner and a glass of port and wait for the next day to see if the bank was right in approving his advice.

However, *numerical bits flying around the world at speed do not lend themselves to thoughtful action*.

Prior to the Club's Annual Meeting I made up a series of questions about Internet technology. I was hoping to get some answers. Once present at the Meeting, I pocketed my questions. They were unsuitable for the festive occasion. They were meant for lazy day-dreaming, when one was not pressed for time. Are we better off now, than we were then in seeing the emerging architecture of financial transactions? I think so, but there new ways to wash money, and plenty of ruffians to "suss them out." During these undiscovered times, attention to new financial regulations serve as protection for those bankers who prefer not to risk jail.

I looked for and found the questions on my computer, and now send them forth.

* * *

March 2011, at the Harvard Club of Boston:

Questions proposed for our guest, Lawrence H. Summers

INTERNET TECHNOLOGY

1. **The Nick Leeson Effect**

Barings Bank, an old and well-established firm in London, collapsed catastrophically in 1995, thus fulfilling Stephen Jay Gould's "*Great asymmetry*" (Gould, 2002, p. 1145).

The general public lay the blame for the collapse at the feet of Nick Leeson. Do you view that collapse as a mere failure of risk management, or do you view it as symptomatic of an Internet technology financial architecture that has not yet been fully revealed?

Can a financial architecture be regulated before it has been revealed?

Is it possible that Alan Greenspan felt that Barings was a lesson learned, and that banks would adjust their risk management accordingly, when, in reality, financial architecture had changed so entirely, risk management was unable to see the dimensions of risk?

2. **Speed of Transactions**

When I graduated in 1957, I was employed by THE FIDUCIARY TRUST COMPANY of NEW YORK, as a trainee. One of my duties involved replacing a vacationing expert in "*The securities cage*" for two weeks. Great fun! We had three days, business days, to "*execute*" or complete a trade. That included the signing and transferring of the stock in trade. Today a transaction is "*Completed*" in three to five milliseconds.

Do you believe our regulations have kept up with the speed of a trade?

With brokers striving for "*Net Zero*", where are we in trade speed?

With photon entanglement the new golden boy of physics, where will we be in trade speed?

3. **Worldwide Financial Entanglements**

Our regulators are skilled in closing down USA banks in USA. They have a protocol to shut down all branches at the same second, regardless of the time frame.

We have some banks (at least one) that have 30,000 employees in USA, and 300,000 employees outside of USA. How are our regulators able to craft rules that are applicable to each, the international banks, the very local banks, and the midsized, so-called American banks?

4. **Recording Transactions**

Short of a geosynchronous satellite, to which all transactions of any significance must pass through and be recorded, are there ways to record the activities of money that is traveling around the world at about 186,000 MPS?

Is all money, in effect, in "*dark pools*"?

5. **Expansion in the Use of Credit, and Debit Cards**

It is non-proprietary information for you to guess the yearly transaction cost to an issuing bank, for an individual person's (not a company) credit, or debit card. That cost includes yearly postage, sending out accounts, receiving and recording payments, and so forth. Would you guess $30, $300, or two six-packs of beer? This is before "*stuffers*". For them, you may take a bottle of beer from the well.

How "*new*" is this expansion? To phrase it differently, in 1992, the Fed considered credit cards to be appropriate for the Division of Consumer Affairs *(DCA),* referred to as the last stop before one gets off the train. Do you think the financial impact of credit cards is still of minor interest to the Fed?

Do you believe that the reduced cost of servicing credit cards is indicative of the impact of Internet technology on the entire employment structure of our (the world's) banking system? Or to put it differently, do you think that our (USA) productivity gain is an accurate description of the speeded up gains of our individual employee?

6. **Politician Awareness**

Do you believe that our politicians are politically able to answer the above questions?

Do you believe that our professional government financial staff is free of constraints to answer the above?

Thank you very much,

Phillip M. Williams '57

* * *

Now, in 2017, at our age, we have time for leisure thought. Maybe these questions are appropriate for RECOLLECTIONS and REFLECTIONS.

Looking back, some questions seem antique, and others appear yet to be answered.

Philip M. Williams writes: "Formerly married. Four children. Learned much at Fiduciary Trust Company of New York one year, but was found unsuitable. School teacher 13 years, coach 13 years, novelist off and on during some summers. Moved to Cataumet on Cape Cod, spent a year writing a children's sailing novel. Went to work as a common laborer at a construction site for FHA housing. Moved to carpenter (I'm not very handy), promoted to supervisor and used horizontal skills (easy). Promoted again to a housing project in Plymouth, MA. Promoted again to condominium project in Stoughton, MA. Fun and easy. Housing funding collapsed and was let go. Bought four lots in Falmouth, MA, with Mike Robertson's help. Designed houses, built them, and sold them. Good work for ten years, or more, and travel to Europe. And again a collapse. Refused to go bankrupt and lost everything. No big deal. Worked as a security guard and wrote on off days. That job phased out. Did enough building on the side to put dinner on the table. Children grown up. Got Social Security. One child, a lawyer in DC, supports me. Son-in-law, married to another daughter, does his bit.

I'm happily ensconced in a comfortable house, reading PG Wodehouse at the fireside, with a single glass of Whiskey to ward off evil spirits. Very little to complain about. Now it's mostly writing poetry . . . . I guess it would be called old-fashioned. Try not to be Narcissistic, like that fellow Whitman. Try to have rime and rhythm, like the recent Nobel poetry winner."

Income Distribution

(Song)

"Billionaire's Lament"

John R. Menninger

Music:
"Nobody Knows You When You're Down and Out"
(apologies to Jimmy Cox, 1923)

(https://www.youtube.com/watch?v=6MzU8xM99Uo)

Once I lived the life of a billionaire,
Contributing to super-PACs and I didn't care.
Taking senators out for a mighty fine time,
Buying high-priced liquor, champagne and wine.

Dumping sub-prime loans into pension plans,
Flogging derivatives; there were no bans.
Bond-rating agencies ate out of my hand;
Regulators' backs scratched, all over this land.

Everybody knows you, when you're flying high.
You get invited to all the best places,
News photos feature you with famous faces.
Congress waits on your every word.
Since you're rich you're sure to be heard.
It's common knowledge that you're the guy;

Everybody loves you when you're flying high.
The real estate collapse then sealed my doom;
I found myself hiding in a tiny dark room.
I liquidated assets without a thought;
Sold my Lamborghini, then my yacht.

My spouse left me to rue my day.
My broker bailed out 'cause I couldn't play.
Folks down in DC wouldn't pay attention.
What the press called me, I won't mention.

Income Distribution

Nobody knows you,
When you're down and out.
Your margin account? Not one penny.
And your friends; well, you ain't got many.
Staring at those padded walls;
The Koch brothers won't even return your calls.

Yes it's tragic, without a doubt;
Nobody knows you when you're down and out.

But banks revive after they're bailed out
Speculators survive a stock market drought.
Business losses stay off the book;
Taxpayer money is what's on the hook.

The laws protect the bankers so they cannot fail
No matter how guilty, none has gone to jail.
Campaign contributions make a lot of sense;
Buying up Congress is just a business expense.

Now everybody loves me; I'm back in the game.
The question is, how long will this last?
Will the future repeat the past?
How many recessions can the US stand
Before my bad behavior is finally banned?
I'm sure to survive, without a doubt; unless
Voters decide to throw the rascals out.

I said, throw the rascals out.
Oh, yeah; throw the rascals out!

John Menninger is a retired professor of biology. After graduation he received his PhD from Harvard and also attended Harvard Medical School and Caltech. He did post-doctoral research in the UK in Cambridge and London. His research studied the mechanisms of cellular protein synthesis, especially errors during synthesis; the mechanism of inhibition of MLS antibiotics, and cellular aging in yeast. Among the subjects he taught at the Universities of Oregon and Iowa were cellular and molecular biology, and genetics, physiology, and mechanisms of aging. At Iowa he was chair of the department and program director of an NIH Training grant.

While an undergraduate, Menninger was program director at WHRB and was captain and "John Harvard" with the football cheerleaders, wearing the traditional crimson pilgrim costume. After one questionable referee decision he encouraged the Harvard stands to "*Give me a 'Hmmm'*". Memorial Drive was the scene of a kidnap attempt by over-zealous Tufts fans, but "John Harvard" was saved by Dunster colleagues.

John and his wife, Lesley Margaret Hiller, who died in 2003, have two daughters. He spends leisure time putting up videos under the *nom de YouTube* of "**RuralRoberts**".

Figures 6.2.1.1 and 6.2.1.2 *Cartoon versions of former iconic head cheerleader John Harvard, taken from different issues of Harvard football game programs*

Artwork by Vic Johnson
Reprinted courtesy of Harvard University

Editor's Note

In the 1960s, John Harvard as cheerleader was banished from the fields and expunged from the records, but no iconic figure has replaced him, not even a bulldog or a tiger.

Investments

Reversion to the Mean

From Aristotle to Jack Bogle, a Statistical Absolute to Keep in Mind When Navigating Life's Shoals and Managing Other People's Money

James L. Joslin

> *"... Jim is not a problem child by any means. He is just a good husky, normal boy who is growing fast and has so much surplus energy he is ready to burst. The things he does are mostly just loud and noisy and thoughtless ..."*

So wrote (in perfect Palmer Method cursive) in 1945 Miss Ethel Ascott, my long-suffering fourth-grade teacher, in a special letter to my distressed mother, who I am certain then thought her ten-year-old son was about to be remanded for special disciplinary action.

From such beginnings we all arise with very little idea of where we wish to go, never mind by what path we will get there. By the time the Edina-Morningside Minnesota, Independent District #17 High School Class of 1953 graduated, that "*surplus energy*" had been put to good use on the gridiron (first team All-State), hardwood (All-Regional), and cinder track (remember cinder tracks?), if not so much in the classroom.

Moving East to Harvard Square

Senior year at EHS when my father was at the HBS Advanced Management Program in Cambridge, it was arranged for me to spend a few days with a number of coaches and the Harvard Admissions staff, as well as Minnesota students then enrolled at Harvard. The flight out was memorable because it was aboard a Northwest Air Boeing double-deck Stratocruiser, my first overnight in the air. Lunch in the Square at Cardullo's with Harvard football coach Lloyd Jordan wasn't exactly an elevating experience, but at that early unaware age my antennae were not yet fully attuned to sort those things out.

A session with Bill Bender, then Dean of Admissions, was a deciding event. As it turned out his "*outreach*" *program* to move Harvard from its status as a regional New England College to a national university directly benefited those of us from Minnesota and others beyond New England. Fifty-seven of us from Minnesota applied that year (1953), and thirty-six were admitted; it was the luck of the draw for us, a tribute to Dean Bender's determination to diversify the student mix.

The Cambridge Years

The early days at Harvard were for me a mixed experience. But by my junior year, things began to sort themselves out. The course catalogue seemed less daunting, although Constitutional Law, a requirement for a Government major, was a real challenge which classmate John Barrett pulled me (and a number of others) through; a "*gentleman's C*" felt like a great achievement.

A painful full year spent in Economics 1 loomed as a monumental stumbling block. Taught by pre-Nobel Laureate Paul Samuelson, who, having been denied tenure at Harvard (an ethnic issue), had moved down the river to MIT, our basic reading was his just-published text (now in its 36th edition). Operating on the theory that if he couldn't see me I might not be called upon during class, I always sat in the back row. Having reduced most economic principles to mathematical equations, at best I was lucky to be able to understand every other word as he droned on through those weekly lectures. It was during one of Professor Samuelson's discourses when he suggested that *investment market return results* were *random* in character and *tended to revert to the mean*. In the end, another "*gentleman's C*" seemed a monumental accomplishment.

Afternoons on Soldiers Field

Contrasted with our high school program at EHS, football at Harvard wasn't a great experience, but by virtue of a few accomplishments on the field was for me, without question, a door-opener. Yale game of sophomore year (see *Sports Illustrated* article below) changed everything. My guess is that the picture taken by *The Boston Globe* photographer at that contest was such a good one that it almost required an article. But there were some other memorable occasions associated with those four fall seasons spent across the river at Soldiers Field. One involved our deceased Senator from Massachusetts.

Pre-season, double-sessions on the practice fields next to the Stadium were boot camp on the Charles, painful to contemplate, as well as

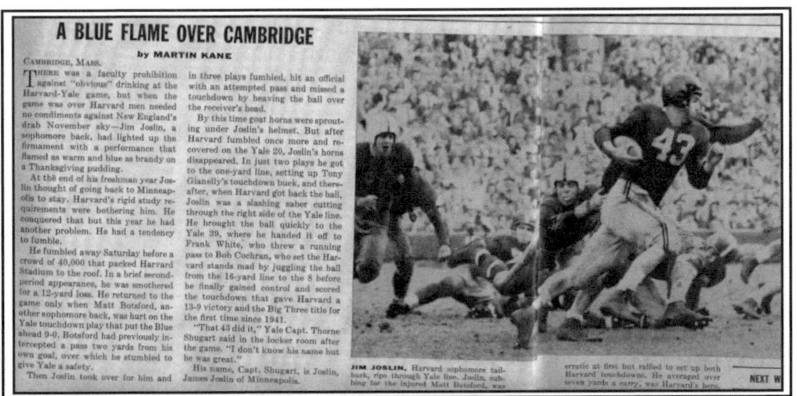

A BLUE FLAME OVER CAMBRIDGE

by MARTIN KANE

CAMBRIDGE, MASS.

THERE was a faculty prohibition against "obvious" drinking at the Harvard-Yale game, but when the game was over Harvard men needed no condiments against New England's drab November sky—Jim Joslin, a sophomore back, had lighted up the firmament with a performance that flamed as warm and blue as brandy on a Thanksgiving pudding.

At the end of his freshman year Joslin thought of going back to Minneapolis to stay. Harvard's rigid study requirements were bothering him. He conquered that but this year he had another problem. He had a tendency to fumble.

He fumbled away Saturday before a crowd of 40,000 that packed Harvard Stadium to the roof. In a brief second-period appearance, he was smothered for a 12-yard loss. He returned to the game only when Matt Botsford, another sophomore back, was hurt on the Yale touchdown play that put the Blue ahead 9-0. Botsford had previously intercepted a pass two yards from his own goal, over which he stumbled to give Yale a safety.

Then Joslin took over for him and in three plays fumbled, hit an official with an attempted pass and missed a touchdown by heaving the ball over the receiver's head.

By this time goat horns were sprouting under Joslin's helmet. But after Harvard fumbled once more and recovered on the Yale 20, Joslin's horns disappeared. In just two plays he got to the one-yard line, setting up Tony Gianelly's touchdown buck, and thereafter, when Harvard got back the ball, Joslin was a slashing saber cutting through the right side of the Yale line. He brought the ball quickly to the Yale 39, where he handed it off to Frank White, who threw a running pass to Bob Cochran, who set the Harvard stands mad by juggling the ball from the 16-yard line to the 8 before he finally gained control and scored the touchdown that gave Harvard a 13-9 victory and the Big Three title for the first time since 1941.

"That 43 did it," Yale Capt. Thorne Shugart said in the locker room after the game. "I don't know his name but he was great."

His name, Capt. Shugart, is Joslin, James Joslin of Minneapolis.

JIM JOSLIN, Harvard sophomore tailback, rips through Yale line. Joslin, subbing for the injured Matt Botsford, was erratic at first but rallied to set up both Harvard touchdowns. He averaged over seven yards a carry, was Harvard's hero.

Figure 6.3.1.1 "A Blue Flame Over Cambridge" by Martin Kane from *Sports Illustrated* November 29, 1954 © Time Inc.
Photograph for the *Boston Post* by John M. Hurley

experience. Starting during the last week in August, the heat was intense, and since the prevailing medical regime dictated that water during exercise was not permitted, the two to three hours twice a day on the practice field in 90-degree-plus heat and dust always ended with the sensation one had just come in from a desert trek. For two weeks, we (100-plus varsity candidates) were lodged, more accurately interned, on the top floor of the Indoor Athletic Building (IAB).

The scene was much like a crowded converted gym floor covered with bunk-beds in an over-full capacity California prison. The massive exhaust fans ran 24/7, the interior temperature never got below the mid-80s, the noise level made uninterrupted sleep almost impossible. A 10:00 p.m. curfew was always being gamed (particularly by the seniors) with endless bed-checks required to enforce. So, when during my sophomore year, Ted Kennedy, who had returned from a few years of Harvard-imposed exile in the Army, invited me, along with Jerry Marsh (Law School student/assistant football coach from Austin, MN), for a short weekend at the compound in Hyannis Port, we both gratefully accepted.

A Weekend in Hyannis Port

Pre-season practice Saturdays were always only a single morning session, so at noon we headed for the Cape immediately in my second-hand Chevy, arriving in time for a late afternoon sail on brother Jack's 28-foot sailboat *Victura*. It was a dreary day with a light prevailing on-shore breeze. Jerry, a brilliant student, who later became Ted's senior Senate staff assistant, and subsequently managing partner of one of Chicago's largest law firms, had virtually no sailing experience. I had had a certain amount of summer camp instruction.

Jack Kennedy and his sailboat

Jack (right) and Ted Kennedy on the sailboat Victura, a gift to Jack from his parents.

By Jan Gardner

Jack Kennedy and the Victura

President John F. Kennedy's beloved sailboat Victura, Latin for "about to conquer," was a birthday gift from his parents when he turned 15. He soon started winning races, eventually becoming one of the best collegiate sailors in New England.

It was on that approximately 25-foot Wianno Senior, built in 1932, that he taught his wife, Jackie, to sail, and the Life magazine photos of them at sea branded the young couple as vital and daring. When Kennedy was on shore, he doodled pictures of the sloop, and the Oval Office at the White House was a shrine to sailing. The biggest piece of seafaring memorabilia was Kennedy's desk, made from the timbers of the HMS Resolute, abandoned by the crew after it got locked in ice in the Arctic.

Every winter Victura is taken from its spot on the lawn of the John F. Kennedy Presidential Library and Museum in Dorchester to winter in the Crosby Yacht Yard in Osterville. The boat yard, founded in 1850, is still building boats like Kennedy's, now out of fiberglass instead of wood.

This year the return of Victura to the Kennedy Library will be celebrated at 1 p.m. May 18 with a talk by James W. Graham, author of **"Victura: The Kennedys, a Sailboat, and the Sea"** (ForeEdge). Bob Oakes, host of WBUR's "Morning Edition," will be the moderator.

Figure 6.3.1.2 *Jack and Ted Kennedy on Jack's sailboat* Victura*, 1946*

We tacked our way out of the harbor against the on-shore prevailing breeze and then reversed course heading back down wind for the mooring. It was low tide as we approached shore, and Ted, smiling at me, instructed Jerry to move to the bow and grab the Styrofoam mooring ball, with the admonition that if he wasn't successful we might not have a second chance at it. Jerry, with all the determination he always brought to everything, grabbed the two-foot-diameter ball, picked it up out of the water, and almost embracing it as we continued down wind, of course went into the bay. As he hit the water, he realized he had been had and let us know it. We picked him out of the water, had a steam bath, were served by the house staff with whatever beverage was desired, watched a movie in the compound theater, and were treated to an elaborate dinner (at least by my standards); it was all a very revealing early exposure to the life of the rich and famous.

Many years beyond, in 1990 I think, Ted on the Senate Floor read a resolution (a framed copy of which is on the wall in daughter Char's downstairs exercise room) celebrating the Harvard Women's Lacrosse NCAA National Division One title win over Maryland. It noted Char's particular role, as well as the fact that he and I had played on the football team together.

The Jordan Years

Junior year in Cambridge, pre-season was interrupted by Hurricane Carol. Vivid memories remain of sitting on the porch of Dillon Field house watching practice-field 6' x 8' solid wood partitions fly about like so many pieces of paper caught in an updraft. Coach Jordan always thought we should hold practice sessions out of sight, excluding any outside observers, in particular the media, since what we were working on was intelligence the opposing scouts would find useful. So, to hold our adversaries at bay, each practice field was enclosed with these solid-wood paneled sections.

Jordan also banned low-cut shoes; some teammates were banished from practice when they had the courage to flaunt that obsession. Jordan was not exactly the right peg for a group of irreverent Harvard types; he had spent 19 years at Amherst, where he had gained tenure, and for some reason Harvard relieved Amherst of the burden of that arrangement. Occasionally, during games in the stadium, two substitutes were sent for the same position. Game strategy sessions, pre-game and half-time locker room talks were often more confusing than inspirational. My game-winning effort against Yale sophomore year ironically probably saved his job, and in the end after our senior season, we (graduating seniors) found it necessary to petition AD Dolph Samborski for his removal.

A Balanced Outcome

As senior year drew to a close, my awareness of how much the previous three-plus years had changed the playing field for me began to sink in. In the early spring prior to Commencement, I was elected Class Marshal-at-Large, along with John Simourian, Charlie McVeigh, and Ed Abramson, and as we began to plan graduation activities, the newly constituted Class Committee, meeting for the first time, voted me Class Secretary. Frankly, the impact of all this did not make an impression until a number of years later when Alumni activities started to find their way onto my calendar.

Eliot House and Dr. Finley

My most memorable and lasting encounters at Harvard were during senior year at Eliot House, to which I was luckily allowed to move by arrangement of House Master Dr. John Finley. He was, of course, a world-renowned classics scholar and just before the Class of 1957 arrived in the fall of 1953, runner-up in the selection for Harvard's next President.

Somehow in my sophomore year, Dr. Finley heard of my desire to leave Lowell House, and after a year living off-campus in Morris Hall at HBS, he arranged for me to move into Eliot with Tony Gianelly, Tony Markella and Chuck Papallia. We were given a suite of rooms at the top of D Entry. This probably rescued my Harvard experience, for which I shall always be grateful. Beyond that, for some reason (and I am sure many other of our classmates harbor similar impressions), although certainly not for academic reasons, Dr. Finley seemed interested in what I was up to.

Figure 6.3.1.3 *Dr. John Finley*
Reprinted courtesy of Harvard University

It goes without saying that for those who knew him, Dr. Finley was drawn to the athletic side (House sports seemed a lasting interest of his), but beyond that there appeared to be a bond of a nature that lasted well beyond Commencement. He often attended the parties we organized in D-5. Perhaps he worried that if he wasn't there, we would do something he would have to deal with in disciplinary proceedings the next day. But I don't think that really was the reason. He also had a habit of characterizing people with Greek classical simile monikers. Tony Gianelly was the "*mighty Ajax*", Jim Damis was "*Adonis*", I was "*puma-like*", etc. His remarks about each of us at the Eliot House Commencement Day Luncheon were individualized in every sense.

His post-graduation letters of recommendation, I am told by classmate Nelie Aldridge, who is writing Dr. Finley's biography, were classics of originality, innuendo and subtlety, requiring the reader to consider carefully the context in what was unsaid and capturing between the lines any concerns the good Doctor might have about the letter's subject. Copies of all these letters today are held underground in the Pusey Library Archives, because in those days Dr. Finley's faithful secretary, whose name escapes me, naturally dropped a carbon into her typewriter every time she turned out an original.

Following my stint in the Navy, Dr. Finley contacted me and asked if I would help him raise money for a travelling stipend he was hoping to set up for Eliot House graduates. Long story shortened, we raised nearly $300,000 (real money in those days) for a fund which today still provides a year's unrestricted travel outside the US and is awarded to a graduating Eliot House resident at the end of each academic year.

We met occasionally while Dr. Finley continued as House master. At such sessions he would always seem to have much more knowledge of our classmates' comings and goings; embarrassing for 1957's Class Secretary. Later Sally and I were invited to a rather poignant dinner at the Master's lodgings on the eve, as it turned out, of his and Magdalena's departure following Dr. Finley's official retirement. Dean Bob Watson and wife, Polly, also attended. We were served a very nice dinner in the formal dining room among the packing crates which were to be removed the next morning. As dessert was put on the table, Dr. Finley produced a small box wrapped in a crimson ribbon and asked me to open it. It turned out to be a Georgian silver gravy boat which was from his family's collection; a lovely, much appreciated gift which sits on the shelf in my home office. The Finleys moved to 1010 Memorial Drive following this, where classmate Peter Scully lived and managed the building at the time. His Dr. Finley stories of this period are the stuff of legend.

As I was putting together the front matter for our 1957 *20th Reunion Class Report*, it struck me it might resonate with the class if I could get Dr. Finley to write a Report Preface ruminating on how Harvard might have changed since we both left. What arrived from his summer retirement retreat on the hill at Tamworth, NH, typed on his trusty Royal portable with corrections and erasures, was a classic piece which opened our *20th Report*. I also had it reprinted in our *55th Report*. In "*Harvard Through the Years*" he concluded that very little had changed in that the student body was still very much the University's main strength. His thoughts on paper were/are still apt and on point. Sadly, Dr. Finley died after succumbing to a seven-year bout with dementia. Such cruel irony.

A few summers back, classmate Peter Davis, Academy-Award-winning documentarian, related to me over lunch in Castine, ME, that during Dr. Finley's 1010 Memorial Drive residence, Peter invited him to a dinner in New York, which took place at Jackie Kennedy's apartment. The other guest, in addition to classmate Nelie Aldridge, was I. F. Stone (*The Trial of Socrates*). Peter has published a story about the dinner, which is included in this book.

The Investment Business Years

As my three-year "*tour*" as an Air Intelligence Officer with the Navy on the coast of Maine and deployment to Sicily with a P2V squadron was ending, I applied to Harvard Summer School and registered for a course in "*The Economics of Taxation*", given by Professor Otto Eckstein. He was one of the early innovators of the *econometric modeling* discipline and the founder of Data Resources *(DRI)*. Although during his presentations he often veered off course, in retrospect his lecture series was one of those experiences which count when considered in the context of how one's investment philosophy was influenced and has evolved over time ever since.

Developing a Philosophy of Investment—*Harvard Summer School, 1961*

Professor Eckstein was then attempting to build a massive *computerized model of the world's macro- and micro-economic relationships* on a mainframe computer. It was to be the development of his version of a *commercially usable econometric model* which was the then competitive rage of others in the economics profession at the time. He sometimes remarked that his development group and programmers had been successful in identifying and coding something like 2,700 micro-economic dependent variables for mainframe manipulation, but they had yet to build algorithms for the interaction of government policy, shifts in investor sentiment and geopolitical inputs.

Looking back, that turned out to be a significant concern, because although he subsequently built DRI into a huge personal commercial success (sold to McGraw Hill for $120 million in the 1960s, $500 million plus in today's dollars), the *model's predictive outcomes never were very useful to its users*, mostly because of their inability to deal with the behavioral aspects of the global macro-economic equation.

Unfortunately, Professor Eckstein died a few years after the DRI sale, and his career at Harvard was cut short of fulfillment. But in many ways he had already come up against the *persistent issue confronting those attempting to predict economic and investment outcomes*—how to factor emotional and behavioral drivers into such models, as well as account for that nagging, inconvenient, recurring statistical phenomenon, *reversion to the mean.*

The significance of this shortcoming evaded my rather superficial understanding of the discipline that summer in the classroom, but as the research and findings in behavioral economics in the early 1990s challenged the rational expectations model of classical economics, Professor Eckstein's dilemma began to resonate. And these conclusions have since been reinforced and validated by the realization that *any attempt to predict economic outcomes is a useful exercise only if the conclusions are intended for use in a broad sense.*

Attempting to achieve superior investment returns because of an *assumed unique information advantage* is inevitably destined to disappoint, an assertion which Jack Bogle impressed on me in the mid-1970s. Even today artificial intelligence-based computerized financial modeling aimed at beating the markets still has yet to develop algorithms able to adjust outcomes for *irrational investor behavior*, which is the rule rather than the exception. This prevailing hubristic basis for much of what masquerades as serious research in Wall Street today will, sadly, continue to line the pockets of Goldman Sachs, hedge fund managers, and other sell-side purveyors at the expense of the individual investor.

TDP&L/Wellington

In 1968, Guido Perera *(Class of 1954)* who had been, like me, part of the New England Merchants National Bank *(NEMNB)* Trust Research Group, was a kind of mentor while I was there in training. He had earlier joined the investment firm of Thorndike, Doran, Paine& Lewis *(TDP&L)*. He called and in so many words said, "*You had better get over here, there are some very exciting developments ahead.*"

IVEST Fund, TDP&L's first and only mutual fund, was a hot performer, at the top of every broker's list, and very much in the financial press headlines. It was in the heady days of "*performance*" *investing* (e.g., Jerry Tsai and the *Manhattan Fund* at Fidelity), and Nick Thorndike, Bob Doran, Steve Paine, and George Lewis were at the forefront of this *new* approach. Walter Morgan, founder of the *Wellington Fund* and his in-the-wings successor, Jack Bogle, sought out Messrs. T, D, P, & L and worked out an acquisition which caught the media's attention. It was consummated just as my employment there started.

For this naïve player in the world of Boston-New York-Philadelphia finance, these were heady times. Away from the comfortable protective umbrella of the NEMNB Trust Department, a taste of the fast track against the background of a rising stock market in which the Nifty Fifty growth stock era and the performance investing game were just unfolding, the possibilities seemed boundless.

The Boston *IVEST Group* was the go-to money management firm of the day and the invitations from prospective clients to present our wares came in from up and down the East Coast, as well as out into the Midwest. We picked up accounts from Chicago, Madison, Philadelphia, New York, and even from Alaska (the Alaskan Tribe Federal Retribution Legislation). We added some $1.8 billion in new, mostly corporate pension accounts during the early days of the merger. I was charged with marketing the firm's separate account investment counseling services.

Unfortunately, after a few years the merger outcome was unsuccessful. The Boston group *(TDP&L)* at the time (1972) was convinced that "*active management*" (i.e., picking stocks through superior research and selection techniques) could continue to beat the market. Not surprisingly, Jack Bogle had in the back of his mind the admonishments of his friend and mentor, Paul Samuelson, as well as the assertions of his Princeton thesis advisor and Wellington Board member, Professor

Figure 6.3.1.4 *Boston IVEST Group. Shown with Jim Joslin (14) are Jack Bogle (6), Guido Perera (3), Nick Thorndike (16), Bob Doran (9), George Lewis (11), and Steve Paine (5) (Jim's mother drew the circle around his head to identify her son for a friend.) Circa 1969*

Courtesy of James L. Joslin

Burton Malkiel (*A Random Walk Down Wall Street*), that *stock market returns were both unsystematic* and *tended to revert to the mean (less fees).* As the understanding of these differences between the Boston and Philadelphia factions surfaced, so were the seeds planted for the *passive, or indexed, approach* to portfolio management which today have become the default and/or opt-out features of many defined contribution retirement plans *(e.g., your 401(k) retirement plan).*

When the break-up became public, acrimonious media gleanings, most inaccurate as always, sensationalized the proceedings, and the separation was difficult for all. Jack has since written some on the subject (*The Clash of the Cultures*). I had then only an employee's view of the events, but through a chance window provided by a distant relative of my mother's in Cooperstown, Chuck Root, who was then on Wellington's Board, I was able to hear the other side from Jack, at times during a game of tennis with Chuck at the Cooperstown Country Club courts. In Jack's retelling of the drama of the collapse, he credits Chuck with providing wise counsel, adult behavior, and important supportive board votes to help resolve the conflict. The split took place in 1973, and both parties went their separate ways without seeing each other for the next 35-plus years.

I stayed in touch with Jack over the years, and certainly followed the growth of his Vanguard offerings throughout. *Passive investing*, in most manifestations, is based on the *statistical principle* that investor equity market return results over the long run, as mentioned, will *invariably revert to the mean* (less fees) for the asset class benchmark being tracked.

TFC Financial

In late 1979, I resolved to form my own firm and joined forces with four others with similar ambitions. We were among the first in the nation to offer comprehensive personal financial planning services for a fee in the high net worth market place, as well as investing our client portfolios only in no-load mutual funds. After a certain amount of missionary selling of this at-the-time novel approach, the market for such services has embraced the format of this offering, and today both fee-based advisors and "sell-side" commission-based purveyors of financial management services make the claim to practice this so called fiduciary model of rendering independent personal financial advice.

Index-tracking, essentially building portfolios of funds arrayed to replicate strategic asset class mixes to fit with a client investment risk profile, and seeking to achieve the *mean return* earned by each asset class included, as Vanguard pursues it, became the *core of our firm's (TFC's) client portfolio strategy*.

Throughout all of this, I had stayed in touch with Jack Bogle in a number of ways. So one day in 2011, knowing Jack was to be in Boston speaking at a National CFA Conference, I called and asked if he might have time after his talk to stop by our offices and meet a group of our clients. A few weeks later, after his speaking engagement with Jason Zweig of *The Wall Street Journal* at the CFA Conference, he joined us for an afternoon reception with a few invited clients.

A year or so later Jack called and asked if I would serve, with Jeremey Grantham, as co-chairman of a dinner to be held in his (Jack's) honor sponsored by the Lown Institute. The dinner at the Boston Mandarin Hotel turned out to be a great success: Jack seemed pleased with the outcome, as did *Nobel Laureate* cardiologist Dr. Bernard Lown who had attended to Jack's many heart troubles. From that chance encounter developed my own association with the Lown Institute.

Figure 6.3.1.5 *Jack Bogle and Jim Joslin at a client reception meeting in 2011*

In May of 2013 I arranged for Jack to present his latest book, *The Clash of the Cultures*, to a Boston Society of Security Analysts luncheon at the Avery Street Ritz Carlton. It was a standing-room-only turnout, and our firm provided all (250 attendees) with a copy of the book. Jack's speech, which he had spent a great deal of time crafting for the occasion (see www.tfcfinancial.com for the full text), was a *tour de force* tracing the history of the mutual fund business in Boston. It was for him a kind of Boston valedictory, and for our firm, a chance to identify with an industry icon in a very favorable setting.

Today, Jack, who at the age of 87 has lived with a transplanted heart for more than 20 years, has had the pleasure of watching the firm he founded in 1977, Vanguard Group, flourish beyond all reasonable expectations. In 2016, Vanguard was the recipient of in excess of 40% of all the mutual fund cash inflows nationally. Recently the firm's combined assets under management crossed the $4.0 trillion mark, ranking it the number two firm in the US by assets under management; a phenomenon for the most part based on the realization that, as is also the case in life's unfolding events, *reversion to the mean (less fees)* is an important precept to keep in mind when managing one's own or other peoples' money.

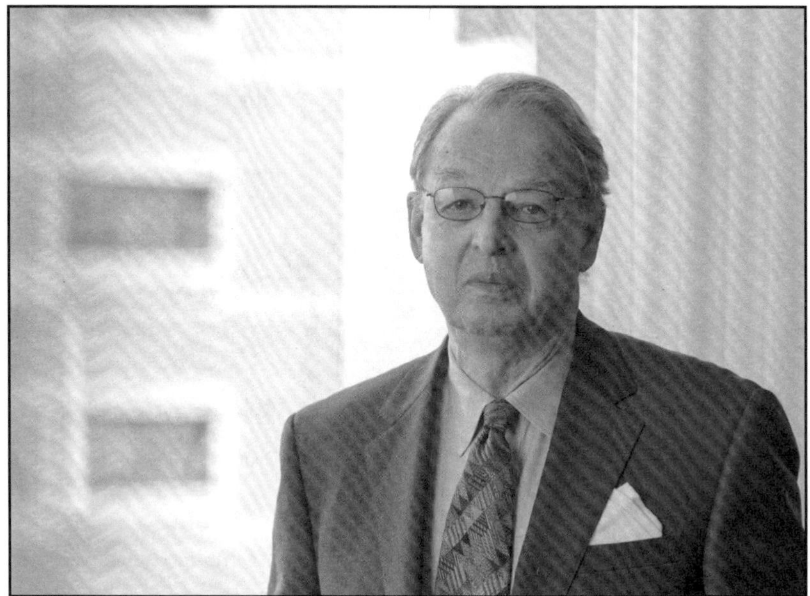

Figure 6.3.1.6 *James L. Joslin in his Boston office at TFC Financial, January 2016*

James L. Joslin, a founding and current principal of Boston's TFC Financial Management, has more than 50 years of experience in private wealth management. Elected 1957 Class Secretary at Commencement, he continues to serve in that capacity, interrupted only by a stint in the Navy as an Air Intelligence Officer in the US and Europe. Currently he serves on the boards of the Maine Maritime Museum, the International Museum of World War II, and the Lown Institute. His daughter, Charlotte, a member of the Class of 1990, was selected as the John Harvard Scholar at Cambridge University, and was the most decorated female athlete in Harvard's annals. Two of her sons are currently enrolled at Harvard and playing varsity lacrosse. Jim resides in Wellesley Hills, MA, with Sally, his wife of 59 years.

Financial Crisis

Robert Lenzner

2008: My Most Frightening Experience as a Journalist

I've been a financial journalist for a long time, and I've seen a lot, but the 2008 financial crisis deeply shook my faith in the financial system. More important, it opened my eyes to the shortcomings of financial journalism. Covering the Great Recession was, I've come to realize, the most sobering, and at times frightening experience of my forty-year career.

In the spring of 2014, I decided I needed to step back and sort out what I'd learned—and why it still troubled me, so I left New York for Harvard's Shorenstein Center on Media, Politics and Public Policy. I spent my time as a Fellow there talking to a lot of people in finance and economics, and read every bit of market history and analysis I could get my hands on. I wanted to figure out how and where my colleagues (and I) had missed the big picture—and how we could do better the next time.

While at Harvard, I spoke with a range of experts. I also read important speeches by Fed officials, dozens of IMF and NBER working papers, as well as a stack of books about the crisis, the role of the Federal Reserve, the "too-big-to-fail" banks, and previous financial crises. (Several current and former central bankers, and Wall Street bankers and investors—as you'll see—also spoke to me, but not for attribution.)

What follows are the conclusions I reached. Most of them are deeply alarming to me as a journalist and a citizen because what became inescapably clear is that we are still living today with the same global financial system we had on the eve of the 2008 crash—which was so complex and opaque that no one understood it. Worse, I've concluded, we don't understand it now.

First, I now realize, in 2008 neither regulators, policymakers, nor leaders had ready access to the information they needed to read the early warning signals of disaster. Most importantly, systemically important financial institutions weren't obligated to report their level of financial leverage, the illiquidity of their assets, their counterparty risk exposures, or other critical risk data they preferred to remain silent about.

Second, I can see now that there were higher levels of dangerous interconnectivity between the most concentrated financial institutions that weren't visible or understood by anyone involved, including the Federal Reserve, the Treasury, the Securities and Exchange Commission and other regulators, or the institutions they were meant to regulate.

Third, I finally understand that, although we are faced today with very nearly the same level of connectivity, no responsible body among the regulators or the regulated is fully able to evaluate developments in the financial system, just as in 2008. We still don't know who owes what to whom, either inside the United States or between American and international financial counterparties. Moreover, there is no coherent regulatory system in foreign financial capitals that is fully coordinated with the (dangerously fragmented) regulators in the United States.

How Did We Ever Get Ourselves into this Situation?

During the meltdown, especially in September 2008, a great many decisions had to be made, some almost instantly, in order to save the financial system as it faced the worst crisis since 1933. But passage of the Dodd-Frank bill hasn't solved the problems we faced in 2008. In fact, some of the bold acts that saved the day in 2008, such as the SEC's guarantee of the money market mutual funds, or the FDIC's guarantee of bank bonds, or the Fed's bailout of AIG, are now prohibited by Dodd-Frank.

But Dodd-Frank's weaknesses, which I'll address shortly, aren't even the biggest problem. As I now see it, the core problem in the traditional banking system is that five too-big-to-fail banks still exist—and they still control 95 percent of the dangerously unregulated derivatives market. No less a wise man than Warren Buffett told me that he can't evaluate the banks' derivative risk levels, and as a result fears that the next catastrophe (he prefers the word "discontinuity") could be worse than 2008.

Outside the regulated traditional banking system lies the so-called "shadow banking system", barely regulated and barely understood—and a huge problem of its own (more on this shortly). For the moment, just understand that financial media have only lately even tried to investigate sectors such as the $2.4 trillion money market funds industry, the $1.9 trillion world of short term repo agreements, or the $2.5 trillion hedge fund business—or biggest of them all, the $240 trillion over-the-counter derivatives trade.

That $240 trillion derivatives trade offers several vivid examples of just how unregulated (or under-regulated) shadow banking really is. One is that no one's really sure whether the market's real size is $240 trillion, or something larger or smaller—a not inconsequential matter, given the sums involved. I challenge anyone, for example, to explain the derivative reports by J.P. Morgan, Goldman Sachs, Citigroup, or Bank of America—the biggest players in the market. Should they show their positions in gross dollars or by netting out their long and short positions to make the amounts at risk seem far less? Jim Stone, a former chairman of the Commodity Futures Trading Commission—which is supposed to, at least minimally, oversee the derivatives market—insists that it's the total exposure that counts, because it's impossible to tell from the banks' information whether the netting operation between long and short positions actually does substantially reduce their risk.

The more I've dug, what has become clear to me—in spades—is just how difficult it is for those of us in the financial press to comprehend all the forces at work in these enormous, and enormously complicated, markets. But the markets themselves—and their biggest private players—are only one side of the problem. Government regulators, meant to represent and protect the public, are the other.

As former Federal Reserve chairman Ben Bernanke explained to an audience of market insiders (to the press and public) at the Brookings Institution in 2014, "It was a big challenge to explain what was going on. I tried where I could to bring the story, not just to markets and to other economists, but to a more Main Street type of audience, on television or in town halls and things of that sort. But it was very challenging, frankly, to do that."

"The goal today, in 2014," Bernanke then went on, should be "to explain what we did, why we did it and try to win back the confidence of the public." Yet, looking back now, I'm not sure even Bernanke initially understood that we were experiencing a systemic crisis, because that very theme was missing in his presentations to Congress, the president, and the media. Officials at the New York Fed admitted to me (but only off the record), that they did a very poor job of clarifying the scale and scope of the systemic problems. As a consequence, all of us suffered as the Great Recession unfolded, institution by institution, event by event, with never a clear overview of the health of the entire financial system—and we have no clearer an understanding today.

Too Big to Fail; Too Big to Manage; Too Big to Regulate

Today, nine years after the frightening start of the Great Recession in September 2008, the giant financial institutions of Wall Street are still an unparalleled elite of wealth and power. Since 1970 their share of total US corporate profits has risen from 24 to 37 percent. Second quarter profits on Wall Street in 2014 totaled more than $40 billion, their second highest in the past quarter century. At the apex of this system, the six largest banks, whose revenues equaled 17 percent of GDP in 1995, now count revenues equal to 58 percent of GDP. How, you ask, could that be possible?

The explanation is disarmingly simple: Wall Street is more concentrated today than it was before the crisis; in fact it's more concentrated today than at any time in US history. Altogether the five largest financial firms control 68 percent of all the commercial bank deposits in the US and hold on their balance sheets over $10 trillion in assets—an amount roughly equal to two-thirds of the entire American economy.

Mind you, this was all done by institutions that obtain more than 90 percent of their funding from debt. Even after the passage of the ostensibly reformist Dodd-Frank legislation and all the deliberations over Basel III, the amount of equity to debt of the major banks remains essentially what it was in 2008. True, Basel III is supposed to increase bank equity, but it has a transition period that will last until 2019, when banks will still only be required to have equity equal to seven percent of their assets.

"This is an unnecessarily long transition period," warn Anat Admati and Martin Hellvig, authors of *The Banker's New Clothes*. They add that Basel III's equity requirements even then will be far too low, because for the most part, the required equity will be related not to a bank's total assets but to what are called "risk-weighted assets", which are in fact a fraction of total assets. Translation? Basel III hasn't made the banks safe from insolvency.

These machinations are, frankly, I've reluctantly concluded, the result of the "crony capitalism" (or "regulatory capture") that defines the financialization which has replaced industry as the American economy's most prominent activity since the 1980s. Yet despite the painful losses of the 2008 meltdown, I discovered that some 35 percent of Harvard Business School grads went into finance in 2012, with J.P. Morgan Chase and Goldman Sachs still considered two of the ten most sought-after employers in the US. In short, finance, and its premium compensation opportunities, still rules the business culture. Wall Street, in short, houses the new "power elite" of America, reflecting the influence amassed by the major banks, investment banks, private equity empires, hedge funds, and formidable investment management firms such as BlackRock—which by itself oversees $4.3 trillion of other people's money, an astounding amount equal to the assets of the entire Federal Reserve system today. Today the evidence is overwhelming that "some financial institutions have grown beyond the point where they can efficiently monitor themselves," writes Luigi Zingales, a finance professor at the University of Chicago's Booth School of Business.

Mind you, most financial experts from Stanley Fischer, vice chairman of the Fed, to Warren Buffett, America's most highly respected investor, to MIT economist Stanley Lo, are all quite confident that sooner or later we will have another crisis. Yet as long as we have financial firms that are too big to fail, warns William Dudley, president of the New York Federal Reserve Bank, "the goal of financial stability will remain elusive." So, I believe that too big to fail is target number one for reformers of the financial system. Yet the *realpolitik* of finance so far seems to have stymied all but the most ardent reformers, implying that we will require another catastrophe to force any truly meaningful reform.

What I've additionally learned from my extensive research and interviews in the past year is that too big to fail also means that these are institutions that are too big to manage, too big to regulate, and too opaque for the press, public, and even their regulators to comprehend. Too big to fail means that the nation is faced with a highly concentrated oligopoly of banks that keeps getting larger and more powerful politically, and that when these banks next get into financial trouble, they will once again become expensive wards of the state.

Warren Buffett, when I talked to him, had much more than "a healthy fear of the unknown." The "Oracle of Omaha" flatly predicted that "there will be a huge discontinuity some day. I can't say when. But the numbers on the balance sheets of J.P. Morgan Chase and Goldman Sachs will mean nothing." Buffett admitted that even with his decades of experience, he couldn't understand J.P. Morgan Chase's presentation of its derivatives positions, which he noted represent a very large share of the assets on the giant bank's balance sheet. "There is no risk system that is effective if the numbers get big enough," he added quietly. Buffett says he fears that the next financial crisis will develop from the year-after-year increase in concentrated holdings by just five banks, which possess 95 percent of all the outstanding derivative contracts.

The notional amounts (i.e., the total value) of derivative contracts quintupled between 2001 and 2009, according to the Office of the Comptroller of the Currency, and today are over $240 trillion—an amount 15 times the size of the US economy. Yet the intricate details of these huge derivative positions, the identity of their counterparties, the nature and amounts of collateral backing the contracts, the degree of leverage employed, and the duration of the contracts are not known to the four giant accounting firms, the credit rating agencies, or banking industry analysts.

The banks don't even have to reveal how much capital they've used in derivative operations or what portion of their overall revenues or profits these operations represent. (Some, like Goldman Sachs, tend to obfuscate by reporting different derivative operations in separate segments of their business.) Derivative prices and volumes of trading are not reported on any public securities exchange or regularly reported in the financial press.

Back in 2003, Buffett noted that positions the banks report publicly each quarter "are often wildly overstated . . . the parties to derivatives also have enormous incentives to cheat in accounting for them." During the 2008 financial crisis, former Treasury Secretary Geithner has since admitted, it was impossible for regulators to understand "what exposures they (the banks) had, what counterparties might be in trouble"—then described the ways the large banks expanded their derivative positions in 2008 as "the Wild West." According to Geithner, "We couldn't persuade enough of them to reduce their leverage or manage their risks more carefully, because they didn't think that was in their interest. That was the real danger to the system."

We keep learning about the never-ending mischief the banks' derivative operations can cause. A Senate committee found last year that as a part of J.P. Morgan's "London Whale" derivative fiasco, the bank hid "hundreds of millions of losses", obstructed government oversight, lied and misinformed regulators, investors, and the public about the nature of the risks it was taking.

Shadow Banking

Beyond the too-big-to-fail banks and their virtual monopoly on derivatives trading stands a parallel financial colossus called the "shadow banking system", which entails a whole group of disparate financial firms, products and functions that have each added complexity and their own risks to order in the marketplace. Shadow banking isn't banking as we understand it, with a vast network of ATMs, retail branches and debit cards. Instead it is a profusion of clever financial products like money market mutual funds, commercial paper, short-term repurchase notes, and credit default swaps, as well as firms such as hedge funds and investment banks. These shadow banks performed the dangerous act of borrowing vast amounts of money short-term, and then lending it or investing it—just like regulated banks.

By 2008, money market mutual funds had grown to $3.4 trillion, the use of commercial paper to $600 billion, the use of short-term repurchase agreements to $3.9 billion, and credit derivatives globally to a notional value of $600 trillion. Taken together, the products and firms of shadow banking had grown larger than traditional banking—all without the capital requirements and other regulatory safeguards imposed on banks to limit risk. As shadow banking outpaced regulated finance, the gross debt of the US financial system grew from 20 percent of GDP in 1979 to 120 percent of GDP by 2008. In fact, the unstoppable sequence of events in September 2008 illustrates exactly how shadow banking now affects traditional banking and created the disintegration of financial markets across the globe.

In short, shadow banking's weaknesses were crucial to 2008's gargantuan market failures, first in the US and then globally, as banks in Europe and elsewhere sought their own local bailouts. Despite the passage of both nine years and Dodd-Frank, I'm far from alone in thinking too little has changed in regulatory oversight of most aspects of the shadow banking system. Former Treasury Secretary Larry Summers told me point-blank that the regulatory gap he worries about most is shadow banking oversight, especially in the $2.4 trillion money market mutual fund industry. Even more worrisome, Summers believes that the web of linkages between shadow banks and traditional banks still prevent the Fed from ever knowing in advance when a major bank might be becoming insolvent.

In other words, there are still so many obstacles and challenges to a properly functioning financial system that no one—including the media—can understand precisely the problems hidden in the plumbing of the financial markets. To mix metaphors, in short, we are still flying blind.

The Whole vs. the Sum of the Parts

"One of the great pre-crisis mistakes was to look at risk in the financial system institution by institution, atom by atom. Doing so resulted in regulators missing the systemic crisis of a lifetime," says Andrew Haldane, one of the top officials of the Bank of England. "Yet an asset by asset, atom by atom approach to risk management still lies at the heart of the post-crisis regulatory framework." Former Fed governor Kevin Warsh is even more explicit: there is still no way to "compare a firm's exposures against one another in a timely and effective manner.

Warsh's remedy is no less explicit: "Those interconnected firms that find themselves dependent on implicit government support do not serve our economy's interest. Their continued existence should not be countenanced. The risks associated with our largest firms must never again be underwritten by taxpayers."

Yet I've come to conclude—despite my deep respect for professionals like Haldane, Warsh, and Yellen—that lack of data or data analysis isn't the only problem. The problem, quite frankly, is that when too-big-to-fail bankers want to oppose some reform that damages their bottom line, they can usually block such a change by dint of the influence their money can buy. The banks are no less determined to block public oversight of the $10 trillion market in credit default swaps that are arranged bilaterally between one bank and another. As a consequence, this gargantuan—and exceptionally profitable—trading business is still not subject to even the oversight and reporting requirements of a market-based clearing house like ICE (Intercontinental Exchange, Inc.).

Dodd-Frank was supposed to reorganize regulation to prevent another 2008, but in seven years of rule-making has grown from a 1,400-page bill into an 8,843-page rule book—and could grow to 30,000 pages or more, in the estimate of Martin Wolf. "This manic rule-making," he writes, "is designed to disguise the fact that the thrust of it all has been to preserve the system that existed prior to the crisis: it will still be global; it will continue to rely on the interaction of vast financial institutions with free-wheeling capital markets; it will continue to be highly leveraged; and it will continue to rely for profitability on successfully managing huge maturity and risk mismatches."

Stunning to most of us, Wolf believes "the authorities want largely to preserve a system they also mistrust." "We can now see that the largest, most powerful banks came out of the crisis even larger and more powerful," writes MIT economist Simon Johnson. When the future of the financial industry appeared dire in September 2008, "Washington came to its rescue—not because of personal favors to a handful of powerful bankers, but because of a belief in a certain kind of financial sector so strong not even the ugly revelations of the financial crisis could uproot it." That's why, even though trust between Washington and Wall Street is still in a state of unease and disrepair, Wall Street's interest in the bottom line, rather than the public's in proper regulation, is winning.

Seven years after the passage of Dodd-Frank, the financial system still contains enormous, unsolved inherent risks. The whole structure of modern finance still suffers from the fragility of being a nontransparent global network—in which lending and trading and borrowing constantly raises the degree of interconnectivity in the system, thereby amplifying strategic risks, which in turn offers yet more opportunities for turbulence, vulnerabilities, and shocks.

And if I've seemed only a Cassandra, let me close by noting that there has been some progress toward modernization of the financial system, although it has been steadily diluted by the political power of Wall Street. Dodd-Frank and Basel III, for example, have forced the banks to increase their capital—and even more significantly their liquidity. Some of the major banks such as J.P. Morgan Chase, Goldman Sachs and Citigroup, as I've noted, do now hold highly liquid assets including cash equal to between 20 and 30 percent of their entire assets on the balance sheet. Moreover, these banks are by no means presently over-leveraged as dangerously as they were in 2007 and 2008. The "plumbing" of what I still consider the dangerous derivative markets has also been improved by placement of many transactions on publicly accessible clearing houses like the CME and ICE.

One Closing Fusillade: Make Markets Safer

Let me finish not as Cassandra but hopefully as Paul Revere here, by saying what needs to happen to make markets safer.

(1) It is absolutely absurd that no Federal Reserve forecasting model "captures what's going on", as former Fed governor Kevin Warsh told me. It makes no sense that monetary management today includes not a single input from domestic financial markets which are affected by every Fed decision.

(2) Dodd-Frank now prohibits many of the techniques government used in 2008 to protect Wall Street and America from complete chaos. The Fed is prohibited from bailing out a single institution

without the approval of Congress. The Treasury is prohibited from guaranteeing the value of money market mutual fund shares. The FDIC is prohibited from guaranteeing the fixed income securities of major banks, the strategy that helped Citigroup keep its doors open in 2008. These are dangerous mistakes—and must be corrected.

(3) Rumors about the financial health of a too-big-to-fail bank can still lead to "contagion risk", where a threat to parts of a derivatives portfolio can lead to a "run" on the entire portfolio, which is exactly what happened with Lehman Brothers as it approached bankruptcy.

(4) Before he retired from the Fed, Ben Bernanke exclaimed that his goal as chairman of the central bank had been to "explain what we did, why we did it and try to win back the confidence of the public." A noble goal, to be sure, but one the Fed has never achieved because the public (supported in part by the press) has made it abundantly clear that most Americans believe that since 2008 the Feds have done more to bail out Wall Street than Main Street.

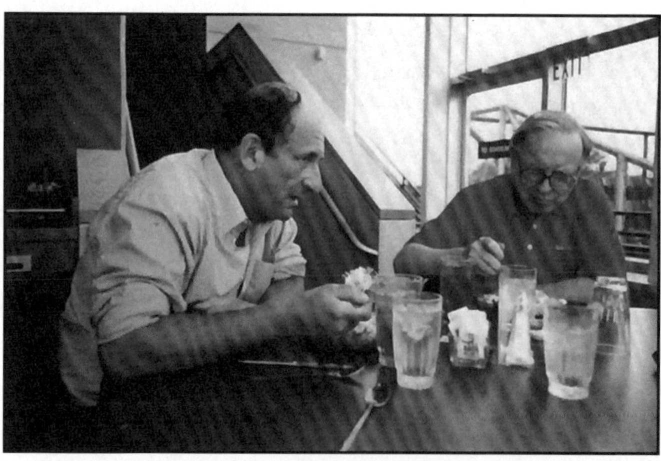

Figure 6.3.2.1 *Financial journalist Robert Lenzner interviewing Warren Buffett, in Omaha, NE, 1993*

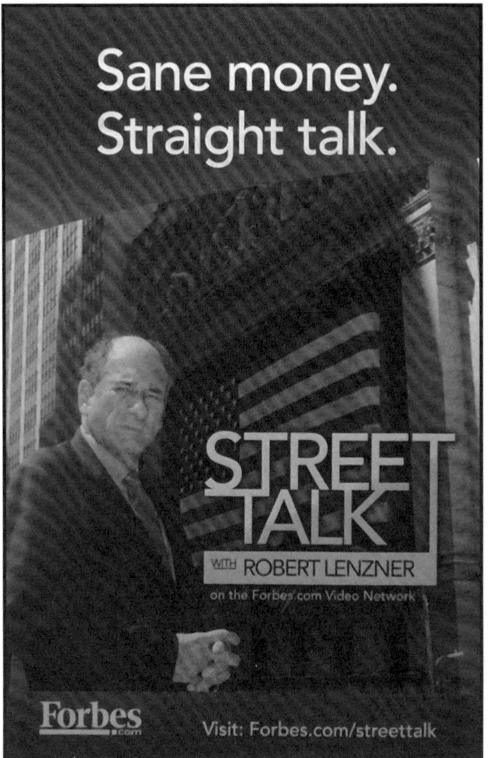

Figure 6.3.2.2 Forbes' *advertisement featuring the author, shown in front of the New York Stock Exchange*
Photo courtesy of the author

Robert Lenzner learned about finance in his six years at Goldman Sachs & Co. in the 1960s. By the early 1970s he had joined *The Boston Globe* as New York correspondent. As well he was approached by the London *Economist* to become its Wall Street correspondent. He worked for both publications simultaneously until 1990. He also wrote a best-selling biography of oil billionaire J. Paul Getty, *The Great Getty*, which was on *The New York Times* best-seller list for 13 weeks and translated into 21 languages. In 1992 Lenzner joined *Forbes* magazine as Senior Editor, subsequently becoming National Editor and worked there 23 years until leaving at the end of 2014.

Figure 6.3.2.3 *Kenneth Joseph "Ken" Arrow (1921–2017)*
American economist, writer, and political theorist, in 1972 and 2004

In 1972 Kenneth Arrow shared the Nobel Memorial Prize in Economics with John R. Hicks and later received the von Neumann Theory Prize (1986) and the National Medal of Science (2004). The latter recognized his research on decision-making when using imperfect information and on bearing risk.

Professor of economics at Harvard (1968–1978) and Stanford (1979–1991), he made significant contributions to social choice theory, notably "Arrow's impossibility theorem", and general equilibrium analysis, and to post-WWII neo-classical economic theory with his theory of endogenous growth and economics of information.

His first publication, On the Optimal Use of Winds for Flight Planning, *came from his research during World War II as a weather officer (1942–1946) in the United States Army Air Corps.*

Kenneth Arrow was brother-in-law of economists Paul Samuelson and Robert Summers. His sister, economist Anita Summers, was the mother of former Harvard President Larry Summers.

Sources:
Text: https://en.m.wikipedia.org/wiki/Kenneth_Arrow, http://www.nobelprize.org/nobel_prizes/economic-sciences/laureates/1972/arrow-bio.html

Images: 1972—https://www.nobelprize.org/nobel_prizes/economic-sciences/laureates/1972/arrow.jpg; 2004—https://en.m.wikipedia.org/wiki/File:Kenneth_Arrow,_Stanford_University.jpg,
Credit: Linda A. Cicero, Stanford News Service, Kenneth_Arrow,_Stanford_University.jpg

Chapter Seven
ENVIRONMENT

Figure C7 *Dunster House in winter, fronting on the frozen Charles River. Within this century, will this winter scene be only a memory preserved in a photograph?*

Reprinted courtesy of Harvard University

Chapter Seven
ENVIRONMENT

Architecture

Harvard Reflections

Edward "Ted" McCagg

My first architectural assignment was remodeling a dormitory at Wellesley College while working for Shepley, Bulfinch, Richardson & Abbott in Boston. I had interviewed there but received no offer. I was later hired while waiting in the elevator lobby. (Those elevators were really slow, fortunately.) Other assignments, mostly remodels in Boston, included Harvard houses and the aquarium. These kept me in Boston for two years. I could see my future clearly: marriage, move to the North Shore, kids, rise at Shepley. So clear, so ordered .... So, in 1963, I fled.

I interviewed at five or six major firms as I headed West. It was a good information gathering opportunity: research, and short list interviews, but I was asking the questions. It was a great learning experience. I also wanted to try again for the US Olympic rowing team after coming in second in the pairs in 1960. Same results this time, taking second. I ended up in Seattle as I didn't want to go to Alaska at that time. I was hired by a 25-person architectural design and engineering firm, Young, Richardson and Carleton. Y,R&C had just been hired to plan and design the expansion for Seattle/Tacoma international Terminal Area (excluding taxiways, runways), and I ended up as the head of that firm!

My career was underway, and I enjoyed all of the subsequent flying, plus years of airport planning, concept development, design, and construction overview. The Sea-Tac expansion allowed me to practice all aspects of terminal expansion. Initially it was concourse expansion and airline clubs. Then we continued into terminal design, baggage handling, concessions, curb and traffic design, culminating in an eight-level parking garage. I couldn't have had a broader or better introduction to airport planning and design.

I stayed in the airport field for the next 50 years and recently retired.

An overview of airports I worked on:

Over 100 in the US, 15 in the Middle East and Europe, and 15 in the Far East and Pacific region. Lots of airline miles, most not used, and way too much time away from home.

Scale of airports, but not necessarily projects: Seattle, Portland, Chicago, JFK, LaGuardia, Boston Logan, Denver, Detroit, Philadelphia. International airports included: Qatar, Dubai, China, Israel, several in Saudi Arabia, Hong Kong, and others. Smaller airports, same challenges on a different scale and great fun included: Billings, MO, Casper, WY, Providence, RI, and others plus some really small ones to which we flew on our consultants' planes.

Project value is no longer relevant with the changes in dollar value. Range would be from several billion to several hundred thousand dollars.

One of the best parts of this broad geographic range of projects was the people we met: airport operators, airline staff and pilots, concessioners, airport authority members as well as FAA and their counterparts around the world. Some of the most interesting experiences were working with consultants. We often not only worked with them, but were invited home to meet families and share a meal.

A few adventures but mostly work, seven days a week. (Arabs work on Sundays). We had a couple of desert Jeep rides and saw some gazelles; some sailing on the Persian Gulf, some Arabian castle tours. However, the best were the casual conversations with the locals at all levels. My Arabic never got beyond basic greetings, which I now regret. Fortunately my partner on the ventures spoke perfect Arabic.

Over the 50 years, aircraft went from 727 and 707, DC-8, to the 747 and DC-10 to the Super-Sonic. We had one trip on the SST, London to Seattle. Too short a flight to sleep. Many other aircraft, large and small.

All of this meant many days on the road for me. I have the greatest love and admiration for my wife, Sharon, who continued to work as a pediatric nurse while raising twin girls and a son, plus household work, while I was away. She has been wonderful all these years and raised three children all of whom graduated from Harvard, class of '89 and '93. Our daughters rowed at Harvard and continued to row for the USA in three Olympic Games. Our son and family live in Brooklyn. We have a daughter in Cambridge and her twin sister lives near us in Kirkland, WA. All of them are married and we have five grandchildren. Life has been good, and we will work hard to continue the trend.

Figure 7.1.1.1 Left: *TRA's model of McCarran International Airport, Las Vegas, at the time one of 126 airport projects all over the world, including master planning for 1,200 airports for the State of Alaska. The firm also designed office buildings.* Right: *Ted McCagg*

Photos courtesy of *The Seattle Daily Journal of Commerce*, March 30, 1983; Architecture-Engineering – Anthony Dodoye-Alali, Editor

---

Edward K. "Ted" McCagg II after graduation spent 4½ years at the Harvard School of Design, earning a M.Arch. in 1962. He then enjoyed two years as an architect with Shepley Bulfinch in its Boston office before his passion for rowing took him to Seattle for the Olympic trials in 1964. He liked it so much he settled there. Ted joined a firm to do health care design but was soon asked to help design an expansion of the Seattle-Tacoma (Sea-Tac) Airport. Eight years and $100 million later, he was leading an airport planning and design group, TRA Ltd., that over the next 25 years won projects in the US, Iraq, Iran, the Gulf states, Israel, Peru, the Philippines, the Pacific Islands and Korea. He was president of the Airport Consultants Council in 1987. For the Denver Airside Concourses he received a design award from the US Department of Transportation. His twin daughters, Elizabeth '89 and Mary '89, carried on the rowing tradition in a combined five Olympics. Sharon, his wife of more than 50 years, is a retired pediatric nurse. Their son, Ted '93, is in advertising.

Ecology

Land Conservation

Heartland—Conserving Indiana

Warren Buckler

About 18 years ago, on a damp spring morning, my wife, Pat, and I joined a hike at a place called Springfield Fen. The outing was organized by the Shirley Heinze Land Trust, or *SHLT*, whose mission is to acquire, protect and restore natural areas—prairie, forest, wetlands, dunes—in northwest Indiana, where industrial and residential development has claimed a lot of the landscape.

With doctorate in hand, Pat had accepted a job teaching English at Purdue University North Central. We commuted for a time until I retired after years of hard labor as a reporter and editorial writer for *The Louisville Times* (now defunct) and *The Courier-Journal* in Louisville, KY. I had a special interest in environmental issues and didn't mind telling others how to deal with them. Then I became a *Hoosier*, the nickname recently recognized by the feds as the one Indianans prefer.

After reading about the land trust I sent a contribution, was notified of hikes and so there we were. While looking for wildflowers, admiring a rare *massasauga rattlesnake,* groggy from a long winter, or listening to a talk about *thismia*, a plant not seen in years but avidly sought by botanists, I decided this was a group I could happily join.

Pat was way ahead of me. She struck up a conversation with a lean, tanned young woman who was in charge of stewardship, known in the field as *taking care of*, the Shirley Heinze properties, which now total about 2,300 acres. That day she was concerned about finding summer help.

"*Why don't you take Warren?*" said my loving wife. "*He has nothing to do.*"

I was showing signs of incipient geezerhood and doubted I was a promising prospect. But the upshot was that I showed up the following Monday at a place called Hidden Prairie, squeezed between I-65 and a residential area. My boss had discovered prairie plants hidden beneath noxious weeds, mostly "*invasives*" from Europe or Asia. Our job was to get rid of the weeds and revive the prairie.

Members of the work crew were mostly beginners, and we had to learn to recognize the *bad guys* as well as those plants we were hoping to encourage. I am a plant fancier, but by no means a botanist, and worked hard in college to learn as little as possible from a required natural science course, for which I suffer ex-student's remorse. But I could soon identify such *deplorables* as *multi-flora rose*, *autumn olive* and *buckthorn*. And I labored to liberate from their deadly embrace such denizens of the prairie as *prairie dock* with its elephant-ear leaves; *agrimony*, a humble member of the rose family; an untamed sibling of garden variety *black-eyed Susans*; and especially the brilliant *blue bottle gentian*, patches of which I have in my home garden. For six months I cut, pulled and poisoned.

One day a genial man known as *Dan, Dan the Orchid Man* came visiting. It was said of him that if there were an orchid in the vicinity he could find it in short order. I doubted he could pull that off unless he happened to be in the Thai jungle. But after briefly poking around in a wooded area, he shouted that he had found a *tway-blade*, a variety of orchid. I was dumbfounded. Orchids in the wild in Indiana? Yes, there are a number of species, some so small they're hard to find without Dan's help. Others are showier, though probably not big enough to impress your prom date. Thus are the ignorant enlightened. I have since planted yellow *lady slippers* at home.

So I read up on prairies and learned that what was known as the *Grand Prairie*, valued for its fertile "black earth", with grasses and flowering plants tall enough to conceal a man on horseback, once occupied 170 million acres across the Midwest. With hundreds of species of plants, and teeming with birds, butterflies, pollinators and other wildlife, it was surely among the most interesting natural communities on earth. And it stretched as far as the eye could see. An extension called the *Prairie Peninsula* poked into the Great Lakes region. It covered about 15 percent of Indiana, although its extent varied with climate. During hot, dry periods the prairie advanced eastward. Cooler, wetter times favored the hardwood forest. The space in between was savanna.

So where can you visit this fabulous landscape? Alas, most of it has been obliterated. In Indiana about 1,000 of two million acres remain, mostly, with noteworthy exceptions, in small segments. When settlers began arriving in the early 19th century and acquired the equipment to turn over the black earth, the prairie was converted to agriculture. Now rows of corn and soy beans stretch to the horizon. Both are worthy crops. But in a more enlightened age, a large swath of prairie would surely have been set aside so our descendants could appreciate the importance of the *Great Plains* in American life and imagination.

As Lynton Caldwell noted in an essay in a volume entitled "*The Natural Heritage of Indiana*", early settlers were mainly interested in "*prospects for livelihood or profit*". They eliminated whatever stood in the way—trees, wildlife, wetlands, Native Americans. By the end of the 1900s the hardwood forest that occupied two-thirds of the state had been greatly diminished. The few huge trees that remain, mostly in state preserves, are reminders of the grandeur that was.

Well into the 1960s, Caldwell wrote, "*nature lover* was an epithet of scorn in the Indiana State House." "Civic club members," he noted in a wry comment about the paradoxical attitudes prevailing at the time, "could sing '*On the Banks of the Wabash*' at luncheon meetings, then applaud a speaker who urged the river's transformation into an industrial canal."

Change came slowly but has picked up impressive momentum. Indiana's state park system was established in 1916. The *Dunes State Park*, about 2,000 acres, which includes sand hills up to 185 feet high, broad beaches along Lake Michigan, plus woods and wetlands, was among the first. In the mid-1960s the epic battle over the remaining dunelands came to a successful conclusion, though at a high cost. Since before World War I, conservationists had sought federal protection for this scenically stunning, botanically rich, ecologically intriguing stretch of lakeshore.

Finally, with support from Illinois Sen. Paul Douglas of Illinois, but not much from development-minded Indiana politicians, and thanks to the tireless advocacy of a group of local citizens, the feds established the *Indiana Dunes National Lakeshore*. However, a section of the Dunes, considered the best, was leveled for yet another steel mill. Given that the Dunes rank among the top several national parks in botanical diversity, the long delay seems all the more shameful.

In the wake of this struggle came a surge of citizen and governmental activity aimed at protecting natural areas and environmental quality. An organization called *Save the Dunes* was involved in the fight and remains active on a number of fronts. The Indiana chapter of the *Nature Conservancy* has undertaken major restoration projects in our region. In 1966 a new state *Division of Nature Preserves* came into being and has conferred a high degree of protection on some 50,000 acres around Indiana. SHLT traces its ancestry to 1981. Volunteer groups and public agencies work together in pursuit of shared goals.

After a summer battling invasives I was invited to join the SHLT board and later served three years as president. We worked on fund-raising techniques and broadening board membership—a typical nonprofit agenda. But the organization truly flourished after my tenure thanks to an energetic young executive director and growing business and foundation support. Recently the land trust acquired an unused 74-acre Girl Scout camp situated on the Valparaiso Moraine, originally a pile of soil and rock left behind by glacial activity, but now a mostly forested upland. Eighty acres have since been added, and last summer 20,000 native hardwood seedlings were planted there. Reforestation of old farmland is also in progress at the almost 1,000–acre state-owned Moraine Nature Preserve near our home.

Once out of office, a colleague and I started a support group called *Friends of Shirley Heinze* or *FOSH*—but don't call us Foshists!

Our main project, now in its seventh year, encourages and calls public attention to home owners, businessmen and park managers who use native plants in their landscaping schemes. We are impressed by the work of Douglas Tallamy of the University of Delaware, whose book *Bringing Nature Home* and extensive research make a powerful case for greater use of wildflowers, shrubs and trees that have "co-evolved" with native insects and birds over centuries.

We embrace the idea that *yards and public spaces might be converted into functioning natural communities,* replacing some of the 30 million acres of lifeless, chemically saturated lawn that has become America's largest crop and the hallmark of suburbia.

There are many good reasons to back off from current approaches to landscaping. Native wildlife, it seems, finds popular non-native garden plants unappetizing. That's one reason some of the imports can spread unmolested and outcompete the natives, turning woods and wetlands into a monoculture.

When an animal's life cycle is linked to a specific family of plants, a property owner's quest for a weed-free yard or farm can put a desirable species at risk. The monarch butterfly-milkweed connection has captured public attention. *When we banish the milkweed, disliked by many gardeners, the monarch population declines*, provoking widespread lamentation.

In my experience, insects do show little interest in "foreigners" like my beloved *dahlias* and *tree peonies*. I've never seen a caterpillar munching leaves on invasive autumn olive trees that sneak onto my property. But the pinkish floral globes that seem to hover above the native *Joe-Pye weed* in my yard throb with life as pollinators, and bumble bees and swallowtail butterflies jockey for position. Tallamy has calculated how many butterfly and moth species are "supported" by various trees and shrubs. Oaks lead the pack with more than 500. Aliens aren't even in the running. *If you like bees, butterflies and birds, native is the way to go.*

The news in Indiana has been good lately, indicating anew how much attitudes have changed. FOSH attracts a lot of attention and this past year recognized, among others, a county park's prairie planting on 25 acres of former cow pasture. A local woman created an endowment for the 719-acre *Hoosier Prairie*, which in turn was "discovered" by another local woman who spent years successfully lobbying legislators to grant the place state and federal protection.

In celebration of its *2016 Bicentennial*, the state committed $20 million to land protection projects and plans to protect 43,000 acres along the storied Wabash. Last fall, the *Nature Conservancy* introduced 25 bison, missing from the wild in Northwest Indiana since 1824, to a portion of an 8,300-acre prairie restoration.

In 1980, when we still lived in Louisville, Pat and I bought 25 acres of degraded farm and forest near French Lick, IN, a community known for an aging resort hotel, and revered as the hometown of basketball megastar Larry Bird. We planted 700 trees by hand, *Virginia pine* in deep gullies in an eroded hillside corn field and *white pine* in better ground. We girdled old, low-value trees to make room for younger, more vigorous ones. This was my introduction to *environmental repair.*

So why do I get involved in such activities? I like to see things grow, preferably where they belong: *trillium*, *hepatica* and *bluebells* in the spring, *sunflowers* and *liatris* in the summer, *sneezeweed* and *asters* in the fall. I learn stuff, perhaps compensating for my D- in *Nat Sci 1.*

More important, I think historic landscapes are as closely linked to a region's personality, character, individuality and intrinsic beauty as the old buildings and museum artifacts we work to preserve. Whether prairies, forests, rugged seacoast, or purple mountains majesty, we should take care of them all.

Figure 7.2.1.1 *Bumblebees and Eastern swallowtail butterfly jockey for position on native Joe-Pye weed in Warren Buckler's yard, which throbs with life. Swallowtail's larval (caterpillar) hosts include tulip, poplar and black cherry trees, plentiful here in Indiana Heartland. Adults prefer native wildflowers like Joe-Pye weed, though they won't turn up their proboscis at a brightly colored zinnia. Common in fields, woodland edges in midsummer.*

Photo by Warren Buckler

Warren Buckler, a native of Baltimore, MD, following graduation served from 1957–1960 in the US Army with the Army Security Agency, where he first studied Russian at the Army Language School, subsequently renamed the National Defense Language School, in Monterey, CA. He then was stationed on the East-West border, monitoring East German/Russian military communications. From 1961–62 he studied German literature and Russian at the University in Goettingen, Germany, before returning to the US as reporter and editorial writer for six years at the Bennington Banner, Bennington, VT.

In 1968 he was recruited by the *The Louisville Times/The Courier Journal,* where he remained for 27 years as reporter and editorial writer. After retiring, he moved to Valparaiso, IN, where he remains involved in variety of volunteer activities. He and his wife, Patricia Prandini, formerly of Bennington, VT, are parents of two sons and grandparents of one granddaughter. They have been married for 50 years.

Water Conservation

Water: Theme of My Life

John Smith Farlow III

Water has fascinated me all of my life.

Early on, it was just the slippery look of it, as its whirlpools formed around obstructions and then faded, and as it rose magically above its surface while the stream flowed over rocks in its bed. My home was adjacent to my grandparents', on whose land were three small seasonal ponds which fed a small brook for much of the year and provided excellent skating during the winter. The brook was splendid for splashing in and for making small dams. While I was growing up, children were allowed far more freedom than now, and I took full advantage to get happily wet and muddy.

When I was about eight, my father and grandfather bought a kayak kit for me from Sears, Roebuck & Co., and assembled it in our basement. All of eight feet long and of black-painted canvas stretched over a wood frame, it provided hundreds of hours of happiness over the next years. It was small enough to be portable, and could be lugged both up to the three ponds and, later, about a half mile down to the Charles River. The latter was much shallower and narrower near home than it became down in Cambridge and Boston, and it had numbers of exciting, rocky rapids between long quiet stretches. There was even a twelve-foot high dam at a former rug mill several miles upstream, with fast-moving, dangerous rapids just below! And because the river was unpolluted, it provided good habitat for fish, sun turtles, milk snakes, ducks, muskrats and numerous other wildlife: there was always much of interest to watch and enjoy, when one became bored with just paddling.

A couple of years after the end of World War II, my family started spending part of the summer at Ironbound Island, off Bar Harbor, Maine. What a wonderful place, with 100-foot cliffs on its seaward side, against which crashed the waves of the North Atlantic Ocean! Besides learning to row in a pea-pod boat with stand-up oars (and being rocked in larger waves than the quiet Charles River could provide!) and becoming accustomed to the rhythms of the tide, I could also spend many happy hours looking down from the cliff-top at the swirling seas as the waves advanced and retreated over the ledges below. The motions of the water were different for every wave, and were endlessly fascinating. The changes in lighting as clouds came and went provided additional, enjoyable variety. And after the tail of a hurricane swept through, the patterns of the giant waves crashing on the shore were truly marvelous.

Parts of the next two summers were enjoyed in the Canadian forests north of Montreal at a canoe camp, which, besides providing larger lakes, rivers and rapids than the ponds and the stretch of the Charles River near home, introduced me to the concept of rivers as a transportation network for much of the continent (and also to the pains of portaging!). As bowman the first summer and stern man the second, I became much better acquainted with the liquid clues for reading a stream and its submerged hazards.

Admitted to Noble and Greenough School as a ninth-grader, I began to learn to row in their racing shells. In these, one is about as close to the water as you can get without swimming. You can immediately see the effects of your skill (or lack of it!) in handling your oar, and can readily gauge the effects of a stronger or weaker pull by the actions of the little whirlpools coming off the oar blades. In addition, you are part of a crew, of which each member's actions have an immediate effect on the boat and its relation to the water.

When I got to Harvard, I was fortunate to be able to continue rowing for the college for three years, and then for Eliot House in my senior year. Fifty years later I could still identify a specific fellow oarsman on the street from behind: His walk was still the same as back in our college days!

The spring of senior year a professor asked me if I would like a job in the Arctic during the International Geophysical Year: Of course, I said "Yes!" The Professor (Columbus Iselin) was also director of the Woods Hole Oceanographic Institute, where I learned the trade of a physical oceanographic technician, both ashore and on several oceanographic cruises. Here were whole different ways to think about that marvelous fluid! I eventually spent about 4½ months (in two periods) living and working on frozen sea ice at latitudes between 84 and 85 degrees north. The first period was from "sunset" to "midnight" (mid-September to mid-December) and then "sunrise" to "morning" (March to mid-April). Subsequently, I worked at sea between Bermuda and North Carolina, and in the eastern North Atlantic, before entering the Oceanography Department at The Johns Hopkins University to earn a master's degree studying more advanced aspects of things to do with water. My last summer there I was involved in studies of the great Chesapeake Bay Estuary and learned an important truth:You are much less likely to become seasick working on estuaries!

After leaving Hopkins I spent four years working for the US Public Health Service on water quality studies of Lakes Michigan and Erie, studying water currents and dispersion. I observed that the lack of significant tides make the lakes much more boring than the oceans and tidal estuaries. Luckily, I was able to move to a water quality study of Raritan Bay, and then to a National Estuarine study of the region from Delaware north to Canada. While at Raritan Bay I purchased a 17-foot-long sloop, in which I introduced my three sons to the joys of small-boat sailing, and taught them and my wife to sail. We've had many adventures in New Jersey and along the Maine coast, where our family has spent most summer vacations. Getting close to the water is fun and also teaches you a lot about yourself and the real world!

The Federal Government then reorganized again for greater efficiency, and created the US Environmental Protection Agency, with an Office of Research and Development planning to investigate better ways of preventing and cleaning up oil spills. They soon determined that they couldn't evaluate the claims of equipment manufacturers unless they gave them some spilled oil to work with(!), and so they decided to create a facility where oil could be safely spilled, contained and controlled: the Oil and Hazardous Materials Simulated Environmental Test Tank (OHMSETT) near Sandy Hook, NJ. Some 660 feet long, 50 feet wide and filled with water eight feet deep, different types of oil could be laid down at known thicknesses and in the presence of controlled waves or harbor chop. EPA shared the use of the facility in evaluating equipment and techniques with the US Navy, Coast Guard and Minerals Management Service and with Canada, Russia and other foreign countries for some ten years, before a change in mission led EPA to hand it over to the Minerals Management Service (just before the EXXON VALDEZ spill). I was involved in both the building and the managing the facility, and enjoying watching it do its job.

I have since retired to coastal Maine, where I have been lucky enough to have sailed among many of its coastal islands (until my back gave out). However, I still enjoy watching the tide surge in and out among the granite reefs along the shore.

Fluids continue to be fascinating. They are still providing great interest and joy in my life.

Ecology

Water Conservation

Jack Farlow's career in physical oceanography began with a course his senior year at Harvard, following which he was selected to serve as an oceanographic technician on a floating, arctic ice slab for 4½ months during the International Geophysical Year (1957–58). After earning an MA in Physical Oceanography at the Johns Hopkins University, he worked for four years in Lakes Michigan and Erie studying water currents and dispersion for the US Public Health Service, before joining a water quality study of Raritan Bay, NJ. When the EPA was created in 1970, Jack joined as an oceanographer, overseeing contractors constructing the OHMSETT facility for evaluating oil spill cleanup technology and then managing the completed facility. Later promotions to Section Chief and Branch Chief shifted his duties from managing research contractors' efforts to managing EPA personnel.

Since retiring to coastal Maine in 1996, Jack has been serving on his town's conservation commission, on the board of his local land trust, as a docent for the Farnsworth Art Museum, and his local community college in several capacities. In February 2017, he circumnavigated Cape Horn on a cruise ship.

Figure 7.3.1.1 *Hurricane evacuation zones for New York City, showing Hudson and East Rivers, Raritan and Jamaica Bays, and Long Island Sound. When a coastal storm is approaching, the City may order the evacuation of neighborhoods in danger of flooding from storm surge, starting with Zone 1.*

Source: http://www.nyc.gov/html/oem/downloads/pdf/hurricane_map_english.pdf

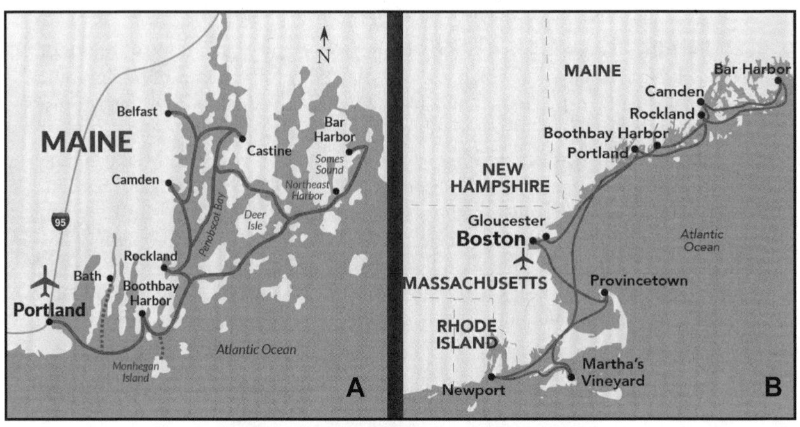

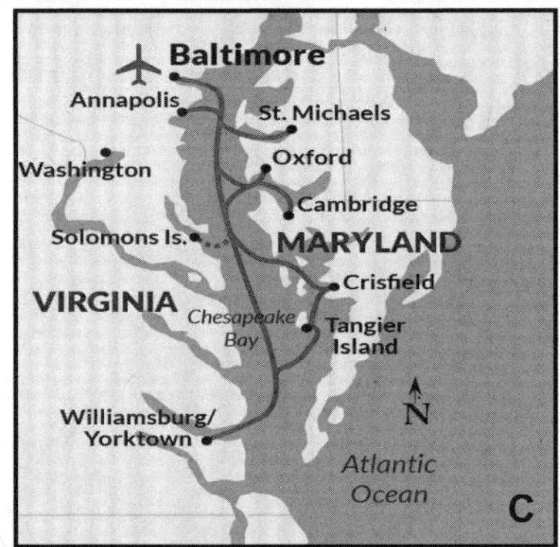

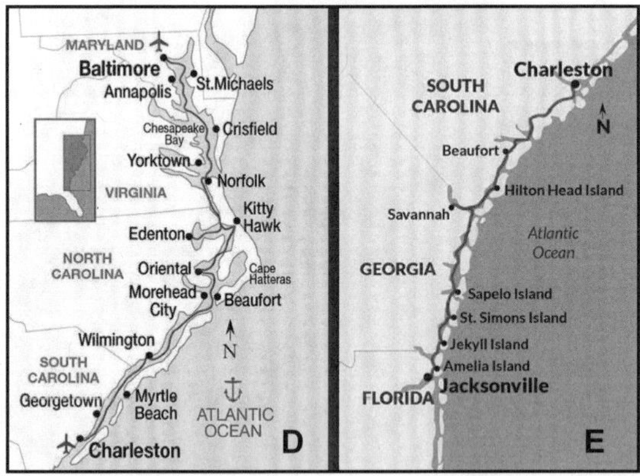

Figure 7.3.1.2 *Coastal cruising routes for exemplary Atlantic Coast ports, showing estuaries, bays, and barrier islands subject to environmental change*

Sources: http://www.americancruiselines.com/cruises/:
A: /new-england-cruises/maine-coast-and-harbors-cruise;
B: /new-england-cruises/grand-new-england-cruise;
C: /southeast-us/chesapeake-bay-cruise;
D: /southeast-us/east-coast-inland-passage-cruise;
E: /southeast-us/historic-south-and-golden-isles-cruise

Chapter Eight

SCIENCE

Figure C8 *Test of hydrogen bomb "Castle Bravo", in March 1954*
That test, one of several H-bomb explosions that month, was the largest in yield of any US nuclear explosion.

Photo source: https://commons.wikimedia.org/wiki/File:Castle_Bravo_(black_and_white).jpg

Chapter Eight
SCIENCE

Technology

Medicine

Technology

Science: 1957–2016

So We Decided Not to Blow Ourselves Up

Victor K. McElheny

In the spring of our freshman year, as most of us focused on our choice of major, we received, along with the rest of the world, a startling announcement. Standing next to President Eisenhower, the Chairman of the US Atomic Energy Commission told a Washington press conference that the hydrogen bomb that had been tested in the Pacific on March 1, 1954, was capable of destroying the entire New York metropolitan area. Across the world, newspapers showed a vast fireball enveloping the Manhattan skyline. In Matthews 37, looking across the Yard to University Hall, I studied the story and pictures with amazement. It was the first clipping for my lifelong collection of popular coverage of science and technology (now in the MIT Archives and Special Collections).

Hydrogen Bombs and Mutually Assured Destruction

The force of the explosion was equal to 15 million tons of TNT, about three times what the designers had expected. Dangerous levels of radioactivity from the blast had forced the evacuation of nearby islanders, and a shower of radioactive coral had spread like snow over the decks of a Japanese tuna boat that failed to receive prior warning to leave the area. One crew member died on the way home to Japan, where panic temporarily froze sales of tuna. The huge explosion swiftly drew an anxious private letter to Eisenhower from British Prime Minister Churchill, a public denunciation from India's Prime Minister

Nehru, and a prediction by Soviet leader Malenkov that an H-bomb war would mean the end of civilization.

None of us knew then that in those same March days, President Eisenhower had responded to the worldwide anxiety by meeting his council of science advisors. He told them that his priority task was to avoid a nuclear Pearl Harbor by the Soviet Union. He asked them to devise a plan for avoiding such a desperate stroke by an essentially weak nation. Under MIT's president James Killian and others such as the Harvard dropout Edwin Land '30, the scientists of the Technological Capabilities Panel complied. Within months, they outlined a rapid, staged buildup to an unanswerable deterrent of bombers and both short- and long-range missiles on land and at sea.

That plan for offense and defense also called for something possibly even more significant for the long run. This was sustained surveillance of the Soviet Union's military preparations from above, first by glider-like U-2 airplanes and then by spy satellites. The idea was to substitute facts for fevered "worst case" imputations from military leaders and their industrial allies, and instead to give us concrete limits on how big our strategic forces had to be. Eisenhower's aim was to defend democracy without bankrupting us or turning us into a garrison state.

So, only nine years after two different nuclear bombs—developed in fear that Hitler would get them first—had destroyed Hiroshima and Nagasaki, humanity faced an explosive 1,000 times as powerful. The chance that civilization would extinguish itself seemed very real. This perception was dramatized in Stanley Kramer's powerful film drama *On the Beach* and Stanley Kubrick's black comedy *Dr. Strangelove*. But humanity pulled back. Somehow, and partly in secret, we decided that we would not destroy ourselves. The task, instead, was survival. Instead of thinking that science would kill us, we would have to pursue science even more intensely than ever as we struggled to grow more food, conserve water, combat diseases of youth and age, detect and slow down climate change, disarm, and intensify the rapid and general flow of information.

But in March 1954, I had little idea how such issues would dominate my journalistic work. I was planning to major in Social Relations (where I eventually did a senior paper on the psychology of political opinions) because I had decided that sociology and psychology helped explain the forces that drove history. Indeed, Harvard's grouping of anthropologists, sociologists, and psychologists was based in good part on a hope that a critical mass of social scientists would help avert another disaster like World War II.

Becoming a Journalist

And, at *The Harvard Crimson* (upstairs as a reporter and editor and downstairs as a paid proofreader), I worked hard to prepare myself for a career as a newspaper reporter in which I could witness and chronicle history as it happened. A highlight was my assignment (by David Halberstam '55) to cover the contempt of Congress trial of a former Harvard psychology researcher, Leon J. Kamin, for refusing to answer questions put by Sen. Joseph R. McCarthy. US District Judge Bailey Aldrich '28 acquitted Kamin on the narrow grounds that McCarthy's committee had no purview over the lab where Kamin worked in World War II.

As with so many of us, my career got going because of the help and example of others. Having headed my prep school newspaper at Phillips Exeter (strenuous training in "localizing" national issues) and covered a complex legal case for *The Crimson*, I did not want to start out as a copy boy, even at *The New York Times*. I wanted to cover something exciting and important. And Halberstam, having gone to Mississippi and then Tennessee to cover civil rights, was already free-lancing for national magazines about such subjects as the murder of Emmett Till.

Just after our Graduation, the head of *Look* magazine and a former chief of the Exeter paper, Gardner Cowles, told me that my job search should be wide. He told me, "Write everybody." So I wrote 150 daily papers, mostly across the South, which I had visited on cross-country summer hitchhiking trips in school and college. Of 60 replies, I judged 30 non-perfunctory and wrote back asking if they'd see me if I dropped by. And 15 wrote back. After one offer (for which I'd turned down another) evaporated, I hitchhiked and bused to Florence, SC, and secured a one-month trial at *The Florence Morning News*. Before reporting for work, I took a weekend to call at *The Winston-Salem Journal and Sentinel* and *The Charlotte Observer* before dropping down to see Halberstam, who was in clerk-typist's school at Fort Jackson, SC. Days after a very happy and busy month at Florence had produced a permanent job, the call from the much-larger *Observer* came.

The Space Race

Meanwhile, almost covertly, scientists on each side of Churchill's Iron Curtain confronted the imperatives of survival. To avert Armageddon, they knew they had to talk constantly to each other over back channels. They found a safe but momentous subject: harnessing the world's science to understanding our home planet. They gave it a name: the International Geophysical Year (actually from July 1957 through 1959). Under IGY's auspices, a California scientist named Charles Keeling began measuring the accumulation of carbon dioxide in the atmosphere at two very isolated places, at the South Pole and on a volcano in Hawaii. (In the 58 years since, those instruments have documented a 30 percent increase in carbon dioxide, to levels not seen in hundreds of thousands of years.)

Also for the IGY, on Oct. 4, 1957, the Soviets pulled off a spectacular Cold War stunt. They used one of their first three intercontinental missile tests to put a small scientific observatory into orbit. It sent radio waves downward through what is called the ionosphere, a layer of particles in the upper air off which we bounce AM radio signals. The Russians called it *Sputnik*.

All of a sudden, by the mysterious emotional processes that seem to underlie history, a new tool of science acquired huge symbolic importance. *Sputnik* seemed to show communist ideology pulling ahead of capitalist. Americans felt that they must dramatically step up their scientific effort. The local effects were immediate and dramatic. Cities like Charlotte, conscious of the link between well-paid teachers and holding onto advanced industries, began beefing up their science courses. The direction of the local science museum became something worth fighting over. Science began looking like a vital subject, alongside politics and economic development and civil rights. During nine months of invaluable training on *The Observer*'s copy desk, I started writing a weekly science news summary for the Sunday paper. I maintained the column until I went off to Harvard for a Nieman Fellowship in 1962–63.

Becoming a Science Reporter

As a young, cheap, and available cub reporter on a vibrant paper recently purchased by the Knight chain, I could be sent to doing stories about new kinds of surgery in local hospitals, or research in a local textile fibers laboratory, or work to develop genetically uniform forests for the paper industry, or fisheries research on the Atlantic coast, or the arrival in Charlotte of direct dialing of long-distance telephone calls.

I could be sent to Antarctica to cover in depth the life of scientists at the very edge of Earth. That assignment led promptly to numerous appearances in local school science classes, and talks at local civic lunch clubs, demonstrating to my editors that science coverage was a crowd pleaser.

I could go to Oak Ridge to see what the pioneers of the Atomic Age were doing now that the Space Age had started, or to Washington, DC, to get at the burgeoning science behind the weather reports, including attempts to forecast farther ahead, to track the migration of clouds of polluted air, and to study the weather from space.

In 1962, it was exciting to pull together for *The Observer* the avalanche of wire-service reporting of the dramatic three-orbit space flights of John Glenn and Scott Carpenter. That same year, I attended in Washington the talks given by Glenn and Soviet cosmonaut Gherman Titov, who orbited the earth 17 times in 1961.

Freeing me for learning my craft was the law many of us benefited from: the Reserve Forces Act of 1955. Under RFA 55, draft-eligible men could serve six months' active duty and then continue for 5½ more years in the Army Reserves. During my active duty in 1958, I had the immense good fortune of attending the excellent Army Information School at Fort Slocum on an island off New Rochelle, NY. The eight-week course provided training in everything from photography to broadcasting—truly a multi-media experience. I was chosen to lead a mock newsroom in a management exercise and became the course's Honor Graduate.

The Quiet Missile Buildup

After 1957, the blazingly public manifestations of the Space Age provided—as Eisenhower intended—a magnificent cover for America's immense and hurried response to what was seen as early as 1954 as a Soviet lead in developing missiles to carry nuclear weapons hundreds or even thousands of miles to hit enemy targets. Eisenhower's Killian panel recommendations energized a multi-front technological response to the Soviet threat, largely out of the public eye. To replace shorter-range jets based in places like Morocco and Spain, America built some

600 B-52s to carry H-bombs from the continental US to Russia. How many of them would be able to return to their bases was not clear. The path to using missiles was cleared with development of bomb-bearing nose-cones that could survive the fierce heat of descent to the target. More than 40 Polaris nuclear submarines, able to stay submerged for months at a time, were built to roam the oceans carrying clusters of 16 quick-launch solid-fuel missiles.

Generations of land-based missiles were developed almost simultaneously. Medium-range Thor and Jupiter rockets were soon superseded by liquid-fuel Atlases in concrete boxes on the surface, Titans in silos, and solid-fuel Minutemans in silos across the Great Plains.

Spy Planes and Satellites

By 1961, flights by US spy planes and spy satellites made it clear that the United States had a more powerful array of ultimate weapons than the Soviet Union. The U-2 spy plane, which spotted the first big Soviet missiles on the launch pad in 1957, flew in secret for nearly four years until one was shot down over Russia on May Day 1960. This spectacularly ended prospects for a summit between Eisenhower and Soviet leader Khrushchev. The downing of Gary Powers on May Day 1960 did not blind the American President for long, however. In August 1960, after a heartbreaking series of failures, the first of America's Corona spy satellites sent down a nose cone with 24 hours of nicely shadowed, near-noontime photos in strips across the Soviet land mass. That fall, a Corona photo showed a small ring of liquid fuel missiles in one location. That's all there were. That photo lay on the desk of Kennedy's Defense Secretary Robert McNamara when he entered his Pentagon office on Jan. 21, 1961.

The US had the drop on Russia, and on October 21, 1961, Roswell Gilpatric, the deputy Secretary of Defense, said so in a blunt speech to the Business Council at the Homestead Hotel in Hot Springs, Virginia. On behalf of the Kennedy Administration, Gilpatric spelled out America's newly assembled arsenal, including the ability to administer a crushing "second strike" after a nuclear attack. He derided the Soviet Union's "bluster and threats of rocket attacks against the free world," adding that these "must be evaluated against the hard facts of United States nuclear superiority." Khrushchev, who had demanded what amounted to a western abandonment of Berlin by the end of the year, had to gulp hard and withdraw his demand. The humiliation was sharp enough to spur the following year's attempt to sneak Soviet nuclear missiles into Cuba.

Peaceful Space Activities

Next to this extraordinary Cold War crash mobilization, the years after *Sputnik* witnessed a more peaceful explosion in space, one that has sunk below the horizon for most people while influencing our lives profoundly every day. It involves something perhaps even more remarkable than human space flight: I refer to human telepresence in space, not only to gather treasures of knowledge but to perform useful work for all humanity. The continuing torrent of space robots transmits huge chunks of data across the oceans, observes the world's weather hour by hour, tells people exactly where they are on the earth's surface, and captures minute details of enemy movements and capabilities. Projecting human curiosity, scientific robots from the United States and other nations continually go into space in search of new knowledge of a universe in which Planet Earth rushes along near one of a hundred billion stars in a galaxy of stars that takes 200 million years to rotate once. That galaxy is just one of a 100 billion stretching across billions of light-years of distance. A light-year, already embraced by the human imagination, is six trillion miles.

On April 1, 1960, less than three years after *Sputnik*, and just a year after a Russian rocket had hit the moon, an American satellite called Tiros aimed its electronic camera toward Earth and beamed down pictures of cloud patterns moving across the planet. This feat opened the era of regular tracking of hurricanes in rich and poor regions alike.

On July 10, 1962, the spherical Telstar communications satellite, speckled with newly-crafted solar electric cells, went into orbit, and, thanks to a dish antenna at Pleumeur Bodou in Brittany and another in Andover, Maine, Yves Montand could sing on live television for viewers in America.

Also in 1962, one of the first of the space robots, *Mariner 2*, whizzed by Venus and told us that this size-twin of earth—shrouded in thick clouds of carbon dioxide, and turning on its axis just once every 243 Earth days—had no detectable magnetic field. The contrast with rapidly spinning Earth, with belts of particles trapped by a strong magnetic field, was stark.

Exploring the Solar System

Like all the succeeding cosmos-exploring spacecraft, the Venus fly-by observatory was piloted from control rooms on Earth. Future explorer craft not only flew by but also orbited or landed on planets and comets and asteroids of our own solar system. Other space robots went into orbit for decades to observe the universe in x-rays and ultraviolet and visible and infrared wavelengths to understand the births and evolution and deaths of planets and stars and star systems. We're at the point today when we get occasional weather reports from Saturn's biggest moon, Titan, relayed by a robot called Cassini that has been orbiting Saturn since 2004 and will crash into the planet, gathering data to the last, in September 2017.

This glorious cascade of discovery, with engineers and researchers on Earth traveling virtually to the edge of the universe, makes it seem strange to me that people constantly complain that human pilots, after six visits to the moon half a century ago, are confined to a Space Station just 250 miles above our planet.

My Commitment to Science Reporting

In Charlotte in the heady days after *Sputnik*, it seemed natural to attend a string of briefings for science reporters staged with support from the US National Science Foundation. The first of these, two weeks in February 1960, was sponsored by New York University. A blizzard of lectures and visits took me on a trip to the mountaintop and helped commit me to science reporting. Newly minted science reporters from around the country met leaders in the field, including the cocky, physics-trained CCNY graduate Earl Ubell of the New York Herald Tribune. We heard from a founder of modern computing machinery, Herman Goldstine of IBM, and visited both Bell Telephone Laboratories in Murray Hill, NJ, and the Brookhaven high-energy physics lab out on Long Island.

Navigating the long, collaboration-spurring corridors of Bell Labs, perhaps the greatest of all industrial research centers, we could hear one of the pioneers of the communications satellite, John Pierce, tell us that the biggest factors in science communication were scientists talking to each other on the telephone, and hopping planes to converse face to face.

Bell Labs glittered with brilliant basic science, but its origins lay in mundane tasks of putting the phone calls through. The first task was to perfect an amplifier for trans-continental long-distance calls in

1915. Light-heartedly, Pierce reminded me that the payoff from investing 2 percent each year of your phone bill in Bell Labs produced a 2.25 percent annual increase in completed telephone calls per Bell System employee. The underlying point was that the volume of phone calls—nerve impulses of the society—kept swelling so fast that you couldn't keep handling them with operators (lovingly mocked by Lily Tomlin) asking, "Number, please." As in most of modern life since the Industrial Revolution began ten generations ago, automation in making the connections was inevitable.

As America, Russia, and other countries rushed into the Space Age, the stories quickly got bigger for me. In 1962, I received a breathless hour's briefing on America's progress in sending men to the moon and back from James Webb, NASA Administrator. It occurred just a year after President Kennedy announced the goal of what became the Apollo moon flights by the end of the decade. Also present was Terry Sanford, Governor of North Carolina, whom Webb was visiting as he planted the multibillion-dollar new space agency, NASA, physically and politically across the country. At the end of the briefing, Governor Sanford smiled, raised his eyebrows ironically and asked me: "Did you get all that down?"

In those same months, the ferocious controversy surrounding Rachel Carson's warnings in Silent Spring about indiscriminate use of pesticides led to my front page interview with North Carolina's commissioner of agriculture, in which he said new regulations were necessary.

In building a science beat in the Carolinas, I could see how global—and local—the issues were. And I could see a lifetime ahead of reporting what was genuinely new about our times even if nothing so exciting as Armageddon was likely to happen.

Impact of Science on Human Affairs

In 1959, C.P. Snow's *Two Cultures and the Scientific Revolution* heightened my sense of the immense impact of science in human affairs. My liberal politician-journalist cousin Elizabeth Fetter of Philadelphia put me onto it. Snow's stunning final chapter predicted that science would be a dominant world influence in the decades ahead, particularly in pushing the developing countries toward far larger geopolitical influence. He was emphatically reminding us that economic development is the major arena, along with medical care, where science intersects with our daily lives.

The force of this point was obvious just a few years later, when I toured India's scientific establishments in 1965 and 1966 for *Science* magazine, covering the gamut from nuclear power to the Green Revolution in agriculture. Focused on economic development, India aimed to get around a highly uneven distribution of coal for electricity by developing its own nuclear industry, including the separation of plutonium from "spent" fuel rods. Hoping to escape a major dependency on imported food grains (which was then a million tons a month), India was building up supplies of short-straw wheat seeds, that is, wheat selected to put more of its mass into grain rather than stalks. Over ten years, Indian wheat varieties were crossed with strains imported from Mexico, site of the pioneer plant breeding of Norman Borlaug and his colleagues. Now India's farmers could plant them for higher yields to feed hundreds of millions of people.

Again, the Green Revolution was one of those profoundly influential movements that started and continued largely out of the public eye, at a pace slower than the grass growing, and covered by few journalists.

Figure 8.1.1.1 *Norman E. Borlaug, PhD, examines wheat stocks at the Rockefeller Agricultural Institute in Atizapan, Mexico, 1970.*

Photo source: Academy of Achievement (AP Images), http://www.achievement.org/achiever/norman-e-borlaug/

Borlaug had just won the Nobel Prize for Peace for his efforts to promote peace through improved agriculture. Planting the same seeds at different altitudes, exposing them to different temperatures, sunlight and rainfall conditions enabled Borlaug to create wheat varieties that flourished under varying environmental conditions. Over time he realized that tall thin stalks of wheat collapsed under the weight of their own grain. In the 1950s, by cross-breeding with a Japanese dwarf strain, he developed a semi-dwarf strain of thicker, stronger stalk, capable of supporting a heavier load of grain. Crossing these with his rust-resistant strains produced ideal wheat for Mexico's needs.

My Approach to Reporting on Science

Just a few years after my accidental beginnings as a science reporter, I had established an approach to journalistic work. First of all, I focused on the material circumstances of human beings, not on ideology or science fiction. I was constantly being pulled toward the applications of science in the world of business, in manufacturing and transportation and energy and communications—changing people's comfort and safety, lengthening life spans, raising a large fraction of humanity above mere subsistence, and creating problematic effects like pollution and climate change.

The industrial revolution in England after 1760, the fountainhead of modern productivity and wealth, continually fascinated me. In basic science, I concentrated on astronomy and the new biology of DNA, giving less attention to the evocative subject of animal behavior. Although trained in sociology and social psychology, I gave more attention to how cells worked and less to the ever-receding frontier of how the brain works. I found myself attuned more to researchers who insisted on attacking "amenable" problems rather than speculating on puzzles without a visible path to solution.

Such attitudes were reinforced over the next two decades. Six months covering science in Swedish industry exposed me over and over to such industrial processes as mining iron ore in the north, converting it into steel in the center of the country, and using the steel to build ships in Gothenburg. Three years based in London for *Science* allowed me to witness a rapid rebirth of European science in response to the American challenge. At *The Boston Globe*, I not only covered advances in life science and astronomy, but also the Apollo missions to the moon, which transformed a Cold War stunt into our first detailed look at another planetary body.

During a year as a Polaroid Corporation consultant, I wrote an account of a radical restatement of instant photography with the SX-70 system. It was brought on by the company's founder Edwin Land (whose biography I wrote many years later after his death). This wrenching "disruption" showed me a vast and intricate project, plunged me into an array of teams of researchers, and brought me into huge factories for coating the SX-70 film negative, assembling positive and negative into the iconic white film units, and the joining of many subunits into the little folding camera with its red start button and whirring motor.

At *The New York Times* for five years, I had a chance to define what a beat labeled "technology" would mean in practice. It was not just the latest copier from Xerox. It meant developments like the falling-off of productivity improvements after 1970, the development of microbes that could detect the cancer-causing potential of various chemicals, communications satellites taking up "stations" 22,300 miles above the equator, rampant increases in the power of tiny silicon chips for handling electronic data, the struggle over the future of nuclear power, Chinese agriculture, and, most spectacularly of all, the total failure of New York City's electric power system on July 13, 1977, when power lines north of the city were struck repeatedly by lightning. The power failure, which lasted more than 24 hours, not only led to a wave of looting in several neighborhoods but also laid bare, like the cut of a surgeon's knife, a huge, almost invisible technical system on which everyone depended for a modern existence.

No wonder I have felt a continual increase in the excitement of the manifestations of science in our daily lives. After a Parris Island stint of four years running a conference center at Cold Spring Harbor Laboratory in 1978–82, I felt ready for the managerial challenge of founding the Knight Science Journalism Fellowships at MIT.

Victor McElheny, born in Boston and raised in Poughkeepsie, NY, was a science reporter at *The Charlotte (NC) Observer* (1957–63), *Science* magazine (European correspondent 1964–66), the *The Boston Globe* (science editor 1966–72), and *The New York Times* (technology reporter 1973–78). After four years as inaugural director of the Banbury Center of Cold Spring Harbor Laboratory (1978–82), he became the founding director of the Knight Science Journalism Fellowship at MIT (1982–98). He is the author of biographies of Edwin Land of Polaroid and James Watson of DNA, and of a general history of the Human Genome Project.

Artificial Intelligence

Artificial Intelligence in Our Lives

From Google to Hands-Off-Parking and Minds-Off-Driving to Robo-Investing and Big Brother: A Liberal Arts Major's View of Burgeoning AI Developments

James L. Joslin

On an iPhone somewhere, the user is asked in a computer monotone: "How can I help you?" User answers . . . "Siri, how long can a Caucasian male aged 81 years, with a college degree and in good health, expect to live?" And Siri replies, "Here's what I found . . . . // Try the Life-Expectancy Calculator at www . . . ."

At the Los Angeles Airport Marriott Residence Inn Hotel, standing next to the registration desk, is a three-foot-high R2–D2-like robot on rollers with bluish eyes blinking. After checking in, as the writer and his wife enter the elevator heading to their eighth floor room, "Wally the Butler" (as he/she/it introduces itself) follows, electronically selects the seventh floor, and announces it is delivering toothpaste and extra facecloths to a guest's room. Wally also suggests that if we would like coffee from the lobby Starbucks, it would be happy to fetch it for us. As we depart the next morning for our flight home, Wally is dutifully standing at the hotel check-out desk, and (enabled by artificial intelligence facial recognition technology) remembers our name and wishes us a safe flight.

Ideas (technologies) that seem unthinkable to a present generation often become conventional with time. Artificial Intelligence (AI), the notion that computers will eventually replicate humans as sensory beings, is one such outlandish assertion.

In almost any direction one turns today, some form of computer-based information-processing technology intrudes, whether to the individual knowingly or not. Artificial Intelligence has already transformed our lives. From the punch-card-driven mainframes of the 1960s to the voice-activated instantaneous cell phone response applications of today, the elusive era of brutish computers armed with chips (number-crunching power is now doubling every 2.5 years according to Intel), designed to facilitate algorithms that replicate the way the human brain processes information, is said to be finally at hand. Whether during a Google search, or while conversing with Siri on an iPhone, Amazon's Echo, or Nuance's Dragon v15 deep learning speech engine, or tracking your travel patterns when using EZPass on the Massachusetts Turnpike, various forms of artificial intelligence programs are at work behind the computerized voice or screen.

Broadly speaking, AI is the branch of computer science that attempts to model the mind and the process by which the mind attempts to diagnose and solve problems, make choices, or resolve conflicts. The ultimate goal for a specific AI application is to replicate the thinking pattern of a sensitive human expert in a selected domain. It would appear that the global golden age of AI is now at hand; or is it?

What Is AI Anyway, and How Pervasive Is It in Our Lives Already?

As indicated, AI is, broadly speaking, software with logic devised, and code written, to approximate human cognitive reasoning patterns. Whether to recognize images, schedule meetings, process human speech, simultaneously translate languages, drive autonomous vehicles, or help doctors and other professionals make diagnoses and remedial decisions, it can be thought of as "... a rational agent that perceives its environment and takes actions that maximize its chances of success at some goal...."[1]

Computers have been used for decades to increase automation tasks and efficiency. Until early in this decade, AI programming has been mostly driven by rules-based (i.e., "if-then") tools of logic and programming language. But as AI enters the real time mainstream, humans and machines are expected to collaborate in new ways, on ever-more sophisticated assignments. Such inferential-reasoning electronic machines, learning from their own experience, we are told, will be able to take on more complex tasks entirely on their own, particularly when repetitive routines are the mode. In perhaps its worst manifestation, personal information-gathering, aggregation, and profiling in personal, corporate, and governmental applications, or deciding whether another human being's life should be ended, Big Brother (back to Orwell's future)[2] may be closer to reality than one thinks.

AI works better in context-limited, defined domains where the challenge is carefully delineated. However, as we know, human behavior is highly variable, depending on the individual's personal psychological profile and the circumstances of a particular incident. But circumstances can vary, the law of unintended consequences seems always to lead to situations and outcomes that are different each time, and humans continually confront occurrences requiring creative responses to new combinations of events.

Today, using leading-edge cameras and imaging technology, AI algorithms can assist law enforcement authorities with non-invasive DUI discovery techniques. In such confined domain space, reading facial expression patterns and corneal configuration may reveal an individual's state of inebriation. Even so, can an online "robo" personal financial planning and/or investment program for an individual investor divine a truly uniquely personal investment portfolio for a financial advisor or online user? Can such technology be a substitute for in-person advisory services in which the human connection is the driving combination behind conclusions which emerge as personal and useful?

Where Is AI Headed?

If AI's paramount goal is programming, data aggregation and analysis that solves problems, makes decisions and/or resolves conflicts replicating how the human brain operates, then that hoped-for state-of-the-art and its capabilities are still a long way from realization.

Neurologists are just beginning to understand the brain's physiology (see John Dowling's concerns in his very timely essay in this volume, "A Neuroscientist Looks at Artificial Intelligence"), and geneticists have only relatively recently successfully mapped the complete human genome.

Complicating the problem is that behaviorists, during the past 25 years, have learned that the classical economic model of "rational expectations", in which individuals always optimize personal financial resources, is flawed. Until science unlocks the secrets of how to account for, and remove (or include) emotional impulses in the human mental process equation, computer scientists will continue to have difficulty devising processing logic that learns from its own experience the way individuals do. "Artificial emotional intelligence" is today where aeronautical science was perhaps in the 1930s. Today's AI applications might be likened to the "smart calculators" of the late 1960s.

AI implementations today are to be found in robotics, attempts to leverage Big Data aggregation and sorting tasks, formulations to optimize Internet search engine performance, scan, interpret, and parse text language as well as assist in narrow-context decision-making tasks. For example, it compares and identifies nuances in the language in successive Federal Reserve Bank bimonthly policy statements.

> "*Operating in the background (of which most users are unaware), narrowly defined AI algorithms have automated many user routines in shopping, net browsing, driving, manufacturing, flying, education, and health care, enhancing user experience and ultimately redefining the rules of how business is done.*"[3]

As we know, most humans tend to learn from experience, particularly from repeated exposure to the same routine and resulting outcomes, and react by modifying future personal behavior accordingly. In its ultimate state, AI's objective is to build algorithms that learn from its observations and modify future processing routines; "machine-learning" aimed at training a system to sift through a vast quantity of data to discern a pattern which might be predictive of a future outcome.

But if the ultimate objective of AI is to exactly replicate human cognition, then AI may never realize that hoped-for, ideal state. Learning from experience and inferential reasoning in unexpected, spontaneously occurring situations are particularly human capabilities. The human psyche is influenced daily by the variety of experiences it continuously confronts and to which it adjusts dynamically in real time. The decision-making environment and emotional framework within which humans decide how to act is loaded with an almost infinite number of dependent variables. "Singularity", "Synchronicity", the era of "Super Intelligence" in which human cognition, true wisdom and inferential machine behavior are identical, remains well off into the future.[4]

Beyond this, computer scientists have had to confront what is termed "NP-complete" problems[5] suggesting that there are some complexities, equations, in computer applications which simply are not resolvable. Landon Clay's Institute is offering a US $1.0 million award to anyone who develops a formal proof solving the NP-complete dilemma. Such intractable combinations of randomly selected starting points, all of which come to bear in problems, are rife when attempting to model human behavior and one of the soft inputs is sentiment. Sentiment, of course, however defined, must be measured, some form of aggregation agreed to, and then quantified for inclusion in the algorithm being developed. Enter, as well, chaos theory: attempting to identify, track and predict outcomes from an initial combination of randomly selected starting points, which compounds the challenge to replicate.

The list of hurdles creators of AI algorithms must contend with is formidable to say the least. In the global financial market domain, for instance, more specifically in the macroeconomic context, there are thousands of dependent variables.

> How can machine-learning algorithms ever expect to disaggregate the full menu of the drivers required to encompass an actionable global macroeconomic framework if the logic cannot incorporate the soft variables of investor sentiment (i.e., emotion and behavior), government policy (i.e., political compromise), and geopolitics (conflict and diplomacy)?

Orwell Was Right: *The Struggle for AI's Soul*

Stealthily, unnoticed by the public, as if it is a conspiracy among neurologists, psychologists, computer scientists, chip manufacturers, and Internet providers, AI has been evolving as a technology which could impact one's freedom of movement, choice, and even the exercise of free will!

In *1984*, the reader is warned of ever-present cameras monitoring movement, thought control police checking citizen attitude profiles, and Big Brother always watching for apostate conduct. The sense of helplessness before the power of Orwell's version of ever-present, overwhelming technology is palpable in the principal character of Winston Smith. Although Orwell in the early 1950s surely knew nothing of the future of computing, nor had any sense of how the Internet would unfold, his intuitive concerns were prescient and on point. Today, privacy issues abound already, and these apprehensions are not only limited to government and corporate intrusions. As information processing technology becomes more innovative and human-like, the advent of the dystopian world Orwell foresaw is moving closer to reality.

Ethical Issues: Dangerous, Biased or Discriminating Algorithms

As AI algorithms with time inevitably move toward replicating human cognitive patterns of conduct, and begin to closely resemble systems that are more capable of inferential reasoning, the greater the concern becomes about who has sponsored the design of the algorithm, and by what moral or ethical compass the logic is guided. Ideally, an AI algorithm should be expected to not disadvantage any party when grinding through to a concluding outcome.

An optimist might ignore the prospect that AI technology could be used for nefarious purposes. But as Einstein and his associates came to realize during World War II when unleashing the atom, the unintended consequences could, and did, have world-shattering potential. So also could AI technology in the wrong hands.

An innate rising sense of distrust of this technology is already possible to detect. Reining in algorithms that discriminate and disadvantage will increasingly be a challenge which all free societies face. Perhaps more immediately concerning are algorithms in the hands of the defense establishment that make life and death decisions without human intervention and sign-off.

This concern has not gone unnoticed in Silicon Valley, around Kendall and Harvard Squares in Cambridge, and elsewhere in the scientific community of the western developed world. Technological futurists are well into how to ward off what Stephen Hawking, when referring to the AI ethics issue, has termed a "... technological catastrophe vastly exceeding the human sort."

The immediate issue is with the development of autonomous weapons tasked with various missions to kill! With the accelerating development of drones, the convergence of instantaneous computer processing, more productive and responsive learning algorithms, as well as expanding usage of an exponentially growing list of applications, keeping the AI genie in the bottle in an interconnected online world becomes an almost impossible undertaking.

Drawing up, gaining universal acceptance, and enforcing ethical rules for AI research, development and applications, never mind global enforcement, would seem almost an insurmountable, possibly quixotic, chore. Will Vladimir Putin, or the Iranian mullahs, abide by rules of conduct drafted in the free world aiming to control the ethical behavior of such programming?

Nonetheless, such a movement is underway at Stanford, MIT, Harvard, the University of Texas, Silicon Valley, and elsewhere, all aimed at compiling a catechism for AI technical development while "keeping society in the loop". An initial report from Stanford titled "Artificial Intelligence and Life in 2030"[6] argues it will be difficult to regulate the development of AI in that "... the risks and considerations are very different in different domains ...."

Just as there is an infinite variety in human cognitive patterns, psychological profiles, and applications to be replicated, guaranteeing freedom of expression while protecting privacy rights needs to underlie an effort to codify any rules of AI development conduct. Some sense of common ground in the Western world might be gained in this challenge, but represented at the global negotiating table will be a vastly different set of going-in philosophical principles in totalitarian, autocratic, East Asian societies.

Is this Smart Gadget Actually Useful?

Computer-programmed robots have taken over automobile production lines in Detroit and throughout the rest of the developed world. Vastly improving quality control, the jobs undertaken by these automatons are performed within precisely constrained domains. Nothing more or less is expected from these machine-driven repetitive routines than a perfect weld, or a screw placed in a designated hole and turned to its optimal torque setting. The individual who once functioned in this role has been replaced; and, of course, has needed to reinvent his/her occupation.

AI-programmed interaction on the Internet between an Amazon customer and Amazon's search engine is more broadly constrained. As Amazon's AI algorithms, or Google's search activity, continually learn from a given user's questions and choices, and build their AI-assembled user profiles, the user's evermore robust file will, in turn, prompt pop-up ads in subsequent online encounters. Additionally, AI-generated targeted, unsolicited e-mails focused on the customer's indicated interests, age, socioeconomic status, location, and any number of other variables that the big data-sifting algorithms have been developed to track will further attempt to lure the beleaguered consumer to part with his/her savings.

In the individual setting, these personal data-parsing systems represent the state-of-the-art of applied consumer AI applications today. The future looms in soon-to-be driverless cars, remote medical diagnostic and treatment techniques, analytical tools to develop and measure the effectiveness of government policy initiatives, and AI applications for the US Defense Department which delegate to inferential machines the decisions to kill. The challenge ahead would, it seems, to be ". . . how to keep society in the loop" as the inevitable, inexorable evolution of AI unfolds and promises to further intrude.

For consumers, techno-jockeys, and leading-edge gadgetiers, questioning whether some of the latest AI applications represent anything more than conspicuous consumption seems appropriate. For example, is a personal hairbrush ($400) with connectivity sensors programmed to communicate with a user's smart phone app enabling an assessment of whether the brush stroke is too fast and damaging, a useful necessity? Or is a smart tooth brush, tracking the time it takes to complete each session, destined to be in everyone's bathroom, or a smart garden umbrella (today priced at $2,000-$3,000) programmed to rotate with the sun certain to become a backyard barbecue must-have?

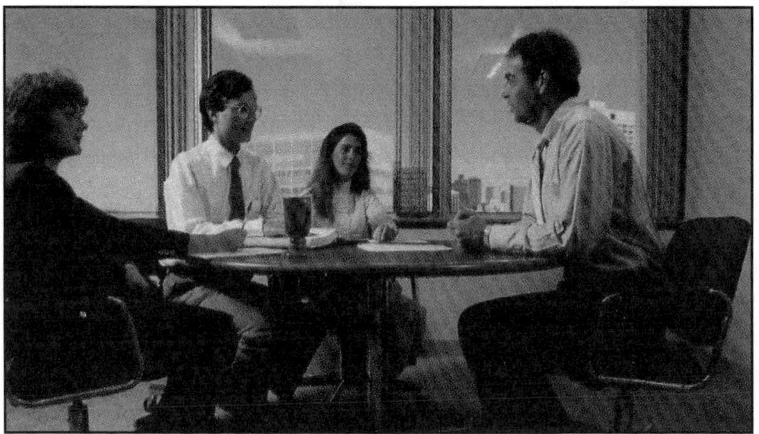

Figure 8.2.1.1 *"How do you . . . ?", Why do you . . . ?", How do others do it . . . ?", If you could start it again . . . ?", With unlimited resources, how would you . . . ?" Knowledge Engineers interrogating financial planning domain "expert" Jim Joslin, building the AI programming logic for expert system PlanPower (c. 1985)*

"A Financial Planner with Nerves of Silicon"

In October 1985 this assertion headed a *Business Week* article describing a pioneering AI program developed during the heady early days of AI's first wave when the technology was thought to be the new era in computing.

It was an early effort in Cambridge to create an expert system replicating this writer's and his collaborators' approach to comprehensive personal financial planning. According to *Business Week*, our effort produced "PlanPower ... one of the most complex 'expert systems' ever built ..."[7] *Forbes*, in its December 30, 1985 edition, "Deus ex Machina", described our PlanPower (a 6,600 what-if-then rules-based, expert system) as "... featuring audited analytical and accounting methodologies, along with computational tax-planning formulas and unique asset class allocation strategies to provide a planner with an optimized framework to interact with clients ... and simulates the thinking patterns of a human expert...."

In the mid-1980s, AI's prospects were thought to be limitless, but in Globe columnist Scott Kirsner's more recent words, "... technology moves blindingly fast—except when it doesn't."[8]

PlanPower, which produced a personalized 50-page lifetime strategic plan document, was a $40 million write-off for a major Hartford insurer for a number of reasons, not the least of which was frustratingly slow computer speed, but just as importantly a lack of understanding of elemental individual behavioral heuristics on the part of both intended planner-user (i.e., insurance agent) and individual client. It goes without saying that in today's IT world, computing power has yielded the instantaneous response times required to remove the hardware speed issue holding back AI in the mid-1980s, but replicating human cognition and the soft inputs of emotion, government policy and geopolitical events still has not been achieved. Neurologists today suggest that a fuller understanding of the brain's physiology remains an elusive goal. Further, for all the reasons cited earlier, expecting dramatic breakthroughs in such broad and all-encompassing domains as comprehensive personal and individual financial planning, and investment portfolio management, would seem beyond reach presently.

How Might AI Play Out in the Future Personal Financial Services Environment?

Jason Zweig, in a recent *Wall Street Journal* column, "An Investing Idea for the Near Future",[9] contends that AI-based platforms effectively program themselves to analyze data and solve problems. He further asserts that "Backed by artificial intelligence, a human advisor should be better able to prevent a change in emotions or circumstances from knocking you off track to meet your goals." As a decision-support tool, Zweig's contention may hold up, but AI remains a fair distance from the time when algorithms can broadly replicate human thinking patterns, particularly in such full-bodied domains as personal finance and global financial market behavior. At best such programs remain decision-support, not decision-making tools.

A futuristic application of AI in the field of personal financial advisory services might have a Registered Investor Advisor's (RIA) client submitting to an fMRI[10] brain scan analysis while the client puts his/her head in the tunnel and responds to 20 questions framed to elicit the client's response to various investment risk situations. This would be supplemented by a genome map uncovering the client's DNA pattern and hereditary propensity to take, or avoid, financial risk. The resulting data aggregation would then be parsed through an AI-based natural-language generation program that crafts a client-specific investment policy statement (IPS).

Armed with such information (never mind the inherent privacy issues in the genome map) and the agreed upon IPS, the financial advisor could then provide a road map for the client to achieve financial independence, or navigate retirement. But the weakness in this picture is that the profile has been compiled in an essentially stress-free setting. Attitudes about personal and financial risk are situation-dependent and not consistent. Financial market circumstances shift daily, if not in nanosecond timeframes. And whereas the human brain can sometimes handle and balance all these inputs and variables, programming computers to deal with this dynamic and almost infinitely interactive range of the dependent variables in this equation is not in the AI technology cards presently. Nor, if neurologists and computer scientists are pushed to opine honestly, is it likely to occur in the near future.

Is There an Online Robo Financial Advisor in Your Future?

In todays and future "robo" advisory online world, what will be the impact of AI-based support programs on the RIA personal financial advisory business? Can these online, "personalized" programs improve the odds for individual investors of achieving at least a mean reversion (less fees) investment return? Can the *Financial Times* (www.ft.com/funds) really help an investor ". . . invest in funds the smart way?" Even if sifting through an all-encompassing global financial market database, an investor or his/her advisor could isolate useful predictive fact patterns, will not ". . . both investors and their agents still fall prey to behavioral biases in interpreting what is happening, the handling of which will probably explain outcomes better than an underlying active management function itself"[11].

If mean reversion, or average (less fees), investment-return outcomes are the expected statistical norm, can an AI algorithm (purporting to learn from its own experience) ever be smarter, or make better investment choices and portfolio structuring decisions, than those who design its logic? And in attempting to find certainty in an uncertain, often irrationally, randomly-behaving domain, such as the global financial markets, in which the fuzzy math of chaos theory prevails, can an AI-driven decision-making process develop practical solutions? How will AI deal with the law of unexpected consequences, which always seems to be the missing variable in most investment equations?

Concluding Thoughts

It will be interesting to observe the inroads of AI into addressing harder-to-quantify questions involving more of a human connection. Human advisors spend much of their time helping clients balance amongst multiple, often-conflicting personal goals that have a financial element as well as heuristic and emotional components. The emotional part, particularly if attempting to predict the effect of a Black Swan occurrence, is much harder to codify and capture for AI than the financial element, and typically requires trust, non-verbal insight and intuition to navigate.

Another interesting dimension involves decision-making when outcomes are uncertain and subject to a high degree of randomness such as in the case of the global financial markets. Investing combines luck and skill, and emotions play a significant part in explaining individual investment performance over short and intermediate periods of time. Will it ever be possible for AI to fully replicate the investment wisdom of a Warren Buffett, or the creativity of a Steve Jobs?

In the end, AI software logic must be translated into an array of binomials and interpreted through hard-wired circuitry. To expect such electronic processing to achieve sentience, at least in today's highly touted "global golden age of AI", would seem a stretch, and not yet a major threat to the human condition.[12]

The real challenge that AI poses for the individual user and personal financial advisory profession is not so much whether AI-based platforms will replace in-person rendered advice, but more importantly, whether users can learn to work with it in a complementary fashion as the science evolves, thereby offering clients and advisors the best of both worlds.

James L. Joslin, a founding and current principal of Boston's TFC Financial Management, Inc., has more than 50 years of experience in private wealth management. Elected 1957 Class Secretary Commencement year, he continues to serve in that capacity, interrupted only by a stint in the Navy as an Air Intelligence Officer in the US and Europe. Currently he serves on the Boards of the Maine Maritime Museum, the International Museum of World War II, the Lown Institute, and as Treasurer of the Pioneer Institute. His interest in Artificial Intelligence dates back to the early 1980s when he first served as a "domain expert" for the nation's most extensive AI-based expert system in the financial services field, PlanPower, developed in Cambridge by Applied Expert Systems (Apex).

Endnotes

1 Wikipedia

2 Orwell's *1984* is today Amazon's top-selling book!

3 Nassib Chamoun: Chairman, Lown Institute

4 Raymond Kurzweil, *The Singularity Is Near: When Humans Transcend Biology*, 2006, takes issue with this conclusion.

5 Wikipedi, ". . . the most notable characteristic of NP-complete problems is that no fast solution to them is known . . ."

6 Stanford, *One Hundred Year Study on Artificial Intelligence* (AI100), 2014

7 *Business Week*, McGraw Hill, October 7, 1985

8 "Watch Out: The AI Bulls Are Running Again", *Boston Globe*, July 7, 2016

9 *The Wall Street Journal*, September 10–11, 2016, p. B-1.

10 fMRI . . . Functional magnetic resonance imaging; a neuroimaging procedure using MRI technology that measures brain activity by detecting changes associated with blood flow patterns

11 *Financial Times*, "Letters", Stuart Fowler, August 8, 2016

12 BCA Special Report, "AI and Deep Learning", October 18, 2016

A Neuroscientist Looks at Artificial Intelligence

John E. Dowling

In Jim Joslin's excellent essay in this volume, "*Artificial Intelligence in Our Lives*", he states,

> "*Broadly speaking, AI is the branch of computer science that attempts to model the mind and the process by which it attempts to solve problems, make choices, or resolve conflicts. The ultimate goal for a specific AI application is to replicate the thinking pattern of a sensitive human expert in a selected domain. It would appear that the global age of AI is now at hand; or is it?*"

As a neuroscientist, I would like to address the "*or is it?*"

The questions being: Is artificial intelligence really intelligence, and is AI likely to replicate the mind? Albert Einstein once remarked, "The true sign of intelligence is not knowledge but imagination." Clearly, AI has knowledge, but can it have imagination?

I continue to teach a Freshman Seminar at Harvard on the brain, and each week I ask the students to write a one-page "thought" essay on a topic relevant to the reading for the week. A recent thought question relates to the question of AI replicating the mind, and it was:

> *Computers have revolutionized our lives and are getting better all the time. Some believe that computers will eventually be able to think and be as good if not better than our brains. Is this likely in your view? How do brains and computers differ in terms of how they process information, respond to experience, and so forth? What kinds of things do brains do that computers don't do (at least so far) and vice versa?*

One of the students wrote an excellent essay and here is what she said:

> "*In spite of the rapid progression of technology, I do not believe that computers will be 'better' or ever become replacements for our brains. While computers may exceed*

brains in many quantitative categories (in speed, precision, and so forth), they lack qualitative aspects present only in humanity—both human consciousness and human conscience. Computers process information and respond to experience based on models. At best, computers are able to analyze problems and determine how to build their own models to solve them. This can come across a whole lot like 'thinking' to the observer, but there are fundamental differences.

One example, of such differences is when it comes to ethics. While brains are capable of emotion, empathy, and complex ethical assessments, such is not the case with computers (at least so far). Computers could be programmed to follow either a completely utilitarian model in assessing value and outcome and eventually determining action (which would not take into consideration non-quantitative values such as inherent values in human life, rights, liberty, and so forth), or a completely categorical model in which it obeys certain 'universal' laws in all circumstances (for example, never lie). However, either program would lack the nuances that humans use to determine ethics and make choices on a daily basis. Needless to say this is a vital function in any 'member of society', rendering computers unable to ever be full-functioning members of society."

In essence, she said that computers and AI can do many of the things the brain does and controls—walking, talking, mathematical and other rule-based operations, remembering and learning things and so forth, but will AI ever have a "mind"—feelings, emotions, awareness, rationality, understanding and creativity—aspects of mental function that most of us believe are emergent properties of the brain, but which remain most mysterious and not at all understood in terms of brain mechanisms.

Where do we stand at present in understanding brain mechanisms? Enormous progress has been made in the past century, but it has focused primarily on two areas: first on cellular and molecular mechanisms that underlie brain function—this is the province of neurobiology—and second, on behavioral phenomenon related to the mind—the province of cognitive science. But as yet these two areas of inquiry have little to say to each other, which clearly must happen if we are to understand fully how our brains work. And even if we get to that point which I suspect may take much or all of the 21st century or even beyond, will we be able to make a machine that can do what a brain does? I wonder!

And I suspect that as we learn more about brain mechanisms, we will discover aspects of neural function that we have no sense of today. Let me expand on this notion. In 2014 then President Obama announced the beginning of a *Brain Initiative*. Its initial objective is to map the connectivity in the human brain—how one part of the brain connects with another. Eventually it is hoped we will map the brain down to the synapse level—how cells talk to one another—using the so-called "connectomics methods" that are becoming available.

If successful, this will give us a wiring diagram or blueprint, if you will, of the brain. An important first step, but then we need to know how the neurons and synapses are functioning, how they change in response to whatever, and what we do know already is that our synapses, neurons, and even overall brain structures are quite modifiable—they are changing all the time. Your brain will be changed a bit by reading this essay, whether you like it or not. And I suspect that there will be surprises along the way—things about brain mechanisms that we have no knowledge of at the present time.

Why do I say this? Because of the other great biomedical initiatives undertaken over the past half-century. First, in the 1960s, there was the *War on Cancer*, which was going to eradicate cancer. Have we succeeded? No, but we have learned an enormous amount about the disease and have had some significant successes in combatting a number of cancers. When the war began, it was generally believed cancer was one disease, but today we know cancer is many diseases, caused by many factors. There is no magic bullet that can prevent or cure all cancers. This much we do know. Virtually every cancer type requires understanding on its own.

Next was the *Genome Initiative* in the 1990s—to analyze the human genome—which, it was hoped, would enable us to deal with all the genetic diseases that mankind suffers. It was then believed that one gene codes for one protein, and the guess was that we had about 100,000 genes in our genome. Indeed, the molecular geneticists had an informal lottery that asked those in the field to guess the number of genes we have, and 100,000 genes was the consensus guess.

Well, how many genes do we have, now that we have succeeded in analyzing the human genome—about 20,000. How can this be? That is not enough to code for all the proteins we have. The answer is that one gene can code for more than one protein through a process called alternative splicing. Indeed, one gene, it has been estimated, could code for as many as 30,000 different proteins, although this is the exception and not the rule. But this was totally unexpected and has made the analysis of the human genome and its protein products much more complicated.

So where do we stand today in our understanding of higher brain function—the mind, if you will? In my view, just at the beginning, and so saying that computers and AI are capable of replicating the human brain is today naïve, at least in terms of our present understanding of higher brain function[1]. I can describe to you in exquisite detail how neurons work—how they receive information, how they carry information, and how they transmit information. We know how they generate electrical and chemical signals, how synapses function and are modified—down to the molecular level, but what can I say about how aggregates of neurons interact to underlie complex behaviors? Precious little. Some simple behaviors, yes, but not behaviors that reflect the enormous number of things that our brains do effortlessly and make us human.

But let me be not too dismissive of our eventual understanding of higher brain function. Do we have any examples of a unique human attribute emerging from brain phenomena that we find in many species, and of which we have some understanding—an example of an emergent property of the human brain that may give us a model to think about. My example is *rationality*—what is involved in making rational decisions?

This example derives from the ideas of Antonio Damasio,[2] a neurologist who noted that patients who have frontal lobe lesions are often disturbed emotionally—they do not respond appropriately to emotional situations. Put in other terms, they have flattened emotions. Damasio describes one such patient named Elliot in his book *Descartes' Error.* Elliot had a sizable tumor that required excision of part of his cerebral cortex—the lower part of the frontal lobes which are known to contain the brain region concerned with the appropriate expression of emotions. Following successful surgery, Elliott, however, was a dramatically different person. Damasio wrote the following about him:

> *"He seemed not to have lost any intelligence, but rather his ability to get things done was severely impaired. He was unable to manage his time appropriately and used poor judgment when trying to accomplish even simple tasks.*

> *After repeated incidents and an apparent refusal to take advice and to do things correctly, he lost his job. He tried other jobs, but failed at them as well. He squandered his savings on inappropriate ventures, and soon his marriage collapsed. A second marriage also failed.*
>
> *Elliot appeared perfectly healthy and intellectually competent, but he was no longer an effective human being.*
>
> *Elliot was aware that something was wrong, but when he talked about his life, he did so dispassionately—like an uninvolved spectator. Never did he express sadness, impatience or even frustration. Seldom did he show any anger—he was constantly calm, relaxed and detached. In short, he had lost his feelings—things that once evoked strong emotions no longer did so. He showed very little reaction—either positive or negative—regardless of the situation.*"

Damasio links the loss of reason and rationality in patients like Elliot to their debilitated emotional state. He continues,

> "*Certain aspects of the process of emotion and feelings are indispensable for rationality. Feelings point us in the proper direction, take us to the appropriate place in a decision-making space, where we may put the instruments of logic to good use.*"

Although at first glance this notion appears counterintuitive—we usually think of emotions as interfering with rational behavior—it is also the case, however, as Damasio points out, that strong feelings incite in us a plan of action. Without emotions and feelings, why bother? And this is the way patients with frontal lobe lesions behave.

An instructive test of these ideas was developed by Damasio and his wife, Hanna. Subjects are presented four decks of cards from which they must make a selection that results in a reward or a penalty involving play money. The amounts of reward and penalty are different for the four decks: the cards from two decks provide higher rewards, but occasionally very high penalties; whereas cards from the other two decks provide smaller rewards, but almost always small penalties. Since the purpose of the game is to make as much money as possible, the trick is to figure out which decks are most advantageous to choose from (namely, those with the lower risk).

Normal individuals soon sense that two of the decks (the ones that have the small penalties) are better, and they then choose most often from these decks. When they occasionally do take a chance and choose from the high-risk decks, they show a prominent skin-conductance change—a physiological indicator of an emotional response—(this is the basis for lie detector tests), and this response builds as the game goes on, or until they no longer choose from the bad decks.

What do patients with frontal lobe lesions do? Although they, too, soon realize which decks are advantageous, they nevertheless tend to pick from the high-risk decks as often or even more often than from the low-risk decks, because the rewards are higher. They usually lose all their money and must borrow money from the investigators to go on with the game. Furthermore, they show no skin-conductance changes throughout the game to any deck choice that they make.

So linking together emotions and rationality is in my view, a nice triumph of cognitive science. But, how do neurons in the brain interact to give rise to our emotions and feelings?

We really do not have a clue as yet. It is an example of the huge chasm that presently exists between neurobiology, the cellular mechanisms underlying brain function; and cognitive science, the behavioral phenomena that relate to the mind. We even know where to look in the brain for some answers; areas involved in emotions, for example, have been identified, but how these areas work to give rise to our emotions is still very much of a mystery.

Thus, when I read or hear of brain-based AI circuits that are mimicking neural circuits of higher brain function, I am skeptical. Are these AI circuits reflective of real brain circuits? We really cannot say at present. We simply do not have that information. Yes, computers are indispensable to us today, but are they replicating our minds? Not at the present time. Will we ever get there, or *do we ever want to get there?* The latter question is for the future, when we have a much better notion on how the brain works.

Let me end by returning to one issue raised by my student in the essay I quoted earlier. This relates to the issue of ethics, AI and driverless cars, about which much has been written lately; indeed, they are even being tested today. This is a variant of the classic ethical issue taught in every introductory class on ethics.

Suppose a driverless car carrying two people sees a deep sinkhole on the highway ahead but cannot stop. What should it do if the only way out is to turn abruptly into a large crowd of people looking on? Either two people could be killed if the car continues on ahead, or as many as 20 if the car swerves into the crowd. Mercedes-Benz, in discussing driverless cars, initially stated that its main objective with driverless cars was to protect the car's occupants, but then it backed away from that statement when this kind of ethical dilemma was raised.

Would we ever entrust a computer or AI to make such a decision for us?

John E. Dowling, PhD, received his AB and PhD in Biology from Harvard University, where he joined the Biology Department. In 1964 he moved to the Wilmer Institute of Johns Hopkins University as Associate Professor of Ophthalmology and Biophysics. In 1971 he returned to Harvard as Professor of Biology, and is presently the Gordon and Llura Gund Professor of Neurosciences. From 1975 to 1978 he was Chairman of the Biology Department and from 1980 to 1984 served as Associate Dean of the Faculty of Arts and Sciences. He is a Fellow of the American Academy of Arts and Sciences and a member of the National Academy of Sciences and the American Philosophical Society.

His research has focused on the vertebrate retina as a model piece of the brain with emphasis on the functional organization of the retina: its synaptic organization, the electrical responses of retinal neurons, and mechanisms underlying neurotransmission and neuromodulation within the retina. More recently he has used zebrafish as a model system to explore the development, genetics and color vision of the vertebrate retina.

The author of over 270 scientific articles, he has written five books—*The Retina: An Approachable Part of the Brain*; *Neurons and Networks*; *Creating Mind: How the Brain Works*; *The Great Brain Debate: Nature or Nurture?*, and in 2016 co-authored with his ophthalmologist brother, *Vision: How it Works and What Can Go Wrong*.

Endnotes

1 Dowling, John E. *Creating Mind: How the Brain Works.* (W.W. Norton, New York, paperback edition, 2000)

2 Damasio, Antoinio R. *Descartes' Error: Emotion, Reason and the Human Brain* (Grosset/Putnam, New York. 1994)

Communications

The Art of Networking—Communications 1957–2017

Hermann Kopp

Growing Up

I was born in Bergen, Norway, where I lived my first 17 years. I had no brothers and sisters, but many friends. In my neighborhood we were eleven boys, just enough to form a soccer team. During WWII and the five years of German occupation, there were no organized sports, and soccer balls were very scarce. Sometimes we made our own "balls" from old newspapers. The nearest park had been converted into a prison camp for Russian POWs, who made wooden birds and other handicrafts that were exchanged for various food items. The hardships of war were part of our experience, with brothers and fathers disappearing, but at least we didn't get the horrors of war into our living rooms like we do today. So in spite of the war, we had a happy childhood.

In post-war Norway, there were naturally a lot of shortages. Housing. Food. All imported goods. Automobiles required a special permit, and sales of new cars were regulated until 1961. Many products were still rationed. One bar of chocolate per week was the limit! I still remember the cartons of food we received from our American relatives. The arrival of a new shipment was almost like Christmas—chocolates, canned peaches, apricots and fruit salad, corned beef, and—best of all—original NIBS licorice.

In 1948, my mother and I left Norway for the land of opportunities—United States of America. After a ten-day voyage on board the freighter, M.S. *Ranenfjord*, we embarked in Baltimore and drove in my uncle's "big" Chevrolet to Orange, NJ. My cousin Chris, whose mother died in a hotel fire in Oslo in 1947, became my "big brother", and I enjoyed my year at Tremont Ave. Junior High School and the summer in Camp Undercliff, Lake Placid, NY. After an exciting time in the US, we returned to Norway in 1949, but I was determined to return.

In 1954, I graduated from high school, and I applied to four American universities—Tufts (where my cousin Chris had just graduated), Princeton, Yale, and Harvard. Believe it or not, they all accepted me. I knew somebody in the three other schools, but not at Harvard. However, the cultural attaché in the American embassy in Oslo (obviously a Harvard man!) convinced me that Harvard was the only place to study political science—or government.

Travel

In the 1950s, there was a huge number of the ships crossing the Atlantic, from Southampton, Le Havre, Rotterdam, Genoa, Bremerhafen, Gothenburg, and Oslo—all heading for the Big Apple. Some of them were competing for the Blue Ribbon for the fastest crossing. My trip to New York in 1954 (I was admitted as a sophomore) included a voyage on the *United States*, the ship that had just been awarded the Blue Ribbon. My trip home in 1957 also went by sea, nine days on board *Bergensfjord* from New York to Oslo.

To fly across the Atlantic was more expensive. During the Christmas recess in 1954, I experienced air travel for the first time. Iceland's Loftleidir offered low-cost flights between New York and various European destinations. The DC4 was the transatlantic workhorse, always stopping to refuel at Gander, Goose Bay, Keflavik, Shannon, or Prestwick (who has even heard of those airports today?).

The British Comet was the first commercial jet, but it was the Boeing 707 (1958) and DC8 (1959) that really shortened the flights, and made air travel more accessible and affordable. However, the first charter flight for Harvard students, organized in 1955, flew from Boston to Paris with Flying Tigers.

Many of the great airlines of the post-war era have disappeared—PanAm, TWA, Eastern, Braniff, Northwest, SwissAir, BOAC, Loftleidir—but others are still going strong. In 2017, Norwegian—a low-cost airline—offers flights from eight US destinations to many cities in Europe and flies Boeing's new Dreamliner for a fraction of what a transatlantic flight cost in the 1950s.

Radio and Television

During the German occupation all privately owned radios were confiscated. The population was simply not allowed to listen to the news, or the coded messages from London. Even after the war, there was a huge shortage of radios.

So why not build your own crystal radio? As described by Wikipedia: "*Crystal radios are the simplest type of radio receiver and can be made with a few inexpensive parts, such as a wire for an antenna, a coil of copper wire for adjustment, a capacitator, a crystal detector and earphones.*" The excitement was huge when we detected the first signals, and could even listen to music!

At that time, I knew nothing about my great-uncle, Anders H. Bull, whom I met in Livingston, NJ, in 1948. According to Wikipedia, "*he became noted in the engineering community for his pioneering work on wireless telegraphy*, and by some sources, I've been told, was really ahead of Marconi. His brother, Fredrik Rosing Bull, gave name to the French computer company Bull when he developed his electromechanical statistics machine, and filed for a patent on a "sorting-recording-adding machine using perforated cards". That ended the domination of the Hollerith (IBM) system, bringing prices down, and giving customers a choice.

In New Jersey, I remember visiting the house of a friend who actually had a TV set in the living room! Wow! In Leverett House, I recall that there was a TV in the basement, and—I believe—Viceroy, the filter cigarette brand, ran a competition for college students where you could actually win a color TV for your dorm.

In Norway, regular TV programming started August 20, 1960, and the Norwegian Parliament debated for years whether we really needed to see everything in color. The first transmission in color took place New Year's Eve 1971, when King Olav spoke to his people.

Telecom

Remember the introduction of direct distance dialing?

It began in 1951 in Englewood, NJ. The first transatlantic direct dial telephone call was made from Dedham, MA, to Dedham, Essex, UK, in 1957. Earlier we had to go through the operator, and sometimes wait for hours. To call long distance was quite expensive, and international calls were almost unthinkable.

In the mid-'70s the cellular telephone was introduced in Scandinavia—NMT, Nordic Mobile Telephone. Many of the world's telephone and consumer electronic giants scrambled to get market access and market shares—Siemens, Ericsson, Nokia, Mitsubishi, NEC, and Motorola—were eager to develop the networks and sell the new telephones. Eventually a European, and later a world network, were established. In Europe, they used the 900 and 1,800 MHz bands; in the US 1,900 MHz became the standard. In order to operate in all networks, the more advanced phones offered triple bandwidths.

The smallest phones were "luggable". Installed in cars, they were called "mobile phones". NEC introduced a phone that was the size of a regular car radio. It was marketed as the "world's smallest" and weighed about 5 lbs. with a battery pack! I remember a visit to NEC's Osaka plant, where the chief designer told me that he expected the cell phone soon to be the same size as his shirt pocket calculator. Unbelievable at the time!

When the first SMART phones entered the market, my son, Alexander (then a Harvard undergraduate), claimed that the new iPhone would be too complicated for his old man!

Today it seems like almost everybody—man, woman, or child—has an iPhone, or something, similar. In Norway, it is quite common that children get their first cell phones before they start school.

The US telephone companies made a major mistake when they decided to charge for incoming calls. This was never the case in Scandinavia. The result is that the fixed phones are practically gone; even in the office the cell phone has become our primary phone.

The Economist has followed the telecom industry closely and has had many special issues. In the early '90s, one of them carried the headline "DEATH OF DISTANCE", indicating that the phone companies would soon discontinue their practice of charging for long distance.

Today we can call anywhere for free! With Viber, Skype, and FaceTime we can even see each other. "Skype for Business" has become a preferred service provider for many international businesses. Video conferencing over the Internet between Oslo, Bergen, Boston, Dubai, Sydney—and where ever the company's management happen to be travelling—is as simple as using the intercom in the old days. All you need is a laptop, iPad or smartphone. Because of the improved bandwidth, the sound quality exceeds by far the quality offered by a regular fixed-line telephone.

Social Networking

During our college years social networking was limited to the telephone, and the Jolly Ups at Radcliffe, the Mixers at Wellesley. If you were really lucky, you also had access to Freshman Registers from Radcliffe or Wellesley.

Mark Zuckerberg's Facebook in 2004 was an alternative to the Freshman Register and spread from Harvard to institutions in the Boston area, the Ivy League, and Stanford in no time. Today Facebook is universally accepted and has become an essential ingredient in the life of people all over the world.

Computers

Harvard's computer power in the 1950s was probably less than a modern-day laptop. While in the Business School, we were exposed to computers once. We were allowed to play a business game in a building near the Law School where Harvard University's computer was located. In 1957, Professor Georges Doriot had invested $70,000 for a 70% share in Ken Olsen's new venture. Olsen, who was working at MIT, had told the General (he preferred General to Professor) about his new computer, and Doriot said he would support him as long as he didn't put "computer" in the company name, as he would never sell more than one a year. Thus DEC—Digital Equipment Corporation—was launched, and in the '80s DEC became one of the pioneers in the PC industry.

We were still writing letters, and IBM's electric typewriter was the market leader. My thesis was printed on one. Word processing preceded the PCs, and Lexitron's screen-based processor was launched in 1973. In the early 1980s Exxon launched a new venture and built a huge plant in Pennsylvania to manufacture QYX—an alternative to IBM's typewriter that even had a memory option. Like Olivetti's TES 410, QYX's most advanced model had a memory of four—*four!*—pages.

Another product that preceded the PC and made networking easier was the fax machine. Every office needed a telefax, and there are good reasons to claim that the fax machine effectively delayed the introduction of e-mail.

The introduction of the PC in the 1980s revolutionized the computer industry.

In 1989–91, I had a sabbatical at University of Washington in Seattle. In spite of having Microsoft around the corner, most of the faculty used Macs, and we had a faculty print room where we could get our documents printed. Frankly, the whole place seemed quite archaic.

In the spring of 1994, I was back at the UW and discovered that the university had made a quantum leap. The most important development was that the UW had given their 34,000 students e-mail addresses. As dean of the MBA program at the Norwegian School of Management, I insisted in September 1994 that the incoming MBA students should get access to e-mail. We all know what has happened since!

Sixty Years Later

In the 1950s, we networked through travel, expensive long-distance telephone calls, and letters that could take from three to ten days to cross the Atlantic. Today—in 2017—letters still take a long time if we use the regular postal service, but now we have our phones, iPads, laptops, e-mails, video-conferencing and Facebook. Our homes and offices, coffee bars, cafés, Teslas, and even entire cities are wired for high-speed Internet.

But we still meet every fifth year for our class reunions.

I believe there is plenty of room for improvement. We still want to meet at least every fifth year! But with all these tools on hand, why aren't we even better at networking?

When did you last give an out-of-town, or out-of the country, class-mate a phone call?

Or send him an e-mail? Or visit?

Last year, I made seven trips to the US, crossing the Atlantic 14 times!

Looking forward to seeing you in Cambridge in May.

When will you visit me in Norway?

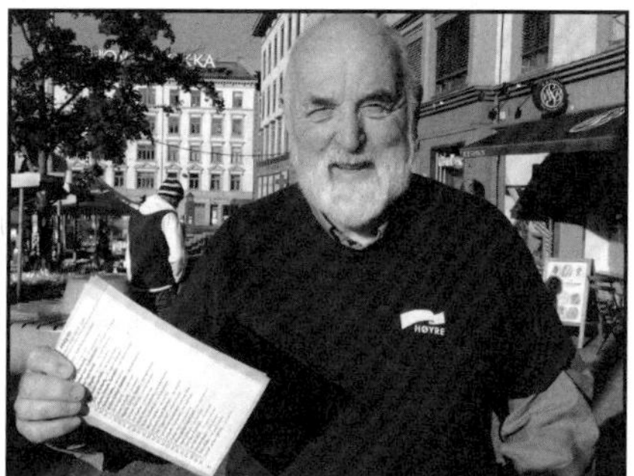

Figure 8.3.1.1 *Hermann Kopp, candidate for re-election to the Oslo City Council, hands out brochures in front of City Hall, Oslo, Norway, to downtown voters in 2015.*

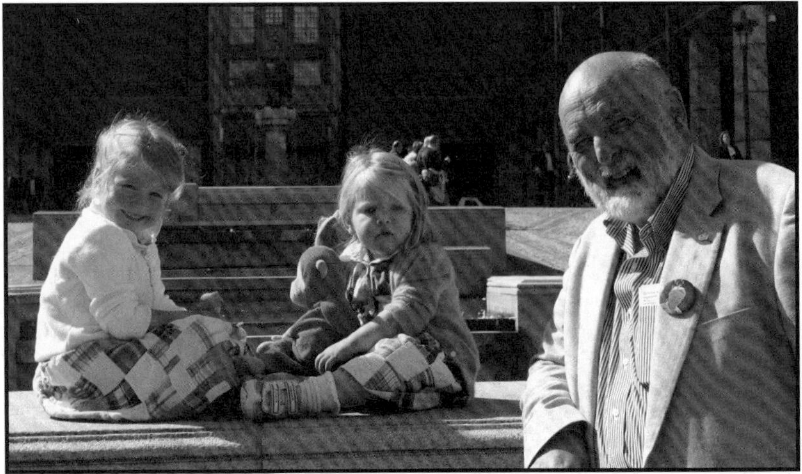

Figure 8.3.1.2 *Hermann Kopp with his granddaughters*

Hermann Kopp after graduation served in the Norwegian Army (from sergeant to captain) and then graduated from Harvard Business School in 1961 before entering his family business for six years. Subsequently he served two terms as Dean of the Norwegian School of Marketing (1967–72 & 1991–92) and from 1992–2007 held various positions at Norwegian Business School. From 1972–85 he participated in several start-up companies, including Peritel Scandinavia. He has been Visiting Professor at the University of Washington (1989–94), Universidad Gabriela Mistral, Santiago-de-Chile, (1992–2004), Babson College (2000–01), Soros Foundation, Moldova (1998), Helsinki School of Management (1997), Fudan University, Shanghai (1995–2015) and Foreign Trade University, Hanoi (2009–10).

His non-professional life has included refereeing soccer games for almost 50 years and holding various positions in Norwegian soccer organizations. Notable is his long service on the Oslo City Council, (1971–83, 2003 to present), where he is the oldest member and planning to seek reelection in 2019. He has also served on various business and non-profit boards, including Chairman of Coast Seafood AS (1999 to present) and in 2017 was appointed Managing Director of its UAE joint venture in Dubai. His son, Alexander, is a graduate in the Harvard Class of 2003.

Computers

The Digital Revolution and the Information Age

George Sadowsky

Introduction

The changes that have occurred during our lifetime in our ability to produce, disseminate and consume information have been enormous. In elementary school, we were taught how to use the library card catalogue to physically locate a limited amount of material stored in one room. Discovery of the existence of information we needed was uncertain, laborious, and often involved long delays. Today, we use search engines that give us access to a world of information consisting of literally billions of documents worldwide, in multiple languages and scripts, and we often follow information discovery by contacting people of interest to us, immediately, anywhere in the world, without difficulty.

I don't think that any of us would have been able to predict the information revolution that we would ultimately observe in our lifetime. Yet some visionaries in the past have been truly prescient. In 1908 Nikola Tesla wrote the following:

> "*It will be possible for a business man in New York to dictate instructions, and have them instantly appear in type in London or elsewhere. He will be able to call up from his desk and talk to any telephone subscriber in the world. It will only be necessary to carry an inexpensive instrument not bigger than a watch, which will enable its bearer to hear anywhere, on sea or land, for distances of thousands of miles. One may listen to or transmit speech or song to the uttermost parts of the world. In the same way any picture, drawing, or print can be transferred from one to another place.*"

In effect, Tesla predicted the information environment that exists today. I wish that we had had his foresight when we were in college.

Computers

When we entered Harvard, computers were known to and understood by a very tiny sliver of the population. The Harvard Computation Center was being run by Howard Aiken, a man who was primarily concerned with automatic human language translation, and who did not support Harvard providing computer access for "ordinary"applications, which he considered mundane. As a result, I remember Ned Benton and I taking a numerical analysis course and having to program a donated Univac I, a behemoth of a machine and the first commercial computer, to get our work done. Now some 60 years later, any of our smart phones have millions of times the power of either of these machines, and sections of Aiken's Mark I are being restored and displayed as historical artifacts in Harvard's applied science labs. Howard Aiken did not live to realize his dream, as reasonably good general automatic language translation has only been realized in the last five to ten years.

Communications

Similarly, communication of any kind was slow and expensive. When we attended Harvard, minimum long-distance voice charges, even for short distances such as between New York and Boston, cost three 1950 dollars for the first three minutes, and the calls had to be set up by a human operator. Fidelity over those original analog long-distance lines was a matter of luck. Telex, the first global e-mail, operated at a speed of ten characters per second. Facsimile transmission, or fax, was not in common use until the mid-1970s, and is itself now being largely surpassed as an intermediate technology. Fax did represent a breakthrough in that it relied upon the digitization of images and the transmission of a stream of digital information to the recipient machine, a capability that would become essential in enlarging the scope of information types that would feed the digital revolution.

History

The roots of the digital revolution and the information age started long before we entered Harvard. Digital representations of numbers, essential for any computing device, date back to two thousand years ago in the Orient with the invention of the abacus. As early as the 17th century mechanical calculators, designed by Pascal and others, used gear positions to represent digits and could perform basic arithmetic operations. Charles Babbage built two very large mechanical calculators in the 19th century, so large that they would have to be "powered by steam" .The gear position model was used in all electromechanical calculators until the 1960s.

Punch Cards

One breakthrough leading to the digital representation of information required by modern computers was made by a French weaver, Joseph Jacquard, who in 1804 built a loom run by punch cards, much like the "*computer IBM cards*" that were in common use until recently. Each position on Jacquard's cards would serve to raise or not raise an element in the Jacquard loom for one pass of the weaving shuttle, depending upon whether there was a hole in that position or not. Sequences of cards fastened together would run through the loom to produce complex patterns in the fabric being woven.

Jacquard's punch card concept was adopted by a Columbia University engineer, Herman Hollerith, in the 1880s. With the explosion of population in the US in the late 19th century, the Census Bureau estimated that it would take eight years to finish tabulating the results of the 1880 census, and they looked for viable alternatives for the future. Hollerith convinced the Bureau to use machines that he had designed to tabulate their results. Using punch cards to record data for each person enumerated, Hollerith's machines finished the census tabulations for the 1890 census in two years. Hollerith's company evolved into the IBM Corporation, and Hollerith's punch card became the dominant manner of recording text and numbers for automatic data processing for many years.

Digital Computers

Three inventions were instrumental in launching digital computers.

The invention of the digital circuit, made feasible initially by using vacuum tubes as electronic on-off switches, made possible high-speed electronic circuits that could be combined to perform arithmetic operations.

The invention of digital storage, initially mostly tiny magnetic cores that could be magnetized in either of two directions, allowed rapid storage and retrieval of digital information.

Finally, the invention of multi-use memory by John Van Neumann, in which instructions could be co-located with data and treated as data, made possible the general purpose stored program computer.

Waves of technological inventions brought the computer to where we are today. Vacuum tubes were replaced by solid-state transistors, which were in turn replaced by integrated circuits, which halved in their price-performance ratio about every two years. Advances in photolithography allowed components to continually shrink to today's microscopic dimensions. Today's "*smart phone*" has more power than a warehouse of computers at the time of our graduation.

Communications Technology

Advances in communications technology piggybacked on advances in computer circuitry. The need to transmit digital data, as opposed to traditional low bandwidth analog voice information, led to the development of techniques for the modulation of copper circuits of increasing bandwidth, but had clear limits. Geosynchronous satellites used for communication, popularized in a 1945 science fiction story written by Arthur Clarke for *Wireless World*, became a reality in the late 1960s.

Two major advances in communications paved the way for modern data communication networks, including today's Internet. The first was the invention of the laser in 1964 and the efficient manufacture of optical fiber in the early 1980s, which could transmit digital information at enormous bandwidths over long distances with very low signal loss. The second was a conceptual advance: development of packet switching technology as an alternative to conventional circuit switching, that recognized the bursty nature of much data communication and allowed many such independent communication sessions to share common circuits and thus dramatically lower the cost of transmission.

Digital Representation of Content

As the power of digital logic became apparent, so did the need to represent more classes of information in digital form. Music, captured in analog waveforms pressed into vinyl disk, evolved into rapid digital samplings of those wave forms, first stored on CDs and then on solid state devices such as the iPod. Images, historically captured on light sensitive chemical film, evolved to become a series of rectangular pixels translated into digital information identifying the intensity and color of each pixel. Video, captured initially upon film, became a series of linked digitized images with digital compression technology applied to successive frames for efficient representation.

Perhaps the most important digital representation of matter was discovered not by engineers, but by molecular biologists Francis Crick and James Watson. In 1962, they received the Nobel Prize for the discovery of DNA and RNA, the two fundamental structures that underly living matter. We humans ourselves are fundamentally digital; any of us can have our genetic material sequenced to provide a very large collection of alphabetic strings that determine our biological makeup uniquely.

It is now becoming possible to design a hypothetical living organism by creating its DNA equivalent on a computer, using cut, copy and paste as the fundamental operations to manipulate a string of alphabetic characters corresponding to the DNA of the organism. The string can then be sent to a fabrication plant and the organism can be created and sent to the designer. This capability is now in its infancy but, given the rate of increase of both computational power and knowledge of molecular biology, it may ultimately be the most important product of the digital revolution. It is no longer completely unthinkable to think that, given a complete sequencing of our genes, we could be cloned exactly in the distant future.

The Internet

The confluence of advances in both computer technology and communications technology provided the fertile soil needed for the creation of the Internet. Started in 1969 by linking four western US universities, it has expanded to currently link about three billion people in every country in the world. Created by the academic and scientific community, the values of trust, openness and sharing of information were central to its implicit value system. These values promoted the rapid spread of the initial Internet and are still important in the Internet community. However, the lack of attention to sender authentication and security of transmission in its initial design have emerged to be very serious problems as the Internet has scaled up to encompass the entire world. Vint Cerf, one of the fathers of the Internet, observed in this context that "*the Internet was an experiment that escaped from the laboratory before its time.*"

The conventional wisdom now is that the Internet is in its adolescence. What that characterization means is that we as a global community are in our adolescence with regard to how we use and misuse it. The Internet is one of a series of *disruptive technologies* with which we are now dealing. Earlier disruptive technologies, such as the printing press, the Industrial Revolution, gunpowder, the telephone, the automobile, television, atomic energy, and pharmacological birth control have caused major changes in societies, and have resulted in both short-run disruptive effects and longer-run changes. Disruptive changes can be both positive and negative, and there are many examples of both with respect to the Internet.

Robotics and Automation

When we graduated from Harvard, computers were just beginning to enter the public consciousness. One of the concerns in the conventional wisdom of the time was that these "giant brains", as they were often described, would take over jobs and that they would create massive unemployment. Such a process of substitution has clearly occurred over the years, but at an evolutionary scale, and the labor supply has generally been able to adjust to the rate of technological progress in information technology. This progress has been responsible for the growth of entire new industries as well as weakening others through enabling *disintermediation* and *product and service substitutions.*

The fear of the 1950s regarding displacement by machines seems to apply more today than then. During the last 60 years, the US economy has shifted from being primarily a manufacturing economy to a service economy. The reversal of the relative costs of labor and capital in the last 60 years has been profound, and has encouraged the substitution of capital in place of labor. Robotics has made substantial progress in the last several decades, thanks in part to the growth and sophistication of both artificial intelligence techniques and the ability to embody that intelligence, in a complex form, in machines.

This trend is likely to continue and even intensify. Unskilled and semi-skilled labor are being increasingly replaced by robotic mechanisms using local digital intelligence in the mechanisms coupled with overall networked direction and control. This trend has been made quite visible during the last US election and is causing political turbulence at present, as political pressure mounts to keep jobs within the US. However, repatriating manufacturing capacity is much more likely to increase investment in robotic technology in the US rather than replacing foreign jobs. It is not clear at present how this dimension of structural employment will resolve itself. However, given the initial actions of the new administration, this is almost certain to remain an important political issue for some time.

Assessment

Given all of the change that has accompanied us since we graduated from Harvard, what's our assessment of where we are now, and what can we reasonably expect in the future? What are the important issues with which we as a global society should concern ourselves?

The Positives

We now live in an information-rich world, and for many of us *information overload is much more prevalent than information poverty*. The Unicode Consortium and various technical organizations have made it possible to use all known linguistic scripts to communicate using computers and the Internet. No previous form of information dissemination comes close to those provided by the Internet, which supports one-to-one, one-to-many, and many-to-many communication equally easily. Users can communicate privately and they can post content that can be read by millions almost instantly. "Good enough" automatic language translation is a reality and is improving. Online education opportunities multiply and are available to anyone in the world with a connection to the Internet. In the last ten years, advances in mobile telephony have enabled connectivity within entire continents. Artificial intelligence is increasingly distributed and aiding us in more and larger niche industries. Access to information is now approaching a level playing field worldwide.

The Negatives

While the benefits of the digital revolution are momentous, widespread, and well recognized, its negative consequences are significant and a cause for real concern. The reality is that almost all aspects of human behavior have migrated to our new and shared information space. The Internet is a playground, a workspace, an entertainment arena, a world-class library, and a large collection of special interest communities, but also an arena in which misogynists, criminals, sexual predators and intelligence agencies can prowl just as well, and they do. The disintermediation of much of journalistic reporting has provided an arena rich in possibilities for the distortion of information, both unintentional through rumor propagation and intentional for nefarious purposes.

Evolving Information Technology

The constant in the evolution of information technology is that things are never constant. Reductions in cost and size continue and have enabled an important trend called the "*Internet of Things*", characterized by objects that have computing capability and that can generally be connected directly or indirectly to the Internet. Current such "things" include industrial process controls, law enforcement devices, thermostats, webcams, children's toys, wearable clothing, utility meters, parking meters, cars and trucks, home appliances, home and office buildings, military equipment, airplanes, trains, and yes, even the proverbial refrigerator. The Internet of Things also includes things in our bodies and things that care for our health. Pacemakers are programmed using external controllers. CAT and MRI scanners and other medical devices are controlled by computers and have online capability. Future medical devices are more likely to be connected than not.

Governance of Digital Technology

The governance of our digital communications world has evolved in a decentralized manner, initially under the radar of the standard telecommunications regulatory bodies such as the Federal Communications Commission and the International Telecommunications Union. The initial partners in its evolution came from research and education, and the culture that derived from that beginning was one of openness and equal and shared responsibility. The organizations that evolved from that beginning, the Internet Engineering Task Force for standards, the Regional Internet Registries for Internet addresses, and ICANN (Internet Corporation for Assigned Names and Numbers) for domain names, adopted governance structures that are now called *multi-stakeholder structures*, as opposed to classical governance through *multilateral structures* dominated by government and international agencies such as those within the United Nations system. The organizations comprising the new model of governance tend to be private sector led, but with significant involvement and some distribution of power to the technical community, civil society organizations, and governments.

Internet Access

Control of access to the Internet within countries around the world is another matter. Ever since the Westphalian system of sovereign states was established in 1648 as part of the Peace of Westphalia, the principle of non-intervention of one state in the internal affairs of another has been recognized. Each nation state is permitted to rule as sovereign within its boundaries. This non-intervention principle limits the extent to which any uniform global Internet access and use policy is possible. As the Internet grew and became more visible, its importance to national governments and the issues of redistribution of power and control that it caused became increasing evident, and nations started to learn how they could control access, either selectively or by brute force. Examples range from China's sophisticated selective filtering system to governments that have simply disconnected their countries from the Internet as required to implement their political and security agendas.

Regulatory Jurisdictional Disputes

Regulatory agencies have found the Internet to be a service that does not fit well into any of the categories with which they are familiar. In the United States at present there is a battle between administrations based upon the issue of whether the Internet is a communications service or an information service, with strong jurisdictional implications. In fact, the Internet is neither and it is both at the same time. The battle for so-called net neutrality, fought during the Obama administration and the result probably to be reversed by the new administration, typifies this discord, along with the shifts in power among industry groups that it implies.

Content and Data Collection Issues

The digital revolution has had a number of dramatic impacts on governments and governmental processes. The Internet and social media played a major part in the Arab Spring of 2011, starting in Tunisia and rippling through the Middle East. Governments are now fully aware of the potential of both the Internet and mobile telephony for rapidly mobilizing concerted social action.

Differences in societies are magnified by the immediacy and ease of digital communication. In the US, personal data collection is a thriving industry, both legally and illegally, while the European Union's data retention and privacy policies are strict. In one of the first classic cases of cross-jurisdictional disputes, the French government took legal action against Yahoo for offering Nazi memorabilia on its auction site for sale to French citizens. Content that is legal in some countries is illegal in others, yet the transmission of that content is invisible and requires only the press of a key.

A "*right to be forgotten*" on the Internet has significant support in Europe, proponents arguing that some negative data about individuals should not be able to persist publicly indefinitely. A combination of free speech advocates and personal data marketers argue that this constitutes an ominous Orwellian editing of history on the fly and should not be legitimized.

As technology that ignores national boundaries, the Internet is creating the need for the boundaries of privacy and confidentiality to be tested in a multinational context.

Economic and Societal Impact

The impact of the digital revolution on both society and business has been enormous. On the business side, one can observe Schumpeterian creative destruction in rapid action, as products and industries replace old products and industries in fairly rapid succession.

Robotics, distributed intelligence and disintermediation are playing a significant part in displacing significant swaths of jobs, leading to a situation of structural unemployment caused by technological change more than by shifting demand. The direction of this structural change is unlikely to be reversed, implying that *an increasing percentage of the potential labor force will not find permanent employment for a long time, if ever.* Public policy needs to address the issue of older workers who are unlikely to recover their former employment prospects and also the issue of ensuring that new entrants into the labor force are more flexibly equipped and trained to be able to keep up with technological changes underlying changes in labor force demand.

Digital technologies have been agents of very significant disintermediation with substantial changes in business models.

Consider the following: AirBnB is the largest supplier of rooms for travelers, yet it owns no rooms; Uber has control of the largest taxi fleet in the world, yet it owns no cars; and AliBaba is the largest seller of merchandise in the world, yet it owns no inventory.

In addition, trade in information products and niche match making become easy if not effortless, so that intellectual property can be copied and redistributed, legally and illegally, with relative ease. The protection of intellectual property, from music and movies to industrial designs and technical innovations, has become a major issue for its creators.

Authentication in a global digital world characterized by transactions with strangers has become an important issue. In financial transactions, the banking system provided legitimacy through various payment instruments including letters of credit for international relationships, but they typically relied upon personal relationships and knowledge of their customers. With the growth of electronic transactions, new business models have emerged to support more frictionless anonymous relationships. They include encryption technologies, online peer review of behavior, and experimental crypto-currencies such as Bitcoin that bypass all central financial intermediaries.

The Dark Side

There is a significant and growing dark side emerging from the ubiquity of the digital revolution. As noted above, almost all kinds of human behavior have moved to the net, causing new modalities of crime to emerge. What was once a playground for hackers is now a digital industry for organized crime of all sorts, and the early open and permissive culture of the Internet has provided a relatively insecure environment in which to expand its business. Cybercrime is a multi-billion-dollar-per-year industry. It is expanding, and has creative and innovative talent driving its operations.

Cybercrime

Some behaviors directly attack us on a personal level. Acts such as cyber bullying, spam, remote takeover of PC microphones and cameras, online harassment, social engineering leading to password theft and account penetration followed by financial theft, ransomware, online sexual exploitation, government surveillance, and child exploitation may be legal or illegal, but as a force they can serve to savage individuals' existence as well as their futures.

Anarchists

Other behaviors attack directly our stability as an economy and a society. Modern-day Luddite attacks on digital infrastructure, optical fiber and submarine cables, occur from time to time. Hackers try to penetrate the control systems of power plants and electric distribution grids, water utilities, financial networks, Internet providers, research and development labs, government offices and even our intelligence agencies, and there are indications of some success. Voting machines have been successfully hacked, and the recently expressed conventional wisdom that voting machines were not hacked in the last election is open to question.

Social Media

Social media has reinforced tribalism in many of us. We feel more comfortable associating with people whose beliefs we share, and as a result, our social media orbits tend in the direction of sameness rather than differences. This makes us vulnerable to believe rumors and incorrect information that are positive about what we think and that are negative and even destructive about what we reject. We tend to form *social media silos* that then serve as echo chambers and amplifiers of our beliefs, generating fertile ground for believing rumors and negative misinformation. Critical thinking has given to a large extent way to the pressures of the tribe.

Social media sites such as Facebook may have inadvertently created a very effective *propaganda polarization* machine that they will not be able to control. Of particular interest recently is the use of social media to spread misinformation in order to influence elections. The ascendancy and popularity of social networks such as Facebook and the believability of information from such sources have been achieved by the gratification of immediate interaction and at the expense of traditional media such as print and television. The Internet has the very desirable property of *letting anyone be a publisher*, but that also allows everyone to publish what they wish, without any test of its veracity or even its legality. Although Facebook admits concern for this, the solution for this state of affairs, if one can call it that, must occur mostly through behavioral change.

Algorithms and Biased Information

When social media, search engines or information providers decide what to show us or how to respond to our queries, they depend upon algorithms that are invisible to us. Yet the results of their actions may depend upon our previous access, introduce bias of which we are unaware, and of which even the authors of the algorithm may be unaware. As artificial intelligence increases in power and ubiquity, we will be ceding control to algorithms that operate autonomously, invisibly and unpredictably. For the most part, this allows us to delegate tasks to processes of which we approve. However, there remains the danger of invisible bias or error, unintentional or deliberate.

Security in the Age of the Internet of Things

A special challenge comes from the anticipated explosive growth of the "Internet of Things". Many of these devices are consumer appliances with limited built-in intelligence. They are fairly inexpensive, and compete in price-sensitive consumer markets. Even though they have as much risk of being infected with malware as any computer or smart phone, the design of their security component is likely to be minimal and their control software is not likely to be updatable. Ownership and location records for such devices are likely to be non-existent, so that when flaws of any kind are discovered, only conscientious owners are likely to find out, much less to take corrective action. With many millions of such devices on the horizon, these "things" are likely to be incriminated in major cybercrime actions without their owners' knowledge unless concerted action is taken to update liability and negligence criteria for the design of such "things".

To Be Continued . . .

The *digital revolution* has brought us many benefits as well as significant problems of adaptation of many aspects of our lives to the new technologies. The results are irreversible except by global catastrophe. The Internet is by far the major people-facing agent of this revolution, and if there ever were a system that could be considered "*too big to fail*", it's the Internet.

This revolution is in its adolescence and will live far longer than we will, and many challenges to its eventual success exist. Like the history of the human race, the digital revolution is in the process of evolving, and the paths that it takes and the goals that it achieves rests in our collective hands and in the hands of future generations. I wish it well.

Figure 8.4.1.1 © *George Sadowsky, February 14, 2017*

George Sadowsky received an AB degree in mathematics from Harvard, and MA and PhD degrees in economics from Yale. He has worked as an applied mathematician and a programmer, and has directed computing centers and networks at Yale University, the Brookings Institution, Northwestern University and New York University.

At the United Nations during 1973–1986, he supported numerous technical assistance projects in ICT, including the Chinese Population Census of 1982, and has worked in more than 50 developing countries. During 2001–2006 he was Executive Director of the Global Internet Policy Initiative with Internet policy projects in 17 countries in transition. He has been a consultant to foundations, governments and international agencies.

He has been a Director of ICANN, the Internet Corporation for Assigned Names and Numbers, since 2009. Previously he served on Boards of Applied Theory Corporation, the Corporation for Research and Educational Networking, the New York State Educational and Research Network and the Internet Society. From 2005–2009 he was a Special Adviser to the chair of the Internet Governance Forum. In 2013 he was inducted into the Internet Hall of Fame.

He and his wife live in Woodstock, VT.

Shared-Memory Multiprocessors

William W. Collier

I joined IBM in 1960 as a programmer. I loved programming. It was car mechanics with clean fingernails. The most fascinating aspect of the work, however, was trying to figure out the constraints which programs should obey, constraints which we did not yet know even existed, much less understand.

> One early example was learning to deal with *deadlocks* in operating systems. From that experience I learned how hard people (myself included) resist understanding new ideas, a lesson of great value in subsequent endeavors.
>
> A second example arose during the transition from uniprocessors (one processor per computer) to multiprocessors (two or more processors per computer). The move was not so simple as initially expected.

Behaviors could be seen on multiprocessors which could not be seen on uniprocessors. Dealing with these behaviors required *new concepts of programs and of machines*. Creation of the concepts came from a discussion which was broad, intense, and long lasting. One early, fundamental paper by Leslie Lamport in 1978 has been cited almost 10,000 times. The discussion continues even today. Here is a very brief *history of that discussion*, as seen from my vantage point in IBM Poughkeepsie.

In the days of uniprocessors, engineers built a machine and published a document telling programmers how it worked. Programmers read the document and wrote programs. Everything was so obvious about how things should work (and how they did work and how they appeared to work) that the two groups had hardly any need to speak with each other.

Effect of *Out of Order* Instructions on Machine Behavior

Engineers found that in certain instances they could *make machines run faster* by *executing instructions out of order*. Of course, this was done only in situations in which programmers could not detect it.

Example 1. Out of order execution on a **uniprocessor**

```
Initial value of operands: A = B = X = 0.
   L1: B = 1
   L2: X = A
Terminal value of operands: A = X = 0, B = 1.
```

In the example the machine has nearby access to operands A and X, but not to operand B (for reasons which space limitations preclude explaining here). While it waits to retrieve operand B, the machine performs the second instruction at L2 before it performs the first instruction at L1. The result is that the machine runs faster, and the *programmer never sees the deception.*

Sharing Memory by Multiprocessor Machines

Beginning in the 1960s machines were built with two (later, many more) processors which could read from and write into the same *shared memory*. The question came up: how should *shared-memory multiprocessing (SMMP)* machines behave when *two processors read and/or write the same data at the same time?* The obvious answer was that the new technology of multiprocessing should not allow SMMP machines to differ visibly in their behavior from uniprocessors.

Then someone noted that, theoretically at least, the *out of order execution* on uniprocessors, when carried over to SMMPs, *could become visible.* Specifically, two processors could interact to compute a result which could not be computed on a uniprocessor.

Example 2. Out of order execution on a **multiprocessor**

```
Initial value of operands: A = B = X = Y = 0.
   P1               P2
L1: B = 1 L1: A = 1
L2: X = A L2: Y = B
Terminal value of operands: A = B = 1, X = Y = 0.
```

Here program P1 sets operand B to 1 and then fetches the value of A to store into operand X. Since it sees a value of 0 for A, this action must have occurred before Program 2 set A to 1. Similarly, Program 2 sets A to 1 and then fetches the (zero) value of B. Since Y is zero at the end, the fetch had to have occurred before P1 wrote a 1 into operand B. Thus, a *seeming impossibility occurs*: event e1 happens before event e2 which happens before event e3 which happens before event e4 which happens before event e1.

The *impossibility argument* above relied on assumptions being made about the *rules of behavior* followed by the machine. One rule was that things happen in the order defined by the programs, P1 and P2. Call this rule *program order.* Another rule is that each write operation appears to take effect instantaneously throughout the machine. Call this rule *write atomicity.* These are just two of the many rules which programmers impute to SMMP machines.

Here are the ideas needed to explain what is happening in *Examples 1* and *2*.

> Programmers expect a machine to follow certain *rules of behavior.* Call this the *expected or apparent behavior* of the machine.
>
> Engineers may implement a machine to behave in a way which differs from what programmers expect. Call this the *actual behavior.*
>
> > A machine is called *strong* if it appears to obey a given set of rules.
> >
> > A machine is called *weak* it if violates all or part of a given set of rules.
> >
> > If a machine's *implementation* is strong, then its apparent behavior will be strong. However, if a machine's *behavior* is weak, then its apparent behavior may be strong or it may be weak.
>
> *Example 1* is the earliest case of the *actual behavior* of a machine *differing significantly* from its *expected behavior.* The actual implementation violated the rule of program order, but only in cases where the behavior could not be seen. Consequently, the machine appeared to be strong.
>
> *Example 2* shows how a *weak implementation* can result in an apparent behavior which is weak.

Seeing, and Coping with, Weak Behaviors

In the next few years others invented half a dozen other small programs which potentially could reveal distinct failures of SMMP machines to be strong. Some argued these programs justified requiring SMMPs to exhibit uniprocessor (strong) behavior.

Others scoffed at the programs, calling them "*toy programs*", and arguing that processor interactions on shared data could never be so perfectly timed as to intentionally reveal a failure of a machine to be strong.

There were three choices on how to proceed.

1) Make SMMPs strong, at least apparently. Compute only results which could also be computed on a uniprocessor.

2) Build weak machines, but claim they were strong. Ignore the possibility of toy program interactions being visible since it would be virtually impossible to prove such interactions occurred.

3) Build SMMPs to be visibly weak.

The industry eventually went with *choice 3*. The argument was that programmers know how to deal with the increased complexity of weak behavior, and that the potential performance improvement was too large to ignore. To be fair, some contemporary machines, though weak, offer massive function to make *parallel programing* easier.

Creating a Logical Model of an SMMP Machine

I was present in one of the early discussions on what the *rules for an SMMP machine* should be. I decided that this was an interesting problem, one that I could solve.

The first step was to *define the various rules of behavior concretely*. I would write out definitions and then put them away. I would come back and find them lacking. This went on for years. In my frustration I likened the effort to elephants picking up egg yolks with their elbows.

Eventually the definitions crystallized, and I published them in a couple of technical reports in 1981 and 1984. On the basis of the first technical report Prentice-Hall approached me to write a book on computer architecture. I said I'd like to, but I had more work to do before I was ready. After some detours, "*Reasoning About Parallel Architectures*" appeared in 1992.

A major argument of the book was that if engineers say that two SMMP machines are logically distinct in their behavior on shared data, then they should be able to demonstrate a program which can calculate a result on one machine which provably cannot be calculated on the other machine. The book offered many examples of such distinguishing programs.

Most *models of events occurring in time* imagine them as points on the real line. I observed that (1) what we start with is information of the form: event e1 happened before event e2, and (2) useful information is thrown away in prematurely projecting events onto the real line. I set out to create a model of events occurring in time on an SMMP in which all the information about happened-before relationships is preserved.

The result, which reifies *nondeterminism*, is a *structure of unseemly complexity*. However, the structure allows for the proof of this gem of a theorem. If all running programs see the exact same order of all changes in the value of all operands, then the result will be as if all running program saw each change in value of an operand at exactly the same instant. This is an SMMP case of a weak, actual behavior appearing to be a strong behavior *(write atomicity)*. Sun Microsystems used the theorem to argue that a machine of theirs was *write atomic*.

Summing Up

And finally, the book showed *how to turn the toy programs into real, long running programs* which consistently and reliably reveal weak behaviors in today's SMMP machines.

The programs have also proven valuable in the very earliest stages of testing models of new chips before they are manufactured, and they offer a low resolution x-ray of behavior in the memory hierarchy.

I am grateful to IBM for its support and for the chance to work with some fascinating people. I know how lucky I was in life to find something so totally consuming.

Gosh, it was interesting. Gosh, it was fun.

William W. Collier writes: "I interrupted college to join the Army, 1954–1957, emerging as a sergeant in the reserves in 1960. I finally graduated in 1960 and joined IBM as a programmer. I left in 1993 and founded Multiprocessor Diagnostics. I got a MA in mathematics in 1964 and a MS in computer science in 1986, both from Syracuse University. I married Yasuko Hatano-Collier in 1984. Children: me 2; her 2; us 0."

Figure 8.4.2.1 *Writing code with enthusiasm in ancient times*
Wikimedia Commons—File: Kunsthistorisches Museum 10th century ivory Gregory the Great 23062013.jpg

My Life since Harvard

Rohit Jivanlal Parikh

Life after Harvard College

My life since Harvard College consists of four stages.

- Four years at Harvard GSAS, receiving a doctorate in Mathematics in 1962
- Short employments: Stanford (1961–63), Panjab University (1964–65), Bristol University (1965–67) and Caltech (1967).
- First extended position: Boston University (1967–82).
- Current position: City University of New York (Distinguished Professor since 1982)

Mathematics

My doctorate was in Mathematical Logic with effectively three advisers: Hartley Rogers of the MIT Mathematics department, Burton Dreben of the Harvard Philosophy department, and Georg Kreisel of the Stanford Philosophy department. I also worked as a research assistant to Noam Chomsky for a year, 1960–61. That work done in 1960 is still widely cited under the title *Parikh map*. The notion *of inherent ambiguity* was also introduced in that work with Chomsky.

Philosophy

I also took some courses with Willard Van Orman Quine, often considered the greatest American philosopher of the 20th century. I remained in touch with him ever since but did not pick him as adviser as he had left mathematical logic long ago.

The philosopher Ludwig Wittgenstein was an early influence, but I came to understand him only when I attended a course on Wittgenstein with Arthur Collins, then the chair of the philosophy program at the CUNY Graduate center (in the 1980s). The main source was Saul Kripke's book *Wittgenstein on rules and private language: An elementary exposition*. Kripke misrepresents Wittgenstein, but Kripke, unlike Wittgenstein, is an extremely clear writer and made it easier to understand the master himself. Wittgenstein's approach has influenced my work more and more as time passed.

Computer Science

I stayed in pure logic until 1977 when, influenced by some friends at MIT, I moved into theoretical computer science. But since coming to CUNY in 1982 my interests have broadened to include philosophy of language, epistemic logic, game theory, and an area which I call *Social Software* (there is a Wikipedia page on that topic[1]).

The work at MIT (as visiting scientist) involved work on *Dynamic Logic*, which is concerned with the analysis of the correctness conditions of computer programs—how to show that a program achieves its desired result. Obviously thinking about this requires not only a knowledge of logic (to prove the correctness) but also a clear understanding of what the program is supposed to achieve in the first place.

With computer programs themselves, the task is usually easy. We know what we want them to do. But with social programs (social software) it is not always clear what we want them to achieve and even whether there is general social agreement on the goal itself. Kenneth Arrow showed in 1950 that there is no electoral procedure which satisfies certain conditions of rationality. List and Pettit showed more recently that it is impossible in general to arrive at what might be called the consensus opinion of a group of people. More about this in the next section.

Social Software

Social Software starts by noticing that while computers are now used to perform algorithms (programs), both *individual and social algorithms* have existed for a long time in society.

An obvious example of an *individual algorithm* is a cooking recipe, for making scrambled eggs, or pasta primavera.

Somewhat different is an *algorithm for going from my apartment to a hotel* in Chicago. The latter consists of various steps like taking a taxi to the airport, taking a flight to Chicago O'Hare, and then taking a taxi from O'Hare to the hotel. Each step has a precondition, and a post-condition. For the first step, the precondition is that a taxi is available, and the post-condition is that I arrive at the airport. The entire algorithm *consists of three steps*, the post-condition of each step becoming the precondition of the next.

But *social algorithms—like arranging a lecture or a conference* or organizing an election—are much more complicated and interesting. *Preconditions* for a lecture include finding a room, advertising the talk, etc. But what is the *post condition?* We do not usually ask, but somehow we expect that information is exchanged, the audience is gratified, etc.

Now what about an *election?* We expect that an election procedure should satisfy some rationality conditions. For instance, if everyone prefers candidate A to candidate B, then it should not be the case that B is elected. Also, the procedure should allow all the voters to vote any way they choose. And the procedure should treat all voters equally.

Kenneth Arrow showed in 1950 that no procedure satisfying such rationality conditions is possible. Arrow showed in effect that the notion, *the people's choice,* is logically contradictory in that it is *not always definable* (sometimes we *do* know what the choice of the people is, just not always). To use an example due to Ludwig Wittgenstein, it is like planning a trip to the East Pole. Unlike the South Pole and the North Pole, there is no such place as the East Pole and you cannot plan a trip to it.

So what is the aim of an election if it cannot be "finding the choice of the people"? Elections do something, that is certain. And hopefully that something is good. But beyond that we are not sure what to say.

Other examples of *social procedures* include auctions. It is known that the so called *Vickrey auction* encourages honesty. In a Vickrey auction, the *highest bidder wins, but pays the price bid by the next highest bidder.* This means that one can just bid the highest one is willing to pay, and need not worry about having bid too much. If Jack bids $100 and Jill bids $200, and Amy bids $75, then Jill will get the object, pay $100 and *need not* have worried how much the others did bid.

A recent result proved by myself and Tasdemir, a female student from Turkey, showed that under certain assumptions, a candidate running for office is best off being as explicit as possible. Why? If there is a question Q to which the answers are "yes" and "no", we show that it cannot be that both answers will do her harm. One of the two answers will either benefit her, or at least do no harm.

But then why are actual candidates cagey? Both George H.W. Bush and Barack Obama won their elections while remaining vague on some issues. One explanation is that "yes" may be inconsistent with what the candidate herself believes. Another is that a yes answer will help her a lot, but only with people who were going to vote for her anyway. But it may displease some other voters who were on the borderline, and they may move from voting for her to voting against her. So she gains in total approval but loses in votes.

A more recent area of interest is the *formation of group beliefs*. It was shown by Marquis de Condorcet in the 18th century that if a group of people have *independent* opinions on some issue, and each of them is slightly more likely to be correct than not, then the majority is almost certain to be correct. This phenomenon has a colloquial name, *The Wisdom of Crowds.*

But the *assumption of independence is crucial.* In practice people form their opinions from their friends, the newspapers they read, etc. And if they find some fact which goes against the beliefs of their group, they may be reluctant to change. The story of the *Emperor's Clothes* illustrates this. Each man could see that the emperor was naked but said, "*If they all think he has beautiful clothes, then I must be mistaken.*" It took a child to say aloud that the Emperor actually was naked.

This phenomenon has important effects and surely is partly responsible for the fact that America is so sharply divided into two (or more) groups with different views of the world. *Clusters of opinions form and people are reluctant to leave their intellectual home.*

Once you identify as a progressive, you may be reluctant to admit that your group, the progressives, might be wrong on some issues. And of course it is the same for conservatives.

How can we get people to think and not blindly follow their group? That is the big question for our times.

Spirituality

Growing up in India means that *religion is everywhere.* Most *religious practices* in India are just that, practices, and they are not always backed up by beliefs. Moreover, there is a heavy overlay of spirituality in the Indian tradition which has produced several major religions: Hinduism, Buddhism, Sikhism, Jainism, and smaller, more recent religions like Arya Samaj and Brahmo Samaj.

Is there anything to spirituality or is it just hokum? I have never quite known, but I am well aware not only that science does not answer all questions; science is not even able to *ask* all questions. Are animals conscious? This is not a scientific question, although we may use science to educate our nonscientific intuition.

Two people who have influenced me are the teacher J. Krishnamurti and the Buddha. Much of Krishnamurti's teaching seems almost anti-religious, certainly iconoclastic. And yet his *Notebooks* reveal an amazing number of experiences which can only be called spiritual.

The *Bhagvadgita* of Krishna is also an influence, although Krishna was more of conventional religious figure than a mystic. Krishna's theory of reincarnation resembles Plato's theory in the *Meno,* but is more detailed.

I will end this part by relating a joke about a Zen master. His disciple asked him what happens after death and received the answer that the master did not know. "*But you are a Zen master!*" said the disciple. "*Yes, but not a dead one!*" was the answer.

So the mystery remains a mystery.

Summing Up

I am 80 now but not yet retired. There was a two-day conference at CUNY to celebrate my 80th birthday.[2] There were talks by former students and colleagues.

I am already lining up speakers for my 90th birthday. I invite you all to come!

Rohit Jivanlal Parikh was born in India and came to Harvard at the age of 17. All his degrees are from Harvard. He is currently distinguished professor of Computer Science, Mathematics and Philosophy at the City University of New York. He is a three-time winner of the William Lowell Putnam prize for mathematics. He married Carol Parikh (née Geris) in 1968, and they were married until 1994. They are still good friends, and have two children, Vikram and Uma. He also has two grandchildren, Sona (girl, 4 years) and Shiva (boy, eight months).

Endnotes

1 https://en.wikipedia.org/wiki/Social_software_(social_procedure)

2 http://eva16968.wixsite.com/parikh80conference

References

Arrow, Kenneth Joseph. "*Social choice and individual values.*" No. 12. Yale University Press, 1963.

Hansen, Pelle G., Vincent F. Hendricks, and Rasmus K. Rendsvig, "*Infostorms.*" Metaphilosophy 44.3 (2013): 301–326.

Krishnamurti, Jiddu. *Krishnamurti's notebook.* Krishnamurti Foundation Trust Ltd, 2016.

List, Christian, and Philip Pettit. "*Aggregating sets of judgments: An impossibility result.*" Economics and Philosophy 18.01 (2002): 89–110.

Parikh, R. (2002). *Social software.* Synthese, *132*(3), 187–211.

Pacuit, Eric, and Rohit Parikh. "*Social interaction, knowledge, and social software.*" In *Interactive Computation*, pp. 441–461. Springer Berlin Heidelberg, 2006.

Parikh, Rohit, and Çagil Tasdemir. "*The Strategy of Campaigning.*" In *Fields of Logic and Computation II.* Springer International Publishing, 2015. 253–260.

Wittgenstein, Ludwig. *Philosophical investigations.* John Wiley & Sons, 2010.

Figure 8.4.3.1 *James Dewey Watson (1928–), American molecular biologist, geneticist and zoologist, in 1962*

In 1953 James D. Watson, with Francis Crick and Rosalind Franklin, discovered the structure of DNA. Their discovery, later described in lay terms by Watson in the The Double Helix *(1968), revolutionized understanding of the chemical basis of biological inheritance.*

In 1962 Watson, Crick, and Maurice Wilkins were awarded the Nobel Prize in Physiology or Medicine "for their discoveries concerning the molecular structure of nucleic acids and its significance for information transfer in living material". Rosalind Franklin had died in 1958 and was therefore ineligible for nomination.

From 1956 to 1976 Watson promoted the field of molecular biology in the Harvard University Biology Department, where he was on the faculty before moving to the Cold Spring Harbor Laboratory. Between 1988 and 1992 he helped to establish the brilliantly successful Human Genome Project at the National Institutes of Health.

Sources:
Text: https://en.wikipedia.org/wiki/James_Watson
Image: https://www.nobelprize.org/nobel_prizes/medicine/laureates/1962/watson_postcard.jpg

Medicine

Medical Research

Basic Science

Turns in the Road before and after Harvard

Ioannis V. Yannas

"*Please, can you show me where is Stoughton Hall?*"

That was my plea to the police officer on that September 1953 evening upon arriving at Harvard Yard. I was still clutching my generously large suitcase with which I had traveled from Athens, Greece.

My room, Stoughton 11, was on the third floor, and it was empty when I entered because my intended roommate had not yet arrived. When I met Fred from Ohio the next day he explained to me that he was a classics major. I figured that this was the method used by the admissions office for pairing roommates (classics major = Greek roommate). Today I rank this approach as a sort of nerdy precursor to finding a date on match.com.

Why Harvard?

Going to Harvard over MIT was the result of my silent consent to the stated preference of a knowledgeable Greek relative: "*Harvard is older, it must be better.*" I had an interest in chemistry and started going to my classes, selected after having read the gossipy *Harvard Freshman's Guide* (was that the title?). Soon I was intrigued by the well-proclaimed choice between classes in Humanities and Natural Sciences in the curriculum. (Remember, this was the era of C. P. Snow's "*two cultures*".) Although I battled briefly with the conceptual distinction, I admit I was relieved that, because of my choice of major, I would not be burdened with taking Nat Sci classes.

A Thesis that Favors Solid-State Biology

But my plans to return to Greece were thwarted, and after four years at Harvard, I found myself entering the MIT chemical engineering department to get an MS. Eventually, I ended at Princeton to do my PhD with the "big man" in polymer science, Arthur Tobolsky. I chose to work not on a synthetic polymer but on a natural polymer, *collagen*, and its alter ego, *gelatin*, the easier-to-study noncrystalline form.

Collagen is a ranking member of the extracellular matrix, the insoluble stuff that lies outside cells in tissues. This insoluble protein, a natural polymer, was widely considered in those years to be biologically inert and mechanically useful but, frankly, a relatively boring presence in tissues. Collagen used to be the *parvenu* guest at the table of biology.

Now, I was interested in medical applications of polymers and in things like tissues and organs. Tissues are constituents of organs. Since tissues are typically insoluble states of matter, it occurred to me that collagen, or even gelatin, had to be studied directly as *protein solids*, not as *protein solutions*. And that is the way I pursued my thesis.

To this day, basic medical researchers still rely almost entirely on the study of proteins, genes, etc. in some kind of dilute solution using the methods of that great discipline, biochemistry (and, increasingly, cell biology as well). Biological activity is still widely studied in dilute solution, as with enzymatic activity, for example. The alternative approach, working directly with tissues and organs, is still relatively underdeveloped and underfunded. Eventually, this choice turned out to be a turn in the road, a paradigm shift in experimental methodology that led to a useful medical discovery.

Working on problems of biology and medicine with solids rather than liquids seems like a matter of esoteric taste, certainly not an earth shaking difference. Yet the dilute solution methodology of the 1940s and '50s was eventually inherited by people later working with cells rather than molecules.

In the 1960s, practically nobody's lab knew how to culture mammalian cells. The drive towards reliable methods of *cell culture* was based on the use of various cell culture media, which were complex versions of the dilute solution used with proteins. Using cell culture media, an investigator had control of the behavior of cells, their interaction with each other, their life cycle. And it is these same cell-culture methods that have led to contemporary efforts to build new tissues and organs in cell culture media.

With minor exceptions, these so-called *in vitro* methods have so far led to synthesis of sophisticated drugs but not to the synthesis of many clinically useful tissues or organs. *What has been quite successful for growing organs was an approach based on a solid surface*, not a dilute solution or cell culture. This discovery was made in my MIT lab where I had been appointed as an assistant professor in 1966.

The Experiment that Failed

One morning in December 1969, I walked into the office of John F. Burke, a renowned Harvard surgeon who specialized in burns, particularly massive burns in children. Dr. Burke had the urgent problem of finding a material for covering massive skin wounds in his young patients.

On my side, I had the problem of locating a source of funds for my lab to get away from projects in biomechanics and instead do medical research, which had been my goal. All I needed was enough money to support a few graduate students and some pieces of equipment. With Burke's participation, I was able to legitimize myself enough as a budding medical researcher to secure a grant from the National Institutes of Health. Burke needed materials for extensive wound cover that would speed up healing of skin and protect his patients as soon as possible from bacteria and water loss. It was a good match.

People studying *wound healing* in those years measured the concentration of various growth factors or other proteins in the healing wounds. Then they used the data to draw hypotheses about the relative importance of these proteins in the process of wound healing. Most still do.

Using my compulsion to design experiments that would lead to *quantitative results*, or not performing them at all, I designed a rather simple study of wound healing with guinea pigs. This study consisted of measuring the effect of a variety of solid and solid-like materials (used as wound covers that we synthesized in my MIT lab) on the *speed of wound closure*, an outcome that I could measure directly.

After trying a plethora of man-made polymeric materials, I realized that none of them had any effect, whether to slow down or speed up, the closure of wounds. In desperation, I turned to the natural polymer of my doctoral thesis, collagen. I remember very clearly the evening when I found out that, rather than speeding up wound closure, a thin porous *collagen sheet* that we had fabricated actually *slowed down* remarkably the *closure of wounds*. Instead of closing in about ten days as usual, the experimental wounds closed in 25 days. For a biological or medical study, this effect was huge, not to be underestimated. But it was in the wrong direction! Burke was very unhappy, and I was even unhappier. We had failed.

Figure 8.5.1.1 *Early photo of author in his MIT lab holding a sample of scaffold that regenerates skin*

Gold Nuggets inside the Experimental Ashes

Yet something really strange was going on. When I looked at results of these experiments in tissue slides with the microscope, I noticed that the group of animals that had been treated with the collagen sheet had *healed their wounds without a scar*. Not even a trace. This result was fundamentally different than anything that had been reported to this date by people working with skin wounds. Burke was delighted and soon decided to graft with the collagen sheets some very deep skin wounds in ten children with massive burns. He got great results, and we both got ourselves articles for publication that are still being cited extensively.

We had no idea how the collagen sheet was working to give *scarless healing* or *regeneration of skin*. In spite of such ignorance, a well-known Harvard neurosurgeon, Dr Nicholas Zervas, encouraged me to extend our approach to the problem of *nerve regeneration*. Could the same method that had restored skin also work to restore nerves that had been severely damaged? Let's find out, I thought, and I asked my doctoral student, Dr. Dennis Orgill (now Professor of Surgery at Harvard) to attempt an experimental series with injured peripheral nerves in rats.

These nerves were cut through, and the two stumps were connected with a tube made of approximately the same collagen material we had used with skin wounds. It was exciting to find out that the wound tissue at each of the two nerve stumps synthesized tissue extensions that led to reconnection of the two stumps across a long distance, leading to nerves with pretty good function. This result was confirmed later and was improved enough to be used with patients suffering from nerve paralysis due to trauma.

Let us take account of what had happened so far: Two organs, skin and peripheral nerves, had been regrown almost from scratch, both in experimental animals and in people. Unbelievably, we had achieved regeneration of these two organs and could even demonstrate these results with patients. Another turn in the road.

How It All Works Out

The embarrassing truth was that we did not understand how regeneration had happened. Unraveling the mechanism of this process, which closes wounds without scar formation, took several years packed with conceptual errors.

For example, at one point we thought that, in line with the prevalent opinion, the scar tissue that normally forms in wounds is itself the reason why mammals, with very few exceptions, do not regenerate their organs. That turned out to be wrong.

Eventually, our search led to an extraordinary full cycle. Remember that the first time we noticed the absence of scar in skin wounds in animals was when we had used a porous collagen sheet as a cover for the wounds? One observation we had made at that time that was neglected for years was that the *animals that healed without scar formation* were also those which *healed by contracting their wound edges much more slowly than normal.* Well, we struck gold when we finally focused on this irritating and apparently unimportant detail.

We now know that the *key to regeneration of skin and peripheral nerves* is the presence of an *appropriate solid surface in the wound.* In order to work, the solid surface must be part of a *porous scaffold* and have the kind of *surface chemistry that goes with strong biological activity.*

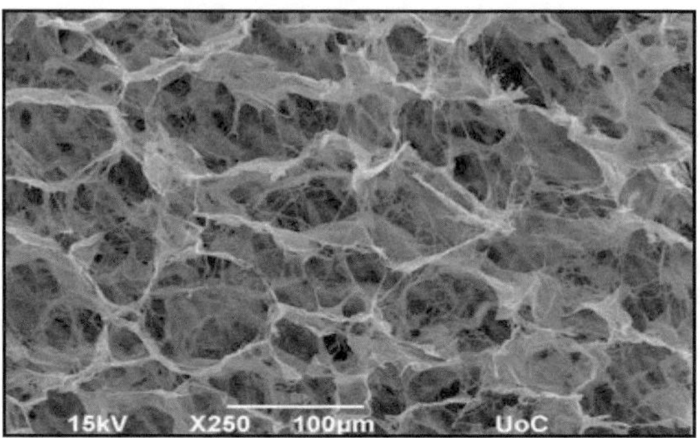

Figure 8.5.1.2 *A microscopic view of the scaffold that used to be known as "artificial skin"*

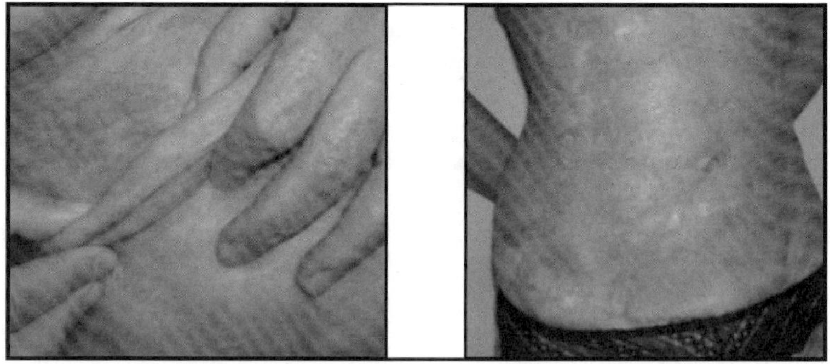

Figure 8.5.1.3 *View of a 40-year-old female patient who had a very large scar on the abdomen from a burn incident. The surgeon removed her scar and grafted the resulting wound with the scaffold that induces regeneration. The photos show the regenerated abdominal skin.*

Photos courtesy of E. Dantzer, MD

Reprinted with permission from I.V. Yannas, *Tissue and Organ Regeneration in Adults*. 2nd edition, Springer: Heidelberg. 2015

The surface of collagen naturally features "ligands" that connect securely with molecular extensions from cells, called integrins. In our experiments, the particular type of cells that were bound on the scaffold surface via integrins were those that specialize in contracting wounds during normal healing, *i.e.,* cells that pull the wound edges together and lead to wound closure.

We now know that when these contractile cells make contact with the surface of the collagen sheet and become attached to it, their behavior changes dramatically. Instead of staying close together and pointing their long axes along the same direction, as they do when the wound heals normally, these cells are instead dispersed and point their axes randomly in the space of the wound. This leads to *cancellation of force vectors*. These and other changes *cause strong delay or even blocking of wound closure by the process of contraction of wound edges.*

Here is the explanation of why we had seen a strong delay of wound closure in our early experiments in the 1970s, rather than the hoped-for speedup that would have given Dr. Burke the rapidly healing wound cover for burned skin surface that he was looking for!

To regenerate an organ requires a paradigm shift, away from conventional notions of a wound healing process that works by contraction and scar formation. To get to this point, many turns in the road were taken, some before and some after my Harvard experience.

Figure 8.5.1.4 *Professor Ioannis Yannas on learning of his election to both the National Academies of Medicine and Engineering*

* * *

I thank my pre-med classmate, Newton Hyslop, for encouraging me to write this report. I am especially hoping that I have reached across the aisle to my Hum 4 classmates.

Ioannis Yannas, PhD, has degrees from Harvard College (AB, chemistry, 1957), MIT (MS, chemical engineering, 1959) and Princeton University (MS, 1965; PhD, 1966, physical chemistry). He has been on the MIT faculty since 1966 and is currently Professor in the Departments of Mechanical Engineering and Biological Engineering.

Professor Yannas and John F. Burke, MD, discovered the principle of scaffolding as necessary for inducing living cells to regenerate tissue. Use of a scaffold in skin wounds led to synthesis of a neodermis, the foundation tissue of skin in animals and humans (1975–81). When this scaffold was seeded with keratinocyte cells from normal epidermal skin surfaces, there followed simultaneous regeneration of the dermis and the epidermis (1981–84). A similar treatment employed by Yannas and Dennis Orgill led to regeneration of peripheral nerves over long distances.

The discovery of the key role of biological scaffolding in tissue regeneration translated into a commercial product used today in treating patients with burns and chronic skin wounds, patients needing plastic surgical repairs, and those whose traumatic nerve damage has caused local paralysis. It has spawned the emerging disciplines of organ regeneration and regenerative medicine.

For his discoveries in organ regeneration Yannas was elected to the National Academy of Medicine, National Academy of Engineering and was inducted in the National Inventors Hall of Fame.

The Revolution in Biomedical Research

Joel Rosenbloom

As I entered Harvard in the fall of 1953, like many of my classmates, I had already made up my mind to become a doctor, but had little understanding of what that really would entail and no knowledge whatsoever of biomedical research. Little could I imagine what the next sixty years would bring in terms of our understanding of how life works and the application of that knowledge to disease processes and treatment. What was to occur over that period of time was a virtual revolution in understanding at all levels, from the molecular to the cellular to the tissue to the organ to the whole organism. The driver behind this revolution was the federal government as carried out by the National Institutes of Health (NIH). In 1953, the NIH consisted of a few buildings surrounded by farmland located near Washington, DC, in Bethesda, MD. Presently, there are 27 separate institutes so that NIH now is a small city with a budget for intra-mural research in the $3.5 billion range.

Introduction to Laboratory Research—Elastin

Unknowingly, what was to initiate my career in biomedical research began in my junior year when I started working in the laboratory of Dr. Paul Zamecnik at the Massachusetts General Hospital under the supervision of Dr. Robert Loftfield. The laboratory was investigating the biochemical mechanisms involved in protein synthesis using homogenates of rat liver as a model system. By present standards, the approach was fairly primitive with reagents being very limited, but the laboratory did have one great advantage: it could obtain radioactive $C^{14}O_2$ from the Oakridge Laboratory. Dr. Loftfield used the $C^{14}O_2$ to synthesize the radioactive amino acid glycine, which was used to trace its incorporation into a complex mixture of proteins by the liver system. This was *one of the first uses of radioactive compounds* which proved to be one of the most powerful technical tools in many aspects of biomedical research.

At the time, very little was known about the detailed *machinery of protein synthesis*. One of the remarkable discoveries made by the group was that of transfer RNAs which act as intermediate carriers of amino acids ensuring their correct positional incorporation into protein. Among Dr. Zamecnik's many interests was that of the *elastic properties of blood vessels* and my project was to investigate the synthesis and turnover of the *protein elastin* in arteries. As it turned out, elastin was found only in a highly insoluble form of elastic fibers that had the characteristics of a rubber band. When radioactive glycine was injected into the tail vein of a young rat, the glycine was rapidly incorporated into the elastic fibers of the aorta. However, when I tried to determine the rate at which the elastin turned over, that is degraded physiologically, there was essentially no turnover, a rather surprising and boring result. However, this was only my initial intersection with elastin which was to play a big part in my scientific life.

New Pathways for Medical Students—MD/PhD

After graduating Harvard, I went to the University of Pennsylvania Medical School where I was one of the first to enroll in a new MD/PhD program. This was a very exciting time for medical research, both for the spectacular advances which were underway and because of the increasing support by the federal government making a research career attractive.

At the time of my entering Penn Med, the oldest medical school in the United States, it consisted of one reasonably large building (named after the school's founder, John Morgan) which housed the administrative offices, the medical library and research laboratories (which contained a laboratory used by Otto Meyerhof!). Very close to the John Morgan Building was the University Hospital, and that was all there was!

I worked in the Biochemistry Department which then had ten faculty members, including some high powered ones including Seymour Cohen, who came close to discovering messenger RNA, and Samuel Gurin, who was competing with Konrad Bloch at Harvard for determination of the pathway for the synthesis of cholesterol. (Bloch won, of course, and received a Nobel Prize.) We graduate students were thoroughly drilled on the precise pathway involved in the biosynthesis of cholesterol and the key role of the rate-limiting step, HmG-CoA reductase, investigation of which subsequently lead to the development of statins and the awarding of the Nobel Prize to Michael Brown (a Penn Med graduate) and Joseph Goldstein.

Another outstanding Penn Med scientist was Britton Chance, who had been involved in development of radar during World War II and had made many contributions to enzyme kinetics, but who was now making great attempts to find the secret intermediate in the formation of ATP during oxidative phosphorylation. Sadly for Chance and others, it turned out that there was no intermediate, and Peter Mitchell finally received the Nobel Prize for his brilliant work in discovering the chemiosmotic process involved.

Fortunately for me, a very talented young biophysicist, Verne Schumaker, took me into his laboratory where I characterized high molecular weight bacteriophage DNA and enzymes by novel hydrodynamic techniques using the Ultracentrifuge. At the time, this was great stuff but now elegant techniques such as x-ray crystallography and nuclear magnetic resonance have permitted much more detailed definition.

Collagen Research

Adjacent to Penn Med was Philadelphia General Hospital, built during the Civil War to care for injured Union soldiers, and it was there that I began research on *connective tissues* in a Clinical Research Center. The focus was on the protein *collagen*, and at the time there was only one type known (presently there are 27 different known collagens). The work centered on the biosynthesis of collagen focusing on the hydroxylation of proline to hydroxyproline, which we found to be necessary for the stabilization of the *collagen triple helix*. This was an interesting result since the reaction required vitamin C, and thus its deficiency in *scurvy* results in weak blood vessels because of poor collagen formation. My work also began in detail on the synthesis of elastin.

Emergence of Molecular Biology

A revolution in technology was beginning to take place with a *blending of biochemistry and microbiology* into a new field coined molecular biology which led to profound insights in the structure and function of living cells. This was particularly true for nucleic acids in which sequencing of DNA enabled determination of the amino acid sequence of proteins through the genetic code, whose structure once understood became the foundation for modern genetics. Such analyses were made possible because fragments of DNA from any species, including human, could be cloned and produced in quantity in bacterial cells.

In my own case, we sequenced the human elastin gene, which led to a better understanding of the structure of the elastic fiber and identification of mutations that caused genetic diseases, including some forms of *cutis laxa*. This technology culminated in the *sequencing of the human genome* while other techniques now permit *alteration of genomes,* including human. Certainly, while mutations in many genes are responsible for heritable diseases, gene variation can increase the susceptibility to acquired diseases such as cancer.

Cell Communication

In the context of the new biology, it was realized that cells communicate with one another not only by *touching*, but through a multitude of *signaling molecules*. Detailed investigation into the mechanisms of such signaling communication has profoundly increased understanding in such diverse areas as developmental and immunobiology. It is through these *signaling pathways* that cells can be induced to differentiate and to integrate their activities. Not surprisingly, *signaling abnormalities* are critical features of many chronic debilitating diseases including cancer. The elements of these signaling pathways provide therapeutic targets and many drugs act either through inhibiting or stimulating their activities. The implementation of such drugs is a major focus of pharmacologic activity.

Funding the Biomedical Revolution

The major increase in the body of knowledge has come about largely through the tremendous increase in NIH funding which is now in the $35 billion range. Of this, 10% is in-house on the NIH campus, and the remainder is passed on through *competitive grants* largely to scientists in US universities.

Effect on Universities

Approximately 85% of university funding for biomedical research is now from federal sources. Due to this immense funding increase, the size of many medical schools has enlarged enormously, as has their university role with a commensurate decrease in the role of the humanities and social sciences. Simultaneously, patient care in university medical centers has become proportionately greater.

The enormity of these two funding streams has resulted in a greater university bureaucracy and the creation of an infrastructure in which business decisions play a predominant role. It can be argued that such changes have altered the fundamental character of universities where freedom of thought is excessively tempered by financial considerations and administrators have assumed larger roles and salaries.

Funding Basic Scientists

These changes have significant consequences for faculty members particularly in the basic sciences. In the 1960s, when NIH began enticing young medical graduates to go into research, their salaries were paid entirely by the institution, and research grants could only pay for support staff, supplies, equipment and so forth. Gradually over the years, universities pushed to change this so that a larger and larger percentage of faculty salaries were covered by grants. New types of faculty positions were devised including "*research professors*" whose entire salaries were on grants. In addition, in order to pay for bricks and mortar, the concept of "*indirect costs*" was created and tied in as a percentage (usually around 60% or more) of the direct costs.

Effect of Funding Shifts on Universities and Faculty

Overall, the shift in funding sources enabled universities to grow to extraordinary sizes. But the foundations rest largely on "soft" money, and there are nasty consequences. Generally, if research faculty lose their grants, they are forced to leave the university unless they can pay their salaries in some other way, such as by seeing patients for those with an MD degree. PhDs are out of luck. The importance of teaching has taken a back seat to funded research.

Up to the present (2017), most major universities have yet to experience threats to their stability because of a shaky financial foundation. However, severe potential difficulties loom on the near horizon. The supply of NIH funding has not kept up with the demand. The fraction of grant applications which are funded is in the 10–15% range and could worsen. This means that faculty have to spend more and more time re-writing grants in a demoralizing environment and to the point that many may opt out. The irony of this situation is that *universities have become heavily dependent on the very individuals to whom they have made no real commitment.*

Loss of Scientific Independence

A direct consequence of this huge expansion of a faculty with an altered composition and role, coupled with the increased power of administrators, is that some universities are now questioning whether tenure should be maintained. Universities are becoming more and more businesses-like with bureaucratic top-down control. I recently heard Jack Welch, who is the retired but highly regarded ex-CEO of General Electric, speak at a faculty meeting at which he half-jokingly questioned whether any sensible organization (business or otherwise) should give a life-time job to a 35–45-year-old. Amazingly, this brought a good laugh. What he and his administrative cohorts fail to realize (or maybe they do realize) is that *without tenure there would be no real academic freedom.* Presidents, vice-presidents, provosts, vice-provosts, associate provosts, deans, vice deans, associate deans, assistant deans would hold all the power, win all the arguments and fire any trouble-making non-tenured faculty in a fashion similar to what occurs in the business world.

Summing Up

Of course, all is not doom and gloom. The tremendous advances made in understanding *the chemistry of life* and the application of sophisticated technology have resulted in effective treatment of many diseases and a marked extension of lifetime expectancy in the United States.

I am still in the game trying to find cures for diseases such as pulmonary and kidney fibrosis. In building on these advances, we must be aware of the true costs and minimize damage to the fundamental strengths of our great universities.

Figure 8.5.2.1 *Joel Rosenbloom, circa 1970, in his laboratory in the University of Pennsylvania Biochemistry Department, is shown assembling a chromatography system to separate different collagen molecules newly synthesized by cultured fibroblasts.*

Joel Rosenbloom, MD, PhD, received his AB degree from Harvard College and MD and PhD from the University of Pennsylvania. He began his career at the University of Pennsylvania as an Assistant Professor of Biochemistry and became full Professor in 1974. From 1975 until 1999 he served as the chair of the Department of Anatomy and Cell Biology and Director of the Center for Oral Health Research in the School of Dental Medicine. He then joined the Faculty of Thomas Jefferson Medical College, first as Professor of Medicine, and currently is Professor of Dermatology and Cutaneous Medicine. He is also the Director of the Joan and Joel Rosenbloom Center for Fibrotic Diseases at Jefferson.

Dr. Rosenbloom's research has centered on the biochemistry and molecular biology of connective tissues. His laboratory found that hydroxyproline, whose formation requires vitamin C, was necessary to stabilize the collagen triple helix, thus partially explaining how vitamin C deficiency causes scurvy. His laboratory was the first to clone the human elastin gene which facilitated studies on the structure of the elastic fiber and its role in disease and on the gene encoding amelogenin, a critical protein found in tooth enamel, mutations in which cause *amelogenesis imperfecta*. His current interest centers on translating recent advances in understanding the pathogenesis of fibrotic reactions into effective therapies for such diseases as abdominal adhesions and fibrosis of lungs and kidneys. He has published extensively, with more than 350 peer-reviewed papers, and served on journal editorial boards and NIH study sections.

Science of the Human Past

Malcolm H. Wiener

I went directly from my graduation at Harvard College and simultaneous commissioning as an Ensign in the United States Navy to the Mediterranean to board the USS *Newport News,* a heavy cruiser on which I was to spend my next three years. I had never been to Europe before, and so literally joined the Navy and saw the world.

I returned to spend three years at Harvard Law School, but afterward had no contact with Harvard for the next 25 years.

In 1985 I reconnected as a Fellow of the Faculty of Government at what is now the Harvard Kennedy School, working with then Dean Graham Allison on the history of the Cuban Missile Crisis. I also became a Member of the Visiting Committee to the Fogg Art Museum. The Director's office at the Harvard Art Museums now bears the name of our family Foundation.

My contact with the Kennedy School deepened, and I participated in the consolidation of several separate but interrelated programs in health and human services, the inner cities, criminal justice and Native American affairs, all of which became part of the Malcolm Wiener Center for Social Policy. Today the Center includes Harvard's outstanding program on inequality, together with a number of other major initiatives in housing, health and human services, criminal justice, immigration and other areas.

Recently, I've been involved in the creation of the Harvard program on the *Science of the Human Past (SoHP)* and the collaboration between SoHP and the Max Planck Institute, known as the Max Planck Harvard Research Center for the Archaeoscience of the Ancient Mediterranean (MHAAM). Forty years of research on Aegean Prehistory, with annual trips to Greece, and over thirty years of service on the Board of Trustees of the American School of Classical Studies at Athens placed me in a position to facilitate the transfer of DNA samples from Greece to the Research Center.

Archaeological science is poised to transform our understanding of the human past. My essay in a recent issue of *Dædalus*, the Journal of the American Academy of Arts & Sciences, noted that:

> "Sudden dramatic breakthroughs in archaeological science, intertwined with new approaches to the understanding of classical texts and of depictions in various media, promise major new insights into both the physical realities and the mentalities of the classical world.
>
> DNA analysis of humans, animals, and pathogens; strontium isotope analysis of movements of individuals over the course of their lives; source analysis of clays and metals; plus technical studies of the *chaîne opératoire* of pottery manufacture establishing whether the inspiration, the pot, or the potter moved, illustrate the rapid advance of archaeological science.
>
> A recent DNA study of a corpse from the time of Justinian revealed a pathogen of the same strain of bubonic plague as that which ravaged Europe from AD 1347–1351.
>
> Holistic analysis of the 430–426 BC burials in the Kerameikos of Athens during the Great Plague, including DNA and strontium isotope analysis, paleopathological and histological analysis, dietary pattern and dental microwear studies, plus calculus biomolecular and biodistance analysis, will add much new information, while new approaches to the study of texts and funerary rituals will shed light on how the survivors in classical Athens understood and reacted to the disaster.
>
> Understanding how societies respond to catastrophes is as relevant to our likely future as to our comprehension of ages past."

Similarly, we have much to learn from about 1,500 bodies found recently in a burial ground on the outskirts of Athens, where the Stavros Niarchos Foundation has constructed a new National Opera house/concert hall, National Library and park stretching to the shore. The burials cover the span from the Geometric period c. 750 BC to about 490 BC, the time of the Battle of Marathon.

About 100 of the bodies were found with hands bound, their heads having been crushed by blows. They may comprise the bodies of those condemned after the first reliably dated event in Athenian history, the Kylonian conspiracy of 632 BC, when the son-in-law of the tyrant of nearby Megara attempted to seize power in Athens. Examination of the bodies has been entrusted to the newly completed Wiener Laboratory of Archaeological Science at the American School of Classical Studies at Athens, a state-of-the-art facility, and I am in the process of attempting to raise the funds required.

My own recent work has focused on the collapse of civilizations, including a lengthy study entitled "*The Interaction of Climate Change and Agency in the Collapse of Civilizations ca. 2300–2000 BC*", which has been cited by parties of varying views in the current debate.

The period encompassed a major climate event which disturbed preexisting patterns of rainfall and led to mass migrations, but the epoch also witnessed the widespread adoption of bronze, including the introduction of bronze weapons, a major advantage over copper weaponry, and the first appearance as well of sailing vessels in the Aegean Sea, where previously sea travel had been accomplished by rowed longboats.

Climate change mattered greatly, but so also did the responses of humans, on the individual, familial and societal levels.

* * *

Most importantly, having married late, my wife, Carolyn, and I are now the proud parents of two Harvard students: Kate, now at the Harvard Law School, and Elizabeth, a senior at the College. We are keeping our fingers crossed for our twin sons, Thomas and Jonathan, now 16.

Figure 8.5.3.1 *Aegean prehistorian and archaeoscientist Malcolm H. Wiener in his study in 2009*

Malcolm H. Wiener is an Aegean prehistorian who has written extensively on the Eastern Mediterranean world in the Bronze Age. He has also published articles on economics, foreign affairs, antiquities law and Picasso. His awards include the honorary doctorates of the Universities of Sheffield, Tübingen, Athens, Cincinnati, University College London, Dickinson College and the University of Arizona, the Gold Cross of the *Order of Honor* of Greece, and the Ring of Honour of the German Academy in Mainz. He is a member of the AAAS, the Royal Swedish Academy, the Austrian Academy and the Society of Antiquaries in London, a Corresponding Member of the Austrian and German Archaeological Institutes, and holds a rank of Chevalier in the *Ordre des Arts et des Lettres* of France. He is a member of the CFR and is a Trustee-Emeritus of the Metropolitan Museum of Art and American School of Classical Studies at Athens.

Malcolm is a graduate of Harvard College and the Harvard Law School, served as an Ensign/Lt. (JG) in the United States Navy, practiced as an attorney, and between 1971 and 1987 was the founder and CEO of related investment management firms.

Figure 8.5.3.2 *"Geometer", c. 1710, by Antoine Pesne (Paris 1683–Berlin 1757)*

Source: Wikimedia Commons—http://www2.maius.uj.edu.pl/uczony/sala4.htm/obiekty/25-s.jpg

HIV/AIDS

The Human Immunodeficiency Virus and AIDS

Newton E. Hyslop, Jr.

The AIDS epidemic, one of the defining events of our time, was first recognized in the United States but soon became the cause of illness and death for millions worldwide and by definition a pandemic. The cause proved to be a virus capable of destroying human immunity and related to viruses previously circulating among subhuman primates.[1] Once the infectious agent, named Human Immunodeficiency Virus (HIV), entered the human population, human behaviors of multiple sex partners and injecting drug use promoted its rapid spread from person-to-person by sexual transmission and exposure to infected blood and its products. Further, the profound immunodeficiency of AIDS fed secondary resurgent outbreaks of tuberculosis, as coughs from persons dually infected with HIV and TB generated infectious aerosols capable of infecting immunodeficient and immunocompetent persons alike.

The international scientific and public health response to the AIDS epidemic has been well chronicled by many authors. This essay briefly reviews early epidemiological research and outlines key steps in the discovery of effective antiviral suppressive therapy. Highly active antiviral therapy brought an end to the uncontrolled epidemic by restoring immunity and reducing transmission. However, it has not eradicated HIV, and transmission continues.

The Warning

On June 5, 1981, the national Centers for Disease Control (CDC), a branch of the US Public Health Service, announced that an epidemic of a previously unknown immune deficiency disease was emerging. CDC subsequently named this deadly scourge *Acquired Immune Deficiency Syndrome*, or *AIDS*.[2]

AIDS was to be the first of a new wave of sinister biomedical developments called "*Emerging and Reemerging Infections*". It was followed a decade later by instances of domestic biological warfare with anthrax immediately after the events of 9/11 and the possible threat that

Saddam Hussein would use smallpox aerosols in response to the invasion of Iraq. Fear of smallpox weaponry reactivated a discontinued national smallpox vaccine program but now targeted military, medical and other first responders in case of attack. Being an infectious disease specialist, helping public health authorities plan local and national responses and educate medical personnel, would become intense and hazardous work.

Initial Definition of AIDS

Without a known cause in the beginning, but suspected of being infectious, AIDS in affected persons was characterized by two primary elements: (1) a measurable deficiency of circulating immune cells in the blood, together with (2) the presence of one or more associated, previously rare, secondary infections and/or malignancies, which could appear singly or in various combinations in one individual. Patients wasted away, feverish, short of breath, the skin of some showing the tell-tale purplish spots of Kaposi's sarcoma. Some reached the end of their lives in an ICU on a ventilator, while others in hospice were eased into the darkness by a morphine drip. In Africa many patients died of overwhelming disseminated tuberculosis. AIDS was a fatal disease.

Transmission of Infection

In the US AIDS initially seemed to target primarily younger men with numerous same-sex sexual partners. However, among the important outliers were children with inherited hemophilia whose defense against spontaneous bleeding required regular dosing with anti-hemophiliac globulin made from pooled blood donations. This fact supported a transmissible infectious etiology and raised concerns over the safety of the nation's blood supply.

As further epidemiological reports came in to the World Health Organization (WHO) from Africa and elsewhere, it was quickly recognized that in much of the world, this rapidly moving pandemic targeted *both* sexes at the age of sexual maturity and, unchecked, threatened to leave behind masses of orphans, cause economic disruption and simultaneous collapse of social order, especially in hard-hit Africa.

Besides sexual transmission, an epidemic of crack cocaine addiction in the US, fomented by a criminal drug cartel, fed a parallel epidemic of needle-sharing among injecting drug users. Residual blood in needles from those infected with HIV, often coinfected with hepatitis and other viruses, transmitted the infection to sharing users, who became part of a growing population of HIV-infected heterosexuals. AIDS became an international emergency at multiple levels.

Thus began a 20-year saga of scientific, medical, social, and political ferment in the United States and overseas generated by the fallout of the AIDS pandemic.

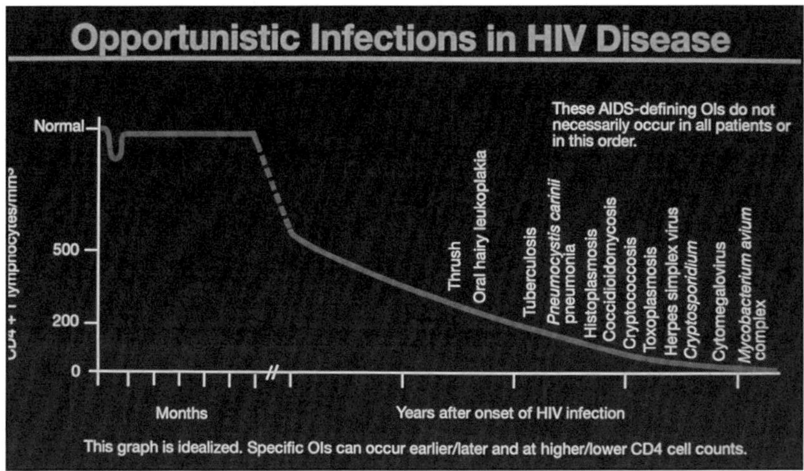

Figure 8.5.4.1 Relationship of CD4 lymphocyte count to clinical stages in the natural history of untreated HIV infection

Progressive immunodeficiency reduces resistance to environmental organisms and also allows latent infections from prior exposures to escape from immune control. Environmental organisms include old and new exposures to tuberculosis, fungi and parasites. Post-infectious latent viruses include Herpes simplex, Varicella zoster *and* Cytomegalovirus.

Source—CDC diagram

The Early Years

The Dark Ages

For more than a decade after the Human Immunodeficiency Virus (HIV) became known in 1984 as the cause of AIDS, although denied by some, there was no effective treatment.

Medical scientists probed the vulnerability of this new retrovirus by reviewing old drugs designed for other purposes and testing them in living cells grown in the laboratory. However, the search for potential targets for antiviral therapy would not accelerate until the pharmaceutical industry committed itself to HIV research and helped define the lifecycle of HIV.

Meanwhile, the frustrations of at-risk and HIV-infected populations with the lack of progress precipitated formation of a revolutionary group called ACT-UP, which mocked and excoriated the CDC, occupied pharmaceutical companies and disrupted AIDS scientific conferences, including the Third World Congress on AIDS held in

Washington, DC, in 1987. There Vice President George H. Bush's welcoming speech was rendered inaudible by dozens of identically costumed protestors who stood at the rear of the auditorium and chanted in unison "Shame" through electric bullhorns until he left the scene; their chant referenced the Reagan administration's unwillingness to fund AIDS research.

ACT-UP continued civil disobedience and even voiced antagonism to the new NIH-sponsored AIDS Clinical Trials Group research program, demanding representatives of AIDS patients be included in all committees responsible for design and testing of drug candidates in clinical trials. Inclusion proved an excellent decision: as ACT-UP representatives came to realize the limits of scientific understanding of the component diseases of AIDS and of HIV biology, they became supportive of investment in quality research, brought practical input to trial design and encouraged participation in trials by persons living with AIDS.

Fear of Contagion

In the US, death and dying among previously healthy young men, 25–44 years old, dominated the early days. Deaths of several Hollywood stars from AIDS highlighted the fact that social standing gave no protection.

Death from opportunistic infections, especially *Pneumocystis carinii pneumonia (PCP),* and malignancies of AIDS provoked immense fear, even among medical personnel. Before the HIV antibody test became available, risk of transmission by casual contact with an infected person was difficult to evaluate without a marker of infection. The paucity of data allowed speculation to run wild. Some medical personnel neglected their AIDS patients, or refused to work in areas with AIDS patients, or to perform diagnostic or therapeutic procedures on them. They worried that HIV might be as highly contagious as the well-known debilitating hepatitis B virus (HBV), which for health care workers—until introduction of an effective vaccine—was a common and potentially chronic, even lethal, infection acquired following unprotected exposure to blood and body fluids from infected patients.

Naturally, certain groups sought to identify scapegoats and demanded isolation of those infected from society. For a period Haitians were suspected to have introduced HIV into the US. A Howard University biology professor repeatedly told his students that HIV was a government-sponsored genocidal tactic designed to eradicate African-Americans.

The level of public fear was epitomized by the story of Ryan White, an Indiana schoolboy with AIDS acquired from HIV-contaminated anti-hemophilic globulin used to treat his hemophilia. In 1985 he was shunned by his friends and neighbors, expelled from middle school and needed a court order for reinstatement. National attention to his plight humanized AIDS, as he had not acquired HIV infection by risky personal behaviors. Following his death from AIDS in 1990, he was memorialized by passage of the Ryan White CARE Act which created HIV/AIDS services programs for persons living with HIV/AIDS throughout the US.

Public Health Education and Interventions

After HIV antibody testing became available in 1985, epidemiological studies of HIV infection documented person-to-person transmission by contact with infected blood or body fluids as the principal source of new infections. Importantly, unlike West Nile and other mosquito borne-viruses, HIV transmission did not involve an intermediate host. Further, there was no risk from casual contact with infected persons. The focus of public health programs turned to transmission prevention.

Public health authorities launched efforts to prevent transmission by introducing public educational programs on *risk reduction*. As their work required they engage all elements of society, they employed advertising in the media, public places and even on city buses. Those political and religious groups opposed to public discussion of transmission risks voiced opposition to proposals for education in public schools, insisting that discussion about risky behaviors would only arouse young people to copy those behaviors. Public health proposals for sex education, free distribution of condoms and of clean needle exchange for injecting drug users met with passionate opposition and often blocked their implementation on state or local levels.

Exiting the Darkness

HIV Antibody Test

Technological advances were critical to being able to move from ignorance to knowledge about HIV and AIDS. At the clinical level, the introduction in 1985 of the HIV antibody test was revolutionary as it allowed detection of HIV infection.

In particular, for persons with infections and/or malignancies compatible with the clinical definition of AIDS, the diagnosis could be confirmed by positive HIV antibody test.

Further, its ability to identify asymptomatic HIV infection among otherwise healthy persons gave epidemiologists a tool to investigate transmission rates among risk groups and define the incubation period between time of infection and onset of symptomatic disease. Importantly, HIV antibody screening of blood donations brought safety to the blood supply and its products.

HIV Epidemiology

In the US, the speed with which HIV could spread after its introduction into a vulnerable high-risk population became apparent from CDC retrospective studies on blood samples stored from a pre-AIDS prospective multiyear study of hepatitis B (HBV) transmission within a cohort of gay males in San Francisco. HIV was found in a few early samples but with the passage of time, HIV prevalence rose rapidly and especially among those who also acquired HBV infection, itself an indicator of sexual and/or injection transmission. Further, longitudinal follow-up of those whose HIV tests converted to positive established the delay between infection and onset of AIDS-related disorders.

While AIDS in the US early on seemed predominantly a disease occurring in men at risk from same-sex partnerships, the availability of the HIV antibody test to detect asymptomatic infection began to show other groups at risk of HIV infection. Epidemiological studies by the World Health Organization (WHO) of commercial sex workers in Nairobi, Kenya and other African cities showed rising HIV infection rates which over time approached prevalence rates of 100%. Worldwide, HIV rates were higher in major cities, and especially seaports, than in surrounding countryside, and higher in certain occupational groups, such as long-distance truck drivers in Africa. Countries closed to tourism, like China at that time, remained reportedly free of invasion by HIV.

Sexual transmission of HIV during unprotected sex was found to be enhanced when the sex partner also transmitted gonorrhea, syphilis or another concurrent sexually transmitted disease (STD) to the unprotected recipient. Persons who shared multiple partners in small "sexual networks" often had STDs; on acquiring HIV infection they became efficient transmission sources to the occasional partner from outside the network. Such networks were not limited to commercial sex workers, but extended to social groups whose numbers increased with the cocaine epidemic, which in New Orleans began in 1988.

These and similar population studies informed establishment of prevention goals, especially behavioral "risk reduction" through condom usage and needle exchanges.

HIV, now added to the list of known *sexually transmitted diseases (STDs)*, would ultimately be isolated from semen, breast milk and other body fluids besides blood.

Later studies on HIV infection in newborn babies demonstrated that transmission to some occurred *in utero* during pregnancy, to others at delivery, or postpartum by feeding breast milk. To define the extent of the population at risk for transmitting *pediatric AIDS*, antibody testing of pregnant women was introduced. At Charity Hospital in New Orleans, the prevalence of HIV positively among pregnant African-American women reached a frightening 2%, or 1 in 50 pregnancies.

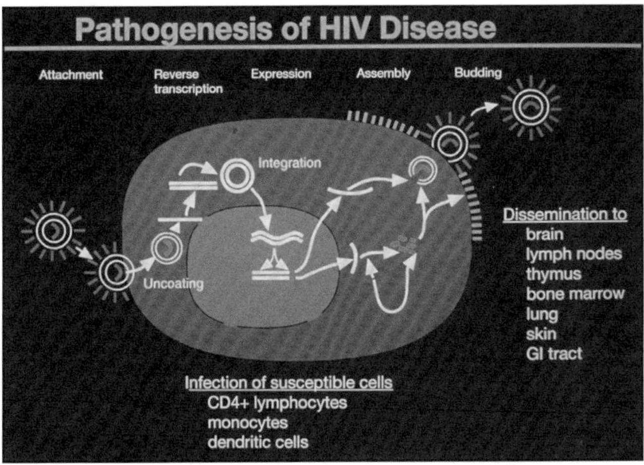

Figure 8.5.4.2 *Life cycle of HIV*

Infectious RNA virions enter CD4 subset of lymphocytes by specific receptor, integrate into DNA of host cell, reproduce vRNA and capsid proteins, and assemble new virion at cell surface for export and dissemination by blood. Each step offers different potential drug targets.

Source—CDC diagram

The Search for Treatment of HIV Infection

Characterizing HIV

Amazingly, it took only three years of basic research in NIH-supported laboratories and the Institute Pasteur to identify the cause of AIDS as a wily RNA retrovirus which entered a specific lymphocyte subpopulation, took over its cellular machinery, copied itself into the host cell's DNA and then spewed out infectious RNA particles into its environment. It would take another decade to understand its full life cycle and develop *effective treatments which turned HIV infection into a chronic disease.*

Progress in antiviral research depended on a full understanding of the biochemical details of these steps in viral replication and export. Viral *reverse transcriptase*, the enzyme responsible for the key first step, was the initial target, and others would follow as they were discovered, among them the viral *protease* enzyme involved in a late stage of the life cycle.

Early Antivirals

Once HIV could be cultivated in cell cultures, drug susceptibility testing began. Candidate drugs emerged first from laboratory shelves storing failed cancer drugs, such as the first HIV drug, AZT, a nucleoside analogue of thymidine, one of the bases in DNA and RNA. Found to inhibit *reverse transcriptase in* culture systems, its effectiveness spurred development of a generation of *nucleic acid analogues* based on the AZT model of *chain termination* to halt viral replication.

Proof of efficacy in patients required clinical trials.[3] To accomplish this, the National Institutes of Health created national AIDS Treatment Evaluation Units (ATEU), later renamed AIDS Clinical Trials Units (ACTU), at multiple sites in the US, of which the Tulane-LSU Unit was one. Similar consortia were organized in Europe, Britain, Australia and Canada.

Figure 8.5.4.3 *The Tulane-LSU ATEU, subsequently renamed an AIDS Clinical Trials Unit, was a successful applicant in the national competition for AIDS Treatment Evaluation Units, sponsored by NIH.*

The scientific staff included faculty from the Tulane and Louisiana State University infectious diseases programs in medicine and pediatrics, Tulane pharmacology, hematology and immunology, Tulane School of Public Health and Tropical Medicine, Tulane Primate Center, and Charity Hospital diagnostic laboratories, pathology and pharmacy.

The author (fourth from the right, front row) *was the founding Principal Investigator of the T-L ACTU.*

Credit: Alan Dufour, Photography Department, Tulane University School of Medicine

Early Clinical Trials

The AIDS epidemic stimulated major improvements in the methodology of clinical trials. However, the first years of clinical trials of HIV treatments were handicapped by a major disability: There was *no method to measure virus concentration (viral load, vL)* in the blood, and *no tests for drug resistance.*

Principal endpoints for demonstrating drug efficacy at that time were limited to (1) *blocking progression to AIDS,* a clinical endpoint, and (2) *reversal of depletion of T4/CD4 helper lymphocytes* in the blood, a laboratory endpoint. Clinical endpoints required long term observation of patients and importantly their retention in multiyear trials. Further, in the absence of alternative treatments, proof of *drug efficacy and safety* required random assignment of patients to drug or to placebo "dummy pills" without the knowledge of patients or investigators, a so-called "*double-blind*" design.

Early trials of AZT monotherapy illustrate the difficulties of using these limited criteria for assessing efficacy. To speed trial completion, the first study enrolled patients with *symptomatic HIV infection*, AIDS Related COMPLEX (ARC), who already had dangerously low helper lymphocyte blood counts and were at high risk for rapid progression to AIDS or death. Initiation of AZT treatment provoked a hopeful initial but brief uptick in CD4 counts, termed the "CD4 bump", and while it seemed to slow the process, did not prevent progression to "full-blown" AIDS and death.

The difficulties of using clinical endpoints as major determinants of drug efficacy were reinforced by two studies on *asymptomatic HIV infected* populations with higher starting CD4 counts. The trial asked if *AZT monotherapy* would prevent clinical deterioration, and a secondary endpoint looked for positive effects on CD4. To gain statistical significance, two large randomized double blinded placebo-controlled landmark trials, one American and one European, enrolled many hundreds of persons. One trial ended at two years and the other at three. Both showed an early but unsustained CD4 bump; but only the longer observation unequivocally demonstrated *equal progression rates* among placebo-controls and those on AZT.

These discouraging clinical results with a drug shown to be effective in the laboratory were not understood until some years later. After studies on HIV plasma viral loads had delineated viral kinetics, and when genetic resistance testing became available, retesting of the original samples showed that in both instances, failure to sustain the CD4 bump was due to selection for AZT-resistant strains which then resumed destroying lymphocytes.

The basis of the failure of AZT monotherapy was a rapidly replicating virus population with high mutation rates which continuously generated a swarm of new strains of virus, from which monotherapy selected mutants of progressively higher drug-resistance. This critical insight led to major revision of treatment strategy, which moved from serial monotherapy to multidrug combination therapy, as described below.

HIV Science Matures

Active Replication vs. Latent Infection

HIV released into the extracellular environment specifically targets uninfected CD4 helper lymphocytes in the blood and tissues. The virion binds to specific receptors and enters the cell. Once inside it chooses one of two alternatives: (1) initiates another round of *viral replication,* called *active infection,* or (2) executes the equally dangerous step of its inserting a DNA *(vDNA)* copy of its viral RNA *(vRNA)* into the host's genome while the cell is in its resting state and *without activating viral replication,* termed *latent infection.*

No drug to date can remove the latent infection form of the virus; it remains a time bomb inside the cell whose DNA it has invaded until the cell is activated, when it makes new virus. Even in the current era of effective drug therapy for active HIV infection, how to exorcise latent infection remains an unsolved problem. Latent HIV infection underlies the need for *chronic suppressive treatment*, since discontinuation of antiviral treatment permits HIV replication whenever latently infected cells are activated.

CD4 Depletion: Laboratory and Clinical Phenotypes

HIV replication in cultures of human isolates in lymphocyte cell cultures exhibits two forms: a "*non-cytopathic*" phenotype which releases infectious particles but does not kill the producing cell, and a "*cytopathic*" phenotype which fuses infected lymphocytes and destroys the cell culture.

These two laboratory variants correlate with two clinical phenotypes of early HIV infection based on rates of CD4 depletion in peripheral blood: "*rapid*" and "*slow progressors*". This useful predictor resulted from long term observational studies in a cohort of asymptomatic HIV-infected persons whose CD4 counts of $\geq$500 at entry indicated intact protective immunity. Depletion rates for each individual were calculated from serial CD4 values obtained over time until they reached <200, the laboratory marker of AIDS.

For "*slow progressors*" the drop in lymphocytes from >500 cells/ml to dangerous immunodeficiency on average took 8 years but only 2 for "*rapid progressors.*" "Slow progressors" were dominant in the cohort studied; presumably they were also predominant in the previously described retrospective HBV/HIV study which had demonstrated a prolonged delay between first evidence of HIV infection and progression to immunodeficiency.

Darwinian Virology

The extent of viral mutation during its reproductive cycles, explored when technology for rapid sequencing of HIV viral RNA became accessible, lent further understanding of the HIV replication cycle. Unlike most viruses affecting humans, HIV replication was found to be "*error-prone*", releasing multiple sequence variants from cells into the blood. Certain sequence changes led to "*defective*" virus, unable to be destructive or to infect other cells or replicate successfully. But HIV's "*replication strategy of high mutation rates*" also churned out variant copies retaining pathological characteristics with a Darwinian advantage: as the host immune response tried to control the infection, the viral target kept shifting, allowing it to escape from immune control and continue to destroy CD4 lymphocytes.

Accordingly, when antiviral drugs were introduced as monotherapy, drug-resistant mutants thrived. One trick to shift the odds in favor of treatment, already known to students of tuberculosis, could be simultaneous administration of several drugs affecting different targets, which required the virus to make three resistance mutations at once to escape the effects of three drugs, a low probability event. As additional classes of antiviral drugs became available, it was possible to test the concept of overcoming selection for resistance by simultaneously targeting more than one step in viral replication. Proof of concept came from benchmark clinical trials and led to the effective "*highly active antiretroviral therapy*" *(HAART)* multidrug cocktail which changed the trajectory of the AIDS epidemic.

Drug Development after AZT

Drug Toxicity

Early explorations of candidate drugs focused on blocking viral replication by interfering with the vRNA-to-vDNA cycle by inhibiting its reverse transcriptase (RT) enzyme. Those first *nucleoside analogues*, azidothymidine (AZT), dideoxycyotosine (ddC) and dideoxyinosine (ddI), all disrupted the viral DNA step in cell cultures, but in patients had unexpected toxic effects on human DNA pathways.

From closely monitored clinical trials of antiviral drugs, it soon became apparent that at the dosing used, AZT caused *anemia* by its nasty suppressive effect on normal red blood cell production, and ddC *interfered with lymphocyte production*, already under attack from HIV. Further, ddC and ddI shared dose-dependent neurotoxicity which caused severe, even disabling, *peripheral neuropathy* characterized by burning pain and abnormal sensitivity in hands and feet. Other side effects of ddI included loss of normal facial fat, called *lipodystrophy*, leading to prominence of facial musculature.

In higher dosages, many of the nucleosides were toxic to liver function. Patients suffered with but tolerated these toxicities because the alternative was death.

Understanding Nucleoside Drug Toxicity

An unexpected biological explanation of these targeted toxicities of nucleoside analogues emerged from animal studies on *mitochondria*, the energy-producing intracellular organelles found in all living tissue and with their own DNA. *Mitochondrial DNA content*, necessary for regular organelle functioning, proved to have been profoundly *depleted by drug therapy*, but could be restored by stopping drug exposure. Further, the organ distribution of DNA depletion varied according to the drug: AZT lowered mitochondrial DNA inside red blood cell precursors, while ddC and ddI depleted mitochondria which maintain axonal flow inside peripheral nerves. With the discovery of *selective mitochondrial toxicity*, the differential toxic effects made sense.

Much later, when the nucleoside analogue Abacavir was introduced, in nearly 8% of individuals it caused a severe, even life-threatening *hypersensitivity reaction*, which almost removed this potent antiviral RT inhibitor from continued clinical use. Wisely, the pharmaceutical manufacturer collected DNA samples from all available patients who experienced this serious adverse reaction and from controls who did not. Since by this point the human genome had been sequenced, it was possible to identify a reliable *gene marker for susceptibility to Abacavir hypersensitivity*, which became the first example of modern individualized patient-specific *pharmacological screening* for susceptibility to adverse events before beginning treatment.

Molecular Discoveries of New Drug Targets

As more pharmaceutical companies established dedicated HIV-drug discovery divisions to supplement research in universities and at NIH, the pace of mapping the HIV genome and discovering all the functioning proteins involved in its full replication accelerated. Definition of the structure and function of HIV lock-and-key mechanism for attachment to the CD4/complement receptors on the lymphocyte stimulated work on *entry-inhibiting drugs*. Isolation, purification and analysis of the *viral protease enzyme,* which cleaves the polyprotein into parts needed for assembly of new virus, offered a *post-transcription drug target* and a type familiar to biochemists.

While the receptor inhibitors failed to make the grade to clinical use, the protease inhibitors soon arrived for testing in clinical trials. By this point, the technology for assessing drug efficacy had outstripped end-points based solely on clinical progression and rates of CD4 depletion.

In the interim, assay techniques for measuring concentrations of HIV in blood had been developed, and now the *impact of treatment on viral replication could be determined directly by following viral load (vL).*

Measuring Drug Efficacy by Effects on HIV Viral Load and CD4 Count Responses

Viral load allowed clinical trials to easily measure drug effects on HIV infection. Now the *laboratory surrogates* of *vL* and *CD4 counts* became the *primary endpoints* for antiviral efficacy. *Drug toxicity* continued to be evaluated by monitoring liver, kidney, bone marrow, muscle, central nervous system and other organs for adverse effects. Regular clinic visits collected data on clinical symptoms and signs.

The FDA could now approve an antiretroviral drug, or combination of drugs, based on (1) *sustained depression of vL,* (2) *sustained reversal of CD4 depletion* and (3) *acceptable rates of adverse reactions attributable to drug use.*

In the new design of clinical trials for HIV therapies, clinical outcomes now were only secondary endpoints. Consequently, trial length could be shorter—48 weeks—and involve as few as 140 patients, instead of 2,000, to reach statistically valid comparison of the new drug. Since those in the blinded control arm now received an approved drug instead of placebo, the new drug would be either *superior, inferior or equivalent to the approved drug.* FDA would license only superior and equivalent drugs with acceptable toxicities.

Outwitting Drug-Resistant Virus with HAART—The Holy Grail

The final step, alluded to earlier, was the introduction of combined therapy—originally two nucleoside analogues and a protease inhibitor—which defeated the Darwinian escape of resistant mutants, as it required two or more *simultaneous mutations* to generate a multidrug-resistant virion.

In 1997, 16 years after the CDC recognized the oncoming AIDS epidemic, multidrug highly active antiretroviral therapy (HAART) became the standard of care. In tailoring individual treatment, technology for sequencing HIV "swarms" in individual patients allowed detection of circulating mutants associated with antiretroviral drug resistance, whether originally acquired from a resistant source, or the residual of prior ineffective therapy.

Proper combinations of HAART drugs miraculously reversed even severe immunodeficiency. The ensuing *immune reconstitution* occasionally disclosed an undetected subclinical OI, revealed when the restored immune system could recognize the invader and generate an active inflammatory response (*immune reconstitution syndrome*).

> *HAART produced durable viral suppression, restored health to the ill, and prevented healthy asymptomatics from progressing to AIDS.*
>
> *Further, lowering vL to undetectable levels converted HIV-infected persons from infectious to non-infections, a prevention program more effective than condoms or needle exchange programs.*
>
> *The discoveries and technological inventions during the AIDS epidemic closely resemble the Manhattan Project and the Moon Shot in terms of their impact on science and humanity. It was a new world in many ways.*

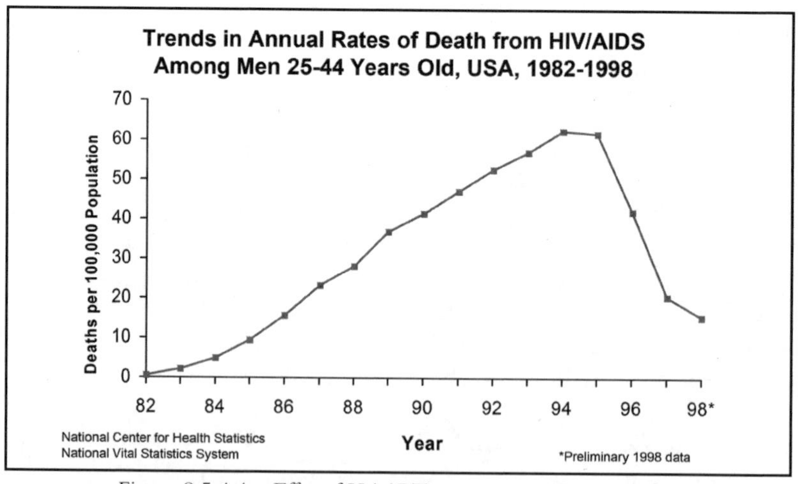

Figure 8.5.4.4 *Effect of HAART treatment on AIDS mortality*

Although initiation of prophylactic medications for PCP and other OIs began to impact death rate, the dramatic drop shown is due to introduction of HAART combination therapy for HIV infection, which became the standard of care.

Source: CDC diagram

Reflections on the Scope of the HIV/AIDS Epidemic

The HIV/AIDS timeline[2] offers some sobering facts about the dimensions of the AIDS pandemic. In 1994, AIDS became the leading cause of death for all Americans aged 25–44 and by 1995 over 500,000 cases of AIDS had been reported. In 1998 CDC reported that 49% of US AIDS-related deaths were African-Americans. By 2007 565,000 persons had died of AIDS in the US since 1981.

In 1997 HAART became the new standard of care for HIV infection, and for the first time AIDS-related deaths declined by 47% compared with the previous year.

In 1999 WHO estimated that worldwide 33 million adults and children were living with HIV infection, and that 14 million had died of AIDS. The UN saw AIDS as a threat to peace and security and adopted the specific goal of reversing the spread of HIV/AIDS.

Following on this important declaration came a series of funding programs to provide antiretroviral therapy to developing countries and other efforts to stem the tide of HIV infection, among them the Global Fund to fight AIDS, Tuberculosis and Malaria; PEPFAR, the US President's Emergency Plan for AIDS Relief; and the Global Health Initiative.

By 2006 over one million people in sub-Saharan Africa were receiving antiretroviral therapy for the first time.

By 2013 35 million worldwide were living with HIV infection, 6.8 million people in South Africa alone, and 1.2 million Americans.

Where Is the HIV Vaccine?

The epidemiological cohort studies which defined fast and slow progressors also noted a small subset of *non-progressors*, presumably immune, who also did not deplete their CD4 cells. The hypothesis of presumed immunity to HIV, a rare event, was confirmed when viral load measurements became available: these individuals had values below detectable, and their lymphocytes could not be coaxed into viral replication, proving absence of latent infection.

Further, there were a group of HIV-negative individuals who although repeated sexually active with an HIV-infected partner, a so-called *discordant couple*, failed to convert to antibody-positive or to show any other evidence of HIV infection. Some of these individuals proved to be congenitally missing one of the coordinate cell surface receptors needed for effective cell docking by HIV before entry into CD4 cells.

Each of these discoveries boosted hope that, like many other viral infections, a new vaccine would soon be developed which would remove the threat of continuing spread of HIV infection. These hopes were doomed, however, by the very complexity and changing nature of the HIV virus in infected and transmitting populations. HIV in different regions of the world gradually acquired signature geographical markers, sorting them into "*clades*", such that one vaccine would not cover all clades.

Further, the search for stable "*immunodominant epitopes*" on the virus to incorporate into non-pathogenic live virus "carrier" vaccines so far has turned out to be less effective than hoped.

We are now 36 years out from recognition of the AIDS epidemic in the US. While occasional candidate vaccines still come to the Phase I and II trial stages and at least one is now in large phase III trials, for the present more hope is vested in reduction of transmission through effective drug therapy by suppressing infectiousness. If successful, it would lower high rates of acquisition through risky behaviors. The fight against HIV/AIDS is not over, and it is still a big challenge.

* * *

Participation in this scientific biomedical revolution as a clinical investigator contributing to design and execution of clinical trials was an exciting and extraordinary privilege for all concerned. It was also a once-in-a-lifetime opportunity to join in a focused effort by basic scientists, clinicians, pharmaceutical companies and government, which unquestionably made a positive difference on human health and has had a worldwide impact on human society.

Endnotes

1 **Simian origin of HIV—the *Simian Immunodeficiency Viruses (SIV)*.** Gene sequencing has shown that two closely related *simian retroviruses* which target T-lymphocytes, but are generally non-injurious to their host species, entered human populations at some point. Mutant variants of the two simian types adapted to their new hosts, giving rise to *two types of human immunodeficiency virus*. The more virulent was the first to be discovered and named HIV in 1984, but changed to HIV-1 on subsequent discovery of its close cousin, HIV-2.

HIV-1 is related to viruses found in chimpanzees and gorillas living in western Africa. HIV-2 viruses are related to viruses found in West African primate sooty mangabey. The primate precursor of HIV-2 was discovered in a sick NASA monkey by virologist S.R.S. Rangan at the Tulane Primate Research Center and named SIV_{delta} in 1986.

HIV-1 is responsible for the AIDS pandemic. HIV-2, originally limited to West Africa and also transmissible by sex and blood, as a result of travel and immigration occasionally appears in Europe and the Americas. While HIV-2 possesses destructive potential for the human immune system, decline in immunity is much slower than with HIV-1, and the virus is not as pathogenic in infected persons, as indicated by the high percentage of asymptomatic infected non-progressors and the lack of maternal-child transmission. Its antiviral drug susceptibility pattern also differs from naive HIV-1 strains.

For more details, see https//en.m.wikipedia.org/wiki/Subtypes_of_HIV; and also McCarthy, KR, Johnson WE, Kirmaier, A: https://doi.org/10.1371/journal.pone.0159281, "Phylogeny and History of the Lost SIV from Crab-Eating Macaques: SIVmfa", *PLOS*, July 14, 2016; https://doi.org/10.1371/journal.pone.0159281.

2 For a **Timeline of HIV/AIDS**, see http://www.aids.gov/hiv-aids-basics/hiv-aids-101/aids-timeline.

3 **AIDS and alternative medicine**. Before testing for drug susceptibility became available for HIV, the Louisiana HIV/AIDS Research Committee received a proposal from the general public recommending a treatment trial of garlic extract, an all-purpose nostrum since antiquity.

Once clinical trials of synthetic antivirals got underway, some participants supplemented prescribed regimens with "*alternative medicine*" programs which promised "immune enhancement" by gazing at crystals or pyramids. Other recommended folk remedies, such as ingesting St. John's wort or blue-green algae, which unknowingly altered metabolism of antiviral drugs. Addition of folk remedies containing biologically active substances not only had potential for harm to the patient but also for the integrity of clinical trials, as strict adherence to prescribed medication is assumed in evaluating results.

AIDS in New Orleans—

A Second Wave City

Newton E. Hyslop, Jr.

At four o'clock on the afternoon of June 28, 1984, my adventurous wife, Debbie, and I drove into New Orleans, LA, after a 2½-day journey from Massachusetts, and just a day ahead of the moving van. We were greeted by the daily late afternoon near-blinding tropical downpour of two hours, which lowers the temperature, floods streets, soaks the below-sea-level soils, replenishes swamps and ensures that for the five months of summer, the atmosphere remains oppressively humid, the environment vibrantly green and richly populated with vertebrates, invertebrates, arthropods and microbial species, some likely still unknown.

Coming from Yankee Land, we were prepared to leave if the natives proved restless, but it would be 29 years before I returned home alone after Hurricane Katrina nearly destroyed what I had built.

In the meantime, my New Orleans medical career of 22 years would be defined by the AIDS epidemic, which is the subject of this essay. But first, a little background.

* * *

Before New Orleans

Choosing a Career

In 1948 my younger brother and I had scarlet fever. The Town of Duxbury Board of Health posted a formal notice on the door announcing that our home was quarantined. My own recovery was complicated by rheumatic fever, and thus at age 12 began my interest in a medical career. The migratory arthritis of rheumatic fever and its other effects left me assigned to bed rest for eight weeks. Our family doctor came each week to examine me and draw blood for testing. There was no treatment, except tincture of time. As rheumatic fever could irreversibly damage heart muscle and valves, he listened carefully to my heart sounds with his stethoscope. After my recovery, he counseled gradual return to full activities. He was my hero.

During second year of medical school, class work in bacteriology and immunology drew my interest. It linked microbial life with human disease and historic epidemics, and the organisms causing infectious diseases could be observed with the microscope and grown in the laboratory. A summer job in the bacteriology laboratory of the Peter Bent Brigham Hospital (PBBH) on a project studying infections in kidney transplant recipients reinforced my interest.

By my internship year, the Massachusetts General Hospital (MGH) had just established a clinical Infectious Diseases (ID) Unit, and during the next year I was encouraged to enter the field.

Becoming an Immunologist

Being subject to the Doctor Draft, I committed to government service in the US Public Health Service (USPHS) for two years following initial clinical training. My application to NIH for a Research Associate position serendipitously matched me with the Laboratory of Immunology in the National Institute of Allergy and Infectious Diseases, thereby launching my career in immunology.

Two years of mentored "bench research" at NIH were followed later by a year as associate in the Oxford immunochemistry laboratory of future Nobelist R. R. Porter.

Becoming an Infectious Diseases (ID) Specialist

My final year of internal medicine training, at PBBH, brought regular exposure to clinical research, after which I was invited to join the MGH ID Unit, merging this neophyte immunologist with the new medical subspecialty of infectious disease.

In 1966, the ID Unit numbered only four staff members, all of whom had research experience, like those in the other few fledging ID programs nationwide. For the first two years, while setting up my laboratory I served simultaneously as Fellow and Staff, and learned on the job how to be a consultant. There were no clinical ID textbooks. Fortunately, requests to consult on patients were infrequent, and there was time to visit the hospital library before handwriting a note in the paper chart.

My clinical subspecialty became care of patients with recurrent infections due to immunodeficiencies. Laboratory studies on antibody transport into secretions (saliva, breast milk), the immunochemistry of penicillin allergy, and locomotion of white blood cells complemented the clinical research.

Over time my ID expertise grew as I grappled with disease, studied problems in the laboratory, learned from my peers and elders, and reviewed the medical literature in preparation for teaching and writing.

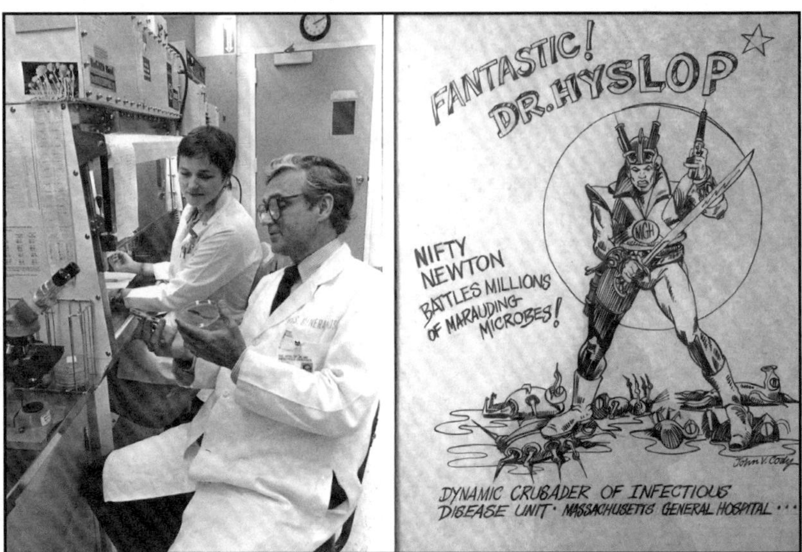

Figures 8.5.5.1 and 8.5.5.2 Left: *Infectious Disease specialist NEH in 1984 reviewing culture plates with technician Wendy Kallas in the MGH Bacteriology Laboratory.* Right: *Cartoon, gift to the author by illustrator John V. Cody, 1982*

Credits: MGH Photography Department *(L)*, Author *(R)*

Unknowingly Preparing for the Gathering Storm

Changes in the Subspecialty of Infectious Diseases

During my 18 years in the MGH ID Unit, the field of clinical infectious diseases blossomed. Multiple factors drove the changes.

New antibiotics came in abundance, both derived from nature and synthetic derivatives designed to enhance performance.

Antibiotic resistance followed widespread use of antibiotics. Resistant microbes first appeared in the hospital and then spread to the community.

> Resistance also resulted from sustained use of antibiotics in mass prophylaxis against invasive bacteria. The most famous example was the emergence of sulfonamide-resistant meningococci among military recruits at Fort Ord, CA, following an atttempt to suppress outbreaks of life-threeatening invasive bacterial infection.

> Resistant organisms then spread into the general population, where they persisted for decades. This failure of antibiotic prophylaxis stimulated the Walter Reed Army Institute of Research to develop effective meningococcal vaccines for protection against infection.

Diagnostic microbiology, the detection and diagnosis of infectious agents, ranging from viruses to bacteria and parasites, was enriched by emerging technology and microbiological research.

Hospital epidemiology developed into a separate discipline. The need to prevent transmission of infections within hospitals spawned *infection control programs* which viewed the environment with an epidemiologist's perspective.

Changes in composition of patient populations increased demand for infectious diseases consultations, as the number of patients with infections increased. These patients came with *(1) travel-associated infections, (2) surgical infections,* especially those complicating implantation of heart valves, vascular grafts and orthopedic hardware; and (3) *opportunistic infections* taking advantage of the immunosuppressive effects of therapies for cancer, autoimmune disorders and organ transplantation.

The changing hospital environment both grew and changed the subspecialty. A need arose for clinicians of broad general medical knowledge who were also knowledgeable about diagnostic microbiology, clinical pharmacology, and the clinical features and epidemiology of infections.

Standardization of training and credentialing of ID specialists became necessary for quality control of staff appointments and reimbursement of clinical services by insurance. Internal medicine and pediatrics added ID as a new subspecialty. The number of trainees and training programs slowly increased until the mid 1980's, when the AIDS epidemic required more practitioners. By 2005, there would be over 100 ID Fellowship training programs in the US, and attendance at the annual educational meeting of the *Infectious Diseases Society of America* rose to over 5,000.

Changes in Immunology

Clinical immunology similarly advanced in the 18 years leading up to 1984.

Cellular mechanisms involved in the immune response were revealed, and the lineage of individual cells could be tracked and their maturation monitored.

Immune competence and incompetence could now be described with blood tests by quantifying each cellular and molecular component of the immune repertoire.

As the epidemic of Acquired Immune Deficiency Syndrome (AIDS) unfolded, even the general public became aware of the two major classes among the *"T-cell"* lymphocytes which regulate the immune response: T4 (or CD4) *"helper"* cells which turn it on, and T8 (or CD8) *"suppressor"* cells which turn it off. Their proportions and numbers among the other white blood cells were critical to intact immunity.

Between 1966 and 1984, three trends—the development of infectious disease as a medical subspecialty, the expansion of diagnostic microbiology, and advances in immunology—were building the clinical and laboratory infrastructure needed to recognize and cope with the oncoming AIDS epidemic *without knowledge of its presence on the horizon.*

Harbingers of AIDS—Opportunistic Infections after Therapeutic Immunosuppression

A steady and notable rise in instances of opportunistic infections (OIs)—unusual infections from normally benign organisms, which can only take hold in an environment of weakened immunity—presaged the onset of the AIDS epidemic. These OIs represented the unavoidable consequence of immunosuppressive drug regimens used for organ transplantation, cancer and autoimmune diseases. The risks and types of infections varied according to the extent of immunosuppression required.

Pneumocystis carinii pneumonia (PCP) was the bellwether OI of the AIDS epidemic. My first encounter with it came 45 years ago, 10 years before the AIDS epidemic, when Mr. Herbert Juster became my patient at the MGH.

The New York Times
Published: January 3, 1972
Copyright © The New York Times

BOSTON, Jan. 2 (AP)—Herbert G. Juster, 49 years old, who underwent heart transplant surgery at the Stanford University Medical Center eight months ago, died today of a lung infection at the Massachusetts General Hospital.

Figure 8.5.5.3 *"Heart Transplant Recipient Dies of Pneumonia at Mass. General Hospital. Special to the New York Times, January 3, 1972."*
Death notice from The New York Times, *January 3, 1972*

In 1971, heart transplantation was still experimental, pre-transplant testing for donor-recipient compatibility was imperfect, and laboratory tests for assessing immune status were yet to be discovered. To prevent immune rejection of the transplanted heart, the Stanford immunosuppressive regimen depended on maximal tolerated dosing.

On returning to Boston, Mr. Juster became feverish and increasingly short of breath. His lung biopsy showed PCP, then a rarely diagnosed infection. The only available treatment was pentamidine, highly toxic in excess and variably effective. CDC controlled the national supply and immediately released the drug on documentation of diagnosis. Despite treatment by protocol, Mr. Juster succumbed, as did many others with far advanced PCP treated with pentamidine.

In the interval between his death in 1972 and the onset of the epidemic in the 1980's, there was minimal progress in development of new drugs for the prevention and treatment of OIs. They effectively became "orphan diseases". While OIs unquestionably caused morbidity and mortality in persons with immunodeficiency acquired from immunosuppressive therapy, the relatively small size of this patient population failed to attract the necessary focused and costly investment in microbiological and pharmaceutical research needed for scientific advancement. The AIDS epidemic removed this obstacle.

PCP and AIDS

Ten years later in 1981, when CDC control of pentamidine supplies was still the practice, suddenly there were multiple requests for the drug. Unlike prior PCP cases, these all occurred in young men *not* on any immunosuppressive medications.

Recognizing the rarity of these events, CDC investigated and alerted the medical community to a new disease soon termed Acquired Immune Deficiency Syndrome. They designated it as predominantly a deficiency of cell-mediated immunity, based on the abnormally low number and percentage of CD4 cells among the blood lymphocytes.

If the AIDS epidemic had started in an earlier era, understanding the immunological nature of AIDS would have been delayed, as would recognition that it was in fact an *infectious immunodeficiency.* Furthermore, if it had occurred before the discovery of a new class of obscure viruses called retroviruses, it would have blocked the rapid discovery that the cause of AIDS was a *retrovirus which attacks and destroys lymphocytes.* Instead, this virus, *Human Immunodeficiency Virus (HIV),* was discovered only three years after the announcement of the AIDS epidemic, and ranks among the great achievements in microbiology.

The New Orleans Years

How did we come to be in New Orleans?

Serendipity again played a role. As a physician, laboratory scientist and teacher, my responsibilities for patient care and teaching of undergraduate and graduates competed for research time in an epoch when NIH funding of medical research was shifting from MD to full-time PhD researchers and to large groups. Although I relished the independence, intellectual challenge and collegial life in MGH's rarified academic medical research environment, by 1980 my status was becoming financially unstable. Finally, the grants ran out, and it was time to move on. Fortunately, the Tulane Department of Medicine was looking for a Chief of Infectious Diseases and saw me as a match.

Tulane needed someone to build a worthy training and clinical research program in infectious diseases for its three affiliated hospitals in New Orleans: Charity Hospital, VA Medical Center and Tulane University Hospital. Given the institutional conditions then present, the move had significant potential for personal hazard. However, at age 49 it would be my only chance to apply my hard-won skills and knowledge on a larger scale.

Our grown children well-launched, and Debbie willing to test out living in the Deep South, *we* accepted the offer. It was a calculated risk, but one worth taking, as became apparent shortly after my appointment. Two months into my new position, the medical attaché of a Middle Eastern country's embassy requested that a Tulane representative accompany the 4-member CDC Plague Team sent to investigate an outbreak of bubonic plague. That week-long expedition was the first indication that the move to Tulane would dramatically change my professional life.

Success in New Orleans would involve coordinating a lot of moving parts, and still require me to bring in external funding from grants and contracts, but now to grow and support young faculty.

Ironically, the AIDS epidemic would bring financial strength and recognition to our embryonic Tulane ID program. The medical center and state needed scientific and medical leadership to organize a clinical response, and we needed to build a financially sound ID training program. The AIDS epidemic brought us opportunities for growth and program development.

AIDS in New Orleans

Before the discovery of HIV in late 1984, AIDS was purely a clinical definition: profound depletion of cellular immunity from unknown cause, together with an opportunistic infection and/or certain highly unusual cancers. Delineation of the stages between HIV infection and progression to AIDS became possible only after HIV antibody testing became available in 1985.

The geographical distribution of the first wave of the AIDS epidemic was confined to the large metropolitan cities of the East and West Coasts, which began to grapple with its consequences in 1982. When defined by case attack rates per 100,000 population, New Orleans was a second wave city when I arrived in 1984.

The disease burden of AIDS began to impact the Tulane-associated teaching hospitals, not only in terms of utilization but also fear of contagion among health care workers. I focused my attention on Charity Hospital.

Figure 8.5.5.4 *Commemorative poster for 250th Anniversary of Charity Hospital, New Orleans, by Danny Frolich (1986)*

The 1830 hospital building (foreground) *was replaced in 1939 by a new hospital* (background) *which remained in use until 2005 when damage by Hurricane Katrina forced its closure. Its replacement, built on another site, opened in 2015 at the cost of $1 billion.*

Source: photograph of the author's print

Settling In

The first few months at Charity Hospital alerted me to the need to have a neutral identity, as the corridors and wards of old Charity were full of people of all ages in white coats with different armorial badges, announcing that they were from Charity Hospital, or from LSU, Tulane, Delgado, Respiratory Therapy, and so forth. In order not to disappear into the sea of white coats, I decided to wear a blue blazer and bow tie at all times when I wasn't at the bedside. This uniform did not align me with any faction and gained me access and trust from others as my own man.

My position as Chief of Infectious Diseases Services at three different hospitals meant learning three different systems and three sets of personnel. Further, there was also the medical school with its own hierarchy. I decided to use 3x5 index cards to collect data on patients, to record my observations and thoughts about the institutions, and to store ideas for my plans. The index cards fit easily in the pockets of my blazer.

The problem list for state-funded Charity Hospital grew into a project of its own, as in the early years there were more problems than administrators could handle. About 15 years later, I rediscovered my stack of cards enumerating Charity's problems. I was pleased to see that most of them had disappeared because the hospital had finally received an infusion of support from the state, which allowed enlightened administrators to upgrade equipment, create isolation beds and increase staffing to needed levels.

Lessons from Patients

Five patients who came to Charity Hospital for medical care exemplify the institution's strengths, its weaknesses, its ability to reshape itself in response to the AIDS epidemic and its central role in infectious diseases programs during my 22 years at Tulane.

Case 1. The Honduran Banana Picker's Swollen Hand—1985

A Honduran banana harvester, working in his native country, injured his dominant hand. Over the course of a year, his hand developed an insidious, disabling and progressive swelling. When local remedies failed, he traveled by banana boat to New Orleans to seek help at Charity Hospital. His massively swollen hand had draining fistulas exuding fluid, and x-rays showed the bones to be dangerously eroded.

Laboratory examination of the fluid revealed the rare organism *Nocardia asteroides*, susceptible to oral antibiotics. Surgery was deferred, and treatment begun. The swelling gradually resolved, and by three months his hand and bones were normal. The published case report[1] would be cited by others writing about this unusual infection.

He would have lost his hand without the superior diagnostic microbiological laboratories at Charity Hospital. The ability of these PhD-led laboratories to identify unusual and difficult-to-grow fastidious organisms causing opportunistic infections in AIDS was critical to patient care and also to our eligibility for clinical research grants.

Case 2. The Dress Designer with Wasting and Persistent Fever of Unknown Origin—1987

A young man with a profitable dress-designing business in the French Quarter, but without medical insurance, developed daily fevers to 105°F, progressive weight loss and wasting of his muscles and body fat. The suspected diagnosis of AIDS was confirmed by his positive HIV test. But only when laboratory cultures from multiple sites grew the environmental fungus *Histoplasma capsulatum* was the OI diagnosis of *disseminated histoplasmosis* established. An entity of which I was aware but had never seen before, it would become commonplace in New Orleans as the AIDS epidemic progressed.

Our ID Consultation Team wrote specific recommendations for his physicians on dosage and IV infusion rate for Amphotericin B, a drug with a narrow margin between therapeutic and toxic effects, but which was then the only treatment for histoplasmosis.

At that time many medical personnel were afraid of acquiring HIV infection, and lack of close following of AIDS patients and even neglect were problems. On the first treatment, although dosing was correct, our recommendation for slow infusion was ignored, and the patient developed dangerously low blood pressure. The next day we reiterated the advice, but he again received the drug rapidly. This time he developed irreversible shock and died.

It was at this moment that it became obvious that the separate Tulane and LSU Infectious Diseases Sections needed to move away from consultative care and join together to become primary care providers to persons with HIV/AIDS. This joint venture was the beginning of the Tulane-LSU Charity Hospital HIV/AIDS Center for patient care, education and research. This partnership brought immense benefits to patients, nurses, technicians, medical students, residents, specialty trainees, Fellows and Faculty of both schools, and trained over 1000 physicians. It also created the perfect environment for clinical research on HIV and AIDS, and made our program attractive for external support by grants and contracts.

Case 3. The Accountant with Progressive Dementia—1988

A young male accountant moved to New Orleans to accept a position in a city agency. After an interval, his behavior concerned his fellow employees, and following a possible convulsion at work, he was sent to Charity Hospital because he had no medical insurance in his job. Found to be HIV-positive, he was admitted to the new HIV/AIDS Unit.

I found him sitting up in bed reading the *Wall Street Journal* upside-down. Not surprisingly he had no recall of what he had read, and neurological examination disclosed severe dementia. Tests of spinal fluid and brain imaging were normal. Over two weeks he lapsed into coma without obvious cause, lost his vital reflexes and died. His family agreed to post-mortem examination of his brain.

At first the neuropathologist could determine no cause, but on microscopic exam found multiple small clusters of fused cells scattered throughout the brain. This clue fit the first report of HIV-associated dementia and encephalitis which the neuropathologist had just read about in the previous week's *New England Journal of Medicine*.

This patient was another instance of the rare disorders that would become common for us as the HIV/AIDS epidemic proceeded. At first we had no weapons to fight this terrifying viral infection and its complications. However, through our participation in the national AIDS Clinical Trials Group and in pharmaceutically sponsored trials of antiretroviral drugs, over time we gained competence in early diagnosis and effective treatment of many of the previously deadly opportunistic infections and, ultimately, over HIV itself.

The AIDS epidemic focused the combined efforts of government, pharmaceutical and academic research on the study and treatment of many hitherto rare and poorly understood infections. Advances in microbiology and pharmacology were permanent dividends from the scientific response to the worldwide devastation of HIV/AIDS.

Case 4. The Pregnant High School Senior with Asymptomatic HIV Infection—1990–1999

At her first visit to the Prenatal Clinic, medical evaluation of this 7-months-pregnant 18-year-old adolescent discovered three asymptomatic sexually transmitted diseases (STDs): *venereal warts, gonorrhea* and *HIV,* each transmitted to her by one or more of her three lifetime sexual partners. All were *asymptomatic infections*, detectable only on screening tests, which in turn made her a risk for sexual transmission of all three infections to others.

Her baby, delivered by C-section, tested positive for HIV due to normal pre-partum transfer of maternal antibody. At risk for HIV infection and pediatric AIDS, he escaped, as after many months maternal antibody disappeared, and his test became negative. His concerned mother brought him regularly to the recently established Maternal-Child HIV Clinic, which provided care for both of them in one-stop visits and offered support services.

Over six years, our patient progressed slowly from normal immunity to immunodeficiency. When her CD4 count dropped below 500, a trial of AZT alone failed to halt the drop, and a second drug was added. Her treatment team was uncertain about how regularly she took the medicine.

At age 23, in her sixth year, she developed an AIDS-defining malignancy—cervical cancer—from her human papilloma virus (HPV) infection, also the cause of her venereal warts. Following surgery to remove her cancerous uterus, for the next two years she was lost to medical follow-up until she returned for treatment of a massive abscess. Shortly afterwards, she developed a second AIDS-defining malignancy—B-cell lymphoma of the abdomen—which proved resistant to multiple rounds of chemotherapy.

She died *just prior to her 27th birthday,* nine years after initial diagnosis of asymptomatic HIV infection at age 18. Her child, then age nine, healthy and growing normally, was being brought up by her parents.

This patient's desperate history illustrates several points:

(1) *Shifting demographics of HIV/AIDS epidemic in the US.*

Initially spread by male-to-male sexual transmission, by 1990 most of new HIV infections occurred among minorities, and were acquired through heterosexual transmission, injecting drug use or both. Our African-American patient did not use drugs, but her partners might have.

(2) *Risk of HIV transmission during unprotected sexual relations.*

In an HIV-infected person the simultaneous presence of another sexually transmitted disease potentiates sexual transmission of HIV to others. Beginning in 1988 in New Orleans, risky behaviors accompanying an epidemic of crack cocaine use nearly tripled rates of gonorrhea and syphilis, and for six years drove rising rates of STDs and HIV among both sexes. Within the vulnerable population, HIV infection rates reached 1 in 50 among pregnant young women who, like our patient, attended the prenatal clinic at Charity Hospital.

The high STD rate only reversed when public health programs made free condoms generally available in high-risk neighborhoods, where users could grab a handful from clear glass bowls placed in grocery stores, beauty parlors, barbershops and clinics. As condom use protected against HIV transmission as well as other STDs, similar risk-reduction programs were introduced worldwide.

(3) *Risk of HIV transmission from infected mother to child.*

Maternal-child transmission risk of HIV, originally 25%, became safely preventable in later years. Antiviral treatment of the mother began during pregnancy. After delivery the baby was treated for an interval, while the mother remained on chronic suppressive treatment. Antiviral prophylaxis of HIV-infected pregnant women only began four years after our patient's son was born; it initially consisted of AZT monotherapy but was later superseded by combination therapy.

(4) *Immunodeficiency allows certain viruses to transform cells into AIDS-defining cancers.*

Under conditions of deficient immunity, potentially oncogenic viruses can spontaneously transform their target cells into cancer. In our patient's case, cells infected by the infectious mononucleosis virus (*Epstein-Barr virus, EBV)* were transformed into B-cell lymphoma, and cells in her cervix became malignant after invasion by venereal wart virus *(human papilloma virus, HPV).*

(5) *Technical advances were needed to assess treatment responses to antiviral drugs.*

When antiviral drugs for HIV first underwent clinical trials, the only laboratory test for clinical response was a rise in CD4 count, usually of brief duration, which did not occur in our patient.

Antiviral therapy was only rationalized after advances in HIV virology unraveled its complex life cycle and added new drug targets. They also provided tools for measuring amount of virus present in blood (*viral load, vL*) and tests for drug resistance. Used together, one could determine whether poor clinical results were due to resistant virus or failure to take the drug.

Importantly, the new tests demonstrated that treatment with only a single drug ("*monotherapy*") results in selecting for drug-resistant virus, which becomes dominant and obliterates the early CD4 recovery. "*Never add a single drug to a failing regimen*" became the mantra for physicians once the danger of monotherapy for HIV was recognized. However, this insight came long after our patient had received a single second drug following her failure to respond to AZT alone.

(6) *The ability to measure vL allowed the strategy of simultaneous treatment with multiple drugs to be tested in clinical trials.*

Highly active antiretroviral therapy (HAART) with three drugs was shown to be dramatically effective in reducing vL to undetectable levels, which in turn generated a steady rise in CD4 counts and slowly restored immunocompetence.

For our young mother, these seemingly miraculous scientific discoveries came too late, but they saved the lives of millions of others.

Case 5. The Carpenter with Early Tuberculosis—1995

A young carpenter from rural Louisiana, married with two young children, was referred to Charity Hospital for evaluation of chronic cough and bloody sputum. His chest x-ray showed a small cavity consistent with tuberculosis (TB), and TB-like organisms were visible on microscopic examination of his sputum. As his HIV test was negative, he did not have AIDS.

When I examined him, he was a healthy-appearing individual and seemed intelligent and responsible. The source of his infection was unknown to him, but during the early days of the AIDS epidemic, undiagnosed patients coinfected with HIV and TB had unknowingly spawned a parallel TB epidemic in many areas of the country, including Louisiana.

He was to begin TB therapy as an outpatient while awaiting culture results to confirm the diagnosis and check drug susceptibility. He was discharged with TB medication and an appointment for outpatient follow-up at the local public health TB Clinic. After six weeks, the Charity Hospital TB/mycology laboratory confirmed drug-sensitive tuberculosis and reported the result to the TB Control Program of the Louisiana Office of Public Health.

Nine months later he was readmitted to the hospital and found to have active TB with severe damage to his previously involved lung, and also spread to the other side. He was highly infectious for his family and other contacts.

How did this happen? He was feeling fine before his two-month supply of TB meds ran out but had not gone to the outpatient TB clinic as instructed. Even though he once again began to lose weight and developed shortness of breath, he said he assumed that since he had not been contacted about his lab results, he did not have TB. In fact, because of the stigma of TB, he was in denial until his worsening symptoms overrode his fears.

This preventable treatment failure and unnecessary risk for others triggered an outcomes study of the local TB Control Program for Public Health Region I which served metropolitan New Orleans. Review of records for the past five years found only 43% of patients completed treatment and 18% died. Fully 25% of TB cases were lost to follow-up, most of them homeless individuals. Of the homeless, 60% received no more than one month of therapy, instead of the minimum nine months recommended at that time. Finally, many of those who completed the designated months of therapy received multiple interrupted short courses of treatment, stretched over a year or more, a condition which favored development of drug-resistant organisms transmissible to contacts in the household, community and workplace.

These findings, published in 1997,[2] led to reforms in management and surveillance of TB outcomes in Public Health Region I. Our intervention coincided with the national push for *directly observed* daily therapy in which outreach workers deliver medicines to patients each day to assure successful completion of TB treatment.

This case and other instances of incomplete initial treatment also led to opening of a long-term care facility for recalcitrant TB patients, and stimulated changes in Louisiana law regarding the management of persons who refused TB treatment.

A strong collaboration developed between the Tulane infectious diseases program and the Regional and State TB Control Programs. They supported training of ID Fellows in TB control and our related research on the molecular epidemiology of TB infection in New Orleans and Louisiana.

Figure 8.5.5.5 *Faculty and Fellows of Tulane Adult Infectious Diseases Section, 1998–99, Tulane University School of Medicine, New Orleans, Louisiana. The author is the one without a white coat.*

Photo by Photography Department, Tulane University School of Medicine

Summing Up

These case vignettes illustrate aspects of my experience at Charity Hospital, which for 22 years was my clinical focus and my teacher. Sometimes the lessons exhilarated and stretched the mind, as we struggled joyfully to learn the biology and new treatments of HIV and to understand their complications. Other times our experiences with patients, families and relationships devastated by AIDS only reinforced earlier lessons on the human condition and the human spirit.

Some lessons were grim, more troubling when seen up close, and unfortunately in Louisiana, repetitious, such as the destructive effects on body and soul of poverty, of physical exploitation, substance use, violent crime, reflex incarceration, and of our society's aversion to supporting those in need, or even providing them with a responsive system of medical care.

Fortunately for us in New Orleans, the AIDS epidemic ultimately forced reassessment of priorities at state and federal levels and brought us improved physical facilities, adequate staffing and resources.

Building effective programs from 1984 to 2006 to meet the twin challenges of the HIV and TB epidemics was the product of many dedicated people at Tulane and LSU Schools of Medicine, at Charity Hospital and its affiliated nursing and technical schools, and those within the State of Louisiana Department of Public Health. And it was my honor and pleasure for 22 years to be an integral part of those achievements.

> *"Look not mournfully into the Past. It comes not back again. Wisely improve the Present. It is thine. Go forth to meet the shadowy Future, without fear, and with a manly heart."*—Henry Wadsworth Longfellow[3]

* * *

In August 2005, Hurricane Katrina flooded Tulane Medical School and Hospital, VA Medical Center and Charity Hospital, scattered staff, and left the future of the AIDS and TB programs in doubt. Fortunately, as the city returned to life, the T-ID program was resuscitated under the leadership of one of my trainees and in 2017 is flourishing in a new and modern version of Charity Hospital. Hurricane Katrina also forced the evacuation of Debbie, then ill, and myself from New Orleans to family in San Jose, CA. There my beloved partner departed to the Great Beyond before I returned to New Orleans to begin a new career.

Newton E. Hyslop, Jr., MD, is Professor of Medicine *emeritus* at Tulane University School of Medicine, where he was Chief of the Adult Infectious Diseases Section and Medical Director of the HIV/AIDS/TB In-Patient Service at Charity Hospital of New Orleans.

A history major in college, after Harvard Medical School (HMS) he trained in internal medicine at Massachusetts General (MGH) and Peter Bent Brigham hospitals and in infectious diseases at MGH. He served two years as a US Public Health Service Officer at the National Institutes of Health (NIH), learning laboratory immunology, and a third year in immunochemistry at Oxford as Moseley Traveling Fellow of HMS. In 1966 he joined the HMS faculty and MGH Infectious Diseases (ID) Unit where he served for 18 years. In 1984 Tulane recruited him as ID Section Chief, a position he held for 22 years until his retirement.

His medical career included patient care, teaching, laboratory and clinical research, administration and authoring journal articles and chapters in text-books of infectious diseases. His research received support from NIH, the Howard Hughes Medical Institute, pharmaceutical and Louisiana sources.

The AIDS epidemic shaped his role in Louisiana where besides his New Orleans activities he also held statewide leadership positions in HIV/AIDS Disease Management and Tuberculosis Control programs. Nationally he participated in the AIDS Clinical Trials Group, the AIDS Subcommittee of the Infectious Disease Society of America, and the task force of the Centers for Disease Control on Prevention of Opportunistic Infections in AIDS. The Medical Center of Louisiana Foundation recognized his contributions with the *Spirit of Charity* award in 2010.

During 48 years of marriage to musician and former medical secretary Deborah Boyer, they successfully raised a daughter and a son before moving to Louisiana. Thereafter Debbie continued to keep Newt sane, grounded, well-traveled and happy until her passing in 2005. In 2013, after 29 years of residence in New Orleans, he returned home to Massachusetts to re-explore his native land.

Endnotes

1 Carlisle JT, Greer DL, Hyslop NE. Actinomycetoma of the hand caused by *Nocardia asteriodes. J Infect Dis* 1988; 158:244–246.

2 Brainard D, Hyslop NE Jr, Mera R, Churchill J. Long-term outcome of inpatients with tuberculosis assigned to outpatient therapy at a local clinic in New Orleans. *J Investig. Med.* 1997 Aug 45 (6):381–7.

3 Henry Wadsworth Longfellow (1807–1892): *Hyperion* [1839], bk. IV, ch. 8; from Beck EM, *John Bartlett, Familiar Quotations*, 15th ed., 1980, Little Brown & Co., Boston, pg. 519.

Vaccines

My Life with Vaccines

Ronald Gold

How I Became a Vaccinologist

Following graduation in 1957, I took a year off, courtesy of Harvard College and a Sheldon Traveling Fellowship. Upon my return, I entered Harvard Medical School and graduated in 1962. I then completed my training with a medical internship and pediatric residency, an MPH in tropical public health from the Harvard School of Public Health, and a final year doing research on schistosomiasis under Tom Weller. I felt prepared to enter a career in tropical public health, starting at the Rockefeller Foundation research project in St. Lucia.

However, 1968 was the year of the major expansion of US forces in Viet Nam, an expansion which included drafting every available doctor. I received orders to report to Fort Sam Houston in San Antonio, TX, in August 1968 to undergo the required basic training for physicians and then proceed to Saigon. Luckily, before reporting for duty, while visiting a friend, I met Dr. Carleton Gadjusek. When I mentioned my Army orders, he suggested that I call him at his office at NIH because he thought there was a position available in the Bacteriology Division at Walter Reed Army Institute of Research. A few days later, I phoned him, and he gave me the number of Dr. Mal Artenstein at WRAIR. As a result, I was offered a research position at WRAIR, working on the new meningococcal vaccines which had been developed and undergone preliminary testing in Army recruits at Fort Dix. However, my orders were not changed until, while at Fort Sam, I agreed to serve three years rather the usual two in order to work at WRAIR. Just a little blackmail.

At WRAIR, I developed a new laboratory method to identify different strains of serogroup C meningococci [MenC], including differentiating the strain causing large outbreaks at recruit training centers of the Army and Navy from strains isolated from cases elsewhere in the world. In addition, I was in charge of the design and conduct of a very large trial of the new group C vaccine in recruits at five recruit training centers in order to determine its safety and its ability to prevent meningitis and other life-threatening meningococcal infections. The

MenC proved to be very safe and 89% effective when given as a single dose within days of arrival of the recruits.

Thus the Army changed my career, and I became *a vaccinologist—a scientist who is involved in the development and implementation of vaccines.*

Including my three years at WRAIR, I have spent nearly 50 years studying the safety and efficacy of old and new vaccines in children. As a result of my experience with vaccines, I propose to review the advances that have been made in the last half century and indicate what the future holds.

My Vaccine Research after the Army

Following discharge from the Army, I spent nine years at the University of Connecticut where I studied the Groups A and C vaccines in infants and older children. The results of the studies at WRAIR and at the University of Connecticut provided the basis of the decision to approve the use of the A and C vaccines.

I then moved to Toronto where I became head of the Division of Infectious Disease. My research there focused on the several *new vaccines*, including acellular pertussis vaccine, *Haemophilus influenzae* type b (the most common cause of meningitis in children less than five years of age), and chickenpox vaccine.

In addition, I became involved in examining *adverse effects of routine childhood vaccines* and, in collaboration with others in Canada, developed a system of surveillance of adverse events following vaccination severe enough to result in hospitalization. This program, called IMPACT (Immunization Monitoring Program, Active), now provides real-time information on severe adverse events reported from all tertiary care pediatric hospitals in Canada. IMPACT has provided important evidence documenting the rarity of severe adverse events following immunization of children with vaccines that make up the routine immunization schedule as well as the rapid decline in disease following the introduction of meningococcal and pneumococcal vaccines in Canada.

Making Vaccine Policy

In addition to research on vaccines, I also became involved in vaccine policy and immunization program issues while serving on the National Advisory Committee on Immunization [NACI]. NACI provides recommendations to Health Canada on the use of all vaccines used in routine immunization programs. Preparing such recommendations entails a review of the epidemiology of the disease; the age distribution of the disease and immunology of the disease in question; the method of preparation and composition of the vaccine; and studies on the safety, immune responses, and effectiveness of the vaccine. The recommendation for use of the vaccine was then submitted to Health Canada and served as the primary position statement used by provincial health ministries in their decision about whether or not to include the vaccine in the routine immunization program and provide the necessary funding.

I also served on the Committee of Immunization and Infectious Diseases of the Canadian Paediatric Society and the Committee on Infectious Diseases of the American Academy of Pediatrics, both of which committees make recommendations to their parent organizations and to practicing pediatricians concerning the use of vaccines. I was a member of expert advisory committees of several vaccine manufacturers during the process of research, development, and introduction of new childhood vaccines.

The Public Health Impact of Vaccines

Vaccination of children has been *one of the ten most important public health achievements of the 20th century.*[1,2] The impact of vaccines is demonstrated in Table 1.

Table 1. Annual Incidence Rates of Diphtheria, Tetanus, Pertussis, Hemophilus Influenza B (Hib) Meningitis, Polio, Measles, Mumps. Rubella. Hepatitis B, Chickenpox, Invasive Pneumococcal Disease, Hepatitis A, and Rotavirus (cases per 100,000)*

Disease	Pre-Vaccine Era	With Vaccination (2009)	Decrease
Diphtheria	600	0	100%
Tetanus	0.3	0.003	99%
Pertussis	4720	12	99.7%
Hib	158	0.1	99.9%
Polio, paralytic	31	0	100%
Measles	10641	0.2	99.99%
Mumps	6205	11.3	99.8%
Rubella	3300	0.01	99.999%
Hepatitis B	72.4	5.5	92%
Chickenpox	9839	394	96%
IPD†	213.6	31.8	85%
Hepatitis A	14.3	2.5	82%
Rotavirus	12750	6209.1	51%

* Modified from Reference 3
† IPD: Invasive pneumococcal disease

As a result of vaccination, smallpox has been eradicated worldwide, paralytic polio has been eradicated in the most of the world, and most other vaccine-preventable diseases have decreased by over 99%. There is unanimous agreement among scientists that *vaccination is responsible for the control or elimination of infections listed in Table 1.* There is, unfortunately, a very active anti-vaccine movement alleging that the risks of vaccines far outweigh the benefits, although such allegations are not supported by any scientific evidence. More on this later.

In my nearly 50 years as a vaccinologist, many new vaccines have been introduced into routine immunization programs (Table 2).

New Vaccines since 1969

Table 2. Year of approval of vaccines in USA since 1969

Vaccine	Year	Vaccine	Year	Vaccine	Year	Vaccine	Year
Rubella	1969	PNC	1983	Varicella	1995	MMRV	2005
MMR	1971	Hib-C	1987	Dtap	1996	MenACYW-C	2005
Flu, split product	1978	Polio-eIPV	1988	Hib-HepB	1996	HPV	2006
MenC-PS*	1978	Typhoid Oral	1989	PCV-7	2000	Rotavirus	2006
MenC-C†	...	DTaP-Hib	1990	HAV-HBV	2001	Zoster	2006
MenA-CYW-P	1981	Typhoid VI	1994	DTaP_ HBV-IPV	2002	DTap_IPV	2008
HBV	1981	HAV	1995	Tdap	2005	Dtap-IPV-Hib	2008

* PS: polysaccharide

† C: conjugate MenC-C not licensed in USA, licensed in Canada 2001

Each new vaccine undergoes a series of required steps in order to be approved for use:

1) Mass production processes used by the manufacturers to make a vaccine;

2) Studies in human adult volunteers to demonstrate safety and ability of vaccine to induce protective antibodies;

3) Large trials in children followed by larger studies in infants to demonstrate safety, antibody production, and effectiveness in preventing the disease.

4) If the vaccine is approved for use, post-marketing surveillance of the vaccine to confirm its safety and demonstrate its efficacy.

All of these steps are monitored and reviewed by the federal regulatory authority (FDA in USA). Finally the results of all of the studies must be submitted to the FDA for approval before a vaccine is licensed for use.

Quality Control

The approval process also requires inspection of the factories where the vaccine is produced in order to assure that good manufacturing processes are followed. Each lot of vaccine must also be tested for toxicity and potency, with results submitted to FDA before it is approved for use.

All of these steps are time consuming and expensive, which accounts for the high price of new vaccines. Almost invariably, if a vaccine is used in routine programs for infant and children, the price drops significantly. In countries such as Canada, vaccine costs are significantly lower in routine immunization programs which are funded by provincial governments, than in countries such as the USA where parents often must pay for the vaccine.

The development of many of the new vaccines has occurred only because of the many advances in immunology, microbiology, molecular biology, manufacturing techniques for mass production, better surveillance programs to identify adverse events after vaccination, and research into the costs of the target disease and the benefits and risks of the vaccine.

Establishing Vaccine Targets

Advances in immunology have greatly improved the ability to identify which of the many molecules on the surface of the microbe are responsible for inducing protective immune responses. If the target molecule or molecules are identified, then advances in microbiology and molecular biology may permit extraction of the target molecules from the microbe after it is grown in the laboratory followed by chemical and physical processes to end up with a highly purified protein or polysaccharide. These steps have led to the development of the new vaccines against Hib, meningococcus, pneumococcus, influenza, and typhoid VI vaccine.

A newer process combines identification of the target molecule of the microbe followed by identification and isolation of the gene responsible for production of the target molecule. Using the methods of molecular biology, the gene can be transferred into another microbe such as yeast or a bacterium. As that microbe grows in the laboratory, it makes large amounts of the target molecule(s) which are then be extracted from the growth medium, purified and made into a vaccine. This is the process that has been used to make the group B meningococcal vaccine, Hepatitis B vaccine, HPV vaccine.

Modifying Vaccines

For other infections, it has not been possible to use these new techniques. The older method of growing the microbe and then killing it with heat and/or formaldehyde is still in use:

- New forms of Inactivated Polio Virus
- The initial influenza vaccine which has been modified by splitting the dead viral particle with detergent and then extracting and purifying the HA and NA proteins and eliminating most of the other viral proteins.
- The acellular pertussis vaccine in which the pertussis bacteria are grown in cultures, killed, and then the surface proteins are extracted, purified, and combined to make the vaccine.

Attenuated Live Viruses and Hybrids

Other new vaccines have been made by attenuating the virus in tissue culture cells so that it is alive, but modified so that it no longer causes symptoms as it grows in the body following immunization. One of the rotavirus vaccines has used a novel attenuation process. The human rotavirus is grown together with a calf rotavirus. In the course of growing together, hybrids are produced containing a mixture of human and calf genes. The vaccine strains contain human proteins on the surface which induce protective antibodies, while the remainder of the vaccine strain consists of calf proteins. The hybrid can multiply in humans and induce immunity, but does not cause symptoms.

Anti-Vaxers

All of the vaccines used in routine immunization programs have overwhelming scientific evidence that they are both safe and effective. *Why then are increasing numbers of parents reluctant to vaccinate their children?*

This is not a new phenomenon. Ever since the development of a vaccine to prevent smallpox by Edward Jenner in 1776, there have those who insisted that the risks of vaccination are much greater than benefits, if any such benefits exist.

The current anti-vaccine promoters have been aided by those in the United States who oppose the mandatory immunization requirements for those attending day care, school, and/or university, believing that such mandatory regulations are an infringement of personal freedom and of the right of parents to make decisions concerning the health of their children. Such beliefs ignore the judgment of the Supreme Court that government has the right to make vaccination mandatory in the interest of protecting public health, even if this overrides individual rights.

Absence of Personal Experience with Vaccine-Preventable Diseases

There are now two generations of parents and physicians who have little or no personal experience with most of the diseases small prevented by vaccines (diphtheria, tetanus, pertussis, measles, mumps, rubella, Hib disease, or paralytic polio) and decreasing experience with meningococcal disease, pneumococcal disease, hepatitis A, hepatitis B, chickenpox, HPV, or rotavirus, Therefore it not surprising that such parents and physicians are unaware of the risks of death or chronic illness or disability resulting from vaccine-preventable diseases.

Fear of the diseases is no longer a potent stimulus for parents to vaccinate their children. Moreover the alleged risks of the vaccines have been greatly exaggerated by stories in the press, on TV, and on numerous anti-vaccine websites on the Internet.

Unsubstantiated Vaccine Risks

Allegations of harm from vaccines used by anti-vaxers are based on case reports of individual children who have problems recognized at some time after immunization. Such problems include autism, mental retardation, brain damage, usually with no cause being identified.

Because vaccination occurred at some point before the recognition of a problem, the vaccine is easy to blame. But well-designed, carefully conducted scientific studies of autism, encephalopathy (a severe brain disorder with coma, seizures, and frequently permanent brain damage), mental retardation, attention deficit hyperactivity disorder, autoimmune diseases, etc. have all failed to find any increased rate of such disorders in vaccinated children compared to unvaccinated children.

Known Vaccine Risks

This is not to say that severe illness never occurs after use of certain vaccines:

- Encephalitis after smallpox vaccine, some forms of rabies vaccine, yellow fever vaccine in infants and elderly;
- Paralytic polio after oral polio vaccine (with a rate of one case in every 400,000 first doses in infants);
- Transient, but sometimes severe decreases in platelet counts after MMR vaccine.

But these severe events are so rare that the benefits of the vaccines outweigh the risks.

Risks for Non-Immune Children

The major impact of the anti-vaccine movement has been the growing number of children who are not immune to the vaccine-preventable infections, resulting in small or large outbreaks of these infections, depending on the proportion of unimmunized children. Unimmunized children are at risk of infection because the diseases do not disappear unless immunization through the world has eradicated the infection. Such eradication has only occurred with smallpox.

If rates of vaccination drop below a critical level so that there are sufficient numbers of unimmunized, susceptible children in a population, then outbreaks will sooner or later occur. This fact has unfortunately been demonstrated with diphtheria (in Ukraine and Russia), pertussis (in USA, England, Australia), measles and mumps (in USA, England), and paralytic polio (in Nigeria, India, Pakistan, Afghanistan).

Better education of parents and physicians and politicians about the true benefits and risks of vaccinating versus not vaccinating is essential if the risks of the anti-vaccine promoters are to be minimized, if not avoided altogether.

The future development of new vaccines depends not only on the application of new techniques of production of vaccine, but also on convincing the public of the safety and effectiveness of such vaccines. The fact that college-educated parents form the largest proportion of those refusing immunization of their children reflects the sad state of understanding of science by the American public.

Future Vaccines

The newest approach to vaccine development (termed *reverse vaccinology*) raises the possibility of many new vaccines. Instead using the whole microbe or molecules extracted from the microbe, reverse vaccinology *starts with the DNA of the microbe* and ends with the vaccine.

This process requires the following steps:

(1) Identify the molecule(s), usually located on the surface of the microbe where our immune defenses can recognize and respond to them;

(2) Identify and isolate the gene responsible for production of the target molecule(s);

(3) Transfer the gene to another bacteria or yeast which is used to make the target molecule(s);

(4) Demonstrate the purified molecule(s) induces protective immune responses, first in laboratory animals and then in humans;

(5) Develop mass production of the target molecule(s);

(6) Isolate and purify target molecule(s) from the growth media;

(7) Demonstrate its safety and ability to induce antibody production) after vaccination;

(8) Prove the vaccine prevents disease.

Reverse vaccinology was the method employed in making the new vaccine against group B meningococcus.

Diseases in Need of a Vaccine

Many old and newly emerging infectious diseases threaten the world with potentially serious problems. There are many important infectious diseases for which we currently lack effective means of prevention, especially *malaria* and *tuberculosis*. *Although treatment may be available, prevention is always less expensive than treatment.*

Other important infections for which vaccines are lacking include: group B streptococcal and E. coli meningitis and sepsis of newborn infants; antibiotic resistant infections due to *Staphylococcus aureus*, *E. coli*, *Pseudomonas aeruginosa*, and other bacteria.

There are also newly emerging infections similar to Ebola virus, avian influenza, Zika, and unknown animal viruses which can develop the ability to infect and cause disease in humans.

The growing volume and speed of international travel increases the ability of new pathogens to spread worldwide easily. Few preventive techniques are as effective as immunization. Hopefully we will be able to develop the vaccines needed to protect all of us against the old and new infectious agents that we will face.

For myself, my career in vaccinology began in 1968 with the group A and C meningococcal vaccine. And seems fitting that it has ended with the approval of the Group B meningococcal vaccine, the last major cause of bacterial meningitis in children and young adults.

Figure 8.5.6.1 *Ronald Gold, MD, MPH, with his staff and Infectious Diseases Fellows in training at the Infectious Disease Division at the Hospital for Sick Children, Toronto, Canada, in 1986*

Figure 8.5.6.2 *Dr. Ronald Gold, pediatrician, vaccinologist, and chief of infectious diseases, at the renowned Hospital for Sick Children in Toronto, Ontario, Canada*

Photo by staff photographer at The Hospital for Sick Children

---

Ronald Gold, MD, a 1962 graduate of Harvard Medical School and Harvard School of Public Health (MPH, 1967), trained in pediatrics at Boston City Hospital, Boston's Children's Hospital Medical Center, and St. Mary's Hospital in London. During his military service in the US Army, he was a research medical officer at Walter Reed Army Institute of Research before becoming professor of pediatrics at UConn Medical School and then chief of the Division of Infectious Disease, the Hospital for Sick Children, and Professor of Pediatrics, University of Toronto, from 1970–1996.

Dr. Gold's research focused primarily on the safety and immunogenicity of vaccines. He directed the first field trials which demonstrated the efficacy of meningococcal group C vaccine in Army recruits and its safety and immunogenicity in infants and children.

For many years he was a member of the National Advisory Committee on Immunization, Health Canada and the Infectious Disease and Immunization Committee of the Canadian Paediatric Society. He was co-principal investigator in the development of the Immunization Monitoring Program, Active [IMPACT], an active surveillance system based at 12 Canadian children's hospitals for detection and investigation of severe adverse events following vaccination.

References

Centers for Disease Control. Ten Great Public Achievements—United States 1900–1998. *Morbidity Mortality Weekly Report*. 1999; 48:241–3. (https://www.cdc.gov/mmwr/preview/mmwrhtml/00056796.htm)

Moore DL. *Your Child's Best Shot; a parent's guide to vaccination*. Canadian Paediatric Society, 4th Edition. 2015, 370 pp.

Myers MG, Pineda D. *Do Vaccines Cause That? A guide for evaluating vaccine safety concerns*. i4ph, Galveston TX. 2008, 267 pp.

National Immunization Program, Centers for Disease Control. Impact of vaccines universally recommended for children—United States, 1990–98. *Morbidity Mortality Weekly Report*. 1999; 48:243–8. (https://www.cdc.gov/mmwr/preview/mmwrhtml/00056803.htm)

Offit PA, Bell LM. *Vaccines: What every parent should know, Revised edition*. IDG Books, New York, NY. 1999, 234 pp.

Zhou F, Shefer, A, Wenger J, et al. Economic evaluation of the routine childhood immunization program in the United States, 2009. *Pediatrics* 2014; 133:85 (http://pediatrics.aappublications.org/content/133/4/577)

Neuroscience

Academic Medicine 1957–2017 and the Explosive Growth of Neuroscience

Edwin H. Kolodny

A Chemistry major at Harvard, I switched to Economics after taking a brilliantly taught course in Ec 1 by then teaching fellow, Otto Ekstein, later to become himself a member of President Johnson's Council of Economic Advisors. With a career in medicine in the back of my mind, my senior thesis topic, National Compulsory Health Insurance, compared American initiatives for a national US health insurance scheme with those already established in England and Israel. Now, 60 years later, it is hard to fathom that there is still political bickering in our great country about the need and means to guarantee health care for every citizen, a priority already well-established in so many other advanced democratic nations around the world.

My fascination in biochemistry and genetics grew with courses taught at Harvard by Konrad Block and George Wald, two subsequent Nobel Prize winners, and led me to the New York University School of Medicine whose superb faculty included Severo Ochoa, another Nobel Prize winner in biochemistry, Homer Smith, a renowned physiologist, and later the immunologist Baruj Benacerraf, a subsequent Nobel Laureate, and a host of other inspiring teachers and experimentalists. Itching to try my hand in research, I enrolled in a "Medical Science Year" program in our Department of Pharmacology to explore with Dr. Norman Altschuler the physiologic responses of dogs to phlorizin, a compound that caused the kidneys to excrete large amounts of glucose from the blood into the urine. A publication in the *American Journal of Physiology* co-authored with Dr. Altschuler, then a following talk before a national scientific meeting in Atlantic City, and I was hooked.

I finished my clinical clerkships and went on to do two years of an Internal Medicine Residency at Bellevue Hospital. By then a career in Genetics beckoned.

Becoming a Neurologist

But as there was no defined pathway, I chose in 1963 to enter a Neurology Residency at the Massachusetts General Hospital (MGH) under Dr. Raymond D. Adams. My reasoning was that so many genetic disorders had neurological sequelae that it was *de rigueur* to understand the nervous system. What a fortuitous choice! Our program included a year of neuropathology study which fostered two publications with my lab partners. One which described a new syndrome of progressive parietal lobe dysfunction in late life became a well-established disorder known as "corticobasal ganglionic degeneration". At the time we could not stain the neuronal inclusions we saw in our autopsy tissues, but over the course of many years these have been shown to be composed of an important brain protein known as "Tau" protein.

Aminoacidopathies and disorders of fatty acid metabolism were beginning to become known to pediatricians, and dietary studies hinted that phenylketonuria and maple syrup storage disease could be controlled. Turning to Dr. Philip Dodge, our Chief of Pediatric Neurology at the MGH, I asked if I could join his training program. His advice has stuck with me ever since:

> "*Don't waste your time with me. You can always learn Pediatric Neurology. Go to a lab where you can learn the techniques that you can use to solve some of the many problems we have in the neurological diseases of children!*"

Becoming an Academic and My Mentors in Translational Medicine: "*From Bench to Bedside*"

Off I went to the NIH in Bethesda, MD, where Dr. Roscoe Brady took me into his lab as a "Special Fellow" in 1967. His lab had just solved the riddle of Gaucher disease and Fabry disease, two lipid-storage diseases affecting children and adults, and my job was to figure out the root cause of Tay-Sachs disease, a killer of children, especially those born to families of Eastern European Jewish parentage. Within three years under the tutelage of Dr. Brady and his associate, Julian Kanfer, using biosynthesized radioactive compounds we found a block in the enzyme cleavage of sialic acid from the Tay-Sachs lipid known as 'G_{M2}-ganglioside'. My essay on this subject won the Weir Mitchell award of the American Academy of Neurology at their 1970 annual convention.

A lab with a faculty position followed at the Harvard Medical School, subsequent appointment to a tenured position in the 1980's, and in 1991 Chairmanship of the New York University School of Medicine Department of Neurology from which I retired in 2012. In reflection on these fast-paced years, I come back repeatedly to the *entrée* given to me by many mentors of whom Drs. Adams and Brady especially deserve mention. Their omnipresence, manner of personal deportment, constant encouragement and support throughout my career have been so influential that their collegiality and spirit were so incorporated into my own manner with my students and patients that I am now not surprised at my own accomplishments in the clinic and laboratory.

By the way, Dr. Dodge's advice proved providential. I eventually set up a very productive laboratory for the study of lysosomal storage diseases (of which Tay-Sachs, Gaucher and Fabry were three of more than 50), passed my Board exams in Genetics without the benefit of a formal residency in the subject, and was the first physician in the US not trained specifically in Pediatric Neurology to be inducted into the Child Neurology Society. Approximately three-quarters of all patients I saw in clinical practice were children or adolescents, and I became very comfortable teaching our fellows Pediatric Neurology. Moral lesson: "*Follow your heart*" and as I instructed our residents, "*Do what you think will make you happiest and is most consistent with your world view and sense of self-worth.*"

The choice of a career in academic medicine has opened vistas to the world not always available to others. The joy of teaching bright students who then go on to achieve their own greatness and stature in the field, meeting and collaborating with colleagues not only in your own university circle but across the city, around the country and around the world, attending scientific colloquia in far-away places, interacting with foreign students at courses, receiving inquiries and challenges from patients across national divides and ultimately *finding answers in nature to human problems* are part of the rewards.

Animal Models of Human Diseases of Metabolism

I have also had the enormously satisfying experience of ending my career (although not yet officially) with a topic with which it started. Over the years, I have collaborated with several veterinarians who have brought to my attention animal models of human diseases of metabolism. My first exposure was at the NIH and was to material sent to us from New Zealand from Black Angus cattle who were dying of some sort of storage disease. They had what proved to be alpha-mannosidosis, a lysosomal storage disease due to accumulation in tissues of glycoconjugates containing the alpha-mannoside linkage on their carbohydrate residues. I missed the diagnosis because my training and focus at the time was concentrated on lipids, and I had disposed of the non-lipid extractable material. Once I learned of my mistake, I was determined never to allow it to happen again!

As the years went by, Dr. Joseph Alroy, a veterinarian pathologist at a neighboring institution, and I successfully identified cats with alpha-mannosidosis and dogs with G_{M1}-gangliosidosis. With the help of the pathologist at the Smithsonian zoo we found two flamingos with Tay-Sachs disease and 13 others in the same flock who were carriers. This set the stage for our discovery of Jacob sheep with Tay-Sachs disease. The Texas farmer owning the sheep and local veterinarian pathologist had been searching for the answer for nine years. One of our lab staff recalled that sheep had branched off of cattle phylogenetically 20 million years ago which enabled us to clone the sheep gene and identify a mutation responsible for Tay-Sachs disease. These sheep are now being bred and used for gene therapy trials. Even more recently we have reported G_{M1}-gangliosidosis, another lipid storage disease, in the brain of New England Black bears.

Recent clinical trial work in which I have participated with one of my former NYU trainees, Dr. Heather Lau, harks back to my early work 40-plus years ago at the NIH with sialic acid which we were then using to radioactively-label the Tay-Sachs ganglioside. The clinical trial involves middle-aged patients with Hereditary Inclusion Body Myopathy (HIBM), an inherited deficiency in the incorporation of sialic acid into muscle tissue causing progressive muscle weakness. Administration of sialic acid daily in an oral preparation is now under active investigation as a therapy for patients with HIBM.

Retooling

The progress in neurology and neuroscience over the past 60 years has been astounding. While subscribing to many scientific journals, maintaining memberships in many societies and attending conferences and invited talks regularly, *there is no substitute for stopping what you are doing at the moment and taking a chunk of time off to retool.* In 1980, I spent a year away from my MGH responsibilities learning about the new tools in genetics at the Department of Genetics across town at the Boston

Children's Hospital and again, between1988 and 1990, I was absent a total of almost 12 months working in the lab of Dr. Mia Horowitz at the Weitzman Institute in Rehovoth, Israel. This is a way not only of gaining newer technical expertise but developing additional collaborations and sharing scientific insights with like-minded colleagues.

Funding Scientific Research

A look back at 60 years of science also includes its resource base. Research cannot thrive without funds to support laboratories, train scientists, pay salaries and purchase equipment and supplies. Older style institutions used to realize some spinoff from patient revenues that helped clinical departments maintain a modest research presence. Moreover, the National Institutes of Health (NIH) at one point was the main support of training grants and individual research grants.

The landscape has dramatically changed so that those institutions with the largest research programs now receive their funding from a mix of private philanthropy, government grants (NIH, National Science Foundation, Department of Defense, etc.) and the pharmaceutical industry. Clinical metrics are now squeezing patient visits into shorter and shorter time slots, and insurance reimbursements are preempting any possibility of patient revenues contributing to scientific progress.

The *Orphan Diseases Act* has provided Federal Government incentives for the biotech industry to develop new pharmaceuticals for some of the 7000 rare genetic diseases that afflict thousands of Americans. Partnerships with academic centers as well as new jobs in pharma are keeping the research enterprise going. Within my own area of interest, the Lysosomal Storage Diseases, this has meant the development of several new and revolutionary approaches to diseases of enzyme deficiency, namely, enzyme replacement therapy (first federally approved in 1991), substrate reduction therapy, and chaperone enzyme enhancement therapy. Bone marrow (BMT) and stem cell research have also shown promising results. (Dr. William Krivit of the University of Minnesota and I were involved in the first successful BMT for Krabbé disease in the late 1980s). New DNA techniques such as DNA gene silencing by mRNA interference and DNA read-through for nonsense mutations are also under intensive scrutiny for gene correction.

Advances in Neuroscience in Our Lifetimes

Finally, without being comprehensive, this essay cannot close without a look back at the vast changes that have entered into every aspect of neuroscience.

Cerebrovascular Disease and Stroke: Tissue plasminogen activator (tPA) is now accepted therapy for the acute treatment of most thrombotic clots causing brain vascular blockage. Clot removing devices are also available and coils can be inserted intravascularly for brain aneurysms. Endovascular clot removal is also common in the case of carotid artery narrowing discovered using ultrasound imaging and angiography.

Dementia: Genes causing Alzheimer disease amyloid protein aggregation have been identified, early cognitive signs are better known, methods for imaging Tau protein neurofibrillary tangles in the living brain are now available and variants such as fronto-temporal dementia have been separated out. At least three approved drugs are available but this *remains the number one disease for the coming decades* where there is neither a preventative nor cure.

Epilepsy: Video-EEG monitoring, use of subdural grids and MRI have helped to localize trigger points amenable to surgical ablation with up to 90% cessation of seizures in appropriate candidates. A major cause of seizures has been shown to result from medial temporal sclerosis. Inherited disorders such as tuberous sclerosis and cerebral dysgenesis are other recognized causes that may be amenable to surgical removal. Newer more effective anticonvulsants have also been added.

Movement Disorders: Both environmental and genetic bases for Parkinson disease have been elucidated, and the genetic causes of Huntington disease, Friedreich's Ataxia, Macado-Joseph disease and many forms of spinocerebellar ataxia are now known. Neurosurgical strategies that have been developed to improve functionality in Parkinson disease include pallidotomy, thalamotomy and deep brain stimulation.

Multiple Sclerosis: The role of hypo-vitaminosis D and late EBV infection are being debated. Drugs are now available that decrease the frequency of new exacerbations. Neuromyelitis optica has been separated out from the more common forms of MS.

Neuroinfectious Diseases: HIV which emerged in the 1980s as a fatal viral disorder that destroyed the immune system can now be stabilized with a cocktail of medications; West Nile virus and Lyme disease are also newer conditions with treatment paradigms.

Neuromuscular Disorders: Genetic causes and underlying mechanisms of spinal muscular atrophy, amyotrophic lateral sclerosis, and the muscular dystrophies are much better understood, and therapeutic trials underway.

Neuroradiology: Major advances in CT and MRI scanning greatly expand our non-invasive diagnostic capabilities. Innovations in MR spectroscopy and PET scanning facilitate analysis of cellular composition and functionality.

Peripheral Nervous System: Many genetic causes of Charcot-Marie-Tooth disease and other hereditary forms of peripheral neuropathies have been elucidated, chemotherapy-induced and hypovitaminosis causes of peripheral neuropathy are better understood, as are factors involved in axon regeneration.

Psychiatry: New neuropharmacologic agents have revolutionized the treatment of psychiatry since the days of prolonged hospitalization.

Tumor: 79,000 new cases of brain tumor are anticipated in 2017 in the US. Therapy for malignant brain tumor remains challenging with surgery and chemotherapy not having changed the survival rate in many years.

Pharmacological Discovery

CNS therapeutics accounts presently for 15% of total pharmaceutical sales. Neuroscientists, clinicians and representatives of the pharmaceutical industry are in agreement with patients that the interval between the discovery of a promising therapeutic agent and its actual approval by the FDA is much too long and therefore many initiatives are underway to hasten such approvals. One approach has been to take off-the-shelf drugs already approved for one indication and test them for efficacy for other indications. Libraries of 10,000 such drugs are now actively being examined using robotic screening against model cell systems for appropriate candidates.

For those with rare diseases, the NIH maintains a data base of clinical trials that should be consulted for those who can meet the entrance criteria and are interested in participating (ClinicalTrials.gov).

Figure 8.5.7.1 *Professor Edwin H. Kolodny, MD* (center), *in 2010 with his lysosomal storage diseases laboratory research team of the Department of Neurology at New York University Medical Center*

Edwin "Ed" Kolodny, MD, attended NYU School of Medicine, interrupting his training to do research for one year and graduating in 1962 with Honors in Pharmacology. After training in internal medicine for two years on the Third and Fourth Divisions of Bellevue Hospital in New York City, he completed a three-year neurology residency at the Massachusetts General Hospital (MGH) and then began his 5½-year service in the US Army Reserves as Captain in the Army Medical Corps. In the first three years he simultaneously pursued research training in neurochemistry at the National Institutes of Health (NIH) while working part-time in the Neurology Clinic at the Walter Reed Army Medical Center. His research at NIH focused on the metabolic defect in Tay-Sachs disease, one of approximately 50 lysosomal storage diseases.

In 1970, he joined the staff of the Eunice Kennedy Shriver Center for Mental Retardation in Waltham, MA, and established a laboratory to study patients with lysosomal storage diseases. From 1970–1991 he held various faculty positions at the MGH and Harvard Medical School (HMS), rising to the rank of Professor at HMS and Director of the Shriver Center.

In 1991 NYU recruited him as Chairman of the Department of Neurology and director of laboratory research on inherited diseases of the nervous system. The Neurogenetics Laboratory also provided state-approved clinical diagnostic services for a variety of inherited neurological diseases, including many of the lysosomal storage diseases.

After 19 years as Chairman, he stepped down in 2010 and officially retired at the end of 2011. However, he continues to consult with pharmaceutical companies interested in developing therapies for rare diseases and serves on scientific advisory boards for disease-specific lay organizations. He is an author of over 300 scientific papers and two books, holds two patents and has received numerous awards for his research. He is a Fellow of the American Academy of Neurology and the American College of Medical Genetics, and a member of AOA, the medical honor society.

Clinical Medicine

Conquest of Cancer

Jack T. Evjy

Introduction

Our class, the Harvard Class of 1957, has lived through a remarkable time in the history of the effort by medical science to understand and conquer cancer. This is a brief description of the illness as it was experienced by the generation that came before us and by our generation with a few thoughts about what may lie ahead for those who will come after us.

Our Parent's Generation—Sara's Story

Sara and her husband lived in Minnesota during the Second World War. She was 39 and pregnant with her second child. One of her breasts enlarged to an alarming degree and became inflamed. Following the delivery of a normal male the breast continued to expand. Her family physician diagnosed breast cancer and a local surgeon removed the breast. Cancer was confirmed. It was said that the pregnancy did not cause the disease but had led to its acceleration. The family prepared for the worst and moved to Chicago, where her parents lived, to manage the inevitable. The child went to live in Kankakee, IL, with Sara's sister-in-law. The elder boy stayed with Sara and her husband.

The chest wall wound never healed. Within a year the cancer spread to her bones and liver; later the lungs, and soon thereafter her brain and spinal cord. Short of morphine for body pain and anxiety, there was little to offer relief.

Sara lived to celebrate the end of the war but died in the hospital within the following year. She often said to her husband, "I hope to live to see our two boys grow up." Her last words to her elder son as she left for the hospital were, "If I do not return home again, be a good boy." Her husband once confided that what made him love her was not her breast. He never spoke of the cancer or of her pending death. It took years for him to accept his wife's passage. Sara's mother never accepted the death of her daughter.

Figure 8.6.1.1 *Sara with her infant son in the early 1940s in the backyard of her parents' Chicago home just before her breast cancer was discovered. Typical for cancer patients before the biological revolution of our time, she died within a few years, and before her son was old enough to remember her.*

Sara's story was typical for this time period. This was, for the Harvard Class of 1957, our childhood. Cancer was seen as masses of bleeding, often infected tissue arising in many different places within one's body and spreading painfully almost anywhere. It seemed to attack anyone anytime, even children. Although cancer is simply cells that multiply and spread uncontrollably, in fact it has a bewildering number of subtypes. Typically its victims suffered, wasted and their life foreshortened. The diagnosis was at the time and continued to be for our generation greatly feared. Cancer patients and their families experienced a sense of helplessness and hopelessness. Sara's generation did not speak of cancer, sadness or death. This was taboo. It was unmanly. There was, compared to today, very little that could be done. Save for surgery, cancer patient care was for the most part a ministry.

Following the war, as our class became teenagers, the combination of fear and resentment toward cancer and the appearance of several new promising treatments opened a door of opportunity and hope. Technical advances in surgery as well as the discovery of anesthesia, blood transfusions and antibiotics enabled surgeons to become very aggressive removing cancer tissue. More often than not the illness invaded beyond the margin of resection and spread to distant organs resulting in death. It was found that radiation might augment and often replace surgery. Hormones and chemotherapy drugs to treat the spread of cancer seemed possible. Additionally, some families appeared prone to cancer. Viruses, radiation and chemicals in our environment often played a role in its initiation, offering opportunities for cancer prevention and early discovery. This was the situation as the 1950s unfolded and we entered Harvard.

Our Generation—The Advance of Medical Science and Building of Clinical Infrastructure

Our generation has made enormous advancements in understanding the basic nature of cancer and its control. As a result, cancer has for the most part become a chronic disease that is more often that not curable or preventable. Suffering can almost always be alleviated. We are no longer helpless and a patient's situation is rarely hopeless. Why and how did this occur?

Had Sara been born 50 years later the outcome might have been the same but her journey likely would have been improved. Indeed, her youngest granddaughter developed breast cancer during the 1990s. This granddaughter lived not three uncomfortable years but almost two decades, much of which was comfortable and meaningful. Sara's eldest granddaughter also developed the disease but with mammography it was found at a less virulent stage. She is apparently disease-free ten years following breast-conserving surgery, radiation therapy, chemotherapy and hormone therapy. This story and millions more like it—of cure, prolonged control, lessened suffering, even prevention—is today commonplace.

During our professional lifetime cancer for the most part has been viewed as a *disease of wayward cells*. Cells that had learned to multiply uncontrollably spread to other parts of the body and lead to illness and death. While it was appreciated that the basic problem is a derangement of the chemistry within the cell, there was little technology to see this process in full detail, let alone manage it. Indeed in 1957 Watson and Crick had just determined the double helix as the structure of DNA, but the details of the genetic code and the means by which the information that determined the structure and function of life were just being discovered. Progress in cancer care during our educational and professional lifetime has been to *prevent* and *find cancer cells; then kill them.*

Soon after the end of the War, the attention of the public came to focus on the carnage caused by cancer and cardiovascular disease. Of these cancer was the most feared and garnered enormous public attention. Although the American Cancer Society had been established early in our century its advocacy efforts now became much more active. The Cancer Society was an organized grassroots community effort that succeeded in increasing public awareness and knowledge about cancer. It funded research in cancer prevention, detection and patient care as well as fostered the training and deployment of specialized oncology physicians. Similarly, on the public side the National Cancer Institute was formed in 1937, and it became part of the National Institutes of Health in 1944. Thus began the US National Cancer Program.

National Focus on Cancer Research and Care of the Cancer Patient

The public effort to support cancer research, education, prevention and patient care since that time has been relentless. The milestones have been too numerous to include here, but listed below are a few.

> President Lyndon B. Johnson established the Commission on Cancer chaired by Dr. Michael E. DeBakey in 1964. This led to the creation of the Heart Disease, Cancer, and Stroke Program which in turn evolved into the Regional Medical Program, an effort that in various forms continued into the early 1970s. The Surgeon General's Report on Smoking and Health was published that year (1964), which linked tobacco use to lung cancer among other illnesses.
>
> Next, President Richard M. Nixon signed the National Cancer Act of 1971, which was called the "War on Cancer". The crusade to kill cancer extended during the years that followed into the far reaches of our country and also became worldwide. In 2009 the International Union Against Cancer of the World Health Organization announced the World Cancer Campaign. Locally the institutionalization of cancer care and research became and remains most visible in the form of the "Jimmy Fund", the Dana Farber Cancer Institute, and Clinical/Academic Cancer Programs at most of the major medical centers. This model has become the norm for our country and the world.

Compelled by this degree of public and institutional interest and support, a *clinical and academic research army* began to mobilize in the early 1950s. This effort was led by the surgical community. Clearly they were the ones most able to remove cancer tissue and in some cases effect cure.

The American College of Surgeons created a national program to encourage hospitals and clinics to establish approved cancer programs. The major elements of each program included consultation services and committees of cancer experts to review and recommend treatment programs for individual cancer patients, cancer patient clinics for continuing follow up after initial surgery, clinical cancer data repositories and clinical records to gather information about the community cancer care experience of patients, as well as educational conferences for all caregivers.

Before long, more adequate funding emerged for patient care. Notable examples include Medicare, Medicaid and Blue Cross/Blue Shield. State-aided cancer clinics, registries and health planning organizations were established.

About this time, radiation therapy surfaced as a modality of treatment that could kill cancer cells. For the most part this started with diagnostic radiologists but soon became a specialty in its own right. Radiology also proved to be helpful for seeing cancer tissue within the patient without having to perform exploratory surgery. Over the last half century both diagnostic and therapeutic radiology have made enormous gains and today are often excellent supplements to or alternatives for surgery.

When our class graduated from Harvard, at the end of the 1950s, it was already very clear that local forms of therapy, no matter how extensive, would not help many patients because their cancer had already spread beyond the organ of origin, invading not only locally but often metastasizing distantly to virtually any place in the patient's body. The malignant cells had entered the lymphatic and vascular system and moved almost everywhere. The challenge was to find other means to chase the malignancy wherever it went and make it go away. The answer to this complication was *systemic therapy*, which could be inserted into the circulation to chase after the disseminating malignant cells. By this time it was already known that changing the patient's hormonal status or administering cytotoxic chemotherapy drugs occasionally caused regression of some forms of cancer. Examples were breast cancer, leukemia, lymphoma and bowel cancer.

Specialization and the Multidisciplinary Approach to Care of the Cancer Patient

During the 1960s it became noticeable that there were increasing numbers of cancer patients not only because of the early successes of the surgeons and radiotherapists but because smoking and other environmental factors were in play. Furthermore, cardiovascular disease and infections were beginning to come under control, allowing patients to live long enough to acquire cancer.

Cancer was seen at this point in time as a multisystem issue coming from and going to virtually all organ systems and causing a legion of medical problems. The side effects of treatment plus the fact that many patients were elderly and had concurrent medical illness expanded the complexity of the medical picture. The caregiver teams began to evolve to encompass the total scope of care needed to manage such complicated patients. Cancer patient care became multidisciplinary, a collaborative effort.

Blood specialists, termed hematologists, were available in some numbers, and they often dealt with patients who had leukemia. There were very few internal medicine physicians fully committed to what was now clearly a general, internal medical set of patient care problems. Someone was needed to coordinate and provide continuity to the care of these patients.

As a young internal medicine physician at the Massachusetts Memorial Hospital (now the Boston University Medical Center), I admired an academic cancer surgeon, Dr. Peter Mozden. He would visit the medical service to consult on patients with complicated cancer problem. His sense of compassion for these patients and the care givers trying to help them was remarkable. Even when patients could no longer hope for cure, much could be done to make their life better and more meaningful until death came. He worked with the American Cancer Society, Dr. Sidney Farber of Harvard and Dr. William Maloney, a Tufts University hematologist, and others to create the Advanced Clinical Fellowship Program.

Organizing the Training of Oncologists and Building Cancer Treatment Centers

Because of this new specialized educational opportunity, I and many with a similar interest became *medical oncologists*. While at first there were few, today there are thousands. In the years that followed many additional specialists and subspecialists emerged dealing with every aspect of medical and surgical care. Nursing and other allied health fields then emerged with special training in cancer patient care.

Clearly by the turn of the 1980s there was an enormous and dedicated army in the making, prepared to fight and control cancer. This growth and diversification continues to this day. To illustrate, in the late 1960s The American Society of Clinical Oncology (ASCO) and The American Association of Cancer Research (AACR) were organizations with a handful of members. Today these and related professional societies have thousands of members in this country and worldwide.

The growth of research financed by the National Institutes of Health *(NIH)* and the evolution of the Jimmy Fund into the Dana Farber Cancer Institute *(DFCI)* locally have been spectacular. Concurrently all medical schools and major academic medical centers have well-developed cancer care, education and research facilities.

When I was a young oncologist on the full-time faculty at Boston University, one of the first multidisciplinary cancer inpatient care units was constructed under the leadership of Dr. Mozden and supported by the American Cancer Society. Because of the work of the academic community and the biotech and pharmaceutical industry over the last half century, all sorts of technology, services and systems have been developed to understand, prevent, detect and treat cancer patients from the routine to the most sophisticated.

Developing Targeted Treatments

New and more effective advances are made daily worldwide. Examples of this include microsurgery, gamma knife radiation therapy, seed implant radiation, proton beam radiation therapy, diagnostic radioactive isotopes, small molecule drug therapy such as Gleevec for chronic myelogenous leukemia, hematopoietic growth factors, multiple forms of immunotherapy, nonsense ribonucleases, vaccines for Hepatitis C and Human papilloma virus, monoclonal antibodies, blood tests for alpha fetoprotein, bone marrow and stem cell transplants, genomic testing and personalized care.

Perhaps the most important contribution has been the technology to begin seeing into the cell to visualize the details of what makes a cell live and also become deranged. Indeed we have much to be grateful for because of this progress. However, to access the full scope of this care, community cancer patients in the early years of cancer care development had to endure the added burden of distant travel.

New Models for Organizing Care of Cancer Patients—Bringing Specialty Care to Communities

Most cancer patients are diagnosed in the community where they live or work. Organized community cancer care designed to meet most of the needs of cancer patients with the exception of the very new and sophisticated procedures (tertiary care) began in earnest about the beginning of the 1970s. Up to this point there were a few itinerant cancer surgeons who traveled a circuit of community hospitals performing cancer surgery with the help of local primary care physicians and general surgeons. The construction of the federal interstate highway system made moving patients and specialists much easier. Perhaps the most transformative next development was the decentralization of radiation therapy machines to the community. This event triggered the routine establishment of comprehensive community cancer care facilities.

While making rounds on cancer patients one Saturday morning in 1969 at the Boston University Medical Center Hospital, a traveling thoracic surgeon, Dr. Irving Madoff, came by and asked if I would be interested in talking with the medical community in Greater Lawrence (Methuen and Lawrence) about helping them organize a community cancer care program. The two local hospitals, Bon Secours, now the Holy Family, and Lawrence General Hospitals had come together to construct in the middle of the Merrimack Valley a radiation therapy facility at Bon Secours. They needed medical oncologists now that many of their patients would be staying in the community and guidance about how to organize and coordinate an overall cancer program. It seemed they needed a formal cancer control program to be accredited by the American College of Surgeons and fulfill the certificate of need requirements of the Massachusetts Department of Public Health.

Over the ensuing three decades this program evolved. A linear accelerator joined the cobalt facility. Medial oncology clinics were established. Diagnostic equipment included routine radiology and nuclear scanning. Then the CAT scan, MRI. and PET scans arrived as well as a large range of medical and surgical subspecialists. Within a couple of years the Lowell medical community established a sister program as well and the two communities worked together to operate the effort together for the good of all the patients and eight hospitals in the Merrimack Valley. The William Lane Cancer Center building was constructed in the 1990s. A similar facility now exists at the Lowell General Hospital and another at the Anna Jacques Hospital in Newburyport. Patients needing tertiary care and/or part of their more routine care in Boston academic centers have traditionally been referred to whichever academic medical center was most proficient in solving that patient's individual needs. It has been gratifying to watch this kind of activity emerge all over Massachusetts, New England and the country. Today it is commonplace.

The academic oncology centers and the community cancer programs are interdependent and have long worked together for the benefit of individual cancer patients and the advancement of medical science. However, until recently they were independent enterprises and physicians were in private community practice.

This *cancer care delivery model* is now rapidly changing. More and more oncology physicians are employed by hospitals or very large multispecialty groups. Increasingly, community hospitals and medical centers are consolidating with one another and with metropolitan academic medical centers. Costs for new equipment and sophisticated drugs have exploded, and the economic risks to deliver state of the art cancer care are beyond the ability of smaller institutions and practices. Furthermore the administrative and regulatory burdens in the new collaborative care systems plus managing modern information and computer systems preclude small-scale operations.

Finally the advance of medical science into the molecular heart of the cell means that new ways of thinking and managing cancer are frequent and highly specialized. As a result of these and other factors now and in the future, cancer care will be by teams of care givers, both those in the laboratory and at the bedside working as one.

At our peak as a private practice providing medical oncology, radiation therapy, palliative care, care coordination and program management services, we were a group of close to 30 physicians and 200 allied professionals, likely the largest organization of its kind in New England. Today we are fully integrating with the Dana Farber Community Cancer Program. Together we share a common set of values and interests which we feel best serves our patients and uses the full talents of our caregivers. This move we feel is the wave of the future.

Future Generations

Despite all the positive progress that has been made, cancer continues to be a major source of suffering and death in our country and the world at large. We still have a way to go before claiming victory.

While Sara's youngest granddaughter never had children, her eldest granddaughter has two sons. One of these young men is married and has a son and daughter. Sara's two sons, who have had prostate cancer, prior to their illness between them fathered seven children: three boys and four girls, now grown to adulthood. Likely this family has a *molecular genomic predisposition to forming cancers*, although the available genomic studies so far have not pinpointed one. Can/could anything be done to prevent future episodes of cancer in this and other families? What improvements might be made in changing the course of the illness, and/or its outcome, should it occur in this family and others?

The children and their progeny of the Class of 1957 can look forward to the ultimate conquest of cancer and unimaginable advances in the broad arena of biological sciences.

First, we should expect more incremental advances in all aspects of cancer biology and care. Simply, there will be more progress along the continuum long established. All aspects of the biological sciences and of other fields are evolutionary. Each step forward leads to other new steps in a process of continuous invention, not unlike the natural evolution of humans and indeed our entire biosphere. Modern cancer care and research has become worldwide.

Second, cancer control, like all aspects of medicine, depends on a healthy economy, an effective educational system, and maintaining safety and security and other activities that create a healthy world, community and health care system. A strong effective public health system is also important. The continued development of effective and efficient health care systems is underway, and efforts to achieve universal coverage are essential because the cost to administer effective modern cancer care is beyond the means of most individuals. Today as in the past the high cost of health care remains a common cause of personal bankruptcy.

Third, the management of human behavior, risk taking, choice making, trust building, assuming personal responsibility and many other attributes of being healthy and living a safe and meaningful life is paramount. Recognizing that the human brain on average reaches maturity of decision making and experience well into the third decade of life is important. Persons who develop a sense of responsibility and take good care of themselves and others rather than engaging in destructive behavior to themselves or to others likely will live longer, more meaningful lives.

Fourth, continued progress in computation, data management and communications is vital. Medicine is essentially a field suffused with information. It's about knowing what to do and having the skills to realize meaningful actions regarding health.

The growth and evolution of the information technology industry, the use of new powerful digital computers, like Watson by IBM, are helping with medical decision-making and keeping track of enormous amounts of medical data (Big Data). The Internet and smart phones are keeping us in touch like never before. In the future all of us and our caregivers will have the ability to have at our fingertips what we need to know and do to be healthy or if ill to become well again. Cancer is no exception.

Fifth, perhaps the area of greatest interest is *genomic analysis* and *engineering*. While it was theorized a hundred years ago by Theodore Boveri that cancer is a disease of the genome (chromosomes) within cells, it is only recently that we know at a molecular level the structural and functional meaning of this hypothesis. It is now possible to know the genetic code and protein composition of normal and ill patients. Cancer cells are no different. Many mutations occur in cell chromosomes over a lifetime; in fact cancer cells are notorious for their genomic instability.

Research has long identified *environmental factors* that create changes in the cell genome. For example, radiation, chemicals, and some viruses may alter genes. Some cells are less able to repair such damage and often the resistance or vulnerability to such change is inherited from one generation to another. Modern technology in recent times can trace the specific molecular elements and pathways leading to loss of control of cell multiplication and movement. These changes have many origins, but all lead to the same result: metastatic cancer.

Finally, many drugs which impact these vulnerable vital points in cell chemistry, especially monoclonal antibodies, are under development. But one of the most exciting developments has been to engineer changes in the genome itself at will and easily (CRISPR-Cas9). The outcome of this type of approach to cancer control is the ability to overcome many other illnesses, like sickle cell disease. However, it is becoming possible to extract, change and insert genes to do almost anything one can imagine.

Genomic Engineering—Its Promise and Caveats

Genomic engineering is the gateway to changing the very nature of life across our planet at will. While the advantages of genomic engineering are enormous, so are its potential dangers, which have stimulated ethical and moral discourse worldwide. Just because we adhere to ethical and safe procedures does not mean all other countries will do the same. The potential hazards are huge.

Furthermore, *what does it mean to be molecular and at the same time a human person?* We need in the end and always to be aware that the human person and not the inanimate anatomic parts are primal. At what point does modifying or deleting genes cross over into some structure that is no longer human. At what point does adding genes result in some being that we would think was no longer just human? Traversing this new gateway is a responsibility larger than human beings have ever confronted. We are entering a new age.

In the end it is impossible to predict the future, but measured by the past it is more hopeful and exciting to think about and work toward than ever before.

Jack T. Evjy, MD, is Clinical Professor of Medicine Emeritus at Boston University School of Medicine. Following graduation from Boston University School of Medicine, he completed his internship, residency, chief residency in medicine, and his specialty training in medical oncology at the Massachusetts Memorial and Boston City Hospitals, now the Boston University Medical Center.

A proponent of local access to high-quality cancer care, he was Board Chair of Commonwealth Hematology Oncology, a regional community-based private practice based in Quincy, and helped establish the Cancer Management Center at Holy Family Hospital in Methuen. He directed the Greater Lawrence and the Greater Lowell Community Cancer Programs and was Chair of the Board of Directors of the Massachusetts Division of the American Cancer Society. He served on the Board of Directors of the New England Division of the American Cancer Society and was a Massachusetts delegate to the American Medical Society (AMA).

A Trustee and Executive Committee Member of the Boston Medical Library, he has been President of the Massachusetts Medical Society, which publishes *The New England Journal of Medicine*. His community activities have been recognized by receipt of the Ingersoll Bowditch award of the Massachusetts Medical Society for his work in public health and in award of an honorary Doctor of Humane Letters by Merrimack College.

He and his wife, Sheila O'Donnell, have four children, two grandchildren, and two great-grandchildren.

Aerospace Medicine

A Dream Realized with Unforeseen Results

Royce Moser, Jr.

The Beginning

On that Sunday my mother and I were listening to the radio when the announcer suddenly broke in to report that Japanese aircraft had attacked Pearl Harbor. We alerted our family and sat listening to the evolving information. We were suddenly at war!

Within a few weeks news reels, comic strips, and even books focused on the conflict, often stressing the victories by our pilots. News of the successes of the American Volunteer Group (Flying Tigers) was one of the few bright spots as Bataan and Corregidor fell.

With this background, it is not surprising I had decided to become an Army Air Corps pilot by the time I entered high school. Unfortunately, it was not to be. My sophomore year vision test revealed that I was near-sighted, and Air Force pilot candidates had to be 20/20 in both eyes. Fortunately, I did have a fall-back option. In the fifth grade, I developed possible rheumatic fever, and I was so impressed by Dr. Jack Gunn and what he did for me and others that I decided to become a physician. Thus, after my disappointing vision test, my career path was "set".

Rapid Advances in Flight Capabilities and in Space

Although not destined to be a pilot, my interest in flying remained strong. I perused flying magazines and closely followed news of rapidly advancing flight capabilities, including "jet" aircraft that were much faster than piston-engine planes. The "Century Series" jet aircraft debuted with the F-100 "Super Sabre" as the first US aircraft that could exceed the speed of sound in level flight.

By the time of our college graduation, there was increased interest in space flight, but we were shocked when the Soviet Union launched *Sputnik* in October 1957, just after I began Medical School. The

Space Race began. *Sputnik II* was in orbit in November, and we had a spectacular explosion on the launch pad as we tried to catch up. Our *Explorer* satellite did not reach orbit until January 1958.

Russians orbited dogs and we orbited Ham, the chimpanzee, in 1961. The animals demonstrated that humans could survive in a "weightless" (actually microgravity) environment. There had been concern that the body's baroreceptors would not work without gravity and the blood pressure would be totally out of control. Others postulated that the stomach contents would be regurgitated if gravity did not 'hold" the contents in place. These animal flights were reassuring and set the stage for the *Mercury*, *Gemini*, and, finally, the *Apollo* moon landing flights. A very exciting time for those of us interested in these aerospace activities! I still recall getting an EKG tracing from an astronaut in space and thinking how useful that capability would be in an ambulance taking a patient to a hospital.

The Dream Has a Second Life

Between my junior and senior years in Medical School, I found that Dr. Ross McFarland, across the road at Harvard School of Public Health, had done studies of high altitude exposure and aviation challenges. I visited him, and we discussed my interest. He asked "Have you considered becoming an Air Force Flight Surgeon?" My brilliant response: "What's that?" He explained a flight surgeon provides care for aircraft crew-members and their families and does research regarding humans in an aerospace environment. Also, flight surgeons have to fly with crews to experience and study the psycho-physiological stressors of flight. HAVE to fly?

Enter the US Air Force

I entered the Air Force after my medical internship, completing the basic flight surgeon course at the USAF School of Aerospace Medicine (SAM) Brooks AFB, TX. My first assignment was at a Strategic Air Command base where we had B-47 bombers, KC-135 tankers (that could refuel aircraft in flight, and Atlas F intercontinental ballistic missiles. I arrived approximately six weeks before the Cuban Missile Crisis occurred, and I rapidly saw what the Air Force was all about. We were at Defense Condition (DEFCON 2), one step below nuclear war. I mentioned in the *Report* that I was so impressed by the dedication and commitment of all of the Air Force members and families that I decided to remain on active duty and specialize in aerospace medicine.

The field had recently been recognized as a specialty by the Accreditation Council for Graduate Medical Education.

The Aerospace Medicine Residency

I was so fortunate to go to Harvard School of Public Health (HSPH) for the first year of my residency and work with Dr. Ross McFarland, one of the "fathers" of aviation medicine. Among his many contributions was his convincing the airlines to pressurize aircraft so they could fly above storms and also helped develop the Human Factors discipline.

Why Do I Need to Study Administration and Management? I Just Want to Make People Well!

One interesting aspect of the residency was the requirement for training in management in all three years. We had no training on the subject in medical school. Initially, I thought I would not need the courses because I was going to practice medicine. Gradually I realized how essential it was that those in charge of a health program, whether individual, group, major medical facility, or population have effective management capabilities.

Application of One Management Technique

During the year at HSPH I learned the concept of "borrowing power." The Aerospace Medical Association was meeting in New York City in May. As the junior officer in our military group Dr. McFarland asked me to contact our funding agency to get funds for the trip. When I contacted the agency, a lieutenant colonel asked me, "Captain, can't you read? If you can read you can plainly see that paragraph XXX, sub-paragraph YYY, sub-sub paragraph ZZZ plainly states there will be no funding of travel during an academic year. Now, don't bother me again!"

I reported my results to Dr. McFarland the next day. As our class ended, I overheard Dr. McFarland ask his secretary to see if General Bohannon was free. I wondered why he was calling the Surgeon General and went to the library. I got to our apartment about 5:30, and Lois told me I had a call from a colonel whom I was to call as soon as I got home, saying, "He will remain in his office until you call." "Dr. Moser, I am so sorry Lieutenant Colonel (---) gave you such misinformation. Of course we will fund the travel. Would you mind calling Dr. McFarland tonight and letting him know?" It took a couple of days for me to put two and two together. I applied the "borrowing power" approach in many ways during my careers, most notably when I was the Commander of the USAF School of Aerospace Medicine and the Director of the 30 year Air Force Agent Orange study evaluating the health of those exposed to dioxin in Vietnam. Follow-up exams were scheduled every two years. I received a call from Air Force Systems Command Budgeting Office to tell me they had to cut our funding for the study by 50%. I attempted to explain the scientific protocol (and emphasized that "their solution to do one-half of the exam on each subject this year and the rest of the exam the following year would not work) but only got, "It's your problem." "Yes, sir. Of course I have to contact Dr. Bernadine Buckley (Healy) in the Office of Science and Technology Assessment at the White House to tell her we will be unable to do the study the way the White House directed and the Surgeon General agreed to do it." Long, long pause. "Sir?" "Could you go over the last part?' I did. "Let us get back to you." Approximately one hour later a major general called to reassure me we would be fully funded and gave me his direct number in case we needed additional funding.

The Dream Becomes Real

The second year of our residency was at SAM and began with flying training in the T-33 jet aircraft to the point of soloing. This was to enhance our understanding of the requirements of piloting aircraft. I practiced on the simulator and finally had my first flight. As rolled down the runway, I applied ever-increasing back pressure on the stick as I had in the simulator so we would climb. Nothing happened even though increased pressure. Finally, the instructor pilot in the back seat took control and, with firm pressure, we were climbing. I soon learned to control the aircraft and do the maneuvers I had read about years before.

As noted in the *Report*, I did gain some ability and could maintain formation position in our F-100 with twenty feet separation from our lead aircraft as we maneuvered at over 450 mph. I realized my dream of controlling high speed USAF aircraft. I was honored when our squadron selected me as one of two in the squadron to fly in the wing's final combat mission in Vietnam. (I completed my Air Force career with over 2,000 flight hours in over thirty different aircraft. What an experience! Flying with crews was not only essential in establishing rapport so essential in providing care but I also became aware of some human factor concerns, including one that could have prevented parachute deployment during ejections.)

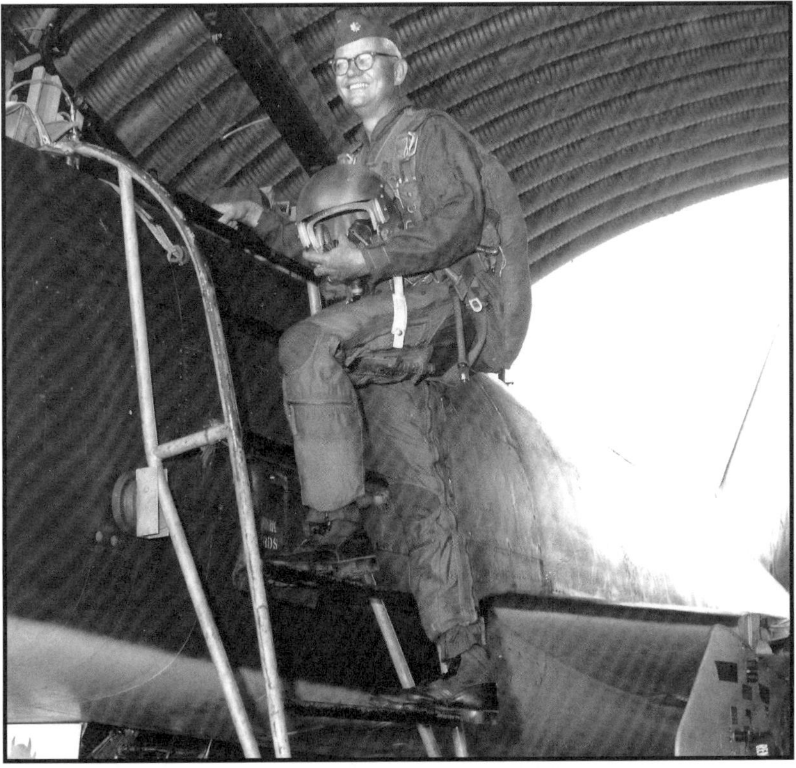

Figure 8.7.1.1 *A Flight Surgeon "Must" Fly.*
Dr. Royce Moser boarding F-100 Super Sabre, Phan Rang Air Base, Republic of Vietnam.
"I flew in the two-seat, one up front, one behind, F-100 F. Max speed for the F model: 871 mph; cruise speed: 584 mph; ceiling 35,000 ft. The bombs are live."
USAF Photo, August 1969

During my residency year at SAM I was a monitor of a group of three subjects who were locked in an altitude chamber for three weeks. The study was to determine if there was any personality or cognitive problems in a group that would have to be together for the duration of moon landing and return trip. (They all did well, but I would be concerned about a trip to Mars.) The final two years of my residency passed too rapidly.

Back to the "*Real World*" Air Force

My first assignment after my residency was a joint position, in the aerospace medicine office at Aerospace Defense Command (ADC) Headquarters and as Medical Officer, Special Weapons Defense, at North American Aerospace Defense Command (NORAD). The former was concerned with the fighter interceptor groups that would respond to nuclear-armed aircraft attacking the US and Canada. NORAD was focused on responding to an attack by intercontinental ballistic missiles.

My role at NORAD was to assist in preparing for nuclear, biological, or chemical attacks, and I was located in Cheyenne Mountain. The debriefings were in the large room with large maps, depicted in movies and TV shows, and I sat through two exercise debriefings. At that time one emphasis was getting a base back up and running (reconstituting) after an attack. The presenters were just finishing when the Major General in charge stated "I haven't heard from the doc yet. Doc, what did you think of the exercise?" I noted there had been some "glitches" but the teams had worked around them so the work went as planned. I still remember my next words. "As long as everyone recognizes the response is totally unrealistic, its fine." There been a few side conversations going on among the groups and suddenly there was dead silence! "Would you care to explain?" "Yes, Sir. You are using the decay curves for a fission weapon in order to determine when it is safe for the workers to begin repairing the base. However, the bases were hit with fusion weapons that have a much longer decay period. Those returning to the base at the specified time will be dead within twenty-four hours due to radiation. "When I returned to ADC I heard the Command Surgeon on the phone, "Yes Sir, I know he is only a captain, but he is absolutely correct." NORAD exercises were stopped for six months until they could be re-scripted.

I mentioned in my *Report* that I accomplished my first research effort while at ADC. It was a study of spatial disorientation accidents, where misleading inputs from the semicircular canals or otolith organ in the ear, from the eyes, or skin and muscles can convince a pilot all is well when the aircraft is actually flying into the earth. My data were used in a study by the Secretary of Defense to justify installing automatic Ground Collision Avoidance Systems that will take control of the aircraft to prevent the collision.

I then had a series of enjoyable assignments, including commander of two medical facilities (one in a combat environment), director of all Air Force aerospace medicine education programs, and director of the Air Force Aerospace Medical Consultation Center. My final Air Force assignment was Commander of the USAF School of Aerospace Medicine. It was a 900-member organization with over 80% of our $35-million budget (1983 dollars) devoted to research and development. Studies involved basic science such as studying the ways the neo-cerebellum controls the speed of transmission of nerve impulses and, hence, decision making (an important consideration in aerial combat). Focused, practical research included developing methods for pilots to withstand the onset of 9 Gs/second in the new F-16. One interesting development was the On-Board Oxygen Generating System (OBOGS) designed to extract oxygen from air rather than relying on liquid oxygen tanks that would explode if struck by a shell. The initial version was approximately 15 feet long and quite heavy. Now, my wife uses an oxygen concentrator that weighs five pounds.

Another Career

After retirement from the Air Force in 1985 I went to the Department of Family and Preventive Medicine, University of Utah School of Medicine. I was Director of the Rocky Mountain Center for Occupational and Environmental Health. I applied my management experience in developing a course, Management of Health and Safety Programs, and have written the third edition of my book, *Effective Management of Health and Safety Programs—A Practical Guide* that is used nationally and internationally. I used my Air Force experience when I was the lead author for Utah's Medical Surge Capacity Plan to respond to mass casualty situations. (The effort involved coordinating inputs from over forty state agencies. The Plan was used as a model by several other states.)

An Unexpected Benefit of Going to Harvard

My most momentous event occurred during "Some Enchanted Evening" in my junior year in college. I attended a Halloween Social at Old Cambridge Baptist Church and was with friends when I saw this strikingly beautiful young lady with deep red hair arrive. I got up my courage, visited with her, and was impressed by her keen intellect as well as with her other attributes. We agreed to meet the next Sunday, and the rest is history.

A graduate of Children's Hospital School of Nursing, Lois had many accomplishments during our careers. She designed, implemented, and was in charge of the first all-pediatric recovery room in the United States. A neonatal nurse, she also was president of volunteer organizations that, for example, funded college scholarships for women and provided new clothes for over 5,000 deprived children each year. She has totally supported all of our career decisions.

Looking Back

I may not have wanted to go to Harvard College, but the unexpected results are exceptional. If I had not gone to Harvard I would not have met Lois. Additionally, I would not have gone to Harvard Medical School, where I learned about flying as a flight surgeon and specializing in aerospace medicine. If I had not gone to Harvard I would not have gone to Harvard School of Public Health. By becoming a flight surgeon I not only realized my dream of controlling high performance aircraft but also experienced so many more professionally and personally satisfying events, with two superb careers (and a truly exceptional wife). I would have missed the opportunity to work with outstanding fellow students and leaders at Harvard and in my subsequent careers. As noted in the *Report*, I would not change a thing if I could get a "do-over"!

I am so fortunate to have had a mother whose effort resulted in my two superb careers.

Royce Moser, Jr., MD, MPH, a native of Versailles, MO, is a graduate of Harvard College, Harvard Medical School and Harvard School of Public Health. Before entering the US Air Force Residency in Aerospace Medicine, he interned in internal medicine at Tufts New England Center Hospital. He is certified in Aerospace Medicine and in Occupational Medicine.

He served 23 years in the US Air Force as a base flight surgeon; Medical Officer Special Weapons Defense for North American Aerospace Defense Command (NORAD), Chief Aerospace Medicine, Office of the Command Surgeon, Aerospace Defense Command, Director Base Medical Services (DBMS) for 35th Medical Group, Phan Rang Republic of Vietnam, and DBMS Tyndall AFB, Florida. He also held a number of positions in the USAF School of Aerospace Medicine, and his final assignment was Commander of the 900-member School.

Following retirement from the USAF, he was Professor, Department of Family and Preventive Medicine, University of Utah School of Medicine, Vice Chair of the Department, and Director of The Rocky Mountain Center for Occupational and Environmental Medicine.

He is past President of the Aerospace Medical Association, past Vice President for Medical Affairs American College of Occupational and Environmental Medicine, past member of the American Board of Preventive Medicine, member Accreditation Council for Medical Education Preventive Medicine Residency Review Committee, and past President, Harvard School of Public Health Alumni Association.

Dr. Moser has published a number of peer-reviewed scientific papers and authored the textbook, *Effective Management of Health and Safety Programs—A Practical Guide*, now in its third edition.

Medical Care

Missions

Lost in the Gobi and Jailed in Nigeria

James E. Standefer

I have always wanted to be a doctor. Prior to WWII, my father was a "*country doctor*" in the small town of Tama, IA. My mother was a nurse.

I can remember gathering around our "*green-eyed*" floor model Zenith radio listening to the account of the Japanese bombing of Pearl Harbor, quickly followed with onset of WWII. My father was a patriot, and within two weeks he had joined the US Navy as a Lt. Medical Officer. On return home, we moved to Des Moines for his pediatric training.

At the age of 14, I began my "*medical career*" by cleaning out the cages of the rabbits used for pregnancy tests. I delivered lab slips to the hospital floors, which at that time were manually glued into patients' charts. At age 16, I pushed the wheeled stretchers taking patients to and from the surgery department. I was on-call to help the pathologist with autopsies. After turning down the scalp, I would remove the upper part of the skull to facilitate the removal and examination of the brain by the pathologist. I even assisted with an appendectomy.

College to Medical School

I did well in high school and was encouraged to apply to Harvard by a Harvard graduate, Hirum Hunn, an attorney in Des Moines. I was most honored to receive a scholarship. I traveled to Boston on the train, the subway to Harvard Square and through the main gate into Harvard Yard. Thus, my new life began.

After graduation from Harvard, I attended Cornell Medical School, graduating in 1961. In exchange for my room in the medical school dorm, I taught anatomy to the first-year nursing students, including dissection of a cadaver. I like to say that "*I met my wife, Sarah, over a dead body.*"

Following medical school I completed a one-year rotating internship followed by one year of internal medicine residency at the University of Vermont.

US Navy Flight Surgeon

The Vietnam War had started. There was a doctor draft, and I was out of money. I joined the Navy, and attended the six-month School of Aviation Medicine in Pensacola, FL. Returning from my solo flight, I learned that JFK had been assassinated while I was in mid-air.

I was assigned as the flight Surgeon to a test pilot squadron, VX-5, in the Mohave Desert. I served as a general medical officer, tended to the pilots, delivered babies and conducted sick calls for the enlisted men. My flight-time was in the rear cockpit of the Mach2 VX-5 Phantom monitoring G-forces during practice weapon delivery.

Drawn to Ophthalmology

While in Flight Surgeon School in Pensacola, I became interested in ophthalmology. Captain Preston described ophthalmology as the "*Queen of the Specialties: you get to know your patients, you can do surgery if you want to, see generations of families and the night call is not bad.*" I was convinced.

Following discharge from the Navy, I did a 3½-year residency at Washington University in St. Louis under Professor Bernard Becker, a world renowned authority on glaucoma.

After my residency in ophthalmology, we moved to Minnesota where I began a private practice with a specialty in glaucoma. I also was invited to join the faculty of the University of Minnesota.

I taught glaucoma diagnosis and treatment to medical students, residents, and private practice physicians. I practiced and taught for 23 years during which the practice grew to four offices and four ophthalmologists.

Volunteerism in Developing Countries

I had always been interested in volunteerism in developing countries. The time had come to follow my interest. I used the American Academy of Ophthalmology International Registry to find opportunities, initially as a cataract surgeon. This began my career as a full-time international volunteer. The large majority of my services were self-funded.

I traveled widely performing ***cataract surgery*** in more than 15 locations, especially in Central America and the Solomon Islands in the South Pacific. I also worked for extended periods of time as a clinical and surgical ophthalmologist in several locations, including a number of extended trips to Mercy Hospital in Abak, Nigeria.

In 2000 I was in Ulaanbatar, Mongolia, with two other ophthalmologists for a SEE International visit. The director of the ophthalmology department, Professor Bassanhu, learned of my special interest in ***glaucoma*** and invited me to return the following summer for a month to teach about glaucoma.

Professor Bassanhu's invitation led me to a turning point in my volunteer career. I realized that my volunteer service would be more valuable as a teacher of glaucoma.

Glaucoma Education for Overseas Physicians

As I had traveled and volunteered as a general ophthalmologist, I had become aware of a troubling knowledge gap for the proper diagnosis and treatment of glaucoma in many countries.

Worldwide glaucoma is the second leading cause of blindness, and more importantly, it is the leading cause of irreversible blindness. Hence I designed a two-week glaucoma workshop using the "*trainer of trainers*" principles.

The participants must agree to teach others upon their return to their home institution. Each work-shop was attended by five post-residency ophthalmologists from five different training centers. I have conducted the workshop 42 times in 36 major ophthalmic training centers of 31 developing countries. Early on, I hand-carried a portable operating microscope and a diode laser loaned by generous equipment companies.

The most fulfilling part of my volunteerism has been to address this knowledge gap as a teacher of the proper diagnosis and treatment of glaucoma.

Adventures Abroad

Over the 20 years of my volunteer service in developing countries, there were many what I call "*adventures*". The following are the ones that stand out.

Security Violation in Nigeria

I had been in Nigeria many times for clinical service or teaching. During one of my visits Dr. Kunle Hassan, his assistant and I were flying from Lagos to Calabar to perform cataract surgery. This was the first air travel for the assistant who had borrowed a video camera from a relative. The plane was in the process of getting ready to leave the gate for takeoff, and during this time the assistant who was sitting next to a window was practicing zoom and more. He did not know that it was unlawful to take photos of an airport. Out of nowhere a man in civilian clothes appeared and ordered the assistant to disembark via the rear drop-down stairway. Kunle, of course, went with him.

I remained on board to stay with the equipment. At the very last moment before take-off, Kunle shoved the camera into the hands of a policeman, and Kunle and the assistant ran up the stairs that had just begun to close and dove into their seats. Whew! However, not so fast! The airport police at our destination had been notified. The plane landed but remained at the end of the runway where we were removed from the plane and driven to the terminal in the paddy wagon. We were immediately put "*behind bars*" in the airport jail. The Captain of the airport police was notified but did not appear for about two hours. Now the near miracle: Kunle had successfully performed cataract surgery on the captain's father a few years previously and was recognized. We were promptly released. The second near miracle was that the camera was returned about a year later.

Lost in the Gobi Desert

Near the end of a teaching visit to Mongolia, Professor Bassanhu asked me if I wanted to visit some outlying clinics. One was in the north, one was in the south. I chose south to one that bordered the Gobi Desert. The duration of the flight was about one hour in a typical passenger jet.

Following a short visit to a local eye clinic, we drove a short way out of town to visit one of Bassanhu's patients. We returned to the airport only to learn that the airplane had departed earlier.

We spent the night on cots in the infirmary and left the next morning in a Russian jeep. There were no roads, not even tire tracks that could return us to our departure city. The plan was to drive north through the Gobi Desert. The estimated driving time was four hours. The jeep was designed for four, and we were six.

We set out in the jeep at about mid-day. Because it was mid-summer with extended daylight, the expected arrival time was between 5 and 6 p.m. If we continued it was expected that we would come across a real road leading to the city.

The terrain in that part of the Gobi is not flat and consists of mostly sand and small to medium rocks. There are some gullies from the infrequent rains, springs and snow melt. The jeep and the driver did well, and we were slowly making progress.

Once or twice we came upon small ponds between two steep slopes, steep enough to prevent driving around. You had to go through the water. It looked very innocent but there was no obvious way to find out how deep it was except to have someone in a prone position on the hood with a long pole, hopefully long enough to estimate the depths.

The driver asked us to get out of the jeep while he crossed in case the pond was deeper than we thought. The driver would back up and take us two at a time through the pond up a small rise. We ate some sandwiches and chocolate bars and headed in the direction we thought was north. However, we later discovered it was not. We later learned that we had drifted to the west.

We continued on but darkness seemed to come quickly. There was no concern about fuel because the jeep carried two full five-gallon jerry cans of gas. It was a clear night with bright star light that actually lit up the terrain enough to see outside the headlights.

At about midnight it became obvious that we were lost. We had no idea where we were. Either the driver or one of the passengers said that sometimes there were sheep herders that lived in remote places in the Gobi. The sheep herders used dogs to herd the sheep.

He got out of the jeep and barked loudly like a dog. No response. We drove on and on with numerous barking dog stops. Finally, after a long time, there was a faint response. We headed in that direction, stopping several times to listen for more barking. Eventually we heard a bark.

The response got louder and much to our surprise we came to the *ger*/ home of a man and his wife. They told us that we were too far to the west. Our driver changed course and eventually we came to a packed dirt road that led us to the city. We arrived about 6 a.m., an 18-hour journey instead of the predicted four to six. It was an adventure that I will always remember.

* * *

I have received many awards for my work as an international volunteer. These have been personally rewarding, but most important to me has been the recognition of my work by having been granted the prestigious International Prevention of Blindness Award by the American Academy of Ophthalmology.

I have been a member of the American Academy of Ophthalmology for 45 years. I have promoted international volunteerism in courses and at Breakfast with the Experts. I also served eight years as the Chairman of the AAO International Educational Development Committee that initiated the popular International Forum.

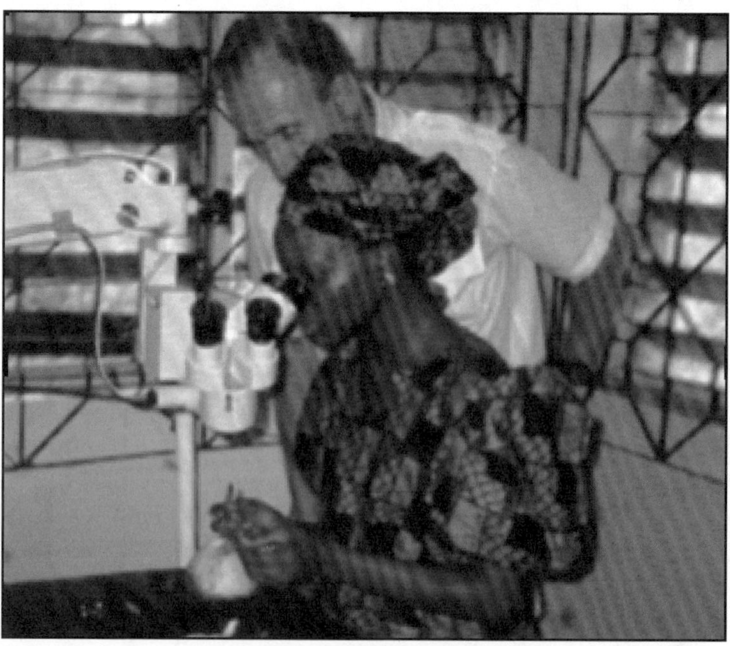

Figure 8.8.1.1 *The author instructs his Nigerian counterpart, Dr. Rosalind Duke, how to perform glaucoma release surgery by practicing on a grapefruit viewed through a dissecting microscope.*

Photo courtesy of James E. Standefer

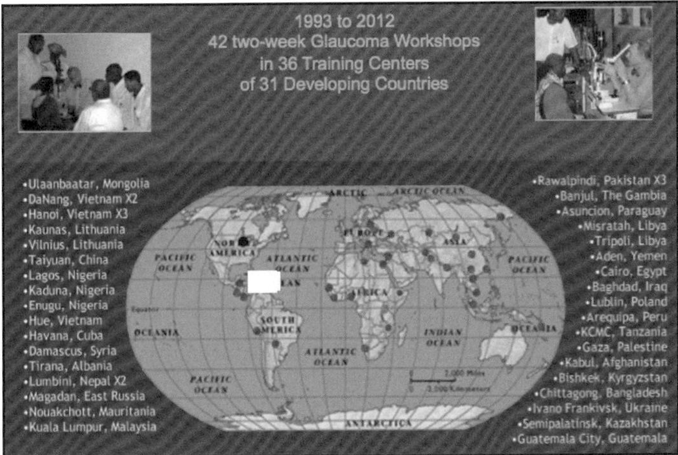

Figure 8.8.1.2 *Locales of 42 Glaucoma Workshops conducted around the globe over 19 years in 31 developing countries: organized and supervised by Dr. James Standefer following his retirement from private practice of ophthalmology in Minneapolis, MN*

James E. Standefer, MD, has been recognized for his many contributions to international service in ophthalmology, including the *Outstanding Humanitarian Service Award* from the American Academy of Ophthalmology (AAO); *The Outstanding Service Award*, from the Vision Foundation, University of Minnesota; *The International Public Service Award* of the Foundation of the AAO; *The Distinguished Alumni Award and Visiting Professor,* Washington University Eye Alumni Association; and *The Presidential Award* of the Ophthalmology Society of Nigeria. He has been an invited speaker at numerous international meetings, including a WHO Regional Workshop in Cairo, Egypt.

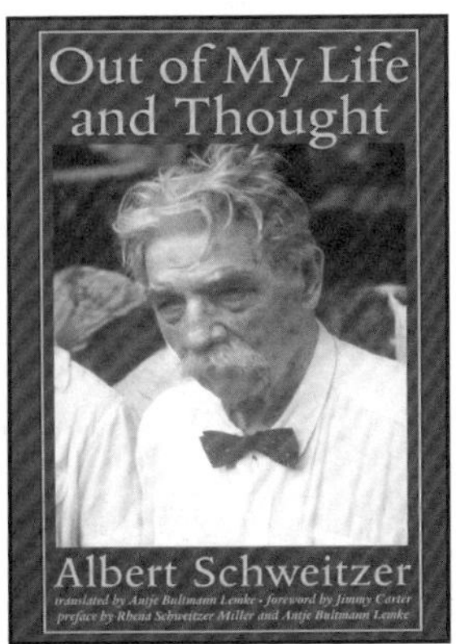

Figure 8.8.1.3 *Albert Schweitzer (1875–1965)*
60th Anniversary Edition, Johns Hopkins University Press, 2009

Evolution of Health Care

Health Care – Past, Present and Future

Some Personal Experiences

Kenneth I. Shine

Polio

It was the late summer of 1955 during one of the last poliomyelitis epidemics in Boston, when the power failed. I was a volunteer on a ward at the Massachusetts General Hospital (MGH) which cared for 12 to 15 pregnant women in Drinker tank respirators. The respirators were used for individuals whose central respiratory center had been damaged by the polio virus. The pregnant women and their families were committed not only to the survival of the mother, but especially that of the baby.

Suddenly one afternoon about 3:00 p.m. the power failed. The Drinker respirators depended upon electricity to function. Emergency generators immediately began operating, but they serviced only outlets in the corridors. The nurses began to wheel the respirators into the corridor as quickly as possible to reestablish power, and an emergency search for extension cords was undertaken.

My responsibility was to hand crank each respirator three or four times in order to ventilate the patient until power could be restored to their machine. I raced around from Drinker to Drinker, terrified that one of the patients might die from lack of ventilation. Fortunately, power was re-established without any serious complications. It was my fledgling introduction to emergency care. That same year, 1955, Jonas Salk introduced his new vaccine.

Polio was eradicated from the United States in 1979 and in the western hemisphere shortly thereafter. Efforts to eliminate the last vestiges of polio in the rest of the world continue today.

The enormous, expensive, and inefficient tank respirators were rapidly replaced by positive pressure respirators.

I have had the opportunity on a number of occasions to speak to medical audiences about advances in health care. When asked *if anyone has seen a case of acute poliomyelitis*, no more than one or two older physicians raise their hands.

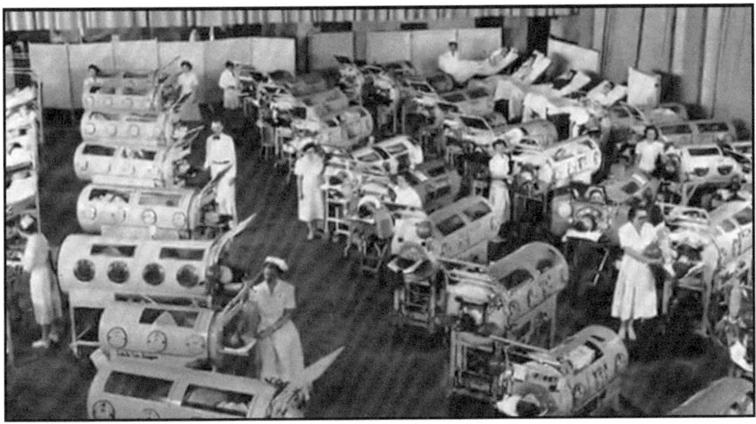

Figure 8.8.2.1 *"Iron lung ward" filled with polio patients, Rancho Los Amigos Hospital, California (1953)*
Photo source: Iron lung—Wikipedia

Heart Attacks

Death from Heart Attack

I became a medical intern at the MGH in July 1961. On the very first day in the emergency room, I admitted a 56-year-old man with an acute myocardial infarction, a heart attack. I had controlled his chest pain with morphine and admitted him with very careful orders for oxygen, pain medications and monitoring his blood pressure, heart rate, and respirations.

I was devastated the next morning to find that he had been discovered by the nurses dead in bed during the night. Almost simultaneously with this experience Dr. Edgar Haber and several of my intern colleagues began monitoring the electrocardiograms of patients with heart attacks.

Much to everyone's surprise, it was discovered these patients had many abnormal heart rhythms which sometimes terminated in death. The discovery lead to the development of coronary care units and the application of technology for monitoring patients, some of which was derived from the NASA space program. I carefully reviewed the orders that I had written for my patient and determined that they had been entirely appropriate at the time.

Compare contemporary treatment for an acute myocardial infarction, which now begins with prophylactic aspirin in the emergency vehicle taking the patient to the hospital. Emergency cardiac catheterizations now open narrow coronaries with balloon catheters—or drugs may be used to dissolve clots.

Effective cardiac surgery to treat coronary artery disease was not available on that day in 1961. Hospital mortality from myocardial infarction exceeded 30% at that time. Today it is unusual to have hospital mortality in excess of three to five percent, principally occurring among individuals brought to the hospital in cardiogenic shock.

Researching Treatment of Heart Attacks

I became Chief Resident in Medicine at the MGH in 1968. I had served a cardiac fellowship, described a newly recognized cardiac rhythm disturbance, and concluded that I would continue my research interests in cardiovascular disease.

I noticed that patients with myocardial infarctions were invariably hospitalized for 21 days. One week was spent at complete bed rest for the patient, frightened to the extent that he/she hardly moved in bed. The patients were fed by nurses or nurses' aides, lifted onto bedpans, and feared that any kind of effort would rupture their heart.

By 1968, Samuel Levine, at the Brigham Hospital, had begun to change care by mobilizing patients to a chair rather than to rigid bed rest, which was complicated by blood clots and infections. But 21 days was the standard. I could find no evidence to support that requirement.

I proposed that we undertake a clinical trial in which patients were randomly assigned to a 14-day hospitalization versus 21 days. Today, 14 days is very long for hospitalization of a routine heart attack, but at the time, a one-third reduction in hospitalization was substantial. There was great resistance from physicians to undertake the trial for fear that patients would drop dead as they left the hospital on the 14th day.

Therefore we undertook a process called sequential analysis in which patients were followed in parallel groups for 21 versus 14 days, with a commitment that we would stop the trial if mortality was higher in the 14-day group. As it turned out, there was absolutely no difference in the biological outcome of the two groups. Indeed, the patients discharged after 14 days had a higher prevalence of returning to work than those who were hospitalized for a longer period.

The paper was published in the *New England Journal of Medicine* and was among the very first examples of what has become known as *health services research.* It became apparent that it was important to study the way in which care is delivered, rather than to continue historical practices which have not been validated.

The actual work of collecting the patients and monitoring the data was conducted by a young cardiology fellow named Adolph Hutter. Ultimately, Hutter became the President of the American College of Cardiology. It is always great fun to develop new knowledge, but it is even more rewarding when it leads to outstanding careers for the students and fellows with whom you work.

Cancer

Hodgkin's Disease

Decreases in mortality of cancer were slower to come than those in heart disease. Hodgkin's disease is a cancer of lymph glands and the spleen. The tumor can also invade other tissues. I can best exemplify developments here by describing three vignettes which had a profound effect upon me.

Case 1. I was a medical intern at MGH. A young woman, aged 25, was admitted for treatment of end stage Hodgkin's disease. She was to receive last-ditch chemotherapy, which produced nausea, headache, and a variety of other symptoms. I attended to her late in the evening. I established an intravenous line to administer her chemotherapy after giving her a sleeping medication and an anti-nausea drug. The intent was to help her sleep through the night and avoid as many of the side effects of the medication.

One evening in February 1962, as I sat on the edge of her bed injecting the medicine into her IV line, she turned to me with a question,

"*Am I going to die?*"

I was rather shaken. She was younger than I and the intimacy of the relationship in the darkened room caused me to pause with a rush of adrenaline. I thought of all the usual platitudes about our desire to do everything we could to help her. Instead I responded,

"*Why do you ask?*"

Without hesitation, she indicated that she was a school teacher with a class of 12 deaf children in Connecticut. She said the students were doing quite well, and if she were going to die, she would like to write to each of them a letter encouraging them to continue their studies. "Do you think it is time to write those letters?" she asked. I said "Yes, it would be a good thing to do." Over the next 2½ weeks, she read to me sections of these letters as I was giving her medication. And then she died.

I learned an enormous amount from this patient.

> First and foremost, was to not insert my own anxieties or thoughts about pivotal questions, but rather to try to really understand what the patient wanted to know.
>
> The second, to realize that the objective of the patient was often to discover information that was in fact not a direct response to the question.

Throughout my career, when patients have asked me whether they were going to die, I have always responded, "Why do you ask?"

Some patients indicate that they had business arrangements to make. Others indicated that they had long thought of a cruise or a trip to take with their significant other. "Is it time to take that trip?" The most unusual response was from a middle-aged man who responded that "I made a killing at the track and buried $10,000 in a tin box beside the garage. If I'm going to die, I better tell the old lady where the money is."

The interaction with this teacher-patient with Hodgkin's disease was an important lesson for me in *caring for patients at the end of life* and being willing to directly discuss their plans, fears, thoughts, apprehensions, and opportunities.

Case 2. In 1969, my wife and I were on our way to California for a post-doctoral fellowship. Before we left, we visited my wife's 28-year-old cousin who had just been diagnosed with stage IVb Hodgkin's disease. That meant that the disease was very widespread and symptomatic, with a very poor prognosis.

I remember vividly commenting to my wife as we drove away that it was unlikely that we would ever see him alive again. However, at that very time new treatments were evolving, particularly led by Dr. Henry Kaplan of Stanford University. Kaplan began aggressive treatment with radiation and removal of the spleen.

What had been until that time a disease with a mortality in excess of 95% now became treatable, indeed curable. My wife's cousin was cured of Hodgkin's disease. He lived 25 years before dying of a heart attack.

Case 3. In 1981 I was the Chair of the Department of Medicine at UCLA Medical Center when an intern came to see me with tears in his eyes. He indicated that he wished to have a leave of absence because of recently diagnosed Hodgkin's disease, pointing to a bandage on his neck where the biopsy had been taken.

I asked why he needed a leave of absence. He indicated he would require extensive chemotherapy and removal of his spleen as part of the Kaplan protocol. He felt it was unfair to his colleagues to require that they cover his duties while he was having these procedures.

However, the leave would cost him at least one year in this training. I told him I was not prepared to give him a leave of absence and thereby set back his long training program by at least one year. Instead, I insisted that he would be cured, and that he work out a coverage plan with his colleagues. He was visibly angry, fearful, and upset about this decision, but he accepted it.

Approximately two years later, as he was leaving his residency program for a fellowship, he approached me at a farewell party, held out his hands to shake mine and thanked me for refusing to grant him the leave.

From February 1962 to September 1981 Hodgkin's disease treatment had progressed to a point that I could in good faith deny leave to a young man in the expectation that he was to be cured. The intern is currently a professor at a major eastern medical school.

Figure 8.8.2.2 *Kenneth Shine, MD, July 1986, newly appointed Dean of UCLA School of Medicine*

Photo courtesy of the author

AIDS

In 1980, I made what was for me the most difficult clinical decision of my career.

Beginning of the Epidemic

In the spring of that year, a medical intern named Robert Wolfe presented a patient to me during the weekly rounds that I made as the Chief of the Medical Service at the University of California at Los Angeles *(UCLA)*. The patient had multiple infections and was clearly immunocompromised from no known cause. I pontificated that one of his infections, cytomegalovirus, was a potential cause for his unusual situation.

I had to give up this diagnosis approximately two weeks later when intern Wolfe presented another patient with multiple infections but no cytomegalovirus. Both of the patients were young gay men, and both of them had a pneumonia caused by an organism called *Pneumocystis carinii*. I recommended that Wolfe consult with a new, young member of our faculty, Dr. Michael Gottlieb. Adding these patients to those referred to him by a local physician, Gottlieb then reported a new gay related immune-deficiency disease *(GRID)* to the CDC, Centers for Disease Control.

These cases were featured in the December 1981 issue of *The New England Journal of Medicine* describing the first patients on the West Coast to be identified with what soon became known as the Acquired Immune Deficiency Syndrome, or AIDS. That *Journal* issue also included a separate report from New York City on a similar group of individuals who were drug users. It became clear that this infection could be transmitted two ways: not only by sexual transmission but also by blood through transfusions and even sharing of used IV needles.

UCLA became a very active center for the treatment of AIDS and its associated infections. The disease itself was frightening to everyone since there was no effective treatment beyond trying to control the infections that these patients incurred. In 1982, large numbers of patients came to the medical center, and I was extremely proud of the staff response, which was to care for every patient or potential patient.

Fear of Contagion

One day early in that year, an Infectious Disease Fellow, i.e., trainee, who was highly respected among the resident staff, became concerned that he might bring this new infection to his newly pregnant wife. At the time there was still enormous speculation as to how the virus was transmitted. This fellow came to work in complete operating room protection—mask, gown, gloves, hair and shoe covering—ostensibly to minimize the possibility that he might carry it home. Seeing the way he dressed, a large number of staff dressed the same way. I was very concerned that the appearance of this kind of protection would frighten other patients from using the emergency room or hospital. It suggested a level of transmittable ability for which I had seen no evidence.

Over the next several days I researched the epidemic as well as I could and consulted a number of experts in the field. I then released a memorandum indicating that precautions dealing with known and suspected patients with this new disease would be the same as for viral hepatitis. As I was the Chairman of the Department of Medicine and considered a leading clinician, my directive was routinely accepted by everyone, *except myself.*

For several months, I would wake up at night in a cold sweat terrorized by the notion that I might have inappropriately exposed a large number of people to this new infection, unsafely. You can imagine my relief when the Centers for Disease Control announced that the precautions for dealing with AIDS would be the same as those for hepatitis.

Assessing Health Care Delivery

As exemplified by the project on length of stay after a heart attack, I have always been interested in the way health care is delivered.

My interest peaked early when, as a medical resident, a Harvard medical student named Michael Crichton approached me and some other residents to let him know when certain patients were admitted. It was his intention to follow these patients throughout their care.

We accommodated Crichton, who then wrote a book entitled *Five Patients*, documenting their experience. The book is very readable and provides insight as what could be done at that time for care of the five conditions which he described. Of particular note was his analysis of health care costs. A day at the Massachusetts General at that time cost approximately $80. Crichton suggested that it could go as high as a $100 per day and provided an explanation as to why the cost was so high. He also speculated that the costs might rise to as much as six percent of gross domestic product in the United States.

Michael Crichton went on to a very distinguished literary career, starting with *The Andromeda Strain*, and a whole series of other science fiction books. He clearly had an uncanny ability to understand the possibilities and implications of science and technology for good and evil. However, his estimates on health care completely missed the rate of change which has brought us close to eighteen percent of gross domestic product and an average cost of hospitalization that approaches $17,000.

Quality of Care Research at the Institute of Medicine—*Reducing Medical Errors*

I continued to work with other investigators on issues related to health care and consulted on subjects such as the routine use of electrocardiograms in the emergency room (unless the patient has cardiac symptoms there is very little additional value) and advising on programs in the Rand Corporation and the Robert Woods Johnson Clinical Scholars Program. It is not surprising, then, that when I became the president of the Institute of Medicine of the National Academy of Science, I suggested that the Institute do an in-depth analysis of the quality of care in the American health care system.

We started with a roundtable, and then with a committee, which produced two early publications. "*To Err Is Human*" was published in 1999 and identified the extraordinarily high number of errors made in the American health care system and the need to substantially improve patient safety. It was followed by a report called "*Crossing the Quality Chasm*", which was a more profound in-depth assessment of quality across the system.

It is of considerable interest that I could not raise any outside money to do these projects. Both governmental and private funders questioned the wisdom of challenging quality of care in the United States. A number of potential donors asked, "*Do you really want to scare people with information about the number of errors that take place?*" The answer is, *of course*, that I did want to give an objective assessment of the situation and introduce methods to improve quality and reduce errors.

The project started as a quality of care initiative, but when our outstanding staff consulted with the print and electronic media at a workshop, they were told that quality is what Ford Motor Company was using to combat the influx of Japanese automobiles, and that everyone believed their physician or hospital was of the highest quality. The media people indicated that we needed another approach if we were to get anyone's attention. It was that feedback which caused the committee to go from quality to medical errors which were more easily understood and undeniable. Periodically newspapers would cover examples of surgery on the wrong limb or wrong side of the body or brain.

As it turned out these episodes were far more extensive than anyone thought. When we estimated that there were *between 40 and 80 thousand lives lost annually from medical errors*, the Institute and the report were soundly attacked and criticized. As it turned out, these were underestimates of the number of inpatient errors and did not include fatal errors in the ambulatory environment or nursing homes.

One criticism by investigators who actually confirmed our findings of the prevalence of errors in hospital mortality was that at least half of the people who died had an end stage illness and would have died within the next six months. Needless to say, I pointed out that most of us who have six months to live would just as soon have that opportunity rather than to have it ended by an error. These reports continue to be among the top ten publications annually of the Institute of Medicine, which later became the National Academy of Medicine.

Organizing Medical Care Delivery

In the last phase of my career, I was responsible for six health campuses in The University of Texas System, including the MD Anderson Cancer Center, The University of Texas Southwestern, and others.

Clinical Effectiveness and Patient Safety

I supported the development of a program in clinical effectiveness and patient safety in The University of Texas System which educated over two thousand medical professionals, of whom almost 40% are physicians. The program completed over 800 projects to improve quality and increase safety in The University of Texas hospitals. This post gave me an opportunity to take academic ideas and apply them in the academic medical center.

I became very active in supporting new reimbursement models and delivery models for health care in order to increase the *value of care: the relationship between patient outcomes and costs.*

I joined the Board of Directors of UnitedHealth Group, the largest health insurer in the United States. This is the first and only for-profit board which I joined, although I had other opportunities. I was particularly attracted by the fact that the substantial portion of the United agenda was not insurance at all, but rather a range of ways to improve delivery of care/quality of care, electronic health records, and other technologies.

Relating Patient Outcomes to Cost

My agenda was to improve care for patients, the way in which providers, particularly physicians, were dealt with, and to support new models of care which would maintain quality while controlling costs. United, through its *Optum* programs, began to buy group practices which were committed to these goals, i.e., controlling costs while maintaining or improving quality.

Many of them adopted total or partial *capitation*, i.e., payments per person per year. Such reimbursement allows the creation of effective health care teams incorporating prevention, wellness, nutrition counseling, physical activity, etc., as well at disease treatment into their programs. *Optum* now provides this kind of care to almost four million individuals and growing. It also includes ambulatory surgical care, rapid community health care, house calls, and a variety of other strategies.

In some way it is ironic that an individual who throughout most of his career served as an academic in not-for-profit settings should end up on the board of a for-profit organization where many of the ideas developed in academia can actually be applied in the real world.

Designing, Funding, and Building New Medical Schools in Texas

In the last portion of my service at The University of Texas, I had the privilege of working on the creation of two new medical schools.

The *Dell Medical School* is located at the University of Texas at Austin, one of a few AAU universities previously without a medical school. For a variety of political reasons, it was not possible to get state support for the creation of a medical school, and we pledged not to take resources from the limited budgets of the academic campuses in order to create a medical school. Instead, the medical school was funded by a combination of $30,000,000 of annual support from The University of Texas Board of Regents and $35,000,000 of support from the central health hospital district. The voters of Travis County, by a 55 to 45 percent margin, voted to increase their taxes in order to support the new medical school. So far as I know, this is a first in America, i.e., a local jurisdiction taxing themselves to produce a medical school, as opposed to many state-supported schools funded by legislatures.

The *University of Texas Rio Grande* was established in south Texas, one of the poorest parts in the United States, originally suffering from a dramatic scarcity of every type of health professional, including physicians, nurses, pharmacists, etc. In that case, it was possible to get state support for a regional academic health center and then for the medical school; however, the resources are dramatically less than those in Austin. For example, in Austin, well over $250,000, 000 in philanthropic support has been raised in just the past two years compared to a few million dollars in south Texas. However, south Texas, which is overwhelmingly Hispanic in population, has prided itself in the creation of this new medical school. Even with limited resources this school has already begun to substantially improve the quality of health care, particularly to some underserved populations in the unincorporated *colonias*, areas in which the poorest individuals live.

Summing Up

I have used these vignettes to dramatize where American medicine was, is, and where it is going. The advances in health care in our time have been beyond belief.

Not only has Hodgkin's disease come under control, but childhood leukemia, testicular cancer, breast cancer, and many other conditions are rapidly responding to the new technologies.

Heart disease care has been revolutionized by surgical and non-surgical interventions but also by drugs which control cholesterol levels, metabolism, rhythm disturbances, hypertension and strokes. The overall mortality from heart disease is now one third of what it was when I became an intern.

At the same time, the health care system has continued to grow without limits on size, space, personnel, or costs. It simply cannot continue to do this. The increasing proportion of Gross National Product *(GNP)* going into health care means that schools, roads, bridges, universities, and a whole variety of other important functions may not be carried out effectively without further exploding the national debt.

Moreover, the health care outcomes in the United States are not substantially better than that of countries which spend far less money. We stand far lower in life expectancy, infant survival, and other parameters of health than other OECD countries. We do excel in the treatment of cancer once it has been discovered, but our prevalence of cancer is no lower than in many other countries.

While the future looks bright for advances in technology to improve the outcome of disease treatment, it is critically important that we *conduct meaningful experiments in how to deliver care which is efficient, effective, patient centered, and with a value that is of high quality and low cost. Health maintenance and disease prevention must be major goals.*

New delivery models such as health homes, accountable care organizations, and bundling of episodes of care are only a few of the interventions which will be required to make this happen. Access to care through adequate health insurances is essential in any system to follow "Obamacare".

* * *

When I entered medical school, we were very sanguine that we knew about health and disease. Little did we anticipate an epidemic such as that produced by human immunodeficiency virus *(HIV)* and the millions of patients and lives lost from AIDS. We did not recognize the extent to which health care would cost so much, and we actually believed that antibiotics had solved the problem of infectious disease forever.

There is no way to tell our students today what will happen within the next 60 years. But at least my own experience has been exciting, rewarding, stimulating, and certainly held my attention. I am sure the same is true with many of my classmates in their own areas of activity.

But to paraphrase Yogi Berra: "*The future is hard to predict since it hasn't happened yet.*"

Figure 8.8.2.3 *Kenneth Shine, MD, joins the University of Texas System as Executive Vice Chancellor for Health Affairs in 2003*

Photo courtesy of the author

Kenneth Shine, MD, after graduation from Harvard Medical School, trained at Massachusetts General Hospital and University of California in Los Angeles (UCLA) and then joined the faculty in 1971, ultimately becoming Dean of the School of Medicine and Provost for Health Sciences at UCLA.

In 1992, Dr. Shine was named President of the Institute of Medicine of the National Academy of Sciences, (now the National Academy of Medicine), a nonprofit, nonpartisan organization chartered to advise the federal government on health science and health care. He addressed the quality of care in America with landmark reports, "*To Err is Human*" in 1999 and "*Crossing the Quality Chasm—A New Health System for the 21st Century*" in 2001.

After 11 years in Washington, in 2003, Dr. Shine became Executive Vice Chancellor for Health Affairs in the University of Texas System with responsibility for six health campuses. He spearheaded a project called "CODE RED, the critical condition of Health in Texas" and laid the groundwork for two new medical schools, in Austin and South Texas. He also served as Professor of Medicine in one of these schools, the Dell Medical School in Austin. He has been married to Carolyn Lois Shine, a retired high school mathematics teacher, for 58 years. They have two children, Daniel and Rebecca.

Figure 8.8.2.4 *Abraham Flexner, MD (1866–1959) was an American educator, best known for his role in the 20th-century reform of medical and higher education in the United States and Canada.*

After founding and directing a college-preparatory school in his hometown of Louisville, KY, Flexner published a critical assessment of the state of the American educational system in 1908 titled The American College: A Criticism. *His work attracted the Carnegie Foundation to commission an in-depth evaluation of 155 colleges and universities across the United States and Canada. It was his resultant self-titled* Flexner Report, *published in 1910, that sparked the reform of medical education in the United States and Canada. Flexner was also a founder of the Institute for Advanced Study in Princeton, which brought together some of the greatest minds in history to collaborate on intellectual discovery and research.*

Source: https://en.m.wikipedia.org/wiki/Abraham_Flexner

Media—Journalism

The Continuous Evolution of Medicine

Gabe Mirkin

When I finished my medical fellowship training in 1965 and was ready to open a practice, I picked my city—the Washington, DC, area—solely because it had the best running program in the country. It was the only city in America that had running races 52 weeks a year. I was passionate about running and worked out three times a day, sandwiched around a full-time, very busy medical practice.

My reputation as a bit of a fanatic spread among the running community and other fitness buffs. I had lots of theories about prevention and treatment of injuries, training and the benefits of fitness, and was eager to share them with other athletes. I was among the first to blame the very high incidence of running injuries on pronation, the way that the foot rolls after hitting the ground.

I was asked to do the first college sports-medicine course in the country for the University of Maryland, which proved to be very popular. My class notes formed the basis of my first book, *The Sportsmedicine Book* (Little Brown, 1978), which became a best seller and led to a column syndicated by *The New York Times*, being the fitness broadcaster for CBS radio, a national call-in radio show syndicated in more than 120 markets, my own TV show on the Learning Channel, being the medical editor for multiple running journals and other media activities.

As my audience grew larger, I found I couldn't just talk about sports all the time, so I needed to become an "expert" on general health issues. When I was on the air and on-the-spot, never knowing what question I would be asked, I had to be confident in my opinions. My medical practice gave me plenty of real-life experience, and I spent all my spare time (when I wasn't running) reading the medical journals so I could always be up-to-date on breakthroughs.

Still, as I look back on nearly 60 years of media activity and medical practice, I am dismayed to realize how many of the theories I believed in turned out to be wrong. Here are some examples:

RICE[1]

When I wrote the *Sportsmedicine Book* in 1978, I coined the term RICE (Rest, Ice, Compression, Elevation) for the treatment of athletic injuries. Ice has been a standard treatment for injuries and sore muscles because it helps to relieve pain caused by injured tissue. Athletes, coaches and even medical texts have used my RICE mnemonic for decades, but now it appears that both Ice and complete Rest may delay healing, instead of helping.

You can't enlarge a muscle unless you damage it so that when it heals, it becomes stronger and larger. So, intelligent athletes train by taking a hard workout that damages muscles on one day, feel sore on the next day, and then go at a less-intense pace until the soreness lessens and then they take their next intense workout. Cooling (ice) delays recovery in athletes who develop exercise-induced muscle damage that causes extensive muscle soreness (*American Journal of Sports Medicine*, June 2013*). A* summary of 22 scientific articles found almost no evidence that ice and compression hasten healing of injuries over the use of compression alone, although ice plus exercise may marginally help to heal ankle sprains *(American Journal of Sports Medicine*, January 2004*;* 32(1): 251–261).

Healing Requires Inflammation

When you damage tissue through trauma or develop muscle soreness by exercising very intensely, you heal by inflammation: using your immunity, the same biological mechanisms that you use to kill germs. When germs get into your body, your immunity sends cells and proteins into the infected area to kill the germs. When muscles and other tissues are damaged, your immunity sends the same inflammatory cells to the damaged tissue to promote healing. The response to both infection and tissue damage is the same. Inflammatory cells rush to injured tissue to start the healing process *(Journal of the American Academy of Orthopaedic Surgery*, 1999; 7(5). *The inflammatory cells called macrophages release a hormone called insulin-like growth factor (IGF-1)* into the damaged tissues, which helps muscles and other injured parts to heal and grow. However, applying ice to reduce swelling actually delays healing by preventing the body from releasing IGF-1.

Ice Keeps Healing Cells from Entering Injured Tissue

Applying ice to injured tissue causes blood vessels near the injury to constrict and shut off the blood flow that brings in the healing cells of inflammation (*Knee Surgery, Sports Traumatology, Arthroscopy*, published online Feb. 23, 2014). The blood vessels do not open again for many hours after the ice was applied. This decreased blood flow can cause the tissue to die from decreased blood flow and can even cause permanent nerve damage.

Anything that Reduces Inflammation Also Delays Healing

Anything that reduces your immune response will also delay muscle healing. Thus, healing is delayed by:

- cortisone-type drugs,
- almost all pain-relieving medicines, such as non-steroidal anti-inflammatory drugs like ibuprofen (*Pharmaceuticals*, 2010;3[5]),
- immune suppressants that are often used to treat diseases such as arthritis, cancer or psoriasis,
- applying cold packs or ice, and
- anything else that blocks the immune response to injury.

Ice Also Reduces Strength, Speed, Endurance, and Coordination

Ice is often used as short-term treatment to help injured athletes get back into a game. The cooling may help to decrease pain, but it interferes with the athlete's strength, speed, endurance and coordination (*Sports Medicine*, Nov. 28, 2011). In this review, most of the 35 studies found a decrease in strength, speed, power and agility-based running. A short re-warming period returned the strength, speed and coordination. The authors recommend that if cooling is done at all to limit swelling, it should be done for less than five minutes, followed by progressive warming prior to returning to play.

Carbohydrate Loading for Runners[2]

Carbohydrate Loading Does Not Increase Endurance

"Carbohydrate loading" the night before a big race can harm your performance and your health, yet athletes have followed this practice for more than 70 years and some athletes still harm their performance by using it today. More than forty years ago, I reported the case of a marathon runner who had a heart attack after carbohydrate loading (*JAMA*, March 26, 1973; 223(13): 1511–1512). A review of 88 studies shows that eating or drinking a source of sugar *during* competitions lasting longer than 70 minutes will prolong your endurance far more than anything you eat *before* a competition. The longer the event, the greater the benefit of eating during competitions (*Sports Medicine* (Auckland, NZ), September 2011; 41(9): 773–92).

How Did Carbohydrate Loading Get Started?

First proposed in 1939, the carbohydrate loading regimen was supposed to increase the amount of sugar stored in your muscles before a race or endurance competition. The process took several days: a four-day depletion phase and a harmful three-day loading phase. We now know that the theory was wrong because your muscles can only store a very limited amount of sugar and all extra carbohydrates are immediately stored as fat. When you load up on refined carbohydrates, such as bakery products, pastas and potatoes, before a competition, you just store more fat which will slow you down during a race. If you already store too much fat, this overloading can make you diabetic or even suffer a heart attack. If you already have blocked arteries leading to your heart, you can kill yourself by loading with sugar or flour.

How Endurance Athletes Can Maximize Sugar in Muscles

Research in the 1980s led to replacement of the old seven-day carbohydrate-loading regimen with a three-day training program that eliminated both depletion and loading. Conditioned athletes can store the maximum amount of sugar in their muscles just by continuing to eat their regular diet and cutting back on the amount of training they do for three days before a competition.

Eating and Drinking during Competition

Athletes start to run out of their sugar stored in muscles after 70 minutes of intense competition, so you need to take sugar during endurance sports that last longer than 70 minutes (*Medicine & Science in Sports & Exercise*, July 2010). However, you can exercise at a relaxed pace for more than three hours without needing sugar. Caffeine can increase the rate that sugar enters muscles by more than 26 percent (*Journal of Applied Physiology*, June 2006), so most athletes take their sugared drinks and foods with some source of caffeine. Ordinary beverages containing both sugar and caffeine are fine; there is no need for special sports energy drinks or gels. On very rare occasions, caffeine can cause some susceptible people to develop irregular heartbeats.

Diets for Longevity[3,4]

Dietary Sugar, Rather than Cholesterol or Saturated Fat, May Cause Heart Attacks

In the late 1940s and early 1950s, Ancel Keys showed that dietary saturated fat and cholesterol were associated with increased risk for heart attacks. Today most of the medical community feels that sugar is the major culprit. Recent data show that the sugar industry paid to exonerate sugar, and I was deceived along with many of my peers. In 1976, I asked Dr. Fred Stare, the chairman of the Department of Nutrition at Harvard, who was a personal friend, to write the introduction to my *Sportsmedicine Book*. It had a section specifically stating that eating too much sugar in foods and drinks is harmful and a probable cause of obesity and heart attacks. Dr. Stare sent me a note telling me that, as an academic, he could not endorse popular books. Now I can see that his real reason could have been that I disagreed with Harvard's well-funded position on sugar. I remember being a guest on Elizabeth Whelan's radio show while I was promoting my book. When I told her that sugar is harmful, she excoriated me for not knowing that "sugar is harmless because it is a natural fuel for all cells in our bodies". (Whelan was a member of Harvard's Department of Nutrition and a cofounder, with Dr. Stare, of the American Council of Science and Health (ACSH).

Worse, like most doctors in the United States, I came to believe that fat was the primary culprit in the obesity and heart-attack epidemic and told my patients to follow a low-fat diet. In 1993, my wife, Diana, and I wrote *Fat Free, Flavor Full*, our first of several popular books based on restricting fat. At least we did advocate limiting sugar and other refined carbohydrates, too. Now I cringe when I remember that I encouraged people to restrict the healthful fats found in plants such as avocados, nuts, olives and coconuts. Today I tell everyone that they should include these fats even if they are trying to lose weight.

Astounding Changes in Medical Paradigms[5]

Stomach Ulcers Are Caused by Infection

In the 1960s I started treating stomach ulcers and rheumatoid arthritis with antibiotics and many doctors called me a quack. Today almost all doctors acknowledge that infection is a common cause of stomach ulcers but they still think that rheumatoid arthritis is not caused by infection.

In 1983, Barry Marshall and John Warren presented a paper to the Australian Gastroenterological Society claiming that stomach ulcers are caused by infection. They never finished their presentation because they were laughed off the stage. Barry Marshall became so upset that he swallowed a vial of the bacterial culture, went into shock and almost died. He had to be hospitalized and was saved by massive doses of intravenous antibiotics. Today, Barry Marshall has the Nobel Prize in

Medicine for discovering that stomach ulcers are caused by bacteria. He is revered worldwide as the person who cured stomach ulcers (*Lancet,* November 6, 1999 pp. 1634).

Many doctors still feel that antibiotics are not effective in treating some cases of rheumatoid arthritis, yet I still get lots of thank-you letters from my former rheumatoid arthritis patients who are doing just fine today because they spent months on antibiotics. In 1939, Thomas McPherson Brown first proposed that rheumatoid arthritis is caused by infection with mycoplasma and he was ignored by his colleagues. He died in 1988, still considered a quack. Now nine prospective double blind studies show that antibiotics are an effective treatment for rheumatoid arthritis and many more studies show benefits from that treatment. Most doctors still criticize the few doctors who treat their rheumatoid arthritis patients with antibiotics. However, today a doctor who refuses to give antibiotics to most ulcer patients is likely to be guilty of malpractice.

Gabe Mirkin, MD, is a retired practicing physician and media personality who still writes a free medical newsletter[6] and does radio shows. At Harvard, he was self-supporting financially and failed to letter in cross-country, but spent his early career competing as a mediocre marathon runner and media personality. When injuries ended his running career, he became a bicycle racer, and at age 81 rides more than 150 fast miles a week with a large group of bicycle racers in the retirement community of The Villages in Florida.

Editors' Note
Dr. Mirkin's summary articles on the Internet, listed below, and statements in his essay reflect his own opinions on medical science and practices.

Endnotes

1 http://www.drmirkin.com/fitness/why-ice-delays-recovery.html

2 http://www.drmirkin.com/fitness/carbohydrate-loading-does-not-work.html

3 http://www.drmirkin.com/histories-and-mysteries/ancel-keys-cholesterol-debunker.html

4 http://www.drmirkin.com/nutrition/big-sugar-paid-harvard-to-say-that-sugar-is-healthful.html

5 http://www.drmirkin.com/morehealth/g123.html

6 www.drmirkin.com

Intellectual Leaders

The Superachievers[1]

Ronald Gerstl

> *"Properly, the Jew ought hardly to be heard of; . . .*
> *His contributions to the world's list of great names in literature, science, art, music, finance, medicine and abstruse learning are also way out of proportion to the weakness of his numbers. He has made a marvelous fight in this world, in all the ages; and has done it with his hands tied behind him. He could be vain of himself, and be excused for it."*

As so quaintly stated by Mark Twain, the Jew ought hardly to be heard of, but is always heard of, and some might say heard of too much. Even Mark Twain would have to be surprised that with only 0.2% of the world's population, Jews have been awarded 25% of all Nobel Prizes in science and medicine. With only 2% of US population, Jewish Americans have received 38% of American awards.

Why are there so many Jewish achievers? After all, Jews constitute a tiny minority. Spurred by this observation, I started by jotting down names of musicians and composers, businessmen and financiers, inventors and scientists. As the list grew, the idea of a book took root.

Should I write about business titans who forged America's financial and industrial might? Should I concentrate on contributions to music? To cover all areas of Jewish achievement would require multiple volumes, something I was not prepared to undertake. Just to compile the works of stellar composers of the American musical theatre, such as Jerome Kern, Irving Berlin, George Gershwin, Richard Rodgers, and Leonard Bernstein—to name a few—would necessitate a book by itself. Their legacy has become part of the fabric of American life.

Unlike other fields of human endeavor, such as the arts or literature, which are often evaluated by subjective criteria, achievements in science can be evaluated with a high degree of objectivity. What's more, there is a universally recognized measure—the Nobel

Prize—the highest distinction that can be bestowed for scientific merit. That's it! My book will focus on Jewish Nobel Prize winners in science, even though personally I am far more familiar with the worlds of business and music.

Except for scientists, physicians, researchers or academicians, most of us, at best, have heard of only a few Nobel science laureates. This is an unfortunate reflection of our society. While most people are obsessed with professional athletes, movie and television personalities, they hardly know—or care—about outstanding scientists who have made a difference. How many kids do you know who collect famous scientist cards? Edward Teller or Isidor Rabi can hardly compete with LeBron James and Lady Gaga.

Jews may be best known for their contributions to medicine. Their discoveries and innovations—frequently made jointly with non-Jewish colleagues—resulted in life saving drugs, inventions and procedures that have benefited mankind.[2]

Contributions by Jews to the scientific and cultural development of the world, in general, and of the United States, in particular, have been vastly out of proportion to their number. By any measure, whether based on demographics or probability theory, it is amazing that such a tiny segment of the population has achieved so much. Jews constitute a minute fraction of the world's population. Their total number is estimated at 14,000,000, less than one-fifth of one percent of the earth's inhabitants.[3] More people live in Mexico City, São Paulo or Seoul than there are Jews in the world. There are 17 times more Indonesians and 13 times more Nigerians. Only one out of 514 people in the world is Jewish.

Nobel Prizes in Science

In the 113 years from 1901—when the Nobel Prizes were first awarded—through 2013, there have been 566 award recipients for medicine, physics and chemistry. Of these prizewinners—25%—one out of four is of Jewish origin.[4] If the prizes had been awarded on a proportionate basis, Jews should have earned one or two. Instead, there were 144 Jewish Nobel Science Prize winners—an over-representation of some 125 times what could be expected statistically.

From an American perspective, Jewish representation is even greater. Through 2013, Americans garnered 254 Nobel science prizes, 45% of the world total, more than any other nation. The American recipients include 97 Jews, 38% of all US awards.[5] Since Jews comprise only about 2% of the US population, or about one out of every 57 Americans, the Jewish American laureates are over represented among US Nobel science prizewinners 22 times. Viewed by categories, Jewish achievement has been particularly noteworthy in medicine, having garnered 43% of all US Nobel Prize awards in that field. Physics follows closely, with 39%, and chemistry, with 30%.[6]

The earlier achievements were all the more remarkable because these prizewinners accomplished them in spite of discrimination. We are all familiar with the anti-Semitism that led to the Holocaust. We may be less familiar with the anti-Semitism that Jews faced in the United States until after World War II. Although in no way comparable to the unspeakable horrors that occurred in Europe, significant restrictions did exist in the United States. Barriers to admissions to top universities, professions, government positions and employment in most of the nation's foremost corporations were part of the American reality.[7]

When examining the lives of Jewish Nobel science laureates, we do not delve into the technical details of their contributions. The scientific breakthroughs, especially in chemistry and physics, are often unintelligible to most non-scientists. To cite an example: Richard Feynman (Physics 1965) received the award for "fundamental work in quantum electro-dynamics, with deep-ploughing consequences for the physics of elementary particles." When a reporter pressed him to describe briefly the work that won the prize, he is said to have replied: "Listen, buddy, if I could tell you in a minute what I did, it would not be worth a Nobel Prize." In a similar vein, Robert Lefkowitz was awarded the Chemistry Nobel in 2012 for "the detailed characterization of the sequence, structure and function of the beta-adrenergic receptors and the discovery of the two families of proteins which regulate them, the G protein-coupled receptor kinases and beta-arrestins."

Lives of the Nobel Laureates

My book's focus is primarily on Jewish Nobel science laureates' ethnic and national origins, socio-economic, and family backgrounds that shaped them[8] and educational background.[9] Harvard and Columbia were by far the leading universities in terms of affiliations as undergraduates, doctoral graduates, researchers, and professors among Jewish Nobel prizewinners in science and medicine. With the rise of Nazism, Jewish laureates and laureates-to-be had to flee Europe: "Germany's Loss, America's Gain".[10]

Recent laureates usually led fairly conventional lives that rarely involved personal and professional struggles of their European pre-World War II counterparts. Such was the life of Fritz Haber, the controversial winner of the Nobel Prize in Chemistry in 1918, who discovered the way to synthesize ammonia to produce fertilizer, greatly increasing food production which benefitted mankind. But he was also the inventor of poisonous gas and a proponent of chemical warfare. In World War I, Germany used the banned poisonous gas, resulting in some 150,000 Allied casualties in the battle of Ypres, Belgium. While he was hailed as a hero in Germany, scientists worldwide abhorred his work, as did his chemist wife, who committed suicide. Despite his services to Germany, he found it necessary to leave for England in 1933. He died shortly thereafter on his way to Tel Aviv to take a post at what was later to become the Weizmann Institute in Tel Aviv. Tragically, during the Holocaust, the Nazis used a formulation of his poisonous gas, Zyklon B, in the gas chambers of the extermination camps.

Reflections[11]

Those who have known me for a long time may be surprised that I would write a book concerning Jews. Even though both my parents were Jewish, I was not brought up in any way practicing Judaism. My parents were indifferent to religion. Neither my grandfather nor my father nor I had a bar mitzvah. During World War II, my aunt's family, who lived in Prague, were deported to the Terezin concentration camp and later found their deaths in the gas chambers of Auschwitz.

There was never a question that we were Jewish. There are those who do not comprehend that one can be at the same time a Jew and a nonbeliever, agnostic, or atheist. Being Jewish is not only a matter of religion. It is also about parentage and ancestry, ethnic and group identification, and cultural values. Many Jews who do not practice the faith are deeply involved in Jewish causes and charities. In my case, through reading, discussion, and observation over the years, my skepticism turned to total disbelief of religion.

With a multinational, multilingual background, I am accustomed to interacting with all kinds of people. I was born in Budapest to a Hungarian mother and a father from Curaçao in the Netherlands West Indies. Shortly after my birth, my parents returned to their home in Curacao, where I grew up. Thereafter, I have lived in Caracas, New England, New York City, and now Miami. Besides English, I am fluent in Spanish and Papiamento (the native tongue of Curaçao) and knowledgeable in Dutch, French, and Portuguese.

I attended a nondenominational prep (high) school, which was actually quite Episcopalian. We had prayers and hymns daily at vespers, and compulsory church services on Sundays. This was quite a contrast from my experience in college at Harvard, where questioning the validity of religion was not uncommon and served to reinforce my views. For additional diversity, my wife happens to be a Protestant from Indiana. These differences in background naturally affected our children as well. A large part of my life, both pre- and post-marriage, was spent in Caracas, Venezuela, where my many cousins and friends were all Catholic. There was no exposure to Jewish life.

My appreciation and interest in the Jewish people came somewhat later in life. Reading opened my eyes to the painful historical trajectory of the Jewish people and, in spite of this, their mind-boggling achievements. Some of the works that influenced me included *My People: The Story of the Jews* by Abba Eban, *O Jerusalem* by Larry Collins and Dominique Lapierre, and Leon Uris's *Exodus*, as well as the movie based on the novel. *The Six-Day War* (1967) instilled in me a great deal of pride for Israel and the Jews.

I would like to reach a broad readership, not only Jews, to help make better known the contributions Jews have made to human well-being. As far as Jews themselves are concerned, it seems to me that few are aware of the extent of the achievements. It is my hope that in this way, "***The Superachievers***" makes a modest, positive contribution.

Ronald Gerstl has a multicultural, multilingual background. Shortly after his birth in Budapest to a Hungarian mother and a father from Curaçao in the Netherlands West Indies, his parents returned to their home in Curaçao. He grew up there speaking Dutch, Papiamento (the local language) and English. Later, he became fluent in Spanish as well as knowledgeable in French and Portuguese

In his early teens, the family moved to Caracas, Venezuela, and he went off to prep school at the Taft School in Connecticut. Thereafter, he attended Harvard, where he received his bachelor degree. Subsequently, he obtained an MBA from Columbia University while residing in New York.

He lived in Caracas off and on for some 30 years. His early career experience was in marketing/advertising with leading multinational consumer products companies, and afterwards as a consultant in the same areas. Thereafter, he founded Maxecon Executive Search Consultants in Caracas to assist multinational corporations in their executive personnel requirements.

In the 1980s, he moved the family to Miami, FL, to expand the geographic scope of his consulting services. Now retired, he lives in Miami with his wife, Suzanne, a native of Indianapolis. Their two children and grandchildren live nearby in Palm Beach County. In 2014, he published his book, *The Superachievers*. Since childhood, Ron has been a geography whiz. He enjoys tennis, golf, travel and reading nonfiction.

Endnotes

1 Excerpt from Chapter 1 of *The Superachievers*, by Ronald Gerstl, published by Amazon, 2014. The book contains the content referenced below, except the personal reflection.

2 List of Jewish contributions to medicine not included for space restrictions

3 Jewish demographics are discussed in Chapter VI.

4 Exhibit I: Jewish Nobel science prizewinners in book

5 Exhibit II

6 Exhibits III, Medicine; IV, Physics; and V, Chemistry

7 Chapter X: "From Barriers to Breakthrough and Success: The American Experience"

8 Chapter IV: "Laureates' National and Ethnic Backgrounds"

9 Chapter IX: "Laureates' University Affiliations"

10 Chapter V: "Germany's Loss, America's Gain"

11 Personal reflection not previously published

Figure 8.10.1.1 *Sigmund Freud (Sigismund Schlomo Freud), May 6, 1859–September 23, 1935*

Austrian neurologist and the founder of psychoanalysis, a clinical method for treating psychopathology through dialogue between a patient and a psychoanalyst

Source: https://en.m.wikipedia.org/wiki/Sigmund_Freud

Figure 8.10.1.2 *Harvard Yard—Bird's-eye View*

Source: https://hspvsketchbook.files.wordpress.com/2015/10/harvard-yard-birds-eye.jpg

Chapter Nine

SOCIOLOGY

Figure C9 *View from William James Building towards Harvard Yard, Charles River, and the hills of Brookline and Newton*

Left: *Cambridge Fire Station, Sever Hall, Widener Library, and Lowell House tower.*
Center: *Memorial Church, Memorial Hall with restored tower, Canaday dormitories, and, in the distance, Indoor Athletic Building (IAB).*
Right: *Thayer Hall*

Chapter Nine

SOCIOLOGY

Mediation

Observations for my Sixtieth Reunion

John G. Wofford

One of the great satisfactions of my professional life has been to help people, organizations and government agencies transform seemingly intractable conflicts into creative opportunities.

Let me begin with my best-known local "claim to fame"—the rejection of a huge, tangled mess of a proposed bridge over the Charles River, and the construction in its place of the Leonard P. Zakim-Bunker Hill Memorial Bridge, the Boston area's latest icon.

The Zakim-Bunker Hill Bridge

Like many Democrats in the election of November 1990 to succeed Michael Dukakis as Governor of Massachusetts, I had supported Bill Weld, moderate Republican, instead of John Silber, conservative Democrat and president of Boston University. Women, environmentalists and gay voters (like me) had given Weld a very close victory. As a result, because of my extensive background in transportation policy at both state and federal levels, I was named to the "transition committee" briefing the new administration on highway, transit, airport and other transportation issues.

One of those issues concerned intense controversy over a proposed new bridge over the Charles River. The new bridge would be part of "The Central Artery/Tunnel (CA/T) Project" (later known as "The Big Dig")—at the time the largest public works project in the United States. The project involved tearing down the elevated "Central Artery" built in the 1950's (during our College years), and construction directly below it of a 3.5-mile tunnel that would tie in with the planned tunnel across Boston Harbor to Logan Airport (the "Ted Williams Tunnel"). On the final day of the outgoing administration, Dukakis' Secretary of Environmental Affairs had filed a certificate that the huge project met all state environmental requirements—subject, however, to convening within 30 days of the Weld administration's taking office an advisory committee to recommend ways to improve the Charles River crossing.

That certificate was in response to widespread controversy, including a well-publicized statement by a regional official of the US Environmental Protection Agency that the bridge, if built in accordance with its planned design, "would be the ugliest structure in New England." In addition, five groups and municipalities had filed formal notices of intent to sue to stop, not just the bridge, but the entire CA/T Project—mainly over the design and scale of the bridge.

In searching for the best design, scale and location for the new bridge, staff for the former administration had developed 31 schemes—A to Z and on to EE—and had settled on what came to be called "Scheme Z." The planners had picked Scheme Z because dense development precluded ramps on the Boston side near North Station, terminus of commuter rail to the north and west, or Boston Garden, home for the Celtics and Bruins. Similarly, historic Charlestown could not have additional ramps. The one place that could accommodate ramps was an industrial and warehouse part of Cambridge, so they decided to put all the ramps there, piled one on top of the other. An easy solution . . . except that it made a lot of traffic—thousands of cars a day—cross the river twice that didn't need to cross it at all, on what would be the widest cable-stayed bridge in the world. The proposed bridge and its ramps came to be called "the double-crossing of the Charles River."

I was named the facilitator of the new advisory committee. By then, I had had extensive experience in transportation policy at state and federal levels, and I was working at a dispute resolution firm in Boston, so was a natural pick to facilitate.

The Bridge Design Review Committee was composed of 42 officials of municipalities and state agencies, representatives of private civic, environmental and business groups, management and labor of the construction industry, neighborhood associations, and professional groups. They were engineers, architects, planners, business people, lawyers, neighborhood activists, and others. I felt the weight of the future of the Big Dig project on my shoulders as I began the work with this to reach conclusions by the end of June—only five months from the committee's first meeting on February 1.

To get started by squarely facing the issues, the Chairman and I structured the first meeting of the new committee so that each member could speak for not more than one minute, expressing concerns about the proposed design, to be followed up with a one-page written version that would be circulated to all members.

Coordinating with the "*Big Dig*". When the representative of the Beacon Hill Civic Association took his turn to speak to the 42 members seated at four conference tables arranged around an open square, he walked over to the design plans for the giant intersection and bridge, pointed to the proposed traffic moves, and said, "With this multi-billion dollar project to put the Central Artery in a tunnel and build a new bridge across the Charles River, I don't understand why we can't do in the future what we can do now—have a direct connection between Storrow Drive and the Central Artery? The Artery is now elevated and in the future will be underground, but why will the new project require that we cross the river twice—crossing to Charlestown and Cambridge, looping around with ramps and eventually making the circuitous connection? Traffic that doesn't want to cross the river at all will have to do it twice! And that makes the bridge have four extra lanes—16 in all, making the new bridge the widest cable-stayed bridge in the world? I don't understand why that has to be."

A simple question—clearly stated—in less than one minute! The answer: Not simple at all. Very complex, in terms of both process and substance. With respect to process, one Committee member asked how we could structure the work so that recommendations on such large issues could be made within five months. "What is our process?" he asked. Finding no ready-made answer in negotiation literature, I presented my own one-page outline for its deliberations. With a not-so-subtle allusion to Woodrow Wilson's attempts at creative peace-making, I called it "14 Points: Approaches and Stages of Consensus-Building and Dispute Resolution." (See the end of the essay.) It described a clear path to make recommendations within a limited time after full discussion but with enough breadth to deal with sharp differences, understand deeper concerns, draw on extensive technical resources to develop new options, develop mutual respect to take each others' perspectives seriously, and make recommendations by the short deadline. The Committee enthusiastically followed the process.

With respect to substance, the Committee needed to free itself from the constraints that limited the elaborate ramp structure to that quadrant in Cambridge, but it also needed to recognize the challenges of one of the most complex urban intersections in the country. We needed engineering help to find a new approach and a new bridge designer to create a design that, as the Chairman frequently said, would make our grandchildren proud.

Solving the Ramp Maze Problem. In fact, a medium-level engineer on the CA/T staff had been working on a design that solved the ramp problem. His scheme had two completely new, land-based tunnels—one way in each direction, going under North Station and its railroad tracks and winding around the supports for Boston Garden. Prior planners had suppressed this scheme because it was more complex, required reconstruction of parts of existing highways, and would create delays. We brought the engineer's scheme to the committee, which greeted the idea with excitement. The 42 members unanimously chose to add the new tunnels to all its bridge options.

Eliminating the double-crossing of the river meant there could be a more slender bridge, but it needed to be designed. By coincidence, a world-renowned bridge designer from Switzerland, Christian Menn, happened to be visiting the Harvard Graduate School of Design to deliver a lecture, and a top consultant for the CA/T project invited him to view the large, three-dimensional physical model of Scheme Z, both bridge and ramps. The BDRC had been meeting and, as it adjourned, members walked out in the hall where the model sat, and gathered around as the Swiss designer pondered the model. "Why, this is a bridge designer's . . ." he paused, and the committee thought he was about to say "nightmare". Instead, he finished his sentence with the word "dream". "This is a bridge designer's dream," he repeated. With his extensive portfolio of great bridges, the committee recommended that he be retained and, within a month, he went to work creating new designs. When *The Boston Globe* featured his preliminary sketches, the large headline read: "Bridge Doctor to the Rescue!"

Finding the Right Bridge Designer. In developing those sketches, Dr. Menn was able to base his drawings on a narrower and simplified bridge made possible by the engineer's new tunnels. With engineering and design resources, the Committee developed 13 new options, and then narrowed to three. The new administration picked one of them.

Because of the engineer's technical perseverance, the Swiss designer's creativity, a focused process, and a hard-working, independent and determined Committee, Boston can enjoy the beauty of today's Zakim-Bunker Hill Bridge. At its ribbon-cutting, more than a million people walked across in celebration. This result was possible in large part because the new administration, with no ego involved, was eager to put its stamp on the project. The legacy of the Big Dig is truly bipartisan, with two Governors making a major, lasting contribution to the Boston area. That result reinforced my view that most major transportation decisions inevitably and properly have major political dimensions.

The "Restudy"—The Boston Transportation Planning Review

Politics was also key to my involvement in an even more complex transportation conflict. I became the state's director of a multiyear Restudy of proposed new expressways and transit lines in the Boston area. The controversy focused on three new expressway spokes inside Route 128, to be joined at the hub by a circular expressway called the "Inner Belt". That highway would have crossed the Fenway and the Charles River and gone through dense neighborhoods in Boston, Cambridge and Somerville. It also included transit extensions and the abandonment of the elaborate commuter rail network. The Restudy had three phases: a Task Force recommending it; a "study design" to define its scope; and an open, participatory process to carry it out.

In November 1968, Richard Nixon was elected President. He chose as his Secretary of Transportation the sitting Governor of Massachusetts, John Volpe, who was succeeded in January 1969 by Francis W. Sargent as Acting Governor. Sargent had been Commissioner of Natural Resources and Commissioner of Public Works before being elected Lieutenant Governor, and was known as a liberal and an environmentalist. As he took the traditional walk down the steps outside the State House following his swearing in, he was greeted by a demonstration against an extensive network of new highways in the Boston area and expansion of Logan Airport. Later that year, he appointed a blue-ribbon task force to advise him on the highway and transit controversies.

Balancing Development and Preservation. I was privileged to be the Executive Director of that Task Force, composed of about a dozen businesses, non-profit and academic leaders. It met confidentially Saturday mornings beginning in October 1969. Building on my lawyerly instincts honed during two years as law clerk to a federal District Judge, I helped structure the meetings to have separate sessions with opponents and proponents of the existing plans. By December, the Task Force recommended that the Governor impose a moratorium on detailed plans for the new expressways and transit lines, and instead order a Restudy of the need for them, their fit within an integrated transportation system, and their impacts on the environment and the quality of urban life—all to be analyzed in an open process, with opportunities for participation by public officials, private groups and ordinary citizens. In early 1970, despite 14% unemployment in the construction industry, Sargent went on state-wide TV to announce the moratorium. Local press greeted the Governor's decision with banner headlines.

By remarkable coincidence, during the same week in December 1969 that the Task Force made its recommendations to Governor Sargent, the US Congress enacted the National Environmental Policy Act (NEPA), which required "environmental impact statements" for all proposed major federal actions, with an emphasis on weighing pros and cons of different alternatives in an open process. Here was a state that wanted to do exactly what NEPA required.

Involving the Community. With the Restudy's purpose recommended by the Task Force and adopted by the Governor, the first step was to define its scope. For that, a small, experienced consultant team was retained. Initially, the idea was to let this new group of three consultants write the scope. I drew upon my background, however, to suggest a different approach: my work earlier work as staff assistant helping to organize the Community Action Program (CAP) of the Office of Economic Opportunity, enacted by Congress to carry out LBJ's *War on Poverty*, I had learned the benefits of developing its programs with "maximum feasible participation" by the poor themselves. So I proposed—successfully—to convene an informal steering group composed of the wide range of opinions about outcome and let them recommend the structure and scope for the Restudy process. Unlike the process for the controversial highway and transit plans that needed to be reexamined, the Restudy was to be open and participatory, so we decided to design the study in an open and participatory manner.

The informal steering group consisted of about 20 representatives of highway and transit, environment and business, inner cities and outer suburban towns, white suburban advocates for open space and black inner city politicians, even "good government" advocacy groups. The group spent two evenings a week during the summer of 1970 wrestling over the shape of the Restudy, with the three outside consultants listening, absorbing, and writing and re-writing drafts of a proposed scope. The discussion, modification, and expansion of those drafts became key to establishing the credibility that was essential if the Restudy were to succeed. One important new concept adopted by the group: 10% of the budget would be for "community liaison and technical assistance", so that new options originating with neighborhoods or municipalities could be developed with technical help. By the end of the summer, all participants agreed on a final draft, which was then advertised as a request for proposals from new consultants to carry out the scope as agreed.

Maintaining Neutrality on Outcomes. I was named the state's director of the newly named Boston Transportation Planning eview (BTPR) from 1971 to 1973. Prior studies had been fraught with assumptions and conclusions that were widely criticized. Given the need for an impartial and open process with objective analysis, I defined my role as being completely impartial as to outcomes so I could focus on running a fair process. At its peak, the BTPR had a consultant team of 75 professionals from many disciplines (planners, engineers, architects, economists, ecologists, lawyers) headed by a manager from the private sector—all committed to developing and analyzing options objectively, and with preferred alternatives.

To watch over this process, the informal "steering group" morphed into a structured Steering Committee, made more formal with a "municipal caucus", an "environmental caucus", and other structured participants, as well as highway and transit, business and labor, and good government interests.

As the Restudy's director for the two years of its active work, I met with the Steering Committee at least every two weeks for a two-hour "brown bag lunch" meeting. At those meetings, the Committee dealt with all major issues of process . . . how balanced options would be assembled, which neighborhood workshops deserved priority, what new ideas deserved rigorous technical analysis, how the written reports would have executive summaries and be in language easily understood, how policy justifications for different approaches would be analyzed, what criteria would be used to evaluate the options, how regional public hearings at the end would be the forum for all sides to express their views on outcome—all as advisory to the Governor. They even named a five-person editing committee to review and revise every word of the voluminous reports before they were released. Remarkably, the Steering Committee reached complete consensus on every issue of process for two years. Fairness, objectivity, completeness, credibility, creativity, and respect for each other's views were shared standards.

Developing Optimal Choices with Financing. A key requirement set by the Steering Committee was that each major option would be developed to an equal level of detail, so that highways of different size and location and transit lines on various routes would all be analyzed in a way that did not favor any one option over others but instead could present choices among equals. Thus the Governor did not have to choose between "build" and "no build", but instead could choose among complete packages, each of which had complex, balanced elements.

After formal regional public hearings focused on a wide range of views about outcome, the Governor adopted an overriding policy for the inner Boston region: enhance its public transportation system as a key support for its already dense and historic downtown and its vibrant neighborhoods. And do not build highways simply to meet "demand;" instead, build facilities, like transit, that will shape that demand. And use the transportation infrastructure to enhance environmental quality. To carry out that policy, he announced the three proposed expressway spokes and the Inner Belt would not be built, believing they would take too many houses and businesses, would undermine public transportation and destroy parkland; supported extending the Red Line beyond Harvard Square through Somerville to a major park-and-ride transit hub at Alewife and relocating the Orange Line from an elevated line into a tunnel in the Amtrak corridor; endorsed a development boulevard and linear park where an expressway would have been; and supported a new harbor tunnel on a new route that that would not require the destruction of either houses or businesses in East Boston but instead would emerge on Logan Airport property.

I had been impartial as to outcome throughout the entire Restudy process, but once our reports were completed and I had conducted the public hearings, the Governor asked a few of us to discuss his options. We knew that not building the expressways would risk losing $1 billion of federal aid to highways, so we pointed out that the Restudy had produced expressway options that were feasible and could be defended, even though picking them would certainly lead to extended litigation. The Governor thought hard as he sat back and said, "Well, I'm thinking of the commuter sitting in a car stuck in traffic on the Southeast Expressway. . . . I don't want to repeat that, aside from all the federal funds." I responded that rather than fighting litigation on behalf of the expressways, my own energies would be more engaged going forward if he would select the non-expressway options, with new transit and parkland opportunities, and coupled that decision with a commitment to fight to change federal law so that the highway money could be used for transit instead. His eyes lit up as he anticipated making that fight.

"The Boston Provision." In late 1972, the Governor went on statewide TV to announce his decisions and said he would go to Washington to change federal law so the highway funds could be used to build the essential transit extensions. Initially known as "the Boston provision", the idea of using highway money for transit gathered support from metropolitan areas around the country, resulting in the passage of the "Interstate Transfer Provision" in the 1973 Federal Aid to Highways legislation. This statute allowed metropolitan areas to transfer federal highway funds to transit if they went through an open process to consider the options and make a decision that met the needs of the area more effectively with transit than with highways.

Thus, money collected from the federal gas tax was used to extend the subway system, build prize-winning linear parks, and improve local roads. Commuter rail was preserved and improved. Boston transportation policy was remade. The combination of an open process, a wide-ranging search for alternatives, extensive professional resources, and strong political leadership made it all possible.

After the Governor had made his decisions but before he announced them, he appointed me Associate Commissioner of the Department of Public Works, in charge of . . . highway construction, "to convey that values have changed," he said. After directing a new transportation planning staff for the region, I ended the 1970s serving for two years in the Carter Administration as the Deputy General Counsel of the US Department of Transportation—a position that stretched my experience from highways and transit to include rail, trucks, aviation, highway traffic safety, maritime affairs, port facilities and the Coast Guard.

After helping the General Counsel advise the Secretary and manage 45 lawyers, I returned to Boston to join the real estate department of a medium size firm to help structure major development. In my first week, I spoke with my senior partner about my inexperience in real estate, and he responded, "We can teach you everything you need to know about real estate. Just remember: in any major real estate development there are many perspectives—the owner, the developer, the municipality, the lender, perhaps a second lender, the architect, the builder, the neighborhood, and others. You need to use the same consensus-building techniques you've developed in the public sector to keep people working together to achieve the result." And then he added: "You can be the glue that will hold the transaction together."

What a great headline for me in my new work in real estate development! I kept consensus-building front and center.

Other Mediations

After seven years as associate and partner at the law firm, I joined a dispute resolution firm but left in 1993 to work independently as mediator, arbitrator and facilitator. I felt I could create more security as my own boss, and I could use the independence to work at my own pace, taking time to work in our garden and ride my bike up and down the paths of the Charles River. I continue learning from every new and challenging engagement.

Recently, I mediated a long-standing dispute between the Commonwealth of Massachusetts and the Town of Medfield over how to clean up severe contamination of a portion of the large but abandoned Medfield State Hospital site, one of the 19th century's state mental hospitals out in the country. Over the hundred years or so, as the state tore down or modified old buildings and built new ones, they put all the debris on the side of the site, letting it rot with its contaminants (lead, asbestos, oil, PCBs and other dangers) seeping into the ground and into the Charles River where it is a narrow stream close to its origins far out in the countryside. Although the state and town had been at impasse for years, the mediation resulted in a creative agreement that produced extensive parkland, new recreation trails, a kayak launch and the largest wetland restoration in the history of the Charles River.

Aside from environmental and transportation disputes, I mediate a wide range of disputes, including conflicts over the operation and future of family-owned businesses, vacation homes, fights over estates, and other highly charged usually multi-party conflicts. I find the similarity in process for all multi-party disputes remarkable, but I learn something new in each engagement, since each process must be specially designed for the issues, context, and people involved. There is no "cookie cutter" approach to mediation as I practice it. My own impartiality as to outcome, however, remains an essential ingredient.

Advocacy

In the midst of these challenging situations in the professional arena I've had major challenges in my personal life. When I went to Washington to serve for two years as the Deputy General Counsel of DOT, I became a commuter, returning each weekend to wife and four growing children in Lincoln, MA. While in Washington, I decided to explore a side of my life that I had kept under wraps for many years . . . my gay side. Upon my full-time return, my wife and I decided to go our separate ways as we continued to be parents closely collaborating on family responsibilities. My kids have adjusted each in his or her own way over whatever time they needed. We have all remained close. I've been in a marvelous relationship with my partner, Michael, now in our 20th year together.

Over the years, I've had an opportunity to exercise some significant leadership in the area of gay rights. Shortly after returning from

Washington, I became an early member of a new organization, "Gay Fathers of Greater Boston", and heard many "coming out" stories of men in circumstances not unlike my own. I was on the board and president of Gay & Lesbian Advocates & Defenders (GLAD) back in the early '90s. At the same time, I was co-chair of the Harvard Gay & Lesbian Caucus, the umbrella group of students, faculty, staff and alumni of the College and all graduate schools. In that capacity, I helped lead the protests in 1993 over Harvard's award of an honorary degree to Colin Powell, who was opposing President Clinton's efforts to open the military to service by gay men and lesbians. On Commencement Day, we floated above the thousands of people in Harvard Yard over 7,500 pink balloons reading "Lift the Ban"—in honor of each gay soldier who had been thrown out of the military. We're thankful the horrible "Don't Ask, Don't Tell" policy was repealed early in the Obama administration.

There has been great progress over the years advancing gay equality, and I am glad to have played a part in it locally. I'm also glad to continue my diverse professional career and rich personal life as the years move on.

"14 Points"

Approaches and Stages in
Consensus-Building and Dispute Resolution

John G. Wofford

(1) From Positions to Interests, Clarity about Basic Concerns and Goals

(2) Confidentiality, Credibility and Openness

(3) Creating not Claiming; Avoiding Either/Or; Enlarging the Pie

(4) Brainstorming—Options; Hypothetical Proposals; "What if . . ?"

(5) Disaggregating the Problem; Untying the Knot

(6) Task Groups and Subcommittees—Focus and Interactions

(7) Understanding Technical, Factual Complexities; Joint Fact-Finding

(8) Narrowing Options; Missions, Objectives and Criteria

(9) Creative Repackaging; Elements; A Single-Text Focus

(10) Impacts and Integration; Long- and Short-Range

(11) Deadlines and Details

(12) Trade-Offs and Negotiations; Reworking the Elements

(13) Compromise and Consensus

(14) Resolution—Agreement or Disagreement? Some or All?

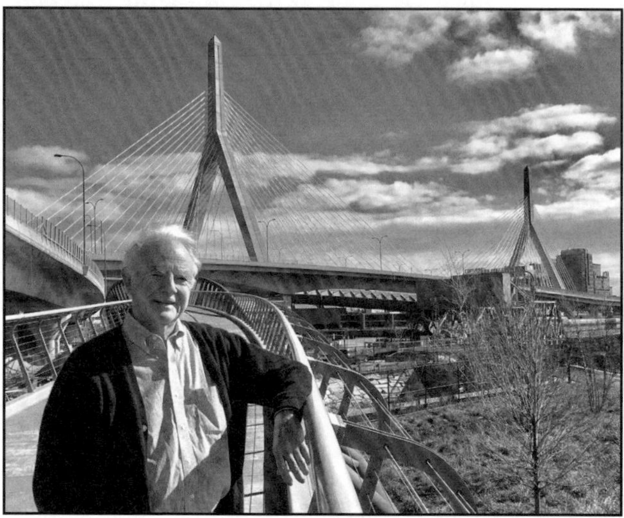

Figure 9.1.1.1 *Author John Wofford in front of the Zakim-Bunker Hill Bridge, February 2017*

Jack Wofford has an LLB from Harvard Law School and BA and MA degrees from Oxford University, where he was a Rhodes Scholar. He was a law clerk; partner in the real estate department of a Boston law firm; Fellow and Associate Director of the Institute of Politics at Harvard's Kennedy School; Associate Commissioner, Massachusetts Department of Public Works; and Deputy General Counsel, US Department of Transportation. From 1999 to 2002, he was a Presidential appointee to the Federal Service Impasses Panel, resolving labor-management disputes.

Jack is a mediator, facilitator and arbitrator. For over 25 years he has provided only impartial services, assisting people and organizations in managing and resolving conflicts. He has extensive experience in complex, highly charged, multi-party disputes in a wide range of subject areas. He has had his own dispute resolution practice since 1993. Jack received several awards for his environmental and transportation consensus-building work: a "*History Makers Award*" from Historic Boston, a "*Hero of the Revolution*" award from the Boston Society of Architects, and an "*Environmental-Energy Award for Outstanding Public-Private Collaboration*" from the Environmental Business Council of New England. In College, Jack was president of *The Crimson*, where he learned the importance of collaboration among strong-minded editors.

Human Relationships

Conflict Resolution

A Mediator's Perspective on Conflict Resolution

Jack Hamilton

My purpose in writing this essay is to bring to the attention of those reading it the practical approach to resolving interpersonal conflicts my fellow mediators and I have been teaching for 25 years. It is a method that has helped people engaged in conflict to creatively tackle tough issues, while treating the other people in the conflicts with consideration and respect. Even though conflict permeates our lives, and taking time to examine and resolve it takes awareness and effort, the ten techniques I've included in this essay have guided many people in conflict to meaningful resolutions.[1]

1. The first step in resolving conflicts is to understand what is going on in our minds and in the minds of the other parties to the conflicts.

A key to resolving interpersonal conflicts involves understanding how the human mind works. People tend to make negative assumptions about who caused a conflict in which they're involved. So a person caught up in conflict often will blame the other individual for having caused the dispute, or will try to put pieces together that don't always lead to a correct view of the whole picture. That may ease anxieties for a time, but it doesn't ultimately resolve the conflict in a way that leaves everyone involved satisfied.

When two people are in conflict, their minds have unconsciously raced up metaphorical ladders of assumptions about each other. By no means do we need to take personally the behavior of another person that is caused by that individual's assumptions about us.

Unless we understand that, we will have difficulty resolving our conflicts with others. The assumptions individuals have made are their own, not ours. They often are based on genetic factors, as well as on environmental ones such as early life conditioning, cultural differences, and even traumatic experiences.

Consider the human brain as a sort of finely tuned computer designed to make quick, survival-oriented decisions based on input from the environment. Understanding people would be an overwhelming process if we had to start from scratch with every human contact. We all are exposed to more input from the world than we can possibly manage. Instead, we classify the infinite variety of human beings into workable groups of types. These generalized images help us define people so we can readily understand them.

In effect, the categories we create determine the assumptions we make about people. Those assumptions affect our understanding of them as well as our relationships with them. For example, for hundreds—if not thousands—of years, people with mental illnesses have been stereotyped as "crazy" people, "kooks", or at the very least "lazy" individuals who could overcome their mental problems if they only tried hard enough.

However, more recently, scientists have discovered that many mental illnesses, including schizophrenia, are caused by biologically based brain disorders rather than by lack of effort or interest on the part of an individual. People with such illnesses can now be more or less effectively treated with drugs and psychotherapy. With such scientific and clinical data available, we are challenged to change our assumptions. We need to remove the stereotypes of the past and view mentally ill people as ordinary people who happen to have illnesses.

From our earliest years, when we first begin to typecast people, we see others in terms of our standardized pictures. For good or bad, our parents and guardians and our earliest teachers help us form these categories. To truly reach an accord after a disagreement, we need to become more aware of what actually motivates us as well as our partners-in-conflict, rather than what our conditioned way of thinking leads us to believe.

- Acknowledge that we often rush to judgment about others based on unconscious assumptions. Consider the people in our backgrounds who have had a major influence on the way we think.
- Consider that our original take, regarding the motive for another person's behavior, is mainly based on our own temperament, biases

and prejudices, which are usually quite different than that of the other person.

- Be open to the possibility that our first reaction to a person or a situation may be incorrect. Be willing to entertain the possibility that people don't always fit the categories in which our minds have placed them.
- Imagine a different but plausible explanation when we're convinced we understand the intent behind a person's behavior. Be open to the possibility of putting aside assumptions that may be invalid and changing our mindsets about people.

2. Make it a daily self-awareness practice to look inward and identify preconceptions that can lead to instant assumptions about others.

Each time we feel the need to be right and make critical judgments about others, we create seeds of conflict. Making negative assumptions instantly about others, and not accepting them the way they are, is self-defeating and adds fuel to the fire of disharmony. We need to observe our behavior toward others in the moment, and check it out by trying to figure out why our minds rush so quickly to making assumptions about them.

- Identify another person's behavior that comes across to us as objectionable, and observe how we reacted to the person. Commit to looking inward and examining the assumptions that may have led to our reactions.
- Bring to the surface of our minds emotions, positive or negative, that we are experiencing in relation to the person, and acknowledge that those emotions are our own—the other person is not causing them.
- Notice that it is our assumptions about the behavior of the person that are triggering our emotions. Be aware that these assumptions have no objective validity; they are our own thoughts.
- Acknowledge the actions we may have taken in the process of reacting to the person.

3. Listen for deep understanding to others, which lets them know we've heard them and enables us to hear their assumptions about our behavior.

Key to listening for deep understanding is a sincere desire to know what is going on with other people. It lets us ask questions we might otherwise not have had the insight to ask. And it allows us to be more open to responses that otherwise would not have found their way into our awareness.

There are four components of listening for deep understanding:

ENCOURAGE the other person to expand upon what was said.

- Remain quiet while others are expressing their assumptions about us. Take a deep breath, and let intruding thoughts fade away.
- Try to be truly open to others' assumptions about us. Be interested in learning more from others regarding their assumptions about our strengths and about our areas that need developing.
- Acknowledge that our assumptions regarding a particular situation are different from everyone else's. Entertain the possibility that others' assumptions are as valid as ours.

CLARIFY our understanding of what the other person told us.

- Be willing to dig deeper to fully grasp the concerns and feelings behind what another person is saying.
- Tell the person that we don't yet have a clear picture of what is bothering them. Such a statement actually indicates we are sincerely trying to gain a deeper understanding of what is going on with the individual.
- Ask questions that let the person know we are seriously interested in getting on the same page with them, such as the following examples:
- "What exactly did I do that caused you to have such negative feelings about me?"
- "I'm not clear about why my statements affected you so negatively. Can you explain again how you felt when I spoke to you?"
- "You said I couldn't care less about what is going on in your life. Can you explain to me what I've said or done that has caused you to feel that way?"

RESTATE and REFLECT what the other person said.

- Work on remembering the essential thoughts expressed by the other person, and restating them in our own words.

- Develop a "third" ear that enables us to hear the deeply felt emotions behind the speaker's thoughts, and to reflect them to the speaker.
- Keep repeating and rephrasing in different ways what the other person has said until the individual expresses confidence that he has been fully heard.

SUMMARIZE main points and feelings expressed by the other person.

- State the main thoughts the other person mentioned, rather than the specific details that were expressed.
- From all the various emotions the other person has expressed, focus strictly on the predominant feelings we heard and communicate those.

4. Ask others with whom we're in conflict if we can discuss with them the assumptions we've made about them.

We need to encourage others to give us their perspectives about the assumptions we've made about them and, though their views may differ from ours, not immediately judge them as being wrong.

- State to the other person the assumptions we've made about their behavior.
- Ask the person whether the assumptions we've made about them are accurate, and listen for deep understanding to their comments.
- Be aware that our assumptions about the person may be faulty, and take responsibility for the effects they may have had.

5. Ask those with whom we're in conflict to discuss with us the assumptions they've made about us.

The other person's assumptions about our behavior are typically their honest impressions. Their assumptions hold important clues that can lead to a better understanding on our part of the effect of our behavior on them and how we contributed to the conflict.

- Be truly open and listen for deep understanding to the other person's statements of their assumptions about our behavior.
- Recognize that the other person isn't purposefully trying to make an incorrect case against us but, rather, has simply made assumptions about us they truly believe to be correct.

- Ask questions in a manner that indicates we are grateful to receive further information, rather than in a way that might come across as blaming the other person.

6. Work together with the person with whom we're in conflict to clarify the validity of our respective assumptions about each other.

When people in conflict are willing to jointly evaluate their respective assumptions about each other, it opens a door for them to seriously consider the idea that it is more important to resolve conflicts and restore relationships than it is for one person to be right and the other to be wrong.

- Work toward being able to entertain two apparently contrary assumptions—our assumptions and those of the other person—at the same time.
- Be willing to revise assumptions each of us have made or even abandon them completely if they don't pass our joint reality checking.

7. Come to a mutual understanding with the person with whom we're in conflict that enables both parties to let go of invalid assumptions.

When people in conflict are willing to let go of assumptions they've made about each other that turn out to be invalid, they are making important strides toward coming to agreement on assumptions that are factually based.

- Assess whether each person sincerely desires to reach common ground with the other person. Don't proceed if there are any vestiges of negative feelings toward one another.
- Jointly explore alternative assumptions about each other's behavior. Together be willing to entertain the possibility that there might be explanations for each other's behavior that haven't yet been considered.
- Acknowledge that each person has sufficient self-confidence to yield to the correctness of another person's assumptions without feeling personally diminished.
- Work together to reconcile differing assumptions and to arrive at mutually acceptable assumptions about each other's behavior.

8. Apologize sincerely to people we have wronged based on incorrect assumptions we've made and actions we've taken that offended them.

Recognize that our assumptions have caused the negative feelings we had about others, and apologize for our behavior that has offended them. It shows that we have chosen the future, not the past, as the focus for our interactions with the offended parties. When we apologize, we should, if possible, include four aspects of an effective apology:

(a) acknowledging our offensive behavior;

(b) explaining our actions;

(c) expressing remorse; and

(d) making amends.[2]

- Take responsibility for the circumstances that caused another person to feel offended by acknowledging what we did.
- State truthfully the reasons for behaving the way we did.
- Express regrets for what we did that was offensive to the other person.
- Make a sincere effort to right any wrongs we committed. Do whatever we can to help the other person recover emotionally from what we said or did.

9. Reach agreement on new, constructive ways to communicate with each other when dealing with issues that may arise in the future.

In our agreements with others, we need to include solutions that will benefit us both. Although it is important to stick up for our own suggestions, in order for an agreement to be balanced, it is equally important for us to be willing to yield to the other person's ideas. Each of us needs to be willing to be part of the solution.

- Seek statements to include in a mutual agreement that transform previously contentious issues into practical steps to resolve them should they reoccur.
- Include explicit steps for implementing the agreement, knowing they will increase the likelihood that the agreed upon changes in each other's behavior spelled out in the agreement will be sustained.

10. Decide to "bury the hatchet", bringing closure to old conflicts and starting new, positive chapters in repaired relationships.

The challenge is to be 100 percent willing to let go of old grudges and move forward expecting the best possible outcomes from a repaired relationship. If one person falters along the way in doing something that was agreed upon, the other person needs to be magnanimous—accepting an apology and a commitment to not let it happen again.

- Acknowledge that a full-fledged effort on the part of both individuals is required to change old habits.
- Recognize that while things don't always work out as planned in an agreement, it doesn't mean that corrections can't be made.
- Anticipate best efforts from both parties in getting back on course.

Even though some interpersonal conflicts we have may seem to be intractable, the techniques I've described in this essay can help us address them in a fresh, creative manner. The techniques are designed to enable us to focus on two sets of assumptions simultaneously—ours and the other person's—and work together with that person to reach agreement on the assumptions that have a factual basis. The techniques have the potential of helping us open a new door to resolving our differences with the person. Putting them into practice hopefully will have given both of us a chance to become more understanding and compassionate people.

Jack Hamilton holds a bachelor of arts from Harvard College, a master of arts from the University of California, and a master of arts and a doctorate from Stanford University. He has taught conflict resolution classes and workshops at the Leadership Training Institute of the National League of Cities, as well as at universities, businesses and nonprofits.[3] He was honored by Santa Clara County, California, for his work as a mediator.

Endnotes

1 Jack Hamilton, Elisabeth Seaman, Sharlene Gee, and Hillary Freeman. *Conflict—The Unexpected Gift: Making the most of disputes in life and work* (Bloomington: iUniverse, 2nd Edition, 2014).

2 Aaron Lazare. *On Apology* (New York: Oxford University Press, 2004).

3 Jack can be seen in a video skit with his partner which demonstrates how mediations work at https://www.youtube.com/watch?v=NHDcsveodLg.

Politics

It's All about Politics!

John R. Thomson

My fascination with politics goes back to 1940 and has lasted a lifetime. Not love but fascination for what many consider the world's second-oldest profession.

It started during Wendell Willkie's foredoomed campaign to deny Franklin D. Roosevelt an unprecedented third presidential term, when I took a bag of "We Want Willkie" pins from my father's stash and walked to every house in the neighborhood handing out buttons to all who would receive them.

My interest has not waned since, whether living for at least a year in the US, Bahamas, Cambodia, Colombia, Cyprus, Egypt, Greece, India, Japan, Lebanon, Saudi Arabia, and Thailand, or our current base in South Africa.

Politics is usually far from being an easy, fun, clean or decent game . . . but it is a critical factor in the lives of most individuals and for society as a whole, whether in Harvard's hallowed halls, the Pentagon, Nuku'alofa, Beijing's Forbidden City, or Timbuktu.

My Larousse dictionary devotes one and a half pages covered with four columns in small type, defining the word "politics". That's because politics define our lives, from the simple to the special and the minor to the massive. Consider:

- gaining a child acceptance at a highly rated school;
- collecting letters of recommendation for a new job;
- raising funds for a church or synagogue;
- sending a note of thanks for a pleasant dinner;
- apologizing for being late to an important meeting.

It's only politic, isn't it?

College Politics

How about Freshman Registration at Memorial Hall? Standing in line to visit the various non-academic organizations, I decided to register for the Young Republican Club, which became a major interest of my undergraduate years. The HYRC grew from less than 50 to more than 500 members. We launched a weekly paper, *The Harvard Times-Republican*, which had the temerity to criticize the folks in Harvard Hall (I was more than an occasional visitor to Dean Watson's office).

The newspaper caught the eye of several Republican officeholders in Washington, making enough of an impression that several luminaries including Speaker of the House B. Carroll Reece of Tennessee and Senate Majority Leader William F. Knowland of California visited Cambridge. (Speaker Reece kindly brought a case of Jack Daniel's that slaked the thirst of our under-21 members!)

I was appointed a Chief Page at the 1956 GOP convention in San Francisco that led to spending most of the campaign in a DC-3 traveling the country as Field Director of Youth for Eisenhower-Nixon—a terrific experience that weighed negatively on my '56 fall semester grades.

Goldwater and Reagan

My activities at college and as a young businessman in New York and Minneapolis eventually led to meeting Ronald Reagan in 1961, who was then a traveling/TV spokesman for 20 Mule Team Borax and an active Hollywood actor. We were again in contact during the 1964 presidential campaign when I called on him to make a speech for the failing campaign of Senator Barry Goldwater.

I was a marketing executive at Colgate-Palmolive at the time and with a colleague from Quaker Oats, we blocked primetime on ABC, CBS, and NBC and Reagan agreed, wrote, and delivered "A Time for Choosing", the speech that two years later opened the door to his active political life. Many observers believe the speech, followed by a nationwide TV talk by John Wayne, at least led to Goldwater winning six states as Lyndon Johnson won by a landslide while the country continued to mourn his predecessor, the assassinated John F. Kennedy.

Expatriate Life

Two years later, I launched my expatriate life as a marketing consultant and political observer in Africa, the Middle East, and Southeast Asia, plus contributor to several publications (*Time, The National Review,*

Advertising Age, The Washington Star and, later, *The Washington Times*). Everywhere I went was a great experience, including covering five wars in the Middle East and Southeast Asia. It all made me realize the breadth and depth of politics, and its vastly diverse meanings.

My wife, Tica, and I had been living in Cyprus for several years, my regional base for serving clients, when I received word in mid-1983 from Washington friends that President Reagan had expressed interest in seeing me. Shortly after getting back in touch, I was appointed Senior Commercial Officer at the American Embassy in Riyadh and director of commercial staff in Africa, the Near East, and South Asia (acronymed by the State Department as ANESA). It was to be the greatest professional period of my life.

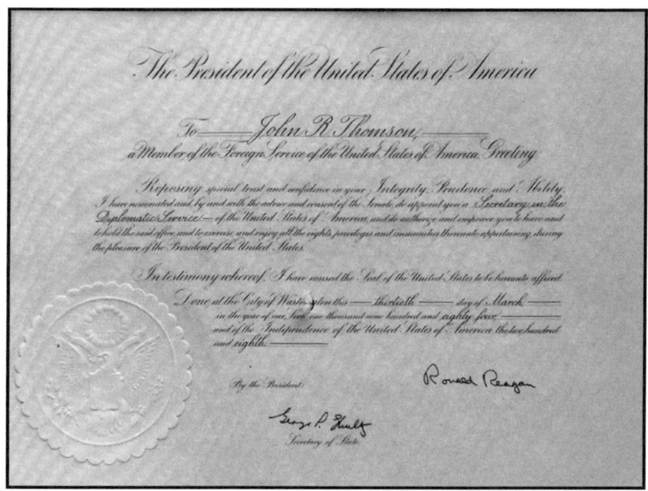

The President of the United States of America

To John R. Thomson, a Member of the Foreign Service of the United States of America Greeting

Reposing special trust and confidence in your Integrity, Prudence and Ability, I have nominated and, by and with the advice and consent of the Senate, do appoint you a Secretary in the Diplomatic Service of the United States of America, and do authorize and empower you to have and to hold the said office, and to exercise and enjoy all the rights, privileges and immunities thereunto appertaining, during the pleasure of the President of the United States.

In testimony whereof, I have caused the Seal of the United States to be hereunto affixed.

Done at the City of Washington this thirtieth day of March in the year of our Lord one thousand nine hundred and eighty four and of the Independence of the United States of America the two hundred and eighth.

By the President: Ronald Reagan

George P. Shultz
Secretary of State

Figure 9.2.2.1 *John Thomson's Presidential appointment*

Trade Missions to Middle East

In four years, our staffs created countless trade missions to the United States, which led to significant trade deficit reductions at a time when America was importing enormous quantities of oil from Saudi Arabia, Kuwait, United Arab Emirates, Iraq, and Egypt. The missions not only led to increased US export trade but also were the key to creation of more than 50 joint ventures between American and Arab firms. (The commercial relationship with Israel was handled by a separate team, in order to contend with the Arab Boycott.)

To supplement tangible business development we launched a bilingual monthly business magazine in two editions—Arabic-English and Arabic-French—that reached virtually all commercial and industrial organizations throughout the Asian-Arab states and the Maghreb nations of North Africa. All commercial staff, American and non-American, attended two regional conferences a year. Moreover, all staff had the option of taking a one-year University of Maryland correspondence course on foreign trade development. The entire staff chose to matriculate, and all successfully passed a rigid study program while continuing to do their work.

Ending the Arab Boycott of American Companies

A particularly interesting challenge was dealing with the Arab Boycott by a Kuwait-centered group of governments that refused to deal with companies who did business with Israel. The boycott effectively kept numerous American multinationals out of the region, among them Ford and Coca-Cola. While this gave rich opportunity to General Motors, Chrysler and Pepsi-Cola, among others, it negatively impacted America's international trade. It took the better part of three years, but extensive discussions and relentless negotiations finally convinced the anti-Israeli boycott enforcers and their home governments that they were losing far more than they gained from their spiteful attitude that had lasted for more than 40 years.

The result was that the White House and the Commerce Department repeatedly cited our regional team as the outstanding group in the US Foreign Commercial Service (USFCS).

The entire experience was replete with politics—with host country ministries, with Washington bureaucrats, and with locally sourced suppliers. There was nothing like negotiating a purchase from a local supplier, or convincing the department Inspector General that we could use the revenue from selling advertising for our magazine for underwriting a team conference.

At the conclusion of my diplomatic tour, I remained in Riyadh as Senior Vice President of the Olayan Group, the leading private business organization in Saudi Arabia and the Gulf Cooperation Council (Saudi Arabia, Kuwait, Bahrain, Qatar, United Arab Emirates, and Oman). The organization, founded by Suleiman Saleh Olayan in 1947 in Dhahran, grew to more than 40 operating companies.

During 55 years in business, Sheikh Suleiman was a significant shareholder in multinationals, including Transamerica, Chase Manhattan and Occidental Petroleum. He was founding chairman of Saudi British Bank, chaired the Saudi Council of Chambers of Commerce, plus director of Saudi Aramco, Riyad Bank and Saudi Arabian Airlines.

Family Politics

My parents passed away when I was 14, and I was fortunate, indeed blessed, to be guided by my older brother Marsh. Our brother-to-brother politics were powerful, as he showed me the ropes as a teenager, doing so deftly and effectively. It has been my great fortune to have experienced the exceptional, indeed outstanding, mentoring provided by three people: Ronald Reagan, Suleiman Olayan, and Marsh Thomson.

Married in 1974, Tica and I developed a close relationship with my elder son, Jim, from my first marriage. Sadly, it was virtually impossible even to communicate with Bob, Jim's younger brother. After lengthy failed efforts, our priest advised us to desist and proceed with our lives, which motivated us to have children, starting with the 1979 birth of Ian in Nicosia, followed by Alexander five years later in Riyadh.

When they were 12 and 7, we decided it was time they became well acquainted with life in the US and moved to Florida, settling in Key Biscayne. Ian spent a difficult first year but eventually adjusted, while Alexander learned about behavioral politics when he and a pal decided to toss bread balls at kindergarten lunch and was banned to sit apart from his class for an embarrassing afternoon. Over the years, both lads have developed their own political chops and become successful international entrepreneurs, Ian and family based in South Africa and Alexander in Angola.

Son Jim became a successful commercial real estate broker and enjoyed bringing up three children: Diana, David, and Catherine Annie. He and I frequently talked about American politics as well as the familial politics of estranged parents raising kids. He contracted leukemia in his late 40s and, after extensive research, decided on treatment at Mount Sinai hospital in New York, where the doctors prescribed chemotherapy and a stem cell transplant.

However, our close Indian friend, Dr. Akhilesh Sharma, urged that Jim take natural ayurvedic medications which he provided from Delhi. In slightly more than two months taking the herbal capsules, Jim's blood tests administered at Mount Sinai showed no live leukemia cells. Their medical team was baffled and insisted Jim receive their allopathic treatment program, despite its eliminating his immune system for 8–12 months, "as an insurance policy".

Jim finally agreed and underwent the treatment. He was in isolation for 12-plus weeks to safeguard him from the absence of his immune system, and was eventually instructed to dress in gown, mask and gloves, and walk in the hospital's halls to get some exercise.

He did as instructed, got an infection, and died within a few days, on his birthday, Easter Sunday 2012.

If the mal-prescribed chemotherapy had not cancelled Jim's immune system, he most certainly would have survived. Mount Sinai practitioners prevailed politically versus Dr. Sharma, only to have their flawed treatment program fail at the cost of my son's life.

Jim's needless passing tested my faith, and it diminished for some time. Finding solace in prayer, I especially focused on a key line in the Lord's Prayer: *"Thy will be done."*

I pondered and came to believe in destiny: Not man but the Almighty is in charge.

Politics Today

Certainly, Donald Trump is not Almighty. Nevertheless, as much as I have doubted his capacity to lead (Google "Trumpaloney" for my March 2016 diatribe), it is my belief that, to date and despite his idiosyncratic behavior, he is showing much-needed leadership, innovation and determination as President. The massive media prejudice against Mr. Trump, with scarcely a positive word before and since his inauguration, is deplorable as he clearly tries his best to make our country great again.

It is very clear: he wants to be a successful, indeed great, president. If he succeeds in reversing the recent lengthy period of leaderless drift, I say more power to him!

* * *

So, from my perspective, life for me has come full circle over the last 77 years, with countless stops, big and little, along the way:

It's All about Politics!

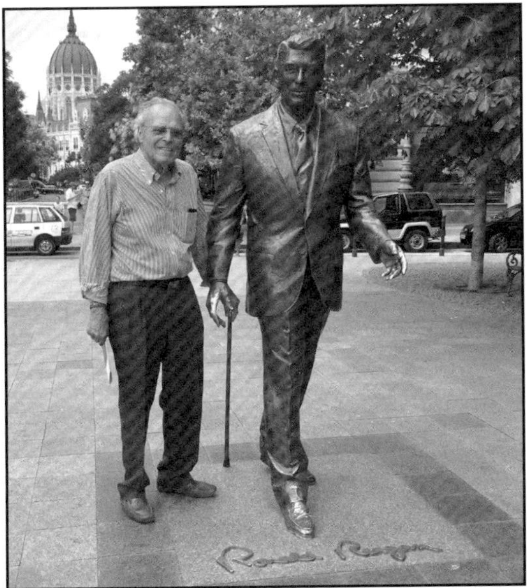

Figure 9.2.2.2 *"Taking a virtual stroll in Budapest with my real-life mentor, Ronald Reagan,"* wrote *John Thomson of his visit to the statue of Ronald Reagan in Budapest, Hungary.*

Photo courtesy of the author

John R. Thomson after graduation spent three years with NYSE member firm Grimm & Co. After three MBA program semesters at Harvard Business School, he left to become Media Director for the Pillsbury Company. He later held marketing positions with General Foods, Colgate-Palmolive, and as Corporate Marketing Director of Aerosol Techniques, a pioneering innovator of the '60s consumer boom.

In 1966, he launched a consultancy to American companies seeking to enter the Middle East and Southeast Asia. Based in Cyprus 1978–82, he partnered with BBDO and directed local advertising agencies in Cyprus, Egypt, Iran, Kuwait, and Lebanon.

Beginning with 1967's six-day Arab-Israeli war and aftermath, he covered five conflicts, becoming increasingly involved in journalism as a frequent geopolitical contributor to *The National Review* and *The Washington Times*, plus contributing editor to *Advertising Age*. During President Reagan's second term, he headed US commercial relations with Saudi Arabia and the Africa, Near East, and South Asia region.

His team received multiple Certificates of Merit and the Thomas Jefferson Medal.

After more than three decades abroad, he lived in the US for 15 years and Colombia for 12, before moving to South Africa, where he currently resides.

Violence

Apologia pro Vita Sua

James Gilligan

In response to the Alumni Association's request for a memoir describing an event in my life that was challenging, motivational and influential in my future life, I cannot avoid referring to the automobile accident in which two of our classmates, Bill Boyden and Bill North, were killed, and the driver of our car, John Fell Stevenson, and I were nearly killed. We were driving home for Christmas vacation in our Junior year, when a semitrailer truck ran headlong into our car. The truck driver, who had been driving nonstop for days (presumably for financial reasons), was so delirious from amphetamine intoxication and sleep deprivation that he did not even know where he was or what he had done. (Following that event, he was convicted of some form or other of vehicular homicide and spent a few years in prison.) While that was not the only event that motivated me to spend the rest of my life attempting to learn about the causes and prevention of violence, it was certainly among the most powerful.

I had spent the previous summer in Chicago, during which Bill Boyden became one of my closest friends, and his parents became like surrogate parents to me. When I met with them after the accident as the parents who had lost a son, while I was still living, I learned how hard it is to avoid "*survivor's guilt*", even when your intellect tells you that it's irrational. Nor did I realize for many years that I would spend so much of my life attempting to do whatever I could to learn how to keep as many people as possible from suffering such an experience—which is, of course, a bit like attempting to bail out the ocean with a teaspoon.

I decided to become a psychiatrist, but my first conscious motives for doing so were merely to help others (and myself) learn how to deal with guilt, trauma and other emotional difficulties. It was only later that I realized that what I really wanted to do was to work with people who had committed lethal violence, in order to learn what the causes of such behavior were, and what we could do (as individuals and as a society) to prevent such violence from happening in the first place. In fact, it was only after I had been doing this for some years that I came to realize how strong an influence the auto accident had played in determining the shape I would give to my career.

The *social-psychological "laboratories"*, so to speak, in which I have investigated the *biological, psychological and social causes of violence* have been primarily the *prisons and jails* in which our legal system has placed the people whom we have identified (or misidentified) as the most violent people our society produces. During my psychiatric training at the Harvard Medical School, I was first given the challenge of attempting to engage violent prisoners in psychotherapy.

To my surprise, I found working with those men the most emotionally moving experience I had had in psychiatry, because I was confronted on a daily basis with the depths of human tragedy: not only the tragedies they had inflicted on their victims, but also the tragedies of which they themselves were the victims. I discovered that the most violent among them were the survivors of their own attempted murder, often at the hands of a parent, or of the actual murder of their closest family members. The degree of *child abuse* these men had suffered was beyond anything that I had realized occurred in our society.

I also found it the most intellectually challenging work to which I had been exposed, namely, how to understand how any human being could have behaved toward another human being in ways that we describe as inhuman. And as soon as I felt I had solved that puzzle with one man, at least partially, another one would walk into my office in one prison or another, and I would have to begin the whole process all over again. Finally, I concluded that *investigating the etiology and prevention of violence was the most socially important problem* to which I could apply my training as a psychiatrist.

Several years later, throughout the 1970s, Massachusetts prisons experienced an epidemic of murders, suicides, riots, hostage-taking and other violence. This led to class action suits against the Department of Correction, as a result of which two US District Courts in Boston concluded that much of this *violence was a consequence of undiagnosed, untreated psychopathology*, and that much of that was *precipitated or exacerbated by the conditions existing in the prisons* (years of solitary confinement, grossly inadequate medical and mental health care, inadequate protection from gang rapes, etc.). Therefore they ordered the Department of Correction to allow a team of mental health professionals from the Harvard Medical School to provide psychiatric services, first to the prison mental hospital and then to all the prisons.

As the Medical Director of this program (by virtue of being Director of the Institute of Law and Psychiatry at McLean Hospital), I decided to use the prisons as a laboratory in which our efforts to reduce the violence and psychopathology of both the *prisoners and the prisons could become a form of clinical research* into the *causes and prevention of violence*, wherever it might occur, much as microscopic research in a microbiology laboratory can lead to knowledge about the etiology, treatment and prevention of epidemics of infectious disease in the macrocosm, the community as a whole.

When I would ask one man after another why he had assaulted or even killed someone, I would almost always get back the same response: "*because he had 'disrespected' me (or my mother, wife, friend, etc.)*". In fact, they used that word so often that they abbreviated it into the slang term, "*he 'dis'ed' me*".

And it occurred to me that whenever people use a word so often that they abbreviate it, it tells you something about how central it is in their moral and emotional vocabulary. I concluded that there is *one emotive force that is necessary* (though not sufficient) to the *production of the motive force that causes violence*, in the same sense that the tubercle bacillus is necessary but not sufficient in the causation of tuberculosis—except that in the case of violence, the pathogenic agent is an emotion, not a bacterium.

For violence the *necessary cause is the feeling of being disrespected* (or any of its many synonyms: being shamed, humiliated, dishonored, disdained, disgraced, demeaned, defeated, insulted, slighted, rejected, ridiculed, subjected to contempt, treated as weak, inferior or inadequate, or any other version of what psychoanalysts call "*narcissistic injuries*"). When I reviewed the literature on the causes of violence I found that there is evidence from every one of the human or behavioral sciences confirming that finding.

Everyone is shamed or humiliated at one time or another, of course, insulted or rejected, and yet most people never commit a serious act of violence in their lifetimes. So clearly *other preconditions need to be in place before violence will result*, even among those who are shamed. One is the absence of sufficient *non-violent means of maintaining or restoring self-esteem*, such as education, knowledge and skills, employment in work from which one can gain respect from self and others, having a family that is respected, and that treats oneself with respect, etc. Most violent offenders do not have access to any of those resources.

In fact, the most powerful *predictors of the rates of individual and interpersonal violence*, meaning homicide and suicide, in the US and other comparable countries, include the various measures of *unemployment, recessions, and social and economic inequality.* But that is understandable, since all of those stressors tend to cause feelings of shame, inferiority, failure, emasculation, etc.

In my last book, *Why Some Politicians Are More Dangerous Than Others,* I summarized the statistical finding that those stressors, and the individual/interpersonal violence that they stimulate, have correlated in the United States with which party was in the White House, from 1900 to the present. Collective political violence, however, such as totalitarianism and terrorism, may have more to do with the collective shame that even those who are not at the bottom of the social hierarchy in their respective countries experience when they feel their nation or religion is being collectively shamed by other comparable groups.

A *second precondition for violence* is the *incapacity to feel guilt and remorse about hurting others.* Freud has commented that no one feels guiltier than the saints. I would add, based on experience with a population that Freud never studied, that *no one feels more innocent than the criminals.* That is, the more heinous the crime, the less likely it is that the offender will feel guilty. But, of course, that would have to be true, for if one had the capacity for guilt feelings (i.e., an internalized conscience), how could one have the capacity to injure or kill people (unless that was the only way to stop them from killing a third party—which is practically never the case in the thousands of murders that occur in this country every year)?

A *third precondition* that enormously increases the likelihood of committing serious violence is to have been *raised as a male* (rather than a female). That is, the *male role in a patriarchal culture or subculture* (which all societies known to me are, to one degree or another) is defined by the requirement that, to *prove that one is a man* (rather than any of the many alternatives, in the dictionary of patriarchy—sissy, wimp, coward, etc.), one has to be willing to commit serious violence in many circumstances. Most homicides, suicides, wars, assassinations, capital punishments, honor killings, duels, feuds, lynchings, acts of terrorism, etc., are committed by men. In fact, that is also true even of most so-called "unintentional" or "accidental" injuries that kill people, from traffic accidents to hazardous vocations or avocations.

The most important *benefit of understanding the causes of violence* is that it can *help us learn how to prevent it.* In the Massachusetts prisons we were able to bring the level of lethal violence to zero for up to a year at a time. And in an intensive, experimental violence prevention program with violent offenders in the jails of San Francisco, we were able to bring even nonlethal violence to zero for up to a year at a time.

Perhaps more importantly, the rate of violent reoffending, after release from the jail, was 83% lower among the members of the experimental group, compared with an otherwise identical "control group" in an ordinary jail. We found that this program not only made the community safer, it even saved the taxpayers $4 for every $1 spent on it, since the costs of incarceration are so high, and the rate of re-incarceration was so much lower, among those in the experimental group. As a result, this program won a major national prize from the Kennedy School of Government at Harvard, for "innovations in American governance."

While I engaged in these and other activities to attempt to prevent violence, throughout this country and around the world, I have to admit that I felt I was doing so as a kind of "closet" religious. That is, even though I have not continued any active membership in the Episcopal Church in which I was raised as a child, I realize that my attitude toward the violent men I have worked with throughout my career was crucially shaped by my earlier religious upbringing.

To summarize that religious influence, I will quote an aphorism summarizing what one author described as the *religious conception of human beings*, namely, that "*none are good but all are sacred*". That is, none of us can claim to be "good", when judged by the highest moral standards; we are all "sinners", to use the religious term for having hurt other people (perhaps especially those we love), and we are all in need of forgiveness.

But *every human being possesses a soul,* by which I mean not something "supernatural", but rather, *a psyche, a mind, a self, a human consciousness*—which is the subject of psychiatric understanding and therapy. And we cannot even begin to help others—in fact, we will only harm them further—unless we are willing to consider each individual's soul or personhood, no matter how damaged it may be, as *something that needs to be given unqualified respect and treated as sacred.*

The term "*psychiatry*", after all, comes from Greek roots meaning "*physician of the soul*". Thus, even though I am not a theologian or a clergyman, nor even a member of any organized religion or church, I consider my work to have been, in the deepest sense, a religious vocation.

Figure 9.2.3.1 *James Gilligan in West Stockbridge, MA, in 2006*

James Gilligan became a psychiatrist after Harvard College and served on the faculty of the Harvard Medical School from 1966 to 2000, studying the causes and prevention of violence. He directed mental health services for the Massachusetts prisons from 1977–1991. He now teaches in the Schools of Medicine and Law at NYU.

He has served as a consultant on violent crime and punishment, including war crimes, to President Clinton, Tony Blair, Kofi Annan, the World Health Organization, the World Court, and numerous other leaders and organizations. A violence-prevention experiment he conducted in California received a major national prize from Harvard's Kennedy School of Government in 2004. He has written widely on the subject of violence in books, textbooks, encyclopedias, and journal articles.

He is a past president of the International Association for Forensic Psychotherapy and has received annual and lifetime achievement awards from numerous violence-prevention advocacy groups.

Social Order

Reflections for the Sixtieth Reunion

Neil Olken

The recent political year with its appeals to racism and other bigotry has me reflecting on some business experiences and some after-retirement experiences.

After Harvard Business School I worked in the investment department of a large insurance company. The year was 1960, and Kennedy was running for President. Most of my contemporaries were JFK supporters. The senior management was disparaging of the idea that this country would elect a Catholic. Needless to say, no junior employee was willing to challenge any of the senior executives.

I joined a family business a few years later. Shortly after I arrived, a supervisor came to me and told me he wanted to make a black man foreman of a department, but that he was worried the other employees would object. I was surprised, but calmly told the supervisor to go ahead with the promotion. That afternoon that department staged a walkout. The supervisor was panicked. I suggested he ignore the employees, and they would come back the next day. That strategy worked, probably because these were low-skilled and low-wage employees who could not afford to lose the pay.

Several years later I was looking for a new factory location. The mayor of a large southeastern Massachusetts town invited me to visit. After personally showing me several sites, we returned to his office where he proudly told me he controlled the unemployment office, and he would make sure they did not send over any "niggers" if I did move a factory to his town. I said nothing and never considered that town.

I sold my business in 2000 and retired. I began doing team consulting as part of Community Action Partners, a Boston HBS Alumni group. I was on a team one year that consulted for a new charter school start-up. I was terrifically impressed with the people and the programs. The founders were Kennedy School graduates. A few months later I was invited to join their board, and I accepted. In my visits to the school I have seen many extraordinary and positive things. I have seen an English teacher integrate a badly disabled student into a class discussion of a difficult novel while keeping the discussion moving at a good pace. I have seen real student diversity achieve success and 100% college acceptance. Unfortunately, I have also seen a student with a full scholarship to college have to postpone and join the Army because his family could not survive economically without the support his income gave them.

Our generation of college students was often called the *Silent Generation.* This description certainly described me, and many others in our class, self-satisfied with our own moral behavior, but not working hard enough to influence a broader population. I have to wonder if this year's political ugliness is partly our legacy.

On the other hand, I am optimistic and view the longer-term outlook as moving in a positive direction despite the current political environment. After all, in 1957 we still had racial segregation of schools and public places in a large part of the country.

After graduating from Harvard Business School in 1960, **Neil Olken** worked for three years at Prudential Insurance Company in their Commercial and Industrial Loan Department. In 1963 he joined a family business, Dyecraftsmen, Inc., remaining with this firm until his retirement in 2000. Neil created an industrial real estate affiliate for the Company, and this combination worked out well. Since retirement he has served on several nonprofit boards, including those of Boston Collegiate Charter School and Cambridge Camping.

Immigrant Experience

Running from Hitler

John M. Stein

I was never supposed to go to Harvard at all.

Born in 1935 into a Viennese Jewish medical family three generations deep, my parents expected stability. . . . Turmoil ensued.

Getting to the USA

My father's oral surgery had flourished with an influx of American patients after a lecture trip to the US in 1928. In 1937 and early 1938 many of those concerned Americans warned my Austrian parents of the danger to our family if we stayed in Europe. These wonderful people provided support for our application to obtain an American visa and an affidavit attesting to our financial stability to allow our legal entry to the United States.

In one of my bits of isolated flashback memory as a three-year-old in 1938 was the flurry of Nazi propaganda leaflets that were dropped from airplanes and flew past our apartment windows like snow in July. With childish innocence, I so wanted to reach out of that window to get one of them.

We were a small core family, just my parents and me as an only child. I had no idea what was going on, but I do remember the disruption to my routine and the sense of urgency to get a lot of things done. Even as a sheltered three-year-old I sensed there was trouble. Strangers were coming into our apartment, and things were disappearing into boxes and crates. I had no idea how my parents managed to get our entire household and my father's entire oral surgical equipment packed up.

I mean, here we were running for our lives, and they had the presence of mind to bring everything they owned to America. First of all, there were the really big pieces. In our Phoenix home today stands a nine-foot-long dining room chest which held their china for 24 with multiple plates and serving pieces, glassware, silverware, a second set of informal china, table cloths and table mats. We call it "the coffin". Each time I pass it, it reminds me of my Austrian heritage and the ones we left behind.

There were other large matching furnishings. They also brought a grand piano, beds, sofas, chairs, chandeliers, wall lighting, the dining room table to seat the 24 guests, radios, a huge free-standing three-part wardrobe . . . so much stuff that they eventually could furnish their entire house in the US with it.

On top of all that they packed an entire oral surgical outfit with x-ray machine, two dental chairs, lights, and all those little instruments needed and chests to hold them. It exhausts me just to think about moving all that stuff locally, but to ship it across the world? It was in storage for over three years, and almost nothing was chipped, cracked or broken.

Now you may wonder why I catalog all the stuff, and believe me, I have mentioned but a fraction of what was shipped. I am trying to convey the frenzy of leaving your home, and your ancestor's home, and the only place you have lived all your life in a matter of about three months. Consider the discussions that my parents must have had. What to take and what to abandon. Make travel plans . . . you could not just go to the computer and book a flight. Where should we go, and how to get there safely? What should we do with the three-year-old, and what do we tell him? What to tell our friends and relatives? What was my father's obligation to his patients?

And as always there was the money. When I became older I asked my father why we brought all the stuff to America. When we were in Austria we were well off and could pay for moving everything. However, as soon we left the country, all money was confiscated, and we had nothing, except for what we could smuggle out.

The paperwork and red tape slowed everything down. When my mother went to the American embassy to pick up our visa, she was told it was missing. We always hoped another family appropriated it and got out too. We imposed on our American sponsor to facilitate a duplicate visa and affidavit. These documents were so vital to escape legally and without a hassle that other Jewish emigrants would steal them.

There were tearful goodbyes to my grandparents and my parents' siblings, friends and employees. Everybody was upset, but we left them in Hell. Some got out and others did not.

This was the last time my mother saw her parents, and she always blamed herself for not getting them out. There was no communication from them during the rest of the war, telling her that they were not alive. She only received confirmation of their death at Auschwitz when the concentration camps were liberated, and the meticulous German documentation was obtained.

My father anonymously left behind all the dental gold and some cash for the Jewish dental lab technician whom he had employed for years. He fled to Venezuela, where he established a dental lab of his own, did well and moved to Israel in 1948 to open the first kosher hotel in Tel Aviv.

After all the packing and goodbyes, we left Vienna in October of 1938 by train to Berlin. In another flashback, I recall thinking, "If the Germans are the bad guys, why are we on a train to Germany?" It was only one month before *Kristallnacht*, when the Nazis broke windows of homes and businesses and trashed everything in Jewish sections . . . after that it was much more difficult to escape.

Other relatives from both my mother's and father's side delayed too long. They no longer could come west, but had to take the trans-Siberian Railway east to Shanghai, where they survived the war years. They escaped with the clothes on their back, as did many Austrian and German Jews. No papers were needed since the Japanese already occupied China and seemed indifferent to the Jewish immigration into Shanghai. Some of the German evacuees took ships around the Cape of Good Hope to Shanghai, avoiding the Suez Canal for fear of capture there.

Our own evacuation train north through Berlin took us to Denmark, evoking a great celebration when we crossed the border and left Germany. My father had a dental colleague in Gothenburg, Sweden, who put us up. It was the first time my parents could unwind a bit, and the colleague's child and I became playmates. They lived on the edge of town, and I remember seeing elephants being used at a construction site, tearing out trees with their trunks to clear the land.

Although I did not know it, our next step was not yet certain . . . London or New York. Dad left Gothenburg after about a month to go to London, leaving Mom and me in Sweden. By phone my parents decided on New York. While in London, Dad and another Austrian physician, Max Schur, consulted on Sigmund Freud, dying of jaw cancer from long-term smoking. Max's son, Peter Schur, would graduate from Harvard Medical School (HMS) a few years before me.

Mom and I left Sweden on December 17, 1938, by boat across the North Sea to meet Dad in London. The North Sea was wild with froth and wind tossing about our small boat. Essentially everyone except me on the ship was sick. On board, Mom and I celebrated the first night of Hanukkah. Mom was prepared with a barf bucket for her and a toy farm for her baby's Hanukkah gift. No candles on the ship, but the farm was ideal. It came in pieces: several animals, a barn, a water trough and separate links of white fencing. This allowed her to mete it out to me item by item for the eight-day holiday. The sea was so rough that we were delayed by 24 hours in reaching London, without a way to contact Dad.

Our time in London was tight. We were booked on the Cunard White Star Liner *Aquitania*, leaving Southampton on December 20. The 4-funnel *Aquitania* was fast and beautiful, built on the Clyde River in Scotland in the *Titanic* style and launched two years after the *Titanic* catastrophe. The *Titanic* had been built in Belfast, Ireland. After an uneventful crossing, we arrived in Manhattan on Christmas Eve, 1938. Able to bypass Ellis Island because we had the legal papers, we were met at the pier by my father's cousin—I called him Uncle Marcy. We wrangled a cab, and I was assigned to sit on a pile of luggage in the back seat, but promptly fell out of the opposite door. Begin with a bang. No harm.

My life in America had started!

I am forever grateful to my parents for getting me out of Hell.

I am forever grateful for the experience of getting out and for having snippets of recollections of some of that experience. That experience has given me a toughness to deal with the difficult parts of life.

I am forever grateful to the United States of America for the opportunities it has given me.

I fly an American flag at our house every day.

I am forever grateful to Harvard for branding me twice.

Being in the USA

Once in the USA, my parents had to work diligently to make a go of it. The Great Depression was waning, but not gone. Work was hard to find and wages were low. I was aware that money was tight. Mom had me, a three-year-old, to care for, and Dad needed to study to take the New York State licensure boards to resume his dental and surgical practice.

Mom was very good at what used to be called "home economics". You remember when the boys went to "shop" and the girls to "home economics". Well, she was good at it. She found herself a job making little hand-sewn doo-dads that could be put on key chains or worn as decorations. Her brother had also escaped, and his wife, Bertha, had found someone who would buy the stuff. So, Mom cranked it out endlessly while minding me and paying the rent on our one-room 82nd Street West Manhattan walkup.

The apartment was just a couple of blocks from Central Park, so Mom took me there for the fresh air. It reminded me of the Viennese Stadt Park, where my nanny took me almost daily, and where I played with Ruthie. (I always had an eye for the girls.) And then suddenly in the middle of Central Park I heard a child's voice speaking German, "*Schau, Mutti, dort ist der Hansi vom Stadt Park*". (Look, Mom, there is Johnny from the Stadt Park.) Indeed, there was Ruthie with a lady whom I had never seen before. Our mothers did not know each other because nannies walked the kids in Vienna. However, the two moms became fast friends, and Ruthie's mom sublet a section of their apartment to us, which seemed to help the economy for both families. Ruthie named her son John after me, and wrote a book of poems about leaving Austria. Her experience mirrored mine; she and her family never talked about the experience of getting out of Austria. Then we lost touch.

Dad was busy studying for the New York State boards so that he could carry on with his practice. Many of his Viennese patients had made the same pilgrimage as we did and ended up in NYC area, so he wanted to get into business as soon as possible. His studies paid off, and he passed the MD boards on the first try. However, he then became aware that he was ineligible to take the Dental boards because he had no dental degree. You see, in Austria at that time dentistry was a specialty of medicine, much like psychiatry and Ear Nose and Thorat (ENT) are medical sub-specialties in the US today. That meant that Dad would have to go to dental school to get that degree.

Mom was a great communicator. She realized that I should go to day care so that I would learn English. Both of my parents spoke English when we arrived, but it was learned at school, and they could get by, but not teach it to me. We spoke mainly German at home. So, Mom found the Children's Colony, a nearby day care. Its mission was free day care for refugees. Perfect! Walking distance from our apartment and free. It was funded by established New Yorkers, largely Jewish, who saw the need and acted. A major contributor was Ruth Tishman, wife of Paul Tishman, a Harvard College graduate and an executive of Tishman Construction, a major New York firm privately held by the Jewish Tishman family. Tishman constructed the World Trade Center and Madison Square Garden. Mom met Ruth Tishman during one of her visits to Children's Colony and told her of my father's problem with the dental degree. As it happened, Ruth was a good friend of Margaret Blumgart, Herrman Blumgart's wife. Herrman Blumgart, MD, was professor of medicine at Harvard Medical School and the Beth Israel Hospital in Boston. Ruth put Margaret Blumgart and my mother in touch, and pretty soon they got a member of the Harvard Dental School faculty involved. Networking succeeded, and Harvard Dental School admitted my father for the two clinical years he needed to award him the DMD and gain New York State licensure.

Margaret Blumgart and my mother remained lifelong friends.

Dad had to work his way through dental school, and Harvard gave him jobs on campus. One of the jobs was to work at the Harvard Medical School library at night. There he befriended Stanley Levenson, who was an HMS student at the time, as I would be from 1957–61, and who later became my mentor when I was a surgical resident in New York.

In October 1941 my father opened his practice at 5th Avenue and 57th Street in New York City. Two months later the United States was attacked at Pearl Harbor on December 7, 1941, while I was playing on the neighbor's swing on a sunny Sunday morning in Larchmont. "Johnny," my mother called from the back door. "Come home, we have something to tell you."

President Roosevelt declared war on Japan the next day, and World War II began. We heard it on the radio and went to the News Reel movie later in the week to see footage of the attack.

Analyzing the Experience

I really did not recognize until recently what a profound effect my early life had on me. As a family we never really talked about it. I have asked other refugee immigrants of my generation who got out of Europe around 1938 whether they talked about it with their families, and they also said it was not discussed. One would think that such life changing experiences would evoke discussion and analysis, but that was not the case. It just never came up as a topic of conversation.

Perhaps it was because we felt there was some shame to being a refugee. For example, we spoke "gemisched" at home, a random mixture of German and English words, and that was the norm for others with similar experiences. Whatever language comes into your head comes out the mouth. But when we went out we spoke only English. Even with an accent, my parents thought that we should not let on that we could speak German. Thanks to Children's Colony and my youth when exposed to English, I could speak both languages without any discernable accent. Perhaps the brain's language center accepted both as first languages. This is not a unique attribute, and I now see it most commonly in Arizonan Latino families who speak English and Mexican Spanish with equal facility.

Our life in Larchmont, NY, was both banal and remarkable. It was banal probably because we were Depression babies and believed in patriotism, obedience and hard work. Don't make waves and be polite was the motto.

It was remarkable because, before World War II, Larchmont was a waspy suburb of 5,000 40 minutes north of NYC by train. There was no Jewish problem because there were no Jews. However, after the first refugee bought a house there, the floodgates opened, and dozens moved in. When we moved to Larchmont there were several Christian churches along the main street. The first synagogue building appeared seven years later, although before that services were held people's houses.

Despite the refugee invasion of Larchmont, I never felt antisemitism from my schoolmates, teachers, shop owners or others. Now, maybe I am not Jewish enough. My family did not observe religious dietary restriction or wear symbolic attire in either Vienna or Larchmont.

Furthermore, although I am an immigrant and a refugee, I could not consider myself a "Holocaust Survivor". We did not survive it, we ran from it and got away. So, that leaves me as a barely recognizable, barely observant, reformed Jew. It leaves me with the asset of a cultural Jewish heritage but the mixed blessing of the Jewish label.

Today I sit on the other side of the fence, viewing images of war-disrupted lives for Syrians and other refugees worldwide, who are largely Muslim. With their numbers overwhelming the rich countries, the US has taken in a substantial number of them. These refugees are running for their lives just as my family and I did, but vetting them is more difficult because of the confounding problem of letting terrorists into the country.

Now I am left with this soliloquy wondering how I should think about myself and having essentially no input from my deceased parents. My father never opened up on the subject. However, after her 100th birthday party, my mother was talking to one of my sons and said angrily, "That Hitler . . . he was a very sick person." That was it!

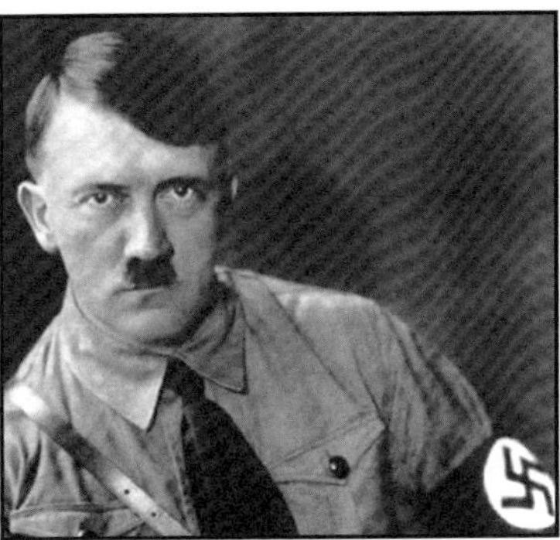

Figure 9.4.1.1 *Adolf Hitler—in Nazi Party uniform, c. 1933*

Photo source: Wikimedia Commons, File: Hitler adolf_33.jpg

John M. Stein, MD, is a partially retired surgeon with a specialty in trauma, burn care and wound healing. A graduate of Harvard College and Medical School, he trained in General Surgery at Cornell University Medical Center and Albert Einstein College of Medicine. From 1967–1969 he served in the US Army as a surgeon stationed at Fort Sam Houston, where he was the Clinical Care Director in the Institute of Surgical Research and Burn Care. He then joined the Einstein faculty, where he established the Burn Unit, and supervised post-graduate training in critical care, trauma and general surgery. Later he joined the Clinical Faculty at the University of Arizona, directed the Maricopa County Burn Center and a trauma center in Scottsdale and helped establish a trauma network for the State. He is the author of 57 journal articles in the medical literature, the father of four children and grandfather of eight.

From Bad Kreuznach to Abu-Dies: A Most Unusual Path

Robert Stern[1]

"I am most grateful to the Pastoral couple, Michel and Ulrike Wohlrat, for this opportunity to speak to you, in this holy city, in this holy place.

My name is Robert Stern, and I am currently a **Professor on the faculty of Al Quds University, in Abu-Dies, in East Jerusalem**. It is the ***first Palestinian School of Medicine***, and I am the only Westerner currently on the faculty. I give, unassisted, as a volunteer, the entire course in Pathology to the third-year medical students, from September until June.

My Family Origins

I stem originally from a Jewish family from a small town in the Rhineland near Bad Kreuznach, from a town originally called Heddesheim, but now called Guldental on the Nahe.

Hildegard of Bingen comes from a nearby town, Boekelheim on the Nahe. So it has to be a fairly decent area to come from. The Nahe, a small stream, flows into the Rhine at Bingen, not far from Guldental. My family had lived there for countless generations, at least since the 17th century, which is as far as it can be traced using local records.

Here are the famous houses on the bridge for which Bad Kreuznach is famous. They still stand. And it is in Bad Kreuznach that I was born in 1936.

Figure 9.4.2.1 *The iconic bridge houses in Robert Stern's birthplace, Bad Kreuznach, Rhineland-Palatine, Germany (from old tinted postcard: "1817. PZ. Kreuznach Bruckshausen")*

We were all peasants then. The men were cattle-dealers, and had been that for many generations. It was a typically Jewish occupation in those days. The wives all came from nearby villages; at the time it was unusual to go more than 30 kilometers from one's birthplace, whether for professional or for family reasons. For example, for their honeymoon, my parents went to Mainz, the nearest big city, for a few days. That was considered a major journey. And perhaps once in lifetime one went to Frankfurt, if at all.

The family was poor. My great-grandfather fought in the Franco-Prussian War of 1870. And my grandfather, born in 1864, stood barefoot in the train station of Bad Kreuznach, selling cigars to the troops returning home from the front, for five pennies each. Those are among the stories that were told and retold in our family.

Village Life in the Early 20th-Century Germany

Here is a picture of my father as a soldier in the Kaiser's Army during the First World War. He was certainly a handsome fellow with black hair and dark brown eyes. He was stationed in the barracks at Kaiserslautern, and saw battle in Forbach and Metz. The jokes that were told in the trenches, he would repeat throughout his life. They are in a sense, a valuable part of history. They provide a flavor and a feeling for the life of that time.

The war was obviously an exciting time for him, and one of the highpoints of his life. Expressions from that era, such as 'Out of Metz, Paris is bigger' [*Aus Metz, Paris ist groesser*] or 'Shut your mouth and sing the watch on the Rhine' [*Halts Maul und sing dem Wacht am Rhein*] were expressions he would use on occasion, though I am not sure what they mean.

Here is a photo of the house in Heddesheim, located on Jew Street [*Judengasse*], though it was not a derogatory term at the time. The house had only one water faucet, and that was in the kitchen. The toilet was located outside, and served the entire street, which was typical for German farming villages at that time.

Here is a picture of my father, as a cattle-dealer, at about age 30.

Figure 9.4.2.2 *Young Robert Stern, sitting on his grandmother's lap in 1938, shortly before his family's departure from his farming village for the USA. "My mother stands behind us, and my father is behind the boy shading his eyes."*

This picture was taken shortly before our departure for the USA, in June 1938. I am sitting on my grandmother's lap. If you look carefully, you can tell she is wearing the same dress that she wore at my father's bar mitzvah in 1913. My mother and father are standing behind her in the photo, as well as other family members, a typical peasant family, not unusual for rural Germany at the time.

The names of most of the people from that last photo can be seen on this memorial tablet, which now stands in the Jewish cemetery of Heddesheim. And here is a photo of a similar tablet with names from my mother's side of the family, from the nearby village of Weinsheim.

Blind to the Coming Societal Changes in Germany

Strangely enough, I recall that once a week, the family had a 'one-pot [*Eintopf*] dinner'. The Jewish families also participated in this German conservation enterprise. They were so naïve. They felt themselves German and wanted to be patriotic. They had no idea what was coming. And they remarked on occasion then that things were never eaten as hot as they are cooked. They did not realize that they would prove to be even hotter. But at the time, no one was able to fathom the unimaginable, the horror of what was coming.

The entire world could not comprehend what was about to occur. Here is a railroad ad from 1938 that I found on the Internet. '*Come holiday in beautiful Germany.*' No one could have anticipated it, or better said, no one wanted to believe it.

Immigration to America—1938

We immigrated to the US in June 1938, just in time. Here is the ship's passenger list.

We landed in Seattle, WA, and stayed with distant relatives that had been our sponsors. My father was able to find work immediately, as a butcher, at Frye and Company, and later at the Armor Meat Packing Plant. He remained a butcher, working until near the end of his life, at 90. My mother found work in a butcher shop, at the Pike Street Market in Seattle, to help support the family. They also took in boarders. And in 1940, my little brother was born. My mother died recently, at age 93. So as you can tell, I had selected my parents very carefully.

German was always the language that we spoke at home. So, in reality, German is my mother tongue. But my parents only went to school until they were 12 years old, which was typical for rural German families at the time. Remarkably, I can imitate any sound I hear, like a parrot, and I have been able to retain the German language. However, my vocabulary and my sense of grammar are very limited. It halts with the language typical for a 12-year-old. Reading and writing continue to be difficult for me.

I can read '*Bild*' or the '*Süddeutsche Zeitung*' with ease. But '*Die Zei*' is too difficult for me. So you can gauge quite precisely what my level of German is.

But I have never had any formal instruction in German. For that, myself, and for many others, we can thank that Austrian corporal, as well as for a great deal else.

I suggest that the 20th century could well have been the German century, as the 19th was the British, the 18th French, and the 17th, the Spanish. Everything was prepared for that, in physics, historiography, classics, biochemistry, medicine, nuclear physics, mathematics, music, film etc. But thanks to the politicians, that opportunity was wasted, irrevocably lost, and everyone present in this room has suffered the consequences.

And it is, similarly, all the politicians that we have to blame that there is no peace currently between the Israelis and the Palestinians.

My American Education, Profession, and Family

I was always very good in school, ever striving, and in 1953, I received a full scholarship to Harvard College in Cambridge, MA. So I left my parents' home at the age of 17.

I became an academic, in Medicine, in Pathology, and was a Professor of Pathology for 32 years at the University of California in San Francisco. With good fortune, I was able to publish 230 articles in scholarly journals, as well as publish a book. Here, for example, is the title page of the book that will be published this month by Academic Press.

I married, have three children, and now, five grandchildren. Here is a photo of the only granddaughter, a remarkably beautiful child, as is typical for the women in my family.

My eldest son, Aaron, is a Nephrologist, a kidney doctor, and he will be coming here to give a 'crash course' in Clinical Nephrology. This is a medical specialty that has never been taught previously at Al Quds University, because there has never been any one available trained in that particular specialty.

It is amusing to be reminded that he is the child that was most opposed to my coming here. He postulated that I was in danger of being kidnapped, shot, or murdered in some other manner. And it is precisely he who is coming now. One never can predict what will happen in life. And if you do what your children oppose, then you know you are doing the right thing.

My Uprooted German Family in America

We Jews came to the Rhineland accompanying the Romans as slaves in the second or third century. But now, after 2,000 years, that story has come to an end. I feel very sad about that, because, basically, I still feel myself to be very German.

It was an exciting period, with very bad periods, but interspersed with some very good times. As my parents used to comment, Germany was a good, even an extraordinarily sweet place to live, that is until 1933. It was a good life that was never again as good, even in the US. There they had gone, without family, without friends, without language. They went to a foreign place with very strange customs to which they never quite became adjusted.

But my parents were very fortunate. My father was able to find work immediately, even in the Depression. As a butcher you can always find work, at any place, at any time. Others were not as fortunate. A Mr. Cassirer, a family acquaintance, who had been a Supreme Court judge in Berlin, had to gather empty bottles at two cents each, in order to support his family.

My children speak no German, have no connection to Germany, and have no interest. That for me is particularly sad. And so, this German journey, that lasted 2,000 years, ends with me. The 2,000 years was apparently not long enough to be accepted as Germans at the tine.

In 1933, all park benches around Bad Kreuznach carried the sign 'Jews and Dogs forbidden' [*Juden und Hunten verboten*]. At that time, much of the Christian world was saying, 'Jews, go back to Palestine.' And now, many from the same group are saying, 'Jews, get out of Palestine.' They apparently have a hard time making up their minds. What can we do? Well, we are here, from where we came originally, and we intend to stay. Where else can we go? We are not really wanted elsewhere.

The Danger of Retirement

As I was saying, I was active for a long time at the University of California. After 32 years, it came time to retire.

But I think the concept of retirement is absolutely absurd. It is not only absurd, but also extremely dangerous. It is important to be constantly faced with new challenges. One can never stand still, not in life, not in social situations, not professionally, nor in relationships, psychologically, physically, or spiritually. If you are not going forward, you are automatically moving backwards.

If you are not making progress, you are deteriorating. Standing still is never an option. Additionally, when you retire, one day you are somebody, and the very next day, you are nobody. That had no appeal for me at all.

I needed to be and wanted to continue to be somebody.

And my presence here now, as happens often in life, has a story attached to it.

> About 17 years ago, in 1992, I was giving lectures on breast cancer at Hadassah, at the Hebrew University School of Medicine in Ein Karem. It then occurred to me that there was another group of people, the Palestinians, that I had not addressed. On a hunch, I telephoned the Biology Department at Birzeit University north of Ramallah, the only university with Western standards in the West Bank at that time. I telephoned,

> someone answered, and I indicated that if there was sufficient interest, I could come to give a lecture on breast cancer. There was a pause, and then someone said, in a very soft voice,
>
> "*No one ever comes to see us.*"
>
> Well, that was heartbreaking. On any particular day, there are scores of American and European visiting doctors and scientists wandering the halls of Hadassah. I told her I would be there in about an hour or an hour and a half
>
> I then went to the Damascus Gate, took one of those shared taxis to Ramallah, and another to Birzeit. When I arrived, the entire university was there to greet me, students and faculty. The auditorium was filled, and there were even people standing in the back, from all possible departments, from fields as far removed as agriculture and soil management; they were all so hungry for contact with the outside world.

This was for me a momentous experience. I returned several times, that is until about 2001, when the second Intifada had started. It was not possible to pass through the checkpoints. It was too dangerous, I was told.

A New Career in Palestine

Interestingly, about that time, the Medical School was being founded, and the basic science faculty at Birzeit University, who knew me, were those involved in setting up the new basic science faculty at Al Quds. They invited me to come and join them.

Therefore, shortly after my retirement on December 31, 2007, one month thereafter, to be precise, on February 1, 2008, I was salvaged.

I started my new career, at the age of 72, teaching Pathology to Palestinian medical students, after a vacation of one month. I am not the kind of person that can lie on the beach, play golf, or go on cruises. I need to stay active, be engaged and to remain involved.

So now I have been at Al Quds for over a year, teaching for the third semester. I live in the guesthouse of Augusta Victoria Hospital. I am also active on the Tumor Board of Augusta Victoria that meets weekly to discuss difficult management problems of all newly referred cancer patients from Gaza and the West Bank.

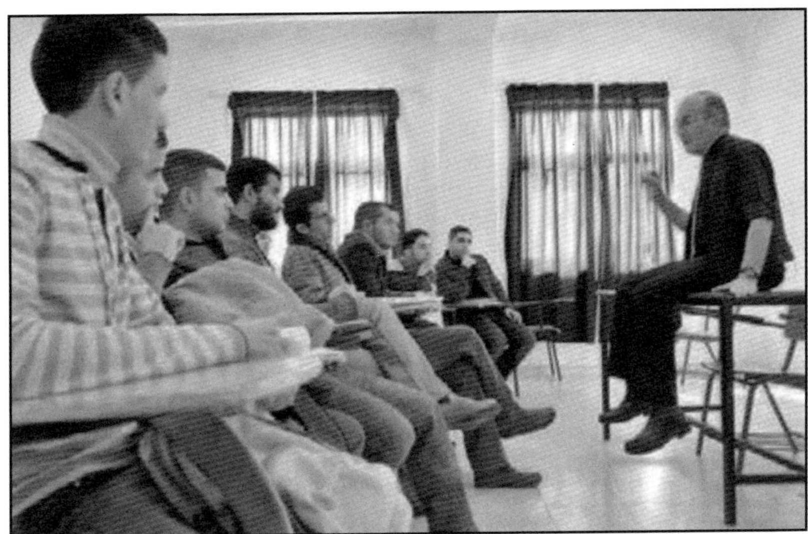

Figure 9.4.2.3 *In his post-retirement career, volunteer Robert Stern, MD, lectures to a class of students at Al-Quds University Medical School, Abu-Dies, East Jerusalem, founded in 1993 and the first in Palestine. The girls are sitting separately behind the boys.*

The Palestinian medical students are really terrific, a wonderful and talented group of people, better than my students in San Francisco. There are 45 in the class, 25 women and 20 men, selected from over 1,000 applicants. They are really very, very good, and I consider it a great honor and a privilege to be their instructor. We get along well, and we understand each other. And they know from the first day that I am Jewish. When I step out of the elevator, they whistle, clap, and cheer.

I also continue to be active in science and in research. My dear colleague, Dr. Maysa Azzeh, who graciously shares her research laboratory with me, is here this evening also.

At the beginning of February, during the semester break, I traveled in Europe, to look for research funding for the Al Quds laboratory, to Brussels and the European Commission, and Germany, to the German equivalent of the NIH, the DFG, while also visiting potential collaborating laboratories. Hopefully, something will come of these efforts. And that is also the reason that the talk this evening had to be delayed. And for that, my sincere apologies.

Summing Up

Finally, I must admit that my time here at Al Quds is an ego trip, as are all sensible human activities. It has turned into an incredible adventure, I get lots of attention, and I continue to be constantly curious. Obviously, there is so much satisfaction on so many levels.

Thus, I have embarked, at the age of 73, on a new career, and with that, Act III of this theater piece that is my life. And that act has to be a good one, even if the first two acts are not up to standards, because it is the last one; not only good, but outstanding. *It is the last opportunity to do something really worthwhile in life, something special.* Not all of us have such an opportunity.

It can be claimed that while Nelson Mandela was in jail all those years, he was the only free person. It was all the others that were really in a prison. Similarly, I feel I have reached the two-state solution. It is all of you out there that are still struggling.

I have my health, and I have energy. I feel that I have been blessed with a second life, and that I must do something special with that extra life. My life began with unspeakable horrors around me. Perhaps my good deeds can balance some of that out.

And in the end, it is important to be a hero, particularly to one's self.

The Dean of the Medical School at Al Quds asked me recently how long I intended to stay? I answered, with some impudence, '*Until you find someone better.*'

When does life begin?

> The Catholics claim at conception.
>
> The Protestants claim at birth.
>
> The Jews say, 'When the children have grown up, left home, the dog is dead, and the house has been paid off.'
>
> Well, I can really claim that my life is now beginning.

Why am I here, specifically? The Jews want the Arabs to go away. And the Arabs want the Jews to go away. But in the end, no one is leaving. That has to be accepted, finally, on both sides. And both sides have to accept that they are not enemies, but that they are each other's best allies. That is why I am here, to promote that concept.

Everyone hates the Jews, and everyone hates the Palestinians, particularly the other Arabs. Both Jews and Palestinians are ambitious, energetic, and intelligent. Most other people are jealous. Both groups care deeply about education. Both groups work hard to ensure that their children obtain the best education possible. The two groups are really so similar. They must really come to understand each other better, even to trust each other, if that were ever possible . . . .

Therefore, here I am. '*Hineini*', as our father Abraham said to God.

* * *

I have to thank each of you for the opportunity to address you, in this holy place, in this holy city, to tell you my story.

I thank you all for your time, and for your patience, and for having to listen to my simple German.

My thanks to each of you."

Robert Stern, MD, graduated in Medicine from University of Washington (Seattle) and then spent 12 years at the National Institutes of Health, where he also obtained training in Anatomic Pathology. On staff at University of California, San Francisco, for 32 years, he published papers in cell biology and anatomic pathology. His laboratory discovered and described the hyaluronidase enzyme family in the Human Genome. He was a Fulbright scholar, won numerous teaching awards, and served on the editorial staff of scientific journals, as well as being on the board of U. California Press. Following retirement, for two years he volunteered as faculty at the first Palestinian School of Medicine. Since 2009, he has continued to teach and do research, albeit at a slower pace, at the Touro College of Osteopathic Medicine in New York City, from which he expects to exit "feet first."

He is currently collecting a series of clinical vignettes for publication gathered over 55 years. "Relaying such stories makes us human, but they can no longer be accommodated in the current 'flipped classroom' video-based mode of medical instruction." He also maintains Belvedere House, an Airbnb in San Francisco, the former family home. He has three children and eight grandchildren.

Endnote

[1] Talk given by Robert Stern, MD, at the Church of the Redeemer in the Old City, Jerusalem, March 3, 2009. Translated from the German. Not all of the photos mentioned in the text were accessible in 2017. All photographs are courtesy of the author.

Figure 9.4.2.4 *"Baruch Spinoza" (1632–1677)*
Dutch philosopher of Sephardi/Portuguese origin
Franz Wulfhagen (1624–1670), ca. 1664

One of the great rationalists of 17th-century philosophy, his magnum opus, Ethics, *published posthumously in Latin in 1677, overturned medieval philosophy and laid the foundation for the 18th-century Enlightenment, modern biblical criticism and modern conceptions of the self and the universe. A leading philosopher with René Descartes during the Dutch Golden Age, he opposed Descartes' philosophy on mind–body dualism. An optical instrument maker, he also contributed to emerging technology in manufacture of microscopes and telescopes.*

Sources: Text: https://en.wikipedia.org/wiki/Baruch_Spinoza
Image: https://commons.wikimedia.org/wiki/File:Baruch_Spinoza_-_Franz_Wulfhagen_-_1664.jpg

Epilogues

Figure E1 *Massachusetts Hall, built in 1764, enlarged in 1842 and 1870, and adjacent to the Johnson Gate, is Harvard College's oldest remaining building. The first floor houses the offices of the President of Harvard. The upper floors are dormitories for Harvard College first-year students, still termed "freshmen".*

Reprinted courtesy of Harvard University

Figure E2 *Charles William Eliot (1834–1926)*
President, Harvard University, 1869–1909

Photographs ca. 1865 (*left*) and 1903 (*right*), reprinted courtesy of Harvard University and the Library of Congress

Selected as Harvard's president in 1869, he transformed the provincial college into the preeminent American research university.[1] *Eliot House, one of the seven original residential houses for undergraduates at the college, was named in his honor.*

Eliot, a Harvard graduate and in 1858 newly appointed as Assistant Professor of Mathematics and Chemistry, aimed for the Rumford Professorship of Chemistry. Fortunately for him and especially for Harvard, it eluded him. Instead, in 1863 he left to spend two years in Europe studying the educational systems of the Old World and the role of education in its national life.

He wrote:

> *"The Puritans thought they must have trained ministers for the Church, and they supported Harvard College—when the American people are convinced that they require more competent chemists, engineers, artists, architects, than they now have, they will somehow establish the institutions to train them . . . .*[2]

In 1865 Eliot returned to Boston to become Professor of Analytical Chemistry at the newly founded Massachusetts Institute of Technology. That same year the government of Harvard University underwent revolutionary change: membership of the board of overseers passed from elected officials in state government and political appointees to election by graduates of the college.

The change brought reforms, including the appointment in 1869 of Eliot at age 35 to the office of President shortly after publication of his views for reform of American higher education.[3]

He believed that a college education could enable a student to make intelligent choices, but should not attempt to provide specialized vocational or technical training. However, it should preserve its traditional functions of spiritual and character education, which were especially important for those who would go on to attain positions of economic and political leadership.

Under Eliot, Harvard became a worldwide university and his influence on education widespread. The expansion of graduate and professional schools and departments promoted specialization and scientific research. For undergraduates a new "elective system" enabled students to discover their "natural bents" and pursue specialized studies. Both private and public high schools reshaped their curricula to meet Harvard's demanding standards, and Eliot became a founding member of the College Entrance Examination Board.

Footnotes

1 Text source: https://en.wikipedia.org/w/index.php?title=Charles_William_Eliot&oldid=796759682

2 James, Henry (1930). Charles W. Eliot, President of Harvard University, 1869–1909, Vol. 1. AMS Press, p. 147

3 Charles W. Eliot, "The New Education," Atlantic Monthly, XXIII, Feb. (Part II in Mar.) 1869

Essay from 20th Reunion Report, Class of 1957

Professor John H. Finley

Chance to share in this report is very welcome. Memory of the class brings back a glad era of the college and of the House that I chiefly knew. Serious rivalry seemed absent then; people expected the future to open. They joyously greeted others' successes, justly imagining that something similar would follow for everyone. Most people got the job or graduate school that they wanted or, if not, one about as good. I remember few or no bad disappointments. Aging memory may be golden, but the mood was bright.

My present top-floor Widener study gives only an airy view of Cambridge reality. Astonishment at my long luck has bred the conclusion that it quite simply reflects ideas of Harvard that were common in my college years. We ignorantly assumed that the visible bond of college with graduate schools had always been such, to learn only later that the Graduate School of Arts and Sciences was not founded until 1878, and that our teachers represented, in any systematic sense, the first or second generation of elaborate instruction in this country. Our Harvard that thus joined the ancient college with these lofty pretensions (needless to say, in the other graduate schools as well) was Mr. Eliot's creation, a kind of second founding. But the resultant unity was to us simply a fact, something fixed and given. Cambridge was smaller; one was occasionally invited to professors' houses. They in turn seemed equally to take for granted both the amiable world of undergraduates and their own exacting sphere. The learned editor of the *Divine Comedy*, Professor C. H. Grandgent, it was said, would supply editors of the *Lampoon* with bright ideas when theirs ran dry; a former editor of the *Advocate* feelingly remembers a kind letter from him about a story. The Latin scholar and medievalist, Professor E. K. Rand, a class secretary for years, adorned menus of class dinners with quotations from the Roman poets; it was observed that no class ever had compulsory Latin so long. Professor Bliss Perry described Thoreau as an undergraduate, seemingly not long before, listening to Emerson's famous Phi Beta Kappa address from the graveyard outside the open windows of what is now the First Unitarian Church. Pleasant as college was for us, it opened to a kind of sky. It was this simple assumption that later suggested no conflict between scholarship and being Master of a House. Each, it seemed, would enhance the other; the two seemed complementary. Whether or not the assumption was correct is another question, which is not for me to answer. The present point that my triple good fortune followed from it, alike in friendship with sparkling generations, in teaching, and in Greek.

Every member of the class will have had cause to know, personally and in his own life, many consequences of the American growth, in population, technology, competition, elaboration. Opportunity is wider, but so is competition. Needless to say, Harvard has not been immune. It characteristically harbored two ideas—that it comprises a wider family and that it is first among American universities—but the ideas become hard to hold together. There are more applicants and from more varied places and backgrounds; as fields grow and change, the faculty is larger, and choice of it more complex; Cambridge is less intimate; other universities challenge. Add the fetching but complicating presence of the other sex, the general American drive toward size and inclusion, and the financial needs of private universities, and the wonder is not that Harvard changes but that it stays so constant. It is less to be judged relatively to its own past than to other more changing institutions.

A personal story may illustrate. Early in Mr. Conant's term I was an assistant professor on a five-year appointment, when our departmental chairman, the austere and tireless C. N. Jackson, decided to end his long reign. The dean, the visionary mathematician George Birkhoff called me in, said that he had in mind a younger chairman, and kindly offered me the job. He seemed surprised when I said that I was only an assistant professor but thought that he could do something about that—which was how I joined the faculty as a permanent member. Mr. Conant, no doubt alarmed by such quaint ways, soon created the present system of so-called ad hoc committees to advise on permanent appointments. The system in turn increasingly reflects Harvard's competitive position among universities here and abroad; it is one means by which the president tries to find and judge emergent talent. In defense of Harvard's position he must surely do so, yet his criteria grow harder. Shall they include, in addition to excellence in a field, loyalty to the college and promise in teaching, and, if so, how be sure? Futures were always unpredictable, but many professors once simply emerged from the college; their double loyalty to it and to scholarship was more easily judged. The issue concerns Harvard's persisting identity—as a whole, separately in the Houses, in research, writing, and teaching—in sum, in its historic double role toward the college and the graduate schools. The powerfully enlisting force of Harvard's history is the great assurance.

A further assurance may grow more visible with age than to people twenty years out, still in strong forward traction. It is, paradoxically, that education does not chiefly look to getting on in the world but first of all to great and permanent things beyond one's own life. Not that courage, intelligence, and generosity are not essential, but that obsession—with career, marriage, esteem, inner and outer doubts—remains to be coped with. Mental interests are not a duty but a privilege, almost a salvation, blessed means of attaching the hot present to cooler, longer processes that help give life direction and decency. Their seed, never fully grown, drew from many sources but not least from college. Its growth in young and old is Harvard's final measure. It clearly persists and, though students and faculty look different from those that we knew, continues to work in them. This progressively discovered, never wholly achieved, allegiance to things beyond the self is our main bond and main assurance.

Figure E3 *Dr. John Finley, Master of Eliot House, seated before the fireplace in the Housemaster's Library, gives his full attention to the unseen speaker.*

Reprinted courtesy of Harvard University

Endnote

1 Reprinted from the 20th Reunion Report of Harvard College Class of 1957. Dr. Finley's essay was written in 1977 at the invitation of Class Secretary James L. Joslin on behalf of the Reunion Committee.

John H. Finley, Jr., 91, Classicist at Harvard for 43 Years, Is Dead

Robert McG. Thomas, Jr.
The New York Times
published June 14, 1995

John H. Finley Jr., the classicist who brought ancient Greece alive and taught a generation of Harvard men how to live, died on Sunday at a Exeter Health Care Center in Exeter, NH. He was 91 and a resident of Tamworth, NH.

There were close to 300 years of Harvard before he came along, and the university has continued for more than a decade since he left. But almost from the moment he joined the faculty in 1933 until 1,000 students, including the university president, gave him two standing ovations at his final lecture in 1976, John H. Finley, Jr., was the embodiment of Harvard.

He wrote the Harvard book. He taught the Harvard course. He lived the Harvard life.

As the principal author of *General Education in a Free Society*, in 1946, Professor Finley laid down the principles—and the handful of required courses—that governed education at Harvard until the 1980s.

None of the courses were more popular than Humanities 103—the Great Age of Athens—in which Professor Finley interpreted Homer, explained Plato and defended Aristotle with a mesmerizing delivery that took wing on unexpected flights of image and notion.

"A single three-by-five card," his son, John III, said yesterday, "would last him an entire lecture."

He was born in New York City at a time when his father, a renowned educator who later became the editorial page editor of *The New York Times*, was serving as president of City College, and he came to Greek early.

As a child he would carry a Greek New Testament to church every Sunday to check on the adequacy of the King James version.

A 1925 *magna cum laude* graduate of Harvard, he continued his studies of Greek literature abroad before obtaining his doctorate from Harvard in 1933, becoming an associate professor that fall and a full professor in 1944.

But for all his achievements at the lectern and for all his scholarly accomplishments, including books on Thucydides and other Greek luminaries, it was in the dining hall and sitting rooms of Eliot House, one of Harvard's residential complexes, that Professor Finley put his most lasting imprint on a generation of students.

As master of Eliot House from 1941 to 1968, Professor Finley took far more pains than his fellow house masters in evaluating the freshmen who applied to live there for their last three years. He not only studied each resume carefully and interviewed every applicant, he also memorized their names and advised them on life's perils. The purpose of college, he would tell them, was to reduce the time they spent thinking about women from 80 percent to 60 percent.

His goal, his son recalled yesterday, was the well-rounded man, one who combined intelligence with a range of social and other skills, especially those that ran to athletic prowess.

"Sports were very important to him," his son said, noting that Eliot House invariably won the most intramural competitions.

The care he took paid off academically, too. During a year Professor Finley spent as a visiting professor at Oxford, his son recalled, his father was pleased to note that something like 12 of the 18 Rhodes scholars in attendance had come from Harvard and that 11 of those 12 had come from Eliot House. "One of the great pleasures of university life," he once said, "is the cheerful company of the young."

As a traditionalist, however, Professor Finley drew the line at admitting women, saying: "I'm not quite sure people want to have crystalline laughter falling like waterfall down each entry way of the house at all hours. I should think it would be a little disturbing if you were taking advanced organic chemistry."

A short, trim man, Professor Finley said his soul was shaped like a shoehorn, the result of getting so many Harvard men into jobs and academic positions for which they did not immediately seem all that qualified, once asking, "How should I have known that God as humorist had in store for me the letter of recommendation as an art form?"

In addition to his son, he is survived by a daughter, Corrina Hammond of Exeter, and five grandchildren.

Harvard through the Ages

Harvard at 375: Celebrating Momentum in the Sciences, Public Service, Diversity, and the Arts

[Adapted from "Harvard at 375", *The Harvard Gazette*, May 25, 2011]

In 1636, Harvard began as an idea—a pledge by the young Massachusetts Bay Colony to build a Puritan college in the wilderness of early New England "to advance Learning and perpetuate it to Posterity".

By 1638, Harvard was a building as well, "very fair and comely within and without". The structure was steep-roofed, with a spacious hall, a parlor, and a lean-to kitchen and buttery out back. Peyntree House stood on one and one-eighth acre in what was called Cowyard Row.

And by 1642, Harvard was a college. It graduated its first class on September 23 that year—nine "young men of good hope", as colonial leader John Winthrop recorded in his journal. Edward Mitchelson, the colony's marshal general, began the ceremony by striking the dais with the butt of his pikestaff. That first Commencement included a long prayer and oration in Latin, followed by "disputations" from the graduates to prove their grasp of Latin, Greek, and Hebrew. Afterward, the school's president made a private appeal for funds. At the time, Harvard—with no rents, annuities, or estates—scraped by on about 55 English pounds a year.

Since that modest beginning, Harvard has grown from a training school for ministers to a global institution that promotes public service; from a school that forbade music outside of chapel services to a university where the arts are integral to scholarship; from an institution where learning "letters" followed strict classical models to one where a rainbow of humanities options reflect a diverse world; and from a place that focused on Latin and Greek to one that embraces science, technology, and innovation.

All this is what Harvard celebrates as it marks its 375th anniversary.

"With this anniversary celebration, we hope to both glance back and leap forward," said Harvard president Drew Gilpin Faust of the festivities, which will span ten months starting in the fall of 2011. "We plan to honor Harvard's rich history and cherished traditions, the great minds that have taught here, and the great minds those teachers have inspired. And we will also focus our energy and attention on the questions that will define our present and our future."

Here are some key areas that Harvard has helped to shape in recent decades, and that in turn have helped to shape the Harvard of today.

The Rise of the Sciences

The present and future depend on the past, and so it is with Harvard and the sciences. But first came centuries of reluctance, as the young College clung to a classical model of education.

French journalist J.P. Brissot de Warville visited Harvard in 1788. He marveled at the College's great library but also said that the "sciences are not carried to any high degree," in keeping with a young nation that he found more interested in commerce than in Newton-like inquiry.

In 1847, Harvard opened the Lawrence Scientific School, the progenitor of today's top-flight engineering and physical sciences departments. (In the physics department alone, there are currently ten winners of the Nobel Prize.) The new school helped to provide the scholarly grist to power the rising nation's manufacturing, mining, and agriculture.

In World War II, Harvard's embrace of the sciences transformed the campus into "Conant's Arsenal", named after President James B. Conant, a chemist by training. Myriad researchers worked on radar jamming, night vision, aerial photography, sonar, explosives, a proto-computer, blood plasma derivatives, synthesized quinine, antimalarial drugs, and new treatments for burns and shock. By 1945, Harvard's income from government contracts was the third highest among US universities. Chemistry professor George B. Kistiakowsky tested new explosives and later led the Manhattan Project's search for a way to trigger a nuclear bomb. Organic chemistry professor Louis Fieser invented napalm, lightweight incendiary grenades, and the M-1 fire-starter used for sabotage.

But the Harvard project that most influenced postwar science was the Mark I Automatic Sequence Controlled Calculator, a protocomputer developed in the Computation Laboratory by Harold Aiken, PhD '39, in cooperation with IBM. Unveiled in 1944, it was 51 feet long, contained 72 tiered adding machines, and had 500 miles of wire. It calculated ballistic tables and Manhattan Project equations.

Now, science and innovation are deeply embedded in the architecture of Harvard, where research has led to the grand (the heart pacemaker), the odd (breathable chocolate), and the futuristic (one of the first multimedia online scholarly journals).

"We can celebrate that Harvard is—but doesn't feel—375 years old," said Jonathan Zittrain, cofounder and faculty codirector Berkman Center for Internet & Society, who has broad-based faculty appointments in law, public policy, engineering, and computer science.

Harvard values traditions and "inspiringly worn pathways from those who have come before," he said, but it is at its best when its sturdy foundations lead academics and researchers "to venture into genuinely new scholarship and teaching." When the old supports the new, said Zittrain, "the University can catalyze activity far beyond campus."

When Faust took office in 2007, she said that higher education had an "accountability to the future." At Harvard, that mission includes pushing ideas out of the laboratory and into the marketplace. From 2006 to 2010, Harvard research spawned 39 start-up companies, 216 patents, and 1,270 faculty inventions. Institutionally, the players include the Wyss Institute for Biologically Inspired Engineering and Harvard's Office of Technology Development, which considers sharing innovation a form of public service.

The Public Service Mission

In his 1923 memoir, longtime president Charles William Eliot said one defining quality lay at the heart of Harvard's traditions: "a spirit of service in all the professions, both learned and scientific, including business," as well as "a desire, a firm purpose, to be of use to one's fellow men."

Eliot's own memory of that service stretched back to the Civil War, in part because of the many participants from Harvard who fought to save the Union. So he would hardly be surprised to find that the

University's sense of self-sacrifice still includes military service. When Faust spoke at a ceremony this March reinstating ROTC after a hiatus of forty years, she said the agreement "recognizes military service as an honorable and admirable calling—a powerful expression of an individual citizen's commitment to contribute to the common good."

During last year's Commencement address, Faust underscored the importance of giving back, announcing creation of the Presidential Public Service Fellowships, which fund ten students annually to spend a summer helping others. She also promised to double funding for student service, including opportunities in the graduate and professional schools, and to create a Harvard-wide public service website.

In recent years, the number of service opportunities at Harvard has grown, taking on an astonishing diversity. Earlier this year, 110 undergraduates fanned out during Alternative Spring Break, going on 11 service trips. They helped to rebuild a burned church in western Massachusetts, worked with AIDS patients in New York City, and constructed affordable housing in El Salvador.

At Harvard Law School, every student must complete forty hours of pro bono work before graduating. Members of the Class of 2010 averaged 556 hours of free legal services apiece. Students in public health, medicine, and dentistry regularly perform aid work. The Harvard Kennedy School regards service as a core mission, and the Harvard Business School supports a Social Enterprise Initiative. Similar service opportunities are open to graduate students in education, divinity, and design.

Undergraduates and faculty regularly volunteer at the Harvard Allston Education Portal, tutoring neighborhood students in science, math, and the humanities. The Phillips Brooks House Association (PBHA), Harvard's oldest and largest public service club, is home to the Public Service Network, which supports independent, student-led service programs, and the Center for Public Interest Careers, which administers paid internships for summers and after graduation.

Helping others can change lives. Emmett Kistler '11 came to Harvard to study chemistry. But during his first Alternative Spring Break two years ago, he not only learned how to swing a hammer but decided to study religion and civil rights. Public service "has been one of the most shaping experiences of my college career," said Kistler.

"Some of Harvard's best souls" use their personal time to help others, said Tim McCarthy '93, lecturer in history and literature and public policy. He led the first such public service trip in 2001 and has since squired hundreds of undergraduates on similar forays. "I'm on my own spiritual journey," said McCarthy. "This is part of it."

Blossoming of the Arts

Across Harvard, a different sort of spiritual journey involves discovering the power of the arts.

"There is much to celebrate, of course," from Harvard's first 375 years, said Stephen Greenblatt, John Cogan University Professor of the Humanities, "principally the fact—so easy to take for granted, so astonishing in reality—that the pedagogical commitment, intellectual power, and spirit of exploration embodied in this University have been renewed for so many generations."

To the University's core values, Greenblatt said, "have more recently been added a vital interest in the role of art-making in the cognitive life of the Harvard community and of the world at large. This development seems to me crucial in furthering the University's project of advancing our best qualities as human beings."

Greenblatt chaired Harvard's 2007 Arts Task Force, which the next year released an influential report that favored making the arts a greater part of the University's intellectual life. After all, "art-making is a way of knowing," said Office for the Arts director Jack Megan at the time. "It has to do with understanding the world around us." The report forcefully echoed one from 1956, when the University's Committee on the Visual Arts released what became known as the Brown Commission Report, urging enhanced arts education for undergraduates. "Talking about knowing" was a medieval model of scholarship, that report said. It argued instead that "knowing and creating" belonged together.

Though the Brown Commission did not turn Harvard on its head, it did make a difference. By 1960, Harvard had built the Loeb Drama Center on Brattle Street, and in 1963 the Carpenter Center for the Visual Arts. Harvard soon created a Visual and Environmental Studies (VES) program. "It comes down to the making," said VES concentrator Julia Rooney '11, a painter. "Making is what I wanted to do."

The arts have come a long way. Making art at a 17th-century Puritan college was considered subversion. Edward Taylor, Class of 1671, eventually went down in literary history as a great poet in the metaphysical tradition—but it took until the 1920s for an American scholar to discover him. In his own day, Taylor kept his poems private.

The first documented concert at Harvard came in 1771, and singing was confined to chapel services. General Oliver, Class of 1818, concealed his flute under his featherbed, fearing the wrath of College officials and of his Puritan father. The first course in music was taught in 1855—a watershed moment, according to music champion John Sullivan Dwight, Class of 1832. It was, he said, "the entering wedge, and we may all rejoice in it."

A century and a half later, that wedge has widened to include today's student painters, filmmakers, poets, actors, dancers, novelists, and photographers, some of whom make the arts their careers. There are so many Harvard graduates in the Los Angeles entertainment industry, for example, that alumni founded Harvardwood, a nonprofit that facilitates their professional networking.

Increasingly, noted arts professionals move in and out of Harvard's academic settings with ease, leaving inspiration in their wake. In late April, famed jazz virtuoso Wynton Marsalis launched a two-year lecture and performance series at Sanders Theatre. The same month, the Office of the Arts and the Music Department sponsored "Forty Years of Jazz at Harvard: A Celebration." Last year, the nonprofit Silk Road Project moved its headquarters from Rhode Island to Harvard, strengthening a partnership between the University and an organization that promotes innovation and learning through the arts.

This fall, art-making will be prominent during the October 14 launch of the University's official 375th anniversary. The celebrations during the academic year will include scholarly panels and symposia. But the opening will be festive and musical, putting Harvard's "vital arts mission" on display, said University marshal Jacqueline O'Neill, MPA '81. "The launch is decidedly and intentionally supposed to be fun." At one point, guests will assemble in the Tercentenary Theatre for orchestral and choral interludes, with a capstone performance by cellist Yo-Yo Ma '76.

A University of the World

The Harvard of the dim past was small, insular, and guardedly parochial. Now it is a university of the world. Some historians say Harvard finally assumed that role in 1936, when it decided to celebrate its 300th birthday on a bright stage presented to the world. Everything about the 1936 celebration was grand and represented "a seismic shift in institutional weight and presence," wrote authors Morton and Phyllis Keller in *Making Harvard Modern* (2001).

That summer, 70,000 visitors toured Harvard Yard, and a light show on the Charles River in September drew 300,000 viewers. The fall convocation was preceded by two weeks of scholarly symposia. About 15,000 guests attended the final day of festivities. Representatives from 502 universities and learned societies gathered to recognize Harvard's three centuries. The climax of the event was a speech by President Franklin D. Roosevelt '04, who sat gamely though heavy rains.

In the decades since, Harvard has cemented its position as a global university. This year, more than 4,300 international students—nearly 20 percent of enrollment—attended, coming from 130 countries. The Web portal Harvard Worldwide lists more than 1,600 activities, and notes that Harvard has offices in nine countries. Last year, nearly 1,500 Harvard College students traveled to a total of 104 countries for research and other activities. Harvard Summer School faculty will lead 28 study abroad programs in 18 countries this year.

"In a digital age, ideas and aspirations respect few boundaries," President Faust told a scholarly audience in Dublin last year. "The new knowledge economy is necessarily global, and the reach of universities must be so as well."

Jorge I. Domínguez, Antonio Madero Professor for the Study of Mexico and vice provost for international affairs, said that most Harvard College seniors have had a significant international experience. Moreover, "roughly two-thirds of the faculty at the Kennedy School, the Graduate School of Design, and the Business School say on their websites that some significant part of their professional work takes place outside the United States."

One Trunk, Many Branches

Modern Harvard also has evolved profoundly in its embrace of diversity. The University of decades ago that one wag described as "male, pale, and Episco-pale" now has a student body that is just over 50 percent white, with 13 percent foreign-born. All male just a generation ago, Harvard College today has a student body that is evenly divided by gender. Women have a full place at the University's table, though it was only in 1971 that they were first allowed to process into Harvard Yard for Commencement. Economically, any student admitted to the College is guaranteed a place in the Class. If money is a factor in attending, the University will provide financial support.

Diversifying the University has been a major aim of Harvard presidents from Eliot to Faust. Eliot, who became president in 1869, has been credited with transforming Harvard from a small college into a true university, and his views on diversity played a large role in that transformation; he envisioned an institution that would bring together scholars from a wide variety of nations, schools, families, sects, political persuasions, and conditions of life, allowing them to experience the "wholesome influence" that comes from observing and interacting with people different from themselves. A decade ago, in his reflective book Pointing Our Thoughts, Harvard's 26th president, Neil L. Rudenstine, wrote: "Diversity is in itself not an absolute value, and it cannot be dissociated from other values that are fundamental to a university: free inquiry, intensive research and scholarship, integrity of mind and thought, devoted teaching and passionate learning."

As President Faust said on the day she was inaugurated, on October 12, 2007:

> *"In the past half century, American colleges and universities have shared in a revolution, serving as both the emblem and the engine of the expansion of citizenship, equality and opportunity—to blacks, women, Jews, immigrants, and others who would have been subjected to quotas or excluded altogether in an earlier era.*
>
> *My presence here today—and indeed that of many others on this platform—would have been unimaginable even a few short years ago. Those who charge that universities are unable to change should take note of this transformation, of how different we are from universities even of the mid-twentieth century. And those who long for a lost golden age of higher education should think about the very limited population that alleged utopia actually served. College used to be restricted to a tiny elite; now it serves the many, not just the few. . . . Ours is a different and a far better world."*

John Winthrop
(1587/1588–1649)
Governor or Lt. Governor, Massachusetts Bay Colony Governor, 1629–1649

Henry Dunster
(1609–1658/1659)
First President of Harvard University, 1640–1654
(his signature)

Charles Chauncy
(1592–1672)
Second President of Harvard University, 1654–1672

Figure E4 *Early influences during the infancy of Harvard University*

John Winthrop *(1587/1588–1649), English Puritan lawyer, born in Suffolk, England, law graduate in 1602 from Trinity College, Cambridge.*

Instrumental in organizing the Massachusetts Bay Colony, the second major settlement in New England after the pioneer Plymouth colony, he was elected the colony's first governor in 1629 while still in England. He sailed for America in April 1630 with a fleet of 11 ships and nearly 700 settlers. By the end of the year over 2,000 immigrants were living in six settlements along the coast, including the new Boston.

Winthrop served as governor for 12 of the colony's first 20 years and was repeatedly elected as Lieutenant Governor between his four terms as Governor. His writings and vision of the colony as a Puritan "city upon a hill" *dominated New England colonial development.*

Henry Dunster *(1609–1658/1659), Puritan clergyman, first president of Harvard University, was later a precursor of the Baptist denomination in America.*

Graduate of Magdalene College, Cambridge, specializing in oriental languages and Hebrew, he was Headmaster of Bury Grammar School in Bury, Lancashire, when invited in 1640 to succeed Nathaniel Eaton, dismissed in 1639 as master of the recently established Harvard College. Dunster remodeled it on Eton College and Cambridge University and for years taught the curriculum alone. In 1642 he graduated the first college class in America.

With approval of the General Court of Massachusetts Bay, he introduced the first corporation charter in America, the Charter of 1650, which still governs Harvard University.

Charles Chauncy *(1592–1672), educated at Westminster School, then at Trinity College, Cambridge, lecturer in Greek, commanded Arabic and other languages. In 1637 he emigrated to America and preached at Plymouth, then Scituate, until appointed president of Harvard College in 1654. He died in office in 1671.*

Like Dunster, he embraced both religious orthodoxy and scientific curiosity, adding a printing press and a telescope to the university. The university press produced materials in both English and Native languages, including the 1,200-page Indian Bible (1663), translated into Algonquian by John Eliot.

Sources: *Text and Images*
Americanantiquarian.org/Inventories/Portraits/bios/153.pdf—portrait of Governor John Winthrop
en.wikipedia.org/w/index.php?title=John_Winthrop&oldid=80408712, =Henry_Dunster&oldid=799393252, =Charles_Chauncy&oldid=798211989
www.harvard.edu/about-harvard/harvard-glance/history-presidency/henry-dunster, charles-chauncy

Signature of President Henry Dunster and portrait of President Charles Chauncy reprinted courtesy of Harvard University.

DREW GILPIN FAUST

28th President of Harvard University
Preceded by Lawrence Henry Summers
Successor Lawrence S. Bacow will begin July 1, 2018

Born in Clark County, Virginia, September 18, 1947

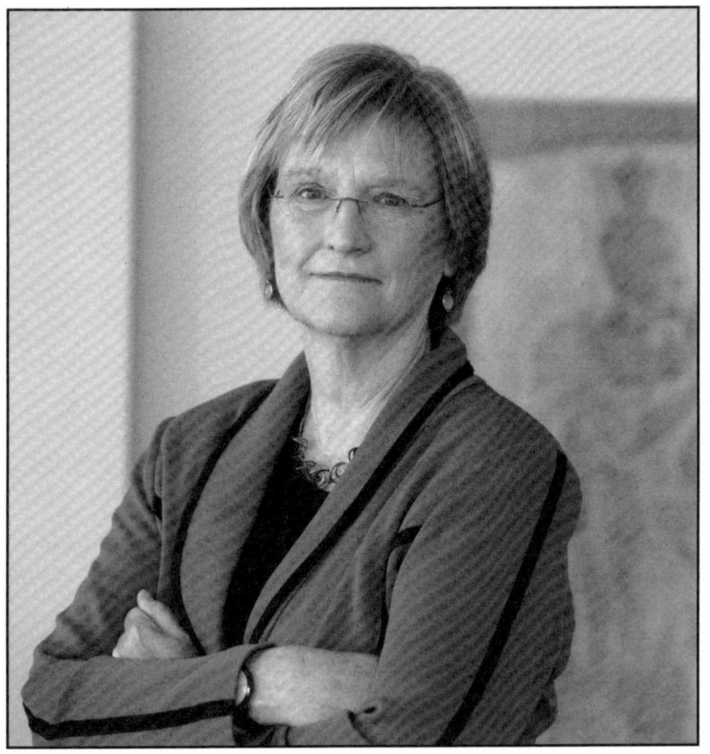

Stephanie Mitchell/Harvard University

Figure E5.1 *The first woman to serve as the President of Harvard University, President Faust's transformational presidency will conclude following graduation of the Harvard College Class of 2018, which is composed of nearly equal numbers of men and women of diverse racial, ethnic, economic and national origins.*

In keeping with the goal of educating the leaders for an increasingly diverse society, 50.8% of the incoming Class of 2021 for the first time will be comprised of individuals who are African-American, Hispanic, Asian-American, Native American, or Native Hawaiian.[1]

Photograph reprinted courtesy of Harvard University

Drew Gilpin Faust

President, Harvard University
2007–2018

Drew Gilpin Faust is the 28th president of Harvard University and the Lincoln Professor of History in Harvard's Faculty of Arts and Sciences.

As president of Harvard, Faust has expanded financial aid to improve access to Harvard College for students of all economic backgrounds and advocated for increased federal funding for scientific research. She has broadened the University's international reach, raised the profile of the arts on campus, embraced sustainability, launched edX, the online learning partnership with MIT, and promoted collaboration across academic disciplines and administrative units as she guided the University through a period of significant financial challenges.

A historian of the Civil War and the American South, Faust was the founding dean of the Radcliffe Institute for Advanced Study at Harvard, guiding its transformation from a college into a wide-ranging institute for scholarly and creative enterprise, distinctive for its multidisciplinary focus and the exploration of new knowledge at the crossroads of traditional fields.

Previously, Faust served as the Annenberg Professor of History at the University of Pennsylvania, where she was a member of the faculty for 25 years.

Raised in Virginia's Shenandoah Valley, Faust went on to attend Concord Academy in Massachusetts. She received her bachelor's degree from Bryn Mawr College in 1968, *magna cum laude* with honors in history, and her master's degree (1971) and doctoral degree (1975) in American civilization from the University of Pennsylvania.

She is the author of six books, including *Mothers of Invention: Women of the Slaveholding South in the American Civil War* (University of North Carolina Press, 1996), for which she won the Francis Parkman Prize in 1997. Her most recent book, *This Republic of Suffering: Death and the American Civil War* (Alfred A. Knopf, 2008), looks at the impact of the Civil War's enormous death toll on the lives of 19th-century Americans. It won the Bancroft Prize in 2009, was a finalist for both a National Book Award and a Pulitzer Prize, and was named by *The New York Times* one of the "10 Best Books of 2008." *This Republic of Suffering* is the basis for a 2012 Emmy-nominated episode of the PBS *American Experience* documentaries titled "Death and the Civil War," directed by Ric Burns.

Faust has been a trustee of Bryn Mawr College, the Andrew Mellon Foundation, and the National Humanities Center, and she serves on the educational advisory board of the Guggenheim Foundation. She has served as president of the Southern Historical Association, vice president of the American Historical Association, and executive board member of the Organization of American Historians and the Society of American Historians. Faust has also served on numerous editorial boards and selection committees, including the Pulitzer Prize history jury in 1986, 1990, and 2004.

Her honors include awards in 1982 and 1996 for distinguished teaching at the University of Pennsylvania. She was elected to the Society of American Historians in 1993, the American Academy of Arts and Sciences in 1994, and the American Philosophical Society in 2004.

Faust is married to Charles Rosenberg, one of the nation's leading historians of medicine and science, who is the Ernest E. Monrad Research Professor of the Social Sciences at Harvard. Faust and Rosenberg have two daughters, Jessica Rosenberg, a 2004 summa cum laude graduate of Harvard College, and Leah Rosenberg, Faust's stepdaughter, a scholar of Caribbean literature.

* * *

A 'Rebellious Daughter' to Lead Harvard [3,4]

Figure E5.2 *Drew Gilpin Faust, the new Harvard president, with Derek Bok, the interim president, at a news conference on campus on Sunday (February 11, 2007)*

Photo credit: Erik Jacobs for *The New York Times*

By Sara Rimer – February 12, 2007

CAMBRIDGE, Mass., Feb. 11 – Recalling her coming of age as the only girl in a privileged, tradition-bound family in Virginia horse country, Drew Gilpin Faust, 59, has often spoken of her "continued confrontations" with her mother "about the requirements of what she usually called femininity." Her mother, Catharine, she has said, told her repeatedly, "It's a man's world, sweetie, and the sooner you learn that the better off you'll be."

Instead, Dr. Faust left home at an early age, to be educated at Concord Academy, then a girls' prep school in Massachusetts, and at Bryn Mawr College, a women's college known for creating future leaders, and to become a leading Civil War scholar. And Sunday, through the convergence of grand changes in higher education, her own achievements and the resignation of Harvard's previous president under pressure, she became the first woman appointed to lead the Ivy League university founded in 1636.

"One of the things that I think characterizes my generation—that characterizes me, anyway, and others of my generation—is that I've always been surprised by how my life turned out," Dr. Faust said in an interview Sunday at Loeb House just after the university announced that she would become its 28th president, effective July 1. "I've always done more than I ever thought I would. Becoming a professor—I never would have imagined that. Writing books—I never would have imagined that. Getting a Ph.D.—I'm not sure I would even have imagined that. I've lived my life a step at a time. Things sort of happened."

Sunday morning, she said, she found herself lying in bed thinking in near disbelief, "Today I think they're going to vote for you for the president of Harvard."

Catharine Drew Gilpin was born on Sept. 18, 1947, and grew up in Clarke County, Va., in the Shenandoah Valley. She was always known as Drew. Her father, McGhee Tyson Gilpin, bred thoroughbred horses.

Dr. Faust has written frankly of the "community of rigid racial segregation" that she and her three brothers grew up in and how it formed her as "a rebellious daughter" who would go on to march in the civil rights protests in the 1960s and to become a historian of the region. "She was raised to be a rich man's wife," said a friend, Elizabeth Warren, a law professor at Harvard. "Instead she becomes the president of the most powerful university in the world."

Race was "not much discussed" in her family, Dr. Faust wrote in an article reprinted in Harvard Magazine. "I lived in a world where social arrangements were taken for granted and assumed to be timeless. A child's obligation was to learn these usages, not to question them. The complexities of racial deportment were of a piece with learning manners and etiquette more generally.

"There were formalized ways of organizing almost every aspect of human relationships and interactions—how you placed your fork and knife on the plate when you had finished eating, what you did with a fingerbowl; who walked through a door first, whose name was spoken first in an introduction, how others were addressed—black adults with just a first name, whites as 'Mr.' or 'Mrs.'—whose hand you shook and whose you didn't, who ate in the dining room and who in the kitchen."

In that world, said one of Dr. Faust's brothers, M. Tyson Gilpin Jr., 63, a lawyer in Clarke County, his sister did some of what was expected of her: She raised a beef cow, joined the Brownies and took dancing lessons. But she resisted other things—becoming a debutante, for example.

"My sister took off on her own track in prep school on," Tyson Gilpin said. "I think she read the scene pretty well. She was ambitious. She wanted to accomplish stuff."

Her father, her two uncles, her great-uncle, two of her three brothers (including Tyson) and numerous male cousins all went to Princeton, but since Princeton did not admit women in the mid-1960s, she went to Bryn Mawr. Majoring in history, she took classes with Mary Maples Dunn, a professor who would become the president of Smith College, the acting dean of the Radcliffe Institute for Advanced Study and a close friend and advocate.

It was significant, Dr. Dunn said, that Dr. Faust had been educated at Concord Academy and Bryn Mawr. "I think these women's institutions in those days tended to give these young women a very good sense of themselves and encouraged them to develop their own ideas and to express themselves confidently," she said. "It was an invaluable experience in a world in which women were second-class citizens."

Dr. Faust graduated from Bryn Mawr in 1968, magna cum laude with honors in history. She went on to the University of Pennsylvania, where she received a master's in 1971 and a doctorate in 1975 in American civilization.

She was a professor at Penn for 25 years, including five years as the chairwoman of the Department of American Civilization. She was director of the Women's Studies Program for four years.

At Penn, Dr. Faust, who was divorced from her first husband, Stephen Faust, in 1976, met Charles Rosenberg, a professor who is regarded as a leading historian of American medicine, and who became her second husband. She and Professor Rosenberg have a daughter, Jessica, a Harvard graduate who works at The New Yorker. She also has a stepdaughter, Leah. Dr. Faust's fifth book, "Mothers of

Invention: Women of the Slave Holding South in the American Civil War," won the Society of American Historians' Francis Parkman Prize for the year's best nonfiction book on an American theme. Her sixth book, to be published by Knopf, explores the impact of the Civil War's enormous death toll on 19th-century Americans.

In 2001, as Dr. Dunn was stepping down as acting dean of the Radcliffe Institute, the remnant of Radcliffe College, which had been absorbed into Harvard in 1999, Dr. Faust became the dean. She made major organizational changes, cut costs and laid off a quarter of the staff, transforming Radcliffe into an internationally known home for scholars from multiple disciplines.

"We used to call her Chainsaw Drew," Professor Warren said.

When Lawrence H. Summers, the Harvard president, stepped in trouble two years ago over his comments about women in science, he asked Dr. Faust to lead an effort to recruit, retain and promote women at Harvard.

Asked Sunday whether her appointment signified the end of sex inequities at the university, Dr. Faust said: "Of course not. There is a lot of work still to be done, especially in the sciences."

What would her mother, who never went to college and died in 1966, have to say about her appointment? "I've often thought about that," she said. "I've had dialogues with my dead mother over the 40 years since she died."

Then she added with a rueful smile, "I think in many ways that comment—'It's a man's world, sweetie'—was a bitter comment from a woman of a generation who didn't have the kind of choices my generation of women had."

Endnotes

1 Source: "In a first, more non-whites get the Harvard nod." *Boston Globe*, August 3, 2017

2 Reprinted courtesy of Harvard University from http://www.harvard.edu/president/biography

3 Source: http://www.nytimes.com/2007/02/12/education/12harvard.html?mcubz=3

4 *Correction, NYT*: February 14, 2007 A Woman in the News article on Monday about Drew Gilpin Faust, the incoming president of Harvard, referred incorrectly in some editions to Concord Academy, the Massachusetts prep school she attended. It was a girls' school when she graduated; it is now co-ed.

A version of this article appears in print on Page A18 of the New York edition with the headline: Coming of Age in a Changed World.

Index of Authors

'57

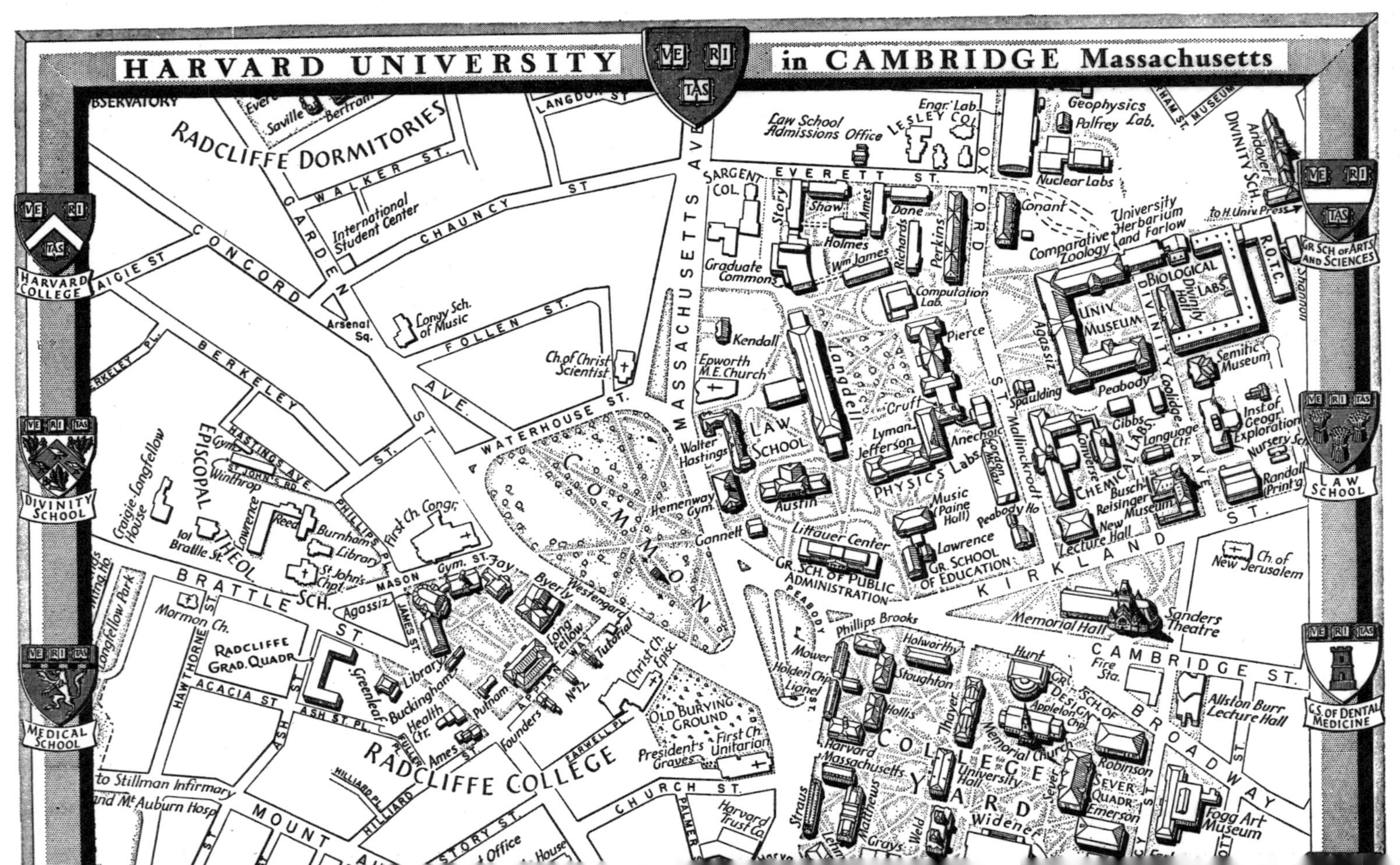
HARVARD UNIVERSITY
in CAMBRIDGE Massachusetts
VE RI TAS
HARVARD COLLEGE
DIVINITY SCHOOL
MEDICAL SCHOOL
GR SCH OF ARTS AND SCIENCES
LAW SCHOOL
G.S. OF DENTAL MEDICINE
RADCLIFFE DORMITORIES
Saville
Bertram
WALKER ST.
International Student Center
CHAUNCY ST
GARDEN
CONCORD
Arsenal Sq.
Longy Sch. of Music
FOLLEN ST.
Ch. of Christ Scientist
BERKELEY
HASTINGS AVE.
EPISCOPAL THEOL. SCH.
Winthrop
Lawrence
Reed
Burnham Library
St John's Chpl.
Craigie-Longfellow House
101 Brattle St.
BRATTLE ST.
Mormon Ch.
RADCLIFFE GRAD. QUADR.
HAWTHORNE
ACACIA ST
ASH ST. PL.
Greenleaf
Library
Buckingham
Health Ctr.
Putnam
Founders
Ames St.
RADCLIFFE COLLEGE
to Stillman Infirmary and Mt Auburn Hosp.
MOUNT AUBURN
HILLIARD
STORY ST.
WATERHOUSE ST.
COMMON
MASSACHUSETTS AVE.
First Ch. Congr.
MASON
Gym. ST.
Fay
Byerly
Westengard
Longfellow
Tutorial
APPIAN WAY
No. 12
Agassiz
JAMES ST.
Christ Ch. Episc.
OLD BURYING GROUND
President's Graves
First Ch. Unitarian
FARWELL PL.
CHURCH ST.
PALMER
Harvard Trust Co.
Hemenway Gym.
Gannett
Walter Hastings
LAW SCHOOL
Austin
Littauer Center
GR. SCH. OF PUBLIC ADMINISTRATION
PEABODY
Kendall
Epworth M.E. Church
SARGENT COL.
Graduate Commons
Story
Shaw
Holmes
Ames
Wm James
Dane
Richards
Perkins
EVERETT ST.
Law School Admissions Office
LESLEY COL.
Engr. Lab.
OXFORD ST.
Langdell
Computation Lab.
Pierce
Cruft
Lyman
Jefferson
PHYSICS Labs.
Anechoic
Gordon McKay
Music (Paine Hall)
Lawrence
GR. SCHOOL OF EDUCATION
Peabody Ho
Mallinckrodt
Spaulding
Agassiz
Conant
Geophysics
Palfrey Lab.
Nuclear Labs
Comparative Zoology
University Herbarium and Farlow
UNIV. MUSEUM
Peabody
BIOLOGICAL LABS.
Divinity Hall
DIVINITY AVE.
Coolidge
Semitic Museum
R.O.T.C.
to H. Univ. Press
Andover
DIVINITY SCH.
Shannon
Gibbs
CHEMICAL LABS.
Converse
Busch-Reisinger Museum
New Lecture Hall
Language Ctr.
Inst. of Geogr. Exploration
Nursery Sch.
Randall (Print'g)
KIRKLAND ST.
Ch. of New Jerusalem
Memorial Hall
Sanders Theatre
CAMBRIDGE ST.
Fire Sta.
Allston Burr Lecture Hall
BROADWAY
Fogg Art Museum
Phillips Brooks
Holworthy
Mower
Holden Chp.
Lionel
Stoughton
Hollis
Thayer
Hunt
GR. SCH. OF DESIGN
Appleton Chp.
Memorial Church
University Hall
COLLEGE YARD
Harvard
Massachusetts
Matthews
Straus
Grays
Weld
Widener
Sever
Robinson
SEVER QUADR.
Emerson
Post Office